THE
ARCHITECTS
OF GOLF

THE ARCHITECTS OF GOLF

A Survey of Golf Course Design from Its Beginnings to the Present, with an Encyclopedic Listing of Golf Course Architects and Their Courses

A COMPLETELY REVISED
AND EXPANDED EDITION OF
The Golf Course

GEOFFREY S. CORNISH
& RONALD E. WHITTEN

HarperCollins*Publishers*

Originally published as *The Golf Course* in 1981 by The Rutledge Press.
Reprinted by arrangement with the authors.

THE ARCHITECTS OF GOLF.

HarperCollins books may be purchased for educational, business, or sales promotional use. For
information, please write: Special Markets Department, HarperCollins Publishers, Inc.,
10 East 53rd Street, New York, NY 10022.

FIRST EDITION

Designed by Irving Perkins Associates, Inc.

Library of Congress Cataloging-in-Publication Data

Cornish, Geoffrey S., and Ronald E. Whitten.
    The architects of golf : a survey of golf course design from its
beginnings to the present, with an encyclopedic listing of golf course
architects and their courses / Geoffrey S. Cornish & Ronald E.
Whitten.—1st ed.
        p. cm.
    Rev. ed. of: The Golf Course, © 1981.
    Includes bibliographical references (p.   ) and index.
    ISBN 0-06-270082-0
    1. Golf courses—Design and construction—History.   2. Golf
courses—Great Britain—Design and construction—History.   3. Golf
courses—United States—Design and construction—History.
4. Architects—Biography.   I. Whitten, Ronald E.   II. Cornish,
Geoffrey S.   Golf course.   III. Title.
GV975.C65   1992   91-58372
712.5—dc20

93 94 95 96 97 PS/CW 10 9 8 7 6 5 4 3 2 1

Contents

Preface

A golf course—being a living, breathing creature—grows old. It may age gracefully, looking and playing better the older it gets, but after a time it begins to show its age. Its holes become too short. Its bunkers no longer seem menacing. Its greens lose character. One of three things must be done. The old course can be reconstructed, completely rebuilt from the ground up with scant homage paid to its original design. It can be restored, faithfully reproducing every nuance, no matter how antiquated, to reflect the original designer's intent and philosophy. Or it can be renovated, changing certain features of the course in order to accommodate modern play but maintaining the original framework.

So it was with *The Golf Course*. When given the opportunity to reissue our history of golf course architecture, which first appeared in 1981 and was reprised in four subsequent editions, we faced three choices. Reconstruct, restore or renovate. Rewrite, reprint or revise.

We chose to revise. We found, a dozen years after its original publication, that our book needed certain updating and correction, but no massive rewriting. We felt then and feel now that we've traced the evolution of the profession of golf course architecture in a concise narrative, and that our biographical section and index of courses will continue to serve as the sole authoritative source on golf architects and courses.

There are changes, to be sure. The title is now *The Architects of Golf*, a more apt description than the original, meant to emphasize that our book deals more with the artists than with the artworks they created.

We've supplemented the text a bit. Our original seemed rather chauvinistic in retrospect. Since 1981, several women have gained prominence in the field of golf course design. Women were active in course architecture even before our first publication, but we, like the rest of the golf world, were blithely ignorant of their contributions. In this volume we seek to atone for their omission.

Also, certain facts have recently come to light that have changed our perspective on the evolution of design. Willie Davis first did Shinnecock, for instance, not Willie Dunn. The original layout of Muirfield did not have returning nines. That sort of thing. So it behooves owners of our original book, especially those who've actually read the textual portion, to browse through our revised presentation. There are no earth-shattering surprises, but some interesting new facts.

We've downsized the book a bit, too. That should make it easier to toss in the briefcase and tote along on those idyllic golf trips, not to pass the hours during a rainstorm, but rather simply to satisfy that burning curiosity about who designed the marvel or monstrosity encountered earlier in the day. Our book was never meant to collect dust on a coffee table anyway.

For those of you new to the subject, we trust you'll find this book a refreshing change from the plethora of golf instruction books and travelogues elsewhere on bookstore shelves. You'll find no tips on whether to pronate or supinate within these pages, nor any recommendation on the best bargains among Great Plains golf resorts. Instead, you'll find a simple celebration of one of the most creative professions known to man, and a catalogue of the accomplishments of nearly every person ever to have practiced that profession.

Only one other book like this has ever been written. We've simply renovated it a bit.

The "Postage Stamp" at Royal Troon, a tiny, treacherous par 3 created from a small corner of spare land during one reconstruction of the course.
COLLECTION RON WHITTEN

PART
ONE

1

Mother Nature

Descendants of the original course maintenance crew at Lahinch Golf Club in Ireland. RON WHITTEN

Games similar to golf have been played in Europe since the Middle Ages. But it was in Scotland that a pastime using a club, a ball and a hole developed, over a period of 500 years or more, into the game we know today as golf. In this same time span, the playing fields of the game evolved into what are today called golf courses. The earliest of these playing fields were found on the Scottish linksland. The location of linksland, often publicly owned, in a northern latitude where summer daylight hours extended from 3 A.M. to 11 P.M. made it possible for persons other than those of a leisure class to use them. Thus, golf established an early democratic tradition in Scotland.

It has been a widely held belief that the term "links" refers to Scottish courses located on sandy deposits left centuries ago along the seacoast by the receding ocean. From a golf architect's point of view this is only partially true. The North Sea may well have deposited rolling dunes of sand along the shoreline, but true linksland consisted of rich alluvial deposits of soil left upon sand dunes by a river as it flowed into the sea. True links, then, would be the golf courses formed by nature on or near river estuaries. Indeed, the game of golf was first played in Scotland along the estuaries of the rivers Eden, Tay and Forth.

The earliest Scottish links were designed entirely by nature. A typical links consisted of high, windswept sand dunes and of hollows where grass grew if the soil was reasonably substantial. The grass was predominantly bent grass with a little fescue interspersed. Its stiff, erect blades, characteristic of turf growing in close proximity to salt-water, were sufficient to support the leather-bound, feather-stuffed golf ball.

The terrain of a linksland usually dictated the route a player would follow. Golfers who batted their "featheries" about a links naturally aimed their shots for the playable sward. The dunes were to be avoided, for the only vegetation that grew there with any regularity was the dreaded whin, a prickly scrub also known as gorse or furze.

There were no trees or ponds on these ancient links, but there were numerous natural hazards. Certain areas of grass would be grazed bare by livestock. Sheep seeking shelter in hollows or behind hillocks would wear down the turf. The nests and holes of small game would collapse into pits. Wind and water would then erode the topsoil from these areas, revealing the sandy base beneath. Such sandy wastelands, sand and pot bunkers dotted the landscape of a links and menaced many a golf shot.

There were no tees or fairways, as such, nor even putting greens. The putting areas were of the same bristly grass that grew everywhere else. It is speculated that the earliest golfers made rabbit holes their putting cups; if this was the case, perhaps the putting areas were nibbled a little closer by rabbits. But since it was customary to tee one's ball within a club length of the previous cup, a well-manicured putting surface was not known on an early links.

Man had little to do even with maintaining the early courses. Bird droppings and periodic showers from the sea kept the turf healthy. The sandy base beneath the soil provided excellent drainage. Grazing sheep and wild game kept the grass clipped, and if it became too lush, the golfer simply abstained from playing. The sandy wastelands and bunkers went unraked, except when smoothed by random gusts of strong wind.

This then was the earliest form of the golf course. It is possible that the original links were single holes, played out and back to a starting point. But as the popularity of the game increased, and because most linksland was common public land unrestricted by boundaries, golfers would wander onward as far as they could find playable ground before turning back. Thus, there was no standard number of holes for a round of golf. The early links at Leith and Musselburgh had five holes each, North Berwick seven, Prestwick twelve, Gullane thirteen and Montrose twenty-five.

The preeminent course of this early period of golf in Scotland (and still preeminent today) was the old links at St. Andrews. Records indicate that it existed in a primitive form as early as 1414. While some argue that the Old Course is no longer a true links because of the rapid recession of the sea during the last century, it nevertheless began as a totally natural links. The playable areas of grass were bordered by

At the intersections of rivers and ocean, rolling sand dunes formed. Over centuries, golf evolved on these deltas, endowing the game with mystical links to sand and sea. RON WHITTEN

thick patches of heather, and a majority of the natural sand bunkers were hidden from a player's view until he went searching for his ball.

The outline of the hole routing at St. Andrews resembled a shepherd's crook. The links had twelve putting areas, ten of which served the player both on his outward trek and again on the homeward one. This arrangement led to the adoption of the terms "out" and "in" to designate which of the common holes a golfer was playing and eventually to describe the front and back sides of any golf course. The remaining two holes were used only once apiece, as the eleventh and the concluding holes. A round of golf at St. Andrews, therefore, consisted of twenty-two holes, eleven out to the farthest point and eleven back.

Around the middle of the eighteenth century, two innovations to the existing game of golf were introduced. One of these was the creation of private golf clubs whose members continued to play on the ancient public links. The three earliest clubs were The Honourable Company of Edinburgh Golfers (established in 1744 on the Links of Leith), The Society of St. Andrews Golfers (established in 1754) and The Honourable Company of Golfers at Blackheath (the first golf club outside Scotland, established in 1766). Continued growth of private golf clubs contributed significantly to the need for course planners after 1850.

The other important innovation of the eighteenth century occurred

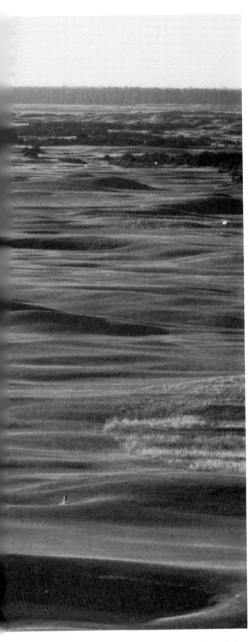

The unmistakable profile of the Old Course at St. Andrews, with a railline hard against one border, broad double greens and wide washboards of fairway pitted with bunkers. COURTESY TAK KANEDA

at St. Andrews. For the first time, man began changing some of nature's handiwork on the Old Course. Many of these changes would have an impact far in the future, when designers began searching for basic principles of golf course architecture.

The first notable change was to the putting areas. Sometime in the 1700s, although it is not known precisely when, greens were instituted at St. Andrews and particular attention was focused on keeping these surfaces adequately turfed.

In 1764, feeling the first four holes were not sufficiently challenging, The Society of St. Andrews Golfers consolidated them into two long holes in order to maintain the integrity of the Old Course. This eliminated two greens and four holes, as each hole was played twice in a round, thus reducing a round of golf at St. Andrews to eighteen holes. (Legend has a more romantic explanation for this change: A bottle of Scotch contained eighteen jiggers. The consumption rate was a jigger per hole. St. Andrews golfers felt the round should conclude with the bottle.)

In 1832 the practice began of cutting two cups into each of the common greens, creating eight "double greens" on which two matches, one heading out and one heading in, could be played at once.

Two years later King William IV was induced to recognize the St. Andrews links to be "Royal and Ancient." The Society of St. Andrews Golfers seized the opportunity to proclaim St. Andrews as the official "Home of Golf" and the Society itself as the foremost authority on the game. Prior to this, the Links of Leith had generally been considered the Home of Golf, but the Honourable Company of Edinburgh Golfers, the true patriarch of private clubs, had disbanded at Leith in 1831. (The Honourable Company reestablished at Musselburgh in 1836 and again at Muirfield in 1891.) Left without its strongest promoter and patron, the Links of Leith soon deteriorated and in 1834 could muster little to dispute St. Andrews's claim to its title.

St. Andrews thus became The Royal and Ancient Golf Club of St. Andrews, and the golfing community afforded it the respect due royalty. Eighteen holes became the standard for any new course because St. Andrews had eighteen holes. Nearly every new course would be compared with St. Andrews to determine its merits and faults. Purists felt it near blasphemy to refer to anything but a linksland course, like St. Andrews, as a links. New terms were invented to describe inland and, by implication, inferior golfing grounds. The first term used was "green," which led to such derivatives as "greenkeeper," "green fee" and "green committee." Later, "golfing-course" became popular, and finally "golf course."

The final hole in an 1858 match of the Society of St. Andrews Golfers. Putting out was Robert Chambers, who, like many prominent golfers in his day, dabbled in course design. He helped stake out the original Hoylake course.
COURTESY *GOLF WORLD*

Its lofty title, however, did not prevent the links at St. Andrews from being further altered. As a public course, in a town devoted to the game, St. Andrews had always seen considerable play. The narrow strip of playable grass was only some forty yards wide, and despite the use of double greens, play became increasingly congested and hazardous. Between 1848 and 1850, the course was widened by replacing the closest crops of heather with turf and by expanding the double greens into huge hundred-yard-wide surfaces. The widened course and huge double greens offered a unique feature: The holes could be played either as the "right-hand" course or in reverse as the "left-hand" course. During the same period of alteration, a new seventeenth green was also built. And in the first recorded instance of such a practice, some artificially created hazards were added to the Old Course.

An accidental but far-reaching result of the course widening was the introduction of the element of strategy into the game of golf. A player was no longer compelled to carry every hazard. He could, if he preferred, play a longer but safer route around a hazard at some sacrifice but without suffering an undue penalty. Previously, St. Andrews, like most links, not only required compulsory carries over most hazards but also penalized, with whins, heather, sandy lies or lost balls, any shot that strayed off line.

Thus, St. Andrews exemplified, in different periods, the two major, competing schools of thought in golf architecture. Originally it was an example of what in modern times is labeled "penal design." But after 1850 the Old Course, despite its blind hazards and fearsome bunkers with equally fearsome names, advanced the theory of "strategic design" by providing direct routes with substantial rewards to the bold player while offering safer but longer routes, at the cost of a stroke or two, to the less daring.

The original natural links of Scotland, especially St. Andrews, form the foundation for the practice of golf course architecture today. Their impressive settings and true golf values exerted a profound influence on golf architecture in the past and no doubt will continue to do so well into the future. In the early development of the game of golf, its players, its rules and its implements all had to adapt to fit the existing conditions of nature as found on the links. As man began laying out and building golf courses, however, the opposite soon resulted. While the avowed purpose of course designers throughout history has been to imitate nature, the actual practice of golf architecture has demanded modifications of existing terrain and soil to create conditions resembling those found on the links.

2
Old Tom and Others

Old Tom Morris, late in life, on the Old Course at St. Andrews. Old Tom did as much as was required of any golf course architect in his day.

Wherever Scots went, they carried their national pastime and the lore of their links with them. The game of golf was introduced sporadically over a number of decades to distant outposts of the British Empire and other parts of the world, first by Scotsmen and later by Englishmen.

It reached England first, where a band of Scots played over a seven-hole course at Blackheath in 1608. By 1758 Molesey Hurst at Hampton was played regularly by the actor David Garrick and was praised as a "very good golfing ground" by a party of his Scottish friends. Another early formal layout was Old Manchester on Kersal Moor, opened around 1818.

Golf was known in America as early as 1779, and a golf club was founded in Charleston, South Carolina, in 1786. A club was formed in Calcutta, India, in 1829 and another at Bombay in 1842. Scottish officers convalescing near the Pyrenees introduced the game to France and built the Continent's oldest course, the Pau Golf Club, in 1856. It was also played in Hong Kong and on the Cape of Good Hope in South Africa by Scottish soldiers and engineers. By the 1870s courses had appeared in Australia and New Zealand, and by 1876 there were five in Canada: at Montreal, Quebec, Toronto, Brantford and Niagara-on-the-Lake.

Most of this early golf was played on rudimentary courses consisting of only a few holes. As golf spread far from Scotland, courses were laid out informally under widely different climatic conditions, in innumerable soil types and on varying terrains. It was soon observed that blind shots, steep climbs, sharp drop-offs, very flat terrain and a superabundance of natural problems such as water and heavy underbrush did not contribute to pleasurable golf. Moreover, none of these early

layouts achieved anything near the golfing satisfaction of the Scottish links, and few lasted beyond their initial season.

Despite its far-ranging introduction, golf was still not widely known or played, even in Scotland, until the first half of the nineteenth century. But by the mid-1800s several events combined to capture the attention of the public in England and Scotland.

A number of widely publicized golf matches were held on the finest of the Scottish links, including St. Andrews and Musselburgh, in the 1840s. The expanding British railway system made it possible for large crowds to travel to and watch such exhibitions. The more venturesome of these spectators soon tried the links themselves.

Then in 1848 the gutta-percha golf ball was invented. The introduction of this rubber-covered ball revolutionized golf. The cost of the old featherie was about four shillings; the new "gutty" cost only a single shilling. In addition, the gutty was much more durable. The featherie would more often than not split open when struck incorrectly; the new gutta-percha would merely dent under the same inexpert blow. Golf thus became a less frustrating and more affordable game.

The gutty led in turn to a revolution in golf club making, for its durability permitted far greater use of ironheaded clubs. Increased use of irons resulted in the unintentional widening of fairways as irons

repeatedly beat down the heather and bent grass grew up in its place.

These factors made golf increasingly popular in the last half of the nineteenth century. Yet its spread was not nearly as rapid as one might expect. By 1857 there were only seventeen golf clubs in Scotland, most of them playing over a handful of ancient, hallowed links. The growth of golf in other parts of Great Britain was even slower. By 1888 there were seventy-three golf courses in Scotland, fifty-seven in England, six in Ireland and two in Wales. More would come in the next decade. The first formal courses in England after the introduction of the gutty were Westward Ho! (1864), Wimbledon (1865) and Hoylake (1869). Early formal courses in Ireland included Royal Belfast (1881), Royal Dublin (1885), Portrush (1888), Lahinch (1892), Portmarnock (1894) and Sligo (1894).

The earliest records of golf course designers and their works date from this period of growth, the latter part of the nineteenth century. The first recognized designer was Allan Robertson, the longtime professional and clubmaker of St. Andrews, who died in 1859. Robertson is usually credited with supervising the widening of the Old Course and with the creation of its seventeenth green. He also did a ten-hole course at Barry, Angus, Scotland, in 1842, which forms the basis for the present championship course known as Carnoustie; and he laid

out links in other parts of Scotland. Allan Robertson's brother David emigrated to Australia in 1848, introduced golf to that continent and planned a few of Australia's earliest courses.

Old records indicate that most people turned to professionals like Allan Robertson to provide them with new golfing grounds. It seemed natural that the men who taught the game, made the implements and were the most proficient players should also lay out the courses. In the 1850s several clubs hired individuals to maintain the turf of their existing links and greens. These "greenkeepers" were soon called upon to help establish new golf courses. More often than not, the professional and the greenkeeper at a course were one and the same person. This person sometimes took on a third hat as a course designer.

Among the greenkeepers and professionals who laid out courses in the British Isles during the last third of the nineteenth century were the twins Willie and Jamie Dunn (of Musselburgh and Royal Black-

heath), Willie's son Tom (of Musselburgh and later Wimbledon), Charles Hunter (of Prestwick), George Lowe (of St. Anne's-on-the-Sea), the brothers Tom and George Morris (of St. Andrews), the brothers Willie and Mungo Park (of Musselburgh), Douglas Rolland (of Elie and later Malvern), Archie Simpson (of Royal Aberdeen) and David Strath (of North Berwick).

These early course planners did their work on the spot, never resorting to a drawing board, with most courses laid out in a few days or less. They selected natural green sites, plotted holes to these sites and then arranged the holes into a circuit. Little construction was undertaken, for the natural contours of the land were seldom altered. Existing hazards, including roads, hedgerows and even stone walls,

Above: The Road Hole at St. Andrews, perhaps the most feared golf hole in the world, and (right) Allan Robertson, the man responsible for its design. Robertson's work in positioning a long shallow green next to the cinder road and guarding it with hillocks and devastating bunker is the earliest recorded expression of golf architecture. COURTESY *GOLF DIGEST*

were incorporated, and existing turf was utilized. Except for assuring that a supply of sand for top-dressing the putting greens was close at hand, these designers rarely considered future maintenance.

Most of these same men were active in modifying existing courses, both the famous links and those rudimentary layouts where golf had been played informally for centuries. As the game gained in popularity, modifications to even the hallowed links became necessary. The courses could not accommodate increasing crowds of players and became dangerous. Alterations were desired when the eighteen-hole course became standard. Greater length was also required because the new gutty outflew the old featherie. Sometimes the professional acted as a consultant, ratifying modifications to existing courses already proposed by club members. Whatever the role, the execution of changes to the ancient links by a select individual was important to the future of golf architecture, for it established the tradition that clubs would seek the talent and expertise of recognized designers.

Despite the knowledge that greenkeepers, professionals and others possessed, and the fact that most of them learned the game on the ancient Scottish links, most of their courses would be at best termed "dismal." Tom Simpson, himself an architect and student of course

Play it as it lies. The rule probably originated at St. Andrews and its dreaded whins. COLLECTION RON WHITTEN

architecture, was prompted to christen the years from 1885 to 1900 the "Dark Ages of Golf Architecture." Simpson wrote:

> They failed to reproduce any of the features of the courses on which they were bred and born, or to realize the principles on which they had been made. Their imagination took them no farther than the conception of flat gun-platform greens, invariably oblong, round or square, supported by railway embankment sides or batters. . . . The bunkers that were constructed on the fairways may be described as rectangular ramparts of a peculiarly obnoxious type, stretching at regular intervals across the course, and having no architectural value whatever. . .

Even the work of Old Tom Morris, called "Old Tom" to distinguish him from his famous son "Young Tom," was sometimes disappointing. A native of St. Andrews, Old Tom apprenticed under Allan Robertson and then served as greenkeeper and professional at the Prestwick links before returning, after Robertson's death, to serve in the same capacity at the Old Course. The most prominent name in the world of golf in the late 1800s, Old Tom Morris was called upon to modify a number of the ancient links. He also created new courses on superb linksland. But his results were sometimes curious. For example, his layout at

The big, deep natural bunkers at St. Andrews were neither raked nor drained. COLLECTION RON WHITTEN

Westward Ho! (Royal North Devon) originally had twelve holes that crossed one another.

In defense of Old Tom, he probably did as much as was required of any golf course designer of that time, and he produced layouts that were functional for the game he knew so well. The statement of Horace Hutchinson in 1898 that the laying out of a golf course was "a wonderfully easy business needing very little special training" was not naive. It reflected the prevailing attitude of the time.

Old Tom Morris did make lasting contributions to the development of golf course architecture. He was apparently the first to ignore the traditional "loop" routing of nine holes out and nine back. For example, his routing of the course at Royal County Down, which opened in 1891, utilized two nines with each starting and finishing at the clubhouse. Moreover, the nines ran in different directions: the front nine counterclockwise, the back clockwise. And only once did three successive holes play in the same direction. Such sophisticated routing took maximum advantage of wind conditions, forcing the player during a round to confront it from all angles.

It is quite possible that Old Tom has been blamed for changes that others made in his courses after they were opened for play. The "gun-platform" greens mentioned by Simpson may not have been Morris's creation; he was known to have utilized natural sites for his greens. The reputations of designers are plagued to this day by changes in their layouts made without their knowledge or consent, which upset strategy, balance and, in extreme cases, the continuity of the round.

Another of the early course designers, Tom Dunn, has been accused of lacking any imagination. In retrospect, it seems reasonable to conclude that Dunn strove for the functional in an age before funds and techniques were available for creating imaginative features. His great contribution was in designing inexpensive layouts for the multitudes who were taking up the game.

The latter half of the nineteenth century did see the introduction of a great many developments in turf maintenance. Foremost, of course, was the creation of the profession of greenkeeper, also called custodian or curator. The first turf cutter used to cut holes for putting cups was invented in 1849 at Royal Aberdeen. Lining the hole with a metal cup to prevent its disintegration began about 1874 at the Crail Golf Club. The lawn mower was invented in 1830 but was not widely used on golf courses until decades later. Prior to its use, most inland courses in climates where bluegrasses predominated could only be played in autumn or winter, or during droughts, for at other times the turf was too lush. The practice of watering the putting surfaces originated in

By the start of the twentieth century, putting surfaces at St. Andrews were remarkably well maintained, considering the primitive equipment available at the time. COLLECTION RON WHITTEN

the 1880s, and by 1894 St. Andrews had sunk a well next to each of its massive greens to insure a steady source of water.

Despite the best efforts of greenkeepers, however, most of the inland golf courses created in this period suffered a common malady. Their turf was rock hard in summer and mushy in winter. The rolling of greens, a beneficial practice on the sandy links, proved disastrous on these clay soils. Except for those laid out in natural linksland, the courses of the late 1880s in the British Isles were built on land totally unsuited for playing the game of golf. And with agronomic knowledge, construction techniques and equipment so primitive, it was impossible to modify existing terrain and soil.

3

The Heathlands Quartet

Herbert Fowler took his time building courses in the Heathlands. Golf design required exhaustive studies of the ground, he later wrote, and badly placed greens would never command the respect of golfers. COLLECTION RON WHITTEN

Dozens of sorry inland courses built on impervious clay soils convinced most golf purists that only the ancient links could provide excellent golf. But a few golf course prospectors were unconvinced and kept searching for suitable inland terrain comparable to the best linksland. Their search was fruitful, for at the turn of the century they unearthed a mother lode of fine golfing land less than fifty miles south and west of London.

Here were the "heathlands," with well-drained, rock-free, sandy soil in gently undulating terrain. This was true golf country, and its discovery was a major step in the development of golf course architecture. Many of the world's greatest courses have since been created on land similar to that of the heaths, which, except for the presence of trees, is not unlike that of the links. The long delay in discovery of the heathlands, despite their proximity to London, is not difficult to understand. The heathlands were covered with an undergrowth of heather, rhododendrons, Scotch fir and pines. Only a fool, it seemed, would spend time building a golf course in such a wasteland when vast meadows were available for the purpose.

The "fools" that did build courses in the heathlands became the most prominent golf architects of their day. Four names in particular stand out: Willie Park, Jr., J. F. Abercromby, H. S. Colt and W. Herbert Fowler. Their prominence was due in part to their vision in recognizing the true potential of this unlikely terrain and in part to their ability to shape the land into splendid golf holes.

And shape the land they did. Heather and other undergrowth were removed from most areas earmarked as playable. Many trees were cleared, although all four architects integrated trees into their designs (a practice unknown before their time) and thus created strategic and aesthetic assets not available to the old links. Earth was moved and contoured into green sites, tees and hazards. These men never moved earth when natural green sites and satisfactory contours could be found; but where nature was deficient, they were not reluctant to make alterations. The cleared areas were then prepared and seeded or sodded, and the architects took special interest in the types of grasses that would be planted.

All these tasks would seem to be modest undertakings in modern times, but in the early 1900s they called for new techniques in course construction. Considering the primitive state of available construction equipment, the results achieved by these designers and builders were extraordinary.

The first pioneering architect of this era was Willie Park, Jr. A superior golfer who won the Open twice, Park had been active in planning and modifying courses since 1890, first with his father, Willie Park, and then on his own. But it was not until 1901 that Willie demonstrated what revolutionary aspects of course design could be accomplished when new methods of course building were used. With the openings of the original course at Sunningdale in Berkshire, England, in the heart of the heathlands, and Huntercombe Golf Club, some fifteen miles northwest, he proved what he had written in 1896:

> The laying out of a golf course is by no means a simple task. . . . Great skill and judgement and a thorough acquaintance with the game are absolutely necessary to determine the best position for the respective holes and teeing grounds and the situation of the hazards.

Sunningdale and Huntercombe stood in stark contrast to the countless geometric layouts with square greens, steep banks and stern cross bunkers previously built on whatever terrain existed. Park's designs featured tees that were built up and landing areas that were lowered. Most of his greens were raised above the fairway level, had gentle shapes, were large and undulating. One green, the thirteenth at Huntercombe, was two-tiered. Both courses featured bold, manmade hazards, clearly visible to a golfer from the tee. Sunningdale even had an artificial pond.

The two courses established a reputation for Willie Park, Jr., that never diminished. Sir Guy Campbell, a fine midtwentieth-century designer, felt Park was the first really capable golf course architect, the man who set the standard by which those who followed developed and amplified the art. Tom Simpson also gave Willie high marks, although he felt that Willie persisted throughout his career in placing bunkers

Right: Willie Park, Jr., perhaps the first true genius of golf course architecture and (below) his first masterpiece, the Old Course at Sunningdale outside London, which featured elevated tees, strategic bunkering, carefully constructed greens and even a manmade water hazard. COLLECTION RON WHITTEN; TOM DOAK

only for the purpose of catching a poor shot. Herbert Warren Wind wrote that Park had a sure touch for "devising golf holes that looked natural and played well."

Park's later works continued to support his reputation. During his wide and active travels as a professional designer, Willie planned courses throughout the British Isles and Europe. He also laid out an estimated seventy courses in the United States and Canada, the best known being Maidstone on Long Island, the North course at the Olympia Fields Country Club near Chicago, Woodway Country Club in Connecticut and Calgary Golf and Country Club in Alberta, Canada. Though at times ably assisted by his brothers, Willie was so busy

as an architect that in the end, it is said, he literally worked himself to death. He died in 1925.

Willie Park, Jr., had done a preliminary routing on another early heathlands course, Worplesdon Golf Club in Surrey. But the course was completed by J. F. Abercromby, considered by midtwentieth-century course designer Frank Pennink and others to be one of the finest golf architects ever to practice in Britain. Like Park, Abercromby built his reputation on the heathlands. Unlike Park, "Aber" did very little work elsewhere.

Besides Worplesdon, Abercromby laid out several other courses in Surrey. Coombe Hill Golf Club, once considered "the finest and most artistic example of artificial construction work," opened in 1908. He also did both the Old Course and, after World War I, the New Course at the Addington Golf Club. Abercromby spent most of his life as president of Addington and constantly sought to improve on his work there. He died just before World War II, and unfortunately his New Course was abandoned by the club just after the war. But Addington's Old Course survived and has been highly regarded even in recent times.

H. S. Colt was the third of the revolutionaries who dared to carve golf courses out of the heather and pines of central England. Colt had his first design experience in 1894, when he laid out the Rye Golf Club on the southeast coast of England. But during the next half-dozen years, he was content to remain a solicitor and play a little competitive golf.

Upon the opening of Sunningdale in 1901, he became the club's secretary, and his interest in course design was soon renewed. Impressed with the basic design of Sunningdale, Colt supervised many changes during his twelve-year stint at the club. He replaced much of the heather that bounded the fairways with planted pines. He also altered and expanded the course to compensate for the greater distances golfers achieved with the rubber-cored golf ball. (This new ball was invented by Coburn Haskell of the United States in 1898 and gained acceptance in Great Britain in 1902 when Alex Herd used it in winning The Open. It flew some 15 to 20 percent farther than the gutty and thus necessitated lengthening and other alterations of existing courses.) In the process of expanding Sunningdale, Colt developed many of the exhilarating elevated tees that still exist on the older course today.

While serving at Sunningdale, Colt began planning courses in the surrounding heathlands for other clubs. Among them were Stoke Poges Golf Club (which opened in 1908), Swinley Forest Golf Club

A rare photograph of another architectural genius, H. S. Colt (second from left), at St. Cloud in France. To Colt's left is construction superintendent Charles Harris, whose nephew John Harris would later become a golf architect. In his day, no architect was more technically proficient that Harry Colt. COLLECTION RON WHITTEN

(1910) and thirty-six holes for St. George's Hill Golf Club (1913), of which eighteen survive. Swinley Forest, one of the first courses ever routed through a thick forest of trees, was considered by Colt himself to be his best design or, as he modestly put it, "the least bad course" he had ever done. He also experimented with the concept of integrating golf courses with housing and planned several such arrangements.

Colt was particularly adept at establishing turf in any environs. He could also be relied upon to make regular inspections of his work long after its completion to assist with the normal problems experienced by infant courses. He is said to have been the first to use a drawing board consistently to plan course designs, and he was apparently also the first to include tree-planting instructions. H. S. Colt was the first full-time golf course architect who had not previously been a professional golfer. He remained an amateur all his life and was a fine amateur competitor.

Colt, like Willie Park, Jr., did not always incorporate strategic concepts into his golf designs; but in his early British courses he did restore a strategic relationship between the placement of fairway and greenside bunkers, a "links" concept missing from most inland courses.

Colt also traveled far and wide to design courses. The majority of his work was done in the British Isles and Europe. Although the partners in his design firm, particularly Charles Alison, did most of the work that bears his name in North America, Colt did make at least two extended trips to the United States and Canada. He had a major part in planning courses for the Toronto Golf Club (1912) and the Hamilton Golf and Country Club (1914), both in Ontario, Canada, and the new course for the Country Club of Detroit, Michigan (1914). At home, his designs include a second eighteen, the New Course, at Sunningdale; two courses for the Wentworth Golf Club; and two remodeled courses for Royal Portrush in Northern Ireland. But perhaps a true measure of the respect in which he was held was his selection to design the third course, the Eden, at St. Andrews, which opened in 1912.

During this era, yet another Briton set out in the heathlands to build an ideal course. In 1902 W. Herbert Fowler, who had longed to design a golf course, was invited by his brother-in-law to do so on property at Tadsworth in Surrey. Fowler spent two years planning his course at a time when two days were still sufficient for many course builders. Initially he rode through the heather on horseback searching for proper green sites and then tracked each hole backward from there.

His creation, which opened in 1904, was called Walton Heath; it attracted even more attention than Park's Sunningdale had three years earlier. A special train brought dignitaries to the course, and its inaugural match was an exhibition by Vardon, Taylor and Braid, golf's "Great Triumvirate."

Fowler soon found his talents in sufficient demand to practice architecture full-time. A somewhat despotic man, he quickly felt the need to put his hand to a traditional linksland course, and in 1908 his total redesign of the Royal North Devon Golf Club at Westward Ho! was completed. It, too, met with immediate acclaim.

Fowler remodeled the Saunton links, across the bay from North Devon, and laid out two more heathlands courses, the Red and the Blue, at the Berkshire Golf Club. All of these opened after World War I, by which time Fowler was busy laying out courses on both coasts of the United States. One of his most impressive American works is Eastward Ho!, which one suspects he had a hand in naming, in Chatham, Massachusetts, on Cape Cod. Eastward Ho! combines the rolling terrain and ocean setting of a links with the tree-lined fairways and elevated greens of a heathlands course.

Before Colt, most golf designers avoided heavily treed sites. But Colt, at places like Swinley Forest, prowled through forests and had thousands of trees felled to expose wonderful golf holes. COURTESY GOLF DIGEST

Herbert Fowler was perhaps the most naturally gifted architect of his time. "I never knew anyone who could more swiftly take in the possibilities of a piece of ground," Bernard Darwin once wrote, "and I think his clients thought, quite unjustly, that he had not taken sufficient pains, because he could see so clearly and work so fast."

The original course at Walton Heath (Fowler built a second one there after the war) particularly impressed one of its first players, James Braid. Braid became the club's first professional upon its opening in 1904 and remained there the rest of his life. While Braid had no hand in changing the courses at Walton Heath, he was a five-time Open champion and thus received a great many requests to design

courses. Though it was always an avocation with him, Braid took his designing seriously and stubbornly refused to change a design once it had been planned. He disliked even the suggestion that some hole be altered. In the beginning he did little more than stake out a rough layout and instruct a committee on how to properly construct and maintain the course. But he soon began conducting inspection trips to his courses, perhaps to insure that no one did change his designs. By the 1920s Braid was considered a most competent architect.

James Braid was responsible for planning hundreds of courses, many of them on paper. His most prominent works, to which he paid personal attention, include the remodeled courses at Carnoustie Golf Club and Blairgowrie Golf Club, the East and West eighteens of Dalmahoy Golf Club, and the King's and Queen's courses at Gleneagles Hotel, all in Scotland.

Another of the Great Triumvirate, John Henry Taylor, also laid out a number of courses in the early 1900s. After the war, Taylor joined forces with Frederic G. Hawtree, a greenkeeper who had founded the British Golf Greenkeepers Association in 1912. The firm of Hawtree and Taylor designed some fifty-five courses in the British Isles and remodeled a similar number. They paid particular attention to the promotion of publicly owned courses, founding the Artisan Golfers Association and the National Association of Public Golf Courses, and they conceived and planned England's first municipal courses before World War I. Their most prominent work was the remodeling of the Royal Birkdale Golf Club into a championship course in 1931.

The third member of the Triumvirate, Harry Vardon, did a number of course designs but fewer than Braid or Taylor, partly because he spent many years before the war in ill health. Two other prominent architects, Alister Mackenzie and C. H. Alison, began their careers as assistants to H. S. Colt during the heathlands era. Their greatest creations would come after World War I.

Although the period lasted only fifteen years, from 1900 to 1914, it was a most important time in the history of golf course architecture. For the first time, golf architecture became a profession rather than simply a sideline for a club professional or greenkeeper.

Men like Park, Abercromby, Colt and Fowler proved on the heaths that exciting and pleasurable golf could be produced in any locale so long as proper techniques in course building were used. These techniques included on-site study of the terrain, detailed plans developed on a drawing board and on-site supervision and inspections once construction began.

They also realized that where a satisfactory natural contour could be

utilized in the design of a hole, it should be so used. But where none existed, natural-appearing sites for greens, tees, landing areas and even bunkers could be created by men.

The competent designers in this period recognized that aesthetics are an intrinsic part of the game of golf. When designing a course, these men subdued harsh natural features. They incorporated trees into the design of certain holes. They abhorred geometrically shaped greens and hazards and built theirs to blend into the surrounding terrain.

Last, it was in this period that the strategic school of golf course design began to influence some people. Most of the courses built in the British Isles between 1900 and 1914, including those of Park, Ab-

ercromby, Colt and Fowler, were still of the penal variety. But particular holes on some of the more prominent courses could certainly have been classified as strategic.

This is attributable in no small part to the enduring influence of the Old Course at St. Andrews. Park, Abercromby, Colt and Fowler all played much of their golf at the Old Course, as did many other designers in the British Isles. It was still the course to which every other course was compared. And its subtle strategies were only then beginning to be realized and appreciated.

The continuing significance of St. Andrews in this period was apparent in revisions of the golf course at Woking. One hole in particular, the fourth, had a considerable influence on at least one golf course architect and did a great deal to educate the golfing public in fundamental design principles.

Woking Golf Club had been originally laid out by Tom Dunn in 1893 in Surrey, England. Ironically, it was right in the center of the heathlands, and had it shown any imaginative design at all, it would surely have attracted the attention that Sunningdale did years later. Instead, it was one of those functional but unexciting courses with square greens, giant cross bunkers bisecting many fairways and pot bunkers peppering the landscape.

But in the early twentieth century, Woking was remodeled by two of the club's more domineering members, Stuart Paton and John L. Low. Neither had previously practiced architecture, but both were fine golfers, especially Low; both had a great interest in the game and were to write eloquently on it; and both had an abiding passion for St. Andrews. They set about to pattern Woking after the Old Course. In doing so, they had sense enough not to try to imitate it but rather to recreate certain playing strategies presented by the Old Course.

Paton paid particular attention to Woking's greens and over the years added various subtle slopes and mounds until finally not a single flat, square green remained. He and Low also did a great deal in rebunkering the course. It was one particular bunker, or pair of bunkers, that made such an impact upon club member Tom Simpson, who would later design many courses himself.

The fourth hole at Woking resembled the sixteenth at St. Andrews in that both were straightaway par 4s with a rail line running along the right. Paton furthered the resemblance by placing a pair of bunkers in the center of the fourth fairway at the landing area, in the manner of the "Principal's Nose" at the Old Course's sixteenth. Many years later Simpson recalled hearing the outrage and condemnation of the revised hole by his fellow members at Woking and wrote:

I went out, fully prepared to find myself in complete agreement with the views which had been so eloquently expressed. So far, however, from agreeing, I realised for the first time, as soon as I saw this much-maligned hazard, that the true line to the hole should not always be the centre of the fairway, and the placing of a bunker had a far more serious and useful purpose than merely the punishing of a bad shot. This led me to see the importance of golf architecture as an art as well as a science.

Paton and Low never designed or remodeled another course, although they spent years refining Woking. Yet they deserve mention in any history of golf course architecture, for they demonstrated, perhaps before anyone else, that it was possible on an inland course to challenge a golfer in more than one way, in much the same fashion as the great links of Scotland.

4

The Emigrants

Young Donald Ross around 1901, fresh from St. Andrews and ready to embark upon what would become an architecture career of nearly fifty years. Throughout it, he never got rid of the hat. COLLECTION RON WHITTEN

It is clear that golf found its way from Great Britain to North America, but when and by whom is not certain. There were golf clubs in South Carolina and Georgia soon after the American Revolution, but there is no definitive evidence that golf was actually played at them despite their titles. The oldest authenticated golf clubs in North America were Canadian—the Royal Montreal formed in 1873 and the Royal Quebec in 1874. There were many hunt, field and polo clubs in America established long before these, but they featured golf at later dates, further complicating claims as America's oldest golf club.

The title of Father of American Golf has generally been given to John Reid, a Scot who settled in Yonkers, New York. In the early spring of 1888 Reid and several hardy friends staked out a rough three-hole golf course near his home. Later that year they built a six-hole course in a nearby pasture and formed a golfing organization that they unabashedly named the St. Andrews Golf Club. Over the years, St. Andrews has persisted in calling itself the oldest golf club in the United States.

The claim of St. Andrews, however, is disputed by many. The Foxburg (Pennsylvania) Country Club maintains it was established on a nine-hole course laid out by Joseph M. Fox in 1887, while the Dorset (Vermont) Field Club was apparently in existence by 1886 and possessed a functional course. Andrew Bell of Burlington, Iowa, who was educated in Scotland, returned home in 1881 with golf clubs under each arm and proceeded to build a four-hole course on his father's property. In 1882 George Grant and his nephew, Lionel Torrin, both English tea merchants, laid out nine holes on the estate of Russell

Montague in White Sulphur Springs, West Virginia, and called their creation the Oakhurst Golf Links.

J. Hamilton Gillespie, a transplanted Scot, batted a gutty about what is now downtown Sarasota, Florida, as early as 1883 and later laid out some of that state's first courses. English golf writer Horace Hutchinson claimed to have introduced the game to members of the Meadow Brook Hunt Club of Hempstead, New York, sometime before 1887— to no avail, he added. At about the same time, Alex Findlay, still another Scot, introduced the game to Omaha, Nebraska.

Charles Blair Macdonald, who had studied as a youth at the University of St. Andrews, told of playing the game at a homemade course on deserted Douglas Field upon his return to Chicago as early as 1875. An avid promoter of the game, Macdonald built a small, seven-hole course at Lake Forest, Illinois, in 1892. He then constructed a nine-hole course for the Chicago Golf Club at Belmont, Illinois, which he rapidly expanded to a modest eighteen. Then, in 1895, he laid out the nation's premier first-rate eighteen-hole course, also for the Chicago Golf Club, at Wheaton, Illinois.

Once golf was introduced to America, its spread was swift and sure. By 1896 there were over eighty courses in the United States, and by 1900 there were 982, with at least one in each of the forty-five states. In fact, by the turn of the century courses in the United States outnumbered those in Britain, although none was comparable in quality to the famous links of Scotland nor to the heathland courses that would appear in England in the early years of the twentieth century.

One professional imported to work on a course in America was Willie Dunn, of the Musselburgh Dunns, called "Young Willie" to distinguish him from "Old Willie," his father. Young Willie, who had been trained by his famous and much older brother, Tom Dunn, was lured over by a rich syndicate to serve as professional and greenkeeper to Shinnecock Hills Golf Club. This club, at Southampton, New York, had been established in 1891, but its twelve-hole course by Scotsman Willie Davis was far from perfect. Soon after his arrival, Dunn added a nine-hole women's course and in 1895 integrated this with the main course to make a full eighteen holes. It included a number of blind shots and a railroad line that came into play. Unfortunately, Willie was never given an adequate budget to maintain it, but Shinnecock Hills was still a cut above the typical layout appearing on the American countryside. It was built on links-type land near the sea and was reconstructed only after Dunn had devised a well-conceived design. It should have served as a model for others wanting to build a course; but because it was inaccessible, located far out on Long Island, few golf

The finals of the 1912 U.S. Amateur at Chicago Golf Club, a course C. B. Macdonald designed to approximate as nearly as possible the arrangement and distances of the Old Course at St. Andrews. COURTESY *GOLF WORLD*

developers spent the time or money to visit Shinnecock to see what a golf course should look like.

It was a shame they didn't, for woeful courses were appearing everywhere. People who could barely play the game and who knew nothing about building a golf course were doing just that to meet the demand. George Wright, for one, laid out a primitive course in Boston's Franklin Park. The owner of a Wright & Ditson sporting goods store, he no doubt felt the availability of a course would increase sales of his newly imported clubs and balls. Henry Hewett, a railroad engineer from Paterson, New Jersey, designed a course for the new Tuxedo (New York) Golf Club, and polo fancier Lemuel Altemus built one for the Devon Golf Club in Philadelphia. In the process of laying it out, he rode around on a polo pony, in order, he said, to secure proper driving distances.

Perhaps because of the abundance of "amateur designers," Young Willie Dunn remained in America, teaching the game, making equipment and laying out several more courses for affluent clientele. He also spread the word back to the Old Country that the United States was a plum waiting to be picked.

Consequently, a good many of Willie's friends and acquaintances flocked to the United States. He even lent some of them the travel fare. Not all came to design golf courses, by any means. Some were club-makers, some greenkeepers, some teachers. A few considered themselves golf Renaissance Men, able to do any task related to the game. Others, being novices to golf, could do none of the jobs. But they came, for Young Willie Dunn became convinced that the real future of golf lay not in Scotland, nor Britain, nor Europe, but in America.

Among those he personally summoned were his two nephews, Seymour and John Duncan Dunn. After working with two sporting goods firms, J.D. landed the job of professional at Ardsley (New York) Country Club and later became golfer-in-chief for the Florida West Coast Railroad. In that capacity he designed and constructed several courses along the railroad's route in Florida, including the original course at what later became known as the Belleview Biltmore Hotel. J.D.'s chief rival at this time was Alex Findlay, the Scot from Omaha,

Early American courses were graded, shaped and contoured by teams of men and flat horse-drawn metal scoops known as pans or scrapers. COLLECTION RON WHITTEN

The Hell Bunker of the original Shinnecock Hills. A rectangular coffin of sand fronted by a mound, it typified the geometric style of early American golf design. COLLECTION RON WHITTEN

who was now golfer-in-chief of the Florida East Coast Railroad. Findlay laid out resort courses up and down his company's route, which stretched from St. Augustine to Palm Beach. Both men later designed numerous other courses across the nation.

Willie's second nephew, Seymour, arrived in New York at the age of twelve and became J.D.'s assistant at Ardsley. After schooling at Lawrenceville, New Jersey, he returned to Europe periodically to occupy professional berths and to plan and build courses with his father's help, among them layouts for the kings of Belgium and Italy. He subsequently built numerous courses in the northeastern United States. He also established the first indoor golf schools in both Britain and America, the latter said to be the largest ever attempted. He eventually settled as professional at the Lake Placid Club in upstate New York.

Willie Dunn also sent for W. H. "Bert" Way, who had served with him on his brother Tom's construction crews in Europe. Way, a native of Westward Ho! in England, brought his brothers Ernest and Jack along. Bert ultimately settled in Ohio and built several Midwestern courses, including the original Detroit Golf Club and Country Club of Detroit courses, the original Firestone Country Club course in Akron, Ohio, and his home course, Mayfield Country Club in Cleveland, where he introduced John D. Rockefeller to the game. Ernest worked as a pro-greenkeeper in Detroit until after World War I, when he took up course design. He planned several courses in Michigan, including Grosse Ile Country Club and Pontiac Country Club. Jack, the youngest, worked as a pro-greenkeeper all his life, although he effected numerous design changes at Canterbury Country Club near Cleveland, where he served for many years.

William H. Tucker, another Englishman who had worked with the

Early seed-bed preparation was also done by intensive hand labor. It wasn't unusual for construction to take two years or longer before a course was ready to play. COLLECTION RON WHITTEN

Dunns in Europe, also came at the behest of Willie. He soon landed jobs designing and building nine holes for the Maidstone Club on Long Island and remodeling the latest layout of the St. Andrews Golf Club. Before his death in 1954, Tucker designed or remodeled over 120 courses. His son, William H. Tucker, Jr., joined him in the business in later years and the firm created courses in the Midwest, the Pacific Northwest and the Southwest. Tucker was also a turfgrass consultant of note.

Of course, not everyone agreed with Willie Dunn that the future of golf would be in America. Willie himself had more than once speculated that its future might rest in France, where his brother Tom devoted a good deal of effort. Alex Findlay's brother Fred went to Australia and designed several courses down under before moving to the United States. Willie Smith of the Carnoustie family came first to the United States but after winning the 1899 U.S. Open, settled in Mexico, where he built that country's earliest courses, beginning with San Pedro. Laurie Waters, a protégé of Old Tom Morris, left St. Andrews for South Africa where, as an expert player, he was a pioneer course designer.

But the destination of a majority of golfing emigrants from Britain at the turn of the century was the United States. Among others that came were:

• Charles Maud, an Englishman who relocated in California. With the assistance of Colonel W. E. Pedley, he designed and built that state's first course, the nine-hole Pedley Farms in Arlington, which ultimately became the Victoria Golf Club.

• Robert D. Pryde, a Scot who settled in Connecticut. Besides coaching the original Yale golf teams, Pryde designed the original New Haven Country Club, Race Brook Country Club and others.

• Robert White, a native of St. Andrews, who would lay out many a course across the United States during a fifty-year career. White originally came to America to study agronomy. He developed a reputation as a fine turfgrass consultant, and many clubs retained him in that capacity. He also served as the first president of the Professional Golfers Association of America when it was organized in 1916.

• H. J. Tweedie, a native of Hoylake, England, who landed a job along with his brother, L.P., running a Spalding sporting goods store in Chicago. Both men were fine amateur golfers, and Herbert James found time to lay out many early Chicago-area courses, including Midlothian, Flossmoor and Glenview country clubs.

• James and Robert Foulis, brothers who were born and raised in St. Andrews and who learned the game from Old Tom Morris. James came to America in 1895, and Robert joined him a year later. James, who won the 1896 U.S. Open, spent most of his time as pro-greenkeeper at a series of Chicago-area clubs. He also designed a number of courses around Chicago, including Hinsdale, and he consulted on Onwentsia. Robert eventually settled in St. Louis, where he designed many area courses, most notably the first version of the Bellerive Country Club, where he served as professional for many years.

• Willie Watson, a Scot who arrived in 1898 to build the Minikahda Club course in Minneapolis to the plans of Robert Foulis. Watson remained at Minikahda as its summer professional, wintering in Pasadena, California. He became a well-known course designer in both regions, creating such courses as Interlachen in Minneapolis and Hillcrest in Los Angeles.

Two Scots who came to America to live and work, Donald J. Ross and Tom Bendelow, deserve special mention. Ross, a onetime golf student of Old Tom Morris, hired on as professional at Oakley Country Club in Boston in 1898, having been persuaded to emigrate by Professor Robert Willson of Harvard during a visit to Dornoch. James

Tufts, of the American Soda Fountain Company, soon convinced Ross to work as winter professional at a new resort he was building in North Carolina. The resort was named Pinehurst; once Ross arrived, he set about rebuilding and expanding the lackluster nine-hole layout that Tufts had installed. He subsequently built three additional courses at Pinehurst, No. 2, which opened in 1907, No. 3 (1910) and No. 4 (1919).

Despite their sand greens, the courses at Pinehurst impressed many affluent patrons from the North, and Donald Ross soon found his talents as a golf course designer in great demand. Ross is often said to have been the first full-time course designer in America, although he retained his position as professional and later golf manager at Pinehurst until his death in 1948. He was to become the most prominent golf architect of his day and one of the most respected.

Tom Bendelow, also from Scotland, quit a steady job with the New York *Herald* in 1895 to join the sporting goods firm of A. G. Spalding & Bros. as a "design consultant." In that capacity Bendelow claimed to

Left: An aerial view of Pinehurst, North Carolina, in the days when its courses still had sand greens. But Donald Ross protected those sand greens (above) with elaborate bunkering, soft mounds and gentle swales. COURTESY *GOLF WORLD*; COLLECTION RON WHITTEN

have laid out hundreds of courses for clients who sought assistance from the huge sporting goods firm. He was, without doubt, the most prolific course builder in America in the early years of the century.

Tom was apparently a character, and quite a few colorful tales have developed concerning him. The most widely circulated but least embroidered concerned his method of design, which was dubbed "eighteen stakes on a Sunday afternoon." In fact, Bendelow did lay out a considerable number of courses somewhat in this manner, although he used more than eighteen stakes. He would stake out a first tee; pace off a hundred yards or so, stake out a cross bunker; pace on farther, stake out another bunker or some mounds; march on farther and stake out his green site. After doing this nine times, he would leave instructions with the club on how to properly build and maintain the course and then be on his way.

Golf historians have been aghast at such an operation, but it is an error to assume that Tom Bendelow was in any way a con artist in an era of otherwise competent, conscientious golf architects. In reality, Tom was widely respected as an architect in his later years and wrote and lectured on the subject at the University of Illinois. The fact is, in the late 1890s and very early 1900s, nearly all the golf courses in America were laid out in such a fashion. Designers of that time, like Alex Findlay, Robert White and even Donald Ross on occasion, practiced this method. It was all club members expected and all they were

willing to pay for: The going rate was $25 per job, regardless of how long it took to stake the layout.

Few designers remained to supervise construction of their designs. The greenkeeper hired by the club, most often a Britisher, would actually build the course and over the years refine it, often changing even the designer's routing concept, which had been recorded only by stakes long since removed. Additional features were undoubtedly added to these courses by Scottish pro-greenkeepers after visits home to the links, for many an early northern professional spent a winter now and again in Scotland. Individual greenkeepers, therefore, had as much to do with this early American course design as did men credited with the designing, for if a designer was even brought in, he often did nothing more than route the layout with stakes.

Consequently, most American courses in this period were primitive compared with those in Britain and Scotland. Most were built quickly and inexpensively. In one of the numerous moves of New York's St. Andrews Golf Club, only two days were required to lay out and "build" a nine-hole course. The Country Club (Brookline, Massachusetts)

The Johnny Appleseed of American golf, Tom Bendelow (far left), toured the country for years sowing golf courses in countless communities. COURTESY TOM AND JACK BENDELOW

Stark earthen berms were a popular hazard utilized on early American courses, including (top right) the St. Augustine (Fla.) Golf Links and (bottom right) the original course at Merion Cricket Club near Philadelphia. COLLECTION RON WHITTEN

budgeted $50 to build its first six-hole course. Construction normally consisted of removing fences, clearing away surface stones and mowing the grass. The stones were often piled into mounds and, when covered with dirt, were thought to make perfectly good hazards. These sharp mounds, nicknamed "chocolate drops," became the fashion for a time and were even added to courses which had no stones to cover. Little islands of unmowed vegetation were often left in the bunkers of these early courses. These "dragon's teeth" added nothing to the aesthetic values but did contribute to player frustration and a high rate of lost balls.

Some early layouts had holes crossing one another. Nearly all greens were indistinguishable from fairways, and most natural obstructions were considered legitimate hazards. "Stone walls, trees, ploughed fields, fences, and chasms," wrote one golf enthusiast in 1895, "present excellent sporting requirements on a course, for variety is the spice of life." In seeking a rationale for placement and style of manmade features at older clubs in the United States, golf architects of later eras were baffled. One explanation for such steeplechase-style layouts was provided by Elmer O. Cappers, historian at The Country Club (Brookline), who pointed out that the coexistence of golfers and horsemen in the early days at his club determined such matters.

For all their shortcomings, American courses at the turn of the century were functional. It is amazing that early greenkeepers were able to build and maintain their courses as well as they did with so little in the way of equipment, materials and skilled help available.

A classic early Bendelow design at Highland Country Club in Indianapolis, with a square green fronted by rectangular crossbunkers and a trio of "dragon's teeth" mounds.
COLLECTION RON WHITTEN

HIGHLAND C.C.-INDIANAPOLIS, IND.

Early tee boxes were literally that, nothing more than platforms of dirt or hard-packed sand. COLLECTION RON WHITTEN

These "sand lot" courses provided adequate training grounds for thousands of beginning golfers. But the expert golfers, and those who fancied themselves as such, clamored for better courses on which to play their beloved game. It was this impetus that led to the advancement of course architecture in America in the early years of the twentieth century. Three courses created during that time—Myopia, north of Boston, Garden City Golf Club, outside of New York City, and the National Golf Links of America on Long Island—advanced the state of the art.

5

The Pioneers in America

Walter Travis was the ultimate quick study. He took up the game of golf at age 35, entered his first tournament a month later, won a national championship within four years and established himself as a golf architect soon thereafter. UNITED STATES GOLF ASSOCIATION

Herbert C. Leeds was one of those dissatisfied with American golf courses at the turn of the century. But he was determined to do something about it. Well-to-do and a fine natural athlete, he had developed into a scratch player within two years of taking up the game and became one of the ruling fathers of the Myopia Hunt Club north of Boston shortly after joining in 1896. Leeds persuaded the membership to build a new course to replace the club's rudimentary nine holes, and soon after they consented he was appointed to lay out the replacement.

Leeds took the task seriously. He visited Shinnecock Hills, which by then had a full eighteen holes, and came away convinced that he could build a comparable course. He started by locating his green sites in natural hollows and on natural plateaus, like those he had observed at Shinnecock. He then gave special attention to the construction of the greens. Not content to simply mow patches of grass, he had each green shaped into rolling surfaces, for he was determined that Myopia would not be cursed with a single flat, lifeless green.

Leeds routed his course to take advantage of the natural terrain. Stone walls, left over from the days when the land served as pastures and fields, were covered with soil and grassed to make them playable. Stone walls were not a legitimate golf hazard, Leeds felt, but mounds were. He later uncovered the walls, heaped the stones into mounds and re-covered them with soil to produce Myopia's giant chocolate drops, still a feature of the course.

Finally, he had bunkers added, several on some short holes, almost none on the holes he deemed were challenging enough already. When his nine-hole layout was completed, it was selected to serve as the site for the 1898 U.S. Open.

The participants in that Open praised Leeds for his efforts and especially for the greens, which were unlike any in the country. But Leeds was not satisfied. He felt Myopia needed another nine to be a "proper links." The club soon purchased adjoining land, and Leeds laid out a second nine on decidedly hilly ground. Again paying particular attention to the greens, he took two years to construct the addition. When completed, Myopia's eighteen holes were termed as fine a test of golf as any in the United States, and the club hosted three National Opens in the next eight years.

Herbert Leeds savored his reputation as a golf course designer. He went abroad in 1902 to study the famous Scottish links. After his return, he laid out a number of courses, including the first Kebo Valley Course at Bar Harbor, Maine, and the original Palmetto Country Club in Aiken, South Carolina. But Myopia was his favorite, and he remained at the club until his death, nurturing and refining the course.

About the time that Leeds was completing his initial nine at Myopia, another man of leisure, Devereux Emmet, began planning a course for his friends in Garden City, New York. His little nine-hole effort was

called the Island Golf Links, and it lasted until 1899. By that time, Emmet and his fellow golfing enthusiasts had decided to establish a more formal organization. They incorporated the Garden City Golf Club, bought the Island Golf Links and surrounding property, and Emmet proceeded to remodel his modest course into a full eighteen.

For a neophyte, Emmet did a remarkably good job laying out the Garden City course on flat, treeless, windswept terrain. He routed the holes so that a player faced differing wind conditions on every hole. There were few parallel holes, so shots drastically off line would end up in unfavorable lies. Several roads ran through the course, but Emmet utilized them as he would creeks, as hazards. He did build several cross bunkers in the fairways, which were popular in that day, but his bunkers were for the most part shallow and provided easy recoveries.

The finest feature of Garden City was its turf. The greens, although basically flat, were hardy and consistent. The fairways were similar, and some felt that Garden City's fairways were superior to the greens on most other courses.

The turf was outstanding because Emmet had the good fortune to work on a piece of land ideally suited for the growing of grass—a large alluvial deposit of loam, like Scottish linksland, resting on layers of gravel and sand. The fine soil and salt air nurtured stiff, thin-bladed grasses, and the underlying strata provided excellent drainage. When the 1902 U.S. Open was played on Garden City, the course was well received by both Americans and Britons.

But as one writer later noted, while Garden City certainly made the reputation of Devereux Emmet as a course architect, it was also nearly his downfall. Emmet would spend the rest of his life designing and building courses all along the Eastern Seaboard. But he would experience several failures trying to duplicate what he had done at Garden City: build a respectable layout with superb turf for under two thousand dollars. He would never again find terrain so perfect for the playing of golf, not even at other nearby sites around Garden City.

Fortunately, once Emmet realized that each course site presented a unique situation, and once he convinced his clientele to provide him with adequate funds, he was able to create a number of notable courses. His list of later accomplishments includes Wee Burn Club in Darien, Connecticut; the original Congressional Country Club course near Washington, D.C.; and Leatherstocking Country Club in Cooperstown, New York.

It may have been beneficial to Emmet that by 1908 people had forgotten that he had designed Garden City. By that time Garden City

Prior to two U.S. Amateurs at Garden City Golf Club in New York, Travis reworked his home course. In 1906 he added dozens of bunkers. In 1913 he added sand mounds and then competed in the event. He lost in the semi-finals.
COURTESY *GOLF WORLD*

Golf Club was being considered the work of Walter J. Travis, whose periodic revisions were to make it a truly outstanding course. Travis had been born in Australia but was raised from an early age in the United States. He didn't take up golf until the age of thirty-five, but by his thirty-ninth birthday he was the top amateur in the country. By 1899 he was also dabbling in golf course design, working in collaboration with John Duncan Dunn on the Ekwanok Golf Club in Manchester, Vermont, and writing about the subject in various periodicals. Travis was also a member of Garden City and was runner-up in the 1902 Open on his home course.

In a 1906 magazine article, Travis analyzed the Garden City course and suggested several improvements. He felt the bunkers on several holes, especially those near the green, should be deepened and cross bunkers filled in. He thought certain fairways should be narrowed, either by allowing the rough grass to grow or by the installation of pot bunkers. And he suggested reworking the famous Garden City greens:

> The dream of having at least a few greens resemble some of the well-known ones in Great Britain is easily capable of realization. All that is necessary is to denude the present greens of their surface of turf, by means of a turfcutting machine which peels it off in continuous rolls of even, uniform depth, arrange the undulations as desired, replace the sod, and fill in the interstices with fine, screened loam mixed with seed.

Travis was able to convince his club to allow him to institute his suggestions; being a three-time U.S. Amateur and British Amateur champion no doubt helped. Over the next two years he reworked every green, carefully preserving the hallowed turf as he did so. He also built some new tees to extend the length of some holes and, in certain cases, to reroute play. He rebunkered each hole, digging some as deep as a man's height so that their faces had to be built up with layers of sod stacked like bricks, as at Muirfield and other courses in Scotland. In all, he added fifty new bunkers.

Garden City, as revised by Travis, hosted the 1908 U.S. Amateur and, just as six years previously, the participants were enthusiastic about the course. "The fairway and the boldly undulating putting-greens were even as velvet," wrote one onlooker, "but those hazards! . . . bunkers, traps and pots lurk on either side of the straight and narrow path, awaiting the pull or the slice of the unwary!"

The "Grand Old Man," as Travis had come to be known, would design or remodel a good many courses in the next twenty years, including the East and West courses at the Westchester Country Club,

Dapper Devereux Emmet, Garden City's original architect. Ultimately, he had the last word on its design and modified it shortly before Travis's death in 1927. COLLECTION RON WHITTEN

Rye, New York; Hollywood Golf Club in Deal, New Jersey; and the original nine holes at the Sea Island Golf Club in Georgia. His true love, however, was the first course he ever had a hand in creating, Ekwanok in Manchester. Ekwanok may have been the country's best golf course in the early 1900s, but it did not receive the early public attention of Myopia or Garden City. Travis touted its merits often, and by 1914 it was selected as the site for the National Amateur. Travis added a second course, Equinox, adjoining Ekwanok in the early twenties. At his death, in accordance with his wishes, Travis was buried near his beloved Vermont courses.

Walter Travis had a certain set of principles that he tried to instill in each of his courses. Hazards should be placed in relation to greens, he believed, so as to require "thinking" golf. Certain holes should necessitate deliberate slices, while others should require deliberate draws. One or two tee shots per round should call for an exceptionally fine carry, as should one or two approach shots. And greens should always be undulating, never flat.

Travis, the "Old Man" of golf, late in his life, with his everpresent cigar. History regards him as a better player than architect, although some of his designs remain classics. COLLECTION RON WHITTEN

Often, perhaps too often, Travis tried to institute his principles by means of a most effective weapon: the small, deep pot bunker. He used the pot bunker to such excess that critics of later years would label him a follower of the penal school of golf design, a master of the "God-fearing approach," a flamboyant but unimaginative architect. Certainly some of the criticism is justified, but Travis never deliberately set out to build a penal course. He had spent his entire golfing career as a notoriously short hitter. He had kept himself alive in countless matches by keeping himself in play and by mastering a deadly putting stroke. That philosophy carried over into his designs. His pot bunkers never hurt players, he said, so long as they stayed out of them.

One final note about Travis's redesign of Garden City Golf Club: He remodeled the eighteenth hole, a par 3 across water, by building a severely tilting green and fronting it with a huge, deep bunker on the left and a smaller, steepfaced bunker on the right. Knowledgeable golfers quickly recognized the hole for what it was: Travis's version of the High Hole, the eleventh hole at the Old Course at St. Andrews. It was not an imitation, Travis would point out, but an adaptation of that highly respected and highly feared par 3.

The idea of modeling a hole on an American course after one from a famous old British links was intriguing. But the idea did not originate with Walter Travis. It started with Charles Blair Macdonald.

Macdonald was the man who had designed and built America's first eighteen-hole course, Chicago Golf Club. He was a wealthy, intelligent man, devoted to the game of golf. He had been one of the founding fathers of the United States Golf Association and was its first Amateur champion. But he was also, in the minds of some, stubborn, egotistical and autocratic.

Certainly Macdonald had the perfect personality to try something different and daring. In 1901, after reading a British magazine survey on the best holes in the United Kingdom, Macdonald resolved to build a classical golf course on American soil, one intended to compare favorably with the championship links abroad and serve as an incentive for improvement of the game in America.

Macdonald established a number of rules for this project. First, the course must be a links. He would only build it near the sea, on land as nearly comparable to the old linksland as could be found. After years of searching from Cape Cod to Cape May, he found two such sites, both on Long Island, New York. He eventually chose a site near Southampton and, coincidentally, adjacent to the Shinnecock Hills Golf Club.

Second, Macdonald's ideal course must contain a full eighteen holes

Charles Blair Macdonald, pontificating in the manner of a dictator, which in many ways he was. COLLECTION RON WHITTEN

of an exemplary nature. Not even St. Andrews, he felt, had eighteen first-class holes, but his course would. To this end, he solicited the opinions of many prominent golfers as to the ingredients of great golf holes. He personally made at least three trips to Great Britain, observing both famous and lesser-known courses. He surveyed and sketched dozens of holes, concentrating only on the features he considered distinctive. "I only approve of the Maiden at Royal St. Georges," he later wrote, "as a bunker, not a hole." He would not be afraid to combine two or three features from different holes into a single hole on his ideal course, and, in the end, more than half would be composites.

Third, he would spare no expense in making his course the best in the world. He spent a great deal of his own money on the project and also solicited subscriptions from seventy enthusiastic friends at a thousand dollars per membership.

Fourth, where nature was deficient, it would have to be improved upon. This was perhaps the most revolutionary action in course building in its time. When he examined the site, Macdonald was delighted to locate natural settings for several of his proposed holes, especially for his versions of Prestwick's Alps and the Redan at North Berwick. But he had a great deal of soil moved around to create "natural" settings for other holes. He also had some 10,000 loads of topsoil hauled in and spread around. He created a turf nursery, one of the first of its kind, and experimented with numerous varieties of grasses to transplant on his course. Since the site was in need of artificial watering, he had a complete irrigation system for greens installed. The greens themselves were built "scientifically," with strata of seaweed, loam and top-dressing to preserve moisture.

Fifth, Macdonald would obtain the assistance of the best experts in their respective fields, for mediocre talent could never result in an ideal course. He sought out Professor C. V. Piper of the United States Department of Agriculture for agronomic help and enlisted the aid of a local surveyor, Seth J. Raynor, to serve as his construction engineer. Raynor was to prove so invaluable that he subsequently constructed all the courses later laid out by Macdonald and designed many of his own as well. In addition, Macdonald invited the opinions of such experienced golfers as Walter Travis, Devereux Emmet and his own son-in-law, H. J. Whigham.

Finally, Macdonald intended that each hole should make a golfer think before he swung. Naturally, the features of the best holes that Macdonald adapted had, for the most part, always required the golfer to place the ball rather than swing aimlessly. But Macdonald went further. Each of his holes provided for an alternative line of play. On each tee the player was called upon to exercise his judgment: Could he carry the bunker in front of the pin, or should he play to the right? Does it accomplish anything to drive over those bunkers, or should the drive be placed down the intended fairway? Macdonald wanted long hitters and short hitters on equal terms when they played a match on his course.

C. B. Macdonald completed his course in 1909, after eight years of planning and two years of actual construction. It was named, somewhat immodestly, The National Golf Links of America. But the course lived up to its name as well as to its advance billing. It was like no other course in the country, and every player, every writer, every course designer who viewed it marveled at it. British observers, too, were astonished at what an ideal links creation Charlie Macdonald had wrought. Horace Hutchinson, Bernard Darwin and Ben Sayers, professional at North Berwick, all wrote laudatory articles about The National Golf Links in British publications between 1910 and 1913, the ultimate tribute to an American course.

Macdonald, who coined the title "golf architect" in 1902, would design fifteen other courses before his death in 1939, adhering to the same principles that made The National Golf Links so successful. But his clients would find his projects expensive. His Yale Golf Club, for instance, cost nearly half a million dollars, and his Lido Golf Club cost three quarters of a million. Macdonald never personally accepted a fee for any of his architectural work, with the exception of a lifetime membership in the club for which he was working.

All of Macdonald's later designs featured the same sort of adaptation of famous holes. He invariably built a Redan on each of his courses and a High. He also built a Cape hole on each layout, patterned after his fourteenth at The National. That hole, a dogleg par 4 across a bay where the player could cut off as much as he dared, was truly a design original by Macdonald. The same hole can be found at the Yale Golf Club (the third), the St. Louis Country Club (the eighth) and, most dramatically, at the Mid Ocean Club in Bermuda, where it appears as the fifth hole.

Macdonald spent the majority of his time at The National Golf Links in his later years and forever tinkered with the bunkering on some holes and the slope of the greens on others. He was uncharacteristically hesitant to join in the acclaim for his magnificent creation; even as late as 1928 he wrote, "I am not confident the course is perfect and beyond criticism today."

But Macdonald was a perfectionist. For the rest of the golfing world, The National was a course without peer. Its excellence would cause the rebuilding of many American golf courses, even some of the best, and would influence the quality of courses yet to be conceived.

Despite his somewhat rigid lines, the work of Macdonald contributed an impressive new style to American course architecture. Certainly Myopia, Garden City and Ekwanok were fine American courses. At the same time, Sunningdale, Walton Heath and Woking, across the Atlantic, were also exceedingly well done. But The National was in a class by itself. It would be accurate to say that Charles Blair Macdonald and The National Golf Links of America revolutionized golf course architecture. Soon after it opened, H. J. Whigham wrote:

> There are many features about the National Links which will make the course famous, for example, the undulating putting greens, the absence of blind holes—nearly every tee commands a view of the entire length of the hole—and the size of the bunkers. But the main achievement is that a course has been produced where every hole is a good one and presents a new problem. That is something which has never yet been accomplished, even in Scotland; and in accomplishing it here, Mr. Macdonald has inaugurated a new era in golf.

6

The Pennsylvanians

A. W. Tillinghast had a simple architectural credo. It costs no more to follow nature than to ignore her, he said, and if you must introduce artificial creations into a golf design, take efforts to make them appear natural. UNITED STATES GOLF ASSOCIATION

By 1910 the scene of important course construction activity had shifted to Pennsylvania. In the years before the First World War, that state was full of men who dreamed of building first-rate golf courses and did so. Their names are now familiar in golf design: Henry C. Fownes and his son, William C. Fownes, Jr.; George C. Thomas, Jr.; A. W. Tillinghast; Hugh Wilson; William S. Flynn and George Crump.

Henry C. Fownes's brainchild was Oakmont Country Club. Fownes, son of a Pittsburgh steel tycoon, conceived the idea of building a links-type course on the plateau overlooking the Allegheny River northeast of the steel town. He organized a golf club in 1903 to fund his project, secured the property and drew the plans for his dream course. Then he set out with a crew of 150 men and two dozen mule teams and spent a year building it.

When Oakmont opened in 1904, it featured eight par 5s, one par 6 (the 560-yard twelfth hole) and a total "par" of 85 (more accurately, a "bogey" of 85, a standard on the scorecard meant to serve as an artificial match play opponent). It had no trees to speak of but did have huge, rolling greens, and its length reflected the acceptance of the Haskell ball.

Henry Fownes was satisfied with his course, but his son, William, was not. The younger Fownes, after he won the 1910 U.S. Amateur, appointed himself permanent course consultant to the Oakmont club and for the next thirty years continually made suggestions on how it could be improved. In summers he lived at the clubhouse and beginning in 1911 spent many an evening walking the course with its greenkeeper, deciding what changes were to be made.

Fownes was determined to make Oakmont the toughest course in the world. "A shot poorly played," he once remarked, "should be a shot irrevocably lost." In order to implement this philosophy, Fownes sought the assistance of two greenkeepers, first John McGlynn and later Emil "Dutch" Loeffler. (Loeffler would remain as greenkeeper at Oakmont throughout his life, but during the 1920s he and McGlynn maintained an active golf design and building practice on the side.)

The revisions made to the Oakmont course by Fownes and his assistants were numerous. Holes were lengthened and the par reduced. Ditches were dug in the rough to improve drainage and to create playing problems. The ditches were played as hazards and were, in fact, almost unplayable. Greens were canted in another effort to improve drainage and were cut very short. And a huge number of bunkers were added throughout the course.

At William Fownes's encouragement, Oakmont Country Club greenkeeper Emil Loeffler (left) concocted a heavy sand rake with wide teeth in order to create deep furrows in Oakmont's sand bunkers. The furrows (right) caused many a furrowed brow. COLLECTION RON WHITTEN

Oakmont became the epitome of the penal style of golf course architecture. At one time, the course is said to have had 220 bunkers, an average of a dozen per hole. Since the heavy clay base upon which the course was built prevented the digging of all but a few deep bunkers, Fownes and Loeffler concocted a device to add to the difficulty of the otherwise flat, shallow bunkers. It was a special rake that, when dragged through the thick, brown river sand in Oakmont's bunkers, left deep grooves or furrows. Many felt it took two special talents to extract a ball from an Oakmont bunker—one if the ball sat on a ridge in the sand, another if it settled in a trough. Others believed that since a ball seldom stayed on the ridges in the sand, Oakmont's bunkers were easier to recover from than those raked in the conventional manner. Indeed, several neighboring courses adopted Oakmont's furrowed rake. In the 1960s, the river sand was replaced, the furrows eliminated and almost a quarter of the bunkers filled in. But that still left some 180 of them, which is sand enough for any challenge.

Oakmont's greens were always clipped exceedingly short, to approximately $^3/_{32}$nds of an inch, and at Fownes's insistence they were watered and rolled with a heavy roller before most golf events. Except for some modifications (most notably the reconstruction of number eight, Fownes's version of a Redan), the club through the years has zealously preserved its greens basically as they were in the days of Fownes and Loeffler and likewise jealously protected their notoriety.

William Fownes certainly achieved what he set out to accomplish. Oakmont has not been revered but feared. For decades, it was a decidedly homely course in appearance, but a long-term tree-planting program eventually converted it into a lovely parkland course. The club has otherwise refrained from any massive facelifting, and Oakmont remains a classic example of the penal school of golf design.

At about the time Henry Fownes was opening Oakmont, George C. Thomas, Jr., was planning a course at the other end of Pennsylvania. Thomas was from one of the state's oldest and wealthiest families. He lived on the family estate, the Bloomfield Farm, in the Chestnut Hill area of Philadelphia. There he dabbled in landscaping and gardening and even wrote a book about roses.

In 1905 a newly formed golf club offered to purchase the Bloomfield Farm as the site for its course. Thomas accepted on condition that he be allowed to design the course. The club agreed, understanding that Thomas had some previous course design experience (in Massachusetts and New Jersey), and, perhaps of greater importance, he didn't want to be paid for his services.

Thomas invited his close friend Samuel Heebner, then president of the Golf Association of Philadelphia, to assist him in the work. Together they routed the course, supervised its construction and refined it with the placement of traps and the planting of trees. The house in which Thomas was born and raised became the clubhouse, and, opening, the club changed its name to the Whitemarsh Valley Country Club. Ever since, the course has remained basically as Thomas and Heebner designed it, with small greens, liberal trapping and unusual balance. One of its par 3s was a monster at 235 yards. Another was a mere 125-yard pitch. Both were difficult to par.

George C. Thomas, Jr. (center), an aristocrat who dabbled in golf course design with considerable success.

Sam Heebner never designed another course, but Thomas, who moved to California after the war, did several more. To George Thomas, golf design was never really a profession, and he rarely accepted a fee for his work. But he took his avocation seriously. He had very definite ideas about how a golf hole should challenge a golfer and how it should not, and he was not always tolerant of others' criticisms of his ideas.

Thomas was one of the few American golf course architects to record his philosophy in a book. That work, *Golf Architecture in*

America, published in 1927, remains one of the finest in the literature of golf. In addition to his book, George C. Thomas, Jr., is best known for his marvelous work in California, which includes the North and South courses for the Los Angeles Country Club (on which English-man Herbert Fowler did the preliminary plans), Ojai Valley Golf Club, Bel-Air Country Club and Riviera Country Club.

Like Thomas, Albert W. Tillinghast was the son of a wealthy Phila-delphian. The elder Tillinghast owned a rubber works, and for the first thirty years of his life Albert was a playboy. He was infatuated with the game of golf and made several trips to Scotland before the turn of the century, specifically to the shop of Old Tom Morris at St. Andrews, where he enjoyed discussions on design philosophy. Back home, "Tillie" belonged to Philadelphia's most fashionable clubs, and he competed in several national amateur championships.

In 1907 a close friend of the Tillinghast family, Charles Worth-ington (developer of water pumps and, later, mower equipment) asked Albert to assist him in laying out a golf course. Worthington was building a resort on the Delaware River and reasoned that a "sporty links" would insure its success. Although he knew absolutely nothing about building a golf course, Tillie accepted the offer.

He soon took complete charge of the project, examining the site, drawing the plans and supervising the construction. The finished project, Shawnee-on-the-Delaware, was a remarkably fine first effort. Tillie had incorporated both the Delaware and Binnikill rivers into his design and built some rather novel teeing areas on several holes. Shawnee quickly became the most popular resort in the Poconos. It remains in existence today, although the course has been radically redesigned and bears little resemblance to the original Tillinghast design.

Nevertheless, A. W. Tillinghast, at the age of thirty-two, had discov-ered his calling. Tillie was determined to be the best in his newfound profession and, with typical intensity, devoted all his energies to it. He established an office in Manhattan, gathered together a construction crew and advertised his availability. He was stubborn enough not to accept any design job unless his firm could also construct the course. This allowed him to insure that his plans would be carried out cor-rectly. It also meant a bigger fee from each client.

There are those who say that, in his time, Albert W. Tillinghast was indeed the best. He was not as prolific as many of his contemporaries, nor did he ever build a breathtaking course on dramatic terrain. But, they argue, his courses have endured the test of time. A look at his list of accomplishments lends support to that view. Among his best-

Top: Thomas used the latest in mechanized equipment, including tractors and even an early bulldozer during construction of Riviera Country Club near Los Angeles in the mid-1920s. Bottom: But the rugged canyon-bottom terrain, while softened, was retained on holes such as the par-4 5th, with its plateau fairway and unusual hillock short of the green.
COURTESY *GOLF DIGEST*

known works are the Upper and Lower courses at Baltusrol and Ridgewood Country Club in New Jersey; the East and West courses at Winged Foot and the Black Course at Bethpage State Park in New York; the East Course of Baltimore Country Club in Maryland; San Francisco Golf Club in California; and Brook Hollow Country Club in Texas. These courses, as well as many others Tillie designed, survived over the years, having been changed very little.

Sad to say, the memory of Albert Tillinghast did not last. By the late 1920s Tillie had made himself well over a million dollars. By the end of the Depression he had lost it all. And by 1937 Tillie had forsaken the game of golf entirely, and he spent his remaining years in obscurity running an antique shop in Beverly Hills, California. Indeed, so totally forgotten was Tillie that for years after his death, writers, when talking of his works, referred to him as "Arthur" or "Archie" Tillinghast. It was not until 1974, when someone noticed that four USGA championships were being held on courses of his design, that the public was rein-

One artist's view of another artist: a 1922 sketch of A. W. Tillinghast.
COLLECTION RON WHITTEN

The masterminds of Merion: Hugh Wilson (right) poses with the club's first two greenkeepers, William S. Flynn (center), who would go on to become a legendary golf architect, and Joe Valentine (left). COURTESY GOLF DIGEST

troduced to Albert Tillinghast. That was accomplished by USGA official Frank Hannigan in a widely circulated magazine article that still stands as the most thorough profile of any American golf architect.

Another Philadelphian who entered golf course architecture by chance was Hugh Wilson. Wilson was a member of Merion Cricket Club (renamed Merion Golf Club in 1942) and was on a 1909 committee appointed to plan a new course when the club decided to move to new quarters. The committee decided a firsthand look at the famous courses of Britain was needed before any attempt to build a course was made. Hugh Wilson was given the honor of making the trip. It has been suggested that Wilson, who suffered from illness throughout his life, was sent to Britain in hopes it would restore his health. It's more likely that he was chosen because his business, insurance brokerage, allowed him an extended leave of absence and because he was the best golfer of the group.

The quarry hole at Merion, the par-4
16th, nicknamed for the abandoned
quarry stretched in front of the green.
The wicker basket flagpoles were a
Hugh Wilson touch, intended to deny
golfers the type of information about
wind conditions that normal flags
provided. COURTESY GOLF WORLD

Before he left, Wilson paid a visit to the site of The National Golf Links of America in Southampton. He not only carefully examined the course under construction there but also discussed an itinerary with C. B. Macdonald, who had made many similar journeys years before.

Wilson spent seven months in England and Scotland, playing and studying courses and sketching the features that most impressed him. When he returned, the committee was content to let Hugh have at it. So, with the aid of committee member Richard Francis, who could read a transit, Wilson plotted out an eighteen-hole course on the L-shaped site Merion had purchased in Ardmore. C. B. Macdonald and H. J. Whigham both offered advice on the endeavor.

But when the new Merion course opened in 1912, it did not attract much public attention. Four of the holes, numbers 1, 10, 11 and 12, originally played across Ardmore Avenue. In the early 1920s they were redesigned to eliminate the road crossings. Over the years, after the course was remodeled and refined, the golfing world came to recognize its virtues.

It started with its only two par 5s among the first four played and finished with three demanding holes routed around an abandoned stone quarry. There were no blind shots to any green. All its bunkers, which eventually numbered some 120, were also clearly visible. Legend has it that Joe Valentine, Merion's legendary greenkeeper, would spread bed sheets on the site of a proposed bunker while Wilson would assure himself, from some vantage point back down the fairway, that the hazard could be seen. Long ago these bunkers were dubbed the "White Faces of Merion."

It has been suggested that Hugh Wilson grasped the basic concepts of British golf design and conveyed them in his work to an even greater degree than Charles Blair Macdonald. It is not quite fair, however, to compare Merion and The National Golf Links. They are two fine courses born of different intentions. Hugh Wilson never meant to duplicate any British golf hole in his design of Merion. Rather, he had hoped to capture the flavor, beauty and playability of a British parkland course. Certain subtle touches at Merion, such as patches of Scotch broom in several bunkers, wicker-basket pins instead of the usual flagsticks and a wild swale in the seventeenth green reminiscent of the Valley of Sin at St. Andrews, leave that impression. But Merion has always been an innovative, thoroughly American original.

Hugh Wilson was involved in the design of only a few other courses. In 1914 he laid out a second course at Merion, the West Course located a few miles down the road, which has always suffered unduly by continual comparison with the original course. In 1925 he began a

complete revision of the East Course's bunkering. But he died unexpectedly that year of pneumonia, at only forty-five years of age.

Another designer closely connected with Merion was William S. Flynn. Flynn had been lured from his home in Massachusetts to the construction site of Merion in 1911 with an offer to become its greenkeeper. He worked on the construction crew and then did serve as greenkeeper for a very short time before leaving for war service. But Flynn made three enduring friendships in this short time at Merion. One was with Joe Valentine, the construction foreman who, on Flynn's recommendation, succeeded him as greenkeeper. Another was with Hugh Wilson himself. Flynn respected Wilson's knowledge, talent and experience in the British Isles, and Wilson provided Flynn with practical suggestions that he was able to apply to his new courses.

Flynn's third friendship was with Howard C. Toomey, a civil engineer who had also worked on the construction of Merion East. When Flynn decided after the war to enter the profession of course architecture, he formed a partnership with Toomey. Howard handled bookkeeping and construction aspects; Bill took care of public relations and the actual designing.

The firm of Toomey and Flynn operated out of Philadelphia for over a dozen years. They created some magnificent layouts, including Philadelphia Country Club; a complete revision of Shinnecock Hills; an additional nine at The Country Club in Brookline, Massachusetts, the Cascades Course at The Homestead in Hot Springs, Virginia; and Cherry Hills Country Club in Denver. They were also chosen to finish bunker revisions at Merion East after Hugh Wilson's death.

One final Pennsylvania contribution to golf architecture in this period was by George A. Crump, although the course he built is actually in New Jersey, some twenty miles southeast of Philadelphia. Crump was the founder of Pine Valley Golf Club in Clementon, New Jersey, generally considered the finest course in the world. Crump, the millionaire owner of the Colonnades Hotel in Philadelphia, conceived his idea to build a dream course in the sandy pine forest of New Jersey in 1912. Although he had the financial backing of many enthusiastic club members, including George C. Thomas, Jr., Crump spent over a quarter-million dollars of his own money on the project.

Crump literally moved to the site and walked every foot of the property in an attempt to devise a basic layout. Finally, in 1913, he secured the services of H. S. Colt, who was touring the Eastern Seaboard, to help him route his course. When Colt visited the site, he surely was struck by its similarity to the land around Sunningdale, the architect's home course in Britain. Countless British visitors to Pine

Above: Bill Flynn's architecture blended old and new. At the Cascades, his stylish crossbunkers turned a short ordinary par 4 into a challenging one. Left: Dumptrucks, such as those used by Flynn during the expansion of The Country Club in Brookline, Massachusetts during the late 1920s, made it much easier to shift earth about and create entire greensites.
COURTESY *GOLF WORLD*; COURTESY DAVID GORDON

Valley have since remarked on the uncanny resemblance of the two settings.

Together Crump and Colt routed a preliminary layout that proved to be so sound that it was altered only twice during construction. Colt, on a later visit, convinced Crump to make the par-3 fifth into a full-wood shot rather than the short pitch originally planned. The fifteenth hole was extended from a par 4 to a par 5 when finally constructed.

In 1914 Crump and his crew began a long, tedious term of construction. Thousands of trees were felled and the stumps removed; they stopped counting at 22,000 stumps. The area was replete with natural springs, which provided much needed water but also necessitated the creation of several concrete dams to form spring-fed lakes. Soil was hauled in for tees, fairways and greens, for the existing land was primarily sand, although with modern irrigation systems the sand would have been ideal.

By the end of 1914 Crump had eleven holes ready for play, the original nine plus the present tenth and eighteenth holes. By 1917 all but four holes, numbers 12 through 15, were complete. But then, in January of 1918, George Crump died. The club raised sufficient funds to finish the eighteen holes, and Hugh Wilson, with his brother Alan, spent the remainder of 1918 completing Pine Valley. The Wilsons made few alterations to the plans of Crump and Colt, most notably the aforementioned extension of the fifteenth hole.

Even before it formally opened as an eighteen-hole course in 1919, Pine Valley had earned a phenomenal reputation, not only among golfers but among golf architects. Travis, Tillinghast and Flynn all visited the course and were enthusiastic about its possibilities. Donald Ross and Charles Blair Macdonald both pronounced it the greatest course in the country.

What garnered Pine Valley such high praise from designers who were normally partial to their own works was perhaps the unique concept of the course. No other American course was like Pine Valley. Its fairways and greens were islands of playable turf, surrounded by natural sandy wastelands. Nearly every hole featured a forced carry over unmaintained sand and brush to the fairway and another such carry to the green. While a great many trees had been removed in building Pine Valley, a great many remained, and over the years more grew back. By midcentury, few other courses in America were as thickly forested. The artificial lakes Crump built also came into play. Certain greens were precariously close to the water, like those of numbers 14 and 18.

Because it required such precise placement of each golf shot, Pine

Valley was punishing to even the finest of players. Its introduction marked the zenith of the penal school of golf course architecture in America. No course quite like it has been built since, and no course has ever been as demanding of every stroke. Pine Valley remains today just as it did when it opened, a monument to its creator, George Crump, who never lived to see its fruition.

Emphasis on the Pennsylvanian influence on this period of golf design history is not intended to imply that other designers were not busy doing impressive things elsewhere. Macdonald tackled a new challenge in 1914, the construction of a links entirely upon land reclaimed from the sea. This course, Lido Golf Club in Long Beach, New York, opened after the war. His assistant Seth Raynor began

Above: Golf's most ferocious hazard, the funnel-shaped "Devil's Asshole" bunker, in front of the short par-3 10th at Pine Valley. Left: That scatological label did not extend to Pine Valley's creator, George Crump, who was universally praised for his efforts. Sadly, he died before the course was completed. RON WHITTEN;
COLLECTION RON WHITTEN

creating brilliant designs of his own, including Fishers Island in New York and Shoreacres near Chicago.

By 1911 Donald Ross, although still the professional at Pinehurst, had embraced the profession almost full-time. His reputation had become widespread that he was called upon to design courses in many parts of the country. Among the dozens of Donald Ross courses that opened in the period before World War I were Brae Burn Country Club near Boston; Wannamoisett Country Club near Providence; Oakland Hills Country Club near Detroit; Scioto Country Club in Columbus; Bob O'Link Golf Club near Chicago; The Broadmoor Golf Club in Colorado Springs and Atlanta Athletic Club (now East Lake Country Club) in Atlanta.

The British invasion of golf talent into the United States also continued in this era. Foremost among the second wave of emigrants who would have an impact on American course architecture were Herbert Strong and Norman Macbeth.

Strong, a professional from St. George's Golf Club in England, came to the United States with his brother Leonard in 1905 to compete in several golf events. Strong remained in the States and, while serving as professional at Inwood Country Club in New York, redesigned and rebuilt that club's course. He soon devoted a majority of his time to course design, and by the 1930s Herbert Strong would be responsible for some of the finest courses in North America: Canterbury Country Club in Cleveland; Metropolis Golf Club in New York; Ponte Vedra Golf Club in Florida; Club Laval Sur Le Lac in Montreal; and Manoir Richelieu in Quebec.

Norman Macbeth, a tall, quiet Scot, ventured to America in 1901 and subsequently settled in Los Angeles. A fine player who would win both the Southern and Northern California Amateur titles, Macbeth had his first design experience assisting in the layout of a new eighteen holes for the Los Angeles Country Club in 1911. He designed several Southern California courses, including San Gabriel Country Club, Annandale Golf Club and his home course, Wilshire Country Club.

There were others who came in the early 1900s: Leslie Brownlee, a Scot who introduced the game to Oklahoma and built that territory's first courses; Grange "Sandy" Alves, who worked primarily as a greenkeeper in Cleveland but also designed several Ohio-area courses; Albert Murray, who moved with his brother Charles from England to Canada at an early age, won the Canadian Open at age twenty and eventually designed several Canadian layouts; William Kinnear, a Scot who settled in Saskatoon in 1910 and did several early courses, including Riverside Country Club in Saskatchewan; and Robert Johnstone, who served as professional at the Seattle Golf Club for many years and did a number of fine courses on the West Coast, including his own club's course.

A disturbing but temporary postscript to this period arose in 1916 when golf architects who accepted fees for their services were stripped of their amateur status under the Amateur Rules of the USGA. Their status was restored in 1921, however, when it was decided that the true definition of professionalism lay in making a profit from exhibiting skill in playing the game.

Steam shovel construction and a preference for British design principles resulted in very geometric architecture by C. B. Macdonald and his associates. Right: A Macdonald plateau green at Sleepy Hollow Country Club in New York. Left: Squarish green and bunker on the 12th at Shoreacres near Chicago, a Seth Raynor design. Below: A blind punchbowl green on the 4th at Fishers Island, New York, by Raynor and Charles Banks. RON WHITTEN

7
The World Travelers

When the Great War in Europe broke out in 1914 it found many Britons who relied upon golf for a livelihood in America. Some of those involved in golf course architecture returned to their native land, while others stayed on in their new homes. Around this time, Herbert Fowler set up offices in the United States; but by the early 1920s he moved back to Britain, where he designed, among other fine courses, thirty-six holes for The Berkshire. Willie Park, Jr., came to North America at about the same time Fowler did, but, unlike Fowler, he remained in America until 1924, when he returned to Scotland because of serious illness. He died a year later.

Among other emigrants who, like Park, chose to stay in America after the war were:

• Wilfrid Reid, who had competed on several occasions in the United States. Reid settled as a club professional but designed over fifty courses and remodeled some forty others in a period of thirty years.

• Tom Winton, who came to America to work for Willie Park and then took a position with the Westchester County (New York) Park Commission. He built and maintained several public courses for that county.

• Harry Robb, of Montrose, Scotland, who built Milburn Golf and Country Club in Kansas City, Kansas, and became its pro. He also laid out several other courses in Kansas.

• James Dalgleish, of Nairn, Scotland, who, like Robb, settled in Kansas City. Dalgleish designed courses all across the Midwest.

Dr. Alister Mackenzie (right) strolls off the first tee at St. Andrews, a walk repeated at least once by most of the world's top golf architects. COURTESY *GOLF DIGEST*

• David Hunter, the son of Charles Hunter of Prestwick, who did several courses in the New Jersey area while serving as professional at Baltusrol and Essex County (New Jersey) Country Club.

• David T. Millar, of Arbroath, Scotland, who settled in Detroit and was responsible for several courses in that area.

• Willard Wilkinson, who came from England and was associated with A. W. Tillinghast before starting a career that continued from the 1920s into the early 1960s.

H. S. Colt also practiced course architecture in America sporadically during the war years. Later he encouraged a new associate, Charles Hugh Alison, to join him. The two had met when Colt was laying out the Stoke Poges Golf Club in Britain where Alison was club secretary.

Perhaps because he had started in the same fashion, Colt was sympathetic to the young Alison's earnest desire to learn the trade. He gave Alison the chance to work with him, and Charles showed himself to be adept at supervising construction and equally talented at designing golf holes. By 1920 the two had formed a full partnership.

Hugh Alison was probably the first truly "worldwide" golf course architect. He was responsible for a majority of the work of the firm of Colt and Alison in the United States, including North Shore and Knollwood Country clubs near Chicago; Burning Tree Club near Washington, D.C.; and Kirtland Country Club near Cleveland. He also worked in Australia and Europe and was the first architect to build first-rate courses in Japan. At the time of his death, in 1952, he was working on yet another course, this one in South Africa.

If Alison was not the first worldwide designer, then the title surely belongs to Alister Mackenzie. Mackenzie was a physician by profession, but he abandoned his medical practice in 1909 after assisting Colt with the design of his home club's course, Alwoodley in Leeds. He worked with Colt on several other courses, most notably the Eden at St. Andrews, and for a time was a partner in the firm of Colt, Alison and Mackenzie. But by 1925 he was on his own and spent the remaining years of his life globetrotting, producing fine courses in such widespread locales as Ireland (where he remodeled Lahinch Golf Club), Uruguay (Golf Club de Uruguay), Australia (where he did several, including the West Course of Royal Melbourne Golf Club), Argentina (Jockey Club at San Isidro) and Canada (the North Course of St. Charles Country Club in Winnipeg). Mackenzie finally settled in the United States, where he did perhaps his finest work.

Tom Simpson, who had obtained a legal degree at Cambridge but found no need to practice law, joined Herbert Fowler's firm in 1910.

When horsepower really was horsepower. Top: Plowing what would become a fairway at Malone in New York. Bottom: Tree clearing during construction of Oak Hills Country Club in San Antonio. COURTESY MALONE G. C.; COLLECTION RON WHITTEN

After the war they were partners in a company that expanded in the 1920s to include J. F. Abercromby and A. C. M. Croome.

Simpson was one of the great characters in the history of golf course architecture. He was a wealthy man and an accomplished writer and artist. He made a major contribution with *The Architectural Side of Golf,* which he authored in 1929 with H. N. Wethered. It featured numerous ink-and-wash sketches of golf holes, all by Simpson.

Simpson was, in fact, eccentric. He traveled from construction site to construction site in a silver, chauffeur-driven Rolls-Royce, invariably dressed in cloak and beret with riding crop in hand. He once selected an assistant on the basis of the young man's suggestion as to how to mount a license plate attractively on a Rolls. Such an artistic eye, Simpson felt, would be valuable in course design. Eccentric or not, Tom Simpson's judgment was sound. The young assistant he hired was Philip Mackenzie Ross, who would prove himself after World War II to be one of Britain's finest designers.

Tom Simpson's abilities as a golf course architect were also sound. During the twenties in Britain, he did such fine work as the remodeled New Zealand Golf Club at Byfleet and the Cruden Bay course in Aberdeen. His finest efforts, however, were found on the Continent, at courses like Deauville (the New Course), Chantilly and Morfontaine in France.

James Braid continued to produce fine layouts during the 1920s. He did, among others, a new course for Royal Musselburgh, and the East and West courses at Dalmahoy, and he remodeled Carnoustie Golf Club into the severe test of golf we know today. His assistant at Carnoustie was John R. Stutt, a landscape contractor who remained associated with Braid through the rest of Braid's design career, getting increasingly involved in course planning as he went along.

Another onetime Braid assistant was Cecil Hutchison, a former British army officer and one of Scotland's finest amateurs. Hutchison learned a great deal from Braid and in the twenties began building

courses of his own design. He worked on occasion with Guy Campbell, another ex-army officer and a descendant of a golfing family.

Sir Guy Campbell was a successful amateur golfer and a superb writer. He worked with Bernard Darwin on the sports staff of the *Times* of London until the mid-1920s, when he resigned, unable to resist the lure of golf course design. His first work was West Sussex Golf Club in England, done with the assistance of Hutchison. Guy Campbell maintained a steady design practice the rest of his life. Among his best works were the revisions of Prince's Golf Club in England (with J. S. F. Morrison) and Killarney Golf Club in Ireland. Sir Guy died in 1960 while laying out his only course in the United States, Tides Inn in Virginia.

One other designer worked with Hutchison and Campbell at West Sussex. He was S. V. Hotchkin, yet another former army officer, who first became involved in course design in 1922 after purchasing and remodeling Woodhall Spa Golf Club. For a time Hotchkin, Hutchison and Campbell were partners in an architectural firm. They later separated and Hotchkin moved to South Africa, ostensibly to retire. But he undertook to plan several of that country's finest courses, including Humewood and Durban Country clubs.

By the 1920s golf course architecture was also a full-time profession for a great many on the western side of the Atlantic. It was a special period of growing prosperity in America. Construction costs, real estate values and interest rates were low. Clients were willing and able to pay for the best and gave designers a free hand. Consequently, the twenties have been called the Golden Age of golf course architecture in America, and these years saw the flair and style of golf courses enhanced immeasurably.

There had been some 742 courses in the United States in 1916. By 1923 there were 1,903. By 1929 there would be 5,648! That was an average increase of nearly 600 new courses per year from 1923 to 1929. Such a rapid growth rate would not be approached again until 1967.

It may seem impossible that a few dozen professional course architects could design so many courses in the United States and abroad, considering the fact that train rides between projects took days and boat trips required weeks. The truth is, professional designers did only a fraction of the courses built in the twenties. A good many courses, perhaps a majority, were still being laid out and built by locals or immigrants who remained indefinitely as pro-greenkeepers. While these men sometimes designed a few other courses in their locale, they never truly practiced course architecture.

Steam shovels became an increasingly popular course construction tool in the 1920s, especially by cut-and-fill designers like Charles Banks and Bill Langford, who relished steep angles and deep bunkers. COLLECTION RON WHITTEN

There were also countless instances of "in-house" planning and design by a member or committee of a private club or by a city or county official for a new public layout.

Even in cases where a professional designer was hired, the architect sometimes provided the client with no more than one or two days at the actual site. In that time he would inspect the land; route the course; prepare an outline, sketches or diagrams of the holes and instruct the members on how to construct and maintain the course. This may have been a step above the practice of "eighteen stakes on a Sunday afternoon," but it was not a very big step. It left many clubs, or public governing bodies, to fend for themselves, and it is doubtful if such procedures ever produced a course as the architect had envisaged it. In some cases, the architect was not even present at the site. James Braid remodeled St. Andrews Golf Club in Mount Hope, New York, without ever setting foot on the property or even in the country. He recommended changes solely by examining topographical maps of the course from his home in England.

The preferable method involved an architect who, after inspecting the site and designing the basic course layout, would leave an experienced construction supervisor to build the course and periodically revisit the site to inspect the evolution of his design and make necessary adjustments. A number of construction supervisors, men like Orrin E. Smith and James Harrison, later entered the field of golf course design.

Toomey and Flynn, Herbert Strong, Walter Travis, A. W. Tillinghast, Devereux Emmet, John D. Dunn and C. B. Macdonald were still very active along the East Coast of the United States during the Roaring Twenties. Macdonald was always assisted by his right-hand man, Seth Raynor, on the dozen or so courses he designed in these years.

Raynor not only constructed all of Macdonald's designs but did some sixty courses of his own. He had established his own practice in 1915 but was most prolific after the war. He played the main role in the remodeling of the Chicago Golf Club, which has been credited entirely, but incorrectly, to Macdonald. Other Raynor originals include Country Club of Fairfield and Greenwich Country Club, both in Connecticut, and Yeaman's Hall Club in Charleston, South Carolina.

Raynor was responsible for luring two academicians into the field of golf design. The first was Charles H. Banks, an English professor at the Hotchkiss School in Salisbury, Connecticut, which hired Raynor to lay out its course. Banks served on the construction committee and worked closely with Raynor; when the latter moved on, Banks resigned and went with him.

The other was Ralph M. Barton, a faculty member at the University of Minnesota. Raynor was hired to design a course for that institution, and Barton volunteered to supervise the construction. When this course was complete, Barton, like Banks, joined Raynor full-time. (Ironically, at least one other math professor became a golf course architect, although, in this case, Raynor had nothing to do with the conversion. He was John Bredemus, a prominent Texas designer of the 1930s.)

The team of Raynor, Banks and Barton, along with C. B. Macdonald, went on to create another university course. In the mid-1920s they designed and built the excellent Yale University Golf Club. It was to be Raynor's last effort, for he died of pneumonia in 1926. Banks, who would die just five years later, finished several of Raynor's designs and did quite a number of fine courses of his own in the East and Bermuda. Barton returned to his native New Hampshire and planned a number of courses in New England, including one nine of the Hanover Country Club owned by Dartmouth College. Macdonald did no more designing (except for endless tinkering with the National Golf Links), preferring to write his memoirs, which were published in 1928 as *Scotland's Gift—Golf.* This book contains several passages concerning his philosophy of golf course architecture.

Also active on the East Coast were:

• Maurice J. McCarthy, an Irish immigrant who is best known for the several courses he did at Hershey, Pennsylvania.

• Fred Findlay, Alexander's brother, who was hired from Australia by a Virginia seed firm and did most of his designing in that state.

• Orrin E. Smith, a former construction superintendent for both Donald Ross and Willie Park, Jr., who opened his own offices in Hartford, Connecticut, in 1924.

• Wayne E. Stiles, a landscape architect, and John R. Van Kleek, a landscape architect and civil engineer, who, as the Boston and Florida firm of Stiles and Van Kleek, did such notable courses as the Taconic Golf Club in Massachusetts.

• Alfred H. Tull, a Walter Travis apprentice who became a partner of Devereux Emmet and his son in the firm of Emmet, Emmet and Tull.

Walter Hagen (far left), one of the first professional golfers who served as a design consultant, with Wayne Stiles (second from left) at the site of Pasadena Golf and Yacht Club, St. Petersburg, Florida. COLLECTION RON WHITTEN

In the Midwest, Chicago was a hotbed of golfing activity. Besides the old Scot Tom Bendelow, at least a dozen other full- or part-time golf course architects could be found in that area. Among them were Robert Bruce Harris, formally trained as a landscape architect; William B. Langford and Theodore Moreau (the firm of Langford and Moreau); C. D. Wagstaff; Leonard Macomber; Frank Macdonald and Charles Maddox (the firm of Macdonald and Maddox); Jack Daray; Harry Collis; Edward B. Dearie, Jr.; Joseph A. Roseman and George O'Neil. In Indianapolis, prominent amateur golfer William H. Diddel opened a practice.

On the West Coast, Willie Watson and William H. Tucker were busy during the 1920s. Tucker also had an active construction firm that built courses for a young Canadian designer, A. Vernon Macan. Macan laid out courses all along the West Coast, including Broadmoor Country Club in Seattle, Fircrest Country Club in Tacoma, California Golf Club of San Francisco and a host of layouts in his home province of British Columbia.

This shot of William P. Bell (left), George C. Thomas, Jr. (center) and Alister Mackenzie (right) led many to conclude that Mackenzie helped Thomas and Bell design Riviera. He did not. The good doctor merely paid them a courtesy visit on opening day.
COLLECTION RON WHITTEN

Watson's construction superintendent for a time was William P. Bell, an Easterner who came west in search of a fortune. Billy, who built most of the courses that George C. Thomas, Jr., designed in California in the 1920s, also had his own design firm. By the end of the decade, Billy Bell was one of the busiest architects of all. His early works include Del Rio Golf and Country Club in Modesto, California, and the fine Stanford University Golf Club in Palo Alto.

Two nationally known amateur golfers became prominent golf designers in the Far West during the twenties. H. Chandler Egan, a two-time U.S. Amateur champion, moved from Chicago to Medford, Oregon, and laid out several courses in the Pacific Northwest, including the original Eugene Country Club in Oregon and Indian Canyon Golf Course in Spokane, Washington. Max H. Behr, a U.S. Amateur runner-up, designed courses in Southern California, including Rancho Santa Fe Golf Club and Lakeside Golf Club of Hollywood.

One area on the West Coast, the Monterey Peninsula in California, was the location of two new courses that captured the attention of the

Max Behr (right) was another Renaissance man of golf who dabbled in golf course architecture during the 1920s. COLLECTION RON WHITTEN

golfing world in the 1920s. The courses, less than a mile apart, were Pebble Beach Golf Links and Cypress Point Club.

Pebble Beach opened for play in 1918. Its designers were two local men, Jack Neville and Douglas Grant. Neville was chosen because he was a fine golfer, several times a California Amateur champion, and because he was employed by the Pacific Improvement Company, the firm that owned the land and wisely chose to develop it into a golf course. Neville asked his friend, Douglas Grant, also a California Amateur champion, to assist him.

Neither man had any previous course design or construction experience. But like Hugh Wilson, George Crump and several other neophyte designers before them, Neville and Grant did a credible job. The course was adapted nicely into the existing terrain, and very little earth was moved. The greens were deliberately kept small and were liberally contoured. Most important, they managed to build seven holes on which the ocean came into play.

Pebble Beach was not a links, for it was located on bluffs overlooking Carmel Bay. But it had a distinctive links feel about it, strung out in loop fashion and subject to the strong ocean winds. It was a resort course from the very start and was available for everyone to play. In fact, its official title for years was Del Monte Golf and Country Club after the Del Monte Lodge located next to it.

Pebble Beach was subsequently modified on several occasions, most notably by a committee consisting of H. Chandler Egan, Robert Hunter and Roger Lapham in 1928 to strengthen the course for the 1929 U.S. Amateur championship. But much of the course remains as Neville and Grant devised it, a dramatic combination of inland and seaside golf. Grant was content to play the game after that and never worked on another course design. Neville worked with several professional architects on other projects and also designed several on his own, only to see the projects fail financially. He remained near Pebble Beach all his life, and in the 1970s he was invited to participate in yet another toughening of the course, this time in preparation of its first U.S. Open.

Ten years after Pebble Beach's opening, the work of the Britisher Alister Mackenzie at Cypress Point was unveiled. Cypress Point did not have a long, exciting stretch of ocean frontage like its neighbor, but its three dramatic ocean holes more than sufficed. The sixteenth hole was the most breathtaking. It was a long, long par 3 over a bay to a green set on a peninsula. The sixteenth has become, over the years, the most photographed and perhaps the most recognizable golf hole in the country. It also graphically demonstrates the strategic philosophy of golf design at its heroic extreme. On the sixteenth the bold player shoots directly to the green, 230 yards away, across pounding surf some 100 feet below. The cautious golfer plays short to dry land on the left and then pitches to the green with hope of putting for a par. Without the alternate route, Cypress Point's sixteenth would have been a terribly penal hole, unreachable to all but a few strong golfers; with it, the sixteenth requires a player to choose his route before swinging.

Dr. Mackenzie teeing off on the ninth at Cypress Point Club, Pebble Beach, California, soon after its opening in 1928. Best known for its oceanfront holes, Cypress also contains a strong stretch of holes in inland sand dunes.

The most photographed hole in golf, the par-3 16th at Cypress Point. This viewpoint is near a back tee that originally made the hole play alternately as a drive-and-pitch par 4. The tee was later abandoned. COURTESY *GOLF WORLD*

Interestingly, Mackenzie's original plan for the course shows the sixteenth as playing both as a dogleg right par 4 from a back tee and as a heroic ocean-carry par 3 from a shorter tee. It apparently was played as a four for a short time, but the back tee was soon abandoned. From the par-3 tee, many still choose to play it as a dogleg.

The fifteenth, which is a par 3 as well, also borders an ocean bay, but it is a short pitch with the green much closer to the precipice. The seventeenth is a dogleg par 4, with the tee shot across the water and the fairway split into two by a stand of cypress trees. The course has several other masterful holes, including the eighth and ninth, both short par 4s, the par-5 fifth and the twelfth and thirteenth, both par 4s playing into the ocean wind.

Cypress Point was possibly Alister Mackenzie's best course. Ironically, the founders of Cypress Point had not originally retained Mackenzie as their architect. They had hired Seth Raynor, who had done the nearby Monterey Peninsula Country Club course. But Raynor died, and, although he had left preliminary plans for the course, they were never used.

Two of Mackenzie's assistants at Cypress Point deserve mention. Robert Hunter, who assisted on several of Mackenzie's California designs, is best known for his dissertation on golf course architecture entitled *The Links,* published in 1925. Jack Fleming, who served as construction foreman on many of Mackenzie's designs, was later active as a course architect on his own in the 1950s and '60s. Mackenzie himself did other courses in California during the 1920s, including Pasatiempo Golf Club in Santa Cruz and Valley Club of Montecito near Santa Barbara.

Mackenzie, Thomas, Bell, Tillinghast and many others made major contributions to course design in the 1920s. But the outstanding figures in course design in this period were probably the veteran Scot Donald Ross and a Scottish-born Canadian, Stanley Thompson.

Donald Ross had been designing courses in the United States since the early 1900s. By 1920 he was probably the most active architect in the country. He had a nationwide reputation and was hired to build courses from coast to coast. Indeed, six of the eight National Opens between 1919 and 1926 were played on courses of his design. Each new course gained him more attention, and it became a symbol of status to have a Donald Ross layout. Northland Country Club in Duluth, Minnesota, turned down a fine Willie Watson design, even after Ross himself had urged them to accept it. They wanted a Donald Ross course, which he reluctantly gave them.

Many of Ross's designs were simply built to his plans and instruc-

tions, without his personal supervision, and the architect often commiserated over the fact that layouts credited to him were not as he had intended. But he continually worked on at least eight courses at a time during the twenties and had a loyal crew of construction supervisors over the years, including Walter B. Hatch, Walter Johnston, James B. McGovern, James Harrison and Henry T. Hughes, all of whom carried out his designs at other sites. The courses he did in this era were of a uniformly high standard.

Among them were Plainfield Country Club in New Jersey; Salem and Winchester Country clubs in Massachusetts; the East and West courses at Oak Hill Country Club and Monroe Country Club, both near Rochester, New York; the East and West courses at Country Club of Birmingham in Alabama; Essex Golf and Country Club and Rosedale in Ontario; Belle Meade Country Club in Tennessee and River Oaks Country Club in Texas.

In the late 1920s, Donald Ross, the architect with more offers than he could ever fulfill, actually pursued a contract to design a course. It is likely this was the only time in his long career that he did so, but he had seen the site for the intended course and was intrigued by its possibilities. Ross's proposal won. Perhaps because it had required an extra effort to get the job, he gave an unusual amount of personal attention to the course.

The result was Seminole Golf Club in North Palm Beach, Florida, possibly Ross's finest creation. Laid out along two small ridges just off the Atlantic, Seminole was an exquisite job. It was heavily bunkered, 187 in all, but the bunkers were positioned and constructed to convey a sense of the nearby rolling surf.

The course was built to provide a challenge for every level of handicap. Each hole had multiple tees and alternate routes to the green, for by this time Ross was a confirmed advocate of strategic golf design. One hole, the fifteenth, featured alternate fairways: a shorter route with tempting water carries and a longer but drier route for those content to play the par 5 in regulation.

The other major force in the twenties was Stanley Thompson. One of a clan of Canadian tournament golfers, Thompson entered the design field following his return from France after the war. He soon became the most conspicuous course architect in Canada, and his reputation spilled over the border to the United States, into the Caribbean and on to South America. Part of his fame was certainly attributable to the magnificent Banff and Jasper courses he constructed in the rugged Canadian Rockies of Alberta. Built in high country devoid of topsoil along a rushing mountain river, Banff had the dubious distinction of being the first course in history to cost a million dollars to construct.

Thompson was most vocal in the 1920s in expounding the merits of strategic design, and his works reflected his philosophy. Besides Banff and Jasper, other impressive courses he did in those years included the Royal York Golf and Country Club in Ontario (now known as St. George's) and Ladies Golf Club of Toronto (today North America's last-surviving "ladies only" golf club).

Thompson also launched the careers of several prominent contemporary designers. At one time or another, Geoffrey S. Cornish, Robert Moote, C. E. Robinson, Howard Watson and Norman Woods all worked for and with Thompson. Robert Trent Jones, fresh out of Cornell, began assisting in the refinement of Banff after it opened. He became Thompson's partner in 1930 and remained a lifelong friend even after he began his own illustrious career.

Paintbrush in hand, Canada's Stanley Thompson fashions a model of one of his flamboyant, ambitious green complexes. COLLECTION GEOFFREY CORNISH

Origin of a mass neurosis. Thompson working on model of a tricky green. He favors overhanging grass flashings.

Important articles by American golf architects were appearing in periodicals of the twenties. Max Behr was a prolific writer, as were Walter Travis, founder and editor of *American Golfer,* and A. W. Tillinghast, who wrote for and later edited *Golf Illustrated.* The first years of the 1920s had also seen the publication in Great Britain of a book on course architecture by H. S. Colt (assisted by C. H. Alison and Alister Mackenzie) and another by Mackenzie on his own.

Seminole Golf Club in North Palm Beach, Florida, was said to be the only design contract Ross ever actively pursued. RON WHITTEN

8

A Changing of the Guard

Bill Flynn's construction crews in the 1930s included young Red Lawrence (left, on horseback) and Dick Wilson (second from right, in cowboy hat). Both would later become prominent architects. COURTESY DAVID GORDON

With readily available capital and an abundance of golf design talent, it seemed that the Golden Age of Golf Course Architecture would last forever. In reality, the era lasted only a scant ten years. The stock market crash of 1929, the bank closings of the early 1930s and the Great Depression brought an abrupt halt to course development in the United States.

Bank closings were especially harmful. Without financing, planned projects were shelved and existing projects abandoned. It was the rare club that had no members who lost fortunes.

Long-established clubs were able to weather the financial storm by implementing austerity measures. But the newer clubs, those born of the boom of the 1920s and patronized by younger men of newfound wealth, were vulnerable because they were overextended financially. Liberal lifetime or single-fee memberships had been handed out as promotional gimmicks. The remaining regular members could not meet the periodic dues. Such new clubs had operation and maintenance expenses to meet, as well as fees to course architects, contractors and subcontractors. With insufficient revenues, they were forced to disband.

In New York, Midvale Golf and Country Club filed for bankruptcy soon after its new golf course was finished. Midvale was the first professional design of architect Robert Trent Jones, and it marked an inauspicious debut to what would be an illustrious career. In California, Lake Norconian Club collapsed, taking with it a fine design of John Duncan Dunn, who had been promoting it as his masterpiece. Real estate development courses, like Norman Macbeth's Midwick

Club near Pasadena and George C. Thomas, Jr.'s El Caballero in Tarzana, also closed, and the land was sold.

Most public and municipal courses managed to stay open, but they were poorly funded and maintained. The feast of the 1920s and the famine that followed in the 1930s clearly demonstrated to architects that the most magnificently designed course would not remain magnificent for very long when adequate funds were not available for upkeep.

Golf course architecture did not become a lost art during the American thirties and the war that followed, but it did become a highly neglected one. In the twenty years between 1932 and 1952, a total of only 200 new courses opened for play. In the same span of time, some 600 courses closed forever.

Times were hard for men in the golf design profession. Full-time architects, especially those who also handled their own construction, were severely affected. With clients defaulting on huge sums of money, many of these architects lost fortunes while trying to settle their accounts honorably from their own resources. Mackenzie, Tillinghast and Strong, among others, were never able to recoup their losses, and all three died in straitened circumstances.

Part-time architects fared somewhat better. Some, like Fred Findlay and Edward Dearie, were able to make a living working as greenkeepers or club managers. Others, like Wilf Reid, Jack Daray and Harry Collis, served as club professionals. Some, like Alfred Tull, entered the maintenance equipment business, and many others practiced professions unrelated to golf, like Norman Macbeth, who operated a cement firm.

A number of America's most prominent architects would die during the thirties. Tom Bendelow, Charles Banks, H. Chandler Egan, Devereux Emmet, Charles Blair Macdonald, Alister Mackenzie, Maurice McCarthy and George C. Thomas, Jr., were among them.

But there were some bright spots on the bleak American landscape of the Depression. In 1932 the long-awaited "dream course" of golfing phenomenon Robert Tyre "Bobby" Jones, Jr., opened in Augusta, Georgia. Jones called it the Augusta National Golf Club, and from its beginning the course was something very special. Jones had asked the renowned Alister Mackenzie to help design his course, and together they routed a stunning layout through the grounds of an old arboretum.

Augusta National was specifically designed with tournament golf and the spectator in mind. Several greens were situated to provide vantage points from nearby hillsides. Several mounds were created to

The legendary amateur golfer Robert Tyre Jones, Jr. (known to the world as Bobby, though he personally hated the nickname) during construction of the masterful Augusta National Golf Club. Jones assisted Mackenzie in its design.
COLLECTION RON WHITTEN

serve as seats for viewers, and over the years many more would be added. But Augusta National was also a player's course. The fairways were broad, and little rough existed. Instead, Mackenzie and Jones utilized natural hazards of trees (there were thousands of tall Georgia pines lining the fairways) and water (two streams and a pond came into play on five holes on the front nine). The greens were large, with flowing contours. And the very few bunkers, only twenty-two at the beginning, were expertly placed.

Soon after Augusta opened, its nines were reversed, for it was felt that the water holes, including the now famous Amen corner of eleven through thirteen, should be tackled later in the round. Augusta National was in some ways the first uniquely American golf course. It was a model of strategic design, reflecting the principles of Mackenzie and Jones. Mackenzie had codified his principles in his book, *Golf Architecture*, in 1920, and he was able to express all those "essentials of an ideal course" at Augusta National.

Jones, who like Mackenzie was a devout admirer of St. Andrews, strongly felt alternative routes should be provided for players of lesser ability. But he also felt there should be rewards, especially on par-5 holes, for those who took a chance and succeeded.

At Augusta every hole looked deceptively simple, and indeed a high handicap golfer could keep the ball in play for an enjoyable round. But every hole had a preferred target, a spot from which it was most advantageous to play the next stroke. Augusta National could yield low rounds, but only to a golfer who thought his way around the course.

By the fifties Augusta National emerged as a standard for American golf course architecture. This was due in no small part to those progressive ideas of Alister Mackenzie and Bobby Jones.

Mackenzie was responsible for other courses in the States during the 1930s, most of which were completed after his death. His associate on several projects, especially Crystal Downs Country Club and the University of Michigan Golf Course, both in Michigan, was a former Oklahoma-banker-turned-course designer, Perry Maxwell. Maxwell was probably the most prolific golf architect in America during the Depression.

This was ironic, for Maxwell did the bulk of his work in the so-called Dust Bowl area of Kansas, Oklahoma and Texas. But those very areas contained industries unaffected by the generally depressed economy of the United States. Oil interests in Tulsa hired Maxwell to build them a course, and in 1935 he gave them Southern Hills Country Club. The Carey Salt people of Hutchinson, Kansas, also hired Maxwell, and in 1937 he built Prairie Dunes Country Club.

Prairie Dunes, featuring striking linkslike qualities, was originally planned as an eighteen-hole course. Only nine were built, however, and for twenty years the course had the reputation of being the best nine-hole course in the country. Perry's son, J. Press Maxwell, added nine more holes in 1957, following his father's routing plan and adding some touches of his own.

In 1936 Perry Maxwell lost the bid to lay out Colonial Country Club for oilman Marvin Leonard in Fort Worth, Texas (architect John Bredemus was hired), but he was later retained to build three new holes at the course in preparation for the 1941 U.S. Open. Those holes are now perhaps the best at Colonial, the third, the fourth and the infamous fifth.

Perry Maxwell was especially noted for his severely contoured greens, which long ago were dubbed the "Maxwell rolls," a play on words on two prominent automobiles of the day. The best example of

Perry Maxwell, looking more like a banker than a golf architect in this formal portrait. In truth, he was both, though he gave up banking early in his life to build courses. COURTESY JESSIE PALIK

the Maxwell rolls is Augusta National, which hired Perry in the late 1930s to rebuild some of its holes. Greens like the first, the tenth and the fourteenth are the result of Maxwell's handiwork. Among other courses for which Maxwell rebuilt greens into rolling terrors were Pine Valley Golf Club (George Crump's masterpiece), Saucon Valley Country Club and Gulph Mills Golf Club, all three in the vicinity of Philadelphia.

The latter course was another of Donald Ross's great creations. Ross was still active in the 1930s, although the Depression curtailed his travels and he stayed closer to his home in Pinehurst, North Carolina. This allowed him to concentrate on his pet project, the Pinehurst courses.

By 1936 Ross had successfully converted the old sand greens of its three courses to Bermuda grass and had sculptured them into visible,

The Maxwell style of heavily rolling greens and gaping sand bunkers demonstrated (above) on the 11th at the Old Course at Saucon Valley Country Club, Bethlehem, Pennsylvania, a Herbert Strong design Maxwell remodeled, and (left) on the 8th at Prairie Dunes Country Club in Hutchinson, Kansas. For years Prairie Dunes was only a nine-hole course. This was the fifth hole in those days.

raised putting surfaces with undulating approaches, a style by that time widely recognized as his trademark. Ross then set about rearranging the courses, rebunkering nearly every hole and adding strategic mounds and hollows. When he finished (although truthfully he was never finished and was forever refining the courses), Pinehurst had two pleasant resort courses, Numbers 1 and 3, and one long, deceptive, topflight layout, Pinehurst No. 2. No. 2 was so good it hosted the national PGA Championship a year after it opened.

At Pinehurst No. 2, Donald Ross demonstrated a brilliantly deceptive form of strategic design. The course appeared to be straightforward. Its fairways were not particularly wide, but there was little rough. The greens were small and undulating, but very few of them were protected by more than a single bunker.

But the illusions soon vanished once a round at Pinehurst No. 2 was begun. A ball off the fairway was either in the pines on a mat of pine needles or on the soft, sandy soil cluttered with clumps of snarly wire grass. An errant driver at Pinehurst seldom found a good lie.

And the tiny greens required a great deal of concentration. Some bunkers were well forward of the green, and the careless player could find his approach land over the bunker but short of the putting surface. Many holes had only one bunker at the corner or side of the green. Yet to follow one's natural inclination and play away from the bunker was often a mistake. Ross counterbalanced most bunkers with greenside mounds and hollows, most of which posed more difficult recovery problems than the sand.

Donald Ross considered his Pinehurst No. 2, with all its subtleties, to be his finest achievement.

Strangely enough, although the Great Depression was worldwide, golf course construction outside the United States continued at a steady pace. In the British Isles an average of forty new courses opened every year in the thirties and professional architects were kept busy remodeling other British layouts into exciting tests of golf. In this period, Taylor and Hawtree rebuilt Royal Birkdale Golf Club into such a fine course that it was proposed as the permanent site of The Open. C. K. Hutchison planned major changes to the thirty-six holes at Turnberry Hotel to bring play closer to the nearby ocean. Sir Guy Campbell revised Killarney Golf Club of Ireland into a lovely lakefront course. Tom Simpson remodeled Ballybunion Golf Club into a dramatic oceanside test that was probably the best in Ireland.

New layouts were also appearing in other parts of the British Empire. In Canada the firm of Thompson and Jones kept busy, producing such solid courses as Digby Pines and Cape Breton Highlands (known also as Keltic Lodge) in Nova Scotia, Green Gables Golf Club on Prince Edward Island and Capilano in British Columbia, In Australia Alex Russell, who had assisted Alister Mackenzie in designing Royal Melbourne, laid out a second eighteen, the East Course, for that club as well as many others throughout the country.

In Japan Kinya Fujita, who had attended college in America and had studied golf course architecture under C. H. Alison, was creating many fine layouts: the East and West courses at Kasumigaseki, the King's and Queen's courses at Narashino and Nasu Golf Club. Alison was also busy in Japan, creating such courses as Hirona and a new Tokyo Golf Club, and he inspected his pupil Fujita's work at Kasumigaseki. The deep bunkers he installed at those courses, including Kasumigaseki, with Fujita's blessing, so awed Japanese golfers that they derived from his name a word for them, "Alisons."

By the mid-1930s it appeared that golf course construction, both in the United States and abroad, might be on the rise again. In America, the federal WPA program allowed many municipalities to hire course architects to design and build public courses. Men like Robert Trent Jones, who had established a U.S. practice separate from Thompson's by the mid-1930s, Robert Bruce Harris, Perry Maxwell and Donald

Like Ross, many architects felt green contours had to be shaped by hand. Top right: Bill Langford painstakingly staked out the elevation changes of his greens and bunkers. Bottom right: William F. Gordon (on left in hat and tie) scratches out the outline of a green during construction of Bill Flynn's Normandy Shores layout in Florida. Gordon served as construction boss for Flynn on many projects. COLLECTION RON WHITTEN; COURTESY DAVID GORDON

The subtle pitches of Donald Ross's greens at Pinehurst No. 2 and the equally subtle rolls off their edges have been nearly impossible to capture on film. They must be experienced firsthand. GIL HANSE

Ross took advantage of this program. Since the purpose of the WPA and similar programs in the United States and Canada was to create jobs, each course employed 200 or more men during construction. Use of earth-moving equipment was limited, and these WPA courses were literally hand-built by men using only hand tools and wheelbarrows.

Actually, this method of construction was not entirely alien to the practices of the time. Although the bulldozer, which appeared in the 1920s, and the steam shovel, which was developed much earlier, had become major earth-moving tools, many architects before World War II preferred older methods, using horses, mules and scrapers for green and bunker construction, feeling that more natural lines could be achieved in this manner.

American architects also began to find employment remodeling existing courses. Many of the courses created in the boom of the 1920s were slapdash jobs, especially those laid out and built by organizations without professional design help. Little attention had been paid to strategy, balance and bunker placement. Some had pretentious features. Dozens of courses boasted a green with two large, symmetrical mounds, invariably dubbed "Mae Wests." Competent architects were hired to rectify the problems and eliminate such features.

Tillinghast, who was hired in the 1930s by the PGA to advise member clubs on alterations, claimed to have eliminated some 7,427 useless bunkers in a two-year period. Many of these were penal fairway bunkers and others were obnoxious cross hazards. The effects of their elimination were dramatic, both in money saved and in enhanced player enjoyment.

But just as the profession seemed on the road to recovery, the Second World War erupted in Europe in 1939. It abruptly altered the plans of those who thought a second golf boom was on the horizon. World War II put a great many men and women back to work, but it curtailed the golfing industry to an even greater degree than had the Great Depression.

Petroleum products became precious commodities. Courses outside metropolitan areas found themselves isolated and, without sufficient revenues, soon closed. Maidstone Club on the far point of Long Island, summer playground of the very rich, and Boca Raton Club near Palm Beach, Florida, winter playground of the same group, both folded for lack of patronage, closing four courses in the process. But so did Olympia Fields near Chicago, with its self-contained community, including its own schools and fire department, and its four courses.

Even clubs without financial difficulties found it hard to maintain

Those golf courses that managed to stay open during the Depression years were often in primitive shape. This was the 5th at Portland's Eastmoreland Golf Course in the early 1940s. COLLECTION RON WHITTEN

their courses without oil, fertilizer and manpower. Clubs like Augusta National and Interlachen in Minneapolis, which was to have held the 1942 U.S. Open, closed for the duration, and their fairways became pastures.

But the fate of North American courses was minor compared to the physical destruction inflicted upon European and Far Eastern countrysides. Some seaside courses, like Turnberry, were deliberately paved over and used as airfields, while others in Britain became training grounds for the British and the millions of American, Canadian, Continental and overseas troops pouring into England. Other courses, from Prince's in England to Biarritz in France, from Oahu in Hawaii to Kawana Fuji in Japan, became pockmarked battlefields or bombed-out rubble. In a life-or-death struggle, the preservation of golfing grounds was of no importance.

The war would end, of course, and reconstruction began once more. By the late 1940s golf would again become one of the preferred pastimes of millions and golf course design would reemerge as a vigorous profession. Among the prominent architects who would not live to see that day were Herbert Fowler, Cecil Hutchison, Norman Macbeth, William S. Flynn, Herbert Strong and Albert Tillinghast. And as was the case in the First World War, a number of promising but unknown associate architects would not survive combat and would never have the chance to prove their talents.

9

The Trent Jones Era

A flurry of course reconstruction followed the Second World War. In North America courses that had been left idle for as long as five years required extensive reconditioning before they could be reopened. Many clubs used this opportunity to remodel their layouts, and, as a result, architectural business was fairly brisk. A brief recession in 1949–50 and the outbreak of the Korean War slowed this activity for a time. But by 1953 course architecture was once again a healthy profession in the United States, with an average of 100 new courses opening yearly in the final eight years of the decade, as well as numerous remodeled or reconditioned layouts. By the 1960s, over 400 new courses were opening annually.

Up until the early sixties there were still many nonarchitect-designed courses coming into play. But with more sophistication required in planning and construction, new clubs and course promoters turned increasingly to professional course designers. By the late 1960s, except for modest layouts, the majority of new courses in the United States were architect-designed.

The era after World War II was one of transition. Golf course construction was revolutionized by modern earth-moving equipment. Where once it took up to 200 men, with horse-drawn scrapers, wheelbarrows and hand tools, two or three years to build an eighteen-hole course, by 1960 a dozen workers with modern equipment could construct a more elaborate eighteen in a few months.

The decade of the 1920s had seen the introduction of new techniques for the preparation and maintenance of golf courses. The practice of cultivating and carefully smoothing fairway seed beds became common. Prior to that time, often pastures had simply been

*"Give your course a signature,"
proclaimed the ads of Robert Trent
Jones. Trent's signature became the
most recognizable around the globe.*
COLLECTION RON WHITTEN

111

mowed to use as fairways and areas previously in other crops or cleared from forests were seeded with a minimum of fine grading. The greenkeeper then had to level these rough areas over a period of decades to achieve "billiard table" fairways. In the early twenties, gang units for mowing fairways were developed and horses to pull them were replaced by the golf course tractor. A mower with extra blades was used for putting greens, while quick coupling green, tee and fairway irrigation systems were introduced by the latter part of the decade.

Greater technical and scientific developments occurred in the 1950s and '60s. The production of improved grasses, such as hybrid Bermudas and ryegrasses, bluegrass cultivars and bent grasses, did much to advance the state of course maintenance. So did new fertilizers and chemicals. Research into turfgrass propagation and management led to a better understanding of how grass grows. It was not until the 1950s, in fact, that soil scientists really understood how water moved through turfgrass soils and how such soils became compacted. In 1960 the USGA method for putting green construction was introduced, and in 1966 Dr. William Daniel introduced a method for retaining underground water within a green through use of a layer of plastic.

In the 1950s the men who maintained golf courses had adopted the title "course superintendent" and turfgrass management became increasingly scientific as an increasing array of quality materials and equipment became available to the superintendent. By the 1950s automatic irrigation of courses had been introduced. It was continually improved over the years to replace hose and sprinklers as well as snap valves. Universal adoption of fairway irrigation also occurred in the 1950s, adding to golfing enjoyment and playing uniformity over an entire season.

But the transition was greatest in the profession of golf course architecture itself. The decade following World War II saw the deaths of nearly all the pioneer golf course designers. Foremost, of course, was the grand master Donald J. Ross, who died at Pinehurst in 1948. In 1950 the great James Braid passed away, and in 1951 H. S. Colt, John Duncan Dunn and Robert Pryde. In 1952 Colt's partner, C. H. Alison, Willie Dunn, Jr., and Perry Maxwell all died, as did the other giant designer of his time, Canadian Stanley Thompson. They were followed a year later by Wayne Stiles and Billy Bell. William H. Tucker died in 1954 and the Briton Frederic G. Hawtree in 1955. With few exceptions, all had courses on their drawing boards at the time of their deaths.

But there were course architects to carry on the traditions estab-

One aspect of that signature was the Trent Jones bunker, each a giant sandy jigsaw puzzle piece pressed into the landscape. These were among his earliest, done in 1934. COLLECTION RON WHITTEN

lished by these and other pioneer designers. Preeminent among the new wave of designers in the fifties was Robert Trent Jones, and in the next quarter century he was to exert an influence on golf architecture unparalleled in its history.

Of course, Trent Jones was not a new face in the golf world. He had been an assistant, and later partner, to Stanley Thompson. In the midthirties Jones established his own practice, building a series of municipal courses with WPA labor in upstate New York. He managed a few jobs during the war but, of greater significance, made several contacts with influential people and important organizations so that by the end of the war, Jones was busy preparing courses for the IBM Corporation and the West Point Military Academy. A great deal of what he did in the forties and fifties attracted nationwide attention, and by 1960 his name was known worldwide by golfers. Astonishingly, it was also recognized by nongolfers.

In 1946 Jones was hired by the Augusta National Golf Club to recondition its course and to remodel several holes. He altered greens numbers 8, 11, 12 and 13, and affected drastic changes to the entire eleventh hole. Originally a slight left-to-right dogleg with the teeing area to the right of the tenth green, number 11 played a maximum of 375 yards. Jones made it straightaway by cutting a slot deep in the trees to the left of the tenth green to increase the hole's yardage to 445. He also dammed Rae's Creek, which meandered alongside the left side and in back of the green. This formed a pond that embraced the entire left side of the green. It also elevated the water level to make it visible from the fairway.

Jones also completely reshaped Augusta's 16th hole. Instead of a short par 3 over a creek, Jones dammed the creek, rotated the direction of the hole ninety degrees and created the present 16th, a mid-to-long iron shot over the pine-lined pond to a kidney-shaped green. Both 11 and 16 attracted much attention at the annual Masters Tournament, but the 16th drew the most praise. Over the years the hole has been featured in nearly every golf publication. It also captured the fancy of one American president, Dwight D. Eisenhower, who painted an oil view of it from the tee.

In 1948 Trent Jones collaborated with Bobby Jones (who, with Alister Mackenzie, had originally laid out Augusta National) on a new course in Bobby's hometown of Atlanta. The course was named Peachtree, and while it was perhaps intended to be another expression of Robert Tyre Jones's golfing philosophy, it in fact became an expression of Robert Trent Jones's design philosophy. Peachtree's features were unprecedented. Its tees were huge, some the size of normal greens and one a long, serpentine 80 yards. Such tees, Jones reasoned, permitted exceptional flexibility, allowing the course to play from under 6,000 yards to over 7,400 by the simple readjustment of the tee markers. Broad tees also spread out wear, Jones felt, thus easing the demands on maintenance men. Peachtree's greens were also enormous. They averaged some 8,000 square feet, twice the size of the typical green of the day. One in particular, number 10, was considered the largest in the country at over 10,000 square feet.

Trent Jones deliberately created five or six definite pin positions on each green. These smaller areas were intended to be the true targets of the approach shot, but each large green surface spread out the play and the wear. Peachtree's greens have always been its most controversial feature, with some players terming the undulating surfaces "elephant burial grounds." Yet the club is protective of its greens; in the 1970s, when all eighteen were converted from Bermuda to bent grass, each green was mapped on a grid and reconstructed to preserve every hump and hollow.

Other aspects of Peachtree were also unique. The second hole had a pond stragically splitting the fairway near the green. Some holes were severely bunkered, while others featured mounds and hollows rather than traps. Peachtree was what Trent Jones called "modern golf course architecture." It was a broad, sweeping layout that, by simply changing pin and tee marker locations, could be played an infinite number of ways. Peachtree had its promoters and its critics, but all agreed it was a uniquely American product and would probably be a standard for future courses.

In 1949 Robert Trent Jones was retained by the Oakland Hills Country Club to revise their Donald Ross layout for the 1951 United

Another aspect was the Trent Jones tee box, a long "landing strip" tee that often stretched, as here at Pauma Valley, nearly 100 yards from end to end. RON WHITTEN

States Open Championship. Jones followed the routing of the old layout, but he altered almost every hole. He totally rebunkered some holes, reshaped greens on others and modified mounds and side slopes on the few holes where he retained Ross putting surfaces. Jones practiced what he dubbed "target golf," establishing specific targets for tee shots, second shots and approach shots. His flanking fairway bunkers pinched in the driving zones for most professionals. His multilevel greens with multiple pin positions and severe bunkering put a premium upon accuracy. When the 1951 Open was conducted, not a single golfer was able to crack its par 70 until the final round, when only two did so. Ben Hogan, the champion of that Open (with a closing 67), termed Oakland Hills "a monster" and apparently had a few choice words off the record for its architect. Some astute observers realized the condition of the course for the Open, with its ankle-deep rough and closely mowed greens, was responsible in part for the high tournament scores. But in the mind of the public at large, Robert Trent Jones was the villain or the hero, depending on one's philosophy.

The eminent writer Herbert Warren Wind did a lengthy article on Robert Trent Jones in *The New Yorker* at about this time, and he definitely came off as a hero in that piece. Publicity of this type was particularly beneficial for an American golf architect, for although both Travis and Tillinghast had been associated with leading American golf magazines of their day, British publications generally gave more attention to course architects and architecture than did American periodicals. Some notable exceptions to this rule were articles by Herb Graffis, author of several books and founder and longtime editor of *Golfdom*. Two books written in the late forties did have chapters devoted to golf architecture, and these helped spotlight the profession in both Britain and America. *The History of Golf in Britain* was coauthored by architect Sir Guy Campbell, and Wind's *The Story of American Golf* appeared first in 1948 and had subsequent editions in 1956 and 1975.

In the 1950s and '60s, articles by Wind dealing with the role of the golf course architect appeared in several publications, including *The New Yorker*. A further elaboration on the subject appeared later in his widely read two-part series in *Golf Digest*. Wind's articles did much to kindle the interest of the American golfing public in course architecture, and, as a likely result, many golfers became interested in knowing who planned the course on which they played.

But it took more than a few isolated incidents of national publicity to create the enormous force in golf course architecture that Robert Trent Jones became. Trent Jones was a talented, artistic man, a good

In the 1950s Trent Jones and golfing great Sam Snead embarked upon a joint venture to develop a nationwide chain of "Sam Snead" golf courses. Only a few were built. COLLECTION RON WHITTEN

administrator able to seek out and surround himself with capable assistants, and apparently a master salesman who could attract men like Laurance Rockefeller for backing. But his most significant attribute was that, throughout his career, Robert Trent Jones was a student of golf architecture.

He was the first architect who expressly entered the field without having first trained in another profession or been involved in another golf-related business. He had been a fine amateur golfer, but he was never a professional golfer with preconceived notions on how to punish the fade, the draw or some such shot. Nor was he a superintendent, concerned primarily with laying out eighteen holes that could be mowed entirely with gang mowers. Yet he was keenly aware of the interaction of the three professions.

Trent Jones was a student. He literally created his own major, golf architecture, while at Cornell University, taking classes he recognized would be imperative for his profession. He took not only the obvious courses, like landscape architecture, surveying, hydraulics, horticulture, agronomy and turfgrass science but also audited courses in philosophy, history and the classics.

He also inspected as many golf courses as he could and sought out experts in the field. Even the great Tillinghast, after he had apparently lost much of his zest for golf architecture, found himself on more than one occasion confronted by the eager young Jones seeking an explanation or, some say, an argument. And Jones landed a position in 1929 working for Stanley Thompson on the refining of the magnificent Banff course.

As early as 1935 Trent Jones was writing about a third school of golf architecture. Besides the penal and strategic schools, Jones said, there existed a "heroic school" of course design. The heroic was a blend of the best of the penal and strategic schools. He explained:

> The trapping (in the heroic) is not as profuse as in the penal, nor as scarce as in the strategic. Traps vary from ugly, treacherous-looking ones to small insignificant pot bunkers. The line of flight is usually blocked by some formidable looking hazard placed at a diagonal and involving a carry of from 170 to 220 yards in which the player is allowed to bite off as much as he feels he can chew. If his game . . . is not equal to the task, a safe alternate route to play round it is provided. The same principle is used in the green design, in which the green is placed at an angle to the line of flight with an opening allowed for the cautious.

In other words, as in strategic design, a heroic hole gives the golfer a choice of routes, but as in penal design, the player is punished if he gambles and fails by playing a poor shot. At first, the most common diagonal hazard Jones utilized for such purposes was the deep bunker, so steep-faced that a shot had to be wasted to get out. He was very fond of Tillinghast's bunkering at Winged Foot, two courses that the young designer cited as examples of heroic architecture. Over the years, Jones increasingly utilized water as the heroic hazard, and nearly every Trent Jones course would feature one or more greens perched ominously over a pond or creek.

But Jones was never an advocate of a strictly heroic or strategic or penal course. The trend, he felt, was to courses that featured all three philosophies blended into an appropriate combination depending on whether the course was intended as a municipal operation, a resort, a private layout or a tournament host. The course Jones always felt best reflected this trend was Jasper Park in Alberta, which was designed by Stanley Thompson and opened in 1925. In the forties and fifties, when Jones was on his own, he continued to popularize this blend or style of architecture, and he felt Peachtree boasted holes of all three philosophies.

Jones has maintained that he absorbed much of his feeling for contemporary design from Thompson, but there is evidence, as well as the belief of other Thompson associates, that Trent Jones also exerted considerable influence on Thompson.

Robert Trent Jones produced in the 1950s such renowned courses as The Dunes in South Carolina (with the ultimate heroic hole, the par-5 thirteenth that horseshoes around a lake); Old Warson Country Club and Bellerive Country Club, both in St. Louis; Coral Ridge Country Club in Florida; Shady Oaks Golf Club and Houston Country Club, both in Texas; and Point O' Woods Golf and Country Club in Michigan. Abroad he created Cotton Bay Club in the Bahamas, the original Dorado Beach course in Puerto Rico and Brasília Country Club for the new capital of Brazil.

Trent Jones's chief rival in the fifties, at least in terms of publicity, was Louis S. "Dick" Wilson, an associate of Toomey and Flynn in the late twenties and early thirties. Like many others, Dick Wilson abandoned design work during the Depression and managed a course in Florida until after the war. Then he formed his own firm and designed the West Palm Beach Country Club in 1949. This course, one of the first of what would be an explosion of courses in Florida, garnered fine reviews, and Wilson soon located other clients.

One of Bill Flynn's last construction crews included two of his main lieutenants, Red Lawrence (far right) and Dick Wilson (far left). COURTESY DAVID GORDON

By the late 1950s Dick Wilson had created a small empire of courses in Florida, laying out such notable clubs as DeSoto Lakes (later renamed Palm Aire of Sarasota), Tequesta and Cypress Lake. In the early sixties he created some of his best work in that state with the original thirty-six holes at Doral, Bay Hill and Pine Tree. Wilson also presided over development of major golfing resorts in the Bahamas, at Arawak (later called Paradise Island), Princess Hotel and Lucayan. Among his other clients was National Cash Register of Dayton, Ohio, for whom Wilson laid out two courses, the North and South, in the early fifties. Wilson also designed courses at new sites for the very old Meadow Brook Club and Deepdale Club, both on Long Island. Meadow Brook attracted special attention since its old course, forced to move due to rising taxes and encroaching suburbs, was so well respected. Wilson's Meadow Brook was greeted with immediate acclaim, and some went so far as to declare it the best course in the United States at the time.

Dick Wilson was not the Cornell-trained student of classics that Robert Trent Jones was, but he was certainly talented. Having learned his craft through on-the-job training, Wilson was proud of the fact that he could personally build the courses he designed. Whether Jones and Wilson ever had a personal rivalry is conjecture now, although it was

La Costa, a quintessential Dick Wilson design, featured several water hazards and heavily bunkered greens. COURTESY LA COSTA HOTEL & SPA

Some twenty years later, Flynn's mantle passed to Dick Wilson (right) and his young associate Joe Lee (left). COLLECTION RON WHITTEN

rumored that the very busy and selective Wilson accepted the commission to design Royal Montreal's new 45-hole complex in 1958 partly because he had heard that Trent Jones was after it. In the fifties, countless comparisons were made of the two architects and their works. One article written during these years said they were producing the best courses ever built.

As it turned out, Dick Wilson shared the spotlight with Trent Jones for only fifteen years, for he died in 1965 at age 61. Wilson died with half a dozen courses under construction and plans for many more at his office. He wrote very little about his profession and so left very little concerning his philosophy of design other than his magnificent courses. They remain outstanding examples of the art. With the exceptions of Donald Ross and Robert Trent Jones, no architect has such an impressive list of consensus topflight courses to his credit.

With Wilson's death, his associate Joseph Lee, whom Wilson had recruited back in the National Cash Register days in Dayton, assumed the firm's practice. Two other Wilson-trained designers, Robert von Hagge and Robert A. Simmons, had already gone out on their own, with Wilson's blessing, before 1965.

Robert Trent Jones and Dick Wilson were not the only architects active in the fifties, of course. There were a great many others, and many of them created courses of substantial merit.

Besides Trent Jones, Stanley Thompson's stable turned out the following:

• Clinton E. Robinson, who established his practice in Canada after the war. Robinson designed the 18-hole addition for Sunningdale Country Club in Ontario, Brudenell Golf and Country Club on Prince Edward Island and Upper Canada Village course in Ontario, among other magnificent layouts.

• Howard Watson, who began working for Thompson the very day that Clinton Robinson did. Watson started on his own in 1950, and much of his early solo work was in the Caribbean at courses like Caymanas Golf and Country Club in Jamaica and Country Club de Medellin in Colombia. But Watson soon had excellent work in Canada to his credit, too, like Pinegrove Country Club and Carling Lake Golf Club in Quebec, Board of Trade Country Club in Ontario and many others. He also trained his son, John, who started his own practice in the 1970s.

• Geoffrey S. Cornish, who, after a stint as an instructor at the University of Massachusetts, set up a practice in the early fifties. By the late sixties Cornish, with his associate, William G. Robinson, a graduate landscape architect who joined him in 1964, had designed more courses in New England than any other person. Crestview Country Club in Massachusetts, two courses for Quechee Lakes Country Club in Vermont, Eastman Lakes Golf Course in New Hampshire, Stratton Mountain Club in Vermont, York Downs in Toronto, Cranberry Valley on Cape Cod, the new Ashburn Golf Club in Nova Scotia, the Porto Carras Links in Greece and two courses for Summerlea Golf and Country Club near Montreal were among the 170 new courses designed by Cornish and Robinson and in play by the late seventies.

• Norman H. Woods, who based his practice in western Canada after Thompson's death. Woods designed many fine courses, including Kokanee Springs Golf Club in British Columbia, Rossmere Golf and Country Club in Manitoba, Lords Valley Country Club in Pennsylvania and the fine nine-hole Hilands Country Club in Montana.

Dick Wilson, of course, began with the old Pennsylvania firm of Toomey and Flynn. Among other assistants of that firm who established their own practices after the war were:

• William F. Gordon, who formed his company in 1941 to seed military installations but was very busy as an architect by the late 1940s. His son, David, a pilot in the war, finished college at Penn State and then joined the firm. By the fifties the two were full partners, and together they were responsible for such superior layouts as the Grace course at Saucon Valley Country Club in Pennsylvania, Stanwich Club in Connecticut, Buena Vista Country Club in New Jersey and Indian Spring Country Club in Maryland. William Gordon died in 1973 at age 80, and David Gordon continued the work of the firm. Before entring the firm of Toomey and Flynn, Bill Gordon had supervised golf course construction for Willie Park, Jr., Leonard Macomber, Donald Ross and others. Probably no other architect in history received such broad practical experience before setting up his own practice, nor was any more imbued with the history of the art.

Another Flynn associate, William F. Gordon (right), teamed for years with his son David (left) in a highly successful course design partnership.
COURTESY DAVID GORDON

• Robert F. Lawrence, who had also worked for Walter Travis and who, like Dick Wilson, had settled as a course manager in Florida

during the war. Lawrence produced such works as Plantation Golf Club and the South Course of Fort Lauderdale Country Club while in that state but did his best-known designs after moving to the Southwest in the early sixties. There he did Desert Forest Golf Club and Camelback Country Club in Arizona, and the South Course of the University of New Mexico in Albuquerque. "Red" Lawrence died in 1976, and associates Jeff Hardin and Greg Nash continued the practice in the Southwest.

Many designers trained under Donald Ross. Those active in the fifties included:

• The Hughes brothers, Lawrence, Frank and Henry. Lawrence and Frank originally worked on Ross construction crews supervised by their father, Henry T. Hughes, while young Henry herded the sheep that would clip long grass along fairway edges. The three brothers worked as a team in the late forties, producing as one of their first works the magnificent Club de Golf de Mexico in Mexico City. Henry B. Hughes eventually located in Denver, Colorado, where he created many of that state's fine courses, including Columbine Country Club, Bookcliff Country Club and Country Club of Fort Collins. Lawrence preferred the rapidly developing Southern California area; with Frank supervising the construction, he built beautiful layouts in wasteland areas, like Thunderbird Country Club and Eldorado Country Club in Palm Springs and Desert Inn Country Club in Las Vegas. At the time of his death in 1975, Lawrence Hughes was busy again in Mexico, where he had completed, among others, Santa Anita and San Isidro golf clubs.

• Eugene "Skip" Wogan, one of Massachusetts's most revered professional golfers. Although he maintained the professional's position at Essex Country Club in Manchester, Massachusetts, he laid out several fine courses in New England. His son, Philip, later became prominent in course design.

• Ellis Maples, who had the good fortune to be the son of a close friend of Donald Ross. Ellis's father, Frank, was the longtime superintendent of the Pinehurst Country Club courses and a sometime course architect himself. Young Maples worked on construction crews for Ross and was supervising construction of the Raleigh (North Carolina) Country Club at the time of the architect's death. Maples finished that course and spent the next few years debating whether to become a touring professional, a pro-superintendent or a course designer. By 1954 he had decided on design and by the mid-1960s he was the most

Bulldozers made it possible for architects like Ellis Maples to carve golf holes from previously hostile terrains, such as Grandfather Mountain in North Carolina's Smoky Mountains. COLLECTION RON WHITTEN

Ellis Maples (right) with his young protégé Ed Seay. COLLECTION RON WHITTEN

prolific architect in the Carolinas since Ross. Maples created the No. 5 Course at Pinehurst, Grandfather Golf and Country Club near Linville, Country Club of North Carolina and Country Club of South Carolina. He also started Edwin B. Seay in the business, as well as his own son, Dan Maples, who became his partner.

• Orrin E. Smith, who had served as a construction superintendent for Willie Park and Donald Ross, and later established his own firm in the twenties. He resumed his practice in the late forties. Smith died in 1958, but he left his own group of protégés who continued the practice. That group included:

• William F. Mitchell, of the prominent Mitchell greenkeeping family of New England. Mitchell, who passed away in 1974, did such courses as Old Westbury Golf and Country Club in New York; Country Club of New Seabury on Cape Cod; Longboat Key Club and President Country Club, both in Florida; Tanglewood Golf Club in Ohio; and Mount Pleasant Country Club in Massachusetts. Mitchell's brother Sam was associated with him for several years in the 1950s before establishing his own design firm.

• Albert Zikorus, who finished Smith's works after his death. On his own, Zikorus designed, among many others, Glastonbury Hills Country Club and Tunxis Plantation in Connecticut, Twin Hills Golf Club and Walpole Country Club in Massachusetts and Punta Borinquen Golf Club in Puerto Rico.

• James Gilmore Harrison, who organized his own business just after the war. Harrison hired a Penn State agronomy student named Ferdinand Garbin as one of his first associates. Garbin later became Harrison's son-in-law and then his partner. In the late sixties Garbin went out on his own, but in the fifties and sixties the two produced such courses as Sewickley Heights Country Club in Pennsylvania and Lakeview Country Club in West Virginia.

Departed pioneer designers William H. Tucker, Perry Maxwell and Billy Bell all left sons to carry on their work. William H. Tucker, Jr., was 59 years old at the time of his father's death, but he had assisted the elder Tucker in course design and construction all his adult life. Tucker Jr. died in 1962 after a relatively short period of practice on his own.

J. Press Maxwell had done all of his father's construction work from the late forties onward due to Perry's failing health. After his father's death, Press Maxwell designed many fine layouts of his own in the Southwest, including Oak Cliff in Dallas; East Ridge in Shreveport; Farmington in Memphis; and Hiwan Golf Club, Boulder Country Club and Kissing Camels, all in Colorado.

William P. Bell's son was William F. Bell, who built a practice in the fifties and sixties that was even larger than his productive father's. William F. Bell worked mainly in Southern California on courses like Torrey Pines, Saticoy Country Club, Industry Hills and Sandpiper Links, and in Hawaii on courses like the Makaha Inn complex. Other associates of the elder Bell also went to work for themselves in California. They included Robert E. Baldock (the Shore Course of Monterey Peninsula Country Club and San Joaquin Country Club) and William H. Johnson (Pala Mesa Golf Club and Knollwood Country Club).

Some "old-time" architects reactivated their practices after the war, and men like Jack Daray, William H. Diddel, Jack Fleming, William B. Langford, Charles Maddox, Sr., Harold Paddock, Alfred Tull and C. D. Wagstaff, all of whom had been active in the 1920s, were busier than ever. They all had young protégés eager to try their own skills, but none had more than Robert Bruce Harris. From Harris's Chicago office came David Gill, Edward Lawrence Packard (whose son, Roger, a graduate landscape architect, joined him in 1971), Kenneth Killian,

William F. Bell, at a Hawaiian
construction site in the early 1960s,
was the son of William P. Bell, George
Thomas's associate at Riviera and
elsewhere. Both father and son were
called Billy. COURTESY GOLF WORLD

Richard Nugent, William James Spear and Richard Phelps, each of
whom formed his own business in the fifties or sixties.

Harris himself was very productive in this period and created such
courses as Signal Point in Michigan, Hillcrest in Illinois and the
Country Club of Florida, which he personally considered his best
effort. Harris died in 1976 after a fifty-year career as a golf course
architect and sometime landscape designer.

In Mexico famed Mexican Amateur champion Percy Clifford started
a course design practice in the 1950s. Clifford, who had worked
closely with the Hughes brothers in the creation of Club de Golf de
Mexico, established himself as the premier course architect of his
country with such works as Bellavista in Mexico City, Pierre Marques
in Acapulco and the links-type Bajamar Country Club in Baja. By the
mid-1970s almost half the courses in Mexico were Clifford-designed.

The list of designers who began in the 1950s is too long to give
adequate justice. For each man named, a dozen or more have had to be
omitted. Here it must suffice to note that in North America for twenty

years following the Second World War, the golf boom was such that over one hundred full- or part-time course architects could remain busy and productive and still not satisfy the demand.

The same could be said for Britain and the Continent. Activity after the war included reconditioning old courses and creating new ones from the ruins of many abandoned golfing grounds. Sir Guy Campbell continued to practice in this period until his death in 1960. A major project of Campbell's at this time was the complete remodeling of Prince's in Sandwich.

John S. F. Morrison, the former associate of Colt and Alison, worked with Campbell at Prince's and then built his own business on the Continent, designing such courses as Le Betulle and La Mandria in Italy. His assistant, John Hamilton Stutt, son of John R. Stutt, continued the practice in Europe after Morrison's death in 1961.

Scottish architect Philip Mackenzie Ross, who had worked for Tom Simpson before going out on his own in the 1930s, also practiced in this era until his death in 1974. He developed his most prominent reputation in the late forties by rebuilding the Ailsa course at Turn-

Trained as a landscape architect, Chicago designer Robert Bruce Harris (right) brought a new concern about course maintenance to his profession.

berry into a dramatic oceanside layout after it had been paved over as a wartime airport.

Frederick W. Hawtree assumed his father's business upon the death of F. G. Hawtree in 1955. A talented designer who had learned the trade well from his father, Hawtree designed the superb courses at Royal Waterloo in Belgium and Saint Nom la Brêteche in France as well as many others.

Also active on the Continent in this era were Britons John D. Harris (who worked extensively in the Caribbean and Far East as well), Donald Harradine, Henry Cotton and the firm of Cotton, Pennink and Lawrie, composed of C. K. Cotton (no relation to Henry), J. J. F. Pennink and C. D. Lawrie. Donald Steel, golf correspondent for the London *Sunday Telegraph,* joined this firm as a partner in 1971 after a six-year "trainee" period.

Native European designers were rare, but two of the more success-

Right: In the 1960s, European designers C. K. Cotton (left), Pier Mancinelli (second from right) and John Harris (far right) contemplated the virtues of Western golf architecture. Below: They incorporated many Western ideas into their work, as at Harris's design for Tobago Golf Club in the Caribbean. COLLECTION RON WHITTEN; COURTESY PIER MANCINELLI

ful were German Bernard von Limburger, who did the Bremen, Lindau and Dusseldorf courses, and Spaniard Javier Arana, who did the El Prat, Rio Real and Guadalmina courses. Irish designers by the mid-1960s included Eddie Hackett of Ireland and Tom Macauley of Northern Ireland.

The dominant influence on British and European golf course architecture in this period was American course design. F. W. Hawtree attributed a "panache and style" to American courses previously unknown on the eastern side of the Atlantic. Some felt the influence began as early as the twenties, at a time when American competitive golf began to dominate the world golf scene. Others felt it was a natural result of the postwar use of more inland "American-type" terrain and American construction methods in Britain and Europe. Still others attributed it to the worldwide fame of Robert Trent Jones. Whatever the source, the influence was real, and by the early 1970s the transition was complete. Such far-flung courses as Woburn in Britain, Tobago in the Caribbean and Mount Mitchell in North Carolina all featured broad, sweeping fairways, large, undulating greens, long tees, yawning bunkers of glistening white sand and finely manicured playing areas. Unknowing observers would be hard-pressed to believe the courses were not the works of major American golf course architects. But, in fact, they were all the creations of Britons. Woburn was done by C. D. Lawrie, Tobago by John D. Harris and Mount Mitchell by F. W. Hawtree, the self-proclaimed admirer of American golf course design.

10

The New Breed

Until the late 1960s, real estate, construction and financing costs were favorable, and golf course design and development was a thriving worldwide enterprise. But by the mid-1970s costs had skyrocketed and the picture changed. Inflation took its toll, and the costs of building and maintaining a golf course multiplied drastically in a decade's time. New laws, including environmental regulations in America and land-use policies in Japan, further increased the expense, and quite often planned projects could not meet the regulations. High-quality construction, including fully automated irrigation systems, special drainage systems and new formulas for building greens, also increased costs.

The price of an average course in this period came to at least a half-million dollars for construction alone, without any consideration for other development costs. Unfortunately, many golfers were unable or unwilling to pay fees commensurate with these higher costs. By 1974 tight money had greatly curtailed construction and forced a number of shakily financed golf developments into bankruptcy. But by the late seventies American course development had picked up somewhat, particularly in the Sun Belt. British architects, with their far-flung practices sometimes stretching over several continents, remained busy. In Canada golf construction kept a steady pace, particularly in the oil-rich West. It was also fairly brisk in Europe and the Far East.

But while many an American course architect found himself as busy as ever planning courses and preparing specifications, an astonishing number of projects fell victim to raging inflation or unyielding regulations. As a result, the number of courses actually built and opened for play in the United States annually was less than a quarter of what it had

Desmond Muirhead, one of golf's great iconoclasts. COLLECTION RON WHITTEN been in the sixties. Development of new, strictly private country clubs all but ceased, although some existing clubs remodeled their layouts or added nines. But few courses could generate enough cash to cover expenses, let alone a profit, especially in regions with short playing seasons. Consequently, the majority of new courses in the late sixties and seventies were built either as municipally owned courses or as part of larger integrated real estate or resort developments. Courses at year-round resorts like Stratton Mountain in Vermont, which caters to golfers in summer and skiers in winter, became especially popular with investors.

Private clubs still in existence were sometimes forced by high taxes and reduced membership to move to new sites. Fortunately, sale of their valuable in-town land would normally pay for the development of a more elaborate facility on less expensive land farther out. The old Colonial Country Club in Memphis, Tennessee, for example, whose tight, 6,400-yard course had been the site of many tournaments, sold its prime location to developers. In exchange, it obtained sufficient land out in the country to build two courses. These were designed by Joseph Finger, a Houston-based architect who also did The Concord in New York and Pleasant Valley in Arkansas.

The ever-increasing value of land also affected the development of golf course architecture. Not only would dramatic, oceanfront courses become the exception in this period, but so, too, would courses on gently rolling, tree-lined terrains. Designers were increasingly confronted with the worst possible property, often the "left-over" land of a developer, on which to build their courses.

Yet any number of course architects rose to the challenge of less-than-desirable sites. Courses in this period were constructed on sanitary landfills (Mangrove Bay Municipal Golf Course, St. Petersburg, Florida, by William Amick, where marsh gas is piped off for city lighting), rocky, cactus-covered land (Picacho Hills Country Club in New Mexico by Joseph Finger), marshlands (Hilton Head Golf Club by George W. Cobb), strip-mined gravel pits (Laurel Green Country Club in western Pennsylvania by Xen Hassenplug), slag heaps (Blyth Golf Club in England by J. H. Stutt) and even on ledge rock (Connecticut Golf Club by Cornish and Robinson). Of all the traits necessary and desirable in a first-rate course architect, perhaps none was more important in this period than imagination. The ability to hew silken courses from sow's pens surely separated the poor designer from the successful one in the seventies.

The ranks of golf course designers had continued to expand in the late 1950s as more men felt the need to express themselves through

Even in modern times, golf construction often requires hand labor. Hand-sprigging a Bermuda-grass green at Kauai Surf Golf Club in Hawaii. COLLECTION RON WHITTEN

molding of the landscape. Some new designers came directly from related professions, like Robert Muir Graves, a landscape architect, Ted Robinson, a land planner, Jack Kidwell, a pro-superintendent, and Jack Snyder, a landscape architect and second-generation superintendent. But most had worked for established architects, as had Francis J. Duane, who was with Robert Trent Jones from 1945 until 1963.

Prior to hiring Duane, Jones had worked almost alone, but from then on his office gradually expanded. In 1961 Yale engineering graduate Roger Rulewich entered the firm, taking over after Duane's departure as a major figure in the eastern office. Robert Trent Jones, Jr., joined his father in 1962 and was responsible for setting up a Pacific branch of the business, based in California. Jones's younger son, Rees, signed on with the organization in 1965. In 1968 graduate landscape architect Cabell Robinson started in the New Jersey office, establishing a permanent Jones branch in Spain in 1970 after Ronald Kirby (who had represented Jones in Europe from 1965 to 1969) formed his own design firm with touring professional Gary Player.

By 1980 there were over 400 Trent Jones courses located in forty-two states and twenty-three countries. Robert Trent Jones, Jr., established his own practice in 1972 with loose ties to his father's. Rees Jones started his own separate practice in 1974 and in the same year wrote *Golf Course Developments*, an influential book in collaboration with landscape architect Guy L. Rando. Both Trent Jr. ("Bobby") and Rees developed individual styles unique from their famous father, and each was the architect of many topflight layouts.

Although the fame of Robert Trent Jones had not abated nationally or internationally, other architects began to influence the field of course design. In the 1970s, three designers began to overshadow Trent. They were Desmond Muirhead, George Fazio and Pete Dye.

Desmond Muirhead, a Scot who trained in Britain as a land planner, moved to the United States via Canada, where he attended the University of British Columbia and planned a golf course in Vancouver. In the early sixties he assisted in the development of the Sun City retirement village in Arizona and became intrigued with the relationship of its golf course to the housing plan.

By 1963 Muirhead had formed his own course design and construction firm, and the courses he developed attracted immediate attention. His distinctive style resembled that of few other architects. It could almost be said that Muirhead sculpted his courses from the terrain. His tees were parabolic, serpentine or pronged and nearly always dozens of yards in length. Some of his greens appeared to flow into the horizon; others were so severely contoured as to resemble rolling surf. His water hazards, which were numerous, were free form in design, and he routed his holes around them in unique fashions. On one hole a green would be located on an island; on another, a fairway would be. Sometimes a tee, other times a landing area, would be perched on a peninsula. Muirhead's bunkers featured exaggerated capes and bays, long fingers of white sand pressed against green slopes of grass.

Muirhead also prided himself on combining his courses into pleasing arrangements with the surrounding environment, be it a housing development or a desert wasteland. He abhorred architects who deliberately routed several holes in one direction so as to maximize the available frontage land for housing developers. He also crusaded for

Papa Jones and his boys. Right: Young Rees Jones reviews a plan with his father, Robert Trent Jones. Below: Robert Trent Jones, Jr., garbed in an Oriental kimono, poses near his "Zen bunker" at Princeville in Hawaii.

COURTESY *GOLF WORLD*

more rational routing of courses to protect players from one another and adjoining landowners from errant shots.

Muirhead's critics argued that his style was really nothing more than contemporary landscape architecture demonstrated for over twenty years by course architect Edward Lawrence Packard. They also claimed Muirhead's designs were sterile, well-manicured lawns devoid of any true golfing values. But the architect maintained his courses followed modern-day principles of strategic design and maximum flexibility. Among his creations were the Old Course at Mission Hills Golf and Country Club in Palm Springs, California; Baymeadows Country Club in Jacksonville, Florida; McCormick Ranch Golf Club in Scottsdale, Arizona; and Bent Tree Golf Club in Dallas, Texas.

In the mid-1970s Muirhead disappeared from the golf design scene entirely. There were reports he relocated in Australia, where he engaged in city planning instead of course design. But he reemerged in America a decade later, and produced a couple of startling designs that sparked a national debate on the merits of his work.

The first was Aberdeen Golf and Country Club in Boynton Beach, Florida, with holes symbolic of art, literature and the meaning of life. A par 3 was shaped like a fire-breathing dragon, with bunkers serving as its eyes and puffs of smoke. A par 5 was shaped like a mermaid, with a fantail teebox, angular earthen scales dotting the fairway, a pair of fish-shape bunkers floating along the waistline and two bosomy mounds just below a putting surface framed by a flowing bunker of tresses. Another hole featured concentric circular mounds around a circular green, representative of the cosmos. Still others were built as tributes to the British sculptor Henry Moore and the Japanese artist Hokusai.

Muirhead was even more fanciful in his next project, Stone Harbor Golf Club in Cape May, New Jersey. He built bunkers in the shape of flowers, a bear's foot, an eagle's head and dragon's teeth. One hole had a green representing the state of New Jersey fronted by a Pennsylvania-shaped bunker and edged by an island bunker shaped like Manhattan. Another hole was symbolic of a Viking warrior, with a helmet-shaped green, complete with a horn bunker on each flank and a long sword-like bunker dividing the fairway before it. Its par-3 12th was a tomahawk hole, with a long rectangular bunker running from the tee to the wedge-shaped green.

His fans argued that Muirhead was expanding golf architecture into a true art form, open to varying interpretations. His critics blasted him for sacrificing fundamental design principles and creating blatantly artificial holes. One competitor suggested that perhaps Muirhead was

Desmond Muirhead, before the bear or the beard. At the height of his career, Muirhead teamed with the Golden Bear, Jack Nicklaus, on several designs. COLLECTION RON WHITTEN

simply poking fun at the entire profession. Whatever his motivation, one thing was clear. Aberdeen and Stone Harbor announced to the golf world that Desmond Muirhead had returned.

At another end of the spectrum was the work of George Fazio, who had been a successful club professional and competitive golfer in the 1940s and '50s. When he retired, he intended to operate a car dealership and a few daily-fee courses in Pennsylvania, but friends lured him into designing a course. By the time he had completed the design of Atlantis Country Club in Tuckertown, New Jersey, Fazio was hooked on course design as a new career. His early works, like the Jackrabbit Road Course of Champions Golf Club in Texas and Moselem Springs Country Club in Pennsylvania, were warmly received. But it was not until the late 1960s that George Fazio was recognized as a major force in American course design.

By then it was apparent that Fazio had steadily, through a progression of works, developed into a fine classical course architect. His designs were not modernistic like Muirhead's nor as stylized as those of Trent Jones. They were, instead, reminiscent of the grand old courses of the Golden Era. Fazio's courses had a graceful and appeal-

Muirhead's return to golf design after a ten-year absence was marked by highly symbolic designs, including this "Norseman" hole at Stone Harbor Golf Club in New Jersey. The large bunker represented a sword and shield, the green a helmet with flanking horn bunkers. RON WHITTEN

ing appearance that belied their youthfulness. And they were challenging without being repetitive in the process. One Fazio hole might feature a huge bunker in the inside corner of a dogleg and a tightly bunkered green. The next might feature a trap on the outside of a dogleg and a green devoid of sand.

George Fazio certainly had a wealth of experience and observation upon which to draw. He learned the game in Philadelphia, amidst the bright collection of courses by Hugh Wilson, Donald Ross, William Flynn, William Gordon and others. Merion was a particular favorite of Fazio, and he nearly won a U.S. Open there. He also served as head

Often mistaken as father and son, George Fazio (left) and Tom Fazio (right) were actually uncle and nephew. COLLECTION RON WHITTEN

professional for several years at Pine Valley, and he not only played the course on countless occasions but absorbed its nuances. With this background, Fazio was able to instill in his own works the distinctive qualities of many of the great American courses.

The works of George Fazio include Jupiter Hills in Florida, which contains a series of holes seemingly appropriated from Pine Valley, Edgewood Tahoe Golf Club near Lake Tahoe, Butler National Golf Club in Chicago, Devil's Elbow Golf Club at Moss Creek and The National Golf Club in Toronto.

Fazio also became a favorite architect of clubs hosting major tournaments in the seventies. In this capacity he made major revisions, including creation of several new holes at such hallowed courses as Oak Hill in New York and Inverness in Ohio. One of Fazio's nephews, Tom Fazio, ably assisted him on most of his works almost from the beginning and became his partner in 1973. A decade later, the two went their separate ways. Tom's brother Jim then joined forces with George Fazio. The two produced a few more subtle, finely hewn designs before George's death in 1986. Tom Fazio, meanwhile, demonstrated his talents at Wild Dunes near Charleston, South Carolina, The Golf Club of Oklahoma near Tulsa and a new 54-hole PGA National golf complex in Florida.

Pete Dye entered the profession about the same time as Muirhead and Fazio. An insurance salesman-turned-golf architect, Dye spent the first few years of his design career without conspicuous success. But in the mid-1960s, after he and his wife, Alice, a wonderful amateur golfer and partner in his design firm from the start, made a tour of the grand old courses of Scotland, Dye began to develop his own style of design, a style as unique as Muirhead's or Fazio's but far different than either.

Dye felt that graceful mounds and undulations on a golf course were artificial. True natural features, he observed, were characterized by abrupt change. Those were the features that most impressed him on the Scottish links, the swales and hollows and pits around fairways and greens, the jagged sandhills and steep bunker faces shored up by railroad ties.

Respectful, too, of the works of many of the great early American architects like Ross, Tillinghast and Macdonald, Pete Dye began to develop a philosophy that disdained the typical features of modern American golf courses, the same features, ironically, that British designers at this time were wholeheartedly embracing.

Dye's new courses sported tight, swiggly, undulating fairways with small, wildly contoured greens surrounded by mounds, swales, hollows or pot bunkers. His roughs were maintained in indigenous vege-

Origins of inspiration (right): A snapshot of Alice Dye playing from a Prestwick bunker in 1963. Soon after this extended tour of Scottish courses, Peter Dye began incorporating Old World touches into his designs, including bunkers shored up by planks. Below: Case in point, the 13th hole at The Golf Club, New Albany, Ohio, finished by the Dyes in 1967.

tation. Many of his tees, bunkers and even water hazards were lined with upright railroad ties, so many that the railroad tie came to be known as Dye's trademark. One Dye course, Oak Tree Golf Club near Edmond, Oklahoma, had over 8,000 ties running about it.

His courses were also shorter than most, often less than 6,200 yards from the regular tees, not over 6,500 from the back and less than 5,000 yards from the forward tees. Alice Dye was especially influential in positioning forward tees. While she often made major contributions to his designs, her biggest triumph was to convince her husband not to locate front tees as an afterthought but rather deliberately position them to provide women with the opportunity to play each hole as designed but within their capabilities.

Dye's most prominent early works included The Golf Club near Columbus, Ohio, Crooked Stick near Indianapolis, Indiana, Harbour Town Golf Links on Hilton Head Island, South Carolina, and Teeth of The Dog, a dramatic seaside layout in the Dominican Republic.

Dye's critics most often complained that his designs were exceedingly difficult to maintain. His severely contoured greens, small deep bunkers, huge wasteland bunkers and other novel features were not suited for modern maintenance equipment, they said. An elevated tee surrounded by a bank of railroad ties was charming, but it required daily hand-mowing and the lifting and lowering of the mower at that.

In reality, few features on a Pete Dye layout were truly revolutionary, even in America. C. B. Macdonald, for instance, lined several of his bunkers with railway ties at The National Golf Links. Perry Maxwell was notorious for his small, treacherous greens. Devereux Emmet had long experimented with mounds and hollows as substitutes for greenside bunkers, and Donald Ross did much the same at times. But in the late 1960s and early 1970s, no other golf course architect had the courage and the tenacity to try such different approaches to course design; Dye's results caused immediate and widespread attention, probably because they were so opposite to the style ushered in by Robert Trent Jones in the 1950s and adopted and modified by nearly all contemporary American and British architects.

In the early seventies Pete's brother Roy Dye joined him in the business and was responsible for such typical "Dye designs" as the revised Country Club of Montreal and Waterwood National Golf Club in Texas. Pete Dye was also responsible for employing, training and inspiring a new generation of golf course designers, most without formal landscaping education but all with a burning desire to design-and-build courses in the same hands-on manner as their mentor.

They included the two sons of Pete and Alice. Perry Dye, the elder son, located in Denver, but established a lucrative overseas business, especially in Japan. He did relatively little work in conjunction with Pete, most notably the Dunes Course at Riverdale Golf Club in Brighton, Colorado, and Karsten Golf Club for Arizona State University in Tempe.

P. B. Dye, the Dyes' younger son, remained with his father for a longer time, collaborating on DeBordieu and Prestwick, both near Myrtle Beach, before establishing his own reputation at courses like Loblolly Pines in Hobe Sound, Florida, and Cross Creek Plantation near Greenville, South Carolina.

Among other longtime "Dye-sciples" who eventually began designing courses on their own were Bill Coore, Tom Doak, Gary Grandstaff,

David Pfaff, Scott Pool, David Postlethwait, Lee Schmidt, Bobby Weed and Rod Whitman.

As contradictory as it might seem, the multitalented Jack Nicklaus worked at separate times with both Pete Dye and Desmond Muirhead. With Dye, he collaborated on Harbour Town, and with Muirhead, he assisted on several courses, including Mayacoo Lakes in Florida. In the mid-1970s, Nicklaus formed a course-design firm that planned, among others, Muirfield Village in Ohio (with the advice and counsel of Muirhead), Glen Abbey near Toronto and Shoal Creek in Birmingham, Alabama.

It was a sign of the times that in the mid- and late 1970s, relative newcomers like Desmond Muirhead and George Fazio garnered more publicity than Robert Trent Jones. Even more significantly, it was Pete Dye who changed the face of late-twentieth-century course architecture. The era of Robert Trent Jones faded as that of Pete Dye arose.

11
The Pete Dye Influence

Pete Dye, a very hands-on golf architect, in the field during construction of Kings Mill Golf Club, Williamsburg, Virginia. COLLECTION RON WHITTEN

The 1980s can be called the Pete Dye era. Not because he dominated the decade, for he did not. Dye had his strong years and lean ones. Other talented designers also produced outstanding products during the same period. But Pete Dye's designs, few though they were in comparison to many high-powered firms, established new standards in how golf courses could look and play. Pete Dye's style of golf architecture, much of it produced by associates and even imitators, pervaded the entire decade. Even his chief competitors were building courses that were either a reflection of his style or a response to it.

For instance, every architect sooner or later incorporated some wooden bulkheading into his or her design, usually around water hazards, to create a "sink or swim" finality to the edge of a hole. A few designers even bulkheaded the faces of bunkers with railroad ties or timber. Some lined their elevated tees with planks. All of this was old hat to Dye, who had been doing the same thing for over fifteen years, beginning at courses like The Golf Club and Harbour Town, and who had appropriated the idea himself from the grand old links of Scotland. But the increasing popularity of his target-golf philosophy (that required pinpoint accuracy rather than low, bouncing golf shots) and the astonishing visual contrasts of Dye's courses caused other architects to try similar features.

Railroad ties so proliferated golf course design in the 1980s that Dye himself ultimately declined to use them anymore. Feeling stereotyped, he sought alternative methods to achieve his "abrupt change" design style. On some courses, he simply used near vertical walls of turfgrass, which proved difficult to mow and maintain, even when slow-growing grasses were utilized. On a few sites, he experimented with rocks and

147

boulders as bulkheads. He brought back the old Scottish riveted bunker, with a vertical face of stacked bricks of sod. In the South, he edged water hazards with a framework of vertical wire mesh, down which runners of Bermuda grass would grow. The more Dye experimented, the more others would follow.

That was true even at the start of the decade. In 1980, Dye and PGA Tour commissioner Deane Beman (who himself had dabbled in golf architecture during his playing days) ushered in the era of "stadium golf" with the advent of the Tournament Players Club at Sawgrass in Ponte Vedra Beach, Florida. It was not the first golf course to be designed for spectator convenience. It was simply the most complete. Its routing moved away from the clubhouse and back toward it again and again. Every hole had spectator viewpoints, huge earthen bleachers dubbed "spectator mounds" positioned around the tees, fairways or greens. There were no uphill shots or elevated greens where viewers couldn't see the action. The finishing hole was meant to be one giant amphitheater, capable of holding 50,000 people, the entire audience of a typical tournament's final round, so that every paying customer could witness the climatic final putts.

But while press and fans marveled over its countless vantage points, players complained about the difficulty of the course. Meant to be a southern version of Pine Valley, with vast waste areas of sand and tiny tilted greens, TPC at Sawgrass added acres of unforgiving water to its formula and proved to be even more intimidating than its inspiration. Because the PGA Tour owned the facility, the players got their way,

Typical of the Dye inventiveness: The basket trap on the 17th at Harbour Town Golf Links, Hilton Head Island, South Carolina. COURTESY *GOLF WORLD*

The par-5 11th of the Stadium Course at TPC at Sawgrass, Ponte Vedra, Florida, typifies the Dye style of abrupt change, with a huge waste area, native grass roughs, a pedestal green, steep banks and a vertical bulkhead along the water. RON WHITTEN

Another view of the course that introduced amphitheater golf to America. Above: The 18th at TPC at Sawgrass, with spectator mounds, just after grassing. Left: The finished hole hosted its first Players Championship in 1982. COLLECTION RON WHITTEN

and TPC at Sawgrass was subsequently revised on several occasions, mainly in modification of green contours and elimination of many waste areas.

One hole that successfully avoided reconstruction was the par-3 17th. Ironically, this short-iron shot to an island green proved to be especially controversial. With its stark profile—a simple putting surface edged in plank, encircled by water and connected to the shoreline by a narrow isthmus—this frying pan of a hole popularized anew the notion of the island green. It was certainly a far cry from the island green Herbert Strong had done at nearby Ponte Vedra Club back in 1932, or the one Dev Emmet had done at Wee Burn in the 1920s or the couple that Tillinghast had designed. This island green was clearly ominous, for it offered no margin for error. A shot was either on or off, dry or wet. It was Pete Dye target-golf in its most basic form.

Tour players feared and hated it, complaining that it was totally unplayable in heavy winds common to its location, that no lead was too large until that hole was encountered. But if players despised it, fans loved it.

Perhaps the protests solidified the general public's admiration for the hole. Whatever the reason, island greens began popping up with regularity on courses in the 1980s. Architects claimed course owners demanded them. Others suspected that at least some designers secretly hoped to outdo Pete Dye. Island greens certainly became the star attractions at many new courses and focal points for countless photographs and advertisements.

For a time, nearly every Jack Nicklaus design seemed to contain an obligatory island green. He not only built single island greens, he built double island greens serving two separate holes. He built island greens surrounded by sand. At Valhalla near Louisville, Kentucky, he built one atop a 15-foot-high stack of boulders. Curiously, he rarely put his island greens on par 3s, preferring instead to use them on short par 4s or par 5s. Few other designers followed that lead, feeling that an island green on anything but a par 3, where the length and angle of approach could be anticipated, was simply unfair.

Even designers with relatively conservative philosophies, men such as Joe Lee and Rees Jones, began featuring island greens in their work. True to their philosophies, their island greens were only on par-3 holes and offered a buffer, a wide ring of rough and a bunker or two between the putting surface and the water. But they produced them nonetheless, proving that golf design, like other forms of fashion, was in part a reaction to the latest trend.

Other designers unabashedly imitated Pete Dye's infamous 17th at

The evolution of the island green. Top left: Not the earliest, but a granddaddy nonetheless, the par-3 9th at Ponte Vedra Golf Club, Ponte Vedra Beach, Florida, by Herbert Strong. Bottom left: A Trent Jones version at Golden Horseshoe Golf Club, Williamsburg, Virginia, dating from 1957. Top right: The 18th green at the Old Course at Mission Hills Country Club, Rancho Mirage, California, by Desmond Muirhead during his graceful parabolic period. Bottom right: The infamous 17th at TPC at Sawgrass (Stadium Course). Other architects provided buffers around their island greens. Pete Dye made it a distinct hit-or-miss proposition. COURTESY *GOLF WORLD;* COLLECTION RON WHITTEN; RON WHITTEN; RON WHITTEN

*The evolution of the island green,
continued. Top left: A near duplicate of
Dye's target island green, by Dye
himself at PGA West's Stadium
Course, La Quinta, California in 1986.
He simply substituted a boulder
bulkhead. Center left: Another
variation on the target island green, by
von Hagge and Devlin, on a par 5 at
TPC at The Woodlands near Houston.
Bottom left: At the Cochise Course of
the Golf Club at Desert Mountain,
Scottsdale, Arizona, Jack Nicklaus
provided a double island green, serving
both the par-5 7th and the par-4 15th.
Top right: Muirhead's fanciful
"Clashing Jaws" island green with
flanking island bunkers proved too
difficult for members. They ultimately
remodeled it to provide for some
margin for error. Bottom right: With
the 1990s came perhaps the ultimate
in island greens, a movable floating
island green at Coeur d'Alene Resort
Golf Club in Idaho.* RON WHITTEN;
COLLECTION RON WHITTEN; RON WHITTEN;
COURTESY STONE HARBOR G. C.; COURTESY
COEUR D'ALENE RESORT G. C.

TPC. Dye himself was among the imitators, building another 17th hole island green at his Stadium Course at PGA West, near Palm Springs, in 1986. Instead of timber, he surrounded the green with sharp-edged boulders (stained to the shade of the backdropping Santa Rosa Mountains), adding another ominous dimension to the shot. And heeding one Sawgrass criticism, he installed a series of elevated tees around this island green so that players could better see the target and the water behind the green.

Two attempts to outdo a Dye island green stand out. At Stone Harbor Golf Club in Cape May, New Jersey, Desmond Muirhead produced an island green shaped like a football pointed at the player and flanked it by twin jagged-edged island sand bunkers. It proved to be not only outlandish, but too difficult, and in the end club officials rebuilt the hole into a larger inviting island, with green and flanking bunkers hugged by mounds and slopes. Meanwhile, in Coeur d'Alene, Idaho, developer Duane Hagadone conceived the idea of the ultimate island green, a floating movable one completely detached from the rest of the course. Designed by golf architect Scott Miller and engineered by a shipbuilding firm at an expense in excess of $1 million, the floating 14th became the flagship of the Coeur d'Alene Resort Golf Course. As ingenious as it was, it had its limitations. It would be moved closer to shore or farther out, but not moved side to side. It was a novelty that few expected would be duplicated because of the cost involved and its potential for slow play. Besides the inevitable dunked shots and reloads, all players had to be shuttled to and from the island in a small custom-built ferry.

Besides spectator golf and island greens, the Tournament Players Club at Sawgrass may well be remembered as one of the last courses of its kind, a layout built from land reclaimed from a swamp by draining the water into lateral lagoons and reshaping the muck. Even during its conception, swamps and bogs became protected wetlands under a series of state and federal regulations. The definitions were very strict and narrowly construed. A wetlands did not need to be wet (except for a small number of consecutive days) in order to be off limits. Even in the arid Southwest, federal Corps of Engineer officials would painstakingly identify wetland areas on a potential golf site. At the time, it seemed like bureaucratic overkill. Upon reflection, it perhaps made sense, for it was even more essential to preserve small water pockets in desert areas than along the Mississippi Delta or a South Carolina bayou.

In some locales, wetlands couldn't be touched at all. In others, mitigation became the keyword. Portions of wetlands could be altered only if the developer mitigated the damage by creating new wetlands of concomitant area elsewhere on the property.

The challenge to golf architects working in areas of protected wetlands was to shoehorn golf courses into wetland areas. Their efforts further promulgated the Pete Dye concept of target golf, golf played through the air to specific target fairways and target greens. Such golf was challenging for the bold and skilled, deflating for the foolhardy and miserable for the hack.

Architects persevered in such hostile environments. There were some failures but some notable triumphs:

• Haig Point Golf Club on Daufuskie Island, South Carolina, woven through ancient tree plantation and along the ocean sound by Rees Jones, younger son of Trent Jones.

The versatility of Rees Jones showcased at the par-3 15th at Haig Point Golf Links on Daufuskie Island, South Carolina. From the back tee, scratch players must carry marsh and bunker to reach the green. The front set of tees, tucked well forward and into the trees, affords a shorter, easier tee shot. RON WHITTEN

• The Witch Golf Club in Myrtle Beach, South Carolina, by Dan Maples, son of Ellis Maples, with holes linked by miles of nearly a mile of bridges.

• The Hampton Club, on St. Simons Island, Georgia, by veteran architect Joe Lee, who expanded upon the art of his mentor Dick Wilson.

• Elk Ridge Golf Course in Atlanta, Michigan, with holes worked through an attractive northern savannah by veteran architect Jerry Matthews, son of Bruce Matthews.

• Bonita Bay Club, Bonita Springs, Florida, by classically trained Arthur Hills, perhaps the most extensive wetlands design of all.

• Shattuck Inn Golf Club in Jaffrey, New Hampshire, featuring a stretch with tees on natural ledge-rock peninsulas and targets on the far sides of an eerie bog. Shattuck was the product of Brian Silva, a talented new associate of veteran Geoffrey Cornish, who replaced Bill Robinson in the partnership when Robinson moved to the West Coast.

• Old Marsh Golf Club near West Palm Beach, by Pete Dye, who made Old Marsh an engineering marvel by devising an internal drainage system designed to prevent any runoff from the course into the surrounding marsh.

There were other legacies established by Pete Dye and the original TPC at Sawgrass. The concept proved so alluring that it spawned several networks of Tournament Players courses. One popped up in the Far East, another in Europe. In America, the TPC family of stadium golf courses expanded and contracted with regularity during the decade. Dye produced another at Sawgrass, called the Valley Course, which hosted one Senior PGA Tour event and then drifted into obscurity, inevitably overshadowed by his prominent big brother. Dye also designed one in Castle Rock, Colorado, which, after several annual Senior events, left the TPC network and operated as the semiprivate Plum Creek Golf and Country Club.

Other architects were hired to do Tournament Players courses. Arthur Hills was asked by the Tour at the last minute to convert his nearly completed residential development in Coral Springs, Florida, into a spectator course. The resulting TPC at Eagle Trace received major criticism over its playability in heavy coastal winds, which left the impression that design flaws rather than lack of course maturity were to blame. Other TPC layouts at Scottsdale, Hartford, Memphis and Dallas/Fort Worth proved functional if not inspirational. As TPC courses slowly replaced older designs on the PGA Tour schedule and became the mainstay for the newly developed Senior PGA Tour, many players expressed dismay that the courses were too homogenized, that each one looked like the previous and all were patterned after Pete Dye's original.

There was perhaps some justification for the dismay. The PGA Tour had its own construction crew building each TPC course, headed by Bobby Weed and David Postlethwait, two former Pete Dye construction supervisors. The green complexes and bunkers at most TPC layouts were essentially the same regardless of site. And every TPC course adhered to the same philosophy of accommodating gallery views. No uphill shots, no elevated greens, no trees that could interfere with a spectator's view. Tournament Players layouts each had their own personality, but all were unmistakably children sired within the same clan.

By the end of the decade, some changes occurred within that family. The Tournament Players Club of Connecticut, renamed TPC at River Highlands, was remodeled by Bobby Weed using an old-style design. There were deliberate uphill shots and perched greens, even a couple of blind tee shots. The bunkers, perhaps overdone, were not the garden-variety flat-sand, steep-faced ones, but instead were sweeping bunkers with capes and bays. TPC at River Highlands contained the ideal amphitheater finish, a huge bowl around which the final four holes were rerouted. Even more than at Sawgrass, the River Highlands finish seemed the perfect stage for the closing act of a PGA tournament. Ironically, despite all the attention paid to the gate, network television still dictated that a sudden-death playoff on any TPC layout be returned to the far reaches of their stationary cameras rather than on the arenas of the closing hole.

Even more intriguing were revisions at the Tournament Players Club at Avenel in Potomac, Maryland. Originally designed by veteran architect Ed Ault, his son Brian and associates Tom Clark and Bill Love, but constructed by the Tour's crew, it looked more like a Pete Dye product than an Ed Ault one when it first opened. Parts of the course in hilly, wooded terrain contained beautiful natural holes. But the closing holes were on barren open land with artificial mounding. The Tour, however, rejected Ault's proposed tree-planting program, feeling that no trees should be planted that would interfere with gallery view of the action. Years later, the Ault firm was informed that the course bunkering had quietly been remodeled to conform to Ault's original plans. And, they were told, trees were being planted on the closing holes. But rather than follow the architects' planting plans,

Tour players were invited to make the selections and locate the plantings by marking their preferences on photographs of the holes.

Because every Tournament Players Club was assigned a prominent Tour player as a design consultant, many professional golfers suddenly discovered golf design as a lucrative avocation. A few seemed genuinely convinced that little more was required of them than to insure the design fit the demands of their particular game. A few others, smitten by the creative process, became more heavily involved in golf design following a TPC experience. Whether ego- or agent-dictated, the sad fact is that far too many touring professionals allowed public relations firms and sportswriters to misinform the general public that they were the designers of the course. The true designers, golf course architects less well known than the players, were given little or no credit.

By the end of the 1980s, over a dozen touring professionals headed full-time golf design firms. The wisest of tour pros affiliated with a prominent architect before forming a firm in order to learn the ropes and afterward staffed his own firm with talented full-time architects. Jack Nicklaus, of course, was the prime model, going from greatest golfer of all time to one of the leading architects in a nearly seamless transition, first teaming with Pete Dye, then with Desmond Muirhead and finally opening his own design firm. His first team of designers were Jay Morrish and Bob Cupp, who served him well for several years before establishing very successful practices of their own.

Morrish formed his own business in 1983 and subsequently teamed with former British Open champion Tom Weiskopf to produce a succession of high-ranking courses, including Troon Golf and Country Club in Scottsdale, Arizona; Troon North, its sister club; Forest Highlands Golf Club in Flagstaff, Arizona; Shadow Glen Golf Club near Kansas City, Kansas; The Kings Golf Club at Waikaloa Village in Hawaii and Double Eagle Golf Club in Columbus, Ohio.

Cupp left the Nicklaus organization a few years after Morrish and quickly garnered his own following. Enjoying the input of a variety of touring professionals, including Jerry Pate, Tom Kite, Fuzzy Zoeller and Hubert Green, Cupp was more willing than most to play occasional second fiddle to a Tour pro on a design project. By the end of the decade his resumé included Port Armor Club on Lake Oconee in Georgia, Settindown Creek north of Atlanta and the Tournament Players Club at StarPass near Tucson, Arizona. With Jerry Pate as consultant, he did Old Waverly Golf Club in West Point, Mississippi, the New Course at Indianwood Golf and Country Club near Detroit and The Grasslands in Lakeland, Florida.

Among the other touring pros who invested considerable time in golf course architecture:

• Arnold Palmer, who teamed with Frank Duane in the early 1970s, then formed a design firm with Ed Seay at the end of the decade. By the mid-1980s the Palmer Course Design Company was one of the busiest. The company reached a new frontier when it constructed the first golf layout in the People's Republic of China in 1985.

• Gary Player, who worked on several South African courses with Sid Brews, then later formed an American partnership with veteran designers Ron Kirby and Arthur Davis. When that company dissolved, Player teamed for a time with Karl Litten, a former associate of Robert von Hagge. By the end of the 1980s Player's firm bore only his name.

• Bruce Devlin, who worked with Robert von Hagge, the onetime Dick Wilson associate, for nearly twenty years starting in the late 1960s. The pair produced such notable designs as Key Biscayne Golf

In the 1970s Robert von Hagge (left) and partner Bruce Devlin (right) were golf design's glamor boys. COLLECTION RON WHITTEN

Links near Miami, Crown Colony Country Club in Lufkin, Texas, and the Tournament Players Course at The Woodlands near Houston.

• Ben Crenshaw, who formed a partnership with ex Dye-sciple Bill Coore in the middle of the decade but spent several frustrating years on failed projects before finally debuting original designs at the close of the decade.

• Hale Irwin, who worked on a few designs with Gary Kern and then established his own company in affiliation with veteran Colorado architect Dick Phelps. Phelps's son Richard served as in-house course architect in Irwin's firm.

• Mark McCumber, who expanded his family's course construction business into a turnkey design-and-build company that handled several jobs in the Southeast, including Windance in Mississippi and Osprey Cove in Georgia.

But it was Jack Nicklaus who achieved the most attention as a player turned architect, no doubt in part because of his phenomenal record as a player and in part because of his reported million-dollar-per-course design fee. While Nicklaus took his design career seriously, he was also willing to risk criticism by experimenting in the field.

His designs at Grand Cypress and Loxahatchee, both in southern Florida, were prime examples. Searching for a novel way of reshaping flat, lifeless Florida terrain, Nicklaus ringed each hole on both courses with randomly placed knobby mounds of varying sizes. These giant chocolate drops, which provided a distinct landscape for their venues, were immediately praised, scorned and even copied by other architects on other courses. But the mounds proved harder to maintain than to play and ultimately proved to be more fad than fashion.

About the same time, Nicklaus's golf equipment company perfected a lightweight golf ball that maintained all the feel and playing characteristics of a regular ball yet only traveled half the distance. It was not a novel idea. Architect Bill Diddel had proposed such a golf ball as far back as the forties. But it wasn't until the mid-1980s that such a ball became economically feasible.

To promote its acceptance, Nicklaus and his team designed a few courses specifically for use with the lightweight ball. The first was a short course on the Cayman Islands in the Caribbean, which quickly led the media to christen the new ball as the "Cayman ball." Nicklaus hedged his bet a bit on his Britannia course in the Caymans. While it was a regular par-72 course for golf balls that would only travel 150

The par-5 16th at the Nicklaus Private Course of PGA West is a classic Jack Nicklaus design, with a dual fairway split by a bunker and a three-level green especially accessible by a high fade. RON WHITTEN

Jack Nicklaus (right) sketching instructions to assistant Jim Lipe during a site visit in Michigan. Among PGA Tour stars, few took as much interest or spent as much time on golf architecture as Nicklaus. RON WHITTEN

yards at most, he also designed additional tees and greens so it could play as a precision course for use with a regular ball.

The Cayman ball, despite its obvious appeal to developers who lacked sufficient land to build a regulation 18 holes, never gained widespread support. At the end of the 1980s it was still considered a novelty or golf substitute, despite the efforts of designer Bill Amick (a former Diddel student) to promote its widespread use. Amick even designed the first golf course created exclusively for use with a Cayman ball, Eagle Landing near Charleston, South Carolina.

Perhaps the greatest impact Jack Nicklaus made on golf course architecture occurred with the opening of Desert Highlands in Scottsdale. Desert Highlands issued in another facet of course architecture, the blending of golf into the hostile terrain of an arid desert. Strict governmental restrictions, which included the transplantation of virtually every desert plant disturbed during construction and a limitation upon the acreage that could be irrigated, forced Nicklaus and his design team to create a state-of-the-art layout that ultimately opened avenues for many desert-area communities.

Desert Highlands didn't prove that golf could be successfully integrated into a desert. Red Lawrence's Desert Forest had done that two decades earlier. What Desert Highlands did was mesh the game into a desert better than anyone had done before. The key was the use of "transition areas," a buffer between manicured turf and native desert of unplayable pebbles and coarse rock. The transition areas were wide troughs of native sand (or playable sand tinted to resemble the surrounding desert) on each side of the fairway. These troughs collected errant shots, prevented balls from bounding out into unplayable (or unfindable) lies and afforded opportunities to hit decent recovery shots. Nicklaus utilized the transition areas on other desert layouts, most notably at nearby Golf Club at Desert Mountain.

Nicklaus will also be remembered for the opulent look he demanded of all his courses. In direct contrast to Pete Dye's designs, which were intentionally a bit scruffy around the edges, Nicklaus wanted his courses to look almost perfect. No expense was spared. Bunkers were hand-raked and then the rake marks smoothed over. Greens were hand-mowed. Fairways, often of bent grass, were mowed with small triplex mowers rather than large fairway gang mowers. Water hazards featured elaborate cascading waterscapes made from artificial rock and recirculation equipment. Feeling bent grass was the optimum putting surface, Nicklaus prescribed it for all his greens, regardless of location. It was extremely stressful in hot weather Sun Belt areas, but combined with sophisticated programmable irrigation

The short, natural par-4 10th at Wild Dunes, Isle of Palms, South Carolina. When it opened in 1980, it immediately catapulted Tom Fazio's popularity above that of his uncle.
COURTESY WILD DUNES GOLF LINKS

systems and supplemented by separate misting systems, bent grass greens were successfully propagated by Nicklaus's company at Loxahatchee near West Palm Beach, Shoal Creek in Birmingham, Alabama, and Hills of Lakeway in Texas. Only on Kiawah Island, where the Atlantic's salt-saturated mists took their toll, did his bent-grass experiment fail.

But by the end of the 1980s, the opulent designs of Jack Nicklaus were clearly overshadowed by those equally as lavish by Tom Fazio. After splitting from his uncle's firm around 1980, Tom assembled a firm of talented associates, including Jan Beljan (after Alice Dye, the second female member of the American Society of Golf Course Architects), Andy Banfield and Tom Marzolf, and produced a succession of courses that captured the nation's imagination.

First came Wade Hampton Golf Club in the Great Smoky Mountains of North Carolina, in an easy-flowing, tree-dotted valley. Then came Ventana Canyon near Tucson, Fazio's answer to Nicklaus's desert masterpieces. Black Diamond Ranch in northern Florida soon followed, with 13 hilly pined-lined holes and five cliffhangers routed around and through an abandoned quarry. Lake Nona in Orlando and Hammock Dunes, on the edge of the Atlantic, south of Jacksonville, continued to elevate the Tom Fazio mystique.

This mystique culminated with Shadow Creek, an ultraexclusive course north of Las Vegas. Reportedly the most expensive American course ever built, at an estimated cost of over $37 million, it was as if part of western North Carolina had been deposited in the middle of the Nevada desert. Bulldozers dug down 60 feet and piled sand up 60 feet. Thousands of mature pine trees were transplanted. An entire stream system was created to continuously circulate throughout the layout. Fazio credited the course owner, Vegas casino owner Steve Wynn, with many of Shadow Creek's unique design features, including holes that lined up with distant mountain peaks and dark lagoons of water that reflected only the pines and not the sky. It was perhaps the least natural course ever created. Its genius was that it looked totally natural.

At the close of the 1980s, it was difficult to determine which direction golf course architecture would follow to close out the century. The Fazio juggernaut seemed destined to continue. Nicklaus showed indications of reducing his tournament play even further to devote more time to architecture. Pete Dye was regaining attention, with no less than four major events scheduled in 1991 on courses of his design, including the Ryder Cup at The Ocean Course, his version of a links in the subtropical locale of Kiawah Island.

There were indications that other architectural styles were regaining favor, too. The renovation of The Country Club, Brookline, Massachusetts, by Rees Jones for the 1988 U.S. Open renewed appreciation for early twentieth-century architecture and expanded Jones's following. His brother, Robert Trent Jones, Jr., showed remarkable versatility in creating Spanish Bay in Pebble Beach, California, and The Prince in Kauai, Hawaii, two totally different courses bonded only by the Pacific Ocean, which edged them both. Arthur Hills showed new range with the Pine Valley–like Seville in north Florida and the Augusta National–like Golf Club of Georgia, near Atlanta.

But the trend, if it could be called that, at the close of the eighties seemed to be an attempt to create something different from anything being built by Dye, Nicklaus, Fazio, Hills or the Jones boys. Less well known architects, young and old, were rediscovering low-profile architecture, the kind practiced eighty years before when courses were designed to fit the lay of the land with as little earth movement as possible. Tom Doak, a former Dye employee, accomplished it at High Pointe and Black Forest, both on wonderful properties in northern Michigan. High Pointe had some holes reminiscent of an old Scottish highlands layout, while others brought to mind Garden City Golf Club. Veteran Algie Pulley laid out Chardonnay atop the rock-strewn foothills of Napa, California, with so little clearing that vineyards remained between many holes. Michael Hurdzan espoused a low-profile philosophy at Devil's Paintbrush near Toronto, Canada, on an open rolling field he dotted with pot bunkers. The team of Bill Coore and Ben Crenshaw perhaps did it best of all at new courses at Barton Creek in Austin, Texas, and Kapalua in Hawaii, where some holes look amazingly as if they had been done by old C. B. Macdonald himself.

If that is the future direction of golf course design, it looks very much like the past.

12

The Special Few

In reviewing the history of golf course architecture, we found it possible to divide those who practiced it into three groups: those who provided the functional, inexpensive layouts demanded by their times; those who constructed attractive, enjoyable golf courses that advanced the state of the art; and those who created superior designs, often pioneering trends in the process.

Little credit has been given to the first group, the functional designers, yet the world of golf owes them a great debt. These are the planners—men like Tom Dunn of Britain and Tom Bendelow of America—who provided scores of courses that enabled legions of newcomers to play the game. They did what their times and locales required of them, building "sandlot" layouts for communities that could afford nothing more. Occasionally, one of their layouts developed into a well-regarded course, but for the most part the functional designers dealt in quantity and economy rather than quality. Functional designers had a profound effect on the game of golf itself, if not upon the practice of architecture. Yet, as Horace Hutchinson once said of Tom Dunn, no man should be criticized for not being in advance of his time.

The second group consists of the accomplished designers, men like Seth Raynor and Dick Wilson. They were masters of their craft, routinely creating above-average courses and the occasional outstanding layout. It could well be said that a majority of the 500 or so men throughout history who practiced golf course design as a profession or devoted avocation attained this position. The early accomplished architects established a very high standard for golf design, and succeeding generations maintained and improved upon it. Because of their

A common architectural experience rarely recorded. George Cobb (right) reviewing a proposed golf course routing even before clearing.

169

The architectural equivalent of being hoisted upon one's own petard is being trapped by one's own bunker. It happened to (top left) Dr. Alister Mackenzie at Cypress Point; (bunker far left) Robert Trent Jones at Spyglass Hill; (bottom left) Robert von Hagge at Doral Golf Club; (top right) George Fazio at Jupiter Hills Club; and (bottom right and far right) Pete Dye at The Ocean Course, Kiawah Island, South Carolina. COLLECTION RON WHITTEN; COLLECTION GEOFFREY CORNISH; COURTESY *GOLF DIGEST*; COLLECTION RON WHITTEN; RON WHITTEN; RON WHITTEN

Joe Lee at the drawing board, where most architects developed many of the strategies and creativities of their designs. COURTESY *GOLF DIGEST*

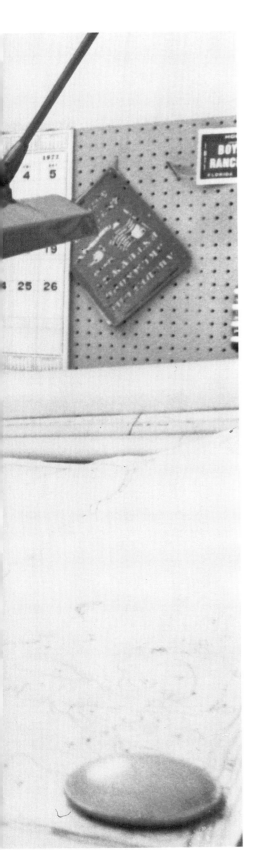

sheer numbers, many such architects never achieved widespread recognition, although their works often did.

The final group is the smallest. It comprises the virtuosos of golf course architecture, the perfectionists who designed and built outstanding courses, often masterpieces of design. Nearly all virtuosos received the accolades due them in their lifetimes, although even then they were often overshadowed by their own works. Their best courses were ahead of their times. Every virtuoso set new standards in some aspect of golf design or construction.

What has distinguished one group from another, the functional from the accomplished and the latter from virtuosos, are the playing qualities contained in problems. Generally, if the target is of generous size, or can be reached with a short shot, the problems that must be surmounted can be more punishing than if the target is very small or far away. For instance, because most golfers are less accurate with a driver than a wedge, most architects don't bunker fairway landing areas nearly as heavily as they do a green on a short pitch-shot hole.

Fundamental to most architects' view of shot values is not the severity of the hazards, but whether such hazards are fair under the circumstances. An uphill target usually has fewer hazards than a downhill one because uphill hazards are often hidden from view. If used at all, a hidden bunker is considered fairer than a hidden water hazard because the latter leaves the unsuspecting golfer with no chance of recovery.

Shot values will vary, not only from hole to hole, but from golfer to golfer. The challenge posed to every golfer is to decide what type of shot is required in each situation (for instance, high or low, maneuvered from right to left or left to right) and then to execute the shot. If the golfer fails to recognize the shot, or simply can't pull it off, he may feel the hole has poor shot values. But in truth, the best shot values are those that reward both each individual golfer's thought process and his or her skill. Poor shot values exist on holes that require no thought to play or reward even the most dreadful of golf shots.

Functional architects usually create 18 holes with easily reachable objectives and relatively few problems. For scratch players, such courses are considered mediocre, devoid of genuine shot values. For high handicappers, such courses may contain genuinely fair shot values, posing just enough difficulty to make the round enjoyable but not frustrating.

Accomplished architects, striving for shot values that test low handicappers but don't overwhelm duffers, mix up the shot values on their courses. They avoid uniformity in lengths of holes, bunkering placement and patterns and the size and shape of greens. They try always to balance shot values, not only from hole to hole but from shot to shot. A difficult teeshot along a lake might be followed by a relatively easy second shot to the green. A teeshot to a generous fairway might be followed by a very testing second to a narrow uphill putting surface. Constant change of pace is considered essential to providing pleasure to a round of golf. A course of extremely difficult shot values, with each target nearly unreachable and each fraught with problems, is no better than a functional course with easy targets and no hazards.

Virtuoso architects take it one step further. While accomplished architects feel it essential to design their courses so that golfers can identify each required shot after a bit of examination and thought, virtuoso designers delight in the occasional use of deception and misdirection. With a virtuoso, the obvious shot might not be the preferable one on a particular hole. From the tee, a left-hand fairway bunker may look ominous, forcing the golfer to intentionally drive away from it. But then the golfer may find, from the right side of the fairway, that the approach must carry a greenside hazard that could have been avoided had the teeshot hugged the left-hand bunker.

Likewise, a bunker seemingly just in front of a green might turn out to be well short of it on a virtuoso's hole, or perhaps a benign fairway seems to invite a long teeshot, until the long hitter discovers a hidden swale and awkward lie that could have been avoided by laying back.

The difference between accomplished and virtuoso architects is in presentation of shot values. Accomplished architects try to make the routes to most holes fairly obvious, using such things as directional bunkers placed to convince golfers to aim in a different direction, saddled fairway contours that seem to funnel a teeshot and/or greens devoid of rear bunkers to encourage aggressive approach shots. But virtuoso designers, rather than dictating how a hole should be played, consider how each hole could be played from many different angles and distances and then position obstacles appropriate to the particular shot. There are preferable angles of attack, to be sure, but more often than not there is more than one way to successfully play the virtuoso's hole. Robert Trent Jones described the goal:

As far as possible, there should be problems for each class of golfer to solve according to his mechanical skill and mental keenness. These problems should be interesting; there should always be something for each golfer to do, and that something should lie within the realm of his particular repertoire.

On a virtuoso design, there will be some fairway bunkers that never come into play for the scratch players and others that never come into play for an average golfer. And each group will consider the others' bunkering to be superfluous.

The virtuoso designer, being a perfectionist, strives to create shot values in every single shot within each golf hole, not just a drive to the landing area or an approach shot to the green, but also a second stroke on a par 5, a chip-and-run from off a green or even a putt. Clever mounding can often be found on the far flanks of a green of a virtuoso architect, or out in the far roughs or in the exact center of a fairway. A lone tree in the hands of a virtuoso can end up being more strategic in the design of a hole than an entire forest on others' designs.

The virtuoso has long examined even the shot values of the green itself. James Braid wrote with some foresight in 1908:

> The greens should be large when they are expected to be reached in good play by a long shot and correspondingly small when it is generally an iron club that will be used to get to them. It will be noted that the size of the green is not at all dependent on the length of the hole . . . As to the undulations, they may be of all kinds, and a pronounced knob, not in the very centre of the green but a few yards to one side, is generally an excellent thing; but the hole should never be cut either on the knob or very close behind it, because that would make it next to impossible to hole out from the other side. The purpose of the knob is to make the player avoid it or to play his approach to the side on which the hole is; and if he fails to do that and gets the knob in between his ball and the hole, he will have an unusually difficult putting problem to think out.

To both accomplished and virtuoso architects, the cardinal sin of golf architecture is predictability. A designer who always insists on bunkering the inside of a dogleg is just as rigid and dogmatic as another who refuses ever to do so. Not only do predictable designs spoil some of the pleasure of a round, they can soil the reputation of a designer. The architect who simply selects a green plan from a raft of standardized contour plans deserves to be labeled unimaginative, regardless of how clever his standard set of green plans may have originally been.

So who are the virtuoso among golf course architects? It's a question open to plenty of debate, especially when the decision must be based upon the rather limited qualifications established here. Among the historical figures, strong arguments can be made for James Braid, Willie Park, Jr., H. S. Colt, George Crump, C. B. Macdonald, Alister

Mackenzie, Donald Ross, Stanley Thompson and A. W. Tillinghast. As for architects active since World War II, Robert Trent Jones and Pete Dye would clearly fit the criteria, with Tom Fazio, Jack Nicklaus, Rees Jones, Robert Trent Jones, Jr., and perhaps Desmond Muirhead deserving strong consideration for inclusion.

Such a limited selection obviously leaves out such legendary designers as Dick Wilson, Hugh Wilson, Seth Raynor, William S. Flynn, Perry Maxwell, George C. Thomas, Jr., Walter Travis, Joe Lee, George Fazio and many others. Such a small list is not meant to detract from the quality or pleasure of any other architect's works. It is simply meant to identify that special few, the virtuosos of the profession of golf course design who were always willing to press forward, to push the envelope of standard design, to try new and different things, to design golf holes that seemed exciting, imaginative and alluring.

The game of golf owes a great deal to all golf course designers. To those few virtuosos, it owes the most. They've kept the game forever fresh.

Two of the virtuosos of golf course architecture, Robert Trent Jones (left) and Pete Dye in 1988. RON WHITTEN

Shapes of things to come. Top left: Arthur Hills incorporated natural dunes as hazards at Seville Golf and Country Club in western Florida. Bottom left: Perry Dye left no earth unmoved in converting a flat site into a jumble of hillocks at Rancho Santa Fe Farms Golf Club, California. Top right: Gary Panks deliberately prescribed gentle mounding on the par-3 10th at Sedona (Arizona) Golf Resort to complement rather than compete with the spectacular backdrop. Bottom right: Robert von Hagge's undulating landscape at Crystal Springs Golf and Country Club, New Jersey. COURTESY ARTHUR HILLS; COURTESY PERRY DYE; COURTESY GARY PANKS; COURTESY CRYSTAL SPRINGS G. & C. C.

Few holes demonstrated the value of width quite as well as the downhill, double-fairway gambling par-5 1st at Devil's Pulpit in Caledon, Ontario, Michael Hurdzan's first big-budget extravaganza. COURTESY MICHAEL HURDZAN

Robert Trent Jones, Jr. teamed with PGA Tour legend Tom Watson and former USGA President Sandy Tatum to create The Links at Spanish Bay, a seemingly authentic links along the Pacific shores at Pebble Beach, but in truth a manmade links created over bare rock with imported sand and lots of imagination. COURTESY ROBERT TRENT JONES, JR.

Top left: One of Tom Fazio's favorite whims, alternate greens, here serving the short par-3 13th at Pelican Hill Golf Club, Newport Coast, California. Top right: A flat cornfield transformed into an endless sea of mounds by Bob Lohmann at Fox Hills National Golf Club, Mishicot, Wisconsin. Bottom left: An amphitheater effect tastefully created by Arthur Hills at the 6th at Golf Club of Georgia near Atlanta. Bottom right: In the late 1980s lay-of-the-land architecture was reintroduced to golf by, among others, the team of Bill Coore and Ben Crenshaw. The first green at their Plantation Course at Kapalua Golf Club, Maui, Hawaii, accepts a low bouncing approach from the left apron, but rejects high shots thrown right at the flag. COURTESY PELICAN HILL G. C.; COURTESY G. C. OF GEORGIA; COURTESY FOX HILLS NATIONAL G. C.; COURTESY KAPALUA G. C.

PART TWO

Profiles

These biographical profiles of golf course designers and others who have made an impact on the history of golf course design were prepared using a multitude of sources and records.

Attribution of any design is sometimes difficult. Often the architect of record assigns principal responsibility for a design to one or more associates. In such a case, the course will appear in Part Two, both under the profile of the architect of record and under the profile of the associate. Please note, however, to designate those instances where a designer worked on a course under the employ of an architect of record, we have used either the phrase "As assistant to . . ." or the abbreviation "ass't," depending upon the particular architect. Also please note that only architects of record are listed in Part Three. The contributions of the associates of such architects are only listed under the profiles of such associates.

The course lists following each profile contain only works verified by the authors. None of the lists is intended to represent the complete work of any particular designer. In many cases, architects (especially the pioneers) did many more courses than are listed, but the names of some of those courses are yet to be determined.

As this book goes to press, many present-day designers have designs on their drawing boards, which, for a variety of reasons are not listed.

Abbreviations used include:

ASGCA for American Society of Golf Course Architects

BIGCA for British Institute of Golf Course Architects

ESGCA for European Society of Golf Course Architects

FAGCA for French Association of Golf Course Architects

GCSAA for Golf Course Superintendents Association of America
CGCSA for Canadian Golf Course Superintendents Association
ASLA for American Society of Landscape Architects
CSLA for Canadian Society of Landscape Architects
USGA for United States Golf Association
LPGA for Ladies Professional Golfers Association
NGF for National Golf Foundation
PGA for Professional Golfers Association
A. for added holes (Example: A.9 indicates added nine holes.)
R. for remodeled holes (Example: R.4 indicates remodeled four holes. Remodeling runs the gamut from minor revisions to total creation of a new lay-out. No attempt has been made to distinguish the extent of remodeling.)
FKA for formerly known as
NKA for now known as
NLE for no longer exists
GC for Golf Club
G Cse for Golf Course
Muni for Municipal Golf Course
C for Club
CC for Country Club
C de G for Club de Golf
G&BC for Golf and Beach Club
G&CC for Golf and Country Club
RC for Racquet Club
TC for Tennis Club
YC for Yacht Club
TPC for Tournament Players Club
AFB for Air Force Base
NAS for Naval Air Station

"Par 3" refers to a course consisting solely of par-3 holes.

"Precision" indicates a precision course, those shorter courses consisting mainly of par-3 and par-4 holes, commonly called "executive courses."

"Reversible" indicates a golf course with additional tees and greens so positioned that the course can be played both forward and backward.

"With" indicates a collaborative effort between design partners.

"*Solo*" indicates a design done without the involvement of other partners mentioned in the designer's profile or list of works. It **does not** mean that the entire creation of the course was done solely by that architect. Obviously, many people are involved in the creation of every course. "*Solo*" is simply used to distinguish between sole efforts by an architect and collaborative efforts with a design partner.

The number of holes is indicated within parentheses. Example: (9), (27), etc. If no number is given, it is presumed the course or project consisted of eighteen holes.

A name listed in *italics* on any list indicates that the architect is not profiled in Part Two.

The designation of membership in an architectural organization is indicated by a listing beside the name of the architect. Such designation merely indicates the architect was at some time during his or her career a member of the organization and not necessarily a member at the time of the publication of this book.

JOHN FREDERICK ABERCROMBY
(1861–1935)

BORN: Felixstowe, Suffolk, England.
DIED: Addington, Surrey, England, at
age 74.

J. F. Abercromby, a doctor's son, took up golf in his youth and eventually became a scratch player, competing successfully in matches around London. At the turn of the century he was hired as private secretary to a financier at Bridley Manor, southwest of London. Impressed with three new golf courses in the area (Sunningdale, Walton Heath and Woking), his employer instructed Abercromby to provide him with a course.

Somewhat audaciously, "Aber" decided to lay out the course himself. He consulted with Willie Park, Jr., and Jack White during the initial stages, but the final product, Worplesdon GC, was basically Abercromby's design. Choosing to pursue a career in golf architecture, he soon landed the commission for Coombe Hill GC and then laid out a course for Addington GC, built just before World War I. Abercromby settled at Addington, serving as its secretary and "benevolent despot" for the remainder of his life. He eventually built a second course there and was constantly refining both.

In 1920, Abercromby joined Herbert Fowler, Tom Simpson and Arthur Croome in the design firm of Fowler, Abercromby, Simpson and Croome. Most of his work for the firm, done primarily in collaboration with Fowler, was in the London heathlands area. Abercromby was considered a totally free-hand artist, never measuring distances nor sketching designs, but laying out golf holes on-site and supervising their creation. Contemporary critics felt he made the most natural-looking hazards of any architect of the day, and some considered him the finest British designer of the era before World War I.

Courses by J. F. Abercromby:

England: Addington GC (New Cse 1933; Old Cse 1914); Coombe Hill GC (1909), with Willie Park, Jr.; Cowdray Park GC, with Herbert Fowler; Knole Park GC (1924), with Herbert Fowler; Liphook GC (1922), with A. C. M. Croome; Manor House Hotel GC (1930), with Herbert Fowler; Mill Hill GC (1924); West Kent GC (1916),
with Herbert Fowler; Worplesdon GC (1908).
France: Golf de Chantilly (Old Cse 1906).

Courses remodeled or expanded by J. F. Abercromby:

England: Worplesdon GC (R.), with Willie Park, Jr.
Netherlands: Haagsche GC (A.9, NLE).

CHARLES HENRY ADAMS

BORN: Parkersburg, West Virginia.

"Chic" Adams began his golf career working for his father, who for many years held the position of course superintendent at Cherokee (Iowa) CC. Turning professional in the 1940s, Adams served as pro-superintendent at Sioux City (Iowa) CC for over a decade. A member of both the PGA of America and the GCSAA, he began designing courses as a sideline in the early 1950s and eventually resigned his club job to devote full time to golf architecture. In the late 1950s he moved his design and construction business to Atlanta and concentrated on building courses in the Southeast. He retired in the early 1970s, moving first to southern Florida and then to the Myrtle Beach area of South Carolina.

Courses by Chic Adams:

Alabama: Skyline CC (1962).
Florida: Airco GC (1962); Bay West Lodge & CC (1968); Diamond Hill GC (1959); Portage Y&CC (1959); Scenic Hills G&CC (1959); Seminole Lake G&CC (1962); Top of the World GC (27 Precision 1971); Turf and Surf GC (9 1956); Yacht C Estates GC (1965).
Georgia: Castle View T&CC (1960); Dobbins AFB GC (9 1959); Golfland GC (9 Par 3 1959); Monroe G&CC (9 1958); Pinetree CC, Marietta (1961); Riverside G&CC (1961).
Iowa: American Legion GC (9 1956).
Kansas: Brookridge G&CC (27 1963).
Kentucky: Hurstbourne CC (27 1967).
Maine: Fairlawn CC (1960).
Missouri: North Shore CC (27 1959), with Homer Herpel; St. James Muni (9 1966).
Tennessee: Fox Meadows CC (1957); Valleybrook G&CC (1957).

Courses remodeled or expanded by Chic Adams:

Georgia: East Lake CC (Cse No. 2, R. NLE).
Iowa: Ottumwa G&CC (A.9 1959).

ROKURO AKABOSHI

BORN: Japan.

Rokuro Akaboshi took up golf in his native Japan and was later educated in the U.S. at Princeton University, where he served as captain of the golf team and won an invitation tournament at Pinehurst. Returning to Japan after college, Rokuro became a pioneer of the game in that country. He was an accomplished teacher and introduced the game to many. He was a talented competitor and won the inaugural Japanese Open in 1927. He was also a golf course designer and designed over sixty courses in Japan, most in collaboration with his brother Shiro, also a Princeton graduate and a highly regarded golf instructor.

The Akaboshi brothers were generally considered Japan's first native golf architects. They also laid out courses in other parts of Asia, including Taiwan. In the early 1930s Rokuro made an extensive trip to Scotland to study the famous old links.

Courses by Rokuro Akaboshi (All with Shiro Akaboshi):

Japan: Abiko GC (1930); Hakone CC (1954); Naruo CC; Sagami CC (1931); Sengoku GC (1927).
Taiwan: Taiwan G&CC.

Courses remodeled or expanded by Rokuro Akaboshi (All with Shiro Akaboshi unless otherwise indicated):

Japan: Fuji CC (R.); Hodogaya G&CC (R.).

JAMES ALEXANDER

James Alexander, superintendent of British Transport Hotels, assisted golf architect Philip Mackenzie Ross with the re-planning of the Ailsa course at Turnberry, Scotland, after World War II. He then re-planned the Arran course at Turnberry himself. He also planned major changes to the Queen's course at Gleneagles in the 1950s (in order to make it more equal to the King's course as a test of golf) and collaborated on the Prince's course at Gleneagles with I. Marchbanks and T. Telford. In addition, Alexander made extensive changes at Manor House Hotel Golf Club in Devonshire, England.

C. H. Alison, circa 1932 COLLECTION RON WHITTEN

CHARLES HUGH ALISON
(1882–1952)

BORN: Preston, Lancashire, England.
DIED: Johannesburg, South Africa, at age 70.

Hugh Alison was educated at Malvern and Oxford University, where he was an outstanding cricket player and golfer. He was the youngest member of the Oxford and Cambridge Golfing Society team that toured the U.S. in 1903. He won every match he played during that tour.

After college Alison worked for a time as a journalist and then served as club secretary for the newly formed Stoke Poges GC near London. There he met H. S. Colt, who was laying out the course. Intrigued by course design since his early golfing days, Alison assisted Colt with the completion of Stoke Poges and then worked for Colt in the construction of several other London-area courses.

After service with the British army during World War I, Major Alison rejoined Colt. They formed a partnership that lasted the remainder of their lives and included, for a short time, Alister Mackenzie, and then J. S. F. Morrison. Colt handled most of the design work in Britain and on the Continent, while Alison worked extensively in North America and the Far East. Nearly all the courses built by the firm of Colt and Alison in the United States during the 1920s and '30s were designed by Hugh Alison.

Alison made an extensive tour of the Far East in the early 1930s and designed and remodeled a number of Japanese courses. Colt never made any claim to these. Alison also mapped out a number of topographic jobs for sites in Australia and India that he never visited, a practice that Colt did not condone. By the time of Alison's return to Britain in the mid-1930s, Colt had all but retired, and though Alison and Morrison continued the partnership name, they each worked on projects individually, although they kept the other abreast of their earnings. In 1949 Alison and his wife visited South Africa for what was to be an extended business trip. He ended up consulting on several remodelings, laying out another course and continually postponing his return to Britain. Hugh Alison never made it back home. He was finishing up a course in South Africa when he died in 1952.

Alison was coauthor with Colt of *Some Essays on Golf Course Architecture,* first published in 1920. He also contributed to *Golf Courses: Design, Construction and Upkeep* (edited by M. A. F. Sutton), both the 1933 version and the revised 1950 edition which he wrote while in South Africa. An extended set of his correspondence with J. S. F. Morrison from the last years of his life is reproduced in *Colt & Co.,* the biography of H. S. Colt written by golf architect Fred W. Hawtree and published in 1991.

Courses by C. H. Alison (All with H. S. Colt unless otherwise indicated):

Georgia: Sea Island GC (Seaside Nine 1928).
Illinois: Briarwood CC [FKA Briergate CC] (1921); Knollwood C (1923); North Shore CC (1924).
Iowa: Davenport CC (1924).
Maryland: Burning Tree C (1924).
Michigan: Orchard Lake CC (1926).
New Jersey: Canoe Brook CC (North Cse 1924, NLE).
New York: Century GC (1926); Colony CC (1923); Fresh Meadow CC [FKA Lakeville CC] (1925); Old Oaks CC (1927); Park CC (1928); Timber Point CC (1927).
Ohio: Kirtland CC (1921); Westwood CC (1924).
Wisconsin: Milwaukee CC (1929).
Ontario: St. George's G&CC (NLE); York Downs CC (1921, NLE).
Australia: Huntingdale GC (1941), with S. Berriman.
Belgium: Royal Waterloo GC (27 1923, NLE).
Denmark: Copenhagen GC (1926), and J. S. F. Morrison.
England: Brancepeth Castle GC (1924), and Alister Mackenzie; Cuddington GC (1929), and J. S. F. Morrison;

Effingham GC (1927); Fulwell GC (1947 *solo*); Ham Manor GC (1936), and J. S. F. Morrison; Kingsthorpe GC (9 1908, NLE); Leamington and County GC (1909); Leckford GC (9 1929), and J. S. F. Morrison; Moor Park GC (West Cse 1923), and Alister Mackenzie; Stoke Poges GC (27 1908; 9, NLE); Sunningdale GC (New Cse 1922); Trevose G&CC (27 1926), and J. S. F. Morrison; Wentworth GC (East Cse 1924; West Cse 1924), and J. S. F. Morrison.
France: GC de Chantaco (1928), and J. S. F. Morrison; GC de Granville (1922); GC de St. Cloud (Yellow Cse 1931), and J. S. F. Morrison; Le Touquet GC (Sea Cse 1930), and J. S. F. Morrison.
Germany: Aachener GC (1927), and J. S. F. Morrison; Falkenstein GC (1930), and J. S. F. Morrison; Frankfurter GC (1928), and J. S. F. Morrison; Hamburger Land und GC (1935), and J. S. F. Morrison.
Ireland: Dunlaoghaire GC (1910).
Japan: Fuji CC (1932 *solo*); Hirona CC (1932 *solo*); Kawana GC (Fuji Cse 1936 *solo*); Tokyo GC (1932 *solo*).
Netherlands: Eindhoven GC (1930), and J. S. F. Morrison; Haagsche G&CC (1939), and J. S. F. Morrison; Kennemer G&CC (1929), and J. S. F. Morrison; Utrecht GC (1929), and J. S. F. Morrison.
New Zealand: Auckland GC (1941 *solo*); Maungakiekie GC (1946 *solo*).
Northern Ireland: Belvoir Park (1927); Cairndhu GC (1929), and J. S. F. Morrison; Royal Belfast GC (1927).
Scotland: Longniddry GC (1921).
South Africa: Bryanston CC (1951 *solo*); Glendower CC (1938 *solo*); Vereeniging CC (1938 *solo*).
Spain: Real C de la Puerto de Hierro (Old Cse 1915); Real G de Pedrena (1928), and J. S. F. Morrison.
Sweden: Stockholm GC (1932), and J. S. F. Morrison.
Wales: Pyle and Kenfig GC (1922).

Courses remodeled or expanded by C. H. Alison (All with H. S. Colt unless otherwise indicated):

Georgia: Sea Island GC (Plantation Nine, R. 1928).
Illinois: Bob O'Link CC (R. A.4 1924); Highland Park GC (R. 1924).
Maryland: Chevy Chase CC (R. 1924).

Michigan: CC of Detroit (R. 1927);
   Lochmoor C (R. 1920).
Ohio: Columbus CC (A.4 1923).
Pennsylvania: Baederwood GC (R. 1927).
England: Blackmoor GC (A.5 1918; R.
   1924); Burnham & Berrow GC (R.
   1947 *solo*); Lansdown GC (A.2 1947);
   Northumberland GC (R. 1924); Royal
   Lytham & St. Annes GC (R. 1930);
   Royal St. Georges GC (R.9 1930); Sun-
   ningdale GC (Old Cse, R. 1922).
Ireland: County Sligo GC (R. 1922); Fox-
   rock GC (R. 1908); Greystones GC (R.
   1910); Rosapenna GC (R. 1932); Royal
   Dublin GC (R. 1921).
Japan: Kasumigaseki GC (East Cse, R.
   1930 *solo*; West Cse, R. 1930 *solo*);
   Kawana GC (Oshima Cse, R. 1936
   solo); Naruo GC (R., 1930 *solo*).
Malaysia: Royal Selangor GC (Old Cse R.
   1931 *solo*).
Morocco: Tangier GC (R. 1939 *solo*).
New Zealand: Auckland GC (R. *solo*);
   Germiston GC (R. 1953 *solo*).
Northern Ireland: Belvoir Park GC (R.
   1927).
Scotland: Muirfield GC (R. 1925).
South Africa: Bulawayo GC (R. 1948
   solo); Crown Mines GC (R. 1949 *solo*);
   East London GC (R. 1923 *solo*);
   Johannesburg CC (R. 1948 *solo*, NLE);
   Pretoria CC (R. 1948 *solo*); Royal Cape
   GC (R. 1951 *solo*); Royal Johannes-
   burg CC (East & West Cses, R. 1948
   solo); Wingate Park GC (R. 1947 *solo*).

PETER ALLISS
(1931–   )

BORN: Berlin, Germany.

Peter Alliss, the son of famed British
professional golfer Percy Alliss, won numerous tournaments after turning professional in 1946. He was an eight-time
member of the British Ryder Cup team
and wrote several books on golf, including
one novel.

In the 1970s Alliss began regular com-
menting on televised golf broadcasts in
Britain and the U.S. He also teamed with
David Thomas in a design-and-build firm
that handled several projects in the U.K.
and the Continent, most notably thirty-six
holes at The Belfry, which became the new
home of the British PGA and later a three-
time Ryder Cup site. In the mid-1980s, the

*Peter Alliss, circa
1965* COLLECTION RON
WHITTEN

team broke up. Alliss then formed a design
alliance with former British Amateur
champion and fellow television commentator Clive Clark, while Thomas became
partner with former Open champion Tony
Jacklin.

**Courses by Peter Alliss (All with David
Thomas unless otherwise indicated):**

Brazil: Golf Hotel do Frade (1980).
England: [The] Belfry GC (Brabazon Cse
   1979; Derby Cse 1979); Dewsbury
   District GC; Hessle GC; Hill Valley
   G&CC (27 1975); King's Lynn GC
   (1975); Thorpe Wood GC (1975).
France: Cannes-Mougins GC (1978).
Ivory Coast: President CC (1980).
Northern Ireland: Clandeboye GC (Duf-
   ferin Cse 1973), and T. J. A. Macauley.
Scotland: Blairgowrie GC (Lansdowne
   Cse, 9 1974).

**Courses remodeled or expanded by
Peter Alliss (All with David Thomas
unless otherwise indicated):**

France: Golf de La Baule (R. 1977); Le
   Touquet GC (Forest Cse, R. 1991),
   with *Clive Clark*.
Ireland: Dundalk GC (R. A.9 1975).
Northern Ireland: Ballyclare GC (R.9 A.9
   1973) and T. J. A. Macauley.
Scotland: Blairgowrie GC (Rosemount
   Cse, R. 1974); Haggs Castle GC (R.);
   Turnberry GC (Ailsa Cse, R. 1976).

GRANGE GORDON ALVES
(1885–1939)

BORN: Aberdeen, Scotland.
DIED: Cleveland, Ohio, at age 54.

Grange Alves, called "Sandy" after his
hair color, learned golf from his father and

was a successful amateur player before
emigrating to the United States at age
nineteen. He worked as a stonemason's
apprentice in Barre, Vermont, until 1909
when he landed a position as pro-
greenkeeper at French Lick Springs, Indiana. While there, a flood ravaged the
course and Alves supervised its reconstruction, redesigning several holes in the
process.

Donald Ross was hired soon afterward
to design a second course and Alves constructed it. Impressed with his work, Ross
recommended Alves to Shaker Heights
CC of Cleveland, Ohio. He was hired to
supervise construction of its Donald Ross
course and stayed on in 1915 as the club's
first professional. Eight years later he was
chosen by fellow Masons to design and
build a course for the Masonic organization in Cleveland. With Ross's help he created the Acacia CC, which opened in
1923. Alves remained there as pro-
greenkeeper until his death.

While at Acacia, Alves designed a number of Cleveland-area courses on the side.
He was highly regarded as a golf instructor
and continued to be a good player, winning the Ohio Open in 1922 and 1925. In
addition, he served as vice president of
both the GCSAA and the PGA of America.

Courses by Sandy Alves:

Indiana: French Lick G&TC (Country
   Club Cse 1922), ass't Donald Ross.
Ohio: Acacia CC (1921), with Donald
   Ross; Highland Meadows CC (1928);
   Highland Park GC (Blue Cse 1929;
   Red Cse 1927); Lyndhurst GC (1925);
   Madison CC (27 1926); Meadowlands
   GC (9 1930); Middle Bass Island GC
   (1930); Ridgewood Muni (1924);
   Shaker Heights CC (1915), ass't Don-
   ald Ross; Twin Lakes CC (1925);
   University Heights GC (9 1929).

*Sandy Alves, circa
1933* COURTESY
ROBERT ALVES

Courses remodeled or expanded by Sandy Alves:

Indiana: French Lick G&TC (Valley Cse, R. 1911).

Ohio: East Liverpool CC (A.9 1928); Oakwood C (A.6 1928); Sylvania CC (R.6 1929).

WILLIAM WALKER AMICK
(1932–), ASGCA, PRESIDENT 1977

BORN: Scipio, Indiana.

Bill Amick received his B.A. degree from Ohio Wesleyan University (where he played on the golf team) and was then employed as a graduate assistant in Turfgrass Management at Purdue University. After two years as an officer in the U.S. Air Force, Amick returned to Indiana to train under golf architect William H. Diddel.

After stints with Diddel and designer Chic Adams, Amick formed his own practice in Ohio in 1959. Within a few years he moved to northern Florida.

A low-handicap golfer and thoughtful architect, Bill Amick established himself in several facets of the profession. His residential development layouts helped establish standards of integrating housing with golf. He did considerable research on conversion of sanitary landfills into golf courses and designed several model landfill course projects. He helped popularize shorter courses consisting of par-3 and par-4 holes, the so-called executive or precision layouts that Amick preferred to call "challenge courses."

In the 1980s Amick was at the forefront of a movement to reintroduce a shorter golf ball, an idea Diddel had promoted some forty years earlier. Amick served as first president of the American Modified Golf Association, an organization dedicated to the experimentation and evaluation of "modified" golf balls, those that flew only half the distance of normal compression balls. In 1986, Amick laid out Eagle Landing G&RC in Hanrahan, South Carolina, the first Cayman-style course designed solely for use of such modified golf balls.

Courses by Bill Amick:

Alabama: Chattahoochee CC (9 1964); Cumberland Lake CC (1968).

Florida: A. C. Read GC (Seaside Cse 1962, A.3rd 9 1992); Alhambra G&CC (1970); Beacon Woods CC (1974); Fairgreen CC (Precision 1978); Fair

Bill Amick, 1990
COURTESY BILL AMICK

way GC (1972); Fort Walton Beach Muni (1962); Foxwood CC [FKA Crestview CC](9 1961); Halifax Plantation GC (1991); Havana CC (9 1963); Hollywood GC (1966); Island GC (1985); Jefferson CC (9 1965); Killearn G&CC (1967, A.3rd 9 1975); Mangrove Bay GC (1977); Meadow Oaks G&CC (Precision 1985); Monsanto Employees GC (1961); Ocean G Links (10 Par 3 1982); Palm Harbor GC (1973); Panama City Beach GC (1968); Pelican Bay G&CC (1979); Perdido Bay CC (1963); Pineview G&CC (1968); Rocky Bayou CC (1973); Sawgrass GC (Oakbridge Cse 1972); Seminole Valley GC (1986); Seven Rivers CC (1968); Shalimar Pointe CC [FKA Lake Lorraine CC](1968); Sherwood G&CC (9 1968); Spruce Creek GC (1974); St. Joseph's Bay CC (1962); Tiger Point G&CC (East Cse, 9 1979; West Cse 1965); Vineyards G&CC (South Cse 1987).

Georgia: Briar Creek CC (9 1963); Donalsonville CC (9 1970); Green Meadows CC (1962); Pineknoll CC (9 1968).

Illinois: Chester CC (9 1969).

Missouri: Deer Lake GC (1990).

New Hampshire: Sky Meadow CC (1989).

North Carolina: Highlands Falls CC (9 1962).

Ohio: Homestead GC (1973).

South Carolina: Eagle Landing G&RC (Cayman 1987); Three Pine CC (1969).

Tennessee: Chestuee G&CC (1971); Windyke CC (West Cse 1963).

Belgium: Golf de la Tournette (American Cse 1991).

Italy: GC Di Montegallo (1991); Sansicario GC (1991).

Portugal: Vasco da Gama G Resort (1992).

Courses remodeled or expanded by Bill Amick:

Florida: A. C. Read GC (Mainside Cse, R. 1970); Harbor City Muni (R. 1970); Magnolia Valley G&CC (R. A.4 1986); Melbourne G&CC (R. 1977); Patrick AFB GC (R.); Seminole GC (A.9 1969).

Georgia: Monroe G&CC (A.9 1971); Rivermont G&CC (R. 1983).

Kentucky: Pine Valley GC (A.9 1986).

Louisiana: City Park GC (Cse No. 1, R.3 1983).

Missouri: Hillcrest CC (R. 1984).

New Hampshire: Wentworth-by-the-Sea GC (R. 1987).

Ohio: North Olmstead GC (R.).

Belgium: Golf de Reginee (R. 1991).

ROY ALBERT ANDERSON
(1918–)

BORN: Hot Springs, Arkansas.

R. Albert Anderson, the son of a club professional and nephew of two golf course superintendents, was raised and educated in Racine, Wisconsin. He took up golf architecture following the Second World War, operating from a summer residence in Racine and a winter home in Sarasota, Florida. Among numerous courses he designed and built were six that he owned and operated.

Courses by R. Albert Anderson:

Alabama: Rolling Green CC (1967).

Florida: Bird Bay Executive GC (Precision 1974); Clewiston CC; CC of Brevard (1959); Englewood G&CC (1966); Forest Lakes CC (1964); Futurama GC (Par 3 1963); Golden Tee GC (Par 3 1970); Green Valley CC (9

R. Albert Anderson, 1971 COLLECTION RON WHITTEN

1966); Harbor City Muni (1963); Heather Hills GC (1963); Lehigh Acres CC (North Cse 1958; South Cse 1960); Little Cypress G&CC (9 1965); Red Lake CC (1959); Rolling Green G&CC (1968); Santa Rosa G&CC (1970); Seminole GC (9 1959); Sorrento Par 3 GC (9 Par 3 1975); Starke G&CC (9 1959); Sunnybreeze Palms GC (27 1971); Sunrise National CC (1971); Venice East GC (Precision 1961); Woodcrest Par 3 GC (Par 3 1970).

Georgia: Cairo CC (1962); Four Seasons CC (9).

Illinois: Shady Lawn GC (1971).

Indiana: Broadmoor CC; Cedar Lake GC (1957); Hollow Acres GC (9); Pheasant Valley GC.

Missouri: Terre du Lac CC (1969); Tower Tee GC (Par 3 1969).

Ohio: Copeland Hills CC; Golden Tee GC (Par 3 1966); Orchard Hills CC (9 1955); Puckerbrush GC; Tippecanoe CC [FKA Southern Hills GC].

Tennessee: Carrol Lake GC; Shelbyville CC; Smithville Muni.

Wisconsin: Oak Hill GC (1962); Spring Valley GC (9 1959).

Courses remodeled or expanded by R. Albert Anderson:

Florida: Bobby Jones Muni (American Cse, R. 1963); Capital City CC (R. 1960); Keystone G&CC (R. 1959); Palm-Aire West CC (Champions Cse, R. 1969); Palma Sola GC (R. 1968); Punta Gorda CC (R. 1966).

Indiana: Gary CC (R.).

Minnesota: Wilmar CC (A.9 1960).

CHARLES F. ANKROM
(1936–), ASGCA

BORN: West Virginia.

Chuck Ankrom attended West Virginia University. An excellent golfer, he became Director of Golf at Sandpiper Bay in Port St. Lucie, Florida, in 1962. Sandpiper was the flagship of a new set of Florida clubs by General Development Corporation, and Ankrom became Director of Golf over all GDC course operations. Having taken classes in golf course turf management and real estate at the University of Florida, he soon expanded his duties to include supervision of golf course development for GDC. During the last half of the sixties, Ankrom supervised creation of several

GDC courses and designed Port Malabar CC.

In 1970 Ankrom headed west, taking a similar position as national Director of Golf Operations for the Boise Cascade Recreation Communities Group. But the Idaho-based firm divested itself of most of its recreational developments during the recession of 1972, so Ankrom resigned the same year and formed his own golf architecture firm. In 1974, he moved back to Florida, where he established his practice.

In 1990 Paula J. McGhee joined Ankrom's business as a design associate.

Courses by Chuck Ankrom:

Florida: Big Cypress at Royal Palm CC (1982); Boca Raton Muni (27 1982); Bulldog Sport Complex (3 1991); Club Med Sandpiper GC (Family Cse [9 Par 3] 1981); Cocoa Beach CC (27 1992); Crystal Lakes GC, Okeechobee (9 Precision 1977); [The] Habitat GC (1992); Indian River Plantation GC (Precision 1978); Martin Downs CC (Crane Creek Cse 1976, with Arthur Young; Tower Cse 1982); Meadowood CC [FKA TPC at Monte Carlo](1984); Naples Shores CC (1978); Port Malabar CC (1967); Sabal Trace G&CC [FKA North Port Charlotte CC](1970); Savanna C (Precision 1985); Sebastian Muni (1982).

Courses remodeled or expanded by Chuck Ankrom:

Florida: Boca Del Mar G&TC (R.); Boynton Beach Muni (R.); C at Emerald Hills (R. 1990); Club Med Sandpiper GC (Sinners Cse, R. 1982); Eglin AFB GC (A.3rd 9 1988); Fort Lauderdale CC (North Cse, R. 1988; South Cse, R. 1992); Frenchman's Creek CC (South Cse, R.); Heritage Ridge GC (R.9 A.9

Chuck Ankrom, 1991 COURTESY
CHUCK ANKROM

1981); Piper's Landing CC (R.); Port Charlotte CC (R. 1970); Sun 'n Lake CC (A.3rd 9); Tequesta CC (R.); Vero Beach CC (R. 1985); [The] Yacht & CC (R.).

Javier Arana, circa 1945 COURTESY ALVARO ARANA

JAVIER ARANA
(1904–1975)

BORN: Bilbao, Vizcaya, Spain.
DIED: Marbella, Spain, at age 70.

Renowned Spanish golfer Javier Arana began designing courses in 1936. Although he confined his work to his native Spain, he was recognized as a leading contemporary golf course architect. His characteristic trademarks were an isolated tree found in one or more fairways of nearly every course he built and a par 3 as the seventeenth hole on each of his designs.

Arana trained his nephew Álvaro Arana in the business, and following Javier's death in 1975 Álvaro continued the course design practice.

Courses by Javier Arana:

Spain: Aloha Golf (1976); Campo de G El Saler (1967); C de G Cerdana (27 1945); C de G Los Monteros; C de G Ulzama (9 1965); Golf Guadalamina (North Cse 1959; South Cse 1959); Golf Río Real (1965); Real Automóvil C de España (1967); Real C de G El Prat (1954); Real Sociedad de G Neguri La Galea (1960); Real Sociedad Hípica Española (27 1956); Reina Cristina GC.

ROWLAND ARMACOST
(1916–)

A graduate of Western Maryland University with postgraduate studies in art at North Carolina University, Rowland Armacost planned several golf courses both stateside and overseas for the U.S. military while serving as a pilot during World War II. After the war he formed a landscape contracting firm in Berkshire County, Massachusetts.

Armacost became course superintendent in 1959 at Wahconah CC in Dalton, Massachusetts, where, in collaboration with Geoffrey Cornish, he planned and built a nine-hole addition. In the mid-1960s he designed and built Waubeeka Springs in Williamstown, Massachusetts, and then became its manager. He continued to design several courses as a sideline even after his retirement.

Courses by Rowland Armacost:

Massachusetts: General Electric A.A. GC; Rolling Hills Par 3 GC (NLE); Skyline GC; Waubeeka Springs G Links.

Courses remodeled or expanded by Rowland Armacost:

Massachusetts: Bas Ridge GC (R.); Wahconah CC (A.9 1959), with Geoffrey Cornish.

BRIAN T. AULT
(1947–), ASGCA

BORN: Washington, D.C.

Brian Ault, son of golf architect Edmund B. Ault, earned an associate degree in civil engineering and for a short time served as an inspector for the Washington, D.C., Highway Department. In 1973 he

became an associate architect in his father's design firm. In 1984 he became a full partner with his father and Tom Clark in the newly organized firm of Ault, Clark & Associates.

Courses by Brian Ault:

Arkansas: Mountain Ranch GC (1984), with Tom Clark and Edmund B. Ault.
Indiana: West Boggs Muni (9 1978), ass't Edmund B. Ault.
Iowa: Sundown GC (9 Par 3 1978), ass't Edmund B. Ault.
Louisiana: Eden Isles CC (1976), ass't Edmund B. Ault.
Maryland: [The] Beach C (1991); Clustered Spires G Cse (1991), with Bill Love; Heritage Harbour GC (9 1982), ass't Edmund B. Ault; TPC at Avenel (1986), with Ed Ault, Tom Clark, Bill Love and *Ed Sneed.*
Missouri: Paradise Pointe GC (1984), with Tom Clark; Poplar Bluff Muni (1980), ass't Edmund B. Ault.
Mississippi: Mississippi State Univ. G Cse (9 1986, A.9 1989).
New Jersey: Concordia GC (1986), with Tom Clark and Bill Love; Mercer Oaks GC (1991), with Bill Love; Quail Brook GC (1982), ass't Edmund B. Ault.
Pennsylvania: Bavarian Hills GC (1989), with Bill Love; Clinton CC (9 1972, A.9 1977), ass't Edmund B. Ault; Mountain View GC (1987), with Edmund B. Ault and Tom Clark.
Texas: Twin Wells G Cse (1988), with Bill Love.

Virginia: Cypress Point CC (1986), with Tom Clark; Hollows GC (1984), with Tom Clark; Penderbrook GC (1979), ass't Edmund B. Ault.
West Virginia: Sheraton Lakeview Resort & CC (Mountainview Cse 1984), with Tom Clark.

Courses remodeled or expanded by Brian Ault:

Connecticut: Rolling Hills CC (R.5 1984), with Tom Clark; Woodbridge CC (R.1 1986).
Delaware: Brandywine CC (R.7 1987), with Bill Love.
Maryland: Manor CC (R.4 1986), with Edmund B. Ault and Bill Love; Sherwood Forest GC (R.4 1986).
Massachusetts: Pleasant Valley CC (R.3 1984), with Tom Clark.
Mississippi: Columbus CC (R.9 1985); Northwood CC (R.2 1985).
Nevada: Tropicana CC (R. 1984, NLE), with Tom Clark.
New Jersey: Greenacres CC (R.2 1984), with Tom Clark.
New York: Ridgemont CC (R.2 1984).
North Carolina: Duck Woods GC (R.7 1986), with Tom Clark; Paradise Point GC (Gold Cse, R.7 1979), ass't Edmund B. Ault.
Pennsylvania: Chambersburg CC (A.9 1977), ass't Edmund B. Ault; Oak Tree GC (R.2 1983), ass't Edmund B. Ault.
Tennessee: Woodmont CC (A.9 1977), ass't Edmund B. Ault.
Virginia: Army-Navy CC (Fairfax Cse, R.2 1984), with Edmund B. Ault; Kingsmill GC (River Cse, R.5 1982), ass't Edmund B. Ault; Westwood CC (R. 1984), with Edmund B. Ault.

EDMUND B. AULT
(1908–1989), ASGCA

BORN: Washington, D.C.
DIED: Silver Springs, Maryland, at age 81.

Edmund Ault studied construction engineering at Columbia (Md.) Technical Institute and for a time was employed in that field. He then trained for several seasons with golf architect Fred Findlay and entered private practice as a course designer in 1946. For several years in the late 1950s he partnered with club professional Al Jamison.

A onetime scratch golfer, Ault played in the National Amateur on several occasions. He served in the Green Section of the USGA, was a past president of the

Brian Ault (right), with partners Tom Clark (center) and Bill Love (left), 1983 COLLECTION RON WHITTEN

Edmund B. Ault, circa 1968 COURTESY BRIAN AULT

District of Columbia Golf Association and chaired the Design Standards Committee of the ASGCA. Long an advocate of flexibility in courses, Ault pioneered the systematic coordination of pin placements with tee marker locations.

A most prolific designer, Ed Ault once estimated that he had designed or remodeled one quarter of all the courses in the Maryland and Virginia suburbs around Washington, D.C.

Ault was made a Fellow of the ASGCA in 1984. That same year he reorganized his company by forming a partnership with his son Brian and Tom Clark, both longtime design associates. Ault continued to actively design courses as a member of Ault, Clark and Associates until his death in 1989.

Courses by Edmund B. Ault:

Arkansas: Balboa GC (1987), with Tom Clark; Berksdale GC (1977); Branchwood GC (9 Par 3 1983); Cherokee Village CC (North Cse 1973; South Cse 1962); Coronado GC (Precision 1983); Cortez GC (1977); DeSoto GC (1972); Kingswood GC (1977); Maumelle G&CC (1969); Metfield CC (Precision 1983); Mountain Ranch GC (1984), with Brian Ault and Tom Clark; Scotsdale GC (1987), with Tom Clark.

Delaware: Delcastle GC (1971); Eagle Creek G Cse (9 1961), with Al Jamison; Garrisons Lake GC (1965); Shawnee CC (9 1960, with Al Jamison; A.9 1984); Sussex Pines CC (1966); Three Little Bakers CC [FKA Pike Creek Valley GC](1972).

Florida: Carrollwood Village G&TC (27 1971); CC of Coral Springs (1969).

Indiana: Christmas Lake G&CC (1968); Wesselman Par 3 GC (18 Par 3 1970); West Boggs Muni (9 1978).

Iowa: Sundown GC (9 Par 3 1978).

Louisiana: Eden Isles CC (1976).

Maryland: Aberdeen Proving Ground GC (9 1965); All-View GC (1968); Baltimore CC (West Cse 1962); Bay Hills GC (1968); Bretton Woods GC (1968); Caroline CC (9 1963); Chartwell G&CC (1961), with Al Jamison; Crofton GC (1963); Diamond Ridge GC (1968); Dwight D. Eisenhower Memorial GC (1969); Falls Road Muni (1960), with Al Jamison; Generals GC (1969); Hawthorne CC (9 1960), with Al Jamison; Henson Creek GC (Precision 1963); Heritage Harbour GC (9 1982); Hobbit's Glen GC (1965); Hunt Valley Inn & CC (1970); Lakewood CC (1960), with Al Jamison; Montgomery Village CC (1966); Northwest Park GC (27 1964); Oakcrest CC (1969), with Al Jamison; Oakland CC (9 1965); Paint Branch GC (1965); Piney Branch GC (1969); Poolesville GC (1959), with Al Jamison; Ralph G. Cover Estate GC (1962); Sligo Park GC (9 1956), with Al Jamison; Turf Valley CC (North Cse 1959, with Al Jamison; South Cse 1963; Woods Cse, 9 1959); TPC at Avenel (1986), with Brian Ault, Tom Clark, Bill Love and *Ed Sneed*; Western Maryland College GC (1968); Wocomico Shores G&CC [FKA Aviation Y&CC](1962).

Missouri: Meadow Lake Acres CC (1961), with Al Jamison; Poplar Bluff Muni (1980).

Nevada: Las Vegas CC (1965).

New Jersey: Quail Brook GC (1982); Ramblewood CC (27 1961); Spooky Brook GC (1969).

New York: McGuire AFB GC (9 1967); Riverton GC (1974).

North Carolina: Etowah Valley CC (1967); Wedgewood CC.

Ohio: Lakeside Greens GC (9 1963); Mayfair CC (East & West Cses, 1968); Town & Country GC (1970); Windmill Lakes GC (1972).

Pennsylvania: Belles Springs GC (1969); Center Square GC (1963); Charnita CC (1967); Clinton CC (9 1972, A.9 1977); Corry Muni; Great Cove GC (1967); Hidden Valley CC (1964); Honey Run G&CC (1971); Iron Masters CC (1965); Juniata GC (Precision 1965); Lewiston CC (1973); Middleburg GC (1969); Monroe Creek GC (1967); Mountain View GC (1987), with Brian Ault and Tom Clark; North Hills Muni (1964); Northampton Valley CC (1964); Oak Tree GC (1967); Olde Hickory GC (9 1966); Olmstead AFB GC; Outdoor CC; Pennsylvania

National G&CC (1967); Pleasant View GC (1960), with Al Jamison; Sinking Valley CC (1962); Toftrees CC (1971); Tyoga CC; Tyrone CC; Waynesboro CC (9 1971).

South Carolina: Cane Patch Par 3 GC (18 Par 3 1982); Midway GC (27 Par 3 1984); Myrtlewood CC (Palmetto Cse 1972).

Virginia: Bolling AFB GC (1960), with Al Jamison; Broad Bay Point G&CC (1986), with Tom Clark; Bryce Resort GC (1972); Bushfield CC (9 1962), with Al Jamison; Chantilly National G&CC (1960), with Al Jamison; CC of Petersburg (1968); CC of Virginia (Tuckahoe Cse, 9 1972, NLE); Deer Run GC (Cardinal Cse 1969; Deer Run Cse, 9 1969); Edwin R. Carr Estate GC (1959), with Al Jamison; Hermitage CC (1986); Herndon Centennial Muni (1979); Hidden Creek CC (1969); Holston Hills CC (9 1968); Lake Fairfax GC (1959), with Al Jamison; Langley AFB GC (1965); Loudoun G&CC (1959), with Al Jamison; Mill Quarter Plantation GC (1979); Penderbrook GC (1979); Reston South GC (1969); River Bend G&CC [FKA Forest Lake CC](1960), with Al Jamison; Shannon Green GC (1971); Sigwick Inn & GC; South Wales G&RC (1957); Spotswood CC (9 1960, A.9 1964); Springfield G&CC (1960), with Al Jamison; Sterling GC (18 Par 3 1963); Stonehenge GC (1969); [The] Summit GC (1987), with Tom Clark; Westpark Hotel & GC (1969); Winton CC (1972).

West Virginia: Green Hills CC (1962); Pines CC (1968); Preston CC (9 1965); Sandy Brae G&CC (1969).

Wisconsin: Brighton Dale GC (27 1971).

British West Indies: Belham River Valley GC (9 1968).

Courses remodeled or expanded by Edmund B. Ault:

Arkansas: Bella Vista CC (R. 1977); CC of Little Rock (R. 1968, R. 1980); Indian Hills GC (R. 1981); Newport CC (A.9 1978).

Delaware: Dover CC (R.9 1969); Green Hill Muni (R. 1971).

Florida: Bardmoor CC (East Cse, R. 1986, NLE), with Tom Clark; Broken Woods G&RC (R. 1973; R.2 1980); Miles Grant CC (R. 1975); Sawgrass GC (Oceanside Cse, R. 1982).

Indiana: Fendrich GC (R. 1968).

Kentucky: Highland CC (R. 1961).

Louisiana: Eden Isles GC (R. 1 1983).

Maryland: Argyle CC (R. 1960), with Al Jamison; Bethesda CC (R.9 A.9 1966); Bethesda Naval Hospital GC (R.9 1961); Bonnie View CC (R. 1961); Burning Tree C (R. 1963); Chester River Y&CC (A.9 1972); Congressional CC (Gold Cse, R.2 1981); Elkridge CC (R. 1974); Fountain Head CC (R. 1968); Hillendale CC (R. 1962); Indian Head Naval Ordnance GC (R.9 1966); Indian Spring C (Chief Cse, R. 1976); Kenwood G&CC (R. 1962); Longview Muni (R.3 1981); Manor CC (R.4 1986), with Brian Ault and Bill Love; Norbeck CC (R. 1965); Silver Springs GC (R. 1958), with Al Jamison; Suburban CC (R. 1964; R.4 1982); Swan Creek CC (R.9 1978); U.S. Navy Medical Center GC (R.); Woodholme CC (R. 1964, R. 1975).

Mississippi: CC of Jackson (R.9 1979).

Missouri: Hickory Hills CC (R. 1974).

New York: Blue Hill GC (R. 1963); Hampshire CC (R. 1962).

North Carolina: Paradise Point GC (Gold Cse, R. 7 1979).

Ohio: Marietta CC (R. 1970); Oakwood CC (R. 1960); Squaw Creek CC (R. 1990).

Pennsylvania: Bucknell University GC (A.9 1963); Butler CC (R. 1963); Chambersburg CC (A.9 1977); Conewango Valley CC (R. 1972); Indiana CC (R. 1969); Nottingham CC (R. 1962); Oak Tree GC (R.2 1983); South Hills GC (R. 1973); VFW GC (A.9 1969).

Tennessee: Woodmont CC (A.9 1977).

Virginia: Army-Navy CC (Arlington Cse, R.3 1985; R.5 1986, with Tom Clark and Bill Love; Fairfax Cse, R. 1962; R.2 1984, with Brian Ault and Bill Love); Belle Haven CC (R. 1969); Belmont Park GC (R. 1971); Eastern Shore Y&CC (R. 1962); Fort Belvoir GC (R.9 A.9 1975); Hampton GC (R. 1972); International Town & CC (R. 1975); Kingsmill GC (River Cse, R.5 1982); Meadowbrook CC (R. 1975); Salisbury CC (R. 1967); Shenvallee Lodge & GC (R.9 A.9 1961); Washington G&CC (R. 1988), with Brian Ault and Tom Clark; Westwood CC (R. 1984), with Brian Ault and Tom Clark; Winchester GC (R. 1966).

West Virginia: Clarksburg CC (R.9 A.9 1964); Parkersburg CC (R. 1965).

Puerto Rico: Dorado del Mar GC (R. 1973).

Switzerland: Caslano GC (R. 1966).

H. G. Babbage

Native New Zealander H. G. Babbage turned to golf course architecture after World War II, first renovating several courses that had closed during the war, then trying his hand at several original designs. Among his best was Muriwai, a genuine links considered by many to be New Zealand's best layout or, at the very least, "the longest short course in the world."

Courses by H. G. Babbage:

New Zealand: Muriwai GC (1959); North Shore GC (27 1964); Taihape GC.

Courses remodeled or expanded by H. G. Babbage:

New Zealand: Manawatu GC (R. 1954); Remuera GC (R. 1974); Te Awamutu GC (R.); Waitomo GC (R.).

Gary Roger Baird
(1941–   ), ASGCA

BORN: Glendale, California.

Gary Baird received a Bachelor's degree in landscape architecture from California Polytechnic Institute in Pomona. In 1969 he joined the West Coast branch of the firm of Robert Trent Jones Inc. and worked as a design associate to both Robert Trent Jones and Robert Trent Jones, Jr. When Trent Jr. formed his own business in the early 1970s, Baird joined him as a senior designer. Baird remained until 1977, when he formed his own design firm.

After several remodeling jobs along the Pacific coast, Baird relocated to Nashville, Tennessee. In the mid-1980s Baird designed a novel course in Japan that utilized common fairways with tees and greens at

Gary Baird, 1990
COURTESY GARY BAIRD

each end. This "two-way" system allowed the course to be played both ways, in one direction toward summer bent-grass greens and in the opposite direction to winter korai-grass greens. In 1990 he became the first American architect to design a course in Turkey.

Courses by Gary Roger Baird:

Alabama: [The] Oaks GC (1991).

Arizona: Rio Rico G&CC (1971), ass't Robert Trent Jones.

California: Bodega Harbour GC (9 1977), ass't Robert Trent Jones, Jr; Lake Shastina G&CC (1972), ass't Robert Trent Jones; Mountain Shadows GC (North Cse 1974); Rancho California GC (1970), ass't Robert Trent Jones; Rancho Solano G Cse (1990); Spring Valley Lake CC (1971), ass't Robert Trent Jones.

Colorado: Arrowhead GC (1974), ass't Robert Trent Jones, Jr; Steamboat Village CC (1974), ass't Robert Trent Jones, Jr.

Georgia: Windstone G Cse (routing 1988).

Hawaii: Princeville Makai GC (27 1971), ass't Robert Trent Jones, Jr; Waikoloa Village GC (1972), ass't Robert Trent Jones, Jr.

Idaho: Elkhorn GC (1975), ass't Robert Trent Jones, Jr.

Michigan: Inkster Valley G Cse (1992).

Montana: Mission Mountain CC (9 1988).

Nevada: Incline Green GC (Precision 1971), ass't Robert Trent Jones.

North Dakota: Oxbow CC (1974), ass't Robert Trent Jones, Jr.

Oregon: Heron Lakes GC (27 1971), ass't Robert Trent Jones.

Tennessee: Brentwood CC (1988); Forrest Crossing GC (1988); Heatherhurst G Cse (1989); Hermitage G Cse (1986); Shaftsbury GC (1987).

Texas: El Dorado CC (1982); Horseshoe Bay CC (Slick Rock Cse 1973), ass't Robert Trent Jones.

Fiji: Pacific Harbour G&CC (1977), ass't Robert Trent Jones, Jr.

Indonesia: Pondok Indah GC (1977), ass't Robert Trent Jones, Jr.

Japan: Shishido International CC (Reversible 1986); Shishido Kokusai GC (Shizu Cse 1990).

Korea: Chung-Nam CC (1992).

Mexico: Ista de la Piedra GC (9 1972), ass't Robert Trent Jones, Jr; Palma Real GC (1977), ass't Robert Trent Jones,

Jr; Pok-Ta-Pok GC (1978), ass't Robert Trent Jones, Jr.

Taiwan: Xen-Wie G&CC (1992).

Thailand: Barrington GC (1992); Kristall Lake CC (27 1992); Navatanee CC (1975), ass't Robert Trent Jones, Jr.; Royal Gems & Sport C (1991).

Turkey: GC at the Mediterranean (1992).

Courses remodeled or expanded by Gary Roger Baird:

Alabama: Gulf Shores GC (R. 1992).

California: Bel-Air CC (R.1 1975), ass't Robert Trent Jones, Jr; Birnam Wood GC (R. 1977), ass't Robert Trent Jones, Jr; Bishop CC (A.9); Corral De Tierra CC (R. 1983); Del Paso CC (R. 1981); Glendora CC (R. 1970), ass't Robert Trent Jones; Green Hills CC (R. 1983); Menlo CC (R. 1970), ass't Robert Trent Jones; Palo Alto Hills G&CC (R. 1982); Palo Alto Muni (R. 1980), ass't Robert Trent Jones, Jr; Pasatiempo GC (R. 1984); Petaluma G&CC (R. 1983).

Hawaii: Mauna Kea Beach Hotel GC (R. 1976), ass't Robert Trent Jones, Jr.

Michigan: Warren Valley GC (East Cse, R. 1990; West Cse, R. 1990).

Oregon: Eugene CC (R. 1983); Roseburg CC (R.9 A.9 1980).

Tennessee: Belle Meade CC (R. 1981); Chattanooga G&CC (R. 1983); Montgomery Bell State G Cse (R. 1989).

ROBERT EARL BALDOCK (1908–   )

BORN: Omaha, Nebraska.

California-based golf architect Bob Baldock planned more than 350 courses in his career. A former Class A PGA golfer, he worked at one time for golf architect William P. Bell. His career lasted from the 1950s into the 1990s. In 1984, Baldock was honored with an Outstanding Service Award by the NGF in recognition for the many occasions that he donated architectural services to Veterans Administration Hospitals, air force bases and small communities that could not afford professional assistance in building their courses.

Courses by Bob Baldock:

Alabama: Jetport GC (Jetport Cse 1968), with Robert L. Baldock; Skypark GC (9), with Robert L. Baldcock.

Arizona: Desert Lakes G Cse (1990), with Robert L. Baldock; Elden Hills

Bob Baldock (left), with son and design partner Robert L. Baldock, 1984
COURTESY *GOLF DIGEST*

GC (1960); General Blanchard GC, Davis Monthan AFB.

California: Alta Sierra CC (1965); Anaheim "Dad Miller" GC (1965); Auburn Valley G&CC (1965); Azuza Greens GC (1965); Baywood G&CC (1958); Bear Valley GC (1962); Bethel Island GC (1966); Blue Lake Springs GC (1966); Butte Creek G&CC (1965); Chimney Rock GC (1966); College of the Sequoias GC (4 1953); Comstock CC (1965); Corral de Tierra CC (1959); Diablo Creek GC (1963); El Macero CC (1961); Eureka Muni (9 1957, A.9 1966); Exeter Muni (9 1963); Fairway Glen GC (9 1961); Fresno West G&CC (1966); Gold Hills CC (1979), with Robert L. Baldock; Hacienda Hotel Par 3 GC (1957); Heather Farms GC (1966); Horse Thief G&CC (1974), with Robert L. Baldock; King City GC (9 Precision 1953); Lazy H GC (9); Leland Meadows Par 3 GC (1962); Lenmoore Muni (9 1963); Lew Galbraith Muni (1966); Lindale Greens GC (1965); Lindsay Muni (9 1963); Livermore VA Hospital GC (9 Par 3); Lone Tree G Cse (1957); Los Banos CC (9 1963); Los Robles Greens GC (9 1964); Madera G&CC (9 1955); Mariposa Pines GC (1973), with Robert L. Baldock; Merced G&CC (1961); Moffett Field GC (9 1956); Monterey Peninsula CC (Shore Cse 1961), with Jack Neville; Mount Whitney CC (9 1959); Mountain Shadows GC (South Cse 1963); Napa Muni (1958), with Jack Fleming and Ben Harmon; Oakdale G&CC (9 1963); Palo Alto VA Hospital GC (9 Par 3); Paradise Pines GC (1972), with Robert L. Baldock; Pariso Springs CC (9 1955); Peach Tree G&CC (1960); Ponderosa G Cse

(9 1961); Rancho del Ray GC [FKA Castle AFB GC](9 1955, A.9 1963); River Island GC (1963); Selma Valley CC (1958); Sherwood Forest GC (1968), with Robert L. Baldock; Shingle Lake GC [FKA Beale AFB CC]; Sierra Sky Ranch GC (9 1954); Skywest Public GC (1964); Swallow's Nest GC (Par 3 1964); Tall Pines GC (9 1972), with Robert L. Baldock; Teaford Lake GC (1972), with Robert L. Baldock; Tracy G&CC (9 1956); Tulare CC (1956); Turlock G&CC, with Jack Fleming; Valley Gardens CC (1971), with Robert L. Baldock; West Winds GC, George AFB (9 1965); Westside GC (9 Par 3 1947); Willow Park GC (1966); Yolo Fliers C (9 1950); Yosemite Lakes GC (1965).

Colorado: Lowry AFB GC (1961).

Florida: Tyndall AFB GC (9 1964).

Hawaii: Hickam AFB GC (1966); Mililani GC (1966); Olomana G Links (1969), with Robert L. Baldock; Pukalani CC (1979), with Robert L. Baldock; Ted Makalena GC (1971), with Robert L. Baldock.

Idaho: Cascade GC (9); Cherry Lane GC (9 1979), with Robert L. Baldock; Crane Creek CC (1962); Kimberland Meadows GC (9 1985), with Robert L. Baldock; Lewiston CC (1974), with Robert L. Baldock; Nampa Muni (9 1985), with Robert L. Baldock; Silver Sage GC (9 1956).

Kansas: Forbes GC (9 1962).

Kentucky: Lexington VA Hospital GC (9 Par 3); Warren Meadows CC (9 1983), with Robert L. Baldock.

Maine: Tagus VA Hospital GC (9 Par 3).

Massachusetts: Otis GC (9 1972).

Michigan: Kinchelo Memorial GC (9); Sawyer AFB GC (1968).

Missouri: Belton Muni (1965).

Montana: Glacier View GC (1972), with Robert L. Baldock; Glasgow AFB GC; Red Lodge CC (9 1983), with Robert L. Baldock.

Nevada: Aladdin Hotel GC (9 Par 3, NLE); Black Mountain G&CC (9 1959); Brookside GC (1964, NLE); Carson City Muni (9 1956); Casa de Mar G&CC (9); Hacienda Hotel Par 3 GC (9 Par 3 1956, NLE); Stead AFB GC (1965); White Pine GC (9 1957); Winnemucca Muni (9).

New Mexico: Four Hills CC (1961); Los Altos Muni (1960).

Oregon: Emerald Valley GC (1966); Illinois Valley GC (9 1977), with Robert L. Baldock; Ontario Muni GC (1965); White City VA Hospital GC (9 Par 3).

Pennsylvania: Hideout GC (9).

Washington: Hangman Valley Muni (1968), with Robert L. Baldock; Swallow's Nest GC (9 1964); Whispering Firs GC, McChord AFB (9 1961).

Wyoming: Jackson Hole G&TC (1961); Olive Glenn GC (1970), with Robert L. Baldock.

Mexico: San Antonio Shores GC (1970), with Robert L. Baldock.

Philippines: Manila G&CC (1961); Philippines CC (1961).

Tahiti: Golf D'Atimaona CC (1967).

Courses remodeled or expanded by Bob Baldock:

California: Belmont CC (R. 1956); Bermuda Dunes CC (A. 3rd 9 1986), with Robert L. Baldock; Fort Washington G&CC (R. 1956); Indian Hills CC (R. 1968), with Robert L. Baldock; Kings River G&CC (R. 1961); Polvadero G&CC (R.9); Plumas Lake G&CC (R.9 A.9 1962); San Joaquin CC (R. 1961); Santa Maria GC (R. 1965); Shorecliffs CC (R. 1985), with Robert L. Baldock; Sierra View CC (A.9 1966); Soule Park GC (A.9 1970), with Robert L. Baldock; 1001 Ranch GC (R. 1972), with Robert L. Baldock.

Hawaii: Ala Wai GC (R. 1962); Mid-Pacific CC (R. 1968), with Robert L. Baldock; Waialae CC (R. 1966).

Idaho: Eagle Hills GC (A.9 1975), with Robert L. Baldock; University of Idaho GC (R.9 A.9).

Nevada: Black Mountain G&CC (R. 1990), with Robert L. Baldock.

Oregon: Bend G&CC (A.9 1972), with Robert L. Baldock; Grant's Pass CC (R.4 A.14), with Robert L. Baldock; Reames G&CC (A.9 1966).

Washington: Edgewater Muni (R., NLE).

Wyoming: Casper CC (R.9 A.9 1960).

ROBERT LEE BALDOCK (1945–)

BORN: Avalon, California.

As a student at Fresno State College in California, young Bob Baldock assisted his golf architect father, Robert E. Baldock, on weekends and during summers. He became a partner with his father in the business in 1968.

Courses by Robert L. Baldock (All with Bob Baldock unless otherwise indicated):

Alabama: Jetport GC (Jetport Cse 1968); Skypark GC (9).

California: Alta Sierra CC (1965), ass't Bob Baldock; Azuza Greens GC (1965), ass't Bob Baldock; Bethel Island GC (1966), ass't Bob Baldock; Butte Creek G&CC (1965), ass't Bob Baldock; Chimney Rock GC (1966), ass't Bob Baldock; Fresno West G&CC (1966), ass't Bob Baldock; Gold Hills CC (1979); Horse Thief G&CC (1974); Lindale Greens GC (1965), ass't Bob Baldock; Mariposa Pines GC (1973); Sherwood Forest GC (1968); Tall Pines GC (9 1972); Valley Gardens CC (1971); Vineyards GC (1985); Willow Park GC (1966), ass't Bob Baldock; Yosemite Lakes GC (1965), ass't Bob Baldock.

Hawaii: Olomana G Links (1969); Pukalani CC (1979); Ted Makalena GC (1971).

Idaho: Cherry Lane GC (9 1979); Kimberland Meadows GC (9 1985); Lewiston CC (1974); Nampa Muni (9 1985).

Kentucky: Warren Meadows CC (9 1983).

Montana: Glacier View GC (1972); Red Lodge CC (9 1983).

Oregon: Illinois Valley GC (9 1977).

Washington: Hangman Valley Muni (1968).

Wyoming: Olive Glenn GC (1970).

Mexico: San Antonio Shores GC (1970).

Courses remodeled or expanded by Robert L. Baldock (All with Bob Baldock):

California: Bermuda Dunes CC (A. 3rd 9 1986); Indian Hills CC (R. 1968); Shorecliffs CC (R. 1985); Soule Park

GC (A.9 1970), 1001 Ranch GC (R. 1972);

Hawaii: Mid-Pacific CC (R. 1968).

Idaho: Eagle Hills GC (A.9 1975).

Nevada: Black Mountain G&CC (R. 1990).

Oregon: Bend G&CC (A.9 1972); Grant's Pass CC (R.4 A.14).

JAMES ANDREW BANFIELD (1949–)

BORN: Haileybury, Ontario, Canada.

The son of a noted geologist, Andy Banfield moved to the United States at an early age. He grew up in Norwalk, Connecticut, where he excelled in junior and amateur golf tournaments. Banfield attended the University of Arizona and, after graduating with a degree in mining engineering, worked for a time with a mine-exploration firm in Idaho. But his heart was in golf, and, soon after he returned to Connecticut, a friend and fellow resident of Norwalk, *Golf Digest* editor Cal Brown, arranged for him to meet with Tom Fazio. Banfield soon went to work for George and Tom Fazio as a tractor operator, field assistant and eventually a foreman. He learned his craft quickly, and by the late 1970s Banfield had developed a reputation as an expert shaper.

After serving as construction superintendent on several Fazio projects, Banfield moved to the drafting table and began assisting the Fazios in the routing and design of courses. When George and Tom Fazio separated their design businesses, Banfield stayed with Tom and became his chief designer. He continued to work in the field, too, both in supervising construction of his designs and even in handling shaping on occasion.

Andy Banfield, 1991

Courses by Andy Banfield (All as assistant to Tom Fazio):

Arizona: Ventana Canyon G&RC (Canyon Cse 1988; Mountain Cse 1984).
California: Pelican Hill GC (Canyon Cse 1993; Ocean Cse 1992).
Florida: Black Diamond G&CC (1987); John's Island C (West Cse 1988); Lake Nona C (1986); Old Trail GC (Fazio Cse 1987).
Illinois: Conway Farms GC (1991); Stonebridge CC (1989).
Kansas: Hallbrook CC (1988).
Nevada: Shadow Creek GC (1990).
New Jersey: Pine Valley GC (Short Cse, 10 1992).
North Carolina: Champion Hills G&CC (1991); Treyburn CC (1989).
South Carolina: Wachesaw Plantation GC (1986).
Texas: Barton Creek C (Fazio Cse 1986).

Courses remodeled or expanded by Andy Banfield (All as assistant to Tom Fazio):

New Jersey: Pine Valley GC (R.2 1989).
Pennsylvania: Philadelphia CC (A.3rd 9 1992).
South Carolina: Cotton Dike GC (A.2 1990).

Charles Henry Banks (1883–1931)

BORN: Amenia, New York.
DIED: New York City, New York, at age 48.
INTERRED: Salisbury, Connecticut.

Charles Banks graduated from Yale University in 1906. He then returned to his preparatory school, Hotchkiss in Salisbury, Connecticut, where he served as English instructor and track coach for fifteen years. While a member of the school's construction committee, he met Seth J. Raynor, who had been hired to design and build a new golf course at Hotchkiss. He worked closely with Raynor on the job and in 1921 resigned his teaching position to join Raynor's firm. "Josh" Banks stayed with Raynor until Raynor's death in 1926, assisting him (and, on a few projects, C. B. Macdonald) in the design and construction of such courses as Fox Chapel in Pennsylvania and Yale University GC in Connecticut.

Banks finished ten of Raynor's projects and designed or remodeled over thirty other courses in the late 1920s. Nick-

Charles Banks, circa 1902

named "Steam Shovel" Banks by his colleagues, he was an enthusiastic believer in massive earth moving to create huge elevated greens and deep bunkers. Legend has it that at Whippoorwill Club in Armonk, New York (a Ross course he completely redid and claimed by many to be Bank's masterpiece), this enthusiasm for depth was dampened when a steam shovel excavating an exceptionally deep pond disappeared in the ooze. Fortunately, the operator was rescued, but the steam shovel is said to still lie deep beneath the sixth fairway a half century later.

Banks also carried on the Macdonald/Raynor tradition of including adaptations of famous holes in each design. Invariably a "Redan," "Alps" or other renowned hole can be found on a Banks layout.

Charles Banks died of a heart attack in 1931. His last project was Castle Harbour GC in Bermuda, which abutted the famous Mid Ocean Club, a course he had helped to construct a decade earlier.

Courses by Charles Banks:

California: Monterey Peninsula CC (Dunes Cse 1926), with Seth Raynor.
Connecticut: Yale University (1926), with Charles Blair Macdonald, Seth Raynor and Ralph Barton.
Georgia: Lookout Mountain GC [FKA Fairyland CC](1925), with Seth Raynor.
Hawaii: Mid-Pacific CC (9 1927), with Seth Raynor; Waialae CC (1925), with Seth Raynor.
Maryland: Annapolis Roads GC (9).
New Jersey: Essex County CC (West Cse 1930); Forsgate CC (East Cse 1931); Hackensack CC (27 1930); Knoll GC (1929); Rock Spring CC (1927).

New York: Southampton GC (1927), with Seth Raynor; Tamarack CC (1929); Westhampton CC (Oneck Cse 1929, NLE).
Pennsylvania: Fox Chapel GC (1925), with Seth Raynor.
Virginia: Cavalier G&YC (1930).
Bermuda: Castle Harbour GC (1932); Mid Ocean C (1924), with Charles Blair Macdonald, Seth Raynor and Ralph Barton.
Colombia: CC of Bogotá (NLE).
Venezuela: Caracas CC (1931); Junko CC.

Courses remodeled or expanded by Charles Banks:

Connecticut: Hotchkiss School GC (R. 1930).
Massachusetts: Wyantenuck GC (R.3).
New Jersey: Forest Hill Field C (R. 1927); Montclair GC (A.4th 9 1930).
New York: Knollwood CC (R. 1927); Whippoorwill CC (R. 1930).

Cecil Barcroft

BORN: County Tyrone, Ireland.

Secretary of Royal Dublin GC in Ireland at the beginning of the twentieth century, Cecil Barcroft laid out many Irish golf courses. His contemporaries admired the expert manner in which he routed courses around hilly sites, but Barcroft himself preferred his works on natural linksland.

Courses by Cecil Barcroft:

Ireland: Castle GC (1913), with *Tom Hood* and *W. C. Pickeman;* Howth GC (9 1914).

Courses remodeled or expanded by Cecil Barcroft:

Ireland: Bray GC (R.9 1914); County Louth GC (R.), with *N. Halligan;* Waterford GC (A.9).

Richard A. Baril (1957–)

BORN: Nampa, Idaho.

Rick Baril obtained a degree in landscape architecture from the University of Idaho, then went to work full-time for Sterling Landscape Architects, a firm he

Rick Baril, 1991
COURTESY RICK BARIL

had interned with during college. In 1982, after receiving a call from a former classmate, Mike Smelek, he joined Smelek in the Texas-based golf design firm of von Hagge and Devlin. With the departure of Bruce Devlin in 1987, Baril was elevated to an associate architect position, with principal responsibility for von Hagge Associates' work in Europe and the United States. He participated extensively in every von Hagge design from that time on.

HERBERT H. BARKER
(–1924)

BORN: England.
DIED: England.

After winning several tournaments in Great Britain in the early 1900s, including the Yorkshire Amateur in 1904 and 1906, the Irish Open in 1906 and the Dartmouth Bowl for three consecutive years starting

Herbert Barker, circa 1910
COLLECTION RON WHITTEN

in 1905, Herbert Barker moved to America and served as head professional at Garden City (New York) Golf Club from 1908 to 1911. He found golf to be more competitive in America and failed to win any events. But he also discovered less-challenging courses and soon began designing and remodeling layouts with the intention of elevating the game in the United States.

Barker moved to the South after leaving Garden City, laid out Roebuck Country Club in Alabama and stayed on as its pro for a time. But then he renounced his professional standing and worked solely as a golf architect. After designing several Southern courses, Barker returned to Britain in 1915 to enlist in the military. Although he told friends he intended to return after the war, Barker never returned to America. He died after an extended illness, reportedly related to injuries he sustained in the war.

Courses by Herbert Barker:

Alabama: Don Hawkins Muni [FKA Roebuck CC](9 1914).
Georgia: Capital City C (1911); Druid Hills CC (1912).
Maryland: Columbia CC (1910).
New Jersey: Arcola CC (1909); Rumson CC (1910).
Ohio: Mayfield CC (1911), with Bert Way.
Virginia: CC of Virginia (Westhampton Cse 1908, NLE).

Courses remodeled or expanded by Herbert Barker:

North Carolina: Grove Park Inn CC (R.9 A.9 1911).

RALPH MARTIN BARTON
(1875–1941)

BORN: Newport, New Hampshire.
DIED: New Hampshire at age 66.

Ralph Barton attended Phillips Exeter Academy and Dartmouth College and also took courses at Harvard and the University of Chicago. From 1904 until the early 1920s he pursued a career in the academic world, teaching mathematics and holding administrative posts at Dartmouth College, the University of New Mexico, Lombard College and the University of Minnesota. While at Minnesota he undertook supervision of the university's golf course, designed by Seth Raynor.

This experience left Barton permanently enamored with golf architecture, and he subsequently resigned his university post and, at age 48, became an apprentice to Raynor and C. B. Macdonald. He participated in the design and engineering of such famous Macdonald courses as Yale Golf Club in Connecticut and Mid Ocean Club in Bermuda. The full extent of his participation is open for debate. Late in his life Barton claimed to have handled the major aspects of the design and construction of those courses. Macdonald, in his autobiography, credits Raynor and Charles Banks with substantial assistance, but doesn't mention Barton.

In 1926, the year of Raynor's death, Barton entered private practice, establishing a golf course architecture and engineering firm in New Hampshire that he maintained until his death. In 1932 he donated his time and added a third nine to Dartmouth College's Hanover Country Club. Sadly, the nine was eventually closed, though four holes were preserved and used for years as a practice course.

Barton was married and widowed three times. His design practice was never prolific, and he apparently discontinued it sometime during the Depression. In the months before his death in 1941 he was working for the bridge division of the New Hampshire State Highway Department.

A member of the American Mathematical Society, Ralph Barton was buried at the Dartmouth Cemetery in Hanover.

Courses by Ralph Barton:

Connecticut: Sleeping Giant GC (9); Yale University GC (1924), with C. B. Macdonald, Seth Raynor and Charles Banks.
Maine: Bridgton Highlands GC (9 1926).
Massachusetts: Greenfield CC; Magnolia GC.
New Hampshire: Concord CC (9 1927); Lakeport CC (9, NLE); Lancaster CC

Ralph Barton, circa 1925 COURTESY *THE AEGIS,* DARTMOUTH COLLEGE, NEW HAMPSHIRE

(9, NLE); Lisbon Village CC [FNA
Ammonoosuc INN & GC](9 1929);
Mackenzie's GC (9 1933, NLE);
Mountain View House GC (9 1939);
Pecketts CC (9, NLE); Plymouth GC
(9, NLE).
Vermont: Kingsbery Club (NLE); New-
port CC (9); Wilmington CC (NLE).
Bermuda: Mid Ocean C (1925), with
C. B. Macdonald, Seth Raynor and
Charles Banks.

**Courses remodeled or expanded by
Ralph Barton:**

Massachusetts: Greenfield CC (R. 1931).
New Hampshire: Hanover CC (A.3rd 9
1932); John H. Cain GC [FKA New-
port CC] (R.); Laconia CC (A.9 1927);
North Conway CC (R.9); Profile C
(R.9 1930); Sugar Hill CC (R.);
Waumbek GC (R. 1928).

GENE D. BATES
(1947–   )

BORN: Cambridge, Ohio.

Gene Bates was one of those golf architects who rose through the ranks, going
from field work to the front office. He
graduated from Colorado State University
in 1969 after a year at Ohio University.
During summers in college, he learned to
operate heavy equipment working on coal
strip mining and highway construction
projects. After college he returned to his
native Ohio and worked in heavy construction. In 1977 he used his experience
to gain work on a golf course construction
crew and soon proved to be a talented
finish shaper.

From 1978 to 1983 he was project administrator for his father-in-law, Ron
Kirby, in the Kirby/Player & Associates
design firm, mainly handling its overseas
projects. Bates then joined Jack Nicklaus
Design Services, and his first assignment
was the construction of the unique Cayman ball course in the Cayman Islands. He
became so interested in the concept that
he later created several other courses designed primarily for the shorter Cayman
ball.

Bates eventually became a vice president of the design and construction services division in Nicklaus's organization,
but he left the company in 1988 and
formed Gene Bates & Associates, based in
Florida and staffed by, among others, Robert E. Cupp, Jr., son of golf architect Bob
Cupp. Bates served as architectural part-

Gene Bates, 1991
COURTESY GENE BATES

ner to former U.S. Open champion Johnny
Miller in many of Miller's designs. Bates
also used PGA Tour player Jerry Heard as
a consultant on some projects.

Courses by Gene Bates:

California: Brighton Crest CC (1990),
with Johnny Miller; PGA West GC
(Nicklaus Private and Nicklaus Resort
Cses 1987), ass't Jack Nicklaus.
Colorado: Breckenridge GC (1987), ass't
Jack Nicklaus; Ptarmigan G&CC
(1988), ass't Jack Nicklaus.
Florida: Binks Forest CC (1990), with
Johnny Miller; Riverwood G&CC
(1992).
Georgia: CC of the South (1988), ass't
Jack Nicklaus.
Hawaii: Kauai Lagoons G&CC (Kiele
and Lagoon Cses 1988), ass't Jack
Nicklaus.
Indiana: [The] Players C at Woodland
Terrace (1992).
Kentucky: Triple Crown CC (1992);
Vahalla GC (1986), ass't Jack
Nicklaus.
Louisiana: CC of Louisiana (1986), ass't
Jack Nicklaus; English Turn G&CC
(1988), ass't Jack Nicklaus.
North Carolina: [The] Falls G&RC (9
Cayman 1989).
South Carolina: Long Bay C (1988), ass't
Jack Nicklaus; Pawleys Plantation GC
(1988), ass't Jack Nicklaus.
Tennessee: Richland CC (1989), ass't Jack
Nicklaus.
Utah: Green Spring G Cse (1989).
Wisconsin: Missing Links GC (9 Cayman
1987).
Austria: GC Gut Altentann (1988), ass't
Jack Nicklaus.
Bophuthatswana: Gary Player CC (1979),
ass't Ron Kirby and Gary Player.
Cayman Islands: Britannia GC (Cayman
1985), ass't Jack Nicklaus.
England: Collingtree Park GC (1989),
with Johnny Miller; St. Mellion G&CC
(New Cse 1987), ass't Jack Nicklaus.

Japan: Sunnyfield CC (1988), ass't Jack
Nicklaus.
Sweden: Mauritzberg Slotts G Resort.
Switzerland: GC Crans (1988), ass't Jack
Nicklaus.

**Courses remodeled or expanded by
Gene Bates:**

Florida: Mayacoo Lakes CC (R. 1988),
ass't Jack Nicklaus; South Seas Planta-
tion GC (R. 1990), with *Jerry Heard;*
Forest G&CC (Bobcat Cse, R.); Well-
ington GC (R. 1989), with Johnny
Miller.
Hawaii: Seamountain GC (R. 1992), with
Johnny Miller.
Kentucky: Summit Hills CC (R. 1990).
Ohio: Stillwater Valley (R.).
Philippines: Wack Wack G&CC (East
Cse, R. 1980), ass't Ron Kirby and
Denis Griffiths.

ROBERT D. BEARD
(1914–   )

A native of Indiana, Robert Beard established a golf course design-and-build firm
in Fort Wayne in 1959. His course design
work, done over a 25-year period, was
mainly in Indiana, Michigan and Ohio.

Courses by Robert Beard:

Indiana: Big Pine GC; Canterbury Green
GC (Precision 1971); Cedar Creek
GC; Crestview GC (9); Havenhurst
GC (1967); Lake James CC; Lakeside
GC (27); Pond A River GC (9); Tri-
County GC; Zollner GC, Tri-State
University (1971).
Michigan: Case Leasing GC (9); Cedar
Creek GC; Coldwater CC (1971); Ev-
ergreen CC (9); Katke GC, Ferris State
University (1974); Katke Cousins GC,
Oakland University; Manley's GC; Ma-
ple Hill GC (9); Stony Creek GC
(1978); Tomac Woods GC.
Ohio: Marvin Rupp GC.

MICHAEL BEEBE
(1958–   ), ASGCA

BORN: Indianapolis, Indiana.

Mike Beebe received degrees in environmental design and landscape architecture from Ball State University of Indiana
in 1982. He then worked as a landscape
architect in south Florida for a short time

Mike Beebe, 1991
COURTESY MIKE BEEBE

before joining the staff of golf architect Chuck Ankrom. In 1985 he joined the Jacksonville-based course architecture firm of PGA Tour star Mark McCumber. As a vice president and chief project architect, he assumed responsibility for the design and daily coordination of all the firm's course projects.

Courses by Mike Beebe (All as assistant to Mark McCumber):

Florida: Burnt Store Marina GC (South Cse [9 Precision] 1988); Cutter Sound CC (1985); Deep Creek GC (1985); Dunes GC (Precision 1983); Embassy Woods at Bretonne Park (Precision 1991); Magnolia Point G&CC (1986); Marsh Creek CC (1988); Queen's Harbour Y&CC (1991); Summer Beach G Cse (1987); Vineyards G&CC (North Cse 1988).
Georgia: Osprey Cove GC (1990).
Mississippi: Timberton GC (1991); Windance G&CC (1986).
Alberta: Edmonton Petroleum G&CC (1992).
Japan: Ohtake GC.
Korea: Dae Jeon CC.

Courses remodeled or expanded by Mike Beebe (All as assistant to Mark McCumber):

Florida: North Palm Beach CC (R. 1990).
Michigan: Great Oaks CC (R. 1989).

MAX HOWELL BEHR
(1884–1955)

BORN: New York City, New York.
DIED: Los Angeles, California, at age 71.

Max Behr attended the Lawrenceville School in New Jersey and graduated in 1905 from Yale University, where he had been a member of the golf team coached by pioneer golf designer Robert Pryde. He had learned golf at Morris County CC in New Jersey and as a youth had competed in several father-son tournaments with his father, Herman.

Behr was a perennial bridesmaid in competition, losing the 1907 and 1908 New Jersey Amateurs and the 1908 U.S. Amateur, all to the same golfer, Jerome Travers. He finally won the New Jersey title in 1909 and successfully defended it in 1910, gaining his only victory over Travers in the final of the New Jersey event. In 1914 Behr became the first editor of the New York–based magazine *Golf Illustrated*. He resigned from the publication after the death of his first wife in 1918 and moved to California, where he continued to write on golf, especially on the design and construction of courses. He remained active as an author well into his sixties. In the early 1920s Behr also began designing and remodeling courses, but his business was curtailed during the Depression, and, after World War II, when others resumed course design careers, Behr had lost interest.

Max Behr was something of a radical. In golf he was a strong advocate of the floating golf ball, petitioning the USGA for over 15 years to adopt it. He didn't believe in rough on his course designs, preferring instead to defend his greens from every conceivable approach shot. He was outspoken on politics and religion and late in his life developed his own religion based on his interpretation of numbers, although he disavowed any connection with numerology, to which he was opposed.

Courses by Max Behr:

California: Hacienda CC (1922); Lakeside GC of Hollywood (1924); Montebello GC; Montecito CC (1922);

Max Behr, circa 1915 COLLECTION RON WHITTEN

Oakmont CC (1924); Pasadena GC (1920, NLE); Rancho CC (1922, NLE); Rancho Santa Fe CC (1927).

Courses remodeled or expanded by Max Behr:

California: Brentwood CC (R.); California CC (R.9 A.9, NLE); Olympic C (Lake Cse, R. 1926; Ocean Cse, R. 1926); Victoria GC (R.9 A.9 1923).

Ed Beidel, 1990
COURTESY ASGCA

EDWARD M. BEIDEL, JR.
(1954–), ASGCA

BORN: Pittsburgh, Pennsylvania.

Ed Beidel's interest in golf began at an early age, when he caddied at Fox Chapel Golf Club, Pittsburgh Field Club and Oakmont Country Club. He graduated from Penn State University in 1976 with a Bachelor of Science degree in landscape architecture and shortly thereafter joined the Pittsburgh golf design firm of X. G. Hassenplug. He eventually became the senior designer and project manager for the firm.

Courses by Ed Beidel (All as assistant to X. G. Hassenplug):

New York: Chautauqua GC (Cse No. 2 1985).
Ohio: Fairway Pines GC (1988).
Pennsylvania: Five Ponds G Cse (1988); Sheraton Inn GC (9 Precision 1981).

Courses remodeled or expanded by Ed Beidel (All as assistant to X. G. Hassenplug):

New York: Chautauqua GC (Cse No. 1, R. 1986).
Pennsylvania: Lenape Heights GC (A.9 1983); Lone Pine GC (R. 1986); Pittsburgh Field Club (R. 1985); Pleasant Valley CC (R. 1984); Seven Oaks CC (R. 1977); Skippack GC (R. 1988); Skytop C (R. 1985); South Hills CC (R. 1979).

JAN BELJAN
(1953–), ASGCA

BORN: Pittsburgh, Pennsylvania.

A career in golf seemed inevitable for Jan Beljan, for her father, George Beljan, was a longtime club professional and golf superintendent and four of her uncles were also well-known Pittsburgh-area club professionals. When she was a youngster, her father designed, built and maintained a course. Jan worked on a course as a laborer in the mornings, then changed clothes and moved into the pro shop during the afternoons.

When her family moved to West Virginia, Beljan attended West Virginia University on a GCSAA scholarship and also worked as an assistant golf superintendent at Preston Country Club. She graduated cum laude in landscape architecture in 1976 and went to work for Davey Tree Co.'s lawn-care division in Pittsburgh. At the 1978 PGA Championship at Oakmont, Jan was introduced to Tom Fazio. Later that same year he hired her as a design associate. Based in Fazio's Florida office, Beljan was originally assigned to creation of working drawings but soon progressed to field work, construction supervision and ultimately to primary responsibility on several Fazio designs as a senior designer in the firm. Beljan also traveled extensively in the United States, Europe and the Far East to study golf design.

In 1990 Jan Beljan became the second female elected to membership in the ASGCA.

Courses by Jan Beljan (All as assistant to Tom Fazio):

California: Pelican Hill GC (Ocean Cse 1992).
Florida: [The] Bayou C (1991); Black Diamond Ranch G&CC (1988); Emerald Dunes GC (1990); Gateway GC (1989); Hammock Dunes GC (1988);

Hunter's Green CC (1989); Pelican's Nest GC (1987, A.3rd 9 1990); Walt Disney World GC (Osprey Ridge Cse 1992); Windstar CC (1983).
Georgia: Eagle's Landing CC (1988); [The] Farm GC (1988); St. Ives G&CC (1989).
New York: Oyster Bay G Cse (1988).
North Carolina: Champion Hills G&CC (1991); Porters Neck Plantation GC (1991); Treyburn CC (1989).
South Carolina: Wild Dunes G Links (Yacht Harbor Cse 1986).

Courses remodeled or expanded by Jan Beljan (All as assistant to Tom Fazio):

Florida: Bluewater Bay GC (A.3rd 9).
North Carolina: Hendersonville CC (R. 1990).
Pennsylvania: Philadelphia CC (A.3rd 9 1992).

ALEXANDER BELL

A native of Scotland who trained under Ben Sayers at North Berwick, Alex Bell settled in Hawaii around the turn of the century. He designed several of Hawaii's earliest golf courses. Bell's son Art was a distinguished competitive golfer and club professional who served at several California clubs, including the famed Pebble Beach Golf Links.

Courses by Alex Bell:

Hawaii: Maui CC (9 1927), with William McEwan; Oahu CC (1912); Palolo Muni (9 1931, NLE).

EARL LEE BELL
(1899–1955)

BORN: Lenexa, Kansas.
DIED: Kansas City, Missouri, at age 56.

"Smiley" Bell began his career in golf running horse-drawn mowers for his father, Henry Bell, greenkeeper at Mission Hills CC in Kansas City, Kansas. He later worked as caddy master at the club and in the midtwenties formed a course construction and management firm in Kansas City.

Bell opened his first commercial driving range, "Smiley's Sportland" (the first operation of its kind in the Midwest), in 1928. He also worked on several Kansas- and Missouri-area courses reconstructing

Smiley Bell, 1953
COLLECTION RON WHITTEN

greens, often converting them from sand to grass. In the mid-1920s he also built Armour Fields GC, a daily-fee course that he operated until it was subdivided in the early fifties. This led to other course design projects, and until his death Bell was busy planning and constructing Midwestern courses with the avowed intent of bringing golf to as many communities as possible.

Courses by Smiley Bell:

Kansas: Coffeyville CC (9 1954); El Dorado CC (9 1950); Hillcrest Muni (9 1923); Manhattan CC (1949); Smiley's Sportland GC (Par 3 1930, NLE).
Missouri: Armour Fields GC (1923, NLE); Camp Crowder GC; Columbia Muni (9 1954); Twin Hills CC (9).

Courses remodeled or expanded by Smiley Bell:

Arkansas: Hot Springs G&CC (Arlington Cse, R. 1949; Majestic Cse, R. 1949).
Kansas: Garden City CC (R.); Independence CC (R.); Park Hills CC (R. 1953).
Missouri: Columbia CC (R.); Excelsior Springs CC (R. 1951); Shifferdecker CC (R.9 A.9).

Jan Beljan, 1990
COURTESY JAN BELJAN

WILLIAM FRANCIS BELL
(1918–1984), ASGCA, PRESIDENT 1957

BORN: Pasadena, California.
DIED: Pasadena, California, at age 66.

William F. Bell, son of golf architect Billy Bell, trained and worked with his father after graduating from the University of Southern California. He took over the practice upon his father's death in 1953 and retained the firm name of William P. Bell and Son in his honor.

Bell, often called Billy Bell, Jr., laid out over 200 courses in his lifetime, most of them along the Pacific coast and Hawaii.

Ironically, he died in the same manner as his father, of a heart attack in Pasadena, at almost the same age.

Courses by William F. Bell:

Arizona: Forty-Niner CC (1961); Maryvale GC (Precision 1961); Mesa CC (1950), with William P. Bell; Papago Park GC (27 1963); Pima G Resort (1959); Randolph Park GC (South Cse 1961); Rolling Hills GC (Precision 1962); Tucson CC (1949), with William P. Bell; Wickenburg CC (1950), with William P. Bell; Yuma G&CC (1951), with William P. Bell.

California: Alameda Muni (Jack Clark Cse 1957); Alhambra Muni (1955); Alisal GC (1955); Ancil Hoffman GC (1965); Antelope Valley CC (1957); Apple Valley CC (9 1951, with William P. Bell, A.9 1963); Bakersfield CC (1949), with William P. Bell; Banning Muni; Bermuda Dunes CC; Blue Skies CC (1957); Blythe Muni (1969); Bonita GC (1958); Buenaventura GC (1949), with William P. Bell; California CC (1957); Calimesa G&CC (1958); Canyon CC (1962); Canyon South G Cse (1962); Carmel Highland G&TC [FKA Rancho Penasquitos GC](1964); Chevy Chase CC, with William P. Bell; China Lake GC (1956); Costa Mesa G&CC (Los Lagos Cse 1968; Mesa Linda Cse 1968); Crystalaire CC (1958); DeBell GC (1958), with William H. Johnson; Diamond Bar GC (1964); Dryden Park Muni (1961); Eaton Canyon GC (6 1959); Fullerton G&CC (27 1963); Green Tree GC (27 1963); Heartwell GC (Par 3 1962); Hesperia G&CC (1957); Hidden Valley Lake G&CC (1970); Hillcrest CC (Par 3 Cse [9 Par 3] 1950, with William P. Bell; Industry Hills GC (Eisenhower Cse 1979;

Zaharias Cse 1980); Irvine Coast CC (1954), with William P. Bell; Ivey Ranch CC (1985); Jurupa Hills GC (1960); Kern River CC (1953), with William P. Bell; Kern Valley GC (9); Knollwood CC (1957), with William H. Johnson; Lake Arrowhead CC (1963); Lake Don Pedro G&CC (1971); Lake Wildwood GC (1971); Lomas Santa Fe GC (1964); Los Coyotes CC (27 1958); Los Verdes G&CC (1965); Malibu CC (1980); Marina GC (1963); Mesa Verde CC (1959); Monterey Hills GC (9 Par 3 1949), with William P. Bell; Newport Beach CC (1954), with William P. Bell; Newporter Inn GC (9 Par 3 1962); North Kern CC (1959); North Ridge CC (1954), with William P. Bell; Palm Desert CC (1962); Palm Meadows GC; Palm Springs Muni; Palo Alto Muni (1954), with William P. Bell; Pine Mountain Lake CC (9 1971); Rancho Bernardo Inn & CC (West Cse 1962); Rancho Duarte GC (9 1982); Rancho San Joaquin CC (1969); Recreation Park GC; River Ridge GC (1986); Riviera Marin GC; Rolling Hills GC, with William P. Bell; San Luis Rey GC (1965); Sandpiper G Links (1972); Saticoy CC (1964); Sepulveda GC (Balboa Cse 1953; Encino Cse 1953), with William P. Bell and William H. Johnson; Shoal Canyon GC (9 Precision 1979); Silver K GC (9 1975); Singing Hills CC (Willow Glen Cse 1953), with William P. Bell and William H. Johnson; Skylinks GC (1959); Soule Park GC (9 1962); South Hills CC (1954), with William P. Bell; Sunset Oaks CC (1963); Tamarisk CC (1953), with William P. Bell; Tony Lema Memorial GC (1983); Torrey Pines Muni (North Cse 1957; South Cse 1957); Valle Grande GC (9 1954, with William P. Bell, A.9 1964, A.3rd 9 1973); Valley Hi CC (1961); Victoria Muni (1962); Whittier Narrows GC (27 1960).

Colorado: Valley CC (1960).

Hawaii: Hawaii Kai CC (Championship Cse 1973); Keauhou Kona CC (1971; A.3rd 9 1986, with Robin Nelson); Makaha Valley CC (1969); Sheraton Makaha Resort & CC (1968).

Idaho: Idaho Falls CC (1970); Sand Creek Muni (1974).

Montana: Bitterroot River CC (1974).

Nevada: Calvada Valley G&CC (1979); Dunes Hotel CC (1964); Hidden Valley CC (1958).

Oregon: Forest Hills GC (1953), with

William P. Bell; Illahee Hills CC (1961); Kah-nee-ta GC (9).

Utah: Bonneville Muni (9 1952, with William P. Bell; A.9 1956); Dugway GC; Glendale Park Muni (1973); Hidden Valley CC (1960); Hobble Creek GC (1973); Mountain Dell GC (1960); Oakridge CC (1957); Riverside CC (1960).

Guam: Windward Hills G&CC.

Courses remodeled or expanded by William F. Bell:

Arizona: Encanto Muni (A.3rd 9 1952), with William P. Bell.

California: Bel-Air CC (R. 1968); Coronado GC (R. 1968); Crystal Springs GC (R. 1964); Del Paso CC (R. 1958); DeBell GC (R. 1966); Furnace Creek GC (A.9 1967); Irvine Coast CC (R. 1966); La Cumbre G&CC (R. 1957); Lake Arrowhead CC (R.2 1977); Los Alamitos GC (R. A.12 1960); Montebello GC (R.5 1962); Oakmont CC (R. 1967); Ojai Valley Inn & CC (R. 1948), with William P. Bell; Riverside G&CC (A.9); San Clemente Muni (R.9 A.9 1957); San Gabriel CC (R. 1958).

Colorado: Overland Park Muni (A.9 1956).

Hawaii: Hawaii Kai CC (Executive Cse, R. 1973).

Nevada: Las Vegas GC (A.9 1955).

Oregon: Columbia-Edgewater CC (R. 1970); Riverside G&CC (R. 1970); Rogue Valley CC (R.9 A.9 1949), with William P. Bell.

Utah: [The] Country Club (R.9 1952), with William P. Bell; Rose Park GC (A.9 1960).

William F. Bell, 1960 COURTESY GOLF WORLD

WILLIAM PARK BELL
(1886–1953) ASGCA, CHARTER MEMBER, PRESIDENT 1952

BORN: Canonsburg, Pennsylvania.
DIED: Pasadena, California, at age 67.

Billy Bell studied agriculture at Duff's Business College in Pittsburgh, Pennsylvania. In 1911 he moved to California, where he became caddiemaster at Annandale GC in Pasadena and then greenkeeper at Pasadena Golf Club.

Bell served as construction superintendent for golf architect Willie Watson on a number of Southern California courses before going into private practice as a

William P. Bell,
1952 COLLECTION RON
WHITTEN

course designer in 1920. In his early years he often collaborated with architect George C. Thomas, Jr., and while Thomas is listed as architect of record (and Bell as construction superintendent) for these courses, Billy made major contributions.

By the 1930s Bell had earned a reputation as the most prolific architect in the West. During World War II he served as a turf consultant to the U.S. Army Corps of Engineers, and in 1946 he was awarded a commendation by the Southern California chapter of the PGA for his efforts in creating courses for wounded servicemen. After the war, Billy was joined in practice by his son William F. Bell.

Billy Bell died of a heart attack at age 67 in Pasadena, the town where he had begun his career.

Courses by William P. Bell:

Arizona: Arizona Biltmore GC (Adobe Cse 1928); El Rio GC; Encanto Muni (1936, A.3rd 9 1952, with William F. Bell); Mesa CC (1950), with William F. Bell; Randolph Park GC (North Cse 1930); Tucson CC (1949), with William F. Bell; Wickenburg CC (1950), with William F. Bell; Yuma G&CC (1951), with William F. Bell.
California: Alameda Muni (Earl Fry Cse 1927); Alondra Park GC (Cse No. 1 1947), with William H. Johnson; Altadena GC (9 1939); Apple Valley CC (9 1951), with William F. Bell; Bakersfield CC (1949), with William F. Bell; Balboa Park GC (1921); Baldwin Hills GC (1926, NLE), with George C. Thomas, Jr; Bayside CC; Bel-Air CC (1927), with George C. Thomas, Jr., and Jack Neville; Birmingham VA Hospital GC (9 Par 3); Brookside Muni (Cse No. 1 1928; Cse No. 2 1928); Buenaventura GC (1949), with William F. Bell; Castlewood CC (Hill Cse 1923; Valley Cse 1923); Chevy Chase CC, with William F. Bell; Circle J GC

(1954); Del Rio G&CC (1926); El Caballero CC (1926, NLE), with George C. Thomas, Jr.; Fox Hills GC (1926, NLE), with George C. Thomas, Jr.; Furnace Creek GC (9 1939); Hillcrest CC (Par 3 Cse [9 Par 3] 1950), with William F. Bell; Irvine Coast CC (1954), with William F. Bell; Kern River CC (1953), with William F. Bell; La Jolla CC (1927); Laguna CC; Lakewood GC (1933); Los Angeles Royal Vista GC; Marine Memorial GC, Santa Ana; Marine Memorial GC, Camp Pendleton; Meadowlark CC (1922); Mission Trails G Cse (9); Monterey Hills GC (9 Par 3 1949), with William F. Bell; Mountain Meadows G&CC (1922, NLE); Newport Beach CC (1954), with William F. Bell; North Ridge CC (1954), with William F. Bell; Ojai Valley Inn & CC (1925), with George C. Thomas, Jr.; Palo Alto Muni (1954), with William F. Bell; Palos Verdes CC (1924), with George C. Thomas, Jr.; Rancho Park GC (1947), with William H. Johnson; Riviera CC (1927), with George C. Thomas, Jr.; Rolling Hills GC, with William F. Bell; San Clemente Muni (9 1928); San Diego CC (1921); San Pedro Community Hotel GC (9 Par 3); San Pedro CC; Santa Susana CC; Sepulveda GC (Balboa Cse 1953; Encino Cse 1953), with William F. Bell and William H. Johnson; Singing Hills CC (Willow Glen Cse 1953), with William F. Bell and William H. Johnson; South Hills CC (1954), with William F. Bell; Stanford University GC (1930); Sunnyside CC; Sunset Fields GC (NLE); Tamarisk CC (1953), with William F. Bell; Tilden Park GC (1937); Valle Grande GC (9 1954), with William F. Bell; Ventura Muni (1930); Virginia CC (1939); Western Avenue GC (1950); Willowick GC (1928); Woodland Hills CC (1925).
Hawaii: Kanehoe Klipper GC (1947); Navy–Marine GC, Pearl Harbor (1947).
Idaho: Sun Valley GC (9 1939, A.9 1947).
Nevada: Las Vegas GC (9 1938).
Oregon: Forest Hills GC (1953), with William F. Bell.
Utah: Bonneville Muni (9 1952), with William F. Bell; Hidden Valley CC (1928, NLE).
Wisconsin: Wrigley Estate GC.
Mexico: Tijuana CC [FKA Agua Caliente GC](1928).

Courses remodeled or expanded by William P. Bell:

California: Annandale CC (R.2 A.2 1948); Crystal Springs GC (R.); Hacienda CC (R. 1947); Indian Hill GC (R.); La Cumbre G&CC (R.9 A.9 1920), with George C. Thomas, Jr.; Los Angeles CC (North Cse, R. 1928); Oakmont CC (R. 1934); Ojai Valley Inn & CC (R. 1948), with William F. Bell; Pasadena GC (R. 1926, NLE); Red Hill CC (A.9 1947); Riverside of Fresno GC (R.9 A.9 1939); San Francisco GC (R. 1947); Valley C of Montecito (R. 1946); Victoria GC (R. 1949).
Oregon: Rogue Valley CC (R.9 A.9 1949), with William F. Bell.
Utah: [The] Country Club (R. 1952), with William F. Bell.

PETER BELLCHAMBERS
(1951–), BIGCA

BORN: Totnes, Devon, England.

Peter Bellchambers received a degree in landscape architecture from Heriot-Watt University in Edinburgh, Scotland, in 1980. After landscape design experience in Scotland and in the Middle East, he joined the English golf design firm of Hawtree & Son in 1986. After training under both Fred W. Hawtree and his son Martin Hawtree, Bellchambers was made a design associate in 1987. In 1989 he moved to Fontainebleau, France, to direct the Hawtree Continental branch office.

Courses by Peter Bellchambers (All as assistant to Martin Hawtree):

England: China Fleet GC (1991); Hintlesham Park GC (1990), and Fred W. Hawtree.
France: Anjou G&CC (1990), and Fred W. Hawtree; Golf du Château d'Avoise (1991); Golf de Teoula (1990).
Portugal: Pine Cliffs G&CC (1990).

Courses remodeled or expanded by Peter Bellchambers (All as assistant to Martin Hawtree):

England: Teignmouth GC (R.).
France: Golf de Fontainebleau (R. 1990); Golf de Quimper et de Cornouaille (A.9 1991), and Fred W. Hawtree.
South Africa: [The] Country Club, Johannesburg (R.12 1991).

Thomas M. Bendelow
(1872–1936)

BORN: Aberdeen, Scotland.
DIED: River Forest, Illinois, at age 64.

Tom Bendelow, one of America's pioneer golf course architects, learned the game as a youngster in Scotland and made several trips as a teenager to St. Andrews. He became a good enough player to join Harry Vardon in an exhibition match in 1900, shortly before Vardon won the U.S. Open.

Bendelow moved to the United States in 1885 and went to work as a typesetter for the New York *Herald*. In 1895, he noticed an advertisement in the classified section seeking a young golfer willing to teach the game to a family. He answered the ad and was hired by the Platt family, whose patriarch was a co-founder of Standard Oil. As part of his duties, Bendelow laid out a short golf course on the grounds of the Platt estate on Long Island. It was the first of over 400 layouts Bendelow planned in his career.

Bendelow soon was laying out many rudimentary courses in the New York area. He also became manager at the nation's first municipal golf course, Van Cortlandt Park in the Bronx. In that capacity, he remodeled its nine-hole course and added a second nine, organized America's first public golfers association and instituted the first system of reserved starting times during peak periods.

Later, as a salaried employee of A. G. Spalding sporting goods concern, Bendelow staked out modest layouts through the country, as far south as Florida and as far west as California.

He was transferred by Spalding to Chicago after World War I and in 1920 left the company to become chief golf architect for the American Park Builders, taking over for designer William B. Langford, who had formed a partnership with Theodore Moreau.

Principally a functional architect, Bendelow refined his procedures in Chicago, producing elaborate detailed plans and molding plaster scale models to demonstrate proposed green contours. He lectured about golf architecture at the University of Illinois and wrote about it for national publications.

Despite such credentials, Bendelow's reputation after his death centered on the primitive staking method Bendelow (as well as many of his contemporaries) utilized around the turn of the century. This

Tom Bendelow, circa 1930 COURTESY TOM BENDELOW II

simple method was labeled pejoratively "eighteen-stakes-on-a-Sunday afternoon." Ironically, Bendelow, a deeply religious man, never laid out a course on a Sunday. He refused even to play golf on a Sunday, so strict was his personal doctrine. He never drank alcohol, never swore and never told off-color jokes. His only apparent weakness was for the huge cigars he constantly smoked. None of his relatives could recall if he smoked them on Sundays.

Courses by Tom Bendelow:

California: Griffith Park GC (Wilson Cse 1914); La Cumbre G&CC (9 1918); Lincoln Park GC (9); Paso Robles GC (9, NLE); Point Loma GC (1912); Redondo Beach GC (9); Santa Barbara CC (NLE); Santa Cruz G&CC (9).

Colorado: Boulder CC (9 1918, NLE); City Park GC (1914); Greeley CC (9); Lakewood CC (1908).

Connecticut: Manchester CC (9); Ridgefield GC (NLE); Stonybrook GC (9).

Florida: Dubsdread CC (1923); Palma Ceia G&CC (1917); Temple Terrace G&CC (1921); West Orange CC (NLE).

Georgia: CC of Savannah (NLE); East Lake CC [FKA Atlanta Athletic C (Cse No. 1)](1910).

Illinois: Abingdon CC (9); Aurora CC (1914); Automobile C of Peoria (9, NLE); Bel-Mar GC (9 1919); CC of Decatur (9); Champaign CC (1904); Chevy Chase CC (1925); Columbus Park GC (9 1921); Crawford County GC (9 1919); Cross Roads CC (9 1915); Dempster GC (9, NLE); Diversey GC (9 1916, NLE); Dixon CC (9); Edgewood CC, Polo (9); Garfield Muni (9 1911); Glen Oak GC (1911); Glendale CC (NLE); Greenview GC

(1922); Harlem GC (NLE); Hillsdale GC (9); Hillside Muni (NLE); Illini CC (9); Ingersoll Muni (1920); Jacksonville CC (9 1925); Joliet CC (9 1905); Kankakee CC (9 1915); Kishwaukee CC (9 1923); La Grange CC (1913); Lake Shore CC (1909); Lake Waneawega GC (9); Leroy CC (9); Lincoln Elks GC (9); Lincolnshire CC (Cse No. 1 1929; Cse No. 2 1929); Madison Park Muni; Maywood CC (NLE); Medinah CC (Cse No. 1 1924; Cse No. 2 1926; Cse No. 3 1928); Midland CC (9 1911); Monmouth CC (9); Naperville CC (1920); Nelson Park GC (1917); North Shore GC (9 1905, NLE); Oakville CC (9); Olympia Fields CC (Cse No. 2 1920, NLE; South Cse 1916); Peoria North Shore CC (9, NLE); Pine Hills GC (9 1923); Rock Island CC (9 1926, NLE); Rock Springs CC (9 1912); Roselawn GC (9); St. Charles CC (1928); Sinnissippi Park GC (1914); Skokie CC (1904); Soangetaha CC; South Shore CC (9 1906); Sunnyside GC (1921); Urbana G&CC (1922); Villa Olivia CC (9 1926); Wing Park GC; Woodlawn CC (9); Woodstock GC (9 1916).

Indiana: Boonville GC (9); Clear Creek GC (9); Clermont GC (9 1914); CC of Connersville (9); CC of Indianapolis (1914); CC of Terre Haute (9); French Lick GC (Valley Cse 1907); Garrett CC (9); Hammond CC (9); Hazelden CC (9 1915); Helfrich Muni (1923); Highland G&CC (1906, NLE); Kendallville CC (9); Kentland GC (9); Kokomo CC (9 1906); Lafayette CC (9); Mississinewa CC (9); Potowatomi CC (9); Tolliston GC (9); Wawasee GC (9); Wicker Park GC.

Iowa: Cedar Rapids CC (1904, NLE); Centerville G&CC (9); Clinton CC (1920); Dubuque G&CC (1923); Ellis Park Muni (9 1920, NLE); Elmhurst CC (9); Elmwood G&CC (9); Fort Dodge CC; Geneva G&CC (9, NLE); Hickory Grove CC (9); Hyperion Field C (1901); Iowa City CC (NLE); Keokuk CC (9); Mason City CC (9 1918); Ottumwa G&CC (9); Sioux City CC (9); Sunnyside CC (NLE); Wapsipinicon GC (9); Waveland GC (9 1910).

Kansas: Hutchinson CC (NLE); Kansas City CC (1922); Leavenworth CC (1922); Mission Hills CC (1915); Topeka CC (9 1906, NLE).

Kentucky: Audubon CC (1908, NLE); Cherokee GC (1903); CC of Paducah (9, NLE); Fort Mitchell CC (9); Highland CC (9 1914, NLE); Lexington CC (1906).

Louisiana: Aurora CC; Baton Rouge Muni (9, NLE); West End CC (1921).

Maryland: Elkridge CC (9).

Michigan: Atlas Valley GC [FKA Flint GC]; Birmingham CC (9 1916, A.9 1920); Bloomfield Hills CC (1909); Cascades GC (1929); Charlotte CC (9); Duck Lake GC (9 1922); Escanaba CC (9); Grand Beach CC (9 1912); Green Ridge CC (1922, NLE); [The] Highlands CC (9); Hillsdale G&CC (9 1909); Huron Hills GC (9 1922); Kalamazoo CC (9 1909); Ludington Hills GC (9 1920); Manistee G&CC (9 1901); Marshall CC (9, NLE); Meadow Heights CC (9); Mullet Lake G&CC (9); Northport Point C (9); Owosso CC (9); Palisades Park GC (9, NLE); Plymouth Park GC (9); Rochester GC; Saginaw CC (9); South Haven GC (9); Spring Lake CC; Stag Island GC (9); Traverse City CC (9); Wawonowin GC (9).

Minnesota: Detroit CC (9 1917); Edina CC; Lafayette C (9 1915); Minneapolis GC (1917).

Mississippi: Alexandria G&CC (9); Biloxi CC (9 1918, NLE); CC of Jackson (9, NLE); Pass Christian CC (9).

Missouri: Carthage Muni (9); Columbia CC (9 1921); Evanston GC (9 1903, NLE); Excelsior Springs CC (1915); Hannibal CC (9 1909, NLE); Joplin CC (1922, NLE); Oakwood CC (9 1912); Westborough CC (1908).

Montana: Billings G&CC (9).

Nebraska: Beatrice CC (9); Elmwood Park Muni (1916); Fremont GC (9 1930).

New Jersey: Colonia CC (9); East Orange Muni (9 1926); Essex County CC (East Cse 1898); Forest Hill Field C (NLE); Glen Ridge CC (9 1900, NLE); Hackensack CC (9 1900, NLE); Hendricks Field GC (9 1897); Hillside G&TC (1898, NLE); Hollywood GC (1902, NLE); Montclair GC (9 1898, NLE); Morris County GC (1897); Plainfield GC (West Cse, 9 1898, NLE); Point Pleasant GC (9 1910); Somerset Hills CC (9, NLE); Suburban GC (9 1896, NLE); Yountakah CC (9 1899, NLE).

New Mexico: Santa Fe CC.

New York: Auburn CC (9); Chappaqua CC (NLE); Dyker Beach GC (9 1897); Dyker Meadow GC (9 1899, NLE); Flushing GC (9, NLE); Forest Park GC (1910); Fort Erie GC (9); Fox

Hills GC (1899); Huntington GC (9 1899, NLE); Mahopac GC (9 1900, NLE); Mohawk GC (1900, NLE); Oakland GC (9 1896, NLE); Onondaga G&CC (NLE); Oswego CC (9, NLE); Pelham Manor GC (9 1898, NLE); Pratt Estate GC (9 1895); Sunset Park GC (NLE); Yahnundasis GC (9, NLE).

North Carolina: Tryon CC (9 1916).

Ohio: Butler County GC (9); Columbus CC (9 1907); Coshocton T&CC (9); Hamilton County GC (1911); Hyde Park CC (1903, NLE); Kettenring CC (9 1921); Lorain CC (9); Losantiville CC (1906); Moundbuilders CC (1927); Mount Vernon CC (9); Plum Brook GC (9 1914); Rosemont GC; St. Mary's CC; Shawnee CC (9); Union CC (9, NLE); Western Hills GC; Wyoming CC (9).

Pennsylvania: Allegheny CC (1902); Butler CC (9 1906); Greensburg CC (9 1904); Grove City CC (1917); Lake Shore GC; Monongahela Valley CC (9); St. Clair CC (1916); Sharon CC; Stanton Heights CC (1909); [The] Country Club, Donora (9); Union City GC (1915).

South Carolina: Anderson CC; CC of Charleston (1901, NLE).

South Dakota: Minnehaha CC (9, NLE).

Texas: Breckenridge GC (9); Corpus Christi CC (9, NLE); Dallas CC (1908); El Paso CC (1910); Fort Worth GC (1911, NLE); Lakewood CC, Dallas (1912); River Crest CC (1911); Sherman GC (9 1907).

West Virginia: Huntington CC (9 1919).

Wisconsin: Big Foot CC; Blue Mound G&CC (1903, NLE); Chenequa GC (9); CC of Beloit (9 1909, NLE); Fox River CC (9 1911); Lake Lawn GC; Lincoln Park GC (9 1922); Meadow Links GC; Nakoma CC (1920); Northernaire CC (9); Old Hickory GC (9 1920); Oshkosh CC (9 1916); Quit-Qui-Oc GC (9); Racine CC (9 1909, NLE); Town & Country C (9); Tripoli CC (1920); Tuscumbia CC; Washington Park Muni (9 1917).

Wyoming: Casper CC (9, NLE); Cheyenne CC (NLE).

Alberta: Calgary Muni; Lethbridge GC (9); Medicine Hat GC (9).

British Columbia: Vernon G&CC (9 1913).

Manitoba: Birds Hill GC; St. Charles CC (West Nine), Winnipeg (9 1904, NLE).

Ontario: Sundrim GC (9); Thunder Bay CC (9).

Quebec: Royal Ottawa GC, Hull (1917).

Courses remodeled or expanded by Tom Bendelow:

Illinois: Elgin CC (R.9 A.9, NLE).

Minnesota: Northland CC (R.9 A.9 1912, NLE).

New York: Apawamis C (A.9 1896); Nassau CC (R.9 A.9 1900, NLE); Rockaway Hunting C (A.9 1900, NLE); Van Cortlandt Park GC (A.9 1899).

Ohio: Oakwood C (A.9 1915).

Pennsylvania: Wanango CC (A.9 1914).

Tennessee: Memphis CC (A.9, NLE).

Wisconsin: Geneva Lake Y&GC (R.); Milwaukee CC (A.9, NLE).

Dave Bennett, 1990
COURTESY DAVE GENNETT

DAVID W. BENNETT (1935–   ), ASGCA

BORN: Dallas, Texas.

After graduating from Texas Tech in 1958 with a degree in landscape architecture, Dave Bennett worked as a landscape architect with the Texas Highway Department for seven years. In 1965 he joined the staff of golf architect Leon Howard, and two years later Bennett, Howard and Howard's brother Charles became equal partners in the firm of Leon Howard Inc. Bennett handled most of the design work, Leon the client consultations and Charles the irrigation systems. In 1970, Bennett left to form his own practice, based in Austin, Texas.

At different times in the 1970s, Bennett utilized PGA Tour golfers Terry Dill and Lee Trevino as consultants.

Courses by Dave Bennett:

Arizona: Arthur Pack GC (1977), with *Lee Trevino*; Canoa Hills GC (1983); Desert Hills CC (1978).

Arkansas: Hindman Park GC (1967), with Leon Howard.

Colorado: Peaceful Valley CC (1972), with *Lee Trevino*.

Florida: Hurlburt Field GC (9 1972, A.9 1982); Shoal River G&CC (1983).

Kentucky: Woodson Bend CC (9 1975), with *Lee Trevino*.

Montana: Billings Muni (Par 3 1978).

Nebraska: Applewood G Cse (1970), with Leon Howard; Tiburon GC (1990), with *Lee Trevino*.

New Mexico: Santa Teresa CC (Spanish Dagger Cse 1976; Yucca Cse 1976), with *Lee Trevino*.

Tennessee: Two Rivers Muni (1968), with Leon Howard.

Texas: Cimarron CC (1984); DeCordova Bend GC (9 1968), with Leon Howard; Diboll Muni (1968), with Leon Howard; Grover Keaton Muni (1978); Harker Heights Muni (1967), with Leon Howard; Harlingen CC (1968), with Leon Howard; Highland Lakes GC (1967), with Leon Howard; Lago Vista CC (1967), with Leon Howard; Laredo AFB GC (1967), with Leon Howard; L. B. Houston Muni (1969), with Leon Howard; Lost Creek GC (1973), with *Terry Dill*; Maxwell Muni (New Cse 1979); Plantation CC (1982); Prestonwood CC (Hills Cse 1986); Shady Oaks CC, Baird (1967), with Leon Howard; Sotogrande G&TC (Par 3 1969), with Leon Howard; Webb Hill CC (1968), with Leon Howard.

Virginia: Burke Lake Park GC (Par 3 1969), with Leon Howard.

Alberta: Country Hills GC (Links Cse 1992; Ridge Cse 1993); Harvest Hills GC (9 1980), with *George Browning*.

Mexico: Taboada GC (1980).

Venezuela: C de G de Caracas (1979).

Courses remodeled or expanded by Dave Bennett:

Arizona: Oro Valley G&CC (R. 1983).

Mississippi: Castlewood CC (A.9 1982); East Ridge CC (R. 1987); Shreveport CC (R. 1990).

Nebraska: Omaha CC (R. 1983); Elmwood Muni (R. 1979).

Oklahoma: Arrowhead State Park GC (R.9 A.9 1981).

Texas: Highland Lakes GC (R. 1990); Landa Park GC (A.9 1969), with Leon

Howard; L. B. Houston Muni (R. 1982); Pecan Valley Muni, Fort Worth (Hills Cse, R.9 A.9 1981); Sinton Muni (A.9), with Leon Howard.

BRADFORD L. BENZ (1946–), ASGCA

BORN: Oelwein, Iowa.

Bradford Benz attended Iowa State University, receiving a Bachelor's degree in 1968 and a Master's degree in 1970, both in landscape architecture. After college he went to work for golf architect Dick Phelps and became his partner in 1973. In 1980, Benz struck up a friendship with Mike Poellot while the two, along with many fellow ASGCA members, toured several classic Scottish links. Poellot soon joined Phelps and Benz in their Colorado operation, and three years later Benz and Poellot formed their own design partnership, based in California.

Drawing on Poellot's contacts in the Far East, Benz and Poellot laid out several courses in the Pacific Basin in the 1980s. Perhaps their most significant work was Beijing Golf Club, the first private golf club ever built in the People's Republic of China. In 1988 Benz and Poellot established separate practices, with Poellot continuing to work the Pacific Basin while Benz branched into British and European markets.

Courses by Brad Benz:

Arizona: Fred Enke Muni (1983), with Dick Phelps; Gainey Ranch GC (27 1986), with Mike Poellot.

Colorado: Copper Mountain GC (9 Precision 1980, A.9 1984, NLE), with Dick Phelps; Englewood Muni (1982), with Dick Phelps and Mike Poellot; [The] Meadows GC (1984), with Dick Phelps and Mike Poellot; Raccoon Creek GC (1984), with Dick Phelps and Mike Poellot.

Missouri: Longview Lakes G Cse (27 1986), with Mike Poellot.

Montana: Briarwood CC (1985), with Mike Poellot.

Nebraska: Heritage Hills GC (1981), with Dick Phelps.

Nevada: Northgate GC (1988), with Mike Poellot; Rosewood Lakes G Cse (1991 solo); Wildcreek GC (27 1980), with Dick Phelps.

New Mexico: Elephant Butte G&CC (9 1975), with Dick Phelps; Ladera GC (27 1980), with Dick Phelps.

Brad Benz, 1990
COURTESY ASGCA

North Carolina: Lost Diamond Valley CC (9 Precision 1979), with Dick Phelps.

North Dakota: Prairiewood GC (9 Precision 1976), with Dick Phelps.

South Dakota: Southern Hills CC (1979), with Dick Phelps.

Texas: Firewheel G Park (Old Cse 1983), with Dick Phelps and Mike Poellot; Indian Creek G Cse (Creek Cse 1983), with Dick Phelps and Mike Poellot.

China: Beijing GC (1987), with Mike Poellot.

Hong Kong: Clearwater Bay CC (1984), with Mike Poellot.

Japan: Glen Oaks CC (1988), with Mike Poellot; Joeltsu Kokusai GC (Tokamachi Cse 1987), with Mike Poellot; Prestige CC (East and West Cses 1988), with Mike Poellot; Shizukuishi GC (1988), with Mike Poellot; Tomisato GC (1989), with Mike Poellot.

Courses remodeled or expanded by Brad Benz:

California: Claremont CC (R. 1989), with Mike Poellot.

Colorado: Dos Rios CC (A.9 1982), with Dick Phelps and Mike Poellot; Grand Lake GC (R.9 A.9 1978), with Dick Phelps; Meadow Hills GC, Denver (R. 1983), with Dick Phelps; Springhill GC (Precision 1977, A.9 R.9), with Dick Phelps.

Montana: Riverside CC (A.9 1981), with Dick Phelps.

New Mexico: Riverside CC (R.9 A.9 1984), with Mike Poellot.

North Dakota: Heart River GC (R.9 A.9 1984), with Dick Phelps and Mike Poellot.

South Dakota: Huron CC (R.9 A.9 1975), with Dick Phelps.

Wyoming: Riverton CC (R.9 A.9 1982), with Dick Phelps and Mike Poellot.

Malaysia: Subang GC (R. 1986), with Mike Poellot.

ROBERT BERTHET
(1952–) BIGCA, FAGCA PRESIDENT 1991

BORN: France.

A former Junior and university golf champion, Robert Berthet graduated as a professional golf teacher in 1973. Two years later he obtained an Ecole Speciale d'Architecture degree from the University of Paris. In 1976 Berthet formed his own golf design firm called Archigolf, which handled projects on the Continent and Northern Africa.

Berthet served as editor of the French golf magazine *Golf Pro*, as a technical consultant to the French Golf Association and as honorary secretary for the French PGA. Berthet's designs were often fanciful, usually unique thematic designs, stylized to reflect the particular site. One course, La Salle, featured holes fashioned after parts of the female anatomy. Another, Digne, was a tribute to archaeology and featured bunkers shaped like fossils as well as free-form statuary. Still another had bunkers shaped to imitate the wave movement of the ocean.

Courses by Robert Berthet:

France: Académie De G Du Tremblay (1989); Benodet-de-L'Odet GC (1987); Bois le Roe GC (9 1983); G D'Ammerschwihr (1989); G D'Avrille (1987); G de Bournel (1989); G de Cap Skirring (9 1986); G de Castelnaud (1987); G de Courchevel (1988); G De Digne (1989); G de Dunkerque (1986); G de L'Odet (1986); G de la St. Baume (1986); G de La Salle (1988); G de Metz (1989); G de Nice (1988); G de Niort-Romagne (9 1988); G de Perigueux (1988); G de Rennes St. Jacques (1989); G de Rougemont (1989); G de Villennes (1989); G du Petit Chene-Mazieres (1987); G du Techonopole Metz; Flaine Les Carroz GC (1986); L'Isle d'Abeau GC (1983); Othain GC (9 1983); Royan GC (9 1982).

Courses remodeled or expanded by Robert Berthet:

France: Evian GC (R. 1976); G de Cannes (R. 1981); International C du Lys (Bouleaux Cse, R.9 A.9); Nampont St. Martin GC (A.9 1982).

RICHARD A. BIGLER

BORN: Utah.

As a teenager Richard Bigler worked on several course construction projects in Utah for architect William H. Neff. After a stint in the U.S. Navy and a mission for his Mormon Church, Bigler obtained a landscape architecture degree from the University of California at Berkeley in 1959. Bigler worked for several years as an irrigation specialist and then as a draftsman on several Southern California projects for course designer Larry Hughes. In the mid-sixties Bigler opened his own landscape design office in Southern California, handling city and county parks as well as some public golf courses.

Courses by Richard Bigler:

California: Anaheim Hills GC (1972); La Contenta CC (1973); Oceanside Muni (1973); Palm Lakes GC (Precision 1986); Ridgemark G&CC (Diablo Cse; Gabilan Cse); Valley Oaks GC.
Nevada: Meadow Valley GC (9 1986).

Courses remodeled or expanded by Richard Bigler:

California: DeBell GC (R. 1984); Hillsview GC (A.9); Visalia Plaza GC (R. 1984).
Nevada: Desert Inn CC (R. 1990).

Sandy Bigler, 1992
COURTESY SANDY BIGLER

SANDY BIGLER, NÉE SANDY RICE
(1966–)

BORN: Lancaster, Pennsylvania.

While attending Penn State University as an agronomy student in the early 1980s, Sandy Bigler spent her summers working on the grounds crew at Lancaster Country Club in her hometown. It was there she met golf architect Fred Garbin, who had been hired to make some revision to the

course. After completing the job, Garbin invited Bigler to join his design firm as an associate. She moved to Pittsburgh and, after a period of apprenticeship, became Garbin's principal design associate.

CLARENCE RILEY BLANKENSHIP
(1906–)

"Buck" Blankenship operated a dairy farm in Kentucky until retiring in the early 1950s. A fine golfer, he became a member of the PGA of America in 1955 and served as pro-superintendent at several Kentucky courses. He also began designing and constructing golf courses on a part-time basis in the 1960s and by the early 1970s had designed or remodeled some 35 layouts.

Courses by Buck Blankenship:

Kansas: Village Greens GC (9 1968).
Kentucky: Anderson GC (1948), with *Morgan Boggs*; Bowling Green CC; Bright Leaf GC (1963); Burlington GC (1960); Dix River CC (1966); Glenwood Hall CC (9); Hickory Hills CC (9); Juniper Hills GC; Lakeshore CC (9 1971); Lone Oak CC (1969); Oldham County CC; Park Mammoth GC (1964); River Hills GC (1969), with *Morgan Boggs*; Spring Lake CC (1949); Tanglewood G Cse; Tates Creek GC (1959); Woodford Hills CC (1969).

Courses remodeled or expanded by Buck Blankenship:

Indiana: Valley View GC (A.9 1968).
West Virginia: Riviera CC (A.9 1960).

JAMES W. BLAUKOVITCH
(1947–)

BORN: Northampton, Pennsylvania.

James Blaukovitch graduated from Penn State University with a Bachelor of Science degree in landscape architecture, then worked for Chicago-based golf course architects Killian and Nugent from 1973 until 1979. He next returned to his native state and was employed as an irrigation designer for Philadelphia Turf Company for seven years. In 1986 Blaukovitch started his own golf course design and irrigation practice.

Courses by James Blaukovitch:

Pennsylvania: Stone Hedge GC (1991).

Courses remodeled or expanded by James Blaukovitch:

New York: Putnam GC (1990).
Pennsylvania: Doylestown CC (1989); Kimberton GC (1990); Paxon Hollow CC (1991).

FREDERICK C. BLISS
(1944–   ), ASGCA

BORN: Colby, Kansas.

As a youngster, Fred Bliss played his early golf with boyhood friend Mike Hayden, who would later become governor of Kansas. After obtaining an undergraduate degree in education from Fort Hays State University, he enrolled at Kansas State University to study landscape architecture. Spending the summer back home. Bliss was approached by young Greg Nash, a friend of his sister. Nash, like Bliss, wanted someday to become a golf course architect. The two spent the summer playing golf together, and Bliss convinced Nash of the necessity of a landscape architecture degree.

Once he obtained his landscape architecture degree in 1969 (graduating first in his L.A. class), Bliss spent three years with the U.S. Corps of Engineers. He then returned to Kansas and worked for a Wichita landscaping firm before moving to Colorado Springs. As a park planner for the city, Bliss got his first taste of golf course architecture.

In 1979 he moved to the West Coast and was hired by golf architect Ronald Fream, who was establishing his own firm. After five years, Bliss became Fream's senior designer and a vice president in the firm.

Fred Bliss, 1991
COURTESY FRED BLISS

Fred Bliss started his own design practice in 1989, when he established Bliss Golf Design based in Santa Rosa, California.

Courses by Fred Bliss (All as assistant to Ronald Fream unless otherwise indicated):

California: Carmel Mountain Ranch GC (1986); [The] Charter C (1992 *solo*); Desert Falls CC (1985); McInnis Park G Cse (9 Precision 1992 *solo*); Oakhurst CC (1990); Redhawk GC (1991); Windsor GC (1989).
Borneo: Jerudong Park GC.
Finland: Kerigolf (1990).
France: Golf du Cap d'Agde (1989).
Japan: Palm Hills GC (1991); Tohbetu GC.
Malaysia: Saujana G&CC (Orchid Cse 1986; Palm Cse 1985).
Portugal: Carvoeiro GC (27 1991).
Singapore: Tanah Merah CC (1983).
Tunisia: El Qortine International GC (1988); Hammamet GC (1987); Montazan Tabarka G Resort (27 1992).

Courses remodeled or expanded by Fred Bliss (All as assistant to Ronald Fream unless otherwise indicated):

California: Bing Maloney G Cse (A.3rd 9 [Precision] 1985); Castlewood CC (R.); Los Altos G&CC (R.); Mesa Verde CC (R. 1991); Napa Valley CC (R.9 A.9 1987); Palo Alto Hills CC (R.); Peninsula CC (R.); Richmond CC (R.); San Diego CC (R.); Santa Rosa CC (R. 1991 *solo*); Seacliff CC (R. 1985); Tamarisk CC (R. 1981).
Texas: El Paso CC (R. 1986).
Washington: Manito G&CC (R. 1979).
South Korea: Dragon Valley GC (A.9).
Tunisia: El Kantaoui GC (A.3rd 9 1985).

BRUCE E. BORLAND
(1958–   ), ASGCA

BORN: Peoria, Illinois.

A 1981 graduate of the University of Illinois in landscape architecture, Bruce Borland worked in succession for golf architect David Gill, the golf design firm of Killian and Nugent and the Hitchcock Landscape Architecture Design firm. In early 1984 Borland rejoined Dick Nugent, who had formed his own design business the previous year. After a brief attempt at design practice on his own in 1989, Borland joined Jack Nicklaus's corporation as a senior designer.

Bruce Borland,
1991 COURTESY BRUCE BORLAND

Borland was among the first golf architects to utilize a computer in the actual design of a golf course. In the mid-1980s he adapted a computer program in order to analyze golf designs in terms of optimum shot values, club selection sequence and balance.

Courses by Bruce Borland (All as assistant to Dick Nugent unless otherwise indicated):

Illinois: Glendale Lakes GC (1987); GC of Illinois (1987); Ivanhoe C (1990); Oak Brook Hills GC (1987); Seven Bridges GC (1991).
Ohio: Glenmoor CC (1992), ass't Jack Nicklaus.
South Carolina: Colleton River Plantation GC (1992), ass't Jack Nicklaus.

Courses remodeled or expanded by Bruce Borland (All as assistant to Dick Nugent unless otherwise indicated):

Illinois: Chicago GC (R. 1989 *solo*).
Iowa: Wakonda C (R. 1987).
Oklahoma: Dornick Hills CC (R. 1985).
South Dakota: Westward Ho! CC (R.1 1985).

K. WARNER BOWEN
(1935–   )

BORN: Crystal, Michigan.

Following military service during the Korean War, Warner Bowen received an A.A. degree from Ferris State College and a B.A. degree from Michigan State University. He later did graduate work under Dr. James Beard, then head of Turfgrass Science at Michigan State. At his father's urging, Bowen entered private practice in Sheridan, Michigan, as a course architect and builder in 1964. He involved himself in all phases of the design and construction of a golf course, including personally sculpting tees, greens and other features with his own bulldozer.

Courses by Warner Bowen:

Arizona: Arroyo Dunes G Cse.
Florida: Reservation GC [FKA Jekyll-Hyde GC](9 Precision).
Michigan: Alpena GC (9); Benona Shores GC (1979); Centennial Acres GC (9 1979); Highland Burne GC (9 1971, NLE); Holland Lake GC (9); North Kent GC (1979); Prairiewood G Cse (1991); Rogue River GC; Rolling Hills GC; Schuss Mountain GC (1977); Spring Valley GC (9); Twin Oaks GC (9); Walnut Woods CC; Western Woods GC (1971).

Courses remodeled or expanded by Warner Bowen:

Michigan: Dearborn Hills GC (R. 1991).

HARRY F. BOWERS
(1957–)

BORN: Detroit, Michigan.

A low-handicap golfer most of his life, Harry Bowers was a three-time All-State golfer at his South Lyon, Michigan, high school. He also played college golf at Schoolcraft College in Livonia, Michigan, and at Michigan State, where he graduated with dual majors in park planning and turfgrass science.

Harry Bowers, 1991 COURTESY HARRY BOWERS

Bowers spent several years employed by Robert Trent Jones as an associate designer, supervising construction on nine Jones courses and remodeling six others. During that time, he qualified in the New Jersey Amateur and the U.S. Mid-Amateur championships.

In 1988, Bowers returned to South Lyon and established his own golf design business. He preferred a small operation that allowed him to control all facets of the process by personally constructing his own designs.

Courses by Harry Bowers:

Illinois: Odyssey GC (1991), with *Curtis Strange*.
Michigan: Marion Oaks GC (routing 1990); [The] Rock GC (1990).
South Carolina: Falcon's Lair GC (1992).

JAMES BRAID
(1870–1950)

BORN: Earlsferry, Fife, Scotland.
DIED: London, England, at age 80.

James Braid, who learned golf at age four and won his first tournament at age eight, played his early golf with such prodigies as Jack and Archie Simpson and his cousin Douglas Rolland. He left school as a teenager, obtained work as an apprentice carpenter at St. Andrews and honed his golfing skills on the side. He played in his first professional tournament in 1894. In 1896 Braid became professional at Romford GC in England and in 1904 moved to the newly opened Walton Heath GC, where he served as its professional for the rest of his life.

Braid, along with John Henry Taylor and Harry Vardon (the "Great Triumvirate"), dominated competitive golf during the first two decades of the twentieth century. He won most of his prestigious titles within a span of ten years: the British Open in 1901, 1905, 1906, 1908 and 1910, the News-of-the-World match play championship in 1903, 1905, 1907 and 1911 and the French Open in 1910.

Braid had worked on the design of a course or two as a young professional at Romford. He was called upon to design several courses soon after his initial victory in the British Open, and he wrote knowledgeable articles about course design as early as 1908. But it was not until after his active competitive days were over that Braid devoted much of his time to golf course architecture.

James Braid, 1912
COLLECTION RON WHITTEN

Fearing the ocean, he seldom ventured even as far as the Continent; thus, most of his work was done in the British Isles. He did design one course in America and one in Singapore, but both were done solely from topographic maps. Braid was greatly respected for accurate and detailed working drawings of the courses he laid out. Many of his designs were constructed by contractor John R. Stutt, and the two reached a nearly perfect accord. Often subject to motion sickness, Braid dreaded travel by car, so Stutt's on-site work was invaluable to him. Braid also started C. K. Hutchison in design and collaborated with him on several projects.

Shortly before his death, James Braid was granted membership in the Royal and Ancient Golf Club of St. Andrews, making him one of the first professional golfers ever to be so honored.

Courses by James Braid (All with John R. Stutt unless otherwise indicated):

England: Arcot Hall GC (1909 *solo*); Barnehurst GC (9 1903 *solo*); Basingstoke GC (1927); Bognor Regis GC (*solo*); Bridport and West Dorset GC (*solo*); Budock Vean Hotel GC (9 1922 *solo*); Charnwood Forest GC (9 1891 *solo*); Church Stretton GC (1898 *solo*); Clitheroe GC; Colchester GC (1909 *solo*); Copthorne GC (*solo*); Croham Hurst GC (1912), with F. G. Hawtree; Dorking GC (9 1897 *solo*); Drayton Park GC; Dunstable Downs GC (1907 *solo*); Eaglescliffe GC (1914 *solo*); Ellesborough GC (1906 *solo*); Exeter G&CC; Finchley GC (1929); Fulford Heath GC (1934); Hoylake Muni (1933); Henley GC (1908 *solo*); Home Park GC (*solo*); Ipswich GC (9 1927); Kedleston Park GC (1947), and J. S. F. Morrison; Kingswood GC (1928); Luffenham Heath GC (1911 *solo*); Mere G&CC (1934), and George Duncan; Middlesborough GC (1908 solo); Newton Abbot CC (1930); North Hants GC (1904 solo); North Shore GC (1910 solo); North Worcestershire GC (1906 solo); Northumberland GC (solo); Orsett GC; Oswestry GC (1930); Perranporth GC (1927); Petersborough Milton GC (1938); Romford GC (solo); Royal Blackheath GC (1923); St. Austell GC (1912 solo); St. Enodoc GC (solo); Scarborough North Cliff GC (1927); Sherborne GC (solo); Shipley GC (1896 solo); Southport and Ainsdale GC (1907 solo, NLE); Stinchcombe Hill GC (solo); Theydon Bois GC (9 1897 solo); Thorpeness GC (1923 solo); Tiverton GC (1932); Torquay GC; Tyrrells Wood GC (1922 solo); Weir Park GC (solo); West Hove GC (Old Cse 1910 solo); Wildernesse GC (solo); Workington GC (1922 solo); Worsley GC (9).

France: Vittel GC (1910).

Ireland: Dundalk GC (1905 solo); Limerick GC (9 1920 solo, A.9 1928); Mullingar GC (1932); Newlands GC (1926); Rosapenna GC (1906), with Harry Vardon.

Isle of Man: Ramsey GC (1935).

Northern Ireland: Carnalea GC (1927); Kirkistown Castle GC (1902 solo).

Scotland: Airdrie GC (solo); Balmore GC (1906 solo); Belleisle GC (1927); Blairgowrie GC (Wee Cse); Blairmore and Strone GC (9 solo); Boat-of-Garten GC; Brechin GC (solo); Brora GC (solo); Buchanan Castle GC (1936); Carnoustie GC (Burnside Cse 1926); Cawder GC (Cawder Cse 1933; Keir Cse 1933; Colville Park GC (1922 solo); Cowal GC (solo); Crow Wood GC (1925); Dalmahoy GC (East Cse 1926; West Cse 1926); Deaconsbank GC (1922 solo); Downfield GC (1932); Dullatur GC (solo); Forfar GC (solo); Fort Augustus GC (9 1930); Glenbervie GC (1932); Glencruitten GC (1905 solo); Gleneagles Hotel GC (King's Cse 1919; Queen's Cse 1919), with C. K. Hutchison; Greenock GC (27 solo); Hamilton GC; Hayston GC (1926); Hilton Park GC (Allender Cse 1937); Ingliston GC; Kelso GC (solo); Kingsknowe (1908 solo); Kirriemuir GC (solo); Musselburgh GC (1937); North Berwick East Links (9 1894, A.9 1906), with Ben Sayers; Peebles GC (solo); Powfoot GC (1903 solo); Ratho Park GC (1928); Ravelston GC (9 1912 solo); Rothesay GC (solo); Routenburn CC (1920 solo); Royal

Musselburgh CC (1926); Seafield GC (1930); Southfield GC (1920 solo); Stranraer GC (1906 solo); Taymouth Castle GC (1928); Turnhouse GC (1909 solo); Williamwood GC (solo); Wishaw GC (solo).

Singapore: Singapore Island GC (Bukit Cse 1924 solo).

Wales: Flint GC (solo); Holyhead GC (1912 solo); Machynlleth GC (9 1905 solo); Monmouthshire GC (solo); Portmadoc GC (solo); Rhyl GC (9 solo); St. Deiniol GC (1905 solo); Weishpool GC (1929).

Courses remodeled or expanded by James Braid (All with John R. Stutt unless otherwise indicated):

New York: St. Andrews GC (R. 1930).

Channel Islands: La Moye GC (R. 1938).

England: Berkhampsted GC (R.12 A.6 1927); Berwick-upon-Tweed GC (R. 1925); Bramley GC (R.); Brighton and Hove GC (A.9 1910 solo); Bush Hill Park GC (R.); Cockermouth GC (R.2); Denham GC (R.); Enfield GC (R.); Ganton GC (R. 1919 solo); Hankley Common GC (R.9 A.9 1922 solo); Hunstanton GC (R.9 A.9 1910 solo); Leamington and County GC (R.); Littlestone GC (R.); Northamptonshire County GC (R. 1920 solo); Northumberland GC (R. 1911 solo); Parkstone GC (R. 1927); Queens Park GC (R.); Royal Cromer GC (R.); Ruislip GC (A.9 1938); Sherwood Forest GC (R. 1935); Thetford GC (R.); Verulam GC (R. 1910 solo); Wallasey GC (R. 1929).

Ireland: Ballybunion GC (Old Cse, R.9 A.9 1927); Howth GC (R.9 A.9 1929); Rosapenna GC (R. 1906), with Harry Vardon; Tullamore GC (R. 1938); Waterford GC (R.9 A.9 1934).

Isle of Man: Peel GC (R. solo).

Northern Ireland: Bangor GC (R. 1932).

Scotland: Alyth GC (R.); Blairgowrie GC (Rosemount Cse, R.10 A.8 1934); Broomieknowe GC (R.); Bruntsfield Links (R.); Carnoustie GC (R. 1926; R. 1936); Cochrane Castle GC (R. A.10 1949); Crieff GC (R.); Darley GC (R. solo); Edzell GC (R. 1934); Elie Golf House C (R. 1921 solo); Forres GC (R.); Fortrose and Rosemarkie GC (R. solo); Lochgreen GC (R. solo); Murcar GC (R.); Nairn GC (R. 1938); Newtonmore GC (R.); Prestwick GC (R. A.4 1918 solo; R. 1930); Royal Burgess G Society of Edinburgh (R. 1932); Royal Troon GC (R. 1923 solo); St.

Andrews (New Cse, R.; Old Cse, R.); Scotscraig GC (R.).

Wales: Aberdovey GC (R. solo); Bull Bay GC (R. solo); Pwllheli GC (R.9 A.9 1909 solo); Royal Porthcawl GC (R. 1910 solo).

JEFFREY D. BRAUER
(1955–), ASGCA

BORN: Albany, New York.

Jeff Brauer graduated with honors and an ASLA National Merit Award from the University of Illinois in 1977 with a Bachelor's degree in landscape architecture. He immediately went to work for the design firm of Killian and Nugent on the design of such prominent layouts as Kemper Lakes GC near Chicago. Brauer's largest involvement during that period was the design and construction supervision of Lake Arrowhead GC in Nekoosa, Wisconsin.

When the Killian and Nugent firm dissolved in 1983, Brauer remained with Ken Killian for a year. He then formed his own design company, Golfscapes, Inc., based in Arlington, Texas. On several of his early solo projects, Brauer worked with PGA Tour veteran Jim Colbert on jobs related to Colbert's daily-fee course lease/management business.

Beginning in 1987 Brauer teamed with former U.S. Open champion Larry Nelson to codesign a series of well-received designs, notably Springhouse GC in Nashville and Centennial near Atlanta. They worked together on many domestic projects. Brauer also maintained a separate practice, staffed by young architects Jeff Blume, John Colligan, Derek Hanks, Eric Nelson and Steven Plumer.

Courses by Jeff Brauer:

Georgia: Brookstone G&CC (1988), with Larry Nelson; Centennial GC (1990), with Larry Nelson; Windstone G Cse (1990).

Illinois: Kemper Lakes GC (1979), ass't Ken Killian and Dick Nugent; Robert A. Black GC (9 Precision 1979), ass't Ken Killian and Dick Nugent.

Nebraska: [The] Champions C (1992); Eagle Run GC (Precision 1990); Woodland Hills GC (1991).

New Mexico: Links at Sierra Blanca (1991).

Tennessee: Springhouse GC at Opryland (1990), with Larry Nelson.

Texas: Bluebonnet Hills GC (1990); Chester W. Ditto Muni (1982), ass't

Jeff Brauer, 1991
COURTESY JEFF BRAUER

Ken Killian and Dick Nugent; Colonial Bend GC (9 Par 3 1985); Mission CC (1983), ass't Ken Killian and Dick Nugent; Ratliff Ranch G. Links (1988), Squaw Creek GC (1992).

Virginia: Poplar Forest GC (9 1980), ass't Ken Killian and Dick Nugent.

Wisconsin: Lake Arrowhead GC (1984), ass't Ken Killian and Dick Nugent.

Guam: Lonfit New Towne GC (1992), with Larry Nelson.

Indonesia: Talvas G & Resort Batam (Private Cse 1992; Resort Cse 1992), with Larry Nelson.

Courses remodeled or expanded by Jeff Brauer:

California: San Bernardino CC (A.1 1986), with *Jim Colbert*; San Dimas Canyon GC (R. 1991).

Kansas: Manhattan CC (R.1 1985)

Louisiana: Northwood CC (A.9 1987).

Nebraska: Fairbury CC (R.2 1985); Holdredge CC (A.9 1985); Oak Hills CC (R.2 1984); Pioneer Park GC (R. 1989).

Nevada: Desert Rose GC (R. 1985), with *Jim Colbert*; Las Vegas GC (R. 1986), with *Jim Colbert.*

Texas: Brookhaven CC (Masters Cse, R. 1991) with Larry Nelson; Eastern Hills CC (R. 5 1989); Grapevine Muni (R.1); Great Southwest GC (R. 1983), ass't Ken Killian and Dick Nugent; Lady Bird Johnson GC (A.9 1992); Lost Creek CC (R. 12 1991); Plano Muni (R. 1986), with *Jim Colbert:* Weeks Park GC (R. 10 1986); Wichita Falls CC (R.2 1986).

JOHN BREDEMUS
(1884–1946)

BORN: Flint, Michigan.
DIED: Big Spring, Texas, at age 61.

The son of Luxembourg immigrants, John Bredemus attended public schools in South Bend, Indiana, until the death of his father. He finished his primary education at Phillips Exeter Academy in New Hampshire, attended Dartmouth for a year, then switched to Princeton University and graduated with a degree in civil engineering in 1912. All the while, he established himself as a fine athlete, winning the AAU National All-Around competition in track and field in 1908 and playing varsity football at Princeton. In 1912, Bredemus competed again in the AAU Nationals, finishing second to the legendary Jim Thorpe, who earlier in the year had won both the decathlon and pentathlon in the Summer Olympics. But in 1913 Thorpe was stripped of both his Olympic and AAU titles for having played semipro baseball a few years earlier. Thorpe's AAU medals were sent to Bredemus, the runner-up, and while Bredemus accepted them, it would prove not to be an honor. Thorpe's popularity was such that Bredemus was criticized for keeping the medals, as if he had something to do with disqualifying Thorpe.

After college, Bredemus taught college mathematics, served as athletic director in Stamford, Connecticut, and took up golf. By 1914, he was competing in local tournaments around New York City. Two years later, he turned professional. Bredemus moved to San Antonio, Texas, after World War I and spent a few years as a high school principal. In 1920 he designed and built his first golf course, San Felipe Springs CC in Del Rio, west of San Antonio, and gave up teaching forever. He spent the remainder of his life as a golf professional and course architect.

In 1922 he cofounded the Texas PGA and proposed a Texas Open as part of a winter schedule of professional golf events. The winter golf tour, through Texas and Louisiana, became the forerunner to the PGA Tour, and the Texas Open became the PGA Tour's oldest continuous event. In 1928, Bredemus established the first bent-grass greens in Texas, at San Angelo CC.

Toward the end of his career, he was assisted in his designs by Ralph Plummer, a young professional golfer who went on to make a name for himself as a course architect following World War II.

Bredemus was one of the more obscure figures in golf course architecture, the subject of many legends. It was true he received Jim Thorpe's medals, but they were not Thorpe's Olympic ones. It was true that he once took his shoes off before entering a client's office, but it was not true that he preferred to play barefoot. He did once consider viewing a potential golf course site from atop some tall trees on the site, but he was not so eccentric as to design every course from a treetop.

In the late 1930s Bredemus moved to Mexico, reportedly following a dispute with the U.S. government over income taxes. He designed over a half-dozen fine Mexican layouts, but returned to Texas to complete one last course. Bredemus died of a coronary occlusion in Big Spring, Texas, in 1946. In 1991 he was posthumously inducted into the Texas Golf Hall of Fame.

Courses by John Bredemus:

Texas: Brae Burn CC (1927); Cherokee CC (1930); Colonial CC (1936); Corpus Christi G&CC (9 1926, NLE); Ebony Hill GC [FKA Edinburg CC](9 1927); Galveston CC (1933); Hermann Park GC (1923); Hillcrest CC, San Antonio (9 1926, NLE); Llano Grande GC [FKA Mercedes CC](9 1926); Max Starcke Park GC [FKA Sequin CC](9 1936); Memorial Park GC (1936); Odessa CC (9 1939); Offats Bayou Park G Cse (1932, NLE); Oso Beach GC(1939); Pine Forest CC (1946, NLE); Ridglea CC (North Cse 1928); Rockwood Muni (1933); San Angelo CC (1928); San Felipe CC (9 1921); Scott Schreiner Muni [FKA Kerrville CC](9 1924); Shore Acres CC (9 1925, NLE); Temple Jr. College GC (9 1946); Tenison Muni (West Cse 1924); Tony Butler Muni [FKA Harlingen CC](1926); Victoria CC (9 1923); Westwood CC (9 1930); Z. Boaz GC.

Mexico: Acapulco CC; Churubusco CC; C de G Hermosillo (NLE); Guadalajara CC (9 1942; A.9 1948); Monterrey CC; Tampico CC (9).

John Bredemus, circa 1930 COURTESY FRANCES TRIMBLE

Courses remodeled or expanded by John Bredemus:

Texas: Austin CC (R. A.9 1924, NLE); Big Spring CC (R.9 A.9 1946, NLE); Brackenridge Park GC (R.6 1926); Cedar Crest GC (R. 1927); Glenbrook GC (R. 1924); Glen Garden CC (R.9 A.9, NLE); Gus Wortham Muni [FKA Houston CC](R.4); Meadowbrook G Cse (R.9 A.9 1928); Willow Springs CC (R.9 A.9 1925).
Mexico: Mexico City CC (R. 1939).

RUSSELL F. BREEDEN
(1917–)

BORN: Alvamar County, Virginia.

Russell Breeden entered private practice as a golf course designer in 1961 after training under golf architect Fred Findlay. By 1990 he had designed over 85 courses, personally supervising construction of most of them. He was joined in his work during the 1980s by his son Dan Breeden.

Courses by Russell Breeden:

North Carolina: Beechwood CC; Montgomery CC (1963); Ocean Isle Beach GC (1986), with *Dan Breeden*; Pawtuckett GC (1973); Pinewood CC (1970); Quaker Meadows GC (1969); Raintree CC (North Cse 1971: South Cse 1971); Rock Barn GC (1969); Sapphire Lakes CC (9 1984), with *Dan Breeden*; Scotch Meadows CC (1968).
South Carolina: Bay Tree G Plantation (Gold Cse, routing 1972; Green Cse, routing 1972; Silver Cse, routing 1972); Bonnie Brae GC (1961); Carolina Spring G&CC (1970); Chester GC (1971); Chickasaw Point GC (1973); Cypress Bay GC (1972); Eagle Ridge G&CC (1980), with *Dan Breeden*; Hejaz Shrine Recreation C; Hidden Valley CC (1965); Kings Grant GC (1988); Lan-Yair GC (1962); Linrick GC (1972); Mid Carolina CC (1968); Pawpaw CC (1981); Pine Ridge CC (1969); Pineland Plantation G&CC (1974); Pleasant Point Plantation CC (1972); Possum Trot GC (1968); Ramsgate GC (1983), with *Dan Breeden*; Robber's Roost GC (1968); Sedgewood CC (1965); Shadowmoss G&TC (1971); Village Green G&CC (1969); Village Greens CC (1983), with *Dan Breeden*; Widow Maker GC (1979), with *Dan Breeden*; Wildewood CC (1974).

Virginia: Chestnut Creek CC (1991); Hanging Rock GC (1992); Jordan Point CC (9 1974); Sleepy Hole Muni (1972).

Courses remodeled or expanded by Russell Breeden:

North Carolina: Asheboro CC (A.9 1970); Fox Squirrel CC (R.); Grove Park Inn (R. 1988); Kinston CC (R. 1983), with *Dan Breeden*.
South Carolina: CC of Newberry (R.); Greenville CC (Riverside Cse, R. 1971); Lancaster CC (R. 1969); Woodlands CC (R. 1980), with *Dan Breeden*.
Virginia: Halloud Muni (A.9); Suffolk CC (R.).

Sid Brews, circa 1965 COURTESY *GOLF DIGEST*

SIDNEY FRANCIS BREWS

BORN: Blackheath, England.

Talented tournament golfer Sid Brews emigrated to South Africa in the 1920s. While serving as club professional at Durban Country Club, he played extensively throughout the country and abroad. He nearly won the 1934 British Open, won twice on the U.S. PGA Tour in 1935 and won successive French and Holland opens in 1934 and 1935. But he was best remembered for winning eight South African Opens between 1925 and 1952.

Brews, who served for years as president of the South African PGA, designed a number of courses in that country after his competitive career wound down. In the 1960s he teamed with a new rising South African star, Gary Player, and Dr. Van Vincent in a design team.

Courses by Sid Brews (All with Gary Player and Dr. Van Vincent unless otherwise indicated):

South Africa: Four Ways GC; Glenvista CC (1973); Randpark GC (Randpark Cse 1964 *solo*).
Zimbabwe: Elephant Hills GC.

Courses remodeled or expanded by Sid Brews (All with Gary Player and Dr. Van Vincent unless otherwise indicated):

South Africa: Crown Mines GC (R.); St. Michaels GC (R.).

WILLIAM H. BRINKWORTH

William Brinkworth served as pro-greenkeeper and manager at Jasper Park GC in Alberta, Canada, from 1920 until his retirement in 1959. He designed several western Canada courses during that time.

Courses by William Brinkworth:

Alberta: Derrick C (1959); Edmonton G&CC; Elk Island National Park GC; Highlands GC; Prince Rupert GC; Sherwood Park GC.
Saskatchewan: Regina GC; Wascana G&CC.

Courses remodeled or expanded by William Brinkworth:

Alberta: Jasper Park GC (R. 1948).
Saskatchewan: Elmwood G&CC (R.).

ERNEST BROWN

Canadian designer Ernie Brown planned several courses in his home province of British Columbia in the 1960s and '70s. His projects emphasized the family aspect of the country club by providing some form of outdoor activity for every member of the family. On a couple of his courses, Brown experimented with the covering of a portion of each tee for play on rainy days.

Courses by Ernest Brown:

British Columbia: Chilliwack G&CC (1958); McCleery GC; Prince George CC; Shuswap Lake Estates G&CC (9); Sparwood GC (9 1984); Sunshine Coast G&CC (9 1970), with *Roy Taylor*; Sunshore GC (9 Precision 1968).

Courses remodeled or expanded by Ernest Brown:

British Columbia: Vernon G&CC (R.5 1968).

LESLIE BROWNLEE

A native of Scotland, Leslie Brownlee emigrated to America, where he served for several years as professional at the Fort Smith (Arkansas) CC. He designed the first golf courses in Oklahoma, including nine holes each for Muskogee CC (1907) and Lakeview CC in Oklahoma City (1907). Brownlee's stepbrother, Arthur Jackson, was also a pioneer golf architect in Oklahoma.

JOHN G. BULLA
(1914–   )

BORN: Newell, West Virginia.

Veteran PGA touring pro Johnny Bulla was best known as the "Po-Do pro" as a result of his long-running contract with a cut-rate golf ball manufacturer. Twice a runner-up in the British Open and once a second-place finisher at the Masters, Bulla dabbled in course design in the late 1940s and early 1950s. After retiring from active competition and taking a club professional job, Bulla laid out several courses as a sideline in the Southwest.

Courses by Johnny Bulla:

Arizona: Leisure World GC (Precision 9); Orange Tree CC (1958), with Lawrence Hughes; Thunderbird CC (1957), with *Clarence Suggs*.
Colorado: Fairfield Pagosa GC [FKA Pagosa Pines GC](1980).

Courses remodeled or expanded by Johnny Bulla:

Arizona: Arizona CC (R. 1962).

STEPHEN R. BURNS
(1958–   )

BORN: Troy, Ohio.

After graduating from Ohio State with a degree in landscape architecture in 1981, Stephen Burns worked for a short time for golf architect Chuck Ankrom, then joined the Fazio design firm in Florida. Over the next seven years, he ran clearing operations and served as a designer's representative in the field. In 1988, Burns formed his own design company based in northern Florida.

Stephen Burns, 1991
COURTESY STEPHEN BURNS

Courses by Stephen Burns:

Florida: Hammock Dunes GC (1988), ass't Tom Fazio; John's Island C (West Cse 1988), ass't Tom Fazio; Long Point C (1987), ass't Tom Fazio.
Georgia: Laura S. Walker State Park G Cse (1992).
Ohio: Hawk's Nest GC (1992).
South Carolina: Cotton Dike GC (1985), ass't Tom Fazio; Wachesaw Plantation GC (1986), ass't Tom Fazio.
Mexico: C de G Malinalco (1992).

Courses remodeled or expanded by Stephen Burns:

Ohio: Brookside G Cse (A.9 1992).

THOMAS JEFFRYES BURTON, JR.
(1966–   )

BORN: Freeport, Grand Bahama Island, Bahamas.

The grandson of renowned turf specialist Glenn W. Burton and the son of a golf course superintendent, Jeff Burton spent three summers interning with golf archi-

Jeff Burton, 1991
COURTESY JEFF BURTON

tect Cabell Robinson in the European office of Robert Trent Jones and then became the principal design associate of Rocky Roquemore in Georgia. At the same time, Burton completed studies at the University of Georgia, where he obtained a landscape architecture degree in 1991.

Courses by Jeff Burton (All with Rocky Roquemore):

Georgia: Noname GC (9 1990).
Pennsylvania: CC at Woodloch Springs (1991).
France: Makila GC (1992).
Portugal: Golden Eagle GC (1992); Quinta do Peru GC (1992).

Courses remodeled or expanded by Jeff Burton (All with Rocky Roquemore):

Georgia: Sconti GC (A.3rd 9 1991).

C. S. Butchart, circa 1925 COLLECTION RON WHITTEN

CUTHBERT STRACHAN BUTCHART
(1876–1955)

BORN: Carnoustie, Scotland.
DIED: Ossining, New York, at age 79.

Cuthbert Butchart, one of twin sons of golf club maker John Butchart, became a professional golfer in his teens and at age twenty-three took a position as professional at Royal County Down in Northern Ireland. He remained there for several years, staking out or reconstructing a number of Irish courses before returning to Scotland in 1904.

After working as a professional and laying out a few courses in Scotland, Butchart moved on to Germany. There he designed and built Berlin GC, served as its professional and became golf teacher to German royalty. A fine golfer, he also won the 1913 German PGA Championship. Several courses of his design were under construction in Germany when World War I broke out. Butchart was interned and spent the next two years in a German prisoner-of-war camp.

Upon his release, Butchart returned to Scotland but soon moved to the United States, where he became head professional at the newly opened Westchester Biltmore CC in New York. He lived in America for the remainder of his life, spending summers in New York and winters in Florida. As an avocation, he began marketing handmade woods bearing his famous clubmaking family name. He also designed and remodeled several American courses, many of them in Florida during the boom of the 1920s.

Courses by C.S. Butchart:

Florida: Eustis CC (NLE); Mayfair CC (1927).
New York: Hessian Hills CC (1923, NLE).
England: North Middlesex GC; Porters Park GC (1899); West Byfleet GC (1904).
Germany: Bad Kissingen GC; Berlin G&CC (1911); Opperdorf Estate GC.
Ireland: Bundoran GC.
Northern Ireland: Belvoir Park GC; Fortwilliam GC; Royal County Down GC (Cse No. 2); Whitehead GC (1904).

Courses remodeled or expanded by C.S. Butchart:

England: Highgate GC (R. 1904).
Northern Ireland: Royal County Down GC (R.).

WILLARD C. BYRD
(1919–   ), ASGCA

BORN: Whiteville, North Carolina.

Following military service in the U.S. Navy during World War II, Willard Byrd attended North Carolina State, receiving a B.S. degree in landscape architecture in 1948. He worked first in recreational site planning with the U.S. Army Corps of Engineers and later as a planning consultant for the Federal Housing Administration in North Carolina and Florida. He then served as assistant manager and designer in the southeastern office of a large landscape architecture and city planning firm.

In 1956 he founded Willard C. Byrd and Associates, Landscape Architects, Town Planners and Golf Course Architects. By 1979 Byrd's Atlanta, Georgia–based firm had completed some 900 projects, including work on 100 golf courses. Because he was also involved in land planning and

Willard Byrd, 1989
COURTESY WILLARD BYRD

master planning, his contributions as a golf architect were often overlooked. He designed both eighteens for the Country Club of North Carolina, for example, although Ellis Maples is often credited with that club's Dogwood Course and Robert Trent Jones with its Cardinal Course. In truth, Maples was brought in as a consultant during the completion of the Dogwood Course by Byrd, and a Trent Jones crew completed the second nine of the Cardinal Course to Byrd's plans. Likewise, he designed and constructed Atlanta Country Club, but credit is usually given to Joseph Finger, a design consultant brought in during construction by club members.

A member of the ASLA as well as the ASGCA, Byrd served for five years as an assistant professor in the graduate school of the Georgia Institute of Technology. Over the years, his associates in golf design included Clyde Johnston and Lee Chang.

Courses by Willard Byrd:

Alabama: Indian Oaks CC (1976).
Florida: Bay Point Y&CC (Club Meadows Cse 1972); Breakers West GC (1970); Lake City CC (1970); Longboat Key C (Harborside Cse 1983); [The] Oaks G&CC (Blue Heron Cse 1984; Eagle Cse 1984).
Georgia: Atlanta CC (1965), with Joseph S. Finger; Cherokee Town & CC (Pineside Cse, 9 1977); Country Oaks GC (1976); Dunwoody CC (1966); Fairfield Plantation CC (1973); Francis Lake GC (1973); [The] Landings at Skidaway Island (Plantation Cse 1984); Northwood G&CC; Southland CC (1990); Spring Hill CC; Sugar Hill G Cse (1991); Thomaston CC (9); White Path CC.
North Carolina: Beech Mountain GC (1969); Brunswick Plantation GC

(1992); Carolina Sands GC; CC of North Carolina (Cardinal Cse, 9 1968, A.9 1979, with Robert Trent Jones; Dogwood Cse 1963, with Ellis Maples); Gates Four G&CC (1974); Happy Valley CC (1973); Lake Hickory CC (27 1968); Lion's Paw G Links (1992); Lockwood G Links (1988); MacGregor Downs CC (1967); Mountain Harbour G&YC (1991); Willow Creek CC (1964); Wilson CC (1974).
South Carolina: Heather Glen G Links (1987); Indigo Creek GC (1990); Indigo Run GC (27 1992); Litchfield CC (1966); Patriots Point G Links (1984); Port Royal GC (Planters Row Cse 1984); River Hills CC (1969); Seabrook Island GC (Ocean Winds Cse 1973); Timberlake Plantation GC (1988); Verdae Greens GC (1991); Wexford GC (1984); Wild Wing Plantation GC (Hummingbird Cse 1992; Wood Stork Cse 1991).
Tennessee: Fox Den CC (1969).

Courses remodeled or expanded by Willard Byrd:

Alabama: CC of Mobile (R.).
Florida: Deerwood CC (R. 1977); Longboat Key C (Islandside Cse, R. 1984); Ponce de Leon Resort & CC (R.2 A.2 1977).
Georgia: Cherokee Town & CC (Hillside Cse, R.); Griffin CC (A.9); Idle Hour CC (R.); Sheraton Savannah Resort & CC (R. 1966).
Kentucky: Highland CC (R.).
North Carolina: Alamance CC (R.); Emorywood CC (R. 1980); Forsyth CC (R.); Sedgefield CC (R. 1977).
South Carolina: Heron Point GC (R.9 A. 9 1987); Port Royal GC (Barony Cse, R. 1984; Robbers Row Cse, R. 1984); Shipyard GC (A.3rd 9 1982).
Tennessee: Green Meadow CC (R. 1984).

CHARLES RAYMOND CALHOUN

While studying horticulture at Iowa State University, Charles Calhoun opened a landscape contracting business. He continued in that business for nearly 20 years, specializing in grounds management. After obtaining a Master's degree in agronomy and plant physiology from Iowa State in 1964, Calhoun began designing golf courses in small central Iowa communities. Stressing the importance of

Charles Calhoun, circa 1975 COURTESY CHARLES CALHOUN

properly constructed greens, Calhoun converted many small sand green courses to grass.

Courses by Charles Calhoun:

Iowa: Gowrie G&CC (9 1965); Jesup G&CC (9 1967); River Bend GC (9 1970); Waukon G&CC (1975).

Courses remodeled or expanded by Charles Calhoun:

Iowa: Appanoose G&CC (R. 1973); Colfax GC (R. 1973); Kalona GC (R.9); Oak Leaf CC (R.); Pella G&CC (R. 1976); Silvercrest G&CC (R.); Wildwood Muni (R. 1976).

ALEXANDER CAMPBELL
(1879–1942)

BORN: Troon, Scotland.
DIED: Dayton, Ohio, at age 63.

The oldest of seven golfing brothers, Alex Campbell came to the United States in 1896. His diminutive stature earned him the nickname "Nipper" at an early age, and it stuck all his life. A fine competitive player, he lost the 1907 U.S. Open to

Nipper Campbell, 1932 COURTESY *GOLF WORLD*

Alex Ross (Donald Ross's brother) when his golf ball exploded after a shot in the final round, costing him two shots.

Campbell emigrated to America and became club professional at The Country Club in Brookline, Massachusetts, in 1899, a position he maintained until World War I. He was generally credited with discovering Francis Ouimet, a youngster who lived along the 12th fairway of The Country Club. It was Campbell who refereed the famous playoff when amateur Ouimet stunned the golfing world by defeating veteran professionals Harry Vardon and Ted Ray for the 1913 U.S. Open title on that very course.

While at Brookline, Campbell laid out several Eastern courses and remodeled several others, including some holes at Cape Arundel in Maine, although apparently his job was given to Walter Travis when Alex failed to appear for an inspection trip.

From Brookline, Nipper moved on to the club professional's job at Baltimore Country Club. While there, he did at least one course, a public layout for the city of Baltimore.

In the late 1920s, one of Campbell's students, former Ohio governor and unsuccessful U.S. presidential candidate James Cox, lured Nipper to Dayton to serve as pro at Losantiville Country Club. While there, Campbell designed and built Moraine CC, where he served as head professional until his death. At Moraine, Nipper taught extensively, constructed clubs and continued to design golf courses. He did over thirty original designs in his lifetime.

Courses by Alex "Nipper" Campbell:

Maryland: Forest Park Muni.
Ohio: Madden GC; Meadowbrook CC (9); Miamisburg Muni (9); Moraine CC; Northmoor CC.
Vermont: Basin Harbor C (9 1927).

SIR GUY COLIN CAMPBELL
(1885–1960)

BORN: England.
DIED: Irvington, Virginia, at age 75.
INTERRED: St. Andrews, Scotland.

Sir Guy Campbell, great-grandson of Robert Chambers (an early British golf historian and codesigner of the original nine-hole course at Hoylake), was educated at Eton and at the University of St.

Andrews. He was a fine oarsman and cricket player. As a golfer, he won several medals in competition at St. Andrews and was a semifinalist in the 1907 British Amateur Championship.

During World War I, Campbell served in the infantry and was wounded in action. He also served in World War II as a member of the Royal Rifle Corps, even though he was in his late fifties at the time. Campbell joined the staff of *The Times* of London in 1920 as a special correspondent and later as editor of sports under the legendary Bernard Darwin. He also wrote countless magazine articles on golf and several books. Most notable was his contribution to *A History of Golf in Britain* (1952), edited by Darwin, in which Campbell outlined the history of course architecture in Britain.

Campbell assumed the hereditary rank of baronet upon the death of his father, Sir Guy T. Campbell, in 1931.

He began designing golf courses in the late 1920s, working in conjunction with Cecil K. Hutchison and S. V. Hotchkin on a series of layouts. He maintained a steady practice during the early 1930s in partnership with Hutchison. Hutchison bowed out due to ill health in the late thirties, and Campbell found little work until after the Second World War, when he teamed with talented golfer Henry Cotton on several course restorations and worked with veteran J. S. F. Morrison on an expansion at Prince's. Campbell was working on his first design in America at the time of his death in 1960.

Courses by Sir Guy Campbell (All with Cecil K. Hutchison and S. V. Hotchkin unless otherwise indicated):

Virginia: Tides Inn & CC (Tartan Cse, 9 1960 *solo*).
England: Ashridge GC (1932); Beamish Park GC (1950), with Henry Cotton; Kington GC (1926); Leeds Castle GC; Prince's GC (Red Cse, 9 1951), with J. S. F. Morrison; Shoreham GC; Warsash GC; West Sussex GC (1930).
Ireland: Killarney G & Fishing C (Killeen Cse, 6 1939 *solo*; Mahony's Point Cse, 12 1939 *solo*).

Courses remodeled or expanded by Sir Guy Campbell (All with Cecil K. Hutchison and S. V. Hotchkin unless otherwise indicated):

England: Felixstowe Ferry GC (R. 1949), with Henry Cotton; Prince's GC (Blue Cse, R. 1951), with J. S. F. Morrison;

Royal Cinque Ports GC (R. 1946), with Henry Cotton; Royal West Norfolk GC (R. 1928); Rye GC (R. *solo*); Seacroft GC (R. *solo*); Seascale GC (R. *solo*); Sundridge Park GC (East Cse, R. 1927); Trevose G&CC (R. A.3rd 9 *solo*); Woodhall Spa GC (R. 1926).
Ireland: Royal Dublin GC (R. 1950), with J. S. F. Morrison.
Netherlands: Haagsche G&CC (R. 1947 *solo*).
Scotland: Machrihanish GC (R. *solo*); North Berwick GC (R. 1930).

WILLIE CAMPBELL
(1862–1900)

BORN: Musselburgh, Scotland.
DIED: Manchester, Massachusetts, at age 38.

Born in Musselburgh, Scotland, Willie Campbell planned courses in the British Isles before emigrating to the United States in the early 1890s. He quickly gained fame as an instructor and as a player. He lost the first unofficial U.S. Open in 1894 by two shots to Willie Dunn. That same year he became the first professional at The Country Club, Brookline, Massachusetts, where he established the foundations of its present course and presided over one of its expansions. Later, while serving as summer pro at Essex CC in Manchester, Massachusetts, he planned other courses in the Northeast.

Willie Campbell's designs were very basic routings, done in a matter of hours or days, but he was among the earliest to design golf courses in America.

Courses by Willie Campbell:

Massachusetts: Oakley CC (9 1898, NLE); Tatnuck CC (9 1899, NLE); [The] Country Club (9 1893, A.3 1895).
New Hampshire: Beaver Meadow GC (9 1897).
Pennsylvania: Torresdale-Frankford CC (9 1895).
Rhode Island: Wannamoisett CC (9 1899, NLE).
England: Seascale GC (9 1892).
Scotland: Machrie Hotel GC (9 1891).

Courses remodeled or expanded by Willie Campbell:

Massachusetts: William F. Devine GC [FNA Franklin Park GC] (R. 1900).

Warren Cantrell, 1964 COURTESY *GOLF WORLD*

WARREN DAVID CANTRELL
(1905–1967)

BORN: Hillsboro, Texas.
DIED: Irving, Texas, at age 61.

Warren Cantrell attended Armour Institute of Technology in Chicago and Texas A&M, earning degrees in engineering and architecture. Following graduation he formed a contracting business in Texas. It evolved into a large operation, headed by his brother, which handled such major projects as the roof for the Houston Astrodome.

Cantrell himself left the firm in 1940 because of ill health. A fine golfer, he turned professional and became a club pro in Lubbock, Texas. He soon became involved in local and sectional PGA activities and was eventually elected treasurer and later president (1964–1965) of the PGA of America. He also served as the golf coach at Texas Tech University from 1953 to 1958.

Cantrell designed his first course after World War II and by the 1950s was busy planning on a part-time basis throughout West Texas and New Mexico. He designed some 30 courses in his career. His son William, a Texas Tech graduate, finished several Cantrell designs after Warren's death and later tried his hand at some designs of his own in Texas.

Courses by Warren Cantrell:

New Mexico: Colonial Park CC (9); Farmington CC (9); Lovington Muni (9 1954); Ocotillo Park GC (9 1955); Zuni Mountain GC (9 1961).
Texas: Andrews CC (1955); Big Spring CC (1960); Caprock G&CC; Farwell CC (9); Lake Oaks CC (Executive Cse 1960; Regulation Cse 1960); Old Elm

GC; River Hills CC (9 1960); San Angelo CC; Tascosa CC; Treasure Island GC (1964).

Courses remodeled or expanded by Warren Cantrell:

New Mexico: Albuquerque CC (R. 1959); Hobbs CC (R.9 A.9 1957).
Texas: Amarillo CC (R. 1960); Lubbock CC (R.9 A.9); Meadowbrook Muni (Cses No. 1 & 2, R. 1955).

DOUGLAS A. CARRICK
(1956–   ), ASGCA

BORN: Toronto, Ontario.

A low-handicap golfer, Carrick competed in many major Canadian national and provincial tournaments. A 1981 graduate of the University of Toronto's School of Landscape Architecture, Doug Carrick collaborated on several golf course projects and developed a close working relationship with C. E. "Robbie" Robinson, one of Canada's best-known architects. In 1985 Carrick established his own practice, but in 1987 he became partners with Robinson in the firm of Robinson and Carrick Ltd.

Upon Robinson's death, Carrick continued the business and the corporate name. In 1990 he was joined in his practice by landscape architect Ian C. Andrew.

Courses by Doug Carrick:

British Columbia: Qualicum Highlands G&CC (1992).
Ontario: Farringdon Place G Cse (9); Glenway CC (1987); Greystone GC (1991); King Valley GC (1990); Laurel Heights G&CC (1992); Mandarin

Doug Carrick, 1991 RON WHITTEN

G&CC (1991); Osprey Valley G Links (1992).

Courses remodeled or expanded by Doug Carrick:

Newfoundland: Twin Rivers G Cse (R.9 A.9 1991).
Ontario: Briars G&CC (R. 1989); Summit GC (R. 1990); Sunningdale CC (R. 1989).

Lee Chang, 1990

NAI CHUNG CHANG (1947–), ASGCA

BORN: China.

After obtaining a degree in architecture in his native China, "Lee" Chang moved to Atlanta, Georgia, in 1970, where he attended Georgia Tech and obtained a Master's degree in city planning in 1976. During his schooling, Chang worked in the offices of the Atlanta firm of Willard Byrd, who handled both land planning and golf course architecture. After teaching land-use planning to graduate students at Georgia for two years, he joined Byrd full-time. Originally hired as a land planner, Chang soon developed an interest in golf course design while working with Byrd on several residential-development courses. After the departure of Clyde Johnston from Byrd's firm in 1988, Chang became Byrd's chief design associate. In 1990 Chang became the first Oriental member of the ASGCA.

Courses by Lee Chang (All as assistant to Willard Byrd):

Florida: Longboat Key C (Harborside Cse 1983); [The] Oaks G&CC (Blue Heron Cse 1984; Eagle Cse 1984).
Georgia: [The] Landings at Skidaway Island (Plantation Cse 1984); Southland

CC (1990); Sugar Hill G Cse (1991).
North Carolina: Brunswick Plantation GC (1992); Lion's Paw G Links (1992); Lockwood G Links (1988); Mountain Harbour G&YC (1991).
South Carolina: Heather Glen G Links (1987); Indigo Creek GC (1990); Indigo Run GC (27 1992); Patriots Point G Links (1984); Port Royal GC (Planters Row Cse 1984); Timberlake Plantation GC (1988); Verdae Greens GC (1991); Wexford GC (1984); Wild Wing Plantation GC (Hummingbird Cse 1992; Wood Stork Cse 1991).

Courses remodeled or expanded by Lee Chang (All as assistant to Willard Byrd):

Florida: Longboat Key C (Islandside Cse, R. 1984).
South Carolina: Heron Point GC (R.9 A. 9 1987); Port Royal GC (Barony Cse, R. 1984; Robbers Row Cse, R. 1984).
Tennessee: Green Meadow CC (R. 1984).

SHANNON BRUCE CHARLTON (1957–), ASGCA

BORN: Manchester, Iowa.

Bruce Charlton grew up in Iowa, where he took up golf at an early age and enjoyed a fine amateur career. After working as an assistant golf course superintendent at Manchester (Iowa) CC part-time over a six-year period, Charlton graduated from the University of Arizona in 1980 with a Bachelor of Landscape Architecture degree. The following year he joined the Palo Alto, California–based design firm of Robert Trent Jones, Jr., where he became a design associate and later a vice president.

Courses by Bruce Charlton (All as assistant to Robert Trent Jones, Jr.):

Arizona: Falcon Ridge CC (1992).
California: Brookside CC (1991); Coto de Caza GC (1987); Desert Dunes G Cse (1989).
Illinois: Crystal Tree GC (1990); DuPage G Cse (1992).
Maine: Sugarloaf GC (1986).
Minnesota: Edinburgh USA G Cse (1987).
Nevada: Spanish Trail G&CC (Canyon Cse 9 1985, A.9 1992, Sunrise Cse 1985).

Bruce Charlton, 1991

Ohio: Jefferson G&CC (1992); Wedgewood G&CC (1991).
Wisconsin: University Ridge GC (1991).

Courses remodeled or expanded by Bruce Charlton (All as assistant to Robert Trent Jones, Jr.):

Hawaii: Waikoloa Beach GC (R. 1988).

ALEX CHISHOLM (1886–1961)

BORN: Peabody, Massachusetts.

Born of Scottish ancestry, Alex Chisholm spent his professional life in service to several Maine golf clubs, including a long stint as the head professional at the Portland CC. His competitive record included winning the 1928 and 1929 Maine Open and placing as runner-up five times. He served as teaching pro to Helen Payson, winner of the Canadian Ladies Amateur title in 1927.

Courses by Alex Chisholm:

Maine: Lakewood GC (9 1925); Old Orchard Beach CC (9 1920); Sanford GC (9 1923); Shore Acres GC (9 1926).
New Hampshire: Androscoggin Valley CC (9 1921).

THOMAS E. CLARK (1948–), ASGCA, PRESIDENT 1991

BORN: Broomall, Pennsylvania.

Tom Clark attended Penn State University, receiving a B.S. degree in landscape architecture in 1971. He joined the Maryland-based firm of Edmund B. Ault, Ltd., that same year. Over the next dozen

Tom Clark, 1990
COURTESY TOM CLARK

years Clark had primary responsibility for several hundred design projects along the Eastern Seaboard, Southeast and Midwest. In 1984 Clark became a full partner with Edmund Ault and Brian Ault in the reorganized company called Ault, Clark and Associates. He handled certain designs on his own and others in collaboration with one or more of the company partners.

Courses by Tom Clark:

Arkansas: Balboa GC (1987), with Edmund B. Ault; Berksdale GC (1977), ass't Edmund B. Ault; Branchwood GC (9 Par 3 1983), ass't Edmund B. Ault; Coronado GC (Precision 1983), ass't Edmund B. Ault; Highlands G Cse (1989); Kingswood GC (1977), ass't Edmund B. Ault; Metfield GC (Precision 1983), ass't Edmund B. Ault; Mountain Ranch GC (1984), with Edmund B. Ault and Brian Ault; Ponce de Leon CC (1991); Scotsdale G Cse (1987), with Edmund B. Ault.
Georgia: Barrington Hall GC (1991); [The] Landings GC (1987), with Bill Love.
Indiana: West Boggs Muni (9 1978), ass't Edmund B. Ault.
Iowa: Sundown GC (9 Par 3 1978), ass't Edmund B. Ault.
Louisiana: Eden Isles CC (1976), ass't Edmund B. Ault; Lake D'Arbonne G&CC (9 1984).
Maryland: Heritage Harbour GC (9 1982), ass't Edmund B. Ault; TPC at Avenel (1986), with Ed Ault, Brian Ault, Bill Love and *Ed Sneed*.
Missouri: Paradise Pointe GC (1984), with Brian Ault; Pointe Royale CC (1986); Poplar Bluff Muni (1980), ass't Edmund B. Ault.
Nevada: Emerald River G Cse (1990).
New Jersey: Quail Brook GC (1982), ass't Edmund B. Ault; Concordia GC (1986), with Brian Ault.
Pennsylvania: Mountain View GC (1987),

with Edmund B. Ault and Brian Ault.
South Carolina: Cane Patch Par 3 G Cse (18 Par 3 1982, ass't Edmund B. Ault; A.9 1986); Midway Par 3 G Cse (Par 3 1980), ass't Edmund B. Ault; Myrtlewood GC (Palmetto Cse 1972), ass't Edmund B. Ault; Tara CC (1991).
Tennessee: Three Ridges G Cse (1991); Toqua GC (1987).
Virginia: Broad Bay Point G&CC (1986); Cypress Point CC (1987); Herndon Centennial Muni (1979), ass't Edmund B. Ault; Kiln Creek CC (1991); Penderbrook GC (1979), ass't Edmund B. Ault; [The] Summit GC (1987), with Edmund B. Ault.
West Virginia: Sheraton Lakeview Resort & CC (Mountainview Cse 1984), with Brian Ault.

Courses remodeled or expanded by Tom Clark:

Arizona: Arizona CC (R. 1986), with Bill Love; Skyline CC (R. 1989).
Arkansas: Bella Vista CC (R. 1989); CC of Little Rock (R. 18 1980), ass't Edmund B. Ault.
Connecticut: Rolling Hills CC (R.5 1984), with Brian Ault.
Florida: Bardmoor CC (East Cse, R. 1986), with Edmund B. Ault; Broken Wood G&CC (R.2 1980), ass't Edmund B. Ault; Sawgrass GC (Oceanside Cse, R. 1982), ass't Edmund B. Ault.
Kansas: Mission Hills CC (R.5 1984); Indian Hills (R.2 1984); Leawood South (R.5 1984).
Louisiana: Eden Isles CC (R.1 1983), ass't Edmund B. Ault.
Maryland: Chester River Y&CC (A.9 1972), ass't Edmund B. Ault; Congressional CC (Gold Cse, R.2 1981), ass't Edmund B. Ault; Chevy Chase CC (R. 1990); Elkridge CC (R. 1974), ass't Edmund B. Ault; Indian Spring C (Chief Cse, R. 1976), ass't Edmund B. Ault; Swan Creek CC (R.9 1978), ass't Edmund B. Ault; Woodholme CC (R. 1975), ass't Edmund B. Ault.
Massachusetts: Pleasant Valley CC (R.3 1984), with Brian Ault.
Mississippi: CC of Jackson (R.9 1979), ass't Edmund B. Ault; Gulf Hills GC (R. 1985).
Missouri: Hickory Hills CC (R. 1974), ass't Edmund B. Ault.
Nevada: Tropicana CC (R. 1984, NLE), with Brian Ault.
New Hampshire: Kingswood CC (R.6 1990).

New Jersey: Greenacres CC (R.2 1984), with Brian Ault.
North Carolina: Duck Woods GC (R.7 1986), with Brian Ault; Paradise Point GC (Gold Cse, R.7 1979), ass't Edmund B. Ault.
Oklahoma: Walnut Creek CC (R.9 1983).
Pennsylvania: Chambersburg CC (A.9 1977), ass't Edmund B. Ault; Clinton CC (A.9 1977), ass't Edmund B. Ault; Host Farms GC (R.8 1988); Manufacturers G&CC (R. 1988); Tyoga CC (A.9 1979).
Tennessee: Woodmont CC (A.9 1977), ass't Edmund B. Ault.
Virginia: Army-Navy CC (Arlington Cse, R.5 1986), with Edmund B. Ault and Bill Love; Cavalier G&YC (R.18 1986); Cedar Point C (R. 1986); City Park GC (R.1 1988); Hampton GC (R. 1972), ass't Edmund B. Ault; Lake of the Woods GC (R.1 1988); Kingsmill GC (River Cse, R.7 1982), ass't Edmund B. Ault; Princess Anne CC (R.18 1986); Roanoke CC (R.7 1985); Sewells Point GC (R.18 1986); Washington G&CC (R. 1988), with Edmund B. Ault and Brian Ault; Westwood CC (R.18 1984), with Edmund B. Ault and Brian Ault; Winchester GC (R. 1973), ass't Edmund B. Ault.
Ontario: Hamilton G&CC (R.2 1989).

PERCY CLIFFORD
(1907–1984), ASGCA, FELLOW

BORN: Mexico City, Mexico.
DIED: Chicago, Illinois, at age 77.

Percy Clifford, the son of British citizens, was born and reared in Mexico City but attended school in England. Clifford was an outstanding amateur golfer, winning six Mexican Amateur and three Mexico Open titles.

Percy Clifford, circa 1976 COLLECTION RON WHITTEN

Clifford's first experience in course design came in the late 1940s, when he assisted golf architect Lawrence Hughes in planning Club de Golf de Mexico. Envisioning a topflight course, Clifford did much to organize the club and spent months personally selecting the site and reviewing the plans. After that experience, Clifford felt confident that he could handle design on his own.

By 1980 Clifford had designed nearly half of Mexico's golf courses. His layouts, comparable to some of the best in Britain and America, contributed significantly to the advancement of golf in his native country. Most were done on relatively modest budgets, for throughout his career Percy deplored the extravagance in both construction and maintenance of North American courses.

Clifford's daughter Sandra Fullmer was a former Women's Amateur Champion of Mexico, Spain and Germany. His son-in-law Paul Fullmer served as the first executive secretary of the ASGCA. The first Mexican citizen admitted to the ASGCA, Clifford was granted Fellow status in that society in 1977. He spent his last years in retirement at Rancho Santa Fe, California, where he routinely shot his age. In late 1984, Percy Clifford succumbed to cancer.

Courses by Percy Clifford:

Colombia: C de G Baru (1973).

Mexico: Bahía de Banderas (1974); Bajamar GC (1974); Campestre de Lagunero (1957); Centro Deportivo GC (9 1947); Chihuahua CC (1956); Club Campestre Aguncro (1951); Club Campestre de Morelia (9); Club Campestre de Queretaro (9 1951); Club Campestre de Torreón (1974); C de G de Mexico (1949), ass't Lawrence Hughes; C de G Avandara (1950); C de G Bellavista (1955); C de G Bugambillian (1964); C de G Campestre Del Lago (1970); C de G Certo Alto (9 1963); C de G Dos Mares (1962); C de G Erandeni (1975); C de G Hacienda (1956); C de G La Canadá (1972); C de G La Villa Rica (9 1971); C de G Monte Castillo (1963); C de G Morelia (9 1960); C de G Obregón (1953); C de G Pirámides (1966); C de G Ranchitos (1967); C de G Río Seco (9 1961); C de G San Carlos (1968); C de G San Gasper; C de G San Luis (1958); C de G Tabashines (1973); C de G Vallescondido (1974); C de G Xalapa (9); Del Bosque CC; El Bosque CC (1960); Laguna CC (1969); Las

Huertas CC (1965); Los Flamingos CC (1975); Pierre Marqués GC (27 1969); Queretaro CC (1955).

Courses remodeled or expanded by Percy Clifford:

Mexico: Acapulco CC (R.9 A.9); Chapultepec CC (R. 1972).

Lloyd Clifton, 1991
COURTESY LLOYD CLIFTON

LLOYD M. CLIFTON, SR. (1924–)

BORN: De Land, Florida.

After graduating from the University of Florida in 1950 with a degree in ornamental horticulture, Lloyd Clifton worked for the city of Daytona Beach until 1953, when he became superintendent of Daytona Beach G&CC. In the late 1950s he supervised construction of Rio Pinar CC in Orlando to the design of Mark Mahannah, then remained as its superintendent until 1961.

He then joined other family members in a successful fern-production business and served as an agronomic consultant to various Florida businesses. He designed his first golf course in 1964 and practiced course architecture on the side for nearly two decades.

In 1987 Clifton decided to concentrate solely upon golf course design. He formed a full-time business, the Clifton, Ezell and Clifton Design Group, with a son, George, and former club professional Kenneth Ezell. Clifton and his partners concentrated their design-and-build operation in the Southeast.

Courses by Lloyd Clifton (All in association with *Kenneth Ezell* and *George Clifton* unless otherwise indicated):

Florida: Bella Vista GC (1989); CC of

Mount Dora (1991); Cypress Creek CC (1970 *solo*); DeBary Plantation GC (1989); Eastwood G&CC, Orlando (1989); Grey Oaks CC (1992); Hacienda Hills G&CC (1990); Harbor Hills G&CC (1989); Highland Lakes GC (27 Precision 1980 *solo*); Hunter's Creek CC (1986 *solo*); Indigo Lakes CC (1976 *solo*); Kissimmee Bay CC (1990); Pelican Bay G&CC (South Cse 1984 *solo*); Plantation Bay CC (1987); River Bend GC (1990); Rosemont G&CC (1973 *solo*); Silver Pines GC (9 Precision 1980 *solo*, NLE); Sweetwater Oaks CC (1976 *solo*); West Chase GC (1992); West Orange CC (1964 *solo*); Willow Lakes G&CC (Troon Cse 1974 *solo*); Winter Pines GC (Precision 1967 *solo*).

North Carolina: Highland Creek CC (1992).

Courses remodeled or expanded by Lloyd Clifton (All in association with *Kenneth Ezell* and *George Clifton* unless otherwise indicated):

Florida: Casselberry GC (R.9 A.9 1973 *solo*); Deer Run CC (R. 1982 *solo*); Dubsdread CC (R. 1990); Green Valley GC (A.9 1989); Indigo Lakes CC (R. 1990); Ocala Muni (R. 1989); Ocean Palm GC (R. 1974 *solo*); Riviera CC (R.); Sherwood G&CC (A.9 1985 *solo*); Tuscawilla CC (R. 1990); Windermere CC (R. 1990).

PAUL N. COATES, JR.

For over 30 years, Ramsey (Minnesota) county engineer Paul Coates maintained a part-time golf design practice, laying out public layouts in Minnesota and neighboring states.

Courses by Paul Coates:

Minnesota: Bloomington CC; Cedarholm Muni (9); Cokato Town & CC (9 1959); Gem Lake GC (9 1955); Hastings CC; Hyland Greens CC; Keller GC (1929); Madden Inn & GC (West Cse); Mendota Heights Par 3 GC (9 Par 3 1929); Northfield GC; Stillwater CC (1957).

Courses remodeled or expanded by Paul Coates:

Iowa: Waveland GC (R. 1937).
Minnesota: Midland Hills CC (R.).

George Cobb, 1957
COLLECTION RON WHITTEN

GEORGE W. COBB
(1914–1986), ASGCA

BORN: Savannah, Georgia.
DIED: Greenville, South Carolina, at age 71.

George Cobb attended the University of Georgia, graduating in 1937 with a degree in landscape architecture. He was employed by the National Park Service as a landscape architect until 1941, when he entered the U.S. Marine Corps as an engineering officer.

The Marine Corps recognized in Cobb, a scratch golfer as well as a landscape architect, the makings of a golf course architect. So he was assigned to design and build a golf course for Camp LeJeune, North Carolina. Unsure of his abilities, Cobb asked and got permission to retain Fred Findlay as course architect, for, as he later put it, "I didn't want to be court-martialed if it turned out badly." Cobb acted as construction superintendent on this and a second layout built by Findlay at Camp LeJeune.

Cobb's first solo project was at the Cherry Point (North Carolina) Marine Corps Air Station in 1946. He entered private practice as a golf architect in 1947 but was recalled to active duty in 1951. Following his second tour in the Marines, Cobb reentered private practice as a golf architect and land planner, opening an office in Greenville, South Carolina, in 1956. In the 1950s and 1960s he served as design consultant to Augusta National GC and developed a close friendship with Bobby Jones. When the club decided to install a nine-hole par-3 course, Cobb was asked to design it. When Jones authored an autobiography, *Golf Is My Game* in 1959, Cobb drafted the attractive hole-by-hole diagrams of Augusta National used as illustrations.

Though several of his designs were used as professional tournament sites, Cobb prided himself in providing attractive, playable layouts that resort players found enjoyable, not frustrating.

During the last 15 years of his career, Cobb was assisted by talented associate John LaFoy.

Courses by George W. Cobb:

Alabama: Burningtree CC (1966); Fort McClellan GC (9 1971); Goosepond Colony GC (1971); Inverness CC (1973); Pine Tree CC (1969); Still Waters CC (1972).

Florida: Deerwood CC (1961); Gainesville G&CC (1963).

Georgia: Augusta National GC (Par 3 Cse 1960), with Robert Tyre "Bobby" Jones, Jr; Brookfield West G&CC (1972); Browns Mill GC (1970); Doublegate Plantation CC (1964); Forest Heights CC (1966); Green Island CC (1960); Hunter Army Base GC (9); Lakeside CC (1960); Mary Calder GC (9 1967); Milledgeville CC (1961); Sea Palms G&CC (1967); Waynesboro CC (9 1963, A.9 1984 with John LaFoy); Windsor Forest CC (9 1962).

Maryland: Fort Eustis GC (1956); Fort Meade GC (Parks Cse 1956); Glenn Dale GC (1956); Laurel Pines CC (1957); Prospect Hill CC (1956); University of Maryland GC (1956).

New York: Eisenhower College GC (9 Precision 1972).

North Carolina: Bald Head Island CC (1972); Bryan Park GC (Players Cse 1973), with John LaFoy; Cabarrus CC (1966); Carmel CC (North Cse 1950); Cherry Point GC (1946); Cleghorn Plantation G&CC (1972); Connestee Falls CC (1972); Croasdaile CC (1965); CC of Sapphire (1958); Finley GC, University of North Carolina (1951); Forest Hills CC (9 1971); Green Valley GC (1947); High Meadows GC (1964); Hound Ear CC (1963); Jacksonville CC (1951); Linville Ridge CC (1983), with John LaFoy; Mountain Glen GC (1963); Mountain Valley GC (9 Par 3 1961); North Ridge CC (Oaks Cse, 9 1967; Lakes Cse, 9 1967); Oak Island CC (1962); Quail Hollow CC (1961); Raleigh G Association (9 1958); Rolling Hills CC (9 1964, A.9 1967); Wildcat Cliffs CC (1962); Willow Haven CC (1958); Willow Lakes GC, Pope AFB (9 1970, A.9 1975, with John LaFoy).

Ohio: Sharon C (1965).

South Carolina: Adventure Inn GC (9 1965, NLE); Berkeley CC (1961); Botany Woods GC (9 Par 3 1963); Cat Island CC (1985), with *Byron Comstock*; Charleston AFB GC (9 1966); Clemson University GC (1976), with John LaFoy; Cobb's Glen CC (1975), with John LaFoy; Fort Jackson GC (1949); Green Valley CC (1958); Greenwood CC (9 1950, A.9 1958); Holly Tree CC (1973), with John LaFoy; J. C. Long Estate GC (9 1957); Keowee Key CC (1977), with John LaFoy; Myrtlewood GC (Pines Cse 1966); Ocean Point G Links [FKA Fripp Island CC](1964); Port Royal GC (Barony Cse 1964; Robbers Row, Cse 9 1965, A.9 1974, with John LaFoy); Santee Cooper CC (1968); Sea Pines Plantation GC (Ocean Cse 1967; Sea Marsh Cse 1961); Shipyard GC (Clipper and Galleon Nines 1970); Snee Farm CC (1970); Spanish Wells CC (9 1970); Spring Valley CC (1961); Star Fort National GC (1969); Surf GC (1960); Woodlands CC (1975), with John LaFoy.

Tennessee: Clarksville CC (1966); Frank G. Clement GC; Stonebridge GC (1974); Warriors Path State Park GC (1970).

Virginia: Lynwood G&CC (1965); New Quarter Park GC (1977), with John LaFoy; Pohick Bay GC (1978), with John LaFoy; Red Wing Lake GC (1971); Tides Inn & CC (Golden Eagle Cse 1976), with John LaFoy.

West Virginia: Edgewood CC (1970); Glade Springs CC (1973).

Bahamas: Andros Island CC (9 1965, NLE).

Courses remodeled or expanded by George W. Cobb:

Alabama: CC of Birmingham (East Cse, R. 1964); Green Valley CC (R.9 A.9 1963); Mountain Brook C (R. 1968); Vestavia CC (R. 1962).

Florida: Beauclerc CC (A.9 1961); Indian Lakes CC (R.9 A.9 1974); Timuquana CC (R. 1963).

Georgia: Athens CC (A.3rd 9 1985), with John LaFoy; Augusta National GC (R. 1967; R. 1977, with John LaFoy); Capital City C (R. 1962); Coosa CC (R. 1973); Dublin CC (R.9 A.9); East Lake CC (R. 1960); Fort McPherson GC (R. 1965); Savannah GC (R. 1963; R.3 1977, with John LaFoy).

Maryland: Wicomico Shores GC [FKA Aviation Y&CC](R. 1967).

Minnesota: Somerset CC (R. 1976), with John LaFoy.

North Carolina: Chapel Hill CC (R. 1957, NLE); Greensboro CC (Irving Park Cse, R. 1968); High Hampton Inn GC (R. 1958; R. 1980, with John LaFoy); Hillandale CC (A.2 1956; R.13 A.3 1960); Starmount Forest CC (R. 1972).

South Carolina: CC of Spartanburg (R.9 A.9 1959); Greenville CC (Riverside Cse, R. 1960); Ocean Point G Links (R. 1976), with John LaFoy; Springs Mill CC (A.9 1960).

Virginia: Army-Navy CC (Fairfax Cse, R. 1959); Belle Haven CC (R. 1959); Tides Inn & CC (Tartan Cse, A.9 1968).

West Virginia: Twin Falls State Park GC (A.9 1981), with John LaFoy; Western Greenbrier Hills GC (R. 1976), with John LaFoy.

JOHN N. COCHRAN
(1913–1985)

BORN: Mississippi.
DIED: Denver, Colorado, at age 72.

John Cochran received his undergraduate degree in engineering and did graduate study on turfgrasses at Abraham Baldwin College in Georgia and Penn State University. He turned professional in 1937 and played the PGA Tour for ten years, winning the 1939 Mississippi Open and 1940 Southeastern PGA. He also laid out his first course around that time, though it was over 20 years before he did another. Cochran was a club pro in Georgia and Mississippi until 1957, when he became professional at Columbine CC near Denver, Colorado, and later at Denver CC.

In 1962 Cochran resigned to found Golf Club Operations Inc., a turnkey organization that designed, built and operated country clubs. Press Maxwell served as the firm's golf architect, and Cochran worked as the company's agronomist. When Maxwell resigned after two years, Cochran continued the business by taking on the full responsibilities of golf course architect.

In the last years of his life, Cochran worked on building what he considered his best design, Fox Acres CC. Cochran died of a heart attack at his home in Denver.

Courses by John Cochran:

Colorado: Boulder CC (27 1965), ass't Press Maxwell; Dos Rios CC (9 1966); Fox Acres CC (1983); Hiwan GC (1965), ass't Press Maxwell.
Iowa: Crow Valley CC (1970).

Courses remodeled or expanded by John Cochran:

Colorado: City Park GC (R. 1966); CC of Fort Collins (R.); Denver CC (R.3 1966); Snowmass GC (A.9 1973).
Louisiana: Bayou de Siard CC (R. 1973).

MILTON COGGINS
(1902–   ), ASGCA, FELLOW

BORN: Arizona.

Milt Coggins studied economics at the University of Redlands in California, receiving a B.A. degree in 1926. Having played basketball, baseball, tennis and golf, he sought a sports-oriented profession. He operated a sporting goods store in the 1930s, then played professional tennis for 11 years and in 1950 became sports director at Camelback Inn in Phoenix. Coggins then served as golf professional at Encanto Municipal GC, where he remained until 1961. While at Encanto, he designed his first course in 1956. After 1961, Coggins practiced golf architecture on a full-time basis until his retirement in the mid-1970s.

Courses by Milt Coggins:

Arizona: Camelot CC (1967); Christown G&CC (9 1962); Fort Huachuca GC (9 1971); Glen Lakes GC (9 1968); Kingman GC (9 1973); Lakes West GC (1968); Paradise Valley Park GC (9 1972, NLE); Pine Meadows GC (9 1970); Pinetop CC (1961); Pinetop Lakes G&CC (1973); Prescott CC

Milt Coggins, 1980
COURTESY *GOLF WORLD*

(1972); Rio Verde CC (Quail Run Cse, 9 1973); White Wing Cse, 9 1973), with *Fred Bolton*; Rolling Hills GC (Precision 1961, NLE); Sun City CC (1966); Sun City North GC (1960); Sun City South GC (1962); Sunland Village GC (Precision 1975), with Jeff Hardin and Greg Nash; Villa Monterey CC (9 1965, NLE).
California: Cherry Hills GC (1963).
Colorado: Ranch at Roaring Fork GC (9 Precision 1973).
Florida: Sun City Center G&CC (North Cse, 9 1961).
New Mexico: Alto Lakes G&CC (9 1968).
Texas: Clear Lake CC (Routing 1963).

Courses remodeled or expanded by Milt Coggins:

Arizona: Apache Wells CC (A.9 1966); Camelot CC (A.9 1974); Coronado GC (A.9 1976).

Neil Coles, circa 1980 COLLECTION RON WHITTEN

NEIL COLES
(1934–   )

BORN: London, England.

Neil Coles turned professional in 1950 and played successfully on the British and European tours for over twenty years. A three-time British PGA Match Play champion, Coles was a member of eight Ryder Cup teams.

In the late 1970s Coles teamed with fellow touring pros Brian Huggett and Roger Dyers in a golf design partnership. In the 1980s, he established his own design business, working both in Britain and on the Continent.

Courses by Neil Coles (All with Brian Huggett and Roger Dyer unless otherwise indicated):

England: Hickleton GC; Tilgate Forest GC (1982); Warmley GC (1985).
Iran: Ahwaz GC (1977).
Scotland: Hazelhead Muni (Cse No. 2 1975).

Harry Collis, circa 1925 COLLECTION RON WHITTEN

Courses remodeled or expanded by Neil Coles (All with Brian Huggett and Roger Dyer unless otherwise indicated):

England: West Wiltshire GC (R. 1972).

HARRY J. COLLIS (1878–1937)

BORN: London, England.
DIED: Chicago Heights, Illinois, at age 59.

Harry Collis was a talented soccer player in London in his youth. He emigrated to America in late 1889 and became greenkeeper at Indianapolis CC. In 1906 he moved to the Chicago area to work as pro-greenkeeper for Flossmoor CC. While at Flossmoor, Collis remodeled the course into a popular tournament site, developed a turf cutter that was eventually patented and created a strain of bent grass named after the club.

The remodeling at Flossmoor led to other course design jobs, and after World War I Collis worked steadily on a part-time basis planning courses all across the United States. On occasion he collaborated with his friend Jack Daray, professional at nearby Olympia Fields CC. Collis also operated the Flossmoor Turf Nurseries of Chicago, specializing in Flossmoor bent grass.

In 1929 Collis resigned from Flossmoor to pursue his own activities full-time. But the Depression intervened, and he was never able to develop a prosperous business. He struggled through the 1930s to maintain his turf farm and other Chicago-area properties before ultimately losing them to bankers and tax men. Flossmoor CC then rehired Collis as its greenkeeper, but he died in 1937, just after his return to the club.

Courses by Harry Collis:

Arizona: La Palma CC (1919, NLE); Phoenix CC (1919); San Marcos Hotel & C (1922).
Florida: Homosassa CC (NLE).
Illinois: Cherry Hills CC (1932), with Jack Daray; Dundee CC, with *Jack Croke*; Freeport CC; Glenwoodie GC (1923), with Jack Daray; Harlem Hills CC; Indian Wood G&CC; Laramie CC (NLE); Navajo Fields CC (NLE); Normandy CC; Park Forest GC (NLE); Pistakee Hills CC; Richton Park GC.
Indiana: Casa Del Mar CC; Longwood CC.

Iowa: Newton CC (9).
Maryland: Manor CC (1923); U.S. Naval Academy GC (9 1928).
Michigan: Chickaming GC; Walled Lake CC (NLE).
Mississippi: Rainbow Bay GC [FKA Edgewater GC](1930), with Jack Daray.

Courses remodeled or expanded by Harry Collis:

Colorado: Denver CC (R.).
Illinois: Flossmoor CC (R.); Medinah CC (Cse No. 3, R. A.5 1932).
Michigan: Meadowbrook CC (R.6 A.12 1921), with Jack Daray.
Wisconsin: Rhinelander CC (A.9).

HARRY SHAPLAND COLT (1869–1951)

BORN: St. Amands, England.
DIED: St. Amands, England, at age 82.

H. S. Colt studied law at Cambridge University, where he became captain of the golf team. After admission to the bar, Colt practiced for several years as a solicitor in Hastings. But his first love was golf. He was a member of the Royal and Ancient Golf Club of St. Andrews and won the Jubilee Vase on the Old Course in 1891 and 1893. In 1894 he assisted golf professional Douglas Rolland in the design of a new course for Rye GC. He served from 1901 to 1913 as the first club secretary for the newly opened Sunningdale GC.

Colt was a fine golfer all his life. He was a semifinalist in the 1906 British Amateur and played for the English team against the Scottish two years later. His skills and previous design experience led to an invitation to lay out a course near London in the early 1900s. Other contracts soon followed, and Colt ultimately abandoned the practice of law for the practice of course architecture. By World War I he had established himself as one of the world's leading designers.

Colt trained a number of men who later developed into first-rate golf architects themselves, including C. H. Alison (his partner for over twenty years), Alister Mackenzie (a partner for a short time), J. S. F. Morrison (who worked with him during the last 30 years of his life) and John Harris (nephew of Charles Harris, one of his construction supervisors).

Several firsts in golf course design are generally attributed to H. S. Colt. He was the first designer not to have been a professional golfer. He was the first to consis-

H. S. Colt, circa 1900 COLLECTION RON WHITTEN

tently use a drawing board in preparing his course designs. He was the first to prepare tree-planting plans for his layouts.

Colt outlined his philosophy of architecture in *Golf Course Architecture*, which he coauthored with Alison in 1920. He also contributed to *The Book of the Links*, edited by Martin H. F. Sutton (1919), and *Golf Courses: Design, Construction and Upkeep*, also edited by Sutton (1933).

Golf architect Fred W. Hawtree's biography, *Colt & Co.* (1991), describes the life and achievements of Harry Colt, together with his three partners: Alison, Morrison and Mackenzie. It gives a far different picture of Colt than previously revealed. During World War I Colt served as a deputy commissioner for the Ministry of Food and then as a justice of the peace. After the war he, Alison and Mackenzie formed a design partnership, but he apparently was not on good terms with Mackenzie. Although they remained in a partnership until 1928, they did no work together and actually competed for some jobs.

Alison, though he remained loyal to Colt during his entire career, did little work with his mentor either, preferring to travel to the United States, Japan and South Africa to design courses. Alison also laid out several "paper jobs" without visiting sites, a practice Colt did not condone.

Sadly, H. S. Colt outlived most of his family and friends and at the time of his death at age 82 was deaf and lonely. Alison and Morrison lamented how very little attention the golfing world paid to the passing of one of the true geniuses of golf course architecture.

Courses by H. S. Colt (All with C. H. Alison unless otherwise indicated):

Georgia: Sea Island GC (Seaside Nine 1928).
Illinois: Briarwood CC [FKA Briergate CC](1921); Knollwood C (1923); North Shore CC (1924); Old Elm C (1913), with Donald Ross.
Iowa: Davenport CC (1924).
Maryland. Burning Tree C (1924).
Michigan: CC of Detroit (1914 *solo*); Orchard Lake CC (1926).
New Jersey: Canoe Brook CC (North Cse 1924, NLE); Pine Valley GC (routing 1914), with George Crump.
New York: Century GC (1926); Colony CC (1923); Fresh Meadow CC [FKA Lakeville CC](1925); Old Oaks CC (1927); Park CC (1928); Timber Point GC (1927).

Ohio: Kirtland CC (1921); Westwood CC (1924).
Wisconsin: Milwaukee CC (1929).
Manitoba: Pine Ridge G&CC (NLE).
Ontario: Hamilton G&CC (1914 *solo*); Hamilton G&CC (Ladies Cse, 9 1915 *solo*); St. George's G&CC (1920 *solo*, NLE); Toronto GC (1912 *solo*); York Downs CC (1921, NLE).
Belgium: Royal Waterloo GC (27 1923, NLE).
Denmark: Copenhagen GC (1926), and J. S. F. Morrison.
England: Alwoodley GC (1907), with Alister Mackenzie; Beaconsfield GC (1914 *solo*); Betchworth Park (1913 *solo*); Blackmoor GC (13 1914 *solo*, A.5 1924, R. 1930); Brancepeth Castle GC (1924), with Alister Mackenzie; Brockenhurst Manor GC (1920); Calcot Park GC (1930), and J. S. F. Morrison; Camberley Heath GC (1913 *solo*); Canterbury GC (1927); Chadwick Manor GC (1936, NLE), with J. S. F. Morrison; Churston GC (1924); Clyne GC (1921); Cuddington GC (1929), and J. S. F. Morrison; Denham GC (1910 *solo*); Edgbaston GC (1909); Effingham GC (1927), and J. S. F. Morrison; Folkestone GC (*solo*, NLE); Ham Manor GC (1936), with J. S. F. Morrison; Harborne GC (1921 *solo*); Hendon GC (1926); Hopewood GC; Kingsthorpe GC (9 1908, NLE); Ladbroke Park (1910 *solo*); Leamington and County GC (1909); Leckford and Longstock GC (9 1929), and J. S. F. Morrison; Lilleshall Hall GC (1937), with J. S. F. Morrison; Manchester GC (1913 *solo*); Maylands GC (1936), with J. S. F. Morrison; Moor Park GC (High Cse 1911 *solo*; West Cse 1923); Northamptonshire County GC (1909 *solo*); Oxhey GC (1923, NLE); Prenton GC (1905 *solo*); Prestbury GC (1920), and J. S. F. Morrison; Rickmansworth Public GC (1923); Ringway GC (1909 *solo*); Robin Hood GC (1914 *solo*); Rye GC (1894), with *Douglas Rolland*; Sandy Lodge GC (1910), with Harry Vardon; Southport Muni (1932), with J. S. F. Morrison; St. George's Hill GC (36 1913, 9 NLE); Stoke Poges GC (27 1908, 9 NLE); Sunningdale GC (New Cse 1922), and J. S. F. Morrison; Swinley Forest GC (1910 *solo*); Tandridge GC (1925); Trevose G&CC (27 1926), and J. S. F. Morrison; Truro GC (1937), with J. S. F. Morrison; Tyneside GC (1910 *solo*); Ulverston

GC (1910 *solo*); Wentworth GC (East Cse 1924); West Cse 1924).
France: GC de Chantaco (1928), and J. S. F. Morrison; GC de Granville (1922); GC de St. Cloud (Green Cse 1913 *solo*; Yellow Cse 1931, and J. S. F. Morrison); Golf Club de St. Germain (1922); Le Touquet GC (Forest Cse 1908 *solo*; Sea Cse 1930, and J. S. F. Morrison.
Germany: Aachener GC, and J. S. F. Morrison; Falkenstein GC (1930), and J. S. F. Morrison; Frankfurter GC (1928), and J. S. F. Morrison; Hamburger Land und GC (1935), and J. S. F. Morrison.
Ireland: Dun Laoghaire GC (1910).
Netherlands: Eindhoven GC (1930), and J. S. F. Morrison; Haagsche G&CC (1939), and J. S. F. Morrison; Kennemer G&CC (1929), and J. S. F. Morrison; Utrecht CC (1929), and J. S. F. Morrison.
Northern Ireland: Belvoir Park (1927); Cairndhu GC (1929), and J. S. F. Morrison; Royal Belfast GC (1927); Royal Portrush GC (Dunluce Cse 1932).
Scotland: Longniddry GC (1921); St. Andrews (Eden Cse 1913), with Alister Mackenzie.
Spain: Real C de la Puerto de Hierro (Old Cse 1915); Real G de Pedrena (1928), and J. S. F. Morrison.
Sweden: Stockholm GC (1932), and J. S. F. Morrison.
Trinidad and Tobago: St. Andrews GC (1940, NLE), with J. S. F. Morrison.
Wales: Clyne GC (1921); Pyle and Kenfig GC (1922); St. Mellons GC (1937), with J. S. F. Morrison.

Courses remodeled or expanded by H. S. Colt (All with C. H. Alison unless otherwise indicated):

Georgia: Sea Island GC (Plantation Nine, R. 1928).
Illinois: Bob O'Link CC (R. 1924); Highland Park CC (R. 1924).
Maryland: Chevy Chase CC (R. 1924).
Michigan: CC of Detroit (R. 1927); Lochmoor C (R. 1920).
Ohio: Columbus CC (A.4 1923).
Pennsylvania: Baederwood GC (R. 1927).
Quebec: Royal Montreal GC (South Cse, R. 1913).
England: Abercrombie CC (R.); Barton-on-Sea GC (A.9 1893 *solo*); Broadstone GC (R. A.8 1920); Burhill GC (A.9 1913 *solo*); Chelmsford GC (R. 1921); Chesterfield GC (R.9 A.9 1937); Churston GC (R. 1918); Copt

Heath GC (A.9 1912 *solo*); Crow-borough Beacon GC (R.2 1924); Formby GC (R.2 1937); Ganton GC (R.); Handsworth GC (R. 1912 *solo*; R. 1919 *solo*); Hankley Common GC (R. 1922); Hastings & St. Leonards GC (A.9 1908 *solo*, NLE); Hendon GC (R. 1926); Isle of Purbeck GC (Purbeck Cse, A.9 1925); Lansdown GC (R. 1935); Little Aston GC (R. 1925); Mill Hill GC (R. 1931); Moseley GC (R. 1918 *solo*); Nevill GC (R. 1926); New quay GC (R. 1909 *solo*); Northumberland GC (R. 1924); Robin Hood GC (R. 1930); Rowlands Castle GC (R.9 A.9 1922); Royal Liverpool GC (R.1 1912 *solo*; R.5 1920 *solo*); Royal Lytham & St. Annes GC (R.12 1923; R.5 1932; R. 1936, with J. S. F. Morrison); Royal St. Georges GC (R.9 1930); Royal Wimbledon GC (R. 1924); Royal Winchester (R. *solo*); Royal Worlington GC (R.9 1906 *solo*); Sandiway GC (R. 1938); Sandwell Park GC (R. 1925); Southfield GC (R. *solo*); Sunningdale GC (Old Cse, R. 1922); Tyneside GC (R. 1910); Whittington Barracks GC (R. 1923); Woodhall Spa GC (R. 1912 *solo*); Worplesdon GC (R. 1932); Worthing GC (Lower Cse, R. 1923; Upper Cse, R.9 A.9 1923).

France: Cannes GC (R. 1908 *solo*); Golf de Biarritz (R. 1908 *solo*).

Ireland: Castle GC (R. 1918); County Sligo GC (R. 1922); Foxrock GC (R. 1908); Greystones GC (R. 1910); Portmarnock GC (R.3 A.1 1919 *solo*); Rosapenna GC (R. 1916 *solo*; 1932); Royal Dublin GC (R. 1921).

Northern Ireland: Royal Portrush GC (Valley Cse, R. 1933, with J. S. F. Morrison).

Scotland: Muirfield GC (R.11 A.7 1925); Peebles GC (R. 1925).

Wales: Aberdovey GC (R. 1910 *solo*); Bargoed GC (A.9 1921), and J. S. F. Morrison; Borth and Ynslas GC (R. *solo*); Royal Porthcawl GC (R.6 A.8 1913 *solo*); Southerndown GC (R. 1919 *solo*).

JAMES CHRISTOPHER COMMINS (1955–) ASGCA

BORN: Chicago, Illinois.

Chris Commins graduated in 1978 from the University of Florida with a degree in landscape architecture. He practiced landscape architecture in Florida for a short

Chris Commins, 1991 COURTESY CHRIS COMMINS

time and then joined the Jacksonville-based design firm of PGA Tour player Mark McCumber as a senior designer and chief of operations.

WILLIAM CONNELLAN

William Connellan, a former construction foreman for architect Donald Ross, was associated with Wilfrid Reid in the golf design firm of Reid and Connellan during the 1920s and 1930s.

Courses by William Connellan (All with Wilfrid Reid):

Michigan: Bald Mountain GC; Bob O'Link CC; Brae Burn GC; Flushing Valley GC; Harsens Island GC; Indian River GC (9); Indianwood G&CC (Old Cse 1928); Plum Hollow G&CC; Port Huron CC; Tam O'Shanter CC.

Courses remodeled or expanded by William Connellan (All with Wilfrid Reid):

Michigan: Birmingham CC (R. 1928); Black River CC (A.9); Grosse Ile G&CC (R.); Orchard Lake CC (R. 1928).

EDWARD HOLLIS CONNOR III (1942–)

BORN: Fort Benning, Georgia.

After graduating from the University of California at Berkeley in 1964, civil engineer Ed Connor worked for six years for a California engineering firm. As many of his housing development projects included golf, Connor worked with golf architects and contractors and eventually

discovered golf courses to be much more intriguing than streets and sewers. In 1973 he established his own golf course irrigation business in California and later branched into golf course construction. After handling the reconstruction of The Greenbrier in West Virginia for Jack Nicklaus prior to the 1979 Ryder Cup, Connor moved to Florida, where he worked exclusively in course construction.

It was on another Nicklaus reconstruction project, the rebuilding of the famed greens at Pinehurst No. 2 in 1987, that Ed Connor stumbled upon the equipment that would make him unique among golf architects. Faced with the demands of recreating all contours of Pinehurst's storied greens, Connor invested in a laser theodolite, a computer and a computer modeling program. With those items he was able to create accurately computer grids of each green, rebuild each green and restore their contours in precise detail. Before Pinehurst, Connor never gave much thought to golf course restoration, what he termed the "stepchild of the industry." After Pinehurst, he was convinced that he could make a living at it.

Practicing what he termed "stealth architecture" because his efforts would not be detected if he were successful, Connor at first concentrated on rebuilding the subbases of greens to USGA specifications without destroying their previous character. He later began restoring old courses to their original bunkering styles, again using his laser and computer technology. Although he worked with a number of golf architects on projects, he also handled some restorations on his own. "I get along very well with dead architects," he once joked. "I find we have very few disagreements in philosophy."

Connor never attempted to restore a course to its original state, feeling that changes in equipment, techniques, player skills, tree growth and maintenance practices made it impossible to turn back the clock. But he could stop the clock by "archiving" a particular course, recording for posterity the contours of its greens and bunkering. Once on computer, he reasoned, future generations of club members, superintendents and architects would have actual detailed knowledge with which to preserve a course design.

Courses restored by Ed Connor:

California: Pebble Beach G Links (R. 3 1991).

Florida: Pine Tree GC (R. 1 1990); Seminole GC (R. 1991).

North Carolina: Pinehurst CC (No. 2, R. 1987), ass't Jack Nicklaus; Sedgefield CC (R. 1990).

Graham Cooke, 1991 COURTESY GRAHAM COOKE

GRAHAM COOKE
(1949–   )

BORN: Toronto, Ontario, Canada.

While attending Michigan State University, where he received a degree in landscape architecture in 1971, Graham Cooke starred on its golf team and was honored as an all-American in his senior season. After college, he returned to Canada and trained for six years under Quebec golf architect Howard Watson.

Cooke entered private practice in 1974, based in Montreal. He later established satellite offices in Vancouver, Nova Scotia and Italy. Despite his active design business, Cooke maintained his fine competitive game and won over 30 amateur tournaments. He also represented Canada on five separate international golf teams.

In 1989 Stephen C. Miller, a University of British Columbia graduate, joined his firm as an associate.

Courses by Graham Cooke:

British Columbia: Crown Isle GC (1992).
Newfoundland: Pippy Park GC (1992).
Nova Scotia: Bridgewater G&CC (1992).
Quebec: Atlantide GC; C de G Baie Comeau (New Cse 1992); C de G Beattie; C de G Belvedere (1992); C de G St. Césaire; C de G Le Mirage (Nord & Sud Cses 1992); C de G St. François; Dorval Muni (Gentilly & Oakville Cses); Le Blainvillier GC (Le Royal & L'Heritage Cses); Le Ricochet GC (9); Owls Head GC; Parcours du Cerf; Royal Bromont GC.

Ontario: Balmoral GC; Emerald Links GC; Greeley Glen G&CC.
Italy: Santa Croce GC (1992).

Courses remodeled or expanded by Graham Cooke:

Vermont: Champlain GC (R.9 A.9).
Ontario: Lambton G&CC (R.); Mississippi GC (A.9); Pembroke GC (A.9); Petawawa GC (A.9).
Quebec: C de G Des Pins (A.9); Laval-sur-le-Lac GC (A.9 1992); Richelieu Valley GC (Blue & Red Cses, R.); Royal Montreal GC (Blue & Red Cses, R.); Royal Ottawa GC (R.); Royal Quebec GC (Quebec Cse, R.);

WILLIAM ERNEST COORE
(1945–   )

BORN: Richmond, Virginia.

Bill Coore grew up in the Pinehurst area of North Carolina and played for Wake Forest University, which he attended on an academic, not an athletic, scholarship. After graduating in 1968 he decided to pursue a career in golf design, so he worked on construction crews of several Pete Dye projects in the Southeast.

In the mid-1970s Coore helped build Waterwood National GC in Texas (a Roy Dye design) and then worked as assistant to its course superintendent, Gary Grandstaff. When Grandstaff joined Dye on a

Bill Coore (left), with design partner Ben Crenshaw, 1985 RON WHITTEN

Mexican project, Coore took over as superintendent and over the next several years rebuilt and modified most holes at Waterwood. In the early 1980s Bill Coore spent two years designing and building his first solo layout. The result, Rockport (Texas) CC, so impressed popular PGA Tour golfer (and avid course design historian) Ben Crenshaw that he asked Coore to join him in a golf design partnership.

Although they announced their partnership in late 1985, it was not until 1991 that the team produced their first original designs. Their early years were spent handling a few remodeling jobs and planning several designs on select sites that, for a variety of reasons, stopped during one stage of construction or another. Undaunted, Coore and Crenshaw persisted in doing it the old-fashioned way, keeping a team of personally trained graders and shapers on call, designing in the field with very few formal drawings, and emulating the early American "bump-and-roll" designs of Seth Raynor and C. B. Macdonald. At the close of the decade of the eighties, Coore and Crenshaw's work had attracted both admiration and debate.

Courses by Bill Coore (All with Ben Crenshaw unless otherwise indicated):

Hawaii: Kapalua GC (Plantation Cse 1991).
Texas: Barton Creek C (Crenshaw/Coore Cse 1991); Kings Crossing G&CC (1987 *solo*); Rockport CC (1984 *solo*); Waterwood National CC (1980), ass't Roy Dye.
France: Golf du Médoc (1989), with Rod Whitman.

Courses remodeled or expanded by Bill Coore (All with Ben Crenshaw unless otherwise indicated):

Colorado: Denver CC (R. 1986 *solo*).
Kansas: Prairie Dunes CC (R.2 1989).
Oklahoma: Southern Hills CC (A.3rd 9 1992).
Texas: Houston CC (R. 1988); Waterwood National GC (R. 1981 *solo*).

GEOFFREY ST. JOHN CORNISH
(1914–   ), ASGCA, PRESIDENT 1975; BIGCA, HONORARY MEMBER

BORN: Winnipeg, Manitoba, Canada.

Geoffrey S. Cornish received a Bachelor's degree from the University of British

Geoffrey S. Cornish,
1990 COLLECTION
GEOFFREY CORNISH

Columbia and a Master's from the University of Massachusetts, both in agronomy. His interest in golf course architecture developed after his graduation in 1935, when he was hired to evaluate soils for Capilano Golf Club, then under construction by architect Stanley Thompson in West Vancouver. Cornish joined Thompson and trained under him for four years before becoming greenkeeper at St. Charles Country Club in Winnipeg.

During World War II Cornish served with the Canadian Army overseas, then returned to become an associate of Thompson in 1946. This was followed by a five-year association with pioneer turfgrass scientist Lawrence S. Dickinson at the University of Massachusetts. In 1952 Cornish entered private practice as a golf architect.

During his first years as a designer, Cornish was assisted in artwork and drafting by his wife, the former Carol Burr Gawthrop. He soon established himself as a competent designer and in 1964 took on a partner, young Penn State graduate William G. Robinson. Robinson moved to the Pacific Northwest in 1977, and in 1983 Cornish was joined in the business by Brian M. Silva, a graduate landscape architect and agronomist.

By 1980 Geoffrey Cornish had planned more courses in the New England area than any other architect in history. He had also designed or remodeled layouts in many other parts of the United States, Canada and Europe.

Cornish wrote numerous articles on course design and turfgrass as well as two books. The first, *Golf Course Design—An Introduction*, was prepared with Robinson in 1975 and was widely distributed by the National Golf Foundation. The other was *The Golf Course*, coauthored with Ronald E. Whitten and first published in 1981.

In the 1980s and 1990s Cornish and fellow golf architect Robert Muir Graves conducted scores of design seminars across the continent under separate auspices of the Harvard Graduate School of Design, the GCSAA and the PGA.

Numerous awards were bestowed upon Geoffrey Cornish during his career. He received a Distinguished Service Award from the GCSAA in 1981, the Donald Ross Award from the ASGCA in 1982 and an Outstanding Service Award from the National Golf Foundation in 1984. In 1987 he was awarded an honorary doctorate from the University of Massachusetts. In 1991 he received the John Reid Lifetime Achievement Award from the Metropolitan GCSA. He is an honorary member of several golf course superintendents associations as well as the BIGCA.

Courses by Geoffrey S. Cornish (All with William G. Robinson unless otherwise indicated):

Connecticut: Blackledge CC (1966); Cedar Knob CC (1963 *solo*); Century Hills CC (1974); Cliffside CC (1959 *solo*); Clinton CC (1967); [The] Connecticut GC [FKA GC at Aspetuck] (1966); Crestbrook CC (9 1962 *solo*); Ellington Ridge CC (1959 *solo*; R. 1990, with Brian Silva); Farms CC (1961 *solo*); Hop Meadow CC (1961 *solo*); Laurel View Muni (1969); Millbrook C (9 1963 *solo*); Minnechaug GC (9 1959 *solo*); Neipsic Par 3 GC (Par 3 1974, NLE); Oak Lane CC (1961 *solo*); Patton Brook GC (Precision 1967); Pautipaug CC (1960 *solo*); Portland GC (1974); Short Beach GC (9 Par 3 1987), with Brian Silva; Simsbury Farms Muni (1971); South Pine Creek GC (9 Par 3 1968); Sterling Farms Muni (1971); Westwoods CC (Precision 1964).

Maine: Bangor Muni (1963, A.3rd 9 1988, with Brian Silva); Falmouth CC (1988), with Brian Silva; Frye Island GC [FKA Running Hills CC](9 1971); Sable Oaks GC (1989), with Brian Silva.

Maryland: Towson G&CC (1971).

Massachusetts: Allendale CC (1961 *solo*); Bayberry Hills G Cse (1988), with Brian Silva; Blue Rock GC (Par 3 1961 *solo*); Bradford CC (1988), with Brian Silva; Butternut Farm GC (1991), with Brian Silva; Captains GC (1985), with Brian Silva; Chicopee Muni (1964 *solo*); Cranberry Valley CC (1974); Crestview CC (1957 *solo*); Crestwood CC (1959 *solo*); Crystal Springs GC (1960 *solo*); Dunfey's GC (Par 3 1966); Edgewood CC (1963 *solo*); Far Corner Farm GC (1967); Farm Neck GC (9 1976); Foxborough CC (9 1955 *solo*, A.9 1970); Grasmere GC (9 Par 3); Greylock Glen CC (1973); Heritage Hills GC (Par 3 1970); Hickory Ridge CC (1969); Holly Ridge GC (Par 3 1966); Indian Meadow CC (1960 *solo*); Indian Ridge CC (1961 *solo*); International GC (1956 *solo*; R. 1990, with Brian Silva); Iyanough Hills GC (1975); Kingsway GC (Precision 1986), with Brian Silva; Little St. Andrews GC (9 Par 3 1961 *solo*); Middleton GC (Par 3 1965); Midway GC (9 Par 3 1953 *solo*); Nashawtuc CC (1961 *solo*); Oak n' Spruce GC (9 1954 *solo*); Ocean Edge GC (1986), with Brian Silva; Olde Barnstable Fairgrounds GC (1991), with Brian Silva; Pine Oaks GC (9 1966); Poquoy Brook GC (1963 *solo*); Powder Horn GC (Par 3 1964 *solo*); Quashnet Valley CC (9 1976); Rehoboth GC (1966); Sea View Village GC (9 Par 3 1953 *solo*); Shaker Farms CC (1954 *solo*); Shaker Hills GC (1990), with Brian Silva; Spring Valley CC (1960), with Samuel Mitchell; Stow Acres CC (North Cse 1965); Sun Valley GC (1956 *solo*); Swansea GC (1962 *solo*); Thomson C (1963 *solo*); Thunderbird GC (Par 3 1963 *solo*); Trull Brook GC (1962 *solo*); Veterans Memorial GC (1960 *solo*); Wampatuck CC (9 1957 *solo*); White Cliffs GC (9 1961 *solo*, NLE).

New Hampshire: Bretwood GC (1967); Eastman G Links (1975); [The] Links of Amherst (9 Precision 1988), with Brian Silva; Passaconaway GC (1989), with Brian Silva; Perry Hollow GC (9 1989), with Brian Silva; Shattuck Inn GC (1990), with Brian Silva; Sunningdale GC (9 1961 *solo*); White Mountain CC [FNA Cold Spring GC](1976).

New Jersey: Bowling Green GC (1966); Hillman's GC (9 Par 3 1962 *solo*).

New York: Adirondack G&CC (1991), with Brian Silva; Addison Pinnacle CC (9 1969); Colonie CC (1963 *solo*); CC of Ithaca (1958 *solo*); Endwell Greens GC (1965); GC of Newport [FNA Honey Hill CC](1967); Grassy Brook GC (9 1974); Heritage Hills C (East Hills Cse, 9 1974; West Hills Cse 1986 *solo*); Higby Hills CC (1966); Manhattan Woods GC (1991), with M. Kubayashi and Brian Silva; Vesper Hills CC; Vestal Hills CC (1957 *solo*).

Ohio: Darby Creek GC (1992), with

Brian Silva; Firestone CC (West Cse 1989), with Brian Silva; Westfield CC (North Cse 1974); Zoar Village GC (1974).

Pennsylvania: Center Valley C (1992), with Brian Silva; Host Farms GC (Executive Cse [9 Precision] 1967); Mill Race GC (9 1973, A.9 1977); Mountain Laurel GC [FKA Hershey Pocono GC](1970); River Valley CC (9 1962 *solo*); Standing Stone GC (1972); Sugarloaf GC (1966); Wilkes-Barre Muni (1967).

Rhode Island: Alpine CC (1960 *solo*); Cranston CC (1974); Exeter CC (1964 *solo*); Hillsgrove GC (9 Par 3 1954 *solo*); Kirkbrae CC (1961 *solo*); Quidnesset CC (9 1959 *solo*; A.9 1974); Richmond CC (1991), with Brian Silva; Woodland CC (9 1963 *solo*).

Vermont: Farms Resort GC (Par 3 1970); Killington GC (1983, A.3rd 9 1985, with Brian Silva); Manchester CC (1969); Mount Snow GC (1970); Quechee Lakes CC (Highland Cse 1970; Lakeland Cse 1975); Stratton Mountain G Academy (1972); Stratton Mountain GC (1969, A.3rd 9 1984, with Brian Silva).

West Virginia: Canaan Valley State Park GC (1966); Pipestem State Park GC (27 1966); Twin Falls State Park GC (9 1966).

New Brunswick: Campobello Provincial Park GC (9).

Nova Scotia: Halifax G&CC (New Ashburn) (1969).

Ontario: York Downs G&CC (27 1970).

Quebec: Summerlea G&CC (Cascades Cse 1960 *solo*; Dorion Cse 1960 *solo*).

Greece: Links at Porto Carras (1975).

Courses remodeled or expanded by Geoffrey S. Cornish (All with William G. Robinson unless otherwise indicated):

Arizona: Paradise Valley CC (R. 1984), with Gary Panks.

Connecticut: Avon CC (R.18 A.3rd 9 1966); CC of Darien (R.3 1983 *solo*); CC of Fairfield (R.2 1963 *solo*); CC of Farmington (R.1 1960 *solo*); Glastonbury Hills CC (R.4 1973); Hartford GC (R.2 1972); Innis Arden GC (R.3 1983), with Brian Silva; Keney Park GC (R.3); Madison CC (R. 1985), with Brian Silva; New London CC (R.5); Orange Hills GC (A.9 1957 *solo*); Pequabuc CC (A.3); Quinnatisset CC (A.9 1967); Stanley GC (R.27 1975);

Stanwich C (R.3 1985), with Brian Silva; Wampanoag CC (R.5), with Brian Silva; Watertown CC (A.9 1970); Wee Burn CC (R.4 1978); Wethersfield CC (R.1 1978; R. 1983, with Brian Silva); Woodway CC (R.4).

Delaware: Du Pont CC (Du Pont Cse, R. 1980; Louviers Cse, R. 1980; Montchanin Cse, R. 1980; Nemours Cse, R. 1980); Hercules CC (A.4), with Brian Silva.

Florida: CC of Orlando (R.), with Brian Silva.

Georgia: Idle Hour CC (R.2), with Brian Silva.

Maine: Bethel Inn & CC (A.11 1989), with Brian Silva; Biddeford and Saco CC (A.9 1986), with Brian Silva; Bridgton Highlands GC (A.2), with Brian Silva; Brunswick GC (A.9 1964); Green Meadow GC [FKA Meadowhill C](R. A.9 1991), with Brian Silva; Martindale CC (R.), with Brian Silva; Prouts Neck GC (R. 1959 *solo*); Purpoodock C (R.2 1985), with Brian Silva; Samoset GC (R.), with Brian Silva; Riverside Muni (A.3rd 9 1967); Waterville CC (A.9 1966); Webhannett GC (R.4 1970).

Maryland: Baltimore CC (Five Farms Cse, R. 1991), with Brian Silva.

Massachusetts: Bedford AFB GC (R. 1985), with Brian Silva; Berkshire Hills CC (R.4); Blue Hill CC (R. 1985), with Brian Silva; Brae Burn CC (R.2 1970, R., with Brian Silva); Brewster Green GC (A.2 1979, NLE) Cohasset GC (R.), with Brian Silva; [The] Country Club (R.2 1960 *solo*; R.2 1969); Dedham Hunt & Polo C (R.2); Duxbury YC (A.9 1969); Ellinwood CC (A.9 1969); Fall River CC (A.9 1975); Framingham CC (A.2); Franconia Muni (R.7 1973); Fresh Pond Muni (A.9 1967); Hopedale CC (R. *solo*); Juniper Hills GC (A.9 1952 *solo*); Kernwood CC (R.5 1968; R. 1991, with Brian Silva); Longmeadow CC (R. 1990), with Brian Silva; Marlborough CC (A.9 1969); Marshfield CC (R.), with Brian Silva; Meadow Brook GC (R.9 1964 *solo*); Myopia Hunt C (R. 1962 *solo*, R. 1985, with Brian Silva); Needham CC (R.), with Brian Silva; Norton CC (R.9 A.9 1989), with Brian Silva; Oak Hill CC (R.5 1966); Pine Brook CC (R. 1985), with Brian Silva; Quaboag CC (R.2); Ridder's GC (A.9 1963 *solo*); Segregansett CC (A.9 1976); Springfield CC (A.7 1985), with Brian Silva; Stow

Acres CC (South Cse, R.9 A.9 1965); Tatnuck CC (R.5); Wahconah CC (A.9 1959), with Rowland Armacost; Wellesley CC (A.9 1961 *solo*); Weston GC (R.2 1982 *solo*); Wilbraham CC (R.), with Brian Silva; Woodland CC (R. 1964 *solo*); Worcester CC (R.2 *solo*).

Michigan: Crystal Downs CC (R. 1985), with Brian Silva; CC of Detroit (R. 1986), with Brian Silva.

Minnesota: Edina CC (R. 1985), with Brian Silva; Interlachen CC (R. *solo*); Golden Valley CC (R.), with Brian Silva; Minneapolis GC (R. 1985), with Brian Silva; Rochester G&CC (R.2), with Brian Silva; Somerset CC (R. 1979); Wayzata CC (R. 1985), with Brian Silva; Woodhill CC (R. 1979).

Missouri: Algonquin CC (R. 1986), with Brian Silva.

New Hampshire: Abenaqui C (R.); Beaver Meadows Muni (R.9 A.9 1968); Hanover CC (R. 1970); Mt. Pleasant GC (A.9 1990), with Brian Silva; Plausawa Valley CC (A.9 1989), with Brian Silva; Province Lake CC (A.9 1988), with Brian Silva; Wentworth-by-the-Sea GC (A.11 1965).

New Jersey: Brook Lake CC (R. A.5), with Brian Silva; Echo Lake CC (R.3 A.3 1968); Fiddler's Elbow CC (South Cse, A.9 1988), with Brian Silva; Green Brook CC (R.), with Brian Silva; Hollywood GC (R. 1990), with Brian Silva; Howell Park GC (R. 1985), with Brian Silva; Knickerbocker CC (R.6 1973); Navesink CC (R. 1986), with Brian Silva; Packanack GC (A.9 1963 *solo*); Preakness Hills CC (R. 1984), with Brian Silva.

New York: Albany CC (R.2), with Brian Silva; Bedford G&TC (R.9 *solo*); Blind Brook Club (R.), with Brian Silva; CC of Buffalo (R. 1965); Garden City CC (R.), with Brian Silva; Highland Park CC (A.9 1973); Ives Hill CC (A.9 1974); Monroe CC (R.2 1965); Nassau CC (R. 1984), with Brian Silva; Ontario GC (R.), with Brian Silva; Oswego CC (A.9 1977); Powelton C (R.4 1985), with Brian Silva; Rockaway Hunting C (R. 1985), with Brian Silva; St. Lawrence University GC (A.12 1971); Schuyler Meadows C (R. 1985), with Brian Silva; Shepard Hill CC (A.9 1970); Siwanoy CC (R.); Sodus Point GC (R.9 A.9 1966); Thendara CC (R.1 1968); Twin Hills GC (Precision, A.9 1967); Westwood CC (R. 1959); Whippoorwill CC (R.

1984), with Brian Silva; Wildwood GC (R. 1985), with Brian Silva; Wiltwyck CC (R.2), with Brian Silva; Wolferts Roost CC (R.), with Brian Silva; Woodmere C (R.), with Brian Silva.

Ohio: Avon Oaks CC (R.6 1978); Canterbury CC (R. 1978); Columbus CC (R. 1990), with Brian Silva; CC of Hudson (R. 1982 *solo*); Dayton CC (R. 1965); Miami Valley CC (R. 1965); Portage CC (R.); Salem GC (R. 1981 *solo*); Shaker Heights CC (R. 1982 *solo*); Sharon C (R. 1986), with Brian Silva; Tippecanoe CC (R. 1980 *solo*); Westfield CC (South Cse, R. A.11 1967); Worthington Hills CC (R.2 1985), with Brian Silva; Youngstown CC (R. 1984 *solo*).

Pennsylvania: Concordville CC (A.4 1974); CC of Scranton (R. 1983), with Brian Silva.

Rhode Island: Agawam Hunt C (R. 1963 *solo*); Metacomet CC (R.2 1957 *solo*); Point Judith CC (R.9 1964); Rhode Island CC (R. 1960 *solo*); Valley CC [FKA Valley Ledgemont CC](A.9 1963 *solo*); Warwick CC (A.9 1953 *solo*); Woonsocket CC (A.9 1961), with Samuel Mitchell.

Vermont: Basin Harbor C (R. *solo*); Ekwanok CC (R.8 1957 *solo*); Montague GC (R. A.3).

West Virginia: Guyen G&CC (R.), with Brian Silva.

British Columbia: Point Grey G&CC (R. 1973); Quilchena G&CC (R.6 1979).

Manitoba: Breezy Bend CC (R. 1973); Elm Ridge CC (Cse No. 1, R. 1978); St. Charles CC (North 9, R.; West 9, R. 1983).

New Brunswick: Fredericton GC (R.2 1967).

Donald H. Cottle, Jr. (1962–)

BORN: Tifton, Georgia.

Don Cottle studied two years at Abraham Baldwin Agricultural College, then graduated from the University of Georgia with a degree in landscape architecture. He next worked for 15 years in golf course construction, building such Georgia courses as Atlanta Athletic Club and Horseshoe Bend. In the early 1980s Cottle joined the Palmer Course Design Company as a construction foreman and in 1985 formed his own design firm based in tiny Ty Ty, Georgia.

Don Cottle, 1991
COURTESY DON COTTLE

Courses by Don Cottle:

Georgia: Greystone GC (1989); Orchard Hills GC (1990); Waterford GC (1992).

Courses remodeled or expanded by Don Cottle:

Alabama: Eufaula CC (A.9 1991).
Georgia: Douglas G&CC (A.9); Monroe G&CC (R. 1990).

Charles Kenneth Cotton (1887–1974), BIGCA, founding member, president 1974

BORN: Sonning-on-Thames, England.
DIED: Reading, England, at age 86.

C. K. Cotton, a graduate of Cambridge University, took up golf after college and quickly developed into a fine player. He was a scratch golfer for over 30 years.

Cotton worked for nearly 20 years as club secretary at a series of British golf clubs. After World War II he decided to assist in reconstruction of the many war-torn layouts in Britain and the Continent. He soon began planning original designs, too, first on his own and then in partnership for some 10 years with Commander John D. Harris.

Through the years, Cotton started a number of aspiring designers in the business, including J. J. F. Pennink, Charles Lawrie and Donald Steel. Ultimately he headed the firm of Cotton (C. K.), Pennink, Lawrie and Partners Ltd.

Courses by C. K. Cotton:

Denmark: Randers GC (9 1958); St. Knuds GC (1954), with J. J. F. Pennink.

England: Brickendon Grange G&CC (1964), with J. J. F. Pennink; Lamberhurst GC, with J. J. F. Pennink; Lee Park GC (1954), with J. J. F. Pennink; Marsden Park CC (9 1969); Ross on Wye GC (1967), with J. J. F. Pennink; Stressholme GC, with J. J. F. Pennink; Tunbridge Wells GC (9); Wentworth GC (Short Cse, 9 1948), with J. J. F. Pennink.

France: CC du Château de Taulane, with John Harris; Le Coudray GC (1957).

Ireland: Courtown GC, with John Harris.

Italy: Olgiata CC (27 1961), with J. J. F. Pennink.

Wales: St. Pierre G&CC (Old Cse 1962), with J. J. F. Pennink; Tenby GC.

Courses remodeled or expanded by C. K. Cotton:

England: Army GC (R. 1965), with J. J. F. Pennink; Frilford Heath GC (Green Cse, R.9 A.9 1968; Red Cse, R.9 A.9 1968), with J. J. F. Pennink; Ganton GC (R. 1948); Hexham GC (R. 1956), with J. J. F. Pennink; Louth GC (R.), with J. J. F. Pennink; Mendip GC (A.9 1965), with J. J. F. Pennink; Northamptonshire County GC (R.); Royal Lytham & St. Annes GC (R. 1952), with J. J. F. Pennink; Saunton GC (East Cse, R. 1952), with J. J. F. Pennink; Sunningdale GC (Old Cse, R.; New Cse, R.); West Lancashire GC (R.).

Ireland: Athlone GC (R.); Cork GC (R. 1975), with J. J. F. Pennink and C. D. Lawrie.

Italy: Bergamo l'Albenza GC (A.9), with John D. Harris; Lido di Venezia GC (R.9 A.9 1958), with John Harris.

Scotland: Downfield GC (R. 1964).

Singapore: Singapore Island CC (Island Cse, R. 1965), with J. J. F. Pennink.

Switzerland: Patriziale Ascona GC (R.), with John Harris.

C. K. Cotton, circa 1960 COLLECTION RON WHITTEN

Wales: Ashburnham GC (R. A.1 1947); Brynhill GC (R.); Royal Porthcawl GC (R. 1950).

Henry Cotton, 1985
COURTESY *GOLF WORLD*

SIR THOMAS HENRY COTTON (1907–1987), BIGCA, HONORARY MEMBER

BORN: Holmes Chapel, Cheshire, England. DIED: London, England, at age 80.

Henry Cotton was the greatest British golfer of his day. He won three British Opens and half a dozen other national titles. He trained as a golf architect under Sir Guy Campbell, initially providing war-damage appraisals following World War II. He later worked with J. Hamilton Stutt before establishing his own business in the late 1950s. Cotton designed many layouts in Britain and the Continent, working in a variety of terrains ranging from swamps and rice fields to pine forests. His layout at Penina in Portugal, which involved the planting of tens of thousands of trees, was his particular favorite, and he maintained a homesite on the course for years.

He was assisted during the last 20 years of his career by golf course contractor Alec Swan, who built nearly all his courses in Britain and Portugal.

In the course of his sixty-year golfing career, Cotton wrote 10 books and contributed to countless golf journals and newspapers. He claimed never to have counted the number of courses he designed nor tournaments he won, but he could remember each vividly.

Late in his life, Cotton founded the Henry Cotton Golf Foundation, dedicated to constructing low-cost simple golf designs, with little rough, no bunkers and minimal maintenance, to encourage beginners to take up the game and make it affordable to all. The first courses financed by the foundation did not open until after his death.

It was shortly before his death in 1987 that he was granted knighthood by the Queen of England.

Courses by Henry Cotton:

England: Abridge GC (1964); Ampfield Par 3 GC (Par 3 1963); Beamish Park GC (1950), with Sir Guy Campbell; Canons Brook GC (1962); Ely City GC (1961); Farnham Park GC (Par 3 1966); Gosfield Lake GC (27 1986), with Howard Swan; Sene Valley, Folkestone and Hythe GC (1960); Windmill Hill GC (1972).
France: Mont D'Arbois GC (1968).
Italy: Bologna GC (1959); Tirrenia CC (1968).
Madeira Islands: Santo da Serra GC (9).
Portugal: Monte Gordo GC; Penina GC (1964, A.3rd 9 1975); Vale do Lobo GC (1969, A.3rd 9 1975); Quinta da Benamor GC (1987), with Howard Swan.
Scotland: Gourock GC; Moray GC (New Cse 1970); Windyhill GC.
Wales: St. Mellons GC (1937), with H. S. Colt and J. S. F. Morrison.

Courses remodeled or expanded by Henry Cotton:

Channel Islands: La Moye GC (R. 1966).
England: Castle Eden and Peterlee GC (R.); Eaglescliffe GC (R.); Felixstowe Ferry GC (R. 1949), with Sir Guy Campbell; Royal Cinque Ports GC (R. 1946), with Sir Guy Campbell; Temple GC (R.).
France: New GC (A.3rd 9 1965).
Italy: Campo Carlo Magno GC (R.); Lido di Venezia GC (R.).
Scotland: Stirling GC (R.).
Spain: Real C de la Puerto de Hierro (New Cse, R. 1964).

ARCHIBALD CRAIG

"Pete" Craig served as pro-superintendent at Penfield CC in New York until the late 1950s, when he resigned to design and build golf courses on a full-time basis.

Courses by Pete Craig:

Florida: Monastery GC.
New York: Blue Heron Hills CC (1988), with *Richard Bator*; Clifton Springs CC (9 1962); College GC (9); Deerfield CC (27 1966); Francourt Farms GC (1963); Green Hills CC, with *Joseph Demino*; Island Valley GC (1961); Janley Hills GC (9); Northway Heights G&CC; Penfield CC; Salmon Creek CC; Shadow Lake G&RC (27); Sunnycrest CC (27); Thunder Ridge CC (1973), with *Joseph Demino*; Twin Hills GC (1970); Victor Hills GC (9); Whispering Hills GC; Wildwood GC (Precision 1973); Winged Pheasant GC (1963).

Courses remodeled or expanded by Pete Craig:

New York: Ballston Spa & CC (R.9 A.9 1965).

Ben Crenshaw, 1990 RON WHITTEN

BEN DANIEL CRENSHAW (1952–)

BORN: Austin, Texas.

An easygoing manner and smooth putting stroke garnered PGA Tour star Ben Crenshaw the nickname "Gentle Ben." After a spectacular college record, Crenshaw won the very first professional event he entered, the 1973 Texas Open, and a stellar career was predicted for him. But victories were infrequent, with a green jacket at the 1984 Masters his main highlight and losses in the 1975 U.S. Open, the 1978 British Open and 1979 PGA Championship the lowlights.

From an early age, Crenshaw was a student of golf history and golf course architecture. Through the years he accumulated an impressive golf book collection. He also took the time to play and study obscure courses around the globe, sacrificing some of the sidelight income available to Tour players in favor of his architectural education.

Crenshaw's goal was to become a golf architect, and in 1985, after meeting young designer Bill Coore and playing Coore's first solo effort, he formed a golf course design partnership with him.

Courses by Ben Crenshaw (All with Bill Coore unless otherwise indicated):

Hawaii: Kapalua GC (Plantation Cse 1991).

Texas: Barton Creek C (Crenshaw/Coore Cse 1991).

Courses remodeled or expanded by Ben Crenshaw (All with Bill Coore unless otherwise indicated):

Kansas: Prairie Dunes CC (R. 2 1989).
Oklahoma: Southern Hills CC (A.3rd 9 1992).
Texas: Houston CC (R. 1988); Las Colinas Sports C (TPC Cse, R.9 A.9 1987), with Jay Morrish and Byron Nelson.

ARTHUR CAPEL MOLYNEUX CROOME (1866–1930)

BORN: Stroud, Gloucestershire, England.
DIED: Maidenhead, Berkshire, England, at age 64.

Educated at Wellington and Oxford, A. C. M. Croome was one of Britain's great sportsmen, playing cricket, rugby and track at school and golf, curling and billiards later. Following graduation, he accepted a post as schoolmaster, athletic coach and house parent at Radley School, where he remained until 1910. It was during this period that Croome took up golf, and he was soon competing in the British Amateur and other championships.

At the turn of the century, Croome founded the Oxford and Cambridge Golfing Society with his friends John L. Low and R. H. DeMontmorency. The group played exhibition matches on both sides of the Atlantic and numbered C. H. Alison among its early members. "Crumbo," as Croome was called by his friends, served as captain and later president of the society.

Croome supplemented his income at Radley by writing articles on golf for London newspapers, notably the *Evening Standard* and *Morning Post*. Following his retirement from Radley, he turned to journalism full-time, covering cricket for *The Times* of London as well as continuing his golf columns.

While a newspaperman, Croome met and formed a lasting friendship with golf architect J. F. Abercromby. Fascinated by the design aspect of the sport, Croome assisted "Aber" on the design of several British courses and after World War I became a partner in the architectural firm of Fowler, Abercromby, Simpson and Croome. His role was primarily that of business manager and publicist for the company, but he was entirely responsible for the design of at least one course, Liphook GC in the heathlands. The excellence of this course caused it to be considered a design milestone, but Croome was prevented from further participation in course designs by the ill health that plagued the last years of his life.

MARCO CROZE (1940–), ESGCA

BORN: Venice, Italy.

After obtaining a degree in architecture from Venice University in 1965, Marco Croze worked for noted English golf course architect John D. Harris as his Italian representative from 1967 until Harris's death in 1977. He then established a design business of his own and also served as course superintendent at Venice Golf Club and worked in his family's jewelry business. In the 1980s Croze was appointed by the Italian Golf Federation as a consultant on various projects aimed at increasing golf tourism in Italy.

Courses by Marco Croze:

Italy: Adriatic GC; Albarella GC (1975), ass't J. D. Harris; Cà Amata GC (9); Carezza GC (9); Cento GC; Conero GC (27); Folgaria GC (9); Franciacorta GC (27 1992); Frassanelle

Marco Croze, 1991
COURTESY MARCO CROZE

GC; GC Castel d'Aviano (9); GC Colli Berici; GC des Iles Borromees; GC Lignano; GC Matilde di Canossa; Golf La Margherita; La Rocca GC; La Vecchia Pievaccia GC; Le Chiocciole GC; Le Fronde GC (1974), ass't J. D. Harris; Le Rovendine GC (9); Mediolanum GC; Monte S. Pietro GC; Nettuno GC; Porto d'Orra GC; Prà delle Torri GC (9); Riva dei Tessali GC (1972); Udine GC (9), ass't John D. Harris; Versilia GC.

Courses remodeled or expanded by Marco Croze:

Italy: Bergamo l'Albenza GC (A.9), ass't John D. Harris; Croara GC (A.9 1987); La Mandria GC (A.9 1966), ass't John D. Harris; Villa Condulmer (A.9).

George Crump, 1914 COLLECTION RON WHITTEN

GEORGE ARTHUR CRUMP (1871–1918)

BORN: Philadelphia, Pennsylvania.
DIED: Merchantville, New Jersey, at age 46.
INTERRED: Philadelphia.

George Crump, the wealthy owner of the Hotel Colonnades in Philadelphia, was an avid hunter and fisherman. He was also an accomplished golfer and finished as runner-up in the 1912 Philadelphia Amateur. He was among the founders of Philadelphia CC before the turn of the century and played most of his golf there. But he harbored a dream of building his own golf course in the sand hills of New Jersey and in 1912 convinced a syndicate of friends to invest in the project.

Crump sold his hotel, purchased 184 acres of sandhills near Clementon, New Jersey, and moved to the site to create his dream. His Pine Valley GC became one of the world's toughest courses and certainly the most ferociously penal golf course of its time. Crump spent the last six years of his life and over a quarter million of his own dollars developing it. Many professional golf architects examined the work in progress, but only Britisher H. S. Colt, who had assisted Crump in the original routing, was allowed to make recommendations. Colt, impressed by Crump's carefully planned holes, suggested few modifications.

George Crump died suddenly in January 1918. Fourteen holes at Pine Valley were completed at the time, but numbers 12 through 15 had only been roughed out. It took time to raise the necessary funds and four more years to complete construction, but under the guidance of Hugh Wilson, aided by his brother Alan and British architect C. H. Alison (H. S. Colt's partner), the full 18 holes of Pine Valley finally opened in 1922.

George Crump's creation has long been considered a landmark in course architecture, today admired more for the strategic nature of its holes than for its ferocity. Pine Valley is generally acknowledged to be among the world's finest. From 1985 through 1991, it was ranked the top course in both the country and the world in separate periodic polls conducted by *Golf Digest* and *Golf*.

GEORGE CUMMING
(1878–1949)

BORN: Bridge of Weir, Scotland.
DIED: Toronto, Ontario, Canada, at age 71.

George Cumming emigrated to Canada as a young man and soon landed a position as club professional at Toronto GC. It was a job he would retain the rest of his life.

A fine golfer, Cumming won the 1905 Canadian Open and was a runner-up in the event four times. Generally regarded as the dean of Canadian golf professionals, Cumming helped found the Canadian PGA and served as its president on five occasions.

Aside from his teaching and clubmaking duties, Cumming found time to design dozens of golf courses throughout Canada.

Courses by George Cumming:

Ontario: Brantford G&CC (1920), with *Nicol Thompson*; Mississauga G&CC, Port Credit (1906), with *Percy Barrett*;

Sarnia GC (9 1915); Windemere House GC (9 1920).
Quebec: Green Valley GC.

ROBERT ERHARD CUPP
(1939–), ASGCA

BORN: Lewistown, Pennsylvania.

After graduating in 1961 from the University of Miami with a degree in art, Bob Cupp served in the military. During that stint, he obtained a Master's in fine arts from the University of Alaska. After discharge, Cupp returned to Florida, worked for a short time in advertising, then took a job as a pro shop manager at a daily-fee operation near Miami. He soon found himself assisting the rebuilding of portions of the golf course. When other clubs in the area requested his services, Cupp returned to school and obtained an associate degree in agronomy from Broward Community College. In 1968 he received his first contract as a course architect—the revision of one nine and addition of a second nine to the Homestead Air Force Base golf course.

In the next four years Cupp designed and constructed several South Florida courses. In 1973 a friend introduced him to Jack Nicklaus, who was at the time forming his own design firm. Cupp accepted Nicklaus's offer to work as a senior designer in the firm. Cupp worked on all Nicklaus projects in the East and in Europe for over a decade. During the same time, Cupp and another Nicklaus employee, Jay Morrish, collaborated on other designs under the corporate name Golforce, Inc.

In 1985 Bob Cupp left the Nicklaus organization and established his own design firm in South Florida. A few years later he moved his headquarters to Atlanta and opened a West Coast office in Portland.

Perhaps because of his long association with Nicklaus, Cupp felt comfortable working with a variety of PGA Tour pros on design jobs. He designed a series of highly regarded courses with 1976 Open champion Jerry Pate. He also used former Open champions Hubert Green and Fuzzy Zoeller and all-time leading money winner Tom Kite as consultants. Former U.S. Amateur champion John Fought so impressed Cupp with his talent that Cupp put him in charge of his Oregon office. Also on his team was design associate Mike Riley, a

Bob Cupp, 1990
COURTESY BOB CUPP

Clemson graduate, and former Augusta National superintendent Billy Fuller as the design firm's full-time agronomist.

Courses by Bob Cupp:

Alabama: Greystone GC (1992), with *Hubert Green*; Shoal Creek (1977), ass't Jack Nicklaus.
Arizona: Desert Highlands GC (1984), ass't Jack Nicklaus; La Paloma GC (27 1985), ass't Jack Nicklaus; Tatum Ranch GC (1987); TPC at StarPass (1986).
California: Bear Creek GC (1982), ass't Jack Nicklaus; [The] C at Morningside (1983), ass't Jack Nicklaus; Spanish Hills G&CC (1992).
Colorado: Breckenridge GC (1987), ass't Jack Nicklaus; Castle Pines GC (1981), ass't Jack Nicklaus; CC of Castle Pines (1986), ass't Jack Nicklaus; CC of the Rockies (1984), ass't Jack Nicklaus; Meridian GC (1984), ass't Jack Nicklaus; Singletree GC (1981), with Jay Morrish.
Florida: Bear Lakes CC (Lakes Cse 1985), ass't Jack Nicklaus; Bear's Paw CC (1980), ass't Jack Nicklaus; Boca Pointe CC (1982), with Jay Morrish; Cheeca Lodge GC (9 Par 3 1981), with Jay Morrish; Costa Del Sol G&RC (1971); Crooked Creek G&CC; Emerald Bay G&CC (1992); Frenchman's Creek (North and South Cses 1982), with *Gardner Dickinson*; Grand Cypress GC (East & West 9s, 1984; A.3 Golf Academy, 1985; A. North 9 1986), ass't Jack Nicklaus; [The] Grasslands G&CC (1991), with Jerry Pate; Hidden Valley GC (Precision 1972); Loxahatchee C (1985), ass't Jack Nicklaus; Mayacoo Lakes GC (1973), ass't Jack Nicklaus and Desmond Muirhead; Sailfish Point CC (1981), ass't Jack Nicklaus; Walden Lake Polo & CC (1978), with Jay Morrish.
Georgia: Jennings Mill CC (1987); Mar-

ietta CC (1990); Port Armor C (1986); Reynolds Plantation GC (1988), with *Fuzzy Zoeller* and *Hubert Green*; Settindown Creek GC (1988).

Kentucky: Valhalla GC (1987), ass't Jack Nicklaus.

Louisiana: CC of Louisiana (1986), ass't Jack Nicklaus.

Michigan: Grand Traverse GC (The Bear Cse 1985), ass't Jack Nicklaus; Indianwood G&CC (New Cse 1988), with Jerry Pate.

Mississippi: Annandale GC (1981), ass't Jack Nicklaus; Old Waverly GC (1988), with Jerry Pate.

North Carolina: Elk River GC (1984), ass't Jack Nicklaus; Horseshoe GC (1986); Laurel Ridge CC (1986).

Ohio: CC at Muirfield Village (1982), ass't Jack Nicklaus; Muirfield Village GC (1974), ass't Jack Nicklaus and Desmond Muirhead.

Oregon: Pumpkin Ridge GC (Ghost Creek Cse 1992; Witch Hollow Cse 1992).

South Carolina: Palmetto Hall Plantation GC (Bob Cupp Cse 1992); Melrose GC (1988), ass't Jack Nicklaus; Turtle Point G Links (1981), ass't Jack Nicklaus; Woodside Plantation GC (Plantation Cse 1990; Short Cse [9 Par 3] 1990).

Tennessee: Council Fire GC (1991); [The] Legends C of Tennessee (1992), with *Tom Kite*.

Texas: [The] Hills of Lakeway GC (1980; A.3 Golf Academy 1985), ass't Jack Nicklaus; Lochinvar GC (1980), ass't Jack Nicklaus.

Utah: Park Meadows GC (1983), ass't Jack Nicklaus.

Ontario: Beacon Hall GC (1988); Deerhurst Highlands GC (1990), with Tom McBroom; Glen Abbey GC (1976), ass't Jack Nicklaus; Mad River G&CC (1991).

Cayman Islands: Britannia GC (9 Cayman/18 Precision 1985), ass't Jack Nicklaus.

England: East Sussex National GC (East Cse 1989; West Cse 1990); St. Mellion G&CC (New Cse 1984), ass't Jack Nicklaus.

Japan: New St. Andrews GC (1976), ass't Jack Nicklaus and Desmond Muirhead.

Spain: La Moraleja GC (1975), ass't Jack Nicklaus and Desmond Muirhead.

Courses remodeled or expanded by Bob Cupp:

Connecticut: Farmington CC (R. 1988);

GC of Avon (R. 1989).

Florida: Crooked Creek G&CC (R. 1970); Falcon Fairways GC (R.9 A.9 1969); Feather Sound CC (R. 1990); Frenchman's Creek GC (North Cse, R. 1983; South Cse, R. 1983), with Jay Morrish; Lost Tree C (R. 1980), with Jay Morrish.

Georgia: Atlanta CC (R. 1980, with Jay Morrish; R. 1990); Augusta CC (R. 1983); Augusta National GC (R. 1982, with Jay Morrish; R. 1984, ass't Jack Nicklaus); Capital City C (R. 1990).

Illinois: Bryn Mawr GC (R. 1982), with Jay Morrish; Evanston GC (R. 1982).

Maryland: Baltimore CC (West Cse, R. 1990), with *Tom Kite*; Swan Point Y&CC (R. 1990); Woodmont CC (R. 1988).

Massachusetts: Weston GC (R. 1986).

Michigan: Grand Traverse Resort GC (Resort Cse, R. 1983); Indianwood G&CC (Old Cse, R. 1988), with Jerry Pate.

Nevada: Royal Kenfield GC (R. 1992), with *Hubert Green*.

New York: Brooklea CC (R. 1984); St. Andrews GC (R. 1985), ass't Jack Nicklaus; Wanakah CC (R. 1983), with Jay Morrish.

Ohio: Scioto CC (R. 1983).

Oregon: Tualatin CC (R. 1990).

Tennessee: Colonial CC (South Cse, R. 1984).

Texas: Colonial CC (R. 1982), with Jay Morrish; Preston Trail GC (R. 1982), with Jay Morrish.

West Virginia: [The] Greenbrier (Greenbrier Cse, R. 1978), ass't Jack Nicklaus.

Australia: Australian GC (R. 1977), ass't Jack Nicklaus.

Japan: Kiokawa GC (East Cse, R. 1983; West Cse, R. 1985), with Jay Morrish.

Ontario: Rosedale GC (R. 1988); Summit GC (R.).

BRIAN CURLEY

BORN: Pebble Beach, California.

Growing up at Pebble Beach, Brian Curley was certain to pursue a career involving golf. Brian Curley graduated in 1982 from California Polytechnic State University of San Luis Obispo with a Bachelor of Science degree in planning from Cal Poly's School of Environmental Design. After college he went to work for

Brian Curley, 1991

golf architect Ronald Fream and in 1984 joined the Palm Springs–based Landmark Land Company. At Landmark he assisted Pete Dye and Lee Schmidt in the design and construction of several courses. In 1991, when Schmidt resigned to join the Nicklaus organization, Curley was named director of golf course design and construction for Landmark.

Courses by Brian Curley: (All as assistant to Pete Dye unless otherwise indicated):

California: La Quinta Hotel GC (Citrus Cse 1987); Mission Hills G&CC (Dinah Shore Cse 1988); Mission Hills Resort GC (1987); Moreno Valley Ranch (27 1988); Mount Woodson GC (1991), with Lee Schmidt; Oak Valley GC (1990), with Lee Schmidt; PGA West GC (Stadium Cse 1986).

Louisiana: Oak Harbor Y&CC (1991), ass't Lee Schmidt.

South Carolina: [The] Ocean Cse (1991).

GEORGE C. CURTIS

After decades as head professional and course superintendent at various Tennessee country clubs, George Curtis took up golf architecture in 1960. For over ten years Curtis divided his time between laying out courses throughout the Southeast and running a cattle ranch in Jackson, Tennessee.

Courses by George Curtis:

Louisiana: Pine Hills GC (1974).

Mississippi: Fernwood CC (1969); Liveoaks CC; Pine Hills CC (1969); Rolling Hills CC.

Tennessee: Houston Levee CC (1971); Milan G&CC (9 1960); Weakley County CC (9 1966).

DAVID M. DALE
(1962–)

BORN: Missoula, Montana.

While a student at Washington State University, David Dale received an ASLA honor award for excellence in the study of landscape architecture. In 1988, after graduating with honors in landscape architecture, Dale joined the California-based firm of Ronald Fream and found himself handling many of Fream's far-flung projects. In 1990, Dale was made a senior architect in the firm.

Courses by David Dale (All as assistant to Ronald Fream):

Finland: Kerigolf (1990); Midnight Sun G Center (1991); Oulu Golfkerho (1992).
France: Set C (9 1990).
Guam: Guam International CC (1992).
Japan: La Rainbow CC (1991); Palm Hills GC (1991).
Taiwan: Orient G&CC (1992).
Thailand: Panya Hill GC (1992); Panya Park CC (1992).
Tunisia: Hammamet II CC (1992).

Courses remodeled or expanded by David Dale (All as assistant to Ronald Fream):

California: Mesa Verdê CC (R. 4 1991).
France: St. Nom la Brêteche (Blue Cse, R. 6 1991).

David Dale, 1991
COURTESY DAVID DALE

JAMES DALGLEISH
(1865–1935)

BORN: Berkshire, England.
DIED: Kansas City, Missouri, at age 70.

James Dalgleish was one of many young British golfers who moved to America in the late 1890s. The son of a forester, Dalgleish knew a bit about both landscaping and clubmaking, and soon after arriv-

James Dalgleish, circa 1925
COLLECTION RON WHITTEN

ing he landed a job managing the golf department for the A. G. Spalding & Bros. Sporting Goods Store in New York City, where he remained for five years. After brief stints at Shinnecock Hills in New York and Hyde Manor in Vermont, Dalgleish moved to Kansas City, Missouri, where he designed and built Evanston GC and remained as its pro-greenkeeper. When the club opted to move up a hill to new property, Dalgleish again constructed the new course, but this time to the design of Donald Ross. When completed, Dalgleish remained as pro-greenkeeper to the club, renamed Hillcrest, for a short time. In 1922 he resigned to operate a series of clubs that he both designed, constructed and owned.

Dalgleish became the dean of golf professionals in the Kansas City area and in 1927 was a charter member of the organization now known as the GCSAA. He laid out a number of courses across the Midwest, but much of his work, done in the early days of American golf development, was later replaced or abandoned.

Dalgleish was very much an innovator. He built an early precision course consisting of par 3s and 4s specifically to speed play. He created several "vest pocket" courses, miniature layouts in five acres or less. In 1928, Dalgleish installed lights on one of his public courses, Eastwood Hills, making it one of the first night-lighted courses in the country. In 1930 a Midnight Open tournament was held on the course to formally open it. Famous Kansas City golfer Jug McSpaden won the event.

Courses by James Dalgleish:

Kansas: Bellevue CC (9); Homestead CC (NLE); Macdonald Park Muni (1911); Victory Hills CC (1927); Winfield CC (9).

Minnesota: Madden Inn & GC (East Cse 1926); Ruttger's Bay Lake GC (9 1920).
Missouri: Blue River G Cse (1906); Bruce Dodson Estate GC (9 1919, NLE); Chevy Chase CC (1931, NLE); Crane Athletic C (9 1923, NLE); Eastwood Hills G Cse (1930, NLE); Evanston GC (1906, NLE); Frank Seested Private Cse (9, NLE); Log Cabin GC (1924, NLE); St. Andrew GC (1925, NLE); Santa Fe Hills GC [FKA Ivanhoe CC](Precision 1922, NLE); South Ridge GC [FKA Automobile C](1921, NLE); Swope Park GC (1917).
Nebraska: Valley View GC (1926, NLE).

Jack Daray, circa 1930 COURTESY JACK DARAY, JR.

JACK L. DARAY, SR.
(1881–1958), ASGCA, CHARTER MEMBER

BORN: Louisiana.
DIED: Coronado, California, at age 76.

Jack Daray turned professional in 1901 and served briefly as club pro at Highland CC in Grand Rapids, Michigan, and then at Olympia Fields CC near Chicago for many years. For fifteen years he also worked winters as teaching pro at the Biloxi Golf Club on the Mississippi Gulf Coast. Among Daray's students were then Princeton University president Woodrow Wilson (later President of the United States) and baseball great Ty Cobb.

Daray was one of a number of Chicago professionals who designed courses on the side during the 1920s. He kept active in the thirties and resumed his design work after World War II. Although ill health necessitated his move to Southern California in the early 1950s, he was still designing courses at the time of his death. Daray was a charter member of the PGA of America in 1916 and a charter member of the ASGCA in 1948.

Courses by Jack Daray:

Alabama: Old Spanish Fort CC.

California: Castle Creek CC [FKA Circle R Golf Ranch CC](1956); CBC Port Hueneme GC (9 1958); Coronado GC (1957); Navy GC, Mission Gorge (North Cse 1956); Sail Ho GC (9 Par 3 1957); Sea 'n Air GC (Precision 1959, NLE).

Illinois: Cherry Hills CC (1932), with Harry Collis; Glenwoodie GC (1923), with Harry Collis; Mellody Farm CC (1928, NLE), with George O'Neil and *Jack Croke;* White Pines CC (East Cse 1930; West Cse 1930).

Louisiana: Metairie CC (1925); Tchefuncta GC (1925).

Michigan: Big Rapids CC (1921); Cascade Hills CC (1927); Hastings CC (9 1922); Hy Pointe CC (1928).

Mississippi: Gulf Hills GC (1922); Greenville CC (1950): Oak Shore CC (NLE); Pine Hills GC (NLE); Rainbow Bay GC [FKA Edgewater GC](1930), with Harry Collis.

Courses remodeled or expanded by Jack Daray:

Alabama: Don Hawkins Muni [FKA Roebuck CC](R.9 A.9 1923).

Illinois: Olympia Fields CC (North Cse, R. 1946; South Cse, R. 1946).

Michigan: Meadowbrook CC (A.12 R.6 1921), with Harry Collis.

Mississippi: Biloxi CC.

JACK L. DARAY, JR.
(1919–   )

BORN: Grand Rapids, Michigan.

The elder son of golf architect Jack Daray, Jack Daray, Jr., followed his father into the profession only as a second career. Young Daray attended Tulane University in New Orleans, graduated with an M.B.A. and then enlisted in the navy, where he became a commissioned officer just before the outbreak of World War II.

After 26 years of service, Daray retired in 1966 as a naval captain to manage his family's golf course interests in the Chicago area. After directing resort and golf course development for the Chicago-

Jack Daray, Jr. (right), with design partner Stephen Halsey, 1990
COURTESY JACK DARAY, JR.

based Branigar Organization, Daray moved to San Diego and began consulting on golf developments. His first design jobs were remodeling his father's original works and courses for the U.S. Navy. In 1978 Daray teamed with landscape architect Stephen Halsey and formed Halsey Daray Golf, Inc. Starting with a new Sea 'n Air GC along the Pacific, Daray and his young partner developed an active practice in the 1980s and 1990s.

Courses by Jack Daray, Jr. (All in association with Stephen Halsey unless otherwise indicated):

California: [The] Alisal Ranch G Cse (1992); Eagle Crest CC (1990); Golden Era GC (9 1989); Golden Hills Muni (9 Precision 1992); Miramar Memorial GC (1964), with *Kenneth Welton;* Modesto Creekside G Cse (1992); Navy G Cse, Mission Gorge (South Cse 1984); Sea 'n Air GC (1981); Willowbrook CC (9 1985).

Montana: Pryor Creek GC.

Virginia: Cheatham GC (9).

Courses remodeled or expanded by Jack Daray, Jr. (All in association with Stephen Halsey unless otherwise indicated):

California: [The] Alisal GC (R. 1991); Balboa Park GC (R. 1992); Carmel Highland CC (R. A.3 1987); Castle Creek CC (R. 1983); CBC Port Hueneme GC (R.9 A.9); Chula Vista Muni (R. *solo*); Coronado GC (R.9 A.9 1966, ass't William F. Bell, R. 1991); Dryden Park Muni (R. 1991); Navy

GC (North Cse, R. 1984); Rancho Bernardo GC (R. 1991); Salinas CC (R. 1991); Torrey Pines Muni (North & South Cses, R. 1988); Village CC (R. 1989).

JOHN R. DARRAH
(1903–1971), ASGCA

BORN: Chicago, Illinois.
DIED: Matteson, Illinois, at age 68.

John Darrah received a degree in engineering from Crane College in Chicago, worked as an engineer for a coal firm in Wyoming and then returned to Illinois to work for the Union Fuel Company. He resigned in 1931 due to ill health. After his recovery he took a position as greenkeeper at Beverly CC near Chicago, where he remained until 1947. He then moved to Olympia Fields CC and restored the two remaining courses after the complex had been nearly abandoned during the war.

John Darrah, 1967
COURTESY LARRY PACKARD

In 1949 Darrah left Olympia Fields to form a golf course construction business. After rebuilding and renovating many Chicago-area courses, he began designing as well as building. In the 1960s he planned several dozen courses in the Midwest.

Courses by John Darrah:

Illinois: Arispie Lake CC (9 1968); Morris CC (1970); Wyaton Hills GC (9 1968).

Indiana: Arrowbrook CC.

Kentucky: Hopkinsville G&CC (1971); London GC (1969).

Courses remodeled or expanded by John Darrah:

Illinois: Kankakee CC (R.8 A.10 1963).

Indiana: Valparaiso CC (R.9 A.9 1962); Youche CC (R.9 A.9 1963).

Mississippi: Back Acres CC (R.9 A.9 1967).

Mike Dasher, 1991
COURTESY MIKE DASHER

ROBERT MICHAEL DASHER
(1951–   ), ASGCA

BORN: Atlanta, Georgia.

Mike Dasher attended Georgia Tech University, receiving a Bachelor's degree in civil engineering in 1973 and a Master's in civil engineering in 1980. From 1973 to 1979 Dasher was employed as a project superintendent for The Wadsworth Company, one of the largest golf course contractors in the United States. In 1980 he joined the golf design firm of Arthur Hills and Associates, running the Orlando, Florida, branch. Dasher was a leading character in John Strawn's *Driving the Green*, published in 1991.

Courses by Mike Dasher (All as assistant to Arthur Hills):

Florida: Bonita Bay C (Creekside Cse 1991; Marsh Cse 1985); Coral Oaks G Cse (1988); Cross Creek CC (Precision 1985); Foxfire CC (1985); Gator Trace GC (1986); Ironhorse G&CC (1987); Tampa Palms CC (1987); TPC at Eagle Trace (1984); Vista Plantation GC (Precision 1985); Willoughby GC (1989).

Georgia: GC of Georgia (Creekside Cse 1992; Lakeside Cse 1991); [The] Landings at Skidaway Island (Palmetto Cse 1985; Oakridge Cse 1988); [The] Standard C (1986).

Louisiana: Southern Trace CC (1986).

Michigan: Oak Pointe GC (Honors Cse, 9 1987).

South Carolina: Palmetto Dunes CC (Hills Cse 1986).

Courses remodeled or expanded by Mike Dasher (All as assistant to Arthur Hills):

Florida: Vista Royale GC (A.9 1981).

Georgia: Capital City C (R. 1985); Druid Hills CC (R. 1985).

Kentucky: Highland CC (A.9 1985); Summit Hills CC (R. 1985).

Michigan: Orchard Lake CC (R. 1984).

Ohio: Fremont CC (R. 1985); Terrace Park CC (R. 1984).

ARTHUR L. DAVIS
(1939–   ), ASGCA

BORN: Georgia.

Arthur Davis attended Abraham Baldwin College in Tifton, Georgia, where he worked part-time for Southern Turf Nurseries, which specialized in newly developed hybrid Bermuda grasses. In the course of his work, Davis met golf architects Robert Trent Jones, George Cobb, Dick Wilson, William Mitchell, Alfred Tull and others. The experience convinced him to change his major from agronomy to landscape architecture, and he received a Bachelor's degree in landscape architecture from the University of Georgia in 1963.

Following graduation, Davis was employed with the firm of Willard C. Byrd and Associates until 1967, when he established his own practice in Atlanta. In 1970 he formed a partnership with Ron Kirby, and soon thereafter the pair negotiated to include professional golfer Gary Player in their firm. Davis, Kirby and Player, Inc., existed for three years. Davis then sold his interest to Kirby and established his own course design business based in Rome,

Arthur Davis, 1990
COURTESY ARTHUR DAVIS

Georgia. He later moved his headquarters to nearby Gainesville and his son Lee joined him in the business.

Courses by Arthur Davis:

Alabama: Heatherwood GC (1986).

Florida: Summertree GC (9 1983).

Georgia: Arrowhead CC (9 1968); Berkeley Hills CC (1971), with Ron Kirby and Gary Player; Cross Creek CC (1967); Fields Ferry GC (1992); Green Acres GC (9 1969); Pebble Brook CC (9 1970), with Ron Kirby; Pine Isle CC (1972), with Ron Kirby; Pines GC (1968); River North G&CC (1973), with Ron Kirby and Gary Player; Royal Lakes G&CC (1990); Royal Oaks GC (9 1971), with Ron Kirby and Gary Player; Twin Creek CC (1970).

Illinois: Holiday Inn GC (9 1970), with Ron Kirby.

Maryland: Swan Point Y&CC (9 1985, A.9 1988).

South Carolina: Dolphin Head GC (1973), with Ron Kirby and Gary Player; Fort Jackson GC (New Cse 1992).

Tennessee: Bent Creek G Resort [FKA Cobbly Nob G Links], Gatlinburg (1972), with Ron Kirby and Gary Player; Centennial CC (1977); Concord GC (1977).

Ivory Coast: Riviera Africaine GC (9 1972), with Ron Kirby and Gary Player.

Japan: Odawara CC (1973), with Ron Kirby and Gary Player.

Puerto Rico: Palmas del Mar GC (1973), with Ron Kirby and Gary Player.

Spain: El Paraiso GC (1974), with Ron Kirby and Gary Player.

Courses remodeled or expanded by Arthur Davis:

Alabama: Arrowhead GC (R.9 A.9 1990); Tuscaloosa CC (R. 1986).

Georgia: Cartersville CC (R.9 A.9 1972), with Ron Kirby and Gary Player; Coosa CC (R. 1979); Evan Heights GC (R.9 1977); Green Island CC (R. 1989); Little Mountain CC (R. 1970), with Ron Kirby; Sandy Run GC (R. 1970), with Ron Kirby; [The] Standard C (R.1 A.1 1971, NLE), with Ron Kirby and Gary Player; Warner Robbins AFB GC (R. 1970), with Ron Kirby.

New Mexico: Alto Lakes G&CC (A.9 1973), with Ron Kirby and Gary Player.

Tennessee: Chattanooga G&CC (R.4 1975); Lawrenceburg CC (R.4 A.9 1967); Montclair CC (R.9 A.9); Paris Landing State Park GC (R.18); Stones River CC (R.9 1977).

Texas: Royal Oaks CC (R. 1982); Stevens Park GC (R. 1983); Tenison Muni (East Cse, R. 1983; West Cse, R. 1983).

William F. Davis, circa 1900
COLLECTION RON WHITTEN

WILLIAM F. DAVIS
(1863–1902)

BORN: Scotland.
DIED: New York at age 39.

When William Davis left Hoylake, England, to take up duties as pro-greenkeeper at Royal Montreal Golf Club in 1881, he became the first golf professional to travel to America. His stay was short-lived, however, and he was unceremoniously fired the following year. He returned to Britain, presumably to another club professional job. Strangely enough, in 1889 he returned to Canada to the very same club, Royal Montreal. This time, he lasted five years, making clubs and balls, giving lessons and on the side laying out a couple of Canada's earliest courses.

In 1894 he was lured to the United States to become golf professional at the newly formed Newport Country Club in Rhode Island. He built the club a nine-hole members' course and a six-hole beginners' course, both replete with rambling stone walls, artificial mounds and deep pot bunkers. While at Newport, Davis laid out several other courses in the New England and New York area, the most notable being the original 12-hole course at Shinnecock Hills, historically credited to Willie Dunn. In 1896 he moved to Apawamis Club in New York, expanded its course and took over its clubmaking and teaching duties, while serving as professional until his death in 1902.

Courses by William F. Davis:

New York: Shinnecock Hills GC (White Cse, 12 1895, NLE).
Rhode Island: Newport CC (9 1894); Newport CC (beginners' cse, 6 1894, NLE); Point Judith CC (9 1894).
Ontario: Ottawa GC (1891, NLE).

Courses remodeled or expanded by William F. Davis:

New York: Apawamis C (A.9).

EDWARD B. DEARIE, JR.
(1888–1952)

BORN: Philadelphia, Pennsylvania.
DIED: Evanston, Illinois, at age 64.

Ed Dearie was a noted authority on golf course construction and maintenance. He began his career as greenkeeper at Wanango CC in Reno, Pennsylvania, and later spent several years building courses for golf architect Donald Ross in Pennsylvania and Illinois.

In 1921 Dearie settled at Ridgemoor CC in Chicago. Ten years later he moved to Oak Park CC, where he served as course superintendent until his retirement in 1951. During the 1920s and '30s he built a dozen new courses and remodeled an equal number in the Greater Chicago area.

Dearie was a charter member of both the GCSAA and the Midwest Association of Greenkeepers. He wrote extensively on the construction and upkeep of golf courses for national periodicals in the 1920s and '30s.

Courses by Edward B. Dearie, Jr:

Illinois: Big Oaks CC; Fort Sheridan GC (9 Par 3); Lincoln Park Muni; Rob Roy

Edward B. Dearie, Jr., 1928 COLLECTION RON WHITTEN

GC; Sportsman G&CC; St. Andrews G&CC (Cse No. 1 1928; Cse No. 2 1929).

Courses remodeled or expanded by Edward B. Dearie, Jr:

California: Virginia CC (R. 1927).
Illinois: La Grange CC (R. 1926); Oak Park CC (R. 1936); Ridgemoor CC (R. 1933); Waveland GC (R.9 1932).

Jimmy Demaret, circa 1960 COURTESY *GOLF WORLD*

JAMES NEWTON DEMARET
(1910–1983)

BORN: Fort Worth, Texas.
DIED: Houston, Texas, at age 73.

Three-time Masters champion Jimmy Demaret was coowner with Jack Burke of Champions GC in Houston, Texas. He and Burke collaborated with Ralph Plummer on the creation of its Cypress Creek course and with George Fazio on its Jackrabbit eighteen. The pair also worked with Joe Finger in designing The Concord in New York. On his own, Demaret designed Onion Creek CC in Austin, Texas, a few years before his death.

DAVID JOHN DeVICTOR
(1953–   )

BORN: Columbus, Ohio.

D. J. DeVictor graduated with a Bachelor of Science degree in landscape architecture from Ohio State University in 1977. While in college he apprenticed with Toledo golf architect Arthur Hills. Upon graduation, he worked for a land-planning firm in Portland, Oregon, and then for landscape architect Bill Oliphant in Knoxville, Tennessee, for whom he handled some course-remodeling projects. After a few years, DeVictor joined the Tennessee-based Fairfield Development Company as director of its Resorts and Golf Development Division. In that capacity, DeVictor handled the expansion of some of Fairfield's courses. In 1987 he left Fairfield and established a golf design firm in partnership with landscape architect Peter Langham. In 1990, the partnership was expanded by the addition of former U.S. Amateur champion and noted television commentator Steve Melnyk.

Courses by D. J. DeVictor:

Florida: Rotonda G&CC (Pebble Beach Cse 1989).
Georgia: [The] Champion's C of Atlanta (1991), with *Steve Melnyk*.
South Carolina: Oak Hills GC (1991), with *Steve Melnyk*.
Tennessee: Egwani Farms GC (1991); Royal Oaks G Cse (1992).

Courses remodeled or expanded by D. J. DeVictor:

Colorado: Fairfield Pagosa (A.9 1985).
Georgia: Lake Spivey GC (A.3rd 9 1987).
North Carolina: Harbour Pointe GC (A.9 1989).
Tennessee: Knoxville Muni (R. 1983).
Virgin Islands: Carambola Beach GC (R. 1987).

BRUCE DEVLIN
(1937–)

BORN: Armidale, New South Wales, Australia.

Bruce Devlin took up golf at the age of thirteen. While receiving training as a plumber by his father (and eventually attaining the rank of master plumber), Devlin also played a great deal of amateur golf. After winning the 1959 Australian Amateur and the 1960 Australian Open he turned professional, moved to the United States and over the next dozen years won nine tournaments on the PGA Tour as well as many events around the world.

In 1966 Devlin was asked by members of The Lakes GC in New South Wales to

Bruce Devlin, 1970
COURTESY *GOLF WORLD*

recommend an architect to redesign their course. He had always admired the work of American Dick Wilson, who had died the previous year, so he suggested a former Wilson associate, Robert von Hagge. Devlin worked closely with von Hagge on remodeling of The Lakes, and the two soon formed a partnership in Australia. In 1969 they expanded into the United States as the firm of von Hagge and Devlin.

From the beginning Devlin took an active role in the construction supervision of the firm's courses. As his professional career slowed, he assumed increased design responsibilities. He left his partnership with von Hagge in 1987 to compete full-time on the Senior PGA Tour, but the lure of architecture was too great to give up entirely. In the late 1980s and early 1990s Devlin worked on some projects with Karl Litten, an old von Hagge and Devlin employee, and then with young designer Derrell Witt.

Courses by Bruce Devlin (All with Robert von Hagge unless otherwise indicated):

California: Blackhawk CC (Lakeside Cse 1981); Tierra Del Sol GC (1978).
Colorado: Eagle Vail CC (1975).
Florida: Bay Point Y&CC (Lagoon Legend Cse 1986); Bayshore Muni (1969); Boca Del Mar G&TC (1972); Boca Lago G&CC (East Cse 1975; West Cse 1975); Boca West CC (Cse No. 3 1974); Boynton Beach Muni (27 1984); Briar Bay GC (9 Precision 1975); Card Sound GC (1976); Carolina CC [FKA Holiday Springs CC](1975); C at Emerald Hills (1969); Colony West GC (Cse No. 1 1970; Cse No. 2 [Precision] 1974); Doral CC (Gold Cse 1969); Doral Park CC (Silver Cse 1984); East Lake Woodlands G&CC (North Cse 1979); Eastwood Muni (1978); Fountains G&RC (North Cse 1970; South Cse 1972; West Cse 1981); Hunters Run GC

(East Cse 1979; North Cse 1979; South Cse 1979); Indian Spring CC (East Cse 1975; West Cse 1980); Key Biscayne GC (1972); Marco Shores CC (1974); Ocean Reef C (Harbor Cse 1976); Palm-Aire CC (Palms Cse 1969; Sabals Cse [Precision] 1969); Poinciana G&RC (1973); Sandalfoot Cove G&CC (27 1970); Sherbrooke G&CC (1979); TPC at Prestancia (Club Cse [FKA CC of Sarasota] 1976); Winter Springs GC [FNA Big Cypress GC](1973); Woodlands CC (East Cse 1969; West Cse 1969; Woodmont CC (Cypress Cse 1976; Pines Cse 1976); Wycliffe G&CC (1989), with Karl Litten.
Idaho: Quail Hollow GC [FKA Shamanah GC](1983).
Missouri: [The] Oaks GC (1980).
New Mexico: Tanoan GC (27 1978).
North Carolina: Brandywine Bay GC (1983).
Ohio: Quail Hollow Inn & CC (1975).
Oklahoma: Shawnee G&CC (9 1982).
South Carolina: Secession GC (1991).
Tennessee: Nashville G&AthleticC [FKA Crockett Springs National G&CC](1972).
Texas: Chase Oaks GC (Blackjack Cse 1986; Sawtooth Cse, 9 1986); C at Falcon Point (1985); C at Sonterra (North Cse 1985); Crown Colony CC (1979); Gleneagles CC (King's Cse 1985; Queen's Cse 1985); Hollytree CC (1982); Northgate CC (1985); Northshore CC (1985); Raveneaux CC (1980); TPC at The Woodlands [FKA The Woodlands Inn & CC (East Cse)] (1982); Vista Hills CC (1975); Walden on Lake Conroe CC (1976); Walden on Lake Houston GC (1985); Willow Creek GC (1982).
Wisconsin: Brookfield Hills GC (Precision 1971).
Australia: Campbelltown GC (1976); [The] Lakes GC (1970); Magnolia Hills CC (1975); Ocean Shores GC.
Bahamas: Cape Eleuthera GC (1971, NLE).
France: G International Les Bordes (1987).
Japan: Daisifu Central CC (1971); Kawaguchi-ko GC (1979).
Tahiti: Travelodge GC (9 1972).

Courses remodeled or expanded by Bruce Devlin (All with Robert von Hagge unless otherwise indicated):

Arizona: Tucson National GC (R. A.3rd 9 1979).

Florida: Doral CC (Blue Cse, R. 1971;
    Gold Cse, R. 1982; Red Cse, R. 1985);
    Ocean Reef C (Dolphin Cse, R. 1969).
Texas: Ranchland Hills GC (R. 1983);
    Rayburn G&CC (A.3rd 9 1984); [The]
    Woodlands Inn & CC (North Cse, A.9
    1983; West Cse, A.9 1983).

MARK DEVRIES
(1927–)

Mark DeVries attended Michigan State
University, receiving a B.A. degree in landscape architecture in 1949. He was employed as a landscape architect with the
Grand Rapids (Michigan) Department of
Parks until 1963, when he entered private
practice. His company handled the design
of many golf courses from the 1960s to the
1980s.

Courses by Mark DeVries:

Michigan: Alpine CC (1965); Brayside
    GC at Courtland Hills (1979); Broad-
    moor GC (1963); Chase Hammond
    Muni (1969); English Hills GC (9 Pre-
    cision 1973); Fox Creek G Cse (1988);
    Fox Run Muni (South Cse 1986);
    Hickory Hills CC (1980); Meadowood
    GC (1985, A.3rd 9 1986); Mount
    Pleasant CC (9 1975); Saskatoon GC
    (Blue Cse 1970; Red Cse, 9 1970, A.9
    1991); Springfield Oaks GC (1974);
    Tyler's Creek GC (1973); Western
    Greens GC (1963); Whispering Wil-
    lows Muni GC (1968).

Courses remodeled or expanded by
Mark DeVries:

Michigan: Broadmoor GC (R.); Forest
    Hills GC (A.10 R.8 1986); Silver Lake
    CC (R.3 A.2 1988).

WILLIAM HICKMAN DIDDEL
(1884–1985), ASGCA, CHARTER MEMBER,
PRESIDENT 1954, 1965

BORN: Indianapolis, Indiana.
DIED: Zionsville, Indiana, at age 100.

A graduate of Wabash College in Indiana, Bill Diddel lettered in baseball, basketball, football and track. He was a
member of a national collegiate championship basketball team and later coached
basketball for one season at Wabash.
    Diddel was also an excellent golfer, but
unfortunately Wabash never fielded a golf

*William H. Diddel,
1952* COURTESY GOLF
WORLD

team. Still, Diddel achieved individual
success, winning the Indiana Amateur in
1905, 1906, 1907, 1910 and 1912. He retained his golfing skills throughout his life
and shot his age more times (over 1,000
rounds in all) than any golfer in history.
    His first design experience occurred in
1921, when, as a member of Highland
G&CC in Indianapolis, Diddel finished a
new course routed by Willie Park, Jr.
Buoyed by the experience, Diddel began
full-time practice as a golf course architect
in 1922. He designed over 75 courses in a
career that spanned more than 50 years.
    Bill Diddel loved to experiment. He
built one course, Woodland CC in Carmel, Indiana, where he and his wife lived
for years in a log cabin, without any sand
bunkers. Instead, Diddel shaped and contoured the fairways and greens to provide
what he felt was sufficient challenge to low
handicappers. In the late thirties he developed and patented a "short" golf ball,
which traveled about half the distance of a
regular ball. It took over 30 years before
others realized the potential of such an
invention.
    Diddel was confined to a wheelchair
during the last decade of his life. He died
in a nursing home in his native Indiana
just a few months short of his 101st
birthday.

Courses by William H. Diddel:

Arkansas: Hot Springs G&CC (Arlington
    Cse 1932).
Florida: Bardmoor CC (East Cse 1968,
    NLE; North Cse 1974; South Cse
    1974); CC of Naples (1963); Jupiter
    Island C (1958); Melbourne G&CC
    (1926); Sunset G&CC (1926); Sunset
    Hills CC (1926).
Illinois: Danville CC (9 1928); Edgewood
    Valley CC (1926); Midland Hills GC
    (9 1929); Rolling Green CC (1930);
    Sunset Ridge CC (1924).
Indiana: Beechwood GC (1930); Beeson
    Park GC (9 1932); Brookshire GC

(1971); Coffin Muni (1931); Columbus CC (9 1946); Connersville CC (9);
Crawfordsville Muni (1931); CC of Indianapolis (1923); Elcona CC (1955);
Elks CC, West Lafayette (1928); Elks
CC, Marion (1961); Erskine Muni
(1934); Evansville CC; Fendrich GC
(1945); Forest Hills CC (1931); Forest
Park GC (9 1935); Fort Harrison GC
(1970); Fox Cliff CC (1970); Green
Hills G&CC (1951); Greentree CC
(1959); Hamilton Muni (1951); Hawthorne Hills CC (27 1963); Hendricks
County GC (1927); Highland G&CC
(1921); Hillcrest CC (1924); Honeywell GC (9); Kilbuck GC (1965);
Marion CC (9 1927); Martinsville CC
(1925); Meridian Hills CC (1923);
Mineral Springs GC (1953); Min-
nestrista GC (9 1930); Oak Grove CC
(9 1941); Oak Hill GC (1962); Oak
Lawn GC (1962); Parke Country G
Cse (9 1959); Purdue University GC
(South Cse 1934); Riverside Muni
(1935); Rockville GC (9 1959); Roll-
ing Hills CC; Rozella Ford GC;
Rushville Elks CC (9 1950); Shady
Hills GC (1957); Shelbyville Elks CC
(9 1930); Speedway 500 CC (1928,
A.3rd 9 1956); Sun Blest GC (1940);
Tipton Muni (9 1963, A.9 1967); Twin
Lakes GC [FKA Elks Green Tree GC];
Ulen CC (1924); Valley View GC
(1962); Walnut Grove GC (1969);
Woodland GC (1951).
Kansas: Wichita CC (1950).
Kentucky: Frankfort CC (1949); High-
    land CC (9 1954); Wildwood CC
    (1952).
Michigan: Echo Lake CC (1927); Forest
    Lake CC (1926); Hidden Valley C
    (1957); Lake St. Clair CC (1929);
    Shanty Creek GC (Deskin Cse 1968).
Missouri: Crystal Lake CC (1929).
Montana: Lewistown Elks CC (9 1948);
    Meadow Lark CC (1949).
Ohio: California GC (1936); Fairborn CC
    (1961); Greene CC; Indian Valley GC;
    Kenwood CC (Kendale Cse 1930; Ken-
    view Cse 1930); Miami View GC
    (1961); Neumann Park GC (1965);
    Potter Park GC (1958); Reeves Memo-
    rial GC (9 1965); Sharon Woods GC
    (1935); Swaim Fields GC (9 1933, A.9
    1955); Twin Base GC, Wright-
    Patterson AFB (1953); Twin Run GC
    (1965); Walnut Grove GC (9 1962);
    Western Row GC (1965); Winton
    Woods GC.
Oklahoma: Mohawk Park Muni (Wood-
    bine Cse 1934).

Texas: Northwood C (1948).
Wisconsin: Brynwood CC (1954); Lakeside CC (1956).

Courses remodeled or expanded by William H. Diddel:

Arkansas: CC of Little Rock (R. 1929); Hot Springs G&CC (Majestic Cse, R. 1932).
Colorado: Denver CC (R. 1957).
Florida: Mountain Lake C (R. 1961); Oceanside G&CC (R.9 A.9); Ponce de Leon Resort & CC (R. 1955).
Illinois: Oak Park CC (R. 1955); Westmoreland CC (R. 1963).
Indiana: Anderson CC (R.9 A.9 1935); Coffin Muni (R. 1954); CC of Indianapolis (R. 1930); CC of Terre Haute (R.9 A.9 1928); Fort Wayne CC (R. 1950); Green Hills G&CC (R. 1951); Hillcrest G&CC (R.9 1933); Kokomo CC (R.9 A.9 1925); Lafayette CC (R.9 1924); Meshingomesia CC (R. 1955); Sarah Shank Muni (R.9 A.9 1941); South Shore CC (R.9 A.9 1927); Wawasee GC (R.9 A.9 1927); Woodmar CC (R.9 1967).
Kansas: Macdonald Park Muni (R. 1950); Mission Hills CC (R. 1957).
Kentucky: Big Spring CC (R. 1951); Louisville CC (R. 1955).
Michigan: Barton Hills CC (R. 1952); Birmingham CC (R. 1930); Black River CC (R.9 A.9 1956); Forest Lake CC (R. A.4 1959); Orchard Lake CC (R. 1954).
Missouri: Midland Valley CC (R. 1928); Oakwood CC (R. 1961); Westwood CC (R. 1961).
Montana: Harve Elks CC (R. 1950).
Nebraska: Happy Hollow C (R. 1946).
Ohio: Avon Fields GC (R. 1933); Clovernook CC (R. 1962); Kenwood CC (Kendale Cse, R. 1966; Kenview Cse, R. 1966); Meadowbrook C (A.9 1956); Still Meadow CC (R. 1956); Western Hills GC (R. 1931).
Pennsylvania: Shawnee CC (R.18 A.3rd 9 1963).
Tennessee: Millington NAS GC (R. 1966).
Ontario: Hamilton G&CC (R. 1966).

WILLIAM H. DIETSCH, JR.
(1928–)

BORN: Atlanta, Georgia.

Bill Dietsch graduated from Staunton Military Academy in 1946 and attended the University of Pennsylvania, where he majored in mechanical engineering. He then served with the U.S. Army and was a witness to the first test of the hydrogen bomb in the South Pacific.

Following military duty, Dietsch started in course maintenance in 1955 under superintendent Scott Tuppen. Shortly thereafter, Tuppen was hired to build courses for Robert Trent Jones, and he took his assistant with him. Dietsch worked for the Jones organization for twelve years and for a time was closely associated with Jones's chief assistant Francis Duane. In 1967 Dietsch entered private practice as a course architect based in Florida.

Courses by Bill Dietsch, Jr.:

Florida: CC of Miami (South Cse 1968, NLE); GC of Delray (Precision 1983); Lakeview GC (Precision); Oriole G&TC (27 1982); Springtree GC (Precision 1972); Sunrise Lakes Phase 3 GC (9 Precision 1981).

Courses remodeled or expanded by Bill Dietsch, Jr.:

Florida: Miami Springs GC (R.10 1982); Pasadena GC (R.); Rolling Green G&CC (A.9); Rolling Hills CC (A.3rd 9 1983).

Tom Doak, 1989
RON WHITTEN

THOMAS H. DOAK
(1961–)

BORN: New York, New York.

In order to become a golf architect, Tom Doak followed the footsteps of Robert Trent Jones by attending Cornell University. Unlike Jones, Doak graduated, receiving a degree in landscape architecture in 1982. He then spent eight months touring and studying classic courses of the British Isles, funded by a postgraduate grant from Cornell's Floriculture Department. Following that, he apprenticed under Pete Dye and then Perry Dye, working on construction crews, drafting routing plans and even handling final shaping. Deeming his education complete, Doak struck out on his own in 1987, intent on building courses the old-fashioned way. To emphasize that fact, he named his company Renaissance Golf Design, Inc.

His first project, High Pointe GC in Williamsburg, Michigan, reflected his philosophy of lay-of-the-land architecture, employing natural contours to the utmost effect. Working with superintendent Tom Mead, Doak grassed both fairways and greens with drought-tolerant fescues to provide firm playing surfaces and minimal maintenance. It was the first such major effort in the field since the 1920s.

Starting in his college days, Doak freelanced design articles for *Golf* magazine and later became a contributing editor and handled the publication's rankings of golf courses and golf holes. He also developed a reputation as a topflight golf course photographer. He authored and self-published *The Confidential Guide to Golf Courses* in 1988, what one observer called "a no-holds-barred" rating of all courses Doak had played. Others more critical felt it could be called the "controversial guide to golf courses." For a more mainstream audience, Doak put both his design philosophy and his photography into *The Anatomy of a Golf Course* (1992).

In 1990 Doak was joined by Gilbert Hanse, another graduate landscape architect from Cornell who had studied in the British Isles on the very same grant that Doak had utilized. While in Britain, Hanse apprenticed with the famous Hawtree design firm.

Courses by Tom Doak:

Michigan: High Pointe GC (1989); Wilderness Valley GC (Black Forest Cse 1992).
South Carolina: [The] Legends GC (Heathland Cse 1990; Parkland Cse 1992).

Courses remodeled or expanded by Tom Doak:

New York: Garden City GC (R. 1990).
Ohio: Camargo C (R. 1990).

FRANCIS J. DUANE
(1921–), ASGCA, PRESIDENT 1972

BORN: Bronx, New York.

Frank Duane studied landscape architecture at the State University of New York, graduating in 1944. He was employed for a

Frank Duane, circa 1970 COURTESY *GOLF WORLD*

short time as a landscape architect with the New Hampshire Department of Forestry and Recreation, then in 1945 went to work for golf architect Robert Trent Jones. He became chief assistant to Jones and remained with him until 1963, when he went out on his own.

In 1965 Duane was stricken with Guillame-Barré Syndrome, a debilitating disease that confined him to a wheelchair. Undaunted, Duane continued his design practice. For a three-year period in the early 1970s he worked in partnership with legendary golfer Arnold Palmer. By the late 1970s his health was such that he was unable to continue an active architectural practice.

Courses by Frank Duane (All as assistant to Robert Trent Jones unless otherwise indicated):

Alabama: Turtle Point Y&CC (1964).
California: El Dorado Hills GC (Precision 1964); Half Moon Bay CC (1973), with Arnold Palmer.
Colorado: Eisenhower GC (Blue Cse 1959).
Florida: Apollo Beach G & Sea C (9 1962); GC of Miami (East Cse 1962; North Cse [Par 3] 1962, NLE; West Cse 1962); Mariner Sands GC (Green Cse 1973), with Arnold Palmer; Meadows CC (Highlands Cse, 9 1976 solo; Meadows Cse, 9 1976 solo); Patrick AFB GC (9 1961); Ponte Vedra C (Lagoon Cse, 9 1962); Royal Palm Y&CC (1960); Spring Lake G&CC (1979 solo).
Georgia: Chattahoochee GC (1959); [The] Landings at Skidaway Island (Magnolia Cse 1973), with Arnold Palmer.
Hawaii: Honolulu CC (1976), with Arnold Palmer; Kapalua GC (Bay Cse 1974), with Arnold Palmer.
Louisiana: Timberlane CC (1959).
Michigan: Point O'Woods G&CC (1958).
Missouri: Bellerive CC (1959).

Montana: Big Sky GC (1974), with Arnold Palmer; Yellowstone G&CC (1959).
New Hampshire: Portsmouth G&CC (1957).
New Jersey: Goldman Hotel GC (9 solo); Howell Park GC (1971 solo); Montammy CC (1966 solo); Preakness Valley Park GC (solo); Tamcrest CC (9 1970 solo); Tammy Brook CC (1962).
New York: Brae Burn CC (1964 solo); Fallsview Hotel GC (9 1962); Glimmerglass State Park GC (solo); Golf Hill G&CC (1966 solo); Hampstead GC at Lido (1956); Hampton GC (solo); Merrick Road Park GC (9 1967 solo); North Hills CC (1961); Osiris CC (9 1965 solo); Pines Hotel GC (9 1960); Pleasant View Lodge GC (9 1968 solo, A.9 1978 solo); Rock Hill G&CC (1966 solo); Seven Oaks GC (9 1955); Sound Shore GC (solo); Spook Rock GC (1969 solo); Sycamore GC (1973 solo); Tall Timbers CC (1967 solo); Tuxedo Park C (1947); Wildwood CC (1964 solo).
North Carolina: Duke University GC (1957); Sugar Hollow GC (Precision 1974 solo); Tanglewood GC (West Cse 1957).
South Carolina: Myrtle Beach National GC (North Cse 1973; South Cse 1973; West Cse 1973), with Arnold Palmer; Sea Pines Plantation GC (Club Cse 1976), with Arnold Palmer.
Tennessee: Scona Lodge GC (9 1957).
Texas: Corpus Christi CC (1965).
Vermont: Fox Run GC (9 1968 solo); Sugarbush GC (1963).
Virginia: Massanutten Village GC (9 1972 solo); Stumpy Lake GC (1957).
Ontario: London Hunt & CC (1960).
Colombia: El Rincon C (1963; Par 3 Cse 1964).
Jamaica: Half Moon–Rose Hall GC (1961).
Puerto Rico: Dorado Beach GC (East Cse, 9 1958, A.9 1961; West Cse, 9 1958, A.9 1966).

Courses remodeled or expanded by Frank Duane: (All as assistant to Robert Trent Jones unless otherwise indicated):

Connecticut: CC of New Canaan (R. 1960); Innis Arden GC (R. 1964 solo); Millbrook C (R.3 1964 solo); Patterson C (R.1 1965 solo); Ridgewood CC (R. 1959).
Florida: CC of Orlando (R. 1959).
New Jersey: Arcola CC (R. 1960); Cherry Valley CC (R.12 1978 solo); Colonia

CC (R. 1970 solo); Crestmont CC (R.3 1963 solo); Essex County CC (West Cse, R.9 1967 solo).
New York: Bartlett CC (R. 1960); Bellevue CC (R.14 A.4 1972 solo); Bethpage State Park GC (Blue Cse, R. solo; Green Cse, R. solo; Red Cse, R. solo; Yellow Cse, R. solo); Blue Hill GC (R. 1970 solo); Century GC (R. 1959); Cherry Valley CC (R. 1962); Douglaston Park GC (R.5 1964 solo); Elmwood CC (R.1 1977 solo); Engineers GC (R.3 1970 solo; R.18 1977 solo); Garden City GC (R. 1958); Garden City CC (R.6 1970 solo); Hampshire CC (R.4 1964 solo); Huntington CC (R. 1960); Inwood CC (R. 1972 solo); IBM CC (R.1 1978 solo); La Tourette Muni (R.4 1964 solo); Mill River CC (R.4 1971 solo); Moonbrook CC (R. 1959); Muttontown G&CC (R.1 1964 solo); Nassau CC (R. 1970 solo); Old Oaks CC (R.6 1968 solo); Old Westbury G&CC (R.2 1972 solo); Plandome CC (R. solo); Quaker Ridge CC (R. 1964 solo); Richmond County CC (R.4 1970 solo); Ridgeway CC (R.9 1976 solo); Rockville CC (R.1 1965 solo); Sands Point CC (R. 1961: R. 1964 solo); Scarsdale GC (R.4 1965 solo); Seawane C (R. 1964 solo); South Fork CC (R.3 1974 solo); Towers CC (R. 1976 solo); Woodcrest CC (R. 1976 solo).
Pennsylvania: Westmoreland CC (R. 1958).
Vermont: Marble Island G&YC (R.9 1964 solo).

J. F. Dudok Van Heel, 1985 COURTESY D. M. A. STEEL

JOAN FREDERIK DUDOK VAN HEEL (1925–), BIGCA

BORN: Naarden, The Netherlands.

After obtaining a Master's at Law from Leiden University, J. F. Dudok Van Heel worked as an apprentice banker and then in the oil, petrochemical, pharmaceutical and real estate industries. A noted Continental golfer, Dudok Van Heel won 14 national titles and represented the Netherlands in international competition for 25 years.

After handling the financing and management of several European projects, Dudok Van Heel founded Golf Development International, based in Brussels, Belgium, in the 1970s. He subsequently designed over 35 courses throughout Europe.

Courses by J. F. Dudok Van Heel:

Austria: Goldegg GC; Mürstatten GC.
Belgium: GC de Pierpont; Louvain-la-Neuve GC; Ypres GC.
France: St. Omer GC.
Germany: Bad Neuenahr-Ahrweiler G&CC (1979); Im Chiemgau GC (1983); Kohlerhof GC; Olching GC; Rohrenfeld GC.
Netherlands: Almere GC; Best GC; Biltse Duinen GC; Brunssum GC (9); Crossmoor GC; De Dommel GC; De Schoot GC (9 1973); Hoge Dijk GC (9); Noordhollandse GC; Oosterhout GC; Reymerswael GC; Rozenstein GC; Sluispolder GC (9 1985); St. Oedenrode GC; Tongelreep GC; Welschapse Dyk GC; Wijchen GC (9); Wijde Wormer GC; Zoetermeer GC.

Courses remodeled or expanded by J. F. Dudok Van Heel:

Austria: Murhof GC (A.9 1973).
Germany: Chiemsee GC (A.9); Kronberg GC (R.)
Portugal: Palmares GC (R.).
Spain: El Paraiso GC (R.).

GEORGE DUNCAN
(1893–1964)

BORN: Aberdeen, Scotland.
DIED: Scotland, at age 70.

George Duncan won the British Open in 1920 and was runner-up in 1927. A member of several Ryder Cup teams, he served as captain in 1929.

Duncan laid out several courses on his own and in collaboration with his friends James Braid and Abe Mitchell. His most highly regarded architectural work was the restoration of the course at Royal Dornoch to 18 holes after World War II. Duncan added four new holes to replace four lost to the RAF. The four "lost" holes were

George Duncan, circa 1925 COURTESY *GOLF WORLD*

later returned to Royal Dornoch and made into the short, nine-hole Struie course.

Courses by George Duncan:

England: Hallowes GC; Mere G&CC (1934), with James Braid and John R. Stutt; Tapton Park GC (1936).
Scotland: Stonehaven GC.

Courses remodeled or expanded by George Duncan:

England: Harrogate GC (R.); Wheatley GC (R.).
Scotland: Royal Dornoch GC (R. A.4 1947).

John Duncan Dunn, circa 1925 COLLECTION RON WHITTEN

JOHN DUNCAN DUNN
(1874–1951)

BORN: North Berwick, Scotland.
DIED: Los Angeles, California, at age 77.

John Duncan Dunn trained as a professional greenkeeper and course builder under his father Tom Dunn. After laying out a few courses in Britain and on the Continent, he followed his uncle Young Willie, only nine years his senior, to the United States in 1894. He worked briefly with the sporting goods firms Slazengers and Bridgeport Arms and then acquired the post of professional at the newly opened Ardsley-on-Hudson CC in New York.

By 1900 J.D. was in charge of planning, building and operating golf courses for the Florida West Coast Railroad. Around the same time, he collaborated with Walter Travis on the design of several courses in the Northeast. Throughout these years he made numerous trips back to Britain and the Continent, often in the company of his brother Seymour, who had joined him in America.

J.D. settled in California after World War I, where he was hired as professional at Los Angeles CC. He continued to reside in that state until his death. An excellent teacher of golf, Dunn ran a series of golf schools at which he extolled the virtues of the baseball grip. During the 1932 Olympics in Los Angeles, he gave Babe Zaharias her first golf lessons. Dunn was also a competent landscape artist and the author of numerous magazine articles and books on golf instruction.

Courses by John Duncan Dunn:

California: Atascadero CC (1927, NLE); Catalina GC (1925); Idyllwild CC; Lake Elsinore GC (NLE); Lake Norconian C (1928, NLE); Los Serranos Lakes CC (North Cse 1925); Parkridge CC; Peter Pan CC (NLE); Rio Hondo CC; Santa Ana CC (1924); Woodvista GC [FKA Brockway GC](9 1924).
Florida: Belleair CC [FKA Belleview–Biltmore Hotel & C](West Cse, 9 1899); El Merrie Del CC (NLE); Fairmede CC (NLE); Gables GC (9 1898, NLE); Ocala Muni (9); Winter Park GC (1900, NLE).
New York: Catskills Village GC (1900, NLE); Interstate Park GC (9 1900, NLE); Long Beach Hotel GC (1900, NLE); Muirfield G Links (1931, NLE); Quaker Ridge CC (9 1915).
Ohio: Elks CC, Hamilton.
Vermont: Ekwanok CC, with Walter J. Travis.
England: Lee-on-the-Solent GC (1905).
France: Hardelot GC (Pines Cse 1907); Hendaye GC.
Netherlands: Clingendael GC; Doornsche GC (1894, NLE); Hilversumse GC (1910); Noord Nederlandse G&CC; Rosendaelsche GC (1896).

Courses remodeled or expanded by John Duncan Dunn:

Maine: Cape Arundel GC (R.9 A.9 1922), with Walter J. Travis.
Massachusetts: Essex CC (R.), with Walter J. Travis.

MAY DUNN

See May Dunn Hupfel.

SEYMOUR DUNN
(1882–1959)

BORN: Prestwick, Scotland.
DIED: Lake Placid, New York, at age 77.

Seymour Dunn traveled to America at age 12 to work as assistant to his brother John Duncan Dunn at Ardsley-on-Hudson. He later held numerous professional and golf teaching positions on both sides of the Atlantic, among them at the Griswold Hotel and Stevens Hotel in America, Ealing in England, La Boulie in France and Royal County Down in Northern Ireland. Seymour finally settled down in 1908 at Lake Placid Club in New York to raise a family. There he served as director of golf, won the Adirondack Open 12 years in a row and established a mail-order club factory. He also designed or reworked nearly every golf course in the Adirondacks.

Throughout his career, Dunn traveled back and forth to Great Britain on a number of business ventures, sometimes accompanied by his brother John. The brothers established in 1900 the world's first indoor golf school at Bournemouth, England, and in 1929 Dunn founded in New York City's Madison Square Garden the world's largest indoor golf school, complete with an 18-hole pitch and putt course, practice nets and thirty instructors.

Dunn ranked among the great teachers of golfing fundamentals, numbering Jim Barnes, Walter Hagen, Gene Sarazen and Joe Kirkwood among his students. He was the author of *Golf Fundamentals, Elementary Golf Instruction, Standardized Golf Instruction* and *Golf Jokes.* Dunn designed numerous courses as an avocation, both in Europe and America.

Seymour Dunn, 1927 COLLECTION RON WHITTEN

Courses by Seymour Dunn:

Florida: Lake Placid C (NLE); Silver Spring GC (NLE); Tampa Bay Hotel GC (9 1899, NLE).
Mississippi: CC of Laurel (1917).
New Jersey: Beacon Hill CC (1899); Fort Monmouth GC.
New York: [The] Antlers G Cse (9 1925, NLE); Ausable Valley G Cse (9 1920); Cazenovia CC (9); Chautauqua GC (9); Craig Wood CC [FKA Lake Placid CC](9 1925, A.9 1932); Fawn C G Cse (9 1923, NLE); Lafayette CC; Lake Placid C (Lower Cse 1909; Practice Cse, 9 1909); Locust Hill CC (9 1928); Paul Smith's Adirondack C (9); Saranac Inn G Cse (9 1907, A.9 1910); Schroon Lake CC (9 1905, NLE); Schroon Lake G Cse (9 1918); Tuscarora CC.
Belgium: Antwerp GC; King Leopold Private Cse; Royal GC de Belgique (1906); Royal Zoute GC (1908).
France: Chemay Estate GC; D'Allegre Estate GC (9); Rothschild Estate GC.
Italy: King Emmanual Private Cse; Ugolino GC.

Courses remodeled or expanded by Seymour Dunn:

New Jersey: Red Bank G&CC (R.).
New York: Ticonderoga CC (R.9 A.9 1932).
France: Racing C de France (Valley Cse, R.).
Northern Ireland: Royal County Down GC (R. 1905).

TOM DUNN
(1849–1902)

BORN: Royal Blackheath, England.
DIED: Blagdon, England, at age 52.

Tom Dunn became professional at Wimbledon (London Scottish) in 1870. Its course had originally been laid out by his father, Old Willie Dunn, with 18 holes, but over the years it had been reduced to seven. In his first year, Tom extended it again to 18 holes. He later held posts of professional at North Berwick, Tooting Bec near London, Meyrick Park in Bournemouth and other courses.

Tom Dunn was the most prolific course designer of his day. He produced layouts that were inexpensive and serviceable, making it possible for increasing numbers of golfers from all social classes to take up

Tom Dunn, 1897 COLLECTION RON WHITTEN

the game. A great salesman, he was quoted as telling each of his clients, "God meant this site to be a golf course." The first designer to work on inland rather than links sites, Tom Dunn was a firm believer in a cross bunker requiring a forced carry from the tee, another for the approach and an even third on a three-shot hole. Dunn himself considered Broadstone in England, where he was "not stinted for men, money or materials," to be his best effort. He always felt Meyrick Park to be his greatest challenge because of its dense cover of heather, furze and pine forest.

Tom was married to Isabel Gourlay, "the greatest woman golfer of her day" and descendant of the Gourlays of Musselburgh (renowned golf instructors to the Kings of Scotland and ball makers to the Royal Family of Great Britain). Tom traveled to America on several occasions, visiting brother Young Willie, sons John Duncan and Seymour and daughter May, who was a pioneer woman professional golfer.

Despite his presence in the United States, it is doubtful that Tom ever laid out an American golf course. While many a club in the States claimed to have a Tom Dunn course, those layouts were all designed by one of the other Dunns. Tom's work in Great Britain and on the Continent, however, was extensive, and he claimed to have some 137 courses to his credit.

Courses by Tom Dunn:

Canary Islands: Ralara GC.
England: Ashley Wood GC (9 1893); Bath GC (1880); Beckenham Place Park GC (1907); Bramshaw GC (Manor Cse 1880); Brighton and Hove GC (9 1887); Broadstone GC (1898);

Bromley GC; Bude and North Cornwall GC (1890); Bulwell Forest GC (1902); Burhill GC (9 1907); Buscot Park GC; Chiselhurst GC (1894); Eltham Warren GC (1890); Enfield GC (1893); Erewash Valley GC (1905); Felixstowe Ferry GC (9 1880, NLE); Frinton GC (1896); Ganton GC (1891), with Harry Vardon; Hampstead GC (9 1894); Hastings and St. Leonards GC (1893); Hastings GC (1893, NLE); Huddersfield GC (1891); Kinsdown GC (1880); Lansdown GC (1894); Lindrick GC (1891); Maidenhead GC (1898); Meyrick Park GC (1894); North Oxford GC (1908); Northwood GC (1891); Nottingham City GC; Penwortham GC (1908); Richmond GC (1891); Royal Cinque Ports GC (9 1892); Royal Mid-Surrey GC (1892); Royal Worlington and Newmarket GC (9 1892); Royston GC (1893); Saunton GC (East Cse 1897); Seacroft GC (1892); Seaford GC (1887, NLE); Sheringham GC (9); Sherwood Forest GC (1904); Surbiton GC (1895); Tooting Bec C (1890); Ventnor GC (9 1892); Weston-Super-Mare GC (1892); Whickham GC (1911); Woking GC (1893).

France: Coubert GC; Golf de Biarritz (1888), with Willie Dunn, Jr; Golf de Dinard (1887).

Netherlands: Haagsche GC (1893, NLE).

Scotland: Blairgowrie GC (Rosemount Cse, 9 1889).

Courses remodeled or expanded by Tom Dunn:

England: Littlestone GC (R.); London Scottish GC (A.9 1870, R. 1901).
Ireland: Cork GC (R.9 1880).
Scotland: North Berwick GC (R. 1883).

WILLIE DUNN, SR.
(1821–1878)

BORN: Musselburgh, Scotland.
DIED: North Berwick, Scotland, at age 57.

Old Willie Dunn was the patriarch of a distinguished line of professional golfers and course designers. He was born into a golfing family, although his father was a plasterer by trade. Legend has it that a Dunn was partly responsible for King James I's interest in golf at Leith. Whether or not this is true, the name of Dunn has been renowned in the world of golf for centuries.

Old Willie was partnered with his twin brother Jamie in a famous challenge match played over St. Andrews, Musselburgh and North Berwick for the then huge purse of 400 pounds. The twin Dunns were losers to the pair of Allan Robertson and Old Tom Morris.

In 1850 Willie undertook the duties of greenkeeper and professional at Royal Blackheath in England, where he was joined two years later by Jamie. After 20 years they returned to Scotland, working first at Leith, later at Musselburgh and finally at North Berwick. Old Willie is known to have rebuilt several holes at Royal Blackheath, to have designed the first Wimbledon course for the London Scottish Regiment in 1865 and to have planned a number of three-hole layouts on private estates.

Four golf course designers who became famous on both sides of the Atlantic were sons or grandsons of Old Willie: Tom Dunn, Young Willie Dunn, John Duncan Dunn and Seymour Dunn. Several of Willie's other descendants became well-known professional or amateur golfers in Great Britain and the United States. Cameron and Robert Dunn, both sons of Seymour, became prominent American professionals, while Norman "Dick" Dunn, Young Willie's son, returned to England, served in the British army during World War I and later became a well-known amateur golfer in Great Britain.

Courses by Willie Dunn, Sr.:

England: London Scottish GC (9 1865).
France: Pau GC (1856).

Courses remodeled or expanded by Willie Dunn, Sr.:

England: Royal Blackheath GC (NLE).

Willie Dunn, circa 1865 COLLECTION RON WHITTEN

Willie Dunn, Jr., circa 1894
COLLECTION RON

WILLIE DUNN, JR.
(1865–1952)

BORN: Musselburgh, Scotland.
DIED: Putney, England, at age 87.

Young Willie Dunn trained as a professional, greenkeeper and course builder under his brother Tom, sixteen years his senior and well established in England. Young Willie served as professional at Westward Ho! for a few months in 1886, then laid out the Chingford course near London before moving to Biarritz in France. While working as professional at Biarritz, which he had helped his brother build, Willie met American W. K. Vanderbilt and was persuaded to try his hand at an American course as greenkeeper and professional.

The club he came to was Shinnecock Hills on Long Island, a 12-holer by William F. Davis, a fellow Scot. Dunn soon added a ladies course and then in 1895 combined the two into 18 holes. Willie remained at Shinnecock for several years as pro-greenkeeper and won an unofficial U.S. Open in 1894. As a golfer, he was among the first to experiment with the Haskell ball and cardboard tees. As a clubmaker, he developed a set of steel shafts in 1904.

As a designer, Young Willie was ahead of the heathlands architects in utilizing an occasional lateral bunker in place of the traditional cross bunker. He was also the first of a group of colorful designers in America of fluctuating fortune. He experienced periods of great wealth followed by periods of near penury. During lean times his family would be dispatched home to England to await improved circumstances. Young Willie numbered John D. Rockefeller, John L. Sullivan, Buffalo Bill Cody and Zane Grey among his close friends and taught the game to, among others, Teddy Roosevelt, W. K. Vanderbilt and Stewart Maiden, who later introduced young Bobby Jones to golf.

Until 1910 Willie remained on the Eastern Seaboard, laying out courses and working as a pro-greenkeeper, making only occasional trips back to Britain and the Continent. He was then employed as a club designer with the firm of Crawford, MacGregor and Canby Company of Dayton, Ohio. In the early 1920s Willie moved to St. Louis and later to Menlo Park, California. He returned to England in 1940 and remained there until his death in 1952.

Courses by Willie Dunn, Jr.:

Georgia: Jekyll Island GC (9 1894, NLE).
Iowa: Algona CC (9 1920).
Maryland: Baltimore CC (Roland Park Cse 1898, NLE).
New Jersey: Lakewood CC (9 1892); Lawrence Harbour CC.
New York: Apawamis C (1898), with *Maturin Ballou*; Ardsley CC (1895); Eagles Nest CC (9 1900, NLE); Elmira CC (9 1898); Rockaway Hunting C (9 1894, NLE); Scarsdale GC (9 1898); Shinnecock Hills GC (Red Cse, 9 1896, NLE); Westbrook CC (1893).
Pennsylvania: Bala GC [FKA Philadelphia CC](9 1893).
Quebec: Royal Montreal GC (South Cse 1900).
England: Chingford GC (1888); John O'Gaunt GC (Carthagena Cse).
France: G de Biarritz (1888), with Tom Dunn.

Courses remodeled or expanded by Willie Dunn, Jr.:

New York: Shinnecock Hills GC (White Cse, R.12 A.8 1896, NLE).

ROBERT CHARLES DUNNING
(1901–1979)

BORN: Kansas City, Kansas.
DIED: Emporia, Kansas, at age 78.

Bob Dunning attended military academies, where he excelled at all sports and for a time played semipro baseball. He then attended Kansas University and Emporia State College, receiving a B.A. degree in 1921. Following college, he

Bob Dunning, circa 1964 COURTESY BOB DUNNING

became a professional golfer and after apprenticing under Art Hall of Kansas City became pro-greenkeeper at McAlester (Oklahoma) CC. He worked on several course-remodeling jobs while at McAlester and in the mid-thirties attended the Massachusetts Turfgrass School, where he met Dr. John Monteith. He joined Monteith as an assistant in 1940.

Dunning spent World War II with the Army Corps of Engineers developing Bermuda-grass runways in Texas. After the war he assisted Ralph Plummer in establishing several veterans' hospital courses in the South and then formed a successful turf-equipment business in Tulsa, Oklahoma. During the 1950s, Dunning was highly regarded as a turfgrass expert and greens consultant. His Texas experience had convinced him that golf greens could be built on bases consisting almost entirely of sand, and he converted several sand green courses in Oklahoma to sand-base grass greens with great success.

Dunning retired from his equipment business in 1960 and, with the assistance of his wife, Inez, devoted the next 15 years to the full-time design and construction of golf courses. The death of his wife and his own health forced him to retire in 1978.

Courses by Bob Dunning:

Kansas: Alvamar Hills GC (1968); Dubs Dread GC (1963); Happy Hunting C (9); Leawood South CC (1969); Pawnee Prairie Muni (1970).
Louisiana: New Orleans VA Hospital GC (9 Par 3 1946), with Ralph Plummer.
Missouri: Blue Hills CC (1964); Holiday Hills CC.
Oklahoma: Elk City G&CC (9 1953); Falconhead GC (1953), with *Waco Turner*; Hobart CC (9 1965); Pauls Valley Muni (9 1951); Sunset CC; Sunset Hills GC; Woodward Muni (9 1954).

Texas: McKinney Muni (9 1946), with Ralph Plummer.

Courses remodeled or expanded by Bob Dunning:

Kansas: Coffeyville CC (R. 1965); Indian Hills CC (R. 1965); Kansas City CC (R. 1964); Macdonald Park Muni (R. 1963); Meadowbrook G&CC (R. 1966); Mission Hills CC (R. 1964); Sim Park Muni (R. 1963).
Missouri: Hickory Hills CC (R. 1962); St. Joseph CC (R.1 1973).
Oklahoma: McAlester CC (R.9 1960).

ALICE O'NEAL DYE
(1927–   ), ASGCA

BORN: Indianapolis, Indiana.

Alice O'Neal met her future husband, Pete Dye, while both were students at Rollins College in Winter Park, Florida. They married in 1950 and moved to her hometown of Indianapolis, where both became life insurance salespersons. They also worked on their golf games. Pete had some competitive success, but never came close to matching his wife's impressive record. Over the years, Alice Dye won seven Indiana Women's Amateur titles (including three prior to their marriage), three Florida State Women's Amateur titles, five Women's Western Senior Championships and two USGA Women's Senior Amateur Championships. She was named to the 1970 Curtis Cup team at age 42, was selected as Florida Senior Woman Golfer of the Year five years in succession and was voted to the Indiana Hall of Fame.

Alice left the insurance business after the birth of their first son, Perry, in 1952, but Pete continued until 1959, when he quit to pursue a career in golf design. Pete and Alice formed a company and began designing and building small-town layouts around central Indiana. Theirs was an extremely low-budget operation in the beginning; for one project, Alice propagated a stand of bent grass in their front yard and transported it to the course site in the trunk of their Oldsmobile.

In those early days, Alice handled all the drafting for Pete. "Pete couldn't read a contour map. I had to teach him," she later recalled. "And he never did learn to draw." While their sons were young, Alice handled projects close to home while Pete went out on the road, and for a time she mainly handled the paperwork of the busi-

Alice Dye (left), with husband and design partner Pete Dye COURTESY *GOLF WORLD*

ness. Once the boys reached their teens, she again took a more active role in the design aspect of their projects.

Alice Dye considered her most valuable contribution to golf architecture to be the expert attention she devoted to the planning and placement of tees and hazards to create proper challenges for female golfers. For years she spoke and wrote extensively on the need for more than a single set of tees for women. The wide variance in women's skills at any course, she contended, dictated forward and back (and sometimes even middle) tees for women, just as had been provided for years for men. In 1982 Alice Dye became the first woman member of the ASGCA.

Courses by Alice Dye (All as assistant to Pete Dye):

California: La Quinta Hotel GC (Citrus Cse 1987; Mountain Cse 1981); Mission Hills G&CC (Dinah Shore Cse 1988); PGA West GC (Stadium Cse 1986).

Florida: Delray Dunes GC (1969); John's Island Club (North Cse 1973; South Cse 1970); [The] Moorings GC (1972); TPC at Sawgrass (Stadium Cse 1980).

Indiana: Crooked Stick GC (1964); Forest Park GC, Brazil (1963); Heather Hills CC (1961); Monticello CC (1963); Royal Oak CC [FKA El Dorado CC](9 1960); William S. Sahm Muni [FKA North Eastway Muni](1963).

South Carolina: Harbour Town G Links (1969); [The] Ocean Cse (1990); Long Cove Club (1982).

Texas: Austin CC (1984).

Dominican Republic: Casa de Campo (Links Cse 1976); La Romana CC (1990).

KENNETH E. DYE, JR. (1953–), ASGCA

BORN: San Antonio, Texas.

The only golf architect named Dye who was not part of the Pete Dye clan, Ken Dye received a landscape architecture degree from North Carolina State University in 1976, after lettering on the golf team (and often playing as number one man) for four years. Dye joined the Houston-based golf design firm of Joseph S. Finger and Associates in 1976. In 1985 he became a full partner with Finger in the firm, and the company's name was changed to Finger, Dye and Associates to reflect the partnership. In 1987, associate Baxter Spann was

Ken Dye, 1990 COURTESY KEN DYE

also made a partner in the firm, and in 1991 Joe Finger retired from active design. Dye and Spann continued as principal architects, teaming on some designs and handling others on their own.

Courses by Ken Dye (All with Joe Finger unless otherwise indicated):

Colorado: Battlement Mesa GC (1988); Dalton Ranch GC (1992 *solo*); Thorncreek GC (1992), with Baxter Spann.

Georgia: Lake Acworth GC (1992 *solo*).

Mississippi: Deerfield CC (1980), ass't Joseph S. Finger.

New Mexico: Piñon Hills G Cse (1990 *solo*).

Texas: Cedar Creek Muni (1990 *solo*); Clear Creek G Cse (1988), and Baxter Spann; Cottonwood Creek Muni (1985); Deerwood GC (1983), ass't Joseph S. Finger; Grapevine Muni (1980), ass't Joseph S. Finger and Byron Nelson; Hackberry Creek CC (1986); Kingwood CC (Kings Crossing Cse 1992 *solo*); Painted Dunes Desert G Cse (1991 *solo*); Stonebriar CC (1988), and Baxter Spann.

Alberta: D'Arcy Ranch GC (1991 *solo*).

Argentina: Martindale CC (1989 *solo*).

Courses remodeled or expanded by Ken Dye (All with Joe Finger unless otherwise indicated):

Florida: Shalimar Pointe CC (R. 1986).

Louisiana: England AFB GC (A.9 1989), and Baxter Spann; Oakbourne CC (R. 1985).

South Carolina: Whispering Pines GC, Myrtle Beach AFB (A.9 1987), and Baxter Spann.

Texas: Hearthstone CC (A.9 1985), and Baxter Spann; Lubbock CC (R.); Panorama CC (R. 1985); Preston Trail GC (R. 1985); Prestonwood CC (Creek Cse, R. 1979); Tanglewood-on-the-Texoma GC (R. 1988), and Baxter Spann.

Alberta: Valley Ridge CC (A.9 1991 *solo*).

PAUL BURKE DYE (1955–), ASGCA

BORN: Indianapolis, Indiana.

P. B. Dye, the younger son of golf architects Pete and Alice Dye, took his first golf lesson at age four, won his first tournament at age six and played on a high school golf team that went undefeated for three straight seasons. Although he was a

P. B. Dye, 1990
COLLECTION RON
WHITTEN

member of the University of Tampa (Florida) golf team for several years, golf course design, not competitive golf, was always his career choice. He learned more about the subject at home and working on various family projects than he did at any school.

Some of his earliest work with his father attracted immediate national attention. Long Cove Club, on Hilton Head Island, South Carolina, was named one of America's 100 Greatest Courses by *Golf Digest* only two years after it opened. The Honors Course, near Chattanooga, Tennessee, was named the Best New Private Course of 1984 by the same publication.

By the mid-1980s P. B. Dye was handling course designs entirely on his own, patterning his business after that of his father, with no office, full-time employees or working drawings. In 1990 he joined two Canadian investors to form Brassie Golf, a company intended to develop and manage low-cost daily-fee courses.

Courses by P. B. Dye:

Florida: Harbour Ridge G&CC (River Ridge Cse 1989), with Pete Dye; [The] Links at Fisher Island (9 1990); Loblolly Pines GC (1989); Palm Beach Polo & CC (Cypress Cse 1988), with Pete Dye.
Georgia: Atlanta National GC (1987), with Pete Dye; Sterling Bluff GC (1989), with Pete Dye.
Illinois: Ruffled Feathers GC (1992), with Pete Dye.
Kentucky: Kearney Hill G Links (1989), with Pete Dye.
Missouri: Boone Valley GC (1992).
North Carolina: [The] Gauntlet G&CC (1991); Landfall C (Dye Cse 1988), with Pete Dye.

Pennsylvania: Montour Heights CC (1987), with Pete Dye.
South Carolina: Cross Creek Plantation GC (1990); DeBordieu GC (1987), with Pete Dye; [The] Legends GC (Moorland Cse 1990); Long Cove C (1982), ass't Pete Dye; Northwoods GC (1990); Prestwick GC (1989), with Pete Dye; Secession GC (routing 1989); Windemere GC (1990).
Tennessee: [The] Honors Cse (1983), ass't Pete Dye.
France: G de Barbaroux (1989).

Courses remodeled or expanded by P. B. Dye:

Alabama: CC of Birmingham (West Cse, R. 1986), with Pete Dye.
Ohio: Urbana CC (A.9 1992).
Pennsylvania: Rolling Rock GC (R.9 A.9 1992).

Perry Dye, 1990
COURTESY PERRY DYE

PERRY O'NEAL DYE
(1952–   ), FAGCA

BORN: Indianapolis, Indiana.

Perry Dye, Pete and Alice Dye's older son, first accompanied his golf architect parents to course construction sites at age 12. While still a teenager, he absorbed enough knowledge to be heavily involved in the initial routing of the first course at John's Island, Florida. During college, he served as project manager for a number of his father's designs, including Harbour Trees near Indianapolis. After graduating from the University of Denver with a degree in real estate marketing, Perry left the family business to pursue a career in housing development and construction. The recession of the late 1970s caused him to abandon his plans, and he rejoined his father in the course design business.

In 1982 Perry Dye formed his own course design company, Dye Designs Inc. Based in Colorado, with a branch office for a time in Arizona, the firm first concentrated on real estate development courses, then diversified with financial backing from a Japanese group into several fields related to golf. Dye continued to occasionally collaborate with his father on certain designs well into the 1980s. Their most notable joint effort was Karsten G Cse for Arizona State University.

Courses by Perry Dye:

Arizona: Ancala CC (1991); Karsten G Cse at ASU (1989), with Pete Dye; Red Mountain Ranch GC (1986).
California: Cypress GC (1992); Rancho Santa Fe Farms GC (1988), with Pete Dye.
Colorado: Glenmoor GC (1984); Riverdale GC (Dunes Cse 1986); Plum Creek G&CC (1984), with Pete Dye.
Florida: John's Island C (South Cse 1970), ass't Pete Dye; [The] Moorings GC (Precision 1972), ass't Pete Dye.
Hawaii: Royal Hawaiian GC (1992).
Indiana: Harbour Trees GC (1971), ass't Pete Dye.
Oklahoma: Oak Tree GC (1975), ass't Pete Dye.
Japan: Edelweiss GC (1988); CC Glenmoor (1990); Kannami Springs CC (1988); Maple Point GC (1992); Mariya CC (1987); Olympic Staff CC (1992); Pete Dye Royal GC (1988); St. Lakes CC (1988); West One's CC (1992).

Courses remodeled or expanded by Perry Dye:

Colorado: Copper Creek GC [FKA Copper Mountain GC](R.9 A.9 1987).
California: Carlton Oaks CC (R. 1989); Rancho Santa Fe CC (R. 1990).
Indiana: Eagle Creek G Cse (R. 1989).
Minnesota: Izaty's G&YC (R. 1989).

PETE DYE, NÉE PAUL DYE, JR.
(1925–   ), ASGCA, PRESIDENT 1988

BORN: Urbana, Ohio.

Though his given name was Paul, he was known as Pete from an early age because everyone called him "pee-dee," from his initials, to distinguish him from his father, Paul Sr. After attending Rollins College and Stetson University in Florida,

Pete Dye, 1991
COLLECTION RON
WHITTEN

Pete Dye married Alice O'Neal and both worked as life insurance salespersons in Indianapolis. A fine amateur golfer, Dye won the Indiana Amateur in 1958 after being runner-up in 1954 and 1955. He also served as chairman of the green committee at CC of Indianapolis, where he guided the club through a major replanting of its course.

In 1959 Dye left the insurance business after becoming one of the youngest members of the "Million Dollar Round Table" in his company. With his wife, Alice, he laid out his first course that same year and soon embarked on a career in course design.

Dye had done a series of low-budget courses in the Midwest by 1963, when he and Alice toured the great courses of Scotland. When they returned, Pete began to incorporate into his designs several of the features and principles they had observed in Scotland, including small greens, undulating fairways, pot bunkers, railroad tie bulkheads and deep native roughs. The characteristic Pete Dye style that evolved had a profound impact on late-twentieth-century course architecture. In fact, it ushered in a links style with a North American flair.

Dye created some of the world's top courses, including Teeth of the Dog in the Dominican Republic, The Golf Club near Columbus, Ohio, Harbour Town Golf Links on Hilton Head Island, South Carolina, and the original Tournament Players Club at Ponte Vedra, Florida. The latter ushered in an era of "stadium courses" designed with massive spectator mounds.

A second wave of Pete Dye designs further defined and elevated his art, including The Honors Course, PGA West's Stadium Course and The Ocean Course on Kiawah Island, South Carolina, scene of the much ballyhooed 1991 Ryder Cup matches.

Dye started countless architects in the business. He and Alice were business partners during his entire career, and she actively participated in his early designs and many more after their sons were raised. The Dye sons, Perry and P.B., both worked for and with their father before establishing successful practices on their own. Other "Dye-sciples" included Pete's brother Roy, William Newcomb, David Pfaff, Lee Schmidt, Bill Coore, Bobby Weed, Tom Doak, David Postlethwait and Scott Pool. All went on to design courses on their own.

Courses by Pete Dye:

Arizona: Karsten G Cse at ASU (1989), with Perry Dye.
California: Carmel Valley Ranch GC (1980); La Quinta Hotel GC (Citrus Cse 1987; Dunes Cse 1981; Mountain Cse 1980); Mission Hills G&CC (Dinah Shore Cse 1988); Mission Hills Resort GC (1987); Moreno Valley Ranch GC (27 1988); PGA West GC (Stadium Cse 1986); Rancho Santa Fe Farms GC (1988), with Perry Dye.
Colorado: Plum Creek G&CC (1983), with Perry Dye.
Florida: Amelia Island Plantation GC (27 1973); Bonnet Creek GC (Eagle Pines Cse 1991); Cypress Links (1988); Delray Dunes G&CC (1969, R. 1978); Harbour Ridge Y&CC (River Ridge Cse 1989), with P. B. Dye; John's Island C (North Cse 1973; South Cse 1970, with Jack Nicklaus); [The] Moorings GC (Precision 1972); Old Marsh GC (1987); Palm Beach Polo & CC (Cypress Cse 1988), with P. B. Dye; [The] River C at Grand Harbor (1988); TPC at Sawgrass (Stadium Cse 1981, R. 1983; Valley Cse 1987, with Jerry Pate).
Georgia: Atlanta National GC (1987), with P. B. Dye; Sterling Bluff GC (1989), with P. B. Dye.
Illinois: Yorktown GC (Par 3 1963); Oakwood CC (1963); Ruffled Feathers GC (1992), with P. B. Dye.
Indiana: Crooked Stick GC (1964, R. 1978, R. 1986, R. 1990); Eagle Creek Muni (27 1974); Forest Park GC, Brazil (1963); Harbour Trees GC (1973), Heather Hills CC (1961); Monticello CC (1963); Plainfield Elks GC (9 1962); Royal Oak CC [FKA El Dorado CC](9 1960); William S. Sahm Muni [FKA North Eastway Muni](1963).

Iowa: Des Moines G&CC (Blue Cse 1968; Red Cse 1967).
Kentucky: Kearney Hill G Links (1989), with P. B. Dye.
Maryland: Martingham G&TC (1971), with Roy Dye.
Michigan: Radrick Farms GC (1965, R.1 1984); Wabeek CC (1971), with Roy Dye and Jack Nicklaus.
Mississippi: Pine Island GC (1974).
Nebraska: Firethorn GC (1985).
North Carolina: Cardinal GC (1974); Landfall C (Dye Cse 1988), with P. B. Dye; Oak Hollow GC (1972).
Ohio: Avalon Lakes GC (1967); Fowler's Mill GC [FKA TRW GC](27 1972), with Roy Dye; [The] Golf Club (1967); Little Turtle C (1971), with Roy Dye.
Oklahoma: Oak Tree CC (East Cse 1982; West Cse 1978); Oak Tree GC (1975).
Pennsylvania: Montour Heights CC (1987), with P. B. Dye.
South Carolina: DeBordieu GC (1987), with P. B. Dye; Harbour Town G Links (1969, with Jack Nicklaus, R. 1984); [The] Ocean Cse (1990); Long Cove C (1982); Prestwick GC (1989), with P. B. Dye.
Tennessee: [The] Honors Cse (1983).
Texas: Austin CC (1983); Stonebridge CC (1988).
Virginia: Kingsmill GC (River Cse 1974).
West Virginia: Pete Dye G Cse (9 1985).
Wisconsin: Americana Lake Geneva GC (Briarpatch Cse)[FKA Playboy Club Hotel](1971), with Jack Nicklaus; Blackwolf Run GC (Meadow Valleys Cse, 9 1988, A.9 1989; River Cse, 9 1988, A.9 1990).
Dominican Republic: Casa de Campo (Links Cse 1976; Teeth of the Dog Cse 1971, R. 1979); La Romano CC (1990).

Courses remodeled or expanded by Pete Dye:

Alabama: CC of Birmingham (West Cse, R. 1986), with P. B. Dye.
Arizona: Randolph Park GC (North Cse, R.4 1980).
Connecticut: TPC at River Highlands [FKA TPC of Connecticut](R. 1984).
Florida: Marco Island CC (R. 1979).
Indiana: CC of Indianapolis (R. 1957); Speedway 500 GC (R. 1992).
Nebraska: CC of Lincoln (R.3 1963).
New York: En-Joie CC (R.2 1984); Piping Rock C (R. 1985).
Ohio: Kirtland CC (R. 1961).
Texas: Preston Trail GC (R.1 1981).

Roy Dye, 1975
COURTESY *GOLF WORLD*

ROY A. DYE
(1929–   ), ASGCA

BORN: Springfield, Ohio.

Roy Dye graduated from Yale University with a Bachelor's degree in chemical engineering. After a career in that profession for almost twenty years, Roy joined his brother Pete in the practice of golf course design in 1969. After working with Pete on several projects, Roy handled several designs on his own, though many of them—including Waterwood National in Texas and CC of Colorado—were still credited as Pete Dye designs.

In the 1970s Dye moved to the Southwest and designed a series of courses in Mexico and the Phoenix area. Plagued by ill health, his work was curtailed through much of the 1980s, but in the 1990s he began working in architecture once again.

Courses by Roy Dye:

Arizona: Gambel G Links (9 1983, NLE); Stonecreek GC [FKA Anasazi GC](1983).
Colorado: CC of Colorado (1973).
Maryland: Martingham G&TC (1971), with Pete Dye.
Michigan: Wabeek CC (1971), with Pete Dye and Jack Nicklaus.
Ohio: Fowler's Mill G Cse [FKA TRW CC](27 1972), with Pete Dye; Little Turtle C (1971), with Pete Dye.
Texas: Waterwood National GC (1976).
Mexico: C de G Santa Fe; La Mantarraya GC (9 1974, A.9 1984); San Carlos G&CC (1980); San Gil GC (1977).

Courses remodeled or expanded by Roy Dye:

Quebec: CC of Montreal (R. 1975).

HENRY CHANDLER EGAN
(1884–1936)

BORN: Chicago, Illinois.
DIED: Everett, Washington, at age 51.
INTERRED: Medford, Oregon.

H. Chandler Egan graduated from Harvard in 1905. He was one of the top early college amateur golfers in America, winning the NCAA in 1902, the U.S. Amateur in 1904 and 1905 (finishing runner-up in 1909) and the Western Amateur in 1902, 1904, 1905 and 1907.

In the early 1910s Egan retired from national competition and moved to an apple farm in Medford, Oregon. From there he introduced golf to southwestern Oregon and competed successfully along the West Coast, winning the Pacific Northwest Amateur title in 1915, 1920, 1923, 1925 and 1932. He is perhaps best known for his 1929 "comeback" on the national level, when he reached the semifinals of the U.S. Amateur at the age of 45 at Pebble Beach, a course he had significantly remodeled in preparation for that event. He was subsequently selected as a member of the 1930 and 1934 Walker Cup teams.

Egan became involved in golf course design shortly after his move to Medford. He laid out his first course there in 1911 and over the next 20 years designed and built several other Pacific Northwest courses. After working with Robert Hunter on the revisions to Pebble Beach, Egan partnered for a short time with Hunter and his design partner Alister Mackenzie. Egan was constructing a course in Washington at the time of his unexpected death from pneumonia.

Courses by H. Chandler Egan:

California: Bayside Muni (1933); Green Hills CC (1930), with Alister Mackenzie and Robert Hunter; Pacific Grove G Links (9 1932).

H. Chandler Egan, 1930 COLLECTION RON WHITTEN

Georgia: North Fulton Muni (1935).
Oregon: Bend G&CC (9 1926); Coos CC (9); Eastmoreland GC (1921); Eugene CC (1926, NLE); Hood River GC (1922), with *Hugh Junor*; Oswego Lake CC (1926); Reames G&CC (9 1924); Rogue Valley CC (1911); Seaside CC (9); Tualatin CC (1912), with *George Junor*; West Hills Muni (1924, NLE).
Washington: Indian Canyon GC (1935); Legion Memorial GC (1934); West Seattle GC (1939).

Courses remodeled or expanded by H. Chandler Egan:

California: Pebble Beach G Links (R. 1928), with Robert Hunter and *Roger Lapham*.
Oregon: Riverside G&CC (A.9 1928); Waverley CC (R. 1930).

ROBERT L. ELDER
(1927–   )

BORN: DuBois, Pennsylvania.

A graduate of Penn State with degrees in agronomy and agricultural engineering, Bob Elder spent three years working for the USGA Green Section. He then formed a golf course construction business and built over 75 courses for other architects along the mid-Atlantic Seaboard.

In the late 1970s, he was afforded the chance to try his hand at course design. He soon engaged in designing as well as constructing courses, working mainly in his native Maryland.

Courses by Bob Elder:

Maryland: Black Rock GC; Enterprise Muni; Geneva Farm G Cse (1990); Glade Valley G Cse (1991); Greencastle CC; Laytonsville GC (1973); Marlton GC.
Pennsylvania: Callemont Resort GC; Greencastle Greens GC (1992).
West Virginia: Cress Creek G&CC (1990); Opequon CC (1976).

Courses remodeled or expanded by Bob Elder:

Maine: Samoset Resort GC (R.9 A.9 1978).
Maryland: Montgomery CC (R.); Twin Shields GC (R.); Wicomico Shores GC [FKA Aviation Y&CC](A.9).

*Richard Elliott,
1991* COURTESY
RICHARD ELLIOTT

RICHARD R. ELLIOTT
(1963–   )

BORN: Easton, Maryland.

While attending the University of Maryland, Rick Elliott spent his summers on the maintenance crews at Hog Neck and Talbot CC and during the school years assisted Dr. Mark Welterlen on various turfgrass research projects. After graduating with degrees in landscape architecture and agronomy in 1986, Elliott became course superintendent at Echo Mesa G Cse in Sun City West, Arizona. A year later, he joined California golf architect Cal Olson as a project manager, and a year after that he joined Ronald Fream's design firm. For Fream, Elliott handled projects in Europe, North Africa and Southeast Asia. In 1990, he was made a senior architect in the firm.

Courses designed by Rick Elliott (All as assistant to Ronald Fream):

France: EuroDisney GC (27 1992); Golf de Fregate (27 1992); Golf de Gassin (27 1992).
Portugal: Carvoeiro GC (27 1992).
Thailand: Panya Indra GC (27 1992).

DEVEREUX EMMET
(1861–1934)

BORN: New York, New York.
DIED: Garden City, New York, at age 73.

Devereux Emmet was the son of a judge and a descendant of Thomas Addison Emmet, a founder of Tammany Hall. The Emmet family was listed in Ward McAllister's *First Forty Families in America.* Dev and prominent architect Stanford White married sisters who were nieces of financier A. T. Steward.

Emmet was a golfer and huntsman. For two decades he routinely bought hunting dogs in the South in the spring, trained them on Long Island through the summer, sold them in Ireland in the autumn and spent the winter hunting and golfing in the British Isles. One such winter was devoted to measuring British golf holes for his friend C. B. Macdonald, who was then planning The National Golf Links of America. Emmet was a founding member of The National. Emmet was also a talented golfer, making the quarterfinals of the 1904 British Amateur and winning the Bahamas Amateur at age 66.

Emmet designed his first course, the Island Golf Links (a forerunner to Garden City GC), upon his return from an extended trip to the great links of Scotland. His other early design work, including one for his own family's estate at Sherewogue and Cherry Valley (built on property belonging to his father-in-law), was done at no charge. But later he became a professional golf course architect and accepted fees for his work.

In 1929 he formed a design partnership with his associate Alfred H. Tull. A year later, Emmet's son, Devereux Emmet, Jr., joined the firm. But despite the name Emmet, Emmet and Tull, there is little evidence that Devereux Jr. actively participated in any design work. Alfred Tull continued the practice on his own after Emmet's death in 1934.

Courses by Devereux Emmet (All with Alfred H. Tull unless otherwise indicated):

Connecticut: Farmington CC (*solo*); Fulton Estate GC (1933); Hob Nob Hill GC (1934, NLE); Keney Park GC

*Devereux Emmet,
circa 1925*
COLLECTION RON
WHITTEN

(1927 *solo*); Ridgewood CC (*solo*); Wee Burn CC (1923 *solo*).
Delaware: Henry F. Du Pont Private Cse (*solo*, NLE).
Maryland: Congressional CC (Blue Cse, 9 1924 *solo*; Gold Cse, 9 1924 *solo*).
Massachusetts: Cape Cod CC (9 1929); Lenox GC (*solo*).
New Jersey: Cooper River CC (1929, NLE); Greenacres CC (1932).
New York: Albany CC (*solo*, NLE); Bethpage State Park GC (Green Cse) [FKA Lenox Hills CC](1924 *solo*); Briar Hall CC [FKA Briarcliff CC](1923 *solo*); Broadmoor CC (1929, NLE); Cherry Valley CC (1916 *solo*); Coldstream GC (1925 *solo*); Edison CC (1926 *solo*); Eisenhower Park GC (Red Cse)[FKA Salisbury G Links](1914 *solo*); Garden City GC (1901 *solo*); Glen Head CC [FKA Women's National G&CC] (1923 *solo*); Glenwood CC (*solo*); Grassy Sprain CC (*solo*, NLE); Hampshire CC (1927 *solo*); Harrison Williams Private Cse (3 1932); Huntington Crescent CC (1931; West Cse 1931, NLE); Huntington CC (1911 *solo*; R. 1928 *solo*); Intercollegiate GC (9 1926 *solo*, NLE); Island G Links (9 1899 *solo*, NLE); Lake Isle CC (1926 *solo*); Laurelton GC (North Cse 1925 *solo*, NLE; South Cse 1924 *solo*, NLE); Lawrence GC (1924 *solo*); Leatherstocking CC [FKA Cooperstown CC](1909 *solo*); Leewood GC (1926 *solo*); Mahopac GC (*solo*); Manhattan CC (1917 *solo*); Mayflower GC (1930, NLE); McGregor G Links (1921 *solo*); Meadow Brook C (1914 *solo*, NLE); Mechanicsville CC (*solo*, NLE); Mohawk GC (*solo*); Nassau CC (1927 *solo*); Northport CC (1921 *solo*); Old Westbury CC (*solo*, NLE); Pelham CC (1921 *solo*); Pomonok CC (1921 *solo*, NLE); Queensboro Links (1917 *solo*); Queen's Valley GC (1923, NLE), with W. H. "Pipe" Follett; Rockaway Hunting C (1919 *solo*); Rockville Links C (1924 *solo*); Rockwood Hall CC (1929); Rye CC (1920 *solo*); Schenectady CC (*solo*); Schuyler Meadows C (1928 *solo*); Seawane C (1927 *solo*); Sherewogue Estate G Cse (*solo*, NLE); Stephen C. Clark Private Cse (*solo*, NLE); St. George's G&CC (*solo*); St. Lawrence University GC (9 1900 *solo*); Vanderbilt Estate GC (9 1929, NLE); Vernon Hills CC (1928 *solo*); Wheatley Hills GC (1913 *solo*; R. 1929).
North Carolina: Hog Back Mountain C (9 1931, NLE).

Ohio: Belmont Hills CC (*solo*).
Pennsylvania: Charles M. Schwab Estate
  GC (*solo*, NLE); Elk County CC (*solo*);
  St. Mary's CC (*solo*, NLE).
Virginia: Thomas Fortune Ryan Private
  Cse (*solo*, NLE).
West Virginia: Wheeling CC (*solo*).
Bahamas: Bahamas CC (*solo*, NLE); Car-
  nival's Crystal Palace GC [FKA Cable
  Beach Hotel & GC](1928 *solo*).
Bermuda: Belmont Hotel & C (9 1924,
  A.9 1928 *solo*); Castle Inn GC (9 Par 3
  solo, NLE); Hotel Frascati GC (9 Par 3
  1930 *solo*, NLE); Riddell's Bay G&CC
  (1922 *solo*).
Cuba: CC of Santiago (*solo*, NLE).

**Courses remodeled or expanded by
Devereux Emmet (All with Alfred H.
Tull unless otherwise indicated):**

Connecticut: Hartford GC (R. A.7 1921
  solo).
Delaware: Henry F. Du Pont Private Cse
  (R. 1929).
New York: Bedford G&TC (R.9 A.9 *solo*);
  Bonnie Briar CC (R. 1928 *solo*); Engi-
  neers GC (R. 1921 *solo*); Old Country
  Club (R. 1928 *solo*, NLE); Powelton C
  (R.6 A.12 1921 *solo*).
Bermuda: St. George Hotel GC (R. 1928
  solo).

Jim Engh, 1991
COURTESY JIM ENGH

**JAMES J. ENGH
(1958–   )**

BORN: Dickinson, North Dakota.

Jim Engh, who played golf on his high
school and college teams, learned golf architecture from the ground up. After earning a Bachelor of Science degree in
landscape architecture from Colorado
State University in 1981, Engh worked on
a series of golf course construction crews.
He then hired on with the design firm of
Joseph Finger and Ken Dye and after a
year went to work as an associate of Chicago golf architect Dick Nugent.

In 1987, seeking broader exposure to
the game's roots, Engh moved to Great
Britain, where he met A. H. Buckley, a
large British land developer and owner of
the well-established British golf design
firm of Cotton, Pennink and Associates.
Shortly after Engh agreed to serve as director of design for Cotton, Pennink, Buckley
formed a partnership with German golf
star Bernhard Langer and named the firm
Langer Buckley. Engh then designed several courses for which Langer served as
consultant.

A year later Buckley became managing
partner for the recreational development
division of International Management
Group, the sports management group
founded and headed by Langer's agent,
Mark McCormack. Since golf courses
were expected to be a focal point of any
recreational development, Engh was
asked to create and head a golf course
design division for IMG. In that role he
collaborated on European and Asian designs with other McCormack clients, primarily Nick Faldo and Isao Aoki.

In 1991 Engh returned to the United
States, to the foothills of Colorado, where
he founded his own golf design business.
To reflect his international experience in
the field, Engh called his firm "Global Golf
Design."

Courses by Jim Engh:

Illinois: Glendale Lakes GC (1986), ass't
  Dick Nugent.
Austria: Dachstein Tauern GC (1990),
  with *Bernhard Langer*.
England: Duxhurst Farm GC (1992);
  Kenwick Hall GC (27 1992).
France: Bethemont GC (1989), with
  Bernhard Langer; Vichy G&CC (27
  1993).
Germany: Ludersburg GC (1992), with
  Bernhard Langer; Schloss Nippenburg
  GC (1993), with *Bernhard Langer*.
Italy: Ca' Degli Ulivi GC (1990); Modena
  G&CC (1991), with *Bernhard Langer*.
Thailand: Dragon Hills GC (1992), with
  Isao Aoki.

**Courses remodeled or expanded by Jim
Engh:**

Oklahoma: Dornick Hills CC (R. 1985),
  ass't Dick Nugent.
South Dakota: Westward Ho! CC (R.
  1986), ass't Dick Nugent.
Wisconsin: La Crosse CC (R. 1985), ass't
  Dick Nugent.
Germany: St. Eurach GC (R. 1990), with
  Bernhard Langer.
Jamaica: Tryall GC (R. 1991).

Paul Erath, 1965
COURTESY GOLF WORLD

**PAUL E. ERATH
(1905–   )**

BORN: Beaver County, Pennsylvania.

Paul Erath became a member of PGA of
America in 1933 and served as both club
pro and superintendent at several Pennsylvania clubs before joining the construction staff of golf architect Dick Wilson in
the 1950s. After supervising Wilson's reconstruction of Dunedin CC in Florida,
Erath returned to Pennsylvania to build
Laurel Valley CC to Wilson's plans. He
then remained at Laurel Valley as its
course superintendent and designed a
number of local golf courses as a sideline.

Courses by Paul Erath:

Pennsylvania: Champion Lakes GC
  (1965); Pleasant View CC (1967); Port
  Cherry Hills CC (1966); Saranac GC
  (9 1964); Venango Valley GC (1973).

**Courses remodeled or expanded by Paul
Erath:**

Pennsylvania: Fox Chapel GC (R. 1968);
  Laurel Valley CC (R. 1965).

**LINDSAY B. ERVIN
(1942–   ), ASGCA**

BORN: Brownwood, Texas.

Lindsay Ervin, who graduated in landscape architecture from Purdue University
in 1968, trained for several years under
golf architect David Gill. He then joined
an East Coast landscape architecture firm.
In 1976 he designed his first solo design,
Hog Neck GC in Easton, Maryland, which
soon gained acclaim as one of the nation's
top public courses.

In 1979 Ervin established his own landscape and golf design practice based in
Maryland and subsequently produced

Lindsay Ervin, 1990
COURTESY ASGCA

other topflight public layouts, including a second 18 at White Deer in Pennsylvania and Queenstown Harbor on Maryland's Eastern Shore. Ervin's firm was among the first to apply computer AutoCadd technology to golf course design.

Courses by Lindsay Ervin:

Maryland: Cove Creek CC (9 1980); Hog Neck GC (27 1976); Needwood GC (Precision 1985); Old South CC (1991); Queenstown Harbor G Links (27 1991).

New York: Villa Roma CC (routing 1987).

Pennsylvania: GC at Hidden Valley (routing 1988); White Deer Park & G Cse (New Cse 1990).

Virginia: Birdwood GC (1984); Lake Ridge GC (9 Par 3 1992).

Courses remodeled or expanded by Lindsay Ervin:

Maryland: Bethesda CC (R.1); Walden GC (R.9 A.9 1990).

New York: Forest Park GC (R. 1986).

Pennsylvania: White Deer Park & G Cse (Old Cse, R. 1990).

Dave Esler, 1991
COURTESY DAVE ESLER

DAVID A. ESLER
(1963–)

BORN: Wauconda, Illinois.

While attending Ohio State University, Dave Esler was a member of four consecutive Big Ten golf championship teams. He

also qualified for four USGA National Championships, won two Lake County (Illinois) Amateur titles and received three OSU Athlete/Scholar awards. For three summers he worked part-time for Chicago golf architect Dick Nugent. After graduating in 1985 from Ohio State with a degree in landscape architecture, he toured Great Britain and studied its great courses on an Ohio State Landscape Architecture Traveling Fellowship.

Upon return to the States, Esler went to work full-time for Nugent and continued to play in national Amateur events. But in 1987 the lure of the Tour led him to turn professional. He took a swing at both the American and Canadian PGA Tours for two seasons with little success.

In 1989 Esler returned to the Chicago area and formed his own golf design firm based in St. Charles.

Courses by Dave Esler (All as assistant to Dick Nugent unless otherwise indicated):

Illinois: Arboretum GC (1990); Bull Valley GC (1989); Glendale Lakes GC (1987); GC of Illinois (1987); Ivanhoe C (1991); Oak Brook Hills GC (1987); Royal Fox GC (1990).

Texas: Mission CC (1983).

Courses remodeled or expanded by Dave Esler (All as assistant to Dick Nugent unless otherwise indicated):

Illinois: Antioch GC (R.2 1990 *solo*); Big Run GC (R.); Bowes Creek G Cse (R. 1991 *solo*); Briarwood CC (R. 1991 *solo*); Joe Louis the Champ GC (R. 1987); Northmoor CC (R.); Ruth Lake CC (R. 1984).

Indiana: Youche CC (R.).

Iowa: Wakonda C (R. 1987).

CHARLES EVANS
(1890–1979)

BORN: Indianapolis, Indiana.
DIED: Chicago, Illinois, at age 89.

"Chick" Evans, winner of the 1916 U.S. Open and Amateur, wrote extensively about golf architecture for periodicals in the 1920s. For a short period during this time he was associated with Tom Bendelow, who instructed him in course design. In 1927 Evans was hired by the Cook County (Illinois) Board of Parks to "dot the forest preserves with golf." He set up a design office in Chicago, but his output

Chick Evans, circa 1960 COURTESY *GOLF WORLD*

was severely curtailed by the Depression. Evans did do at least one course unrelated to the Cook County project, Cutten Fields Country Club in Guelph, Ontario, Canada, which he designed and built in the late 1920s.

Keith Evans, 1990
COURTESY ASGCA

KEITH E. EVANS
(1944–), ASGCA

BORN: Plymouth, Michigan.

Keith Evans graduated from Michigan State University with a B.A. degree in business administration in 1966. Following military service, during which he was a member of the U.S. Army European Rifle Team, he was employed by Lever Brothers and later with Capital Irrigation.

In 1973 Evans returned to Michigan State to study landscape architecture and received his degree in 1976. He then worked for a year with golf architect Joseph S. Finger in 1977 and in 1978 built courses for golf designer Dick Watson. In 1979 Evans joined the staff of Rees Jones and over the next dozen years rose to become a senior associate in the firm.

Courses by Keith Evans (All as assistant to Rees Jones unless otherwise indicated):

Georgia: Jones Creek GC (1986); Southbridge GC (1989).

Kansas: Rolling Meadows GC (1981), ass't Richard Watson.
Nebraska: Tara Hills GC (9 Precision 1978), ass't Richard Watson.
New Jersey: Pinch Brook GC (Precision 1984).
North Carolina: Bryan Park GC (Champions Cse 1990); Harbour Pointe GC (9 1986); Pinehurst CC (Cse No. 7 1986).
Pennsylvania: Eagle Lodge GC (1982).
South Carolina: Woodside Plantation GC (Wysteria Cse 1987).
Virginia: Hell's Point GC (1982); Stoney Creek GC (1989).

Courses remodeled or expanded by Keith Evans (All as assistant to Rees Jones unless otherwise indicated):
Florida: Crystal Lago CC (R. 1981).
Illinois: Skokie CC (R. 1981).
New Jersey: Flanders Valley GC (White & Blue Cse, R.4 A.9 1982); Ridgewood CC (R. 1981).
New York: Westchester CC (South Cse, R. 1983; West Cse, R. 1982).

Floyd Farley, 1966
COURTESY FLOYD
FARLEY

**FLOYD FARLEY
(1907–), ASGCA, PRESIDENT 1966**

BORN: Kansas City, Missouri.

Floyd Farley began his career in golf as a caddy in 1919. He was later employed as professional at Crestwood Country Club in Kansas, Dundee Golf Club in Omaha, Nebraska, and Twin Hills Golf and Country Club in Oklahoma City.

He designed and built his first course, Woodlawn GC in Oklahoma City, in 1932 and then operated it until 1947. During that period Farley won the Oklahoma PGA Championship (in 1936 and 1942) and the Oklahoma Match Play Open in 1937. He also escorted A. W. Tillinghast around the state during the legendary architect's review of courses on behalf of the PGA of America in 1936.

In 1941 Farley designed and built Meridian Golf Club in Oklahoma City, which he owned until 1961. While operating his daily-fee courses, Farley had helped many small Oklahoma communities construct golf courses. In 1947 Farley decided to devote himself full-time to golf course architecture and developed a decided preference for par-70 layouts, with three par-3 and two par-5 holes per nine. Farley felt his own style to have been most influenced by golf architects William P. Bell and Perry Maxwell. In the early 1980s Farley and his wife, Betty, retired to Sedona, Arizona.

Courses by Floyd Farley:

Kansas: Clay Center CC (9 1964); Hidden Lakes CC (1958); Lake Forest GC (9, NLE); Leroy King Private Cse (3 1956); McConnell AFB GC (9 1959); Overland Park Muni (27 1971); Salina Muni (1970).
Missouri: A. L. Gustin Jr. Memorial GC (1957); Ava G&CC (9 1966); Cabool-Mountain Grove GC (9 1969); Current River CC (9 1970); Green Hills CC (9 1969); Jamestown CC (9 1969); Lake Valley G&CC (1969); Marceline CC (9 1970); Piney Valley GC [FNA Fort Leonard Wood GC](1958); Salem CC (9 1969); Sedalia CC (1970); Twin Oaks CC (1956), with *Horton Smith*; Wedgewood CC (9); Willow Springs GC (9 1970).
Nebraska: Holmes Park Muni (1964); James H. Ager Jr. GC (9 Par 3 1964); Knolls GC (Par 3 1962); Mahoney GC (1975); Meadowbrook GC (9 Par 3 1963); Miracle Hill GC (1963).
New Mexico: New Mexico Military Institute GC (1957); New Mexico State University GC (1962).
Oklahoma: Adams Park Muni (1962); Alva G&CC (9 1950); Arrowhead State Park GC (9 1960); Atoka Muni (9 1964); Beavers Bend State Park GC (9 1976); Broadmoore CC (1962); Brookside GC (9 1956); Cedar Valley GC (27 1974); Dr. Gil Morgan G Cse [FKA Wewoka Muni](9 1949); Earlywine Park GC (1976); El Reno CC (9 1948); Fort Cobb Lake State Park GC (1965); Fountainhead State Park GC (1965); Hook & Slice GC (9 Par 3 1972); John Conrad GC (Precision 1971); Kickingbird GC (1971); Kingfisher GC (9); La Fortune Park Muni (1961, Par 3 Cse 1965); Lake Hefner GC (South Cse 1962); Lake Texoma State Park GC (1958);

McAlester CC (9 1956); Meridian GC (1947); Midwest City Muni (9 Precision 1957); Mohawk Park Muni (Pecan Valley Cse 1957); Nemaha G&CC (1957, NLE); Quail Creek G&CC (1961); Recreation GC (9 1961); Roman Nose State Park GC (9 1960); Sand Springs Muni (1958); Sequoyah State Park GC (1959); Seth Hughes GC (9 Par 3 1958, NLE); Shattuck GC (9 1970); Sulphur Hills CC (9 1960); Tinker AFB GC (9 1961); Walnut Hills CC (1954); Western Village GC (9 Par 3 1954, NLE); Westwood Muni; Westwood Park GC (9 1949, A.9 1968); Woodlawn GC (1932).

Courses remodeled or expanded by Floyd Farley:

Kansas: Crestwood CC (R.3 A.9 1978); Four Oaks GC (A.9 1980); Indian Hills CC (R. 1958); Kansas City CC (R.2 1959); Lake Quivira CC (R. 1958); Milburn G&CC (R. 1957); Mission Hills CC (R.2 1959); Rolling Hills CC (R. 1963).
Missouri: Metro GC (R. 1958, NLE).
Nebraska: Norfolk CC (R.13 A.5).
Oklahoma: Altus GC (A.9); Elks CC, Duncan (A.9 1950); Hillcrest CC (R.9 1960); Lake Hefner GC (North Cse, R.); Lawton CC (A.9 1957); Lew Wentz Memorial GC (R.9 A.9); Lincoln Park Muni (East Cse, R. 1965; West Cse, R. 1965); Mohawk Park Muni (Woodbine Cse, R. 1957); Oklahoma City G&CC (R.10); Rolling Hills CC (R. 1957); Tulsa CC (R. A.3 1968); Twin Hills G&CC (R.1).

**GEORGE FAZIO
(1912–1986), ASGCA**

BORN: Norristown, Pennsylvania.
DIED: Jupiter, Florida, at age 75.

George Fazio played on the PGA Tour in the 1930s and 1940s, winning the 1946 Canadian Open, tying Ben Hogan and Lloyd Mangrum in the 1950 U.S. Open (losing to Hogan in the playoff) and placing fifth and fourth respectively in the 1952 and 1953 Opens. During the same years, he also served as resident professional at several clubs, including the famed Pine Valley in New Jersey.

George Fazio, circa 1975 COURTESY TOM FAZIO

Fazio entered private practice as a course architect in 1959 quite by chance, when a friend asked for his help in routing a golf course. He soon began designing courses on the side, but at the same time continued operating a car dealership and a series of golf courses in the Philadelphia area. Among the young laborers who worked on maintaining his courses were two nephews, Jim and Tom, both of whom would later work with him in golf course architecture.

George Fazio did a series of courses that garnered national acclaim. Moselem Springs served as host to a U.S. Women's Open and then quickly made *Golf Digest*'s list of America's 100 Greatest Golf Courses. Jupiter Hills in Florida captured the golf world's imagination with a series of holes reminiscent of Pine Valley. Butler National became the new home of the PGA Tour's Western Open and proved to be a difficult test for the world's best.

George Fazio also worked as a consulting architect for a number of major golf tournaments, including the Masters and several U.S. Opens. In 1974 George made Tom a full partner in his firm. A decade later the two split up. George did one last course with Jim and was planning others at the time of his death.

Courses by George Fazio (All with Tom Fazio unless otherwise indicated):

Arizona: Willowbrook GC (1973); Willowcreek GC (1973).
Connecticut: Ridgefield Muni (1974).
Florida: East Lakes GC (1981); Eastpointe CC (1976); Jonathan's Landing GC (1978); Jupiter Hills C (Hills Cse 1970 solo, R. A.3 1974; Village Cse 1979); Palm Beach Polo & CC (Olde Cse 1979, 9, NLE); Palm-Aire CC (Cypress Cse 1979; Oaks Cse 1973); [The] Reserve G&CC (1984), with Jim Fazio; Riverbend CC (Precision 1978).
Hawaii: Turtle Bay GC (Old Cse 1971).

Illinois: Butler National GC (1974); Marriott Lincolnshire GC (1975).
Massachusetts: Oak Ridge GC; Wollaston CC (1976).
Nevada: Edgewood Tahoe CC (1968 solo).
New Jersey: Great Gorge GC [FKA Playboy Club/Hotel GC](27 1970); Ocean County G Cse [FKA Atlantis GC](1961 solo).
North Carolina: Pinehurst CC (Cse No. 6 1976).
Ohio: Sawmill Creek GC (1972).
Oklahoma: Indian Springs CC (River Cse 1968 solo).
Pennsylvania: Bristolwood GC (Par 3 1963 solo); Downingtown Inn GC (1967 solo); Hershey CC (East Cse 1970 solo); Kimberton GC (1962 solo); Moselem Springs CC (1964 solo); Pocono Manor Inn & GC (West Cse 1965 solo); Silver Spring GC (Precision 1969 solo); Squires GC (1961 solo); Tanglewood GC (1965 solo); Waynesborough CC (1965 solo).
South Carolina: Bay Tree G Plantation (Gold Cse 1972; Green Cse 1972; Silver Cse 1972); Moss Creek Plantation GC (South Cse 1975); Palmetto Dunes CC (Fazio Cse 1974).
Texas: Champions GC (Jackrabbit Cse 1964 solo); Clear Lake GC (9 1961 solo); El Dorado GC (1964 solo).
Ontario: National GC (1976).
Bahamas: Coral Harbour GC, Nassau (1964 solo, NLE).
Costa Rica: Cariari International CC (1973).
Panama: Coronado Beach GC (1974).
Puerto Rico: Rio Mar GC (1976).
Virgin Islands: Mahogany Run GC (1979).

Courses remodeled or expanded by George Fazio (All with Tom Fazio unless otherwise indicated):

California: Bel-Air CC (R.1 1967).
Connecticut: Tumble Brook CC (A.9 1975).
Florida: Everglades C (R. 1979); Jupiter Island C (R.).
Georgia: Atlanta Athletic C (Highlands Cse, R. 1975); Augusta National GC (R. 1972 solo).
Indiana: Meridian Hills CC (R. 1980).
Maryland: Columbia CC (R.); Congressional CC (Gold Cse, A.9 1977); Hillendale CC (R. 1968 solo).
Massachusetts: Presidents GC [FKA Wollaston CC](R. 1976).

New Jersey: Greate Bay CC (R. 1970 solo).
New York: Apawamis C (R. 1977); Nevele GC (R.); Oak Hill CC (East Cse, R. A.3 1979); Winged Foot GC (West Cse, R. 1973).
Ohio: Inverness C (R. A.4 1978).
Oklahoma: Southern Hills CC (R. 1976).
Pennsylvania: Aronimink GC (R. 1978); Chester Valley CC (R. 1964 solo); Langhorne GC (R. 1958 solo).

Tom Fazio, 1991 COURTESY TOM FAZIO

THOMAS JOSEPH FAZIO (1945–), ASGCA

BORN: Norristown, Pennsylvania.

Tom Fazio entered the business of golf course architecture as a teenager in 1962, assisting his uncle George Fazio in course construction. His on-the-job training and experience gave him intimate knowledge of engineering, landscape design, soils and accounting as well as the business side of the trade.

In 1974 he became a full partner with George, and the partnership gradually became one of the nation's leading course design firms. By the end of the decade, Tom was handling most of the firm's work, with George in semi retirement. Eventually the two went their separate ways. Tom continued to practice under the firm name of Fazio Golf Course Designers, while George did one last course before his death in 1986 in association with Tom's brother Jim Fazio.

His 1979 remodeling of Inverness and his 1980 remodeling of Oak Hill garnered Tom Fazio his first real national attention, but most of it was unfavorable. But the opening of his Wild Dunes course along the Atlantic in South Carolina in 1980 quickly changed that. Next came rave reviews for the opulent Vintage Club near Palm Springs, California. But it was a series of private courses in the late 1980s, starting with Wade Hampton in North Carolina, that elevated Tom Fazio in both public esteem and net worth. Wade Hampton was named Best New Private Course of 1987 by *Golf Digest*. The following year, Fazio's Black Diamond Ranch was accorded the same honor, and two years after that his Shadow Creek Golf Club (reportedly one of the most expensive courses ever constructed in America) nailed down the award for a third time. During the same time frame, Fazio was rated as the top golf architect in separate polls conducted by *Golf Course News* and *Golf Digest*.

Through it all, Fazio retained his humility and his popularity among his peers. He surrounded himself with a strong, talented staff of designers and construction supervisors that included Andy Banfield, Jan Beljan, Steve Burns, Dana Fry, Tom Marzolf, Maury Miller and Dennis Wise, and he was never hesitant to credit them for much of his success. After years of commuting from his home in Hendersonville, North Carolina, to an office in Jupiter, Florida, in 1990 Fazio moved his base of operations to Hendersonville.

Courses by Tom Fazio (All with George Fazio unless otherwise indicated):

Alabama: Liberty Park GC (1992), with Jerry Pate.

Arizona: Ventana Canyon G&RC (Canyon Cse 1988 *solo*; Mountain Cse 1984 *solo*); Willowbrook GC (1973); Willowcreek GC (1973).

California: Pelican Hill GC (Canyon Cse 1993 *solo*; Ocean Cse 1992 *solo*); [The] Vintage C (Desert Cse 1984 *solo*; Mountain Cse 1981 *solo*).

Connecticut: Ridgefield Muni (1974).

Florida: [The] Bayou C (9 1986, A.9 1991 *solo*); Black Diamond Ranch G&CC (1987 *solo*); Bluewater Bay GC (1981 *solo*, A.3rd 9); Bonnet Creek GC (Osprey Ridge Cse 1991 *solo*); East Lakes GC (1981); Eastpointe CC (1976); Emerald Dunes GC (1990 *solo*); Gateway GC (1989 *solo*); Golden Eagle GC (1986 *solo*); Hammock Dunes GC (1988 *solo*); Hunter's Green CC (1989 *solo*); John's Island C (West Cse 1988 *solo*); Jonathan's Landing GC (1978); Jupiter Hills C (Hills Cse 1970, ass't George Fazio, R. A.3 1974; Village Cse 1979); Lake Nona GC (1986 *solo*); Long Point C (1987 *solo*); Mariner Sands CC (Gold Cse 1982 *solo*); Old Trail GC (Fazio Cse 1987 *solo*); Palm Beach Polo & CC (Olde Cse 1979, 9, NLE); Palm-Aire CC (Cypress Cse 1974; Oaks Cse 1973); Pelican's Nest GC (1987, A.3rd 9 1990 *solo*); PGA National GC (Haig Cse 1980 *solo*; Squire Course 1981 *solo*; Champion Cse 1981 *solo*); Riverbend CC (Precision 1978); Windstar C (1983 *solo*).

Georgia: Eagle's Landing CC (1989 *solo*); [The] Farm GC (1989 *solo*); [The] Landings at Skidaway Island (Deer Creek Cse 1991); St. Ives CC (1989 *solo*).

Hawaii: Turtle Bay GC (Old Cse 1971).

Illinois: Butler National GC (1974); Conway Farms GC (1991 *solo*); Marriott Lincolnshire GC (1975); Stonebridge CC (1989 *solo*).

Kansas: Hallbrook CC (1988 *solo*).

Maryland: Caves Valley GC (1991 *solo*).

Massachusetts: Oak Ridge GC; Wollaston CC (1976).

Michigan: Treetops North GC (Fazio Cse 1992 *solo*).

Nevada: Edgewood Tahoe CC (1968), ass't George Fazio; Shadow Creek GC (1990), with *Steve Wynn*.

New Jersey: Great Gorge GC (27 1971); Pine Valley GC (Short Cse, 10 1992 *solo*).

New York: Oyster Bay G Cse (1988 *solo*).

North Carolina: Champion Hills C (1991 *solo*); Old North State C (1992 *solo*); Pinehurst CC (Cse No. 6 1978); Porters Neck CC (1991 *solo*); Treyburn CC (1989 *solo*); Wade Hampton GC (1987 *solo*).

Ohio: Sawmill Creek GC (1973).

Oklahoma: GC of Oklahoma (1982 *solo*).

South Carolina: Bay Tree G Plantation (Gold Cse 1972; Green Cse 1972; Silver Cse 1972); Cotton Dike GC (1985, A.2 1990 *solo*); CC of Callawassie (1986, A.3rd 9 1991 *solo*); Moss Creek Plantation GC (North Cse 1979 *solo*; South Cse 1975); Osprey Point G Links (1988 *solo*); Palmetto Dunes CC (Fazio Cse 1974); Thornblade CC (1989 *solo*); Wachesaw Plantation GC (1986 *solo*); Wild Dunes G Links (Links Cse 1980 *solo*, R. 1990 *solo*; Yacht Harbor Cse 1986 *solo*).

Tennessee: GC of Tennessee (1991 *solo*).

Texas: Barton Creek C (Fazio Cse 1986 *solo*).

Virginia: Governors Landing CC (1992 *solo*).

Ontario: National GC (1976).

Costa Rica: Cariari International CC (1973).

Panama: Coronado Beach GC (1974).

Puerto Rico: Rio Mar GC (1976).

Virgin Islands: Mahogany Run GC (1979).

Courses remodeled or expanded by Tom Fazio (All with George Fazio unless otherwise indicated):

Arizona: McCormick Ranch GC (Palm Cse, R. 1981 *solo*; Pine Cse, R. 1981 *solo*).

Connecticut: Tumble Brook CC (A.9 1975).

Florida: Everglades C (R. 1979); Jupiter Island C (R.).

Georgia: Atlanta Athletic C (Highlands Cse, R. 1975; R. 1980 *solo*); Augusta National GC (Par 3 Cse, A.2 1986 *solo*).

Indiana: Meridian Hills CC (R. 1980).

Maryland: Columbia CC (R.); Congressional CC (Gold Cse, A.9 1977).

Massachusetts: Presidents GC [FKA Wollaston CC](R. 1976).

New Jersey: Pine Valley GC (R.2 1989 *solo*).

New York: Apawamis C (R. 1977); Nevele GC (R.); Oak Hill CC (East Cse, R. A.3 1979); Winged Foot GC (West Cse, R. 1973, R. 1989 *solo*).

North Carolina: Hendersonville CC (R. 1990 *solo*); Highlands Falls CC (R.1 1985 *solo*).

Ohio: Inverness C (R. A.4 1978).

Oklahoma: Southern Hills CC (R. 1976).

Pennsylvania: Aronimink GC (R. 1978); Philadelphia CC (A.3rd 9 1992 *solo*).

South Carolina: CC of Edisto Island (R. 1988 *solo*).

Texas: Columbia Lakes CC (R. 1981 *solo*); Tennwood C (R. 1979 *solo*).

VINCENT JAMES FAZIO (1942–)

BORN: Norristown, Pennsylvania.

Jim Fazio was the older brother of Tom Fazio, and the two of them worked for their famous uncle George Fazio in the golf business for over 20 years, first in club operations and then in golf course construction. While Tom chose to remain in architecture, Jim pursued a career as a golf professional and club manager for a time. But in the 1970s he returned to the employ of his uncle.

In 1984, after Tom and George had dissolved their partnership, Jim joined his uncle to establish the George and Jim Fazio Design Company. Together they designed one course, The Reserve G&CC in

Jim Fazio, 1991
COURTESY JIM FAZIO

Fort Pierce, Florida, before George took ill. The elder Fazio died in 1986, and Jim continued the practice in his own name, with an office in Florida and later one in Switzerland. He personally built as well as designed his courses, with the intention of creating golf courses that appeared to have evolved from the ground they occupied. In the late 1980s Fazio expanded his business with a construction branch and was joined by his sons James and Thomas.

Overshadowed in most of his design career by both his uncle and brother, Jim Fazio achieved some international success in 1991 when his LaQuerce GC in Rome hosted the World Cup.

Courses by Jim Fazio:

Florida: Emerald Dunes GC (routing 1989); Fairwinds G Cse (1991); Hawk's Nest CC (1987); St. Lucie West GC (1987); [The] Reserve G&CC (1984), with George Fazio.
Indiana: [The] Legends of Indiana (1992).
Maine: [The] Woodlands C (1988).
Texas: Riverchase GC (1988).
Italy: LaQuerce GC (1987); Marco Simone GC (1989).
Japan: Nyu GC (1988); Old Orchard GC (1988).

FRED FEDERSPIEL

Fred Federspiel served for many years as superintendent of several courses, including Oswego Lake CC in Oregon. He laid out a number of courses in the Pacific Northwest in the 1950s and '60s.

Courses by Fred Federspiel:

Oregon: Marysville GC (9 1958); McNary GC (1962), with *Fred Sparks*; Meriwether National GC (1962); Ocean Dunes G Cse [FKA Rhodo Dunes GC](9 1960); Pineway GC (9 Precision 1958); Salishan G Links (1965); Santiam GC (1957); Spring Hill CC (1960); Sunriver CC (South Cse 1969).
Washington: Briarcliff G&CC (1969); Royal Oaks CC (1952).

Courses remodeled or expanded by Fred Federspiel:

Oregon: Agate Beach GC (R.9 1965); Corvallis CC (A.9 1957).
Washington: Olympia G&CC (A.9 1959).

A. H. Fenn, circa 1900 COURTESY BOB LABBANCE

ARTHUR H. FENN
(1858–1925)

BORN: Waterbury, Connecticut.
DIED: Lewiston, Maine, at age 67.
INTERRED: Hartford, Connecticut.

After a brief spell as a competitive bicyclist and a try at professional baseball, talented sportsman A. H. Fenn took up golf at age 36 while wintering in Aiken, South Carolina. Within a year he was playing at scratch and captured the first of three successive Lenox Cup championships, a high honor for U.S. amateur golfers at the time. In 1895 he laid out his first golf course in his hometown of Waterbury, Connecticut. A year later he took a job managing the Waumbek Hotel in New Hampshire's White Mountains and soon expanded and improved its nine-hole course. An invitation to design a course for the Poland Spring House in Maine soon followed, and after routing its first nine-hole layout in the fall of 1896, Fenn remained at Poland Spring for 25 years, serving as its course manager and teaching professional while doing similar duty in the winter months at the Palm Beach (Florida) Golf Club and later the Palm Beach Country Club.

Fenn was generally considered to be the first American-born golf professional. Although primarily a club professional, he maintained his competitive edge for decades and won the inaugural Maine Open in 1918. One of his keenest golfing rivals was Alex Findlay, against whom Fenn played countless matches in the early twentieth century. He also competed against Harry Vardon during Vardon's 1900 tour of America. A daughter, Bessie Fenn, became the first female golf professional in America and assumed Fenn's duties at Palm Beach Country Club upon his death.

Although Fenn's course-design work was rudimentary in nature and his efforts were confined to New England states before the turn of the century, he was one of the pioneer golf architects in America.

Courses by A. H. Fenn:

New Hampshire: Abenaqui GC (6 1899); Crawford Notch GC (6 1899, NLE); Mount Washington GC (9 1899); Portsmouth Navy Yard GC (9 1896, NLE); Profile C (9 1899); Twin Mountain GC (9 1899, NLE).
Maine: Oquossoc GC (1899, NLE); Poland Spring GC (9 1896).
Massachusetts: Fall River CC (6).

Courses remodeled or expanded by A. H. Fenn:

Florida: Palm Beach Golf Club (R.)
New Hampshire: Waumbek GC (R.9 A.9 1896).

MICHAEL GEORGE FENN
(1915–1982), BIGCA

BORN: England.
DIED: Lyon, France, at age 67.

As a youngster Michael Fenn moved with his family to France, where his father constructed homes. Michael attended school in Paris, but when his family moved back to Britain in 1937, he transferred to Dover College. After graduation, he began horticultural work, but enlisted with the Royal Navy in 1939 and later fought as a naval commando during World War II. At the end of the war Fenn restored a war-torn 9-hole course in Leckford, England, then remained at the club until 1952, when, in answer to a magazine advertisement, he returned to France to participate in the restoration of a course in Mont-Louis. He then worked at re-creating other war-damaged courses in that country and Belgium. A talented golfer who played to a two handicap, Fenn soon tried some original designs and, over the next 25 years, did over two dozen courses on the Continent while serving as club professional at Evian and then Valcros. He was aided in all his designs by his wife, Nina, who handled the drafting and working drawings. Fenn died in 1982 of a heart attack suffered while playing a round of golf.

Courses by Michael Fenn:

France: Assoc. Sportive du G de Méribel (9); Brest-Iroise GC (1976); C de Palmola; G de Besançon (1967); G de Bourgogne (9); G de Claris; G de Clermont-Ferrand; G de Touraine (1972); G du Clair Vallon; GC de Brotel; GC de Quiberon; GC de Villette-d'Anthon; G Puy de Dome; Lann Rohou GC (9); St. Laurent Ploemel GC (1975); Toulouse-Palmola GC (1974).

Courses remodeled or expanded by Michael Fenn:

England: Leckford and Longstock GC (R. 1946).
France: C de Lyon (R. 1953, NLE); Evian GC (R.); GC de Reims (A.9 1977); G de Nancy-Aingeray (R. 1964); G de Lyon (A.9); Vieille Toulouse GC (A.9 1970).

MARVIN H. FERGUSON (1918–1985), ASGCA

BORN: Texas.
DIED: Bryan, Texas, at age 66.

Dr. Marvin Ferguson graduated from Texas A&M University and received a Ph.D. degree from the University of Maryland. From 1940 until 1969 he was engaged in turfgrass research with the USGA Green Section and Texas A&M. Ferguson played a major role in developing the USGA method of green construction. In 1973 he was presented the USGA's Green Section Award for his extended turfgrass research.

In 1969 Ferguson began to design golf courses. While he did relatively few in his career, they were characterized by well-thought-out strategic holes and excellent turfgrass conditions. His daughter, Judy Ferguson Gockel, became a prominent analyst of sand and soil for golf courses.

Marvin Ferguson, 1958 COLLECTION RON WHITTEN

Courses by Marvin Ferguson:

Arkansas: Ben Geren GC (1970).
Kansas: Wolf Creek GC (1972).
Louisiana: Les Vieux Chenes GC (1977); Mississippi State University G Cse (routing 1980).
Missouri: Bahnfyre GC (1981, NLE); CC of Missouri (1974); West Plains CC (1977).
Tennessee: Holly Hills CC (1972).
Texas: Briarcrest CC (1971); Cielo Vista GC (1977).

Courses remodeled or expanded by Marvin Ferguson:

Arkansas: Hardscrabble CC (R. 1970).
Missouri: Hillcrest CC (R.4 1975); Westwood CC (R.1 1969).
New Mexico: Ocotillo Park GC (A.9 1969).
Pennsylvania: Carrollton CC (R.9 1969).
Texas: Abilene CC (R.1 1975); Brae Burn CC (R.4 1969); Bryan Muni (R.6 1971); Coronado G&CC (R. 1972); Eastern Hills CC (R.5 1986); Northwood C (R.5 1974).

Willie Fernie, circa 1912 COLLECTION RON WHITTEN

WILLIE FERNIE (1858–1924)

BORN: St. Andrews, Scotland.
DIED: Troon, Scotland, at age 66.

Willie Fernie was one of several golfing brothers who grew up at St. Andrews. His siblings were George (a longtime pro-

---

greenkeeper at Dumfries who laid out Hunstanton in 1898), Tom, Harry and Eddie. Willie was the best golfer of the lot, winning the 1883 British Open in a playoff after finishing second the year before. In all he had five runner-up finishes in The Open.

Fernie served as pro-greenkeeper at several Scottish clubs, ultimately settling at Troon (which he laid out) in 1887. He remained there the rest of his life, staking out many courses on the side. Among his best-known were the Ailsa and Arran courses at Turnberry.

Courses by Willie Fernie:

England: Aldeburgh GC (1894); Whitsand Bay Hotel GC (1909).
Scotland: Cardross GC (1895); Darley GC; Lochgreen GC; Pitlochry GC (1908); Shiskine GC; Troon Portland GC (1905); Turnberry GC (Ailsa Cse 1909; Arran Cse 1909); Whitecraigs GC (1905).
Wales: Southerndown GC (1905).

Courses remodeled or expanded by Willie Fernie:

England: Felixstowe Ferry GC (R., NLE).
Scotland: Cochrane Castle GC (R. 1921); Royal Troon GC (R. 1900).

Leo Feser, circa 1963 COLLECTION RON WHITTEN

LEO J. FESER (1900–1976)

BORN: Minnesota.
DIED: Mesa, Arizona, at age 76.

Leo Feser served as superintendent at Woodhill CC, Wayzata, Minnesota, for 30 years. He was a charter member of the GCSAA and served as a national director and vice president in the mid-1930s. He also edited the association's trade journal, and after his retirement an annual golf writing award was established by the GCSAA in his honor.

Feser's first experience in course design was in 1924, when he laid out Minnesota's first privately owned daily-fee course at Orono. He did no other design work until after leaving Woodhill in 1951. He and his sons then began purchasing and operating daily-fee layouts, which Feser remodeled. During this period Feser also designed a couple of new small layouts.

Courses by Leo Feser:

Minnesota: Normandale GC (1956); Orono Public GC (1927).
Wisconsin: Hudson CC.

HOMER D. FIELDHOUSE

Based in Wisconsin, Homer Fieldhouse designed courses throughout the Midwestern states from the mid-1950s on.

Courses by Homer Fieldhouse:

Illinois: Braidwood GC (9 1965); Gibson Woods Muni (1966).
Iowa: Lake Creek CC (1972).
Minnesota: Valley High GC (9 1970).
Ohio: Candywood GC (1966); Ponderosa CC (1966).
Wisconsin: Camelot CC (1966); Cedar Springs GC; Clifton Highlands GC (1972); Dodge Point GC (9); Eagle Bluff CC (1967); Golden Sands GC (1970); Golf Village GC (9 Precision); Lake Breeze GC (1991); Rock River Hills GC (1965).

Courses remodeled or expanded by Homer Fieldhouse:

South Dakota: Hillcrest G&CC (A.9 1972).
Wisconsin: Fox Lake CC (A.9 1965).

ALEXANDER H. FINDLAY
(1865–1942)

BORN: Scotland.
DIED: Philadelphia, Pennsylvania, at age 76.

Alex Findlay emigrated to the United States in the early 1880s to manage a ranch in Nebraska. There he introduced the game of golf and laid out a golf course in 1885. Findlay was later in charge of planning, constructing and operating courses for the Florida East Coast Railroad, the same position as that held by

Alex Findlay, 1940
COLLECTION RON
WHITTEN

John Duncan Dunn with the rival Florida West Coast Railroad.

Findlay was for a time associated in course development with Wright and Ditson and later with Wanamaker's, both prominent East Coast sporting goods firms. In addition, he continued to plan courses on his own, designing over 100 layouts in his design career, many of them constructed by his sons Norman, Ronald and Richard.

Alex Findlay was one of the genuine pioneers in the game. He played a series of American exhibitions with the great Harry Vardon, played some 2,400 courses during his lifetime and established dozens of course records. In 1926 he visited the Vatican, where he tried unsuccessfully to establish a six-hole golf course.

Courses by Alex Findlay:

Arkansas: Fort Smith CC (9).
Connecticut: Hartford GC (1909, NLE).
Florida: [The] Breakers GC (9 1905); Miami G Links (9, NLE); Oceanside G&CC (9 1911); Palm Beach GC (1900, NLE); St. Augustine CC (9 1908, NLE).
Maine: Belgrade Hotel GC (9 1903, NLE); Grindstone Inn GC (9); Megunticook GC (9); Summit GC (9).
Maryland: Chester River Y&CC (1924); Royal Swan CC (1924).
Massachusetts: Bear Hill GC (9); Brockton CC (9); Dedham Hunt & Polo C; Forest Park GC (1901); Great Island GC; Greenfield CC (9 1896); Long Meadow GC, Lowell (9); Meadow Brook GC (9); Miacomet G Links; Northfield GC (9 1912); Siasconset GC (9); Vesper CC (9).
Montana: Butte CC (1909).
New Hampshire: Ferncliffe CC (NLE); Granliden Hotel GC (9, NLE); Intervale GC (9 1899); Maplewood GC (9); Mont Vernon GC (NLE); Russell Cottage GC (9, NLE); Soo Nipi Park GC

(9 1897, NLE); Wentworth-by-the-Sea (9 1899, NLE).
New Jersey: Basking Ridge GC [FKA Pennbrook GC](1927); Blackwood CC (1929); Cohanzick CC (1917); Medford Lakes CC (1930); Moorestown Field C (9); Newark Athletic C (1900, NLE); Pitman GC (1929); Tavistock CC; Woodbury CC (9).
New York: CC of Rochester (NLE); Glenburnie G Cse (9 1909, NLE); Lake George CC (9 1909, NLE); Lake Placid C (Upper Cse 1910); Saranac Lake G Cse (9 1920).
North Carolina: Eseeola Lodge GC (1912, NLE).
Oklahoma: Guthrie CC (9).
Pennsylvania: Aronimink GC (1913, NLE); Centre Hills CC (9); Clearfield-Curwensville CC (1924); Clinton CC (9 1910, NLE); Coatesville CC (1921); Galen Hall GC (1910); Green Pond CC (1931); Langhorne GC; Lebanon CC (NLE); Llanerch CC; Luden Riverside CC (1930); Manor CC; Phillipsburg CC (9 1924); Pittsburgh Field C; Reading CC (1923); Roseneath Farms GC (9 Par 3 1936); Shamokin Valley CC (9); Tredyffrin CC; Tyrone CC (1925); Walnut Lane GC (1935).
Tennessee: CC of Bristol (9, NLE).
Texas: Beaumont CC (1907); San Antonio CC (1908).
Vermont: Old Pine GC (NLE).
Virginia: Roanoke CC (1907, NLE).
West Virginia: [The] Greenbrier GC (Lakeside Cse, 9, NLE).
Bahamas: Nassau G Links (6, NLE).

Courses remodeled or expanded by Alex Findlay:

Maine: Tarratine C of Dark Harbor (R.9 1914).
New Hampshire: Mount Washington GC (A.9 1902); Soo Nipi Park GC (R. 1899, NLE).
New Jersey: Essex County CC (East Cse, A.9 1900, NLE).

FREDERICK A. FINDLAY
(1872–1966)

BORN: Scotland.
DIED: Charlottesville, Virginia, at age 94.

Fred Findlay, the son of a British army officer, joined the army at the age of 14 and served for 21 years, most of them as a

Fred Findlay, circa 1955 COLLECTION RON WHITTEN

bandmaster. Upon retiring from the service he moved to Australia, where he spent 13 years as a club professional and did his first golf design work.

After the First World War, Findlay moved to the United States, following older brother Alex who had emigrated there as a young man and become a pioneer golf promoter and course designer. Fred settled in Virginia, where he served as professional and superintendent at various clubs and designed a number of courses over the next 30 years. In his later years he was partnered with his son-in-law, Raymond F. Loving, Sr., in a course design and construction firm later maintained by his grandson, Raymond "Buddy" Loving, Jr.

Findlay remained active as a golf architect into the early 1960s. A fine landscape artist and poet as well as golfer, he consistently shot his age during the last 20 years of his life. Although an artist, he detested blueprints and claimed the land was his drawing board.

Courses by Fred Findlay:

Maryland: Bethesda CC (9 1927).
North Carolina: Chapel Hill CC (1940, NLE); Paradise Point GC, Camp LeJeune (Green Cse 1939; Gold Cse 1945).
Pennsylvania: Yardley CC (1929).
South Carolina: Parris Island GC (1947).
Virginia: Augusta CC (1927); Bide-A-Wee CC (1955), with *R. F. Loving, Sr.;* Boonsboro CC (1927); Carper Valley GC; Crater CC (1934); CC of Culpepper (9 1960), with *R. F. Loving, Sr.;* Falling River CC, with *R. F. Loving, Sr.;* Farmington CC (1928); Glenwood CC (1925); Hopewell CC (1940); Hunting Hills CC (1965), with *R. F. Loving, Sr.,* and Buddy Loving;

Ingleside Augusta CC (1926); Keswick C of Virginia (1938); Lakeview CC, with *R. F. Loving, Sr.,* and Buddy Loving; Laurel GC (1926); Lawrenceville CC (1960), with *R. F. Loving, Sr.;* Luray GC (1934, NLE); McIntire Park GC (9 1952), with *R. F. Loving, Sr.;* Meadowbrook CC (1959), with *R. F. Loving, Sr.;* Ole Monterey CC (1925); Shenandoah CC; South Boston CC (1942); South Hill CC; Spotswood CC (1935, NLE); Swannanoa GC (1926); Tides Inn & CC (Short Cse [9 Precision]); Waynesboro CC (1950); Williamsburg CC (1935, NLE); Williamsburg Inn GC (9 Par 3 1946, NLE); Winchester GC (1960), with *R. F. Loving, Sr.;* Wytheville CC (9).
Virginia: CC of Virginia (James River Cse, R. 1931; Westhampton Cse, R. 1931); Washington G&CC (R.); Woodberry Forest GC (R.), with *R. F. Loving, Sr.*

Joe Finger, 1971 COLLECTION RON WHITTEN

JOSEPH S. FINGER (1918–)

BORN: Houston, Texas.

Joseph Finger received a Bachelor's degree in engineering in 1939 from Rice University, where he had been captain of the golf team under coach Jimmy Demaret. He continued his education at the Massachusetts Institute of Technology, receiving his Master's degree in 1941. Finger was employed for five years in oil refining and then became president of a plastics manufacturing company, where he developed a corrugated plastic building panel. During these years he also operated a dairy farm and a small commercial turf nursery.

In 1956 Finger planned his first golf course, a nine-hole addition to a course near Houston. His early work included a

number of courses for the U.S. Air Force as well as several jobs where he had received leads from former coach Demaret. Finger wrote the first publication examining golf design as a business, *The Business End of Building or Rebuilding a Golf Course,* distributed by the National Golf Foundation in 1973. He also developed a device he named a Percolometer, which was useful for on-the-job control of seed-bed mixtures for greens.

In 1985 Joe Finger added Ken Dye as a partner, and in 1987 Baxter Spann was invited to become a partner, too. Finger retired from active design work in 1990 to his home in Kerrville, Texas. He then worked to establish a regular golf architecture curriculum at several universities.

Courses by Joseph Finger:

Alabama: Cypress Tree GC, Maxwell AFB (West Cse); Oak Hills CC (1975), with Byron Nelson.
Arkansas: Bella Vista CC (1966); Pleasant Valley CC (27 1969); Riverlawn CC (9 1988).
California: Cypress Lakes GC (1960).
Colorado: Battlement Mesa GC (1988), with Ken Dye.
Georgia: Atlanta CC (1965), with Willard Byrd; Moody AFB GC (9 1968).
Louisiana: Ellendale CC (1967).
Mississippi: Deerfield CC (1980); Keesler AFB GC (9 1964).
New Jersey: Princeton Meadows GC (1972).
New Mexico: Picacho Hills CC (1979).
New York: Concord Hotel GC (Championship Cse 1964); Glen Oak C (27 1971).
Oklahoma: Cedar Ridge CC (1969).
Tennessee: Colonial CC (North Cse 1971; South Cse 1971).
Texas: Amarillo Public G Cse (1962); Bayou GC (1973); Baywood CC; Blue Lake Estates GC (9 Par 3 1962); Clear Creek G Cse (1988), with Baxter Spann and Ken Dye; Cottonwood Creek Muni (1985), with Ken Dye; Deerwood GC (1983), with Ken Dye; Golfcrest CC (1970); Grapevine Muni (1980), with Ken Dye and Byron Nelson; Hackberry Creek CC (1986), with Ken Dye; Kingwood CC (Island Cse 1974; Marsh Cse 1976); Laredo CC (1985), with Baxter Spann; Las Colinas CC (1964); Laughlin AFB GC (9 1960); Perrin AFB GC (9 1962); Piney Point GC (9 Par 3 1961, NLE); Riverhill C (1974), with Byron Nelson;

Starr Hollow GC (9 Precision 1967);
Tejas GC (1966, NLE); Valley International CC (1966).

Mexico: Bosques Del Lago CC (East Cse 1974; West Cse 1974); C de G Tequisquiapan (1985); C Atlas Campo de Golf (1970); Hacienda San Gaspar GC (1984); C de G Marina Vallarta (1986); Pulgas Pandas CC (9 1985).

Courses remodeled or expanded by Joseph Finger:

Arizona: Arizona CC (R.4 1960).
Arkansas: Blytheville CC (R.9 A.9 1968); Burns Park Muni (R. 1961); CC of Little Rock (R.3 1965); Meadowbrook CC (R.); Pine Bluff CC (R.9 A.9).
Florida: Shalimar Pointe CC (R. 1986), with Ken Dye.
Georgia: Atlanta Athletic C (Highlands Cse, A.9 1971); Augusta National GC (R.1 1979), with Byron Nelson; Bacon Park GC (R. 1973); Capital City CC (R.9); Highland CC (A.9); Peachtree GC (R. 1973).
Louisiana: Baton Rouge CC (R. 1973); England AFB GC (A.9 1989), with Baxter Spann and Ken Dye; Oakbourne CC (R. 1985), with Ken Dye; Shreveport CC (R.15 A.3 1960).
New Jersey: Montammy CC (R.4 1971).
New York: Grossinger's GC (R. A.3rd 9 1970); Lawrence Park Village GC (R. 1970); Metropolis CC (R.2); Muttontown G&CC (R. 1971); Westchester CC (West Cse, R. 1971).
Pennsylvania: Westmoreland CC (R. A.12 1967).
South Carolina: Whispering Pines GC, Myrtle Beach AFB (A.9 1987), with Baxter Spann and Ken Dye.
Tennessee: Richland CC (R.9 1967, NLE).
Texas: Brae Burn CC (R.4 1966); Columbian C (R.6 1971); Galveston CC (R.6 1972); Hearthstone CC (A.9 1985), with Baxter Spann and Ken Dye; Kinwest GC (R.); Lackland AFB GC (R.); Lakeside CC (R.14 1968); Lubbock CC (R.), with Ken Dye; Oak Hill CC (R.6 A.3 1961); Panorama CC (R. 1985), with Ken Dye; Preston Trail GC (R. 1985), with Ken Dye; Prestonwood CC (Creek Cse, R. 1979), with Ken Dye; Randolph Field GC (R.3 A.9 1958); River Oaks CC (R. 1969); San Antonio CC (R.15 1959); Victoria CC (R. 1985), with Baxter Spann; Westwood CC (R.3 A.5 1970); Willow Brook CC (R.9 1953, R. 1980).
Mexico: Club Campestre de Leon (A.9 1985).

Larry Flatt, 1991
COURTESY LARRY FLATT

LARRY W. FLATT (1942–   )

BORN: Wichita Falls, Texas.

While attending Texas Tech University, where he earned a B.S. degree in parks administration in 1965, Larry Flatt worked summers as a draftsman for a landscape-golf architect in Wichita Falls, Texas. Upon graduation, he took a golf superintendent job in Kansas City, Missouri. Over the next 15 years Flatt advanced to the position of director of parks and recreation for Overland Park, Kansas, and later became director of community development for the same city. During that time, Flatt moonlighted as a course architect, laying out a few courses in the Midwest. In 1989 he formed his own golf design and consulting firm and began designing golf courses on a full-time basis.

Courses by Larry Flatt:

Iowa: West Hills G Cse (1992).
Kansas: Cimarron Valley G Cse (9 1992); Lake Shawnee GC (1970).
Missouri: Minor Park G Cse (1965).
Texas: La Vista CC [FKA Skyline CC](1966).

Courses remodeled or expanded by Larry Flatt:

Kansas: Colly Creek GC (A.9 1992); Deer Trace G Links (R. 1991); Mariah Hills G Cse (R. 1990); St. Andrews G Cse (R. 1991).
Missouri: Marshfield CC (A.9 1992).

JOHN FRANCIS FLEMING (1896–1986)

BORN: Tuam, County Galway, Ireland.
DIED: San Francisco, California, at age 90.

Jack Fleming left his native Ireland at the age of 18 bound for Manchester, England, in search of a position as a gardener

to some wealthy Briton. After classes in agriculture and a stint tending a soccer grounds, he landed a job as a "pick and shovel" man at a golf course being built by Dr. Alister Mackenzie.

Working his way through the ranks, Fleming became a construction foreman for Mackenzie in 1920. In 1926 he was sent to Marin County, California, where he supervised the building of Meadow Golf Club to a design by Mackenzie and Robert Hunter.

Mackenzie, who also moved to California, designed a number of layouts built by Fleming, among them the dramatic Cypress Point Club. When the Depression hit, at his mentor's urging Fleming accepted a position as superintendent of grounds for the San Francisco Parks Department. Fleming stayed there until his retirement in 1962.

Following Mackenzie's death in 1934, Fleming completed some of his unfinished courses and then built a few of his own. In the late 1940s he designed and built a number of par-3 and precision courses in the San Francisco area, and by the late 1950s he had developed a flourishing practice. He continued, until his retirement in 1975, to be an active course architect in northern California.

Courses by Jack Fleming:

California: Adam Springs G&CC (9); Almaden G&CC (1955); Baymeadows GC (9 Precision 1960); Blue Rock Springs GC (9 1961); Boulder Creek GC (9 Precision); Buchanan Fields GC (9 Precision 1962); Calero Hills CC; Cypress Hills GC (27 1963); Dry Creek GC (1963); Gleneagles International GC [FKA McLaren Park GC](9 1962); Glenhaven G&CC (1961); Golden Gate Fields GC (9 Precision 1954); Golden Gate GC (9 Par 3 1950); Harding Park GC (Fleming

Jack Fleming, 1957
COURTESY JACK FLEMING

Nine, 9 1962); IBM GC (9 Par 3 1959); Lake Chabot Vallejo GC (Precision 1955); Mace Meadows GC (9); Manteca Park GC (9 1966); Mather AFB GC (1963); Meadowood Resort GC (9 1965); Mount St. Helena GC (9); Napa Muni (1958), with Bob Baldock and Ben Harmon; Pruneridge Farms GC (9 Precision 1967); Riverbend G&CC (1967); Riverside G&CC (9); Roseville Rolling Green GC (Par 3); Salinas CC [FKA Salinas Fairways GC](1957); Santa Rosa G&CC (1958), with Ben Harmon; Sharon Heights G&CC (1962); Sierra View CC (9 1956); Spring Creek G&CC (9); Swenson Park Muni (1952); Tanforan GC (Precision); Turlock G&CC, with Bob Baldock; Warm Springs GC (9).
Colorado: Centennial GC (9 Par 3, NLE).

Courses remodeled or expanded by Jack Fleming:

California: Harding Park GC (R. 1934); Lincoln Park GC (R.); Olympic C (Ocean Cse, R.).

William S. Flynn, circa 1920

COLLECTION RON WHITTEN

WILLIAM S. FLYNN (1890–1945)

BORN: Milton, Massachusetts.
DIED: Philadelphia, Pennsylvania, at age 54.

William Flynn graduated from Milton High School, where he played interscholastic golf and competed against his friend Francis Ouimet. He was also an excellent tennis player and taught the game professionally one summer in Lake Placid, New York. He even loved spectator sports and for a time was part owner of football's Philadelphia Eagles.

Flynn laid out his first course at Hartwellville, Vermont, in 1909 and was then hired to assist Hugh Wilson with completion of the East Course at Merion GC in Pennsylvania.

Flynn remained at Merion after it opened and served as its greenkeeper for a time. But he also found steady work laying out courses, and he soon resigned to pursue a career as an architect. He and Wilson had hoped to form a design partnership, but Wilson's failing health prevented it. Instead, Flynn practiced on his own.

He proved to be a shrewd businessman, one who drank, played bridge and hobnobbed with wealthy industrialists who would become clients. Clarence Geist hired him to build courses for his Boca Raton hotel in Florida. Juan Trippe, founder of Pan American Airlines, helped Flynn get the contract to redo Shinnecock Hills. From all accounts, Flynn had both an Irish wit and an Irish temper. He was apparently fearless and would take a flight on the most improbable homemade aircrafts simply on a dare.

After World War I, Flynn formed Toomey and Flynn, a golf construction firm with Howard Toomey, a prominent civil engineer. Flynn would design a course and Toomey would handle the engineering, construction and financial aspects of the project. Toomey and Flynn also trained several assistants in the art of course construction. William Gordon, Robert Lawrence and Dick Wilson all started out as assistants in the firm, and all later became prominent designers in their own right.

Flynn's second love was the art of greenkeeping. He lectured at Penn State and wrote many articles and pamphlets on the subject. He also started a number of men in the profession, including the great Joe Valentine, longtime superintendent at Merion. Flynn was forever experimenting with turfgrasses, trying over fifty separate strains on one project in Chicago.

As a golf architect, William Flynn was an innovator. He routinely installed three separate sets of tee boxes on his designs as early as the 1920s and insisted the shortest set be labeled "forward tees" rather than "ladies' tees" so men would not be discouraged from using them. He also designed a nine-hole reversible course for John D. Rockefeller, Jr., that could be played both forward and backward. And he advocated a limit on the distance a golf ball could travel, fearing that someday technology would compromise design, necessitating courses in excess of 8,000 yards.

Courses by William S. Flynn:

Colorado: Cherry Hills CC (1923).

Florida: Boca Raton Hotel & C (North Cse 1928, NLE); Boca Raton Resort & C[FKA Boca Raton Hotel & C [South Cse](1928); Cleveland Heights G&CC (1925); Floridale GC (1925); Indian Creek CC (1930); Normandy Shores GC (1916, NLE).
Illinois: Mill Road Farm GC (1927, NLE).
Massachusetts: Kittansett C (routing).
New Jersey: Atlantic City CC (1923); Seaview GC (Pines Cse, 9 1931); Springdale CC (1928); Woodcrest CC.
New York: Pocantico Hills GC (9 Reversible); Shinnecock Hills GC (1931).
North Carolina: Plymouth CC (9 1937).
Ohio: Elyria CC; Pepper Pike C; [The] Country Club, Cleveland (1931).
Pennsylvania: CC of Harrisburg (1916); Doylestown CC (1916); Green Valley CC (1924); Huntingdon Valley CC (1927); Lancaster CC (1920); Lehigh CC (1926); Manufacturers G&CC; Philadelphia CC (1927); Philmont CC (North Cse 1924); Rolling Green CC (1926).
Vermont: Hartwellville CC (1911, NLE).
Virginia: Cascades GC (1923); CC of Virginia (James River Cse 1928); Sewalls Point GC [FKA Norfolk CC](1925).

Courses remodeled or expanded by William S. Flynn:

Colorado: Denver CC (R. 1923).
Delaware: Hercules Powder C (R.)
Florida: Miami Beach Polo C (R., NLE).
Illinois: Glen View GC (R.).
Maryland: Burning Tree C (R.); Columbia CC (R.); U.S. Naval Academy GC (A.9 1943); Woodmont CC (R.).
Massachusetts: [The] Country Club, Brookline (R.2 A.3rd 9 1927).
New Jersey: Pine Valley GC (R. 1929); Springdale CC (R. 1938).
New York: [The] Creek C (R.); Glen Head CC (R.); Tuxedo Park C (R., NLE); Westchester CC (South Cse, R.; West Cse, R.).
Pennsylvania: Bala CC (R.9 A.9); CC of York (R.); Eaglesmere CC (R.); Gulph Mills GC (R. 1932); Manor CC (R.); Merion GC (East Cse, R. 1925); Philadelphia CC (R. 1938), with Perry Maxwell; Plymouth CC (R.); Spring Haven CC (R.9 A.9); Whitemarsh Valley CC (R.).
Virginia: [The] Homestead GC (R. 1924); Washington G&CC (R. 1919); Yorktown CC (R.).
Washington, D.C.: East Potomac Park GC (R.); Rock Creek Park GC (R.).

WILFRED H. FOLLETT

BORN: England.

A genial Englishman, graduate of Oxford and resident of Staten Island, Wilfred "Pipe" Follett was editor of *Golf Illustrated* in the early 1920s, succeeding Max H. Behr, who went on to design many courses in California, and preceding golf architect A. W. Tillinghast, who later worked as its editor during the Depression. Follett wrote extensively about course architecture in the magazine and dabbled in it, too, though he was not nearly as prolific as either of the two editors-cum-architects.

Courses by W.H. "Pipe" Follett:

New York: Queen's Valley GC (1923, NLE), with Devereux Emmet; Towers CC [FKA Glen Oaks C](1925).
Massachusetts: Andover CC.
Rhode Island: Valley CC [FKA Valley Ledgemont CC](9).

RICK FORESTER

BORN: Texas.

Rick Forester was a member of one of Houston University's powerhouse golf teams in the mid-1960s. After an unsuccessful try at the pro tour, Forester joined his father to create Bear Creek Golf World in Houston. In 1970 they hired Ralph Plummer to design a second 18 for the club, but during the planning stage Plummer became ill and left the job. Jay Riviere was then hired to complete the course, and Forester served as construction supervisor. Once the course opened, Forester assumed the role of director of golf. In 1980 he remodeled the course in preparation for the 1981 USGA Public Links.

In 1985, Forester sold his club, which by then contained 54 holes, and began designing courses on his own. In 1989 he formed a partnership with former PGA champion John Mahaffey, based in Houston.

Courses by Rick Forester:

Texas: Cypresswood GC (Creek Cse 1988; Cypress Cse 1988).

Courses remodeled or expanded by Rick Forester:

Texas: Bear Creek G World (Masters Cse, R. 1980); Bluebonnet CC (R. 1983).

Steve Forrest, 1990
COURTESY STEVE FORREST

STEVEN P. FORREST
(1956–), ASGCA

BORN: Marion, Virginia.

Steve Forrest graduated from Virginia Tech in 1979, earning a Bachelor's degree in landscape architecture. He immediately became a design associate of Toledo, Ohio, golf architect Arthur Hills. John Strawn, in *Driving the Green*, relates how Hills confessed that, after interviewing two applicants, he awarded the job to Forrest over the phone. When Forrest showed up in the office, Hills realized he had been speaking to the wrong applicant. "Please don't ever tell Steve about this," Hills said to Strawn. But it turned out Forrest had learned about the mixup long ago and found it amusing.

Hills's error turned out to be his gain, for Forrest proved to be a talented and adept golf course designer. Working out of the firm's main office in Toledo, Forrest handled a large number of Hills's East Coast and Midwest products during the 1980s and into the 1990s.

Courses by Steve Forrest (All as assistant to Arthur Hills):

Florida: Bonita Bay C (Creekside Cse 1990; Marsh Cse 1985); Coral Oaks G Cse (1988); Cross Creek CC (Precision 1985); Foxfire CC (1985); Gator Trace GC (1986); Ironhorse G&CC (1989); Meadows G&CC (Groves Cse 1987); Pine Lakes GC (Precision 1979); Quail Creek CC (Creek Cse 1982; Quail Cse 1981); Seville G&CC (1987); Tampa Palms CC (1987); TPC at Eagle Trace (1984); Vista Gardens GC (Precision 1985); Wyndemere G&CC (27 1980).
Georgia: GC of Georgia (Creekside Cse 1992; Lakeside Cse 1991); [The]

Landings at Skidaway Island (Palmetto Cse 1985; Oakridge Cse 1988); [The] Standard C (1986).
Indiana: Hamilton Proper GC (1992).
Kentucky: [The] Champions GC (1988); Persimmon Ridge GC (1989).
Louisiana: Southern Trace CC (1986).
Michigan: Oak Pointe GC (Honors Cse, 9 1987); Pine Trace GC (1988); Taylor Meadows GC (1989).
Ohio: Brookledge GC (1992); Maumee Bay State Park GC (1991); Turnberry G Cse (1991); Winding Hollow CC (1991).
South Carolina: Morgan River GC (9 1988, A.9 1992); Palmetto Dunes CC (Hills Cse 1986).
Tennessee: River Islands C (1991).
Texas: [The] Ranch CC (1987); Trophy C (Creek Cse, 9 1984).

Courses remodeled or expanded by Steve Forrest (All as assistant to Arthur Hills):

Florida: Club at Pelican Bay (A.3rd 9 1990); Cypress Lake CC (R. 1982); CC of Florida (R. 1987); Vista Royale GC (A.3rd 9 1981).
Kentucky: Big Spring CC (R. 1982); Fort Mitchell CC (R. 1982); Highland CC (A.9 1985); Summit Hills CC (R. 1985).
Michigan: Barton Hills CC (R. 1983); Birmingham CC (R. 1985); Bloomfield Hills CC (R. 1981); CC of Detroit (R. 1981); CC of Jackson (A.9 1991); Forest Lake CC (R. 1981); Grosse Ile G&CC (R. 1981); Indianwood G&CC (Old Cse, R. 1984); Lochmoor C (R. 1981); Oakland Hills CC (South Cse, R. 1987); Orchard Lake CC (R. 1984); Plum Hollow G&CC (R. 1984); Riverview Highlands GC (A.9 1980); Western G&CC (R. 1984).
New York: CC of Rochester (R. 1982); Monroe CC (R. 1984); Park CC (R. 1983).
Ohio: Belmont CC (R. 1990); Heather Downs CC (North & South Cses, R. 1990); Inverness C (R. 1983); Sylvania CC (R. 1983).
Pennsylvania: Edgewood CC (R. 1990).

RONALD ERIK FORSE
(1956–)

BORN: Glen Ridge, New Jersey.

Ron Forse grew up caddying, playing and admiring an old Donald Ross design,

Ron Forse, 1991
COURTESY RON FORSE

Mountain Ridge Country Club in eastern New Jersey. The course convinced him that his future would lie in golf course architecture. While still in high school, Forse trained informally with golf architect Hal Purdy. In 1979 he received a Bachelor of Science degree in landscape architecture from West Virginia University. He then spent ten years working for a Pittsburgh engineering and planning company as its in-house landscape architect and golf course designer. During that time Forse served for two years as a part-time instructor of engineering at the Fayette campus of Penn State University.

In 1989, Ron Forse hung up his own shingle as a golf course architect based in western Pennsylvania. Bruce Hepner, a civil engineer and former auto designer from Michigan, soon joined him.

Courses by Ron Forse:

North Carolina: Old Wake GC (1992).
Pennsylvania: Beck Creek GC (1991); Deer Run GC (1992); Donegal Highlands GC (1991); Royal Oaks GC (1991); Wyndon Links (9 1991).
West Virginia: Timberline Resort GC (1992).

Courses remodeled or expanded by Ron Forse:

Massachusetts: Hyannisport C (R. 1992).
New York: Bluff Point GC (R. 1991).
Ohio: Grantwood GC (R. 1992); Lancaster CC (R. 1992); Shady Hollow CC (R. 1991).
Pennsylvania: Lebanon CC (R. 1991); Nemacolin CC (R. 1989); Nemacolin Woodlands GC (A.3 R.3 1988); Seven Springs GC (R.2 1992); Westmoreland CC (R. 1992); Wildwood CC (R.3 1989).
West Virginia: Alpine Lake Resort GC (A.6 1992).

KEITH FOSTER
(1958–   ), ASGCA

BORN: Philadelphia, Pennsylvania.

Starting his career in golf as an assistant superintendent, Keith Foster worked in Florida at three separate courses. In 1980 he joined Wadsworth Golf Construction Company as a project superintendent and over the next five and a half years handled eight course-construction projects, several of which were designed by Arthur Hills.

In 1986 Foster joined Hills's Toledo-based golf design firm. A few years later, in order to help the firm handle western projects, he relocated to Phoenix and operated a western branch office. While there, he played a major role in the design and completion of several Hills projects, including Harbour Pointe Golf Course near Seattle, which was named Best New Public Course of 1991 by *Golf Digest*.

In late 1991 Foster left the Hills firm and formed his own company, Keith Foster and Associates, based in Mesa, Arizona.

Courses by Keith Foster (All as assistant to Arthur Hills unless otherwise indicated):

Arizona: San Ignacio G Cse (1989).
California: Bighorn CC (1990).
Colorado: Walking Stick G Cse (1991).
Kentucky: [The] Champions GC (1988).
Nevada: [The] Legacy GC at Green Valley (1989).
Tennessee: River Islands C (1991).
Texas: Bay Oaks CC (1988).
Utah: Wingpointe G Cse (1991).
Washington: Harbour Pointe GC (1990).
Thailand: Vintage C (1992).

Courses remodeled or expanded by Keith Foster (All as assistant to Arthur Hills unless otherwise indicated):

Arizona: Oro Valley (R. 1987); Stonecreek GC (R. 1989).
California: Palos Verdes GC (R. 1990).

Keith Foster, 1991
COURTESY KEITH FOSTER

JOHN FOUGHT
(1954–   )

BORN: Portland, Oregon.

John Fought culminated a successful college golf career at Brigham Young University by winning the 1977 U.S. Amateur. After graduating with a degree in accounting, Fought turned pro, joined the PGA Tour the following year and won two events in 1979. Many lean years followed, however, and Fought, a talented artist, gravitated to golf architecture as a more satisfying career. In the late 1980s he began working with designer Bob Cupp, operating a branch office in Portland and serving as his principal West Coast design associate.

Courses designed by John Fought (All as assistant to Bob Cupp):

Oregon: Pumpkin Ridge GC (Ghost Creek Cse 1992; Witch Hollow Cse 1992).

Courses remodeled or expanded by John Fought (All as assistant to Bob Cupp):

Oregon: Tualatin CC (R. 1990).

JAMES FOULIS, JR.
(1870–1928)

BORN: St. Andrews, Scotland.
DIED: Chicago, Illinois, at age 58.
INTERRED: Wheaton, Illinois.

James Foulis and his brothers David, Robert, John and Simpson all grew up on the links at St. Andrews. Their father, James Sr., was foreman of Old Tom Morris's golf shop for some 35 years. Old Tom taught the game to each of the boys, and the three eldest helped him in constructing courses. All of the brothers except John were avid golfers, but James was the best, eventually winning the second U.S. Open in 1896.

James Foulis emigrated to the United States in 1895 to serve as the first professional at C. B. Macdonald's Chicago GC. He remained as clubmaker and professional until 1905, routing a number of Midwestern courses during the period. His brother David joined him in the early 1900s, and together they developed the first mashie-niblick club, which they patented in 1905. Marketing this and other clubs under the name J & D Foulis Company, they operated a highly successful club-manufacturing firm until the 1920s.

After working at several clubs in Chicago and St. Louis, Foulis became pro-greenkeeper at Olympia Fields CC in 1917. He supervised construction of the four courses laid out there, then left in 1922 to pursue a golf design career. He worked part-time as an architect until 1927, when he and engineer Ralph Wymer formed the short-lived Pioneer Golf and Landscape Company, which disbanded when Foulis died the following year.

Courses by James Foulis:

Colorado: Denver CC (1902).
Illinois: Bonnie Brook CC; Edgebrook GC (1921, NLE); Hickory Hills CC (1923); Joe Louis the Champ GC [FKA Pipe O'Peace GC](1927); Onwentsia C (9 1896, with Robert Foulis, A.9 1898, with Robert Foulis, H. J. Tweedie and H. J. Whigham).
Minnesota: Meadowbrook GC.
Missouri: Glen Echo CC (1901), with Robert Foulis; St. Louis CC (9 1898, NLE); Sunset CC (1910), with Robert Foulis.
Tennessee: Memphis CC (9 1905, NLE).
Wisconsin: Burlington CC; Hillmoor CC (1924); Milwaukee CC (9, NLE); Nippersink Manor CC.

Courses remodeled or expanded by James Foulis:

Illinois: Calumet CC (R. 1911, NLE).
Michigan: Kent CC (R.9 1900).

ROBERT FOULIS (1873–1945)

BORN: St. Andrews, Scotland.
DIED: Orlando, Florida, at age 71.
INTERRED: Wheaton, Illinois.

Robert Foulis worked from an early age in Old Tom Morris's golf shop at St. Andrews and assisted in the construction of a few courses designed by Morris. Though he had learned the game from Old Tom, Foulis never played much competitive golf because of poor eyesight, the result of two childhood accidents.

In 1895 Robert's brother James accepted a position in the United States. Following him to the States in 1896, Robert assisted James in laying out and building Onwentsia Club in Lake Forest, Illinois, and stayed on as its first professional. Soon after the turn of the century, the remaining Foulis brothers, their sister and

parents all moved to America and settled in Wheaton, Illinois. By this time James was a renowned competitive golfer and course designer. Robert was well known, too, having toured the small towns of the Midwest teaching golf and staking out courses.

In 1902, James and Robert designed and built Glen Echo Country Club in St. Louis, and Robert again stayed on as professional. He then created a number of St. Louis-area golf courses, including the original Bellerive Country Club in 1910. Becoming Bellerive's first pro-greenkeeper upon its completion, Foulis remained there until his retirement in late 1942.

Robert Foulis, who practiced course architecture on a part-time basis for many years was an early member of both the PGA of America and the GCSAA.

Courses by Robert Foulis:

Illinois: Onwentsia C (9 1896, with James Foulis, A.9 1898, with James Foulis, H. J. Tweedie and H. J. Whigham).
Minnesota: Minikahda C (9 1906), with William Watson.
Missouri: Algonquin CC (1904); Bellerive CC (1910, NLE); Bogey CC (1910); Forest Park Muni (1913); Glen Echo CC (1901), with James Foulis; Jefferson City CC (9 1922); Log Cabin C (1909); Meadow Brook CC (1911, NLE); Midland Valley CC (1911); Normandie GC (1901); North Shore CC (NLE); Riverview CC; Sunset CC (1910), with James Foulis.
Wisconsin: Lake Geneva CC (9 1897).

Courses remodeled or expanded by Robert Foulis:

Minnesota: Town & Country C (R.)
Missouri: Glen Echo CC (R. 1904); Log Cabin C (R. 1935); Triple A CC (R.).

WALTER G. FOVARGUE

After serving as head professional at Skokie CC near Chicago for ten years, Walter Fovargue moved to the West Coast in 1916, where he established a retail golf sales business, regained his amateur status, won the 1917 Pacific Northwest Championship and, with Midwest friends Wilfrid Reid and James Donaldson, laid out the Lakeside G&CC in San Francisco on the site of what later became the Olympic Club. Fovargue laid out and re-

Walter Fovargue, 1911 COLLECTION RON WHITTEN

modeled a few other courses in California, but in late 1918 he inexplicably sold his business to Del Monte club professional Harold Sampson and moved to Aberdeen, Washington, where he took a job in the shipyards. A few years later, Fovargue turned up in Japan, where he helped spread popularity of the game and laid out some early Japanese courses.

Courses by Walter Fovargue:

California: Lakeside G&CC (1917, NLE), with Wilfrid Reid and *James Donaldson*; Wawona Hotel GC (9 1917).
Washington: Willapa Harbor GC (9 1927).
Japan: Hodogayo G&CC (1921).

Courses remodeled or expanded by Walter Fovargue:

California: Annandale GC (R.); Santa Barbara CC (R., NLE); Victoria GC (R.9).
Washington: Grays Harbor CC (R. 1921).

WILLIAM HERBERT FOWLER (1856–1941)

BORN: Edmonton, England.
DIED: London, England, at age 85.

Herbert Fowler, born into an affluent family, was educated at Rottingdean and at Grove House School, Tottenham. He was an excellent cricket player in his youth, his size and stature making him an intimidating opponent.

Fowler took up golf at the age of 35 and was soon a successful scratch amateur. He was a member of both the Royal and Ancient Golf Club of St. Andrews and the Honourable Company of Edinburgh Golfers. His first course-design opportunity came when a group headed by his

*Herbert Fowler,
circa 1920*

COLLECTION RON
WHITTEN

brother-in-law agreed to finance construction of Walton Heath Golf Club in the early 1900s.

Walton Heath opened to critical acclaim, and while Fowler remained a lifelong director of the club, he was soon busy with other courses. In the early 1920s he partnered with Tom Simpson in the firm of Fowler and Simpson. Simpson did most of the firm's work on the Continent, while Fowler concentrated on British courses. He also spent a considerable amount of time in the United States during World War I and designed several American courses. The firm later expanded to include J. F. Abercromby and Arthur Croome, who acted primarily as consultants.

Courses by Herbert Fowler:

California: Ambassador Hotel GC (1921, NLE); Burlingame CC (1922), with *Harold Sampson*; Crystal Springs GC (1920); Los Angeles CC (South Cse 1911).
Massachusetts: Eastward Ho! CC (1922).
England: Abbeydale GC (1922); Beau Desert GC (1921); [The] Berkshire GC (Blue Cse 1928; Red Cse 1928), with Tom Simpson; Blackwell GC; Bradford GC; Cowdray Park GC, with J. F. Abercromby; Delamere Forest GC (1910); Knole Park GC (1924), with J. F. Abercromby; Lord Mountbatten Estate GC, with Tom Simpson; Manor House Hotel GC (1930), with J. F. Abercromby; Mortimer Singer Estate GC; North Foreland GC (1919), with Tom Simpson; Royal Automobile C (27); Saunton GC (New Cse 1935, NLE); Walton Heath GC (New Cse 1915; Old Cse 1904); West Kent GC (1916), with J. F. Abercromby; West Surrey GC (1909, NLE); Woodcote Park GC (1912); Yelverton GC (1905).
Scotland: Cruden Bay G&CC (27 1926), with Tom Simpson.
Wales: Bull Bay GC (1913).

Courses remodeled or expanded by Herbert Fowler:

California: Del Paso CC (R. 1921); Lincoln Park Muni (R.9 A.9 1922); Menlo CC (R.); Old Del Monte G&CC (R.9 A.9 1912; R. 1923); Presidio GC (R. 1921); Riverside GC (R.); Sacramento CC (R., NLE); Sequoyah CC (R.).
Pennsylvania: Allegheny CC (R. A.3 1922).
England: Broadstone GC (R.); Cowdray Park GC (R.2); Ganton GC (R.); Huddersfield GC (R.); Royal Lytham & St. Anne's GC (R.); Royal North Devon GC (R. 1908).
Wales: Aberdovey GC (R.); Southerndown GC (R.).

*H. C. Fownes, circa
1930* COLLECTION RON
WHITTEN

HENRY CLAY FOWNES
(1856–1935)

BORN: Pittsburgh, Pennsylvania.
DIED: Pittsburgh, Pennsylvania, at age 79.

H. C. Fownes began working in the iron-manufacturing business with his brother-in-law, William Clark. He later formed the Carrie Furnace Company with his own brother, William C. Fownes, operating it until 1896, when it was bought out by the Carnegie Steel Corporation. By then Fownes was a wealthy man, content to serve as director of several steel firms and two banks and to play a great deal of golf. He was an accomplished golfer, qualifying at age 45 for the 1901 U.S. Open with a score one stroke less than that of his son.

In 1903 Fownes formed Oakmont Country Club in countryside outside Pittsburgh and laid out its course. He participated actively in the refinements of the course in its early years, but Oakmont remained in its basic routing just as he planned it. H. C. Fownes served as president of Oakmont for over 20 years until his death from pneumonia in 1935.

*William Fownes,
circa 1930*

COLLECTION RON
WHITTEN

WILLIAM CLARKE FOWNES, JR.
(1878–1950)

BORN: Chicago, Illinois.
DIED: Oakmont, Pennsylvania, at age 72.

William C. Fownes, Jr., was the son of Henry Clay Fownes, but was named after his uncle. He followed in his father's footsteps in both business and pleasure, working in his father's steel business, taking up golf and assisting his father with the original design of Oakmont Country Club. William became a premier golfer in the early 1900s, winning four Pennsylvania Amateurs and the 1910 U.S. Amateur. He was also selected as captain of the first American Walker Cup team in 1922 and served as president of the USGA in 1925 and '26.

William Fownes served for many years as chairman of the Green Committee at Oakmont and in that capacity worked closely with legendary greenkeeper Emil "Dutch" Loeffler in turning Oakmont into an increasingly fearsome course. Together, they created countless bunkers and a special rake to groom them. They also experimented with the greens until they were lightning-fast. Fownes tinkered, groomed and promoted the course all his life, becoming a leading turfgrass authority in the process. He was made an honorary member of the GCSAA in 1932 for his efforts at Oakmont, but he never showed an inclination to work on any other course.

MANUEL L. FRANCIS
(1903–)

Born aboard a Brazilian steamship bound for Portugal, Manny Francis came to America at age sixteen. Francis worked on construction crews building courses on Long Island for Donald Ross and other architects in the 1920s and was promoted

Manny Francis, 1980 COLLECTION RON WHITTEN

to construction foreman when it was discovered he was the only man who could start the tractors. When the Depression made construction work scarce, Francis became greenkeeper at South Portland (Maine) CC and later at Haverhill (Massachusetts) CC.

Francis then moved on to Vesper CC in Lowell, Massachusetts, where he served as superintendent from 1950 through 1974. During his tenure, he developed Vespers, a velvet bent grass with special putting qualities, and became widely known in the United States and Mexico as a turfgrass consultant. He also designed or redesigned a number of golf courses on the side, including Green Harbor CC at Marshfield, Massachusetts, which he operated (after his retirement) with his son Manny Jr. In 1980 Francis was presented with a Distinguished Service Award by the GCSAA in recognition of his contributions to golf and turfgrass development.

Courses by Manny Francis:

Massachusetts: Bedford AFB GC (9 1957); Dun Roamin GC (9); Green Harbor CC; Hickory Hill GC; Westminster GC (9 1955).
New Hampshire: Whippoorwill CC (9 1959).

Courses remodeled or expanded by Manny Francis:

Massachusetts: Blue Hill CC (R.6 1956); Framingham CC (R.); Ould Newberry CC (R. 1955); Vesper CC (R.).
New Hampshire: Abenaqui CC (R.3 1954); Exeter CC (R.); Keene CC (R. 1957); Rochester CC (R.).
Mexico: Churubusco CC (R.); C de G Bellavista (R.).

RONALD WARREN FREAM
(1942–)

BORN: Hawthorne, California.

Ronald Fream received a B.S. degree in ornamental horticulture from California

Polytechnic Institute in Pomona in 1964. He also did graduate work in turfgrass management at Washington State University. In 1966 Fream was employed as a construction laborer by Robert Trent Jones Inc. Four years later he became a construction superintendent for Robert F. Lawrence in Arizona. He then worked for two years in the field on courses designed by golf architect Robert Muir Graves.

In 1972 Fream decided to leave the construction end of the business and pursue a career in golf architecture. He formed an international partnership with veteran British designer Commander John Harris and Australian professional golfer (and five-time British Open champion) Peter Thomson.

Fream had primary responsibility for projects of the firm in the United States and the Caribbean. He also worked in Europe and Africa on some projects. After Harris's death in 1977, design associate Michael Wolveridge became a full partner in the firm.

In 1980 Fream left the partnership and formed his own company, Ronald Fream Design Group, based in California. His productivity within the United States was limited. Fream preferred the challenges of equatorial rain forests in Borneo, desert sands in Tunisia, subarctic birch forests in Finland and other exotic, far-flung locales. He later renamed the firm Golfplan, Inc. It was staffed with associates who also enjoyed globe-trotting, including Fred Bliss, David Dale, Rick Elliott and Terence McNally.

Courses by Ronald Fream (All with Peter Thomson unless otherwise indicated):

California: Bixby Village GC (9 Precision 1980); Carmel Mountain Ranch GC (1986 *solo*); Desert Falls CC (1985 *solo*); Oakhurst CC 1990 *solo*); Redhawk CC (1991 *solo*); Windsor GC (1990 *solo*).
Washington: Canyon Lakes G&CC (1981); Kayak Point GC (1974); Mint

Ronald Fream, 1989 COURTESY RONALD FREAM

Valley Muni (1976); Tapps Island GC (9 1981).
Argentina: Pilar GC (*solo*); Marayui G&CC (*solo*).
Borneo: Pantai Mentiri GC (1984 *solo*); Royal Brunei GC (1986 *solo*).
China: Guilin-Lijiang G&CC (1987 *solo*).
Estonia: Pirata GC (1992 *solo*).
Fiji: Fijian Hotel GC (9 Precision 1973).
Finland: Kerigolf (1990 *solo*); Midnight Sun G Center (1991 *solo*); Nordcenter G&CC (*solo*); Oulu Golfkerho (1992 *solo*); Outokumpu GC (*solo*); Peurunka G Center (*solo*).
France: EuroDisney GC (27 1992 *solo*); Golf d'Arcangues (1991 *solo*); Golf du Cap d'Agde (1989 *solo*); Golf de Fregate (27 1992 *solo*); Golf de Gassin (27 1992 *solo*); Golf de Massane (1990 *solo*); Green River G Cse (9 *solo*); Set C (9 1990 *solo*).
Guam: Guam International CC (1992 *solo*).
Indonesia: Bali Handara CC (1975), and John Harris; Jagorawi G&CC (1978); National GC; Nongsa Indah CC (*solo*).
Japan: Hanshin CC (*solo*); Happy Valley CC (*solo*); Korakuen CC (27 1974), and John Harris; La Rainbow CC (1991 *solo*); Riverside G Center (Par 3 *solo*); Tohbetu GC (*solo*).
Malaysia: Kelab Golf di Raja Darul Ehsan (9 1984 *solo*); Pilmoor Estate GC (*solo*); Rantau Petronas GC (Links Cse, 9 1984 *solo*); Saujana G&CC (Orchid Cse 1986 *solo*; Palm Cse 1985 *solo*); Taman Tun Abdul Razak GC (9 1984 *solo*); Tioman Island Resort (*solo*).
Okinawa: Palm Hills G Resort (1991 *solo*).
Portugal: Carvoeiro GC (27 1991 *solo*); Estoril Sol GC (9 Precision 1976), and John Harris; Gramacho C (*solo*); Pinheiros Altos CC (1991 *solo*).
Singapore: Sentosa Island GC (Serapong Cse 1983); Tanah Merah CC (1983 *solo*).
South Korea: Asiana GC (*solo*); Dragon Valley GC (27 *solo*).
St. Kitts: Royal St. Kitts GC (1977), and John Harris.
Sweden: Askersunds GC (1987 *solo*); Molndals GC (*solo*); Soderkoping GC (*solo*).
Taiwan: Orient G&CC (1992 *solo*); Sun City G&CC (*solo*).
Thailand: Panya Hill GC (1992 *solo*); Panya Indra GC (27 1992 *solo*); Panya Park CC (1992 *solo*).
Trinidad and Tobago: Balandra Beach GC

(1982); St. Andrews GC (1975), and John Harris.

Tunisia: Dunes de Morjane GC (1992 *solo*); El Kantaoui GC (1977, and John Harris; A.3rd 9 1985 *solo*); El Qortine International GC (1988 *solo*); Hammamet GC (1987 *solo*); Hammamet II GC (1992 *solo*); Monastir International GC (1989 *solo*); Montazan Tabarka G Resort (27 1992 *solo*).

Courses remodeled or expanded by Ronald Fream (All with Peter Thomson unless otherwise indicated):

California: Almaden G&CC (R. 1979); Bing Maloney G Cse (A.3rd 9 [Precision] 1985 *solo*); Brentwood CC (R.3 1983 *solo*); Castlewood CC (R. *solo*); Costa Mesa GC (R. *solo*); DeLaveaga CC (R.2 1983 *solo*); Hacienda CC (R. 1978); Los Altos G&CC (R. *solo*); Los Lagos GC (R. *solo*); Marine Memorial GC (R. 1980); Mesa Verde CC (R.4 1991 *solo*); Miramar Memorial GC (R. 1981); Napa Valley CC (R.9 A.9 1987 *solo*); Palo Alto Hills CC (R. *solo*); Peninsula CC (R. *solo*); Richmond CC (R. *solo*); San Diego CC (R. *solo*); San Juan Hills CC (R. 1981); Santa Ana CC (R. 1983 *solo*); Seacliff CC (R. 1985 *solo*); Shadow Mountain GC (R. 1981 *solo*); Tamarisk CC (R. 1981 *solo*).

Montana: Glacier View GC (R. 1975 *solo*).

Nevada: Edgewood Tahoe GC (R. 1980).

Oregon: Sunriver CC (South Cse, R. 1978).

Texas: El Paso CC (R. 1986 *solo*).

Washington: Broadmoor GC (R.2 1982); Cedarcrest GC (R. 1982); Manito G&CC (R. 1979); Seattle GC (R.2 1981); West Seattle GC (R. 1979).

Alberta: Glendale G&CC (R.3 1981).

Argentina: Jockey C (Blue Cse, R. 1983 *solo*; Red Cse, R. 1983 *solo*); Marayui G&CC (R. 1985 *solo*); San Isidro GC (R.3 1983 *solo*).

Australia: Willunga GC (R. *solo*).

France: St. Nom la Brêteche GC (Blue Cse, R.6 1991 *solo*).

Indonesia: Kebayoran GC (R. 1980).

Japan: Chitose Airport GC (R *solo*).

Malaysia: Awana GC, Gentling Highlands (R. 1984); Royal Selangor GC (New Cse, R. 1983 *solo*); Old Cse, R. 1983 *solo*).

New Zealand: Willunga GC (R.3 1983 *solo*).

Singapore: Jurong CC (R. 1982 *solo*); [The] Keppel Club (R. 1983 *solo*);

Singapore Island GC (Sime Cse, R. 1982 *solo*); [The] Warren C (R.6 A.12 1983 *solo*).

Sweden: Linkopings GC (R. *solo*); Ljunghusens GC (R. *solo*); Skelleftea GC (R. *solo*).

KINYA FUJITA
(1889–1969)

BORN: Tokyo, Japan.
DIED: Kasumigaseki, Japan, at age 80.

Kinya Fujita, son of a wealthy Japanese banking family, was educated at Waseda University, where he excelled at several sports. He worked for three years in his family's bank and then traveled to the United States for graduate studies. He attended the University of Chicago, Miami of Ohio and Columbia University. For a time he worked for a silk-importing firm in New York City before returning to Tokyo to organize and operate an import-export firm with American backing.

Fujita's interest in golf course design was roused when he met C. H. Alison, who was laying out Tokyo GC in 1914. Fujita traveled to Britain in 1919 to meet again with Alison and to study his techniques. Returning to his own country, he organized Kasumigaseki CC in the 1920s and built its first course, the East 18. He also served as the club's captain, its secretary and chairman of its board of directors. For good measure Fujita was the club champion in 1929, 1933 and 1935. After laying out a second course at Kasumigaseki, Fujita invited Alison to inspect both courses and recommend changes. Alison made only slight alterations to each course, mainly adding its now famous deep bunkers.

Fujita designed several courses before World War II, and his services were in

Kinya Fujita, circa 1950 COLLECTION RON WHITTEN

demand during the reconstruction period after the war. He remained a lifelong patriarch at Kasumigaseki and died on its grounds while making plans to remodel its highly respected East Course.

Courses by Kinya Fujita:

Japan: Chiba CC (Noda Cse 1954; Kawama Cse 1957); Higashi Matsuyama GC; Ito International GC; Kasumigaseki GC (East Cse 1929; West Cse 1932); Narashino CC (Kings Cse; Queens Cse); Nasu GC; Oarai GC, with Seichi Inouye; Sanrizuka GC; Shiun CC; Shizuoka CC; Yahata CC.

Courses remodeled or expanded by Kinya Fujita:

Japan: Kawana GC (Fuji Cse, R.).

PAUL FULLMER
(1934–), ASGCA

BORN: Evanston, Illinois.

Paul Fullmer received his Bachelor's degree in journalism from the University of Notre Dame in 1955. He worked for two years as a sports columnist with the Aurora (Illinois) *Beacon News* and then began a career in public relations with the Chicago firm of Selz, Seabolt and Associates. He became president of the firm in 1979.

Fullmer became the first executive secretary of the ASGCA when it retained Selz, Seabolt in 1970. He assisted in executing numerous changes in the society's policies that made it one of the most influential forces in the world of golf. His wife, Sandra (daughter of golf architect Percy Clifford), was a former Women's Amateur champion of Mexico, Spain and Germany (winning all three in one year) as well as a four-time Chicago District champion. In 1992 he was awarded the ASGCA's Donald Ross Award for his contributions to the society and the profession.

LES FURBER

BORN: Saskatchewan, Canada.

Les Furber worked as a field supervisor and project director for golf architect Robert Trent Jones for 14 years, handling on-site constructions of courses in the United States, Europe and Africa. In 1978 Furber returned to his native Canada and assumed responsibility for the development of the 36-hole Kananaskis Country Golf Club for Trent Jones. When that was completed, Furber chose to remain in his homeland and practice architecture.

So in 1980 Furber left the Jones organization and formed his own golf architecture business, Golf Design Services Ltd., with Jim Eremko, another Saskatchewan native and former project manager for Robert Trent Jones. They were later joined by Bob Kains, who became a third design partner in GDS. Over the next decade, based in Canmore, Alberta, Furber and his partners designed and remodeled dozens of western Canadian courses.

Courses by Les Furber (All with *Jim Eremko* unless otherwise indicated):

Alberta: Barrhead GC (1991); Carmoney G&CC (1991); Gilwood G&CC (9 1988); Graham Acres GC (1991); Ironhead G&CC (1991); Land-O-Lakes G&CC (1987); Last Hill G&CC (9 1985); Nanton GC (9 1986); Picture Butte G & Winter C (9 1986); Wabamun Lake G Cse (9 1987); Westlock GC (9 1992).
British Columbia: Balfour G&CC (9 1990); Belmont GC (1992); Fairview Mountain GC (9 1991); Fairwinds G&CC (1989); Hirsch Creek GC (9 1991); Kelowna Springs GC (1990); Mayfair Lakes GC (1988); Morningstar GC (1991); Myrtle Point GC (1990); Powell River GC (9); Predator Ridge GC (1991); Salmon Arm GC (9 1986); Storey Creek GC (1990); [The] Springs G&CC (1988); Trickle Creek GC (1991).
Manitoba: Minnewasta G&CC (1989); Quarry Oaks GC (1991).
Saskatchewan: Elbow Harbour GC (1989); Moon Lake GC (1991); York Lake GC (9 1990).
Sardinia: Pevero GC (1972), ass't Robert Trent Jones.
Spain: C de G Mijas (Los Lagos Cse 1976), ass't Robert Trent Jones; El Bosque GC (1975), ass't Robert Trent Jones; Nueva Andalucia GC (Los Naranjos Cse 1977), ass't Robert Trent Jones.
Portugal: Troia GC (1980), ass't Robert Trent Jones.

Courses remodeled or expanded by Les Furber (All with *Jim Eremko* unless otherwise indicated):

Alberta: Hanna G&CC (R.9); Leduc G&CC (R.8); Maple Ridge GC (A.9 1991); Mayfair G&CC (R.); Medicine Hat G&CC (R.16); Silver Springs G&CC (R.); Turner Valley G&CC (R.10).
British Columbia: Christina Lake GC (A.9 1992); Ledgeview GC (R.14); Penticton G&CC (R.7); Spallumcheen Estates GC (R.); University GC (R.5).
Saskatchewan: Meadow Lake GC (R.9).

Pepe Gancedo, 1989
COLLECTION RON WHITTEN

**JOSE GANCEDO
(1938–)**

Spanish businessman "Pepe" Gancedo won the Spanish Amateur five times, was six times a member of Spain's World Cup team and once reached the quarterfinals of the British Amateur. He entered the field of golf course architecture in 1975 and made an immediate impact with the opening of his first course, Torrequebrada. A very difficult championship course, it was hailed as the best in Marbella, better even than the famous Trent Jones Sotogrande course. Gancedo's subsequent designs retained his penchant for difficult courses, but also featured unconventional, sometimes bizarre holes. He perched tees on the edges of canyons and built greens atop huge rock outcroppings, prompting one writer to proclaim that Gancedo's designs induced vertigo. A British writer dubbed Gancedo "the Picasso of golf course architecture" because of the designer's extroverted nature coupled with his creation of fantasy golf holes.

Courses by Pepe Gancedo:

Portugal: Parque de Floresta GC (1987).
Spain: C de G Costalita (1977); Canyamel GC (1989); El Chaparral GC (1992); Monte Mayor GC (1990); Pollensa GC (9 1988); Santa Ponsa GC (1975); Torrequebrada GC (1977).
Tenerife: Golf del Sur.

Fred Garbin, 1991
COURTESY FRED GARBIN

**FERDINAND GARBIN
(1928–), ASGCA, PRESIDENT 1968**

BORN: Linhart, Pennsylvania.

"Fred" Garbin studied agronomy under H. Burton Musser at Penn State University, receiving a Bachelor of Science degree in turfgrass science in 1959. He was associated for a number of years with golf architect James G. Harrison and married Harrison's daughter Joan. In the mid-1960s Garbin entered private practice on his own, based near Pittsburgh.

An avowed fan of Donald Ross, Garbin worked on restoration of several Ross courses in Pennsylvania courses. He also sympathetically remodeled courses of other old designers. His subtle reworking of Oakmont Country Club prior to the 1983 U.S. Open drew praise from both club members and competitors.

In 1983 Garbin became one of the first architects to employ a female designer full-time when he hired Sandy Rice Bigler, trained her and made her a design associate in his firm.

Courses by Ferdinand Garbin (All with James Gilmore Harrison unless otherwise indicated):

Michigan: Warwick Hills G&CC (1957).
New Jersey: Knob Hill CC.
New York: Cragie Brae GC (1962); Happy Acres CC (1958); Peek 'n Peak GC (1973 solo).
Ohio: Chippewa CC (9 1964; A.9 1967 solo); Hidden Valley GC (1960); Pleasant Vue GC (9 1964; A.9 1967 solo); Spring Hill CC (1963); Tannenhauf GC (1957).
Pennsylvania: Beaver Lakes CC (1974 solo); Blairsville CC (1963); Blueberry Hill GC (9 1961; A.9 1969 solo); Blue Knob Resort GC (9 1974 solo); Bradford GC (1964); Carradam CC (1962); Cedarbrook GC (1963); Chestnut

Ridge CC (1963); Cumberland CC (1961); Downing Muni (1962); Folmont Resort GC (1975 *solo*); Four Seasons GC (Executive Cse [Precision] 1974 *solo* Par 3 Cse [18 Par 3] 1976 *solo*); Glen Oak CC (1961); Hidden Valley GC; Highland Springs GC (1960); Indiana CC (1963); Lake Lawn GC (Precision 1971 *solo*); Lakeview CC (1957); Lenape Heights GC (9 1966 *solo*); Logo de Vita GC (9 1980 *solo*); Meadowwink GC (1970 *solo*); Mount Cobb Muni (1958); Mulberry Hill GC (1984 *solo*); Penn State University GC (White Cse 1965); Pine Ridge GC (9 1960); Rolling Acres CC (9 1960; A.9 1986 *solo*); Rolling Hills CC (1961); Sewickley Heights CC (1960); Shamrock GC (9 1980 *solo*); Silver Lake School GC (1975 *solo*); Sportsman's GC (1964); Valley Brook CC (27 1966 *solo*); Windber CC (1961).

Virginia: Beaver Hill CC (1972 *solo*); Blacksburg CC (1969 *solo*); Castle Rock GC (1971 *solo*).

West Virginia: Bridgeport CC (1957); Sheraton Lakeview Resort & CC (Lakeview Cse 1955).

Puerto Rico: Dorado del Mar GC (1962); Punta Borinquen CC (1960 *solo*).

Courses remodeled or expanded by Ferdinand Garbin (All with James Gilmore Harrison unless otherwise indicated):

Kentucky: Bellefonte CC (R. 1960).

New Jersey: Tavistock CC (R. 1954).

New York: Elmira CC (R. A.5 1971 *solo*).

Ohio: Alliance CC (R. 1983 *solo*); Birchwood GC (R.9 A.9 1974 *solo*); Hilltop GC (R. 1986 *solo*); Steubenville CC (R.9 A.9 1970 *solo*); Sunnyhill G&RC (R. A.9 1967 *solo*).

Pennsylvania: Alcoma CC (R. 1984 *solo*); Beaver Valley CC (R.9 A.9 1958); Blue Ridge CC (R. 1964); Brookside CC (R. 1959); Butler CC (R. 1986 *solo*); Chippewa CC (R.9 A.9 1964); Churchill Valley CC (R. 1960); Conestoga CC (R. 1986 *solo*); [The] Country Club, Meadville (R. 1978 *solo*); Cross Creek GC (R.9 A.9 1971 *solo*); Duquesne GC (R. 1985 *solo*); Edgewood CC (R. 1960); Emporium CC (R.9 A.9 1970 *solo*); Frosty Valley CC (R. 1986 *solo*); Greenville CC (R.9 A.9 1970 *solo*); Hanover CC (R. 1986 *solo*); Hidden Valley CC (R.9 A.9 1958); Highland CC, New Kensington (R. 1975 *solo*); Highland CC, Pittsburgh (R. A.3 1986

solo); Latrobe CC (A.9 1963); Lebanon CC (R. 1986 *solo*); Longue Vue C (R. 1980 *solo*); Meadia Heights CC (R. 1985 *solo*); Montour Heights CC (R.9 A.9 1962); Oak Lake GC (A.9 1985 *solo*); Oakmont CC (R. 1983 *solo*); Oakmont East GC (R. 1962); Penn State University GC (Blue Cse, R. 1965); St. Clair CC (R. 1960); St. Jude CC (A.4 1985 *solo*); Seven Springs GC (R.9 1980 *solo*); Sewickley Heights CC (R. 1986 *solo*); Shannopin CC (R. 1986 *solo*); Somerset CC (A.9 1986 *solo*); Suncrest GC (R. *solo*); Sunnehanna CC (R. 1980 *solo*); Wanango CC (R. 1986 *solo*); Youghiogheny CC (R.3 1985 *solo*).

West Virginia: Black Knight CC (R. 1986 *solo*); Skyline GC (R. A.9 *solo*); Tygart Lake GC (R. 1957).

RONALD M. GARL
(1945–)

BORN: Alabama.

A native of Alabama, Ronald Garl attended the University of Florida on the first scholarship ever granted by the Florida State Golf Association. He graduated in 1967 with a B.S.A. degree in turfgrass science and, after working on the construction crew of one Robert Trent Jones–designed golf course, entered private practice as a golf course architect based in Lakeland, Florida.

While the bulk of his work was concentrated within the confines of Florida, he experimented with all sorts of layouts. He did a series of challenging precision courses. He designed "Scottish-style" links designs. He even successfully reproduced some of the great holes from St. Andrews, Augusta National, Pine Valley and other courses at Golden Ocala G&CC.

In 1979 Garl served as president of the Florida State Golf Association. In the 1980s he worked on a few designs with former U.S. Open champion Jerry Pate. Over the years, his associates included Steve Smyers and Phil Sheldon.

Courses by Ron Garl:

Alabama: CC of Ozark (9).

California: Palm Springs RV Resort & CC (Par 3 1985); Sands RV CC (9 Par 3 1984).

Florida: Avila G&CC (1979); Babe Zaharias GC (1972); Big Cypress GC (1987); Bay Palms GC, MacDill AFB

Ron Garl, 1991
COURTESY RON GARL

(South Cse 1985); Bloomingdale Golfers C (1985); Buffalo Creek GC (1988); Burnt Store Marina GC (Marina Cse [Precision] 1981); Clearwater G Park (Precision 1971); C at Hidden Creek (1988); Continental CC (1972); CC of Sebring [FKA Prairie Oaks GC](9 1985); Cypress Greens CC (9 1981); Cypresswood G&RC (1974); Del Tura CC (Precision 1983); Del Vera GC (1991); [The] Eagles GC [FKA Nine Eagles GC](1986, A.3rd 9 1988); Fiddlesticks CC (Long Mean Cse 1982; Wee Friendly Cse 1982); Glen Lakes CC (1989); Golden Ocala G&CC (1986); Golf Hammock CC (1976); Grenelefe G&RC (South Cse 1983); [The] Great Outdoors G Cse (1988); Heathrow CC (1985); Hideaway CC (Precision 1984); Imperialakes CC, Mulberry (1976); Kingsway CC (1978); La Cita G&CC (1982); Lake Fairways GC (Precision 1981); Martin County G&CC (New Cse 1988); Northdale G&CC (1978); Oak Ford CC (27 1991); Palm Beach Polo & CC (Dunes Cse 1985), with Jerry Pate; Pine Lakes Venture GC; Plantation G&CC (Panther Cse 1980; Bobcat Cse [Precision] 1984); [The] Ravines GC (1979); [The] River C (1989); River's Edge Y&CC (1986); Rocky Point GC (1983); Sandridge GC (1987); Schalamar GC (1988); Seven Springs G&CC (Cse No. 2 [Precision] 1978); St. Andrews South GC (1981); Sugarmill Woods G&CC (1975); Summerfield CC (1987); Sun City Center GC (North Cse 1989); Tall Pines GC (9 Precision 1985); Timacuan G&CC (1987); Timber Pines GC (Hills Cse [Precision] 1982; Lakes Cse [Precision] 1982); TPC at Prestancia (Stadium Cse 1987); University Park CC (1991); Valle Oaks GC (1979); Walt Disney World GC (Wee Links 6 1982).

Indiana: Stonehenge GC (1988).
Mississippi: Northbay CC (9 Precision 1991).
Pennsylvania: Mayapple G Links (1991).
South Carolina: Brays Island Plantation GC (1990); Golden Hills G&CC (1988); Links at Stono Ferry (1989).
Tennessee: Thunderhollow GC (1988).
Texas: Country View G Cse (1989); Fairway Oaks G&CC (1980).
Alberta: Hidden Valley GC; Heritage Pointe GC (27 1992).
Puerto Rico: Dorado Sands CC (1988).

Courses remodeled or expanded by Ron Garl:

Alabama: Lakewood GC (Azalea Cse, A.9 1986).
Florida: Bay Palms GC, MacDill AFB (North Cse, R. 1984); Bobby Jones GC (American Cse, R. 1988); Cleveland Heights G&CC (R.3 A.9 1982); Lakeland Par 3 GC (R. Par 3 1987); Martin County G&CC (Old Cse, R. 1982); Naples Beach Hotel GC (R. 1979); Pine Oak GC (R.9 A.18 1987); Rogers Park GC (R.); Seven Springs G&CC (Cse No. 1, R. 1978); Spruce Creek CC (R. 1985); Tiger Point G&CC (East Cse, R.9 A.9 1984), with Jerry Pate; University of Florida GC (R.); Walden Lake Polo & CC (A.3rd 9 1987); Wedgewood G&CC (R. 1984).
Nevada: Las Vegas CC (R. 1981).
New Jersey: Greate Bay CC (A.3 1989).
New York: Cedar Brook CC (R. 1985).

MICHEL GAYON
(1961–), FAGCA

BORN: France.

A golfer since age 10, Michel Gayon played to a scratch handicap through his school years, appeared on several French amateur teams and competed in the British Open at age 18. His love of golf led him at an early age to chose golf architecture as a career, and he designed and built his first course at age 24. Soon thereafter he established his own golf design firm based in Paris.

Courses designed by Michel Gayon:

France: GC Clement Ader; GC d'Esery (27); GC d'Etiolles (27); GC de Cergy Pointoise; GC de Chambon sur Lignon; GC de Epinal; GC de Fontenailles (27); GC de Forez (1985); GC de La Domangere; GC de

La Vaucouleurs (River Cse 1989; Valley Cse 1987); GC de Les Dryades; GC de L'île d'Or; GC de Lou Roucas; GC de Maintenon (27); GC de Marseille La Salette; GC de Meaux Boutigny (1986); GC de Pornic; GC de Sable (27); GC de Valmartin; G Public de L'Ailette; G Public de Savenay (27).
Reunion Island: GC de Bourbon; GC de St. Denis.

J. PORTER GIBSON
(1931–), ASGCA

BORN: Charlotte, North Carolina.

J. Porter Gibson attended Carlisle Military School in South Carolina and received B.S. and Civil Engineering degrees from Belmont Abbey College in North Carolina. He later earned an additional C.E. degree from Clemson University. From 1958 to 1960 Gibson designed golf courses for the Sam Snead Golf and Motor Lodge franchise. The following several years he planned courses for the R & G Construction Company.

Between 1971 and 1974, Gibson was a partner in the firm of Tait-Toski-Gibson Inc., involved in golf course and community planning and construction. This firm, which included well-known golf teacher Bob Toski, was a pioneer in the use of waste water for irrigation. In the late 1970s Gibson began practicing course design in North and South Carolina on his own.

Courses by J. Porter Gibson

Florida: Palm Beach National G&CC (1962); Tomoka Oaks G&CC (1964).
Maryland: Breton Bay G&CC; White Plains GC (1974).
North Carolina: Elizabeth City GC (1965); Flagtree CC (1982); Gastonia National GC; Mallard Head CC (1980); Mooresville GC (1978); Northgreen Village GC (1974); Piney Point CC (1964); Riverside CC (1983); Westport GC (1968); Woodbridge CC (1971).
South Carolina: Cherokee National G&CC (1967); Deer Track CC (North Cse 1974; South Cse 1982); Santee National GC (1989); Stone Creek Cove GC (9 1975); Wedgefield Plantation GC (1974).
Virginia: Ivy Hill CC (1975); Round Meadow CC (9).

Courses remodeled or expanded by J. Porter Gibson:

Georgia: Bacon Park GC (R.9 A.3 1971); Toccoa G&CC (R.).
North Carolina: Pine Lake CC (R.9 A.9 1965).
South Carolina: Rock Hill CC (A.9 1974).

Simon Gidman, 1991 COURTESY SIMON GIDMAN

SIMON RICHARD GIDMAN
(1953–), BIGCA

BORN: Nottingham, England.

Simon Gidman began his career as an assistant club professional in Great Britain. In 1979, he entered Leeds Polytechnic Institute to study landscape architecture with the avowed goal of becoming a golf course architect. After graduating in 1982, Gidman worked as a self-employed consultant to golf architect Martin Hawtree and assisted on the design, redesign or construction of over forty courses in Britain and elsewhere.

In 1991 Gidman joined land-planning expert Nicholas Blakemore to form a golf architectural firm of their own called The Golf Design Partnership. Gidman handled the golf designs and Blakemore the planning and project management.

Courses by Simon Gidman (All with Martin Hawtree unless otherwise indicated):

North Carolina: Reems Creek GC (1989).
England: Calverton G Centre; Hoebridge GC (Short Cse [18 Par 3]); Hylands Park GC; Marlwood G Centre; Moors Valley GC (9); Puckrup Hall GC (1993 *solo*); Rother Valley GC; Sandford Springs GC; Seedy Mill GC; West Hove GC (New Cse); Wrag Barn GC.
France: Club Med Montargis; Golf de Bombequois (9); Golf de Carquefou; Golf des Baux de Provence (9).

Ireland: Downpatrick GC (R. A.8).
Portugal: Pine Cliffs G&CC (9).
Turkey: Izmir Hilton International GC (1991), with Algie Pulley.

Courses remodeled or expanded by Simon Gidman (All with Martin Hawtree unless otherwise indicated):

England: Brampton Park GC; Bedale GC (A.6); Bury St. Edmunds GC (R.); Salisbury & South Wilts GC (A.3rd 9); Southwood GC (R.5 A.13); St. Michael Jubilee GC (A.9); Western Park GC (R. A.8).
France: Golf de Fontainebleau (R.)

David Gill, circa 1975 COLLECTION RON WHITTEN

DAVID ARTHUR GILL (1919–1991), ASGCA

BORN: Keokuk, Iowa.
DIED: Hinsdale, Illinois, at age 72.

David Gill attended Iowa State University and obtained a degree in landscape architecture in 1942 from the University of Illinois. After distinguished service in the South Pacific theater during World War II, he obtained a license as a civil engineer in Illinois. He then went to work for golf architect Robert Bruce Harris, assisting in the design and construction of several Midwestern courses.

Gill opened his own office in Illinois in 1950 but was stricken with polio in 1953. After a lengthy rehabilitation, he made a remarkable recovery and was able to resume the practice of golf architecture on a full-time basis. Gill was one of the most learned students of old British architects and links courses among his brethren and went to extraordinary lengths to train and assist young people interested in entering the profession, including one son, Garrett Gill, and Steve Halberg, with whom he shared a design partnership at the end of his life. Gill died in late 1991 from complications following quadruple-bypass surgery.

Courses by David Gill;

Arizona: Royal Palms Inn & C (9 Precision 1970); Valley CC (1957, NLE).
Florida: Tides GC (1972); Vinoy Park C (9 1962).
Georgia: Cherokee Town & CC (Hillside Cse 1957).
Illinois: Arlington GC (1966, NLE); Arlington Lakes GC (Precision 1979); Arlington Park GC (Precision 1963); Cress Creek CC (1961); Hillcrest Acres GC (1964); Kenloch G Links (9 Precision 1963); Links at Nichols Park (1979); Palos Hills GC (9 1990); Tamarack GC (1989); Village Links of Glen Ellyn (27 1966).
Indiana: Hulman Links of Terre Haute (1977).
Iowa: Geneva G&CC (1980); Green Valley Muni (1960); Highland Park GC (9 1965); Spencer G&CC (1966).
Minnesota: Bunker Hills G Cse (East Cse 1968; West Cse 9 1968); Dwan GC (1970).
Missouri: Eagle Springs G Cse (27 1989); Mosswood Meadows GC (9 1984).
Nebraska: Lochland CC (1964).
North Dakota: Tom O'Leary GC (9 1983).
South Dakota: Meadowbrook GC (1976).
Wisconsin: Cherokee CC (1964); Ives Groves GC (1971); North Shore CC (27 1965); Villa Du Parc CC (1963).

Courses remodeled or expanded by David Gill:

Alabama: Decatur CC (R.9 A.9 1959).
Illinois: Apple Orchard CC (R.4 1960); Arrowhead GC (A.9 1969); Cherry Hills CC (A.9 1966); Downers Grove GC (R.3 1976); Glen Oak CC (R.4 1965); Jackson CC (A.9 1967); Kishwaukee CC (A.9 1964); Naperville CC (R.5 1969); Park Ridge CC (R.4 1964); Rochelle CC (R.9 A.9 1965); Rock Island Arsenal C (R. 1966); Rolling Green CC (R.6 1968); Sandy Hollow Muni (R. 1973); St. Charles CC (R. 1967); Sunset CC (R.4 1963).
Iowa: Lakeshore CC (A.9 1969); Westwood GC (A.9 1967).
Michigan: Cascade Hills CC (R.); Harbor Point GC (R.15 A.3 1972); Marquette G&CC (A.9 1967).
Minnesota: Green Haven GC (R.3 1971).
Missouri: Cape Girardeau CC (R.9 A.9 1969).
Nebraska: CC of Lincoln (R.2 1960); Fremont GC (A.11 R.7 1961); Happy Hollow C (R. 1964); Highland CC (R. 1973).

Wisconsin: Blue Mound G&CC (R.3 1960); Brown's Lake GC (R.2 1963); Brynwood CC (R.6 1964); Meadowbrook Town & CC (R. 1962); Ozaukee CC (R.3 1968); Racine CC (R.); West Bend CC (A.9 1959); Westmoor GC (R.9 1973).

GARRETT D. GILL (1953–   ), ASGCA

BORN: Chicago, Illinois.

Garrett Gill, the son of golf architect David Gill, received a Bachelor's degree in landscape architecture from the University of Wisconsin and earned a Master's degree in the same subject at Texas A&M. During his school years Gill authored a 40-page thesis, "Golf Course Design and Construction Standards," which soon entered select golf course bibliographies. He trained under his father while still in college and upon graduation joined his father's firm for a time.

During the recession of the early 1980s, Gill returned to Texas A&M, this time to teach. After teaching for several years, Gill returned to golf course design, forming a golf design partnership with former classmate George B. Williams in 1986, based in Wisconsin.

Courses by Garrett Gill (All with George B. Williams unless indicated otherwise):

California: David L. Baker GC (1987); Micke Grove G Links (1992).
Illinois: Arlington Lakes GC (Precision 1979), ass't David Gill; Links at Nichols Park (1979), ass't David Gill.
Indiana: Hulman Links of Terre Haute (1977), ass't David Gill.
Iowa: Geneva G&CC (1980), ass't David Gill.

Garrett Gill, 1990 COURTESY ASGCA

Minnesota: Inverwood G Links (27 1991); Majestic Oaks GC (South Cse 1991); Willinger GC (1991).
Missouri: Mosswood Meadows GC (9 1984), ass't David Gill.
North Dakota: Tom O'Leary GC (9 1983), ass't David Gill.
South Dakota: Meadowbrook GC (1976), ass't David Gill.

Courses remodeled or expanded by Garrett Gill (All with George B. Williams unless indicated otherwise):

California: Aptos Seascape GC (R.); Camarillo Springs CC (R.); Chula Vista Muni (R.); El Dorado Park GC (R.); El Toro G Cse (A.9 1991); Mountain Shadows GC (North and South Cses, R.); MountainGate CC (R.); Yorba Linda CC (R.).
Colorado: Applewood GC (R.).
Georgia: Alfred "Tup" Holmes G Cse (R.); Bobby Jones GC (R.); North Fulton Muni (R.).
Iowa: Ottumwa Muni (R.).
Minnesota: Brookview GC (R.); Keller GC (R.).
Nevada: Sahara CC (R.).
New Jersey: Brigantine G Links (R.); Rancocas GC (R.).
New Mexico: Tanoan CC (R.).
Texas: Maxwell GC (R.); Mesquite Muni (R.); Pecan Valley CC (R.); World Houston GC (R.).

JOHN HAMILTON GILLESPIE (1852–1923)

BORN: Moffat, Dumfrieshire, Scotland.
DIED: Sarasota, Florida, at age 71.

By 1886 Colonel J. Hamilton Gillespie, a transplanted Scot, was hitting golf balls around a two-hole course he had hacked from thick woods on what is now downtown Sarasota, Florida. Gillespie, who became the first mayor of Sarasota, was instrumental in popularizing the city at the turn of the century. He established a railroad running between Sarasota and nearby Bradenton. In 1902 he laid out a nine-hole course, later known as Sarasota GC, and built a clubhouse on the site two years later. It is generally considered to be Florida's first real golf course. He later added a second nine holes to it and did a rudimentary course in Kissimmee, Florida.

Gillespie moved back to Scotland during World War I after a dispute with locals

J. Hamilton Gillespie, circa 1920 COLLECTION RON WHITTEN

over the closing of his Sarasota course, but after the war he returned to Florida and reestablished the course. A few years later, Gillespie died of a heart attack while playing there. The course was abandoned in 1927 when a new Donald Ross–designed municipal complex opened. After some debate, city fathers chose to name the new complex after Bobby Jones, who played in its inaugural foursome, rather than after Colonel Gillespie. But in 1977, when a new nine was added to the club, the city rectified the oversight and named it the Colonel John Hamilton Gillespie Executive Golf Course.

CARLTON E. GIPSON

BORN: Texas.

Carlton Gipson attended Texas A&M University on a Trans-Mississippi Golf Association scholarship. After graduating with a degree in agronomy in 1958, Gipson worked for a short time with the U.S. Soil Conservation Service, then became superintendent of Shreveport (Louisiana) Country Club. In the early 1960s he moved to Mexico City, where he served for several years as superintendent of the Mexico City Country Club.

In the 1970s he returned to his native Texas and worked as superintendent at a succession of clubs. He also began designing golf courses on the side. In 1977 he joined Benchmark Management Company as in-house architect, handling the development company's golf projects, including revisions to its 54-hole Woodlands complex.

Courses designed by Carlton Gipson:

Texas: April Sound CC; First Colony GC (1990); Greatwood GC (1990); Old Orchard GC (27 1991); Pecan Grove Plantation CC; Weston Lakes GC; Westwood Shores GC.

Courses remodeled or expanded by Carlton Gipson:

New Jersey: Forsgate CC (East Cse, A.3 1989).
Texas: Pirates Muni (R. 1989); TPC at The Woodlands (R. 1986); The Woodlands Inn & GC (North Cse, R. 1986; West Cse 1987).

Clark Glasson, 1982 RON WHITTEN

FRANK CLARK GLASSON (1913–)

BORN: San Jose, California.

As a youth, Clark Glasson caddied at Los Altos Golf and Country Club for eight years while he starred in baseball, football and track at the local high school. After graduating from San Jose State College with a degree in engineering, Glasson worked in Oakland, California, for the Railway Express Agency. During that seven-year stint, he worked seriously on his game and at one time had a two handicap.

In 1946, after four years working for an ironworks in Sunnyvale, California, Glasson returned to his beloved Los Altos as its superintendent and worked with retired Los Altos professional (and part-time golf architect) Tom Nicoll in restoring the course. He found he enjoyed the work, and in 1950 Glasson resigned and formed a course-construction firm. By the mid-1950s he was designing as well as building courses.

In 1961 he completed Deep Cliff Golf Club, which he owned and operated for a decade. An inner-ear imbalance forced him to move to the mountains of northern California for his health in the late 1970s. There he designed, built and operated another daily-fee course, Fall River Valley.

Courses by Clark Glasson:

California: Arrowhead CC; Deep Cliff GC (1961); Emerald Hills Elks GC (9 Precision 1959); Fall River Valley G&CC (1980); Indian Pines G&TC (9); Little Knoll GC (9); Los Gatos G&CC (9 Precision 1959); Palo Alto Hills G&CC (1957); San Ramon Royal Vista GC (1962); Shasta Valley CC (9); Sunken Gardens GC (9); Sunol Valley GC (Cypress Cse 1967; Palm Cse 1967); Tularcitos G&CC; Twain Harte GC (9 Precision 1961); Wikiup G&TC (9 Precision 1964).

Colorado: Lake Arbor GC.

Nevada: Royal Kenfield GC [FKA Showboat CC](1959).

Courses remodeled or expanded by Clark Glasson:

California: Los Altos G&CC (R. 1946, with Tom Nicoll; R. 1978); Pasatiempo GC (R. 1977); Peninsula G&CC (R.); Rio del Mar GC (R.).

MICHAEL E. GLEASON
(1959–), ASGCA

BORN: Detroit, Michigan.

After receiving a Bachelor of Science degree from Thornton Community College in South Holland, Michigan, Mike Gleason attended the University of Illinois and obtained a degree in landscape architecture. After his graduation in 1983 Gleason joined the North Carolina firm of golf architect Dan Maples as chief design associate.

Courses by Mike Gleason (All as assistant to Dan Maples):

Georgia: Orchard G&CC (1991).

Hawaii: Oneloa GC (North and South Cses 1992).

North Carolina: Apple Valley GC (1986); Cramer Mountain CC (1986); Longleaf CC (1988); Pearl G Links (East and West Cses 1987); [The] Pit G Links (1984); Providence CC (1989); Sandpiper Bay G&CC (1987); Sea Trail G Links (Maples Cse 1986); [The] Sound G Links (1990); Woodlake CC (Green Cse 1992).

South Carolina: Heritage Plantation GC (1986); [The] Witch G Links (1989); Willbrook Plantation GC (1988).

Virginia: Birkdale GC (1990); Ford's Colony CC (Red Cse 1986; Gold Cse 1991).

Germany: CC of Hanover (1992).

Spain: C de G Capadepera (1992).

Mike Gleason, 1990
COURTESY ASGCA

Courses remodeled or expanded by Mike Gleason (All as assistant to Dan Maples):

North Carolina: Bermuda Run G&CC (A.3rd 9 1986); Deep Springs CC (R. 1991); Forsyth CC (R.); Hope Valley CC (R. 1986).

Tennessee: Cherokee CC (R. 1985).

Virginia: Glenrochie CC (A.9).

Harold Glissmann, 1961 COLLECTION RON WHITTEN

HAROLD W. GLISSMANN
(1909–)

BORN: Douglas County, Nebraska.

Harold Glissmann began his career in golf in the 1930s helping his father, Henry, and brother Hans construct and operate three daily-fee courses near Omaha, Nebraska. When these courses closed during World War II, Glissmann became grounds superintendent at the famed Boys Town community near Omaha.

In the 1950s Glissmann formed a golf design and construction firm and built many small-town courses in Nebraska and Iowa. He also owned and operated several daily-fee layouts in Omaha, including Miracle Hill GC. He retired from his design work in 1965 but continued to serve as a turfgrass consultant for clubs and businesses during the 1970s.

Courses by Harold Glissmann:

Iowa: Emmettsburg G&CC (9 1951), with *Henry C. Glissmann;* Five-by-80 GC (9 1965); Ida Grove G&CC (9); Lakeview GC (9 1966).

Nebraska: Cedar Hills GC (9 Precision 1959, NLE); Dundee GC (NLE), with *Henry C. Glissmann;* Harrison Heights GC (1933, NLE), with *Henry C. Glissmann;* Indian Hills CC (1934, NLE), with *Henry C. Glissmann;* Lakeview GC (9 1968); Maple Village GC (9 Par 3 1962); Ralston GC (NLE), with *Henry C. Glissmann;* Ryan Hill GC (9 1969); Seward CC (9 1964); Valley View GC, Central City (9); Valley View GC, Fremont (9); Westwood Heights GC (9 Par 3 1964).

Courses remodeled or expanded by Harold Glissmann:

Iowa: Council Bluffs CC (R. 1935, NLE), with *Henry C. Glissmann.*

Nebraska: Fremont GC (R.); Kearney CC (R.).

JOEL GOLDSTRAND
(1939–)

BORN: St. Paul, Minnesota.

A member of two University of Houston NCAA Championship teams, Joel Goldstrand played on the PGA Tour during the 1960s and then served as head professional at Minneapolis (Minnesota) Golf Club. As a sidelight to his club professional duties, Goldstrand laid out a series of fine low-budget courses in rural Iowa and Minnesota. He then resigned to practice architecture full-time, teaming with civil engineer Ron Bloom, who handled construction, as Fairway Architects Inc.

Goldstrand was among the most creative of architects. He incorporated ancient Indian burial mounds as hazards on

Joel Goldstrand, 1991 COURTESY JOEL GOLDSTRAND

one course. On another course he positioned a green atop an abandoned bridge so water flowed under the putting surface. His most novel design was a nine-hole reversible layout designed to be played both forward and backward. He introduced it at Double Eagle GC in Eagle Bend, Minnesota, and utilized the same concept at several other courses.

Courses by Joel Goldstrand:

Iowa: Alton CC (9 1980); Heritage Park GC (9 1984).

Minnesota: Bonanza Valley GC (9 Reversible 1990); Bunker Hills G Cse (Executive Cse [9 Par 3] 1971, NLE); Chippendale GC (1989); Fox Hollow GC (1988); Double Eagle GC (9 Reversible 1984); Farmer's G & Health C (9 1975); Hidden Greens GC (1986); Jerry's Farm C (9 Reversible 1990); Le Sueur CC (1972); Montgomery GC (9 1969); Mountain Lake GC (9 1970); Owatonna CC (9 1973); [The] Pines at Grand View GC (1990); Prairie View G Cse (1981); Red Wing CC (1987); Rum River Hills GC (1989); Tipsinah Mounds CC (9 1982); Vallebrook GC (9 1976); Watona Park G Cse (1978); Whispering Pines GC (9 1985); Woodland Creek G Cse (9 Reversible 1988).

North Dakota: Memorial CC (9 1983).

South Dakota: Madison Park CC (9 1975); Willow Run GC (1986).

Courses remodeled or expanded by Joel Goldstrand:

Iowa: Quail Creek CC (A.9 1986).

Minnesota: Benson GC (A.9 1978); Bunker Hills G Cse (West Cse, A.9 1990); Burl Oaks GC (R. 1989); Cannon GC (A.9 1990); Chisago Lakes GC (R. 1989); Island View CC (R. 1987); Luverne GC (R. 1989); Monticello CC (A.9 1988); Moorhead CC (R. 1983); Ortonville GC (A.9 1974); Perham Lakeside CC (A.9 1989); Purple Hawk CC (R. 1987); Rose Lake GC (A.9 1986); Worthington CC (R. 1974).

North Dakota: Fargo CC (R. 1990).

DAVID W. GORDON
(1922–   ), ASGCA, PRESIDENT 1959

BORN: Mt. Vernon, New York.

Son of golf architect William F. Gordon, David Gordon served as a pilot with the U.S. Army Air Force in World War II.

David Gordon, 1959
COURTESY *GOLF WORLD*

He then completed his education at Penn State University, receiving a B.S. degree in agronomy. From 1947 to 1952 he worked in the field as a construction superintendent for his father's firm.

David became a partner in the Gordon firm in 1952 and was involved in all aspects of the business. He continued to maintain the practice after his father's death in 1974, retiring from active work in the mid-1980s.

Courses by David Gordon (All with William Gordon unless otherwise indicated):

Connecticut: East Mountain Muni (1955); Stanwich C (1963); Western Hills GC (1960).

Delaware: Du Pont CC (Louviers Cse 1955; Montchanin Cse [Precision] 1955).

Florida: Hidden Hills CC (1967 solo).

Maryland: Hillendale CC (1954); Indian Spring C (Chief Cse 1955; Valley Cse 1955); Ocean City G&YC (Seaside Cse 1958); Sparrows Point CC (1954); Willow Brook GC (1969).

New Jersey: Buena Vista CC (1957); Eagles Nest GC [FKA Tall Pines GC]; Green Knoll GC (27 1960); Lake Lackawanna GC (9 Precision 1955); Medford Village CC [FKA Sunny Jim GC] (1964); Oak Hill GC; Princeton CC (1964); Rockleigh GC (Bergen Cse, 9 1963).

New York: Bay Park GC (9 solo); Bethlehem Steel C (27 1956); Finger Lakes GC (solo); North Woodmere GC (9 solo); Rockland Lake GC (North Cse solo; South Cse [Precision] solo).

Ohio: Browns Run CC (1958).

Pennsylvania: Bethlehem Muni (1955); Blackwood CC (1970); Blue Mountain GC (solo); Bon Air CC (1954); Bucks County GC; Colonial CC, Harrisburg (1956); Colonial GC, Uniontown (1973); Conestoga CC; Cornwells

CC (1960); Danville CC; Edgewood in the Pines GC (solo); Fairways GC (1958); Frosty Valley CC (1960); Glenhardie CC (9 solo); Hawk Valley GC (1971); Hershey's Mill GC (solo); Host Farms GC (1964); Indian Valley CC (1954); Locust Valley CC (1963); Mahoning Valley CC (1962); Saucon Valley CC (Grace Cse, 9 1953, A.9 1958; Junior Cse, 6 1955); South Hills GC (1960); St. Clair CC (1954); Sunnybrook CC (1956); Upper Main Line CC (1962); Warrington CC (1958); Wedgewood GC (1963); Weyhill GC (1967); White Manor CC (1963); Whitford CC (1958).

Virginia: Ethelwood CC (1957); Newport News Park GC; Williamsburg CC (1960); Willow Oaks CC (1959).

West Virginia: Clinton Springs CC (1959); Oglebay Park GC (Par 3 Cse [18 Par 3] 1957).

Quebec: Elm Ridge CC (Cse No. 1 1958; Cse No. 2 1958); Richelieu Valley CC (Blue Cse 1963; Red Cse 1963).

Bermuda: Queens Park GC (9 Precision 1958 solo).

Courses remodeled or expanded by David Gordon (All with William Gordon unless otherwise indicated):

Connecticut: Hartford GC (R. 1965).

Delaware: Du Pont CC (DuPont Cse, R. 1955; Nemours Cse, R. 1955).

Florida: Timuquana CC (R. 1969 solo).

New Jersey: Canoe Brook CC (North Cse, R. 1955; South Cse, R. 1955); Greenacres CC (R. 1955); Hackensack GC (R. 1961); Lawrenceville School GC (R. 1954); Little Mill CC (A.9 solo); Newton CC (A.9); Raritan Valley CC (R. solo); Rockleigh GC (Rockleigh Cse, R. 1963); Seaview GC (Bay Cse, R. 1957; Pines Cse, A.9 1957).

New York: Engineers GC (R. 1958); Hyde Park Muni (North Cse, R. 1962; South Cse, R.9 A.9 1962); Moonbrook CC (R. 1958); Yahnundasis GC (R.5 1960).

Pennsylvania: Brookside CC (R.9 A.9 1955); Buck Hill Inn & CC (R. 1956); Chambersburg CC (R. 1955); Galen Hall GC (R. 1955); Gulph Mills GC (R.7 1958); Hanover CC (R.); Lancaster CC (R.12 A.6 1959); Lehigh CC (R. 1959); Manufacturers G&CC (A.9 1963); Meadowlands CC (R. 1958); Northampton County (R.12 A.6 solo); Philmont CC (North Cse, R. 1956); Radnor Valley CC (R.4 A.14 1968); Saucon Valley CC (Old Cse, R. 1956);

Susquehanna Valley CC (R. 1955);
Twin Lakes GC, Souderton (A.9 *solo*);
Twin Lakes GC, Mainland (R. *solo*);
Wildwood GC (R. 1955); Williamsport
CC (R. 1964 *solo*).
Virginia: Hermitage CC (R. 1963 *solo*).

WILLIAM F. GORDON
(1893–1973), ASGCA, CHARTER MEMBER;
PRESIDENT 1953, 1967

BORN: Rhode Island.
DIED: Abington, Pennsylvania, at age 80.

William Gordon was an outstanding
track star in his youth and served as an
athletic instructor with the U.S. Navy during World War I. Upon discharge he took
a job as salesman with the Peterson Seed
Company and in 1920 joined the Carter's
Tested Seed Company as superintendent
of its golf course-construction division. In
this capacity he constructed courses for
such well-known golf architects as Willie
Park, Jr., Donald Ross and Devereux
Emmet.

In 1923 Gordon joined the firm of
Toomey and Flynn, where he remained
until 1941. During the Depression, he was
also part owner and manager of Marble
Hall GC in Philadelphia. Gordon founded
the Pennsylvania Public Golfers Association and served as its first president from
1936 to 1940. He was also a member and
president (in 1940) of the Philadelphia
Public Golfers Association.

In 1941 Gordon formed his own corporation, which was involved until 1945 in
the seeding of military installations. For
the next five years the firm constructed
golf courses for Donald Ross and J. B.
McGovern. From 1950 to 1973 Gordon
designed and built courses on his own
under the incorporated name of William
F. Gordon Co. Most of his layouts planned
after 1953 were done in collaboration with
his son David. Bill Gordon served as first
chairman of the ASGCA's Historical Committee and was in part responsible for per-
suading Geoffrey Cornish and Ronald
Whitten to collaborate on *The Golf Course.*

Courses by William Gordon (All with David Gordon unless otherwise indicated):

Connecticut: East Mountain Muni (1955);
Stanwich C (1963); Western Hills GC
(1960).
Delaware: Du Pont CC (Louviers Cse

*William F. Gordon,
circa 1960* COURTESY
DAVID GORDON

1955; Montchanin Cse [Precision]
1955).
Florida: Ocala Muni (1947 *solo*).
Maryland: Hillendale CC (1954); Indian
Spring C (Chief Cse 1955; Valley Cse
1955); Ocean City G&YC (Seaside Cse
1958); Sparrows Point CC (1954);
Willow Brook GC (1969).
New Jersey: Buena Vista CC (1957); Ea-
gles Nest GC [FKA Tall Pines GC];
Green Knoll GC (27 1960); Lake
Lackawanna GC (9 Precision 1955);
Medford Village CC [FKA Sunny Jim
GC](1964); Oak Hill GC; Princeton
CC (1964); Rockleigh GC (Bergen
Cse, 9 1963).
New York: Bethlehem Steel C (27 1956).
North Carolina: Washington Y&CC (9
1949).
Ohio: Browns Run CC (1958).
Pennsylvania: Bethlehem Muni (1955);
Blackwood CC (1970); Bon Air CC
(1954); Bucks County GC; Colonial
CC, Harrisburg (1956); Colonial GC,
Uniontown (1973); Conestoga CC;
Cornwells CC (1960); Danville CC;
Fairways GC (1958); Frosty Valley CC
(1960); Hawk Valley GC (1971); Host
Farms GC (1964); Indian Valley CC
(1954); Locust Valley CC (1963); Ma-
honing Valley CC (1962); Saucon
Valley CC (Grace Cse, 9 1953, A.9
1958; Junior Cse, 6 1955); South Hills
GC (1960); St. Clair CC (1954); Sun-
nybrook CC (1956); Upper Main Line
CC (1962); Warrington CC (1958);
Wedgewood GC (1963); Weyhill GC
(1967); White Manor CC (1963);
Whitford CC (1958).
Virginia: CC of Fairfax (9 1946 *solo*);
Ethelwood CC (1957); Goose Creek
CC (1953 *solo*); Newport News Park
GC; Williamsburg CC (1960); Willow
Oaks CC (1959).
West Virginia: Berry Hills CC (1952
solo); Clinton Springs CC (1959);
Oglebay Park GC (Par 3 Cse [18 Par
3] 1957).

Quebec: Elm Ridge CC (Cse No. 1 1958;
Cse No. 2 1958); Richelieu Valley CC
(Blue Cse 1963; Red Cse 1963).
Washington, D.C.: Fort Du Pont Muni (9
1948 *solo*).

Courses remodeled or expanded by William Gordon (All with David Gordon unless otherwise indicated):

Connecticut: Hartford GC (R. 1965).
Delaware: Du Pont CC (Du Pont Cse, R.
1955; Nemours Cse, R. 1955).
New Jersey: Alpine CC (R. 1953 *solo*);
Canoe Brook CC (North Cse, R. 1955;
South Cse, R. 1955); Greenacres CC
(R. 1955); Hackensack GC (R. 1961);
Lawrenceville School GC (R. 1954);
Newton CC (A.9); Rockleigh GC
(Rockleigh Cse, R. 1963); Seaview GC
(Bay Cse, R. 1957; Pines Cse, A.9
1957).
New York: Engineers GC (R. 1958); Hyde
Park Muni (North Cse, R. 1962; South
Cse, R.9 A.9 1962); Moonbrook CC
(R. 1958); Yahnundasis GC (R.5
1960).
Pennsylvania: Brookside CC (R.9 A.9
1955); Buck Hill Inn & CC (R. 1956);
Chambersburg CC (R. 1955); Galen
Hall GC (R. 1955); Gulph Mills GC
(R.7 1958); Hanover CC (R.); Lancas-
ter CC (R.12 A.6 1959); Lehigh CC
(R. 1959); Manufacturers G&CC (R.1
1952 *solo*; A.9 1963); Meadowlands
CC (R. 1958); Philmont CC (North
Cse, R. 1956); Radnor Valley CC (R.4
A.14 1968); Saucon Valley CC (Old
Cse, R. 1951 *solo*; R. 1956); Sus-
quehanna Valley CC (R. 1955);
Wildwood GC (R. 1955).
Washington, D.C.: Langston GC (A.9
1953 *solo*).
West Virginia: Southmore CC (R. 1952
solo).

JEFFERY JOHN GORNEY
(1947–)

BORN: Jackson, Michigan.

Jeff Gorney attended Michigan State
University and obtained a Bachelor's degree in landscape architecture in 1975.
The following year he completed the
school's turfgrass management program
and soon became the head superintendent
at Grand Rapids (Michigan) Elks Country
Club. He remained there for nearly twelve
years, during which time he became a certified golf course superintendent under

the auspices of the GCSAA. In 1988 he resigned and established his own golf course architecture firm based in Grand Rapids. His former assistant superintendent, Brian Hamilton, soon joined him in the practice. Not surprisingly, the two emphasized design for maintenance in their work.

Courses by Jeff Gorney:

Michigan: Fox Run CC (1990); Greenbriar GC (1992); Lakeview Hills CC (North Cse 1991); Little Traverse Bay CC (1991); Snowsnake GC (1992).

Courses remodeled or expanded by Jeff Gorney:

Indiana: Crawfordsville CC (A.9 1991).
Michigan: Charlotte CC (R. 1989); CC of Jackson (R. 1989); Goodrich CC (R. 1988); Grayling CC (R.2 A.9 1990); Hill's Heart of the Lakes GC (A.9 1992); Indian Trails G Cse (R. 1988); Manistee G&CC (R. 1988); Meceola GC (A.9 1989); Petoskey Bay View CC (R. 1991); Spring Lake CC (R. 1989); University Park GC (R. 1988); Walnut Hills CC (R. 1990).

Roy Goss, circa 1980 COLLECTION RON WHITTEN

ROY L. GOSS

Dr. Roy Goss, a Washington State University turfgrass specialist, was best known for the turfgrass research and assistance he gave course superintendents. He was instrumental in establishing one of the nation's largest turfgrass-variety testing programs, conducted extensive research into the effects of sulfur upon turfgrass and performed countless experiments on the light intensities necessary to propagate putting green turf. In 1978 he was awarded a Distinguished Service Award by the GCSAA, and in 1988 he received the USGA's Green Section Award.

As a sideline, Goss designed a handful of courses in the 1970s with course superintendent Glen "Manny" Proctor.

Courses by Roy Goss (All with *Glen Proctor* unless otherwise indicated):

Washington: Alderbrook G&CC (1970); Hi Cedars GC (1971); Kahler Glen GC (9 1989 *solo*); Lake Padden Muni (1970); Tumwater Valley GC (1970).

Courses remodeled or expanded by Roy Goss (All with *Glen Proctor* unless otherwise indicated):

Washington: Riverside G Cse (A.9).

MARY PERCEVAL GOURLAY, OBE (1898–1990)

BORN: Basingstoke, Hampshire, England.
DIED: England at age 92.

Famed amateur golfer "Molly" Gourlay helped organize the Curtis Cup, the biennial competition between teams of British and American women golfers, and played on the 1932 and 1934 Curtis Cup teams for Great Britain. She also won two English Ladies Amateur Championships, three French Ladies Amateurs, three Swedish Ladies Amateurs and two Belgian Ladies Amateurs.

During the height of her competitive career, Gourlay collaborated with golf architect Tom Simpson on the design and redesign of several courses, making her one of the earliest females to engage in golf course architecture. She did not pursue it as a career, however, preferring to work on furthering women's golf in Britain. She helped organize and chaired the Ladies Golf Union of Great Britain and the English Ladies Golf Association and was still serving as a vice president of each organization at the time of her death.

Courses by Molly Gourlay (All with Tom Simpson):

Austria: Schloss Mittersill GC (1936).

Courses remodeled or expanded by Molly Gourlay (All with Tom Simpson):

Ireland: Ballybunion GC (Old Cse, R. 1936); Carlow GC (R. 1937); County Louth GC (R. 1938).

GARY JAMES GRANDSTAFF (1948–)

BORN: Massillon, Ohio.

After graduating from Penn State University with a degree in agronomy and turf

management, Gary Grandstaff worked as a golf course superintendent at various Ohio courses for five years. In 1971 he joined the construction crew at Wabeek CC in Michigan, being built by Roy Dye. Grandstaff worked on several Dye projects, then served for a time as course superintendent at Waterwood National in Texas after it opened in 1975. His assistant was Bill Coore, who also became a golf course architect.

In 1977 Grandstaff left Waterwood and rejoined Roy Dye in Mexico. The two constructed layouts in the Southwest during the next five years. By 1983 ill health had curtailed Roy Dye's activities and Grandstaff formed his own course-design business, based in Phoenix. By 1990 Grandstaff had moved his headquarters to Bridgeport, West Virginia.

Courses by Gary Grandstaff:

Arizona: Brookview CC (1985); Gambel G Links (9 1983, NLE), ass't Roy Dye; Paradise Peak West GC (9 Precision 1985); Stonecreek GC [FKA Anasazi GC](1983), ass't Roy Dye.
Illinois: Pond Down Woods GC (1992).
Ohio: Castle Shannon GC (1992).
Texas: Waterwood National GC (1974), ass't Roy Dye.
West Virginia: Morris Wells GC (1992).
Mexico: La Mantarraya GC (9 1974, A.9 1984), ass't Roy Dye; San Carlos G&CC (1980), ass't Roy Dye.

Courses remodeled or expanded by Gary Grandstaff:

Arizona: Pinnacle Peak CC (R. 1985); Royal Palms GC (R. 1986); Shalimar GC (R. 1985).
Colorado: Valley CC (R. 1989).
West Virginia: Fairmont Field C (R. 1991); Glenville GC (R. 1991); Pete Dye GC (A.9 1992), ass't Pete Dye.

DOUGLAS S. GRANT (1887–1981)

BORN: Irvington, New York.
DIED: England at age 95.

California Amateur champion Douglas Grant was invited by Samuel Morse to assist Jack Neville in the design of the course that became the famous Pebble Beach Golf Links. Although he did no other design work, Grant was consulted on some later changes at Pebble Beach.

CHARLES M. GRAVES
(1905–)

BORN: Topeka, Kansas.

Born in the Midwest, Charles Graves moved with his family to Birmingham, Alabama, at age five. Graves was one of the first to specialize in parks and recreation planning, having studied it in college and graduate school at Birmingham Southern University, the University of Birmingham and Georgia Tech. He opened his own landscape design company in 1933. Over the years Graves planned hundreds of city, county and state parks.

In the 1960s he began to incorporate golf courses into park complexes and handled the design and construction supervision himself. After a forty-five-year career as a park planner, Graves retired in 1979.

Courses by Charles M. Graves:

Alabama: Lagoon Park GC (1978); Point Mallard Park GC (1969).
Georgia: Westwood GC (1971).
Tennessee: Buford Ellington GC (1963); McKellar GC (1972).

ROBERT MUIR GRAVES
(1930–), ASGCA, PRESIDENT 1974

BORN: Trenton, Michigan.

Robert Muir Graves attended Michigan State University and received a B.S. degree in landscape architecture from the University of California at Berkeley in 1953. He entered private practice as a licensed landscape architect in 1955 and gradually concentrated on golf design within the next four years. After 1959 he was involved in designing, remodeling or consulting on some 650 golf courses throughout the United States and abroad, working in all major vegetative and climate zones.

Although he was not the first landscape architect to become a golf course planner, Graves was generally felt to have ushered in the era of landscape architecture as the preferred academic background for course designers. He wrote extensively on a number of topics relating to golf course architecture and lectured on the subject at the University of California, University of Massachusetts, Utah State University and Harvard Graduate School of Design. With Geoffrey Cornish he conducted two-day seminars on course design under the auspices of Harvard University, the GCSAA

*Robert Muir Graves,
1990* COURTESY
ROBERT MUIR GRAVES

and the PGA, and attendees came from around the world.

In the 1990s, his firm, then known as Robert Muir Graves Ltd., included Damian Pascuzzo as principal associate as well as Michael Stark, Neal Meagher, John Bush and Daniel Bucko as assistants.

Courses by Robert Muir Graves:

California: Big Canyon CC (1971); Blackberry Farm GC (9 Par 3 1962); Boundary Oaks GC (1969); Brooktrails GC (9 1974); Chalk Mountain Muni (1980); Cherry Island GC (1989); Diablo Hills GC (9 Precision 1974); El Cariso GC (1977); Franklin Canyon GC (1968); GC at Quail Lodge [FKA Carmel Valley G&CC](1964); Lake Merced G&CC (1965); La Purisima GC (1987); Las Positas GC (1967, R. A.3rd 9 1990); Moffett Field GC (9 1959, A.9 1964); Moraga CC (9 Precision 1974); Mountain Springs G&CC (1990); Navy Postgraduate School GC (9 1961, A.9 1972); Northstar at Tahoe GC (1979); Paradise Valley GC (1992); Parkway G Cse (Par 3 1970); Rio Bravo GC (1982); Royal Oaks GC (9 Par 3 1961, NLE); San Jose Muni (1968); Santa Clara G&TC (1987); Sea Ranch GC (9 1973); Seven Oaks CC (1991); Van Buskirk Muni (1967); Villages G&CC (27 1970).
Idaho: Bigwood GC (9 1971); Whispering Forest GC (9 1983, A.9 1990).
Montana: Bill Roberts Muni (9 1978).
Nevada: Jackpot GC (9 1970, A.9 1981).
Oregon: Alder Creek GC (9 1983, NLE); Black Butte Ranch GC (Big Meadows Cse 1972); Cedar Links (9 1986); Michelbook CC (9 1984); River's Edge GC (9 1989); Seventh Mountain GC (1991).

Utah: Murray Parkway GC (1983); Twin Lakes GC (9 Precision 1983).
Washington: Avalon GC (27 1991); Canterwood G&CC (1988); Meadowood GC (1987); Port Ludlow GC (1975); Sun Willows GC (1982); Three Rivers GC (1982); Washington State University GC (9 1971).
Malaysia: Labuan GC (9 1975); Mount Kinabalu GC (9 1973); Sabah G&CC.

Courses remodeled or expanded by Robert Muir Graves:

Alaska: Fairbanks CC (R. 1989).
California: Alameda Muni (Jack Clark Cse, R. 1978); Almaden G&CC (R.1 1968); Arrowhead CC (R. 1981); Baywood G&CC (R. 1980); Brentwood CC (R. 1986); Buchanan Field GC (R. 1986); Burlingame CC (R. 1981); Canyon CC (R. 1987); Claremont CC (R. 1987); Contra Costa CC (R. 1976); Corral de Tierra CC (R. 1988); Crystal Springs GC (R. 1964); Del Paso CC (R. 1985); Del Rio CC (R. 1978); Desert Island GC (R. 1987); Diablo Creek GC (R.5 1974); Diablo G&CC (R.2 1964); Elkhorn CC (R. 1978); El Macero CC (R. 1985); Galbraith Muni GC (R. 1980); Gleneagles International GC (R. 1982); Green Hills CC (R. 1965); Green Tree GC (R. 1986); Green Valley CC (R. 1965); Half Moon Bay G Links (R. 1986); Hayward GC (R. 1968); Hillcrest CC (R.6 1974); La Cumbre G&CC (R. 1988); La Rinconada CC (R. 1972); Laguna Hills GC (R.); Lake Chabot GC (R. 1989); Lake Wildwood GC (R. 1977); Lakeside GC of Hollywood (R. 1972); Leisure Town GC (R. 1979); Lew Galbraith Muni (R. 1980); Lomas Santa Fe CC (R. 1983); Los Altos G&CC (R.9 1973); Los Angeles CC (R. 1982); Mare Island GC (R. 1985); Marin G&CC (R. 1986); Meadow C (R. 1964); Merced G&CC (R. 1977); Mira Vista G&CC (R.1 1967); Mission Trails G Cse (A.9 1986); Morro Bay GC (R. 1987); Napa Valley CC (R. 1973); Navy Postgraduate School GC (R.4 1968); North Ridge CC (R. 1986); Northwood GC (R. 1964); Oaktree CC (R. 1983); Olympic C (Ocean Cse, R. 1989); Orinda CC (R. 1977); Pajaro Valley CC (R. 1965); Palm Desert CC (Executive Cse, R. 1982); Palo Alto Hills G&CC (R.5 1968); Palos Verdes CC (R. 1987); Pasatiempo GC (R. 1968); Peninsula

CC (R. 1985); Pittsburg G&CC (A.9 1990); Presidio GC (R. 1964); Rancho Mirage CC (R. 1989); Rancho San Joaquin CC (R. 1972); River Island GC (R. 1975); Rossmoor GC (North Cse, A.9 1977); Round Hill G&CC (R. 1975); San Geronimo Valley GC (R. 1989); San Joaquin CC (R. 1988); San Jose CC (R. 1968); San Luis Bay Inn & CC (R. 1984); San Luis Obispo CC (R. 1984); Sandpiper G Links (R. 1986); Santa Maria CC (R. 1965); Santa Rosa Muni (R. 1971); Santa Teresa GC (R. 1982); Saratoga GC (R. 1966); Saticoy CC (R. 1982); Sequoyah CC (R.13 1968); Sharon Heights CC (R. 1977); Sharp Park GC (R. 1972); Silverado GC (R. 1972); Sonoma GC (R. 1990); Stockdale CC (R.9 A.9 1975); Stockton G&CC (R.); Sunken Gardens GC (R. 1980); Swenson Park Muni (A.9 1970); Tilden Park GC (R. 1963); Tom Fry GC [FKA San Mateo Muni](R.); Twin Lakes GC (R. 1985); Villages G&CC (R. 1982); Virginia CC (R. 1989); Visalia CC (R. 1963); Woodbridge G&CC (R. 1985).

Idaho: Bigwood GC (R. 1979); Buhl CC (R. 1983); Crane Creek CC (R.2 1982); Hillcrest CC (R.6 1968); Plantation GC (R. 1975); Silver Sage GC (A.9 1970).

Montana: Buffalo Hill GC (R.9 A.9 1977); Green Meadow CC (R. 1975); Hilands GC (R. 1978); Laurel G&RC (R. 1979); Marias Valley G&CC (R. 1976); Miles City Town & CC (R. 1976); Missoula CC (R. 1977); Yellowstone G&CC (R. 1980).

Nevada: Glenbrook CC (R.); Incline Village GC (R. 1980).

Oregon: Brandon-by-the-Sea GC (R. 1977); Columbia-Edgewater CC (R. 1966); Emerald Valley CC (R. 1981); Illahe Hills CC (R. 1981); McNary GC (R. 1982); Oswego Lake CC (R. 1973); Portland GC (R. 1985); Rogue Valley GC (R. 1983); Salishan G Links (R.); Santiam GC (R. 1978); Springfield CC (R. 1979); Tualatin CC (R. 1978); Waverley CC (R.1 1978).

Washington: Birch Bay Village GC (R. 1978); [The] Cedars GC (R. 1988); Gig Harbor G&CC (R. 1979); Kelso Elks GC (R., NLE); Lake Wilderness CC (R. 1986); Meadow Springs GC (R.9 A.9 1973); Overlake G&CC (R. 1989); Royal Oaks CC (R. 1982); Sahalee CC (R.); Sands Point CC (R. 1981); Sham-Na-Pum GC (R. 1978); Spokane CC (R. 1986); Tumwater Val-

ley GC (R. 1977); Walla Walla CC (R. 1980).

Wyoming: Casper CC (R. 1973); Casper Muni (R. 1973).

England: Henley GC (R. 1974).

Denis Griffiths, 1990 COURTESY ASGCA

DENIS GRIFFITHS
(1947–), ASGCA

BORN: Marshalltown, Iowa.

Denis Griffiths received a Bachelor's degree in landscape architecture in 1970, then immediately went to work for the Atlanta, Georgia, golf design firm of Davis, Kirby, Player and Associates.

In 1980 Griffiths became a full partner with Ron Kirby in Kirby, Griffiths and Associates. One of Griffiths's designs, Pole Creek GC in Winter Park, Colorado, was selected by *Golf Digest* as the Best New Public Course in 1984. In 1987, when Kirby dissolved the partnership to work full-time for Jack Nicklaus in Europe, Griffiths continued the practice as Denis Griffiths and Associates. Among his associates were Glenn Boorman, Barry Edgar, Alan Hamilton and Tom Johnson.

Courses by Denis Griffiths (All with Ron Kirby unless otherwise indicated):

Alabama: CC of Alabama (1986); Huntsville Muni (1986); North River GC (1978), ass't Ron Kirby and Gary Player.

Colorado: Pole Creek GC (1983).

Florida: Chi Chi Rodriguez Youth Foundation GC (1989 *solo*); Seven Hills GC (1989 *solo*).

Georgia: Château Elan GC (1989 *solo*); Chicopee Woods G Cse (1991 *solo*); Georgia Veterans Memorial State Park G Cse (1991 *solo*); Grimball GC (5 1986); Nob North GC (1978), ass't Ron Kirby; River Pines GC (9 Par 3 1991 *solo*).

Ohio: Bent Tree GC (1988 *solo*); Heatherwoode GC (1991 *solo*).

South Carolina: CC of Callawassie (Putting Cse 1988 *solo*); Eastport Marina

& CC (1988 *solo*); Marsh Point GC (1976), ass't Ron Kirby and Gary Player.

Texas: Fair Oaks Ranch G&CC (1979, ass't Ron Kirby and Gary Player; A.3rd 9 1985); Mission del Lago Muni (1989).

Virginia: Brandermill CC (1976), ass't Ron Kirby and Gary Player.

Bophuthatswana: Gary Player CC (1979), ass't Ron Kirby and Gary Player.

Canary Islands: Maspalomas GC (North Cse 1974), ass't Ron Kirby and Gary Player.

Japan: Niigata Forest GC (1975), ass't Ron Kirby and Gary Player; Nishi Nihon GC (1975), ass't Ron Kirby and Gary Player; Press CC (1992); Sasakami Cayman G Park (Cayman 1990 *solo*); Sun Lake CC (1986).

Philippines: Kamirag GC (1982); Lake Paoay GC (1980); Puerto Azul GC (27 1980), ass't Ron Kirby and Gary Player.

South Africa: Roodepoort Muni (1985); Welkom Muni (1987).

Spain: Almerimar GC (1975), ass't Ron Kirby and Gary Player; Escorpion GC (1975), ass't Ron Kirby and Gary Player.

Thailand: Chiang Mai CC (1991 *solo*); Phoenix G&CC (27 1992 *solo*).

Courses remodeled or expanded by Denis Griffiths (All with Ron Kirby unless otherwise indicated):

Alabama: Riverchase CC (R.3 1989 *solo*).

Florida: [The] Everglades C (R. 1984).

Georgia: Bacon Park GC (R. A.3rd 9 1985); Chattahoochee CC (R.2 1988 *solo*); Dalton CC (R. 1977), ass't Ron Kirby; Horseshoe Bend CC (R.17 1989 *solo*); Newnan CC (A.9 1987 *solo*).

Louisiana: New Orleans CC (R. 1985).

Missouri: Bellerive CC (R.1 1985); Forest Hills CC (R.2 1987 *solo*).

North Carolina: Twin Valley CC (R.9 1982).

Texas: Hogan Park GC (A.3rd 9 1978), ass't Ron Kirby; Midland CC (R. 1979), ass't Ron Kirby; Oak Hills CC (R.2 1978), ass't Ron Kirby.

Virginia: Deer Run GC (Cardinal Cse, R. 1986; Deer Run Cse, R.9 A.9 1986).

West Virginia: Shawnee GC (R.9 1979), ass't Ron Kirby.

Philippines: Wack Wack G&CC (East Cse, R. 1980).

South Africa: Kensington GC (R. 1980); Royal Johannesburg GC (West Cse, R. 1985).

Robert Grimsdell,
1958 COLLECTION RON
WHITTEN

ROBERT G. GRIMSDELL

BORN: Amersham, Bucks, England.

A fine competitive golfer in his youth and a devotee of H. S. Colt, Bob Grimsdell moved to South Africa in the late twenties to establish himself in a year-round golf career. He became pro-greenkeeper at several South African clubs, including Royal Johannesburg, whose East Course he laid out in 1933. A talented player, Grimsdell won the Orange Free State Open and Match Play Championships as well as the Belgian and German Opens.

After World War II, Grimsdell became a full-time golf course architect based in Scottburgh, South Africa. Over the next 30 years he established himself as the leading designer in South Africa and surrounding nations.

Courses by Robert Grimsdell:

South Africa: Defence GC (9); Emfuleni CC (1949); Gold Fields West GC (1947); Huddle Park GC (Blue Cse 1940; Yellow Cse 1940; White Cse 1964); Killarney GC [FKA Transvaal Automobile C](1929, NLE), with *Tommy Tomsett*; King David CC (1956); Maritzburg GC (1970); Orkney GC (9 1940); Plettenberg Bay CC (9, NLE); Randpark GC (Windsor Park Cse 1952); Royal Johannesburg CC (East Cse 1933); Swartkop CC (1948); Wedgewood Park GC (1950).
Zimbabwe: Bancroft GC (1954); Sherwood GC (1959); Warren Hills GC (1957).

Courses remodeled or expanded by Robert Grimsdell:

South Africa: Durban CC (R. 1959); Germiston GC (R. 1940); Grahamstown GC (R.); Hermanus GC (R.); Pretoria GC (R. 1948); Royal Johannesburg CC (West Cse, R. 1933); Scottburgh GC (R.).

KARL F. GROHS
BIGCA, ESGCA

German civil engineer Karl Grohs formed a golf design and construction business, Deutsche Golf Consult, in partnership with Rainer Preissmann in 1978. The two had previously been partners in the long-established German landscape architecture firm, Gruppe Ökologie und Planung). After constructing a few courses designed by other architects, the two began designing as well as building courses in the early 1980s. Grohs and Preissmann emphasized ecological considerations aesthetically linked with existing landscapes in their designs. While at Deutsche Golf Consult, Grohs published a number of technical journals regarding the planning, construction and maintenance of specialized golf projects.

Courses by Karl F. Grohs (All with *Rainer Preissmann*):

Germany: Ahaus G&CC (1990); Am Sachsenwald GC (1989); Bad Neuenahr-Ahrweiler G&CC (1982), ass't Joan Dudok Van Heel; Bad Rappenau GC (1992); Bielefelder GC (9 1980), ass't Donald Harradine; Bochumer GC (9 1982); Burg Overbach GC (1986); Castrop-Rauxel GC (1990); Dinslaken-Hünxerwald GC (9 1989); Franken-Abenberg GC (1989); Gelsenkirchen GC (9 1990); International GC Düsseldorf (1989); Kirchbrombach GC (9 1992); Kurhessischer GC Oberaula (1989); Leverkusen GC (1990); Markgräflerland GC (9 1987); Mülheim GC (1992); Obere Alp G&CC (1992); Schloss Moyland G&CC (9 1989); Schmallenberg GC (9 1988); Seeburg GC (1992); Stromberg GC (Par 3 Cse [9 Par 3] 1986); Stromberg-Schindeldorf GC (1991); Telgta-Hof

Karl Grohs, 1991
COURTESY KARL GROHS

Hahnes GC (9 1991); Unna Fröndenberg GC (18 Par 3 1989); Vechta GC (9 1991); Würzburg-Heidingsfeld GC (1992).
Spain: Cala Serena G Training Center (1988).
Switzerland: GC Erlen (1992).

Courses remodeled or expanded by Karl F. Grohs (All with *Rainer Preissmann*):

Germany: Darmstadt Traisa GC (R.9 1990); Eifel-Hillesheim GC (A.9 1991); Essen-Heidhausen GC (R. 1980); Essen-Kettwig Haus Oefte GC (R. 1989); Frankfurter GC (R. 1982); Freiburger GC (A.9 1983); Heilbronn Hohenlohe GC (A.9 1990); Hubbelrath GC (East Cse, R. 1986); Konstanz GC (A.9 1985); Neu-Ulm GC (R.9 A.9 1990); Schloss Georgshausen GC (R. 1987); Siegen-Olpe GC (A.9 1983); Varmert GC (A.9 1992); Vestischer GC (R. 1991).

EDWIN DEWITT GUY
(1910–1981)

BORN: Mississippi.
DIED: Brandon, Mississippi, at age 70.

Longtime Mississippi club professional "Sonny" Guy served as a director of the Southern Turfgrass Association in the 1950s and helped organize the Mississippi Chapter of the PGA. Over the years the "Dean of Mississippi Golf," as he was known, designed over twenty golf courses within his home state. Shortly after his death, the city of Jackson renamed Livingston Park GC, one of his first designs, in his honor.

Courses by Sonny Guy:

Mississippi: Grove Park GC (9); Lakeside GC, Mississippi State University; Robbinhead Lakes GC (1977); Sonny Guy Muni [FKA Livingston Park GC](1949); Starkville CC (9 1966); University of Mississippi GC; University of Southern Mississippi GC (1959).

HERMAN C. HACKBARTH
(1883–1974)

BORN: Oconomowoc, Wisconsin.
DIED: Little Rock, Arkansas, at age 91.

Herman "Hack" Hackbarth began his nearly fifty-year golf career as professional

*Herman Hackbarth,
circa 1950*
COLLECTION RON
WHITTEN

and greenkeeper at Little Rock CC, Arkansas, in 1907. At that time the club had only a six-hole sand greens course, but over the years Hackbarth enlarged and remodeled it into one of the best in the state. He was a well-respected golf teacher, and although he himself was never successful in competition, several of his pupils won state titles.

Hackbarth was also prominent as a golf architect in Arkansas, planning over forty courses, including such fine layouts as Hardscrabble CC and Pine Bluff CC. A turfgrass expert, he introduced bent-grass greens to Arkansas in 1939, when he installed them at Little Rock CC. He was also instrumental in organizing a state greenkeepers association. Hackbarth remained at Little Rock CC until 1956 and even after retirement lived on the course and played it almost every day.

Courses by Herman Hackbarth:

Arkansas: Belvedere CC (1949); Carroll County GC (9 1965); CC of Little Rock (1910); Hardscrabble CC (1926); Helena CC; Magnolia CC (9 1953); Pine Bluff CC (9 1936); Pla-Mor GC (1933); Rebsamen Park Muni (27 1953); Riverdale GC (1932); War Memorial Park GC (1931); Western Hills CC (1961).
Missouri: Dogwood Hills GC (9 1963, A.9 1969).

EDDIE HACKETT
(1910–   ), BIGCA

BORN: Dublin, Ireland.

Eddie Hackett attended the Catholic University School in Dublin, Ireland, and then worked as a golf professional for nearly fifty years, beginning as an assistant at Royal Dublin. He also worked at Johannesburg CC in South Africa and at Elm Park and Portmarnock in Ireland.

During these years he also worked closely with Henry Cotton in England and Belgium and with Fred W. Hawtree, who was designing the second course at Killarney GC and the Westport course.

Hackett designed his first golf course in 1964 and over the next twenty years designed and remodeled scores of Irish layouts. He was also consulting golf architect to the Golfing Union of Ireland, Bord Failte and Great Southern Hotels.

Courses by Eddie Hackett:

Ireland: Ashford Castle GC (9 1984); Bantry GC (9 1974); Beaverstown GC (1985); Beech Park Rathcoole GC; Blacklion GC (9); Bodenstown GC (1973); Boyle GC (9); Cahir Park GC (9 1968); Ceann Sibeal GC (9); Clongowes Wood College GC (9 1966); Connemara GC (1973); Donegal Town GC; Dublin and County GC (1972); Dublin Sports C (9 1977); Dungarvan GC (9); Enniscrone GC (9); Killarney Racetrack GC (Precision 1986); Letterkenny GC; Lismore GC (9); Mahon Muni; Rockwell College GC (9); Stepaside GC (9 1981); Trabolgan GC (9); Tuam GC (9); Waterville G Links (1972).

Courses remodeled or expanded by Eddie Hackett:

Ireland: Abbey Leix GC (R.); Ardee GC (R. A.9 1985); Arklow GC (A.9); Balbriggan GC (R.); Ballina GC (R.); Ballinasloe GC (R.); Ballinrobe GC (R.); Ballybofey & Stranorlar GC (A.9); Ballybunion GC (Old Cse, R. 1964); Ballyliffin GC (R.); Baltinglass GC (R.); Bandon CC (R.); Birr GC (R.); Blacklion GC (R.); Borris GC (R.); Brandon GC (R.); Callan GC (R.); Carlow GC (R.); Carrick-on-Shannon GC (R.); Carrick-on-Suir GC (R.); Castle GC (R.); Castlebar GC (R.9 A.9); Castlerea GC (R.); Castletroy GC (R.); Charleville GC (R.); Claremorris GC (R.); Clonmel GC (A.9); Clontarf GC (R.); Coollattin GC (R.); Corballis GC (R.); County Caven GC (A.9); County Longford GC (A.9); County Sligo GC (R. 1983); Courtown GC (R.); Donabate GC (R.); Dooks GC (R.); Douglas GC (R.); Dun Laoghaire GC (R.); Dungarvan GC (R.); East Cork GC (R.); Edmondstown GC (R.); Elm Park G & Sports C (R.); Ennis GC (R.); Enniscorthy GC (R.); Fermoy GC (R.); Forest Little GC (R.); Foxrock GC (R.); Gort GC (R.); Greenore GC

(R.); Greystones GC (R.); Gweedore GC (R.); Heath GC (R.); Hermitage GC (R.); Island GC (R.); Killiney GC (R.); Limerick GC (R.); Lismore GC (R. 1965); Loughrea GC (R.); Lucan GC (R.); Malahide GC (R.); Milltown GC (R.); Mitchelstown GC (R.); Monkstown GC (R.); Mountrath GC (R.); Mullingar GC (R.); Mulrany GC (R.); Muskerry GC (R.); Nenagh GC (A.9 1970); New Ross GC (R.); Newcastle West GC (R.); Newlands GC (R.); North West GC (R. A.9); Nuremore GC (R.); Oughterard GC (A.9); Parknasilla GC (R.); Portmarnock GC (R. 1); Portumna GC (R.); Rathfarnham GC (R.); Roscommon GC (R.); Roscrea GC (R.); Rossmore GC (R.); Royal Dublin GC (R.2 1984); Royal Tara GC (R.); Rush GC (R.); Skerries GC (A.9); Slade Valley GC (R.); St. Anne's GC (A.9 R.9); Strandhill GC (R.); Swinford GC (R.); Thurles GC (R.); Tralee GC (R., NLE); Trim GC (R. 1970); Tullamore GC (R.); Waterford GC (R.); Westport GC (R.); Wicklow GC (R.).
Northern Ireland: Cairndnu GC (R.); Castlerock GC (R.); City of Derry GC (A.9); Enniskillen GC (R.); Massereene GC (R.); Omagh GC (R.); Strabane GC (A.9).

*Walter Hagen, circa
1925* COURTESY *GOLF
WORLD*

WALTER CHARLES HAGEN
(1892–1969)

BORN: Rochester, New York.
DIED: Traverse City, Michigan, at age 76.

Famed professional golfer Walter Hagen, who won two U.S. Opens, four British Opens and five PGA Championships, worked as a consultant to the design team of Stiles and Van Kleek during the Roaring Twenties. "The Haig" also laid out a couple of courses on his own in the 1930s.

Courses by Walter Hagen:

Florida: Pasadena GC (1923), with Wayne Stiles and John Van Kleek.
Michigan: Dearborn Hills CC, with *Mike Brady*; Lakeview Hills GC (South Cse, 9 1935).
Japan: Koganei CC (1937).

STEVEN M. HALBERG
(1954–)

BORN: Princeton, Illinois.

Steven Halberg practiced landscape design for over ten years after graduating from the University of Illinois in 1976 with a Bachelor's degree in landscape architecture. In the mid-1980s he assumed management and operation of a municipal golf course in the Chicago area and became acquainted with golf architect David Gill. After training under Gill, in 1990 he became his partner in the firm of Gill and Halberg, Ltd. Gill died the next year but Halberg retained the partnership title and continued Gill's design practice.

Courses by Steve Halberg (All as assistant to David Gill unless otherwise indicated):

Illinois: Palos Hills GC (9 1990); Tamarack GC (1989).
Missouri: Eagle Springs GC (27 1989).

Courses remodeled or expanded by Steve Halberg (All as assistant to David Gill unless otherwise indicated):

Wisconsin: Brighton Dale GC (R. A.2 1990 *solo*).

STEPHEN L. HALSEY
(1946–)

BORN: Whittier, California.

Trained in environmental design and landscape architecture, Stephen Halsey worked for two years for the Peridien Group in California planning residential golf developments. He then formed his own park planning and landscape design firm in Southern California and subsequently won two ASLA landscaping awards.

After preparing several clubhouse landscaping plans, Halsey joined retired navy officer Jack Daray, Jr., son of golf architect Jack Daray, to form Halsey Daray Golf,

Inc., a golf design and construction business. They did their first course in 1978 and worked actively in Southern California throughout the 1980s and into the 1990s.

Courses by Stephen Halsey (All in association with Jack Daray, Jr.):

California: [The] Alisal Ranch G Cse (1992); Eagle Crest CC (1990); Golden Era GC (9 1989); Golden Hills Muni (9 Precision 1992); Modesto Creekside G Cse (1992); Navy G Cse, Mission Gorge (South Cse 1984); Sea 'n Air GC (1981); Willowbrook CC (9 1985).
Montana: Pryor Creek GC.
Virginia: Cheatham GC (9).

Courses remodeled or expanded by Stephen Halsey (All in association with Jack Daray, Jr.):

California: [The] Alisal GC (R. 1991); Balboa Park GC (R. 1992); Carmel Highland CC (R. A.3 1987); Castle Creek CC (R. 1983); CBC Port Hueneme GC (R.9 A.9); Coronado GC (R. 1991); Dryden Park Muni (R. 1991); Navy GC (North Cse, R. 1984); Rancho Bernardo GC (R. 1991); Salinas CC (R. 1991); Torrey Pines Muni (North & South Cses, R. 1988); Village CC (R. 1989).

Gene Hamm, 1989
COURTESY GENE HAMM

EUGENE HAMM
(1923–)

BORN: North Carolina.

After service in the U.S. Navy during World War II, Gene Hamm trained in golf management at Pinehurst, North Carolina, under the GI Bill. Following admission to the PGA, he became assistant to club pro Ellis Maples, who later became a golf course architect himself. In the mid-1950s Hamm left a head professional

job to supervise construction of Duke University GC in Durham to the design of Robert Trent Jones.

In 1959, after assisting on a second Jones project, Hamm opened his own course-design firm and was active in the Carolinas and Virginia for more than thirty years. Always a fine competitive golfer, he won both the 1978 and 1979 Carolinas Seniors on courses of his own design.

Courses by Gene Hamm:

North Carolina: Beacon Ridge G&CC (1988); Cape G&CC (1984); Caswell Pines CC (1991); Cedar Grove GC (1973); Chapel Hill CC (1973); Cheviot Hills GC (1968); Echo Farms G&CC (1974); Falling Creek GC (1970); Foxfire CC (East Cse 1968; West Cse, 9 1973, A.9 1980); Green Valley GC (9 1960); Lochmere GC (1985); Lynrock GC (9 1959); Pilot Knob Park GC (1962); Pine Lake CC (9 1963); Pine Tree GC (1972); Pinewild CC (1989); Reedy Creek GC (1988); River Bend GC (1977); Sandy Ridge CC (1972); Silver Creek GC (1986); Wake Forest CC (1967); Wildwood CC (1958, NLE); Wil-Mar GC (9 1960); Yadkin CC (1962).
South Carolina: Azalea Sands GC (1972); Beachwood GC (1968); Burning Ridge GC (East Cse 1983; West Cse 1979); Eagle Nest GC (1972); Indian Wells GC (1984); Pineland CC (1971); Quail Creek GC (1970); Raccoon Run GC (1976); River Oaks G Plantation (Oaks Cse 1987); Rolling Hills G Cse (1988); Rose Hill Plantation GC (27 1982); Sea Gull GC (1970).
Virginia: Cedars CC (1958); Chatham CC (9 1960); Floyd CC (9 1969); Gay Hill CC (9 1963); Glen Oaks GC (1962); Goodyear GC (9 1981); Green's Folly CC [FKA South Boston CC] (1972); Lynchburg CC (1960); Ringgold CC (1962); Roanoke CC (1977); Spooncreek GC (9 1962); Tuscarora CC (1960).

Courses remodeled or expanded by Gene Hamm:

New York: CitiCorp G Cse (R.9 1987); North Fork CC (R. 1972).
North Carolina: Carolina G&CC (R. 1985); Colonial CC (R. 1973); Henderson CC (R.9 A.9 1970); North Ridge CC (Lakes Cse., A.9 1972; Oaks Cse, A.9 1972); Richmond Pines CC (A.9 1961); Roanoke CC (A.9 1974);

Sedgefield CC (R. 1961); Sippihaw CC (A.9 1968, NLE); Washington Y&CC (R.2 A.9 1973); Williamston CC (R.4 A.9 1980).

Tennessee: Cleveland CC (R. 1968).
Virginia: Bassitt CC (R.9 1960); Danville CC (R. 1958; R. 1961); Du Pont GC (R.9 A.9 1965); Forest Park CC (R.9 A.9 1964); Gypsy Hill GC (A.9 1962).

GEORGE HANSEN
(1891–1951)

BORN: Milwaukee, Wisconsin.
DIED: Milwaukee, Wisconsin, at age 60.

George Hansen was superintendent of the Milwaukee (Wisconsin) Parks Department for over thirty years. He literally built the public golf system in that city. Starting with one nine-hole course in 1920, which he remodeled, Hansen designed and constructed five new layouts for Milwaukee, including the highly regarded Brown Deer Park GC. Largely because of his efforts, Brown Deer hosted the USGA Publinks Championship in 1951. Sadly, Hansen died shortly before the event.

Courses by George Hansen:

Wisconsin: Brown Deer Park GC (1929); Currie Park GC (1927); Grant Park GC (1920); Greenfield Park GC (1923); Whitnall GC (1932).

Courses remodeled or expanded by George Hansen:

Wisconsin: Lincoln Park GC (R. 1920).

WALTER S. HARBAN
(1857–1938)

DIED: Washington, D.C., at age 81.

Dr. Walter S. Harban was a dentist to several presidents of the United States. In his spare time, he planned the first version of Columbia CC in Maryland and collaborated with golf architect William H. Tucker on the design of Bannockburn Club in Glen Echo, Maryland. Harban, while serving as a club official at Columbia, sought professional assistance on turfgrass problems from the U.S. Department of Agriculture. That effort led Harban and others to propose to the USGA that a formal turfgrass consulting body be created. The USGA's Green Section was formed in

Walter S. Harban, circa 1920 COURTESY *GOLF WORLD*

1920, and Harban served as a member until his death. After retiring from dentistry, Harban dabbled in course design and experimented in developing new putting grass strains.

Courses by Walter Harban:

Maryland: Argyle CC, with William H. Tucker; Bannockburn G&CC (NLE), with William H. Tucker; Columbia CC (NLE).
Washington, D.C.: West Potomac Park GC (9 1920), with Walter J. Travis.

Jeff Hardin, 1990 COURTESY ASGCA

JEFF D. HARDIN
(1933–   ), ASGCA

BORN: Tolleson, Arizona.

Jeff Hardin received a Bachelor of Science degree in civil engineering from the University of Arizona in 1959 and was employed for eleven years as a civil engineer, construction manager and golf course designer with the Del E. Webb Corporation in Arizona and California. In this capacity he collaborated on projects in Arizona, California, Hawaii and Spain with such well-known golf architects as Red Lawrence, George and Tom Fazio and Milt Coggins.

In 1972 Hardin formed his own course design and engineering management company. Hardin used an engineering approach to integrate golf and housing,

providing detailed drainage plans of courses and subdivisions, grading plans, cost estimates and quantities all checked by computer. Shortly after establishing his firm, Hardin made young architect Greg Nash a partner.

Courses by Jeff Hardin (All with Greg Nash unless otherwise indicated):

Arizona: Aspen Valley GC (9 1973, A.9 1981); Bellaire GC (Precision 1973), and Red Lawrence; Briarwood GC (1979); Continental CC (Precision 1978); Cottonwood CC (1983); Country Meadows GC (9 Precision 1978); Dobson Ranch GC (1974), and Red Lawrence; Gold Canyon CC (1982); Hillcrest GC (1978); Lakes East GC (Precision 1970 *solo*); Lakes West GC (1968), ass't Milt Coggins; Leisure World GC (Championship Cse 1979; Executive Cse [Par 3] 1979; Los Caballeros GC (9 1979, A.9 1981); Palmbrook CC (1971 *solo*); Paradise Valley Park GC (9 Precision 1986); Pebblebrook GC (1979); Quail Run G Cse (9 Precision 1977); Riverview GC (1972 *solo*); Sheraton El Conquistador GC (Sunrise Cse 1982; Sunset Cse 1985); Stardust GC (Precision 1979); Sun City CC (1966), ass't Milt Coggins; Sun Lakes CC (9 1973, A.9 1979); Sunland Village GC (1975), and Milt Coggins; Union Hills CC (1974); Verde Valley Ranch GC (1991 *solo*); Villa de Paz CC (1976); Wigwam G&CC (West Cse 1974), and Red Lawrence.
Hawaii: Turtle Bay GC (Old Cse 1971), ass't George Fazio and Tom Fazio.
Nevada: Los Prados GC (1987 *solo*).
New Mexico: Las Sierras GC (1991 *solo*).
Colombia: La Colina CC (1974).

Courses remodeled or expanded by Jeff Hardin (All with Greg Nash unless otherwise indicated):

Arizona: Arizona CC (R. 1976 *solo*); Rio Verde CC (Quail Run Cse, A.9 1981; White Wing Cse, A.9 1983).

THOMAS BENJAMIN HARMON
(–1974)

Ben Harmon earned a degree in engineering at Washington State University and in 1952 was hired by Patrick Markovich to serve as his assistant professional at Richmond (California) CC. A few years later, Markovich bought a large ranch and invited Harmon to lay out and construct a golf course on it. The result was the original Silverado CC. Harmon later constructed a few courses for golf architect Lawrence Hughes and designed several projects of his own in California in the 1960s before his death in a fishing accident at sea.

Courses by Ben Harmon:

California: Bennett Valley GC (1970); Glenn G&CC (9 1960); Napa Muni (1968), with Bob Baldock and Jack Fleming; Santa Rosa G&CC (1958), with Jack Fleming; Silverado CC (North Cse 1955), with *Johnny Dawson*; Spring Hills GC (1963); Wilcox Oaks CC (1956).

DONALD HARRADINE
(1911–), BIGCA, FOUNDING MEMBER; CHAIRMAN 1980; ASGCA, CORRESPONDING MEMBER; ESGCA, HONORARY PRESIDENT 1991

BORN: Enfield, England.

Donald Harradine was educated at Woolwich Polytechnic and trained as a golf professional, greenkeeper and clubmaker under his stepfather, J. A. Hockey, who had himself designed three courses. Harradine's first golf design experience came in 1930, when he remodeled a course at Ragaz Spa, Switzerland. He then worked for and with British golf architects John Morrison, Sir Guy Campbell, C. K. Cotton and Fred Hawtree.

In his career, Harradine worked on some 300 courses in Angola, Austria, Canary Islands, Cyprus, France, Germany, Greece, Italy, Liechtenstein, Poland, Portugal, Rumania, Spain, Switzerland and Yugoslavia. He also wrote numerous articles on course maintenance and with the assistance of his wife founded the International Greenkeepers Association. In the 1980s his son Peter Harradine joined him in the golf design business.

Courses by Donald Harradine:

Austria: Bad Kleinkirchheim GC (1985); Europa Sport Region GC (1984); Kaprun-Zell Am See GC (1984); Linz GC (1960); Seefeld-Wildmoos GC (1968).
France: GC de Campagne; GC de Coulandres (27 1986); Golf de Chaumont en Vexin (1963); Golf de Strasbourg;

Donald Harradine, 1985 COURTESY D. M. A. STEEL

Golf de Valbonne (1966); Golf du Rhin (9 1985).
Germany: Bad Worishoffen GC (1980); Bayerwald G und Land C (9 1970); Bielefelder GC (9 1980); Beuerberg GC (1983); Chiemsee GC (9); Erding-Grunbach GC (9); Goettingen GC (9); Hohenhardter Hof GC (1983); Hohenstaufen GC (9); Klingenburg-Gunzberg GC; Oberau GC (1974); Byrmonter GC (9); Regensburg G und Land C (1966); Schloss Klingenburg-Gunzburg (1980); St. Eurach GC (1973); Tegernseer GC (9 1960); Vestischer GC.
Greece: Afandou GC (1973); Corfu G&CC (1972); Glyfada GC (1964); Island of Rhodes GC (1966).
Italy: Arenzano G&CC (1959); Barlassina CC (1957); Cervino GC (9 1955); Lanzo Intelvi GC (9 1962).
Romania: Diplomatic C (9).
Switzerland: Bonmont GC (1984); Interlaken-Unterseen GC (1965); Ostschweizischer GC (1948); Schoenenberg G&CC (1969).
Yugoslavia: Bled GC (1972).

Courses remodeled or expanded by Donald Harradine:

Austria: Schloss Pichlarn GC (A.9 1978).
France: Montreux GC (R.).
Germany: Augsburg GC (R. 1982), with *Peter Harradine*; Garmisch-Partenkirchen GC (R.); Heidelberg G & Sports C (R.); Kassel-Wilhelmshohe GC (A.9 1980), with *Peter Harradine*; Oberschwaben Bad Waldsee GC (R.); Schloss Myllendonk GC (A.9).
Italy: Varese GC (R.).
Switzerland: Bad Ragaz GC (R. 1930, NLE); Breitenloo GC (R. 1964); Davos GC (R.9 A.9); Geneva G&CC (R., NLE); Lausanne GC (R.); Lugano GC (R.); Villars GC (R.9); Zumikon G&CC (R.).

WILLIAM E. HARRIES

Between the wars, William Harries operated a landscape and golf course design firm called Harries and Hall based in Buffalo, New York. After World War II Harries was associated with A. Russell Tryon in the firm of Tryon and Schwartz & Associates Inc. of East Aurora, New York. In the 1960s the firm handled several course designs in upstate New York.

Courses by William Harries:

New York: Amherst Audubon GC; Beaver Island GC (1963), with *A. Russell Tryon*; Brighton Park GC (1962), with *A. Russell Tryon*; Brookfield CC (1927); Byrncliff CC; Byron Meadows CC; Elma Meadows GC (1959), with *A. Russell Tryon*; Hyde Park Muni (North Cse 1928; South Cse, 9 1928); Normanside CC (1927); Oneonta CC; Sheridan Park GC (1933); Shorewood CC (9); Turin Highlands GC; Westwood CC (1954).

Courses remodeled or expanded by William Harries:

New York: Brooklea CC (R.); East Aurora CC (A.9 R.9), with *A. Russell Tryon*; Moonbrook CC (A.9 1928); Orchard Park CC (R. 1950); Thendara CC (A.9 1959), with *A. Russell Tryon*.

JOHN DERING HARRIS
(1912–1977)

BORN: Chobham, Surrey, England.
DIED: Puttenham, Surrey, England, at age 64.

John Harris, a low-handicap golfer nearly all his life, was educated in civil engineering at Nautical College in Berkshire, England. His father, Franks, and uncle Charles operated a construction firm

John Harris, 1970 COLLECTION RON WHITTEN

specializing in golf courses. Joining the firm after college, Harris had the opportunity to work with most of the leading British golf architects. He became director of the business after his father's death in the 1930s but discontinued operations when war broke out.

Harris served with the Royal Navy during World War II, attaining the rank of commander. He returned to golf design in the late 1940s, working with architect C. K. Cotton, with whom he formed a partnership in the early 1950s. In 1960 Harris left to establish his own firm and began worldwide operation. By the 1970s his associates included Bryan Griffiths and Michael Wolveridge of Great Britain. During the same time period, five-time British Open champion Peter Thomson of Australia and Ronald Fream of the United States teamed with Harris for a time in a world-wide partnership.

Although many of the courses bearing Harris's name were designed and built by members of his staff, most were his own designs, and he traveled the globe to supervise their construction. It was noted after his death that he may have been better known abroad than in Great Britain, for he did relatively little work in his native land. Harris himself once estimated that he had participated in the design, remodeling and construction of over 450 courses.

Courses by John Harris:

Australia: Royal Canberra G (1960); Southport GC.
Austria: Enzesfeld G&CC (1972).
Barbados: Barbados G&CC (1974).
Canary Islands: Costa Teguise GC (27 1978).
England: Cirencester GC; Cranbrook GC (1969); Gatton Manor Hotel & GC (1969); Panshanger GC (1975); Southwood GC (9 1977); Staverton Park GC (1977); Telford Hotel G&CC (1979), with Peter Thomson; Washington GC (1969).
France: Chevry I! GC (1977); Club de Valescure; CC du Château de Taulane, with C. K. Cotton; Golf d'Ormesson (1968); Golf des Château de Villarceaux; Lacanau-L'Ardilouse GC (1980), with J. J. F. Pennink.
Germany: Bonn-Godesberg GC (1960).
Hong Kong: Royal Hong Kong GC (Eden Cse 1968), with Peter Thomson.
India: Gulmarg GC (1973), with Peter Thomson.

Indonesia: Bali Handara CC (1975), with Peter Thomson and Ronald Fream.
Ireland: Courtown GC, with C. K. Cotton; East Cork GC (9 1971); Fermoy GC; Lahinch GC (Castle Cse [9 Precision] 1971); Shannon GC (1966).
Italy: Alassio GC; Albarella GC (1975); Garlenda GC (1965); Le Fronde GC (1974); Margara GC (1975); Menaggio E. Cadenabbia GC; Padova GC (1966); Piandiscole GC (1964); Verona GC (1963); Villa Condulmer GC (9 1961).
Jamaica: Runaway Bay CC (1961).
Japan: Chigusa GC (27 1973), with Peter Thomson; Korakuen CC (27 1974), with Peter Thomson and Ronald Fream; Nambu Fuji GC (1974), with Peter Thomson; Tokuyama GC (1975), with Peter Thomson.
Mauritius: Case Noyale GC (1972), with Peter Thomson.
New Zealand: Flaxmere GC (1966); Harewood GC (1967), with Peter Thomson; Karori GC (1968), with Peter Thomson; Maramarua GC (1969), with Peter Thomson; Taieri GC (1967), with Peter Thomson; Wairakei International GC (1975), with Peter Thomson.
Northern Ireland: Bushfoot GC (9).
Portugal: Estoril Sol GC (9 Precision 1976), with Peter Thomson and Ronald Fream.
Scotland: Dougalston GC (1977); Inverness GC (1968), with Peter Thomson; Renfrew GC.
Singapore: Singapore Island GC (New Cse 1963), with J. J. F. Pennink.
Spain: Campo de Golf Somosaguas (1971); C de G Poniente Magaluf (1978); Penas Rojas GC (1973); Playa Granada GC (9 1974); Real Club de la Puerto de Hierro (New Cse 1962); Real C de G de Menorca (9 1976); Son Servera GC (9 1967); Vista Hermosa GC (9 1975).
St. Kitts: Royal St. Kitts GC (1977), with Peter Thomson and Ronald Fream.
Trinidad and Tobago: St. Andrews GC (1975), with Peter Thomson and Ronald Fream; Tobago GC (1969).
Tunisia: El Kantaoui GC (1977), with Peter Thomson and Ronald Fream.

Courses remodeled or expanded by John Harris:

Denmark: Aalborg GC (A.9); Copenhagen GC (R.).
England: Chelmsford GC (R.).
Fiji: Nadi GC (A.9).

Hong Kong: Royal Hong Kong GC (New Cse, R. 1970; Old Cse, R. 1976), with Peter Thomson.
India: Delhi GC (R. A.9 1974), with Peter Thomson; Royal Calcutta CC (R. 1969), with Peter Thomson.
Ireland: Elm Park G & Sports C (R. 1963); Mallow GC (R.9 A.9); Royal Tara GC (R.9 A.9); Tramore GC (R.); Youghal GC (R.9 A.9).
Italy: Barlassina CC (R.); Bergamo L'Albenza GC (A.9), with C. K. Cotton; La Mandria GC (A.9 1966); Le Betulle GC (R.); Lido di Venezia GC (R.9 A.9 1958), with C. K. Cotton; Milano GC (R.); Villa D'este GC (R.).
Netherlands: Rotterdamsche GC (R.).
New Zealand: Hastings GC (R. 1965); Hutt GC (R. 1966); Nelson GC (R. 1967), with Peter Thomson; North Shore GC (R. 1969), with Peter Thomson; Russley GC (R. 1967), with Peter Thomson; Timaru GC (R. 1968), with Peter Thomson.
Spain: Real C de la Puerto de Hierro (Old Cse, R. 1962); Real Sociedad Hípica Espanola (R.).
Switzerland: Patriziale Ascona GC (R.), with C. K. Cotton.

Robert Bruce Harris, 1950
COLLECTION RON WHITTEN

ROBERT BRUCE HARRIS
(1896–1976), ASGCA, CHARTER MEMBER;
PRESIDENT 1947, 1948

BORN: Gilman, Illinois.
DIED: Chicago, Illinois, at age 80.

Following service in the U.S. Navy during World War I, Robert Bruce Harris attended the University of Illinois, earning a degree in landscape architecture. In 1919 he opened a landscape design business in Chicago and planned a number of school grounds and parks. An avid golfer, he laid out his first course, Old Channel Trail GC in Michigan, in 1926. Although his firm continued to specialize in landscape design in the 1930s, he did design and build several more courses during that period. Harris had faith in the future of golf even during the Depression and the postwar years, and he successfully renovated several abandoned courses and operated them as daily-fee facilities. His firsthand experiences as a course operator during the Depression and the Second World War, coping with labor and material shortages, were responsible for his emphasis on economical maintenance requirements in his designs. According to his detractors, he emphasized maintenance almost to a fault, resulting in oval bunkering placed too far from putting surfaces.

Following World War II, Harris devoted virtually full time to golf architecture and rapidly became a leader in the profession. By the 1950s he was busy designing courses throughout the Midwest and the South and estimated that he planned or remodeled over 150 during his career. He was also responsible for training a number of men who became successful course architects, including Edward Lawrence Packard, David Gill, Dick Nugent, Ken Killian and William James Spear.

Harris was the first to conceive a professional society for golf architects, patterned after the ASLA. Together with Stanley Thompson, Harris organized such an association. He was a charter member and the first president of the group, called the American Society of Golf Course Architects. Harris was coauthor with Robert Trent Jones of an influential chapter on course design that appeared in the first edition (1950) of H. Burton Musser's *Turf Management*. He spent his final years in retirement at CC of Florida, his personal favorite design.

Courses by Robert Bruce Harris:

Alabama: Azalea City GC (1957); Huntsville CC (1959).
Arizona: Oro Valley G&CC (1958); Tucson National GC (1963).
Colorado: Flatirons CC (1933).
Florida: CC of Florida (1957).
Illinois: Benton CC (9 1961); Clay County G&CC (9); Flora CC (9 1953); Glenbard GC (1930, NLE); Glen Flora GC; Hillcrest CC (1964); Illinois State University GC (1963); Indian Lakes CC (Iroquois Trail Cse 1965; Sioux Trail Cse 1965); Lake of the Woods GC (1954); Lincoln Greens GC (1957); Lockhaven CC (1955); Maplecrest GC (9 1958, NLE); Mid-

lane CC (1964); Orchard Hills G&CC (1930); Sullivan CC (1954); Timberlake GC (9); Timber Trails CC (1931); Valley Green CC (9 1962); Village Greens of Woodridge (1959); Virginia CC (9); Western Illinois University GC (9 1942, NLE).
Indiana: Clearcrest CC (9 1955, NLE); Decatur GC (9).
Iowa: Canyon Creek GC (9); Finkbine GC (1953); Gates Park GC (1949); Valley Oaks GC (1965).
Kentucky: Iroquois GC (9 1949); Standard CC (9 1950).
Louisiana: Lakewood CC (1962).
Michigan: Heather Highlands GC (27 1966); Old Channel Trail GC (9 1926); Signal Point C (9 1964).
Minnesota: Breckenridge GC; Wayzata CC (1958).
Missouri: Meadowbrook CC (1961); Ruth Park GC (9 1931).
North Dakota: Apple Creek G&CC; Bois de Sioux GC; Grand Forks CC (1964); Jamestown CC (9).
Ohio: Belmont CC (1968); Kittyhawk Muni (Eagle Cse 1962; Hawk Cse 1961; Kitty Cse [Precision] 1961; Riverbend GC (1962).
South Dakota: Chamberlain CC (9 1952).
Tennessee: Bluegrass CC (1961).
Wisconsin: Americana Lake Geneva GC (Brute Cse 1968); Gateway GC (9); Riverside Muni (1946); Village Green GC (9).

Courses remodeled or expanded by Robert Bruce Harris:

California: Monterey Peninsula CC (Shore Cse, R. 1962).
Florida: Delray Beach G&CC (R. 1962); Sanlando G&CC (R., NLE).
Illinois: Acacia CC (R. 1951, NLE); Briarwood CC (R. 1958); Freeport CC (R.2); Illini CC (A.9 1950; R.9 1962); Itasca CC (R. 1953); Macomb CC (R.); Midwest CC (East Cse, R. 1954; West Cse, R.9 A.9 1954); Parkview Muni (R.9 A.9 1956); South Side CC (R.); Thorngate CC (R. 1951); Timber Trails CC (R. 1966).
Indiana: La Fontaine GC (R. 1946).
Iowa: Duck Creek Park GC (R. 1957); Sunnyside CC (R. 1938, NLE).
Michigan: Bay City CC (A.9 R.9 1951, NLE).
Minnesota: Somerset CC (R. 1958).
New York: Douglaston Park GC (R.1 1949).
North Dakota: Edgewood Muni (R. 1951); Fargo CC (A.9).

Ohio: Columbus CC (R.2 1960); Inverness C (R. 1957); Toledo CC (R. 1960).
Tennessee: Bluegrass CC (R. A.2 1966).
Wisconsin: North Hills CC (R.1).

Jim Harrison, 1952
COURTESY *GOLF WORLD*

JAMES GILMORE HARRISON
(1900–), ASGCA, PRESIDENT 1955, 1969; FELLOW

BORN: Wilkins Township, Pennsylvania.

Jim Harrison worked for golf architect Donald Ross, first as a teamster and later as a foreman, between 1921 and 1927. He was then associated for a short time with Hartford (Connecticut) golf architect Orrin Smith. In the late 1920s Harrison entered private practice, planning and building his own course, Pennhurst, at Turtle Creek, Pennsylvania. Between 1955 and 1964 he was joined in practice by his son-in-law, Ferdinand Garbin.

Courses by James Gilmore Harrison (All with Ferdinand Garbin unless otherwise indicated):

Kentucky: Cedar Knoll CC (9 *solo*).
Maryland: Maplehurst CC (9 1955 *solo*).
Michigan: Warwick Hills G&CC (1957).
New Jersey: Battleground CC (routing 1963 *solo*); Knob Hill CC.
New York: Cragie Brae GC (1962); Happy Acres CC (1958).
Ohio: Geneva-on-the-Lake GC (9 1954 *solo*, A.9 1966 *solo*); Hidden Valley GC (1960); Springdale CC (1950 *solo*); Spring Hill CC (1963); Tannenhauf GC (1957); Walnut Hill CC (1955 *solo*).
Pennsylvania: Beaumont CC (1967 *solo*); Blairsville CC (1963); Blueberry Hill GC (9 1961); Bradford GC (1964); Carradam CC (1962); Cedarbrook GC (1963); Chestnut Ridge CC (1963); Cumberland CC (1961); Downing Muni (1962); Erie MacCaune CC

(1964 *solo*); Foxbury CC (1968 *solo*); Glen Oak CC (1961); Greenville CC (9 *solo*); Hidden Valley CC, Reading (*solo*); Hidden Valley GC, Pottstown; Highland Springs GC (1960); Indiana CC (1963); Johnstown Elks CC (*solo*); Lakeview CC (1957); Mount Cobb Muni (1958); Mount Lebanon CC (1947 *solo*); North Fork CC (1948 *solo*); Park Hills CC (1966 *solo*); Penn-hurst GC (1931 *solo*, NLE); Penn State University GC (White Cse 1965); Pine Acres CC (1970 *solo*); Pine Ridge GC (9 1960); Punxsutawney CC (1969 *solo*); Range End GC (1955 *solo*); Rittwood CC (1966 *solo*); Rolling Acres CC (9 1960); Rolling Hills CC (1961); Scotch Valley GC (*solo*); Sewickley Heights CC (1960); Sportsman's GC (1964); Suncrest GC (9 1948 *solo*, A.9 1966 *solo*); Tamarack CC (1966 *solo*); Venango Trails GC (1955 *solo*); VFW GC (9 1963 *solo*); Wave Oak CC (1954 *solo*); Willowbrook CC (1949 *solo*); Windber CC (1961).
Virginia: Fredericksburg CC (A.9 *solo*).
West Virginia: Bridgeport CC (1957); Cheat Lake GC (1954 *solo*); Sheraton Lakeview Resort & CC (Lakeview Cse 1955); Sleepy Hollow GC (1955 *solo*).
Puerto Rico: Dorado del Mar GC (1962).

Courses remodeled or expanded by James Gilmore Harrison (All with Ferdinand Garbin unless otherwise indicated):

Kentucky: Bellefonte CC (R. 1960).
New Jersey: Tavistock CC (R. 1954).
Ohio: Lake Forest CC (R. 1965 *solo*).
Pennsylvania: Beaver Valley CC (R.9 A.9 1958); Bedford Spring CC (R. 1966 *solo*); Bloomsburg CC (R. 1948 *solo*); Blue Ridge CC (R. 1964); Brookside CC (R. 1959); Centre Hills CC (R. 1948 *solo*); Chippewa CC (R.9 A.9 1964); Churchill Valley CC (R. 1960); Edgewood CC (R. 1960); Fox Chapel GC (R. *solo*); Grandview GC (R. 1979 *solo*); Hidden Valley CC (R.9 A.9 1958); Highland CC (R. 1954 *solo*); Hill Crest CC (A.9 1950 *solo*); Irwin CC (R. 1950 *solo*); Latrobe CC (A.9 1963); Montour Heights CC (R.9 A.9 1962, NLE); Oakmont East GC (R. 1962); Penn State University GC (Blue Cse, R. 1965); Pike Run CC (R. 1955 *solo*); St. Clair CC (R. 1960).
West Virginia: Tygart Lake GC (R. 1957); Woodland CC (R. 1953 *solo*).

X. G. Hassenplug, 1969 COURTESY ROBERT DEAN PUTMAN

XENOPHON G. HASSENPLUG (1908–1992), ASGCA, FELLOW

BORN: Bellevue, Ohio.
DIED: Pittsburgh, Pennsylvania, at age 84.

Xen Hassenplug attended Ohio Wesleyan University and Toledo University, majoring in civil engineering. His first experience in golf course construction came in 1946, when he was involved in planning irrigation and seeding of an 18-hole course planned by J. B. McGovern at Overbrook CC near Philadelphia. McGovern became ill during construction of the course, and Hassenplug went on to complete the 18 holes and then to assist golf architect Dick Wilson on two other Pennsylvania projects, Radnor Valley near Philadelphia and Westmoreland CC near Pittsburgh. Upon completion of these layouts, Hassenplug entered private practice, combining golf course design, land planning, irrigation and civil engineering. He was joined in his practice in the 1980s by Ed Beidel.

Courses by X.G. Hassenplug:

New York: Chautauqua GC (Cse No. 2 1989); Shelridge CC (1974).
Ohio: Brookside Park GC (9 1969); Buckeye Hills CC (1971); Fairway Pines GC (1987); Glenwood Muni (9).
Pennsylvania: Alanwood GC (Precision 1980); Five Ponds G Cse (1988); Hampton Valley GC (9); Laurel Greens GC (Precision 1979); Lone Pine GC (1969); Lucky Hills CC (9 1979); Mayfield CC (1968); Overbrook CC (1947), ass't J. B. McGovern; Radnor Valley CC (1953), ass't Dick Wilson; Ridgeview GC (9); Rivers Bend GC (1966); Seven Springs GC (1968); Sheraton Inn GC (9 Precision 1981); Timberlink GC (1964); Valley Green GC (1964); Westmoreland CC (1948), ass't Dick Wilson.
West Virginia: Brooke Hills Park GC (1977); Coonskin Park GC (Par 3 1973); Esquire CC (1973); Huntington Elks CC (1975); Marshall Park GC (Par 3 1974); St. Mary's GC (9 1968); Waterford Park GC (9 1968).

Courses remodeled or expanded by X.G. Hassenplug:

Maryland: Cumberland CC (R.11 1966).
New York: Chautauqua GC (R. 1980).
Ohio: Bowling Green University GC (R.9 A.9 1972).
Pennsylvania: Chartiers CC (R. 1969); Deep Valley GC (R.); DuBois CC (R.9 A.9 1968); Elk County CC (R.9 1966); Fox Chapel GC (R.); Indian Lake GC (A.9 1968), with Arnold Palmer; Lenape Heights GC (A.9 1983); Ligonier CC (R.9 A.9 1965); Lone Pine GC (R. 1983); Mount Odin Park GC (R.9 A.9 1967); North Park GC (R. 1969); Pittsburgh Field C (R. 1962; R. 1970; R. 1985); Pleasant Valley CC (R.9 1968; R. 1984); Seven Oaks GC (R. 1977); Skippack GC (R. 1988); South Hills GC (R. 1979); South Park GC (R. 1969).
West Virginia: Guyen G&CC (R.3 1974).

WALTER B. HATCH (1884–1960)

BORN: Brockton, Massachusetts.
DIED: Amherst, Massachusetts, at age 75.

Walter Hatch graduated from the Massachusetts Agricultural College in 1905 and went to work for Donald Ross, eventually becoming his associate. He is said to have introduced Ross to the use of topographical plans in course design. Hatch traveled widely in the United States and Canada, supervising construction for Ross and sometimes entering into construction contracts. He also planned a number of layouts, although Ross was the architect of record for all except two: Amherst GC and Thomas Memorial GC at Turners Falls. Both were in the vicinity of Amherst, where Hatch maintained an office in the Ross name.

Walter Hatch left the field of golf architecture during the Depression as a result of financial difficulties. He became collector of taxes in Amherst and a researcher for a local attorney, Bruce Brown.

Courses by Walter Hatch (All as assistant to Donald Ross unless otherwise indicated):

Colorado: [The] Broadmoor GC (East Cse, 9 1918; West Cse, 9 1918); Wellshire GC (1926).

Connecticut: Wampanoag CC (1926).
Maryland: Fountain Head CC (1925).
Massachusetts: Amherst GC (*solo*); Ellinwood CC (9 1920); Greenock CC (9 1927); Toy Town Tavern GC (9 1908, NLE); Thomas Memorial GC (*solo*); Whitinsville CC (9 1925).
New York: Thendara CC (9 1920).
New Hampshire: Kingswood CC (1926).
Ohio: Hawthorne Valley CC (1926); Springfield CC (1921).
Rhode Island: Warwick CC (9 1924).
Tennessee: Brainerd Muni (1925).
Nova Scotia: Liverpool GC [FKA White Point Beach GC] (1928).

GEROLD HAUSER
ESGCA, PRESIDENT 1991

Together with his brother Günther Hauser, Gerold Hauser operated a landscape architecture firm founded by their father, Friedrich Hauser, in 1930. In 1970, the Hausers, both registered landscape architects but also golf nuts, designed and built their first golf course, and as they began concentrating upon course designs the firm was renamed G. G. Hauser Golf Company to reflect their primary interest.

Besides handling conventional golf course designs, Hauser and his brother developed and patented Ziel Golf, "target golf" practice areas intended to simulate all the various shots encountered during an actual round of golf. They created several Ziel Golf centers in Austria.

In 1990, the Hausers helped found the ESGCA, and a year later Gerold served concurrently as president of the ESGCA and the European Landscape Contractors Association.

Courses designed by Gerold Hauser (All with Günther Hauser):

Austria: Am Wienerberg G Cse (9 1992); Bad Gleichenberg GC (9); Brunn GC; Kaisergolf Ellmau (9 Par 3); Kitzbühel-Schwarzsee GC (1990); Moosburg GC; Pörtschacher GC (1989); Red Bull G Cse (9 Par 3); Schloss Goldegg GC (1989); Schönfeld GC (27 1991); Wels GC (9 1981); Wiener Neustadt-Föhrenwald GC (1968); Wienerwald GC (9 1981).
Germany: Gut Neuhof GC (1991).
Hungary: Birdland G&CC (Championship Cse 1991; Short Cse [9 Par 3] 1991).

Norway: Dröbak GC (1992); Greverud G Cse (1990); Nes GC (27).

Courses remodeled or expanded by Gerold Hauser (All with Günther Hauser):

Austria: Innsbruck-Igls GC (Lans-Sperberegg Cse, R. 9 1970; Rinn Cse, R.9 A.9 1970); Salzkammergut GC, Bad Ischl (A.9 1988).

FREDERIC GEORGE HAWTREE
(1883–1955)

BORN: Ealing, Middlesex, England.
DIED: Hayes, Kent, England, at age 72.

F. G. Hawtree, the first of three generations of British golf course architects, started out as a greenkeeper. He began designing courses around 1912. Following service with the British army during World War I, he practiced on his own until 1922, when he formed the partnership of Hawtree & Taylor with J. H. Taylor, one of British golf's "Great Triumvirate." The firm continued until World War II, when it was voluntarily liquidated.

As managing director of the firm, Hawtree was responsible for the day-to-day details and design work, while Taylor handled early interviews with clients and appeared at official openings. At one time, Hawtree had four highly regarded Irish foremen (Regan, Ryan, Brick and Ward)

working under him. Each had a special flair for shaping golf courses, and they were widely known throughout the British Isles and on the Continent.

Hawtree and Taylor created some fifty new courses and remodeled another fifty, including the famous Royal Birkdale Golf Club. They also produced one of the world's first all-weather driving ranges, in London. In 1931 Hawtree built twenty-seven holes for himself at Addington and thus established Britain's first privately owned daily-fee course.

F. G. Hawtree was instrumental in founding the British Golf Greenkeepers Association and the National Association of Public Golf Courses, and he served as president of both. He was also on the board of the Sports Turf Research Institute and the council of the English Golf Union.

Courses by F. G. Hawtree (All with J. H. Taylor unless otherwise indicated):

England: Addington Court GC (Lower Cse 1931; Old Cse 1931); Addington Palace GC (1923); Batchwood Hail GC (1936); Bigbury GC (1923); Chigwell GC (1925); Cock Moor Woods GC (1926); Croham Hurst GC (1912), with James Braid; Easingwold GC (1930); Elfordleigh GC (1932); Gorleston GC (1926); Harborne Church Farm GC (1926); Harpenden GC (1931); Hartsbourne CC (1946), with Fred W. Hawtree; Heysham GC (1910), with Sandy Herd; High Post GC (1922); Highwoods GC (1925);

F. G. Hawtree (right), with partner J. H. Taylor, circa 1925 COURTESY FRED W. HAWTREE

Hill Barn GC (1935); Hollingbury Park GC (1922); Ifield G&CC (1927); Knowle GC; Marston Green Muni; Maxstoke Park GC (1948), with Fred W. Hawtree; Norwich Muni; Pinner Hill GC (1929); Pype Hayes Muni (1932); Richmond Park GC (Dukes Cse 1923; Princes Cse 1923); Rose Hill GC (1927); Ruislip GC (1938); Selsdon Park Hotel GC (1929); Southampton GC (27 1935); Southcliffe and Canwick GC; Stratford-on-Avon GC (1928); Swinton Park GC (1926); Tinsley Park GC (1922); Wells GC (9 *solo*); Wells-by-the-Sea GC (9 Par 3); Welwyn Garden City GC (1922); White Webbs Muni (1932); Woodlands Manor GC (1928); Woolacombe Bay Hotel GC (9 Par 3); Wyke Green GC (1928).

France: Vieille Toulouse GC (9 1951 *solo*).

Ireland: Arklow GC (1926).

Italy: Pallanza GC (*solo*).

Portugal: Lisbon Sports C (9 1922 *solo*).

Scotland: Hilton Park GC (Hilton Cse 1922).

Sweden: Bastad GC (1928).

Wales: Abergele and Pensare GC, with Fred W. Hawtree; Rhuddlan GC (1930).

Courses remodeled or expanded by F. G. Hawtree (All with J. H. Taylor unless otherwise indicated):

England: Boyce Hill GC (R.9 *solo*); Dyke GC (R. 1947), with Fred W. Hawtree; Filton GC (R.9 A.9); Freshwater Bay GC (R. *solo*); Hainault Forest GC (Cse No. 1, A.9); Henbury GC (R. *solo*); Hull GC (R.); Ipswich GC (A.9 1931); Littlehampton GC (R.9 A.9); Rickmansworth Public GC (R. 1937); Rochford Hundred GC (R. *solo*); Royal Birkdale GC (R. 1932); Royal Mid-Surrey GC (R. 1928); Sonning GC (R.9 A.9); West Middlesex GC (A.9).

Monaco: Monte Carlo CC (R. *solo*).

Scotland: Williamwood GC (R.).

Wales: Ashburnham GC (R. 1914); Royal Porthcawl GC (R. A.4 1925).

FREDERIC WILLIAM HAWTREE (1916–), BIGCA, FOUNDING MEMBER; CHAIRMAN 1974, PRESIDENT 1975

BORN: Bromley, Kent, England.

Fred W. Hawtree, son of golf architect Frederic G. Hawtree, joined his father's

Fred W. Hawtree, 1985 COURTESY D. M. A. STEEL

firm, Hawtree & Taylor, upon graduation from Oxford in 1938. During World War II, he served with the Royal Artillery in the Far East, where he was captured as a Japanese POW. On his return to England he reentered private practice with his father in the firm of Hawtree & Son.

After his father's death in 1955, Hawtree continued the firm and completed numerous courses over the next twenty-five years. He was joined in 1969 by A. H. F. Jiggens and in 1974 by his own son, Martin, the third generation of Hawtree golf architects. Hawtree & Son created courses in Britain, Ireland, France, Italy, Spain, Belgium, Holland, Germany, Switzerland, Iran, South Africa, El Salvador, Morocco and the United States.

F. W. Hawtree remained active in the golfing organizations founded by his father and was himself influential in forming the BIGCA in 1970. He also participated from its beginnings in the Golf Development Council, for whom he wrote *Elements of Golf Course Layout and Design.*

In his later years, Hawtree reduced his design activities and spent time researching and writing two successful books. He summed up his own design philosophy in *The Golf Course: Planning, Designing, Construction and Maintenance,* published in 1983. *Colt and Co.*, his definitive account of Harry Colt's life and times as well as those of Colt's associates Charles Alison, Alister Mackenzie and J. S. F. Morrison, was published in 1991.

Courses by Fred W. Hawtree:

North Carolina: Mount Mitchell GC (1973).

Belgium: Limburg GC (1966); Royal Waterloo GC (La Marache Cse 1961; Le Lion Cse 1961).

El Salvador: Casino C; CC of Cuzcatlan (9).

England: Addington Court GC (New Cse); Bedwell Park GC (1983), with Martin Hawtree; Bowring Park GC; Brackenwood Muni; Braintree GC; Broome Manor GC (1976), with Martin Hawtree; Chester GC (1973), with A. H. F. Jiggens; Chestnut Park GC; Chipping Sodbury GC (27 1971); Cold Ashby GC (1974); Cold Norton GC; Congleton GC, with A. H. F. Jiggens; Deangate Ridge GC (1972); Downshire GC (1973); Duxbury Park GC (1975), with Martin Hawtree and A. H. F. Jiggens; Eastham Lodge GC (9 1975), with Martin Hawtree and A. H. F. Jiggens; Easthampstead Park GC (1973); Eaton GC (1965); Enmore Park GC (9 1975, A.9 1979), with A. H. F. Jiggens; Foxhills GC (Chertsey Cse 1973; Longcross Cse 1973); Hartsbourne CC (1946), with F. G. Hawtree; Hatchford Brook Muni; High Elms GC (1969), with Martin Hawtree; Hilltop & Manwood Farm GC (1979), with Martin Hawtree; Humberstone Heights GC (1977), with Martin Hawtree; Ingestre GC (1977), with Martin Hawtree; Kings Norton GC (27), with Martin Hawtree; Little Hay GC (1977), with Martin Hawtree; Lullingstone Park GC (27 1967); Malkins Bank GC (1980), with A. H. F. Jiggens; Maxstoke Park GC (1948), with F. G. Hawtree; Minchinhampton GC (New Cse 1975); Mowsbury Muni (1975), with Martin Hawtree; Newcastle-under-Lyme GC, with Martin Hawtree; Normanby Hall GC (1978), with A. H. F. Jiggens and Martin Hawtree; P L London CC (1976), with Martin Hawtree; Port Sunlight GC (9); Portsdown Hill GC; Poult Wood GC (1974); Risebridge GC (1972); Scunthorpe GC, with A. H. F. Jiggens; St. Michael Jubilee GC (9); Stockgrove GC (9); Tamworth Muni (1975), with Martin Hawtree and A. H. F. Jiggens; Wellingborough GC (9, with A. H. F. Jiggens, A.9, with Martin Hawtree); Western Park GC (1973); Widnes Muni (9 1977), with A. H. F. Jiggens; Woodbridge GC; Worsley GC, with A. H. F. Jiggens.

France: Golf de Bondues (Red Cse 1967); Golf de Domont; Golf de Fiac (1989); Golf de Lyon (27 1968); Golf de Metz Cherisey (9); Golf de Quimper de Cornouaille (9 1959, A.9 1984, with Martin Hawtree); Golf de Rochefort en Yveline (1964); Golf de Seraincourt; Golf de St. Samson; Golf de Valcros;

Golf de Vaudreuil; Golf du Prieure (East Cse; West Cse); La Herliere CC (1973); St. Andres de Bruges GC (1988); St. Nom La Brêteche GC (Blue Cse 1959; Red Cse 1959).

Germany: Düsseldorfer GC (1972).

Iran: Imperial Sports C.

Ireland: Brainroe GC (1978), with Martin Hawtree; Corballis GC, with A. H. F. Jiggens; Forest Little GC (1972), with A. H. F. Jiggens; Howth Castle GC; Portmarnock GC (New Cse, 9 1964); Westport GC, with Martin Hawtree and A. H. F. Jiggens.

Netherlands: Wittem G&CC (9).

Northern Ireland: Killymoon GC; Lisburn GC; Malone GC (27).

Scotland: Balnagask GC, with Martin Hawtree; East Kilbride GC; Grangemouth Muni (1973); Torrance House GC (1979), with Martin Hawtree.

South Africa: [The] Country Club, Johannesburg (27); Plettenberg Bay CC.

Spain: GC de Pals (9 1966, A.9 1970); La Penaza GC (1972); Roca Llisa GC (9 1971); Son Vida GC (1964); Vallromanas GC (1969).

Switzerland: Bad Ragaz GC.

Wales: Abergele and Pensare GC, with F. G. Hawtree; Anglesey GC (1982), with Martin Hawtree; Fairwood Park GC; Glynhir GC (1967); Penrhos GC (9 1986), with Martin Hawtree.

Courses remodeled or expanded by Fred W. Hawtree:

Belgium: Royal GC Les Buttes Blanches (R.3 1953).

England: Ashton-in-Makerfield GC (A.9); Bebington GC (A.9); Berwick-upon-Tweed GC (A.9); Bromborough GC (R.), with A. H. F. Jiggens; Burnham and Berrow GC (A.9 1973); Chorley GC (R.), with A. H. F. Jiggens; Delamere Forest GC (R. 1962); Doncaster GC (R.7 1979), with Martin Hawtree; Dyke GC (R. 1947), with F. G. Hawtree; Farnham Park GC, Coventry (R.9 A.9 1983), with Martin Hawtree; Finham Park GC (R.3); Gog Magog GC (A.9); Grimsby GC (R. 1973); Hillside GC (R.9 A.9 1967); Huyton & Prescot GC (R.), with A. H. F. Jiggens; Immingham GC (A.9 1981), with Martin Hawtree; Ipswich GC (A.9 Precision), with A. H. F. Jiggens; John O'Gaunt GC (Carthagena Cse, R.); Lindrick GC (R.); Lutterworth GC (A.9); Malton & Norton GC

(A.9), with Martin Hawtree; Malvern GC (A.9); Marsden Park GC (A.9); Nelson GC (A.9), with A. H. F. Jiggens; Oakdale GC (R.7 1977), with A. H. F. Jiggens; Prenton GC (R.); Pyecombe GC (R.4 1980), with Martin Hawtree; Royal Birkdale GC (R. 1967; R. 1974); Royal Liverpool GC (R. 1967); Royal Mid-Surrey GC (R.3 1982), with Martin Hawtree; Salisbury & South Wilts GC (R.6 1983), with Martin Hawtree; Sandiway GC (R.3 1959); Theydon Bois GC (A.2 1976), with Martin Hawtree; Wellingborough GC (R. 1983), with Martin Hawtree and A. H. F. Jiggens; Welwyn Garden City GC (R.), with Martin Hawtree; West Lancashire GC (R.); Worcestershire GC (A.9), with A. H. F. Jiggens.

France: Golf de Fontainebleau (R. A.4 1965); Golf de la Barouge (A.9 1985), with Martin Hawtree; Golf de Toulouse (A.9 1981).

Ireland: Killarney G & Fishing C (Killeen Cse, R.6 A.12 1971; Mahony's Point Cse, R.12 A.6 1971); Woodbrook GC (R. A.2), with Martin Hawtree and A. H. F. Jiggens.

Italy: Cervino GC (A.9).

Monaco: Monte Carlo CC (R. A.2).

Northern Ireland: Massereene GC (A.9); Tandragee GC (A.9), with Martin Hawtree.

Portugal: Lisbon Sports C (A.9).

Scotland: Bruntsfield Links (R. A.7 1972); Mortonhall GC (R.9 A.9 1979), with Martin Hawtree; Western Gailes GC (R.4 1975).

Spain: C de G Llavaneras (R.); C de G San Andres de Llavaneras (R.); C de G Terramar (A.9).

Switzerland: Lenzerheide Valbella GC (A.9).

Wales: Nefyn and District GC (R.), with A. H. F. Jiggens; Royal St. Davids GC (R. 1960); Swansea Bay GC (R.6 1984), with Martin Hawtree.

Zimbabwe: Royal Salisbury GC (R. A.2 1968).

MARTIN HAWTREE
(1947–   ), BIGCA

BORN: Beckenham, Kent, England.

After receiving an arts degree at the University of Liverpool, Martin Hawtree remained at Liverpool for three years doing research in the history of modern town

Martin Hawtree, 1985 COURTESY D. M. A. STEEL

planning for his doctorate. He joined his father's firm, Hawtree & Son, in 1973. The following year the firm hired scratch golfer John Davis as another partner.

While families such as the Dunns and the Maples may have worked longer in the business world of golf in general, the Hawtree dynasty—Frederic G., Fred W. and Martin—was probably involved in the longest continuous practice of golf course architecture on record, dating from 1912.

Upon his father's retirement, Martin took over and expanded the Hawtree firm. He did a series of courses in conjunction with former European PGA Tour player Simon Gidman and also trained several new associates, including Stephen McFarlane.

Courses by Martin Hawtree (All with Fred G. Hawtree unless otherwise indicated):

North Carolina: Reems Creek GC (1989), with Simon Gidman.

Belgium: Golf d'Avernas (9 solo).

England: Bedwell Park GC (1983); Broome Manor GC (1976); Calverton G Centre, with Simon Gidman; Cobtree Manor GC (solo); Duxbury Park GC (1975), and A. H. F. Jiggens; Eastham Lodge GC (9 1975), and A. H. F. Jiggens; High Elms GC (1969); Hilltop & Manwood Farm GC (1979); Hintlesham Hall GC (solo); Hoebridge GC (Short Cse [18 Par 3]), with Simon Gidman; Humberstone Heights GC (1977); Hylands Park GC, with Simon Gidman; Ingestre GC (1977); Kings Norton GC (27); Little Hay GC (1977); Marlwood G Centre, with Simon Gidman; Moors Valley GC (9), with Simon Gidman; Mowsbury Muni (1975); Newcastle-under-Lyme GC; Normanby Hall GC (1979), and A. H. F. Jiggens; P L London CC (1976); Rother Valley GC, with Simon Gidman;

Sandford Springs GC, with Simon Gidman; Seedy Mill GC, with Simon Gidman; Tamworth Muni (1975), and A. H. F. Jiggens; West Hove GC (New Cse), with Simon Gidman; Wrag Barn GC, with Simon Gidman.

France: Club Med Montargis, with Simon Gidman; Golf de Bombequoils (9), with Simon Gidman; Golf de Carquefou, with Simon Gidman; Golf de Caen (*solo*); Golf de la Ramée (*solo*); Golf de l'Isle Fleurle (9 *solo*); Golf de Teoula (*solo*); Golf des Baux de Provence (9), with Simon Gidman; Golf des Etanges de Flac (*solo*); Parc de Loisirs GC (*solo*).

Ireland: Brainroe GC (1978); Westport GC, and A. H. F. Jiggens.

Portugal: Pine Cliffs G&CC (9), with Simon Gidman.

Scotland: Balnagask GC; Torrance House GC (1979).

Spain: Golf Girona (*solo*); Royal Bendinat GC (9 1986 *solo*).

Wales: Anglesey GC (1982); Llangefni GC (9 1983 *solo*); Penrhos GC (9 1986).

Courses remodeled or expanded by Martin Hawtree (All with Fred G. Hawtree unless otherwise indicated):

Belgium: Royal Hainaut GC (A.9 *solo*).

England: Bedale GC (A.6), with Simon Gidman; Brampton Park GC (R.), with Simon Gidman; Bury St. Edmunds GC (R.), with Simon Gidman; Doncaster GC (R.7 1979); East Dorset GC (R. *solo*); Farnham Park GC, Coventry (R.9 A.9); Immingham GC (R.9 A.9); Malton & Norton GC (A.9); Pyecombe GC (R.4 1980); Royal Mid-Surrey GC (R.3 1982); St Michael Jubilee GC (A.9), with Simon Gidman; Salisbury & South Wilts GC (R.6 1983, A.3rd 9, with Simon Gidman); Southwood GC (R.5 A.13), with Simon Gidman; Theydon Bois GC (A.2 1976); Wellingborough GC (A.9), and A. H. F. Jiggens; Welwyn Garden City GC (R.); Western Park GC (R. A.8), with Simon Gidman.

France: Golf de Fontainebleau (R.), with Simon Gidman; Golf de la Barouge (A.9 1985); Golf de Quimper et de Cornouaille (A.9 1984).

Ireland: Downpatrick GC (R. A.8), with Simon Gidman; Woodbrook GC (R. A.2), and A. H. F. Jiggens.

Northern Ireland: Downpatrick GC (A.8 *solo*); Tandragee CC (A.9).

Scotland: Aboyne GC (R. *solo*); Broomieknowe GC (A.4 *solo*); Mortonhall GC (R.9 A.9 1979).

Wales: Swansea Bay GC (R.6 1984).

ROBERT VERNON HEASLIP (1956–)

BORN: Toronto, Ontario.

Robert Heaslip graduated from the University of Toronto in 1980 with a degree in landscape architecture. He established his own golf design business based in Thornhill, Ontario, in 1982, advocating a basic design philosophy of integrating golf into the natural landscape features of the particular region in which the course is located.

Courses by Robert Heaslip:

Ontario: Bloomington Downs G Centre (9 1989); Fawn Brook GC (1989); Sutton Creek G&CC (1989); Willow Springs G&CC (1992).

Courses remodeled or expanded by Robert Heaslip:

Ontario: Deer Creek GC (R. 1988); Lindsay Arms GC (A.9 1990); Meaford GC (R.2 1984); Rivendell GC (A.9 1990); Summerheights G Links (A.3rd 9 1986).

RANDALL J. HECKENKEMPER

A graduate of Oklahoma State University in landscape design, Randy Heckenkemper began in 1980 working for Pittman-Poe & Associates, a Tulsa-based land-planning group, and conducted land-planning projects for several Jack Nicklaus–designed courses, including Castle Pines and Bear Creek. Heckenkemper later became senior land planner for Nicklaus's Tulsa office, headed by Jay Morrish. When Morrish established his own practice in 1983, Heckenkemper handled the land planning for several Morrish and Weiskopf courses, notably Troon in Scottsdale, Arizona. In 1985, he cofounded Planning Design Group in Tulsa with two fellow Oklahoma State graduates, but delegated the land planning to others in the firm and began concentrating on golf course design. His first works

were local daily-fee courses, low-profile designs intended to emphasize natural terrain and indigenous vegetation.

Courses by Randy Heckenkemper:

Oklahoma: Forest Ridge GC (1989); Silverhorn GC (1992); South Lakes G Cse (1989).

Sandy Herd, circa 1910 COURTESY GOLF WORLD

ALEXANDER HERD (1868–1944)

BORN: St. Andrews, Scotland.
DIED: London, England, at age 76.

"Sandy" Herd won numerous major golf tournaments, including the 1902 British Open, in which he used the new rubber-core Haskell ball, and the British Professional Matchplay at age 58. He served as head professional for years at Coombe Hill, where he garnered thirteen of his nineteen lifetime holes-in-one. During his golf career, Sandy Herd participated in the design of several courses.

Courses by Sandy Herd:

England: Aspley Guise & Woburn Sands GC, with *Charles Willmott*; Harrogate GC (1897); Heysham GC (1910), with F. G. Hawtree; Lees Hall GC (1909); Malden GC (1926), with *H. Bailey*; Pannal GC (1906); Ulverston GC (1894); Wakefield GC (1912).

Isle of Man: Peel GC (1895).

DONALD WAYNE HERFORT (1925–), ASGCA

BORN: Green Bay, Wisconsin.

Don Herfort was employed as senior accountant with the 3-M Corporation in St. Paul, Minnesota, in the mid-1960s, when he was appointed to a committee in charge of building the company's golf course. After consulting with two professional architects, the committee elected to design its own course, and Herfort was chosen to lay it out and supervise the construction of Tarten Park Golf Course.

About the same time, Herfort was involved in the conversion of Lisbon Bissell GC in nearby North Dakota from sand to grass greens. With these experiences behind him and several prospective projects awaiting him, Herfort left 3-M to devote full time to course architecture.

Based in the Twin Cities, Herfort remained active well into the 1990s designing and remodeling courses in the upper Midwest.

Courses by Don Herfort:

Minnesota: Birnamwood GC (9 Par 3 1969); Chromonix CC (9 1970); Cimarron GC (9 Par 3 1971); Country View GC (9 Par 3 1970); Dellwood National GC (1970); Indian Hills CC (1971); Little Crow CC (1969); Oak Glen GC (27 1983); Pebble Creek GC; Purple Hawk CC (1969); River Oaks Muni (1992); Superior National GC (1991); Tartan Park GC (1965).
North Dakota: Mandan G Cse (1989); Underwood GC (9).
South Dakota: Kuehn Park GC (9 1975).
Wisconsin: NorthWoods G Cse (1989); Royal Scot CC (1970).

Courses remodeled or expanded by Don Herfort:

Iowa: Oneota CC (R.9 A.9).
Michigan: Pine Grove CC (R. 1982).
Minnesota: Bent Creek GC (R. 1972); Brookview Muni (R.); Cleary Lake GC (R. 1986); Como Park Muni GC (R. 1986); Cuyuna CC (R.9 A.9); Detroit CC (A.9 1969); Falls CC (R.); Galls GC (R.); Hastings CC (R. 1986); Interlaken GC (R.9 A.9 1968); Keller GC (R.1 1970); Madden Inn & GC (East

Don Herfort, 1990
COURTESY ASGCA

Cse, R. 1981); Manitou Ridge GC (R. 1978); Minnetonka CC (R.3 1968); New Prague GC (A.9 1967); New Ulm CC (A.9 1966); Northfield GC (R.9 A.9 1976); Northland CC (R. 1968); Phalen Park GC (R. 1976); Red Wing CC (R.9 1967); Ridgeview CC (R. 1988); Wadena GC (R.9 1977); White Bear Lake YC (R.1 1971); Whitefish GC (A.9 1981).
North Dakota: Apple Creek CC (R.); Enderlin GC (R.9 1968); Lincoln Park Muni (R.); Lisbon Bissell GC (R.9 1965).
South Dakota: Elmwood Park GC (R. 1977).
Wisconsin: Amery GC (R.9 A.9 1988); Cumberland GC (R.9 A.9 1988); Eagle River GC (R.3 A.9 1986); Hudson CC (R.9 A.9 1969); Nemadji Muni (A.9 1984); New Richmond GC (R.5 A.9 1982).

HOMER G. HERPEL
(1906–1977)

BORN: St. Louis, Missouri.
DIED: University City, Missouri, at age 71.

After working as a newspaper cartoonist in his youth, Homer Herpel turned to golf as a career. He became a member of the PGA of America in 1937 and served as professional at several St. Louis clubs. After retiring as a club professional in 1955, he began designing and supervising construction of courses in the St. Louis area. Herpel worked first in association with golf architect-contractor Chic Adams and later did over a dozen layouts of his own in greater St. Louis and other sections of Missouri.

Courses by Homer Herpel:

Missouri: Ballwin Muni (9); Fox Creek CC; [The] Lodge of Four Seasons GC (Executive Cse [9 Precision] 1957); North Shore CC (27 1959), with Chic Adams; Paddock CC (1964); Union Hills GC (9).

ARTHUR WRIGHT HILLS
(1930–   ), ASGCA, PRESIDENT 1992

BORN: Toledo, Ohio.

Art Hills first became interested in golf as a youngster, when he worked on the maintenance crew at Meadowbrook

Arthur Hills, 1991
COURTESY ARTHUR HILLS

Country Club near Detroit. He later studied agronomy at Michigan State University, where he played on the golf team and earned a Master's degree in landscape architecture.

Hills owned a landscape contracting firm in Toledo for a short time before entering private practice as a golf course architect in 1966, based in Toledo. He later established offices in Florida and Arizona and by the 1990s was one of the nation's most active golf architects.

Hills, like many active architects in the 1980s and 1990s, had a small, select crew of talented designers supporting him. His team included Steven Forrest, Michael Dasher, Brian Huntley and Keith Foster.

In 1991 two Arthur Hills designs were honored by *Golf Digest*. His Lakeside Course at the Golf Club of Georgia was declared the Best New Private Course of that year, and his Harbour Pointe in Washington was selected Best New Public Course. Hills thus became the first golf architect to win two separate categories in the same year in the magazine's then nine-year history of the competition. That same year saw the release of John Strawn's *Driving the Green*, a nonfiction work on golf course design and construction that focused on Arthur Hills and his design of Ironhorse in Florida.

Courses by Arthur Hills:

Arizona: San Ignacio G Cse (1989).
California: Bighorn GC (1991).
Colorado: Tamarron GC (1975); Walking Stick GC (1991).
Florida: Bonita Bay C (Marsh Cse 1985; Creekside Cse 1990); [The] Club at Pelican Bay (1980, A.3rd 9 1990); Coral Oaks G Cse (1988); Countryside at Berkshire Lakes (Precision 1987);

Cross Creek CC (Precision 1985); Foxfire CC (1985); Gator Trace GC (1986); Imperial GC (East Cse 1973); Ironhorse G&CC (1990); Meadows G&CC (Groves Cse 1987); Myerlee CC (Precision 1972); Old Trail GC (Hills Cse 1990); Palmetto Pines CC (1970); Pine Lakes GC (Par 3 1979); Quail Creek CC (Creek Cse 1982; Quail Cse 1981); Quail West G&CC (1992); Seville G&CC (1988); Tampa Palms CC (1987); TPC at Eagle Trace (1984); Vista Plantation GC (Precision 1985); Vista Royale GC (1974, A.3rd 9 1981); Wilderness CC (1974); Willoughby GC (1989); Windsor Parke GC (1990); Wyndemere G&CC (27 1980).

Georgia: GC of Georgia (Lakeside Cse 1990; Creekside Cse 1992); [The] Landings at Skidaway Island (Palmetto Cse 1985; Oakridge Cse 1988); [The] Standard C (1986).

Indiana: Hamilton Proper G Cse (1992).

Kansas: Tallgrass C (1983).

Kentucky: Champions GC (1988); Fox Run G Cse (1991); Persimmon Ridge GC (1989).

Louisiana: Southern Trace CC (1988).

Michigan: Egypt Valley CC (Ridge Cse 1991; Valley Cse 1991); Fox Hills CC (Golden Fox Cse 1989); Giant Oak CC (1971); Millrace CC (9 1970); Moors of Portage GC (1979); Oak Pointe GC (Honors Cse, 9 1988); Oaks CC (1968); Pine Trace GC (1989); Stonebridge CC (1992); Taylor Meadows GC (1989).

Nevada: [The] Legacy GC at Green Valley (1989).

Ohio: Brandywine CC, Maumee (27 1967); Brookledge GC (9 1988, A.9 1992); Detwiler GC (1969); Dunham Muni (9 Precision 1977); Glenview Muni (1974); Maumee Bay State Park GC (1991); PipeStone GC (1992); Shaker Run GC (1979); Turnberry G Cse (1991); Weatherwax GC (Highlands Cse 1971; Meadows Cse 1971); Winding Hollow CC (1991).

South Carolina: Cedar Creek GC (1992); Dunes West GC (1991); Morgan River G Cse (1992); Palmetto Dunes CC (Hills Cse 1986); Palmetto Hall Plantation GC (Arthur Hills Cse 1991).

Tennessee: River Island C (1991).

Texas: Bay Oaks CC (1988); [The] Ranch CC (1988); Trophy C (Creek Cse, 9 1984).

Utah: Wingpointe G Cse (1991).

Washington: Harbour Pointe GC (1990).

Japan: Higashi Ibaragi CC (1974).

Thailand: Vintage C (1992).

Courses remodeled or expanded by Arthur Hills:

Arizona: Oro Valley CC (R. 1987); Stonecreek GC [FKA Anasazi GC] (R. 1989).

California: Palos Verdes GC (R. 1990).

Florida: CC of Florida (R. 1987); Cypress Lake CC (R. 1982); Dunedin CC (R. 1974); Hole-in-the-Wall GC (R. 1984).

Georgia: Capital City C (R. 1985); Druid Hills CC (R. 1985).

Indiana: Elcona CC (R. 1986); Fort Wayne CC (R. 1986); Honeywell GC (A.9 1979).

Kentucky: Big Spring CC (R. 1982); Fort Mitchell CC (R. 1971; R. 1982); Highland CC (A.9 1985); Hunting Creek CC (R. 1988); Hurstborne CC (R. 1986); Summit Hills CC (R. 1985).

Michigan: Barton Hills CC (R. 1983); Birmingham CC (R. 1985); Bloomfield Hills CC (R. 1981); CC of Detroit (R. 1981); CC of Jackson (A.9 1991); Chemung Hills CC (R. 1986); Detroit GC (North Cse, R. 1978); Edgewood CC (R. 1986); Forest Lake CC (R. 1981); Grosse Ile G&CC (R. 1981); Indianwood G&CC (Old Cse, R. 1984); Lochmoor C (R. 1981); Meadowbrook CC (R. 1974); Oakland Hills CC (South Cse, R. 1987); Orchard Lake CC (R. 1984); Plum Hollow G&CC (R. 1984); Riverview Highlands GC (A.9 1980); Tam-O-Shanter CC (R. 1986); Walnut Creek CC (R. 1989); Western G&CC (R. 1984).

New York: CC of Rochester (R. 1982); Monroe CC (R. 1984); Park CC (R. 1983).

Ohio: Belmont CC (R. 1974; R. 1990); Bowling Green University GC (R. 1968); Brown's Run CC (R. 1988); Clovernook CC (R. 1984); Fairlawn CC (R. 1973); Heather Downs CC (North Cse, R. 1990; South Cse, R. 1990); Highland Meadows CC (R. 1974); Hyde Park CC (R. 1984); Inverness C (R. 1970; R. 1983); Orchard Hills CC (R.9 A.9 1967); Ottawa Park GC (R. 1974); Sycamore Creek CC (R. 1969); Sylvania CC (R. 1983); Terrace Park CC (R. 1977; R. 1984); Toledo CC (R. 1974); Wildwood CC (R. 1970).

Pennsylvania: Chartiers CC (R. 1986); Edgewood CC (R. 1990); Oakmont

CC (R. 1988); Pittsburgh Field C (R. 1986).

South Carolina: Bear Creek GC (R. 1986).

Virginia: Hermitage CC (A.3rd 9 1989).

Ontario: Board of Trade CC (West Cse, R.9 A.9 1975); Essex G&CC (R. 1969).

REUBEN P. HINES, SR. (–1964)

Reuben Hines, a golf course superintendent for most of his life, was a member of the GCSAA. In the late 1940s and early 1950s he held the post of Superintendent of Parks in Washington, D.C., and was in charge of five golf courses as well as numerous parklands. He also served as a turf consultant to several area golf clubs. Hines owned and operated a turf nursery in Maryland during the 1950s, and his close contact with golf course contractors and builders led to several remodeling jobs. By the late 1950s he had also designed a half-dozen courses.

Courses by Reuben Hines:

Maryland: Beaver Creek CC (1956); Oxon Run GC (9 1956).

Virginia: Courthouse CC (1955); Fauquier Springs CC (1959); Oak Hills CC (1959).

Courses remodeled or expanded by Reuben Hines:

Maryland: Manor CC (R. 1958).

DONALD HOENIG

Donald Hoenig planned several courses in New England in the 1960s, both on his own and in collaboration with his father. Among them were the widely known Pleasant Valley Country Club at Sutton, Massachusetts (a longtime PGA Tour site), Raceway Golf Course in Thompson, Connecticut (which he owned and operated), and a floodlit 18-hole precision course, Firefly Golf Club in Seekonk, Massachusetts (for legendary LPGA golfer Joanne Gunderson Carner and her husband Don).

George A. Hoffman
(1892–1977)

BORN: Hackensack, New Jersey.
DIED: Big Springs, Texas, at age 84.

George Hoffman moved with his parents to a ranch in West Texas at the turn of the century. He gained experience in golf course construction by helping build a course in the Dominican Republic in 1919. Returning to Texas in the 1920s, Hoffman entered private practice as a golf architect and designed numerous courses in the western part of the state. With a working knowledge of Spanish, he also landed jobs in Mexico and Central and South America. He remained active until his retirement in the 1970s.

Courses by George Hoffman:

Texas: Ascarte Park Muni (27 1955); Lady Bird Johnson Muni (9 1969); Olmos Basin GC (1963); Riverside GC (20 Precision 1962); Riverside Park (NLE); Victoria CC; Windcrest GC (9 1964).
Mexico: Club Campestre de Saltillo (9); Juarez CC.

Karl Hoffmann

Educated as an architect and engineer, Karl Hoffmann was involved in building reconstruction and renovation in his native Berlin, Germany, after World War I. An avid golfer, he also assisted golf architect Tom Simpson in the design of Bad Ems, which became Germany's main championship layout during the 1930s.

The experience led Hoffmann to pursue many golf design projects. In the mid-1930s he took young Bernhard von Limburger as a partner. World War II forced Limburger to flee the country, but Hoffmann remained in Germany and after the war restored many courses, including Bad Ems. For a short time before his death in the 1950s, Hoffmann worked in partnership with Herbert E. Gaertner, a former club secretary who also dabbled in course architecture.

Courses by Karl Hoffmann (All with Bernhard von Limburger unless otherwise indicated):

Germany: Bad Driburger GC (9); Breslau GC (9 *solo*); Chemnitzer GC; Cologne G und Land C; Donaveschingen GC (*solo*); Essen-Kettwig Haus Oefte GC (1959); Feldafing GC (1926); Garmisch-Partenkirchen GC; Gaschwitz GC; Krefelder GC (1930); Mannheim-Viernheim GC (9); Mittelrheinscher GC (1924), ass't Tom Simpson; Neustadt GC (9); Stuttgarter GC (1927); Wittenberg GC (9).
Switzerland: Basel G&CC (1928); Neuchatel GC (9 1928).

Courses remodeled or expanded by Karl Hoffmann (All with Bernhard von Limburger unless otherwise indicated):

Germany: Hanover GC (R.); Mittelrheinscher GC (R. *solo*).

Ben Hogan, circa 1960 COURTESY *GOLF WORLD*

William Benjamin Hogan
(1912–)

BORN: Dublin, Texas.

Ben Hogan, winner of all four major professional golf championships and four U.S. Opens, was a perceptive golf course critic throughout his career. He especially admired the works of Dick Wilson and shortly before the architect's death had talked of doing a course with him. Ten years later, Hogan finally did collaborate on the design of a layout, Trophy Club CC near Fort Worth, Texas. He worked with Wilson's chief associate Joe Lee on the design. Typical of Hogan's intensity, he attacked each phase of the project with painstaking detail, even going so far as to personally hand-rake all the green contours. The course received only a lukewarm reception, and Hogan later disassociated himself with the club. Sadly, except for suggesting changes at Colonial and Shady Oaks in Fort Worth, Hogan did no other golf course design work.

Cecil B. Hollingsworth

A high school football and golf star in Los Angeles, Cecil Hollingsworth attended UCLA and was employed as assis-tant football coach and physical education instructor there in the early 1930s. He then purchased and operated a daily-fee golf course in the 1940s and in the 1950s began a large golf complex in El Cajon, Singing Hills CC. Hollingsworth designed most of the courses he owned.

Courses by Cecil B. Hollingsworth:

Arkansas: Twin Lakes GC (1978).
California: Alondra Park GC (Cse No. 2 [Par 3] 1950); Singing Hills CC (Oak Glen Cse 1967; Pine Glen Cse [Precision] 1967).

Frederic Clark Hood
(1866–1942)

BORN: Chelsea, Massachusetts.
DIED: Boston, Massachusetts, at age 76.

Although A. C. M. Croome (Liphook), H. C. Leeds (Myopia) and Hugh Wilson (Merion) are often referred to as "one-time architects," the truth is that each was active in the design of several layouts. In contrast, Frederic C. Hood, who designed Kittansett, was truly a "one-timer."

Founder and president of the Hood Rubber Company, F. C. Hood was responsible for planning The Kittansett Club at Marion, Massachusetts, built in 1923. While credit for the design is sometimes given to William S. Flynn and his friend Hugh Wilson, and while club records indicate that several experts, including Donald Ross, were consulted, no construction contract was ever awarded to any architect. Instead, Hood, working from preliminary plans prepared by Flynn, completed specifications and acted as construction superintendent of a crew of local men with Kittansett's future greenkeeper, Elliot "Mike" Pierce, as foreman. Most of Flynn's plans were changed by Hood, but he did give credit to Wilson and Flynn for creation of the famous third hole that plays over a beach and ocean cove. F. C. Hood should not be confused with F. G. Hood, who designed several courses in New Zealand.

Charles Hook

"Gus" Hook was the director of parks and recreation for Baltimore, Maryland, for several decades. In this capacity he designed three new municipal courses and remodeled two others.

Courses by Gus Hook:

Maryland: Carroll Park Muni; Mount Pleasant Muni (1933); Pine Ridge Muni (1959).

Courses remodeled or expanded by Gus Hook:

Maryland: Clifton Park Muni (R.); Forest Park Muni (R.).

S. V. Hotchkin, circa 1930 COURTESY NEIL HOTCHKIN

STAFFORD VERE HOTCHKIN (1876–1953)

BORN: Woodhall Spa, Lincolnshire, England.
DIED: Woodhall Spa, Lincolnshire, England, at age 77.

S. V. Hotchkin served in the Leicestershire Yeomanry during World War I. An officer in the 17th Lancers, he attained the rank of colonel by the time of his retirement from the military. In 1922–23 he served as a Conservative Member of Parliament and for many years held the post of alderman in the Lincolnshire County Council.

Hotchkin's first golf design experience was the remodeling of his home course, Woodhall Spa, which he purchased in 1920. He then formed Ferigna Ltd., a firm that dealt with all phases of the golf course business, including design, construction, maintenance, equipment and seed. In the mid-1920s he made an extended tour of South Africa, designing or remodeling a number of the nation's top courses, and many considered him the best architect to have worked there.

In 1930 Hotchkin was joined by fellow military officers Cecil Hutchison and Guy Campbell in a golf design partnership. After a few years, Hutchison and Campbell went into business for themselves and Hotchkin continued designing on his own

until World War II. He then retired to serve as secretary at Woodhall Spa, a position later held by his son Neil.

Courses by S. V. Hotchkin:

England: Ashridge GC (1932), with Sir Guy Campbell and C. K. Hutchison; Grimsby GC (1923); Kington GC (1926), with C. K. Hutchison and Sir Guy Campbell; Leeds Castle GC, with Sir Guy Campbell and C. K. Hutchison; Links GC; Purley Downs GC; RAF Cranwell GC; Sandilands GC; Shoreham GC, with Sir Guy Campbell and C. K. Hutchison; Stoke Rochford GC (1924); Warsash GC, with Sir Guy Campbell and C. K. Hutchison; West Sussex GC (1930), with Sir Guy Campbell and C. K. Hutchison.
South Africa: Humewood CC (1929); Maccauvlei CC (1926); Port Elizabeth GC.

Courses remodeled or expanded by S. V. Hotchkin:

England: Royal West Norfolk GC (R. 1928), with C. K. Hutchison and Sir Guy Campbell; Woodhall Spa GC (R. 1922; R. 1926, with Sir Guy Campbell and C. K. Hutchison).
Scotland: North Berwick GC (R. 1930), with Sir Guy Campbell and C. K. Hutchison.
South Africa: Durban CC (R. 1928); East London CC (R.); Mowbray CC (R. 1923); Royal Port Alfred GC (R.).

HUGH LEON HOWARD (1928–)

BORN: Graham, Texas.

Leon Howard studied agronomy at Texas A&M University, receiving a Bachelor's degree in agronomy in 1954 and a Master's degree in soil physics in 1959. While in graduate school, he worked part-time remodeling greens on local golf courses. The experience formed the basis for his Master's thesis, "Compaction Problems in Putting Green Soils," which was later incorporated by the USGA Green Section Committee in its specifications for greens construction.

Howard's first design experience was a remodeling of the Texarkana CC in 1959. The same year he formed a Texas-based soils laboratory that ultimately provided testing services on the construction of

Leon Howard, 1970
COLLECTION RON WHITTEN

over a thousand courses. In 1965 he formed a golf and park design firm and concentrated on the design and construction of golf courses in the southwestern United States. In 1965 he hired Dave Bennett as an associate. In 1967 Howard formed a three-way partnership with his brother Charles (who handled the irrigation work for his designs) and Bennett. Bennett left the company in 1970, but Charles remained and eventually began handling course designs as well as irrigation systems. In 1977 Charles formed a separate business, and Leon closed his practice.

Two years later, Howard resumed designing courses and was joined in 1986 by his son Warren Howard. In 1991 Howard joined International Sports Turf Research Center, based in Olathe, Kansas, as its chief agronomist. Later that year he formed yet another firm, Sports Turf Services, which offered both agronomic consultations and golf design expertise.

Courses by Leon Howard:

Alabama: Albertville G&CC; Willowbrook CC (1966).
Arkansas: DeGray State Park GC (1976), with *Charles Howard*; Hindman Park GC (1967), with Dave Bennett; Indian Hills GC (1976), with *Charles Howard*; Jaycee Memorial G Cse.
Colorado: Eagle CC (9 1961).
Florida: Hollybrook G&TC (18 Par 3 1970); Monterey Y&CC (9 Precision 1970).
Illinois: Brookhills GC (9 Precision).
Kansas: Schilling AFB GC (9 1965, NLE).
Mississippi: Greenville Muni (1968); Mississippi Valley State University GC (9 1973).
Nebraska: Applewood Muni (1970), with Dave Bennett.
New Mexico: Conchas Lake GC (1967); Gallup Muni (9 1965); Sierra Vista GC (9).

North Carolina: Prestonwood CC (27 1988), with *Vance Heafner.*

Oklahoma: Durant CC (9); Page Belcher G Cse (Olde Page Cse 1977); Pawnee Bill State Park G Cse (9); Trails GC (1979), with *Charles Howard.*

Tennessee: Country Hills G Cse (1990); Druid Hills GC (1971); Mill Creek GC (9 Par 3 1973); Old Fort GC (1985); Two Rivers Muni (1968), with Dave Bennett.

Texas: Babe Didrikson Zaharias Muni; Bar-K GC (9 Par 3); Bowie Muni (9); Brownwood CC (1970); Buckner Children's Home G Cse (9 Par 3); Casa Blanca GC (1967); Casaview CC (9, NLE); Castro CC (9); Chambers County GC (9); Chaparral CC (1970); Clear Creek GC (1970); Cleburne Muni; Country Gold CC; Deer Trail CC (9); DeCordova Bend CC (9 1968), with Dave Bennett; Diboll Muni (9 1968, with Dave Bennett; A.9 1986); Dyess AFB GC (9); Freestone CC (9); Gabe Lozano Sr. G. Center [FKA Corpus Christi G Center](27 1965); Garden Valley G. Resort; Granbury GC (9); Grayson County G Cse; Harker Heights Muni (1966), with Dave Bennett; Harlingen CC (1968), with Dave Bennett; Hempstead GC (9); Highland Lakes GC (1967), with Dave Bennett; Holly Lake Ranch GC (1971); Hurricane Creek CC (1970); John C. Beasley Muni (9); L. B. Houston Muni (1969); Lago Vista CC (1967), with Dave Bennett; Lake Kiowa CC; Lakeway GC (Live Oak Cse 1966; Yaupon Cse 1971); Lake Whitney CC (1969); Lakewood Recreation C (9); Laredo AFB GC (1967), with Dave Bennett; Lost Pines GC (9 1973); Madisonville GC (9); M & W GC (1970); Mesquite Muni (1965); Morris Williams Muni (1965); Nocona Hills CC (1974), with *Charles Howard;* Oak Ridge CC (9); Olney G&CC (9); Pecan Plantation GC (1971); Pedarnales CC (9 1967); Pinewood GC (1961); Red Oak Valley GC; Riverview CC (1964); Rockdale CC (9 1965); Rolling Hills CC; Ross Rogers Muni (East Cse 1968; West Cse 1977, with *Charles Howard*); Runaway Bay GC; Shady Oaks GC, Baird (1967), with Dave Bennett; Sherill Park Muni (East Cse 1973; West Cse 1980, with *Charles Howard*); Sotogrande G&TC (18 Par 3 1969), with Dave Bennett; Spring Lake CC (9 1967); Van Zandt CC (1966); Webb Hill CC (1968),

with Dave Bennett; Western Hills GC (1969); Wildflower CC (1987), with *Charles Howard;* Wildwood CC (1966); Woodcreek CC (Cypress Creek Cse 1977, NLE); Woodhaven CC (1969); World of Resorts GC (1976), with *Charles Howard.*

Virginia: Burke Lake Park GC (18 Par 3 1970), with Dave Bennett; Greendale Muni (1977), with *Charles Howard;* Pinecrest GC (9 1973).

Courses remodeled or expanded by Leon Howard:

Arkansas: Texarkana CC (R. 1958).
Louisiana: Shreveport CC (R.9 1958).
Missouri: Swope Park GC (R. 1990).
New Mexico: Albuquerque CC (R. 1964).
Tennessee: Carnton CC (R.9 A.9 1991); Temple Hills CC (A.3rd 9 1973).
Texas: Columbian C (A.9 1960); Crane County CC (R.9); Hilltop Lakes GC (A.9 1970); Holiday Hills CC (R.); Lakewood CC, Dallas (R. 1964); Landa Park GC (A.9 1969), with Dave Bennett; Lion's Muni (R.); Point Venture Y&CC (A.9 1974), with *Charles Howard;* River Hills CC (A.9 1965); Sinton Muni (A.9), with Dave Bennett.

MELVIN A. HUESTON
(1895–1978)

DIED: Seattle, Washington, at age 83.

A PGA professional for over fifty years, Mel "Curley" Hueston served at a succession of courses in the state of Washington, including fifteen years at Indian Canyon GC in Spokane. Curley also designed a number of golf courses in the Pacific Northwest.

Courses by Melvin "Curley" Hueston:

Idaho: Avondale-on-Hayden GC (1968); Coeur d'Alene GC (1956).
Washington: Liberty Lake GC (1955); Moses Lake GC (1956); Othello G&CC (9 1968); Sham-Na-Pum GC (1966); Westwood West GC (9 1964).

HENRY BARRY HUGHES
(1908–   )

BORN: Chillicothe, Missouri.

Henry B. Hughes was the son of Henry T. Hughes, a construction superintendent for Donald Ross at The Broadmoor in Col-

Henry B. Hughes, 1974 RON WHITTEN

orado. While Henry was too young to join brothers Lawrence and Frank on their father's construction crew, he did herd the sheep used in those days to clip grass around the fairways.

In 1924 the senior Hughes moved his family to Denver, where he constructed Cherry Hills CC for William S. Flynn and remained as its greenkeeper. While Lawrence and Frank went to work for Ross, Henry served on his father's crew until 1933, when he took over the head greenkeeper position.

Hughes remained at Cherry Hills until 1947, then traveled to Mexico City to construct Club de Golf de Mexico for Lawrence. He returned to Denver in 1950 and for the next thirteen years served as superintendent at Green Gables GC and designed courses in the Rocky Mountain area.

By the mid-1960s he was devoting full time to golf architecture and retained an associate, Richard Watson of Lincoln, Nebraska. Hughes retired from design work in 1970 but remained active in golf, operating a course in Denver that catered to senior play.

Courses by Henry B. Hughes:

Colorado: Aurora Hills GC (1969); Bookcliff CC (9 1958); Columbine CC (1955; R. 1966); CC of Fort Collins (9 1960, A.9 1969); Estes Park GC (1958); Glenwood Springs GC (9 1953); Hyland Hills CC (1959); John F. Kennedy Muni (27 1968); Lake Estes GC (9 Precision); Limon GC (9 1967); Loveland GC (9 1960); Meadow Hills GC (1957); Meeker CC (9 1971); Montrose GC (9 1961); Paradise Valley CC (27 1961); Riverdale GC (Knolls Cse 1965); Sterling CC (1956); Twilight GC (9 Par 3 1960); Valley Hi GC (1958); Windsor Gardens GC (9 Precision 1963).

Kansas: Belleville CC (9 1968), with Richard Watson; Scott City CC (9 1968), with Richard Watson.

Nebraska: Ashland CC (9 1968), with Richard Watson; Atkinson-Stuart GC (9 1969), with Richard Watson; Bloomfield-Wausa GC (9 1969), with Richard Watson; Colonial GC (9 Par 3 1964, NLE), with Richard Watson; Friend CC (9 1967), with Richard Watson; Mid-County GC (9 1968), with Richard Watson; Skyview Muni (1953); Wayne CC (1969), with Richard Watson.

Texas: Hunsley Hills CC (1962); Sinton Muni (9 1968), with Richard Watson.

Utah: Willow Creek CC (1959).

Wyoming: Midway GC (9 1970), with Richard Watson; Old Baldy C (1964); Paradise Valley CC (1958); Rolling Green CC (9 1967).

Courses remodeled or expanded by Henry B. Hughes:

Colorado: Fort Morgan Muni (R.9 A.9); Hillcrest CC (R.9 1954; R.9 1969); Overland Park Muni (R. 1966); Pueblo CC (R.9 A.9).

Lawrence Hughes, 1974 COURTESY *GOLF WORLD*

LAWRENCE MARION HUGHES (1897–1975), ASGCA

BORN: Chillicothe, Missouri.
DIED: San Diego, California, at age 78.

Lawrence Hughes's father, Henry T. Hughes, was employed as construction supervisor for Donald Ross, and in their late teens Larry and brother Frank went to work for him on The Broadmoor. After his discharge from the army following World War I, Hughes returned to work for Ross, building a number of courses for him before settling down upon completion of Holston Hills CC in Knoxville, Tennessee, to serve as its manager and greenkeeper.

During the Depression, Hughes operated a garage in Denver, Colorado, and did a little course design work on the side. But it was not until after World War II that he was offered the opportunity to establish a full-time business. In 1946 he met Johnny Dawson, prominent amateur golfer, member of a golfing family and avid real estate promoter. Dawson was sure of the value of development in Southern California and convinced Hughes that there were sufficient underground springs to support golf courses on its desertlike terrain. With Dawson raising the financial backing, Hughes began designing. In 1947 his first course, Mission Valley CC in San Diego (later renamed Stardust CC), opened for play. For the next two decades he continued to create courses in the Southwest and in Mexico, beginning with Club de Golf de Mexico, done with the help of Mexican golfer Percy Clifford in 1950. Hughes was assisted on many of his jobs by his brothers Frank and Henry and apprentice Harry Rainville. Henry Hughes and Harry Rainville both went on to form successful golf design businesses of their own.

Courses by Lawrence Hughes:

Arizona: Antelope Hills GC (North Cse 1956); London Bridge GC (1970); Orange Tree CC (1958), with Johnny Bulla; Paradise Valley CC (1957); Pinewood CC (1958); Scottsdale CC (1954).

California: DeAnza Desert CC (1959); El Dorado CC (1958); Green River CC (Orange Cse 1959); Indio Muni (Par 3 1964); La Canada-Flintridge CC (1962); La Quinta CC (1959); Las Posas CC (1958); Marin GC (1954); Marine Corps GC (Par 3 1952); Roadrunner Dunes GC (9 1964); Round Hill G&CC (1960); Santa Barbara Community GC (1955); Stardust CC (27 1947); Thunderbird CC (1951); Via Verde CC.

Nevada: Desert Inn & CC (1952); Reno CC (1958).

South Dakota: Tomahawk Lake GC (9).

Texas: Coronado G&CC (1961); Shady Oaks CC (1959), with Robert Trent Jones and Ralph Plummer.

Mexico: Bosques de San Isidro GC (1973); C de G Acozac (1973); C de G Chiluca (1975); C de G de Mexico (1949), with Percy Clifford; C de G Santa Anita (1969); Club Campestre de Hermosillo (9 1949); Club Jurica; Club Santiago (1975); Mexicali G&CC (1960); Valle Alto GC (1955).

Courses remodeled or expanded by Lawrence Hughes:

California: Barbara Worth GC (R.).
Mexico: El Cid G&CC (A.9 1971); Guadalajara CC (R. 1974).

Frank Hummel, 1969 COURTESY ROBERT DEAN PUTMAN

T. FRANK HUMMEL (1926–)

BORN: La Junta, Colorado.

Frank Hummel attended Willamette University and Colorado University, receiving a B.S. degree in engineering in 1948. During the early 1950s he won many regional Amateur golf titles while working as a combustion engineer in Pueblo, Colorado. Turning professional in 1956, he served as club pro in Fort Morgan and later in Greeley.

In the early 1960s Hummel designed and built a second nine at Highland Hills Muni in Greeley. After a few additional projects, he resigned his professional position in 1968 to form a course design firm with Theodore Rupel, superintendent of famed Cherry Hills CC in Denver. In 1970 Hummel formed his own golf design and construction business with offices in Colorado and Arizona. A licensed pilot, he created courses in some of the more remote areas of the Great Plains.

Courses by Frank Hummel:

Colorado: Aspen Muni (1970); Bunker Hill CC (9); Cedar Ridges GC (9 1986); Collindale CC (1970); Eisenhower GC (Silver Cse 1977); Foxhill CC (1973); Gleneagle CC (1973); Hillcrest GC; Riverview Muni (9 1972); South Ridge Greens GC (1984); Twin Peaks Muni (1978); Wray CC (9 1970).

Kansas: Buffalo Dunes Muni; Emporia Muni (1970); Hesston Muni (1976); Mariah Hills Muni (1974); Prairie Dog GC (9 1969).

Montana: Jawbone Creek GC (9 1980); Madison Meadows GC (9 1982); Pine Ridge G&CC (9 1982); Powder River CC (1982).

Nebraska: Chadron CC (9); Chappell CC (9 1973); Grand Island Muni (1977); Quail Run G Cse (1991); Scottsbluff CC (1976).

Wyoming: Buffalo G Cse (9); Gillette CC; Lusk GC (9); Red Butte CC (9 1981); Westview Park GC (9); Wheatland CC (9).

Courses remodeled or expanded by Frank Hummel:

Colorado: Highland Hills Muni (A.9 1963); Hollydot at Colorado City GC (A.3rd 9 1988); Hyland Hills CC (A.3rd 9 1984); Loveland GC (A.9 1977); Valley Hi GC (R.).

Montana: Mission Mountain CC (A.9 1991); Polson CC (A.9 1990).

Wyoming: Kendrick Muni (A.9 1984).

CHARLES HUNTER
(1836–1921)

BORN: Prestwick, Scotland.
DIED: Prestwick, Scotland, at age 84.

Charles Hunter worked as a caddy and clubmaker under Old Tom Morris at Prestwick Golf Club and succeeded Old Tom as Prestwick's greenkeeper and professional in 1864. He planned several Scottish courses, including the original Macrihanish, St. Nicholas Prestwick and the original five holes at Troon. His son David emigrated to the United States, where he became professional at Baltusrol and laid out several New Jersey courses.

WILES ROBERT HUNTER
(1874–1942)

BORN: Terre Haute, Indiana.
DIED: Santa Barbara, California, at age 68.

Robert Hunter attended Indiana University, receiving a B.A. degree in 1896. He was a world-renowned sociologist and author and wrote such works as *Poverty* (1904), *Labor in Politics* (1915), *Why We Fail as Christians* (1919) and *Revolution* (1940). He spent his life addressing and attempting to solve serious social problems, was among the organizers of the Chicago Bureau of Charities in the late 1890s and lived for a time at Jane Ad-

Robert Hunter, circa 1928 COLLECTION RON WHITTEN

dams's Hull House and later at Toynbee Hall in England.

In the early 1900s Hunter served as chairman of the New York Commission for the Abolition of Child Labor. He also participated in a campaign against tuberculosis. In 1910 he ran unsuccessfully for governor of Connecticut on the Socialist ticket. He later resigned from the party and in 1917 moved to California, where he taught and wrote for years at the University of California at Berkeley.

Ironically, Robert Hunter was also an avid enthusiast of golf, in those days considered an elitist sport. During his stays in Great Britain, he studied the great courses. While at Berkeley, Hunter helped establish Berkeley CC (later renamed Mira Vista) and recruited Willie Watson to design the course. He then served for several years as chairman of the club's green committee.

Hunter's fascination with course design led him to write one of the classic books in the literature of golf architecture, *The Links* (1926), still considered one of the finest essays on the subject and containing some remarkable illustrations of genuine links.

Hunter was also instrumental in luring Alister Mackenzie to California and, shortly after publication of *The Links*, began assisting the talented Britisher with most of the courses he did in that state. The two teamed as partners in a course design firm that later included former U.S. Amateur champion H. Chandler Egan. Ironically, Egan and Hunter collaborated, along with amateur golfer Roger Lapham, in the remodeling of Pebble Beach in preparation for the 1929 U.S. Amateur. Mackenzie, for unknown reasons, was not invited to participate, but news reports indicate he did stop by and discuss the work with his compatriots.

But Hunter was never a golf architect in the true sense. He served more as a con-

ceptualist, assisting Mackenzie with his deep understanding of the game and its links.

Courses by Robert Hunter (All with Alister Mackenzie unless otherwise indicated):

California: Cypress Point C (1928); Green Hills CC (1930), and H. Chandler Egan; Meadow C (1927); Mira Vista G&CC [FKA Berkeley G&CC](1921), ass't Willie Watson; Northwood GC (9 1928); Pittsburgh GC (9); Valley C of Montecito (1928).

Courses remodeled or expanded by Robert Hunter (All with Alister Mackenzie unless otherwise indicated):

California: Monterey Peninsula CC (Dunes Cse, R. 1928); Pebble Beach G Links (R. 1928), with H. Chandler Egan and *Roger Lapham.*

MAY DUNN HUPFEL, NÉE MAY DUNN
(1880–1948)

BORN: Wimbledon, England.
DIED: California at age 68.

May Dunn was the daughter of Tom and Isabella Gourlay Dunn. "Queenie," as she was called throughout her life, learned golf at an early age and competed against her brothers John Duncan and Seymour on makeshift golfing grounds.

When World War I erupted, May traveled to the United States in hopes of making a living teaching golf to wealthy women. Almost immediately she landed a job writing an instruction series for the New York *Herald.* Her subsequent efforts at promoting women's golf in America caused many to consider May Dunn as America's first woman professional, though she was not.

As a Dunn, it was inevitable that sooner or later she would design a course or two. In 1916, she visited Nevada and laid out Reno Golf Course and Tahoe Tavern Golf Course. She also served as pro-manager at both. Her design and golf professional careers ended in 1920 when she married Californian Adolf Hupfel, but her short foray into golf architecture made her the first woman to actively engage in the golf design business.

May received acclaim in Ron Crowley's article "The Dunns of Musselburgh" in *Golf Journal* of January 1991. She was also the subject of a feature article by Kristine Baer in the same publication in July of 1984.

MICHAEL JOHN HURDZAN, PH.D. (1943–), ASGCA, PRESIDENT 1984

BORN: Wheeling, West Virginia.

Dr. Michael Hurdzan graduated from Ohio State University in 1966 and earned an M.S. in turfgrass physiology and a Ph.D. in environmental plant physiology at the University of Vermont. From 1957 to 1966 Hurdzan worked as a youngster for golf architect Jack Kidwell of Columbus, Ohio, from time to time. After college, Hurdzan began practicing golf design with him on a full-time basis. In 1976 they formed the partnership of Kidwell and Hurdzan, Inc.

Although Hurdzan once stated that the chances of becoming a golf course architect were about equal to that of being struck by lightning, the progress of his own career proved it could be done. During his years at the University of Vermont, he operated a ski and sports shop. He also established the University Tree Service, which engaged in course construction as well as other landscape services. The firm added new nines to Barre (Vermont) CC and Newport (Vermont) CC and had twenty-eight employees by the time Hurdzan sold it to return to Ohio.

By the late 1970s Kidwell and Hurdzan was one of the most active course-design firms in the nation. In addition to his practice, Hurdzan completed a Bachelor of Science degree in landscape architecture at Ohio State University and taught an advanced turfgrass course there, became a major in the Special Forces Reserves and wrote monthly columns for *Weeds, Trees and Turf* and *Golf Business* magazines. He also found time to establish an extensive

Mike Hurdzan,
1990 RON WHITTEN

library of golf books and a large collection of clubs and balls from past eras.

While serving as ASGCA president, Hurdzan wrote a four-part series, "Evolution of the Modern Green," for *PGA Magazine*, later reprinted and distributed by the ASGCA.

In the late 1980s Hurdzan was selected to design two courses in the Toronto area for the developers of Trivial Pursuit, the board game whose popularity swept the country in the 1980s. The first of the courses, Devil's Pulpit, was declared Best New Course of Canada by *Golf Digest*.

Courses by Michael Hurdzan (All with Jack Kidwell unless otherwise indicated):

Georgia: Silver Leaf GC (1991 *solo*).
Illinois: Annbriar GC (1992 *solo*).
Indiana: Grand Oak GC (1989 *solo*); Hidden Valley GC (1976).
Kentucky: Frances Miller Memorial GC (1982); Kenton County GC (North Cse 1981).
Maryland: Eagle's Landing G Cse (1991 *solo*).
Massachusetts: Dennis Highlands GC (1984); Sterling CC (1991 *solo*); Willowbend CC (1988 *solo*).
Minnesota: Baker National GC (1990 *solo*).
Missouri: Crystal Highlands GC (1988 *solo*).
New York: Cobblestone Creek CC (1991 *solo*).
North Carolina: Renaissance Park G Cse (1988 *solo*).
Ohio: Beckett Ridge G&CC (1974); Blue Ash GC (1979); Buttermilk Falls GC (1981); Cliffside GC (1988 *solo*); Deer Creek State Park GC (1979); Eaglesticks GC (1990 *solo*); Hickory Hills CC (1979); Oxbow G&CC (1974); Ridenoor Park GC (9 Precision 1976); Royal American Links (1991 *solo*); San Dar Acres GC (Precision 1976); Shamrock GC (1989 *solo*); Shawnee Lookout GC (1976); Shawnee State Park GC (1979); [The] Vineyard GC (1986).
Pennsylvania: Cedar Brook GC (27 1988 *solo*); Glenmaura GC (1992 *solo*); Hickory Heights GC (1989 *solo*).
Texas: Oak Ridge CC (1986).
Virginia: [The] Hamptons GC (27 1991 *solo*).
West Virginia: Riverside GC (1976).
Ontario: Devil's Paintbrush G Links (1992 *solo*); Devil's Pulpit GC (1990 *solo*); Royal Woodbine GC (1991 *solo*).

Courses remodeled or expanded by Michael Hurdzan (All with Jack Kidwell unless otherwise indicated):

Connecticut: Shorehaven GC (R. 1989 *solo*).
Illinois: Antioch GC (R. *solo*).
Indiana: Hillcrest G&CC (R.9 1984; A.9 1989 *solo*).
Kentucky: Boone Links (A.3rd 9 1988 *solo*); Kenton County CC (South Cse, R. 1974); Summit Hills CC (R.10 A.1 1980); World of Sports GC (R. A.10 1979).
Minnesota: Minikahda Club (R. 1990 *solo*).
Missouri: Sunset CC (R. *solo*).
New Jersey: Copper Hill CC (R. *solo*).
Ohio: Brookside CC (R.2 1977); Brookside Park GC (A.9 1977); California GC (A.5 1975); Elyria CC (R.2 1975); Fairfield CC (R. 1990 *solo*); Foxfire GC (A. Silver Fox Nine 1984); Groveport GC (R. 1977); Kenwood CC (Kendale Cse, R. 1981; Kenview Cse, R. 1977); Lakewood CC (R. 1 1975); Marion CC (R. 1977); Miami Shores GC (R.9 1977); Miami Valley CC (R. 1980); Mohican Hills GC (A.9 1975); Mount Vernon CC (R. 1977); Neumann Park GC (A.9 1975); Shawnee CC (R. 1978); Table Rock GC (A.9 1976); Troy CC (R.9 A.9 1975); Westwood CC (R. 1984); WGC GC (A.9 1982); Wildwood GC (R.3 1977); Winton Woods GC (A.3rd 9 Precision 1992); York Temple CC (R. 1 1975); Zanesville CC (R.5 1981).
Pennsylvania: CC of Scranton (A.9 1991 *solo*); Honesdale GC (R. 1990 *solo*).
South Carolina: Myrtle Beach National GC (South Cse, R. 1990 *solo*).
Vermont: CC of Barre (A.9 1968 *solo*); Newport CC (A.9 1968 *solo*).
West Virginia: Deerfield CC (R.9 A.9 1978).

HORACE G. HUTCHINSON (1859–1932)

BORN: London, England.
DIED: London, England, at age 73.

Horace Hutchinson, renowned British golfer, won the first two British Amateur championships in 1886 and 1887. He was a prolific golf writer whose numerous publications included the first instruction book on the game, *Hints on Golf* (1886), *The Badminton Book of Golf* (1886) and *Fifty Years of Golf* (1919). Passages in his books provide insight into the development of golf course design during the years when the game was spreading from Scotland to England, throughout the British Empire and to the United States. His references to The National Golf Links of America and Myopia Hunt Club were especially laudatory and helped establish those courses as landmarks in course architecture.

Around 1886 Hutchinson assisted the owner of Royal Eastbourne GC in planning the course. This was the site of the notorious "Paradise Green," with contours so severe that if a player missed the hole on his first putt he might putt forever. Hutchinson was also the designer of Royal West Norfolk in England and the nine-hole Isles of Scilly GC.

*C. K. Hutchison,
circa 1905*
COLLECTION RON
WHITTEN

CECIL KEY HUTCHISON
(1877–1941)

BORN: East Lothian, Scotland.
DIED: London, England, at age 64.

C. K. Hutchison was educated at Eton College, Windsor, where he excelled at all sports. He played on the cricket team, won the school mile and competed in golf and skating. The son of a locally prominent golfer, he learned the game on the links at Muirfield. By the turn of the century he was one of the top amateurs in Britain, winning the St. George's Challenge Cup in 1903 and 1910 and the *Golf Illustrated* Gold Vase in 1909. Hutchison represented Scotland in the annual England-Scotland matches each year from 1904 to 1912. He was also runner-up in the 1909 British Amateur Championship, where he tragically bogied the home hole at his own home course, Muirfield, to lose one down.

Hutchison joined the Coldstream Guards, fought in the Boer War and later joined the Royal Scots, attaining the rank of major. Captured by Germans during World War I, he was confined to a POW camp for several years.

After the war, his competitive game having suffered, Hutchison turned instead

to golf course design. He served as assistant to James Braid during the construction of Gleneagles and the reconstruction of Carnoustie. In the mid-1920s he formed a firm with Colonel S. V. Hotchkin, who had assisted him in remodeling Woodhall Spa. Guy Campbell, a former *Times* sportswriter whose background was remarkably similar to Hutchison's, also joined the firm. Together the three designed and built many impressive courses in Great Britain during the period from the late 1920s to mid-1930s, when golf development was at a near standstill in the United States. Hutchison was highly regarded in his time for his refreshing approach to golf design and his eagerness to incorporate innovations in his works.

Courses by C.K. Hutchison:

England: Ashridge GC (1932), with Sir Guy Campbell and S. V. Hotchkin; Kington GC (1926), with Sir Guy Campbell and S. V. Hotchkin; Leeds Castle GC, with Sir Guy Campbell and S. V. Hotchkin; Shoreham GC, with Sir Guy Campbell and S. V. Hotchkin; Warsash GC, with Sir Guy Campbell and S. V. Hotchkin; West Sussex GC (1930), with Sir Guy Campbell and S. V. Hotchkin.
Scotland: Gleneagles Hotel GC (King's Cse 1919; Queen's Cse 1919), with James Braid.

Courses remodeled or expanded by C.K. Hutchison:

England: Ganton GC (R.); Prince's GC (Blue Cse, R.); Royal West Norfolk GC (R. 1928), with Sir Guy Campbell and S. V. Hotchkin; Sundridge Park GC (East Cse, R. 1927), with Sir Guy Campbell; Tadmarton Heath GC (A.9 1923); Woodhall Spa GC (R. 1926), with Sir Guy Campbell and S. V. Hotchkin.
Scotland: North Berwick GC (R. 1930), with Sir Guy Campbell and S. V. Hotchkin; Pitlochry GC (R.); Turnberry GC (Ailsa Cse, R. 1938).

SEICHI INOUYE
(1905–)

One of Japan's leading golf course architects, Seichi Inouye worked under Kinya Fujita for many years before going out on his own. Inouye designed over thirty-five courses in the Far East during his career.

Courses by Seichi Inouye:

Japan: Aichi CC (1953); Funabashi GC (9 1956); Hirakata CC (1959); Ibaraki GC (East Cse 1960); Kasugai CC (East Cse; West Cse); Kawasaki Kokusai CC (1954); Kyushu Shima CC (1964); Musashi CC (Sasai Cse 1959; Toyooka Cse 1959); Nasu GC (1936), with Kinya Fujita; Nikko CC (1950); Nishinomiya CC (1955); Oarai GC (1953), with Kinya Fujita; Sapporo GC (1958); Takanodai CC (1954); Totsuka CC (West Cse 1961); Yamaguchi CC (9); Yomiuri CC, Tokyo (1964); Yomiuri CC, Osaka (Blue Cse; Red Cse).
Philippines: Holiday Hills GC (27).

HALE S. IRWIN
(1945–)

BORN: Joplin, Missouri.

The 1967 NCAA golf champion, as well as a star football defensive back at the University of Colorado, Hale Irwin enjoyed a successful career as a touring pro after turning professional in 1968. Irwin gained the reputation of playing especially well on tough courses, and his victories included three U.S. Open titles, at Winged Foot in 1974, Inverness in 1979 and Medinah in 1990. He also won at Harbour Town, Riviera, Butler National, Muirfield Village, Pebble Beach and Pinehurst No. 2, where he established a course-record 62.

Besides playing the great courses well, Irwin studied their architecture, and upon turning forty he formed a course design and club-management firm, Hale Irwin Golf Services, based in St. Louis. His first

Hale Irwin, 1990
COURTESY HALE IRWIN

courses were done in association with golf architect Gary Kern. He then formed a partnership with Colorado designer Dick Phelps. While Phelps maintained his Denver-area office, his son Rick worked full-time in Irwin's St. Louis office as in-house course designer, as did other Phelps design associates, Tom Kane and Emil Perret.

Courses by Hale Irwin (All with Dick Phelps unless otherwise indicated):

California: Cerro Plata CC (1992).
Colorado: Cordillera Resort GC (1992); Lafayette GC (1992).
Florida: Southern Woods CC (1992).
Idaho: Valley Ranch GC (1992).
Illinois: Panther Creek CC (1992).
Indiana: [The] Lakes at Sycamore GC (1992).
Massachusetts: New England CC (1991), with Ron Kern and Gary Kern.
Missouri: Quail Creek GC (1987), with Gary Kern.
North Carolina: Blackrock CC (27 1992).
Texas: Weston Lakes CC (1986), ass't Carlton Gipson.
Japan: Chiba Sports Chinko GC (1989 solo); Nara Sports Shinko CC (1988 solo).

Courses remodeled or expanded by Hale Irwin (All with Dick Phelps unless otherwise indicated):

Hawaii: Kapalua GC (Bay Cse, R. 1986; Village Cse, R. 1987), with Robin Nelson and Rodney Wright.
Missouri: Lakewood GC (R.3 1991 solo).

ARTHUR J. JACKSON
(1894–1981)

BORN: Scotland.
DIED: Oklahoma City, Oklahoma, at age 87.

Born in Scotland, Arthur Jackson traveled to America in the early 1900s to join his stepbrother Leslie Brownlee in the Oklahoma Territory. After constructing the first golf courses in Oklahoma to Brownlee's designs, Jackson served as professional at a succession of clubs. While at Tulsa CC just before World War I, he laid out his first course on the Ponca City estate of E. W. Marland, oil magnate and later governor of Oklahoma.

In 1920 Jackson designed and built Lincoln Park Municipal in Oklahoma City. He remained as its pro until his retirement

in 1952. He continued to design courses throughout his tenure at Lincoln Park and even did a few in the Oklahoma City area after retirement.

Jackson organized the Oklahoma section of the PGA of America. He was an outstanding teacher and trainer of young professional golfers, and among his assistants at Lincoln Park were U. C. Ferguson (who succeeded him at the course), Ralph Hutchinson (who served for many years at Saucon Valley) and Ralph's brother, Willard.

Courses by Arthur Jackson:

Oklahoma: Airport GC (NLE); Lew Wentz Memorial GC (9 1951); Lincoln Park Muni (East Cse 1932; West Cse 1921); Marland Estate GC (9 1915, NLE); McAlester CC (NLE); Northwest Park Muni (1933, NLE); Southwest Park Muni (1932, NLE); Trosper Park GC (1958); Woodson Park GC (NLE).

Courses remodeled or expanded by Arthur Jackson:

Oklahoma: Frederick GC (R. 1949).

THOMAS RIDGEWAY JACKSON, JR.
(1941–   )

BORN: Kennett Square, Pennsylvania.

Tom Jackson graduated from the State University of New York at Farmingdale with a degree in ornamental horticulture, then obtained a second degree in landscape architecture from the University of Georgia. In 1965, he was hired by golf architect Robert Trent Jones and was involved in the construction of several Jones courses in the Southeast. Three years later, Jackson became an assistant to designer George Cobb, and after a three-year apprenticeship, he entered private practice in 1971. Over the next twenty years, working from headquarters near Greenville, South Carolina, Jackson designed or remodeled over fifty courses in the Southeast. He also personally supervised the construction of most of his designs.

Courses by Tom Jackson:

Alabama: Terri Pines CC (1984).
Florida: East Lake Woodlands G&CC (South Cse 1974); Sandestin GC (Baytowne Cse 1985, A. 3rd9 1987; Links Cse 1976).

Tom Jackson, 1990
COURTESY TOM JACKSON

North Carolina: Carolina Shores GC (1975); Granada Farms CC; High Vista CC (1978); Holly Forest GC; Hyland Hills GC (1974); Land Harbour GC (Precision 1982); [The] Lodge GC (1984); Midland Farms CC; Willow Creek GC (9 Precision).
South Carolina: Buck Creek G Plantation (27 1989); Carolina CC (1985); Cheraw State Park GC (1992); [The] Cliffs at Glassy GC (1992); CC of Edisto [FKA Oristo G&RC](1973); Crowfield G&CC (1990); Hickory Knob State Park GC (1982); Links O'Tryon (1988); Myrtle West GC (1989); Pebble Creek CC (27 1976); [The] River C (1983); River Hills G&CC (1988); Stoney Pointe G Cse (1992).

Courses remodeled or expanded by Tom Jackson:

Georgia: Sea Palms G&CC (A.3rd 9 1974).
North Carolina: Blowing Rock CC (R.); Hound Ear CC (R.); Oakwoods CC (R.); Quail Hollow CC (R. 1974); Pinewood CC (R.); Sapphire Lakes CC (A.9 1987); Waynesville CC (R. A.3rd 9 1989).
South Carolina: River Oaks G Plantation (A.3rd 9 1990); Summersett CC (R. 1979).

FRANCIS L. JAMES
(–1952)

DIED: Moscow, Idaho.

Frank James served as western states representative for William H. Tucker & Son in the Northeast during the 1910s and early 1920s and then handled projects in the Pacific Northwest beginning in 1925. In that capacity, James supervised construction of many Tucker layouts as well as the designs of other architects built by Tucker's company.

By 1924 James formed his own design-and-build company. When the economy curtailed course construction in the early 1930s, James worked as pro-manager of a series of clubs, laying out courses on the side during those years. He returned to full-time course design after World War II and remained active until his death in 1952.

Courses by Frank James:

Idaho: Pinecrest Muni; Rolling Hills GC (9 1947); University of Idaho GC (9 1937).
Montana: Missoula CC (9 1949).
Oregon: Pendleton CC (9 1957).
Washington: Earlington G&CC; Jackson Park Muni (1928), ass't William H. Tucker; Lakeway G Cse; Linden G&CC (9), ass't William H. Tucker; Mapleview G&CC (1933); Olympia G&CC (9), ass't William H. Tucker; Roche Harbor GC, ass't William H. Tucker; Sand Point CC (1928), ass't William H. Tucker; Veterans Memorial GC.

Courses remodeled or expanded by Frank James:

Washington: Everett G&CC (A. 9 1928); Walla Walla CC (A.9 1947); Yakima CC (R. 1929).

ALFRED JAMISON
(1908–   )

BORN: Wilmington, Delaware.

Following a long career as a professional, Al Jamison was associated with golf architect Edmund B. Ault in the 1950s. After the firm of Ault and Jamison was dissolved in the latter part of the decade, Jamison designed a few courses on his own before his retirement.

Courses by Al Jamison (All with Edmund B. Ault unless otherwise indicated):

Delaware: Eagle Creek G Cse (9 1961).
Maryland: Chartwell G&CC (1961); Falls Road Muni (1960); Hawthorne CC (9 1960); Lakewood CC (1960); Oakcrest CC (1969); Poolesville GC

(1959); Sligo Park GC (9 1956); Turf Valley CC (North Cse 1959).
Missouri: Meadow Lake Acres CC (1961).
Pennsylvania: Pleasant View GC (1960).
Virginia: Bolling AFB GC (1960); Bushfield CC (9 1962); Chantilly National G&CC (1960); Edwin R. Carr Estate GC (1959); Gordon Trent GC (1962), with *Claude Bingham*; Lake Fairfax GC (1959); Lake Wright GC (1966 *solo*); Loudoun G&CC (1959); Pinecrest CC (Cse No. 2 *solo*); River Bend G&CC [FKA Forest Lake CC](1960); Springfield G&CC (1960).

Courses remodeled or expanded by Al Jamison (All with Edmund B. Ault unless otherwise indicated):

Delaware: Shawnee CC (A.9 1960).
Maryland: Argyle CC (R. 1960); Silver Springs GC (R. 1958).
Virginia: Washington G&CC (R. *solo*).

ALYN J. JANIS

After attending Florida Southern College and North Carolina State University, where he majored in landscape architecture, Al Janis studied design under Dick Wilson and Alfred Tull. He then joined his father, James E. Janis, a former golf course superintendent, in a construction firm. In 1973 he formed Golf by Janis, which became a design-and-build firm. In 1990 he was joined by Alyn Janis, Jr., making three generations in the business.

Courses by Al Janis:

Maryland: Pine Shore GC (27 Precision 1985); Willow Springs GC (Precision 1991).

Courses remodeled or expanded by Al Janis:

Delaware: Sussex Pines CC (A.9).
New Jersey: Seaview GC (Pines Cse, R. A.3 1990).
Pennsylvania: Limekiln GC (A.9 1987); Pocono Farms (A.9 1982).

DONALD RAY JANUARY
(1929–   )

BORN: Plainfield, Texas.

Well-known touring professional Don January, the 1967 PGA champion, collab-

Don January, circa 1985 COURTESY DON JANUARY

orated with Billy Martindale on the planning of several courses in the Southwest between 1972 and 1975. The partnership dissolved when January resumed playing the Tour in 1976. In the 1980s January was one of the early mainstays of the lucrative Senior Tour full-time. But he quit competitive golf in 1987 and in 1990 formed a new firm in partnership with his son Tim, a former employee of Wadsworth Construction. January's new company, which included designer Craig Curry, who had previously worked for Jack Nicklaus and Larry Nelson, sought to return old-style principles to modern golf design.

Courses by Don January (All with Billy Martindale unless otherwise indicated):

Oklahoma: Walnut Creek CC (1976).
Texas: Great Hills GC; Los Rios CC (1974); Oakmont CC (1986), with Roger Packard; [The] Pinnacle C (9); Plano Muni; Royal Oaks CC (1970); Walnut Creek GC; Woodcrest CC; Woodland Hills GC (1973).

Courses remodeled or expanded by Don January (All with Billy Martindale unless otherwise indicated):

Texas: Lake Country Estates GC (A.9 1975).

ALFRED HARRY FRENCH JIGGENS
(1908–1985), BIGCA

BORN: England.
DIED: Chester, England, at age 76.

A chartered surveyor and civil engineer, A. H. F. Jiggens served in local governments for over fifty years. Retiring in 1968, "Jigg" joined the golf design firm of

Fred W. Hawtree. Concentrating primarily on the business aspects of the firm and engineering problems of courses, Jigg personally handled the designs of a dozen layouts in the late 1970s. Jiggens was a founding member of the British Association of Golf Course Architects, the forerunner to the BIGCA, and was inducted as a senior member shortly before his death.

Courses by A. H. F. Jiggens (All with Fred W. Hawtree):

England: Chester GC (1973); Congleton GC; Duxbury Park GC (1975), and Martin Hawtree; Eastham Lodge GC (9 1975), and Martin Hawtree; Enmore Park GC (9 1975, A.9 1979); Malkins Bank GC (1980); Normanby Hall GC (1978), and Martin Hawtree; Scunthorpe GC; Tamworth Muni (1975), and Martin Hawtree; Widnes Muni (9 1977).
Ireland: Corballis GC; Forest Little GC (1972); Westport GC, and Martin Hawtree.

Courses remodeled or expanded by A. H. F. Jiggens (All with Fred W. Hawtree):

England: Bromborough GC (R.); Chorley GC (R.); Huyton & Prescot GC (R.); Ipswich GC (A.9); Nelson GC (A.9); Oakdale GC (R.7 1977); Wellingborough GC (R.9 A.9 1983), and Martin Hawtree; Worcestershire GC (A.9); Worsley GC (A.9).
Ireland: Woodbrook GC (R. A.2), and Martin Hawtree.
Wales: Nefyn and District GC (R.).

LEO I. JOHNSON
(1918–   )

BORN: Homer, Nebraska.

In 1935 Leo Johnson began working at Sioux City (Iowa) CC, where he eventually became course superintendent. He designed, built, owned and operated a nine-hole par 3 course, Sun Valley GC, in Sioux City in the 1950s. Johnson left Sioux City in 1958 to pursue a career in course design and was still active in the 1970s, based in the Phoenix-Tucson area.

Courses by Leo Johnson:

Iowa: Ankeny G&CC (9); Brookside GC (1965); Emerald Hills GC (1973); Quail Creek GC (1970); River View C (1970); Sun Valley CC (9 Par 3 1961).

Kansas: [The] Highlands GC [FKA Lakewood CC](1972).
Minnesota: Brightwood Hills GC (1969); Worthington CC.
Montana: Cottonwood CC (9 1962).
North Dakota: Cando GC (1968); Riverwood Muni (1969).

Courses remodeled or expanded by Leo Johnson:

Kansas: Council Grove CC (R.9 1970); Elkhart GC (R.9 1969); Eureka GC (R.9 1969).
Nebraska: Kearney CC (R.9 A.9 1972).

Tom Johnson, 1990
COURTESY ASGCA

THOMAS SIDNEY JOHNSON, JR.
(1955–   ), ASGCA

BORN: Charlotte, North Carolina.

Tom Johnson obtained a turfgrass management degree in 1976 and a Bachelor of Science degree in landscape architecture in 1981 from North Carolina State University. He then worked on golf course construction crews throughout the southeastern United States for six years. In 1987 he was hired by the Atlanta-based firm of Denis Griffiths and Associates and soon progressed from construction supervisor to design associate.

Courses by Tom Johnson (All as assistant to Denis Griffiths):

Georgia: Château Elan GC (1989); Chicopee Woods G Cse (1991); Georgia Veterans Memorial State Park G Cse (1991); River Pines GC (9 Par 3 1991).
Ohio: Bent Tree GC (1988); Heatherwoode GC (1991).
South Carolina: CC of Callawassie (Putting Cse 1988); Eastport Marina & CC (1988).
Japan: Sasakami Cayman G Park (Cayman 1990).
Thailand: Chiang Mai CC (1991); Phoenix G&CC (27 1992).

Courses remodeled or expanded by Tom Johnson (All as assistant to Denis Griffiths):

Alabama: Riverchase CC (R.3 1989).
Georgia: Chattahoochee CC (R.2 1988); Horseshoe Bend CC (R.17 1989).

WALTER IRVING JOHNSON, JR.

Walter Johnson was associated with golf architect Donald Ross as a construction superintendent. He also practiced golf architecture on his own on a part-time basis during his years with Ross. Following Ross's death in 1948, Johnson became a full-time golf course architect.

Courses by Walter Johnson (All as assistant to Donald Ross unless otherwise indicated):

Florida: Palma Sola GC (1924).
Massachusetts: Fresh Pond Muni (9 1932); Sun Valley GC (routing).
Rhode Island: North Kingstown Muni (1944).

Courses remodeled or expanded by Walter Johnson (All as assistant to Donald Ross unless otherwise indicated):

North Carolina: CC of Salisbury (R.).
Rhode Island: Potowomut CC (A.9 1928).

WILLIAM H. JOHNSON
(1898–1979), ASGCA

BORN: Pittsburg, Kansas.
DIED: Los Angeles, California, at age 80.

Bill Johnson, who had worked on a number of railroad crews as a youth, joined Willie Watson's construction crew

William H. Johnson, circa 1965
COLLECTION RON WHITTEN

at Lake Arrowhead, California, in 1924. After working on other course construction projects for Watson and William P. Bell, Johnson became greenkeeper of the Los Angeles County Parks System in 1931. He remained in that position until 1958, gaining a wide reputation as a turfgrass expert. Johnson designed his first golf course, a new nine-hole "Roosevelt" layout at Griffith Park, when the original course was taken over by an expansion of the nearby zoo. Johnson began designing courses steadily after World War II, working first on a series of collaborations with William P. Bell and later on his own. An honorary member of the Southern California PGA, Johnson belonged to the GCSAA and served as its president in 1951.

Courses by William H. Johnson:

California: Alondra Park GC (Cse No. 1 1947), with William P. Bell; Arroyo Seco GC (Par 3 1960); Big Tee GC (9 Par 3 1947); Compton GC (9 Par 3 1952); DeBell GC (1958), with William F. Bell; Devonshire GC (27 Par 3 1959); Donneybrook GC (Par 3 1961, NLE); El Caballero CC (1957); El Camino CC (1953); Glen Avon GC (Par 3 1959); Griffith Park GC (Coolidge Cse, 9 Par 3 1941; Los Feliz Cse, 9 Par 3 1944; Roosevelt Cse, 9 1933); Harbor Park GC (9 1957); Knollwood CC (1957), with William F. Bell; Massacre Canyon Inn & CC (River Cse, 9 1958, NLE); Oceanside Center City GC (1957); Pala Mesa G&TC (1961); Pedley Par 3 GC (Par 3); Rancho Park GC (1947), with William P. Bell; Roy Rogers GC (9 Par 3 1956); San Fernando VA Hospital GC (9 Par 3); San Gorgonio GC (9 Par 3 1962); Sepulveda GC (Balboa Cse 1953; Encino Cse 1953), with William F. Bell and William P. Bell; Sepulveda VA Hospital GC (9 Par 3); Silver Creek GC (9 1960); Singing Hills CC (Willow Glen Cse 1953), with William F. Bell and William P. Bell; South Gate GC (9 Par 3 1948); Squires GC (9 Par 3 1961); Twin Lakes GC (Par 3 1954).

Courses remodeled or expanded by William H. Johnson:

California: Bel-Air CC (R.3 1958); Glendora CC (R.9); Griffith Park GC (Harding Cse, R.9 1948; Wilson Cse, R. 1948); Victoria GC (R.3 1958).

Johnny Johnston, circa 1960 COURTESY KAREN PHILLIPS

CLEMENT B. JOHNSTON (1922–1982)

BORN: North Carolina.
DIED: Enfield, North Carolina, at age 60.
INTERRED: Wake Forest, North Carolina.

A longtime PGA professional, "Johnny" Johnston served as golf coach for Wake Forest in the late 1940s and early 1950s for teams that included the young Arnold Palmer. Johnston later served as head professional at several North Carolina clubs, including Sea Scape GC in Kitty Hawk and Echo Farms G&CC in Wilmington. A former officer in the Carolinas PGA and its "Pro of the Year" in 1975, Johnston became a Quarter Century member of the PGA of America shortly before his death in 1982.

Johnston dabbled in golf course design throughout his professional life. His first design was at Reidsville, North Carolina, which he did after leaving Wake Forest. Over the years he handled several low-budget layouts around North Carolina. In his last years he was assisted by his son Clyde, who subsequently pursued a full-time career in golf architecture.

Courses designed by Johnny Johnston:

North Carolina: Sumner Hills GC, with Clyde Johnston; Tamarac GC (1956); Wolf Creek GC (9 1953).

Courses remodeled or expanded by Johnny Johnston:

North Carolina: Echo Farms G&CC (R. 1978), with Clyde Johnston; Scotfield CC (R.), with Clyde Johnston.

CLYDE B. JOHNSTON (1952–   ), ASGCA

BORN: Houston, Texas.

The son of onetime Wake Forest coach Johnny Johnston, Clyde Johnston learned

the game at an early age. As a teenager he assisted his father in pro shop operations and in several course-remodeling projects.

Johnston obtained a Bachelor of Landscape Architecture degree from North Carolina State University in 1973. He then worked for two years as a landscape architect for Willard C. Byrd and Associates in Atlanta. After a year with the golf design firm of Kirby, Player and Associates, Johnston rejoined Byrd in 1977, this time serving as both a landscape and golf course architect. Johnston operated a branch of the firm from the South Carolina coast, where he supervised several golf design projects on Hilton Head Island and the Charleston area.

In 1988, Clyde Johnston formed his own golf design practice, based on Hilton Head Island. On some of his early solo projects, former Masters and U.S. Open champion Fuzzy Zoeller served as his design consultant.

Courses by Clyde Johnston:

California: Shadowridge Creek CC (1992).
Florida: Jacksonville G&CC (1989), with Fuzzy Zoeller; Longboat Key C (Harborside Cse 1983), ass't Willard Byrd.
Georgia: [The] Landings at Skidaway Island (Plantation Cse 1984), ass't Willard Byrd; Southerness GC (1991).
Kentucky: Andover G&CC (1990).
North Carolina: Ocean Harbour G Links (1989); Sumner Hills GC, with Johnny Johnston.

Clyde Johnston, 1990 COURTESY CLYDE JOHNSTON

South Carolina: Heather Glen G Links (1987, ass't Willard Byrd; A.3rd 9 1990); Hope Plantation G&CC (1989); Island West GC (1991), with Fuzzy Zoeller; Old South G Links (1991); Patriots Point G Links (1984), ass't Willard Byrd; Port Royal GC

(Planters Row Cse 1984), ass't Willard Byrd; Wexford GC (1984), ass't Willard Byrd.

Courses remodeled or expanded by Clyde Johnston:

Alabama: CC of Mobile (R.) ass't Willard Byrd.

Florida: Longboat Key C (Islandside Cse, R. 1984), ass't Willard Byrd; Ponce de León Resort & CC (R.2 A.2 1977), ass't Willard Byrd.

Georgia: Griffin CC (A.9), ass't Willard Byrd.

Maryland: Chestnut Ridge CC (R. 1988).

North Carolina: Alamance CC (R.), ass't Willard Byrd; Echo Farms G&CC (R. 1978), with Johnny Johnston; Emory-wood CC (R. 1980), ass't Willard Byrd; Scotfield CC (R.), with Johnny Johnston.

South Carolina: Palmetto Dunes Resort (Fazio Cse, R. 1989); Port Royal GC (Barony and Robbers Row Cses, R. 1984), ass't Willard Byrd; Sea Pines Plantation GC (Sea Marsh Cse, R. 1990); Shipyard GC (A.3rd 9 1982), ass't Willard Byrd.

WILLIAM JOHNSTON
(1925–   )

BORN: Donora, Pennsylvania.

Bill Johnston grew up in Ogden, Utah. After service in the navy during World War II, he attended the University of Utah, where he played on the golf team. Upon his graduation in 1950, he became a professional golfer and that same year participated in his first golf course design.

Johnston spent fifteen years on the PGA Tour, during which he won the Texas and Utah opens. He then served as head professional at a series of Arizona golf clubs and resumed designing golf courses. After turning 55, Johnston divided his time between golf design and competition on the newly formed Senior PGA Tour.

Courses by Bill Johnston:

Arizona: Arizona Biltmore GC (Links Cse 1978); Eagle Creek GC (1989); [The] Pointe at Lookout Mountain GC (1989).

Texas: Dominion CC (1985); Feather Bay G&CC (1989); Tapatio Springs CC (1981).

Utah: Dinaland GC (9 1950).

Bill Johnston, circa 1985 COLLECTION RON WHITTEN

Courses remodeled or expanded by Bill Johnston:

Arizona: Elden Hills GC (R. 1979).

ROBERT JOHNSTONE
(–1937)

BORN: North Berwick, Scotland.
DIED: Seattle, Washington.

In 1905 Robert Johnstone became professional at Seattle GC, a position he held for the rest of his life. He helped lay out a new course for the club in 1907, then did several other designs in the Pacific Northwest.

Courses by Robert Johnstone:

California: Ingleside GC (1925, NLE); Mountaindale CC (NLE); Potrero G&CC (1909, NLE); Presidio GC (1914).

Washington: Inglewood CC (1923), with A. Vernon Macan; Jefferson Park Muni (1917), with *Jim Barnes*; Lake Ridge GC (1930); Mercer Island G&CC; Rainier G&CC; Seattle GC (1907), with *John Ball*; Spokane CC, with *Jim Barnes*.

Courses remodeled or expanded by Robert Johnstone:

Washington: Seattle GC (R.).

ALEXANDER H. JOLLY
(1882–1948)

BORN: St. Andrews, Scotland.
DIED: Michigan at age 66.

A. H. Jolly was one of six brothers who were active in the business world of golf in the United States and Canada between 1901 and 1965. Jolly designed several

courses in the States and at each stayed on for a time as full-time summer or winter professional.

Courses by A. H. Jolly:

Arizona: Douglas G & Social C (1947).
Michigan: Gladstone CC (9 1936); North Shore GC, Menominee (1928); Riverside CC (1923).
Wisconsin: Oconto GC (9 1929).

Courses remodeled or expanded by A. H. Jolly:

Arizona: Nogales CC (R. 1945, NLE).

Rees Jones, 1987 COURTESY REES JONES

REES LEE JONES
(1941–   ), ASGCA, PRESIDENT 1978

BORN: Montclair, New Jersey.

Rees Jones graduated from Yale University with a degree in history in 1963 and went on to study landscape architecture at Harvard University's Graduate School of Design. In 1965 he joined his father's firm, Robert Trent Jones Inc., where he was involved in the design or supervision of over fifty golf courses. Rees Jones entered private practice in golf course design in 1974 and subsequently planned numerous layouts that rivaled his father's for beauty, challenge and attention.

In 1974 Jones coauthored the influential Urban Land Institute publication *Golf Course Developments*. Jones himself designed, collaborated on the design of or supervised the construction of each of the developments described in the book. In 1978 he became the youngest person to serve as president of the ASGCA.

In the 1980s Rees Jones became a leading figure in golf architecture, in part because of a series of well-received remodeling projects. His first triumph was his sensitive restoration of The Country Club at

Brookline, Massachusetts, for the 1988 U.S. Open. Then came modifications to Hazeltine National GC for the 1991 U.S. Open, followed by a major remodeling of Congressional CC's Blue Cse.

His original designs also set new standards for clarity and playability in design. Jones preached and practiced what he termed "definition in design." He wanted his holes to indicate clearly to golfers how they should play them. His hazards were visible, his bunkering directional, his targets accessible and his mounds deflected errant balls back into play.

Courses by Rees Jones:

Alabama: Alpine Bay Y&CC (1973), ass't Robert Trent Jones.

Connecticut: Fairview CC (1969), ass't Robert Trent Jones.

Florida: Inverrary CC (East Cse 1970; South Cse [Precision] 1970; West Cse 1971), ass't Robert Trent Jones; Key West Resort GC (1983); Kings Point Executive G Cse (Cse No. 1 [Precision] 1973, Cse No. 2 [Par 3] 1974), ass't Robert Trent Jones; Sun City Center G&CC (Kings Point Cse [Precision] 1974), ass't Robert Trent Jones; Turnberry Isle G&CC (North Cse 1972; South Cse 1971), ass't Robert Trent Jones.

Georgia: Gordon Lakes GC (1975), ass't Robert Trent Jones; Jones Creek GC (1985); Metropolitan G&TC [FKA Fairington G&TC](1968), ass't Robert Trent Jones; Southbridge GC (1989).

Illinois: [The] Rail GC (1974), ass't Robert Trent Jones.

Kentucky: Marriott's Griffin Gate GC (1981).

Maryland: Ocean Pines G&CC (1971), ass't Robert Trent Jones.

Massachusetts: Sheraton Tara Hotel & GC [FKA Tara Ferncroft & Topsfield CC](1970), ass't Robert Trent Jones.

New Jersey: Cherry Valley C (1992); Panther Valley CC (1969), ass't Robert Trent Jones; Pinch Brook GC (Precision 1983).

New York: Atlantic GC (1992); Bristol Harbor Village GC (1975), ass't Robert Trent Jones; Crag Burn C (1971), ass't Robert Trent Jones; Montauk Downs G&RC (1968), ass't Robert Trent Jones; Ransom Oaks CC (1971), ass't Robert Trent Jones.

North Carolina: Bryan Park GC (Champions Cse 1990); Carolina Lakes CC (1980); Greenbrier GC (1988); Harbour Pointe GC (9 1986); [The]

Peninsula C (1990); Pinehurst CC (Cse No. 7 1986); Sea Trail G Links (Rees Jones Cse 1989); Talamore GC (1991).

Pennsylvania: Eagle Lodge GC (1982).

South Carolina: Arcadian Shores G&RC (1974); Bear Creek GC (1980); Charleston National CC (1989); CC of Hilton Head (1986); Gator Hole GC (1980); Greenville CC (Chanticleer Cse 1969), ass't Robert Trent Jones; Haig Point C (20 1986, A.9 1989); Oyster Reef GC (1982); Palmetto Dunes GC (Jones Cse 1969), ass't Robert Trent Jones; Waterway Hills GC (27 1975); Woodside Plantation C (Wysteria Cse 1987).

Tennessee: Graysburg Hills GC (1979).

Texas: Rayburn G&CC (Blue Nine 1973), ass't Robert Trent Jones; Sugar Creek CC (1970, A.3rd 9 1974), ass't Robert Trent Jones.

Virginia: Glenwood GC (1985); Golden Horseshoe GC (Green Cse 1991); Greenbrier CC (1987); Hell's Point GC (1982); Honey Bee GC (1988); Stoney Creek GC (1989).

West Virginia: Cacapon Springs GC (1974), ass't Robert Trent Jones.

Wisconsin: [The] Springs GC (1969), ass't Robert Trent Jones.

England: Oxfordshire GC (1992).

South West Africa: Swakopmund GC (9 1977).

Courses remodeled or expanded by Rees Jones:

California: La Jolla CC (R. 1983).

Connecticut: Redding CC (A.9 1980).

Florida: Crystal Lake CC [FKA Crystal Lago GC] (R. 1981).

Georgia: Sea Island GC (Plantation and Seaside Nines, R. 1992).

Illinois: Skokie CC (R. 1984).

Indiana: Fort Wayne CC (R. 1978).

Kansas: Kansas City CC (R. 1978; R. 1988).

Maryland: Congressional CC (Blue Cse, R. 1989).

Massachusetts: [The] Country Club, Brookline (R. 1985); CC of New Seabury (Blue Cse, R. 1988; Green Cse, R. 1986).

Michigan: Leland CC (R.9 A.9 1979).

Minnesota: Hazeltine National GC (R. 1990).

New Jersey: Baltusrol GC (Lower Cse, R. 1992); Canoe Brook CC (North Cse, R. 1973, ass't Robert Trent Jones; South Cse, R. 1984); Flanders Valley GC (White & Blue Cse, R.4 A.9 1982);

Forest Hill Field C (R. 1986); Montclair GC (R. 1977; R. 1983); Morris County GC (R. 1987); Ridgewood CC (R. 1988); Woodcrest CC (R.1 1983).

New York: Cold Spring G&CC (R. 1968), ass't Robert Trent Jones; Crag Burn Club (R. 1988); Muttontown G&CC (R. 1968), ass't Robert Trent Jones; Rye GC (R. 1982); Tam O'Shanter GC (R. 1967); Westchester CC (South Cse, R. 1983; West Cse., R. 1982).

North Carolina: Carmel CC (North Cse, R. 1988; South Cse, R. 1988); CC of North Carolina (Dogwood Cse, R. 1979); Myers Park CC (R. 1978, R. 1983); Pinehurst CC (Cse No. 4, R. 1982).

South Carolina: Palmetto GC (R. 1989); Pinetuck GC (R. 1976).

Tennessee: Meadowview GC (R. 1978).

Vermont: Equinox CC (R. 1991).

Virginia: Boonsboro CC (R. 1981); Salisbury CC (R. 1988); Shenandoah Valley CC (R. 1984).

Ontario: Hamilton G&CC (R. 1982).

ROBERT TRENT JONES
(1906–), ASGCA, CHARTER MEMBER; PRESIDENT 1950

BORN: Ince, England.

Robert Trent Jones moved to the United States with his parents in 1911. He became a scratch golfer while still a teenager and set a course record at the age of sixteen while playing in the Rochester City Golf Championship. He was low Amateur in the 1927 Canadian Open. Jones attended Cornell University, where he followed a course of studies personally selected to prepare himself for a career in golf course architecture. Completing this program in 1930, he undertook additional courses in art. At Cornell he designed several greens at the Sodus Bay GC in New York. The course was subsequently remodeled, but two of his greens were retained by the club as the earliest examples of Jones's work.

In 1930 Jones became a partner with Canadian golf architect Stanley Thompson in the firm of Thompson, Jones & Co., with offices in Toronto and New York. These two architects were profoundly influential in the nearly universal acceptance of strategic design in North America. Jones's often quoted philosophy was that every hole should be a hard par but an easy bogey.

By the mid-1960s Robert Trent Jones had become the most widely known and probably the most influential course architect in history. He served as architectural consultant to numerous courses hosting major championship tournaments, many of them courses of his own design. By 1990 he had planned over 450 courses in play in forty-two states and twenty-three countries and had remodeled many others, logging an estimated 300,000 miles by air annually in the process.

Jones and his wife, the former Ione Tefft Davis of Montclair, New Jersey, raised two sons, Robert Jr. and Rees, both of whom followed their father in the practice of golf architecture. He was the author of many essays of golf course architecture, including contributions to Herbert Warren Wind's *The Complete Golfer* (1954), Will Grimsley's *Golf—Its History, Events, and People* (1966) and Martin Sutton's *Golf Courses—Design, Construction and Upkeep* (2nd ed., 1950). The Sutton work featured several of Jones's freehand sketches of golf holes. In 1989 his long-awaited autobiography, *Golf's Magnificent Challenge*, coauthored with Larry Dennis, was published.

He was also the subject of countless articles, the most significant of which was Wind's profile in *The New Yorker* of August 4, 1951, which established the profession of golf course architecture on a higher level of public awareness.

Robert Trent Jones was the first recipient of the ASGCA's Donald Ross Award for outstanding contributions to golf course architecture. He became an advisory member of the National Institute of Social Science, a member of the American Academy of Achievement and recipient of its 1972 Golden Plate Award, and was granted membership to the Royal and Ancient Golf Club of St. Andrew. In 1981 Jones was given the William D. Richardson Award by the GWAA in recognition of his consistent outstanding contributions. That same year the Metropolitan Golf Association presented him with its Distinguished Service Award. In 1987 the GCSAA honored him with its Old Tom Morris Award.

By 1990 Trent Jones had been engaged in golf course architecture for sixty years, a record that exceeded even that of Old Tom Morris. By then, his principal associate, golf architect Roger Rulewich, was handling the bulk of the workload. But the name Robert Trent Jones was still the most recognizable in golf, and that year two courses were named in his honor, one a

Robert Trent Jones, 1968 COLLECTION RON WHITTEN

new design, one an existing course. Also that year Jones's company was awarded the largest golf design contract in history, a series of 54-hole daily-fee complexes in Alabama for Sunbelt Golf, Inc., financed in part by that state's public-employee retirement system. By 1991 the first four sets of the Robert Trent Jones Trail of Golf were under construction in various parts of Alabama.

Courses by Robert Trent Jones:

Alabama: Alpine Bay GC (1972); Grand National GC (Auburn Cse 1993; Opelika Cse 1992; Short Cse [Par 3] 1992); Hampton Cove GC (Highland Cse 1992; Short Cse [Par 3] 1992; Lowland Cse 1992); Magnolia Grove GC (Crossings Cse 1992; Falls Cse 1992; Short Cse [Par 3] 1992); Oxmoor Valley GC (Ridge Cse 1992; Short Cse [Par 3] 1992; Valley Cse 1992); Turtle Point Y&CC (1964).

Alaska: Eagleglen G Cse, Elmendorf AFB (1972).

Arizona: Rio Rico GC (1971); Village of Oak Creek CC (9 1967, A.9 1977); Wigwam G&CC [FKA Goodyear G&CC] (Blue Cse 1965; Gold Cse 1965).

California: Birnam Wood GC (1968); Calabasas Park CC (1968); El Dorado Hills GC (Precision 1964); Laguna Seca G Ranch (1970); Lake Shastina G&CC (27 1972); Mission Viejo CC (1966); Pauma Valley CC (1960); Rancho California GC [FKA Murrieta CC](1970); Silverado CC (South Cse 1967); Spring Valley Lake CC (1971); Spyglass Hill G Links (1966); Sunset Dunes GC (Par 3 1963); Tecolote Canyon GC (Precision 1964); Valencia GC (1969).

Colorado: Eisenhower GC (Blue Cse 1959).

Connecticut: Black Hall C (1967); Bruce Memorial GC (1966); Fairview CC (1968); Lyman Meadow GC (1969); Patterson C (1946); Rockrimmon CC (9 1949).

Delaware: Wilmington CC (South Cse 1960).

Florida: All-American GC (Par 3 1964); American Golfers C (Precision 1958); Apollo Beach G & Sea C (9 1962); Beauclerc CC (9 1955); Coral Ridge CC (1956); GC of Miami (East Cse 1962; North Cse [Par 3] 1962, NLE; West Cse 1962); Flamingo Island C (1990); Grenelefe G&RC (West Cse [Routing] 1971); Inverrary CC (East Cse 1970; South Cse [Precision] 1970; West Cse 1971); Kings Point Executive G Cse (Cse No. 1 [Precision] 1972; Cse No. 2 [Par 3] 1973); MacDonald Estate GC (2 1955); MetroWest CC (1987); Patrick AFB GC (9 1961); Ponte Vedra C (Lagoon Cse, 9 1962); Royal Palm Y&CC (1960); Sun City Center G&CC (Kings Point Cse [Precision] 1974); Turnberry Isle G&CC (North Cse 1974; South Cse 1971).

Georgia: Atlanta Athletic C (Highlands Cse, 9 1967; Riverside Cse 1967); Chattahoochee GC (1959); Fort Benning G&CC (Pineside Cse, 9 1950); Gordon Lakes GC (1975); Metropolitan G&TC (1968); Peachtree GC (1948), with Robert Tyre Jones, Jr; Standard C (1951, NLE); Stone Mountain GC (Stonemont Cse 1968); Sunset Hills CC (9 1949); University of Georgia GC (1968).

Hawaii: Hawaii Kai G Cse (Executive Cse [Precision] 1960); Mauna Kea Beach Hotel GC (1965); Royal Kaanapali GC (North Cse 1962).

Idaho: Elkhorn GC (1975).

Illinois: Hilldale GC (1972); Norris Estate GC (9 1935, NLE); Pottawatomie Park GC (9 1936); [The] Rail GC (1974).

Indiana: Otter Creek G Cse (1959).

Kansas: Crestview CC (North Cse 1969; South Cse, 9 1969); Custer Hill GC (9 1960).

Kentucky: CC of Paducah (1979).

Louisiana: Santa Maria GC (1987); Timberlane CC (1959).

Maine: Evergreen Valley GC (9 1975, NLE).

Maryland: Camp David GC (1 1954); Ocean Pines G&CC (1972); Walden GC [FKA Golden Triangle GC](9 1969).

Massachusetts: Crumpin-Fox C (9 1978, A.9 1989); Ipswich CC (1989); Round Hill C (9 routing); Tara Ferncroft CC (1970).

Michigan: Boyne Highlands GC (Heather Cse 1968); Point O'Woods G&CC (1958); Treetops GC (Jones Cse 1987).

Minnesota: Hazeltine National GC (1962); Jonathan Par-30 GC (9 Precision 1974).

Missouri: Bellerive CC (1960); CC at the Legends (1989); [The] Lodge of Four Seasons GC (1974); Old Warson CC (1955).

Montana: Yellowstone G&CC (1959).

Nebraska: Willow Lakes GC (1964).

Nevada: Incline Green GC (Precision 1971); Incline Village GC (1964); Lake Ridge G Cse (1971).

New Hampshire: Portsmouth G&CC (1957).

New Jersey: Duke Estate GC (9 1940, NLE); Hominy Hill GC (1965); Lyons VA Hospital GC (9 1947); Metedeconk National GC (1987, A.3rd 9 1990); Panther Valley CC (1969); Rancocas CC (1966); [The] Spa GC ([9 Precision] 1988); Tammy Brook CC (1962); Upper Montclair CC (27 1956); Wayne CC (1951, NLE).

New York: Albany CC (1963); Amsterdam Muni (1938); Bristol Harbor Village GC (1975); Crag Burn C (1971); Durand-Eastman Park G Cse (1934); Eisenhower Park GC (Blue Cse 1951; White Cse 1950); Fallsview Hotel GC (9 1962); Fox Hills G&CC (1966); Frear Park G Cse (9 1963); Glen Oak GC (1971); Green Lakes State Park G Cse (1935); Hancock Muni (9 1947, NLE); Hempstead GC at Lido (1956); IBM CC, Poughkeepsie (9 1945, A.9 1948); James Baird State Park G Cse (1948); Malone GC (New Cse 1986); Marine Park GC (1963); Midvale G&CC (1931), with Stanley Thompson; Montauk G&RC (1968); North Hills CC (1961); Pines Hotel G Cse (9 1960); Quaker Hill GC (9 1935); Radisson Greens GC (1976); Robert Trent Jones G Cse, Cornell University (9 1937, A.9 1953); Seven Oaks GC (9 1955; A.9 1965); Sodus Point GC (9 1926); Tuxedo Park C (1947); West Point GC (1949); Wiltwyck CC (1955).

North Carolina: Carolina Trace G&CC (Lake Cse 1971; Creek Cse, 9 1979, A.9 1986); Duke University GC (1957); Tanglewood GC (East Cse, 9 1965, A.9 1970; West Cse 1957).

Ohio: Arthur Raymond G Cse (1949); Champions of Columbus G Cse [FKA Winding Hollow CC](1952); Firestone CC (North Cse 1969; South Cse 1959).

Oregon: Eugene CC (1967); Heron Lakes G Cse (27 1971).

Pennsylvania: Tamiment CC (1947).

South Carolina: Dunes G&BC (1949); Greenville CC (Chanticleer Cse 1970); Palmetto Dunes CC (Jones Cse 1969); Seabrook Island GC (Crooked Oaks Cse 1981).

Tennessee: Link Hills CC (1947); Scona Lodge CC (9 1957).

Texas: Corpus Christi CC (1965); Horseshoe Bay CC (Applerock Cse 1985; Ram Rock Cse 1981; Slick Rock Cse 1973); Houston CC (1957); Rayburn G&CC (Blue Nine, 9 1973); Shady Oaks CC (1959), with Lawrence Hughes and Ralph Plummer; Sugar Creek CC (27 1970).

Vermont: Sugarbush GC (1965).

Virginia: Fort Belvoir GC (9 1949); Golden Horseshoe GC (Gold Cse 1964; Spotswood Cse [9 Precision] 1965); Lower Cascades GC (1961); Robert Trent Jones GC (1991); Stumpy Lake GC (1957).

West Virginia: Bel-Meadow G&CC (1967); Cacapon Springs GC (1973); Speidel GC (1972).

Wisconsin: Madeline Island G Links (1967); [The] Springs GC (1969).

Alberta: Kananaskis Country GC (Mount Kidd Cse 1984; Mount Lorette Cse 1983).

British Columbia: Rivershore GC (1981).

Ontario: London Hunt & CC (1962).

Bahamas: Cotton Bay C (1955).

Belgium: G de Bercuit (1968).

Bermuda: Port Royal GC (1970); St. George's GC (Precision 1985).

Brazil: Brasília GC (1970); Teresopolis GC (9 1934), with Stanley Thompson.

Colombia: El Rincon C (1963).

Dominican Republic: Playa Dorada GC (1979).

England: Moor Allerton GC (27 1970).

France: Chamonix GC (1983); Golf de Bondues (Blue Cse, 9 1968); Golf de la Côte d'Argent Moliets (27 1988); Golf de la Grande Motte (Long Cse 1988; Short Cse [Precision] 1988); Golf de Riviera (1991); Golf de Sperone (1990); Golf de Valescure (1989); Golf de Vidauban (1992); Golf Esterel (1992).

Germany: Bodensee GC (1987).

Guadeloupe: Golf de St. François (1978).

Ireland: Ballybunion GC (New Cse 1985).

Italy: CC Castelgandolfo (1988); GC Castelconturbia (27 1987); I Roveri GC (27 1976).

Jamaica: Half Moon-Rose Hall GC (1961).

Japan: Karuizawa Golf (Higashi Cse 1972; Kita Cse 1972; Minami Cse 1972; Nishi Cse 1972).

Martinique: Empress Josephine GC (1977).

Mexico: Tres Vidas en la Playa (East Cse 1969, NLE; West Cse 1969, NLE).

Morocco: Golf de la Palmeriae (1991); Royal Palace GC d'Agadir (1987); Royal G Dar es Salaam (Blue Cse 1974; Green Cse [9] 1974; Red Cse 1971).

Philippines: Luisita GC (1968).

Portugal: Quinta da Marinha GC (1985); Troia GC (1979).

Puerto Rico: Cerromar Beach GC (North Cse 1972; South Cse 1972); Dorado Beach GC (East Cse, 9 1958, A.9 1961; West Cse, 9 1958, A.9 1966).

Sardinia: Pevero GC (1972).

Spain: C de G Mijas (Los Lagos Cse 1976; Los Olivos Cse 1984); El Bosque GC (1975); Golf La Duquesa (1987); La Canada GC (9 1991); Marbella G&CC (1990); Nueva Andalucía GC (Las Brisas Cse 1968; Par 3 Cse 1968; Los Naranjos Cse 1977); Sotogrande GC (Old Cse 1964; Short Cse [9 Par 3] 1964); Valderrama GC [FKA Sotogrande GC (New Cse)](1975).

Switzerland: Geneva G&CC (1973).

Virgin Islands: Carambola Beach GC [FKA Fountain Valley GC](1967).

Courses remodeled or expanded by Robert Trent Jones:

Alabama: CC of Birmingham (West Cse, R. 1959); Lakewood GC (Dogwood Cse, R. 1949).

Arkansas: North Hills CC (R. 1979).

California: Annandale CC (R. 1970); California GC of San Francisco (R. 1968); El Caballero CC (R. 1964); Glendora CC (R. 1970); Hacienda CC (R. 1971); Menlo CC (R. 1970); Olympic C (Lake Cse, R. 1954); San Gabriel CC (R. 1972); Silverado CC (North Cse, R. 1967); Stanford University GC (R. 1968).

Colorado: Broadmoor GC (East Cse, A.9 1954; West Cse, A.9 1965).

Connecticut: CC of Fairfield (R. 1960); CC of New Canaan (R. 1960); Greenwich CC (R. 1963); Hartford GC (R.2

1966); Innis Arden GC (R. 1960); Ridgewood CC (R. 1959); Round Hill C (R. 1952; R. 1970).

Florida: Boca Raton Hotel & C (R. 1963); CC of Orlando (R. 1959); La Gorce CC (R. 1953); Melreese GC (R. A.4 1966); Ponte Vedra C (Ocean Cse, R. 1954).

Georgia: Augusta National GC (R.3 1946; R. 1950); Sea Island GC (Plantation and Seaside Nines, R. 1949).

Illinois: St. Charles CC (R. 1936).

Maine: Portland CC (R. 1951).

Maryland: Burning Tree C (R. 1963; R. 1977); Chevy Chase CC (R. 1948); Congressional CC (Blue Cse, A. 9 1957; R. 1962; R. 1969); Elkridge CC (R. 1956); Green Spring Valley Hunt C (A.9 R.9 1958); Suburban CC (R. 1949).

Massachusetts: International GC (R. 1969).

Michigan: Bloomfield Hills CC (R. 1968; R. 1978); CC of Detroit (R. 1950; A. 9 Precision 1968); Detroit GC (North Cse, R. 1953; South Cse, R. 1953); Oakland Hills CC (North Cse, R. 1969; South Cse, R. 1950; R. 1972; R. 1984).

Minnesota: Hazeltine National GC (R. 1982); Interlachen CC (R. 1962).

Missouri: Bellerive CC (R. 1990); St. Louis CC (R. 1952).

New Jersey: Arcola CC (R. 1960); Baltusrol GC (Lower Cse, R. 1952); Canoe Brook CC (North Cse, R. 1973); Crestmont CC (R. 1978); Essex County CC (East Cse, R. 1960); Galloping Hills GC (R. 1949); Glen Ridge CC (R. 1949; R. 1978); Green Brook CC (R. 1948); Montclair GC (R. 1935; R. 1959); North Jersey CC (R. 1979); Rockleigh GC (Bergen Cse, R. 1964); Tavistock CC (R. 1959).

New York: Bartlett CC (R. 1960); Bellport GC (R. 1965); Bonnie Briar CC (R. 1936), with Stanley Thompson; CC of Buffalo (R. 1954); CC of Ithaca (R. 1939, NLE); CC of Rochester (A.3 R. 1960); Century GC (R. 1959); Cherry Valley CC (R. 1962); Cold Spring G&CC (R. 1968); Colonie Muni (A.9 1980); Dellwood CC (R. 1956); Garden City CC (R. 1935; R. 1958); Huntington CC (R. 1960); IBM CC, Port Washington (R. 1954); IBM CC, Poughkeepsie (R. 1985); Locust Hill CC (R. 1931); Moonbrook CC (R. 1959); Muttontown G&CC (R. 1968); National G Links of America (R. 1948; R. 1969); New York Hospital GC (R.

1960); Niagara Falls CC (R. 1938); North Hempstead CC (R. 1960); Oak Hill CC (East Cse, R. 1956; R. 1967); Powelton C (R. 1953); Quaker Ridge CC (R. 1962); Rockland CC (R.); Sands Point CC (R. 1961); Scarsdale GC (R. 1944; R. 1962); Siwanoy CC (R. 1953); Sleepy Hollow GC (R. 1966); Stafford CC (R. 1931), with Stanley Thompson; Tam O'Shanter GC (R. 1967); Valley View GC (R. 1940); Vestal Hills CC (R. 1938, NLE); Winged Foot GC (West Cse, R. 1958); Woodmere C (R. 1952).

North Carolina: CC of North Carolina (Cardinal Cse, A.9 1980; Dogwood Cse, R. 1977); Charlotte CC (R. 1962; R. 1984); Pinehurst CC (Cse No. 4, R. 1973; Cse No. 5, R. 1974); Tanglewood GC (West Cse, R. 1973).

Ohio: Brookside CC (R. 1982).

Oklahoma: Southern Hills CC (R. 1957).

Oregon: Portland GC (R. 1950).

Pennsylvania: Aronimink GC (R. 1989); Centre Hills CC (A.9 1967); Gulph Mills GC (R.4 1966); Oakmont CC (R. 1964); Pittsburgh Field C (R. 1952); Valley Brook CC (R. 1978); Westmoreland CC (R. 1958).

South Carolina: Dunes G&BC (R. 1979).

Tennessee: Belle Meade CC (R. 1951).

Texas: Colonial CC (R. 1960).

Vermont: Woodstock CC (R. 1969, R. 1975, R. 1987).

Virginia: CC of Fairfax (A.9 1952); Cascades GC (R. 1961).

Wisconsin: Milwaukee CC (R. 1975).

Wyoming: Jackson Hole G&TC (R. 1966).

Bermuda: Mid Ocean C (R. 1953).

Brazil: Itanhanga GC (R. 1958).

Columbia: El Rincon C (A. Par 3 1964).

France: G de Bondues (Red Cse, R. 1968).

Greece: Glyfada GC (R. 1979).

Italy: Olgiata CC (R. 1984).

Japan: Sobhu CC (R. 1971).

Mexico: Pierre Marqués GC (R. 1982).

Portugal: Vilamoura II GC (R. A.5 1986).

Spain: Valderrama GC (A. 9 Par 3 1989).

West Germany: Hamburg-Ahrensburg GC, Hamburg (R. 1978).

Robert Trent Jones, Jr., 1990
COURTESY ROBERT TRENT JONES, JR.

Stanford for a year, Robert Trent Jones, Jr., joined his famous father's golf design firm in 1960. Eventually he took over the California office and acquired full responsibility for the firm's Western and Pacific Basin practice. In 1972 Bobby left his father's firm and formed Robert Trent Jones II Group, based in California.

Bobby Jones long advocated the concept of golf courses as works of art blended within the environment and built specific examples of that philosophy, such as Sentryworld in Wisconsin (where he designed a widely photographed "flower" hole, a par 3 surrounded by formal flower beds), Spanish Bay (where he and co-designers Sandy Tatum and Tom Watson re-created oceanfront linksland upon bare rock) and The Prince in Hawaii (where fairways edge cliffs and plunge through valleys edged with thick tropical undergrowth).

Throughout his career, Jones was committed to international relations and numbered among his friends and acquaintances several heads of state. He and his wife, Clairborne, were members of the United States delegation to the Helsinki Accords in 1975. He was a friend of Premier Sadat of Egypt and Benigno Aquino, whose wife, Corazon, later served as president of the Philippines.

By the 1990s Bobby Jones had assembled a talented staff that included Donald Knott, Gary Linn, Bruce Charlton and Kyle Phillips. His firm was so prolific and worked in so many countries around the globe that, like his father, he could boast that the sun never set on his designs.

Courses by Robert Trent Jones, Jr.:

Alaska: Eagleglen GC (1972), ass't Robert Trent Jones.

Arizona: Falcon Ridge CC (1992); Rio Rico G&CC (1975); Village of Oak

ROBERT TRENT JONES, JR.
(1939–   ), ASGCA, PRESIDENT 1989

BORN: Montclair, New Jersey.

After receiving a Bachelor's degree from Yale University, and trying law school at

Creek CC (1972), ass't Robert Trent Jones.

Arkansas: Chenal CC (1990).

California: Adobe Creek G&CC (1991); Birnam Wood GC (1968), ass't Robert Trent Jones; Bodega Harbour GC (9 1977; A.9 1987); Brookside CC (1991); Calabasas Park CC (1968), ass't Robert Trent Jones; Coto de Caza GC (1987); Desert Dunes G Cse (1989); Forest Meadows GC (Precision 1980); Laguna Seca Golf Ranch (1970), ass't Robert Trent Jones; Lake Shastina Resort (27 1972), ass't Robert Trent Jones; [The] Links at Monarch Beach (1984); [The] Links at Spanish Bay (1987), with *Frank "Sandy" Tatum* and *Tom Watson*; Poppy Hills GC (1986); [The] Pyramids GC (1992); Rancho California CC [FKA Murrieta CC](1970), ass't Robert Trent Jones; Shoreline G Links (1983); Silverado CC (South Cse 1967), ass't Robert Trent Jones; Spring Valley Lake CC (1971), ass't Robert Trent Jones; Squaw Creek G Resort.

Colorado: Arrowhead GC (1974); Beaver Creek GC (1982); Keystone Ranch GC (1980); Sheraton Steamboat Springs GC (1974); Skyland GC (1984).

Florida: Weston Hills CC (1991); [The] Windsor C (1991).

Hawaii: Kiahuna GC (1983); Makena GC (New Cse 1992; Old Cse 1981); Poipu Bay G Resort (1991); [The] Prince Cse (1990); Princeville Makai GC (27 1971); Waikoloa Beach GC (1981); Waikoloa Village GC (1972).

Idaho: Elkhorn GC (1975), with Robert Trent Jones.

Illinois: Crystal Tree G&CC (1990); DuPage G Cse (1992).

Kansas: Crestview CC (North Cse 1969, ass't Robert Trent Jones; South Cse, 9 1969, ass't Robert Trent Jones; A.9 1977); Deer Creek GC (1989).

Louisiana: Le Triomphe GC (1986).

Maine: Sugarloaf GC (1986).

Michigan: Orchards G Cse (1992).

Minnesota: Edinburgh USA G Cse (1987).

Missouri: Highland Springs CC (1989).

Nevada: Incline Green GC (Precision 1971), ass't Robert Trent Jones; Lakeridge CC (1971), ass't Robert Trent Jones; Spanish Trail CC (Canyon Cse, 9 1985, A.9 1992; Sunrise Cse 1985).

New Mexico: Cochiti Lake GC (1980).

North Dakota: Oxbow CC (1974).

Ohio: Jefferson G&CC (1992); Wedgewood G&CC (1991).

Oregon: Eugene CC (1967), ass't Robert Trent Jones; Heron Lakes GC (Red Cse 1971, ass't Robert Trent Jones; White Cse, 9 1971, ass't Robert Trent Jones, A.9 1991); Sunriver GC (North Cse 1980).

Texas: Horseshoe Bay GC (Slick Rock Cse 1973), ass't Robert Trent Jones; Las Colinas Sports C (Cottonwood Valley Cse, 9 1983; TPC Cse, 9 1983).

Virginia: Lansdowne G Resort (1991).

Wisconsin: Madeline Island G Links (1967), ass't Robert Trent Jones; SentryWorld GC (1982); University Ridge GC (1991).

Alberta: Glencoe G & CC (Forest Cse 1984; Meadow Cse 1985).

Australia: [The] Cape GC (1991); Hyatt Regency Coolum GC (1990); Joondalup CC (27 1985); Meadow Springs GC (1990); [The] National G&CC of Australia (1988).

British Columbia: Château Whistler GC (1992).

China: Shanghai International CC (1992).

England: Wisley GC (27 1992).

Fiji: Pacific Harbour GC (1977).

Finland: Ruuhikoski GC (1992).

France: Golf de Bresson (1992); Golf de St. Donat (1992); Les Terrasses de Geneve G&CC (1985).

Hong Kong: Discovery Bay GC.

Indonesia: Kapuk G Cse (1991); Pondok Indah CC (1977).

Japan: Cherry Hills GC (27 1992); Eastwood GC (1991); Golden Valley GC (1987); Hiroshima GC (1989); Hokkaido CC (Ohnuma Cse 1981); Karuizawa Golf (Higashi, Kita, Minami & Nishi Cse 1972, ass't Robert Trent Jones; Karuizawa Cse 1976); Katsura G Cse (1990); Kinojo GC (1992); Miho CC (1992); Nasu Highlands GC (1991); Oak Hills CC (1982); Pine Lake GC (1984); Sapporo CC (1976); Springfield GC (1986); Sun Hills CC (27 1992); Zuiryo CC (1992).

Malaysia: Bukit Jambul CC (1983); Desaru Resort GC (1982); Mines Resort GC (1992).

Mexico: C de G Palma Real (1977); Isla de la Piedra GC (9 1972, A.9 1987); Pok-Ta-Pok GC (1978).

Philippines: Alabang G&CC (1969); Calatagan GC (1983); Canlubang GC (1978); Luisita GC (1968), ass't Robert Trent Jones; St. Elena G&CC (1990).

Portugal: Penha Longa GC.

Singapore: Raffles CC (1986).

South Africa: Wild Coast CC (1983).

South Korea: Yongpyeong GC.

Spain: Bonmont Catalunya GC (1990).

Taiwan: Royal CC (1992); Sun Rise CC (1991).

Thailand: Eastern Star CC (1992); Green Valley GC (1992); Navatanee GC (1975); President CC (1991); Santiburi CC (1992).

Russia: Nahabino G Cse (1992).

West Indies: Four Seasons Nevis Resort GC (1990).

Courses remodeled or expanded by Robert Trent Jones, Jr.:

California: Annandale CC (R. 1970), ass't Robert Trent Jones; Bel-Air CC (R.1 1975); California GC of San Francisco (R. 1968), ass't Robert Trent Jones; Glendora CC (R. 1970), ass't Robert Trent Jones; Hacienda CC (R. 1971), ass't Robert Trent Jones; Menlo CC (R. 1970), ass't Robert Trent Jones; Palo Alto GC (R. 1980); Pasatiempo GC (R.); San Gabriel CC (R. 1972), ass't Robert Trent Jones; Santa Rosa G&CC (R. 1979); Silverado CC (North Cse, R. 1967), ass't Robert Trent Jones; Stanford University GC (R. 1968), ass't Robert Trent Jones.

Hawaii: Kuilima GC (R.); Mauna Kea Beach Hotel GC (R. 1976); Royal Kaanapali GC (North Cse, R.); Waikoloa Beach GC (R. 1988); Wailea GC (Blue Cse, R. 1992; Orange Cse, R. 1992).

Idaho: Sun Valley GC (R. A.4 1979).

Nevada: Incline Village GC (R.).

Texas: Mill Creek G&CC (R.5 A.13 1981).

Wyoming: Jackson Hole G&TC (R. 1966), ass't Robert Trent Jones.

France: Golf de Bondues (Blue Cse, A.9 1992).

Mexico: Churubusco CC (R.).

ROBERT TYRE JONES, JR. (1902–1971)

BORN: Atlanta, Georgia.
DIED: Atlanta, Georgia, at age 69.

Bobby Jones was one of the greatest golfers of all time, winning fifteen major titles in the world of golf during an amateur career. While he never practiced course architecture himself, he consulted with Alister Mackenzie on Augusta National in the early 1930s, with Robert Trent Jones on Peachtree in the early 1950s and with George Cobb on the par 3 course at Augusta National in 1959. All three courses

Bobby Jones, circa 1925 COLLECTION RON WHITTEN

were originally conceptualized by Jones. The first two exerted a profound influence on the golf design profession throughout North America, and Augusta's nine-hole par 3 course started a modest nationwide boom in par 3 courses.

TAKEAKI KANEDA (1931–)

BORN: Tokyo, Japan.

Takeaki Kaneda graduated from Waseda University and attended graduate school at Ohio State and then the University of Maryland as a graduate assistant. As an amateur golfer he represented Japan in several worldwide events. He served as captain of the Japanese team at the 1961 Singapore Open.

Trained as a journalist, Kaneda served as Japanese correspondent for the American magazine *Sports Illustrated* for many years. He also wrote several books about golf and golf course design in Japan and translated several classic golf books into Japanese, including Byron Nelson's *Shape Your Swing the Modern Way*. He also served as a producer and commentator for programs on Japanese television, including the first Japanese TV broadcast of golf, the 1957 Canada Cup.

Tak Kaneda, 1991 COURTESY TAK KANEDA

In the early 1980s, Kaneda had the good fortune to work with golf architect Robert Trent Jones, Jr. on the creation of Oak Hills Country Club in Japan. Kaneda was soon hooked on golf architecture, and shortly after the opening of Oak Hills, he tried his hand at a course design himself. Over the next decade Kaneda did several fine designs in his homeland.

Courses by Tak Kaneda:

Japan: Akaigawa CC (1990); Hijiri Meadow CC (1991); Kobuchizawa CC; Kochi Kuroshio CC; Koga G Links (1990); Maple CC (1986); North Point GC (1989); Oak Hills CC (1982), ass't Robert Trent Jones, Jr.; Otaki-Jo GC (Castle Cse 1990); Senshu CC (1991); Tahya-Ko Resort GC (1990); Yatsugatake GC (1991).

SHUNSUKE KATO

BORN: Japan.

After spending ten years designing numerous Japanese golf courses while employed by the design department of the Taiheiyo Corporation, Shunsuke Kato resigned and opened his own golf design practice in Japan in 1985. Starting with Izu Golf Club, he developed a distinctly American style of architecture, with endless mounds, pot bunkers and bulkheaded water hazards patterned after those of Pete Dye, whom he admired. Though criticized by some for the difficulty of his courses, Kato became one of the country's most popular and busiest course architects, producing over forty courses in five years.

In 1991 Kato completed what had been, by his own admission, a lifelong goal, a links-style course. His Setonaikai Golf Club in the Okayama Prefecture afforded that rare opportunity, for it was one of the few pieces of flat, treeless land in all of Japan.

Courses by Shunsuke Kato:

Japan: Asuka CC (1990); [The] CC of Japan (1988); Cypress CC (1988); Gifu Inaguchi GC (1986); Goldwin GC (1991); Hokkaido GC (Eagle Cse 1990; Lion Cse 1990); Ikaho GC (1984); Izu GC (1986); Kiire CC (1989); Koryo CC (1975, A.3rd 9 1985); Kujigawa CC (1987); Kunu CC (1989); Liberal Hills GC (1990); Midono CC (1990); Misugi GC (1988); Nachi Katsuura GC (1986); New Nanso GC (1985); Odakyu Nishifuji

GC (1989); Ryugasaki GC (1990); Setonaikai GC (1991); Seven Lakes GC (27 1989); Shirakawa Meadow GC (1990); Taiheiyo C, Chiba (Ichihara Cse 1984); Taiheiyo C, Gunma (Karuizawa Cse 1975; Takasaki Cse 1976); Taiheiyo C, Kanagawa (Sagami Cse 1977); Taiheiyo C, Shizuoka (Gotemba Cse 1977); Taiheiyo C, Tochigi (Mashiko Cse 1976); Takinomiya CC (1987); Talvas GC (1990); Tojo GC (1990); Tokyo Kita CC (1989); Tone GC (1988); Uraku GC (1989); Wilson Royal GC (Mashiko Cse 1989); Wingfield GC (1988).

Korea: Chung Ju CC (1990).
Taiwan: Toyo Rantan CC (1990).

Ken Kavanaugh, 1991 COURTESY KEN KAVANAUGH

KENNETH MARSHALL KAVANAUGH (1952–)

BORN: Lawrenceville, Illinois.

After undergraduate work at Southern Illinois University, Ken Kavanaugh moved to Arizona in order to work on his four handicap year-round. He finished his degree at Arizona State, then received a B.A. in landscape architecture from the University of Arizona in 1976.

Kavanaugh worked as a landscape architect for a number of years. But in 1981, while serving as quality control engineer for the city of Tucson on the creation of Fred Enke Municipal, Kavanaugh met and worked with the project's course architects, Dick Phelps and Brad Benz. Kavanaugh was hooked, and after the Enke course was completed, he resigned his job and entered private practice as a golf course architect.

Although based in Tucson, Kavanaugh found work in Chicago, Missouri, Texas and elsewhere. In 1990, he teamed with PGA Tour player Peter Jacobsen on a design in Jacobsen's hometown of Portland, Oregon.

Courses by Ken Kavanaugh:

Arizona: Foothills West GC (1991); Gold Canyon GC (9 1985); Happy Trails G Cse (9 1985); Oakwood CC (9 1988); Quail Creek CC (9 1985); [The] Vistas C (1990).
Illinois: Orchard Valley GC (1992).
Missouri: Seasons Ridge GC (1991).
Oregon: [The] Oregon GC (1992), with Peter Jacobsen.
Texas: Southwyck GC (1988).

Course remodeled or expanded by Ken Kavanaugh:

Illinois: Lawrence County CC (R.1 1990).
Kansas: Alvamar CC (R.1 1986).
Texas: Raveneaux CC (R. 1986).

Stephen Kay, 1990
COURTESY STEPHEN KAY

STEPHEN KAY, NÉE STEPHEN KACHMARCHYK (1951–)

BORN: New York City, New York.

A member of the Flushing (New York) High School golf team in the mid-1960s, Stephen Kay became enamored with golf architecture when he read a definitive article on the subject by Herbert Warren Wind. After obtaining a Bachelor of Landscape Architecture degree from the State University of New York's College of Environmental Sciences and Forestry at Syracuse (where he played for one year on the golf team), Kay attended the Turfgrass Management Program at Michigan State University, completing the normal two-year program in one year.

While at Michigan State, he met golf architect William Newcomb and joined his firm in 1977. He was made an associate in 1980. In the fall of 1983 Kay returned to the metropolitan New York area, where he established his own golf architecture practice. He spent his first several years tastefully updating classic, old metropolitan-area courses. He developed a healthy respect for older architects, especially Devereux Emmet and Donald Ross.

He also promoted the virtues of nine-hole courses. Among his earliest solo projects was a nine-hole course in the tiny Kingdom of Bhutan in the Himalayas. He designed a nine-hole estate course at Boston Corners, New York, that played differently the second time around. He also worked on restoring an ancient nine-hole course at Quogue Field Club on Long Island.

Courses by Stephen Kay;

Illinois: Fox Run G Links (1983), ass't Bill Newcomb.
Michigan: Boyne Mountain GC (Monument Cse 1986), ass't Bill Newcomb; Grand Traverse Resort (Resort Cse 1979), ass't Bill Newcomb; Holiday Greens GC (Precision 1982), ass't Bill Newcomb.
New Jersey: Blue Heron Pines GC (1993).
New York: Boston Corners G Cse (9 1988); Hamlet G&CC (1992); Hiland GC (1989); Leonard Litwin Private Cse (1 1987).
Bhutan: Royal Bhutan GC (9 1986).
India: Eagle GC (9 1988).

Courses remodeled or expanded by Stephen Kay:

Connecticut: Burning Tree CC (R.1 1991); H. Smith Richardson G Cse (R.2 1991); Millbrook C (R. 1984); Patterson C (R.2 1991); Rolling Hills (R.2 1986).
Louisiana: Briarwood CC (R.2 1987).
Massachusetts: Kittansett C (R.1 1991); Oyster Harbors C (R. 1991); Winchester CC (R. 1991).
Michigan: Chemung Hills GC (A.9 1983), ass't Bill Newcomb; Lakes of the North (A.9), ass't Bill Newcomb; Port Huron CC (R. 1982), ass't Bill Newcomb; Schuss Mountain GC (R.2 1980), ass't Bill Newcomb; Traverse City CC (R. 1982), ass't Bill Newcomb; Westland GC (R.3 1982), ass't Bill Newcomb.
New Jersey: Bedens Brook CC (R.3 1989); Cranbury GC (R.1 1991); Greenacres CC (R.3 1989); Hopewell Valley GC (R.1 1990); Paramus G&CC (R.3 1991); Pascack Brook GC (R.7 1988); Tamcrest CC (R.5 1984).
New York: Ardsley CC (R.1 1986); Blind Brook GC (R.1 1989); Blue Hill GC (R.18 1991); Brae Burn CC (R.2 1987); Cherry Valley C (R.2 1990); Crab Meadow GC (R.3 1986); Dix Hills GC (R. 1986); Elmira CC (R.2 1991); Glen Head CC (R.3 1987); Hempstead GC at Lido (R. 1990); Huntington Crescent CC (R.2 1986); IBM CC, Poughkeepsie (R. 1988); Kissena GC (R. 1986); Knollwood CC (R.1 1984); Lake Success GC (R.1 1989); Lawrence GC (R. 1982); Mahopac GC (R.2 1985); Middle Bay CC (R.2 1984); Mosholu GC (R. 1989); North Hills CC (R. 1989); Noyac G&CC (R.5 1991); Old Oaks CC (R. 1981), ass't Bill Newcomb; Old Westbury G&CC (R.5 1990); Pelham CC (R.2 1991); Quoque Field C (R.2 1987); Ridgeway CC (R.3 1991); Rockland Lake State Park (North Cse, R. 1989); Rye GC (R.7 1989); Sands Point GC (R.3 1987); Seawane C (R. 1988); Smithtown Landing GC (R.1 1987); Southern Dutchess CC (R.1 1990); Southward Ho CC (R.7 1991); Spook Rock G Cse (R.7 1991); Tam O'Shanter C (R.1 1990); Tuxedo GC (R.3 1991); Westchester CC (South Cse, R. 1990); Westchester Hills CC (R.8 1991); Wykagyl CC (R.2 1990).
Wisconsin: Kenosha CC (R. 1991).

GARY KERN (1937–), ASGCA

BORN: Indianapolis, Indiana.

Gary Kern studied engineering at Texas A&M and Purdue universities, then became a licensed land surveyor in Indiana, Ohio and Kentucky. He was employed from 1960 to 1975 by a civil engineering firm that specialized in land planning for single-family subdivisions and multi-family developments.

In 1969 a company client hired golf architect Bill Diddel to lay out a course for

Gary Kern, 1990
COURTESY ASGCA

which Kern handled the land plan. Kern worked closely with Diddel during the initial planning and found course architecture fascinating. He continued to visit Diddel during the actual course construction, looking over his shoulder, picking his brain and gaining some practical insights into the business.

At Diddel's urging, Kern decided to moonlight as a golf designer. Diddel helped him land his first job in Jamestown, Indiana, in 1969. By 1975 Kern had enough work to practice course design and renovation full-time. In the 1980s he moved his base from Indianapolis to St. Louis, where he teamed for a time with former U.S. Open champion Hale Irwin. In 1986 Kern was joined in the practice by his son Ron, who ran a branch office in Indiana.

Courses by Gary Kern:

Illinois: Fox Creek CC (1991), with Ron Kern; Rolling Hills GC (9 1991), with Ron Kern.

Indiana: Brook Hill GC (9 1975); Hanging Tree GC (1989), with Ron Kern; Mohawk Hills GC (9 1972); Nappanee Muni (9 1979); Pebble Brook G&CC (North Cse 1989), with Ron Kern; Riley Village GC (9 Par 3 1974); Royal Hylands GC (1977); Sky Valley GC (9 1972); Sunblest G&CC (1992), with Ron Kern; Tomahawk Hills GC (9 1971); Turkey Run GC (1973).

Massachusetts: New England CC (1990), with Hale Irwin and Ron Kern.

Missouri: Bent Creek GC (1990), with Ron Kern; Casey G Cse (3); Fourche Valley GC (9 1992), with Ron Kern; Fox Run GC (1991), with Ron Kern; Quail Creek GC (1987), with Hale Irwin; Sugar Creek GC (1990), with Ron Kern; Sun Valley GC (1988), with Ron Kern.

Courses remodeled or expanded by Gary Kern:

Arkansas: Maumelle CC (R.9 1989).

Illinois: Cardinal Creek GC, Scott AFB (R. 1985); Cherry Hills CC (R. 1985); Green Hills CC, Mount Vernon (A.9 1979); Rolling Hills GC (A.9); Sunset Hills CC (R. A.6 1990), with Ron Kern; Sycamore Hills CC (R.8, A.10 1976).

Indiana: Coffin GC (R.9 1987), with Ron Kern; Crawfordsville Muni (R.5 A.13 1988); Delaware GC (R. 1985); Greenfield CC (R.9 A.9 1976); Harrison Lake CC (R. 1989), with Ron Kern;

Hillcrest G&CC (R.); Hillview CC (R. 1990), with Ron Kern; Jasper Muni (A.9 1987); Maplecrest CC (R. 1984); Plymouth CC (R. 1983); Royal Hylands GC (R. 1990), with Ron Kern; Royal Oak CC [FKA El Dorado CC](R.9 1976); Rozella Ford GC (R.4 1985); Tippecanoe Lake CC (R.); Wabash Valley GC (R.8, A.10 1991), with Ron Kern; Westwood CC (A.9 1989), with Ron Kern; Woodland GC (R. 1983).

Missouri: Cape Girardeau CC (R. 4 1988), with Ron Kern; Cherry Hills CC (R.5 1985); Lake Forest G&CC (R.9 A.9 1986); Lake Valley CC (R. 1988), with Ron Kern; Meadowbrook CC (R. 1988); Norwood Hills CC (East Cse, R.3 1987), with Ron Kern; Union Hills GC (A.9 1988), with Ron Kern; Westborough CC (R. 1990), with Ron Kern.

Oklahoma: Kicking Bird GC (R.6 1989), with Ron Kern.

RONALD KERN
(1958–   ), ASGCA

BORN: Indianapolis, Indiana.

Ron Kern took up the game of golf at the age of four and competed in countless amateur events during high school and college. As he grew up watching his father, Gary Kern, develop golf courses, it was natural that he would eventually enter the profession of golf architecture, although after he graduated with a B.S. in civil engineering from Purdue University in 1980, Kern worked as a road designer and hydraulic engineer for the Indiana Department of Highways. It wasn't until 1986 that he joined his father in a design partnership. The elder Kern maintained an office in St. Louis, while Ron ran a branch operation near Indianapolis.

Courses by Ron Kern (All with Gary Kern):

Illinois: Fox Creek CC (1991); Rolling Hills GC (9 1991).

Indiana: Hanging Tree GC (1989); Pebble Brook G&CC (North Cse 1989); Sunblest G&CC (1992).

Massachusetts: New England CC (1990), with Hale Irwin.

Missouri: Bent Creek GC (1990); Fourche Valley GC (9 1992); Fox Run GC (1991); Sugar Creek GC (1990); Sun Valley GC (1988).

Ron Kern, 1990
COURTESY ASGCA

Courses remodeled or expanded by Ron Kern (All with Gary Kern):

Illinois: Sunset Hills CC (R. 1990).

Indiana: Coffin GC (R.); Harrison Lake CC (R. 1989); Hillview CC (R. 1990); Royal Hylands GC (R. 1990); Wabash Valley GC (R.8, A.10 1991); Westwood CC (A.9 1989).

Missouri: Cape Girardeau CC (R.4 1988); Lake Valley CC (R. 1988); Norwood Hills CC (R. 1987); Union Hills GC (A.9 1988); Westborough CC (R. 1990).

Oklahoma: Kicking Bird GC (R.6 1989).

WILLIAM H. KIDD, SR.
(1885–1967)

BORN: Monteith, Scotland.
DIED: Minneapolis, Minnesota, at age 81.

Talented young amateur golfer Willie Kidd emigrated to the United States in 1908 and became professional at the Charlevoix (Michigan) G Cse. From 1911 to 1920 he served as club professional at Algonquin CC in St. Louis. He then took the head professional position at Interlachen CC in Minneapolis, where he had finished second in the 1914 Western Open. When he arrived, Interlachen's course had just been expanded and remodeled to the de-

Willie Kidd, circa 1950 COLLECTION RON WHITTEN

sign of Donald Ross, but after Interlachen was awarded the 1930 U.S. Open, Kidd was called upon to remodel two of the club's weakest holes. He converted the 16th from a short par 3 into a dogleg par 4 and changed the 17th into a long, difficult par 3. Both holes were completed in time for the memorable 1930 Open, the third leg in that year's unprecedented completion of golf's Grand Slam by Robert Tyre Jones, Jr.

Kidd remained at Interlachen until his retirement in 1957, when he was succeeded by his son Bill. Willie was an active competitive golfer throughout his life, winning the 1934 Minnesota PGA, and a fine teacher, training among other youngsters young Patty Berg. Beginning in the 1950s Kidd once again dabbled in golf design, laying out a series of small-town courses in Minnesota and neighboring Wisconsin. He was especially active in architecture following his retirement.

Courses by Willie Kidd:

Minnesota: Elk River CC (1962); Faribault CC (1956); Island View GC (9); Rum River GC (9 1956).
Wisconsin: New Richmond GC (9).

Courses remodeled or expanded by Willie Kidd:

Minnesota: Albany CC (A.9 1960); Interlachen CC (R. A.2 1929).

JACK KIDWELL
(1918–   ), ASGCA, PRESIDENT 1979

BORN: Ohio.

Jack Kidwell graduated from Columbus (Ohio) Central High School and studied at Utah State Agriculture College. In 1938 he and his father purchased Beacon Light GC, a nine-hole layout in west Columbus, and Jack served as its pro-superintendent for twenty-eight years. Kidwell became a Class A PGA professional and a Class A golf superintendent during that time. He also rebuilt all the greens at Beacon Light, an experience that led him to accept an offer to design a full 18-hole course in 1957.

Kidwell left Beacon Light and entered the field of course architecture on a full-time basis in 1959. He built many public layouts and gained a reputation for designing courses that were both playable and maintainable. In 1976 he and Michael Hurdzan, who had worked for him as a

Jack Kidwell, 1980
COLLECTION RON WHITTEN

youngster and later became his design associate, founded the partnership of Kidwell and Hurdzan, Inc.

A low-handicap golfer all his life, Jack Kidwell served as director of golf at Hickory Hills Country Club, a course he considered among his finest designs, after its opening in 1979. In 1984 the Golf Course Association presented him with an Award of Merit.

Ill health forced Kidwell to curtail his activities in the mid-1980s, but he continued to consult with Hurdzan on selected projects. In 1990 he came out of semiretirement to handle the design and construction of Indian Springs, a public course near Columbus that opened to fine reviews.

Courses by Jack Kidwell (All with Michael Hurdzan unless otherwise indicated):

Florida: River Greens GC (1969 *solo*).
Indiana: Hidden Valley GC (1976).
Kentucky: Frances Miller Memorial GC (1982); Kenton County GC (North Cse 1981).
Massachusetts: Dennis Highlands GC (1984).
Ohio: Airport G Cse (1968 *solo*); Bash Recreation GC (Precision 1965 *solo*, NLE); Beckett Ridge G&CC (1974); Blackhawk GC (1964 *solo*); Blacklick Woods GC (Cse No. 1 1964 *solo*, A.13 1972 *solo*; Cse No. 2 [Precision] 1972 *solo*); Blue Ash GC (1979); Bolton Field GC (1969 *solo*, A.3rd 9 1991 *solo*); Broadview GC (9 1968 *solo*); Buttermilk Falls GC (1981); Deer Creek State Park GC (1979); Hiawatha GC (9 1961 *solo*); Hickory Flat GC (1968 *solo*); Hickory Hills CC (1979); Hueston Woods State Park (1969 *solo*); HVJAC GC (9 Precision 1968 *solo*); Indian Springs GC (1990 *solo*); Kings Mill GC (9 1960 *solo*); Larch Tree CC (1971 *solo*); Lee Win GC

(1967 *solo*); Licking Springs G & Trout C (1963 *solo*); Mohican Hills GC (9 1972 *solo*, A.9 1975); Oakhurst CC (1958 *solo*); Oxbow G&CC (1974); Pickaway CC (*solo*); Pine Hills GC (1962 *solo*); Pleasant Hill GC (1970 *solo*); Pleasant Valley GC (1969 *solo*); Punderson Lake GC (1969 *solo*); Reeves GC (9 Par 3 1973 *solo*); Reid Memorial GC (North Cse 1965 *solo*; South Cse 1966 *solo*); Ridenoor Park GC (9 Precision 1976); River Greens GC (1967 *solo*); Salt Fork State Park GC (1972 *solo*); San Dar Acres GC (Precision 1976); Shawnee Lookout GC (1976); Shawnee State Park GC (1979); Sugar Isle GC (9 1972 *solo*); Table Rock GC (9 1973 *solo*; A.9 1976, A.3rd 9 1978); Tanglewood GC (1968 *solo*); Thornapple CC (1966 *solo*); Twin Lakes GC (1959 *solo*); Upper Landsdowne CC (9 1962 *solo*); [The] Vineyard GC (1986); Vista View Village GC (1973 *solo*); Willow Run GC (1963 *solo*); Wilson GC (9 Precision 1972 *solo*).
Texas: Oak Ridge CC (1986).
West Virginia: Riverside GC (1976).

Courses remodeled or expanded by Jack Kidwell (All with Michael Hurdzan unless otherwise indicated):

Indiana: Hillcrest G&CC (R.9 1984).
Kentucky: Kenton County CC (South Cse, R. 1974); Summit Hills CC (R.10 A.1 1980); World of Sports GC (R. A.10 1979).
Ohio: Brookside CC (R.2 1977); Brookside Park GC (A.9 1977); California GC (A.5 1975); Camargo C (R.1 1965 *solo*); Elyria CC (R.2 1975); Fostoria CC (R. A.10 1972 *solo*); Foxfire GC (A. Silver Fox Nine 1984); Galion CC (A.9 1967 *solo*); Groveport GC (A.9 1973 *solo*; R. 1977); Kenwood CC (Kendale Cse, R. 1981; Kenview Cse, R. 1977); Lakewood CC (R. 1 1975); Lakota Hills CC (R.9 A.9 1971 *solo*); Lancaster CC (A.9 1961); Marion CC (R. 1977); Miami Shores GC (R.9 1977); Miami Valley CC (R. 1980); Mount Vernon CC (R. 1977); Neumann Park GC (A.9 1975); Ohio University GC (A.9 1963 *solo*); Piqua CC (A.9 1974 *solo*); Shawnee CC (R. 1978); Snyder Park CC (R.4 1962 *solo*); Troy CC (R.9 A.9 1975); Twin Base GC, Wright-Patterson AFB (R.4 1971 *solo*); Westwood CC (R. 1984); WGC GC (A.9 1982); Wildwood GC (R.3 1977); Woodland GC (A.9 1976

solo); York Temple CC (R. 1 1975); Zanesville CC (R.5 1981).
West Virginia: Deerfield CC (R.9 A.9 1978).

Ken Killian, 1990
COURTESY ASGCA

KENNETH K. KILLIAN
(1931–), ASGCA, PRESIDENT 1986

BORN: Chicago, Illinois.

Ken Killian graduated in 1957 from the University of Illinois with a Bachelor of Science degree in landscape architecture. From 1957 to 1964 he was employed with golf architect Robert Bruce Harris. In 1964 he formed the partnership of Killian and Nugent Inc. with Dick Nugent, another Harris assistant. The two worked together for nearly twenty years, collaborating on such designs as Kemper Lakes, site of the 1989 PGA, and Forest Preserve National, one of the country's top public courses.

In 1983 Killian and Nugent formed individual firms. While remaining based in the Chicago area, Killian handled projects in the Southeast and Southwest as well as the Midwest.

Courses by Ken Killian (All with Dick Nugent unless otherwise indicated):

Arizona: Pueblo El Mirage CC (1985 solo).
Hawaii: Molokai Highlands GC (1992 solo).
Illinois: Buffalo Grove GC (1968); Concord Green GC (9 Par 3 1964); Eagle Creek Resort & GC (1989 solo); Edgebrook GC (1967); Forest Preserve National GC (1981); Greenshire GC (1964); Kemper Lakes GC (1979; R. 1987 solo); Moon Lake GC (1973); River Oaks GC (1971); Robert A. Black GC (9 Precision 1979); Vernon Hills GC (9 1979); Warren Park GC (Precision); Weber Park GC (9 Par 3 1973); Western Illinois University GC (9 1971).

Indiana: Oak Meadow G&TC (1972); Sand Creek C (1979); Woodmar CC (1982).
New Mexico: Valle Grande G Cse (27 1991 solo).
Ohio: Shelby Oaks GC (1964); Sugar Creek GC.
South Carolina: Crickentree G Cse (1989 solo).
Texas: Chester W. Ditto Muni (1982); Mission CC (1983).
Virginia: Poplar Forest GC (9 1980).
Wisconsin: Abbey Springs GC (1972); Evergreen GC (1973); Lake Arrowhead GC (1984); Tuckaway CC (1967).

Courses remodeled or expanded by Ken Killian (All with Dick Nugent unless otherwise indicated):

Illinois: Bartlett Hills G&CC (R.1 1985 solo); Bob O'Link CC (R. 1968); Butterfield CC (R. 1969); Chevy Chase CC (R.); Countryside GC (R. 1978); Crystal Lake CC (R. 1980); Deerpath Park GC (R. 1971; R. 1981); Elgin CC (R. 1978); Evanston GC (R. 1972); Exmoor CC (R. 1969); Fox Lake CC (R. 1973); Glencoe GC (R. 1964; R. 1982); Glen Oak GC (R. 1983 solo); Glenview Park GC (R. 1985 solo); Green Acres CC (R.1 1982); Highland Park GC (R.5 1977); Hillcrest CC (R. 1979); Lake Shore CC (R. 1971); Lansing Sportsman's C (A.9 1976); Lincolnshire CC (Cse No. 1, R. 1964; Cse No. 2, R.); Marriott Lincolnshire GC (R.2 1981); McHenry GC (R.1 1970); Medinah CC (Cse No. 3, R. 1970); Midlothian CC (R.); Naval Training Center GC, Great Lakes (A.9 1971); North Shore CC (R.); Onwentsia C (R. 1969); Park Ridge CC (R.3 1966); Pinecrest G&CC (R. 1979); Ravinia Green CC (R. 1973); Ridge CC (R. 1972); Ruth Lake CC (R. 1980); Silver Lake GC (North Cse, R.1 1978); Skokie CC (R. 1973); Sportsman G&CC (R.); Spring Creek GC (R.9 A.9 1966); Sunset Valley GC (R. 1977); Twin Orchards CC (Red Cse, R.); Villa Olivia CC (R. 1975); Westmoreland CC (R.); White Pines CC (East Cse, R. 1982; West Cse, R. 1982); Wilmette Park GC (R. 1979).
Indiana: Burke Memorial GC (R. 1966).
Michigan: Berrien Hills CC (R. 1965); Lost Lake Woods GC (A.9 1974).
Minnesota: Meadowbrook GC (A.9 1966).
Ohio: Lancaster CC (R. 1986 solo).

South Dakota: Minnehaha CC (R.6 1976).
Texas: Great Southwest GC (R. 1983).
Wisconsin: Blackhawk CC (R. 1982); Blue Mound G&CC (R. 1980); Brynwood CC (R. 1968); Hartford CC (R.9 A.9 1969); Maple Bluff CC (R. 1973); Reedsburg CC (A.9 1978).

WILLIAM KINNEAR
(–1945)

BORN: Leven, Scotland.
DIED: Saskatchewan, Canada.

A professional golfer from Scotland, William Kinnear designed several courses and revised a number of established layouts in western Canada between the wars while serving as professional at Riverside CC in Saskatoon. His designs included the East Course at Saskatoon G&CC, Riverside CC, Kindersley GC and several nine-hole courses in Saskatchewan.

RONALD KIRBY
(1932–), ASGCA

BORN: Beverly, Massachusetts.

Ron Kirby, a member of the 1949 Massachusetts State High School Championship Golf Team, studied at the Boston Museum School of Fine Arts in 1946–47. He then attended the University of Massachusetts Stockbridge School of Agriculture on a Francis Ouimet Scholarship, receiving an associate degree in agronomy in 1953.

Kirby served as superintendent on a number of golf courses, including one in the Bahamas designed by Dick Wilson. In the mid-1960s he was employed by Robert Trent Jones Inc., building courses in the United States and England. In 1970 he

Ron Kirby, 1983
COLLECTION RON
WHITTEN

formed a partnership with golf architect Arthur Davis, based in Georgia. Soon thereafter famed golfer Gary Player was signed to serve as a consulting partner in the firm.

In 1973 Davis left the firm, and a few years later Player dissolved his interest in the business. In 1980 longtime associate Denis Griffiths became Kirby's design partner. In 1987 Kirby turned the business over to Griffiths and joined Jack Nicklaus's Design Services. He moved to Monte Carlo and handled Nicklaus's European projects until 1992, when he returned from Europe and settled in suburban Georgia.

Courses by Ron Kirby (All with Denis Griffiths unless otherwise indicated):

Alabama: CC of Alabama (1986); Huntsville Muni (1986); North River GC (1978), with Gary Player.

Colorado: Pole Creek GC (1983).

Georgia: Atlanta Athletic C (Highlands Cse, 9 1967; Riverside Cse 1967), ass't Robert Trent Jones; Berkeley Hills GC (1971), with Arthur Davis and Gary Player; Grimball GC (5 1986); [The] Little Cse (3); Nob North GC (1978 solo); Pebble Brook CC (9 1970), with Arthur Davis; PineIsle CC (1972), with Arthur Davis; River North G&CC (1975), with Arthur Davis and Gary Player; Royal Oaks GC (9 1971), with Arthur Davis and Gary Player; University of Georgia GC (1970), ass't Robert Trent Jones.

Illinois: Holiday Inn GC (9 1970), with Arthur Davis.

Michigan: Boyne Highlands GC (Heather Cse 1968), ass't Robert Trent Jones.

South Carolina: Dolphin Head GC (1973), with Arthur Davis and Gary Player; Marsh Point GC (1976), with Gary Player.

Tennessee: Bent Creek G Resort [FKA Cobbly Nob G Links](1972), with Arthur Davis and Gary Player.

Texas: Fair Oaks Ranch G&CC (1979, with Gary Player; A.3rd 9 1985).

Virginia: Brandermill CC (1976), with Gary Player.

West Virginia: Bel-Meadow G&CC (1967), ass't Robert Trent Jones.

Austria: GC Gut Altentann (1988), ass't Jack Nicklaus.

Belgium: Domaine des Princes GC (1992), ass't Jack Nicklaus.

Bophuthatswana: Gary Player CC (1979), with Gary Player.

Canary Islands: Maspalomas GC (North Cse 1974), with Gary Player.

England: Moor Allerton GC (27 1971), ass't Robert Trent Jones.

France: Cely GC (1992), ass't Jack Nicklaus; Golf de Paris International C (1991), ass't Jack Nicklaus.

Ireland: Mt. Juliet G&CC (1991), ass't Jack Nicklaus.

Ivory Coast: Riviera Africaine GC (9 1972), with Arthur Davis and Gary Player.

Japan: Niigata Forest GC (1975), with Gary Player; Nishi Nihon GC (1975), with Gary Player; Odawara CC (1973), with Arthur Davis and Gary Player; Sun Lake CC (1986).

Philippines: Kamirag GC (1982); Lake Paoay GC (1980); Puerto Azul GC (27 1980), with Gary Player.

Puerto Rico: Palmas del Mar GC (1973), with Arthur Davis and Gary Player.

Sardinia: Pevero GC (1972), ass't Robert Trent Jones.

Scotland: Gleneagles Hotel GC (Monarch's Cse 1991), ass't Jack Nicklaus.

South Africa: Roodepoort Muni (1985); Welkom Muni (1987).

Spain: Almerimar GC (1975), with Gary Player; El Paraiso GC (1974), with Arthur Davis and Gary Player; Escorpion GC (1975), with Gary Player.

Courses remodeled or expanded by Ron Kirby (All with Denis Griffiths unless otherwise indicated):

Florida: [The] Everglades C (R. 1984).

Georgia: Bacon Park GC (R. A.3rd 9 1985); Cartersville CC (R.9 A.9 1972), with Arthur Davis and Gary Player; Dalton CC (R. 1977 solo); Druid Hills CC (R.); Little Mountain CC (R. 1970), with Arthur Davis; Sandy Run GC (R. 1970), with Arthur Davis; [The] Standard C (R.1 A.1 1971, NLE), with Arthur Davis; Warner Robins AFB GC (R. 1970), with Arthur Davis.

Louisiana: New Orleans CC (R. 1985).

Missouri: Bellerive CC (R.1 1985).

New Mexico: Alto Lakes G&CC (A.9 1973), with Arthur Davis and Gary Player.

North Carolina: Twin Valley CC (A.9 1982).

Pennsylvania: Centre Hills CC (A.9 1967), ass't Robert Trent Jones.

Texas: Hogan Park GC (A.3rd 9 1978 solo); Midland CC (R. 1979 solo); Oak Hills CC (R.2 1978 solo).

Virginia: Deer Run GC (Cardinal Cse, R. 1986; Deer Run Cse, R.9 A.9 1986).

West Virginia: Shawnee GC (R.9 1979 solo).

Philippines: Wack Wack G&CC (East Cse, R. 1980).

South Africa: Kensington GC (R. 1980); Royal Johannesburg GC (West Cse, R. 1985).

BENJAMIN KNIGHT

BORN: Scotland.
DIED: Florida.

Ben Knight emigrated from Scotland to Minnesota in 1909. In 1919 he laid out Winona Golf Club in Minnesota, remaining as its professional until his retirement in 1952. He also laid out courses as a sideline, designing the original nine at Burlington (Iowa) Golf Club and some thirty-two courses in Wisconsin and Minnesota.

Don Knott, 1990
COURTESY ASGCA

DONALD JOSEPH KNOTT (1946–), ASGCA

BORN: Alameda, California.

Don Knott attended the University of California at Berkeley, receiving a Bachelor of Landscape Architecture degree in 1969 and a Master of Architecture degree in 1973. He immediately went to work for Robert Trent Jones Inc. and worked closely for a year with Robert Trent Jones, Jr.

After three years with Trent Jones Sr. in Malaga, Spain, in 1977 Knott rejoined Bobby Jones, who had formed his own company. In 1979 Don married Victoria Susan Graves, eldest daughter of golf architect Robert Muir Graves. In the 1980s Knott was the chief designer and project architect for Robert Trent Jones, Jr., and became the company's first vice president.

Courses by Don Knott (All as assistant to Robert Trent Jones, Jr.):

California: Coto de Caza GC (1987); Desert Dunes G Cse (1989); [The] Links at Spanish Bay (1987); Poppy Hills GC (1986); [The] Pyramids GC (1992).

Colorado: Beaver Creek GC (1982); Keystone Ranch GC (1980).

Florida: [The] Windsor C (1991).

Hawaii: Kiahuna GC (1983); Makena GC (Old Cse 1981; New Cse 1992); Poipu Bay G Resort (1991); [The] Prince GC (1990).

Maine: Sugarloaf GC (1986).

Nevada: Spanish Trail G&CC (Canyon Cse, 9 1985, A.9 1992; Sunrise Cse 1985).

Oregon: Sunriver GC (North Cse 1980).

Alberta: Glencoe G & CC (Forest Cse 1984; Meadow Cse 1985).

Australia: [The] Cape GC (1988); Hyatt Regency Coolum GC 1989); Joondalup GC (27 1990); Meadow Springs GC (1986); [The] National G&CC (1986).

China: Shanghai International CC (1991).

France: Les Terrasses de Geneve G&CC (1985).

Indonesia: Kapuk GC (1991).

Japan: Eastwood CC (1991); Katsura CC (1992); Miho CC (1992); Pine Lake GC (1984); Shizukuishi GC (1984); Springfield GC (1986); Sun Hills CC (1990); Zuiryo CC (1990).

Philippines: Calatagan GC (1983).

Singapore: Raffles GC (1986).

South Africa: Wild Coast CC (1983).

Thailand: Eastern Star CC (1992); Green Valley GC (1988).

Courses remodeled or expanded by Don Knott (All as assistant to Robert Trent Jones, Jr.):

Idaho: Sun Valley GC (R. A.4 1979).

RICHARD WILLIAM LaCONTE
(1931–)

After working for years as a golf course superintendent, Richard LaConte was associated with golf architect William F. Mitchell for a short time before Mitchell's death in 1974. He then practiced on his own and, for one year, in partnership with Ted McAnlis. In the 1980s LaConte left course design to concentrate on housing developments. On two such developments, he worked with McAnlis on the layouts.

Courses by Richard W. LaConte (All with Ted McAnlis unless otherwise indicated):

Florida: Lone Pine GC (Precision 1981).

Ohio: Briardale Greens Muni (1977); Chapel Hills GC (*solo*); Dorlon Park GC (1972 *solo*); Duck Creek CC (1972 *solo*); Leaning Tree GC (Precision 1972); Parkview Heights GC (Precision 1971 *solo*); Rolling Green GC (1967 *solo*); Whetstone CC (1972), ass't William F. Mitchell.

Courses remodeled or expanded by Richard W. LaConte (All with Ted McAnlis unless otherwise indicated):

Florida: Suntree CC (North Cse, R. *solo*).

Louisiana: Brechtel Memorial Park GC (R.9 A.9 1978).

Ohio: Grandview CC (R.); Willard CC (A.9 1971).

John LaFoy, 1990
COURTESY ASGCA

JOHN B. LaFOY
(1946–), ASGCA

BORN: Forest Hills, New York.

A native of New York, John LaFoy was raised in Greenville, South Carolina, where he was a schoolmate of George Cobb, Jr., son of prominent golf architect George W. Cobb. After receiving a Bachelor of Arts degree in architecture from Clemson University in 1968, LaFoy went to work for Cobb. His early duties included accompanying Cobb on frequent consultations at Augusta National, an experience much envied by other course architects.

A three-year stint in the U.S. Marine Corps interrupted LaFoy's employment with Cobb. When he returned, he soon became a full partner in the business. LaFoy assumed much of the design responsibilities when illness slowed Cobb in the early 1980s. Several courses credited to George Cobb, including the dramatic mountaintop Linville Ridge CC in North Carolina, were done almost entirely by LaFoy, who maintained the design business in Greenville after Cobb's death in 1986.

Courses by John LaFoy (All with George W. Cobb unless otherwise indicated):

Florida: Cape Haze GC (Precision 1987 *solo*); [The] Moors GC (1992 *solo*).

Georgia: Foxcreek GC (Precision 1986 *solo*); Stone Mountain GC (Lakemont Cse, 9 1987, A.9 1991 *solo*).

North Carolina: Bryan Park GC (Players Cse 1973); Devil's Ridge GC (1991 *solo*); Lane Tree GC (1992 *solo*); Linville Ridge CC (1983).

South Carolina: Clemson University GC (1976); Cobb's Glen CC (1975); Holly Tree CC (1973); Keowee Key CC (1977); Woodlands CC (1975).

Tennessee: Windtree GC (1991 *solo*).

Virginia: Glenmoor CC (1992 *solo*); New Quarter Park GC (1977); Pohick Bay CC (1978); Tides Inn & CC (Golden Eagle Cse 1976).

Courses remodeled or expanded by John LaFoy (All with George W. Cobb unless otherwise indicated):

Alabama: CC of Birmingham (East Cse, R. 1990 *solo*); Coosa Pines CC (A.11 1984 *solo*); Grayson Valley CC (R. *solo*); Huntsville CC (R. 1991 *solo*); Montgomery CC (R. 1987 *solo*); Mountain Brook C (R. 1985 *solo*); Riverchase CC (R.15 1990 *solo*); Valley Hill CC (R.27 1985 *solo*); Vestavia CC (R. 1989 *solo*).

Florida: Palma Ceia G&CC (R.4 1986 *solo*).

Georgia: Athens CC (A.3rd 9 1982); Augusta National GC (R. 1977); Savannah CC (R.3 1977); University of Georgia GC (R. 1990 *solo*); Waynesboro CC (A.9 1984); West Lake CC (R. 1991 *solo*).

Minnesota: Somerset CC (R. 1976).

Mississippi: CC of Jackson (R. 1988 *solo*).

North Carolina: CC of Sapphire (R. 1 1985 *solo*); Cape Fear CC (R. 1986 *solo*); Carolina CC (R. 1990 *solo*); Cleveland CC (R. 1986 *solo*); Finley GC (R.3 1979); Greensboro CC (Carlson Farms Cse, R. 1. 1985 *solo*); High Hampton Inn GC (R.6 1980); High Meadows GC (R. 1985 *solo*); North Ridge CC (R. 1989 *solo*); Pine Lake

CC (R. 1986 *solo*); Rolling Hills CC
(A.9 1967); Rolling Hills CC (R. 1986
solo); Southern Pines CC (R. 1988
solo); Willow Lakes GC, Pope AFB
(A.9 1974).

South Carolina: CC of Charleston (R.
1990 *solo*); CC of Spartanburg (R.
1985 *solo*); Florence CC (R. 1986
solo); Forest Lake CC (R. 1991 *solo*);
Fort Jackson GC (R.4 1986 *solo*);
Ocean Point G Links (R. 1976); Port
Royal GC (Robbers Row Cse, A.9
1974).

Tennessee: Jackson CC (R. 1991 *solo*);
Johnson City CC (R. 1987 *solo*); Mem-
phis CC (R. 1988 *solo*); Ridgefields CC
(R. 1986 *solo*).

Virginia: Lonesome Pine CC (R.10 1987
solo); Tides Inn & CC (Tartan Cse, R.
A.3 1984 *solo*).

West Virginia: Fincastle CC (R. *solo*);
Twin Falls State Park GC (A.9 1979);
Western Greenbrier Hills GC (R.
1976).

Bermuda: Mid Ocean C (R. 1987 *solo*).

Harold B. Lamb

A professional golfer based in Salt Lake
City, Utah, Hal Lamb won the 1922 Utah
Open. He designed several of his home
state's earliest courses, including The
Country Club, Salt Lake City.

William Boice Langford
(1887–1977), ASGCA, CHARTER MEMBER;
PRESIDENT 1951, 1963

BORN: Austin, Illinois.
DIED: Sarasota, Florida, at age 89.

William B. Langford suffered from polio
as a child and took up golf as part of a
rehabilitation program. He developed into
a fine amateur player and was a member of
three Yale University NCAA Championship teams from 1906 to 1908.

After earning a Master's degree in mining engineering at Columbia University,
Langford returned to Chicago and worked
as course architect for the American Park
Builders. He formed his own course-
design firm in 1918 in partnership with
engineer Theodore J. Moreau. Langford
and Moreau were active in course design
and construction throughout the Midwest
from the 1920s to World War II. They

*William B.
Langford, circa
1935* COURTESY TOM
LANGFORD

produced detailed engineering drawings
and balanced cuts and fills for construction as early as the 1920s. Late in his career, Langford estimated that he had
designed some 250 courses and had at one
time employed eighty men, including
three survey crews to prepare topographic
maps and set grading stakes.

Langford also owned and operated several daily-fee courses in the Chicago area
and was a strong promoter of public
courses. He served for many years on the
USGA Public Links Committee, as well as
on local and regional public golf associations. During and after the Depression, he
wrote several articles advocating six-hole
courses with multiple tees to speed play
and accommodate play for the average
working man.

The Langford and Moreau firm dissolved in the early 1940s, but after World
War II Langford again developed a golf
design business. In the 1960s, in semiretirement, he served as consulting golf
architect to the landscape architecture
firm of McFadzean and Everly of Winnetka, Illinois. Langford retired to Florida
in the late 1960s. He died there in 1977,
just a few weeks short of his ninetieth
birthday.

Courses by William B. Langford (All
with Theodore J. Moreau unless
otherwise indicated):

Arkansas: Al Amin Temple CC; Texarkana CC (1927).

Florida: Eglin AFB GC (1925); Granada
GC (9 1925); Kelsey City GC (1924,
NLE); Key West GC (1923, NLE);
Lake Worth Muni (1924); Parkhurst
CC (1925, NLE); St. Lucie River CC
(1924, NLE); Valparaiso CC (1927,
NLE); West Palm Beach CC (1921,
NLE).

Illinois: Acacia CC (1924); Aroma Park
GC (*solo*); Bloomington CC (1917
solo); Bryn Mawr GC (1921); Butter-

field CC (1922); Doering Estate GC (6
1931); Franklin County CC (9 1922);
Golden Acres CC (27 1928); Kankakee
Elks CC (1936); Maple Crest GC (9
Par 3 1951 *solo*); Marquette Park GC
(1917 *solo*); Mid City GC (1924,
NLE); Morris CC (9 1925, NLE);
Northmoor CC (*solo*, NLE); Oaklawn
GC (9 Par 3 1952 *solo*); Ridgemoor
CC (1921 *solo*); Riverside GC (1917
solo); Ruth Lake CC (1926); Skokie
Playfield GC (9 Par 3, NLE); South
Bluff CC (9 *solo*); St. Clair CC (1927);
Twin Orchard CC (1924, NLE); Vil-
lage Green CC (1955 *solo*).

Indiana: Buena Vista CC (9 1921 *solo*);
Christiana CC (9 1925, A.9 1945 *solo*);
Culver Military Academy GC (1920
solo); Dykeman Park Muni (9); East
Shore CC (1922); Gary CC (1921);
Harrison Hills CC (9 1923); La Porte
CC (9 *solo*); Maxwelton GC (*solo*);
Oakland City GC (9 1946 *solo*).

Iowa: Credit Island GC (1925); Duck
Creek Park GC (1927); Ellis Park
Muni (1949 *solo*); Oneota CC (9
1921); Wakonda C (1922).

Kansas: Meadow Lake CC (1917 *solo*,
NLE); Milburn G&CC (1917 *solo*);
Quivira Lakes GC.

Kentucky: Audubon CC (1921); Bowling
Green CC (NLE); Henderson G&CC;
Indian Hills CC (*solo*).

Michigan: Blythefield CC (1927); CC of
Lansing (1919); Iron River CC (1932);
Marquette G&CC (9 1927); Portage
Park GC (9 1916 *solo*, NLE); Riverside
CC (*solo*).

Minnesota: Mankato GC (9 1925; A.9
1954 *solo*).

Mississippi: Clarksdale CC (1921).

Nebraska: Happy Hollow C (1926);
Highland CC (1924).

North Dakota: Town & Country C (9
1920).

Ohio: Avon Fields GC (1924); Clovernook CC (1924); Fairlawn CC (1917
solo); Hillcrest CC (1925, NLE); Portage CC (1918 *solo*).

South Carolina: Greenville CC (Riverside
Cse 1919 *solo*).

South Dakota: Minnehaha CC (1922).

Tennessee: CC of Morristown (1957
solo); Chickasaw CC (1922 *solo*); Colonial CC (1916 *solo*, NLE); Gatlinburg G&CC (1956 *solo*); Green
Meadow CC (1958 *solo*); Ridgeway CC
(9 1919 *solo*, A.9 1950 *solo*, NLE).

Texas: State Line GC (1930).

Wisconsin: Lawsonia GC (Links Cse
1929); Leathem Smith Lodge GC (9

1930); North Shore Acres CC (*solo*, NLE); Our CC (1927); Ozaukee CC (1922); Spring Valley CC (1927); West Bend CC (9 1922).
Jamaica: St. James GC (9 *solo*, NLE).

Courses remodeled or expanded by William B. Langford (All with Theodore J. Moreau unless otherwise indicated):

Florida: [The] Breakers GC (R.9 A.9 1926); Coral Gables Biltmore GC (R. *solo*); Everglades C (R. 1937); Martin County G&CC (R.9 A.9 1951 *solo*, NLE).
Illinois: Barrington Hills CC (R.1 1946 *solo*); Beverly CC (R.4 *solo*); Biltmore CC (R. 1957 *solo*); Bryn Mawr GC (R. 1951 *solo*); Fresh Meadow G&CC (R. 1956 *solo*); Glen Oak CC (R. 1922); Hickory Hills CC (Par 3, A.9. 1954 *solo*); Highland Park GC (R.3 1939); Idlewild CC (R. *solo*); Mid City GC (R. 1931, NLE); Park Ridge CC (R. 1949 *solo*); Ravisloe CC (R.); Ridgemoor CC (R. 1927); Riverside GC (R. 1951 *solo*); Skokie CC (R. 1938); Tam O'Shanter CC (R. 1948 *solo*, NLE); Westmoreland CC (R. *solo*); Winnetka Park GC (Par 3, A.9 1960 *solo*).
Iowa: Keokuk CC (R. 1951 *solo*).
Kentucky: Louisville CC (R. 1921).
Wisconsin: Westmoor GC (R.5 1955 *solo*).

**ERIK TODD LARSEN
(1954–   ), ASGCA**

BORN: Newton, Iowa.

Erik Larsen graduated from North Carolina State University in 1978 with a degree in landscape architecture and horticulture. After working on several golf course construction projects, Larsen joined Arnold Palmer's design company in 1983 and soon developed into one of three major associate architects in the firm.

Erik Larsen, 1990
COURTESY ED SEAY

Courses by Erik Larsen (All as assistant to Arnold Palmer and Ed Seay):

Alabama: Cotton Creek C (1987).
Florida: Isleworth G&CC (1986); Matanzas Woods GC (1986); Mill Cove GC (1990); Orchid Island G & Beach C (1990).
Georgia: Eagle Watch GC (1989); Whitewater Creek GC (1988).
Hawaii: Hawaii Prince GC (1991); [The] Highlands GC (1992); South Kohala Resort GC at Mauna Kea (1991); Turtle Bay CC (New Cse 1992).
Illinois: Spencer T. Olin Community G Cse (1989); White Eagle GC (1989).
Kentucky: Lake Forest GC (1992).
Nevada: Angel Park GC (Mountain Cse, routing 1989; Palm Cse, routing 1990); Dayton Valley CC (1991).
North Carolina: Cullasaja C (1989).
Pennsylvania: Commonwealth National GC (1990).
South Carolina: Musgrove Mill GC (routing 1988).
South Dakota: Dakota Dunes GC (1991).
Virginia: Kingsmill GC (Plantation Cse 1986).
Wisconsin: Geneva National G&CC (Palmer Cse 1991).
Wyoming: Teton Pines G Cse (1987).
Australia: Sanctuary Cove GC (1989).
Italy: Ca'Della Nave GC (1987).
Korea: Eunhwasam CC (1992).
Malaysia: Damai Beach GC (1992).

Courses remodeled or expanded by Erik Larsen (All as assistant to Arnold Palmer and Ed Seay):

California: Rancho Murieta GC (North Cse, R. 1988).
Florida: Hidden Hills CC (R. 1988).
Pennsylvania: Laurel Valley GC (R. 1988).
Virginia: Keswick C of Virginia (R. 1991).

**ROBERT F. LAWRENCE
(1893–1976), ASGCA, CHARTER MEMBER;
PRESIDENT 1956, 1964**

BORN: White Plains, New York.
DIED: Tucson, Arizona, at age 83.

"Red" Lawrence (so-called because of his hair color) got his first golf design experience working for Walter Travis on the construction of two courses at Westchester CC in 1919. From 1921 to 1932 Red was employed by the firm of Toomey and Flynn as a construction superintendent.

Red Lawrence, 1949
COLLECTION RON WHITTEN

In the late 1920s Lawrence constructed several Toomey and Flynn designs in Florida, including 36 holes at the Boca Raton Hotel. When the design firm dissolved during the Depression, Lawrence became course superintendent at Boca Raton, where he remained for twenty years. While there, he became friends with the club's teaching professional, Tommy Armour. As a joke, Lawrence persuaded Armour to instruct a wealthy patron while sitting under a beach umbrella with drink in hand. Armour did it not once, but often, and this unorthodox teaching arrangement quickly became Armour's trademark.

In the late 1930s Lawrence designed a few courses in the Miami area, but most were not built until after World War II. When business improved after the war, Lawrence resigned from Boca Raton to devote full time to golf course architecture. He worked primarily in Florida until 1958, when he moved to Tucson, Arizona. Continuing his practice in the Southwest, Lawrence did some of his finest work, including Desert Forest Golf Club and the University of New Mexico's South Course. In the 1970s he was assisted on his last projects by civil engineer turned golf architect Jeff Hardin and young apprentice Greg Nash.

Courses by Red Lawrence:

Arizona: Bellaire GC (Precision 1973), with Jeff Hardin and Greg Nash; Boulders GC (9 1969, NLE); CC of Green Valley (1971); Camelback GC (Padre Cse 1970); Desert Forest GC (1962); Dobson Ranch GC (1974), with Jeff Hardin and Greg Nash; Fountain of the Sun GC (Precision 1971); Goodyear G&CC (West Cse 1974), with Jeff Hardin and Greg Nash; Meadow Hills CC (1963); Nautical Inn GC (10 Precision 1974); Santa Cruz CC (1974); Sierra Estrella GC (9 1962, A.9 1967); Tubac Valley CC (1960);

Tucson Estates GC (East Cse [9 Precision] 1972; West Cse [9 Par 3] 1960).

Florida: Dania CC (9 1951); Diplomat CC (1957); Fort Lauderdale CC (South Cse 1951); Miami Beach Par 3 GC (1961); Miami Shores CC (1937); Plantation GC (1951); Pompano Beach CC (Palms Cse 1954); Redland G&CC (1947); Sunset GC (9 1952).

New Mexico: Double Eagle CC [FKA Paradise Hills G&CC](1960); Horizon CC (9 1972); Sunport CC (Par 3 1970); University of New Mexico GC (South Cse 1966).

Courses remodeled or expanded by Red Lawrence:

Arizona: San Marcos Hotel & C (R. 1963); Tucson CC (R.3 1963); Tucson National GC (R.6 1966).

Florida: Bayshore GC (R., NLE); Boca Raton Resort & C (R. 1947); Delray Beach G&CC (A.3rd 9 1962); Fort Lauderdale CC (North Cse, R. 1951); Orange Brook CC (East Cse, R. 1961; West Cse, R.9 1955, A.9 1961).

Charles Dundas Lawrie
(1923–1976), BIGCA

BORN: Edinburgh, Scotland.
DIED: Edinburgh, Scotland, at age 53.

C. D. Lawrie was educated at Fettes and at Oxford, where he was a cricket star. After service with the Coldstream Guards during World War II, he was involved in sports administration and amateur golf. He reached the semifinals of the 1955 Scottish Amateur and won thirty-two consecutive matches with partner Donald Steel in the annual Halford Hewitt tournament. He also served as honorary captain of the 1961 and 1963 Walker Cup teams.

Lawrie, specializing in the administration of golf events, coordinated the activities of many British Open tournaments. His last was in 1972 at Muirfield. He also served as chairman of the Royal and Ancient Selection Committee and chose Walker Cup participants from 1963 to 1967. In the late 1960s Lawrie became a partner in the golf design firm of Cotton (C. K.), Pennink, Lawrie and Partners, Ltd., but had completed only a handful of courses before his untimely death in 1976.

Courses by: C.D. Lawrie (All with J. J. F. Pennink):

England: Abbey Hill GC (1975); Fakenham GC (9 1973); Rookery Park

GC; Royal Lytham & St. Annes GC (Short Cse, Precision); Southwick Park GC, "HMS Dryad" (1977); Twickenham GC (9 1976); Winter Hill GC (1976); Woburn G&CC (Duchess Cse 1976, and D. M. A. Steel; Duke Cse 1974).

Scotland: Livingston G&CC (1978); Westhill GC (1977).

Courses remodeled or expanded by C.D. Lawrie (All with J. J. F. Pennink):

England: Corhampton GC (R.9); Romsey GC (R.); Royal Wimbledon GC (R.).
Ireland: Cork GC (R. 1975), and C. K. Cotton.

Joseph L. Lee
(1922–   )

BORN: Oviedo, Florida.

Joe Lee, an outstanding high school and college athlete, graduated from the University of Miami with a degree in education. He took up golf while still in college and, after teaching math for a year at Delray Beach Junior High School in Florida, decided instead to pursue a professional golf career. Golf architect Dick Wilson, a Delray Beach acquaintance, helped Lee land the job of assistant pro at Moraine CC in Dayton, Ohio, which Wilson was remodeling at the time.

Lee spent two years at Moraine, and, while Wilson was working on the neighboring NCR Country Club courses, Lee lived with Wilson's family. In 1952 Lee left Moraine to assist with the completion of NCR. He went on to supervise construction of several Wilson designs and in the mid-1950s was given major responsibility for design and construction of Villa Real GC in Havana, Cuba.

By 1959 Lee was a full partner with Wilson. He finished four courses Wilson had been building at the time of his death in 1965 and then established his own practice with the assistance of many of the same crew that had been with Wilson for a decade or more. Concentrating at first in the Sun Belt, Lee created top courses throughout America as well as outstanding resort layouts in the Caribbean, Portugal and South America.

In 1971 Lee made Rocky Roquemore a partner in his firm. The two collaborated on many topflight courses over the next twenty years, including Stonehenge in Tennessee and Pine Meadow near Chi-

Joe Lee, 1985
COURTESY JOE LEE

cago. Lee was also assisted during his entire career by Betty Peters, an unsung design associate and business manager.

Though he worked for many years in the shadow of Dick Wilson, Joe Lee eventually eclipsed the legend of his mentor, both in terms of the total number of courses designed and the amount of public acclaim. Lee was a true gentleman of the game.

Courses by Joe Lee:

Alabama: Lakewood GC (Azalea Cse, 9 1967); Riverchase CC (1975); Wynlakes CC (1986), with Rocky Roquemore.

California: Heritage Hills CC (1992), with Rocky Roquemore; La Costa CC (North Cse, 9 1964, with Dick Wilson, A.9 1989; South Cse, 9 1964, with Dick Wilson, A.9 1973); Sunnylands GC (9 1962), with Dick Wilson.

Delaware: Bidermann GC, with Dick Wilson.

Florida: Audubon CC (1989); Ballenisles CC of JDM (East Cse 1964, with Dick Wilson; North Cse, 9 1964, with Dick Wilson, A.9 1969; South Cse, 9 1964, with Dick Wilson, A.9 1970); Banyan GC (1973), with Rocky Roquemore; Barefoot Bay G&CC (Precision 1972); Bay Hill C (1961), with Dick Wilson; Bent Pine GC (1979); Boca G&TC (1986); Boca Greens GC (1979); Boca West C (Cse No. 4 1982); Boca Woods CC (South Cse 1981); Bonaventure CC (East Cse 1970); Broken Sound CC (Old Cse 1976; Club Cse 1987); Camino Del Mar CC (1975); Canongate GC (Precision 1968); Century GC (Precision 1968); Century Village GC (Precision 1976); Del-Aire CC (27 1978); Ekana G&CC (1989); Errol Estates Inn & CC (27 1972); [The] Falls CC (1988); Feather Sound CC (1975); Gadsden CC (1975); Gator Creek GC (1976); GC at Marco (1991); Grand

Harbor GC (1989); Hamlet of Delray Beach GC (1973), with Rocky Roquemore; Harbour Ridge Y&CC (Golden Marsh Cse 1985); Harder Hall Hotel GC (1958), ass't Dick Wilson; High Ridge CC (1982); Hillsboro Pines GC (Precision 1975); Hobe Sound GC (1988); Hole-in-the-Wall GC (1958), ass't Dick Wilson; Interlachen CC (1986); International GC (1987); Island Dunes GC (9 Precision 1983); Lacuna CC (1985); Lake Buena Vista C (1972), with Rocky Roquemore; [The] Little C, Delray Beach (Par 3 1969); Lone Palm GC (1965), with Dick Wilson; Marriott's Orlando World GC (1986); Melreese GC (1962), with Dick Wilson; Orange Lake CC (27 1982); Palisades CC (1991); Palm-Aire West CC (Lakes Cse 1982); Pine Tree CC (1962), with Dick Wilson; Piper's Landing G&CC (1981); Quail Ridge CC (North Cse 1974; South Cse 1977); Rainbow's End G&CC (1979); River Hills CC (1989); River Ranch GC (9 1977); Sugar Mill CC (1970; A.3rd 9 1983, with Rocky Roquemore); Suwannee River Valley CC (9); Tequesta CC (1958), ass't Dick Wilson; Turtle Creek C (1969); Tuscawilla CC (1973); Walt Disney World GC (Magnolia Cse 1970; Palm Cse 1970), with Rocky Roquemore; Woodfield CC (1987).

Georgia: Bent Tree CC (1973); Bull Creek G Cse (1971); Callaway Gardens GC (Gardensview Cse 1969; Mountainview Cse 1963, with Dick Wilson; Skyview Cse 1969); Canongate GC (1965), with Dick Wilson; Canongate-on-Lanier GC (1970), with Rocky Roquemore; Canongate on White Oak GC (Cherokee Cse 1986), with Rocky Roquemore; Flat Creek GC (1970; A.3rd 9 1983, with Rocky Roquemore); [The] Hampton C (1989); Hidden Hills CC (1974), with Rocky Roquemore; Horseshoe Bend CC (1975), with Rocky Roquemore; Indian Hills CC (1970), with Rocky Roquemore; Jekyll Island GC (Indian Mounds Cse 1975, with Rocky Roquemore; Oleander Cse 1961, with Dick Wilson; Pine Lakes Cse 1967); Lake Lanier Islands Hotel & GC (1988), with Rocky Roquemore; Mystery Valley CC (1965), with Dick Wilson; Okefenokee GC (1983), with Rocky Roquemore; Pine Hills CC [FKA Snapfinger Woods GC] (27 1974), with Rocky Roquemore; Polo Fields G&CC

(1989); Rivermont G&CC (1970), with Rocky Roquemore; St. Simons Island C (1975), with Rocky Roquemore; Sconti GC (1974), with Rocky Roquemore; Sea Island GC (Retreat Nine 1959, with Dick Wilson; Marshside Nine 1973, with Rocky Roquemore); Tally Mountain C (1974); Valdosta CC (27 1981), with Rocky Roquemore.

Illinois: Cog Hill GC (Cse No. 3 1964, with Dick Wilson; Cse No. 4 1964, with Dick Wilson; R. 1977); Pine Meadow GC (1985), with Rocky Roquemore; Plum Tree National GC (1970).

Louisiana: Beau Chene G&RC (Magnolia Cse 1985; Oak Cse 1974), with Rocky Roquemore; Eastover CC (1988), with Rocky Roquemore; Squirrel Run G&RC (1987).

Maryland: Greystone GC (1993).

Nevada: Desert Rose GC [FKA Winterwood GC] (1964), with Dick Wilson.

New Jersey: Bedens Brook C (1961), with Dick Wilson.

New York: Cavalry C (1966), with Dick Wilson.

North Carolina: Cross Creek CC (1982), with Rocky Roquemore; Kenmure GC (1983), with Rocky Roquemore.

Ohio: Coldstream CC (1960), with Dick Wilson.

South Carolina: Houndslake CC (1976), with Rocky Roquemore.

Tennessee: Fall Creek Falls State Park GC (1972), with Rocky Roquemore; Montclair CC (9 Precision); Stonehenge GC (1984), with Rocky Roquemore.

Texas: Trophy Club CC (Oaks Cse 1976), with Ben Hogan; [The] Woodlands CC (North Cse, 9 1973; West Cse, 9 1973).

Virginia: CC of Virginia (Tuckahoe Creek Cse 1988), with Rocky Roquemore; [The] Crossings G&CC [FKA Half Sinke GC] (1977).

Bahamas: Bahamas Princess Hotel & CC (Emerald Cse 1965, with Dick Wilson; Ruby Cse 1967); Divi Bahamas GC [FKA South Ocean Beach Hotel GC] (1971); Fortune Hills GC (9 1972); Great Harbour Cay CC (1969); Lucayan G&CC (1964), with Dick Wilson; Lyford Cay C (1960), with Dick Wilson; Paradise Island G&CC (1962), with Dick Wilson; Shannon G&CC (1970); Treasure Cay GC (1966), with Dick Wilson.

Colombia: Club Lagos de Caujarel (1972).

Cuba: Villa Real GC (1957, NLE), ass't Dick Wilson.

Guam: Anderson AFB GC (1968).

Portugal: San Lorenzo GC (1988), with Rocky Roquemore; Vilamoura III GC (1990), with Rocky Roquemore.

St. Marten: Mullet Bay GC (1974).

Venezuela: Barquisimeto CC (1982), with Rocky Roquemore; Guataparo GC (1982), with Rocky Roquemore; Izcaragua CC (1982), with Rocky Roquemore.

Courses remodeled or expanded by Joe Lee:

Florida: Boca Raton Resort & CC (R. 1990); [The] Breakers GC (R. 1966); Clearwater CC (R. 1966); Fernadina Beach GC (A.3rd 9 1975); Gulfstream GC (R. 1958), ass't Dick Wilson; Indian Creek CC (R.), ass't Dick Wilson; John's Island C (South Cse, R. 1984); Lake Buena Vista GC (R. 1991); Orange Tree CC (R.1 1983); Palm Beach National G&CC (R. 1980); Pine Tree GC (R. 1990); Ponce de Leon Resort & CC (R. 1991); Ponte Vedra C (Lagoon Cse, A.9 1981); Riomar CC (R.); Sara Bay CC (R. 1980); Seascape G&RC (R. A.4 1980); Tyndall AFB GC (A.9 1975), with Rocky Roquemore.

Georgia: Berkeley Hills CC (A.3rd 9 1985), with Rocky Roquemore; Callaway Gardens GC (Lakeview Cse, A.9 1963), with Dick Wilson; Cherokee Town & CC (Riverside Cse, A.9 1986), with Rocky Roquemore; Green Island CC (R. 1978), with Rocky Roquemore.

Illinois: Cog Hill CC (Cse No. 1, R. 1963, with Dick Wilson; Cse No. 2, R. 1963, with Dick Wilson); Glenwoodie GC (R. 1978); St. Andrews G&CC (Cse No. 1, R. 1968; Cse No. 2, R. 1968).

Kentucky: Owensboro CC (R. 1978).

Louisiana: Baton Rouge CC (R. 1967); New Orleans CC (R.9 1982); Tchefuncta GC (A.9).

Michigan: Warwick Hills G&CC (R. 1967).

North Carolina: Highlands Falls CC (A.13 R.5 1985), with Rocky Roquemore.

Ohio: Scioto CC (R. 1963), with Dick Wilson.

Pennsylvania: Hidden Valley CC (R. 1968); St. Clair CC (A.9 1971).

Portugal: Quinto do Lago GC (Cse No. 2, A.9 1987), with Rocky Roquemore.

Herbert Corey Leeds
(1854–1930)

BORN: Boston, Massachusetts.
DIED: Hamilton, Massachusetts, at age 76.

Herbert Leeds graduated from Harvard College in 1877 and was awarded a Bachelor of Arts degree in 1891. A lifelong sportsman, he was an excellent baseball and football player in college. He was also a yachting enthusiast and spent three years sailing in the Far East and West Indies. As late as the turn of the century, Leeds was a crew member in several International Cup races, and his book *Log of the Columbia* (1899) related his experiences aboard a racing yacht. He was also an expert card player and wrote *The Laws of Bridge* and *The Laws of Euchre*.

Leeds took up golf when he was nearly 40, but within two years was playing at scratch. Though beyond his prime when national Amateur tournaments became prominent, he did win several club championships and invitation tournaments. He was a member of the USGA Executive Committee in 1905.

Leeds's first golf design experience was the creation of a new 18-hole course for Myopia Hunt Club, replacing its rudimentary nine-hole layout that had been built by R. M. Appleton, master of the club's fox hounds. Leeds, who remained at Myopia all his life and served as captain of its green committee, built the front nine in 1896 and the back nine in 1901. The course exists today, with only minor changes, just as he created and refined it.

Leeds's efforts at Myopia created a landmark course, the scene of many early matches, including four U.S. Opens. It was praised by leading American and British golfers and was written about in publications on both sides of the Atlantic. Myopia's historian, Edward Weeks, once observed about Leeds: "He never ceased digging new traps. It was his habit to carry small white chips in his pocket. . . . When the drive of a long hitter was sliced or hooked Leeds would place a marker on the spot and a new trap filled with soft white Ipswich sand would appear." This resulted in some holes being praised by British professionals as the most skillfully trapped in the United States.

After a tour of the great links of Britain in 1902, Leeds returned to the United States to build several other courses. Although club champion at The Country Club in Brookline, Massachusetts, there is no evidence that he participated in any of its expansions. He did, however, create the original course at Essex CC in Manchester, as well as Bass Rocks GC in Gloucester. He also worked outside his native state, as far north as Maine (the original nine at Kebo Valley Club in Bar Harbor in 1894) and as far south as South Carolina (the original nine at Palmetto CC in Aiken).

Peter W. Lees
(1868–1923)

BORN: England.
DIED: Asheville, North Carolina, at age 55.

Peter Lees, greenkeeper at Royal Mid-Surrey, emigrated to the United States around 1912 to construct and maintain Lido Golf Club on Long Island for architect Charles Blair Macdonald. He had been recommended for the job by J. H. Taylor, one of the "Great Triumvirate" of British golf.

Lees was described in obituaries as a noted golf architect and is known to have designed Hempstead G&CC on Long Island and to have revised Ives Hill CC at Watertown, New York, as well as Royal Mid-Surrey with Taylor. He was better known, however, as a constructor of courses for such architects as Macdonald, Tillinghast and others.

Alan Lenz, 1990
COURTESY ALAN LENZ

Alan S. Lenz
(1955–   )

BORN: San Antonio, Texas.

After majoring in art in college, Alan "Bud" Lenz began working on construction projects for the golf design firm of von Hagge and Devlin in 1979. When Bruce Devlin left the firm in 1987, Lenz was offered the chance to make the transition from field to drawing board. He became an associate architect and worked on all subsequent von Hagge projects with von Hagge and fellow associates Rick Baril, Kelly Moran and Mike Smelek. While some associates focused on particular areas of the globe, Lenz handled over fifty projects around the world.

Stanley Leonard

A well-known professional golfer from Vancouver, British Columbia, Stan Leonard won many tournaments in the United States and Canada. In 1974 he was appointed director of golf at Desert Island CC in California.

Leonard assisted a number of golf architects in planning courses in the 1960s and later did design work in collaboration with Philip Tattersfield of Tattersfield Associates Ltd., a land-design group based in Vancouver.

Courses by Stan Leonard (All with Philip Tattersfield):

Alberta: Red Wood Meadows GC.
British Columbia: Tall Timber GC (1979), and *Wayne Lindberg*; 108 Mile Resort GC (1970).

Courses remodeled or expanded by Stan Leonard (All with Philip Tattersfield):

California: Desert Island CC (R.).
British Columbia: Peace Portal GC (R.).

Gordon G. Lewis
(1950–   )

BORN: Paola, Kansas.

A 1974 graduate of Kansas State University, Gordon Lewis worked summers on course construction crews for Floyd Farley. After college he worked for architect David Gill in St. Charles, Illinois, then joined the staff of park planner Charles Graves.

In 1979 Lewis moved to Clearwater, Florida, and formed his own design business. The bulk of his work was concentrated on the west coast of Florida. In 1990 Lewis agreed to serve as designer for a firm established by PGA Tour golfer Paul Azinger.

Courses by Gordon G. Lewis:

Florida: Alden Pines GC (1981); Deer Run GC (Precision 1983); Eagle Ridge CC (1983); Fairway Woodlands GC (1991); Forest CC (Bear Cse, 9 1980,

Gordon Lewis, 1991
COURTESY GORDON
LEWIS

A.9 1986; Bobcat Cse 1987); Fountain Lakes GC (Precision 1991); Golfview G&RC (Precision 1992); Hunters Ridge CC (1988); Indian River Colony C; Kelly Greens G&CC (1989); Newport GC (Precision); Royal Tee CC (27 1991); Sabal Springs GC (Palm Cse [Precision] 1988); Sabal Cse 1990); Southampton GC (1991); Spanish Wells G&CC (1980); Terraverde G Cse (9 Par 3); Savannahs GC; Villages at Country Creek GC (Precision 1988); [The] Vines CC (1985); Worthington CC (1991).
Pennsylvania: Valley Forge GC.

Courses remodeled or expanded by Gordon G. Lewis:

Florida: Bay Beach (Precision R.); Bradenton CC (R.); Burnt Store Village GC (R.); CC of Naples (R.); Eagle Creek CC (R.); Harder Hall Hotel GC (R. 1985); Lakewood (R.9); Lehigh Acres CC (South Cse, R.); Palma Sola CC (R.); Placid Lakes (R.); Quail Creek CC (Creek Cse, R.1 1990); Seven Lakes G&CC (R.); Sun 'N Lake GC (R.); Whiskey Creek (Precision R.)

WILLIAM B. LEWIS, JR.

A former associate of George Cobb, William Lewis established his own design firm in North Carolina in the 1970s. In the 1980s he moved his office to Pickens, South Carolina, and concentrated his work in the Southeast.

Courses by William B. Lewis:

Florida: Bent Tree G&RC (1975); Peridia G&CC (Precision 1988); Village Green GC, Bradenton (Precision 1971); Village Green GC, Sarasota (Precision 1969); Village Green GC, Tavares (Precision 1976); Whiskey Creek CC (Precision 1972).
North Carolina: Bald Mountain GC [FKA Fairfield Mountains GC] (1973); Blue Mountain GC [FKA Wolf Laurel GC] (1969); Glen Cannon GC (1966); Great Smokies Hilton GC (1975); Meadowbrook GC (1972).
South Carolina: Rolling Green GC (1967); Saluda Valley CC (1963); Tega Cay CC (1971).

BERNHARD VON LIMBURGER
(1901–1981)

BORN: Leipzig, Germany,
DIED: Stuttgart, West Germany, at age 80.

Bernhard von Limburger learned golf in Scotland at age thirteen and won the German Amateur in 1921, '22 and '25. He represented Germany thirty-five times in international golf competition. He earned a degree in law but never practiced, choosing instead to publish a German golf magazine that he edited until the mid-1930s. During this period, he laid out a few courses that were, by his own admission, terrible designs.

In the 1930s Limburger formed a partnership with Berlin golf professional Karl Hoffmann, already an accomplished designer. Hoffmann and Limburger created several top courses in Germany before World War II and also operated a number of them. But their business was terminated by the war, and Limburger returned to his native Leipzig to work as a club manager. In 1943 he fled to south Germany and never returned to Leipzig, which became part of the Communist zone after the war.

Hoffmann and Limburger resumed their practice at the war's close, but Hoffmann died in the early 1950s. Limburger was successful in landing several commissions to build courses for American military bases in the newly created West Germany in the late 1940s, and by the 1950s he was designing full-time. In the 1960s and '70s he was busy designing and constructing courses in many parts of Europe.

Always a strong advocate of strategic design and a strong opponent of water hazards and overbunkering (especially with what he termed "jigsaw-puzzle pieces"), Limburger developed a distinctly European style of golf architecture. All German Open tournaments after World War II through 1978 were played on courses he had designed or revised. Limburger was also the author of three golf books published in West Germany.

Courses by Bernhard von Limburger (All with Karl Hoffmann unless otherwise indicated):

Austria: Badgastein GC (9 1962 *solo*); Bellach GC (*solo*); Murhof GC (9 1962, A.9 1972 *solo*); Schloss Fuschl G&CC (9 Par 3 *solo*); Schloss Pichlarn GC (9 1972 *solo*).
Germany: Augsburg GC (1959 *solo*); Bad Driburger GC (9); Bad Waldsee GC (9 *solo*); Bayreuth GC; Chemnitzer GC; Cologne G und Landclub; Delkenheim GC (1982 *solo*); Dortmunder GC (1956 *solo*); Duren GC (9 1965 *solo*); Essen-Kettwig Haus Oefte GC (1959); Feldafing GC (1926); Freiburger GC (1970 *solo*); Furth im Wald GC (*solo*); Garmisch-Partenkirchen GC; Gaschwitz GC; Gut Steinberg GC (*solo*); Hamburg-Ahrensburg GC (*solo*); Hamburg-Waldorfer GC (*solo*); Harz GC (9 1972 *solo*); Heidelberg G & Sports C (*solo*); Herrenalb-Bernbach GC (9 *solo*); Hubbelrath GC (East Cse 1961 *solo*; West Cse [Precision] 1963 *solo*); Intercontinental GC (9 *solo*); Kassel-Wilhelmhohe GC (9 *solo*); Konstanz GC (9 1965 *solo*); Kornwestheim GC (*solo*); Krefelder GC (1930); Lindau-Bad Schachen GC (1954 *solo*); Lohersand GC (9 *solo*); Mannheim-Viernheim GC (9); Marienburger GC (*solo*); Morsum-Sylt GC (9 *solo*); Munchener GC (*solo*); Neckartal GC (*solo*); Neustadt GC (9); Neu-Ulm GC (9 1964 *solo*); Oberfranken GC (9 *solo*); Oberschwaben–Bad Waldsee GC (*solo*); Oldenburgischer GC (9 *solo*); Ostwestfalen-Lippe GC (9 *solo*); Pfatz GC (9 1971 *solo*); Reichswald GC (*solo*); Saarbrücken GC (1961 *solo*); Sauerland GC (9 *solo*); Schloss Anholt GC (9 *solo*); Schloss Braunfels GC (9 1970 *solo*); Schloss Myllendonk GC (9 1964 *solo*); Schloss Rheden GC (9 *solo*); Siegen-Olpe GC (9 *solo*); Spangdahlem GC (9 *solo*); Stuttgarter GC (1927); Timmendorferstrand GC (Cse No. 1 *solo*; Cse No. 2 [Precision] *solo*); Ulm-Do GC (9 *solo*); Weidenbruck Gutersloh GC (*solo*); Westfaelischer GC (*solo*); Wittenberg GC (9); Wuppertal GC (9 *solo*); Zur Vahr GC (Garlstedt Cse 1966 *solo*).
Spain: Atalaya Park Hotel G&CC (1976 *solo*).

Switzerland: Basel G&CC (1928); Blumisberg G&CC (1959 *solo*); Neuchatel GC (9 1928); Zurich-Hittnau G&CC (1964 *solo*).

Courses remodeled or expanded by Bernhard von Limburger (All with Karl Hoffmann unless otherwise indicated):

Czechoslovakia: Marienbad GC (R. *solo*).
Germany: Bergisch Land und GC (R. *solo*); Falkenstein GC (R. *solo*); Frankfurter GC (R. *solo*); Hamburg-Falkenstein GC (R. *solo*); Hamburg-Waldorfer GC (R. 1973 *solo*); Hanover GC (R.); Kiel GC (R. *solo*); Kitzenberg GC (R. *solo*); Kol-Refrath GC (R. *solo*); Kronberg GC (R. *solo*).
Northern Ireland: Clandeboye GC (Ava Cse, R. 1969), with T. J. A. Macauley.

Al Linkogel, circa 1950 COLLECTION RON WHITTEN

ALBERT ANTHONY LINKOGEL (1907–1982)

BORN: St. Louis, Missouri.
DIED: Marthasville, Missouri, at age 74.

Al Linkogel served as superintendent at Westwood Country Club in St. Louis, Missouri, from the 1930s until 1953, when he resigned to operate a turf nursery, lawn and garden supply business. In the 1950s he began converting sand green courses in Missouri and Illinois to grass. He also designed several original courses in those states.

Courses by Al Linkogel:

Illinois: Columbia GC (1960); Hillcrest GC (Par 3).
Missouri: Cape Girardeau CC (9 1955); Cherry Hills CC, with *Ray Freeborg*; St. Ann GC (9 1951); St. Charles GC (1956).

Gary Linn, 1991
COURTESY GARY LINN

GARY D. LINN (1955–), ASGCA

BORN: Wichita, Kansas.

An early interest in golf was almost unavoidable for Gary Linn, whose parents and siblings were all avid amateur golfers. Linn attended Kansas State University and received a Bachelor of Landscape Architecture degree in 1978. After a short stint with a large architectural/planning firm in his hometown of Wichita, Linn joined Robert Trent Jones, Jr.'s California organization in late 1978 as a design associate. Later he assumed a large role as a vice president of the company, handling projects in the Midwestern United States and the Pacific Rim.

Courses by Gary Linn (All as assistant to Robert Trent Jones, Jr.):

Arkansas: Chenal CC (1990).
California: Shoreline G Links (1983).
Colorado: Skyland GC (1984).
Florida: Weston Hills CC (1990); [The] Windsor C (1991).
Hawaii: Makena GC (New Cse 1992).
Louisiana: Le Triomphe GC (1986).
Missouri: Highland Springs CC (1989).
Alberta: Glencoe G&CC (Forest Cse 1984; Meadow Cse 1985).
British Columbia: Château Whistler G Cse (1992).
Japan: Cherry Hills GC (27 1989); Golden Valley GC (1987); Kinojo GC (1992); Pine Lake GC (1984); Springfield GC (1986); Zuiryo GC (1990).
Korea: Yongpyeong GC (1988).
Taiwan: Sun Rise CC (1991).
Thailand: Santiburi GC (1992).

Courses remodeled or expanded by Gary Linn (All as assistant to Robert Trent Jones, Jr.):

California: [The] Links at Monarch Beach (A.2nd 9 1984).

JAMES W. LIPE, JR. (1946–), ASGCA

BORN: Cary, Mississippi.

James Lipe attended Louisiana State University and obtained a Business Management degree in 1969 and a Master's degree in landscape architecture in 1972. He then moved to Ann Arbor, Michigan, and joined the firm of golf architect William Newcomb. In the early 1980s, after a brief stint in Michigan in solo practice, Lipe was hired by Jack Nicklaus to serve as a design associate. He eventually rose to senior design associate status within the organization, working both on Nicklaus designs throughout the world and handling designs on his own under the Golden Bear Golf Associates banner.

Courses by Jim Lipe (All as assistant to Jack Nicklaus unless otherwise indicated):

Illinois: Wynstone CC (1989).
Michigan: Grand Traverse G Resort (Resort Cse 1979), ass't Bill Newcomb; Indianfield G&CC (1976), ass't Bill Newcomb; TPC of Michigan (1990); Travis Pointe CC (1976), ass't Bill Newcomb.
Mississippi: Castlewoods CC (1991 *solo*).
North Carolina: Governors C (1990); Pinehurst National GC (1989).
South Carolina: Melrose GC (1987); Pawley's Plantation GC (1988).
Tennessee: Richland CC (1988).
Austria: GC Gut Altentann (1988).
England: St. Mellion G&CC (New Cse 1987).

Courses remodeled or expanded by Jim Lipe (All as assistant to Jack Nicklaus unless otherwise indicated):

Michigan: Chemung Hills CC (A.9 1983), ass't Bill Newcomb; Fox Hills CC (R. A.3rd 9 *solo*).

Jim Lipe, 1991
COURTESY JIM LIPE

Bruce Littell, 1970

BRUCE A. LITTELL

Raised in Houston, Texas, Bruce Littell obtained a Bachelor of Science degree in landscape architecture from Texas A&M in 1961. He joined the course-design firm of Jay Riviere in 1965 and formed his own business two years later.

Courses by Bruce Littell:

Texas: Bear Creek Golf World (Executive Cse [Precision] 1978); Cape Royale CC; Clay County CC (9 1970); Goose Island Lake GC; Houston Golf Academy (9 Par 3); Kingwood CC (Lake Cse 1977); Kirbywood CC (9); Padre Isle GC (1971); Point Venture Y&CC (1972); Royale Green GC; Sunnyside CC; Woodcreek CC (Brook Hollow Cse 1973).

Courses remodeled or expanded by Bruce Littell:

Texas: Texas A&M University GC (R. 1973).

Karl Litten, 1991

KARL V. LITTEN
(1933–   )

BORN: Braxton County, West Virginia.

After studying architecture and engineering at Steubenville College and Ohio University, Karl Litten worked as a civil engineer for twelve years, first in Ohio and then in Florida. In 1968 he joined golf architect Robert von Hagge and eventually became a vice president in the firm of von Hagge and Devlin.

In 1979 Litten formed his own golf design firm, based in Florida. From 1987 to 1989 professional golfer Gary Player served as a consulting partner in his firm.

Courses by Karl Litten:

California: Pacific GC (27 1988), with Gary Player.
Florida: Alaqua CC (1988), with Gary Player; Belle Glade G&CC (1987), with Gary Player; Boca Delray G&CC (Precision 1983); Boca Grove Plantation GC (1982); Boca Woods CC (North Cse 1984); Cheval Polo & CC (1986); Gleneagles CC (East Cse 1985; West Cse 1985); Overoaks CC (1986), with Gary Player; PGA National GC (Estates Cse) [FKA Stonewal CC] (1984); [The] Polo C (1991); Polo Trace C&TC (1990); Stonebridge G&CC (1985); Twisted Oaks GC (1991); Westchester G&CC (Regulation Cse 1989; Par 3 Cse 1989); Whisper Lakes GC (Precision 1988); Wycliffe G&CC (1989), with Bruce Devlin.
Kansas: Reflection Ridge CC (1989).
Massachusetts: White Cliffs of Plymouth GC (Precision 1986), with Gary Player.
Michigan: Huron GC (1989).
Missouri: Whitmoor CC (East Cse 1988; West Cse 1990).
New Jersey: Cape May National GC (1991).
England: Leek Wooten GC (1992).
Japan: Bato Korakuen CC (1990); Green Academy GC; Isao Aoki GC (1991), with *Isao Aoki.*
United Arab Emirates: Dubai Creek GC (1992); Emirates GC (1987).

Courses remodeled or expanded by Karl Litten:

Florida: Carolina CC (R.1 1987); Jupiter West GC (R. 1987, NLE).
New Jersey: Bamm Hollow CC (R. 1991).
Texas: Piney Woods CC (A.9 1982); Sleepy Hollow G&CC (Lake Cse, R. 1983; River Cse, R. 1983).

EDWARD G. LOCKIE
(1908–   )

A longtime PGA professional in East Moline, Illinois, "Ted" Lockie designed several courses in the Quad Cities area in the 1960s and 1970s before his retirement to Palm Beach Gardens, Florida, in 1976.

Courses by Ted Lockie:

Illinois: Golfmohr GC (1967); Pinecrest G&CC (1972); Short Hills CC.
Wisconsin: Fox Hills CC (1964; A.3rd 9 1970); Grandview GC (1969).

Courses remodeled or expanded by Ted Lockie:

Iowa: Davenport CC (R.2 1965).

Emil Loeffler, circa 1935

EMIL F. LOEFFLER
(1894–1948)

BORN: Pittsburgh, Pennsylvania.
DIED: Oakmont, Pennsylvania, at age 54.

"Dutch" Loeffler (nicknamed for his German heritage) spent his entire career at Oakmont Country Club in Pennsylvania. He began as a caddy at the age of ten, became caddy master in 1912, greenkeeper in 1913 (when John McGlynn vacated the position) and head professional in 1930. He was a fine golfer, winning the 1920 and 1922 Pennsylvania opens and qualifying for the 1920 and 1921 U.S. opens. He was also a member of the GCSAA and served as its national treasurer in 1929.

Loeffler was best known for his work at Oakmont as course superintendent, a position he held, even while serving as club professional, until his retirement in 1947. He instituted the changes and maintenance practices suggested by William C. Fownes, Jr., to make Oakmont the world's toughest golf course. He had several ideas of his own, including the weighted rake that formed the furrows in Oakmont's bunkers.

In the 1920s Loeffler was associated with John McGlynn in the design-and-build firm of Loeffler-McGlynn Co., which constructed courses of its own design, did reconstructions at established layouts and contracted to execute the work of other architects.

Courses by Emil Loeffler (All with *John McGlynn* unless otherwise indicated):

Pennsylvania: Alcoma CC (1923); Ambridge CC; Beaver Valley CC (9); Cedar Rocks CC; Del Mar CC (9); Greene County GC; Hannastown CC; Highland CC (1920); Hill Crest CC (9); Kittanning CC (1922); Latrobe CC (9); Montour Heights CC (9, NLE); Nemacolin CC; Oakmont East GC (1938); Pleasant Valley CC; Shannopin CC (1920); St. Jude CC; Titusville CC; Uniontown CC; Wildwood GC.
Texas: Willow Springs CC (9 1924).
West Virginia: Williams CC (1931).

Courses remodeled or expanded by Emil Loeffler (All with *John McGlynn* unless otherwise indicated):

Michigan: Red Run GC (R.).
Pennsylvania: Butler CC (R.); Chartiers CC (R.); Edgewood CC (R.); Green Oaks CC [FNA Westmoreland CC] (R.); Huntingdon Valley CC (R. solo, NLE); Monongahela Valley CC (R.9 A.9); Oakmont CC (R. 1920), with William C. Fownes, Jr.; Pittsburgh Field C (R.).

ROBERT M. LOHMANN (1952–), ASGCA

Bob Lohmann graduated in 1974 from the University of Wisconsin with a B.S. degree in landscape architecture. The following year he joined the design firm of Killian and Nugent, handling principal design responsibility for several new courses, including Forest Preserve National in Oak Forest, Illinois, a layout selected by *Golf Digest* as one of the nation's top public courses in 1984.

Lohmann remained for a time as a partner with Dick Nugent when Killian and Nugent disbanded, but in 1984 he struck out on his own in a firm, Lohmann Golf Designs Inc., based in the suburbs of northern Chicago.

Courses by Bob Lohmann:

Illinois: Boulder Ridge CC (1991), with *Fuzzy Zoeller*; Canterbury Place GC (1986); Countryside GC (1991); Forest Preserve National GC (1981), ass't

Bob Lohmann, 1991
COURTESY BOB LOHMANN

Ken Killian and Dick Nugent; [The] Merit C (1990); Oak Knoll GC (1989); Settler's Hill GC (1989); Streamwood Oaks GC (1988).
Indiana: Sand Creek C (1979), ass't Ken Killian and Dick Nugent.
Missouri: Sunset Lakes GC (1987).
Texas: Mission CC (1983), ass't Ken Killian and Dick Nugent.
Wisconsin: Birchwood GC (1987); Cedar Creek CC (1988); Fox Hills National GC (1988); Kettle Hills GC (routing); Spring Creek G Center (par 3 1987).

Courses remodeled or expanded by Bob Lohmann:

Hawaii: Navy Marine GC (R. 1988).
Illinois: Bartlett Hills GC (R. 1986); Beverly CC (R. 1985); Biltmore CC (R. 1987); Briarwood CC (R. 1989); Countryside GC (R. 1985); Crystal Lake CC (R. 1985); Crystal Woods GC (R. 1989); Exmoor CC (R. 1987); Forest Hills CC (R. 1989); Glencoe GC (R. 1982), ass't Ken Killian and Dick Nugent; Hinsdale GC (R. 1990); Kishwaukee CC (R. 1987); La Grange CC (R.2 1990); Mauh-Nah-Tee-See CC (R. 1989); Medinah CC (Cse No. 3, R.3 1986); Midlane CC (R. 1986); Pinecrest G&CC (R. 1985); Poplar Creek GC (R.2 1990); Randall Oaks GC (R. 1985); Ravinia Green CC (R. 1987); Ridgemoor CC (R. 1988); Rockford CC (R. 1988); Schaumburg Park GC (R. 1990); Sunset Valley GC (R. 1989); Villa Olivia CC (R.).
Indiana: Harbour Trees GC (R. 1986); Highland G&CC (R. 1990).
Iowa: Cedar Rapids CC (R. 1985); Davenport CC (R. 1988); Elmcrest CC (R. 1989).
Missouri: Ballwin Muni (R. 1987).
Nebraska: Happy Hollow C (R.3 1990).
Texas: Meadowbrook Muni, Lubbock (Cses No. 1 & 2, R. 1988).
Wisconsin: Blackhawk GC (R. 1986); Blue Mound G&CC (R. 1990); Brynwood CC (R. 1984); Butte des Morts

GC (R. 1985); Cherokee G&TC (R. 1985); Delbrook GC (R. 1987); Hawthorne Hills GC (R. 1988); LaCrosse CC (R.3 1986); Lake Windsor CC (R. 1990); Mayville CC (A.9 1989); Onieda G & Riding C (R. A.2 1985); Ozaukee CC (R. 1984); Racine CC (R. 1986); Reedsburg CC (A.9 1975), ass't Ken Killian and Dick Nugent; Riverside Muni (R. 1986); Rock River Hills GC (A.9 1987); Tripoli CC (R. 1987); Tuckaway CC (R. 1987); West Bend CC (R. 1985); Westmoor CC (R. 1989).

Bill Love, 1989
COURTESY BILL LOVE

WILLIAM ROBERT LOVE (1952–), ASGCA

BORN: Cookeville, Tennessee.

In 1972 Bill Love obtained an Associate Arts degree in graphic arts from Prince George's Community College in Largo, Maryland, and then attended Catholic University of America in Washington, D.C., where he obtained a Bachelor of Science degree in architecture. After practicing in the field of architecture for a time, Love enrolled at the University of Virginia and became the school's first graduate student to base a Master's thesis on golf course design.

He received his Master's degree in landscape architecture from Virginia in 1978 and promptly joined the Wheaton, Maryland, firm of Edmund B. Ault, for whom he had previously worked on a part-time basis. A member of the ASGCA, Love was also a member of the ASLA.

Courses by Bill Love:

Delaware: Wild Quail G&CC (1990).
Georgia: [The] Landings GC (1987), with Tom Clark.
Maryland: Clustered Spires G Cse (1991), with Brian Ault; TPC at Avenel (1986), with Ed Ault, Brian Ault, Tom Clark and *Ed Sneed*.

New Jersey: Concordia GC (1986), with
Brian Ault; Mercer Oaks GC (1991),
with Brian Ault.
North Carolina: Charles T. Myers GC (9
1986).
Pennsylvania: Briarwood West GC, York
(1989); Bavarian Hills GC (1989),
with Brian Ault.
South Carolina: Midway GC (27 Par 3
1984), with Edmund B. Ault.
Texas: Twin Wells G Cse (1988), with
Brian Ault.
Virginia: [The] Dominion C (1992), with
Curtis Strange; Ivy Creek Farm GC (9
1985).

Courses remodeled or expanded by Bill Love:

Arizona: Arizona CC (R. 1986), with
Tom Clark.
Delaware: Brandywine CC (R.7 1987),
with Brian Ault; Shawnee CC (A.9
1984), with Edmund B. Ault.
Kansas: Lake Quivira CC (R.4 1984);
Milburn G&CC (R.6 1985).
Maryland: Congressional CC (Blue Cse,
R.2 1981), with Edmund B. Ault and
Tom Clark; Longview Muni (R.3
1981), with Edmund B. Ault; Manor
CC (R.4 1986), with Edmund B. Ault
and Brian Ault; Suburban CC (R.4
1982), with Edmund B. Ault.
New Jersey: Greenacres CC (R.2. 1983),
with Brian Ault and Tom Clark.
Pennsylvania: North Hills Muni (R.10
1984); Oak Tree GC (R.2 1983), with
Brian Ault.
Virginia: Army-Navy CC (Arlington Cse,
R.5 1986, with Edmund B. Ault and
Tom Clark; Fairfax Cse, R.2 1984,
with Edmund B. Ault and Brian Ault);
Fredericksburg CC (R.1 1985).

RAYMOND FRANKLIN LOVING, JR. (1926–), ASGCA

BORN: Richmond, Virginia.

"Buddy" Loving received a B.A. degree
from the University of Virginia and an additional degree from Phillips College. He
also took courses in landscape architecture, turfgrass science and financial management at Virginia Polytechnic Institute.
He was trained in golf course architecture
by his grandfather Fred Findlay, for whom
he began working part-time in 1946, and
by his father Raymond Sr. who also did
some design work.

Buddy Loving, 1969
COURTESY ROBERT
DEAN PUTMAN

For a period in the late 1960s, Loving
worked in partnership with fellow architect Algie Pulley in a company that handled original designs and constructed
layouts designed by others. That company, GolfAmerica, disbanded in the
mid-1970s and Loving resumed solo practice of golf architecture.

Courses by Buddy Loving:

Maryland: Winters Run GC (1973).
Virginia: Boar's Head Inn GC (9 Par 3
1967); Confederate Hills CC (1972),
with Algie Pulley; Country Club Lakes
(Precision 1971), with Algie Pulley;
Evergreen CC (1968), with Algie Pul-
ley; Greene Hills C (1970); Hunting
Hills CC (1965), with Fred Findlay
and *R. F. Loving, Sr.;* Lake Monticello
GC (1972), with Algie Pulley; Lake-
view CC, with Fred Findlay and *R. F.
Loving, Sr.;* Lakeview Motor Inn GC (9
Precision 1972); Pen Park GC (9
1974); Retreat G&CC (1973); Shenan-
doah Crossings Farm & C (1991);
Shenandoah Valley CC (27 1974); Vir-
ginia Tech GC (1973); Water's Edge
GC (1988); Williamsburg Colony Inn
GC (9 Par 3 1973).

Courses remodeled or expanded by Buddy Loving:

Maryland: Patuxent Greens CC (R.).
North Carolina: Sedgefield CC (R. 1989).
Virginia: Army-Navy CC (Arlington Cse,
R.5 1970; Fairfax Cse, R.2 1970), with
Algie Pulley; CC of Fairfax (R. 1969),
with Algie Pulley; CC of Virginia
(James River Cse, R.3 1974); Farm-
ington CC (A.3rd 9 1965, with *R. F.
Loving, Sr.;* R. 1986); Hunting Hills
CC (R. 1987); Staunton CC (R. 1986);
Tides Inn & CC (Golden Eagle Cse, R.
1987); Washington G&CC (R.5
1969), with Algie Pulley.

GEORGE LOW, SR. (1874–1950)

BORN: Carnoustie, Scotland.
DIED: Clearwater, Florida, at age 76.

Soon after arriving in America, George
Low was joint runner-up in the 1899
United States Open. He soon took a job as
professional at Baltusrol Golf Club in New
Jersey, where he remained until the early
1920s. He then served briefly at Ekwanok
in Vermont and as pro at Huntingdon Valley in Pennsylvania. He also served as golf
instructor to two U.S. presidents, William
Howard Taft and Warren G. Harding.

Low designed several courses in the
northeastern United States. In the 1920s
he formed a short-lived partnership with
golf architect Herbert Strong before moving to Clearwater, Florida. There he served
as professional at Belleview-Biltmore until
poor health necessitated his retirement in
1940. Low's son George Jr. was long associated with the PGA Tour and was a respected putting expert.

Courses by George Low, Sr.:

Maryland: CC of Maryland [FKA Rodgers
Forge CC] (1923), with Herbert
Strong.
New Jersey: Echo Lake CC (1913),
with Donald Ross; Weequahic GC (9
1914).
New York: Blind Brook CC (1916); Yah-
nundasis GC (NLE).
Vermont: Rutland CC (9 1902).

Courses remodeled or expanded by George Low, Sr.:

Florida: Clearwater CC (R.).
New Jersey: Rockaway River CC (A.9
1916).
New York: Bluff Point CC (R. 1920);
Nassau CC (R. A.3 1924), with
Herbert Strong.

George Low, Sr.,
1932 COLLECTION RON
WHITTEN

John L. Low, circa 1910 COLLECTION RON WHITTEN

JOHN LAING LOW
(1869–1929)

BORN: Fife, Scotland.
DIED: Woking, England, at age 59.

John Low learned golf at St. Andrews and was an avid competitor all his life. He reached the semifinals at the British Amateur in 1897 and 1898 and was runner-up in 1901. He also won many tournaments at St. Andrews, including the Silver Cross in 1900 and 1909.

A graduate of Cambridge University, Low assisted in the creation of the Oxford and Cambridge Golfing Society in 1897 and served as its captain for twenty years. He organized the society's first matches in America in 1903 and captained the team that included C. H. Alison. Low was also a respected authority on the rules of golf, serving as chairman of the Rules Committee of the Royal and Ancient until 1921. John Low was on the staff of the *Pall Mall Gazette* and later the *Athletic News* and wrote extensively about golf in those and other newspapers. He also wrote several books on golf, including *Concerning Golf* (1903), the first book to codify the principles of golf course architecture.

In the early 1900s Low and fellow club member Stuart Paton worked together in remodeling Woking Golf Club. Their efforts turned a staid Tom Dunn layout into a remarkably strategic course. Although they did no other design work, the discussion, publicity and controversy arising from their changes at Woking contributed greatly to the development of golf course architecture.

John Low's principles of golf course architecture, which were widely circulated and followed during his lifetime, included these points:

1. A golf course should provide entertainment for the high and medium handicapper while at the same time present a searching and difficult test for the accomplished golfer.
2. The one aim of inventors is to reduce the skill required for golf. Golf architects must wage a battle against inventors by designing courses that emphasize golfing skills over equipment.
3. The shortest, most direct line to the hole, even if it be the center of the fairway, should be fraught with danger.
4. The architect must allow the ground to dictate play. The good architect sees that there is a special interest for the accomplished golfer in each stroke, just as the billiard player always has in mind the next stroke or strokes.
5. The fairway must be oriented to both the tee and the green, thereby stressing the importance of placing the teeshot in a position from which the green can be approached with safety.
6. Bunkers should be used sparingly by the architect. Except on one-shot holes, they should never be placed within 200 yards of the tee. Ridges and depressions are the best way of controlling the entrance to the green. The best hazard on a course is a fairway bunker 200 to 235 yards from the tee, placed five to ten yards off the accomplished player's most favorable line to the green.
7. Whenever possible, putting greens should be of the low, narrow plateau type, with the plateau tilting away, not toward, the player. No green should be higher at the back than it is in front, for that gives a player confidence. Only half the flagstick should be seen from where the approach shot should be played.
8. A course should never pretend to be, nor is it intended to be, an infallible tribunal of skill alone. The element of chance is the very essence of the game, part of the fun of the game.
9. All really great golf holes involve a contest of wits and risks. No one should attempt to copy a great hole because so much may depend on its surroundings as well as some features miles away in the background which influence and affect the play of the hole. If the terrain is suitable, some of the character of the original might be incorporated elsewhere.
10. Inequalities of putting green surfaces should not be exaggerated. A tilt from front to back, or left to right or vice versa is sufficient. There should always be a special position for the flagstick on important days.
11. Committees should leave well enough alone, especially when they have a really fine course.

GEORGE LOWE, JR.

Originally from Carnoustie, George Lowe moved to England, where he became greenkeeper at St. Annes in the early 1890s. In England he planned several layouts, including a new course for his home club, Royal Lytham and St. Annes, when it changed locations in 1896.

Courses by George Lowe, Jr.:

England: Ripon City GC (9 1905); Royal Birkdale GC (1889), with *Charles Hawtree*; Royal Lytham & St. Annes GC (1897); Windermere GC (1892).

Courses remodeled or expanded by George Lowe:

England: Seascale GC (A.9 1902).

ARTHUR VERNON MACAN
(1882–1964), ASGCA

BORN: Dublin, Ireland.
DIED: Victoria, British Columbia, at age 82.

Vernon Macan attended Trinity College in Dublin and earned a degree in law at the University of London. He then emigrated to Canada, living for two years in Quebec before moving to Victoria, British Columbia, in 1910, where he worked as a lawyer in the government's Division of Lands and Forests and became one of the area's top amateur golfers. He won a number of regional events in Canada and across the border was victorious in both the Washington State Amateur and the Pacific Northwest Amateur in 1913.

A. Vernon Macan, circa 1960 COURTESY DONALD HOGAN

His prowess as a player led a local judge to offer Macan the chance to design a course for the newly formed Royal Colwood Club. Soon after completing the course, Macan pondered designing courses full-time. But the war in Europe erupted, and he enlisted.

He was crippled for life during a World War I battle in Vimy, France, losing his left leg beneath the knee. Undaunted, Macan decided to continue golf design, using a cane to assist him in walking sites. Although he continued to work full-time in government service, he successfully moonlighted as an architect, and by the 1920s he was the busiest designer in the Pacific Northwest. He also continued to play the game, too, and maintained a four handicap for years.

Macan, who made detailed clay models of the holes he designed, was still actively involved in course architecture at the time he suffered a fatal heart attack at age 82. He was assisted on his last projects by engineer Donald Hogan and club pro Ken Tyson.

Courses by A. Vernon Macan:

California: California GC of San Francisco (1926); San Geronimo Valley GC (1965).
Idaho: Hillcrest CC (9 1940, A.9 1957); Purple Sage Muni (1963).
Oregon: Alderwood CC (NLE); Columbia-Edgewater CC (1925); Colwood National GC (1929).
Washington: Broadmoor GC (1927); Edgewater Muni (1954, NLE); Fircrest GC (1925); Inglewood CC (1923), with Robert Johnstone; Lake Spanaway GC (1967), with Ken Tyson; Manito G&CC (1922); Overlake G&CC (1953); Sunland CC (9 1964); Yakima CC (1956).
British Columbia: Cowichan G&CC (9 1947); Gleneagles GC (9); Gorge Vale GC; Kelowna G&CC; Langara GC; Marine Drive GC (1923); McCleery GC; Nanaimo G&CC (1961); Pentic-

ton G&CC; Qualicum Beach Memorial GC (9); Queen Elizabeth Park GC (Par 3); Richmond CC; Royal Colwood G&CC; Shaughnessy G&CC (1960); Shaughnessy Heights C (NLE); Stanley Park GC (Par 3).

Courses remodeled or expanded by A. Vernon Macan:

Oregon: Alderwood CC (R. 1949); Waverley CC (R.).
Washington: Seattle GC (R. 1950); Wenatchee G&CC (A.9 1958).
British Columbia: Victoria GC, Oak Bay (R. 1930).

T. J. A. Macauley, 1990 COURTESY T. J. A. MACAULEY

THOMAS JOHN ANDREW MACAULEY (1930–), BIGCA, FAGCA

A graduate of Queens University of Ulster, Northern Ireland, and fellow of the Institution of Civil Engineers and the Institution of Structural Engineers, T. J. A. Macauley worked as an assistant to German golf architect Bernhard von Limburger from 1969 to 1973. He also collaborated with Peter Alliss and David Thomas in course design. He later combined his practice as a golf architect with partnership in a firm of consulting civil and structural engineers located in Belfast, Northern Ireland.

Courses by T. J. A. Macauley:

Belgium: Château de la Bawette GC (27); Golf de Mont Garni.
England: Birchwood GC (1979); Welcombe Hotel GC (1980).
France: Golf de Bruz (27), with *Stephen Quenouille*; Golf de Marivaux, with *Stephen Quenouille*; Loudun–St. Hilaire GC (1985), with *Stephen Quenouille*; Ploemeur Ocean GC (27), with *Stephen Quenouille*.
Kenya: Windsor G&CC.
Netherlands: Comstrijen GC.

Northern Ireland: Clandeboye GC (Dufferin Course 1973), with Peter Alliss and David Thomas; Dunmurry GC (1982); Fort Royal GC (9 1974).
Scotland: Gleneagles Hotel GC (Glendevon Cse 1985, NLE); Letham Grange G&CC (Cse No. 2 1990).

Courses remodeled or expanded by T. J. A. Macauley:

England: Denton GC (R.); [The] Grange GC (R.9 A.9 1989); Hazel Grove GC (R.); Shaw Hill G&CC (R. 1983).
France: Fourqueux GC (Forest Cse, R.9 A.9 1989; Hill Cse, R. 1989), with *Stephen Quenouille*.
Isle of Man: Howstrake GC (R.).
Northern Ireland: Ballyclare GC (R.9 A.9 1973), with Peter Alliss and David Thomas; Bangor GC (R.1 1977); Clandeboye GC (Ava Cse, R. 1969), with Bernhard von Limburger; Enniskillen GC (A.1 1982); Wexford GC (R.).

NORMAN MACBETH (1879–1940)

BORN: Bolton, England.
DIED: Los Angeles, California, at age 61.

Norman Macbeth learned his golf at Lytham and St. Anne's and as a teenager lowered his handicap from 18 to 2 in the space of three seasons. He won Amateur titles in England and India before moving to the United States in 1903. He settled in Los Angeles in 1908. A businessman all his life, including many years as vice president of the Riverside Cement Company, Macbeth remained active in amateur golf, winning the Southern California Amateur on two occasions and the Northern California Amateur once.

In 1910 Macbeth assisted in the design of the old Los Angeles Country Club

Norman Macbeth, circa 1935 COLLECTION RON WHITTEN

course. Following service with the American Red Cross in Europe during World War I, he designed and built a number of Southern California courses, many of which (such as the highly regarded Midwick Country Club and St. Andrews Golf Club of Laguna Niguel) succumbed to the Depression.

Courses by Norman Macbeth:

California: Los Angeles CC (South Cse 1911), ass't Herbert Fowler; Midwick CC (NLE); St. Andrews GC (NLE); San Gabriel CC; Wilshire CC (1919).

Courses remodeled or expanded by Norman Macbeth:

California: Annandale GC (R. 1921).

CHARLES BLAIR MACDONALD (1856–1939)

BORN: Niagara Falls, Ontario, Canada.
DIED: Southampton, New York, at age 83.

Charles Blair Macdonald was the son of a Scottish father and a Canadian mother. Macdonald himself grew up in Chicago but returned to his father's homeland in 1872 to attend the University of St. Andrews. There he learned the game of golf under the tutelage of his grandfather and was able to watch matches involving Old and Young Tom Morris, David Strath, Robert Clark (author of *Golf, A Royal and Ancient Game*), D. D. Whigham (whose son, H. J., later married Macdonald's daughter, Frances) and many other renowned golfers.

The game, the Old Course, the town of St. Andrews and Old Tom made deep and lasting impressions on Macdonald. Returning to Chicago in 1875, he described the next few years as the "dark ages" because of the virtual impossibility of playing golf. He ended up knocking balls around a deserted Civil War training camp. Then in 1892 he laid out the nine-hole Chicago Golf Club in Belmont. This was expanded to 18 holes the next year, making it the first 18-hole course in the United States. In 1895 the club moved to Wheaton, where Macdonald laid out a new 18 holes.

Throughout his life, golf course design was an avocation for Macdonald, and he never accepted a fee for his services. Dur-

C. B. Macdonald, circa 1915
COLLECTION RON WHITTEN

ing his years in Illinois he was with the Chicago Board of Trade. In 1884 he married Frances Porter of Chicago. They had two daughters, Janet and Frances. The family moved to New York in 1900, where Macdonald became a partner in the firm of C. D. Barney & Co., Stockbrokers.

Golf and golf design were C.B.'s abiding passions. Macdonald won the first U.S. Amateur Championship in 1895. He was a founder of the Amateur Golf Association of the United States, which evolved into the USGA. He conceived the Walker Cup Series, coined the title "golf architect" in 1902 and was considered by golf historians as the "Father of American Golf Course Architecture." His protégés in golf design included Seth Raynor. Charles Banks and Ralph Barton.

Macdonald's reminiscences, *Scotland's Gift—Golf*, provide a detailed discussion of his principles of golf architecture. He also wrote extensively about course architecture in other publications. One of his most widely circulated pieces dealt with his ingredients for an ideal golf course. Among the points he listed were:

1. There can be no really first-class golf course without good material to work with. The best material is a sandy loam in gentle undulations, breaking into hillocks in a few places. Securing such land is really more than half the battle. Having such material at hand to work upon, the completion of an ideal course becomes a matter of experience, gardening and mathematics.

2. The courses of Great Britain abound in classic and notable holes, and one has only to study them and adopt their best and boldest features. Yet in most of

their best holes there is always room for improvement.

3. Nothing induces more to the charm of the game than perfect putting greens. Some should be large, but the majority should be of moderate size; some flat, some hillocky, one or two at an angle, but the great majority should have natural undulations, some more and others less undulating. It is absolutely essential that the turf should be very fine so the ball will run perfectly true.

4. Whether this or that bunker is well placed has caused more intensely heated arguments (outside of the realms of religion) than has ever been my lot to listen to. Rest assured, however, when a controversy is hotly contested over several years as to whether this or that hazard is fair, it is the kind of hazard you want and it has real merit. When there is unanimous opinion that such and such a hazard is perfect, one usually finds it commonplace. I know of no classic hole that doesn't have its decriers.

5. To my mind, an ideal course should have at least six bold bunkers, at the end of two-shot holes or very long carries from the tee. Further, I believe such holes would be improved by opening the fair green to one side or the other, giving short or timid players an opportunity to play around the hazards if so desired, but of course properly penalized by loss of distance for so playing. Other than these bold bunkers, no other hazards should stretch directly across a hole.

6. What a golfer most desires is variety in the one-, two- and three-shot holes, calling for accuracy in placing the ball, not alone in the approach but also from the tee. Let the first shot be played in relation to the second shot in accordance with the run of the ground and the wind. Holes so designed permit the player to, if he so wishes, take risks commensurate to the gravity of the situation.

7. Tees should be in close proximity to previous greens. This walking fifty to one hundred fifty yards to the next tee mars the course and delays the game. Between hole and

next teeing ground people sometimes forget and commence
playing some other game.

8. Hills on a golf course are a detriment. Mountain climbing is a sport
in itself and has no place on a golf
course. Trees in the course are also
a serious defect, and even when in
close proximity prove a detriment.

9. Glaring artificiality of any kind de-
tracts from the fascination of the
game.

Late in life, however, Macdonald de-
spaired of both the game of golf and golf
architecture. In one of his last pieces of
correspondence, to golf architect Perry
Maxwell, he wrote, "Young man, you have
the idea of a real golf course, and I am
sorry I can't encourage your enthusiasm
by going to see what is undoubtedly a
most wonderful and ideal location, but I
can't. I tell you I am through. I wouldn't
walk around the block to see it for I don't
want to get interested in another golf project, however fine. But I do wish you the
best of luck."

Courses by Charles Blair Macdonald:

Connecticut: Yale University GC (1926),
with Seth Raynor, Charles Banks and
Ralph Barton.

Illinois: Chicago GC (1895); Downers
Grove GC [FKA Chicago GC] (9
1893).

Maryland: Gibson Island GC (9 1922,
NLE), with Seth Raynor.

Missouri: St. Louis CC (1914), with Seth
Raynor.

New York: Blind Brook C (routing 1915),
with Seth Raynor; [The] Creek C
(1925), with Seth Raynor; Deepdale
GC (1925, NLE), with Seth Raynor; H.
P. Whitney Estate G Cse (NLE), with
Seth Raynor; Lido GC (1917, NLE),
with Seth Raynor; [The] Links GC
(1919, NLE), with Seth Raynor; Moore
Estate G Cse (NLE), with Seth Raynor;
[The] National Golf Links of America
(1911); Otto Kahn Estate G Cse
(1925, NLE), with Seth Raynor; Piping
Rock C (1913), with Seth Raynor;
Sleepy Hollow GC (1914), with Seth
Raynor.

West Virginia: Greenbrier GC (Old White
Cse 1915), with Seth Raynor.

Bermuda: Mid Ocean C (1924), with Seth
Raynor, Charles Banks and Ralph Barton.

*Alister Mackenzie,
1932* COLLECTION RON
WHITTEN

ALISTER MACKENZIE, M.D. (1870–1934)

BORN: Normanton, Yorkshire, England.
DIED: Santa Cruz, California, at age 63.

Dr. Alister Mackenzie, the son of Highland parents, graduated from Cambridge
University with degrees in medicine, natural science and chemistry. In the Boer War
he served as a surgeon with the Somerset
Light Infantry, where he closely observed
and analyzed the ability of Boer soldiers to
hide effectively on treeless veldts. After
the war he returned to Britain to practice
medicine in the city of Leeds.

Just when the good doctor entered the
field of golf architecture is unclear. He apparently dabbled in design somewhat
in the early 1900s. What is known is that in
1907 golf architect H. S. Colt, on a visit to
Leeds, stayed overnight at Mackenzie's
home. Impressed with Mackenzie's models
of greens and bunkers, Colt invited his collaboration on the design of Alwoodley Golf
Club. Over the next few years Mackenzie
gradually gave up his medical practice to
devote full time to golf course architecture.
In 1914 he won first prize in C. B. Macdonald's *Country Life* magazine competition for the best two-shot hole for the
proposed Lido GC on Long Island, New
York. This competition, judged by golf
writer Bernard Darwin, Horace Hutchinson and Herbert Fowler, brought Mackenzie considerable publicity on both sides
of the Atlantic.

With the outbreak of war in Europe,
Mackenzie returned to medicine as an
army surgeon but soon transferred to the
Royal Engineers to develop camouflage
techniques based on the knowledge he
had gained in South Africa. The art and
science of camouflage as developed by
Mackenzie was credited with saving thousands of lives. Years later Mackenzie observed that successful course design, like
camouflage, depended on utilizing natural
features to their fullest extent and creating

artificial features that closely imitated nature.

Shortly after the Armistice in 1918,
Mackenzie formed a partnership with
H. S. Colt and C. H. Alison, but it was
short-lived. Reportedly the egos were too
great on both sides, and Mackenzie and
Colt, though partners on paper, competed
on several commissions. A full rift occurred in 1921, but it wasn't until 1928
that Colt got around to formally dissolving
Mackenzie's name from the firm. Consequently, a good deal of American courses
designed by Colt's partner Hugh Alison
also bear Mackenzie's name as architect of
record, though there is little evidence that
Mackenzie worked on any American designs with either of his partners.

When Mackenzie did finally settle in
the United States, he formed brief partnerships with a number of persons, including
Robert Hunter, H. Chandler Egan and
Perry Maxwell. But despite the tempera-
mental nature of his business acumen,
there was no denying the talent of Alister
Mackenzie. Cypress Point in California finally established his reputation as a golf
course architect and led to his collaboration with the immortal Bobby Jones on the
design of Augusta National.

During the 1920s Mackenzie made an
extended trip through South America,
Australia and New Zealand. He did a number of "paper jobs" that were completed by
hastily arranged associates, most notably
Australian Alex Russell.

Mackenzie authored *Golf Architecture*, a
collection of design lectures he had deliv-
ered that was published in 1920. In it, he
codified thirteen essential features of an
ideal golf course that became standards for
course architecture after World War II.
They were:

1. The course, where possible,
should be arranged in two loops
of nine holes.

2. There should be a large proportion of good two-shot holes, two
or three drive-and-pitch holes,
and at least four one-shot holes.

3. There should be little walking between greens and tees, and the
course should be arranged so that
in the first instance there is always a slight walk forward from
the green to the next tee; then the
holes are sufficiently elastic to be
lengthened in the future if necessary.

4. The greens and fairways should be sufficiently undulating, but there should be no hill climbing.
5. Every hole should have a different character.
6. There should be a minimum of blindness for the approach shots.
7. The course should have beautiful surroundings, and all the artificial features should have so natural an appearance that a stranger is unable to distinguish them from nature itself.
8. There should be a sufficient number of heroic carries from the tee, but the course should be arranged so that the weaker player with the loss of a stroke or portion of a stroke shall always have an alternate route open to him.
9. There should be infinite variety in the strokes required to play the various holes—interesting brassy shots, iron shots, pitch and run-up shots.
10. There should be a complete absence of the annoyance and irritation caused by the necessity of searching for lost balls.
11. The course should be so interesting that even the plus man is constantly stimulated to improve his game in attempting shots he has hitherto been unable to play.
12. The course should be so arranged so that the long handicap player, or even the absolute beginner, should be able to enjoy his round in spite of the fact that he is piling up a big score.
13. The course should be equally good during winter and summer, the texture of greens and fairways should be perfect, and the approaches should have the same consistency as the greens.

Of all the course architects of the Golden Age of Golf Design, Mackenzie probably exerted the greatest influence on contemporary design.

Courses by Alister Mackenzie:

California: Charlie Chaplin Estate GC (9 Par 3, NLE); Cypress Point C (1928), with Robert Hunter; Green Hills CC (1930), with Robert Hunter and H. Chandler Egan; Haggin Oaks Muni (South Cse 1932); Harold Lloyd Estate GC (9 Par 3, NLE); [The] Meadow C (1927), with Robert Hunter; Northwood GC (9 1928), with Robert Hunter; Pasatiempo GC (1929); Pittsburgh GC (9), with Robert Hunter; Sharp Park GC (1931); Stockton G&CC; Valley C of Montecito (1928), with Robert Hunter.

Georgia: Augusta National GC (1933), with Robert Tyre Jones, Jr.

Michigan: Crystal Downs CC (1933), with Perry Maxwell; University of Michigan GC (1931), with Perry Maxwell.

Ohio: Ohio State University GC (Gray Cse, routing 1939; Scarlet Cse, routing 1939).

Manitoba: St. Charles CC (North Nine 1930).

Argentina: Jockey C (Blue Cse 1935; Red Cse 1935).

Australia: Australian GC (27 1926); Lake Karrinyup CC (1927), with Alex Russell; New South Wales GC (1928), with Des Soutar; Royal Melbourne GC (West Cse 1931), with Alex Russell; Victoria GC (1927); Yarra Yarra GC (1929), with Alex Russell.

England: Alwoodley GC (1907), with H. S. Colt; Bingley St. Ives GC (1931); Blackpool–Stanley Park GC (1925); Brancepeth Castle GC (1924), with H. S. Colt and C. H. Alison; Cavendish GC (1925); Darlington GC (1909); Felixstowe Ferry GC (1919); Fulford GC (1909); Grange-over-Sands GC (1919); Hadley Wood GC (1922); Low Laithes GC (1925); Marsden GC (9 1921); Moor Allerton GC (1923, NLE); Moortown GC (1909); Oakdale GC (1914); Reddish Vale GC (1912); Scarborough Southcliff GC (1911); Scarcroft GC (1937); Sitwell Park GC (1913); Teignmouth GC (1924); Walsall GC (1909); Wheatley GC (1913); Worcester G&CC (1927).

Ireland: Island GC.

Isle of Man: Douglas Muni (1927).

New Zealand: Heretaunga GC.

Scotland: Hazelhead Muni (Cse No. 1 1927); Pitreavie GC (1923); St. Andrews (Eden Cse 1913), with H. S. Colt.

Uruguay: GC de Uruguay; Punta del Este GC.

Courses remodeled or expanded by Alister Mackenzie:

California: California GC of San Francisco (R.); Claremont CC (R.); Lake Merced G&CC (R. 1929, NLE); Monterey Peninsula CC (Dunes Cse, R. 1928), with Robert Hunter; Redlands CC (R.).

New York: Bayside Links (R. 1932, NLE); Lake Placid C (Upper Cse, R. 1931).

South Carolina: Palmetto CC (R. 1931).

Argentina: Mar de Plata GC (R. 1930).

Australia: Flinders GC (R. A.2 1926); Kingston Heath GC (R. 1928); Royal Adelaide GC (R. 1926); Royal Queensland GC (R. 1927); Royal Sydney GC (R.).

England: Bolton GC (R.); Buxton and High Peak GC (R.); City of Newcastle GC (R.); Harrogate GC (R.); Headingley GC (R.); Ilkley GC (R.); Manchester GC (R.); Royal St. George's GC (R.); Saddleworth GC (R.9 A.9); Seaton Carew GC (R. 1925); Shipley (R.); West Herts GC (R. 1922); Weston-Super-Mare GC (R.); Willingdon GC (R. 1925); Worcestershire GC (R. 1924).

Ireland: Cork GC (R.9 A.9 1927); Douglas GC (R.9 1927); Galway GC (R.); Lahinch GC (Old Cse, R. A.11 1927); Muskerry GC (R.).

Isle of Man: Castletown GC (R.).

New Zealand: Titirangi GC (R. 1926).

Scotland: Blairgowrie GC (Rosemount Cse, R.9 A.9 1927); Duff House Royal GC (R. 1926), with *Charles A. Mackenzie*; Newtonmore GC (R.); Royal Troon GC (R. 1907); St. Andrews (Old Cse, R.).

GREGOR MACLEOD MACMILLAN

BORN: Montana.

Following graduation in the early 1920s from the University of Washington with a degree in civil engineering, Greg MacMillan worked as a surveyor for the Balcom Canal Lumber Company of Seattle. When Balcom headed a group of businessmen organizing the Olympic Golf and Country Club, MacMillan was assigned to oversee the golf course construction. His knowledge impressed Frank James, the Western states representative of the course's contractor, William H. Tucker & Son, and after Olympic opened, James hired MacMillan to help design and supervise Tucker projects along the West Coast.

James soon resigned to pursue his own golf design career, and MacMillan took his place in the Tucker organization. In the next eight years, he designed and built courses with Tucker in nine Great Plains and Western states. The Depression forced Tucker to close his Western office in 1931, and MacMillan moved to California, where he built miniature golf layouts and ran a landscaping service catering to wealthy patrons in Beverly Hills. On Tucker's recommendation, MacMillan was hired to design and build a nine-hole course for the El Mirador Hotel in Palm Springs. It became one of the first golf courses in the exclusive community, but after one successful season the hotel closed, the course was abandoned and MacMillan found himself unpaid and in debt.

In 1934 MacMillan and wife moved to Montana, where he obtained a position with the U.S. Army Corps of Engineers. He later became director of operations of federal WPA projects in Montana and in that capacity helped organize several golf course projects that put countless numbers back to work and brought the game to small Montana communities. MacMillan prepared the architectural plans for these nine-hole layouts.

Several promotions led to transfers to Colorado and then California, but Mac-Millan returned to Montana after World War II. He served as secretary of the Helena Chamber of Commerce and then as training officer for the seriously disabled in the Veterans Administration.

During this time, MacMillan's interest in golf course design continued. Though it was limited mainly to weekends, he designed and supervised the construction of several Montana courses in the 1940s and 1950s. On most of the projects he accepted no fee.

Courses by Gregor MacMillan:

California: El Mirador Hotel GC (9 1932, NLE).
Montana: Anaconda CC (9); Cabinet View CC (9); Green Meadow CC (9 1946); Hamilton CC (9); Hilands GC (9 1950), with Norman H. Woods; Kalispell G&CC (9 1963); Polson CC (9 1937); University of Montana GC (9 1959); Whitefish Lake GC (9 1935; R.9 A.9 1960).
Nebraska: CC of Lincoln (1923), ass't William H. Tucker; Hillcrest CC (1925), ass't William H. Tucker; Pioneer Park GC (1932), ass't William H. Tucker.
Washington: Linden G&CC (9), ass't William H. Tucker; Roche Harbor GC, ass't William H. Tucker.

Courses remodeled or expanded by Gregor MacMillan:

Montana: Green Meadow CC (R. 1960).

LEONARD MACOMBER (1885–1954)

BORN: Brookline, Massachusetts.
DIED: Washington, D.C., at age 69.

Trained as a civil engineer, Leonard Macomber worked before World War I for Carter Tested Seeds Company. In that capacity he assisted in the construction and grow-in of courses designed by such architects as A. W. Tillinghast, Donald Ross and C. B. Macdonald. Macomber also wrote and edited a monthly turfgrass bulletin called *The Golf Course.* Among regular contributors to the bulletin were Tillinghast and Peter Lees.

After the war, Macomber moved to Chicago and established his own golf design firm. From that base he planned courses throughout the Midwest and from New York to Florida. Always ambitious, in 1929 his firm offered a new branch devoted to the design and construction of airports. The Depression shot down that plan.

In 1937 he traveled to Russia, hoping to interest that country in golf, but was unsuccessful. Undaunted, he toured South America and reportedly laid out several courses for clients during his extended stay.

In 1954, while making an inspection trip on what would become Belle Haven Country Club in Alexandria, Virginia, Macomber was stricken and rushed to a nearby hospital. He died shortly thereafter.

Courses by Leonard Macomber:

Florida: National Town & CC (NLE).
Illinois: Biltmore CC; Breakers Beach CC (NLE); Cedardell GC (1926); Libertyville CC; Mission Hills CC (1926, NLE); Silver Lake GC (North Cse) [FKA Euclid Hill CC] (1928); Waukegan Willow GC (NLE).
Indiana: Curtis Creek CC (1928).
New York: Drumlins GC.
Ohio: National Town & CC (NLE); Poland CC; Tam O'Shanter CC (Dales Cse 1928; Hills Cse 1928); West Hills CC.
Virginia: Belle Haven CC (1954).
Wisconsin: Bulls Eye CC (9); Maple Crest CC; Twin Lakes CC (1929).

Courses remodeled or expanded by Leonard Macomber:

Pennsylvania: Butler CC (R.9 A.9 1928).

CHARLES EUGENE MADDOX (1898–   )

BORN: Centralia, Illinois.

Chuck Maddox spent his early days honing his golf game on Chicago-area courses and working for his father in the Maddox Construction Company. The company had been formed in 1870 as a road-grading firm by Asa Maddox, Chuck's grandfather. Chuck's father, Eugene Maddox, branched out into golf course construction when he took command of the firm in the early 1900s.

After the First World War Maddox became head of the company and concentrated its efforts on golf development. In 1923 he joined forces with Frank Macdonald, a native Scot who had served as a club manager and course superintendent in Chicago. The firm of Macdonald and Maddox created a number of impressive Chicago-area courses, several of them owned and operated by Maddox. They also constructed courses for other prominent architects in the 1920s, including Langford and Moreau, Robert Bruce Harris and C. D. Wagstaff.

During the Depression, Maddox lost most of his course holdings. His construction company abandoned golf and worked instead on oil rigs and government projects. Following World War II, Maddox reorganized the construction outfit and soon found plenty of work restoring and reconstructing courses for other architects. In the 1950s, joined by sons Charles Jr. and William, he began designing courses again, as well as building them.

While constructing some of the best works of architects like Edward Lawrence Packard and Robert Bruce Harris, Maddox has also created some notable layouts of his own, including one of America's few true linksland courses, on Dauphin Island, Alabama.

Courses by Charles Maddox (All with *Frank P. Macdonald* unless otherwise indicated):

Alabama: Isle Dauphin CC (1962 *solo*).
Illinois: Atwood GC (1971 *solo*); Bartlett Hills G&CC; Blackhorse GC (9 Par 3 1966 *solo*); Chicago G & Saddle C

(NLE); Danville VA Hospital GC (9 1951 *solo*); Downey VA Hospital GC (1978 *solo*); DuWayne Motel GC (9 Par 3 1960 *solo*); Edgewood CC (9 1962 *solo*); Forest Hills CC (1976 *solo*); Gleneagles GC (Red Cse 1924; White Cse 1924); Lakeview CC (9 1957 *solo*); Menard GC (9 1964 *solo*); Nordic Hills GC (1932); [The] Oak C [FKA Ellwood Greens CC] (1972 *solo*); Old Wayne GC (1960 *solo*); Orchard Hills CC; Palos CC (1925); Parkview Muni (9 1930); Prestwick CC (1929, NLE); River Forest CC; Shambolee GC (9 1964 *solo*); Silver Lake GC (South Cse); Stonehenge GC (1970 *solo*); Sun and Fun G & Swim C (9 Par 3 *solo*); Terrace Hills GC (1985 *solo*).
Indiana: Beverly Shores CC (1930); Fox Ridge CC (9 1974); Frankfort GC (9 1965 *solo*); GC of Indiana (1974); Hoosier Links (1973); Lake Hills G&CC (27); Old Oakland GC (1964), with William Maddox; Turkey Creek GC.
Michigan: Elks CC (1967 *solo*); Georgetown GC (9 Par 3), with *Charles Maddox, Jr.*; Raisin River CC (1963 *solo*).
Minnesota: Brookview CC (27 1968 *solo*); Majestic Oaks GC (North Cse 1971 *solo*); Olympic Hills GC (1971 *solo*); Rolling Green CC (1969 *solo*).
Missouri: Crackerneck CC (1964), with William Maddox.
North Dakota: Larrimore CC (9 1963 *solo*).
South Dakota: Hillsview GC (9 1966 *solo*); Moccasin Creek GC (1969 *solo*).
Wisconsin: Crandon GC (9); Rhinelander CC (9); Spring Brook CC (9); Trout Lake CC.

Courses remodeled or expanded by Charles Maddox (All with *Frank P. Macdonald* unless otherwise indicated):

Illinois: Brookridge CC (R. 1929).
Indiana: Orchard Ridge CC (R. 1929).
South Dakota: Elmwood Park GC (A.3rd 9 1966 *solo*).

WILLIAM EUGENE MADDOX (1925–)

BORN: Chicago, Illinois.

The son of golf architect and contractor Chuck Maddox, Bill Maddox was associated for many years with his father and

brother Charles Jr., then operated his own golf course construction business. He also took to the drawing board on his own, doing several courses, mainly on the west coast of Florida near the headquarters of his construction firm.

Courses by William Maddox:

Florida: Bonita Springs G&CC (1977); Quail Village GC (Precision); Zellwood Station CC (1974).
Illinois: Pheasant Run Lodge GC (1961).
Indiana: Old Oakland GC (1964), with Charles Maddox.
Missouri: Crackerneck CC (1964), with Charles Maddox.

Mark Mahannah, 1977 COLLECTION RON WHITTEN

CHARLES MARK MAHANNAH (1906–1991), ASGCA, FELLOW

BORN: Delta, Iowa.
DIED: Nakomis, Florida, at age 85.

Born in Iowa, Mark Mahannah was raised in Fort Lauderdale from an early age. He attended the University of Florida at Gainesville, but did not graduate. Instead, he moved around the state from job to job.

One of those jobs was on a golf course construction crew in the late 1920s, working under William S. Flynn, who was building the Boca Raton Hotel's courses. Mahannah worked on a few other course projects, then became a member of the course maintenance crew at Miami Biltmore Country Club and in the early 1940s became its head greenkeeper. The club was closed during World War II, and Mahannah spent the duration as a technical adviser on turf problems at an army post in Pinellas County, Florida.

After the war, Mahannah renovated one 18 at Miami Biltmore. It reopened under the name Riviera CC, and Mahannah served as its superintendent. His experience at restoring the course led to other contracts, which he handled part-time un-

til the early 1950s, when he resigned to practice course design full-time. Preferring local jobs, Mahannah did few designs outside Florida and the Caribbean.

One of his sons, Charles, followed in his footsteps, becoming a superintendent at one of his courses, then eventually joining him in the design business. Mark Mahannah retired from active design in the late 1970s. In 1976 Mahannah was made a fellow member of the ASGCA. He died of cancer at his home near Miami in 1991.

Courses by Mark Mahannah:

Florida: Boca Teeca CC (27 1968); Caloosa CC (1981), with Charles Mahannah; Calusa CC (1969); Club Med Sandpiper GC (Sinners Cse 1961); Cocoa Beach Muni (1968); El Conquistador CC (1973); Falcon Fairways GC, Homestead AFB (9 1961); Fontainebleau Park CC (East Cse 1971; West Cse 1979, with Charles Mahannah); Greynolds GC (9 1964); Haulover Beach GC (Par 3 1964); Hillcrest East GC (Precision); Indian Trail CC; Isla del Sol GC (1977), with Charles Mahannah; Jacaranda CC (East Cse 1970; West Cse 1975, with Charles Mahannah); Jacaranda West CC (1976), with Charles Mahannah; Key Biscayne Hotel GC (Par 3 1954); Key Colony GC (Par 3 1962, NLE); Kings Bay Y&CC (1959, NLE); Lake Venice CC (1959); [The] Little C, Tequesta (9 Par 3); Lost Tree C (1960); Miles Grant CC (Precision 1972), with Charles Mahannah; Mirror Lake CC (1970); Ocean Reef C (Dolphin Cse 1951); Okeechobee G&CC (1966); Plantation G Resort (1958); Presidential CC (1962); Rio Pinar CC (1958); Royal Palm Beach G&CC (1960); Sun City Center G&CC (South Cse 1967); Ventura CC (Precision 1980), with Charles Mahannah.
Bahamas: Grand Bahama Hotel & CC (27 1961).
Chile: Club Campestre de Bucaramanga, with *Jaime Saenz*.
Colombia: Macarena GC; Santa Marta GC (1972).

Courses remodeled or expanded by Mark Mahannah:

Florida: Coral Gables Biltmore GC (R.); Crystal River CC (R. 1958); [The] Everglades C (R. 1958); Gulfstream GC (R.3 1960); Hollywood Beach Hotel CC (R. 1955); Naples Beach Hotel GC (R. 1953); Normandy Shores GC (R.);

Palma Ceia G&CC (R. 1979), with Charles Mahannah; Port Charlotte CC (A.9 R.9); Riviera CC (R. 1954); Sun City Center G&CC (North Cse, A.9 1972), with Charles Mahannah; Tarpon Springs CC (R. 1957); Westview CC (A.9 1955).

Cuba: Havana Biltmore GC (R. 1957, NLE).

CHARLES MARK MAHANNAH, JR. (1941–), ASGCA

BORN: Miami, Florida.

Charles Mahannah, son of golf architect Mark Mahannah, was nearly reared on a golf course and followed much the same route as his father in becoming a golf course architect. He served for a time as course superintendent at Kings Bay in Miami (a course his father designed and built), where he helped develop a special salt-tolerant Bermuda grass blend for greens that are in close proximity to the ocean.

Charles then worked for his father in course design, eventually becoming his partner. In the late 1970s, when his father reduced his active involvement, Charles Mahannah formed his own design company. In the late 1980s Mahannah agreed to serve as consulting course architect for a design group bearing the name of legendary golfer Lee Trevino.

Courses by Charles Mahannah:

Florida: Boca Teeca GC (27 1968), with Mark Mahannah; Bonaventure CC (West Cse 1974); California C; Caloosa CC (1981), with Mark Mahannah; Fontainebleau Park CC (West Cse 1979), with Mark Mahannah; Isla del Sol GC (1977), with Mark Mahannah; Jacaranda CC (West Cse 1975), with Mark Mahannah; Jacaranda West CC, Venice (1976), with Mark Mahannah; Kendale Lakes G&CC; Kendale Lakes West CC (Precision); Miles Grant CC (Precision 1972), with Mark

Charles Mahannah, 1977 COLLECTION RON WHITTEN

Mahannah; Raintree GC (1984); Ventura CC (Precision 1980), with Mark Mahannah.

North Carolina: Blue Ridge CC (1991), with *Lee Trevino.*

Wisconsin: Geneva National G&CC (Trevino Cse 1991), with *Lee Trevino.*

Ontario: Wildflower CC (1992), with *Lee Trevino.*

Colombia: Poinciana Place GC; La Florida GC; Lago Mar el Peñón GC; La Sabana GC.

Japan: Nakatsugawa GC (27 1990), with *Lee Trevino.*

Taiwan: Nanfong GC (1991), with *Lee Trevino;* Royal Host GC (1991), with *Lee Trevino.*

Courses remodeled or expanded by Charles Mahannah:

Florida: Palma Ceia G&CC (R. 1979), with Mark Mahannah; Sun City Center G&CC (North Cse, A.9 1972), with Mark Mahannah.

PIER LUIGI MANCINELLI (1920–), BIGCA

BORN: Treviso, Italy.

Educated at Cambridge University in England and the University of Rome, Pier Mancinelli was studying orchestral conducting at the outbreak of World War II. He enlisted in the Italian air force and became one of its youngest squadron commanders. After the Allies invaded Italy, Mancinelli defected and turned himself over to advancing British forces.

After VE Day, he returned to the University of Rome and did graduate work in civil engineering. Following a stint as music critic for an Italian newspaper, Mancinelli spent eight years supervising the construction of roads in East Africa. There, urged on by fellow employees and golf enthusiasts, he constructed a makeshift golf course in the shadow of Mount Kilimanjaro.

In the late 1950s Mancinelli returned to Italy and took a job with a corporation involved with constructing Olgiata Country Club near Rome to the design of British golf architect C. K. Cotton. Working as site manager at Olgiata, Mancinelli studied golf design under Cotton and on completion of the course followed his mentor's advice and entered the field on a part-time basis.

In the early 1970s, after brief employ-

Pier Mancinelli, 1991 COURTESY PIER MANCINELLI

ment with the World Bank, Mancinelli founded an Italian golf magazine and his own course-design firm, both based in Rome. His designs were even more successful than his magazine. One of his most notable works, Is Molas Golf Club on the island of Sardinia, was selected as the site for the 1976 Italian Open soon after it opened.

Courses by Pier Mancinelli

Brazil: Quinta de Arambepe GC (1978).

France: Gassin GC (1985); Lyon-Charbonnière GC (1985); Sporting C de Beauvallon (9).

Iran: Mehr Shahr GC (1978, NLE).

Italy: Carimate Parco GC (1963); Castlefalfi GC (Blue Cse 1988; Red Cse 1991); Contea di Gradella GC (1986); Elba GC (9 1968); Olgiata GC (27 1961), ass't C. K. Cotton; San Vito de Normanni GC (9 1972); Villa La Motta GC (1992).

Ivory Coast: Abidjan GC (9 1983); Yamoussoukro GC (1981).

Sardinia: Is Arenas GC (1992); Is Molas GC (1975).

Courses remodeled or expanded by Pier Mancinelli:

France: St. Nom La Bretêche GC (Blue Cse, R. 1983; Red Cse, R. 1983).

Italy: Firenze GC (R. 1980).

Switzerland: Lugano GC (R.3 1984).

DAN FRANK MAPLES (1947–), ASGCA, PRESIDENT 1990

BORN: Pinehurst, North Carolina.

Dan Maples was another of those born into an ideal situation to become a golf course architect. Son of designer Ellis Maples and grandson of Frank Maples (longtime construction superintendent for Donald Ross), Maples doodled golf designs at age 6, staked courses as a 10-year-old and handled earth-moving equipment even before he had his driver's license. He received an Associate of Science degree from Wingate Junior College in North Carolina and a Bachelor's degree in landscape architecture from the University of Georgia in 1972. During his summers from 1964 to 1972, he worked in golf course construction and maintenance for his father.

After two years as a club professional at Palmetto Country Club in South Carolina, Maples joined his father's firm and became a full partner two years later. In the early 1980s he went into business for himself, retaining offices in Pinehurst while working throughout the Southeast. One of his first solo designs, Oyster Bay Golf Links, was selected by *Golf Digest* as the Best New Resort Course of 1983. As a hobby, Dan Maples researched the history of course construction at Pinehurst.

Courses by Dan Maples:

Alabama: Sehoy Plantation GC (9 1973), with Ellis Maples.
Georgia: Orchard G&CC (1991).
Hawaii: Oneloa GC (North Cse 1992; South Cse 1992).
North Carolina: Apple Valley GC (1986); Cramer Mountain CC (1986); Green Valley GC (9 1974), with Ellis Maples; Keith Hills CC (1975), with Ellis Maples; Longleaf CC (1988); Marsh Harbour G Links (1980); Mountain Springs G&CC (Precision 1978), with Ellis Maples; Oyster Bay G Links (1983); [The] Pearl G Links (East Cse 1988; West Cse 1987); [The] Pit G Links (1984); Providence CC (1989); Sandpiper Bay G&CC (1987); Sea Trail G Links (Maples Cse 1986); [The] Sound G Links (1990); Whispering Woods CC [FKA CC of Whispering Pines (South Course)] (1974), with Ellis Maples; Woodlake CC (Green Cse 1992).
South Carolina: Heritage Plantation GC (1986); [The] Witch G Links (1989); Willbrook Plantation GC (1988).
Tennessee: Dandridge CC, ass't Ellis Maples; Roan Valley CC (1983), with Ellis Maples.
Virginia: Birkdale GC (1990); Devil's Knob GC (1977), with Ellis Maples; Ford's Colony CC (Gold Cse 1991; Red Cse 1986); Olde Mill GC (1974), with Ellis Maples; Tazewell County CC (9 1978), with Ellis Maples.
Germany: CC of Hanover (1992).
Spain: C de G Capadepera (1992).

Dan Maples, 1985
RON WHITTEN

Courses remodeled or expanded by Dan Maples:

North Carolina: Bermuda Run G&CC (A.3rd 9 1986); Deep Springs CC (A.9 1978, with Ellis Maples; R. 1991); Forsyth CC (R.); Hope Valley CC (R. 1986).
Tennessee: Cherokee CC (R. 1985); Gatlinburg G&CC (R. 1974), with Ellis Maples.
Virginia: Glenrochie CC (A.9).

ELLIS MAPLES
(1909–1984), ASGCA, PRESIDENT 1973

BORN: Pinehurst, North Carolina.
DIED: Pinehurst, North Carolina, at age 75.

Beginning at age 14, Ellis Maples worked during summer months for his father Frank Maples, a longtime construction superintendent for Donald Ross and greenkeeper at Pinehurst Country Club. Ellis attended Lenoir-Rhyne College in North Carolina, then worked as an assistant in the Pinehurst golf shop for a year before spending seven seasons as assistant greenkeeper to his father at two other Pinehurst area courses, Mid Pines and Pine Needles.

In 1937 Maples assisted William S. Flynn and Dick Wilson in the construction of a nine-hole layout in Plymouth, North Carolina. He remained at Plymouth as its pro-greenkeeper until 1942, when he entered war service as an army engineer agronomist and technical adviser.

In 1947, while working as pro-manager at New Bern (North Carolina) Country Club, Maples redesigned the course. He soon remodeled two other local layouts and planned a third. In 1948 he supervised construction of the last design done by Donald Ross, Raleigh (North Carolina) Country Club. Maples worked as pro-

superintendent at Raleigh until 1953 when, deciding against a career as a touring pro, he entered private practice as a golf course architect.

His firm handled over seventy course design projects in the Southeast over the next 30 years, including such top layouts as Forest Oaks Country Club and Grandfather Golf and Country Club. The firm included Ed Seay as a design associate for eight years, and in his last years Maples made one of his sons, Dan, a partner in the business. Another son, Joe, served as longtime head pro at Boone (North Carolina) Golf Club, one of Ellis's first designs, and a third son, David, was a golf course builder.

Ellis Maples was a life member of the PGA of America.

Courses by Ellis Maples:

Alabama: Sehoy Plantation GC (9 1973), with Dan Maples.
Georgia: Goshen Plantation CC (1968); West Lake CC (1968).
North Carolina: Bermuda Run G&CC (1971); Boone CC (1959); Brook Valley G&CC (1967); Carmel CC (South Cse, 9 1962, A.2nd 9 1970); Cedar Brook CC (1965); Cedar Rock CC (1965); Cedarwood CC (1963); Chockoyette CC (1972); Coherie CC (9 1950); CC of North Carolina (Dogwood Cse 1963), with Willard Byrd; CC of Whispering Pines (East Cse 1959; West Cse 1970); Deep Springs CC (9 1971; A.2nd 9 1978, with Dan Maples); Duck Woods GC (1968); Forest Oaks CC (1962); Gaston CC (1959); Grandfather G&CC (1968); Green Valley GC (9 1974), with Dan Maples; Greensboro CC (Carlson Farms Cse 1963); Indian Valley CC (1974); Keith Hills CC (1975), with Dan Maples; Meadow Greens CC (1962); Mountain Creek C (9 1955, A.9 1974); Mountain Springs G&CC (Precision 1978), with Dan Maples; Pine Brook CC (1955); Pinehurst CC (Cse No. 5 1961), with Richard S.

Ellis Maples, 1972
COURTESY *GOLF WORLD*

Tufts; Quarry Hills CC [FKA Piedmont Crescent CC]; Red Fox CC (1965); Roanoke CC (9 1955); Sapona CC (1967); Silver City CC (9 1959); Twin Oaks GC (Par 3 1957); Walnut Creek CC (1968); Westwood G Cse (9 Par 3 1953, NLE); Whispering Woods CC [FKA CC of Whispering Pines] (South Cse 1974), with Dan Maples; Winston Lake Park GC (1964); Woodlake CC [FKA Lake Surf CC] (Gold Cse 1969).

South Carolina: Calhoun C (9 1959); Columbia CC (27 1962); CC of Orangeburg (1960); CC of South Carolina (1969); Midland Valley CC (1961); Wellman CC (1970).

Tennessee: Dandridge GC, with Dan Maples; Ridgeway CC (1972); Roan Valley CC (1983), with Dan Maples.

Virginia: ArrowWood CC [FKA Countryside CC] (1967); Chatmoss CC (1960); Devil's Knob GC (1977), with Dan Maples; Ford's Colony CC (West Cse 1986), with Dan Maples; Kempsville Meadows G&CC (1954); Lexington G&CC (1971); Olde Mill GC (1974), with Dan Maples; Roanoke CC (9); Tazewell County CC (9 1978), with Dan Maples.

Courses remodeled or expanded by Ellis Maples:

North Carolina: CC of Johnston County (R.9 A.9 1963); Deep Springs CC (R.9 A.9 1978), with Dan Maples; Emorywood CC (R.9 1962); Kinston CC (R. 1954); Myers Park CC (R. 1962); New Bern G&CC (R.9 A.9 1954); Reynolds Park GC (R. 1966); Roxboro CC (A.9 1969); Stanly County CC (R. 1966).

Tennessee: Gatlinburg G&CC (R. 1974), with Dan Maples.

LANE LEE MARSHALL (1937–   ), ASGCA

BORN: Rochester, New York.

A graduate landscape architect, Lane Marshall served as president of the ASLA in 1977 and 1978. In addition to his landscape practice, he designed a number of golf courses in Florida.

In the early 1980s Marshall curtailed his course design activities and joined the Department of Landscape Architecture at Texas A&M University. He later moved to Kansas and served as dean of the Landscape Architecture Department at Kansas State University.

Courses by Lane Marshall:

Florida: Bobby Jones Muni (Gillespie Cse [9 Precision] 1977); Capri Isles GC (1973); Foxfire CC (1975); Manatee County GC (1977); Myakka Pines GC (27 1978); Tarpon Lake Village GC (1975); Tarpon Woods GC (1975); Wildflower CC (Precision 1972).

North Dakota: Williston Muni, with *Carl Thuesen* (9).

Jerry Martin, 1986
COURTESY JERRY
MARTIN

JERRY MARTIN (1939–   ), ASGCA

BORN: Phoenix, Arizona.

Jerry Martin grew up in Tucson, Arizona, but attended high school in Morocco. He returned to the United States to study fine arts at the University of Arizona. Following military service, he worked for a year on a surveying crew before returning to the University of Arizona, where he earned a degree in city planning in 1967. Martin was employed for five years with a civil engineering firm as an architect and was then associated with the West Coast branch of Robert Trent Jones Inc. for another five. He then became in-house golf architect and manager of recreational planning with Jack G. Robb Engineering of Costa Mesa, California. In 1980 Martin formed his own design practice based in Tucson. He was instrumental in master-planning resorts for Fonatur, the Mexican government's tourism department.

Courses by Jerry Martin:

Arizona: Rio Rico GC (1971), ass't Robert Trent Jones.

North Dakota: Oxbow CC (1974), ass't Robert Trent Jones, Jr.

Texas: Northbank CC (1992).

Mexico: C de G Los Cabos (9); C de G Palma Real GC (1977), ass't Robert Trent Jones, Jr.

Courses remodeled or expanded by Jerry Martin:

California: Mission Viejo CC (R. 2 1986).

Billy Martindale,
1975 COLLECTION RON
WHITTEN

WILLIAM MARTINDALE

Texas A&M graduate and onetime PGA Tour player Billy Martindale designed several courses in partnership with Don January during the early 1970s. January rejoined the PGA Tour in 1976, but Martindale continued design work in Texas for several years before turning to a career in the oil business. In the late 1980s, when course construction proved more lucrative than oil, Martindale again resumed his design practice.

Courses by Billy Martindale (All with Don January unless otherwise indicated):

Oklahoma: Walnut Creek CC (1976).

Texas: Bentwood CC (1980 *solo*); Great Hills GC; Los Rios CC (1974); Oak Forest CC (*solo*); Pecan Hollow GC (*solo*); Pine Forest GC (1992 *solo*); [The] Pinnacle C (9); Plano Muni; Royal Oak CC (1970); Walnut Creek GC; Woodcrest CC; Woodland Hills GC.

Courses remodeled or expanded by Billy Martindale (All with Don January unless otherwise indicated):

Texas: Lake Country Estates GC (A.9 1975).

THOMAS A. MARZOLF (1960–   ), ASGCA

BORN: Columbus, Ohio.

After completing a thesis on "Stadium Golf Course Design" and graduating cum laude in landscape architecture at Virginia Tech, Tom Marzolf landed a position in Tom Fazio's design operation in 1983. Following a couple of years handling remodelings, Marzolf became a design asso-

Tom Marzolf, 1991
COURTESY TOM
MARZOLF

ciate and participated in the design of several prominent courses, notably Wade Hampton in North Carolina. He eventually directed operations of Fazio's North Carolina office and oversaw construction on most Fazio designs in the Southeast. But his remodeling talents remained, and as Fazio's associate he handled such plush renovations as reconstruction at Pine Valley and installation of a putting green at the U.S. vice president's residence near Washington, D.C.

Courses by Tom Marzolf (All as assistant to Tom Fazio):

Georgia: Eagle's Landing CC (1989); [The] Farm GC (1989); [The] Landings at Skidaway Island (Deer Creek Cse 1991); St. Ives CC (1989).
Maryland: Caves Valley GC (1991).
North Carolina: Old North State C (1992); Wade Hampton GC (1987).
South Carolina: Thornblade GC (1990).
Virginia: Governors Landing CC (1992).

Courses remodeled or expanded by Tom Marzolf (All as assistant to Tom Fazio unless otherwise indicated):

New Jersey: Pine Valley GC (R.1 1989).
New York: Winged Foot GC (West Cse, R.1 1989).
North Carolina: Highlands Falls CC (R.1 1985).
South Carolina: CC of Callawassie (A.3rd 9 1991); CC of Edisto Island (R. 1988).
Virginia: Woodlawn CC (R. 1983 *solo*).

GERALD HERBERT MATTHEWS (1934–   ), ASGCA

BORN: Grand Rapids, Michigan.

Jerry Matthews attended Michigan State University, receiving a Bachelor's degree in landscape architecture as well as Bachelor's and Master's degrees in urban planning. During his schooling, he worked for ten summers in golf course maintenance and also supervised the construction of one course designed by his father, architect Bruce Matthews.

In 1960 Matthews and his father established a golf architectural partnership. Over the years, Jerry took on the active design work of the firm, while his father acted as consultant. When his father retired from active participation in 1985, Jerry established Matthews and Associates, based in Lansing, Michigan. Among his design associates were his nephew Bruce Matthews III and Raymond Hearn.

In the 1990s, Matthews, a registered landscape architect himself, was appointed to the Michigan State Board of Landscape Architects.

Courses by Jerry Matthews (All with Bruce Matthews unless otherwise indicated):

Indiana: Summertree GC (1974).
Michigan: Antrim Dells GC (9 1971, A.9 1975); Birchwood Farm G&CC (1974); Bird Creek GC (1990 *solo*); Candlestone GC (1978); Cracklewood GC (1988 *solo*); Crystal Lake GC (9 1970, A.9 1988 *solo*); Eagle Glen GC; Eldorado GC (9 1966, A.9 1978); Elk Ridge G Cse (1991 *solo*); Fellows Creek GC (1961; A.9 1986 *solo*); Flint Elks CC (9 1960); Godwin Glen GC (27 1972, NLE); Grand Blanc GC (1967); Grand Haven GC (1965); Greystone GC (1992 *solo*); Independence Green GC (Precision 1965); Kaufman GC (1963); Lake of the Hills GC (9 Par 3 1968); Lake Isabella GC (1970); Lake of the North GC (9 1971); Lakewood Shores G&CC (1969); Lincoln Hills GC (9 1963); [The] Links of Novi (27 1991 *solo*); Michaywe Hills GC (Lakes Cse 1988 *solo*); Mitchell Creek GC (1982); [The] Natural GC (1991 *solo*); [The] Players Club (1987 *solo*); Railside G Cse (1991 *solo*); Riverside CC (9 1964); Royal Oak GC (9 1960); St. Clair Shores CC (1974); Salem Hills GC (1961); San Marino GC (9 1965); Sandy Ridge GC (1966); Scott Lake CC (1961); Shenandoah G&CC (1964); Southmoor GC (1965; R.1 1989 *solo*); Sugar Springs GC (1978); Sycamore Hills GC (27 1990 *solo*); Timber Ridge GC (1989 *solo*); University Park GC (9 1966); Wallinwood Springs GC (9 1991 *solo*); West Ot-

tawa GC (1964); Winding Creek GC (1967); Wolverine GC (Old Cse 1965; New Cse, 27 1986 *solo*).

Courses remodeled or expanded by Jerry Matthews (All with Bruce Matthews unless otherwise indicated):

Indiana: Elcona CC (R. 1969); Fort Wayne CC (R.3 1968).
Michigan: Birmingham CC (R.3 1963); Blythefield CC (R.5 1973; R.1 1985; R.1 1988 *solo*; R.1 1990 *solo*); Bonnie View GC (R.4 A.2 1978); Cadillac CC (R.1 1977); Cascade Hills CC (R. 1980; R.9 1984); Cedar Glen GC (R.9 A.9 1991 *solo*); CC of Detroit (R. 1962); CC of Lansing (R.1 1984 *solo*, R.11 1990 *solo*); Crockery Hills GC (R.5 A.9 1976); Crooked Creek CC (R.2 1986 *solo*); Dearborn CC (R.1 1985 *solo*); Elmbrook GC (R.3 1985 *solo*); English Hills GC (A.9 1985 *solo*); Farmington CC (R. 1962); Flint GC (R.1 1988 *solo*); Forest Hills GC (R.1 1984 *solo*); Four Winds GC (R.3 1988 *solo*); Frankenmuth GC (R.2 1985 *solo*, NLE); Grand Hotel GC (R.4 1985 *solo*; R.5 1987 *solo*, R.4 1989 *solo*); Hastings CC (R.3 1986 *solo*); Highland Hills GC (A.9 1963); Holland CC (R.1 1986 *solo*); Indian Hills GC (R. 1968); Indian Lake GC (R.3 1980); Indian Run GC (A.9 1972); Inverness CC (R.9 1986 *solo*); Kalamazoo Elks CC (R.2 1976); Kent CC (R.1 1985 *solo*; R.2 1988 *solo*; R.1 1990 *solo*); Knollwood CC (R.1 A.1 1969); Lakepointe CC (A.6 1964, NLE); Lakeview Hills CC (South Cse, R.1 1983 *solo*); Lincoln GC (A.2 1986 *solo*); Lincoln Hills GC (R.1 1984 *solo*; R.2 1986 *solo*); Ludington Hills GC (R.4 A.9 1975); Maple Hill GC (R.1 1984 *solo*); Meadowbrook CC (R.1; R.2 1985 *solo*); Midland CC (R. 1965; R.5 1988 *solo*); Mission Hill GC (A.9 1986 *solo*); Moravian Hills CC (R.1

Jerry Matthews, 1990 COURTESY JERRY MATTHEWS

1987 *solo*); Mount Pleasant CC (A.9 1981); Muskegon CC (R.3 1979; R.2 1989 *solo*); Old Channel Trail GC (A.11 1966); Pine Lake GC (A.2 1985 *solo*; R.16 1989 *solo*); Pine Ridge CC (A.9 1961); Plum Hollow G&CC (R.1 1966); Portage Lake GC (A.9 1988 *solo*); Rackham Park Muni (R.9 1985 *solo*); Ramshorn CC (A.9 1986 *solo*); Royal Scot GC (R.4 1988 *solo*); Saginaw CC (R.2 1979, R.2 1985); Sault St. Marie CC (A.9 1985 *solo*); Spring Lake CC (R.1 1978; R.2 1985 *solo*); Stonycroft Hills CC (R.5 1979); Traverse City CC (R.); Walnut Hills CC (R.2 1962; R.4 1984 *solo*); Washtenaw CC (R.1 1962; R.4 1987 *solo*; R.1 1986 *solo*); West Shore G&CC (R.5 1988 *solo*); Whitefish Lake GC (A.3 1988 *solo*); White Lake GC (R. 1965); Winters Creek GC (R.9 1980).

Pennsylvania: Sunnehanna CC (R.1 1985 *solo*).

Wisconsin: Brynwood CC (R.1 A.2 1979).

Ontario: Essex G&CC (A.2 1976).

WALLACE BRUCE MATTHEWS (1904–), ASGCA, FELLOW

BORN: Hastings, Michigan.

Bruce Matthews received a landscape architecture degree from Michigan State College in 1925. His first course-design experience was with the golf architecture firm of Stiles and Van Kleek of Boston, Massachusetts, and St. Petersburg, Florida. In 1929 he entered private practice in Michigan, where his first original design was a second nine at Manistee Golf and Country Club.

When the Depression curtailed course construction Matthews became manager-greenkeeper at Grand Ridge CC in Grand Rapids. He remained in that position until 1959 but continued to design golf courses on the side. In 1960 he reentered golf architecture on a full-time basis with his son Jerry as his partner. He also owned and operated a course of his own design, Grand Haven Golf Club, a perennial selection as one of the top public courses in America. In 1991 Matthews was awarded the GCSAA's prestigious Distinguished Service Award.

Courses by Bruce Matthews (All with Jerry Matthews unless otherwise indicated):

Indiana: Summertree GC (1974).

Michigan: Antrim Dells GC (9 1971, A.9

Three generations of golf architects: Bruce Matthews (center), with son Jerry Matthews (left) and grandson Bruce Matthews III (right), 1989
COURTESY JERRY MATTHEWS

1975); Birchwood Farm G&CC (1974); Blossom Trails GC (1952 *solo*); Brookshire CC (9 1955 *solo*); Candlestone GC (1978); Crystal Lake GC (9 1970); Dun Rovin CC (1956 *solo*); Eagle Glen GC; Eldorado GC (9 1966, A.9 1978); Fellows Creek GC (1961); Flint Elks CC (9 1960); Forest Akers GC (West Cse 1958 *solo*); Godwin Glen GC (27 1972, NLE); Grand Blanc GC (1967); Grand Haven GC (1965); Independence Green GC (Precision 1965); Kaufman GC (1963); Lake Isabella GC (1970); Lake of the Hills GC (9 Par 3 1968); Lake of the North GC (9 1971); Lakewood Shores G&CC (1969); Lincoln Hills GC (9 1963); McGuires Evergreen GC (27 1954 *solo*); Mitchell Creek GC (1982); Riverside CC (9 1964); Royal Oak GC (9 1960); St. Clair Shores CC (1974); Salem Hills GC (1961); San Marino GC (9 1965); Sandy Ridge GC (1966); Scott Lake CC (1961); Shenandoah G&CC (1964); Southmoor GC (1965); Sugar Springs GC (1978); Sunnybrook CC (1955 *solo*); Tyrone Hills CC (1958 *solo*); University Park GC (9 1966); West Ottawa GC (1964); White Birch Hills GC (1953 *solo*); Winding Creek GC (1967); Wolverine GC (Old Cse 1965).

Courses remodeled or expanded by Bruce Matthews (All with Jerry Matthews unless otherwise indicated):

Indiana: Elcona CC (R. 1969); Fort Wayne CC (R.3 1968).

Michigan: Birmingham CC (R.3 1963); Blythefield CC (R.5 1973; R.1 1985); Bonnie View GC (R.4 A.2 1978); Cadillac CC (R.1 1977); Cascade Hills CC (R. 1980; R.9 1984); CC of Detroit (R. 1962); Crockery Hills GC (R.5 A.9 1976); Farmington CC (R. 1962); Green Ridge CC (R. 1930 *solo*; R. 1950 *solo*, NLE); Highland Hills GC (A.9 1963); Indian Hills GC (R. 1968); Indian Lake GC (R.3 1980); Indian Run GC (A.9 1972); Kalamazoo Elks CC (R.2 1976); Knollwood CC (R.1 A.1 1969); Lakepointe CC (A.6 1964, NLE); Ludington Hills GC (R.4 A.9 1975); Manistee G&CC (R.9 A.9 1930 *solo*); Meadowbrook CC (R.1); Midland CC (R. 1965); Mount Pleasant CC (A.9 1981); Muskegon CC (R.3 1979); Old Channel Trail GC (A.11 1966); Pine Ridge CC (A.9 1961); Plum Hollow G&CC (R.1 1966); Saginaw CC (R.2 1979; R.2 1985); Spring Lake CC (R.1 1978); Stonycroft Hills CC (R.5 1979); Traverse City CC (R.); Walnut Hills CC (R.2 1962);

Washtenaw CC (R.1 1962); White Lake GC (R. 1965); Winters Creek GC (R.9 1980).

Wisconsin: Brynwood CC (R.1 A.2 1979).
Ontario: Essex G&CC (A.2 1976).

WALLACE BRUCE MATTHEWS III
ASGCA

Bruce Matthews III was another of those for whom a career in golf architecture seemed unavoidable. His namesake and grandfather was golf architect Bruce Matthews. His uncle was golf architect Jerry Matthews.

Still, Matthews spent his early years working on the maintenance crew of his grandfather's golf course, Grand Haven in Michigan, and seemed to prefer maintaining courses to designing them. So he spent 12 years as a golf superintendent in Pennsylvania, Indiana and Michigan, after graduating from Michigan State University in 1975 with a Bachelor's degree in crop and soil science. It wasn't until 1986 that Matthews joined his uncle's golf design firm. He learned the trade quickly and soon participated in all facets of course design and construction supervision.

A member of the GCSAA who received certified superintendent status in 1984, Bruce Matthews became a member of the ASGCA in 1990, marking the first time that three generations from one family held membership in that society.

Courses by Bruce Matthews III (All as assistant to Jerry Matthews):

Michigan: Bird Creek GC (1990); Cracklewood GC (1988); Elk Ridge G Cse (1991); Greystone GC (1992); [The] Links of Novi (27 1991); [The] Natural GC (1991); Railside GC (1991); Sycamore Hills GC (27 1990); Wallinwood Springs GC (9 1991).

*Bruce Matthews III,
1990* COURTESY JERRY
MATTHEWS

Courses remodeled or expanded by Bruce Matthews III (All as assistant to Jerry Matthews):

Michigan: Blythefield CC (R.1 1990); Cedar Glen GC (R.9 A.9 1991); CC of Lansing (R.11 1990); Crystal Lake GC (A.9 1988); Hastings CC (R.3 1986); Kent CC (R.1 1990); Muskegon CC (R.2 1989); Pine Lake GC (R.16 1989); Southmoor CC (R.1 1989); Washtenaw CC (R.1 1986).

CHARLES E. MAUD

Englishman Charles Maud emigrated to California, where he laid out the state's first golf course in 1892. Known as Pedley Farms GC (later Arlington GC and then Victoria GC). It was opened by Colonel W. E. Pedley, who assisted Maud in laying out several other early California courses. Although Max Behr revised the original nine and added an additional nine, Victoria GC retained several of Maud's holes.

Charles Maud was the winner of the first California Amateur in 1899 and served as the first president of the Southern California Golf Association in 1900.

Courses by Charles Maud:

California: Delmar CC (9, NLE); Old Del Monte G&CC (9 1897); Victoria GC, Riverside (9 1892), with *Colonel W. E. Pedley.*

HOWARD L. MAURER
(1958–)

Howard Maurer obtained a Bachelor of Science degree in environmental studies and landscape architecture from the State University of New York at Syracuse and an associate degree in ornamental horticulture from the State University of New York at Farmingdale. He also graduated from the widely known Winter Turf School at the University of Massachusetts.

In 1981 Maurer spent a year as an assistant superintendent at Woodmere Country Club on Long Island. He then worked as a landscape designer, first for a firm in Fayetteville, New York, and then for seven years as design director for Matarazzo Design of Concord, New Hampshire. In 1990 he joined the golf design firm of Cornish & Silva and worked closely with designer Brian Silva on all phases of design and construction.

PERRY DUKE MAXWELL
(1879–1952), ASGCA, CHARTER MEMBER

BORN: Princeton, Kentucky.
DIED: Tulsa, Oklahoma, at age 73.

Perry Maxwell, of Scottish descent, was educated at the University of Kentucky. In 1897 he moved to the Ardmore Indian Territory to recover from an attack of tuberculosis and settled in what would become, in 1907, the state of Oklahoma. He was employed as a cashier and later as vice president of the Ardmore National Bank, becoming one of the town's leading citizens. Around 1909 he took up the game of golf after reading an article by H. J. Whigham, and in 1913, with his wife's assistance, he laid out a rudimentary nine-hole course on their farm north of Ardmore. This course became Dornick Hills G&CC.

Maxwell retired from banking soon after his wife's death in 1919 and spent the next several years touring America's most prominent Southern and Eastern golf courses. He added a second nine to Dornick Hills in 1923 and installed the first

*Perry Maxwell,
1933* COLLECTION RON
WHITTEN

grass greens in the state of Oklahoma at the same time. Shortly thereafter he was hired to build courses in Tulsa and Oklahoma City and by 1925 was working full-time as a golf architect. He worked for three years in the early 1930s in partnership with Alister Mackenzie.

Maxwell was best known for his wildly undulating greens, and his reputation was of such stature that he was hired to rebuild greens at Augusta National, Pine Valley, the National Golf Links and others. His last designs, following the amputation of his right leg in 1946, were supervised by his son J. Press Maxwell, who later became a golf architect himself. It is estimated that during his career Perry Maxwell designed some seventy courses and remodeled fifty others.

Courses by Perry Maxwell:

Alabama: Lakewood GC (Dogwood Cse 1947), with Press Maxwell.

Illinois: Rochelle CC (9 1930).

Iowa: Veenker Memorial GC, Iowa State University (1934).

Kansas: Arkansas City CC (9 1937); Prairie Dunes CC (9 1937).

Kentucky: Kentucky Dam Village GC (1952), with Press Maxwell.

Louisiana: Bayou de Siard CC (1949), with Press Maxwell; Palmetto CC (1950), with Press Maxwell.

Michigan: Crystal Downs CC (1933), with Alister Mackenzie; University of Michigan GC (1931), with Alister Mackenzie.

Missouri: Excelsior Springs CC (Par 3 Cse [9 Par 3], NLE); Grandview Muni (1947), with Press Maxwell.

North Carolina: Old Town C (1928); Reynolds Park GC (1941); Starmount Forest CC (1929).

Oklahoma: Dornick Hills G&CC (9 1913, R.9 A.9 1923); Elks CC (9); Hillcrest CC; Lake Hefner GC (North Cse 1951), with Press Maxwell; Lawton CC (9 1948), with Press Maxwell; Muskogee CC (1924); Oakwood CC (1947), with Press Maxwell; Oklahoma City G&CC (1930); Ponca City CC; Rolling Hills CC (1926); Shawnee Elks CC; Southern Hills CC (1936); Twin Hills G&CC (1926); University of Oklahoma GC (1950), with Press Maxwell.

Pennsylvania: Chester Valley CC (1928); Eugene Grace Estate G Cse; Melrose CC (1927).

Texas: Anderson GC (9 1948), with Press Maxwell; Knollwood GC (1952, NLE), with Press Maxwell; Randolph Field GC (9 1948), with Press Maxwell; Riverside GC [FKA CC of Austin] (1950), with Press Maxwell; Walnut Hills CC (NLE).

Courses remodeled or expanded by Perry Maxwell:

Florida: Clearwater CC (R.).

Georgia: Augusta National GC (R. 1937).

Kansas: Topeka CC (R.9 A.9 1938).

Kentucky: Lincoln Homestead State Park GC (R. 1953), with Press Maxwell.

Nebraska: Omaha CC (R.).

New Jersey: Pine Valley GC (R. 1933).

New York: [The] Links GC (R.); Maidstone C (R.); National Golf Links of America (R.1); Rockaway Hunting C (R. 1946); Westchester CC (South Cse, R.).

North Carolina: Hillandale CC (R. 1930); Hope Valley CC (R.).

Oklahoma: Lincoln Park Muni (East Cse, R.; West Cse, R.); Mohawk Park Muni (Woodbine Cse, R. 1934); Oaks CC (R.).

Pennsylvania: Flourtown CC (R. 1939); Gulph Mills GC (R. 1937); Merion GC (East Cse, R., West Cse, R. 1939); Philadelphia CC (R. 1938), with William S. Flynn; Saucon Valley CC (Old Cse, R. 1947).

Texas: Colonial CC (A.3 1940).

J. Press Maxwell, 1972 COURTESY *GOLF WORLD*

JAMES PRESS MAXWELL
(1916–   ), ASGCA, PRESIDENT 1960

BORN: Ardmore, Oklahoma.

The son of golf architect Perry Maxwell, Press Maxwell started in the business upon graduation from high school. His father put him to work running mule teams and fresno scrapers at such sites as Southern Hills and Augusta National.

After service as a pilot with the U.S. Army Air Force during World War II, Maxwell returned to his father's firm. By this time Perry Maxwell had lost a leg, so Press handled most of the on-site supervision of their designs. Continuing the firm after his father's death in 1952, Maxwell designed and built many courses along the Gulf Coast, flying from course to course in his own Cessna. In the early 1960s he moved his base to Colorado and in the early 1970s retired from full-time practice to maintain a ranch and breed Appaloosa horses.

Courses by Press Maxwell:

Alabama: Lakewood GC (Dogwood Cse 1947), with Perry Maxwell.

California: Seacliff CC [FKA Huntington Seacliff CC] (1965).

Colorado: Applewood GC (1961); Boulder CC (1965); Cherry Hills CC (Par 3 Cse [9 Par 3] 1961); Cimarron Hills GC (1974); Cortez Muni (9 1964, A.9 1974); Hiwan GC (1965); Inverness GC (1974); Kissing Camels GC (1961); Lake Valley GC (1964); Pinehurst CC (27 1960); Rolling Hills CC (1968); Snowmass GC (9 1967); Vail GC (1966); Woodmoor CC (1965).

Kentucky: Kentucky Dam Village GC (1952), with Perry Maxwell.

Louisiana: Bayou de Siard CC (1949), with Perry Maxwell; East Ridge CC (1957); Palmetto CC (1950), with Perry Maxwell.

Mississippi: Hattiesburg CC (1962).

Missouri: Fremont Hills CC (9 1971); Grandview Muni (1947), with Perry Maxwell; Pomme de Terre G&CC (9 1976); Tri-way GC (9 1971).

Oklahoma: Lake Hefner GC (North Cse 1951), with Perry Maxwell; Lawton CC (9 1948), with Perry Maxwell; Meadowbrook CC (9 1954); Oakwood CC (1947), with Perry Maxwell; University of Oklahoma GC (1950), with Perry Maxwell.

Tennessee: Edmund Orgill GC (1970); Farmington CC (1968).

Texas: Anderson GC (9 1948), with Perry Maxwell; Brookhaven CC (Championship Cse 1959; Masters Cse 1959; Presidents Cse 1959); [The] Club at Sonterra (South Cse) [FKA Canyon Creek CC] (1960); Irving CC (9 1957, NLE); Knollwood GC (1952, NLE), with Perry Maxwell; Oak Cliff CC (1955); Pecan Valley CC (1963); Randolph Field GC (9 1948), with Perry Maxwell; Riverbend CC (1958); Riverside GC [FKA CC of Austin] (1950), with Perry Maxwell; Sleepy Hollow G&CC (Lake Cse 1957; River Cse 1957); Village CC (1969).

Courses remodeled or expanded by Press Maxwell:

Colorado: Bookcliff CC (A.5 1967); Cherry Hills CC (R.2 1959); Columbine CC (R. 1958); Denver CC (R. 1964); Greeley CC (R.9 A.9 1962); Lakewood CC (R. 1962); Patty Jewett GC (A.9 1968).

Kansas: Prairie Dunes CC (A.9 1957).

Kentucky: Lincoln Homestead State Park GC (R. 1953), with Perry Maxwell.

New York: Rockaway Hunting C (R. 1955).

Oklahoma: Oklahoma City G&CC (R. 1952).

Texas: Pinecrest CC (R.9 A.9 1959).

Utah: Park City GC (R.9 A.9 1972).

Ted McAnlis, 1990
COURTESY TED MCANLIS

THEODORE MCANLIS

Civil engineer Ted McAnlis entered the golf business by forming a group to finance Briarwood GC in Cleveland, Ohio, a daily-fee layout that he designed and constructed. While serving as Briarwood's manager for eight years, McAnlis designed several courses in Ohio in association with Richard LaConte.

In the early 1970s McAnlis moved to Florida and worked as a design engineer for architects George and Tom Fazio from 1973 through 1975. In 1976 McAnlis teamed once again with LaConte, this time forming a design-and-build business in Florida. LaConte and McAnlis Associates lasted only one year, then McAnlis practiced course design on his own.

Courses by Ted McAnlis:

Florida: Calusa Lakes GC (1991); Greenview Cove GC (1980); Heritage Ridge GC (9 1979); Imperial Lakes GC, Palmetto (1987); Indianwood G&CC (9 Precision 1982); [The] Lakes GC (1986); Lone Pine GC (Precision 1981), with Richard W. LaConte; Misty Creek CC (1985); Palms of Terra Ceia GC (1986); River Wilderness Y&CC (1984); Tara G&CC (1989); Tatum Ridge G Links (1989); St. Andrews CC (East Cse 1982; West Cse 1985); Sorrento Valley GC (1992); Venice G&CC (1991); Waterford GC (1989); Wellington GC (1984).
Ohio: Briardale Greens Muni (1977), with Richard W. LaConte; Briarwood GC (1967, A.3rd 9 1973); Gleneagles GC; Leaning Tree GC (Precision 1972), with Richard W. LaConte; Midway GC (9 1971); Wildwood CC (9 1969).

Courses remodeled or expanded by Ted McAnlis:

Florida: Atlantis GC (R.); Card Sound GC (R.); El Conquistador CC (R.);

Foxfire GC (A.3rd 9 1988); Palm Beach Polo & CC (Olde Cse, R. 1981).
Louisiana: Brechtel Memorial Park GC (R.9 A.9 1978), with Richard W. LaConte.
Ohio: Grandview CC (R.), with Richard LaConte; Oakwood C (R.2 1971); Pine Valley GC (R.9 A.9 1971); Willard CC (A.9 1971), with Richard LaConte.

THOMAS MCBROOM
(1952–)

BORN: Toronto, Ontario.

A third-generation golfer who maintained a 5 handicap for years, Tom McBroom graduated in landscape architecture from the University of Guelph in Ontario and then worked briefly for an environmental planning firm before entering practice as a golf course architect in 1973. He worked for veteran architect C. E. "Robbie" Robinson for five years before establishing his own firm in 1978, based in Toronto. By the early 1990s he was one of the busiest and most prominent of a new generation of Canadian golf course architects.

Tom McBroom, 1991 COURTESY TOM MCBROOM

Courses by Thomas McBroom:

Ontario: Barrie National Pines G&CC; Beacon Hall GC (1988), ass't Bob Cupp; Camelot G&CC (1991); Cranberry Village C (1988); Deerhurst Highlands GC (1990), with Bob Cupp; Deer Ridge GC (1991); Grandview GC (9 1988); Heron Point G Links (1991); Hockley Valley Resort GC (1990); Huron Pines G&CC (9 1983); Millcroft G&CC; Monterra G Cse (1990); Oak Ridge G&CC (1988); Parry Sound G&CC (1982); Pointe West GC; Port Carling G&CC (1991).
Prince Edward Island: St. Peters-Morell GC.

Courses remodeled or expanded by Thomas McBroom:

Ontario: Beech Grove G&CC (R. 1986); Deerhurst Inn & CC (R. 1988); Garrison G & Curling C (A.9 1984); Hamilton G&CC (R. 1986); Humber Valley GC (R. 1990); Islington GC (R.1 1985); Kanata Lakes G&CC (R.9 A.9 1992); Meadowbrook G&CC (R. 1988); Muskoka Lakes G&CC (R. 1988); Oakville G&CC (R. A.2 1987); Ottawa Hunt G&CC (R.); Tam O'Shanter Muni (R. 1982); Toronto Hunt C (R. 1990).

Maurice McCarthy, circa 1930
COLLECTION RON WHITTEN

MAURICE J. MCCARTHY, SR.
(1875–1938)

BORN: County Cork, Ireland.
DIED: Flushing, New York, at age 63.

Maurice McCarthy came to the United States at the age of 15 and obtained a job as a teaching professional in Pittsfield, Massachusetts. A few years later he laid out his first course, Jefferson County Golf Club (later renamed Ives Hill Golf Club) in Watertown, New York. Throughout his life, course design remained a part-time endeavor for McCarthy. He was proudest of his accomplishments as a teacher. His son Maurice Jr. was the 1928 NCAA champion and a topflight amateur in the 1930s.

McCarthy served as professional at several New York-area clubs but in his later years was employed exclusively by A. G. Spalding Sporting Goods Company in New York City, where he gave lessons to all purchasers of golf clubs.

It was once estimated that Maurice McCarthy designed or remodeled about 125 courses during his lifetime, most of them in the Eastern and Middle Atlantic states. His most famous works were at Hershey, Pennsylvania, where he laid out four different courses over the years for his friend

Milton Hershey. They ranged from a short beginner's course, Spring Creek GC, to a nationally recognized championship course, the West Course at Hershey Country Club.

Courses by Maurice McCarthy, Sr.:

Connecticut: E. Gaynor Brennan GC [FKA Hubbard Heights CC].
Michigan: Marywood CC (1926).
New Jersey: Knickerbocker CC (NLE).
New York: Ives Hill CC (9 1899); Old Flatbush CC (9 1925, NLE); Peninsula GC; Willow Ridge CC [FKA Green Meadow CC] (1916).
Pennsylvania: Hershey CC (West Cse 1930); Hotel Hershey GC (9 1928); Kingsport CC; Mahoning Valley CC (NLE); Parkview Manor GC (1927); Spring Creek GC (9 1933).
South Carolina: Forest Lakes C.

Courses remodeled or expanded by Maurice McCarthy, Sr.:

Connecticut: Woodway CC (R. 1925).
New Jersey: Green Brook CC (R. 1925); White Beeches G&CC (R. 1926).

Mark McCumber, 1991 COURTESY MARK MCCUMBER

MARK RANDALL MCCUMBER (1951–), ASGCA

BORN: Jacksonville, Florida.

Mark McCumber grew up on Hyde Park Golf Club in Jacksonville, Florida, where he and his brothers dug crabgrass for free green fees. After high school he attended Brooklyn Bethel College in Brooklyn Heights, New York, and studied for the ministry. Ultimately, he opted for a golf career and, after several attempts, gained his PGA Tour card in 1978. He experienced success as a competitive player, winning two Doral Open titles as well as the Western Open and the Tournament Players Championship.

In the late 1970s McCumber became

involved with his brothers Jim, Gary and Tim in the golf course construction business. They constructed the Ron Garl–designed Ravines GC near Jacksonville and used it as a showcase for their talents. The family business soon gained some design-and-build contracts, with Mark supplying the designs. By the mid-1980s McCumber divided his time between the PGA Tour and golf course architecture. His firm also took on two design associates, Chris Commins and Michael Beebe.

Courses by Mark McCumber:

Florida: Burnt Store Marina GC (South Cse [9 Precision] 1988); Cutter Sound CC (1985); Deep Creek GC (1985); Dunes CC (Precision 1983); Embassy Woods at Bretonne Park (Precision 1991); Magnolia Point G&CC (1986); Marsh Creek CC (1988); Queen's Harbour Y&CC (1991); Summer Beach G Cse (1987); Vineyards G&CC (North Cse 1988).
Georgia: Osprey Cove GC (1990).
Mississippi: Timberton GC (1991); Windance G&CC (1986).
Alberta: Edmonton Petroleum G&CC (1992).
Japan: Ohtake GC.
Korea: Dae Jeon CC.

Courses remodeled or expanded by Mark McCumber:

Florida: North Palm Beach CC (R. 1990).
Michigan: Great Oaks CC (R. 1989).

MICHAEL J. MCDONAGH

BORN: Ireland.

Michael McDonagh, a cousin of golf architect Jack Fleming, came to America in the late 1920s. When McDonagh moved to California, Fleming put him in charge of building Haggin Oaks Golf Course in Sacramento to the design of Alister Mackenzie. After completion of the course, McDonagh remained in Sacramento and eventually became course superintendent for all municipal courses in the city. While in that capacity, McDonagh tried his hand at golf course design on several occasions.

Courses by Michael McDonagh:

California: Bing Mahoney GC (1952); Haggin Oaks GC (North Cse 1956); Yolo Fliers C (A.9 1955).

Steven McFarlane, 1991 COURTESY STEVEN MCFARLANE

STEVEN GEORGE MCFARLANE (1963–), BIGCA

BORN: Troon, Scotland.

Steven McFarlane completed a degree in civil engineering at the University of Glasgow, then obtained a postgraduate diploma in offshore engineering at the Robert Gordons Institute in 1984. In 1987 he joined golf architect Martin Hawtree as an assistant.

Courses by Steven McFarlane (All as assistant to Martin Hawtree):

North Carolina: Reems Creek GC (1989), and Simon Gidman.
England: Marlwood G Centre, and Simon Gidman; Moors Valley GC (9), and Simon Gidman.
France: Club Med Montargis, and Simon Gidman; Golf de Carquefou, and Simon Gidman; Parc de Loisirs GC.
Spain: Golf Girona.

Courses remodeled or expanded by Steven McFarlane (All as assistant to Martin Hawtree):

England: Brampton Park GC (R.), and Simon Gidman.
Scotland: Aboyne GC (R.); Broomieknowe GC (A.4).

JAMES BERNARD MCGOVERN (–1951), ASGCA, CHARTER MEMBER

J. B. McGovern spent most of his design career as an associate of Donald Ross, operating Ross's Wynnewood (Pennsylvania) office beginning in 1916. The two had met when Ross was hired to build a new course for McGovern's home course, Aronimink. For a short period following Ross's death in 1948, McGovern planned several courses on his own.

J. B. McGovern, 1949 COLLECTION RON WHITTEN

Courses by J.B. McGovern (All as assistant to Donald Ross unless otherwise indicated):

Georgia: Callaway Gardens GC (Lakeview Cse, 9 1952 *solo*).
Michigan: Elk Rapids GC (9 1923).
North Carolina: Forsyth CC (1920); Highland CC (1945); Myers Park CC (1930; R. 1945; R. 1947); Pennrose Park GC (9 1945); Raleigh CC (1948).
Ohio: Lancaster CC (9 1926).
Pennsylvania: Aronimink GC (1928); Elk View GC (9 1925); Overbrook CC (1952 *solo*); Rolling Rock GC (9 1917).
South Carolina: Fort Mill GC (9 1946).
Tennessee: Ridgefields CC (1947).
Nova Scotia: Liverpool GC [FKA White Point Beach GC] (1928).

Courses remodeled or expanded by J.B. McGovern (All as assistant to Donald Ross unless otherwise indicated):

Massachusetts: Vesper CC (R.9 A.9 1919).
New York: Irondequoit CC (A.9 1948 *solo*).
North Carolina: Cape Fear CC (R. 1946).
Pennsylvania: Green Valley CC (R. 1946 *solo*); Gulph Mills GC (R. 1946 *solo*); Llanerch CC (R. 1949 *solo*).
Virginia: Woodberry Forest GC (R. 1924 *solo*).

ALEXANDER G. MCKAY (1893–1964)

BORN: Aberdeen, Scotland.
DIED: Nashville, Tennessee, at age 71.

Alex McKay learned golf at Cruden Bay Golf Club in Aberdeen and turned professional at a young age. After spending three years in Egypt, he moved to America following World War I. He worked at odd jobs before landing the position of supervisor of the Louisville (Kentucky) city parks in 1926. He remained for ten years

as professional and greenkeeper for the city's golf courses and in that capacity remodeled two existing courses and designed and built three new ones, including the popular Shawnee Municipal G Cse.

In the mid-1930s McKay designed Meadowbrook CC in West Virginia and became its first pro-superintendent. Following World War II, he took a similar position at Holston Hills in Tennessee. In the late 1940s he began experimenting at Holston Hills with bent-grass greens, then a rarity in the South. His success resulted in commissions to convert other clubs from Bermuda to bent greens, and in the process he often recommended changes to the course layout.

In the early 1950s McKay resigned from Holston Hills to work full-time as a course architect, contractor and turf consultant. He supervised the construction of several courses for other golf architects, notably William B. Langford, and also designed a number of courses himself.

Alex McCay, 1927 COLLECTION RON WHITTEN

Courses by Alex McKay:

Kentucky: Benton G&CC (9); Greenville CC (9); Hillcrest Muni; Indian Springs CC (9 1963); L & N GC; Seneca Muni (1928); Shawnee Muni (1927).
Maryland: Chestnut Ridge CC (9 1956).
New York: Commack Hills G&CC (1955).
North Carolina: Statesville CC (1962).
Tennessee: CC of Bristol (1959); Lake View GC (9 Precision 1963); Nubbins Ridge CC; Pine Oaks Muni (1963); Smoky Mountain CC; Southwest Point G&CC.
Virginia: Glenrochie CC (9 1958); Lake Bonaventure CC (9 1957).
West Virginia: Meadowbrook CC (1937).

Courses remodeled or expanded by Alex McKay:

Kentucky: Cherokee GC (R. 1927); Crescent Hill GC (R. 1926).

Ohio: Military GC, Wright-Patterson AFB (R.9 A.9 1960).
Tennessee: Chattanooga G&CC (R. 1953); Cherokee CC (R. 1950); Holston Hills CC (R.3 1953); Moccasin Bend GC (R.).
Virginia: Spotswood CC (A.9 1965).

Terry McNally, 1991 COURTESY TERRY MCNALLY

TERENCE J. MCNALLY

Terence McNally was recipient of an Outstanding Student Award in the School of Environmental Design in his senior year at California State Poly, Pomona, and graduated in 1973 with a degree in landscape architecture. After a three-year stint with Belt-Collins and Associates in Hawaii, McNally returned to the mainland and worked for a series of landscape architecture firms, including that of Cal Olson, who would later develop his own golf design practice.

In 1980 McNally established his own land-planning and landscape design business in Santa Rosa, California. In 1988 he joined the design group of Ronald Fream, based in the same city. While providing master planning expertise to the firm, he began learning the nuts and bolts of golf course design. By the 1990s McNally was actively involved in course architecture as part of Fream's team of designers.

Courses by Terence McNally (All as assistant to Ronald Fream):

Okinawa: Palm Hills G Resort (1991).
Thailand: Panya India CC (1992); Panya Park CC (1992).

GÖTZ MECKLENBURG (1943–), ESGCA

BORN: Germany.

Götz Mecklenburg obtained a landscape architecture degree from Munich University, where he specialized in landscape ecology. Between 1972 and 1975 he worked in Munich with Professor Haber in scientific research on environmental and ecological problems affecting landscape architecture. In 1975 he founded his own design office, specializing in leisure centers, including landscape-oriented golf courses. His motto was "The creation of a first-rate golf course depends on a good player building it, and letting the landscape win."

Courses by Götz Mecklenburg:

Germany: Altötting-Burghausen GC; Bad Uberkingen GC; Donnersberg GC; Eschenried GC; Grafing-Oberelkofen GC; Hechingen-Hohenzollern GC; Rassbach-Thurnau GC; Spessart GC; Schloss Oberzwieselau GC; Schloss Reichertshausen GC; Schwarzwald-Königsfeld.

Courses remodeled or expanded by Götz Mecklenburg:

Germany: Erding-Grünbach GC.

Chet Mendenhall, circa 1935
COLLECTION RON WHITTEN

CHESTER MENDENHALL (1895–1991)

BORN. Montgomery County, Kansas.
DIED: Overland Park, Kansas, at age 96.

Raised on a farm in Oklahoma, Chet Mendenhall was hired in 1921 to construct Sims Park Municipal GC in Wichita, Kansas. He remained there as greenkeeper until 1929, when he took a similar position with Wichita CC. In 1934 he moved to Mission Hills CC in Kansas City, serving as superintendent until his retirement in 1965. He began designing and remodeling courses as a "second career" after retirement. Mendenhall was the last surviving charter member of the GCSAA and served as its president in 1948. He was also a member for several years of the USGA Green Section Committee. Mendenhall was given the GCSAA's Distinguished Service Award in 1986 and in

1990 received a USGA Green Section Award.

Mendenhall moved to Arizona in the 1980s, but returned to Kansas in 1991 to participate in the ribbon cutting of a new headquarters of the GCSAA. He died a few weeks after the ceremonies.

Courses by Chet Mendenhall:

Kansas: Goodland GC.
Missouri: California CC (9); Centralia CC; Claycrest CC (1969); Emma GC; Linn CC; Richmond CC; Shirkey GC (1968); Tarkio CC; Warrensburg CC.

Courses remodeled or expanded by Chet Mendenhall:

Kansas: Fort Hays CC (R.9); Lake Quivira CC (R. 1968); Medicine Lodge Muni (R.9); Osawatomie Muni (A.9 1972); Shawnee CC (R.); Topeka CC (R.1).
Missouri: Excelsior Springs CC (R. 1965).

FRASER M. MIDDLETON, BIGCA, CHARTER MEMBER

Based in Scotland, golf architect Fraser Middleton was involved in the design and construction of golf courses for over forty years. He built courses for several leading British architects after World War II, including P. M. Ross, C. K. Cotton and J. H. Stutt.

In the 1970s Middleton began designing courses himself. He was a charter member of the BIGCA and was installed as a senior member of the group in 1980.

Courses by Fraser Middleton:

England: Cambridgeshire Hotel GC (1974); Davenport GC; Hounslow Heath GC.
Scotland: Annanhill GC (1957); Balbirnie Park GC (1983); Camperdown GC

Fraser Middleton, 1985 COURTESY
D. M. A. STEEL

(1960); Dale GC; Dalmilling GC (1960); Dunnikier Park GC (1963); Glenrothes GC (1958), with J. Hamilton Stutt.

Courses remodeled or expanded by Fraser Middleton:

Northern Ireland: Greenisland GC (R. A.9 1985).
Scotland: Aberdour GC (A.3 1981); Ballochmyle GC (A.9); Invergordon GC (A.9); Nairn Dunbar GC (A.9); Strathaven GC (A.9); West Lothian GC (A.9).
Wales: Creigiau GC (A.9 1982).

Johnny Miller, 1988
COURTESY JOHNNY MILLER

JOHN LAWRENCE MILLER (1947–)

BORN: San Francisco, California.

Professional golfer Johnny Miller was the winner of over twenty PGA Tour events as well as the 1973 U.S. Open and 1976 British Open. He also set a modern-era PGA Tour record with eight victories during the 1974 season. In 1984 he became involved in course architecture as a design consultant. Five years later he headed his own design firm and worked with design associates of Jack Nicklaus on early projects. When Gene Bates, one of Nicklaus's designers, hung out his own shingle, Miller agreed to utilize Bates's design services on his projects.

Courses by Johnny Miller:

California: Brighton Crest CC (1990), with Gene Bates.
Florida: Binks Forest CC (1990), with Gene Bates.
New Jersey: Shore Oaks GC (1990), with Tom Pearson.
England: Collingtree Park GC (1990), with Gene Bates.
Japan: Nara Wakakusa CC (*solo*); Rotary GC (*solo*); Wing Field GC (*solo*).

Maury Miller, 1991
COURTESY MAURY
MILLER

MAURICE M. MILLER II
(1952–)

BORN: Sacramento, California.

The son of a retired air force officer, Maury Miller grew up in Ames, Iowa, where his father attended and then taught at Iowa State University. A talented athlete, Miller played varsity basketball, ran cross country and was a member of the 1968 Iowa State High School Championship golf team. He enrolled at Louisiana State in 1970 and played on its first team for two years. He graduated with honors and a degree in landscape architecture in 1976.

After a brief association with golf architect Joseph Finger and employment in a civil engineering firm, Miller was hired by golf architect Tom Fazio as a construction supervisor. His first assignment was coordinating the building of Wild Dunes near Charleston, South Carolina. For six years, Miller worked both in the office and the field on such Fazio designs as The Vintage near Palm Springs, Old Trail in Florida and GC of Oklahoma. In the mid-1980s Miller left Fazio's firm to become an in-house architect for Pittman-Poe and Associates, a land-planning firm in Tulsa. Among other employees of the firm at the time was Randy Heckenkemper, who later went into course architecture himself. One of Miller's first projects for Pittman-Poe was the revision of his beloved Veenker Memorial Golf Course, the Iowa State University course that he had not only played countless times as a youngster, but also helped maintain as a member of its maintenance crew while a teenager.

In 1988, after working for architect Desmond Muirhead for eight months, Maury Miller formed his own golf design firm in partnership with veteran PGA Tour player D. A. Weibring. They called their company Golf Resources Inc., based it in Dallas and utilized the consultation services of legendary golfer Byron Nelson on some of their jobs.

Courses by Maury Miller:

California: [The] Classic CC (1992), with *D. A. Weibring*; [The] Vintage C (Desert Cse 1984; Mountain Cse 1981), ass't Tom Fazio.
Florida: Mariner Sands GC (Gold Cse 1982), ass't Tom Fazio; Old Trail GC (1987), ass't Tom Fazio; PGA National GC (Champions Cse 1981; Squire Cse 1981), ass't Tom Fazio.
Oklahoma: GC of Oklahoma (1982), ass't Tom Fazio.
South Carolina: CC of Callawassie (1986), ass't Tom Fazio; Wild Dunes G Links (Links Cse 1980; Yacht Harbor Cse 1986), ass't Tom Fazio.
Japan: Iwaki G & Sports C (1992), with Byron Nelson and *D. A. Weibring*; Le Petaw GC (1992), with *D. A. Weibring*.

Courses remodeled or expanded by Maury Miller:

Iowa: Veenker Memorial G Cse, Iowa State University (R. 1988).
Missouri: Lebanon CC (A.9 1990).

Scott Miller, 1991
COURTESY SCOTT
MILLER

SCOTT R. MILLER
(1956–)

BORN: Wichita, Kansas.

While a student at Colorado State University, Scott Miller spent two summers working on the construction crew at Shoal Creek in Alabama, a Jack Nicklaus design. After graduating with a landscape architecture degree in 1978, Miller worked briefly for a golf course contractor in Florida before joining the staff of Jack Nicklaus and Associates. Miller worked closely with senior designer Jay Morrish (with whom he had developed a friendship at Shoal Creek) out of the company's Western office in Tulsa, Oklahoma. For five years nearly all the Nicklaus projects west of the Mississippi, as well as those in Japan, were handled by Morrish and Miller. When Morrish left the company in 1983 to form his own practice, Miller assumed the vacated position in the Nicklaus organization. He soon moved the base of Western operations to Scottsdale, Arizona.

In 1988 Miller left the Nicklaus organization and formed Scott Miller Design, Inc. His first solo project featured the world's first floating island green at Coeur d'Alene Resort GC in Idaho. The five-million-pound island featured a 7,000-square-foot putting surface built to USGA specifications atop foam-filled concrete cells. A cable and winch system allowed the green to be positioned from 75 to 175 yards off the lakefront tees, and an electronic-yardage calculator determined the precise distance of the teeshot. Golfers were shuttled to and from the island green, which was accented by trees, sand bunkers and flower plantings, aboard a specially built ferry.

Soon after going on his own, Miller hired Michael Asmundson as an associate. A University of Washington graduate, Asmundson had previously worked for golf architect William Teufel.

Courses by Scott Miller:

Arizona: Desert Highlands GC (1984), ass't Jack Nicklaus; GC at Desert Mountain (Cochise Cse 1987; Geronimo Cse 1990; Renegade Cse 1986), ass't Jack Nicklaus; La Paloma GC (27 1985), ass't Jack Nicklaus.
California: Bear Creek GC (1982), ass't Jack Nicklaus; C at Morningside (1983), ass't Jack Nicklaus; Dove Canyon GC (1991), ass't Jack Nicklaus; Palmia Putting Cse (1991 *solo*); Sherwood CC (1989), ass't Jack Nicklaus.
Colorado: Castle Pines GC (1981), ass't Jack Nicklaus; CC of Castle Pines (1986), ass't Jack Nicklaus; Meridian GC (1984), ass't Jack Nicklaus.
Florida: Bears Paw CC (1980), ass't Jack Nicklaus.
Hawaii: Kauai Lagoons G&RC (Kiele and Lagoons Cses 1988), ass't Jack Nicklaus.
Idaho: Coeur d'Alene Resort GC (1991 *solo*).
Mississippi: Annandale GC (1981), ass't Jack Nicklaus.
Texas: Bentwater Y&CC (Cse No. 2 1992 *solo*); Hills of Lakeway GC (1981; Golf Academy 3 1985), ass't Jack Nicklaus.

Japan: Kazusa GC (1985), ass't Jack Nicklaus; Mito International GC (1987), ass't Jack Nicklaus; Numata Forum GC (1992 *solo*); Shimoda Forum GC (1992); Sunnyfield GC (1986), ass't Jack Nicklaus.

Courses remodeled or expanded by Scott Miller:

Georgia: Augusta National GC (R. 1984), ass't Jay Morrish and Bob Cupp.
Missouri: Oakwood CC (R. 1990 *solo*).
Texas: Dallas Athletic C (Blue Cse, R. 1986), ass't Jack Nicklaus.

Harrison Minchew, 1991 COURTESY ED SEAY

HARRISON G. MINCHEW (1956–   ), ASGCA

BORN: Augusta, Georgia.

Harrison Minchew took up the game on an old Donald Ross course at Forest Hills Golf Club in Augusta, Georgia. While in high school he worked on its course-maintenance crew. His interest in golf course architecture developed as he listened to old-timers at Forest Hills describe how the course had been built and altered over the years.

Minchew attended the University of Georgia and worked part-time during his senior year for golf architects Ron Kirby and Denis Griffiths. Upon graduating with a landscape architecture degree in 1979, Minchew went to work on the West Coast for designer Ron Fream. In 1982 Minchew moved back East and became an associate of Ed Seay in the Palmer Course Design Company. He handled major responsibility for a number of the firm's projects, including the remodeling of his beloved Forest Hills Golf Club in Augusta.

Courses by Harrison Minchew (All as assistant to Arnold Palmer and Ed Seay):

Arizona: Arrowhead CC (1986); [The] Legend GC (1988).
California: Aviara GC (1991); PGA West GC (Palmer Cse 1986).
Florida: Deering Bay Y&CC (1991); Isleworth G&CC (1986); Marsh Landing GC (1986); Matanzas Woods GC (1986); Mill Cove GC (1990); Monarch CC (1987); Orchid Island G & Beach C (1990).
Georgia: Eagle Watch GC (1989); Whitewater Creek GC (1988).
Kentucky: Lake Forest GC (1992).
Louisiana: [The] Bluffs on Thompson Creek CC (1988).
Michigan: Shanty Creek GC (Legend Cse 1985).
Missouri: North Port National G&CC (1992).
New Jersey: Laurel Creek CC (1990).
North Carolina: Cullasaja C (1989); Pinehurst Plantation GC (1992); TPC at Piper Glen (1989).
Washington: Semiahmoo GC (1986).
Ireland: Kildare GC (1991).
Japan: Ajigasawa GC (A Cse 1992; B Cse 1993); Aso GC (A Cse 1990; B Cse 1990); Minakami Kogen GC (New Cse 1992; Upper Cse 1986).
Taiwan: Formosa Yangmei G&CC (1992).

Courses remodeled or expanded by Harrison Minchew (All as assistant to Arnold Palmer and Ed Seay):

Georgia: Atlanta Athletic CC (Highlands Cse, R. 1989); Forest Hill GC (R. 1986); Stouffer's PineIsle Resort GC (R. 1988).
Virginia: Keswick C of Virginia (R. 1991).

SAMUEL S. MITCHELL (1909–1986), ASGCA, FELLOW

BORN: Manchester, Massachusetts.
DIED: Canton, Massachusetts, at age 76.

Sam Mitchell was the second of four sons (Robert, Sam, Henry and William) of Robert A. Mitchell, longtime greenkeeper at Kernwood Country Club in Salem, Massachusetts. His uncle Enoch Crombie was one of Donald Ross's first construction superintendents. Not surprisingly, Sam and his brothers all became active in golf course design, construction and maintenance.

Mitchell graduated from the Stockbridge School of Agriculture of the University of Massachusetts in 1928. He worked for a time for the firm of Langford

Sam Mitchell, 1983
COLLECTION RON WHITTEN

and Moreau and was later employed with the Metropolitan District Commission of Boston as greenkeeper at Ponkapoag Golf Course. While in Ponkapoag, he constructed a third nine to the design of Donald Ross.

In the 1950s Mitchell was involved in Mitchell Brothers, a design-and-build partnership with brothers William and Henry. He entered private practice as a golf architect in 1958. Mitchell also operated an extensive sod business and managed a course of his own design, Easton (Massachusetts) Golf Club. Two sons, Samuel Jr. and Philip, became golf course superintendents. A past president of the New England Golf Course Superintendents Association, Mitchell was awarded lifetime fellow status by the ASGCA in 1984. He died in 1986 after suffering a heart attack in his home.

Courses by Samuel Mitchell:

Massachusetts: Brookmeadow GC (1968); Chestnut Hill CC (9 1962); CC of Norwood (1975); Dighton GC (9 Par 3 1963); Easton CC (9 1961; A.9 1967); Little Harbor GC (Par 3 1963); Lost Brook GC (Par 3 9); Norwood CC; Spring Valley CC (1960), with Geoffrey S. Cornish.
Rhode Island: Melody Hill GC (9 1965; A.9 1975).

Courses remodeled or expanded by Samuel Mitchell:

Massachusetts: Braintree Muni (R. A.11); D. W. Field Muni (A.2 1972); Gardner Muni (R.2 1968); Hatherly CC (A.3 1968; R.2 1976); Hollis Memorial GC (R. A.11 1971); Martin Memorial GC (A.9 1963); Natick CC (R.4 A.9 1960).
New York: Onondaga G&CC (R.2 1982), with Phil Wogan.
Rhode Island: Kirkbrae CC (R.3 1969); Woonsocket CC (A.9 1961), with Geoffrey S. Cornish.

WILLIAM FOLLET MITCHELL (1912–1974), ASGCA

BORN: Salem, Massachusetts.
DIED: West Palm Beach, Florida, at age 62.

William F. Mitchell was involved with golf courses from an early age. A son of Robert A. Mitchell, respected course superintendent who taught at the Essex County (Massachusetts) Agricultural School in the 1920s and later became superintendent at Kernwood Country Club, Bill Mitchell obtained his first greenkeeper's job at the age of nineteen. A few years later, while working as greenkeeper at Lake Sunapee Golf Club in North Sutton, New Hampshire, he established a turf farm specializing in velvet bent grass for greens. He operated the business successfully for decades. Through his turf business Bill gained first hand experience in golf course construction and in the late 1930s assisted golf architect Orrin Smith in the construction and reconstruction of several New England layouts.

After serving as a navy pilot during World War II, Mitchell became superintendent at Charles River Country Club near Boston. In the late 1940s he and two of his brothers, Samuel and Henry, formed a golf design and construction firm, Mitchell Brothers, which continued until 1954. Sam then left to design and consult on his own. Henry returned to a superintendent's position and did a little design work on the side (notably Dennis Pines and the second nine of Cummaquid, both on Cape Cod). Bill continued in design full-time.

By the 1960s Mitchell had planned courses as far south as Florida and as far west as Michigan. By the early 1970s he had done some 150 original designs and 200 remodeling jobs. He was an early advocate of separate courses designed specifically for women golfers and shortly

William F. Mitchell, circa 1965
COLLECTION RON WHITTEN

before his death had been retained by the LPGA to build such a course. He is also credited with having coined the title "executive course" to describe shorter precision courses consisting of only par-3 and par-4 holes. Such courses, he said, could be quickly and enjoyably played by business executives at the tail end of a hectic workday.

Courses by William F. Mitchell:

Florida: Atlantis GC (1960); Brooksville G&CC (1972); Deerfield CC (Precision 1964); East Bay CC (1962); Hollybrook G&TC (1968); Lochmoor GC (1972); Longboat Key C (Islandside Cse 1961); Palm-Aire CC (Palms Cse 1960); Palm Beach Lakes CC (Precision 1966); President CC (North Cse 1970; South Cse 1972); Rolling Hills CC, Fort Lauderdale (1961); Southern Manor CC (1962, NLE); Tavares Cove GC (Precision 1971); University of South Florida GC (1967).
Maine: Inland Winds GC, Loring AFB (9 1959).
Maryland: Eaglehead G&CC (1971).
Massachusetts: Billerica GC (9 Par 3 1952); CC of New Seabury (Blue Cse 1964; Green Cse 1965); Green Hill Muni (1968); Hillview CC; Martin Memorial GC (9 1952); Mount Pleasant CC (1959); North Hill CC; Ponkapoag GC (Cse No. 2 1955); Saddle Hill CC (1962); Webb Brook GC (1952).
Michigan: Bedford Valley CC (1965); Gull Lake CC (1967).
New Hampshire: Amherst CC (1962); Goffstown CC (1962); Plausawa Valley CC (1965).
New Jersey: Fairview GC (1954).
New York: Bergen Point Muni (1972); Colonie Muni (1969); Crab Meadow GC (1963); Emerald Green GC (1970); Glen Cove Muni (1970); Hammersley Hill GC (9 1951); Indian Island Park GC (1973); Kutshers Hotel GC (1962); Lido Springs GC (Par 3 1963, NLE); McCann Memorial GC (1973); Noyac G&CC (1964); Old Westbury G&CC (27 1962); Otterkill G&CC (1957); Pine Hollow CC (1954); Putnam CC; Stevensville Lake G&CC (1966); Suffolk County GC at Timber Point (1972); Tarry Brae GC (1958); Waldemere Hotel GC (1959); West Sayville GC (1970); Willows GC (1967); Woodcrest C (1963).
Ohio: Pebble Creek GC (1974); Shady Hollow CC; Tanglewood CC (1966);

Walden G&TC (1974); Whetstone CC (1972).
Pennsylvania: Cedarbrook CC (1962); General Washington CC (1962).
Vermont: Crown Point CC (9 1953, A.9 1959); Stowe CC (1962).
New Brunswick: Mactaquac Provincial Park GC (1970).
Ontario: Maple Downs G&CC (1954).
Quebec: Fort Preval GC (9 1961); Golf du Parc Carleton (9 1963).
Portugal: Quintado de Lago GC (Cse No. 1 1973; Cse No. 2, 9 1973).

Courses remodeled or expanded by William F. Mitchell:

California: Canyon CC (R. 1965); Canyon South GC (R. 1965).
Connecticut: Birchwood CC (R. 1946); Glastonbury Hills CC (R. 1952); Hartford GC (R. 1946), ass't Orrin Smith; High Ridge CC (R.2 1951); High Ridge GC (R. 1946); Meadowbrook CC (R. 1947); Mill Stone CC (R. 1948); Minnechaug CC (R.9 1951); Old Lyme GC (R. 1949); Race Brook CC (R. 1947), ass't Orrin Smith; Rockledge CC (R. 1947); Sleeping Giant GC (R. 1951); Tumble Brook CC (A.9 1948), ass't Orrin Smith; Wampanoag CC (R. 1949); Watertown CC (R. 1950).
Maine: Augusta CC (R. 1939), ass't Orrin Smith; Bridgton GC (R. 1939), ass't Orrin Smith; Mount Kineo GC (R. 1940), ass't Orrin Smith; Portland CC (R. 1940), ass't Orrin Smith; Riverside Muni (R. 1948).
Maryland: Rocky Point GC (R. 1939), ass't Orrin Smith.
Massachusetts: Bear Hill GC (R. 1950); Cedar Glen GC (R. 1931), ass't Orrin Smith; Charles River CC (R. 1946); Colonial GC (R.5 1954; A.9 1963); Concord CC (A.9 1967); Duxbury YC (R. 1951); Framingham CC (A.9 1960); Franklin CC (R. A.2 1949; R. 1956); Furnace Brook CC (R. 1947); Holden Hills GC (R. 1957); Kernwood CC (R. 1950); Leicester Hill CC (R. 1950); Longmeadow CC (R. 1956); Lynnfield Center GC (R. 1949); Needham GC (R. 1935), ass't Orrin Smith; North Adams GC (R. 1939), ass't Orrin Smith; North Andover CC (R. 1947); Oak Hill CC (R. 1938), ass't Orrin Smith; Ould Newberry CC (R. 1939), ass't Orrin Smith; Presidents CC [FKA Wollaston CC] (R. 1956); Red Hill CC (R.9 A.9 1951); Springfield CC (R. 1948); Unicorn CC (R.

1937), ass't Orrin Smith; Vesper CC
(R. 1939), ass't Orrin Smith; Wayland
CC (R. 1952); Wenham GC (R. 1938),
ass't Orrin Smith; Whaling City CC
(R.9 A.9 1958); Winthrop GC (R.
1950).

New Hampshire: Claremont CC (R.
1936), ass't Orrin Smith; CC of New
Hampshire (R.9 A.9 1963); Dover CC
(R. 1940), ass't Orrin Smith; Hanover
CC, Dartmouth College (R. 1937),
ass't Orrin Smith; John H. Cain GC
[FKA Newport CC] (R. 1937), ass't
Orrin Smith; Laconia CC (R. 1938),
ass't Orrin Smith; Lake Sunapee CC
(R. 1934), ass't Orrin Smith; Lebanon
CC (R. 1937), ass't Orrin Smith; Na-
shua CC (R. 1949); Rochester CC (R.
1939), ass't Orrin Smith.

New Jersey: White Beeches G&CC (R.
1953).

New York: College Hill GC (R. 1953);
Dellwood CC (R. 1951); En-Joie CC
(R.); Fresh Meadow CC (R. 1938),
ass't Orrin Smith; Gardiner's Bay CC
(R. 1954); Glen Head CC (R. 1949);
Green Lakes State Park GC (R. 1948);
Grossinger's GC (R. 1959); Hiawatha
CC (R. 1948); Huntington Crescent
CC (R. 1939), ass't Orrin Smith; West
Cse, R. 1939, NLE), ass't Orrin Smith;
Huntington CC (R. 1967); IBM CC,
Endicott (R. 1948); Island Hills CC (R.
1967); Old Oaks CC (R. 1949); Sada-
quada GC (R. 1969); Saratoga Spa GC
(R. A.9); Shinnecock Hills GC (R.
1967); Southampton GC (R. 1965);
Teugega CC (R. 1948); Van Cortlandt
Park GC (R. 1947).

North Carolina: Southern Pines CC (R.
1947).

Pennsylvania: Blue Ridge CC (R. 1965).

Rhode Island: Newport CC (R. 1939),
ass't Orrin Smith.

Vermont: Basin Harbor C (R. 1952); Brattleboro CC (R. 1948); Equinox G
Links (R. 1967).

Quebec: Madge Lake GC (R. 1960).

THEODORE MOONE

A British golf writer of the 1930s, Theodore Moone's best-known publication
was *Golf from a New Angle*, which contained a discussion on golf design. He designed at least four courses in the British
Isles, including Carlisle Golf Club (1938)
in England and Eastwood Golf Club in

Scotland. He also remodeled Dumfries &
Galloway Golf Club and Kilmarnock Golf
Club, both in Scotland.

*Hugh Moore, circa
1930* COLLECTION RON
WHITTEN

HUGH C. MOORE, SR.
(1895–1972)

BORN: Onley, Virginia.
DIED: Albany, Georgia, at age 76.

After helping construct the original
nines of Sea Island Golf Club and Jekyll
Island Golf Club to plans of Walter Travis,
Hugh Moore became superintendent at
Sea Island and later constructed a second
nine designed by Colt and Alison. He resigned in 1933 to work as a baseball um-
pire in Southern semipro leagues but
returned to golf in 1942, remodeling and
operating a course in Georgia. He later
designed Bowden Muni in Macon, Georgia, and remained as its superintendent
until 1953, when he was hired to renovate
the Dunedin (Florida) Country Club into
the national headquarters of the PGA of
America. Moore also designed and remodeled several other courses in the
Southeast.

Courses by Hugh C. Moore, Sr.:

Alabama: Dothan CC (1960).
Georgia: Bowden Muni (1949); Dawson
CC; Sunset CC (1944); Town & CC
(9 1959); Turner Field GC (9 1953);
Warner Robins AFB GC (9 1951).

Courses remodeled or expanded by
Hugh C. Moore, Sr.:

Florida: Lake Region Y&CC (R. 1964).
Georgia: American Legion GC (R. 1954);
Athens CC (R.); Augusta CC (R.);
Glen Arven CC (R.4 1942); Jekyll Is-
land GC (Oceanside Cse, R.3 1952);
Pinecrest CC (R. 1939); Radium CC
(R.).
North Carolina: Charlotte CC (R. 1955).

DAVID L. MOOTE
(1952–   ), ASGCA

BORN: London, Ontario.

David Moote, son of golf architect Robert Moote, received a Bachelor of Arts degree from Ontario's University of Guelph
in 1975. Following several years playing
professional hockey and then several years
in golf course maintenance, including a
stint at the private Ile Perrot Golf & Country Club in Montreal, Moote was employed as a teaching master at Seneca
College in King City, Ontario, instructing
in golf course design, construction and
maintenance.

In 1976 he joined his father's golf
course design firm, first working as a
draftsman and site superintendent and in
1982 becoming a design associate.

*David L. Moote,
1990* COURTESY ASGCA

Courses by David L. Moote (All with
Robert Moote):

Nova Scotia: Dundee Resort GC (9
1983); Le Portage GC (1984).
Ontario: Dorchester G&CC (9); [The]
Maples of Ballantrae GC (1983); [The]
Oaks of St. George GC (1991); Scotch
Settlement GC (1984).

Courses remodeled or expanded by
David L. Moote (All with Robert
Moote):

Ontario: Beechwood GC (R.9 A.9 1985);
Listowel GC (R.8 A.10 1982); Peel Village GC (R. 1986).

ROBERT FREDERICK MOOTE
(1924–   ), ASGCA

BORN: Dunnville, Ontario, Canada.

Bob Moote received a Bachelor of Science degree in agriculture and ornamental
horticulture from Ontario Agricultural
College in 1948. His first job was for golf
architect Stanley Thompson, supervising

projects in Canada, Jamaica and the United States. In 1951 he became assistant landscape supervisor with Central Mortgage and Housing Corporation, where he remained for five years. In his spare time, Moote worked on a series of modest golf projects in Quebec, Ontario and the Maritime Provinces.

In 1957 Moote became construction supervisor of a third nine at Oakdale G&CC near Toronto, then stayed on as its course superintendent for some twenty years. During those years he did part-time work with golf architect C. E. Robinson and served as a greens consultant to the Royal Canadian Golf Association. He also practiced course design with his brother David S. Moote, who served as president of the GCSAA in 1964. In 1976 he entered private practice as a full-time architect under the name R. F. Moote and Associates, Ltd. In the early eighties Moote's eldest son, David L. Moote, joined him in the design business. Robert Moote was a member of ASGCA as well as the ASLA and the CSLA.

Robert Moote, circa 1970 COURTESY GOLF WORLD

Courses by Robert Moote:

New Brunswick: Gowan Brae GC, ass't C. E. Robinson.
Nova Scotia: Dundee Resort GC (9 1983); Le Portage GC (1984), with David L. Moote.
Ontario: Barrie GC (1965), with *David S. Moote*; Beverly GC, ass't C. E. Robinson; Blair Hampton GC (1964), with *David S. Moote*; Cedar Brook GC (Par 3 1985); Craig Gowan GC, ass't C. E. Robinson; Deep River GC (9 1952), ass't Howard Watson; Doon Valley GC, ass't C. E. Robinson; Dorchester G&CC (9), with David L. Moote; Downsview G&CC (27 1955), ass't Howard Watson; Dryden G&CC, ass't C. E. Robinson; Galt G & Curling C (1965), with *David S. Moote*; Georgetown GC, ass't C. E. Robinson; Hawthorne Valley G&CC (Par 3

1961), ass't C. E. Robinson; Hornby Towers GC (1964), with *David S. Moote*; Lynwood GC (9 1962), with *David S. Moote*; Maple City G&CC, ass't C. E. Robinson; [The] Maples of Ballantrae GC (1983), with David L. Moote; Mount Hope G&CC, ass't C. E. Robinson; North Halton GC (1967), with *David S. Moote*; [The] Oaks of St. George (1991), with David L. Moote; Orilla GC (1975), with *David S. Moote*; Pleasure Park GC (Par 3 1961); Richmond Hill G&CC, ass't C. E. Robinson; Scotch Settlement GC (1984), with David L. Moote; Streetsville Glen GC (1967), with *David S. Moote*; Trafalgar G&CC, ass't C. E. Robinson; Twenty Valley G&CC, ass't C. E. Robinson; Wildcat Run GC (1985).
Quebec: C de G Baie Comeau, ass't C. E. Robinson.
Colombia: CC de Manizales (1953), ass't Howard Watson; CC El Rodeo (1953), ass't Howard Watson.
Jamaica: Ironshore CC (1971), with *David S. Moote*.
Martinique: La Pointe du Diamant GC (9 Par 3 1967), with *David S. Moote*.

Courses remodeled or expanded by Robert Moote:

New York: Westwood CC (R. 1986).
Alberta: Shawnee Slopes GC (R. 1979).
New Brunswick: Grand Falls GC (R. 1984).
Nova Scotia: Brightwood G&CC (R. 1983); Seaview GC (A.9 1985).
Ontario: Bay of Quinte GC (A.9), ass't C. E. Robinson; Bayview G&CC (R. 1986); Beechwood GC (R.9 A.9 1985), with David L. Moote; Brantford G&CC (R.), with C. E. Robinson; Brooklea GC (R. 1985); Burlington G&CC (R. 1985); Credit Valley G&CC (R.3 1964), with *David S. Moote*; Goderich GC (R. 1976); Huntington GC (R. 1961), ass't C. E. Robinson; Idlywlyde GC (R.1 1985); Kenora G&CC (R.7 A.11 1986); Kingsville GC (A.9 1973), with *David S. Moote*; Listowel GC (R.8 A.10 1982), with David L. Moote; Lively GC (R.9 A.9 1982); North Halton GC (R. 1984); Oakdale G&CC (A.9, ass't C. E. Robinson; R. 1986); Owen Sound GC (R.9 A.9 1964), with *David S. Moote*; Peel Village GC (R. 1986), with David L. Moote; Port Colborne GC (R. 1966, with *David S. Moote*; R. 1985); Puslinch Lake GC (R. 1984);

St. Catharines G&CC (R.), ass't C. E. Robinson; Thornhill GC (R. 1985); Trehaven GC (R. 1977); Westmount GC (R. A.4, ass't C. E. Robinson; R.3 1970, with *David S. Moote*); Westview GC (R.9 A.9 1964, with *David S. Moote*; R. 1984).
Quebec: C de G Ile Perrot (R. 1980).
Jamaica: Paradise Park GC (R. 1969), with *David S. Moote*.

Kelly Moran, 1991 COURTESY KELLY MORAN

KELLY BLAKE MORAN (1960–)

BORN: Odessa, Texas.

Kelly Moran obtained a degree in landscape architecture from Texas A&M and upon graduation in 1984 joined the Texas golf design firm of von Hagge and Devlin. When Devlin left the firm in 1987, the company was reorganized and Moran was made an associate architect primarily in charge of all North American projects. He then worked closely with von Hagge and the other associates in the company on all von Hagge design projects.

THEODORE J. MOREAU (1890–1942)

DIED: Wilmette, Illinois, at age 51.

Civil engineer Theodore J. Moreau teamed with William B. Langford after World War I in a golf design and construction business based in Chicago. The firm of Langford & Moreau was among the busiest in the Midwest and South during the 1920s and 1930s. While Moreau primarily handled the construction aspects of their projects, he also handled a few designs.

Courses by Theodore J. Moreau (All with William B. Langford):

Arkansas: Al Amin Temple CC; Texarkana CC (1927).

Florida: Elgin AFB GC (1925); Granada GC (9 1925); Kelsey City GC (1924, NLE); Key West GC (1923, NLE); Lake Worth Muni (1924); Parkhurst CC (1925, NLE); St. Lucie River CC (1924, NLE); Valparaiso CC (1927, NLE); West Palm Beach CC (1921, NLE).

Illinois: Acacia CC (1924); Bryn Mawr GC (1921); Butterfield CC (1922); Doering Estate GC (6 1931); Franklin County CC (9 1922); Golden Acres CC (27 1928); Kankakee Elks CC (1936); Mid City GC (1924, NLE); Morris CC (9 1925, NLE); Ruth Lake CC (1926); Skokie Playfield GC (9 Par 3, NLE); St. Clair CC (1927); Twin Orchard CC (1924, NLE).

Indiana: Dykeman Park Muni (9); East Shore CC (1922); Gary CC (1921); Harrison Hills CC (9 1923).

Iowa: Credit Island GC (1925); Duck Creek Park GC (1927); Oneota CC (9 1921); Wakonda C (1922).

Kansas: Quivira Lakes GC.

Kentucky: Audubon CC (1921); Bowling Green CC (NLE); Henderson G&CC.

Michigan: Blythefield CC (1927); CC of Lansing (1919); Iron River CC (1932); Marquette G&CC (9 1927).

Minnesota: Mankato GC (9 1925).

Mississippi: Clarkesdale CC (1921).

Nebraska: Happy Hollow C (1926); Highland CC (1924).

North Dakota: Town & Country C (9 1920).

Ohio: Avon Fields GC (1924); Clovernook CC (1924); Hillcrest CC (1925, NLE).

South Dakota: Minnehaha CC (1922).

Texas: State Line GC (1930).

Wisconsin: Lawsonia GC (Links Cse 1929); Leathem Smith Lodge GC (9 1930); Our CC (1927); Ozaukee CC (1922); Spring Valley CC (1927); West Bend CC (9 1922).

Courses remodeled or expanded by Theodore J. Moreau (All with William B. Langford):

Florida: [The] Breakers GC (R.9 A.9 1926); Everglades C (R. 1937).

Illinois: Glen Oak CC (R. 1922); Highland Park GC (R.3 1939); Mid City GC (R. 1931, NLE); Ravisloe CC (R.); Ridgemoor CC (R. 1927); Skokie CC (R. 1938).

Kentucky: Louisville CC (R. 1921).

Sloan Morpeth, 1927 COLLECTION RON WHITTEN

SLOAN MORPETH

Noted Australian amateur golfer Sloan Morpeth won the New Zealand Open in 1928 and the New Zealand Amateur in 1920, '27 and '28. After his playing days were over, Morpeth turned to golf course architecture, designing and remodeling many courses in Australia and New Zealand.

Courses by Sloan Morpeth:

Australia: Surfer's Paradise GC (1969).
New Zealand: Oreti Sands GC (1970).

Courses remodeled or expanded by Sloan Morpeth:

Australia: Australian GC (R. 1967).
New Zealand: Christchurch GC (R.); Invercargill GC (R.).

TOM MORRIS, SR.
(1821–1908)

BORN: St. Andrews, Scotland.
DIED: St. Andrews, Scotland, at age 87.

"Old Tom" Morris apprenticed under Allan Robertson at the Old Course at St. Andrews from 1839 to 1851. Following a bitter disagreement with Robertson concerning use of the gutta-percha ball (of which Robertson disapproved), Morris moved to Prestwick, where he held the position of pro-greenkeeper until 1865. He then returned to similar duties at St. Andrews, where he remained until his retirement in 1904. Morris won the British Open in 1861, '62, '64 and '67, and his son Tom Jr. had won the Open four times by the age of 22. Together, Old Tom and Young Tom Morris rank among the greatest golfers of all time. Old Tom's life was saddened by his son's sudden death in 1875 at the age of 25.

Those who knew him described Old Tom as a man it was impossible to dislike. Throughout his productive life he refused to play golf on Sundays and kept the Old Course closed on that day, feeling it needed a rest even if golfers didn't. His philosophy in regard to putting surface maintenance embraced "sand and more sand" as top-dressing.

Morris ranked at the top of recognized links designers in the last half of the nineteenth century. He practiced the art in an age when it was virtually impossible to alter existing contours in laying out a new course. A native of the linksland with an eye for every shot in golf, Old Tom developed a skill for utilizing every feature of natural terrain, a talent he passed on to an apprentice, Donald Ross. Old Tom was the first to plan double-loop routings to take maximum advantage of the wind.

Courses by Old Tom Morris:

England: City of Newcastle GC (1890); Northampton GC (1894); Royal Cromer GC (1888); Royal North Devon GC (1874); Wallasey GC (1891); West Herts GC (1897).

Ireland: Lahinch GC (Old Cse 1893); Rosapenna GC (1893).

Isle of Man: Castletown GC (1892).

Northern Ireland: Royal County Down GC (1891).

Scotland: Alyth GC (1894); Askernish GC (1891); Callander GC; Crail GC (1892); Dunbar GC (15 1856); Dunblane GC (1891); Elie Golf House C (1895); Glasgow GC (1904); Helensburgh GC; King James VI GC (1896); Kinghorn GC (1904); Ladybank GC (1879); Lanark GC; Luffness New GC (1894); Moray GC (Old Cse 1889); Muirfield GC (1891); Perth GC (12 1864); Prestwick GC (12 1851, A.6 1883); Royal Burgess Golfing Society of Edinburgh (1895); Royal

Old Tom Morris, circa 1902 COLLECTION RON WHITTEN

Dornoch GC (9 1887); St. Andrews (New Cse 1894); St. Leonard's School for Girls GC (9 1873); St. Michaels G Links (9 1903); Scotscraig GC; Stirling GC (1892); Tain GC (1890).
Wales: Pwllheii GC (9 1900).

Courses remodeled or expanded by Old Tom Morris:

England: Bradford GC (A.13); Cleveland GC (R. A.9 1898).
Scotland: Carnoustie GC (R. A.6 1867); Cullen GC (R. 1892); Machrihanish GC (R. A.6 1879); Nairn GC (R. 1889); Newtonmore GC (R. 1897); St. Andrews (Old Cse, R.); Saltcoats GC (R. 1894).

Jay Morrish, 1990
COURTESY JAY MORRISH

JAY MORRISH
(1936–   ), ASGCA

BORN: Grand Junction, Colorado.

Under a Trans-Mississippi Golf Association scholarship, Jay Morrish obtained a liberal arts education at Mesa Junior College and the universities of New Mexico and Colorado. He later received a landscaping and turf management degree from Colorado State University. After teaching horticulture at Colorado State, Morrish joined a construction crew in California that was building the Spyglass Hill Golf Links to the design of Robert Trent Jones. He then moved to Phoenix to assist in construction of another Jones project, Goodyear G&CC. In 1967 Morrish joined the firm of George Fazio, aiding in layout and construction of several courses, including Jupiter Hills. He then joined architect Desmond Muirhead, working on such jobs as Mayacoo Lakes. When Jack Nicklaus and Muirhead dissolved their relationship in 1973, Morrish accepted Nicklaus's offer to work as a designer in his new firm. He worked on most Nicklaus

designs over the next ten years, operating a branch office in Tulsa, Oklahoma. Morrish also collaborated with another Nicklaus in-house designer, Bob Cupp, on certain courses under the corporate name of Golforce, Inc.

In 1983 Morrish left Nicklaus to pursue a golf design business of his own. Most of his work was done in partnership with PGA Tour player Tom Weiskopf. It proved to be a very successful team. One of the earliest Morrish and Weiskopf collaborations, Troon G&CC in Arizona, was selected as the Best New Private Course of 1986 by *Golf Digest*. Another, Shadow Glen near Kansas City, was the magazine's choice for Best New Private Course of 1989, edging out another Morrish and Weiskopf design, Forest Highlands.

In the late 1980s Morrish and Weiskopf became the first American designers to design a course in Scotland. The layout, Loch Lomond, was considered by both to be their very best work.

Courses by Jay Morrish (All with Tom Weiskopf unless otherwise indicated):

Alabama: Shoal Creek (1977), ass't Jack Nicklaus.
Arizona: [The] Boulders GC (North Cse 1984 *solo*; South Cse, 9 1984, A.9 1991 *solo*); Desert Highlands GC (1984), ass't Jack Nicklaus; Estancia GC (1992); [The] Foothills GC (1988); Forest Highlands GC (1988); TPC of Scottsdale (Desert Cse 1987; Stadium Cse 1986); Troon G&CC (1985); Troon North GC (1990).
California: Bear Creek GC (1982), ass't Jack Nicklaus; [The] C at Morningside (1983), ass't Jack Nicklaus; Marbella G&CC (1989).
Colorado: Castle Pines GC (1981), ass't Jack Nicklaus; CC of the Rockies (1984), ass't Jack Nicklaus; Singletree GC (1981), with Bob Cupp.
Florida: Bear's Paw CC (1980), ass't Jack Nicklaus; Boca Pointe CC (1982), with Bob Cupp; Cheeca Lodge GC (9 Par 3 1981), with Bob Cupp; Sailfish Point CC (1981), ass't Jack Nicklaus; Walden Lake Polo & CC (1978), with Bob Cupp.
Georgia: Harbor C (1991).
Hawaii: [The] Kings' GC (1990).
Kansas: Shadow Glen GC (1989); Willowbend GC (1987).
Mississippi: Annandale GC (1981), ass't Jack Nicklaus.
Missouri: CC of St. Albans (1992).
Nevada: Painted Desert GC (1987 *solo*).

Ohio: CC at Muirfield Village (1982), ass't Jack Nicklaus; Double Eagle C (1992); Muirfield Village GC (1974), ass't Jack Nicklaus and Desmond Muirhead.
Oklahoma: Coves at Bird Island GC (9 Precision 1984 *solo*).
South Carolina: Bloody Point C (1991); Turtle Point G Links (1981), ass't Jack Nicklaus.
Texas: Bentwater CC (1989); Buffalo Creek G Cse (1992); [The] Hills of Lakeway GC (1980; A.3 Golf Academy 1985), ass't Jack Nicklaus; Lochinvar GC (1980), ass't Jack Nicklaus; Mira Vista CC (1987); River Place CC (1986), with *Tom Kite*.
Utah: Park Meadows GC (1983), ass't Jack Nicklaus.
Ontario: Glen Abbey GC (1976), ass't Jack Nicklaus.
Japan: Kazusa GC (1985), ass't Jack Nicklaus; New St. Andrews GC (1976), ass't Jack Nicklaus and Desmond Muirhead; Sunnyfield GC (1986), ass't Jack Nicklaus.
Scotland: Loch Lomond GC (1992).

Courses remodeled or expanded by Jay Morrish (All with Tom Weiskopf unless otherwise indicated):

California: Ojai Valley Inn & CC (R. 1988 *solo*).
Florida: Frenchman's Creek GC (North Cse, R. 1983; South Cse, R. 1983), with Bob Cupp; Lost Tree C (R. 1980), with Bob Cupp.
Georgia: Atlanta CC (R. 1980), with Bob Cupp; Augusta National GC (R. 1982), with Bob Cupp.
Illinois: Bryn Mawr GC (R. 1982), with Bob Cupp.
New York: Wanakah CC (R. 1983), with Bob Cupp.
Oklahoma: Tulsa CC (R.5 1984 *solo*).
Texas: Amarillo CC (R. 1983 *solo*); Brook Hollow GC (R. *solo*); Colonial CC (R. 1982), with Bob Cupp; Dallas CC (R. 1985 *solo*); Las Colinas Sports C (Cottonwood Valley Cse, A.9 1986 *solo*; TPC Cse, R.9 A.9 1987, with Byron Nelson and Ben Crenshaw); Northwood C (R. *solo*); Oak Hills CC (R. 1984); Onion Creek CC (R.1 1985 *solo*); Preston Trail GC (R. 1982), with Bob Cupp; Ridglea CC (Championship Cse, R. *solo*); Royal Oaks CC (R. *solo*); San Antonio CC (R. *solo*).
West Virginia: Greenbrier GC (Greenbrier Cse, R. 1978), ass't Jack Nicklaus.

Australia: Australian GC (R. 1977), ass't Jack Nicklaus.

Japan: Kiokawa GC (East Cse, R. 1983; West Cse, R. 1985), with Bob Cupp.

J. S. F. Morrison, circa 1950 COURTESY MRS. GWEN MORRISON

JOHN STANTON FLEMING MORRISON (1892–1961)

BORN: Deal, England.
DIED: Farnham, England, at age 68.
INTERRED: Woking, England.

J. S. F. Morrison attended Trinity College, Cambridge, where he won blues in cricket and soccer before World War I. After service in the Royal Flying Corps, he returned to Cambridge and won another blue in golf. He later won the 1929 Belgian Amateur. Morrison was especially fond of partners' play and won the Worplesdon Foursomes in 1928 with Joyce Wethered and the Halford-Hewitt Cup five times with Henry Longhurst, the renowned British golf writer and Member of Parliament.

Morrison joined the golf design firm of Colt and Alison in the 1920s and by the early 1930s was made a partner and director of the firm of Colt, Alison and Morrison. He worked closely with H. S. Colt on a number of courses on the Continent and in Britain. Following World War II, he was involved in several restoration projects, including Prince's GC in collaboration with Sir Guy Campbell. Morrison was active well into the 1950s, assisted by J. Hamilton Stutt.

Courses by J. S. F. Morrison (All with H. S. Colt unless otherwise indicated):

Denmark: Copenhagen GC (1926), and C.H. Alison.

England: Allestree Park (1939 *solo*); Calcot Park GC (1930); Chadwick Manor GC (1940); Cuddington GC (1929), and C. H. Alison; Fulwell GC (*solo*); Effingham GC (1927); Ham Manor GC (1936); Kedleston Park GC (1947), with John R. Stutt; Leckford and Longstock GC (9 1929); Lilleshall Hall GC (1937); Marlborough GC (1949 *solo*);

Maylands GC (1936); Prestbury GC (1920); Prince's GC (Red Cse 1950), with Sir Guy Campbell; Southport Muni (1932 *solo*); Trevose G&CC (27 1926), and C. H. Alison; Truro GC (1937); Wentworth GC (East Cse 1924; West Cse 1924).

France: GC de Chantaco (1928); GC de Hossegor (1930), with W. A. Martin; GC de St. Cloud (Yellow Cse 1931); Le Touquet GC (Sea Cse 1931), and C. H. Alison.

Germany: Aachener GC (1927), and C. H. Alison; Falkenstein GC (1930); Frankfurter GC (1928; R. 1952, with J. Hamilton Stutt); Hamburger Land und GC (1935).

Italy: Bergamo l'Albenza GC (9 1959 *solo*); La Mandria GC (9 1956 *solo*); Le Betulle GC (1958 *solo*).

Netherlands: Eindhoven GC (1930), and C. H. Alison; Haagsche G&CC (1939), and C. H. Alison; Kennemer G&CC (1929), and C. H. Alison; Noordbrabantse GC (1929); Utrecht GC (1929), and C. H. Alison.

Northern Ireland: Cairndhu GC (1929), and C. H. Alison.

Spain: Real Golf de Pedrena (1928), and C. H. Alison.

Sweden: Stockholm GC (1932).

Trinidad and Tobago: St. Andrews CC (1940, NLE).

Wales: St. Mellons GC (1937), and Henry Cotton.

Courses remodeled or expanded by J. S. F. Morrison (All with H. S. Colt unless otherwise indicated):

Belgium: Royal Zoute GC (R. *solo*).

England: Alnmouth GC (R. 1938 *solo*); [The] Berkshire GC (Blue Cse, R. 1955 *solo*; Red Cse, R. 1955 *solo*); Chislehurst GC (R. 1950 *solo*); Cleveland GC (R. 1947 *solo*); Crewe GC (R. 1947 *solo*); Fulwell GC (R. 1951 *solo*); Hallamshire GC (R. 1939 *solo*); Liphook GC (R. A.2 1946 *solo*); Moortown GC (R. 1950 *solo*); Nevill GC (R. 1939 *solo*); North Foreland GC (R. *solo*); Prince's GC (Blue Cse, R. 1951), with Sir Guy Campbell; Retford GC (R. 1950 *solo*); Rickmansworth GC (R.1 1949 *solo*); Royal Cinque Ports GC (R.2 1939 *solo*); Royal Lytham & St. Annes GC (R. 1936, R. *solo*); Royal Wimbledon (R.1 1949 *solo*); Sandiway GC (R. 1938); Seaford GC (R. *solo*); Sunningdale GC (New Cse, R. *solo*); Thorndon Park GC (R. 1939 *solo*); West Byfleet GC (R. *solo*); West Surrey

GC (R. 1948 *solo*); Whickham GC (R. *solo*); Whitburn GC (R. *solo*); Whittington Barracks GC (R. *solo*).

France: GC de Vittel (R. 1928), with W. A. Martin.

Germany: Frankfurter GC (R. 1952), with J. Hamilton Stutt.

Ireland: Royal Dublin GC (R. 1950), with Sir Guy Campbell.

Northern Ireland: Royal Portrush GC (Dunluce Cse, R. 1946 *solo*; Valley Cse, R. 1946 *solo*).

Scotland: Royal Troon GC (R. 1957 *solo*); St. Andrews (New Cse, R. 1935 *solo*).

Sweden: Lunds Akademiska GC (R.9 A.9 1951 *solo*).

Wales: Bargoed GC (A.9 1921); Borth & Ynslas GC (R. *solo*).

Desmond Muirhead, 1986 COLLECTION RON WHITTEN

GORDON DESMOND MUIRHEAD (1924–)

BORN: England.

Desmond Muirhead studied architecture and engineering at Cambridge University and horticulture at the University of British Columbia and Oregon University. He worked for several years as a landscape planner in British Columbia before moving to the United States in the late 1950s to work on retirement villages. He planned one course during his years in British Columbia.

Muirhead's interest in golf course design grew while working on the Sun City, Arizona, developments. The son of a Scottish golfer, Muirhead claimed never to have been more than a high handicapper himself, but he recognized the need to make golf courses and housing developments compatible with one another. While he took no part in the routing of the courses at Sun City, he offered many suggestions and jumped at the opportunity to lay out his own design within a real estate project in California in 1962.

By that time Muirhead had made a whirlwind tour of the great courses of America and Britain and came away convinced that he could offer some new ideas in the field of golf design. "Those courses have no mystique whatsoever," Muirhead once said in his outspoken style. "I owe very little allegiance to St. Andrews." Much of his early work involved the remodeling of existing West Coast courses, but as his designs gained national attention, the demand for his services increased. By the early 1970s Muirhead was busy laying out radical designs on both coasts.

Two tournament golfers lent their names to various Muirhead projects. Initially Gene Sarazen was listed as his partner, though he did little more than offer endorsements. Later Jack Nicklaus worked with Muirhead on several projects. Pundits called the pairing "The Bear and the Beard." The two dissolved their association during construction of Muirfield Village GC in Ohio.

In the mid-1970s, Muirhead left America and moved to Australia, where he did virtually no golf design work, saying later that he was "burned out." A decade later he returned to the States and resumed his design practice in Florida. Ever the iconoclast, Muirhead immediately created a stir with highly symbolic designs at Aberdeen and Stone Harbor, with bunkers shaped like various animals, holes shaped like mermaids and tomahawks and design strategies based on bits of Gestalt psychology, Oriental religion and art interpretation. Muirhead was equally as entertaining in a long-running series he wrote for *Executive Golfer* magazine.

Courses by Desmond Muirhead:

Arizona: McCormick Ranch GC (Palm Cse 1972; Pine Cse 1973).
California: Desert Island CC (1970); Disneyland Hotel GC (9 Par 3 1963, NLE); Ironwood CC (South Cse 1974); Mission Hills G&CC (Old Cse 1970); Quail Lake CC (1968); Rossmoor GC (9 1965); San Luis Bay Inn & CC (9 1968); Soboba Springs CC (1967); [The] Springs C (1975).
Connecticut: Farmington Woods CC (1970); Oronoque Village GC (1971).
Florida: Aberdeen G&CC (1987); Baymeadows GC (1969); Boca West C (Cse No. 1 1969, R. 1985; Cse No. 2 1971); CC of Silver Springs Shores (1970); Mayacoo Lakes CC (1973), with Jack Nicklaus.

Maryland: Leisure World GC (Precision 1966).
Michigan: Bay Valley GC (1973), with Jack Nicklaus.
New Jersey: Rossmoor GC (1967).
New Mexico: Rio Rancho G&CC (1970).
New York: River Oaks CC (1972).
Ohio: Jack Nicklaus Sports Center (Bruin Cse [Precision] 1972; Grizzly Cse (1972), with Jack Nicklaus; Muirfield Village GC (1974), with Jack Nicklaus.
Texas: Bent Tree GC (1974); Woodlake CC (1972).
Vermont: Haystack CC (1972).
British Columbia: Quilchena G&CC (1956).
Australia: Kooralbyn Valley GC (1980).
Japan: Fuji-Chuo GC; Hillcrest CC; Oak Village GC (1992); Segovia GC (1988); Shinyo GC; Tokyo Zaishi CC; Wakagi CC.
Korea: Long Lake Hill GC.
Spain: La Moraleja GC (1976), with Jack Nicklaus.

Courses remodeled or expanded by Desmond Muirhead:

California: Alameda Muni (Jack Clark Cse, R. 1967); Big Canyon CC (R. 1976; R. 1992); Brookside Muni (Cse No. 2, R. 1966); Fort Irwin GC (R.); Presidio GC (R. 1973); Santa Ana CC (R.); South Hills CC (R. 1968); Visalia CC (R. 1964).
Maryland: All-View GC (R.).
New Jersey: Stone Harbor GC (R. 1988).
Washington: Overlake G&CC (R. 1964).

Greg Muirhead, 1987 COLLECTION RON WHITTEN

GREGORY B. MUIRHEAD (1961–), ASGCA

BORN: Indianapolis, Indiana.

No relation to the more famous golf architect Desmond Muirhead, Greg Muirhead received Bachelors' degrees in both landscape architecture and environmental

design from Ball State University in Muncie, Indiana. After two years working in real estate development and golf course construction he joined the golf design firm of Rees Jones in 1984. He soon became a senior designer in the company and worked closely with Jones on a number of projects, especially those in the southeastern United States.

Courses by Greg Muirhead (All as assistant to Rees Jones):

Georgia: Southbridge GC (1989).
New Jersey: Cherry Valley (1992).
New York: Atlantic GC (1992).
North Carolina: Bryan Park GC (Champions Cse 1990); Greenbrier GC (1988); Harbour Pointe GC (9 1986); [The] Peninsula C (1990); Pinehurst CC (Cse No. 7 1986); Sea Trail G Links (Rees Jones Cse 1989); Talamore GC (1991).
South Carolina: CC of Hilton Head (1986); Charleston National CC (1989); Haig Point C (20 1986, A.9 1989); Woodside Plantation C (Wysteria Cse 1987).
Virginia: Glenwood GC (1985); Golden Horseshoe GC (Green Cse 1991); Greenbrier CC (1987); Honey Bee GC (1988); Stoney Creek GC (1989).

Courses remodeled or expanded by Greg Muirhead (All as assistant to Rees Jones):

Maryland: Congressional CC (R. 1989).
Massachusetts: CC of New Seabury (Blue Cse, R. 1988; Green Cse, R. 1986).
New Jersey: Forest Hill Field C (R. 1986); Morris County GC (R. 1987); Ridgewood CC (R. 1988).
North Carolina: Carmel CC (North Cse, R. 1988; South Cse, R. 1988).
South Carolina: Palmetto GC (R. 1989).
Vermont: Equinox CC (R. 1991).
Virginia: Salisbury CC (R. 1988).

MARK A. MUNGEAM (1961–), ASGCA

BORN: Marlboro, Massachusetts.

After graduating from Worcester (Massachusetts) Polytechnic Institute with a degree in civil engineering, Mark Mungeam worked in golf course construction. There he made the acquaintance of golf architect Brian Silva and in 1987 joined the firm of Cornish & Silva. Working closely with Silva in his Uxbridge, Massa-

Mark Mungeam,
1990 COURTESY ASGCA

chusetts, office, Mungeam participated in every facet of architecture and was soon given major responsibility for several designs of his own.

Courses by Mark Mungeam (All as assistant to Geoffrey S. Cornish and Brian Silva):

Massachusetts: Bradford CC (1990); Butternut Farm GC (1991); Olde Barnstable Fairgrounds GC (1991); Shaker Hills GC (1991).
New Hampshire: Passaconaway CC (1990); Perry Hollow G&CC (9 1990).
New York: Adirondack G&CC (1990).
Ohio: Darby Creek GC (1992).
Rhode Island: Richmond CC (1991).

Courses remodeled or expanded by Mark Mungeam (All as assistant to Geoffrey S. Cornish and Brian Silva):

Connecticut: Ellington Ridge CC (R.).
Massachusetts: International GC (R.).
New Hampshire: Mount Pleasant GC (A.9 1990).

Albert H. Murray
(1888–1974)

BORN: Nottingham, England.
DIED: Montreal, Canada, at age 85.

Albert Murray emigrated to Canada in 1902, where he joined his older brother Charlie at the Toronto Golf Club. Charlie, who dabbled in course design during his career, took over the head professional job at Royal Montreal Golf Club in 1905 and became a legend in that position before his death in 1930. Albert served as professional at a succession of Montreal-area courses while competing successfully in national events. He won many tournaments, including the Canadian Open in 1908 and 1913 and the Canadian PGA in

1924. Albert Murray also laid out a number of courses in eastern Canada and upstate New York during a long successful professional career.

Courses by Albert Murray:

New York: Massena GC (1958).
Quebec: CC of Montreal (1910); Kanawaki GC (1912), with *Charles Murray*; Montreal Muni (Yellow Cse); Royal Quebec CC (Kent Cse 1914, NLE).

Courses remodeled or expanded by Albert Murray:

New York: Malone GC (A.9 1958).
New Brunswick: Edmundston GC (R. A.11 1947).

Frank Murray

In the late 1940s Frank Murray served as green committee chairman at Congressional CC in Maryland. He became interested in golf course construction at this time. After helping build several courses designed by golf architect Alfred Tull, Murray then decided to build one for himself, and Brooke Manor Farms CC, constructed by Murray to Tull's design, was completed in 1955. Murray was so fascinated with golf course design by this time that he formed a design-and-construction firm with Russell Roberts, who had been in charge of maintenance at Brooke Manor Farms.

Murray soon sold his club in order to devote full time to his practice with Roberts. The two designed and built a number of courses along the Eastern Seaboard in the late 1950s. In 1959 the partnership was terminated and Murray moved to Florida, where he did several resort courses in the 1960s.

Courses by Frank Murray (All with Russell Roberts unless otherwise indicated):

Delaware: Cavaliers CC (1959); Old Landing GC; Rehoboth Beach CC (1962).
Florida: Crooked Creek G&CC (1968 solo); Placid Lakes Inn & CC (1966 solo); Pompano Park GC (Precision 1970 solo); Sabal Palm CC (1968 solo); Tierre Verde GC (1965 solo); University Park CC (1960 solo); Vizcaya CC (1961 solo).
Maryland: Andrews AFB GC (East Cse 1956; West Cse 1961); Bel Aire

G&CC (27 1959); Hagerstown Muni (1957); Maryland G&CC; Swan Creek CC (1956); Washingtonian CC (Country Club Cse 1960; National Cse 1962).
Pennsylvania: Fairview G&CC (1959); Lebanon CC.
Puerto Rico: Berwind CC (1966 solo).

Course remodeled or expanded by Frank Murray (All with Russell Roberts unless otherwise indicated):

Delaware: Newark CC (A.9 1956).

René V. Muylaert

A graduate of the University of Massachusetts Winter School for turfgrass managers, René worked as a course superintendent in Ontario for several years. He began designing courses on a part-time basis in 1960 and entered the field full-time in 1966. When his brother Charles, another Massachusetts turfgrass graduate and experienced superintendent, joined him in 1967, they set up the design-and-build firm of Green–Par Golf Construction Ltd. In addition to courses of their own design, the brothers made major or minor modifications to many established layouts. They also operated an extensive sod business. Charles left the business in the mid-1980s, and René concentrated strictly on golf course design from headquarters in Toronto.

Courses by René Muylaert:

Ontario: Aurora Highlands GC (1980), with *Charles Muylaert*; Bear Creek G&CC [FKA Strathroy CC] (9 1975); Brookside GC (27 1967); Caledon CC [FKA Chinguacousy CC] (1960); Chestnut Hill G&CC (1991); Derrydale GC (Precision 1968); Fire Fighters Gormley Green GC (Creek Cse 1972); Glen Cedars GC (1967); Glen Eagles GC (1961); Greenhills CC (27 1977), with *Charles Muylaert*; Horseshoe Valley GC (1972), with *Charles Muylaert*; Indian Wells GC (1972); Markham G&CC (1980), with *Charles Muylaert*; Nobleton Lakes GC (1974); Oakville Executive GC [FKA Nanticoke GC] (Precision 1977), with *Charles Muylaert*; Pheasant Run CC (1979), with *Charles Muylaert*; Royal Downs GC (Precision 1966); St. Andrews East GC (1986); St. Andrews

Valley G&CC (1991); St. Catherine's Muni (Precision 1973); Scenic Woods G&CC [FKA Binbrook GC] (1963); Spring Lakes GC (Cse No. 1 1976; Cse No. 2 1980), with *Charles Muylaert*; Steed and Evans GC (9 1971); Sunset G Centre (Par 3 1973); Thistledown GC (9 1974); Unionville Fairways (Par 3 1962); Vaughan Valley GC (Precision 1969); Victoria Park GC (East Cse 1967; West Cse 1972); Western Trent GC (9 1974).

Courses remodeled or expanded by René Muylaert:

Ontario: Fire Fighters Gormley Green GC (Circle Cse, R.9 1974), with *Charles Muylaert*.

Torakichi Nakamura (1915–   )

BORN: Kanagawa Prefecture, Japan.

Prominent Japanese golfer Torakichi Nakamura, a three-time winner of the Japanese Open, was individual champion of the 1957 Canada Cup Match held at Kasumigaseki GC. It was during this event that he acquired the nickname "Pete" through mutual agreement with his American competitors, who found Torakichi difficult to pronounce.

Nakamura's victory at Kasumigaseki was credited with initiating a golf boom in Japan. In 1963 he began designing courses to accommodate that boom. Nakamura maintained his golfing skills well into the 1980s, winning the 1981 Japanese Seniors while shooting his age in the process.

Courses by Pete Nakamura:

Japan: Fuji Oyama GC; Kawagoe CC; Kinugawa CC; Mino CC; Mito Lakes GC, with *Shinichi Kodaira*; Murasakizuka GC; Nakura CC; Seinan CC; Stork Hill GC.

Scott M. Nall (1920–   )

A 1941 graduate of Vanderbilt University in Nashville, Tennessee, Scott Nall designed and built a handful of courses in the western tip of Kentucky during the 1960s. One of them, Mayfield Golf and Country Club, became a highly regarded state tournament venue.

Courses by Scott Nall:

Kentucky: Clinton GC; Mayfield G&CC; Oaks CC; South Highland CC.
Tennessee: Dyersburg Muni.

Greg Nash, 1990
COURTESY ASGCA

Gregory Nash (1949–   ), ASGCA

BORN: Hays, Kansas.

At the urging of childhood acquaintance Fred Bliss, Greg Nash attended the University of Arizona and earned a Bachelor's degree in landscape architecture in 1972. He worked for two years as a golf course designer and construction supervisor with the Del E. Webb Corporation in Phoenix, Arizona, then joined fellow Webb employee Jeff Hardin in a golf architecture partnership. In 1983 Nash formed his own business, based in Phoenix.

Courses by Greg Nash (All with Jeff Hardin unless otherwise indicated):

Arizona: Aspen Valley GC (9 1973, A.9 1981); Bellaire GC (Precision 1973), and Red Lawrence; Briarwood GC (1979); Continental CC (Precision 1978); Cottonwood CC (1983); Country Meadows GC (9 Precision 1978); Dobson Ranch GC (1974), and Red Lawrence; Echo Mesa GC (Precision 1985); Gold Canyon CC (1982); Grandview GC (1984); Hillcrest GC (1978); Leisure World GC (Championship Cse 1979; Executive Cse [Par 3] 1979); Los Caballeros GC (9 1979, A.9 1981); Paradise Valley GC (9 Precision 1986); Pebblebrook GC (1979); Quail Run G Cse (9 Precision 1977); Riverview GC, Sun City; Roadhaven GC (9 Precision 1984); Sheraton El Conquistador GC (Sunrise Cse 1982; Sunset Cse 1985); Stardust GC (Precision 1979); Sun City Vistoso GC (1986); Sun Lakes CC (9 1973, A.9 1979); Sunland Village GC (Precision 1975), and Milt Coggins; Superstition Springs GC (1986); Union Hills CC (1974); Villa de Paz CC (1976); Wigwam G&CC (West Cse 1974), and Red Lawrence.
Hawaii: Turtle Bay GC (Old Cse 1971), ass't George Fazio and Tom Fazio.
Nevada: Sun City Summerlin GC (1990).
Colombia: La Colina CC (1974).
Thailand: Mahachia GC (27 1991).

Courses remodeled or expanded by Greg Nash (All with Jeff Hardin unless otherwise indicated):

Arizona: Happy Trails G Cse (A.9 1989); Rio Verde CC (Quail Run Cse, A.9 1981; White Wing Cse, A.9 1983); Stonecreek GC [FKA Anasazi GC] (R. 1984).
Kansas: Smoky Hills CC (A.9 1982).
Nevada: Boulder City GC (A.9 1986).

William H. Neff, 1984 COURTESY WILLIAM H. NEFF

William Henrichsen Neff (1905–   ), ASGCA

BORN: Holladay, Utah.

William H. Neff attended the University of Utah and graduated from the American Landscape School in Des Moines, Iowa. He practiced landscape architecture in Utah and Arizona for over twenty years.

A member of The Country Club in Salt Lake City, Neff was appointed to a committee in charge of remodeling the course in 1952. He hired Californian William P. Bell to design the changes and worked with the architect on the reconstruction. After Bell's death, Neff was hired by the architect's son, William F. Bell, to supervise construction of Riverside CC in Provo, Utah. Neff served as construction boss on three other Bell projects in Salt Lake City and then in 1959 decided to try his own hand at golf design. Over the next twenty years he created a number of Utah's top courses.

Courses by William H. Neff:

Colorado: Yampa Valley GC (9 1983), with William Howard Neff.

Utah: Alpine CC (1960); Bloomington CC (1972); Bountiful Muni (1976), with William Howard Neff; Cascade Fairways GC (1968); Davis Park GC (1968); Fore Lakes GC (9 Precision 1973), with William Howard Neff; Glenmore G&CC (1967); Majestic Oaks GC (9 Par 3 1973); Mountain Dell GC (Cse No. 1 1960), ass't William F. Bell; Mountain View GC (1968); Oakridge CC (1957), ass't William F. Bell; Park City GC (9 1962); Riverside CC (1960), ass't William F. Bell; Stansbury Park CC (1972); Sweetwater GC (9 1974), with William Howard Neff; Wasatch Mountain GC (1966; A.3rd 9 1972, with William Howard Neff); Westland Hills GC (9).

Wyoming: Little America GC (9 Precision 1974).

Courses remodeled or expanded by William H. Neff:

Utah: Bonneville Muni (A.9 1956), ass't William F. Bell; Cottonwood C (R.9 A.9 1963); [The] Country Club (R.9 1952), ass't William P. Bell and William F. Bell; Hidden Valley CC (A.9 1978), with William Howard Neff; Rose Park GC (A.9 1960), ass't William F. Bell; Wasatch Mountain GC (A.3rd 9 1972), with William Howard Neff.

William Howard Neff, 1990 COURTESY ASGCA

WILLIAM HOWARD NEFF (1933–), ASGCA

BORN: Limon, Colorado.

William Howard Neff received a Bachelor's degree in architecture from the University of Utah in 1958. During the next eight years, he worked as a draftsman for a land-planning firm in Denver, for the Salt Lake City and County Planning Commis-

sion and as a planning consultant-graphic designer in Salt Lake City.

In 1966 he embarked on a career as a golf course architect, joining the practice of William Henrichsen Neff (who, despite the similarity in names, was no relation) in Salt Lake City. In the early 1980s Bill Neff established his own design business in Salt Lake City.

Courses by William Howard Neff:

Colorado: Boomerang GC (1992); Yampa Valley GC (9 1983), with William H. Neff.

Montana: Anaconda Hills GC (9 1991).

Nevada: Round Mountain GC (9 1991).

Utah: Bountiful Muni (1976), with William H. Neff; Eagle Mountain GC (1989); East Bay G Cse (27 1986, R.1 1991); Fore Lakes GC (9 Precision 1973), with William H. Neff; Gladstan GC (1987); Mountain Dell GC (Cse No. 2 1991); Mt. Ogden GC (1984; R.1 1990); Sweetwater GC (9 1974), with William H. Neff; West Ridge G Cse (1991).

Courses remodeled or expanded by William Howard Neff:

Utah: Bloomington Hills CC (R. 1986); Davis Park GC (R. 1985); Forest Dale GC (R.9 1988); Hidden Valley CC (A.9 1978, with William H. Neff; R.2 1989); Ogden G&CC (R. 1984); Park City GC (R. 1985); Riverside CC (R.1 1991); Southgate GC (R.3 1986; R.6 1989); St. George GC (R.2 1989); University of Utah GC (R.2 1988); Wasatch Mountain GC (A.3rd 9 1972), with William H. Neff; Willow Creek CC (R. 1981).

JOHN BYRON NELSON, JR. (1912–)

BORN: Fort Worth, Texas.

Legendary professional golfer Byron Nelson, a contemporary of Ben Hogan, Sam Snead and Jimmy Demaret, won one U.S. Open, two PGA Championships and three Masters during a relatively short playing career.

In the 1960s Nelson served as a consultant to golf architect Ralph Plummer on several designs, notably Preston Trail GC near Dallas, which for years hosted a PGA Tour event named in Nelson's honor. After Plummer's death, Nelson served as consultant to another prominent Texan

Byron Nelson, 1991 COURTESY MAURY MILLER

golf architect, Joe Finger. Among their collaborations was the restoration of several holes at Augusta National. Nelson also assisted in the remodeling of a TPC course to serve as host of the Byron Nelson Classic on the PGA Tour in the 1980s.

Courses by Byron Nelson:

Alabama: Oak Hills CC (1975), with Joseph S. Finger.

Texas: Grapevine Muni (1980), with Joseph S. Finger and Ken Dye; Great Southwest GC (1965), with Ralph Plummer; Preston Trail GC (1965), with Ralph Plummer; Riverhill C (1974), with Joseph S. Finger.

Japan: Iwaki G & Sports C (1992), with Maury Miller and D. A. Weibring.

Courses remodeled or expanded by Byron Nelson:

Georgia: Augusta National GC (R.1 1979), with Joseph S. Finger.

Texas: Las Colinas Sports C (TPC Cse, R.9 A.9 1987), with Jay Morrish and Ben Crenshaw.

Larry Nelson, 1991 COURTESY LARRY NELSON

LARRY GENE NELSON (1947–)

BORN: Fort Payne, Alabama.

A baseball and basketball letterman in high school, Larry Nelson attended Southern Tech for a year before being drafted by the army and serving a stint in an infantry platoon in Vietnam during the height of the war. Upon his discharge in 1968, Nelson moved to Atlanta, attended Kennesaw Junior College and worked as an illustrator at a Lockheed aircraft plant.

In 1969, after accompanying friends to a local driving range, twenty-one-year-old Larry Nelson took his first golf lesson. Six months later he was scoring under par with regularity and turned professional. Four years later, with only one 72-hole tournament under his belt, Nelson qualified for the PGA Tour. His success was gradual but impressive, as he won the 1981 and 1987 PGA championships and the 1983 U.S. Open as well as over half a dozen Tour events.

In 1986 Nelson created an architectural firm based in Marietta, Georgia. While the bulk of his design domestic projects were done in collaboration with golf architect Jeff Brauer, Nelson handled all aspects of overseas designs on his own.

Courses by Larry Nelson (All in association with Jeff Brauer unless otherwise indicated):

Georgia: Brookstone G&CC (1988); Centennial GC (1990).
North Carolina: Jefferson Landing GC (1991), with *Dennis Lehmann.*
Tennessee: Springhouse GC at Opryland (1990).
Guam: Longfit New Towne GC (1992).
Indonesia: Talvas G & Resort Batam (Private Cse 1992; Resort Cse 1992).
Japan: Dejima CC (1988 *solo*); Hayakita CC (1991 *solo*).
Saipan: Coral Ocean Point GC (1987 *solo*).

Courses remodeled or expanded by Larry Nelson (All in association with Jeff Brauer unless otherwise indicated):

Texas: Brookhaven CC (Masters Cse, R. 1991).
Japan: Isewan CC (R. 1989 *solo*).

ROBERT DAVID NELSON (1951–), ASGCA

BORN: Kentfield, California.

"Robin" Nelson attended the University of Oregon, Chaminade University of Honolulu and the University of California at Berkeley. Upon graduation from Berkeley, Nelson obtained his landscape architecture license in California in 1973 and soon

Robin Nelson, 1991
COURTESY ROBIN
NELSON

joined the golf design firm of Robert Muir Graves. After three years Nelson joined the Ronald Fream Design Group and supervised the construction of several layouts in the Far East.

In 1983 Nelson became director of golf design for Belt, Collins and Associates, a large landscape design firm based in Hawaii. Three years later, Rodney Wright, a former associate of Ron Kirby and Denis Griffiths, joined the company. Soon thereafter Nelson and Wright formed a subsidiary of Belt, Collins—Nelson and Wright, Golf Course Architects—to handle exclusively all Belt, Collins golf course projects. The team had added Gary Howard, Mark Miller, Lynette Morrison and Neil Haworth, a former apprentice of Graham Cooke, to the firm by 1990.

Courses by Robin Nelson (All with Rodney Wright unless otherwise indicated):

Hawaii: Ewa Beach International GC (1992); Frances I'i Brown GC, Mauna Lani Resort (North Cse, 9 1981, with *Homer Flint* and *Raymond F. Cain,* A.9 1991; South Cse, 9 1981, with *Homer Flint* and *Raymond F. Cain,* A.9 1991); Kona International CC (1992); Waikapu Sandalwood G Cse (1992); West Loch Muni (1990).
Australia: Burswood Island GC (1987 *solo*); Caves Beach GC (Cliffs Cse 1991; Lakeside Cse 1991); Palm Meadows GC, Surfer's Paradise (1987), with *Graham Marsh.*
France: Champs de Bataille GC (1990); Montgriffon GC (Coulonges Cse 1992; Luzarches Cse 1992).
Guam: Guam First Green GC (1993); Mangilao GC (1992); Togcha Beach GC (1992).
Indonesia: Bali G&RC (1991).
Japan: Busena Resort GC (1992).
Thailand: Friendship Meadows CC (1992); Royal Hills GC (1993).

Courses remodeled or expanded by Robin Nelson (All with Rodney Wright unless otherwise indicated):

California: San Geronimo Valley GC (R. 1991).
Hawaii: Ala Wai GC (R. 1986 *solo*); Hana Ranch G Park (R.3 1983 *solo*); Hickam AFB GC (R. 1987); Kapalua GC (Bay Cse, R. 1986; Village Cse, R. 1987), and Hale Irwin; Keauhou Kona CC (A.3rd 9 1986), with William F. Bell; Mauna Kea GC (R.); Mid-Pacific CC (R.); Oahu CC (R. 1986); Pearl CC (R.1 1985 *solo*); Sheraton Makaha Resort & CC (R. 1987); Waialae CC (R. 1986 *solo*).
Australia: Campbelltown GC (R. 1985 *solo*).
France: Chantilly GC (Old Cse, R.); Lann-Rohou GC (A.9 1989).
Malaysia: Kelab Golf di Raja Trengganu (R.9 1986).
Okinawa: Naha CC (R. 1990).
Singapore: Sentosa Island GC (Serapong Cse, R.).

Jack Neville, circa 1925 COLLECTION RON WHITTEN

JOHN FRANCIS NEVILLE (1895–1978)

BORN: St. Louis, Missouri.
DIED: Chino, California, at age 83.

Jack Neville moved to Oakland, California, as a young boy and learned golf from Macdonald Smith and Jim Barnes. He was an excellent competitive golfer, winning the California State Amateur Championship in 1912, 1913, 1919, 1922 and 1929 and defeating H. Chandler Egan for the Pacific Northwest title in 1914. He was also a member of the 1923 Walker Cup team.

In 1915 Neville was a real estate salesman with the Pacific Improvement Company of Monterey, California. When the company's manager, S. F. B. Morse, resigned and purchased some 3,500 acres of land known as the Seventeen Mile Drive for future development, he asked Neville to lay out a golf course along some prime oceanfront property. Neville reportedly had participated in a few previous course designs, but still he enlisted the aid of a friend and fellow California Amateur champion, Douglas Grant, in routing and bunkering the course.

When the course, Del Monte Golf and Country Club, opened in 1918, golfers hailed it as a lovely and testing course. Over the years the course was changed. Its name was changed to Pebble Beach, some of its greens rebuilt and rebunkered and a few holes expanded, notably the 18th, converted from a short par 4 into a stunning par 5 along the edge of the ocean. Jack Neville was not invited to participate in those changes. Instead, a committee that included professional architect H. Chandler Egan handled the remodeling.

Jack Neville prepared designs for a few other courses in the 1920s, but few were ever built. He continued to play competitively and sell real estate but was not active in course architecture. Over the years, however, he would be periodically rediscovered and asked to assist on a design. The last time occurred in the late 1960s, when Pebble Beach was being groomed for its first U.S. Open. Amateur golfer Sandy Tatum, a San Francisco lawyer with no previous design experience but with thirty years' experience playing Pebble Beach, was invited to toughen the course for the Open. Tatum located Neville living in obscurity in nearby Pacific Grove. Together they reviewed the design and made several changes in bunkering. It was a collaboration that Tatum later called one of the most satisfying experiences of his life.

Courses by Jack Neville:

California: Bel-Air CC (1927), with George C. Thomas, Jr., and William P. Bell; Monterey Peninsula CC (Shore Cse 1961), with Bob Baldock; Pebble Beach G Links (1918, with Douglas S. Grant; R. 1971, with *Frank "Sandy" Tatum*).

Courses remodeled or expanded by Jack Neville:

California: Old Del Monte G&CC (R.); Pacific Grove G Links (A.9 1960).

WILLIAM K. NEWCOMB, JR. (1940–)

BORN: Logansport, Indiana.

Bill Newcomb, who won the Indiana Open as an amateur in 1961, attended the University of Michigan, receiving a Bachelor of Architecture degree in 1963 and a Master's in landscape architecture in 1965. From 1965 to 1967 he worked for golf architect Pete Dye, during which time he won the 1967 Michigan Amateur.

In 1968 he formed William Newcomb Associates, based in Ann Arbor. His firm included several associates over the years, including John Robinson, Stephen Kay and James Lipe, who all went on to careers in golf architecture. Newcomb served for years as a lecturer at the University of Michigan's Department of Natural Resources and Michigan State University's Department of Agricultural Technology. He also coached the golf team at the University of Michigan in the 1970s.

Newcomb concentrated his designs in the upper Midwest, especially upstate Michigan, where he did no fewer than five courses for the Boyne resorts, including the routing of the Donald Ross Memorial Course at Boyne Highlands, which featured facsimiles of some of the most famous Donald Ross holes.

Courses by William Newcomb:

Alaska: Anchorage G Cse (1987).
Illinois: Fox Run GC (1983); Oak Run GC (9 1975).
Indiana: Brookville Muni (9 1991); Forest Park Muni (1970); Jasper Muni (9 1970).
Iowa: Des Moines G&CC (Red & Blue Cses 1965), ass't Pete Dye.
Kentucky: Greenbrier G&CC (1971); Maysville CC (9); Polo Fields G&CC (1992).
Michigan: Boyne Highlands GC (Donald Ross Memorial Cse 1989, with *Everett Kircher, Stephen Kircher* and *Jim Flick*; Moor Cse 1975); Boyne Mountain GC (Alpine Cse 1971; Executive Cse [9 Precision] 1973; Monument Cse 1986); Brookwood CC (9); Crystal Mountain GC (1977, A.3rd 9 1991); GC at Saginaw Greens (1991); Grand Traverse G Resort (Resort Cse 1979); Great Oaks CC (1970); Green Hills GC (1970); Hampton Muni (9); [The] Heathers GC (9 1990); Holiday Greens GC (Precision 1982); Huron Breeze G&CC (1991); Indianfield G&CC (1976); Lakeview Hills CC (North

Cse, routing); [The] Lion at Tanglewood GC (1991); Oasis G Cse (Precision 1969); Partridge Point GC (9 1985); Portage Lake GC (9 1972); Prairie Creek GC (9 1972); Riverview Highlands GC (9); Travis Pointe CC (1976); Vassar G&CC; Willow Metro GC (1978).
Ohio: Apple Valley GC (1972); Avalon Lakes GC (1967), ass't Pete Dye; Seven Hills GC (1971); Union CC (1969).

Courses remodeled or expanded by William Newcomb:

Indiana: Elbel Park Muni (R. 1991); Erskine Muni (R. 1991); South Bend CC (R. 1989).
Michigan: Barton Hills CC (R.); Battle Creek CC (R.); Belvedere GC (R. 1968); Chemung Hills GC (A.9 1983); Farmington CC (R.); Green Ridge CC (R., NLE); Hickory Hills GC (R.9 A.9 1977); Kalamazoo CC (R.); Lake of the North GC (A.9 1989); Klinger Lake CC (R.); Pine Mountain GC (A.9 1986); Pine Valley GC (R. 1990); Plum Hollow G&CC (R.); Port Huron CC (R. 1982); Saginaw CC (R.); Schuss Mountain GC (R. 1980); Spring Lake CC, Clarkston (R.); Traverse City CC (R. 1982); West Branch CC (A.9 1971); Westland GC (R.3 1982).
New York: Niagara Falls CC (R.); Old Oaks CC (R. 1981).
Ohio: Cincinnati CC (R. A.4 1969); Congress Lake C (R.); Fonderlac CC (A.9); Kettenring CC (A.9 1974); Mayfield CC (R.); Trumbull CC (R.); Wooster CC (A.9 1974).

WILLIAM JOHN NEWIS (1940–)

Bill Newis received a Bachelor of Engineering degree from the University of Saskatchewan in 1962. He developed golf design skills during tenures with the Canadian National Parks Service in Banff, Alberta, and with the Saskatchewan Provincial and Regional Park system. In 1968 Bill formed a golf architectural firm called GPEC Consulting Ltd, based in Calgary, Alberta. He soon took on an associate, Scottish-born land planner Ken Rattray.

Courses by Bill Newis:

Hawaii: Silversword G&CC (1987).
Alberta: Bearspaw CC; Canmore G & Curling C; Cottonwood G&CC (1990); Fort McMurray GC; Hamptons G&CC; Lloydminster G&CC; McCall Lake GC (27); Paradise Canyon G&CC (1991); Priddis Greens G&CC; Redwood Meadows G&CC; Siksika Resort G&CC (9); Wintergreen G&CC (1991).
British Columbia: Royal Riverside G&CC.
Saskatchewan: Last Oak Resort GC; Long Creek G&CC (9); White Bear Lake GC (9); Willows G&CC (1991).

Courses remodeled or expanded by Bill Newis:

Alberta: Grande Prairie GC (R. A.3rd 9 1991); Mighty Peace GC (A.9 1991); Pinebrook G&CC (R.); Turner Valley G&CC (R.).
British Columbia: Fernie G&CC (R.); Golden and District G&CC (A.9 1992) Kimberley GC (R.); Nelson GC (R.9 A.9 1992).
Saskatchewan: Cowessess G&CC (R.); Regina G&CC (R.).

Jack Nicklaus, 1987
COLLECTION RON WHITTEN

JACK WILLIAM NICKLAUS (1940–   ), ASGCA

BORN: Columbus, Ohio.

Jack Nicklaus was arguably the greatest golfer of all time, winning an unprecedented twenty major championships: six Masters, five PGAs, four U.S. Opens, three British Opens and two U.S. Amateurs. He took an interest in golf course design early in his professional career and started consulting on designs while still in his twenties.

Nicklaus worked first with designer Pete Dye on several projects and later with Desmond Muirhead. In 1974 Nicklaus formed his own golf architecture practice, utilizing the talented Bob Cupp and Jay Morrish as full-time designers. Nicklaus allowed his assistants to prepare plans and then reviewed them in detail, making suggestions on changes to enhance playability and strategy. Something of a workaholic, Nicklaus continued to play the PGA Tour while personally inspecting his course projects before, during and after construction.

Cupp and Morrish eventually left to form their own design companies, and Nicklaus brought aboard new talent to serve as design associates, including Scott Miller, Tom Pearson, Jim Lipe, Gene Bates, Ron Kirby, Rick Jacobsen, Bruce Borland, Andrew Raugast and, for a short time, Paul Clute.

A stickler for high design and maintenance standards, Nicklaus was sometimes criticized for catering only to deep-pocket clients who funded big-budget layouts. His courses, however expensive, attracted widespread attention and admiration. One, Shoal Creek, hosted the PGA Championship soon after it opened, then a U.S. Amateur and then another PGA before it was twenty years old. Several became perennial sites on the PGA or Senior PGA Tours. His original eighteen at Grand Cypress Golf Club was a coselection of the Best New Resort Course by *Golf Digest* in 1984. His Loxahatchee Club was named Best New Private Course by the magazine in 1985, and his Kiele Course at Kauai Lagoons in Hawaii was selected its Best New Resort Course of 1989.

Courses by Jack Nicklaus:

Alabama: Shoal Creek (1976).
Arizona: Desert Highlands GC (1984); GC at Desert Mountain (Cochise Cse 1987; Geronimo Cse 1989; Renegade Cse 1986); La Paloma GC (27 1984).
California: Bear Creek GC (1982); [The] Club at Morningside (1982); Dove Canyon CC (1990); PGA West GC (Nicklaus Resort Cse 1987; Nicklaus Private Cse 1987); Sherwood CC (1989).
Colorado: Breckenridge G Cse (1987); Castle Pines GC (1981); CC of Castle Pines (1986); CC of the Rockies (1984); Meridian GC (1984); Ptarmigan G&CC (1988).
Florida: Bear Lakes CC (Lakes Cse 1985; Links Cse 1988); Bear's Paw CC (1980); Grand Cypress GC (1984, A.3 Golf Academy 1985, A.3rd 9 1986); Ibis G&CC (Legend Cse 1991); John's Island C (South Cse 1970), with Pete Dye; Loxahatchee C (1984); Mayacoo Lakes CC (1973), with Desmond Muirhead; New Cse at Grand Cypress (1988); Sailfish Point CC (1981).
Georgia: CC of the South (1987); Great Waters GC (1992).
Hawaii: Kauai Lagoons G&CC (Kiele Cse 1989; Lagoons Cse 1989).
Illinois: Wynstone CC (1989).
Indiana: Sycamore Hills GC (1990).
Kentucky: Valhalla GC (1986).
Louisiana: CC of Louisiana (1986); English Turn G&CC (1988).
Michigan: Bay Valley GC (1973), with Desmond Muirhead; Grand Traverse Resort (The Bear Cse 1984); TPC of Michigan (1990); Wabeek GC (1972), with Pete Dye and Roy Dye.
Mississippi: Annandale GC (1981).
North Carolina: Elk River GC (1984); Governors C (1990); Landfall GC (Jack Nicklaus Cse 1990); Pinehurst National GC (1989).
Ohio: Barrington CC (1992); CC at Muirfield Village (1982); CC of the North (1992); Glenmoor CC (1992); Jack Nicklaus Sports Center (Bruin Cse [Precision] 1973; Grizzly Cse 1973), with Desmond Muirhead; Muirfield Village GC (1974), with Desmond Muirhead; New Albany CC (27 1992).
Pennsylvania: [The] Club at Nevillewood (1992).
South Carolina: Colleton River Plantation GC (1992); Harbour Town G Links (1970), with Pete Dye; Long Bay C (1988); Melrose GC (1987); Pawleys Plantation GC (1988); Turtle Point G Links (1981).
Tennessee: Richland CC (1988).
Texas: [The] Hills of Lakeway GC (1981; A.3 Golf Academy 1985); Lochinvar GC (1980).
Utah: Park Meadows GC (1983).
Wisconsin: Americana Lake Geneva GC (Briarpatch Cse 1970), with Pete Dye.
Ontario: Glen Abbey GC (1976).
Australia: Pacific City GC (1992).
Austria: GC Gut Altentann (1988).
Belgium: Domaine des Princes GC (1992).
Cayman Islands: Britannia GC (9 Cayman/18 Precision 1985).
England: St. Mellion G&CC (New Cse 1987).
France: Cely GC (1992); Golf de Paris International C (1991).
Ireland: Mt. Juliet G&CC (1991).
Indonesia: Damai Indah GC (1992).

Italy: Napoli G&CC.

Japan: Hananomori GC (1992); Hokkaido GC (Classic Cse); Huis Ten Bosch CC (1992); Japan Memorial GC (1990); Kazusa GC (1984); Komono GC (1992); Mito International GC (1987); New St. Andrews GC (1976), with Desmond Muirhead; Oakmont GC (1990); President GC (27); Saint Creek CC (1989); Sendai Minami GC (1992); Shimonoseki Golden GC (1989); Sunnyfield GC (1988).

Philippines: Manila Southwoods G&CC (1992).

Portugal: Villa Nova de Cacela GC (1992).

Scotland: Drumoig G Cse (1992); Gleneagles Hotel GC (Monarch's Cse 1991).

Spain: La Moraleja GC (1976), with Desmond Muirhead; Sherry Golf Montecastillo.

Switzerland: GC Crans (1988).

Taiwan: Chang An G&CC.

Thailand: CC Khao Yai; Golden Valley CC (1992); Laem Chabang International CC (27 1992); Mission Hills GC (1992); Springfield Royal CC (1992); Winsan GC (1992).

Courses remodeled or expanded by Jack Nicklaus:

California: Pebble Beach G Links (R. 1991).

Florida: Avila G&CC (R. 1989); PGA National GC (The Champion Cse, R. 1990).

Georgia: Atlanta CC (R. 1983); Augusta National GC (R. 1985).

New York: St. Andrews GC (R. 1985).

Ohio: Firestone CC (South Cse, R. 1986).

Texas: Dallas Athletic C (R. Blue Cse 1986; R. Gold Cse 1989).

West Virginia: [The] Greenbrier GC (Greenbrier Cse, R. 1978).

Australia: Australian GC (R. 1977).

JACK WILLIAM NICKLAUS, JR. (1961–   )

BORN: Columbus, Ohio.

The eldest son of Jack Nicklaus, Jackie Nicklaus won the North and South Amateur at Pinehurst in 1985. After graduating from the University of North Carolina, Jackie turned professional and played with little success on the U.S., Canadian and European PGA Tours. He found himself spending more time traveling with his fa-

Jack Nicklaus, Jr., 1991 COURTESY JACK NICKLAUS, JR.

ther on golf design projects and discovered his interest lay more in architecture than competition. In 1990 Jackie joined his father's design firm and was immediately given primary responsibility for several new courses.

Courses by Jack Nicklaus, Jr.:

Florida: Ibis G&CC (Heritage Cse 1992).
North Carolina: Legacy G Links (1992).

Courses remodeled or expanded by Jack Nicklaus, Jr.:

England: Hanbury Manor GC (R.9 A.9 1991).

TOM NICOLL

Scottish-born professional Tom Nicoll designed and built a number of courses in California before and after spending several years in Asia. In 1917 he moved to Manila to build and operate a course there for the U.S. government. In Manila he taught a group of Japanese golfers who persuaded him to become the professional at Komazawa GC in Tokyo. As such, he was one of, if not the first, teaching professional in Japan. He also laid out several courses in Japan and was given credit for popularizing the game in the Orient.

He returned to California in the mid-1920s and served as club professional at Los Altos Golf and Country Club for many years.

Tom Nicoll should not be confused with Thomas H. Nicol, a civil engineer who planned several courses in Alabama in the 1960s.

Courses by Tom Nicoll:

California: Burlingame CC (1905, NLE); Los Altos G&CC; Menlo CC (9); San Jose CC (1915).

Courses remodeled or expanded by Tom Nicoll:

California: Los Altos G&CC (R. 1946), with Clark Glasson.

WARD W. NORTHRUP (1932–   )

BORN: Cedar Rapids, Iowa.

After attending Iowa State as an agriculture major, Northrup moved to Florida and became involved in course maintenance at Delray Beach Country Club. Following work on construction crews for architects Red Lawrence and Mark Mahannah, Northrup worked for Dick Wilson as a construction superintendent. In 1964 he became general manager at Wilson's new Bedens Brook Club in New Jersey, but three years later joined golf architect Joe Lee as an assistant. In the summer of 1972 Northrup formed his own course design firm, based in Florida. In the 1980s, Northrup teamed with veteran PGA Tour golfer Bob Murphy on selected course designs.

Courses by Ward Northrup:

Alabama: Auburn Links (1992); Bent Brook GC (27 1988); Saugahatchee CC (1976).

Florida: Bentley Village CC (9 Par 3 1987); Buenaventura Lakes CC (9 Precision 1983); Deer Creek G&T Resort (Precision 1987); Eaglewood CC (Precision 1983); Grand Palms G&CC (1990); Imperial GC (West Cse 1979); Jupiter West GC (1980); Lake Ajay GC (Par 3); Maple Leaf Estates CC (Precision 1982); Moorings of Manatee GC (1985); River Run Golf Links (1987); Sabal Point CC (1981); Turkey Creek G&RC (1977); Victoria Estates GC (Precision 1989); Wekiva GC (1974); Windermere CC (1986).

Ward Northrup, 1988 COURTESY WARD NORTHRUP

Georgia: Ansley GC (1979); Lands West GC (1974); Summit Chase G&CC (1975); Willowpeg GC (1988).
Mississippi: Highland Lake Estates GC (9 1975).
Colombia: Barranquilla CC (1981); Club Campestre Cartagena (1981).

Courses remodeled or expanded by Ward Northrup:

Alabama: Green Valley CC (R. 1987); Woodward CC (R. 1987).
Florida: CC of Naples (R. 1985); Jupiter Dunes GC (R.); Lake Worth GC (R. 1991); Naval Training Center GC (A.3rd 9 1982); West Palm Beach CC (R. 1991).
Georgia: Bowden Muni (A.9 1974); Bull Creek G Cse (A.3rd 9 1989); Sunset Hills CC (A.9 1975).

Dick Nugent, 1980
COURTESY GCSAA

RICHARD P. NUGENT
(1931–   ), ASGCA, PRESIDENT 1981

BORN: Highland Park, Illinois.

Dick Nugent received a Bachelor's degree in landscape architecture in 1958 from the University of Illinois and then worked for six years with golf architect Robert Bruce Harris. In 1964 he and Kenneth Killian, another Harris assistant, formed a course design partnership that actively experimented with such design techniques as computer planning of automatic irrigation and the use of waste water in turf maintenance. In the early 1980s the two dissolved their partnership and Nugent founded his own practice, based in Long Grove, Illinois.

Aided by a young staff that included, at various times, associates Bob Lohmann, Bruce Borland and Jim Engh, as well as his own son Tim, Nugent adapted computer technology into golf course design. He also tried some daring and unusual designs, including a neo-Scottish layout on flat Illinois farmland outside Chicago and

a sandy Pine Valley-style nine-hole course on the shores of Lake Michigan.

Courses by Dick Nugent (All with Ken Killian unless otherwise indicated):

Florida: Silver Lakes GC (*solo*).
Hawaii: Minami GC (1992 *solo*).
Illinois: Arboretum GC (1990 *solo*); Buffalo Grove GC (1968); Bull Valley GC (1989 *solo*); Channahon GC (1992 *solo*); Concord Green GC (9 Par 3 1964); Edgebrook GC (1967); Forest Preserve National GC (1981); Glendale Lakes GC (1987 *solo*); GC of Illinois (1987 *solo*); Greenshire GC (Par 3 1964); Ivanhoe C (1991 *solo*); Kemper Lakes GC (1979); Moon Lake GC (1973); Norris A. Aldeen G Cse (1992 *solo*); Oak Brook Hills GC (1987 *solo*); Poplar Creek GC; River Oaks GC (1971); Robert A. Black GC (9 Precision 1979); Royal Fox GC (1990 *solo*); Seven Bridges GC (1991 *solo*); Shewami CC (1986 *solo*); Vernon Hills GC (9 1979); Warren Park GC (Precision); Weber Park GC (9 Par 3 1973); Western Illinois University GC (9 1971).
Indiana: Oak Meadow G&TC (1972); Sand Creek C (1979); Woodmar CC (1982).
Michigan: [The] Dunes C (9 1991 *solo*); [The] Fortress GC (1992 *solo*).
Ohio: Shelby Oaks GC (1964); Sugar Creek GC.
Texas: Chester W. Ditto Muni (1982); Mission CC (1983).
Virginia: Poplar Forest GC (9 1980).
Wisconsin: Abbey Springs GC (1972); Evergreen GC (1973); Lake Arrowhead GC (1984); Tuckaway CC (1967).

Courses remodeled or expanded by Dick Nugent (All with Ken Killian unless otherwise indicated):

Arkansas: Pleasant Valley CC (R. *solo*).
Illinois: Big Run CC (R. *solo*); Bob O'Link CC (R. 1968); Butler National GC (R. *solo*); Butterfield CC (R. 1969); CC of Decatur (R. *solo*); Chevy Chase CC (R.); Chick Evans GC (R. *solo*); Countryside GC (R. 1978); Crystal Lake CC (R. 1980); Deerpath Park GC (R. 1971; R. 1981; R. 1984 *solo*); Elgin CC (R. 1978); Evanston GC (R. 1972); Exmoor CC (R. 1969); Fox Lake CC (R. 1973); Geneva GC (R. *solo*); Glencoe GC (R. 1964; R. 1982); Glen View C (R. *solo*); Green Acres CC (R.1 1982); Highland Park GC (R.5 1977); Hillcrest CC (R. 1979); Hinsdale GC (R.

solo); Indian Boundary GC (R. *solo*); Joe Louis The Champ GC [FKA Pipe O'Peace GC] (R. 1987 *solo*); Lake Shore CC (R. 1971); Lansing Sportsman's C (A.9 1976); Lincolnshire CC (Cses No. 1 & 2, R. 1964); Marquette Park GC (R. *solo*); Marriott Lincolnshire GC (R.2 1981); McHenry CC (R.1 1970); Medinah CC (Cse No. 3, R. 1970); Midlothian CC (R.); Naval Training Center GC (A.9 1971); Northmoor CC (R. *solo*); North Shore CC (R.); Oak Park CC (R. *solo*); Onwentsia C (R. 1969); Park Ridge CC (R.3 1966); Pinecrest G&CC (R. 1979); Prestwick CC (R. *solo*); Ravinia Green CC (R. 1973); Ridge CC (R. 1972); River Oaks GC (R. *solo*); Riverside GC (R. *solo*); Ruth Lake CC (R. 1980; R.1 1984 *solo*); Scovill GC (R. 1992 *solo*); Silver Lake CC (North Cse, R.1 1978); Skokie CC (R. 1973); South Side CC (R. *solo*); Sportsman G&CC (R.); Spring Creek GC (R.9 A.9 1966); Sunset Valley GC (R. 1977); Thorngate CC (R. *solo*); Twin Orchards CC (Red Cse, R.); Urbana G&CC (R. *solo*); Vernon Hills GC (R.); Villa Olivia CC (R. 1975); Westmoreland CC (R.); White Pines CC (East & West Cses, R. 1982); Wilmette Park GC (R. 1979).
Indiana: Burke Memorial GC (R. 1966); Youche CC (R. 1992 *solo*).
Iowa: Finkbine GC (R. *solo*); Wakonda C (R. 1987 *solo*).
Kansas: Topeka Public G Cse (R.3 1987, *solo*).
Michigan: Berrien Hills CC (R. 1965); Lost Lake Woods GC (A.9 1974).
Minnesota: Meadowbrook GC (A.9 1966); Tartan Park GC (A.11 1986 *solo*); Town & Country C (R. 1986 *solo*).
Missouri: Algonquin GC (R.); Forest Hills CC (R. *solo*).
New York: Orchard Park CC (R. *solo*).
North Dakota: Fargo CC (R. *solo*).
Oklahoma: Dornick Hills G&CC (R. 1985 *solo*).
South Dakota: Minnehaha CC (R.6 1976; R. 1993 *solo*); Westward Ho CC (R.1 1985 *solo*).
Texas: Bent Tree CC (R. 1990 *solo*); Denton CC (R. *solo*); Great Southwest GC (R. 1983); Harlingen CC (R. 1985 *solo*); Midland CC (R. 1985 *solo*).
Wisconsin: Big Foot CC (R. 1986 *solo*); Blackhawk CC (R. 1982); Blue Mound G&CC (R. 1980); Brynwood CC (R. 1968); Hartford CC (R.9 A.9 1969);

Lacrosse CC (R. 1985 *solo*); Lake Lawn Lodge GC (R. 1990 *solo*); Maple Bluff CC (R. 1973); Nakoma CC (R.); North Shore CC (R. 1985 *solo*); Reedsburg CC (A.9 1978).

Willie Ogg, circa 1935 COLLECTION RON WHITTEN

WILLIAM OGG
(1889–1960)

BORN: Carnoustie, Scotland.
DIED: Tampa, Florida, at age 71.

Willie Ogg emigrated to the United States in 1914 and became professional-greenkeeper at Dedham (Massachusetts) Polo and Hunt Club, remaining there until 1921, when he took a similar position at Worcester Country Club. Ogg was an early graduate of the Massachusetts Agricultural College's Winter School for greenkeepers and a founding member of the PGA of America. An excellent player, he won several state Opens and the New England PGA title. Best known for the carefully balanced golf clubs he handmade and marketed, Willie Ogg also designed and remodeled several golf courses during his career.

Courses by Willie Ogg:

Georgia: James L. Key Muni (9 1921).
Massachusetts: Green Hill Muni (1930, NLE); Wilbraham CC (1927).

Courses remodeled or expanded by Willie Ogg:

Florida: Whispering Oaks CC (R.9 A.9 1958).
Massachusetts: Dedham Hunt & Polo C (R.).
New York: Albany CC (R., NLE).

CLARENCE OLIVER OLSON
(1939–)

BORN: Grindstone, South Dakota.

After obtaining a degree in landscape architecture in 1964, Cal Olson worked as

Cal Olson, 1991
COURTESY CAL OLSON

a land planner and civil engineer for fifteen years. During that time he handled land planning on a number of golf course residential projects, notably The Springs near Palm Springs, California. In late 1978 Olson formed his own golf design business, but handled primarily irrigation jobs until the late 1980s, when he landed several contracts. His design company was among the first to adapt software to assist in course design on computer.

Courses by Cal Olson:

California: Peri GC (1992); Southridge GC (1992); Tres Cerritos CC (1991).
Nevada: Painted Hills GC (1992).
Quebec: Cascade Canyon GC (1991).
Korea: Ichon G&CC (27 1992).
Vanuatu: Tiare G&CC (1990).

George O'Neil, circa 1920 COLLECTION RON WHITTEN

GEORGE O'NEIL
(1883–1955)

BORN: Philadelphia, Pennsylvania.
DIED: Miami, Florida, at age 72.

George O'Neil, one of the early American golf professionals, was employed with several Chicago-area clubs, including Midlothian, Beverly, Lake Shore and Edgewater. He was a fine teacher and helped develop the skills of the young Chick Evans.

O'Neil practiced golf architecture as a sideline for several years and at one time or another worked with Chicago club professionals-course designers Jack Daray,

Sr., Joseph A. Roseman and Jack Croke. He formed his own full-time practice with offices in Chicago and Cleveland in the 1920s, but closed them at the height of the Depression. Undaunted, O'Neil then became active in the promotion of professional football and was part owner of a team for a time.

The last twenty years of O'Neil's life were spent battling serious illnesses. His medical expenses were covered by friend and former pupil Albert D. Lasker, the Chicago advertising magnate for whom O'Neil had built Melody Farms GC.

Courses by George O'Neil:

Florida: El Conquistador GC (1918, NLE).
Illinois: Barrington Hills CC (1920), with *Jack Croke* and Joseph A. Roseman; Cedar Crest GC; Crystal Lake CC, with Joseph A. Roseman and *Jack Croke*; Green Acres CC; Melody Farms CC (1928, NLE), with *Jack Croke* and Jack Daray, Sr.; Robin Hood CC (NLE).
Indiana: South Bend CC.
West Virginia: [The] Greenbrier GC (Greenbrier Cse 1925).
Wisconsin: Maxwelton Braes GC, with Joseph A. Roseman.

Courses remodeled or expanded by George O'Neil:

California: Pasadena GC (R. 1920, NLE), with *Jack Croke*.
Illinois: Glen View GC (R.), with Joseph A. Roseman.
Virginia: CC of Virginia (James River Cse, R. 1938).

EDWARD LAWRENCE PACKARD
(1912–) ASGCA, PRESIDENT 1970

BORN: Northampton, Massachusetts.

Larry Packard received a degree in landscape architecture from Massachusetts State College in 1935 and worked as a landscape architect with the National Park Service in Maine, the U.S. Army Corps of Engineers in Massachusetts and the Chicago Park District.

In 1946 Packard joined the staff of golf architect Robert Bruce Harris, where he remained until 1954, when he formed the design firm of Packard and Wadsworth with Brent Wadsworth. This association later divided into two separate organizations, the design firm of Packard Inc. and

Larry Packard, 1970 COURTESY LARRY PACKARD

the construction firm of The Wadsworth Company.

Packard exerted a powerful influence on design trends, professional policy and innovations in the field of course architecture. He hastened the trend toward gentler sculpturing and pioneered free forms in shaping of course features. He played an important role in establishing his profession's outlook on American society and environmental concerns and was among the earliest advocates of the use of waste water for golf course irrigation.

Packard was joined in his practice by his son Roger in the early 1970s. He retired from the business in 1986 to Innisbrook G&CC in Florida, recognized for years as one of *Golf Digest's* Top 100 courses. That complex of 63 holes was considered by many to be his finest work, a classic example of integration of golf with clusters of condominiums. Like other "retired" golf architects, Packard planned several courses even while in retirement. In 1992 his Nueva CC in Guatemala was under construction.

Courses by Edward Lawrence Packard:

California: Leisure Village GC (9 Par 3 1977).
Florida: Countryside CC (27 1973), with Roger Packard; Cypress Run CC (1982); Eagle Creek G&TC (1982); Hilaman Park GC (1972), with Roger Packard; Innisbrook GC (Copperhead Cse 1974, with Roger Packard; Island Cse 1970; Sandpiper Cse, 27 1972, with Roger Packard).
Illinois: Apple Valley CC (9 Par 3 1959); Belk Park GC (9 1957, with Brent Wadsworth; A.9 1970); Brookhill GC (9 1971); Carlinville GC (9 1960); Chanute AFB GC (9 1959); Coal Creek CC (9 1958, with Brent Wadsworth; Countryside West GC (9 1966); Crestwicke CC (1972), with Roger Packard; Da-De-Co GC (9 Par 3 1960); Deer Creek GC (1974), with Roger Packard; Deerfield Park GC

(1963); Earl F. Elliot Park GC (1965); Elgin CC (1968); Faries Park GC (1964); Granite City GC (9 1958), with Brent Wadsworth; Hickory Point GC (1970); Hinsdale Par 3 GC (9 Par 3 1962); Kellogg GC (27 1974), with Roger Packard; [The] Ledges CC; Lick Creek GC (1972), with Roger Packard; Lincolnshire Fields GC (1969); Milford GC; Mission Hills CC (1975), with Roger Packard; Oak Hills CC (9 1975); Palatine Hills GC (1965); Pekin CC (1963); Prestwick CC (1963); Ravinia Green CC (1962); Rend Lake GC (27 1974), with Roger Packard; Shiloh Park GC (9 1963); Spartan Meadows GC (1972); Springbrook GC (1973), with Roger Packard; Turnberry CC (1972), with Roger Packard; Urban GC (9 Par 3 1962); Urban Hills CC (1962); Vermillion Hills CC (9 1959), with Brent Wadsworth; Wagon Wheel GC (9 Par 3 1961); Wedgewood GC (1970); Westlake CC (9 1958), with Brent Wadsworth; Wildwood Park GC (9 Par 3 1965).
Indiana: Indian Village CC (9 1962).
Iowa: A. H. Blank GC (9 1971; A.9 1980, with Roger Packard); Beaver Hills CC (1971); Echo Valley G&CC (1970); Sunnyside CC (1968).
Kentucky: Audubon State Park GC (9 1965); Boots Randolph GC (1972); Lake Barkley State Park GC; Midland Trail GC (1965); Pennyrile Forest State Park GC (9 1963).
Michigan: Bay City CC (1965); Hampshire CC (1961); L'Anse GC (9 1962); Leslie Park GC (1967); Spring Meadows CC (1965), with Brent Wadsworth.
Minnesota: Theodore Wirth GC (A.9 1970).
Missouri: Westmoreland G&CC (9 1967); Whiteman AFB GC (9 1958), with Brent Wadsworth.
Nebraska: Benson Park GC (1964); Platteview CC (1968).
New Jersey: Leisure Village GC (9 Par 3 1969); Woodlake G&CC (1972).
New York: Riverside CC (9 Par 3 1964); Wayne CC (9 1957, with Brent Wadsworth; A.9 1965).
North Dakota: Maple River GC (9 1966).
Ohio: Burning Tree GC (9 Par 3); Rawiga CC (9 1959); Silver Lake CC (1959), with Brent Wadsworth; Military GC, Wright-Patterson AFB (9 1958), with Brent Wadsworth.
South Dakota: Elmwood Park GC (1960); Westward Ho! CC (27 1958).

Tennessee: McMinnville CC (1969).
Wisconsin: Antigo & Bass Lake CC (1961); Baraboo CC (9 1961); Brown County GC (1966); Chaska GC (1975), with Roger Packard; Iola Community GC (9 1966); Lincoln Hills CC (9); Mascoutin GC (1973), with Roger Packard; Naga-Waukee Park GC (1966); Oakwood Park GC; Peninsula State Park GC (1963); Rib Mountain Lodge GC (9 Par 3 1961); River Island GC (9 1961); Skyline GC (9 1956), with Brent Wadsworth; Stevens Point CC (1968; R. 1975); Tumblebrook GC (1963); Wausau GC (1965); Westview CC (1966).
South Korea: Bomun Lake GC (1978), with Roger Packard.
Venezuela: El Morro GC (1984), with Roger Packard.

Courses remodeled or expanded by Edward Lawrence Packard:

Florida: Seven Lakes CC (R. 1977).
Illinois: Barrington Hills CC (R. 1964); Bergen Park GC (R. 1962); Biltmore CC (R. 1972); Bloomington CC (R. 1970); Bob O'Link CC (R. 1964); Brookwood CC (R. 1976), with Roger Packard; Bryn Mawr GC (R. 1964); Bunn Park GC (R. 1967); Butterfield CC (R. 1962); Calumet CC (R.12 1957), with Brent Wadsworth; Champaign CC (R. 1960); CC of Decatur (R. 1964; R. 1970; R. 1982, with Roger Packard); Danville CC (A.9 1958), with Brent Wadsworth; Deerpath Park GC (R. 1966); Glenview Park GC (R. 1961); Greenville CC (R. 1958), with Brent Wadsworth; Hillsboro CC (R.9 A.9 1974); Hinsdale GC (R. 1975), with Roger Packard; Illini CC (R. 1977); Indian Spring GC (A.9 1971); Inverness GC (R. 1967); Inwood GC (R. 1970); Jacksonville CC (A.9 1964); Knollwood C (R. 1975), with Roger Packard; La Grange CC (R. 1976); Mattoon G&CC (A.9 1971), with Roger Packard; Medinah CC (Cse No. 1, R. 1969); Mount Hawley CC (R. 1981), with Roger Packard; Naperville CC (R. 1982); North Shore CC (R. 1969); Northmoor CC (R. 1965); Olympia Fields CC (North Cse, R. 1982; South Cse, R. 1982); Pontiac Elks GC (A.9); Ridgemoor CC (R. 1967; R. 1976, with Roger Packard); River Forest CC (R. 1968); Riverside GC (R. 1977); Ruth Lake CC (R. 1961; R. 1975, with Roger Packard); Spring Lake CC (A.9 1966); Sunset Hills CC

(A.9 1957), with Brent Wadsworth; Twin Orchards CC (White Cse, R. 1966); Woodridge CC (R. 1962); Woodruff GC (R. 1966).

Indiana: Gary CC (R. 1958), with Brent Wadsworth; Purdue University GC (South Cse, R. 1968).

Iowa: Burlington GC (R.9 A.9 1969); Fort Dodge CC (R.9 1958), with Brent Wadsworth; Waveland GC (R. 1965).

Kentucky: Big Spring CC (R. 1964); Cherokee GC (R. 1962); Cole Park GC (R. 1970); Iroquois GC (A.9 1963); Seneca Muni (R. 1962); Standard CC (A.9 1964).

Michigan: Cascade Hills CC (R. 1967); CC of Lansing (R. 1968; R. 1977, with Roger Packard); Lochmoor C (R. 1960); Midland CC (R. 1965; R. 1970); Pine Grove CC (A.9 1962); Western G&CC (R. 1961).

Minnesota: Columbia Park Muni (R. 1965); Westfield CC (R. 1960), with Brent Wadsworth.

Missouri: Cape Girardeau CC (R.2 A.2 1957), with Brent Wadsworth; Columbia CC (R. 1970); Jefferson City CC (A.9 1964, R. 1968); Sunset CC (R. 1962).

Ohio: Canton Park District GC (A.9 1975); Fairlawn CC (R. 1960); Fremont CC (R. 1960); Rosemont GC (A.9 1959); Twin Base GC, Wright-Patterson AFB (R. 1958).

South Dakota: Minnehaha CC (R. 1961).

Wisconsin: Bulls Eye CC (A.9 1963); Chenequa GC (A.9 1963); Lacrosse CC (R. 1970); Merrill Hills CC (R. 1972); Minocqua CC (R.9 A.9 1964); Muskego Lakes CC (R. 1980), with Roger Packard; Racine CC (R. 1977), with Roger Packard; Watertown CC (A.9 1961), with Brent Wadsworth.

ROGER BRUCE PACKARD (1947–   ), ASGCA

BORN: Chicago, Illinois.

Roger Packard, son of golf course architect Edward Lawrence Packard, graduated from Colorado State University with a degree in landscape architecture. As an undergraduate, he worked summers in course construction for The Wadsworth Company of Plainfield, Illinois, and upon graduation joined his father's golf course design firm. He took an active role in all Packard's designs and gradually took over

major responsibility for the firm. After his father went into semiretirement, Roger designed several notable layouts, including Sweetwater CC in Texas (the first championship layout designed primarily for women and home of the LPGA for a number of years), Eagle Ridge (South) in Galena, Illinois, a corecipient of *Golf Digest*'s Best New Resort Course Award in 1984, and Cantigny Golf Club, *Golf Digest*'s Best New Public Course of 1989.

In the late 1980s Packard enlisted the aid of two-time U.S. Open champion Andy North as a design consultant.

Courses by Roger Packard (All with Edward Lawrence Packard unless otherwise indicated):

Florida: Countryside CC (27 1973); Hilaman Park GC (1972); Innisbrook GC (Copperhead Cse 1974; Sandpiper Cse, 27 1972).

Illinois: Boughton Ridge GC (9 Precision 1981 *solo*); Cantigny GC (27 1988 *solo*); Crestwicke CC (1972); Deer Creek GC (1974); Eagle Brook CC (*solo*); Eagle Ridge GC (East Cse 9 1992 with *Andy North*; North Cse 1977 *solo*; South Cse 1984 *solo*); Ironwood CC (1990 *solo*); Kellogg GC (27 1974); Lake Barrington Shores GC (1977 *solo*); Lick Creek GC (1972); Mission Hills CC (1975); Naperbrook GC (1991 *solo*); Oak Brook G Cse (1982 *solo*); Prairie Vista G Cse (1991 *solo*); Rend Lake GC (27 1974); Springbrook GC (1973); Turnberry CC (1972).

Indiana: Briar Ridge CC (27 1981 *solo*); Clearcrest CC (*solo*).

Kansas: Sunflower Hills GC (1977 *solo*).

Missouri: [The] Players C at St. Louis [FKA Crescent CC] (1979 *solo*).

Texas: Oakmont CC (1986), with Don January; Riverside C (1984 *solo*); Sweetwater CC (27 1983 *solo*).

Wisconsin: Chaska GC (1975); Mascoutin GC (1973); Riverbend GC (9

Precision 1983 *solo*); Timber Ridge CC (1976 *solo*); Trappers Turn GC (1991), with *Andy North.*

South Korea: Bomun Lake GC (1978).

Thailand: Lakeview G&YC (*solo*); Lam Luk Ka CC (*solo*).

Venezuela: El Morro GC (1984).

Courses remodeled or expanded by Roger Packard (All with Edward Lawrence Packard unless otherwise indicated):

Iowa: A. H. Blank GC (A.9 1980).

Illinois: Barrington Hills CC (R. 1982 *solo*); Brookhill GC (A.9 1977 *solo*); Brookwood CC (R. 1976); Bryn Mawr GC (R. 1985 *solo*); CC of Decatur (R. 1982); Edgewood Valley CC (R. *solo*); Green Acres CC (R. *solo*); Hinsdale GC (R. 1975); Knollwood C (R. 1975; R. 1982); La Grange CC (R. 1980 *solo*); Mattoon G&CC (A.9 1971); Medinah CC (Cse No. 3, R. A.3 1986 *solo*); Mount Hawley CC (R. 1981); Naperville CC (R. *solo*); North Shore CC (R. 1982 *solo*); Olympia Fields CC (North Cse, R.3 1984 *solo*); Ridgemoor CC (R. 1976); River Forest CC (R. *solo*); Rolling Green CC (R. *solo*); Ruth Lake CC (R. 1975); Shady Lawn GC (R. 1979 *solo*); Short Hills CC (R. 1982 *solo*); Sportsman G&CC (A.3rd 9 1991 *solo*).

Iowa: Des Moines G&CC (Blue Cse, R. *solo*; Red Cse, R. *solo*); Dubuque G&CC (R.9 1979 *solo*); Hyperion Field C (R. 1976 *solo*).

Michigan: CC of Lansing (R. 1977); Riverside CC (R.9 A.9 1982 *solo*).

Missouri: Columbia CC (A.9 1986 *solo*).

Wisconsin: Big Foot CC (R. 1981 *solo*); Muskego Lakes CC (R. 1980); Racine CC (R. 1977); Spring Green GC (A.3rd 9 1991), with *Andy North*; West Bend CC (R. 1981 *solo*).

Roger Packard, 1980 COURTESY GOLF WORLD

HAROLD D. PADDOCK, SR. (1888–1969)

BORN: San Diego, California.
DIED: Aurora, Ohio, at age 81.

Professional golfer Harold Paddock owned and operated Moreland Hills Country Club and Aurora Country Club in Cleveland, Ohio. He began designing courses in the 1920s and reactivated his practice in the 1950s, doing a number of courses in the Cleveland area. Paddock's son Harold Jr. was a fine amateur golfer and later served as professional at Moreland Hills.

Courses by Harold Paddock:

Michigan: Demor Hills CC (1963).
Missouri: Westwood CC (1928).
Ohio: Astorhurst CC; Avon Oaks CC; Breathnach CC; Butternut Ridge CC (1929); Cherry Ridge GC; Chestnut Hill CC (9); Columbia Hills CC (1928); CC of Hudson; Grantwood CC; Griffiths Park GC; Hawthorne Hills CC (27 1963); Highland Springs CC; Hinckley Hills GC (1964); Homelinks GC; Ironton CC (9 1951); Ironwood GC (1968); Mercer County Elks CC (1960); Par Three GC (Par 3); Pine Hills GC (27 1958); Pine Ridge CC; Riverby Hills GC (1959); Spring Valley CC (1928); Sugarbush CC (1965); Valleaire GC; Valley View GC (1956); Willard CC (1959).

Courses remodeled or expanded by Harold Paddock:

Florida: Mount Dora GC (R.9 A.9 1959, NLE).
Michigan: Hillsdale G&CC (R.9 A.9 1927).

ARNOLD DANIEL PALMER
(1929–   )

BORN: Latrobe, Pennsylvania.

Arnold Palmer, son of the pro-greenkeeper at Latrobe Country Club, won four Masters, two British Opens, one U.S. Open and one U.S. Amateur as well as the hearts of millions of fans. He also became the first golfer to win a million dollars on the PGA Tour. He was generally credited with being a major force in the golf boom of the 1960s through his charismatic appearance and dashing devil-may-care style of play.

In the late 1960s Palmer purchased Bay Hill Club in Orlando, Florida, and over the years remodeled many of its holes. He worked as a design consultant with golf architect Frank Duane from 1969 to 1974, then became associated with architect Edwin Seay, founding the Palmer Course Design Co. with offices in Florida in 1975. While continuing to play on the PGA Tour and later the PGA Senior Tour, Palmer left most design activities to the professional architects in his firm.

Arnold Palmer, 1971 COURTESY GOLF WORLD

In 1984 Palmer's company built the first golf course ever opened in the People's Republic of China.

Courses by Arnold Palmer (All with Ed Seay unless otherwise indicated):

Alabama: Cotton Creek C (1987).
Arizona: Arrowhead CC (1986); [The] Legend GC (1988); Mesa del Sol GC (1982).
California: Aviara GC (1991); Half Moon Bay CC (1973), with Frank Duane; Ironwood CC (Short Cse [9 Par 3] 1975); Mission Hills G&CC (New Cse 1979); PGA West GC (Palmer Cse 1986).
Colorado: Bear Creek GC (1986); [The] Broadmoor GC (South Cse 1976); Lone Tree GC (1986).
Florida: Adios CC (1985); Deering Bay Y&CC (1991); Isleworth G&CC (1986); Mariner Sands GC (Green Cse 1973), with Frank Duane; Marsh Landing GC (1986); Matanzas Woods GC (1986); Mill Cove GC (1990); Monarch CC (1987); Orchid Island G & Beach C (1990); Pine Lakes GC (1980); [The] Plantation at Ponte Vedra GC (1987); PGA National GC (The General Cse 1985); Saddlebrook G&TC (Palmer Cse 1986); Spessard Holland GC (Precision 1977); Suntree CC (Challenge Cse 1987); Wildcat Run CC (1985).
Georgia: Eagle Watch GC (1989); [The] Landings at Skidaway Island (Magnolia Cse 1973, with Frank Duane; Marshwood Cse 1979); Whitewater Creek GC (1988).
Hawaii: Hapuna Beach GC (1992); Hawaii Prince GC (1993); [The] Highlands GC (1992); Honolulu CC (1976), with Frank Duane; Kapalua GC (Bay Cse 1974, with Frank Duane; Village Cse 1980); Turtle Bay CC (New Cse 1992).

Illinois: Spencer T. Olin Community G Cse (1989); White Eagle GC (1989).
Kentucky: Lake Forest GC (1992).
Louisiana: [The] Bluffs on Thompson Creek CC (1988).
Maryland: Prince Georges G&CC (1981).
Michigan: Shanty Creek GC (Legend Cse 1985).
Missouri: North Port National G&CC (1992).
Montana: Big Sky GC (1974), with Frank Duane.
Nevada: Angel Park GC (Mountain Cse, routing 1989; Palm Cse, routing 1990); Dayton Valley CC (1991).
New Jersey: Laurel Creek CC (1990).
North Carolina: Cullasaja C (1989); Pinehurst Plantation GC (1992); TPC at Piper Glen (1989).
Pennsylvania: Commonwealth National GC (1990); Eagle Rock GC (1992).
South Carolina: Musgrove Mill GC (routing 1988); Myrtle Beach National GC (North Cse 1973; South Cse 1973; West Cse 1973), with Frank Duane; Sea Pines Plantation GC (Club Cse 1976), with Frank Duane.
South Dakota: Dakota Dunes GC (1991).
Texas: Barton Creek C (Lakeside Cse) [FKA Hidden Hills GC] (1986); GC at Fossil Creek (1987); [The] Woodlands Inn & CC (Palmer Cse 1989).
Utah: Jeremy Ranch GC (1980).
Virginia: Kingsmill GC (Plantation Cse 1986).
Washington: Semiahmoo GC (1986).
Wisconsin: Geneva National G&CC (Palmer Cse 1991).
Wyoming: Teton Pines G Cse (1987).
British Columbia: Whistler Village GC (1980).
Australia: Sanctuary Cove GC (1989).
China: Chung-Shan GC (1985).
Ireland: Kildare GC (1991); Tralee GC (1985).
Italy: Cà'Della Nave GC (1987).
Japan: Ajigasawa GC (A Cse 1992; B Cse 1993); Aso GC (A Cse 1990; B Cse 1990); Furano GC (1975); Furano Kogen GC (1976); Iga Ueno CC (1974); Kanegasaki GC (1990); Manago CC (1974); Minakami Kogen GC (Lower Cse 1986; New Cse 1992; Upper Cse 1986; Niseko GC (1986); Niseko Kogen GC (1986); Nishi Biwako GC; Shimotsuke CC (1975); Tsugaru Kogen GC (1986).
Korea: Eunhwasam CC (1992).
Malaysia: Damai Beach GC (1992).

Taiwan: Formosa First GC (1987); Formosa Yangmei G&CC (1992).
Thailand: Bangpoo GC (1981).

Courses remodeled or expanded by Arnold Palmer (All with Ed Seay unless otherwise indicated):

Arizona: Scottsdale CC (R. A.3rd 9 1986).
California: Rancho Murieta GC (North Cse, R. 1988).
Colorado: Cherry Hills CC (R. 1977).
Florida: Bay Hill C (R. 1980 *solo*); Hidden Hills CC (R. 1988); Meadowood G&TC (R. 1987); Pasadena Y&CC (R. 1990); Saddlebrook G&TC (Saddlebrook Cse, R. 1986).
Georgia: Atlanta Athletic CC (Highlands Cse, R. 1989); Forest Hill GC (R. 1986); Stouffer's PineIsle Resort GC (R. 1988).
Hawaii: Waialae CC (R. 1991).
North Carolina: Quail Hollow CC (R. 1985).
Oklahoma: Hillcrest CC (R. 1985).
Pennsylvania: Indian Lake GC (A.9 1968), with X. G. Hassenplug; Laurel Valley GC (R. 1988); Oakmont CC (R. 1978).
Virginia: Keswick C of Virginia (R. 1991).

GARY A. PANKS
(1941–)

BORN: Flint, Michigan.

Gary Panks, the son of a golf professional at Sault Ste. Marie, Michigan, received a B.S. degree in landscape architecture in 1964 from Michigan State University, where he had played on the golf team and served as its captain in 1963. A longtime competitive player, Panks by 1980 had won sixteen Amateur tournaments.

Panks worked for a short time as assistant superintendent at Michigan State University's golf courses and then held successive positions as a landscape architect or planning consultant with the New York State Roadside Development Department, Maricopa County (Arizona) Park Department, Bureau of Indian Affairs, Department of the Interior and Phoenix Parks Department. In 1978 he entered private practice as a golf course and landscape architect. In the mid-1980s he attracted national attention with his clever 18-hole putting course for Desert High-

lands GC, patterned after "the Himalayas," the huge practice putting surface at St. Andrews in Scotland.

In 1988 Panks teamed up with former U.S. Open and PGA champion David Graham and established Graham/Panks International. They were joined by Gary Stephenson and Mike Rhoads as design associates and planned courses in the United States, Australia, Canada and Thailand.

Courses by Gary Panks:

Arizona: Ahwatukee Lakes CC (Precision 1980); Antelope Hills GC (South Cse 1992); Casa Grande GC (9 1981); Desert Highlands GC (Putting Cse 1986); Riverview GC (9 1987); Sedona G Resort (1988); Silver Creek GC (1986); Sunbird GC (Precision 1987); Williams CC (9 1990).
Arkansas: Red Apple Inn GC (1981).
Nevada: Angel Park GC (Putting Cse 1991).
Virginia: Virginia Oaks G&CC (1992), with *David Graham.*
Australia: Turtle Point G&CC (1992), with *David Graham.*
Thailand: Burapha GC (1992), with *David Graham.*

Courses remodeled or expanded by Gary Panks:

Arizona: Arizona CC (R.); Aspen Valley CC (R.9 1989); Encanto Muni (R.); Fort Huachuca GC (A.9 1983); Paradise Valley (R.13 1984), with Geoffrey Cornish; Phoenix CC (R.14 1984); Pinetop CC (R. 1985); Rio Verde CC

(White Wing Cse, R. 1989); Rolling Hills GC, Tempe (A.9 1985).
British Columbia: Victoria GC (R.9, 1981; R.6, 1985).

JOHN A. PARK
(1879–1935)

BORN: Musselburgh, Scotland.
DIED: Easthampton, New York, at age 56.

Jack Park supervised construction at the Maidstone (New York) Golf Club in 1898 and then worked with his brothers Willie Jr. in Britain and Mungo II in Argentina before returning to Maidstone to become its professional in 1915. He assisted Willie in the design and construction of some courses following Willie's return to North America in 1916, including expansion of Maidstone.

MUNGO PARK
(1835–1904)

BORN: Musselburgh, Scotland.
DIED: Siloth, England, at age 69.

One of five sons and brother of Old Willie Park, Mungo Park learned golf at an early age, but abandoned it for a period of twenty years while he worked as a seaman. Returning to Musselburgh in the early 1870s, he found his golfing skills were unaffected by the long layoff, and he won the 1874 British Open on the course where he had been taught the game.

Gary Panks (right), with design partner David Graham, 1991 COURTESY GARY PANKS

Mungo Park spent the remainder of his life serving as a clubmaker and teacher at various British clubs. He laid out and remodeled several courses during this time, including Alnmouth Golf Club, where he served as professional for over fifteen years.

Courses by Mungo Park:

Northern Ireland: Tyneside GC, Newcastle (1879, NLE).

Courses remodeled or expanded by Mungo Park:

England: Alnmouth GC (R. 1896).
Scotland: Bruntsfield Links (R. 1898, NLE), with Willie Park.

MUNGO PARK II
(1877–1960)

BORN: Musselburgh, Scotland.
DIED: Musselburgh, Scotland, at age 83.

Mungo Park II, son of Old Willie Park and named for his uncle, served as professional at Dyker Meadow Golf Club in New York and Galveston Country Club in Texas around the turn of the century. Between 1901 and 1904 he returned to England and worked as director of the Chiltern Estates, where his brother Willie Jr. was managing director.

From 1904 to 1913 Mungo was employed as a club professional in Argentina, where he planned several golf courses. Following service with the British army during World War I, he returned to Argentina and laid out more courses, including Adolfo Siro Country Club for the Swift family of meat-packing fame. Altogether he claimed some fifty-nine courses of his own design in that country.

Mungo moved to the United States from Argentina in 1924 to escort Willie Jr., then fatally ill, home to Scotland. In 1925 he returned to the United States, completed Willie's unfinished courses and laid out a couple of his own. After that Mungo filled a number of professional berths in the East and in the Southwest. He returned to Scotland permanently in the 1930s and planned several changes at Musselburgh.

Courses by Mungo Park II:

New York: Hollow Brook G&CC; Port-au-Peck GC.
Vermont: St. Johnsbury CC (9 1923).
Argentina: Adolfo Siro CC; San Andres GC.

Courses remodeled or expanded by Mungo Park II:

Scotland: Royal Musselburgh GC (R. 1933).

WILLIE PARK
(1833–1903)

BORN: Musselburgh, Scotland.
DIED: Musselburgh, Scotland, at age 70.

Old Willie Park won the first British Open at Prestwick in 1860 as well as three subsequent Opens. Old Willie was involved in laying out golf courses on his own, with his brother Mungo and with son Willie Jr. It was difficult to distinguish between the work of Willie Park, Sr., and the earliest courses of his son.

Courses by Willie Park:

England: Berwick-upon-Tweed GC (1892); Headingly GC (1892); Hendon GC (1900), with Willie Park, Jr.; Muswell Hill GC (1893); Newbiggen-by-the-Sea GC (1895); Siloth-on-Solway GC (1894), with Willie Park Jr.; Sundridge Park GC (East Cse 1901; West Cse 1901), with Willie Park Jr.; West Middlesex GC (1891).
Ireland: Killarney GC (9 1883, NLE); Tramore GC (1894), with Willie Park, Jr.
Northern Ireland: Larne GC (9 1894); Portstewart GC (1893).
Scotland: Barberton GC (1893); Bathgate GC (1892); Biggar GC (1895); Crieff GC (1891); Duddington GC (1897), with Willie Park, Jr.; Glencorse GC (1890); Grantown GC (1890); Gullane GC (Cse No. 1 1892); Innellan GC (9 1895), with Willie Park, Jr.; Innerleithen GC (9 1985); Jedburgh GC (9 1892); Lauder GC (1896), with Willie Park, Jr.; Melrose GC (9 1982); Murrayfield GC (1896), with Willie Park, Jr.; Royal Aberdeen GC; Selkirk GC (9 1893); Shiskine GC (12 1896); St. Boswells GC (9 1890); Torwoodle GC (9 1895), with Willie Park, Jr.; West Lothian GC (1892); Western Gailes GC (1897), with Willie Park, Jr.

Courses remodeled or expanded by Willie Park:

England: Berkhamsted GC (R. 1900), with Willie Park, Jr.; Broadstone GC (R. 1898), with Willie Park, Jr.; Frinton GC (R.), with Willie Park, Jr.

Scotland: Bruntsfield Links (R. 1898, NLE), with Mungo Park; Dunbar GC (R. A.3 1880); Forres GC (R.)

Willie Park, Jr., circa 1910
COLLECTION RON WHITTEN

WILLIE PARK, JR.
(1864–1925)

BORN: Musselburgh, Scotland.
DIED: Edinburgh, Scotland, at age 61.

The name of Willie Park, Jr., is one of the most respected in the history of golf. He was a multifaceted personality, a talented and prolific golf architect, one of the greatest golfers of his day, an entrepreneur and businessman, a clubmaker, inventor and author. A big man physically, his influence on the game of golf was equally imposing.

As a boy, Willie often played golf at Musselburgh with Young Willie Dunn, who was also destined to make his mark on the history of course architecture. In 1880 Park served as assistant pro-greenkeeper under his Uncle Mungo at the Tyneside Club at Ryton, England. He took the job full-time in 1892 when Mungo returned to Alnmouth. In 1894 Willie returned to Musselburgh, joining his father in the club and ball-making firm of W. Park and Son. Continuing to refine his golf game, he won the British Open in 1887 and 1889 and also was runner-up in 1898.

Willie was a perfectionist. He believed that matches were settled by putting and would spend twelve hours without a break on a practice green. He brought the same intensity to his design work. He laid out links and courses with his father and uncle and later on his own with construction assistance from brothers Mungo II and Jack. Two of Park's courses, Sunningdale and Huntercombe, became landmarks in the history of golf course architecture. Huntercombe, of which Willie was a major stockholder and promoter, was among the first golf courses planned specifically for integration with housing, though the housing scheme was never executed and the project was a financial problem for Willie for many years.

Willie made two trips to the United States before the turn of the century, a six-month stay in 1895 and a shorter visit in 1896. He promoted the game, played exhibitions and laid out a few courses. When he finally returned to the States in 1916, course design was his main vocation, and he established a base in New York and later a branch office in Toronto. Except for a few visits home, Willie spent the remainder of his professional life in North America, designing or redesigning over seventy courses. He was assisted by a loyal crew of construction bosses and personally visited nearly all of his courses periodically during construction.

In the fall of 1923 Willie, stricken with illness, was taken back to Scotland by his brother Mungo. Little is known of the extent of his illness, but Willie was inactive from that point on, and he died in an Edinburgh hospital in May 1925.

In the course of his indefatigable career, Willie found time to write two books: *The Game of Golf* (1896) and *The Art of Putting* (1920). Part of each was autobiographical. Sir Guy Campbell called him the "doyen" of course architects and credited him with setting the standards adhered to by the countless designers who followed. Willie Park, Jr., was surely one of the virtuoso golf architects.

Courses by Willie Park, Jr.:

Arkansas: Hot Springs G&CC (Majestic Cse 1920).
Connecticut: CC of Farmington; CC of New Canaan (9); Madison CC (1909); New Haven CC; Shuttle Meadow CC (1916); Tumble Brook CC (9); Woodway CC (1916).
Florida: Alton Beach GC (NLE).
Illinois: Olympia Field GC (North Cse 1923).
Indiana: Highland G&CC (routing 1921).
Maine: Castine GC.
Maryland: Rolling Road GC (1921).
Massachusetts: CC of New Bedford (9 1902); Milton-Hoosic GC.
Michigan: Battle Creek CC; Flint GC (1917); Grand Rapids CC; Meadowbrook CC; Pine Lake CC (1921); Red Run GC.
New Hampshire: John H. Cain GC [FKA Newport CC] (9 1921).
New Jersey: Glen Ridge CC; Great Bay CC [FKA Sands CC] (9).

New York: Moonbrook CC (9 1918); St. Albans CC.
North Carolina: Grove Park Inn CC (9 1909).
Ohio: Congress Lake C; CC of Ashland; East Liverpool CC (9 1920); Sylvania CC (1917); Toledo CC.
Pennsylvania: Berkshire CC; Chartiers CC (1919); Green Valley CC (NLE); Indiana CC (1919, NLE); Penn State University GC (Blue Cse 1921); Philmont CC (South Cse 1907); Youghiogheny CC.
Rhode Island: Agawam Hunt C; Pawtucket GC.
Vermont: Shelburne Farms G Links (1895, NLE).
Alberta: Bowness GC; Calgary G&CC (1911); Calgary St. Andrews GC.
Manitoba: Southwood GC (1919); Winnipeg GC; Winnipeg Hunt C.
Nova Scotia: Brightwood G&CC; Kentville GC.
Ontario: Abitibi GC; Ottawa Hunt & GC; Toronto Hunt C (9); Weston G&CC (1920).
Quebec: Beaconsfield G&CC; Islemere G&CC; Laval-sur-le-Lac GC (9); Mount Bruno GC (1918); Royal Montreal GC (North Cse 1922, NLE); Royal Quebec CC (Royal Cse, 9 1925); Senneville CC (1919); Summerlea GC (27, NLE); Whitlock G&CC (1912).
Austria: Vienna GC (1901).
Belgium: Koninklijke GC; Royal Antwerp GC (1910).
England: Acton GC; Alton GC (1908); Barnton GC; Cooden Beach GC (1912); Coombe Hill GC (1909), with J. F. Abercomby; Formby GC; Gog Magog GC (1901); Hartepool GC (1906); Hendon GC (1900), with Willie Park; Huntercombe GC (1901); Knebworth GC (1908); Mid-Kent GC (1909); Notts GC (1900); Parkstone GC (1910); Richmond Park GC (NLE); Sheerness GC (9 1906); Shooter's Hill GC (1903); Silloth-on-Solway GC (1894), with Willie Park; South Herts GC (1899); Stoneham GC (1908); Sudbury GC (1920); Sundridge Park GC (East Cse 1901; West Cse 1901), with Willie Park; Sunningdale GC (Old Cse 1901); Temple GC (1909), with *James Hepburn*; Tynemouth GC (1913); Wembley GC; Wimbledon Common GC (1908).
France: Club de Rouen; Costebelle G Links; Evian GC (1905); Golf de Dieppe.
Ireland: Tramore GC (1894), with Willie

Park; Waterford GC (9 1912).
Monaco: Monte Carlo CC (1910).
Northern Ireland: City of Derry GC (1913).
Scotland: Ashludie GC; Bruntsfield Links, Davidson's Main GC (1923); Duddington GC (1897), with Willie Park; Gullane GC (Cse No. 2; Cse No. 3); Innellan GC (9 1895), with Willie Park; Lauder GC (1896), with Willie Park; Murrayfield GC (1896), with Willie Park; Old Ranfurly GC (1905); Torwoodlee GC (9 1895), with Willie Park; Totteridge GC; Western Gailes GC (1897), with Willie Park.
Wales: Brynhill GC (1920); Glamorganshire GC.

Courses remodeled or expanded by Willie Park, Jr.:

New Jersey: Atlantic City CC (R. A.13, NLE); Cherry Valley CC (R.).
New York: Maidstone C (A.9 1899; R.11 1925), with John A. Park.
Pennsylvania: Pittsburgh Field C (R. A.2 1923).
Quebec: Royal Montreal GC (South Cse, R. 1922, NLE).
England: Aldeburgh GC (R); Berkhamsted GC (R. 1900), with Willie Park; Brighton and Hove GC (R.); Broadstone GC (R. 1898), with Willie Park; Burhill GC (R.9); Chiselhurst GC (R. 1894); Frinton GC (R.), with Willie Park; Maidenhead GC (R.); Northampton GC (R.); Nottingham City GC (R. 1910); Richmond GC (R.); Seaford GC (R. 1906); Tooting Bec C (R.); Worplesdon GC (R.), with J. F. Abercromby.
France: Dinard GC (R.); Racing C de France (Valley Cse, R.).
Scotland: Burntisland Golf House C (R.); Carnoustie GC (R.); Montrose GC (Bloomfield Cse, R.; Medal Cse, R.); Royal Burgess G Society of Edinburgh (R. 1905); Shiskine GC (R.); Turnhouse GC (R.).
Wales: Brynhill GC (R.); Southerndown GC.

DAMIAN PASCUZZO
(1959–), ASGCA

BORN: Pottsville, Pennsylvania.

Damian Pascuzzo graduated from California Polytechnic State University in San Luis Obispo in 1981, receiving a Bachelor's degree in landscape architecture.

Damian Pascuzzo, 1991 COURTESY DAMIAN PASCUZZO

Upon graduation, he joined the golf design firm of Robert Muir Graves of Walnut Creek, California. By 1990 Pascuzzo was the senior design associate for Graves and was instrumental in introducing Computer Aided Design and Drafting (CADD) technology to the practice of golf course architecture. With Graves, he lectured on golf course design principles to members of the PGA of America. In 1992 he became Graves's partner.

Courses by Damian Pascuzzo (All as assistant to Robert Muir Graves):

California: Cherry Island GC (1989); La Purisima GC (1987); Mountain Springs G&CC (1990); Paradise Valley GC (1992); Santa Clara G&TC (1987); Seven Oaks CC (1991).

Oregon: Cedar Links (9 1986); River's Edge GC (9 1989); Seventh Mountain GC (1991).

Utah: Murray Parkway GC (1983); Twin Lakes GC (9 Precision 1983).

Washington: Avalon GC (27 1991); Canterwood G&CC (1988); Meadowood GC (1987).

Courses remodeled or expanded by Damian Pascuzzo (All as assistant to Robert Muir Graves):

California: Brentwood CC (R. 1986); Buchanan Field GC (R. 1986); Del Paso CC (R. 1985); Desert Island GC (R. 1987); El Macero CC (R. 1985); Green Tree GC (R. 1986); Half Moon Bay G Links (R. 1986); La Cumbre G&CC (R. 1988); Las Positas GC (R. A.3rd 9 1990); Mare Island GC (R. 1985); Marin G&CC (R. 1986); Mission Trails G Cse (A.9 1986); Morro Bay GC (R. 1987); North Ridge CC (R. 1986); Sandpiper G Links (R. 1986); Twin Lakes GC (R. 1985); Virginia GC (R. 1990); Woodbridge G&CC (R. 1985).

Washington: Lake Wilderness CC (R. 1986); Overlake G&CC (R. 1989); Royal Oaks CC (R. 1982).

JEROME KENDRICK PATE (1953–)

BORN: Macon, Georgia.

Jerry Pate burst upon the golf scene in the early 1970s by winning the U.S. Amateur in 1974 and the U.S. Open two years later. He also made a splash following his victory in the 1982 Tournament Players Championship by tossing golf architect Pete Dye and Tour Commissioner Deane Beman into a lake beside the 18th green before diving in himself.

A rotator cuff injury that required repeated surgery hampered Pate's playing career in the 1980s. Besides working part-time as a television commentator, Pate served as a consultant on course-design projects with several architects, including Dye, Tom Fazio and Ron Garl. His most successful collaborations were with designer Bob Cupp. In 1988 Pate formed his own design firm, based first in Pensacola and later in Birmingham, Alabama. His elder brother Jeff, a computer technician, made it possible for his firm to acquire and utilize state-of-the-art computer drafting and graphics in its designs. Another brother, Scott, also worked in the firm.

Courses by Jerry Pate:

Alabama: Liberty Park GC (1993), with Tom Fazio.

Florida: Bluewater Bay G&CC (A.3rd 9 1986), ass't Tom Fazio; Grasslands G&CC (1991), with Bob Cupp; Palm Beach Polo & CC (Dunes Cse), with Ron Garl; TPC at Sawgrass (Valley Cse 1987), ass't Pete Dye.

Michigan: Indianwood G&CC (New Cse 1988), with Bob Cupp.

Mississippi: Old Waverly GC (1988), with Bob Cupp.

Courses remodeled or expanded by Jerry Pate:

Florida: Tiger Point G&CC (East Cse, R.9 A.9 1984, with Ron Garl; R. 1989 solo).

Michigan: Indianwood G&CC (Old Cse, R. 1988), with Bob Cupp.

GEORGE A. PATTISON, JR.

"Pat" Pattison worked as pro-superintendent at Buckhannon (West Virginia) CC in the early 1950s. After moving to Florida at the end of the decade, he supervised construction of several courses and went on to form his own design and construction firm in Fort Lauderdale.

Courses by Pat Pattison:

Florida: Cooper Colony CC (Precision 1959); Crystal Lake CC (1969); Hidden Valley GC (Par 3 1957); Whispering Lakes GC (Par 3 1963).

Jerry Pate (right), with designer Bob Cupp, 1988 COURTESY STAN ALDRIDGE

Tom Pearson, 1990
COURTESY TOM
PEARSON

THOMAS PEARSON
(1949–), ASGCA

BORN: Lansing, Michigan.

Tom Pearson studied civil engineering and landscape architecture at Michigan State University. After graduating in 1972 he joined the golf architecture firm of Jack Nicklaus and eventually worked his way up to senior design associate status. As well as working on Jack Nicklaus–designed courses, Pearson did some designs on his own as part of Golden Bear Golf Services, a subsidiary of the Nicklaus corporation.

Courses designed by Tom Pearson (All as assistant to Jack Nicklaus unless otherwise indicated):

California: PGA West GC (Nicklaus Private Cse 1988; Nicklaus Resort Cse 1988).
Florida: Bear Lakes CC (Lakes Cse 1985); Grand Cypress GC (1984, A.3 Golf Academy 1985; A.3rd 9 1986); Ibis G&CC (Heritage Cse 1991, ass't Jack Nicklaus, Jr.; Legend Cse 1991; Tradition Cse 1992 *solo*); Loxahatchee C (1984); New Cse at Grand Cypress (1988).
Georgia: CC of the South (1987).
Illinois: Wynstone CC (1989).
Indiana: Sycamore Hills GC (1990).
Kentucky: Valhalla GC (1986).
Louisiana: CC of Louisiana (1986); English Turn G&CC (1988).
New Jersey: Shore Oaks GC (1990), with Johnny Miller.
South Carolina: Long Bay C (1988); Melrose GC (1987); Pawleys Plantation GC (1988).

Courses remodeled or expanded by Tom Pearson (All as assistant to Jack Nicklaus unless otherwise indicated):

Ohio: Firestone CC (South Cse, R. 1986).

STANLEY F. PELCHAR

Stanley Pelchar was active as a course designer in the 1920s, forming the Chicago firm of United States Architects Inc. with landscape architect Otto Clauss and engineer James Prendergast. In the 1950s Pelchar served as club manager at Biltmore Country Club in Barrington, Illinois.

Courses by Stanley Pelchar:

Illinois: Arrowhead GC [FKA Antlers CC]; Burnham Woods CC (1923); Garden of Eden GC (9); Lake Anna CC (NLE); Walnut Hills GC (9); Women's CC (NLE).
Indiana: Indian Ridge GC (1926); Surprise Park GC (9).
Wisconsin: Beloit CC; Four Seasons GC (9); Krueger Muni; Nemadji GC (9 1932); Oneida G & Riding C (1928); Turtle Lake GC.

*J. J. F. Pennink,
1936* COLLECTION RON
WHITTEN

JOHN JACOB FRANK PENNINK
(1913–1983), BIGCA

BORN: Delft, Netherlands.
DIED: Reading, England, at age 70.

Frank Pennink attended the Tonbridge School and Magdalen College of Oxford University. An excellent golfer, he won the English Amateur in 1937 and '38, the Royal St. Georges Challenge Cup in 1938, the Boy's International in 1930 and many other Amateur tournaments. He was also a member of the 1938 Walker Cup team and was on English international teams for several years, first as a player and later as a nonplaying captain. Pennink authored three golf books, *Home of Sports—Golf, Golfer's Companion* and *Frank Pennink's Choice of Golf Courses*.

In 1954 Pennink joined the established course-design practice of C. K. Cotton. He eventually headed the firm that come to be known as Cotton (C. K.), Pennink, Lawrie and Partners, Ltd. He was the most active designer in the firm, handling courses in Britain, the Continent, Africa and even the Far East. He was a founding member of the BIGCA and served for a time as its president.

Courses by J. J. F. Pennink:

Bangladesh: Dacca GC.
Channel Islands: Alderney GC.
Czechoslovakia: Sklo Bohemia Padebrady GC (9 1967).
Denmark: Kokkedal GC (1971); St. Knuds GC (1954), with C. K. Cotton.
England: Abbey Hill GC (1975), with C. D. Lawrie; Barnham Broom GC (1977); Basildon GC (1967); Bedlingtonshire GC (1972); Billingham GC (1968); Blackhill Wood GC, with D. M. A. Steel; Brandon Wood GC (1977); Brickendon Grange G&CC (1964), with C. K. Cotton; Broome Park GC (1977), with D. M. A. Steel; Bushey G & Squash C (9 1980), with D. M. A. Steel; Crookhill Park GC (1973); Edwalton GC (27 1981); Eton College GC (9 Precision 1973); Fakenham GC (9 1973), with C. D. Lawrie; Farnham Park GC (9 1974), with D. M. A. Steel; Fleming Park GC (Precision 1973); Halifax Bradley Hall GC, with D. M. A. Steel; Harrow School GC (9 Precision 1978), with D. M. A. Steel; Hastings GC; Hawkhurst G & CC (9 Precision 1978); Immingham GC (1975); Ingol G & Squash C (1984), with D. M. A. Steel; Lamberhurst GC, with C. K. Cotton; Lee Park GC (1954), with C. K. Cotton; Lowestoft GC; Oxton GC (1973); Pastures GC (9 Precision 1969); Rookery Park GC, with C. D. Lawrie; Saunton GC (West Cse 1975); Southwick Park GC (HMS Dryad) (1977), with C. D. Lawrie; Stockwood Park CC (1973); Stoneyholme GC (1974); Stowe School GC; Stressholme GC, with C. K. Cotton; Tewkesbury Park GC (1976); Twickenham GC (9 1976), with C. D. Lawrie; Walton Hall GC; Warrington GC; Wentworth GC (Short Nine, 9 1948), with C. K. Cotton; Winter Hill GC (1978), with C. D. Lawrie; Woburn G&CC (Duchess Cse 1976, with C. D. Lawrie and D. M. A. Steel; Duke Cse 1974, with C. D. Lawrie).
France: Club du Mans Mulsame; Golf du Nantes; Lacanau-l'Ardilouse GC (1980), with John Harris.
Germany: Nordsec-Kurhof GC (9); Margarethenhof am Tegernsee GC (1983).
Indonesia: Palembang GC.

Italy: Olgiata CC (27 1961), with C. K. Cotton.

Lebanon: GC of Lebanon (9, NLE).

Libya: Benghazi GC; Tripoli GC.

Malaysia: Royal Selangor GC (New Cse 1972); Sibu GC.

Morocco: Royal CC de Tangier.

Netherlands: Broekpolder GC (1983); Gelpenberg GC (9 1972); Geysteren G&CC (13 1974); Kleiburg GC (9 1974); Sallandsche GC "De Hoek"; Spaarwoude GC (1977).

Norway: Vestfold GC (9 1958).

Poland: Jablonna GC (9).

Portugal: Aroeira C de Campo [FKA Lisbon CC] (1974); Oporto GC; Palmares GC (1976); Vilamoura GC (1969); Vilamoura II GC [FKA Dom Pedro GC] (1975); Vimeiro GC (9).

Scotland: Livingston G&CC (1978), with C. D. Lawrie; Royal Aberdeen GC (Ladies Cse, 9); Westhill GC (1977), with C. D. Lawrie.

Singapore: Sentosa Island GC (Sentosa Cse); Singapore Island GC (New Cse 1963, with John Harris; Sime Cse).

Sweden: Halmstad GC (South Cse); Kungsbacka GC (13 1971); Stannum GC; Stora Lundby GC (1983).

Switzerland: Breitenloo GC (1964).

Wales: Cradoc GC (1967); Langland Bay GC (1982); St. Pierre G&CC (Old Cse 1962), with C. K. Cotton.

Zambia: Lusaka GC.

Course remodeled or expanded by J.J.F. Pennink:

Belgium: Keerbergen CC (R.)

England: Army GC (R. 1965), with C. K. Cotton; Ashbourne GC (R.); Bedale GC (R.); Blackwell Grange GC (R.); Bury St. Edmunds GC (R); Carlisle GC (R.); Chippenham GC (R.); Corhampton GC (R.9 A.9), with C. D. Lawrie; Darlington GC (R.); Dartford GC (R); Doncaster GC (R.); Ellesmere GC (R.); Frilford Heath GC (Green Cse, R.9 A.9 1968; Red Cse, R.9 A.9 1968), with C. K. Cotton; Hexham GC (R. 1956), with C. K. Cotton; Louth GC (R.), with C. K. Cotton; Mendip GC (A.9. 1965), with C. K. Cotton; North Downs GC (R.); Radcliffe-on-Trent GC (R.); Rodale GC (R.); Romsey GC (R.), with C. D. Lawrie; Royal Liverpool GC (R. 1966); Royal Lytham & St. Annes GC (R. 1952), with C. K. Cotton; Royal St. George's GC (R. 1975); Royal Wimbledon GC (R.), with C. D. Lawrie; Rushcliffe GC (R.); Rye GC (A.3rd 9); Saunton GC (East Cse, R. 1952), with C. K. Cotton; Shifnal GC (R.); Shrewsbury GC (R.); Stocksfield GC (R.); Warrington GC (R.); Wigan GC (R.).

France: Borden G&CC (R.9); Calais GC (R.); Marseille-Aix GC (A.9).

Germany: Duren GC (A.9 1975).

Ireland: Bandon GC (R.); Cork GC (R. 1975), with C. K. Cotton and C. D. Lawrie.

Italy: Menaggio E. Cadenabbia GC (R. A.5).

Netherlands: Lurgan GC (R.); Noordwilkse GC (R); Rosendealsche GC (R.9 A.9); Utrecht GC (R.).

Northern Ireland: Castlerock GC (A.9 1985); Dunmurry GC (R.); Newtonstewart GC (R.).

Scotland: Stornoway GC (R.).

Singapore: Singapore Island CC (Island Cse, R. 1965, with C. K. Cotton; Bukit Cse, R.).

Wales: Caernarvonshire GC (R.).

Jeremy Pern, 1991

JEREMY PERN
(1950–   ), BIGCA, ESGCA, FAGCA

BORN: Great Britain.

After graduating from Harper Adams with a National Diploma of Agriculture in 1972, Jeremy Pern worked on golf course construction projects for Southern Golf and Landscape in Great Britain for six years, during which time he worked on such courses as The Belfry in Great Britain and El Kantaoui in Tunisia. After a brief stint away from the golf industry, he returned to Southern Golf in 1980 and became a director and partner. He again handled major course-construction projects for such architects as Robert Trent Jones, Donald Harradine and Joan Dudok van Heel. He also tried his hand at a couple of designs of his own, done under a Southern Golf subsidiary, Sogo Design.

In 1986 Pern resigned and joined the newly formed golf design firm of famous French tournament golfer Jean Garaialde as a golf architect. Serving as his partner and director of architectural services, Pern assisted Garaialde in over a dozen design projects in the following four years.

In 1990 Pern left Garaialde's employ and established his own golf course design firm. Despite being a British subject, he preferred to maintain his base of operations near Paris and work on both the Continent and Great Britain.

Courses by Jeremy Pern (All with Jean Garaialde unless otherwise indicated):

England: Darmouth G&CC (27 1992 *solo*); Hinckley GC (1984), with *Ray Wilson.*

France: Golf d'Ableiges (27 1990); Golf d'Albi Lasbordes (1989); Golf d'Arc-en-Barrois (9 1989); Golf de Château de Pelly (1991); Golf de Cognac (1987); Golf de La Bresse (1990); Golf de Lacanau (9 1990); Golf de La Largue (27 1988); Golf de La Porcelaine (1988); Golf de La Wantzenau (1990); Golf de l'Estajean (6 1988); Golf de l'Esterel (9 1989); Golf de Rouret (4 1988); Golf de Salbris (1990); Golf de Saumane (1989); Golf de Toulouse-Seilh (Red Cse 1988; Yellow Cse [Precision] 1988); Golf de Tour d'Aling (1992 *solo*); Golf de Villare (1990); Golf du Charmeil à St. Quentin (1987); Golf du Pays de Brive (1992 *solo*); Golf du Roncemay (1990).

Switzerland: Golf de Mallamolliere (9 1992).

Courses remodeled or expanded by Jeremy Pern (All with Jean Garaialde unless otherwise indicated):

Austria: Brandlhof G&CC (R. 1983 *solo*).

DAVID PFAFF
(1939–   )

BORN: Urbana, Ohio.

Son of a high school golf coach, David Pfaff was a fine arts major at Ohio University. He was working as an industrial designer for an aircraft industry when he got word that an old family friend—golf architect Pete Dye—was looking for a draftsman. Pfaff caught up with Dye on Hilton Head Island, South Carolina (where Harbour Town was being built). Pete promptly put him to work drawing plans for several projects.

After working with Pete and his brother

Roy for several years, Pfaff was placed in charge of Eagle Creek, a municipal course in Indianapolis. He designed and supervised construction of the layout, which was billed as a Pete Dye design even though Dye had little involvement. The same was true of another Dye project, Carmel Valley Ranch in California. "If Pete likes what I did well enough to put his name on it, I'm pleased," said Pfaff when once asked whether he resented Dye getting credit for his work.

Following work with Dye on the construction of Oak Tree Golf Club in Oklahoma, the first Landmark Land project, Pfaff joined Landmark as an in-house course architect in the late 1970s. While continuing to work with Dye on some Landmark projects, Pfaff also designed and built several of that company's courses. Those, too, were generally advertised as Pete Dye designs, mainly because Pfaff's works closely resembled that of his mentor. In the mid-1980s Pfaff left Landmark and formed his own design business, based in Carmel, California.

Courses by David Pfaff:

California: Carmel Valley Ranch GC (1980), ass't Pete Dye; La Quinta Hotel GC (Dunes Cse 1981; Mountain Cse 1980), ass't Pete Dye; Mission Hills Resort GC (1987), ass't Pete Dye; Wildwing CC (1992).
Indiana: Eagle Creek Muni (27 1974), ass't Pete Dye; Harbour Trees GC (1973), ass't Pete Dye.
Kentucky: Oxmoor G & Steeplechase C (1990); Quail Chase G Cse (1989).
Louisiana: Belle Terre CC (1982).
Mississippi: Pine Island GC (1974), ass't Pete Dye.
North Carolina: Oak Hollow GC (1972), ass't Pete Dye.
Ohio: Fowler's Mill GC (1972), ass't Pete Dye and Roy Dye.

RICHARD MORGAN PHELPS
(1937–), ASGCA, PRESIDENT 1980

BORN: Colorado Springs, Colorado.

Dick Phelps received a Bachelor's and a Master's degree in landscape architecture from Iowa State University, graduating in 1963. He then entered private practice as a course designer in Iowa in partnership with engineer Donald Rippel. In 1966 Phelps joined the land-planning firm of Donald Brauer and Associates in Min-

Dick Phelps, 1980
COURTESY DICK PHELPS

neapolis, headed by landscape designer Donald Brauer. Phelps served as chief golf architect for Brauer and within a year became his partner, moved to Denver and established a branch office of Phelps, Brauer and Associates.

In 1973 Phelps and Brauer dissolved their partnership and Phelps formed a firm with his young design associate Brad Benz. In 1981 Mike Poellot joined the firm, but a year later Benz and Poellot left to form their own company in California. In 1990 Phelps formed a partnership with three-time U.S. Open champion Hale Irwin. Irwin established a St. Louis office, which was staffed by Phelps's son Rick and two other Phelps design associates, Emil Perret and Tom Kane, while Dick remained in the Denver suburb of Evergreen, handling his own designs and collaborations with Irwin.

Courses by Dick Phelps:

Arizona: Alta Mesa CC (1985); Fred Enke Muni (1983), with Brad Benz.
California: Cerro Plata CC (1993), with Hale Irwin.
Colorado: Centennial Downs GC (9 1986); Centre Hills GC (9 Precision); Coal Creek G Cse (1990); Copper Mountain GC (9 Precision 1980, A.9 1984, NLE), with Brad Benz; Cordillera Resort GC (1992), with Hale Irwin; Eagles Nest G Cse (9 1986, A.9 1989); Englewood Muni (1982), with Brad Benz and Mike Poellot; ENT AFB G Cse (9); Foothills GC (Foothills Cse 1971; Par 3 Cse 1971); Greenway GC (9 Par 3 1972); Heather Gardens CC (Precision 1973); Heather Ridge CC (1973); Indian Tree GC (27 1971); Lafayette GC (1992), with Hale Irwin; [The] Links GC (Precision 1986); [The] Meadows GC (1984), with Brad Benz and Mike Poellot; Mechaneer GC (1971); Perry Park CC (1972); Peterson Field GC (1965); Pine Creek G Cse (1987); Pub-Links Par 3 G Cse (9

Par 3); Raccoon Creek GC (1984), with Brad Benz and Mike Poellot; [The] Ranch G&CC (1974); [The] Ridges GC (1992); South Suburban Muni (27 1974); Westbank Ranch G Cse.
Florida: Southern Woods CC (1992), with Hale Irwin.
Idaho: Valley Ranch GC (1992), with Hale Irwin.
Illinois: Panther Creek CC (1992), with Hale Irwin.
Indiana: [The] Lakes at Sycamore (1992), with Hale Irwin.
Iowa: Charles City CC (1964); Dysart G&CC (9 1964); Glenhaven CC (9 1965); Jester Park GC (27 1968).
Minnesota: Braemar GC (27 1963); Orchard Gardens GC (9 Par 3 1965).
Nebraska: Elks CC, Columbus (9 1965); Heritage Hills GC (1981), with Brad Benz.
Nevada: Wildcreek GC (27 1980), with Brad Benz.
New Mexico: Elephant Butte G&CC (9 1975), with Brad Benz; Ladera GC (27 1980), with Brad Benz.
North Carolina: Blackrock CC (27 1992), with Hale Irwin; Lost Diamond Valley CC (9 Precision 1979), with Brad Benz.
North Dakota: Prairiewood GC (9 Precision 1976), with Brad Benz; Rose Creek Muni.
South Dakota: Southern Hills CC (1979), with Brad Benz.
Texas: Firewheel G Park (Old Cse 1983, with Brad Benz and Mike Poellot; Lakes Cse 1987); Forest Creek GC (1992); Indian Creek G Cse (Creek Cse 1983, with Brad Benz and Mike Poellot; Lakes Cse 1987); Iron Horse G Cse (1990).
Wyoming: Kemmerer GC (9).
Alberta: Maple Ridge GC (9 1968), with *Claude Muret*; Silver Springs G&CC (1970), with *Claude Muret*.
British Columbia: Juan de Fuca Muni (9 1990); Stonebridge GC.

Courses remodeled or expanded by Dick Phelps:

Colorado: Alamosa GC (A.9); Colorado Springs CC (A.9 1965); Dos Rios CC (A.9 1982), with Brad Benz and Mike Poellot; Eagle CC (R.9 A.9 1984); Fort Collins CC (R.2); Grand Lake GC (R.9 A.9 1978), with Brad Benz; Hiwan GC (R.); Lincoln Park GC (R.9); Loveland GC (R.); Meadow Hills GC (R. 1983), with Brad Benz; Rifle Creek GC (A.9

1990); Springhill GC (R.9 A.9 Precision 1977), with Brad Benz; Tiara Rado GC (R.9 A.9 1986); Valley CC (R. 1986); Valley Hi GC (R.9 1983).

Iowa: Waverly GC (R.9 A.9 1966); Willow Creek GC (A.3rd 9 1964).

Minnesota: Brookview CC (R. 1965); Enger Park GC (R.18 A.9); Lester Park GC (R.18 A.9); Southview CC (R. 1966).

Missouri: Windbrook CC (R.9 A.9).

Montana: Meadow Lake CC (R.9 A.9 1984); Riverside CC (A.9 1984), with Brad Benz.

New Mexico: Arroyo del Oso (A.3rd 9).

North Dakota: Heart River GC (A.9 R.9 1984), with Brad Benz and Mike Poellot.

South Dakota: Huron CC (A.9 R.9 1975), with Brad Benz.

Wyoming: Riverton CC (A.9 R.9 1982), with Brad Benz and Mike Poellot; White Mountain Muni.

Kyle Phillips, 1991
COURTESY KYLE PHILLIPS

KYLE DONALD PHILLIPS (1958–   ), ASGCA

BORN: Atlanta, Georgia.

Kyle Phillips honed his golfing skills near Kansas City, Missouri, where he played and worked at Swope Park, an A. W. Tillinghast design. In 1981 he graduated with honors from Kansas State University with a Bachelor of Landscape Architecture degree. Upon completion of his golf course remodeling plans for the city of Springfield, Missouri, in 1981, he was hired by Robert Trent Jones, Jr., as a design associate. He later became a vice president in the organization, representing the firm in projects in Europe, Africa and the northeastern United States.

Courses by Kyle Phillips (All as assistant to Robert Trent Jones, Jr.):

California: Adobe Creek G&CC (1991); Squaw Creek G Resort.

Kansas: Deer Creek GC (1989).

Maine: Sugarloaf GC (1986).

Virginia: Lansdowne G Resort (1991).

England: Wisley GC (27 1992).

Finland: Ruuhikoski GC (1992).

France: Golf de Bresson (1992); Golf de St. Donat (1992); Les Terrasses de Geneve G&CC (1985).

Portugal: Penha Longa GC.

South Korea: Yongpyeong GC.

Spain: Bonmont Catalunya GC (1990).

West Indies: Four Seasons Nevis Resort GC (1990).

Courses remodeled or expanded by Kyle Phillips (All as assistant to Robert Trent Jones, Jr., unless otherwise indicated):

California: Bodega Harbour GC (A.9 1987).

Missouri: Grandview Muni (R. 1980 *solo*).

Oregon: Heron Lakes GC (White Cse, A.9 1991).

France: Golf de Bondues (Blue Cse, A.9 1992).

GERALD W. PIRKL, ASGCA

Gerry Pirkl was granted a degree in engineering from the Dunwoody Institute of Minneapolis in 1961. After obtaining a degree in construction engineering by correspondence, he became a registered landscape architect in Minnesota and joined the landscape and golf design firm of Donald Brauer and Associates. As director of golf services for the firm, he was involved in over 100 golf course projects along with other Brauer designers Emil Perret and Paul Fjare. After twenty-eight years with Brauer, in 1989 Pirkl resigned, moved to the San Diego area and opened his own golf design firm.

Courses by Gerry Pirkl (All with Donald Brauer unless otherwise indicated):

California: Palacio del Mar GC (Par 3 1990 *solo*).

Iowa: Pheasant Ridge GC, and *Emil Perret* and *Paul Fjare*.

Minnesota: Arrowhead GC (1971); Bluff Creek GC (1971); Brooktree Muni; Dahlgreen GC (1971); Moorhead Village Green GC; Oak Harbor G&TC (9 1969), and *Emil Perret*; Rich Acres GC (9 Par 3 1979), and *Paul Fjare*; Roseville Cedarholm GC (9 Par 3 1969).

Gerry Pirkl, 1969
COURTESY ROBERT DEAN PUTMAN

Courses remodeled or expanded by Gerry Pirkl:

Iowa: Carroll CC (R.9 A.9).

Minnesota: Alexandria GC (R.9 A.9); Braemar GC (A.3rd 9); Brookview CC (R. A.9 Par 3) and *Emil Perret*; Chomonix GC (R.9 A.9); Highland Park GC (A.9 1971), and *Emil Perret*; Interlachen CC (R. 1968); Mankato GC (R.); Mendakota CC (R.3), and *Emil Perret*; Minneapolis GC (R.), and *Emil Perret*; Owatonna GC (A.9); Ruttger's Bay Lake GC (R.9 A.9); Soldier's Field GC (R.); Southview CC (R.), and *Emil Perret*; University of Minnesota GC (R.); Winona GC (A.9).

Ontario: Chappel G & Recreation C (R.9 A.9 1965).

GARY JIM PLAYER (1935–   )

BORN: Johannesburg, South Africa.

Gary Player turned professional in 1953 and won scores of tournaments throughout the world. One of only four men to complete golf's Grand Slam, he won three British Opens, three Masters, two PGA Championships and one U.S. Open. With Jack Nicklaus and Arnold Palmer, Player was considered one of golf's Big Three in the 1960s.

Gary Player, 1989
COLLECTION RON WHITTEN

Although he was always first and foremost a competitive golfer, Player served as a golf design consultant for over half a dozen different golf architects. At the height of his playing career, Player planned several courses in South Africa and Zimbabwe in collaboration with professional golfer Sid Brews and Dr. Van Vincent. In the early 1970s he was associated with American designers Ron Kirby and Arthur Davis. When Davis left the partnership, Player then teamed with Ron Kirby and Denis Griffiths.

In 1987 Player teamed for a time with Karl Litten, a former associate of von Hagge and Devlin. That relationship lasted two years. Player then formed his own golf design firm, Gary Player Design Co., headquartered in southern Florida. But Player competed full-time on the Senior PGA Tour and assigned the day-to-day architectural duties to Jeff Myers, a former Litten associate, and Joseph Duco III.

Courses by Gary Player:

Alabama: North River GC (1978), with Ron Kirby.

California: Mission Hills North G Cse (1991); Pacific GC (27 1988), with Karl Litten; Steele Canyon GC (27 1991).

Florida: Alaqua CC (1988), with Karl Litten; Belle Glade G&CC (1987), with Karl Litten; [The] Classics G Cse (1992); Cypress Knoll GC (1991); Laurel Oak CC (1990); Overoaks CC (1986), with Karl Litten.

Georgia: Berkeley Hills CC (1971), with Arthur Davis and Ron Kirby; River North G&CC (1973), with Arthur Davis and Ron Kirby; Royal Oaks GC (9 1971), with Arthur Davis and Ron Kirby.

Maryland: River Run GC (1991).

Massachusetts: White Cliffs CC (Precision 1986), with Karl Litten.

Missouri: Tapawingo GC (1992).

South Carolina: Blackmoor GC (1991); Dolphin Head GC (1973), with Arthur Davis and Ron Kirby; Hilton Head National GC (1989); Marsh Point GC (1976), with Ron Kirby; River Falls Plantation GC (1991).

Tennessee: Bent Creek G Resort [FKA Cobbly Nob G Links] (1972), with Arthur Davis and Ron Kirby.

Texas: Fair Oaks Ranch G&CC (1979), with Ron Kirby.

Virginia: Brandermill CC (1976), with Ron Kirby.

Belgium: GC Mean.

Bophuthatswana: Gary Player CC (1979), with Ron Kirby.

Canary Islands: Maspalomas GC (North Cse 1974), with Ron Kirby.

France: G du Château de Taulane; Domaine de Foncouverte GC.

Ivory Coast: Riviera Africaine GC (9 1972), with Arthur Davis and Ron Kirby.

Japan: Fuji CC (Shuga Cse 1989), with *Hirochika Tomizawa*; Fuji Shiokawa CC (1988); Niigata Forest GC (1975), with Ron Kirby; Nishi Nihon GC (1975), with Ron Kirby; Odawara CC (1973), with Arthur Davis and Ron Kirby.

Philippines: Puerto Azul GC (1980), with Ron Kirby.

Puerto Rico: Palmas del Mar GC (1973), with Arthur Davis and Ron Kirby.

South Africa: Four Ways GC, with Sid Brews and *Dr. Van Vincent*; Glenvista CC (1973), with Sid Brews and *Dr. Van Vincent*.

Spain: Almerimar GC (1975), with Ron Kirby; El Paraiso GC (1974), with Arthur Davis and Ron Kirby; Escorpion GC (1975), with Ron Kirby.

Zimbabwe: Elephant Hills GC, with Sid Brews and *Dr. Van Vincent*.

Courses remodeled or expanded by Gary Player:

Georgia: Cartersville CC (R.9 A.9 1972), with Arthur Davis and Ron Kirby.

New Mexico: Alto Lakes G&CC (A.9 1973), with Arthur Davis and Ron Kirby.

South Africa: Crown Mines GC (R.), with Sid Brews and *Dr. Van Vincent*.

RALPH M. PLUMMER
(1900–1982), ASGCA, PRESIDENT 1962

BORN: Smithfield, Texas.
DIED: Fort Worth, Texas, at age 82.

A onetime caddy at Glen Garden Country Club in Fort Worth, Ralph Plummer started his career as golf pro at a small South Texas club in the early 1920s. Several years later he was hired as professional for the new Galveston municipal course being laid out by Houston pro-designer John Bredemus. Impressed with Plummer's interest in course design, Bredemus invited his assistance in laying out several area courses. Plummer resigned his job to work with Bredemus full-time on courses in Texas, where the Depression

Ralph Plummer, circa 1965 COURTESY *GOLF WORLD*

had relatively little effect on golf development.

When Bredemus moved to Mexico, Plummer secured a position as professional at Greenville (Texas) Golf Club. After World War II he designed and built several short courses at Veterans' hospitals and then formed a firm specializing in the restoration of courses. By the 1950s he was once again designing golf courses full-time.

In his most active years Plummer constructed all the courses he designed, but by the 1970s he was content to let other firms build them. He was still active as late as 1979, when he designed and supervised construction of a course near Forth Worth. Plummer was known for the attractiveness of his layouts and for his remarkable ability to estimate cuts and fills by eye and shape greens and bunkers without detailed plans. Plummer designed or remodeled eighty-six courses during his career. He was involved in the design, construction or redesign of all three Texas courses that had hosted the U.S. Open—Colonial, Northwood and Champions.

Courses by Ralph Plummer:

Arizona: Francisco Grande CC (1964).

Louisiana: Lake Charles G&CC (1956); New Orleans VA Hospital GC (9 Par 3 1946), with Bob Dunning; Sherwood Forest CC.

New Mexico: Artesia CC (9 1946); Lincoln Hills CC.

Oklahoma: Altus CC (9 1946).

Texas: Alice CC (1952); Atascocita CC (1956); Buckingham CC (1960); Champions GC (Cypress Creek Cse 1959); Columbian C (9 1955); Dallas Athletic C (Blue Cse 1954; Gold Cse 1962); Denton CC; Eastern Hills CC (1956); Elkins Lake GC (1971); Gainesville Muni (1955); Golfcrest CC (1951, NLE); Grand Prairie Muni (27 1965); Great Southwest GC (1965), with Byron Nelson; Hillcrest CC (1956); Hilltop Lakes GC (9 1963); Indian Creek CC (1966); James Connally GC (1956); Lake Arlington GC (1963); Lake Country Estates GC (9 1973); Lakeside CC (1952); Lakewood CC (1947); Magnolia Ridge CC (9 1951); McKinney Muni (9 1946), with Bob Dunning; Meadowbrook Muni (Cse No. 1; Cse No. 2); Midland CC (1954); Mission CC (1959); Oak Grove CC (9 1979); Palm View Muni (1971); Pecan Valley Muni [FKA Benbrook Muni] (Hills Cse, 9 1962; River Cse 1962); Pharaoh's CC (1964); Port Arthur CC (1955); Preston Trail GC (1965); Prestonwood CC (Creek Cse 1965); Ranchland Hills GC (1950); Ridglea CC (1951); Riverside Muni (9 1951); Shady Oaks CC (1959), with Robert Trent Jones and Lawrence Hughes; Sharpstown CC (1957); [The] Shores CC (1979); Squaw Creek CC (9); Tenison Muni (East Cse 1960); Tennwood C (1956); Texas A&M University GC (1950).

Jamaica: Tryall G & Beach C (1958).

Courses remodeled or expanded by Ralph Plummer:

Louisiana: City Park GC (Cse No. 1, R.); Lafayette CC (R. 1960).

Minnesota: Minikahda C (R. 1962).

Texas: Brae Burn CC (R.); Brook Hollow GC (R. 1956); Dallas CC (R. 1947); Glen Lakes CC (R. 1942); Gus Wortham Muni (R. 1957); Hermann Park GC (R.9 1952); Max Starcke Park GC [FKA Seguin CC] (A.9 1979); Meadowbrook G Cse (R. 1960); Northwood C (R. 1950); Pine Forest CC (R.9 1956, NLE); Ridgewood CC (R. 1962); Ridglea CC (North Cse, R. 1959); River Crest CC (R. 1946); River Oaks CC (R. 1957); Rockwood Muni (R. A.3rd 9 1964); Tenison Muni (West Cse, R. 1960); Westwood CC (A.9 1958); Wichita Falls CC (R. 1964); Willow Brook CC (R.9 A.9 1953); Z. Boaz GC (R. 1962).

Utah: [The] Country Club (R. 1963).

J. MICHAEL POELLOT (1943–), ASGCA

BORN: Pittsburgh, Pennsylvania.

Mike Poellot received a B.S. degree in landscape architecture from Iowa State University in 1966 after undergraduate

Mike Poellot, 1989
COURTESY MIKE POELLOT

work in biological sciences at West Virginia Wesleyan College. He then completed postgraduate courses in turf management at Clemson University.

A third-generation golfer, Poellot took up the game at age 12. While working in Thailand as a U.S. Army Intelligence officer in the early 1970s, he met Robert Trent Jones, Jr., who was planning Navatanee GC in Bangkok. Jones hired Poellot to head his Asian office and direct work in Southeast Asia.

By 1980, as vice president of the Robert Trent Jones II Group and vice president-director of Pacific Planners International, the RTJ II overseas division, Poellot had worked on the design-and-construction supervision of twenty Jones Jr. courses in both the United States and Far East. That year he met architect Brad Benz during an ASGCA sojourn to Scotland. The two found they shared many of the same ideas, and Benz convinced Poellot to join him and partner Dick Phelps in Colorado. Phelps, Benz and Poellot Inc. worked the mountain states for three years. Benz and Poellot then left the company and formed their own partnership, based in California. Drawing on Poellot's contacts they soon landed many contracts in the Far East, including the first private country club in the People's Republic of China, Beijing GC.

In 1988 Poellot purchased Benz's share of the firm and renamed the company J. Michael Poellot Golf Design Group, Inc. He continued to concentrate his efforts on the Pacific Rim.

Courses by Mike Poellot:

Arizona: Gainey Ranch GC (27 1985), with Brad Benz.

Colorado: Englewood Muni (1982), with Dick Phelps and Brad Benz; [The] Meadows GC (1984), with Dick Phelps and Brad Benz; Raccoon Creek GC (1984), with Dick Phelps and Brad Benz.

Missouri: Longview Lakes G Cse (27 1986), with Brad Benz.

Montana: Briarwood CC (1985), with Brad Benz.

Nevada: Northgate GC (1988), with Brad Benz.

Texas: Firewheel G Park (Old Cse 1983), with Dick Phelps and Brad Benz; Indian Creek G Cse (Creek Cse 1983), with Dick Phelps and Brad Benz.

China: Bejiing GC (1987), with Brad Benz.

France: GC de Feucherolles (1991).

Hong Kong: Clearwater Bay CC (1984), with Brad Benz.

Japan: Caledonian GC (1990); Chiburi Lake Resort GC (1992); Glen Oaks CC (1988), with Brad Benz; Ikoma Kogen Kobayashi Miyazaki GC (1991); Imperial Wing GC (1990); Joetsu Kokusai CC (Tokamachi Cse 1987), with Brad Benz; Kawagoe Green Cross GC (1989); King Field CC (1984); Lake View CC (1991); Prestige CC (East & West Cses 1988), with Brad Benz; Sapporo Hiroshima GC (1991); Shizukushi GC (1988), with Brad Benz; Tomisato GC (1989), with Brad Benz; Tori CC (1989).

Thailand: Lake Wood CC (1992).

Courses remodeled or expanded by Mike Poellot:

California: Claremont CC (R. 1989), with Brad Benz.

Colorado: Dos Rios CC (A.9 1982), with Dick Phelps and Brad Benz.

New Mexico: Riverside CC (R.9 A.9 1984), with Brad Benz.

North Dakota: Heart River GC (A.9 R.9 1984), with Dick Phelps and Brad Benz.

Wyoming: Riverton CC (A.9 R.9 1982), with Dick Phelps and Brad Benz.

Japan: Kyu-Karuizawa GC (R.12 1992); Minagawajo CC (R. 1991).

Malaysia: Subang GC (R. 1986), with Brad Benz.

RONALD PRICHARD

BORN: New Jersey.

Ron Prichard, who excelled as a skier and lacrosse player from an early age, became a proficient golfer in his high school years. Prichard graduated from Middlebury College in Vermont, then served two years in the U.S. Army. After studying, sketching and playing many renowned layouts on the East Coast, he decided to pursue a career in golf course architecture. In 1968 he joined the staff of Texan golf architect Joe Finger. Ten years later he joined Desmond Muirhead as an associate and a year later went to work for the firm of von Hagge and Devlin.

Following his long apprenticeship with those three distinguished design firms, Prichard entered his own practice in 1983. He continued annual pilgrimages to play and sketch links and heathland courses of the British Isles, feeling that by doing so he enhanced his own traditional style.

Courses by Ron Prichard:

Missouri: Franklin CC.
Pennsylvania: PineCrest GC (1990).
Tennessee: TPC at Southwind (1988), with *Fuzzy Zoeller* and *Hubert Green.*
Texas: Wedgewood GC (1988), with *Bill Rogers.*

Courses remodeled or expanded by Ron Prichard:

Arkansas: Texarkana CC (R.).
Louisiana: Bayou de Siard CC (R.).
Missouri: Greenbriar Hills CC (R.).
Texas: Lakeside CC (R.).

ROBERT D. PRYDE
(1870–1951)

BORN: Tayport, Fife, Scotland.
DIED: New Haven, Connecticut, at age 80.

Robert Pryde grew up near St. Andrews, where he learned to play golf. He attended Harris Academy in Dundee and the Technical College of Glasgow, qualifying as a drawing instructor. In 1892 he emigrated to the United States, became a cabinet-maker in New Haven, Connecticut, and dabbled in the design of several buildings.

In 1895 Pryde was persuaded to build his first golf course, and from that point on his life was devoted to golf. He laid out a

Robert D. Pryde,
circa 1920
COLLECTION RON
WHITTEN

number of courses in Connecticut as well as a few in other states. Pryde was also an early golf coach at Yale University and from 1922 to 1946 served as secretary-treasurer of the Connecticut State Golf Association. He then held a similar position with the Connecticut State Seniors Association, which he helped form.

His pride and joy was Race Brook CC, where he served as secretary-treasurer from 1937 until his retirement shortly before his death.

Pryde was also a golf journalist. He traveled throughout the world, and his written accounts of the foreign golf courses he played were published in New Haven and Hartford newspapers. In 1941 he was presented with a gold key and the designation of the state's "Mr. Golf" by the Sports Writers Alliance of Connecticut.

Courses by Robert Pryde:

Connecticut: Alling Memorial GC; Hunter Memorial GC; New Haven CC (1895, NLE); Pine Orchards CC; Race Brook CC (27 1912); Wethersfield CC.
Massachusetts: Wyantenuck GC.

Nicholas Psiahas,
1969 COURTESY
ROBERT DEAN PUTMAN

NICHOLAS T. PSIAHAS
(1930–)

BORN: Montclair, New Jersey.

Nicholas Psiahas began his career as an eleven-year-old caddy at Upper Montclair Country Club in New Jersey. After working on the maintenance crew at that course, he joined the golf construction firm of William Baldwin Inc. in 1955. Over the next eight years he served as construction superintendent for several Robert Trent Jones–designed courses built by Baldwin's company, including a new Upper Montclair CC, the Air Force Academy course in Colorado and Half Moon–Rose Hall in Jamaica.

In 1963 Psiahas formed his own business, Golf Construction Inc., and built

courses for golf architects Frank Duane, David Gordon and Hal Purdy. In 1965 he began to design as well as construct courses.

Courses by Nicholas Psiahas:

New Jersey: Berkeley Township GC; Darlington G Cse (1979); Overpeck GC; Rolling Greens GC (1970); Two Bridges CC (Precision); Vernon Valley CC; Wantage G Center (Par 3 1972); Wayne G Centre.
New York: Blackhead Mountain Lodge & CC.
Pennsylvania: Fernwood Resort GC (1968).

Courses remodeled or expanded by Nicholas Psiahas:

New Jersey: Bamm Hollow CC (R.); Beaver Brook CC (R.); Cedar Hill CC (R.); Jumping Brook GC (R.); Lakehurst GC (R.); North Jersey CC (R.); Spring Meadow GC (R.).
New York: Fort Jay GC (R.)

ALGIE MARSHALL PULLEY, JR.
(1940–), ASGCA

BORN: Petersburg, Virginia.

Algie Pulley graduated with a degree in engineering from the University of Virginia, where he was also captain of the golf team. Upon completion of his military service, he worked for golf architect Ed Ault. In the 1960s he formed a golf course construction firm with Buddy Loving and E. H. Coffey and was involved in the genesis of an organization that was to become the Golf Course Builders of America.

In the early 1970s Pulley formed Golf America Inc., a firm based in California that designed, built and operated golf courses on both coasts. A poor economy led to dissolution of that corporation in

Algie Pulley, 1991
COURTESY ALGIE
PULLEY

the 1980s, and Pulley resumed designing courses on his own on the West Coast. In the early 1990s Pulley expanded his practice back to the East Coast.

Courses by Algie Pulley:

California: Chardonnay C (Vineyard Cse 1989; Shakespeare Cse, 9 1989, A.9 1992); Dixon Landing CC (1979, NLE).
Delaware: Cripple Creek G&CC (1984).
Maryland: Century XXI Club (1974); Jefferson Park GC (9 1977); Marlboro CC [FKA Duke of Marlborough GC] (1974).
Virginia: Brookwoods GC (1969); Confederate Hills CC (1972), with Buddy Loving; Country Club Lakes (Precision 1971), with Buddy Loving; Evergreen CC (1968), with Buddy Loving; Lake Monticello GC (1972), with Buddy Loving; [The] Links at Natural Bridge (1992); Montclair CC (1972); Royal Virginia GC (1992).
West Virginia: Polish Pines CC (9 1975).
Turkey: Izmir Hilton International (1991), with Simon Gidman.

Courses remodeled or expanded by Algie Pulley:

California: Alhambra Muni (R.9 A.9 1977); Lake Arrowhead CC (R.2 1976); Moraga CC (A.9 1991); San Bernardino CC (R.5 1976).
Maryland: Hunt Valley Inn & CC (R.9 1976).
Virginia: Army-Navy CC (Arlington Cse, R.5 1970; Fairfax Cse, R.2 1970), with Buddy Loving; CC of Fairfax (R. 1969), with Buddy Loving; Washington G&CC (R.5 1969), with Buddy Loving; Willow Oaks CC (R.1 1972).

HAROLD CHANDLER PURDY (1905–)

BORN: Wabash, Indiana.

Hal Purdy graduated from high school in Wabash, Indiana, and went to work as a surveyor for a local engineering firm. During the Depression, he served as manager at Lost Creek Golf Club in Lima, Ohio, before working for two years as a draftsman. He then purchased and operated a course in Sidney, Ohio, until 1945, when he became executive vice president of a construction firm.

In 1954 Purdy became a construction supervisor for architect Robert Trent Jones. He then entered private practice as a golf course architect in 1956. He was joined by his elder son, Dr. Mal Purdy, in 1967 and was also assisted for a few years by his second son, Chandler.

Courses by Hal Purdy:

Connecticut: Aspetuck Valley CC (1966); Burning Tree CC (1962); H. Smith Richardson Muni (1972), with Malcolm Purdy; Whitney Farms CC (1979), with Malcolm Purdy.
Indiana: Elks CC (9 1964); McMillen Park GC (1971); Norwood GC (1970); Shoaff Park GC (9 1966).
Kentucky: Carter Caves State Park GC (9 1963); General Butler State Park GC (9 1964); Harmony Landing CC (9 1966); Jefferson High School GC (9 Par 3 1964); Jenny Wiley State Park GC (9 1963); Mister Golf G Cse (Par 3 1964).
Maryland: Lighthouse Sound GC, with Malcolm Purdy.
New Jersey: Apple Ridge CC (1966); Arrowbrook CC (1963); Atlantic City Electric Co. GC (9 Par 3 1964); B. L. England GC (9 Par 3 1964); Bamm Hollow CC (27 1972), with Malcolm Purdy; Battleground CC (1967); Bey-Lea GC (1970); Clearbrook GC (9 1974), with Malcolm Purdy; Clearview CC (1966); Deer Park GC (9 Par 3 1966); Fairmount CC (1961); Fiddler's Elbow CC (North Cse 1966; South Cse, 9 1966); Flanders Valley GC (Red & Gold Cse 1963; White & Blue Cse, 9 1963); Forge Pond GC; Forsgate CC (West Cse 1974); Fox Hollow GC (1962); Glenbrook CC (1966); Glenwood CC; Hickman GC (9 Par 3 1970); Knoll East GC (1961); Mays Landing GC (1964); Millburn GC (9 Par 3 1970), Navesink CC (1964); Ocean Acres GC (9 1964); Old Tappan GC (9 1970); Ramsey G&CC (9

Hal Purdy, 1969
COURTESY ROBERT DEAN PUTMAN

1965); Roxiticus CC (1965); Summit Muni (9 Par 3 1968); Sunset Valley GC (1974), with Malcolm Purdy; Tamarack GC (27 1973), with Malcolm Purdy; Warrenbrook CC (1966).
New York: Catatonk GC (9 1966); Central Valley GC (9 1968); Chenango Valley GC (9 1967); Columbia G&CC (9 1962); Dinsmore GC (1957); Greenview GC (1967); Hillandale GC (9 1961); Huquenot Manor GC (9 1971); Kanon Valley CC (1969); Locust Tree GC (1972); Monroe County GC (9 1968); Narrowsburg GC (9 1965); [The] Pompey C (1964); Roxbury Run GC (9 1974), with Malcolm Purdy; Skaneatelas CC (9 1966); Stony Ford GC (1962); Sunny Hill GC (9 Par 3 1967); Tioga GC (1969); Village Green GC (1974), with Malcolm Purdy; West Hill CC (1967); Windham CC (9 1969).
Ohio: Moose CC (9 1945).
Pennsylvania: Mount Airy Lodge & CC (1981), with Malcolm Purdy and *Chandler Purdy.*
Virginia: Luray Caverns CC (1976), with Malcolm Purdy.

Courses remodeled or expanded by Hal Purdy:

California: Thunderbird CC (R. 1973).
Connecticut: CC of Darien (R. 1974), with Malcolm Purdy.
Florida: Belleview-Biltmore Hotel & C (East Cse, R. 1973; West Cse, R. 1973), with Malcolm Purdy.
Indiana: French Lick CC (Hill Cse, R. 1965; Valley Cse, R. 1965).
New Jersey: Brook Lake CC (R. A.9 1972), with Malcolm Purdy; Colonia CC (R. 1969); Covered Bridge GC (R. 1972), with Malcolm Purdy; Essex Fells CC (R. 1971), with Malcolm Purdy; Greenbrook CC (R. 1979), with Malcolm Purdy; Medford Lakes CC (A.9 1969); Morris County GC (R. 1968); North Jersey CC (R. 1965); Raritan Valley CC (R.9 1968); River Vale CC (R. 1968); Rock Spring CC (R. 1965); Rockaway River CC (R.), with Malcolm Purdy; Rutgers University GC (R.9 A.9 1963); Shark River GC [FKA Asbury Park GC] (R. A.5 1967); Somerset Hills CC (R.); Weequahic GC (A.9 1969).
New York: Cazenovia CC (A.9. 1969); IBM CC (R.9 1961); Ironwood CC (R. 1959); Middle Bay CC (R. 1963); Newburgh CC (R.9 1965); Onondaga

G&CC (R. 1965); Wykagyl CC (R. 1966).

Ohio: Brown's Run GC (R. 1962); Losantiville CC (R. 1961); Lost Creek CC (R. 1961).

MALCOLM MILLS PURDY
(1932–1983), ASGCA

BORN: Lima, Ohio.
DIED: New Jersey at age 51.

Dr. Mal Purdy grew up on golf courses managed and operated by his father, Hal Purdy. He earned a doctorate in industrial psychology from Purdue University and worked in that field for 15 years. In 1967 he joined his father's course design firm, which became known as The Purdys. Mal Purdy was tragically killed in an automobile accident in 1983.

Mal Purdy, 1969
COURTESY ROBERT
DEAN PUTMAN

Courses by Malcolm Purdy (All with Hal Purdy):

Connecticut: H. Smith Richardson Muni (1972); Whitney Farms CC (1979).
Maryland: Lighthouse Sound GC.
New Jersey: Bamm Hollow CC (27 1972); Clear Brook GC (9 1974); Sunset Valley GC (1974); Tamarack GC (27 1973).
New York: Roxbury Run GC (9 1974); Village Green GC (1974).
Pennsylvania: Mount Airy Lodge & CC (1981), and *Chandler Purdy.*
Virginia: Luray Caverns CC (1976).

Courses remodeled or expanded by Malcolm Purdy (All with Hal Purdy):

Connecticut: CC of Darien (R. 1974).
Florida: Belleview-Biltmore Hotel & C (East Cse, R. 1973; West Cse, R. 1973).
New Jersey: Brook Lake CC (R. A.9 1972); Covered Bridge GC (R. 1972); Essex Fells CC (R. 1971); Greenbrook CC (R. 1979); Rockaway River CC (R.).

ROBERT DEAN PUTMAN
(1924–)

BORN: Wallace, Idaho.

Trained as a commercial artist, Bob Putman practiced that craft for several years before joining golf architect Bob Baldock as a draftsman in 1955. He later became Baldock's chief design associate and worked on the design or redesign of over fifty courses. In 1967 he established his own course-design firm, based in Fresno, California. Over the next twenty-five years Putman worked primarily along the West Coast, designing and supervising construction of his courses. A majority of his jobs were for municipalities, and he prided himself on designing for ease of maintenance as well as playability.

In the early 1970s Putman became one of the first American architects to invade the European market, creating a series of courses in Spain, including La Manga, a highly regarded tournament venue. Later that same decade his East Course at Rancho Canada GC in Monterey, California, was declared by the NGF to be the 10,000th golf course constructed in America.

Throughout his career Putman retained his artistic hand and depicted his routing plans and individual holes in both vivid charcoal sketches and paintings of oil, watercolor and acrylic. In the mid-1980s Putman was joined in the business by his daughter Gail Putman and by design associate Ken Moore.

Courses by Robert Dean Putman:

Arizona: Elden Hills GC (1960), ass't Bob Baldock.
California: Butte Creek G&CC (1965), ass't Bob Baldock; Corral de Tierra CC (1959), ass't Bob Baldock; Cypress Lakes GC, Travis AFB; Diablo Creek GC (1963), ass't Bob Baldock; El Macero CC (1961), ass't Bob Baldock; Eureka Muni (9 1957), ass't Bob Baldock; Fairway Glen GC (9 1961), ass't Bob Baldock; Fresno Airways G Cse (1989); Fresno West GC (1966), ass't Bob Baldock; Lake Chabot GC (Executive Cse [9 Par 3]); Madera G&CC (9 1955), ass't Bob Baldock; Madera Muni (1991); Merced CC (1961), ass't Bob Baldock; Monterey Peninsula CC (Shore Cse 1960), ass't Bob Baldock; Mountain Shadows CC (South Cse 1963), ass't Bob Baldock; Oakdale CC (9 1963), ass't Bob Baldock; Peach Tree G&CC (1960), ass't Bob Baldock;

Robert Dean Putman, 1990
COURTESY ROBERT
DEAN PUTMAN

Rancho Cañada GC (East Cse 1970; West Cse 1970); Rancho del Rey GC [FKA Castle AFB GC] (9 1955, A.9 1963), ass't Bob Baldock; River Island GC (1963), ass't Bob Baldock; Selma Valley GC (1958), ass't Bob Baldock; Sycamore Canyon G Cse (1992); Three Rivers GC (9 Precision); Turlock CC, ass't Bob Baldock; Valley Oaks GC (1972); Vandenberg AFB GC; Visalia Plaza GC (1973); Wasco Valley Rose G Cse (1991); Willow Park GC (1966), ass't Bob Baldock.
Hawaii: Hickam AFB GC (1966), ass't Bob Baldock.
New Mexico: Four Hills CC (1961), ass't Bob Baldock; Los Altos Muni (1960), ass't Bob Baldock; Sandia Mountain GC (Par 3 1962); Tijeras Arroyo GC, Kirtland AFB (1971).
Washington: Harrington G&CC (9 1957); Hangman's Valley Muni (1968), ass't Bob Baldock; Pasco Muni (NLE), ass't Bob Baldock.
Korea: Eagle's Nest GC.
Spain: Alacante GC; La Bilbania GC (1976); La Manga Campo de G (North Cse 1972; South Cse 1973); Las Lomas el Bosque GC (1973).
Tahiti: Golf d'Atimaona CC (1967), ass't Bob Baldock.

Courses remodeled or expanded by Robert Dean Putman:

California: Belmont CC (R.); Fig Garden GC (R.); Fort Washington CC (R. 1956), ass't Bob Baldock; King City GC (R.); Kings River G&CC (R. 1961), ass't Bob Baldock; La Rinconada CC (R.); San Joaquin CC (R. 1972); Sierra View GC (A.9 1966), ass't Bob Baldock; Sunnyside CC (R. 1973); Visalia CC (R.).
Hawaii: Mid-Pacific G&CC (R. 1968), ass't Bob Baldock.

EVERETT J. PYLE

Everett Pyle worked for golf architect Donald Ross in the 1930s, building Twigg Memorial Municipal Golf Course in Providence, Rhode Island, among other Ross designs. From the 1940s through the 1960s Pyle served as superintendent of parks in Hartford, Connecticut. In that capacity he planned extensive changes at Keney Park and Goodwin Park golf courses. He also designed and revised several Connecticut courses on the side, including Pine Hill GC at Windsor.

David Rainville,
1991 COURTESY DAVID
RAINVILLE

DAVID A. RAINVILLE
(1936–   ), ASGCA

BORN: Deadwood, South Dakota.

At age 12, David Rainville started tagging along to job sites with his father, Harry Rainville, who worked as construction superintendent for golf architect Lawrence Hughes. At age 14 young David spent his summer as waterboy and timekeeper for a crew of eighty workmen on the construction site of Thunderbird Country Club in Palm Springs, California. When the elder Rainville started designing courses on his own in the early 1950s, David worked during the summers helping build his father's courses. After high school he attended Fullerton (California) Junior College and received an associate's art degree in engineering in 1957.

In 1963, following military service, Rainville joined his father in the full-time practice of golf course design. After his father's death, Rainville continued the business, concentrating mainly on Southern California.

Courses by David Rainville (All with Harry Rainville unless otherwise indicated):

California: Birch Hill GC (Precision 1972); Cathedral Canyon CC (1975 *solo*, A.3rd 9 1986 *solo*); [The] Colony GC (Precision 1989 *solo*); Desert Princess CC (27 1986 *solo*); El Prado CC (Butterfield Stage Cse 1976; Chino Creek Cse 1970); Escondido CC (1965); Fountains GC (Precision 1986 *solo*); Imperial GC (1974); Laguna Hills GC (27); Lake San Marcos Executive GC (Precision *solo*); Lake San Marcos G&CC; Lawrence Welk Village GC (Precision 1985 *solo*); Mile Square GC (1969); Needles Muni (1964); Newport Beach GC (9 1966); Oasis CC (Precision 1985 *solo*); Ocean Meadows GC (9 1966); Panorama Village GC (9 Par 3); Rossmoor CC (South Cse 1964); San Juan Hills CC (1966); Seven Hills CC (1973); Shadowridge CC (1981 *solo*); Sun Lakes CC (1987 *solo*); Upland Hills GC (1983 *solo*); Warner Springs Ranch GC (1965); Western Hills CC (*solo*).
Nevada: Boulder City GC (9 1973).
South Korea: Club 700 (*solo*).

Courses remodeled or expanded by David Rainville (All with Harry Rainville unless otherwise indicated):

California: Alta Vista CC (A.9 1973); Annandale GC (R. *solo*); Indian Wells CC (R. *solo*); Irvine Coast CC (R.); Lakeside GC of Hollywood (R. *solo*); Los Serranos Lakes CC (North Cse, R. 1965; South Cse, R. 1965); Mesa Verde CC (R. *solo*); Newport Beach CC (R. 1966); Oakmont CC (R. *solo*); Rancho Santa Fe CC (R.); Red Hill CC (R.); Santa Ana CC (R.); Thunderbird CC (R.); Torrey Pines Muni (North Cse, R. 1975 *solo*; South Cse, R. 1975 *solo*); Whispering Palms CC (A.9 1973).

HARRY M. RAINVILLE
(1905–1982)

BORN: St. Onge, South Dakota.
DIED: Tustin, California, at age 77.

Harry Rainville's early years were spent in a variety of occupations, including ranching, mining, general construction and merchandise sales. In the early 1940s he moved his family to California, where he worked at the Cal-Tech Rocket Assembly Factory until 1944.

A friend of golf architect Lawrence Hughes, Rainville worked for Hughes as his construction superintendent on what became Stardust Country Club in San Diego in 1945. He went on to build five more courses for Hughes, including Desert Inn Country Club in Las Vegas and Thunderbird Country Club in Palm Springs.

In 1952 Rainville entered private practice as a golf course designer. He was joined by his son David in 1963. For a short time professional golfer Billy Casper served as consultant to his firm. In the 1970s the firm began to operate, as well as design and build, golf facilities and by 1979 owned an interest in five successful courses.

Courses by Harry Rainville (All with David Rainville unless otherwise indicated):

California: Alta Vista CC (1961 *solo*; A.9 1973); Birch Hill GC (Precision 1972); Brea GC (9 Precision *solo*); Candlewood CC (*solo*); Chula Vista Muni (1961 *solo*); El Prado CC (Butterfield Stage Cse 1976; Chino Creek Cse 1970); El Rancho Verde CC (1957); Escondido CC (1965); Fallbrook CC (1962); Imperial GC (1974); Laguna Hills GC (27); Lake San Marcos G&CC; Marina del Ray GC (Precision 9 *solo*); Mile Square GC (1969); National City GC (Precision 1961 *solo*); Needles Muni (1964); Newport Beach GC (9 1966); Ocean Meadows GC (9 1966); Panorama Village GC (9 Par 3); Pine Trees GC (9 Par 3 *solo*); Rossmoor CC (South Cse 1964); San Juan Hills CC (1966); Seven Hills CC (1973); Warner Springs Ranch GC (1965); Western Hill G&CC (1963 *solo*); Whispering Palms CC (1965 *solo*; A.9. 1973); Yorba Linda CC (1957 *solo*).
Nevada: Boulder City GC (9 1973).

Courses remodeled or expanded by Harry Rainville (All with David Rainville unless otherwise indicated):

California: Chevy Chase CC (R.9 1960 *solo*); Irvine Coast CC (R.); Los Ser-

Harry Rainville,
1957 COURTESY DAVID
RAINVILLE

ranos Lakes CC (North Cse, R. 1965; South Cse, R. 1965); Newport Beach CC (R. 1966); Rancho Santa Fe CC (R.); Red Hill CC (R.); San Diego CC (R.1 1962 *solo*); Santa Ana CC (R.); Thunderbird CC (R.).

Mark Rathert, 1989
COLLECTION RON
WHITTEN

MARK F. RATHERT
(1953–), ASGCA

BORN: Marion, Kansas.

Mark Rathert attended Butler County (Kansas) Community College on a golf scholarship and later graduated with honors from Kansas State University, receiving a Bachelor of Landscape Architecture degree. While in college Rathert won an ASLA Distinguished Undergraduate Student Award in nationwide competition and redesigned his hometown's 9-hole course when its greens were converted from sand to grass.

After graduation in 1977, Rathert landed a job with Robert Trent Jones, Jr., and served as a design associate for four years. In 1981, at the urging of a former Jones employee, Mike Poellot, he joined the newly formed California branch of Phelps, Benz and Poellot. When the firm became Benz & Poellot, Rathert was made a senior architect. In 1988 Benz and Poellot split up and Rathert remained with Poellot. A year later, he started his own golf design firm, based first in Southern California and then in Denver, Colorado.

Courses by Mark Rathert (All as assistant to Brad Benz and Mike Poellot unless otherwise indicated):

Arizona: Fred Enke Muni, Tucson (1983); Gainey Ranch GC (27 1985).
California: [The] Links at Monarch Beach (1984), ass't Robert Trent Jones, Jr.; Shoreline Park Muni (1983), ass't Robert Trent Jones, Jr.

Hawaii: Kiahuna Plantation GC (1983), ass't Robert Trent Jones, Jr.
Missouri: Longview Lakes G Cse (27 1986).
Nevada: Northgate GC (1987).
New Mexico: Cochiti Lake GC (1980), ass't Robert Trent Jones, Jr.
Oregon: Sunriver GC (North Cse 1980), ass't Robert Trent Jones, Jr.
Wisconsin: SentryWorld GC (1982), ass't Robert Trent Jones, Jr.
China: Beijing GC (1987).
Guam: Guam CC (1992 *solo*).
Japan: Caledonian GC (1990), ass't Mike Poellot; Glen Oaks GC (1988); Imperial CC (27 1992 *solo*); Imperial Wing GC (1990), ass't Mike Poellot; Joetsu Kokusai GC (Tokamachi Cse 1987); Miyakojima G Cse, Takamatsu Resort (1992 *solo*); Prestige CC (1988); Shizukuishi GC (1988); Tomioka CC (1992 *solo*); Tomisato GC (1989).

Courses remodeled or expanded by Mark Rathert (All as assistant to Brad Benz and Mike Poellot unless otherwise indicated):

California: Claremont CC (R. 1989).
Kansas: Marion CC (R. 1976 *solo*).
New Mexico: Riverside CC (R.9 A.9 1984).
Texas: Mill Creek G&CC (R.5 A.13 1981), ass't Robert Trent Jones, Jr.

Andy Raugust, 1991
COURTESY ANDY
RAUGUST

ANDREW M. RAUGUST
(1961–), ASGCA

BORN: Tacoma, Washington.

After obtaining a B.S. degree in landscape architecture from California Poly–San Luis Obispo in 1985, Andy Raugust worked for a succession of golf course architects, including Ronald Fream in California and Robin Nelson in Honolulu. In 1989 he joined the Palm Springs–based

Landmark Golf Course Design Company headed by Lee Schmidt. But within a year Landmark's parent company was experiencing severe financial setbacks and both Schmidt and Raugust left the firm for Jack Nicklaus's company. Schmidt agreed to handle the Golden Bear's Hong Kong office, while Raugust was assigned to work out of the main Florida headquarters.

Courses by Andy Raugust:

Hawaii: Wakapu Sandalwood G Cse (1991), ass't Robin Nelson and Rodney Wright.
Finland: Nordcenter G&CC, ass't Ronald Fream.
France: Golf de Massane (1990), ass't Ronald Fream; Montgriffon GC (Coulonges Cse 1992; Luzarches Cse 1992), ass't Robin Nelson and Rodney Wright.

Seth Raynor, circa 1920 COURTESY MRS.
ELIZABETH JOHNSON

SETH J. RAYNOR
(1874–1926)

BORN: Manorville, New York.
DIED: West Palm Beach, Florida, at age 51.
INTERRED: Southhampton, New York.

A Princeton graduate with a degree in engineering, Seth Raynor operated a comfortable surveying and landscaping business in Southhampton, New York, for many years. His introduction to golf design came quite by accident, when he was hired by Charles Blair Macdonald in 1908 to survey the property that would become The National Golf Links of America. Raynor so impressed Macdonald with his engineering knowledge that he was hired to supervise construction of The National. Once it was completed, Raynor went on to construct several more courses for Macdonald, including Piping Rock, Sleepy Hollow, The Greenbrier and Lido.

In 1915 Raynor joined Macdonald as a partner and in the next ten years designed or remodeled nearly 100 courses that appeared under his own name. Macdonald, by his own admission, concentrated on only a half-dozen pet projects. In 1926 Seth Raynor died of pneumonia, leaving his assistants Charles Banks and Ralph Barton to complete his in-progress projects and to carry on the Macdonald tradition. Before his death Raynor had prepared a route plan for the proposed Cypress Point Club at Pebble Beach, California. However, it was never used by Alister Mackenzie, the designer hired to do the course after Raynor's death.

Courses by Seth Raynor:

California: Monterey Penninsula CC (Dunes Cse 1926), with Charles Banks.

Connecticut: CC of Fairfield (1921); Greenwich CC; Hotchkiss School GC (9); Yale University GC (1926), with Charles Blair Macdonald, Charles Banks and Ralph Barton.

Florida: Babson Park G&YC (9 1921, NLE); Everglades C (9 1919; A.9 1926); Mountain Lake C.

Georgia: Bon Air Vanderbilt Hotel GC (Lake Cse, NLE); Lookout Mountain GC [FKA Fairyland CC] (1925), with Charles Banks.

Hawaii: Mid-Pacific CC (1925), with Charles Banks.

Illinois: Shoreacres (1921).

Maryland: Gibson Island GC (1922, 9 NLE), with Charles Blair Macdonald.

Minnesota: Midland Hills CC (1915); University of Minnesota GC (1921).

Missouri: St. Louis CC (1914), with Charles Blair Macdonald.

New Jersey: Hackensack GC (1928), with Charles Banks; Roselle CC.

New York: Bellport CC (1916); Blind Brook C (routing 1916); Brookville CC (1922); Cold Spring Harbor CC (1923); [The] Creek C (1925), with Charles Blair Macdonald; Deepdale GC (1925, NLE), with Charles Blair Macdonald; Fishers Island GC (1917); H. P. Whitney Estate GC, with Charles Blair Macdonald; Knollwood CC (1927), with Charles Banks; Lido GC (1919, NLE), with Charles Blair Macdonald; Moore Estate GC, with Charles Blair Macdonald; Otto Kahn Estate GC (1925, NLE), with Charles Blair Macdonald; Piping Rock C (1913), with Charles Blair Macdonald; Sleepy Hollow GC (1914), with Charles Blair Macdonald; Southampton GC (1927), with Charles

Banks; Thousand Islands C (1923); Westhampton CC (1914).

North Carolina: Green Park-Norwood GC (NLE).

Ohio: Camargo C (1921).

Pennsylvania: Fox Chapel GC (1925).

Rhode Island: Bayside CC (9 1923, NLE); Ocean Links (9 1920); Wanumetonomy CC (1922).

South Carolina: CC of Charleston (1922); Yeaman's Hall C (1925).

West Virginia: [The] Greenbrier GC (Old White Cse 1915), with Charles Blair Macdonald.

Wisconsin: Blue Mound G&CC (1924).

Bermuda: Mid Ocean C (1924), with Charles Blair Macdonald, Charles Banks and Ralph Barton.

Courses remodeled or expanded by Seth Raynor:

Georgia: Augusta CC (R. 1926).

Illinois: Chicago GC (R. 1923).

New Jersey: Morris County GC (R. A.12 1923).

New York: Crawford CC (R.); Gardiner's Bay CC (R.9 A.9 1915); Nassau CC (R.1); Oakland GC (R., NLE).

CHARLES H. REDHEAD (1874–1944)

BORN: Ireland.
DIED: New Zealand at age 70.

A talented amateur golfer in his native Ireland, C. H. Redhead worked until age 50 as an engineer in government service, where, among other accomplishments, he supervised the installation of underground telephone cables throughout Ireland during World War I.

In 1924 he moved to New Zealand and made his home in Rotorua. Eager to test the courses of his newly adopted country, Redhead was appalled at what he found. After a three-year battle with club members, he was allowed to completely remodel and rebunker his home course at Arikikapakapa. The results were so startling that his services were soon sought by other clubs.

Over the next fifteen years he would reshape the look of New Zealand's golf courses, taking many of the penal layouts and rebunkering them for strategic play. Redhead believed holes should be "reasonable but interesting, not for the benefit of the scratch man or the long handicap man, but for all." He took particular care with

one-shot holes, varying direction, length and size of the putting surface.

He worked on nearly all of New Zealand's best courses, leaving an influence on the game and on Australian and New Zealand architects who followed him. As one author put it, Redhead yanked New Zealand golf from the horse-and-buggy age into the modern era.

Curiously enough, Redhead was not a redhead.

Courses by C. H. Redhead:

New Zealand: Chamberlain Park GC (1934); Feilding GC; Northern Wairoa GC; Opotiki GC; Pukekohe GC; Te Aroha GC; Te Awamutu GC; Thames GC; Waitomo GC [FKA Te Kuiti GC] (1932); Whakatane GC.

Courses remodeled or expanded by C.H. Redhead:

New Zealand: Akarana GC (R.); Arikikapakapa CC (R. 1927); Auckland GC (R. 1930); Avondale GC (R.); Balmacewan GC (R.); Cambridge GC (R.); Glendowie GC (R.); Hastings GC (R. 1934); Hutt GC (R.); Manawatu GC (R. 1928); Maungakiekie GC (R., NLE); Middlemore GC (R.); Napier GC (R. 1928); New Plymouth GC (R. 1933); Otago GC (R. 1928); Poverty Bay GC (R. 1927); Pupuke GC (R.); Rotorua GC (R.); St. Andrews GC (R.); St. Clair GC (R.); Wangawi GC (R.).

Dean Refram, circa 1975 COURTESY *GOLF WORLD*

DEAN REFRAM (1937–1991)

DIED: Tampa, Florida, at age 54.

Dean Refram joined the PGA Tour in 1961 and played with only modest success until the mid-1970s. The only official title he won during his fourteen-year career was a Walt Disney World Team Championship with Jim Colbert.

After leaving the tour, Refram developed a golf course construction company and built courses on the west coast of Florida for Palmer Course Design, Gordon Lewis and others. He also constructed a handful of courses of his own design. In the late 1980s, when many of his contemporaries were finding unprecedented riches on the new Senior PGA Tour, Refram was content to continue in his design-and-construction business. He died of cancer in mid-1991.

Courses by Dean Refram:

Florida: Baytree GC (1988); Clerbrook GC (Precision 1984); [The] Links of Lake Bernadette (1985); Saddlebrook G&TC (Saddlebrook Cse 1976).

Courses remodeled or expanded by Dean Refram:

Florida: Lake Region Y&CC (R. 1984).
Indiana: CC of Indianapolis (R.)

Wilfrid Reid, circa 1930 COURTESY BILL ZMISTOWSKI

WILFRID REID
(1884–1973)

BORN: Bulwell, Nottingham, England.
DIED: West Palm Beach, Florida, at age 89.

Wilfrid Reid studied club and ball making under Tommy Armour's father, Willie, in Edinburgh, Scotland. A scratch golfer at 15, Wilf turned professional at 17 and was a protégé of Harry Vardon, who helped him land a club professional job in Paris, France, in the early 1900s. Reid was a fine competitive golfer despite his diminutive size, and he beat his mentor, Vardon, on several occasions.

Reid competed in the United States during several seasons before moving there at the behest of the Du Pont family after the outbreak of World War I. He became a member of the PGA in 1917 and obtained U.S. citizenship in 1921. Wilf served as professional at several of America's top clubs, including CC of Detroit, Beverly CC, The Broadmoor and Seminole GC. He defeated Gene Sarazen in the 1924 Augusta Open, won the 1926 Michigan PGA

and had twenty-six holes-in-one in his long playing career. Reid began designing golf courses at an early age and laid out courses in Europe and Britain before settling in the United States. He once estimated that he had designed fifty-eight courses and remodeled some forty-three others during his design career. While based in Michigan during the 1920s, he partnered with another club professional, William Connellan. The firm of Reid and Connellan designed some twenty courses in that state alone. Reid retired to Florida in the early 1950s and consistently bettered his age in both social and competitive rounds. In 1985 Reid was posthumously inducted into the Michigan Golf Hall of Fame.

Courses by Wilfrid Reid (All with William Connellan unless otherwise indicated):

California: Lakeside G&CC (1917, NLE), with Walter G. Fovargue and *James Donaldson.*
Delaware: Du Pont CC (1920 *solo*, NLE); Green Hill Muni (*solo*); Newark CC (9 *solo*).
Michigan: Bald Mountain GC; Bob O'Link CC; Brae Burn GC; Flushing Valley CC; Gaylord CC (1949 *solo*); Harsens Island GC; Indian River GC (9); Indianwood G&CC (Old Cse 1928); Plum Hollow G&CC; Port Huron CC; Tam O'Shanter CC.
England: Barnstead Downs GC; Garrats Hall GC.
France: G de Cannes (*solo*); GC d'Aix-les-Bains (*solo*); G Ile de Berder (*solo*); Pont St. Maxence GC (*solo*); Racing C de France (Valley Cse *solo*).

Courses remodeled or expanded by Wilfrid Reid (All with William Connellan unless otherwise indicated):

Michigan: Birmingham CC (R. 1928); Black River CC (A.9); Grosse Ile G&CC (R.); Orchard Lake CC (R. 1928).
Belgium: Royal Belgique CC (R. *solo*).
England: Seacraft GC (R.9 *solo*).

ROBERT A. RENAUD

BORN: Canada.

Robert Renaud became pro-manager at Pickens County CC in South Carolina in the early 1950s. After renovating the course (which had closed during World

War II), he moved on to Thomson CC in Georgia and performed the same task. He later served as head professional at a number of Southern clubs and was twice voted South Carolina Golf Professional of the Year by his peers.

Renaud designed golf courses on a part-time basis during the 1950s and '60s. In 1972 he resigned from his position as head professional at Hillwood CC in Nashville to pursue a full-time career in golf architecture. Renaud retired in 1979 to maintain and manage a course he had built in Crossville, Tennessee.

Courses by Robert Renaud:

Florida: Indian Pines GC (1974); Turtle Creek GC (1973).
Indiana: Indian Lakes GC (1986).
South Carolina: Fairfield CC (1961).
Tennessee: Green Hills CC (9 1968); Green River CC (9 1972); Hunter's Point GC (1966); Tansi Resort GC (1973).

Courses remodeled or expanded by Robert Renaud:

Georgia: Thomson CC (R.9 1954).
South Carolina: Pickens County CC (R. 1953); Spring Lake CC (A.9 1962).

GARRETT J. RENN
(1913–1968)

BORN: Mount Holly, New Jersey.
DIED: Camden, New Jersey, at age 55.

Garry Renn held the position of superintendent of Philadelphia's municipal golf courses from 1950 until his death in an auto accident in 1968. A member of the PGA of America and the GCSAA, he designed several courses on a part-time basis, including Little Mill CC (1968) in New Jersey and Bryn Llawen GC (1969) in Pennsylvania.

EDWARD RICCOBONI

Club professional Ed Riccoboni laid out and built several courses in North and South Carolina in the 1960s. He later served as director of golf at the Santee Cooper golf resort in South Carolina, where he expanded the facilities by 18 holes. Riccoboni also planned a preliminary routing for a resort course on Isle of

Palms. Later, Tom Fazio received the contract and created Wild Dunes on the site of Riccoboni's proposed 18.

Courses by Ed Riccoboni:

North Carolina: Arrowhead GC (1964); Fox Squirrel CC (1962).
South Carolina: Bishopville CC (1960); Carolina Lakes GC, Shaw AFB; Clarendon CC; CC of Lexington (1966); Holly Hill CC (1958); Lake City CC (1960); Lake Marion GC (1978); Lamar CC (1970); Miler CC (9 1965); Pocalla Springs CC (1963); Ponderosa CC (1966).

Courses remodeled or expanded by Ed Riccoboni:

South Carolina: Sunset CC (R.).

Forrest Richardson, 1991 COURTESY FORREST RICHARDSON

FORREST RICHARDSON
(1959–   )

BORN: Burbank, California.

Claiming that he began building golf courses in his backyard at age 8, Forrest Richardson studied golf architecture under the tutelage of Arthur Jack Snyder while attending college. He also published *The Golf Course Designer,* a newsletter devoted to various aspects of course design. In 1976 Richardson studied golf architecture in Dundee, Scotland, as part of an ASLA study group.

After practicing landscape architecture for nearly a decade, Richardson formed Golf Group Ltd., devoted to golf architecture, in 1988. His first designs were collaborations with his old mentor, Arthur Jack Snyder.

Courses by Forrest Richardson:

Arizona: [The] Pointe at South Mountain GC (1988), with Arthur Jack Snyder;

[The] Pointe at Lookout Mountain GC (routing 1988).
California: Las Montañas GC (1992), with Arthur Jack Snyder.

Courses remodeled or expanded by Forrest Richardson:

Arizona: Arizona Biltmore GC (Links Cse, R. 1 1989), with Arthur Jack Snyder; Casa Grande Muni (A. 9 1989), with Arthur Jack Snyder; Concho Valley GC (A.9 1991), with Arthur Jack Snyder.

Mick Riley, circa 1960 COLLECTION RON WHITTEN

JOSEPH MICHAEL RILEY
(1905–1964)

BORN: Burke, Idaho.
DIED: Salt Lake City, Utah, at age 59.

"Mick" Riley competed against George Von Elm as a youngster and turned professional while still in his teens. In the 1920s he helped construct Nibley Park GC in Salt Lake City and stayed on as its first professional. He served as pro at a series of Salt Lake City courses and in 1951 was awarded a citation of merit by the PGA of America for his efforts in promoting the game of golf. He was often called the "Father of Golf in Utah."

Riley was responsible for the design and construction of several Utah golf courses and was especially active in the years just after World War II. After his death, the Salt Lake City County Commission named its newest course, Riley's last design, in his honor.

Courses by Mick Riley:

Utah: Brigham City G&CC; Copper CC (9); El Monte GC (9 1950); Empire G&CC (9); Forest Dale GC (9 1935); Fort Douglas VA Hospital GC (9 Par 3 1957); Logan G&CC (1949); Meadowbrook Muni (1950); Mick Riley GC (1965); Mt. Lomond G&CC (1949); Oquirrh Hills GC (9 1949); Rose Park GC (9); Timpanogas Muni (1950, NLE).
Wyoming: Purple Sage GC (9).

Courses remodeled or expanded by Mick Riley:

Utah: Nibley Park GC (R. 1949).

BERTRAND JAY RIVIERE
(1933–   )

BORN: Houston, Texas.

Jay Riviere was an outstanding high school and college athlete. While playing tackle on the Rice University football team, he was an All-Southwest Conference selection in 1954, '55 and '56. He also lettered on the Rice golf team. After college he worked as an assistant professional under Claude Harmon at Winged Foot GC in New York.

Returning to Texas in 1962, Riviere became involved in golf course construction, working for George Fazio in the creation of the Jackrabbit course of Champions Golf Club. After work on other Fazio projects, Riviere struck out on his own as a golf course architect in 1965. Based in Houston, Riviere made professional golfer Dave Marr a partner in his design firm in 1980. Marr, a former PGA champion, had also been assistant to Claude Harmon in the late 1950s at Winged Foot.

Courses by Jay Riviere:

Missouri: Lakewood Oaks GC (1980).
Texas: Bay Forest G Cse (1988); Bear Creek Golf World (Masters Cse 1973; Presidents Cse 1968); Bluebonnet CC (1973); Club del Lago (1984), with *Dave Marr;* El Campo CC; [The] Falls G&CC (1985), with *Dave Marr;* Frisch auf Valley CC (9); Green Meadows CC; Hearthstone CC (1977); Killeen Muni; Lake Houston GC; McAllen CC; Pasadena Muni; Pine Forest CC (27); Pinecrest GC; Point Aquarius CC; Quail Valley CC (El Dorado Cse, A.9; Executive Cse [9 Precision]); Rayburn G&CC (9 1968); River Plantation G&CC (27 1968); Roman Hills GC; South Shore Harbour GC (1983), with *Dave Marr;* Sun Meadow CC.
Panama: Club de G Panama.

Courses remodeled or expanded by Jay Riviere:

Louisiana: Acadian Hills CC (R.); Bayou Bend CC (R.); Lake Charles G&CC (R.); Oakbourne CC (R.); Pine Hills GC (R.).
Michigan: Blythefield CC (R. 1973).

Texas: Baywood CC (R.); Clear Lake GC (A.9 1965); Inwood Forest CC (A.9); Riverbend CC (R.); Riverside Muni (R.); Sharpstown CC (R.); Stephen F. Austin GC (R.9 A.9 1973); Temple CC (R.9 A.9).

Harry Robb, circa 1930 COLLECTION RON WHITTEN

HARRY ROBB
(1894–1952)

BORN: Montrose, Scotland.
DIED: Kansas City, Kansas, at age 58.

Harry Robb apprenticed under pro James Winton (father of golf architect Tom Winton) on the links at Montrose. Besides learning clubmaking from Winton, he also developed a fine competitive game and won several local Artisan tournaments. In 1912 he emigrated to America with his boyhood friend Tom Clark, who was also seeking work as a golf professional. After serving a short time as assistant pro at the Houston (Texas) CC, Robb moved to the Hutchinson (Kansas) GC, succeeding Clark as head professional. While in Hutchinson, he introduced the game to many small Kansas communities and laid out nine-hole courses in several of them.

In 1916 Robb moved to Kansas City, Kansas, again at Clark's behest. There he supervised construction of Milburn G&CC to the plans of William B. Langford and stayed on as head professional. He remained at Milburn for the rest of his life, except for military service during World War I and a brief trip back to Scotland to marry his childhood sweetheart. He continued to design an occasional course while at Milburn and laid out several in the Kansas City area during the 1920s. Upon his retirement from Milburn in the early fifties, his son succeeded him as professional.

Courses by Harry Robb:

Kansas: Dodge City CC (9); Emporia CC (9); Iola CC (9, NLE); Lake Barton GC; Newton CC (9); Old Mission G&CC (27 1930, NLE); Ottawa CC (9); Tomahawk Hills GC; White Lakes GC (NLE).

RUSSELL ROBERTS
(1922–   )

BORN: Gaithersburg, Maryland.

Russell Roberts studied engineering while serving with the U.S. Navy during World War II. After the war he joined Frank Murray in the construction of several courses to the plans of golf architect Alfred Tull. Between 1955 and 1959 the partnership of Murray and Roberts was involved in designing and building courses of their own. After Murray relocated in Florida, Roberts continued to lay out courses on his own along the Atlantic Seaboard.

Courses by Russell Roberts (All with Frank Murray unless otherwise indicated):

Delaware: Cavaliers CC (1959); Mapledale CC (*solo*); Old Landing GC; Rehoboth Beach CC (1962).
Maryland: Andrews AFB GC (East Cse 1956; West Cse 1960); [The] Bay C (1989 *solo*); Bel Aire G&CC (27 1959); Chantilly Manor CC (1969 *solo*); Hagerstown Muni (1957); Holly Hill CC (1974 *solo*); Maryland G&CC; Nassawango CC (1970 *solo*); Newbridge CC (*solo*); Northampton CC (1972 *solo*); Ocean City G&YC (Bayside Cse *solo*); Rocky Point GC (1971 *solo*); Swan Creek CC (1956); Valley Springs GC (9 *solo*); Washingtonian CC (Country Club Cse 1960; National Cse 1962).
Pennsylvania: Fairview G&CC (1959); GC at Hidden Valley (1988 *solo*); Heri-

Russell Roberts, circa 1970 COLLECTION RON WHITTEN

tage Hills G Resort; Lebanon CC; Penn Oaks CC (1966 *solo*).
Virginia: Eastern Shore Y&CC (9 *solo*); Lakeview CC (27 *solo*); Woodlawn CC (9 1969 *solo*).
West Virginia: Valley View GC (9 1963 *solo*).

Courses remodeled or expanded by Russell Roberts (All with Frank Murray unless otherwise indicated):

Delaware: Newark CC (A.9 1956).
Maryland: Chestnut Ridge CC (R.9 A.9 1966 *solo*); Northwest Park GC (A.3rd 9).

ALLAN ROBERTSON
(1815–1859).

BORN: St. Andrews, Scotland.
DIED: St. Andrews, Scotland, at age 44.

Allan Robertson, a prominent St. Andrews ball maker and the greatest golfer of his day, is considered the first professional golfer in history. In 1858 he became the first person to break 80 at St. Andrews, an incredible feat at that time. He used a gutta-percha ball in his record round, even though as a maker of feathery balls he had previously opposed the gutty.

At the urging of Sir Hugh Playfair (who, as provost of St. Andrews in 1842, had set about improving the town), Robertson exercised a general supervision of the St. Andrews links. He was credited with the 1848 modifications to the Old Course that widened the fairways and created the now famous huge double greens. Robertson also built a new 17th green on the classic Road Hole. Apart from St. Andrews, Robertson laid out links in various districts of Scotland, including a 10-hole course in Barry, Angus, that ultimately became Carnoustie. He was certainly, if unofficially, the first greenkeeper and golf course designer in history as well as the first golf professional.

DAVID ROBERTSON

The elder brother of Allan Robertson, Davie Robertson was a ball maker and senior caddy at St. Andrews. In 1848 he emigrated to Australia, where he introduced golf and later helped establish the Australian Golf Society. He laid out some of that country's first courses.

*Cabell Robinson,
1990* COURTESY ASGCA

CABELL B. ROBINSON
(1941–), ASGCA

BORN: Washington, D.C.

Cabell Robinson received a Bachelor of Arts degree in history from Princeton University in 1963 and then studied design for a year at Harvard, where he was a classmate of Rees Jones, son of golf architect Robert Trent Jones. In 1967 he obtained a Bachelor's degree in landscape architecture from the University of California at Berkeley and in the autumn of that year went to work for Jones in New Jersey. In 1970 Robinson moved to Spain to organize a European office for Robert Trent Jones Inc. Over the next seventeen years, Robinson handled most of the Jones designs done in Britain, Europe and North Africa.

In 1987 Robinson left the Jones firm and set up his own practice, based in Marbella, Spain. He continued to design courses in Europe and North Africa, particularly in Morocco.

Courses by Cabell Robinson (All as assistant to Robert Trent Jones unless otherwise indicated):

England: Stockley Park GC (1992 *solo*).
France: Chamonix GC (1983); Golf d'Ardon (1992 *solo*); Golf de la Côte d'Argent Moliets (27 1988); Golf de la Grande Motte (Long Cse 1988; Short Cse [Precision] 1988); Golf de Sperone (1990); Golf de Vidauban (1992); Golf du Club Med, Cannes (27 1990 *solo*); Golf Esterel (1992 *solo*).
Germany: Bodensee GC (1987).
Ireland: Ballybunion GC (New Cse 1985).
Italy: CC Castelgandolfo (1988); GC Castelconturbia (27 1987); I Roveri GC (27 1976).
Morocco: Golf de Cabo Negro (9 1991 *solo*); Golf de la Palmeriae (1991); Golf du Club Med (27 1991 *solo*);

Royal Golf de Fès (9 1991 *solo*); Royal Golf d'El Jadida (1991 *solo*); Royal Golf d'Erfoud (9 Precision 1990 *solo*); Royal Palace Golf d'Agadir (1987); Qettara GC (1993 *solo*).
Portugal: Quinta da Marinha GC (1985); Trioa GC (1980).
Spain: C de G Mijas (Los Lagos Cse 1976; Los Olivos Cse 1984); El Bosque GC (1975); Golf la Duquesa (1987); La Cala G&CC (Red Cse 1992 *solo*; Yellow Cse 1993 *solo*); Marbella G&CC (1990); Nueva Andulucía GC (Los Naranjos Cse 1977); Palheiro GC (1993 *solo*); Valderrama GC (1975).
Switzerland: Geneva G&CC (1973).

Courses remodeled or expanded by Cabell Robinson (All as assistant to Robert Trent Jones unless otherwise indicated):

France: Evian GC (R. 1989 *solo*).
Germany: Hamburg-Ahrensburg GC (R. 1978).
Portugal: Vilamoura II GC (R. A.5 1986).
Switzerland: Lugano GC (R. 1991 *solo*).

*C. E. "Robbie"
Robinson, 1970*
COURTESY *GOLF WORLD*

CLINTON E. ROBINSON
(1907–1989), ASGCA, PRESIDENT 1961, 1971

BORN: St. Amadee, Quebec, Canada.
DIED: Paris, Quebec, Canada, at age 82.

C. E. "Robbie" Robinson received a B.S.A. degree in 1929 from the University of Toronto's Agricultural College at Guelph, Ontario. He became interested in golf course architecture during his undergraduate years, when he updated and renovated the private course of Sir Joseph Flavelle (a Canadian magnate and prominent World War I statesman) at Fenelon Falls, Ontario. After graduation, he embarked on an apprenticeship of several years' duration with golf architect Stanley Thompson, who arranged a stint as course manager and superintendent at Sun-

ningdale CC in London, Ontario, for Robinson.

In 1936 Robinson returned to the Thompson firm and served with the Royal Canadian Air Force during World War II. Following military service, he was employed in site selection and development of housing with the Canadian government's Central Mortgage and Housing Department.

Robinson entered full-time private practice as a course architect in 1961, having designed and remodeled several courses on a part-time basis prior to that. He became recognized as an authority on turfgrass culture and for several years was director of the Royal Canadian Golf Association's Green Section. Robinson exerted considerable influence on the policies of his architectural profession. The top names in Canadian golf architecture after the death of Stanley Thompson were generally considered to be those of Clinton Robinson and Howard Watson. Ironically, both had started work for Thompson on the same day in 1929. In addition to his native Canada, Robinson worked in the United States, the Caribbean and South America. A few years before his death Robbie took on a young landscape architect, Douglas Carrick, as partner in the firm of Robinson and Carrick Ltd.

Courses by Clinton E. Robinson:

Michigan: Lemontree GC (9).
Pennsylvania: Conewango Valley CC.
Alberta: Windermere G&CC.
Manitoba: John Blumberg Muni (27 1970); Steinback Fly Inn GC (9).
New Brunswick: Gagetown GC (9); Gowan Brae GC; Sussex GC.
Newfoundland: Twin Rivers G Cse, Terra Nova National Park (9 1963).
Nova Scotia: Abercrombie CC (A.9); Ken-Wo G&CC (A.9); Lingan GC (A.9); Northumberland G&CC; Oakfield CC (1965).
Ontario: Antonio GC (Precision); Bayview G&CC; Beverly GC; Blue Mountain G&CC (9); Bowmanville CC (9); Bridgeport Fairways (Precision 1986); Cambridge GC; Cedar Brae G&CC; Chatham G&CC; Conestoga G&TC; Coral Creek G&CC (9); Craig Gowan GC; Dalewood G & Curling C; Deerhurst Inn & CC; Doon Valley GC; Dryden G&CC; East Park GC (Precision); Elgin House GC (1969); Fort Frances GC (9); Galaglades G & CC; Georgetown GC;

Hawthorne Valley G&CC (Par 3 1961); Hidden Valley GC (Precision 1968); Holiday Inn GC (9 Par 3); Huron Pines G&CC; Lido Golf Centre; Maple City G&CC (9); Merry Hill G&CC; Mount Hope G&CC; Oxford G&CC; Parkview GC; Richmond Hill G&CC; Richview G&CC; South Muskoka Curling & GC (1973); Strathcona CC (Precision 1970); Sturgeon Point GC; Sunningdale CC (New Cse 1970); Trafalgar G&CC; Twenty Valley G&CC; Tyandaga Muni; Upper Canada GC (1966); Windermere G&CC.

Prince Edward Island: Brudenell G&CC (1969); Green Gables GC (R. A.3rd 9); Mill River GC (1971); Stanhope G&CC.

Quebec: C de G Baie Comeau.

Saskatchewan: Holiday Park GC.

Colombia: Medellin GC, ass't Stanley Thompson.

Courses remodeled or expanded by Clinton E. Robinson:

Michigan: Dearborn CC (R.); Monroe G&CC (R.); Red Run GC (R.).

Pennsylvania: Melrose CC (R.).

Alberta: Calgary G&CC (R.); Earl Grey CC (R.).

British Columbia: Burnaby Mountain GC (R.); University GC (R. 1985); Vancouver GC (R.)

Manitoba: Assiniboine GC (R.); Elmhurst G Links (R.3); Pine Ridge G&CC (R.); Portage La Prairie GC (R.9 A.9); St. Charles CC (North Nine, R.).

New Brunswick: Fredericton GC (R.1); Miramichi G&CC (A.9); Moncton G&CC (R.); Restigouche G&CC (A.9); Riverside G&CC (R.); Westfield G&CC (R.9 A.9).

Nova Scotia: Amherst GC (A.3rd 9); Oakville GC (R.); Seaview GC (R.9 A.9); Truro GC (R.9 A.9).

Ontario: Barcoven GC (R); Bay of Quinte GC (A.9); Beach Grove G&CC (R.); Belleville G&CC (A.9); Brantford G&CC (R.); Briars G&CC (A.9 1972); Brockville CC (A.9); C. F. B. Borden GC (R.); Cherry Hill GC (R.); Credit Valley G&CC (R.); Dundas Valley G&CC (R.); Glen Lawrence G&CC (R.); Glendale G&CC (R.); Golf Land GC (Par 3, R.); Hamilton G&CC (A.3rd 9 1975); Huntington GC (R. 1961); Lake St. George G&CC (R.9 A.9); Lambton G&CC (R.); Manaki G&CC (R.); Oakdale G&CC (A.3rd 9); Oakland Greens GC (A.9); Oak-

ville G&CC (R.); Oshawa GC (R.6 1981); Pine Lake GC (A.9); Rideau View CC (A.9); Rosedale CC (R.); St. Catherines G&CC (R.); St. George's G&CC (R.4 1967); St. Thomas G&CC (A.9); Sarnia GC (R.); Spruce Needles GC (R.9 A.9); Thornhill GC (R.); Thunder Bay G&CC (R.); Westmount GC (R. A.4); Whirlpool GC (R.).

Prince Edward Island: Belvedere G & Winter C (R.).

Quebec: Beaconfield G&CC (R.); Elm Ridge CC (Cse No. 1, R.); Kanawaki GC (R.); Ki-8-EB GC (R.); Laval sur le Lac GC (R.); Royal Ottawa GC (R.).

Saskatchewan: Kenosee Lakes GC (A.9); Madge Lakes GC (R.9 A.9); Regina GC (R.); Wascana G&CC (R.); Waskesiu Lake GC (R.).

Colombia: Calis GC (R.); Medellin GC (R.); Mennezales GC (R.).

JOHN F. ROBINSON
(1947–)

BORN: Toronto, Ontario, Canada.

John Robinson, younger brother of golf architect William G. Robinson, attended the University of Michigan and received a Bachelor's degree in landscape architecture in 1970. During his college years, he worked summers in Ann Arbor for golf architect William Newcomb. Upon graduation he became a senior associate for Newcomb and assisted in the design and construction of eight courses over a three-year period. Robinson returned to Canada in 1973 and joined an engineering firm in Toronto as a senior landscape architect specializing in golf course design.

Robinson formed his own golf design firm, John F. Robinson & Associates, in 1977 and developed courses throughout Canada. Starting in 1984 his work in western Canada was in association with his brother William. In the late 1980s he established a branch office in Ohio and later moved his headquarters to Huntsville, Ontario.

Courses by John Robinson (All with William G. Robinson unless otherwise indicated):

Kentucky: Greenbrier GC (1971), ass't William Newcomb.

Michigan: Boyne Highlands GC (Moor Cse 1975), ass't William Newcomb; Great Oaks GC (1970), ass't William Newcomb; Green Hills GC (1970), ass't William Newcomb; Oasis G Cse

(Precision 1969), ass't William Newcomb; Prairie Creek GC (9 1972), ass't William Newcomb.

Montana: Glacier Greens GC (9 1991).

Ohio: Apple Valley GC (1972), ass't William Newcomb; Carroll Meadows GC (1988 *solo*); Firestone Farms G&CC (1991 *solo*); New Philadelphia G&CC (1991 *solo*); Union CC (1969), ass't William Newcomb.

Washington: [The] Creek at Qualchan G Cse (1992); Sea Links (Precision 1983).

Alberta: Cardiff G&CC (9 1984; A.9 1990); Douglasdale Estates GC (Precision 1985); Indian Lakes G&CC (Lakes Cse 1991); Lewis Estates GC (1992); [The] Links at Spruce Grove (1984); [The] Ranch G&CC (1989).

British Columbia: Arbutus Ridge G&CC (9 1987, A.9 1991); Brentwood Lakes GC (1991); Matticks Farm GC (1990); Moberly Lake GC (1982); Surrey G Cse (1989).

New Brunswick: Covered Bridge GC (1989 *solo*); Mount Carleton Provincial Park GC (1992 *solo*).

Ontario: Branchton Meadows GC (1990 *solo*); Oak Gables GC (1985 *solo*); Pine Knot G&CC (1990 *solo*); Springfield GC (1988 *solo*); Mill Race G&CC (1991 *solo*); Rock Chapel G&CC (1991 *solo*).

Saskatchewan: Emerald Park G&CC (1990); Mainprize Regional Park GC (1990 *solo*); Oxbow Park G&CC (1991 *solo*); Prince Albert GC (18 Par 3 1982); River Hills G&CC (1990); Saskatoon G&CC (West Cse 1991); Silverwood G Cse (18 Par 3 1987).

Courses remodeled or expanded by John Robinson (All with William G. Robinson unless otherwise indicated):

Michigan: Barton Hills GC (R. 1972), ass't William Newcomb; Pine Lake CC (R. 1970), ass't William Newcomb; West Branch GC (A.9 1971), ass't William Newcomb.

Montana: Buffalo Hill GC (R. 1989).

Ohio: Arrowhead Park GC (A.9 1991 *solo*); Echo Hills GC (A.9 1991 *solo*); Stillwater Valley GC (A.9 1991 *solo*); Wooster CC (A.9 1974), ass't William Newcomb.

Oregon: Willamette Valley G&CC (R. 1989).

Washington: Bellingham GC (R. 1983).

Alberta: Belvedere GC (R. 1982); Edmonton CC (R. 1981); Elks Lodge GC (R. 1981); Innisfail GC (R.9 A.9 1988);

Lacombe GC (A.9 1984); Sturgeon Valley G&CC (A.12 1983); Windemere GC (R. 1983).

British Columbia: Cowichan G&CC (R. 1989); Point Grey G&CC (R. 1989); Quilchena G&CC (R. 1989); Victoria GC (R. 1984).

Manitoba: Elmhurst G Links (R.9 A.9 1991 *solo*); Glendale G&CC (R. 1990).

New Brunswick: Miramichi GC (R. 1990 *solo*); Moncton G&CC (R. 1989 *solo*); Rockwood Park GC (A.9); Westfield G&CC (R. 1990 *solo*); Woodstock G&CC (R. 1990 *solo*).

Nova Scotia: Northumberland Seaside Golf Links (R.9 A.9 1990).

Ontario: Blue Mountain G&CC (A.9 1980); Cedar Green G&CC (A.9 1982 *solo*); Conestoga CC (A.9 1986 *solo*); Ironwood GC (A.9 1987 *solo*); Mississauga G&CC (R. A.3 1991); Pine Grove GC (A.9 1988 *solo*).

Saskatchewan: Long Creek G&CC (A.9 1990 *solo*); Wascana GC (R. 1982).

Ted Robinson, 1980
COLLECTION RON
WHITTEN

THEODORE G. ROBINSON
(1923–   ), ASGCA, PRESIDENT 1983

BORN: California.

Ted Robinson received a B.A. degree in naval science from the University of California in 1944 and a Master's in urban planning and landscape architecture from the University of Southern California in 1948. Following graduation, he was employed with a general land-planning and park-design firm. In 1954 he established his own practice in land planning, subdivisions and park design. He added golf course design to his business in the early 1960s after handling land plans on several residential development layouts.

Robinson had been introduced to golf by his father, who was active and well known in amateur golf circles and had long been involved with the game. Nevertheless, the transition from land planner to golf architect took Ted Robinson nearly

ten years to accomplish. By the late 1970s Robinson concentrated solely on course design and had worked extensively in the western United States, Mexico and the Pacific. Robinson also had planned two courses in Iran, but neither was ever built as a result of political unrest. Ted Robinson pioneered fabulous waterscapes as a feature of course design in the Southwest and Pacific Basin.

Courses by Ted Robinson:

Arizona: Dorado CC (1972); Ocotillo CC (27 1986); Westbrook Village CC (Precision 1982).

California: Bernardo Heights CC (1983); Blackhawk CC (Falls Cse 1988); Braemar CC (East Cse 1963; West Cse 1963); Camarillo Springs CC (1971); Canyon Lake GC (1969); Canyon Lakes CC (1987); Casta del Sol GC (Precision 1974); Cerritos Iron-Wood Nine GC (9 Precision 1976); Chaparral CC (1980); Crow Canyon CC (1976); DeAnza Palm Springs Mobile CC (Precision 1970); Desert Aire CC (1960); Desert Horizons CC (1979); Diamond Oaks CC (1964); Discovery Bay CC (1987); EastLake CC (1991); Fairbanks Ranch CC (1984); Indian Wells G Resort (East Cse 1986; West Cse 1986); Inglewood CC (Par 3 1965); Ironlakes CC (1983); Margarita Village G Cse (1992); Marrekesh CC (1983); Marriott's Desert Springs GC (Palms Cse 1986; Valley Cse 1986; putting Cse 1989); Marriott's Rancho Las Palmas CC (27 1977); Menifee Lakes G&CC (1990); Meridian Valley CC (1967); Mission Bay GC (Par 3 1964); Mission Lakes CC (1972); Monterey CC (27 1979); Mountain Gate CC (1975, A.3rd 9 1981); Mountain Meadows GC (1975); Navy GC (Cruiser Cse, 9 1970); North Ranch CC (1975); Oak Tree CC (1973); Oakmont CC (East Cse [Precision] 1974; West Cse 1964); Oaks North GC (27 Precision 1971); Old Ranch CC (1968); Palm Desert Greens CC (Precision 1971); Palm Valley CC (North Cse [Precision] 1986; South Cse 1984); Porter Valley CC (1968); Rams Hill CC (1982); Rancho Bernardo GC; Rancho Murieta CC (South Cse 1979); Rancho Santa Ynez CC (Par 3 1984); Reflections GC (Par 3 1986); Rolling Hills CC (1969); San Vincente CC (1972); Seven Lakes CC (Precision 1964); Silver Lakes CC (27 1975); Sun 'n Sky CC (9); Sunrise CC (Precision

1974); Sunset Hills CC (Precision 1974); Temecu CC (1992); Tijeras Creek GC (1990); Tustin Ranch GC (1989); Village CC (1962); Vista Valley CC (1979); Westlake Village GC (Precision 1966); Wood Ranch GC (1985).

Hawaii: [The] Experience at Koele (1991), with *Greg Norman*; Kalua Koi GC (1977); Ko Olina GC (1990); Waikapu Valley CC (1991).

Illinois: Royal Melbourne GC (1992), with *Greg Norman*.

Maryland: Tantallon CC (1961).

Nevada: Canyon Gate CC (1989); Sunrise Vista G Cse, Nellis AFB (9 1962, A.9 1970).

New Mexico: Inn of the Mountain Gods GC (1976).

Oregon: Charbonneau GC (27 Precision 1978); Summerfield G&CC (9 Precision 1973); Tokatee GC (1967); Trysting Tree GC (1988).

Texas: Bear Creek G&RC (East Cse 1980; West Cse 1981).

Utah: Sunbrook GC (1991).

Washington: Highland GC (9 Par 3 1968); Mill Creek CC (1974); Sahalee CC (27 1969); Sudden Valley G&CC (1972).

Japan: Lakewood GC (East Cse 1973; West Cse 1970); Sunpark Akeno GC (1992).

Mexico: Acapulco Princess CC (1972).

Courses remodeled or expanded by Ted Robinson:

California: Alondra Park GC (Cse No. 1, R. 1978); Candlewood CC (R.6 1971); El Dorado Park GC (R.12 1962); Fullerton Muni (A.9); Hacienda CC (R.2 1965); Indian Wells CC (R. 1984); Ironwood CC (South Cse, R. 1978); La Jolla CC (R.3 1973); Los Coyotes CC (R.6 1970); Navy GC (North Cse, R.6 1970); Pala Mesa G&TC (R. 1984); Palos Verdes CC (R. 1977); Pauma Valley CC (R.1 1983); Rancho Bernardo Inn & CC (West Cse, R.3 1984); Singing Hills CC (Oak Glen Cse, R. 1981; Pine Glen Cse, R. 1981; Willow Glen Cse, R. 1981); Stardust CC (R.6 1976); Stoneridge CC (R.9 A.9 1971); Tamarisk CC (R. 1972); Temecula Creek G Cse (A.3rd 9 1990); Thunderbird CC (R. 1986).

Washington: Everett G&CC (R.6 1969); Royal Oaks CC (R.2 1970); Seattle GC (R. 1969); Yakima CC (R.5 1974).

Bermuda: Southampton Princess GC (R. 1972).

Bill Robinson, 1985
COURTESY ASGCA

**WILLIAM GRIEVE ROBINSON
(1941–), ASGCA**

BORN: Toronto, Ontario, Canada.

As a young man, Bill Robinson turned down an opportunity to play professional hockey, deciding instead on a career in golf design. He studied landscape architecture at Penn State University and graduated in 1964 after two summers' experience working for the firm of Robert Trent Jones. A scratch golfer, he was a member of the Penn State golf team.

Following graduation, Robinson joined the practice of golf architect Geoffrey S. Cornish. In 1977 he formed and became president of Cornish and Robinson Golf Course Designers Ltd. of Calgary and Vancouver and engaged in designing courses in oil-rich Alberta and surrounding provinces. Robinson pioneered methods for modifying established layouts through long-range planning and researched putting green design and bunker placement. A talented freehand artist, Robinson illustrated many magazine articles dealing with course design and coauthored (with Cornish) the booklet *Golf Course Design—An Introduction*, distributed first by the National Golf Foundation in 1971 and then by the GCSAA. He fully updated the manual in 1989. Robinson was responsible for most of the sketches and diagrams in *The Golf Course*.

In the mid-1980s Robinson established a solo firm and later did a number of projects jointly with his brother John Robinson. In 1990 Robinson moved his headquarters to Oregon and continued to work extensively in western Canada and the Pacific Northwest.

Courses by William G. Robinson (All with Geoffrey S. Cornish unless otherwise indicated):

Connecticut: Blackledge CC (1966); Century Hills CC (1974); Clinton CC (1967); [The] Connecticut GC [FKA Golf Club at Aspetuck] (1966); Laurel View Muni (1969); Neipsic Par 3 GC (1974, NLE); Patton Brook GC (Precision 1967); Portland GC (1974); Simsbury Farms Muni (1971); South Pine Creek GC (9 Par 3 1968); Sterling Farms Muni (1971).

Maine: Frye Island GC [FKA Running Hills CC] (9 1971).

Maryland: Towson G&CC (1971).

Massachusetts: Cranberry Valley GC (1974); Dunfey's GC (Par 3 1966); Far Corner Farm GC (1967); Farm Neck GC (9 1976); Grasmere GC (9 Par 3); Greylock Glen CC (1973); Heritage Hills GC (Par 3 1970); Hickory Ridge CC (1969); Iyanough Hills GC (1975); Middleton GC (Par 3 1965); Pine Oaks GC (9 1966); Quashnet Valley CC (9 1976); Rehoboth GC (1966); Stow Acres GC (North Cse 1965).

Montana: Glacier Greens GC (9 1991), with John G. Robinson.

New Hampshire: Bretwood GC (1967); Cold Spring GC (1976); Eastman G Links (1975).

New Jersey: Bowling Green GC (1966).

New York: Addison Pinnacle CC (9 1969); Endwell Greens GC (1965); Grassy Brook GC (9 1974); Heritage Hills C (East Cse, 9 1974); Higby Hills CC (1966); Honey Hill CC (1967); Twin Hills GC (18 Precision 1967); Vesper Hills CC.

Ohio: Westfield CC (North Cse 1974); Zoar Village GC (1974).

Oregon: Prineville Meadows G Cse (1992 solo).

Pennsylvania: Host Farms GC (Executive Cse [9 Precision] 1967); Mill Race GC (9 1973, A.9 1977); Mountain Laurel GC [FKA Hershey Pocono GC] (1970); Standing Stone GC (1972); Sugarloaf GC (1966); Wilkes-Barre Muni (1967).

Rhode Island: Cranston CC (1974).

Vermont: Farms Resort GC (Par 3 1970); Manchester CC (1969); Mount Snow GC (1970); Quechee Lakes CC (Highland Cse 1970; Lakeland Cse 1975); Stratton Mountain G Academy (1972); Stratton Mountain GC (1969).

Washington: [The] Creek at Qualchan G Cse (1992), with John Robinson; Sea Links (Precision 1983), with John Robinson.

West Virginia: Canaan Valley State Park GCC (1966); Pipestem State Park GC (27 1966); Twin Falls State Park GC (9 1966).

Alberta: Cardiff G&CC (9 1984, A.9 1990), with John Robinson; Douglasdale Estates GC (Precision 1985), with John Robinson; Goose Hummock G&CC (1990 solo); Indian Lakes G&CC (Indian Cse 1988 solo; Lakes Cse 1991, with John Robinson); Lewis Estates G&CC (1992), with John Robinson; [The] Links at Spruce Grove (1984), with John Robinson; Ponoka Community GC (1987 solo); [The] Ranch G&CC (1989), with John Robinson; River Bend G Cse (1986 solo).

British Columbia: Arbutus Ridge G&CC (9 1987, A.9 1991), with John Robinson; Brentwood Lakes GC (1991), with John Robinson; Cordova Bay GC (1991 solo); Gallaghers Canyon GC (1979 solo); James Island GC (1990 solo); Matticks Farm GC (1990), with John Robinson; Moberly Lake GC (1982), with John Robinson; Olympic View G Cse (1990 solo); Pleasant Valley Par 3 G Cse (9 Par 3 1979 solo); Poplar Hills G&CC (9 1979 solo); Surrey G Cse (1989), with John Robinson.

New Brunswick: Campobello Provincial Park GC (9); Old Mill Pond GC (9 1984 solo).

Nova Scotia: Grandview G&CC (1988 solo); Halifax G&CC (New Ashburn) (1969).

Ontario: Clairville GC (1987); York Downs G&CC (27 1970).

Saskatchewan: Emerald Park G&CC (1990), with John Robinson; Prince Albert GC (18 Par 3 1982), with John Robinson; River Hills G&CC (1990), with John Robinson; Saskatoon G&CC (West Cse 1991), with John Robinson; Silverwood G Cse (18 Par 3 1987), with John Robinson.

Greece: Links at Porto Carras (1975).

Courses remodeled or expanded by William G. Robinson (All with Geoffrey S. Cornish unless otherwise indicated):

Connecticut: Avon CC (R.18 A.9 1966); Glastonbury Hills CC (R.4 1973); Hartford GC (R.2 1972); Keney Park GC (R.3); New London CC (R.5); Pequabuc CC (A.3); Quinnatisset CC (A.9 1967); Stanley GC (R. 27 1975); Watertown CC (A.9 1970); Wee Burn CC (R.4 1978); Wethersfield CC (R.1 1978); Woodway CC (R.4).

Delaware: Du Pont CC, Newark (Montchanin Cse, R. 1980); Du Pont CC, Wilmington (Du Pont Cse, R. 1980; Louviers Cse, R. 1980; Nemours Cse, R. 1980).

Maine: Brunswick GC (A.9 1964); Riverside Muni (A.9 1964); Waterville CC (A.9 1966); Webhannett GC (R.4 1970).

Massachusetts: Berkshire Hills (R.4); Brae Burn CC (R.2 1970); Brewster Green GC (A.2 1979, NLE); [The] Country Club, Brookline (R.2 1969); Dedham Hunt and Polo C (R.2); Duxbury YC (A.9 1969); Ellinwood CC (A.9 1969); Fall River CC (A.9 1975); Foxborough CC (A.9 1970); Framingham CC (A.2); Franconia Muni (R.7 1973); Fresh Pond Muni (A.9 1967); Kernwood CC (R.5 1968); Marlborough CC (A.9 1969); Oak Hill CC (R.5 1966); Quaboag CC (R.2); Segregansett CC (A.9 1976); Stow Acres CC (South Cse, A.9 R.9 1965); Tatnuck CC (R.5).

Minnesota: Somerset CC (R. 1979); Woodhill CC (R. 1979).

Montana: Buffalo Hill GC (R. 1989), with John Robinson; Crystal Lakes CC (A.9 1986 *solo*); Valley View GC (A.9 R.9 1986 *solo*).

New Hampshire: Abenaqui C (R.); Beaver Meadow Muni (A.9 1968); Hanover CC, Dartmouth College (R. 1970); Wentworth-by-the-Sea GC (A.9 1965).

New Jersey: Echo Lake CC (R.3 A.3 1968); Knickerbocker CC (R.6 1973).

New York: CC of Buffalo (R. 1965); Highland Park CC (A.9 1973); Ives Hill CC (A.9 1974); Monroe CC (R.2 1965); Oswego CC (A.9 1977); St. Lawrence University (A.12 1971); Shepard Hill CC (A.9 1970); Siwanoy CC (R.); Sodus Point GC (A.9 1966); Thendara CC (R.1 1968); Twin Hills GC (Precision, A.9 1967).

Ohio: Avon Oaks CC (R.6 1978); Canterbury C (R. 1978); Dayton CC (R. 1965); Miami Valley CC (R. 1965); Portage CC (R.); Westfield CC (South Cse, A.11 1967).

Oregon: Ocean Dunes G Links (R.9 A.9 1990 *solo*); Willamette Valley G&CC (R. 1989), with John Robinson.

Pennsylvania: Concordville CC (A.4 1974).

Rhode Island: Point Judith CC (R.9 1964); Quidnesset CC (A.9 1974).

Vermont: Montague GC (A.3).

Washington: Bellingham GC (R. 1983), with John Robinson; Overlake G&CC (R.2 1991 *solo*).

Alberta: Banff Springs GC (A.9 1990); Belvedere GC (R. 1982), with John Robinson; Calgary G&CC (R. 1978 *solo*); Canyon Meadows G&CC (R.

1978 *solo*); Cardiff G&CC (A.9 1990), with John Robinson; Edmonton G&CC (R. 1981), with John Robinson; Elks Lodge GC (R. 1981), with John Robinson; Highwood G&CC (R.18 A.9 1991 *solo*); Inglewood Muni (A.9 1978 *solo*); Innisfail GC (R.9 A.9 1988), with John Robinson; Lacombe GC (A.9 1984), with John Robinson; Lethbridge GC (A.9 1982 *solo*); Red Deer G&CC (A.9 1986 *solo*); Sturgeon Valley G&CC (A.12 1983), with John Robinson; Windemere GC (R. 1983), with John Robinson.

British Columbia: Alberni GC (A.9 1990); Cowichan G&CC (R. 1989), with John Robinson; Mount Brenton G Cse (A.9 1989 *solo*); Point Grey G&CC (R. 1973; R. 1989, with John Robinson); Quilchena G&CC (R.6 1979; R. 1989, with John Robinson); Seymour G&CC (R. *solo*); Vancouver GC (R. *solo*); Victoria GC (R. 1984), with John Robinson.

Manitoba: Breezy Bend CC (R. 1973); Dauphin G&CC (A.9 1985 *solo*); Elm Ridge CC (Cse No. 1, R. 1978); Elmhurst G Links (R.2 *solo*); Glendale G&CC (R. 1990), with John Robinson; St. Charles CC (North 9, R.; West 9, R. 1983).

New Brunswick: Fredericton GC (R.2 1967); Oromocto G Cse (R.9 1987 *solo*); Rockwood Park GC (A.9), with John F. Robinson.

Nova Scotia: Chester GC (A.9 1990); Digby Pines GC (R. *solo*); Hartland Point GC (R. A.3 1989 *solo*); Northumberland G&CC (A.9 1987 *solo*); Northumberland Seaside G Links (R.9 A.9 1990), with John Robinson.

Ontario: Blue Mountain G&CC (A.9 1980), with John Robinson; Mississauga G&CC (R. A.3 1991), with John Robinson.

Saskatchewan: Riverside G&CC (R. 1980 *solo*); Wascana GC (R. 1982), with John Robinson.

WILLIAM JAMES ROCKEFELLER (1864–1932)

BORN: Binghamton, New York.
DIED: Toledo, Ohio, at age 67.

W. J. Rockefeller grew up on his family's farm in New York, studied music for a time and worked as a hospital orderly before being hired as a greenkeeper at the newly formed Inverness Club in Toledo,

William J. Rockefeller, circa 1930 COLLECTION RON WHITTEN

Ohio, in 1903. He remained at Inverness for the rest of his life and in 1918 supervised the construction of the remodeling and expansion of the course by Donald Ross. The experience led him to take on some design-and-reconstruction projects of his own in the Toledo area.

Rockefeller was also known as a fine turfman and teacher of course maintenance. Two of his students became outstanding course superintendents, Joe Mayo of Pebble Beach and Al Schardt of Buffalo. Rockefeller's final project was the preparation of Inverness for the 1931 Open Championship, an exhaustive effort completed only a short time before his death in 1932.

Courses by William J. Rockefeller:

Ohio: Catawba Island GC (9); Lakemont CC; Napoleon Muni (9).

Courses remodeled or expanded by William J. Rockefeller:

Ohio: Inverness C (R.9 A.9 1919), ass't Donald Ross; Kettenring CC (A.9); Mohawk CC (R. A.3rd 9 1927).

JAMES B. ROOT (1939–   )

BORN: Detroit, Michigan.

James Root graduated from Memphis State University in 1960 with a Bachelor's degree in business administration and from the University of Georgia in 1966 with a Bachelor's in landscape architecture. After working in landscape architecture with the Virginia Department of Highways and several private firms, he established his own landscape architecture practice in West Virginia in 1969. In 1975 he relocated to Charlottesville, Virginia, and in the early 1980s authored a college textbook, *Fundamentals of Landscaping and Site Planning*. As a sideline of his business, Root handled a handful of golf course designs during his career: Dogwood Lakes CC (9) and Santa Rosa Golf and Beach Club (9) in Florida, the remodeling of Par-Mar Pines GC in West Virginia and a one-green, multiple-tee personal layout for Mrs. W. Alton Jones in Charlottesville, Virginia.

WILLIAM A. ROQUEMORE, JR.
(1948–   )

BORN: Lakeland, Georgia.

After attending the United States Air Force Academy and Georgia Tech, "Rocky" Roquemore joined his family in the business of building and operating daily-fee golf courses in the Atlanta area. His father had hired Floridian architect Joe Lee to lay out the plans for the first of their projects, and the design process so intrigued Roquemore that he begged Lee for a job. Lee made him a construction foreman in 1969 and stuck him in swamps and atop mountains on various projects. "After I saw he could take it," Lee was to recall some years later, "I brought him into the office."

Roquemore was made Lee's partner in 1970 and while remaining in the Atlanta area, handled most of Lee's course-design projects outside Florida. An experienced and talented designer, Roquemore received little public attention for his efforts, in much the same manner as Lee had been overshadowed by his mentor, the legendary Dick Wilson. One of his collaborations with Lee, Stonehenge Golf Club, in Fairfield Glade, Tennessee, was selected as the Best New Resort Course of 1985 by *Golf Digest* magazine and another, Pine Meadow Golf Club near Chicago, was chosen the magazine's Best New Public

Rocky Roquemore, 1991 COURTESY ROCKY ROQUEMORE

Course of 1986. In the late 1980s Roquemore took on a partner of his own, young Jeff Burton.

Courses by Rocky Roquemore (All with Joe Lee unless otherwise indicated):

Alabama: Wynlakes CC (1986).
California: Heritage Hills CC (1992).
Florida: Banyan GC (1973); Bocaire CC (1985 *solo*); Hamlet of Delray Beach GC (1973); Lake Buena Vista C (1972); Walt Disney World GC (Magnolia Cse 1970; Palm Cse 1970).
Georgia: Braelinn GC (1988 *solo*); Canongate on Lanier GC (1970); Canongate on White Oak GC (Cherokee Cse 1986; Seminole Cse 1990 *solo*); Chapel Hills GC (1992); Hidden Hills CC (1974); Horseshoe Bend CC (1975); Indian Hills CC (1970); Jekyll Island GC (Indian Mound Cse 1975); Lake Lanier Islands Hotel & GC (1988); Noname GC (9 1990), with Jeff Burton; Okefenokee GC (1983); Pine Hills CC (27 1974); Polo Fields G&CC (1989); Rivermont G&CC (1970); St. Simons Island C (1975); Sconti GC (1974; A.3rd 9 1991, with Jeff Burton); Sea Island GC (Marshside Nine 1973); Valdosta CC (27 1981).
Illinois: Pine Meadow GC (1985).
Louisiana: Beau Chene G&RC (Magnolia Cse 1983; Oak Cse 1974); Eastover CC (1988).
New York: WindWatch GC (1991).
North Carolina: Cross Creek CC (1982); Kenmure GC (1983).
Pennsylvania: CC at Woodloch Springs (1991), with Jeff Burton.
South Carolina: Houndslake CC (1976).
Tennessee: Fall Creek Falls State Park GC (1972); Stonehenge GC (1984).
Virginia: CC of Virginia (Tuckahoe Creek Cse 1988).
Wisconsin: Lawsonia GC (New Cse, 9 1983, A.9 1986 *solo*).
France: Makila GC (1992), with Jeff Burton.
Portugal: Golden Eagle GC (1992), with Jeff Burton; Quinta do Peru GC (1992), with Jeff Burton; San Lorenzo GC (1988); Vilamoura III GC (1990).
Venezuela: Barquismeto CC (1982); Guataparo GC (1982); Izcaragua CC (1982).

Courses remodeled or expanded by Rocky Roquemore (All with Joe Lee unless otherwise indicated):

Florida: Sugar Mill CC (A.9 1983); Tyndall AFB GC (A.9 1975).

Georgia: Berkeley Hills CC (A.3rd 9 1985); Cherokee Town & CC (Riverside Cse, A.9 1986); Flat Creek C (A.3rd 9 1983); Green Island GC (R. 1978).
Illinois: Cog Hill GC (Cse No. 4, R. 1990 *solo*).
North Carolina: Highland Falls CC (R.5 A.13 1985).
Portugal: Quinto do Lago GC (Cse No. 2, A.9 1987).

Joe Roseman, circa 1930 COLLECTION RON WHITTEN

JOSEPH A. ROSEMAN, SR.
(1888–1944)

BORN: Philadelphia, Pennsylvania.
DIED: Chicago, Illinois, at age 55.

Joseph Roseman began his career as a caddy at Philadelphia Country Club. In 1907 he was hired as a professional for Des Moines (Iowa) Golf & Country Club and shortly after his arrival took on the additional duties of greenkeeper. Gifted as an inventor, he created a hitch for horses that could accommodate three gang mowers at once, later adopted a Model T Ford to serve as a tractor unit to pull his gang mowers and then invented a hollow mower roller to preserve the turf as it moved.

Following a brief stint as pro-greenkeeper in Racine, Wisconsin, where he staked out the first nine holes for the country club there, Roseman moved to the Chicago area in 1916. In neighboring Evanston he founded the Roseman Tractor Mower Co. A short time later he laid out Westmoreland Country Club in Wilmette and remained there as pro-superintendent until 1928, when he resigned to devote more time to his power equipment company.

While course design was always a part-time endeavor, Roseman estimated that he had worked on more than fifty courses, many in collaboration with Jack Croke and George O'Neil. He also pioneered complete underground watering systems on several Chicago-area courses and built one of the first night-lighted par 3 courses in the country in 1933.

Courses by Joseph A. Roseman:

Florida: Fort Lauderdale CC (North Cse 1925).

Illinois: Barrington Hills CC (1920), with George O'Neil and *Jack Croke*; Crystal Lake CC, with George O'Neil and *Jack Croke*; Glenview Park GC [FKA Elmgate CC]; Grand Marais GC; Naval Air Station GC, Glenview (Cse No. 1 1927; Cse No. 2 1927); Suburban CC; Waveland GC (9 1924); West Wilmette Illuminated GC (Par 3 1933); Westmoreland CC (1927); Wilmette GC (1923); Wilmette Park GC.

Indiana: Tippecanoe CC (1920).

Michigan: Walnut Hills C.

Wisconsin: Maxwelton Braes GC, with George O'Neil; Petrifying Springs GC (1922); Racine CC (9).

Courses remodeled or expanded by Joseph A. Roseman:

Illinois: Glen View GC (R.), with George O'Neil; Green Acres CC (R.); Tam O'Shanter CC (R. 1940, NLE).

DONALD JAMES ROSS
(1872–1948), ASGCA, CHARTER MEMBER; HONORARY PRESIDENT 1947, 1948

BORN: Dornoch, Scotland.
DIED: Pinehurst, North Carolina, at age 75.

Donald Ross, son of the stonemason Mundo Ross, worked as an apprentice carpenter under Peter Murray of Dornoch. On the advice of John Sutherland, secretary of the Dornoch Golf Club, Ross went to St. Andrews, where he learned clubmaking at David Forgan's shop and studied golf with Old Tom Morris. In 1893 he returned to Dornoch and became its pro-greenkeeper. At Dornoch he gained from Sutherland a lifelong interest in the propagation and maintenance of grass for golf and an understanding of the fundamental qualities of a good golf hole.

In 1899, at the urging of Harvard astronomy professor Robert Willson, Ross emigrated to Boston, Massachusetts, where he became pro-greenkeeper at Oakley Country Club, a rudimentary layout that he quickly formalized. At Oakley

Donald Ross, circa 1935 COURTESY PHIL WOGAN

he met members of the wealthy Tufts family of Medford. The Tufts persuaded Ross to become winter golf professional at the resort they were developing at Pinehurst, North Carolina. For several years he continued to work summers at Oakley (and later Essex Country Club) in Massachusetts and winters at Pinehurst.

The planning and refining of courses at the Pinehurst golf complex brought Ross national fame. His services as a golf architect were soon in demand throughout North America, and from 1912 until his death in 1948, Ross was considered by many to be America's best-known and most active course designer. By 1925, 3,000 men were employed annually in the construction of Ross courses. Donald J. Ross Associates Inc. had winter offices at Pinehurst, summer offices at Little Compton, Rhode Island, and branch offices at North Amherst, Massachusetts (headed by Walter B. Hatch), and Wynnewood, Pennsylvania (headed by J. B. McGovern). Despite his extensive practice, Ross continued as golf manager at Pinehurst until his death.

Ross's design style incorporated naturalness and a links touch derived from his Dornoch background and training with John Sutherland. He sculpted his greens with a characteristic style that molded putting surface contours into the existing terrain. His green sites almost always put a premium on short recovery shots.

Ross played a major role in forming the ASGCA and was subsequently considered the society's patron saint. Its official jacket was of the Ross plaid, its annual award for contributions in furthering public understanding of golf architecture was named after him and it was no coincidence that the 1980 annual banquet was held in Dornoch.

Courses by Donald Ross:

Alabama: CC of Birmingham (East Cse 1927; West Cse 1929); CC of Mobile (1928); Mountain Brook C (1929).

California: Peninsula G&CC (1923).

Colorado: [The] Broadmoor GC (East Cse, 9 1918; West Cse, 9 1918); Wellshire CC (1926).

Connecticut: CC of Waterbury (1926); Hartford GC (1914, R.14 A. 4 1946); Norwich Muni (1927); Shennecossett CC (1916, R.3 1919); Wampanoag CC (1924).

Florida: Belleair CC [FKA Belleview-Biltmore Hotel & C] (East Cse 1925); Belleview Mido CC [FKA Pelican GC] (1925); Bobby Jones Muni (American Cse 1927; British Cse 1927); Brentwood GC (1923, NLE); Coral Gables Biltmore GC [FKA Miami Biltmore GC (North Cse)] (1924); CC of Orlando (1918); Daytona Beach G&CC (South Cse 1921; North Cse 1946); Delray Beach Muni (1923); Dunedin CC (1926); Florida CC (1922, NLE); Fort George Island GC (1927, NLE); Fort Myers G&CC (1928); Gulf Stream GC (1923); Hyde Park GC (1925); Keystone G&CC (9 1917); Lake Wales CC (1923); Melbourne GC (1926, NLE); Miami CC (1919, NLE); New Smyrna Beach Muni (1922); Palatka Muni (1925); Palm Beach CC (1917); Palma Sola GC (1924); Panama CC (1927); Pinecrest on Loleta GC (1926); Ponce de Leon Resort & CC [FKA St. Augustine GC (North Cse)] (1916); Riviera CC [FKA Miami Biltmore GC (South Cse)] (1924); San Jose CC (1925); Sara Bay CC (1925); Seminole GC (1929); St. Augustine GC (South Cse 1916, NLE); Timuquana CC (1923); University of Florida GC (1921).

Georgia: Athens CC (1926); Bacon Park GC (1926); Brunswick CC (9 1936); CC of Columbus (1915); Forest Hills GC (1926); Gainesville Muni (9 1920, NLE); Highland CC (9 1922); Roosevelt GC [FKA Warm Springs GC] (9 1926); Saffolds G Cse (1926); Savannah GC (1927); Sheraton Savannah Resort & CC [FKA General Oglethorpe GC] (1927); Walthour GC (1928, NLE); Washington Wilkes GC (routing 1928).

Illinois: Beverly CC (1907); Bob O'Link GC (1916); Calumet CC (1917); Evanston GC (1917); Hinsdale GC (1913); La Grange CC (1921); Northmoor CC

(1918); Oak Park CC (1916); Old Elm C (1913), with H. S. Colt.

Indiana: Broadmoor CC (1921); Fairview GC (9 1927); French Lick GC (Hill Cse 1917).

Iowa: Cedar Rapids CC (1915).

Kansas: Shawnee CC (1915).

Kentucky: Idle Hour CC [FKA Ashland CC] (1924).

Maine: Augusta CC (9 1916); Biddeford and Saco CC (9 1921); Cape Neddick CC [FKA Cliff CC] (9 1919); Lake Kezar GC (1918); Lucerne-in-Maine GC (9 1926, NLE); Paradise Springs GC (9 1920); Penobscot Valley CC (1924); Portland CC (1921).

Maryland: Fountain Head CC (1925); Hagerstown CC (1926, NLE); Indian Spring CC (1922, NLE); Prince George's CC (1921, NLE); Silver Springs GC (1921, NLE).

Massachusetts: Belmont CC (1918); Brae Burn CC (1912, R. 1947); Charles River CC (1921); Cohasse GC (9 1922); Concord CC (1914); CC of Pittsfield (1921); Ellinwood CC (9 1920); Essex CC (1917); George Wright Muni (1931); Greenock CC (9 1927); Kernwood CC (1914); Longmeadow CC (1921); Ludlow CC (1920); Nantucket GC (9 1917, NLE); Newton Commonwealth CC [FKA Commonwealth CC] (1921); North Andover CC (9 1920); Oakley CC (1900); [The] Orchards GC (9 1922, A.9 1931); Oyster Harbors C (1927); Plymouth GC (1908); Pocasset GC (1916); Ponkapoag GC (Cse No. 1 1933; R. 1939); Salem CC (1925); Sandy Burr CC (1924); Springfield CC (1924); Tatnuck CC (9 1930); Tekoa CC (1923); Toy Town Tavern GC (9 1924, NLE); Wachusett CC (9 1911); Waltham CC (9 1921, NLE); Wellesley CC (9 1910); Weston GC (9 1916, A.9 1923); Whaling City GC (9 1920); Whitinsville CC (9 1923); Winchester CC (1903, R. 1928); Worcester CC (1913); Wyckoff Park GC [FKA Mt. Tom CC] (1923).

Michigan: Barton Hills CC (1920); Brightmoor CC (1926, NLE); Dearborn CC (1923); Detroit GC (North Cse 1916; R. 2 1934; South Cse 1916); Elk Rapids GC (9 1923); Franklin Hills CC (1927); Fred Wardnell Estate G Cse (9 Par 3 1920, NLE); Grosse Ile G&CC (27 1919); Monroe G&CC (1919); Muskegon CC (1911); Oakland Hills CC (North Cse 1923; South Cse 1917); Rackham Park Muni

(1925); Rogell GC [FKA Redford Muni] (1910); St. Clair River CC (1923); Warren Valley CC (East Cse 1927; West Cse 1927); Western G&CC (1926).

Minnesota: Northland CC (1927); White Bear Lake YC (1915); Woodhill CC (1916, R. 1934).

Missouri: Hillcrest CC (1917); Midland Valley CC (1919, NLE).

New Hampshire: Bald Peak Colony C (1922); Balsam's Hotel GC (Panorama Cse 1912); Farnum Hill CC [FKA Carter CC] (9 1923); Kingswood CC (1926); Lake Sunapee CC (1927); Lake Tarleton C (1916, NLE); Manchester CC (1923); Tory Pines G Resort [FKA Mt. Crotched CC] (9 1929); Wentworth-by-the-Sea GC (9 1910).

New Jersey: Crestmont CC (1921); Echo Lake CC [FKA Cranford GC] (1919), with George Low; Essex County CC (East Cse 1924); Essex Fells CC (1910); Homestead CC (1920, NLE); Knickerbocker CC (1915); Lone Pine GC (1925, NLE); Montclair GC (27 1919); Mountain Ridge CC (1929); Plainfield CC (1916; R. A.3 1928); Riverton CC (1916).

New York: Bellevue CC (1914); Brook Lea CC (1926); CC of Buffalo (1923); CC of Rochester (1913); Chappequa CC (1929); Elmsford CC (1919, NLE); Fairview CC (1920, NLE); Glen Falls CC (1921); Hudson River GC (1916, NLE); Irondequoit CC (9 1916); Mark Twain GC (1937); Monroe CC (1923); Oak Hill CC (East Cse 1923; West Cse 1923); Rip Van Winkle GC (9 1919); Sagamore GC (1928); Siwanoy CC (1914); Teugega CC (1920); Thendara GC (9 1921); Tupper Lake GC (1915, NLE); Whippoorwill CC (1925, NLE).

North Carolina: Alamance CC (1946); Asheville CC [FKA Beaver Lake GC] (1928); Benvenue CC (1922, R. 1946); Biltmore Forest GC (1921); Buncombe County G Cse [FKA Asheville Muni] (1927); Burlington CC (1928); Cape Fear CC (1924; R. 1946); Carolina G&CC (1928); Carolina Pines GC (1932, NLE); Catawba CC (1946); Forsyth CC (1920); Greensboro CC (Irving Park Cse 1911); Hendersonville CC [FKA Laurel Park CC] (1927); Highland CC (1945); Highlands CC (1926); Hillandale CC (1915); Hope Valley CC (1926); Lenoir CC (9 1928); Linville GC (1924); Mid Pines C (1921); Mimosa

Hills GC (1928); Monroe CC (9 1927); Overhills GC (9 1910, A.9 1918); Pennrose Park GC (9 1945); Pine Needles CC (1927); Pinehurst CC (Cse No. 1, R.9 A.9 1901, R.5 1913, R.18 1937, R.2 1940, R.18 1946; Cse No. 2, 9 1901, R.9 1903, A.9 1906, R.2 1922, R.18 1933, R.3 1934, R.18 1935, R.1 1946; Cse No. 3, 9 1907, A.9 1910, R.18 1936, R.2 1946; Cse No. 4, 6 1912, A.3 1914, A.9 1919, NLE; Cse No. 5, 9 1928, NLE); Raleigh CC (1948); Richmond Pines CC (9 1926); Roaring Gap G&CC (1925); Sedgefield CC (1924); Southern Pines CC (Cse No. 1 1923; Cse No. 2 1928, 9, NLE); Stryker GC (1946); Tryon CC (9 1916); Twin City GC (1929); Waynesville CC (routing 1924); Wilmington Muni (1926).

Ohio: Acacia CC (1920), with Sandy Alves; Aladdin CC (1921, NLE); Athens CC (9 1921); Brookside CC (1922); Dayton G&CC (1919); Delaware GC (9 1924); Elks CC, Columbus (1921); Elks CC, Portsmouth (1920); Granville GC (1924); Hamilton Elks CC (1925); Hawthorne Valley CC (1926); Hyde Park G&CC (1927); Lancaster CC (9 1928); Maketewah CC (1919); Manakiki GC (1928); Miami Shores GC (1926); Miami Valley CC (1915); Mill Creek GC (North Cse 1928; South Cse 1928); Mohawk GC (9 1917); Piqua CC (9 1920); Scioto CC (1916); Shaker Heights CC (1913); Springfield CC (1921); Westbrook CC (1920); Wyandot Muni (1922); Zanesville CC (1932).

Pennsylvania: Aronimink GC (1928, R. 1930); Buck Hill GC (1922); CC of York (1927); Edgewood CC (1921); Elk View CC (9 1925); Green Oaks CC [FKA Westmoreland CC] (1921); Gulph Mills GC (1919); Immergrun GC [FKA Charles Schwab Estate GC] 9 1917); Kahkwa C (1915); Kennett Square G&CC (9 1923); LuLu Temple CC (1912); Overbrook GC (1922, NLE); Pocono Manor Inn & GC (East Cse 1919); Rolling Rock GC (9 1917); St. Davids GC (1927); Sunnybrook CC (1921, NLE); Wanango CC (9 1913, NLE).

Rhode Island: Metacomet CC (1921); Rhode Island CC (1911); Sakonnet GC (1921); Triggs Memorial Muni (1932); Wannamoisett CC (1914, R. 1926); Warwick CC (9 1924).

South Carolina: Fort Mill GC [FKA

Spring Mill CC] (9 1947); Lancaster GC (9 1935).

Tennessee: Belle Meade CC (1921); Brainerd Muni (1925); Chattanooga CC (1920); Cherokee CC (1910); Holston Hills CC (1928); Memphis CC (1910); Richland CC (1920, NLE); Ridgefields CC (1932); Tate Springs GC (1924).

Texas: Galveston Muni (1921, NLE); River Oaks CC (9 1924, A.9 1927); Sunset Grove CC (1923).

Vermont: Burlington CC (1930).

Virginia: CC of Petersburg (1928, NLE); CC of Virginia (Westhampton Cse 1921); Hampton GC [FKA Hampton Rhodes GC] (1921); Jefferson-Lakeside CC (1921); Kinderton CC (1946); Sewells Point GC [FKA Norfolk GC] (1927); Washington G&CC (1915); Woodberry Forest GC (9 1910).

Wisconsin: Kenosha CC (1922); Oconomowoc CC (1915).

Alberta: Banff Hotel GC (1917, NLE).

New Brunswick: Algonquin Hotel & GC (27 1927).

Nova Scotia: Liverpool GC [FKA White Point Beach GC] (1928).

Ontario: Essex G&CC (1929); Roseland G&CC (27 1921, R.9 1924).

Cuba: CC of Havana (1911, NLE); Havana Biltmore GC (1927, NLE).

Scotland: Royal Dornoch GC (R. A.2 1921).

Courses remodeled or expanded by Donald Ross:

Colorado: Lakewood CC (R. 1916).

Connecticut: Greenwich CC (R. 1946).

Florida: Belleair CC [FKA Belleview-Biltmore Hotel & C] (West Cse, R.9 A.9 1915); Palma Ceia G&CC (R. 1923); Punta Gorda CC (R. 1927).

Georgia: Augusta CC (R. 1927); Bon-Air Vanderbilt Hotel GC (Hill Cse, R. 1925, NLE); East Lake CC [FKA Atlanta Athletic C] (R. 1915; R. 1925; Cse No. 2, R. 1928, NLE).

Illinois: Exmoor CC (R. 1914); Indian Hill C (R. 1914); Ravisloe CC (R. 1915); Skokie CC (R. 1915).

Maine: Northeast Harbor GC (A.9 1920); Poland Springs GC (R.9 A.9 1920); York G&TC (R.9 A.9 1923).

Maryland: Chevy Chase CC (R. 1915); Congressional CC (Blue Cse, R. 1930).

Massachusetts: Bass River GC (R. 1914); CC of New Bedford (R.9 A.9 1920); Hyannisport C (R. 1936); Northeast

Harbor GC (A.9 1922); Oak Hill CC (R. 1921); Vesper CC (R.9 A.9 1919); Wianno CC (R. 1913); Woodland GC (R. 1927).

Michigan: Bloomfield Hills CC (R. 1936); [The] Highlands CC (R.9 1922; A.9 1927); Kent CC (R.9 A.9 1921).

Minnesota: Interlachen CC (R. 1919); Minikahda CC (R. 1917).

New Hampshire: Bethlehem CC (R.9 A.9 1910); Maplewood CC (R.9 A.9 1914); Mount Washington GC (R. A.3rd 9 1915).

New Jersey: Englewood CC (R. 1916; R. 1927, NLE); Ridgewood CC (R. 1916, NLE); Seaview GC (Bay Cse, R. 1915).

New York: Apawamis C (A.3); Chautauqua GC (R.9 A.9 1921); Fox Hills GC (R. 1928, NLE); Glenburnie G Cse (R. A.3, NLE); Wykagyl CC (R. 1920).

North Carolina: Blowing Rock CC (R.9 A.9 1922); Charlotte CC (R. 1923; R. 1946); CC of Salisbury (R. 1927); Grove Park Inn GC (R. 1924); Myers Park CC (R. 1947).

Ohio: Columbus CC (R.9 A.9 1914; R. 1920; R. 1940); Congress Lake C (R. 1926); Inverness C (R.9 A.9 1919); Oakwood CC (R. 1915); Willowick CC (R. 1917); Youngstown CC (R. 1921).

Pennsylvania: Allegheny CC (R.3 1923); Bedford Springs GC (R. 1924); Cedarbrook CC (R. 1921, NLE); Flourtown CC [FKA Philadelphia Cricket C] (R. 1914); Torresdale-Frankford CC (R.9 1912; A.9 1930); Whitemarsh Valley CC (R. 1930).

Rhode Island: Agawam Hunt C (R. 1911); Misquemicut GC (R. 1923); Newport CC (R. 1915); Point Judith CC (R.9 A.9 1927); Winnapaug GC (R.9 1921, A.9 1928).

South Carolina: Camden CC (R. 1939).

Vermont: Woodstock CC (R. 1938).

Virginia: Army-Navy GC (Arlington Cse, R. 1944); Bannockburn GC (R. 1924, NLE); Belmont Park GC [FKA Hermitage CC] (R. 1940); [The] Homestead GC (R. 1912); Westwood GC (R. 1926, NLE).

Manitoba: Elmhurst G Links (R.9 A.9 1923); Pine Ridge G&CC (R. 1919); St. Charles CC (South Nine, R. 1920).

New Brunswick: Riverside G&CC (R. 1937).

Nova Scotia: Brightwood G&CC (R. 1934).

Ontario: Rosedale GC (R.9 A.9 1919).

Scotland: Royal Dornoch GC (R. A.2 1921), with John Sutherland.

P. M. Ross, circa 1960 COURTESY P. M. ROSS, JR.

PHILIP MACKENZIE ROSS
(1890–1974) BIGCA, PRESIDENT 1972

BORN: Edinburgh, Scotland.
DIED: London, England, at age 83.

P. M. Ross learned to golf at Royal Musselburgh and won several Amateur medals as a youth. He served with the British army during World War I and upon discharge looked for a golf-related job. By chance he met golf architect Tom Simpson, who hired him as a construction boss in 1920. By the mid-1920s, Ross was a full partner in the firm of Simpson and Ross.

In the late 1930s Ross went to work on his own and developed a fine reputation as a designer in Great Britain and on the Continent. After World War II he demonstrated his talents to a new generation by reconstructing or restoring many war-ravaged courses. In 1972 Ross was elected the first president of the BIGCA.

Courses by P. M. Ross:

Azores: Furnas GC; San Miguel GC.

Belgium: Royal GC des Fagnes (1936), with Tom Simpson.

Canary Islands: Maspalomas GC (South Cse 1957).

Channel Islands: Royal Guernsey GC (1949).

England: Hythe Imperial GC (1950).

France: Borden G&CC; Club d'Amiens (9); Golf de la Barouge (9 1935, with Tom Simpson; R.9 1956); New GC (1929), with Tom Simpson.

Northern Ireland: Balmoral GC.

Portugal: C de G Vidago (1958).

Scotland: Southerness GC (1949).

Spain: Club de Campo de Malaga (1928), with Tom Simpson.

Courses remodeled or expanded by P. M. Ross:

Belgium: Royal Antwerp GC (R. A.9 1924), with Tom Simpson.

England: Alnmouth GC (R.); Carlisle GC (R. 1948); Thetford GC (R.).

France: Hardelot GC (Pines Cse, R. 1931), with Tom Simpson; Le Touquet GC (Forest Cse, R. 1958).
Isle of Man: Castletown GC (R.).
Northern Ireland: Bangor GC (R.).
Portugal: Estoril GC (R.9 A.9 1938).
Scotland: Dumfries and County GC (R. 1949); Glen GC (R.); Longniddry GC (R.); North Berwick Muni (Burgh Cse, R.); Turnberry GC (Ailsa Cse, R. 1951), with James Alexander.
Wales: Pyle and Kenfig GC (A.9).

ROBERT JACK ROSS

A civil engineer and prominent amateur golfer, Robert J. Ross served for years as city engineer of Hartford, Connecticut. In his spare time, Ross designed several Connecticut courses in the 1920s and 1930s. Decades later, most of his works were wrongly attributed to Donald Ross, an understandable if unfortunate consequence for any architect bearing the same name as a legend. The fact that some of his designs were considered those of the other Ross spoke well for the architectural abilities of Robert Ross.

Courses by Robert J. Ross:

Connecticut: Avon CC (9); Canton Public GC; Indian Hills CC; Stanley GC; TPC at River Highlands [FKA Edgewood GC] (1928), with *Maurice Kearney.*

Courses remodeled or expanded by Robert J. Ross:

Connecticut: Keney Park GC (R.); Wethersfield CC (R.9 A.9 1924).

Kurt Rossknecht, 1990 COURTESY KURT ROSSKNECHT

KURT ROSSKNECHT
BIGCA, ESGCA

Kurt Rossknecht studied landscape architecture at the Technical University of Munich. He then established a sports landscape and golf architecture company in Lindau, Germany. In the 1990s he established branch offices elsewhere on the Continent and was assisted in his work in Austria by landscape architect George Erhardt and in Switzerland by landscape architect Wolf Hunziker.

Courses by Kurt Rossknecht:

Austria: Bad Tatzmannsdorf GC (27); Donnerskirchen GC; Himberg Gutenhof GC; Salzkammergut GC (9); Schloss Schönborn GC (27); Ulrichsberg G Cse (27); Velden GC.
Germany: Bad Griesbach G Resort (1990); Bad Türkheim GC; Eichenried GC (24); Marktl-Inn GC (9); Motzener See GC (27); Oberstaufen-Steibis GC (9); Sagmühle GC; Schloss Egmating GC (27); Schloss Pähl GC; Starnberg GC; Wörthsee GC (24 1984).
Nigeria: Abuja GC.
Switzerland: Rheinblick-Lottstetten GC.

Courses remodeled or expanded by Kurt Rossknecht:

Austria: Salzburg Klesheim GC (R.9).
Germany: Furth im Wald GC (R.); Lindau–Bad Schachen GC (A.9 1985); Olching GC (R.).

Roger Rulewich, 1990 COURTESY ASGCA

ROGER G. RULEWICH
(1936–), ASGCA, PRESIDENT 1987

BORN: New Brunswick, New Jersey.

Roger Rulewich received a B.E. degree in civil engineering from Yale University in 1958. Following graduation, he was employed for a time with a firm of consulting engineers and landscape architects. In 1961 he joined the firm of Robert Trent Jones Inc., where he quickly took an active role in the design-and-construction inspection of Jones courses in the United States and abroad.

By the 1970s Rulewich was Jones's chief associate, and though receiving little national attention, he became a major force in the profession of golf architecture and was among the most active course architects in the world. In 1986 his design of the Applerock course of Horseshoe Bay CC in Texas, done in collaboration with Jones, was selected the year's Best New Resort Course by *Golf Digest.* In 1990 the Jones firm was awarded a contract to design at least eighteen courses for one owner in the state of Alabama, probably the single largest golf design agreement in history.

Courses by Roger Rulewich (All as assistant to Robert Trent Jones):

Alabama: Grand National GC (Auburn Cse 1993; Opelika Cse 1992; Short Cse [Par 3] 1992; Hampton Cove GC (Highland Cse 1992; Short Cse [Par 3] 1992; Lowland Cse 1992); Magnolia Grove GC (Crossings Cse 1992; Falls Cse 1992; Short Cse 1992 [Par 3]); Oxmoor Valley GC (Ridge Cse 1992; Short Cse [Par 3] 1992; Valley Cse 1992).
Connecticut: Bruce Memorial GC (1964); Fairview CC (1968); Lyman Meadow GC (1969).
Florida: Flamingo Island Club (1990); MetroWest CC (1987).
Georgia: Stone Mountain GC (1971); University of Georgia GC (1968).
Illinois: Hilldale GC (1972); [The] Rail GC (1974).
Louisiana: Santa Maria GC (1987).
Maine: Evergreen Valley GC (9 1975, NLE).
Massachusetts: Crumpin-Fox C (9 1978, A.9 1989); Ipswich CC (1989); Round Hill C (9 routing); Tara Ferncroft CC (1970).
Michigan: Treetops GC (1987).
Minnesota: Jonathan Par 30 GC (9 Precision 1974).
Missouri: CC at the Legends (1989); [The] Lodge of Four Seasons GC (1974).
New Jersey: Metedeconk National GC (1987, A.3rd 9 1990); Panther Valley CC (1969); [The] Spa GC ([9 Precision] 1988).
New York: Radisson Greens GC (1977).
North Carolina: Carolina Trace G&CC (Creek Cse, 9 1979, A.9 1986); Lake Cse 1971).
Ohio: Firestone CC (North Cse 1969).
South Carolina: Greenville CC (Chanticleer Cse 1970); Palmetto Dunes CC (Jones Cse 1969); Seabrook Island GC (Crooked Oaks Cse 1981).

Texas: Horseshoe Bay CC (Applerock Cse 1985; Ram Rock Cse 1981).
Virginia: Robert Trent Jones GC (1991).
West Virginia: Cacapon Springs GC (1973); Speidel GC (1973).
Wisconsin: [The] Springs GC (1969).
Alberta: Kananaskis Country GC (Mount Kidd Cse 1984; Mount Lorette Cse 1983).
British Columbia: Rivershore GC (1981).
Bermuda: Port Royal GC (1970); St. George's GC (Precision 1985).
Dominican Republic: Playa Dorada GC (1979).
Guadeloupe: G de St. François (1978).
Ireland: Ballybunion GC (New Cse 1985).
Martinique: Empress Josephine GC (1976).
Puerto Rico: Cerromar Beach GC (North Cse 1972; South Cse 1972).
Virgin Islands: Carambola Beach GC [FKA Fountain Valley GC] (1967).

Courses remodeled or expanded by Roger Rulewich (All as assistant to Robert Trent Jones):

Connecticut: Hartford GC (R. 1966).
Missouri: Bellerive CC (R. 1989).
New Jersey: Crestmont GC (R. 1978); Glen Ridge CC (R. 1978); North Jersey CC (R. 1979).
New York: Colonie Muni (A.9 1980); IBM CC, Poughkeepsie (R. 1985).
North Carolina: Tanglewood GC (East Cse, A.9 1970).
Ohio: Brookside CC (R. 1982).
Pennsylvania: Aronimink GC (R. 1989); Valley Brook CC (R. 1978).
Wisconsin: Milwaukee CC (R. 1975).
Puerto Rico: Dorado Beach GC (West Cse, A.9 1966).

ALEX RUSSELL

Australian amateur golfer Alex Russell counted the 1924 Australian Open among several victories in his career. In 1926 he assisted Alister Mackenzie in laying out the original course at Royal Melbourne GC and on a few other Australian designs during the famous architect's only sojourn through Australia. Following Mackenzie's departure, Russell designed and built an additional course at Royal Melbourne, as well as several others in Australia and New Zealand.

Alex Russell, circa 1930 COLLECTION RON WHITTEN

Courses by Alex Russell:

Australia: Lake Karrinyup CC (1927), with Alister Mackenzie; Royal Melbourne GC (East Cse 1932; West Cse 1926, with Alister Mackenzie); Yarra Yarra GC (1929), with Alister Mackenzie.
New Zealand: Paraparaumu Beach GC (1949).

EDWARD RYDER

Ed Ryder attended Hofstra University, studying landscape architecture, engineering and business with the avowed intent of becoming a golf course architect. In 1960, on the advice of golf architect Geoffrey Cornish, Ryder joined the golf course contracting firm of C. B. Carlson & Sons. In that capacity he worked on construction sites of layouts designed by several prominent architects in the Northeast. In the mid-1960s he began designing and remodeling courses in metropolitan New York in partnership with Val Carlson, one of C.B.'s sons. In 1970 Ryder moved to Florida, where he opened his own golf design firm, based in Coral Springs.

Courses by Edward Ryder:

Connecticut: Harry Brownson CC (1964) with *Val Carlson;* Redding CC (9); Richter Park GC (1964).
Florida: Palm Gardens GC (Precision 1979); Suntree CC (Classic Cse).
New York: Back O'Beyond GC (1964), with *Val Carlson;* Salem GC, with *Val Carlson.*

Courses remodeled or expanded by Edward Ryder:

New York: Banksville CC (Precision A.9).

BERNARD SAYERS
(1857–1924)

BORN: Leith, Scotland.
DIED: North Berwick, Scotland, at age 67.

A genuine character in golf history, five-foot three-inch Ben Sayers trained as an acrobat before deciding on a career as a clubmaker and golf professional. Outspoken and flamboyant, Sayers thought nothing of turning a cartwheel on a green in celebration after sinking a putt. After working as an assistant at Musselburgh,

Ben Sayers, circa 1895 COLLECTION RON WHITTEN

Sayers became a professional at North Berwick, succeeding Davie Strath. He remained in that position for the remainder of his life.

A talented player, Sayers played in every British Open from 1880 to 1923, and although he never won it, he came close on several occasions. Ben laid out several golf courses in the North Berwick area and elsewhere. He was best remembered, however, for the handmade clubs and golf balls that bore his name.

Courses by Ben Sayers:

Northern Ireland: Castlerock GC (1901).
Scotland: Broomie Knowe GC (1906); Moffat GC (1904); North Berwick East Links (9 1894, A.9 1906, with James Braid).

MARIO D. SCHJETNAN

Mario Schjetnan, the son of a Norwegian settler in Mexico, became a club professional in that country. He began designing courses there in the late 1950s, and by the seventies he was considered one of Mexico's top course architects. In the 1980s he teamed with fellow Mexican golf architect Pedro Guereca to construct a series of spectacular oceanfront courses for Fonatur, the Mexican national tourism council.

Courses by Mario Schjetnan:

Mexico: Campestre de G Loreto (1990), with *Pedro Guereca*; C Campestre Coazacoalcos; C Campestre de León (9 1960); C Campestre Huatulco (1990), with *Pedro Guereca*; C Campestre Lomas de Cocoyoc (1978); C Deportivo Cocoyoc (9).

HANS CARL SCHMEISSER (1892–1980)

BORN: Ulm, Germany.
DIED: West Palm Beach, Florida, at age 88.

Course superintendent of the Fort Lauderdale (Florida) Country Club in the early 1950s and later superintendent for the Miami Beach Parks Department, Hans Schmeisser designed several Florida courses in the late 1950s and early 1960s, most of them par-3 or precision courses. One of his sons, John, was on the construction staff of Robert Trent Jones for a time, while a second, Otto, served as superintendent of The Everglades Club at Palm Beach. Hans Schmeisser received a GCSAA Distinguished Service Award in 1981.

Courses by Hans Schmeisser:

Florida: Forest Hill GC (Precision 1966); Glen Oaks GC (9 Par 3 1960); Lakeland Par 3 GC (Par 3); Lauderdale Lakes CC (Precision 1960); Madison CC (9); Oak Ridge CC (1962); Par Three GC (Par 3 1960); Pines GC (Par 3 1961); Sebring Shores GC (Par 3 1964); Whispering Oaks CC (9 1956).

Courses remodeled or expanded by Hans Schmeisser:

Florida: Rocky Point GC (R.); Sunset G&CC (R.); Temple Terrace G&CC (R. 1960).

LEE E. SCHMIDT (1947–), ASGCA

BORN: Valparaiso, Indiana.

During his high school summers, Lee Schmidt worked on the maintenance crew at Woodland CC in Carmel, Indiana, where golf architect Bill Diddel made

his residence. Encouraged by Diddel, Schmidt attended Purdue University and graduated in 1970 with a Bachelor of Science degree. He then landed a job as a golf course site coordinator for Pete Dye on several projects, then assisted Dye in the design of a second 18 at Casa de Campo in the Dominican Republic.

When he returned to the States in 1979, Schmidt joined Landmark Land Co., a large California-based real estate development corporation, as vice president of its design-and-construction division. In that capacity, he worked again with Pete Dye, who handled all the early Landmark jobs. In the late 1980s Schmidt headed the design team on a series of Landmark course designs. But when Landmark was struck with economic woes in 1990, Schmidt resigned and joined the Jack Nicklaus organization as a senior designer based in its Hong Kong office. From that location he supervised Nicklaus designs in the booming markets of Japan, Thailand and Taiwan.

Courses by Lee Schmidt (All as assistant to Pete Dye unless otherwise indicated):

California: La Quinta Hotel GC (Citrus Cse 1987; Dunes Cse 1981; Mountain Cse 1980); Mission Hills G&CC (Dinah Shore Cse 1988); Mission Hills Resort GC (1987); Moreno Valley Ranch (27 1988); Mount Woodson GC (1991), with Brian Curley; Oak Valley GC (1990), with Brian Curley; PGA West GC (Stadium Cse 1986).
Louisiana: Oak Harbor Y&CC (1991 solo).
Dominican Republic: Casa de Campo (Links Cse 1976).
Japan: Hananomori GC (1992), ass't Jack Nicklaus; Huis Ten Bosch CC (1992), ass't Jack Nicklaus; Komono GC (1992), ass't Jack Nicklaus; Sendai Minami GC (1992), ass't Jack Nicklaus.

Lee Schmidt, 1987
COLLECTION RON
WHITTEN

Philippines: Manila Southwoods G&CC (1992), ass't Jack Nicklaus.
Thailand: Golden Valley CC (1992), ass't Jack Nicklaus; Laem Chabang International CC (27 1992), ass't Jack Nicklaus; Mission Hills GC (1992), ass't Jack Nicklaus; Springfield Royal CC (1992), ass't Jack Nicklaus; Winsan GC (1992), ass't Jack Nicklaus.

Craig Schreiner, 1990 COURTESY ASGCA

WILLIAM CRAIG SCHREINER (1952–), ASGCA

BORN: Kansas City, Missouri.

Craig Schreiner obtained an associate degree in turfgrass management from Ohio State University at Wooster in 1974, where he played on the golf team and was president of its Student Senate, and a B.S. in landscape architecture from Oregon State the following year. After teaching at Kent State, working in course maintenance and serving on a course-construction crew, Schreiner joined forces with Tulsa golf architect Don Sechrest. From 1985 to 1988 Schreiner was Sechrest's principal designer. His collaboration with Sechrest at Page Belcher's Stone Creek course in Tulsa was named runner-up as the Best New Public Course of 1988 by *Golf Digest*.

In 1988 Schreiner worked as a design coordinator with the Hurdzan Design Group in Columbus, Ohio. In 1990 Schreiner entered private practice, basing his firm, called Golf Design from the Heartlands, in his native Kansas City.

Courses by Craig Schreiner:

Kansas: Terradyne Resort & CC (1987), ass't Don Sechrest; West Links GC (Precision 9 1992).
Minnesota: Baker National GC (1990), ass't Michael Hurdzan.
Missouri: Crystal Highlands GC (1988), ass't Michael Hurdzan.
New York: Cobblestone Creek CC (1991), ass't Michael Hurdzan.

Ohio: Royal American Links (1991), ass't Michael Hurdzan.
Oklahoma: Page Belcher G Cse (Stone Creek Cse 1987), ass't Don Sechrest.
Pennsylvania: Hickory Heights GC (1991), ass't Michael Hurdzan.
Virginia: Hamptons GC (27 1990), ass't Michael Hurdzan.

Courses remodeled or expanded by Craig Schreiner:

Kansas: Clapp Park GC (R.5 1988), ass't Don Sechrest; Mariah Hills G Cse (R. 1987), ass't Don Sechrest; Meadowbrook CC (R.5 1987), ass't Don Sechrest; Sim Park GC (R.16 1987), ass't Don Sechrest.
Minnesota: Hastings CC (R.3 1990); Minikahda Club (R. 1990), ass't Michael Hurdzan.
Missouri: Lakewood Oaks CC (R.4 1987), ass't Don Sechrest.
Ohio: Manakiki GC (R. 1990).
Oklahoma: Bristow CC (R. 1986), ass't Don Sechrest; Fort Cobb State Park GC (A.9 1986), ass't Don Sechrest; Ponca City CC (R. 1987), ass't Don Sechrest.

CHARLES DARL SCOTT

In the mid-1960s Charles Scott assisted his father, Darl Scott, a longtime former course superintendent at Gull Lake Country Club near Battle Creek, Michigan, in the design and construction of Gull Lake View Golf Club. The project, owned and operated by the Scott family, was such a success that Charles added a second course half a dozen years later, then designed and built several others in the Battle Creek area. He was assisted in the operation of the courses, all owned by the Scott family, by his father and mother, his wife, Betsie, and a brother, Jim, and his wife.

Courses by Charles Darl Scott:

Michigan: Binder Park G Cse; Clearbrook GC; Indian Run G Cse; Gull Lake View GC (East Cse 1974; West Cse, 9 1963, A.9 1965, with *Darl Scott*); Lake Doster GC (1967); Stonehedge GC (1989).

Courses remodeled or expanded by Charles Darl Scott:

Michigan: Bedford Valley GC (R. 1988); Gull Lake View GC (West Cse, R. 1980).

Ed Seay, 1990
COURTESY ED SEAY

EDWIN B. SEAY
(1938–), ASGCA, PRESIDENT 1976

BORN: Dade City, Florida.

Ed Seay graduated from the University of Florida with a Bachelor's degree in landscape architecture and was then commissioned as an officer in the U.S. Marine Corps. His architectural career began in 1964 as an associate of golf architect Ellis Maples. Under Maples, Seay was involved in the design and construction of twenty-seven courses.

Seay entered private practice, based in Florida, in 1972. He later joined forces with legendary professional golfer Arnold Palmer in a corporation known as Palmer Course Design Company. Seay handled designs throughout the world as director of design for the firm. It became, in the 1980s, one of the most active and prolific design businesses in the country. In 1984 Palmer Course Design created the first golf course ever built in the People's Republic of China. In 1987 its Semiahmoo Golf and Country Club was selected by *Golf Digest* as the nation's Best New Resort Course of the year.

Courses by Ed Seay (All with Arnold Palmer unless otherwise indicated):

Alabama: Cotton Creek C (1987).
Arizona: Arrowhead CC (1986); [The] Legend GC (1988); Mesa del Sol GC (1982).
California: Aviara G Cse (1991); Ironwood CC (Short Cse [9 Par 3] 1975); Mission Hills G&CC (New Cse 1979); PGA West GC (Palmer Cse 1986).
Colorado: Bear Creek GC (1986); [The] Broadmoor GC (South Cse 1976); Lone Tree GC (1986).
Florida: Adios CC (1985); Deering Bay Y&CC (1991); Isleworth G&CC (1986); Marsh Landing CC (1986); Matanzas Woods GC (1986); Mill Cove GC (1990); Monarch CC (1987); Orchid Island G & Beach C (1990); PGA National GC (The General Cse 1985); Pine Lakes GC (1980); [The]

Plantation at Ponte Vedra GC (1987); Saddlebrook G&TC (Palmer Cse 1986); Sawgrass GC (Oceanside Cse 1974 *solo*, R. 1979 *solo*; A. South Nine 1985 *solo*); Spessard Holland GC (Precision 1977); Suntree CC (Challenge Cse 1987); Wildcat Run CC (1985).
Georgia: Eagle Watch GC (1989); Goshen Plantation CC (1986), ass't Ellis Maples; Landings at Skidaway Island (Marshwood Cse 1979); West Lake CC (1968), ass't Ellis Maples; Whitewater Creek GC (1988).
Hawaii: Hapuna Beach GC (1992); Hawaii Prince GC (1993); [The] Highlands GC (1992); Kapalua GC (Village Cse 1980); Turtle Bay GC (Palmer Cse 1992).
Illinois: Spencer T. Olin Community G Cse (1988); White Eagle GC (1989).
Kentucky: Lake Forest GC (1992).
Louisiana: [The] Bluffs on Thompson Creek CC (1988).
Maryland: Prince George's G&CC (1981).
Michigan: Shanty Creek GC (The Legend Cse 1985).
Missouri: North Port National G&CC (1992).
Nevada: Angel Park GC (Mountain Cse, routing 1989; Palm Cse, routing 1990); Dayton Valley GC (1991).
New Jersey: Laurel Creek CC (1990).
North Carolina: Bermuda Run G&CC (1971), ass't Ellis Maples; Brook Valley G&CC (1967), ass't Ellis Maples; Cedar Brook CC (1965), ass't Ellis Maples; Chockoyette CC (1972), ass't Ellis Maples; Cullasaja C (1989); CC of Johnston County (1967), ass't Ellis Maples; CC of Whispering Pines (West Cse 1970), ass't Ellis Maples; Deep Springs CC (9 1971), ass't Ellis Maples; Duck Woods GC (1968), ass't Ellis Maples; Grandfather G&CC (1968), ass't Ellis Maples; Indian Valley CC (1974), ass't Ellis Maples; Pinehurst Plantation GC (1992); Quarry Hills CC, ass't Ellis Maples; Red Fox CC (1965), ass't Ellis Maples; Sapona CC (1967), ass't Ellis Maples; TPC at Piper Glen (1989); Walnut Creek CC (1968), ass't Ellis Maples; Woodlake CC, ass't Ellis Maples.
Pennsylvania: Commonwealth National GC (1990).
South Carolina: CC of South Carolina (1969), ass't Ellis Maples; Musgrove Mill GC (routing 1988); Wellman CC (1970), ass't Ellis Maples.

South Dakota: Dakota Dunes CC (1991).

Tennessee: Ridgeway CC (1972), ass't Ellis Maples.

Texas: Barton Creek C (Lakeside Cse) [FKA Hidden Hills GC] 1986); GC at Fossil Creek (1987).

Utah: Jeremy Ranch GC (1980).

Virginia: Countryside CC (1967), ass't Ellis Maples; Kingsmill GC (Plantation Cse 1986); Lexington GC (1971), ass't Ellis Maples.

Washington: Semiahmoo GC (1986).

Wisconsin: Geneva National G&CC (Palmer Cse 1991).

Wyoming: Teton Pines G Cse (1987).

British Columbia: Whistler Village GC.

Australia: Sanctuary Cove GC (1989).

China: Chung-Shan GC (1985).

Ireland: Kildare Hotel & CC (1991); Tralee GC (1985).

Italy: Cà della Nave GC (1987).

Japan: Ajigawasa GC (A and B Cses 1992); Aso GC (A and B Cses 1990); Furano CC (1975); Iga Ueno CC (1974); Kanegasaki GC (1990); Manago CC (1974); Minikami Kogen GC (Center Cse 1992; Lower Cse 1986; Upper Cse 1986); Niseko GC (1986); Niseko Kogen GC (1986); Nishi Biwako GC (1987); Shimotsuke CC (1975); Tsugaru Kogen GC (1986).

Korea: Eunhwasam CC (1992).

Malaysia: Damai Beach GC (1992).

Taiwan: Formosa G&CC (1987); Formosa Yangmei G&CC (A and B Cses 1992).

Thailand: Bangpoo GC (1981).

Courses remodeled or expanded by Ed Seay (All with Arnold Palmer unless otherwise indicated):

Alabama: Anniston CC (R. 1975 *solo*).

Arizona: Scottsdale CC (R. A.3rd 9 1986).

California: Rancho Murieta CC (R. 1988); San Jose CC (R. 1977 *solo*).

Colorado: Cherry Hills CC (R. 1977); Denver CC (R. 1975 *solo*); Snowmass GC (R. 1982).

Florida: Hidden Hills CC, Jacksonville (R. 1986); Meadowood G&TC (R. 1987); Oakbridge C (R. 1982); Pasadena Y&CC (R. 1991).

Georgia: Atlantic Athletic C (Highlands Cse, R. 1989); Forest Hill GC (R. 1986); Stouffer's PineIsle Resort GC (R. 1988).

North Carolina: Carmel CC (South Cse, A.9 1970), ass't Ellis Maples; Quail Hollow CC (R. 1985); Reynolds Park GC (R. 1966), ass't Ellis Maples; Rox-

boro CC (A.9 1969), ass't Ellis Maples; Stanley County CC (R. 1966), ass't Ellis Maples.

Oklahoma: Hillcrest CC (R. 1985).

Pennsylvania: Allegheny CC (R. 1975 *solo*); Laurel Valley GC (R. 1988); Oakmont CC (R. 1978).

Virginia: Keswick C of Virginia (R. 1991).

Don Sechrest, 1991

DONALD R. SECHREST
(1933–)

BORN: St. Joseph, Missouri.

Don Sechrest received a Bachelor of Science degree in business in 1956 from Oklahoma State University in Stillwater, where he had played on the golf team coached by Labron Harris, Sr. Turning professional upon graduation, Sechrest worked with his former coach at Oklahoma State for ten years and during that time tried his hand at the PGA Tour. In 1966 he laid out and supervised the building of a course for Stillwater Golf & Country Club and then served a short term as its club pro.

In 1968 Sechrest entered private practice as a golf course architect based in Tulsa. In the 1980s he moved his base of operations to Kansas City, Missouri, where he was assisted by young architect Craig Schreiner.

Courses by Don Sechrest:

Arkansas: Champions G&CC (1990).

Iowa: Ames G&CC (1974).

Kansas: Heritage Park G Cse (1990); Southwind CC (1980); Terradyne Resort & CC (1987).

Missouri: Loch Lloyd CC (1991); Loma Linda CC (North Cse 1978).

Oklahoma: Boiling Springs GC; [The] Greens G&RC (1973); Heritage Hills GC (1977); Indian Springs CC (Windmill Cse 1974); Page Belcher G Cse (Stone Creek Cse 1987); Fire Lake GC

(1982); Shangri-La CC (Blue Cse 1971; Gold Cse 1982); Stillwater G&CC (1966).

Texas: Brownsville CC (1977); Monte Cristo CC (1974).

Courses remodeled or expanded by Don Sechrest:

Kansas: Clapp Park GC (R.5 1988); Dodge City CC (A.9 1982); Independence CC (R. 1989); Leavenworth CC (R.); Mariah Hills G Cse (R. 1987); Meadowbrook G&CC (R. 1988); Pratt CC (R.); Sim Park GC (R. 1988).

Missouri: Carthage Muni (R.9 A.9 1984); Grandview Muni (R. 1990); Greenbriar Hills CC (R.); Horton Smith Muni (R. 1990); Lakewood Oaks CC (R.4 1987); Lawrence CC (R.); Liberty Hills GC (R.); Linn Creek GC (R.); Nevada Muni (R.); Oscar Blom Muni (R. 1990); St. Joseph CC (R. 1988).

Oklahoma: Bristow CC (R. 1986); Eastern GC (R.); Elk City G&CC (R.); Fort Cobb State Park GC (A.9 1986); Fort Sill GC (R.); Indian Springs CC (River Cse, R.); McAlester CC (R.); Meadowbrook CC (R.9 A.9 1970); Miami G&CC (A.9 1985); Muskogee CC (R. 1970); Oak Hills G&CC (R.); Oklahoma City G&CC (R. 1977); Okmulgee CC (R.); Ponca City CC (R. 1980, R. 1987); Seminole GC (R.); Twin Hills G&CC (R. 1974).

South Dakota: Westward Ho CC (R. 1990).

Jan Sederholm, 1990 COURTESY JAN SEDERHOLM

JAN SEDERHOLM
(1924–), BIGCA

BORN: Malmö, Sweden.

Educated as an architect and land planner at KTH (the Royal technical high school in Stockholm), Jan Sederholm planned residential developments and homes for over twenty years. An avid golfer eager to enter the field of golf course architecture, Sederholm was awarded a scholarship to do just that by the Swedish Golf Federation in 1972. He studied course design in England, Scotland and America, then made a survey of over two dozen of Sweden's best courses before laying out his first course in 1977.

Sederholm coauthored *Golf Course Planning*, a 1980 publication distributed by the Swedish Golf Federation. He also served as president of the Golf Union of Scandinavia, was presented an Award of Merit for his contributions to golf by the SGF in 1982, founded the Swedish Association of Golf Course Architects in 1988 and served as its first president.

Courses by Jan Sederholm:

Denmark: Fureso GC (9 1974, A.9 1989); Gilleleje GC (1989); Hedeland GC (1989); Himmerlands G&CC (Cse No. 1 1981; Cse No. 2 1990); Horsens GC (1987); Kalundborg GC (9 1982); Odense GC (27 1982); Roskilde GC (9 1978); Viborg GC (9 1978).
Finland: Aland GC (1989); Espoo GC (1982); Ruka GC; Sarfvik GC (Cse No. 1 1985; Cse No. 2 1991); Teijo GC; Vierumäki GC (21 1988); Vuokatti GC (1991).
Norway: Fjugstad GC; Grenland GC (9 1988); Harstad GC (9); Kjekstad GC (1989); Oppdal GC; Stavern GC.
Sweden: Alingsås GC (1988); Älvkarleby GC (9 1987); Angelholm GC (1984); Ekeröd GC; Fredriksberg GC; Gallivare GC (9 1985); Haninge GC (1986); Hassleholms GC (1977); Herrljunga GC (1990); Hook GC (9); Hulta GC (1981); Hylliekroken GC (9 1988); Karlskoga GC (9 1978); Kiplingeberg GC (27); Krusenberg GC; Kumla GC (1986); Kvarnby GC (1990); Laholms GC (1980); Linde GC (1984); Loholm GC (1980); Malmö GC (9 1980, A.9 1987); Noresund GC; Norrviken GC; Nybro GC (9 1980); Osteraker GC (1990); Partille GC (1988); Rydöbruk (9 1988); St. Arild (1989); Skepptuna GC (1991); Sotenäs GC (1990); Svenljunga GC (1990); Vara GC (1990); Vetlanda GC (1986).

Courses remodeled or expanded by Jan Sederholm:

Denmark: Hillerod GC (R.9 A.9 1977); Holbaek (A.2 1988); Kokkedal GC (R. 1986); Kolding GC (R.9 A.9 1978); Mølleaen GC (R.11 1988); Odsherred GC (R.); Rungsted GC (R. 1988); Son-

derjyllands GC (A.9 1978); Vejle GC (R.).
Finland: Tampere GC (A.7 1988).
Norway: Bogstad GC (R.); Vestfold GC (A.9).
Sweden: Agesta GC (A.13 1976); Boskogens GC (R.5 1984); Carlskrona GC (R. A.8 1988); Falkenberg GC (A.11 1985); Forsbacka GC (R.2 1986); Gävle GC (A.9 1988); Göteborg GC (A.4 1990); Korsloet GC (A.9 1981); Ljunghusens GC (R. 1977); Marks GC (R. A.9 1981); Motala GC (A.9 1981); Pitea GC (A.7 1991); Rya GC (A.9); Straengnaes GC (R.9 1979); Strömstad GC (A.9 1986); Sunne GC (A.9 1990).

WOLFGANG SIEGMANN, ESGCA

Wolfgang Siegmann received a doctoral degree in horticulture and landscape management from the Technical University of Hannover, Germany, in 1962. He then established a garden and landscape architecture firm the next year, based in Hannover. In the 1980s he began designing golf courses as part of the business and by the early 1990s had done over a dozen in Germany. Siegmann served as president of the Regional Golf Association of Lower Saxony and Bremen from 1976 to 1988.

Courses by Wolfgang Siegmann:

Belgium: Charlemagne GC (9).
Germany: Attighof GC (1992); Bad Salzgitter GC (9); Brodauer-Mühle GC (9); Buxtehude GC (1982); Celle-Garssen GC; Coesfeld G und Land C (9); Göttingen GC (9 1969); Langenhagen GC (1992); Markischer GC (27 1992); Prenden GC (27 1992); Schloss Lüdersburg GC; Schwarze Heide GC (9); Soltau GC (27 1983); Weselerwald GC (9); Worpswede GC.

Courses remodeled or expanded by Wolfgang Siegmann:

Germany: Münster-Wilkinghege GC (A.9).

BRIAN M. SILVA (1953–), ASGCA

BORN: Framingham, Massachusetts.

Brian Silva was introduced to golf course construction at an early age by his father, John, a much-sought-after bull-

Brian Silva, 1990
COURTESY ASGCA

dozer operator and shaper of golf course features. The elder Silva often permitted his son to operate a dozer at home, and Brian would push earth around for hours, experimenting with shapes. Silva also studied the plans and specifications of many golf architects and watched as his father executed those plans on the ground.

Silva obtained an associate degree in turf management from the Stockbridge School of Agriculture of the University of Massachusetts in 1973. He then taught at the school under the renowned Dr. Joseph Troll while he worked on his Bachelor's in landscape architecture, which he obtained in 1976. Silva was an instructor of agronomy for three years at the Lake City (Florida) Community College and in 1981 received a Distinguished Service Award from the Florida Turfgrass Association. He then returned to Massachusetts to serve as an agronomist for the USGA Green Section's Northeast region.

In 1983 Silva joined veteran golf architect Geoffrey S. Cornish as a partner and fulfilled his boyhood dream of becoming a golf course designer. His talents were soon recognized when his first original 18-hole design, Captains Golf Course in Brewster, Massachusetts, was selected by *Golf Digest* as the Best New Public Course of 1985. An unabashed fan of Donald Ross, Silva studied the architect's works extensively over the years and authored a comprehensive critique of the man. A spirited and tireless worker, it was once said facetiously that Silva was the first person to find twenty-eight hours in a day.

Courses by Brian Silva (All with Geoffrey S. Cornish):

Connecticut: Short Beach GC (9 Par 3 1987).
Maine: Falmouth CC (1988); Sable Oaks GC (1989).
Massachusetts: Bayberry Hills G Cse (1988); Bradford CC (1988); Butternut Farm GC (1991); Captains GC

(1985); Kingsway GC (Precision 1986); Ocean Edge GC (1986); Olde Barnstable Fairgrounds GC (1991); Shaker Hills GC (1991).

New Hampshire: [The] Links of Amherst (9 Precision 1988); Passaconaway GC (1989); Perry Hollow (9 1990); Shattuck Inn G Cse (1991).

New York: Adirondack G&CC (1990); Manhattan Woods GC (1991), and *M. Kubayashi.*

Ohio: Darby Creek GC (1992); Firestone CC (West Cse 1989).

Pennsylvania: Center Valley C (1992).

Rhode Island: Richmond CC (1991).

Courses remodeled or expanded by Brian Silva (All with Geoffrey S. Cornish):

Colorado: Cherry Hills CC (R. 1990).

Connecticut: Ellington Ridge CC (R. 1990); Innis Arden GC (R.3 1983); Madison CC (R. 1985); Stanwich C (R.3 1985); Wampanoag CC (R.5); Wethersfield CC (R. 1983).

Delaware: Hercules CC (A.4).

Florida: CC of Orlando (R.).

Georgia: Idle Hour CC (R.2).

Maine: Bangor Muni GC (A.3rd 9 1988); Bethel Inn & CC (A.11 1989); Biddeford and Saco CC (A.9 1986); Bridgton Highlands GC (A.2); Green Meadow GC [FKA Meadowhill C] (A.9 1991); Martindale CC (R.); Purpoodock C (R.2 1985); Samoset GC (R.).

Maryland: Baltimore CC (East Cse, R. 1991).

Massachusetts: Bedford AFB GC (R. 1985); Blue Hill CC (R. 1985); Brae Burn CC (R.); Cohasset GC (R.); International GC (R. 1990); Kernwood CC (R. 1991); Marshfield CC (R.); Myopia Hunt C (R. 1985); Needham CC (R.); Norton CC (R.9 A.9 1989); Pine Brook CC (R. 1985); Springfield CC (A.7 1985).

Michigan: Crystal Downs CC (R. 1985); CC of Detroit (R. 1986).

Minnesota: Edina CC (R. 1985); Golden Valley CC (R.); Interlachen CC (R.); Minneapolis GC (R. 1985); Rochester G&CC (R.2); Wayzata CC (R. 1985).

Missouri: Algonquin CC (R. 1986).

New Jersey: Brook Lake CC (R. A.5); Fiddler's Elbow CC (South Cse, A.9 1988); Green Brook CC (R.); Hollywood GC (R.); Howell Park GC (R. 1985); Navesink CC (R. 1986); Preakness Hills CC (R. 1984).

New Hampshire: Mount Pleasant GC (A.9 1990); Plausawa Valley CC (A.9 1989); Province Lake CC (A.9 1988).

New York: Blind Brook C (R.); Garden City CC (R.); Monroe CC (R. 1990); Nassau CC (R. 1984); Ontario GC (R.); Powelton C (R.4 1985); Rockaway Hunting C (R. 1985); Schuyler Meadows C (R. 1985); Whippoorwill CC (R. 1984); Wildwood GC (R. 1985); Wiltwyck CC (R.2); Wolferts Roost CC (R.); Woodmere C (R.).

Ohio: Columbus CC (R. 1990); Sharon C (R. 1986); Worthington Hills CC (R.2 1985).

Pennsylvania: CC of Scranton (R. 1983).

Vermont: Killington GC (1982) ass't Geoffrey Cornish; Stratton Mountain GC (A.3rd 9 1984).

West Virginia: Guyen G&CC (R.).

Bob Simmons, circa 1975 COURTESY MRS. ROBERT A. SIMMONS

ROBERT A. SIMMONS (1908–1985)

BORN: Camden, Indiana.
DIED: Kokomo, Indiana, at age 77.

Bob Simmons became a caddy at the age of 9 at Mississinewa CC in Indiana. He later became its caddymaster, assistant professional and finally head pro. While at Mississinewa, he made scale-model greens of famous golf holes as a hobby and laid out three courses in surrounding Indiana communities.

In 1956 Simmons became a construction supervisor for golf architect Dick Wilson, whom he had met when Wilson was building NCR CC in Dayton, Ohio. Simmons was responsible for constructing a number of outstanding Wilson designs, including Moon Valley in Arizona, Bay Hill and Cypress Lakes in Florida, Coldstream in Ohio, Lyford Cay and Paradise Island in the Bahamas and Royal Montreal

in Canada. In 1961 Simmons formed his own practice as a golf course architect.

Courses by Bob Simmons:

Alabama: Olympia Spa & CC (1968).

Arizona: Moon Valley CC (1958), ass't Dick Wilson.

Arkansas: Blytheville CC (9 1957), ass't Dick Wilson.

Florida: Atlantis Inn and CC (1973); Bay Hill C (1961, ass't Dick Wilson and Joe Lee; A.3rd 9 1969); Orange Tree CC (1972); Palm Beach Par 3 GC (9 Par 3 1961), ass't Dick Wilson; Palmetto GC (1960), ass't Dick Wilson.

Indiana: Arrowhead Park GC (1966); Carl E. Smock GC; Green Acres CC (1967); Harrison Lake GC; Highland Lake GC (1971); Hillview CC; Lafayette City GC (1974); Lafayette CC (Battleground Cse 1968); Logansport CC (9); [The] Pointe CC [FKA Lake Monroe GC] (1973); Prestwick CC (1975); Quail Ridge G&TC [FKA Bloomington CC]; Valle Vista CC.

Kentucky: Bent Creek CC.

Louisiana: Oakbourne CC (1958), ass't Dick Wilson.

Missouri: Bent Oak GC (1980).

Ohio: Arrowhead Park GC (9 1967); Coldstream CC (1960), ass't Dick Wilson and Joe Lee; Crest Hills CC (1968).

Pennsylvania: Laurel Valley CC (1960), ass't Dick Wilson.

Tennessee: Town and Country GC (Par 3 1963), ass't Dick Wilson.

Texas: Long Meadows CC (NLE).

West Virginia: Fincastle CC (1963), ass't Dick Wilson; [The] Greenbrier GC (Lakeside Cse 1962), ass't Dick Wilson.

Quebec: Royal Montreal GC (Blue Cse 1959; Red Cse 1959), ass't Dick Wilson.

Bahamas: Bahama Princess Hotel & CC (Emerald Cse 1965), ass't Dick Wilson and Joe Lee; Lucayan G&CC (1964), ass't Dick Wilson and Joe Lee; Lyford Cay C (1960), ass't Dick Wilson and Joe Lee; Paradise Island G&CC (1962), ass't Dick Wilson and Joe Lee.

Venezuela: Lagunita CC (1958), ass't Dick Wilson.

Courses remodeled or expanded by Bob Simmons:

Florida: Atlantis GC (A.3rd 9 1973).

Indiana: CC of Connersville (A.9 1962).

Kentucky: Glenwood Hall CC (A.9); Idle Hour CC (R. 1968).
Ohio: Salem GC (A.9 1967).
Mexico: Club Campestre, Mexico City (R.), ass't Dick Wilson.

Tom Simpson, circa 1935 COLLECTION RON WHITTEN

THOMAS G. SIMPSON (1877–1964)

BORN: Winkley Hall Estate, Lancashire, England.
DIED: Basingstoke, Hampshire, England, at age 87.

Tom Simpson, who came from a wealthy family, studied law at Trinity Hall, Cambridge, and was admitted to the bar in 1905. A scratch golfer, he was a member of the Oxford and Cambridge Golfing Society and played a great deal at Woking. His interest in golf design developed as he observed the remodeling of Woking's course by club members John Low and Stuart Paton. On more than one occasion, Simpson defended their advanced designs in discussion with members of the club. As a result, Simpson began to develop particular ideas about course architecture himself, and by 1910 he had closed his legal practice and joined golf architect Herbert Fowler in the business.

After World War I, Simpson and Fowler were partners in a firm that in a short time included J. F. Abercromby and A. C. M. Croome. Simpson handled most of the firm's work on the Continent, and some of his best designs were done in France. In the 1920s Simpson hired Philip Mackenzie Ross on a whim to assist him in the construction of courses. By the late 1920s Fowler and Simpson had split up and Simpson made the talented and enterprising Ross a partner. In the 1930s Simpson used famed golfer Molly Gourlay as consultant and thus was the first designer to solicit a woman's architectural suggestions.

Always a colorful figure, Tom Simpson toured the English countryside in a chauffeur-driven silver Rolls-Royce and often appeared for site inspections in an embroidered cloak and beret. Although he experimented with golf holes, he believed the Old Course at St. Andrews to be the only enduring text on course design. He was well known for his excellent essays on the philosophy of golf architecture and, in addition to numerous articles, wrote *The Architectural Side of Golf* with Herbert Newton Wethered (1929; 2nd edition, entitled *Design for Golf,* 1952) and contributed to *The Game of Golf* (1931) and *Golf Courses: Design, Construction and Upkeep* (1933; 2nd edition, 1950). A consummate artist, Simpson illustrated his works with ink sketches in color washes and wrote and illustrated *Modern Etchings and Their Collectors* in 1919. He also practiced silk embroidery.

Simpson prided himself on supervising the construction of his designs, and as a result he was not as prolific as some of his contemporaries. He retired from active course design with the outbreak of World War II. After the war he continued to write about the subject but did no further work in the field, and spent his final years in seclusion at his estate in Hampshire.

Courses by Tom Simpson:

Austria: Schloss Mittersill GC (1936), with Molly Gourlay.
Belgium: Keerbergen GC; Royal GC du Sart Tilman; Royal GC des Fagnes (1936), with P. M. Ross.
England: [The] Berkshire GC (Blue Cse 1928; Red Cse 1928), with Herbert Fowler; Bootle GC (1934); Clark Estate GC; Lord Mountbatten Estate GC, with Herbert Fowler; New Zealand GC (1931); North Foreland GC (1919), with Herbert Fowler; Rank Estate GC (9 Par 3); Roehampton GC; Sir Archibald Birkmyre Estate GC; Sir Mortimer Singer Estate GC; Sir Philip Sassoon Estate GC.
France: Baron Edward de Rothschild Estate GC; Baron Henri de Rothschild Estate GC; Club de la Cordelière; Comte de Rougemont Estate GC; Duc de Gramont Estate GC; GC d'Ozoir-la-Ferrière (27); Golf de Chiberta (1925); Golf de Fontainbleau; Golf de Hossegor; Golf de la Barouge (9 1935), with P. M. Ross; Golf de Memillon; Golf de Morfontaine (27 1927); Golf de Vallière; Golf de Vaux de Cerney;

Golf de Villard-de-Lans; Golf de Voisins; Gramont Estate GC (9); Hyde Estate GC (9 Par 3); International C du Lys (Bouleaux Cse, 9 1927; Chênes Cse 1927); New GC (1929), with P. M. Ross.
Germany: Mittelrheinischer GC "Bad Ems" (1924).
Indonesia: Djakarta GC; Sourabia GC.
Ireland: Kilkenny GC.
Scotland: Cruden Bay G&CC (27 1926), with Herbert Fowler.
Spain: Club de Campo de Malaga (1928), with P. M. Ross; C de G Terramar (1922); Malaga GC (1925); Real C de San Sebastian.
Switzerland: Zurich G&CC (1931).

Courses remodeled or expanded by Tom Simpson:

Belgium: Royal Antwerp GC (A.9 1924), with P. M. Ross; Royal GC de Belgique (R.).
England: Ashbridge GC (R. 1934); Betchworth Park GC (R.); Camberley Heath GC (R.); Felixstowe Ferry GC (R. A.4 1936); Hayling GC (R.); Huddersfield GC (R.); Keighley GC (R.); Knole Park GC (R.); Liphook GC (R.); North Foreland GC (R.), with J. S. F. Morrison; North Hants GC (R.); Royal Lytham and St. Anne's GC (R.); Rye GC (R.); Sunningdale GC (New Cse, R. 1935); Wilmslow GC (R.).
France: Golf de Chantilly (Old Cse, R.); Golf de Dieppe (R.); Hardelot GC (Pines Cse, R. 1931), with P. M. Ross.
Ireland: Ballybunion GC (Old Cse, R. 1936), with Molly Gourlay; Carlow GC (R. 1937), with Molly Gourlay; County Louth GC (R. 1938), with Molly Gourlay.
Scotland: Luffness New GC (R.); Muirfield GC (R. 1933); Royal Aberdeen GC (R.).
Spain: Real C de la Puerto de Hierro (Old Cse, R. 1938).
Wales: Glamorganshire GC (R.); Rhos-on-Sea GC (R.); Royal Porthcawl GC (R. 1937).

JOSEPH BOOTHROYD SLOAN (1886–1958)

BORN: Philadelphia, Pennsylvania.
DIED: Evanston, Illinois, at age 72.

Club professional "Todd" Sloan expanded the Racine (Wisconsin) Country

Todd Sloan, circa 1940 COURTESY MARGARET REYHEART

Club during his tenure there. Then club member Samuel Johnson, head of Johnson Wax Company, asked him to design a city course on land Johnson was donating. Once it was finished, Sloan moved to the course and served as its professional. During the next 15 years, he laid out a number of courses in Illinois and Wisconsin.

After World War II Sloan managed Meadowbrook CC in Racine for a time, then moved to Evanston, Illinois, where he served as pro at another course he had designed.

Courses by Todd Sloan:

Illinois: Peter Jans Community GC (Precision 1922).
Wisconsin: Johnson Park GC (1939).

Courses remodeled or expanded by Todd Sloan:

Wisconsin: Meadowbrook CC (A.9); Racine CC (R.9 A.9 1926).

Mike Smelek, 1991 COURTESY MIKE SMELEK

MICHAEL J. SMELEK (1958–)

BORN: San Jose, California.

Mike Smelek studied landscape architecture at the University of Idaho and graduated in 1980. In March 1981 he joined the golf design company of von Hagge and Devlin, which had recently relocated to Texas. In 1987 Bruce Devlin left

the firm to pursue a second career on the Senior PGA Tour. Von Hagge then made Smelek an associate architect and assigned him primary responsibility for projects in the Pacific Basin. The new von Hagge design team, headed by Robert von Hagge, worked on all projects in concert with one another.

AL SMITH

Seattle-based golf course designer Al Smith constructed courses for several Pacific Northwest architects in the 1920s and 1930s. In the fifties Smith designed several courses on his own in the state of Washington.

Courses by Al Smith:

Washington: Brae Burn CC; Brookdale CC; Cross Roads GC (Par 3); Everett Muni (1971); Glendale CC (1956); Glendale G&CC; Lake Samanish State Park GC (1958); Maplewood CC; North Shore CC (1962); Redmond G Links; Twin Lakes CC; Wayne Public GC (Precision).

Courses remodeled or expanded by Al Smith:

Washington: Jackson Park Muni (R.).

ERNEST E. SMITH (1901–)

BORN: Vestal, New York.

Ernie Smith began caddying at age 9 in Binghamton, New York. At age 20 he became an assistant professional at Binghamton Country Club and became its professional at 25. His first design was Geneganslet GC in Greene, New York, completed in 1926. He then helped the Endicott-Johnson Shoe Co. route and construct a company course, En-Joie Country Club, which opened in 1927.

In the early 1930s Smith designed and constructed Ely Park Golf Course in Binghamton and remained as its pro-superintendent. Although he did no further golf design work for some twenty-five years, he proved himself an able teacher and avid promoter of the game. He served as vice president of the PGA of America in 1941 and was on the executive board of the New York PGA for twenty-eight years.

In the early 1950s Smith wintered in

Ernest E. Smith, circa 1960 COLLECTION RON WHITTEN

Florida, where his interest in course design was renewed. He received commissions on a few Florida projects, and when he retired from Ely Park in 1963 Smith moved to that state to practice golf architecture full-time. He remained active until the late 1960s.

Courses by Ernest E. Smith:

Florida: Hobe Sound CC (NLE); Selva Marina CC (1958); Seven Lakes CC (Precision 1971); Silver Lake G&CC (1962); South Seas Plantation GC (9 1969).
New York: Ely Park GC (1933, A.9 Par 3 1962); En-Joie CC (1927); Geneganslet GC (1926).

Courses remodeled or expanded by Ernest E. Smith:

Florida: Martin County G&CC (R. 1963, NLE); Rio Mar CC (A.9 1964).
New York: Kass Inn & CC (A.9 Par 3 1964).

ORRIN EDWARD SMITH (1883–1958)

BORN: Southington, Connecticut.
DIED: New Britain, Connecticut, at age 75.

Orrin Smith began his career as a construction superintendent for Willie Park, Jr., on Shuttle Meadow Country Club in New Britain, Connecticut. He was later associated with Donald Ross on several projects, including Longmeadow (Massachusetts) Country Club.

Smith entered private practice as a course designer in 1925 and remained active through the mid-1950s, operating from his home in Hartford, Connecticut. He was influential in the early design career of James Gilmore Harrison, who served as a construction superintendent, and also trained William F. Mitchell and Albert Zikorus in the necessary skills of golf course architecture. Zikorus took over Smith's practice upon his retirement in 1955.

Courses by Orrin Smith:

Arkansas: Melbourne CC.
Connecticut: Birchwood CC (9); Deercrest CC (1957); East Hartford GC (1956); Longshore Park GC; Louis Stoner Private Cse (9); Pine Valley GC (1950); Suffield CC (9); Torrington CC; Woodbridge CC.
Kansas: Wyandotte CC (1927, NLE).
Maine: Waterville CC (9 1938).
Massachusetts: Brewster Green GC (9 1957, NLE); Duamyre CC (9, NLE); Framingham CC (9); Ludlow Muni; Packachaug Hills CC (9).
Missouri: Lynnhaven GC (9 1928, NLE).
Nebraska: East Ridge CC (NLE).
New Jersey: River Vale CC (1931).
New York: Embassy C; Hilly Dale CC; Plandome CC (1930); Signal Hill CC; Spring Rock CC (27 1955).
Pennsylvania: Baldoc CC.

Courses remodeled or expanded by Orrin Smith:

Connecticut: CC of Farmington (R.); Hartford GC (R. 1946); Highfield CC (R.9 A.9 1954); Race Brook CC (R. 1947); Rockledge CC (R.9 A.9 1954); Rockrimmon CC (A.9 1953); Salmon Brook CC (R., NLE); Stanley GC (A.3rd 9 1958); TPC at River Highlands [FKA Edgewood GC] (R. 1951); Tumblebrook CC (A.9 1948).
Kansas: Macdonald Park Muni (R. 1938); Milburn G&CC (R. 1925).
Maine: Augusta CC (R. 1939); Bridgton GC (R. 1939); Mount Kineo GC (R. 1940); Portland CC (R. 1940).
Maryland: Rocky Point GC (R. 1939, NLE).
Massachusetts: Belmont CC (R.); Cedar Glen GC (R. 1931); Framingham CC (A.5 1954); Needham GC (R. 1935); North Adams GC (R. 1939); Oak Hill CC (R. 1938); Ould Newberry CC (R. 1939); Quincy CC (R.); Unicorn CC (R. 1937); Vesper CC (R. 1939); Wenham GC (R. 1938).
Missouri: Blue Hills CC (R. 1926, NLE); Joplin CC (R., NLE); Oakwood CC (A.9 1925).
New Hampshire: Claremont CC (R. 1936); Dover CC (R. 1940); Farnum Hill CC (R.); Hanover CC, Dartmouth College (R. 1937); John H. Cain GC [FKA Newport CC] (R. 1937); Laconia CC (R. 1938); Lake Sunapee CC (R.

1934); Lebanon CC (R. 1937); Rochester CC (R. 1939).
New York: Fresh Meadow CC (R. 1938); Huntington Crescent CC (R. 1939; West Cse, R. 1939); Lake Success GC (R.9 A.9 1958).
Ohio: Columbus CC (R. 1937); Zanesville CC (R.).
Rhode Island: Newport CC (R. 1939).

WILLIE SMITH
(1872–1916)

BORN: Carnoustie, Scotland.
DIED: Mexico City, Mexico, at age 44.

Willie Smith, a member of a famous Carnoustie golfing family, won the U.S. Open in 1899. Around that time he laid

Willie Smith, 1907
COLLECTION RON WHITTEN

out Mexico's first golf course, the 9-hole San Pedro Country Club. Smith eventually settled in Mexico, planning the first version of Mexico City Country Club and Chapultepec Country Club. After he died in the Revolution of 1916, his brother Alex completed construction of Chapultepec in 1921.

Courses by Willie Smith:

Mexico: Chapultepec CC (1921), with *Alex Smith*; Mexico City CC (1907); San Pedro CC (9 1905).

STEVE SMYERS
(1953–), ASGCA

BORN: Washington, D.C.

Steve Smyers, a graduate of the University of Florida, played on its golf team throughout college, including the Gators' NCAA national championship team of 1973. After earning a business degree in 1975, Smyers apprenticed under golf course architect Ron Garl. He became an associate architect for Garl and worked on

Steve Smyers, 1991
COURTESY STEVE SMYERS

the design and construction of over sixty projects.

In 1983 Smyers formed Fairway Design International, a design company based in Lakeland, Florida. He later moved his headquarters to Tampa and opened a branch office in Australia. In 1986 he married his wife, Sherrin, a native Australian and rookie member of the LPGA Tour.

Smyers continued to hone his golf game by playing competitively, winning, among other titles, the 1984 Polk County (Florida) Amateur. In 1991 he broke a long winless drought by capturing the Invitational de Avila in Tampa.

Courses by Steve Smyers:

Florida: Cedars G&CC; Crescent Oaks CC (1990); Cypress Creek of Lake Alfred GC (9 1987); GC at Cypress Creek; Highland Ridge CC (1989); Meadowbrook GC (1987); Sandpiper G&CC (1987); Wentworth G&CC (1990).
Kentucky: Nevele Meade GC (1991).
Indiana: Wolf Run GC (1989).
Ohio: Ivy Hills CC (1992).
Virginia: River's Bend CC (1991).
Australia: Cypress Lakes CC (1991).

Courses remodeled or expanded by Steve Smyers:

Florida: Cheval Polo & GC (R. 1990).

ARTHUR JACK SNYDER
(1917–), ASGCA, PRESIDENT 1982

BORN: Rosedale, Pennsylvania.

Jack Snyder received a B.S. degree in landscape architecture from Pennsylvania State University in 1939. From 1939 to 1955 he owned two landscape architecture firms, Arthur J. Snyder Co. and Snyder Inc. During World War II he was involved in defense design and, for a brief period, in land surveying.

Snyder was one of three brothers, all of whom became course superintendents after training by their father, Arthur Snyder. The senior Snyder had himself been trained by Emil Loeffler and John McGlynn at Oakmont CC. Jack served as superintendent at Oakmont in 1951 and 1952 and during that time rebuilt the 8th green. From 1956 to 1959 he was superintendent at White Mountain CC in Pinetop, Arizona. Snyder entered private practice as a golf architect in 1958. Prior to that time he had been involved in a few course-remodeling projects and had designed a course at Jane Lew, West Virginia.

Jack Snyder, 1983
COLLECTION RON
WHITTEN

Courses by Arthur Jack Snyder:

Arizona: Apache Wells CC (9 1963); Arizona City CC (1963); Arizona G Resort [FKA Golden Hills G Resort] (1960); Beaver Creek CC (1962); Black Canyon GC (9 Par 3 1961, NLE); Camelback GC (Indian Bend Cse 1978); Cañon del Oro CC (9 Precision 1961); Canyon Mesa GC (9 Precision 1985); Cave Creek Muni (1984); Concho Valley GC (9 1970, A. 9 1991, with Forrest Richardson); Coronado GC (9 Precision 1965); Desert Sands G&CC (Precision 1969); Haven CC (1965); Ironwood GC (9 Par 3); Ken McDonald Muni (1974); Mountain Shadows CC (Precision 1962); [The] Phoenician G&RC (1981); Poco Diablo GC (9 Par 3 1966); [The] Pointe at South Mountain GC (1988), with Forrest Richardson; Show Low CC (9 1961); Silverbell Muni (1979); Villa Monterey CC (9 Precision 1982); Winslow Muni (9 1980).
California: Kern City GC (9 1961); Las Montanas GC (1992), with Forrest Richardson.
Hawaii: Kaanapali Kai GC (Precision 1970, NLE); Royal Kaanapali GC

(South Cse 1976); Seamountain GC (1973); Wailea GC (Blue Cse 1971; Orange Cse 1977).
Nevada: Chimney Rock GC (9 1976); Eagle Valley Muni (1977); Ruby View Muni (1969).
New Mexico: Arroyo del Oso GC (1965); Citivan Park Muni (9 Precision 1965); Puerto del Sol GC (9 1978); Quail Run GC (9 Precision 1986); Scott Park Muni (9 1962).
Utah: San Juan GC (9 1964).
Virginia: Cedar Point C (1963).
West Virginia: Harmony Farm CC (9 1940, NLE).

Courses remodeled or expanded by Arthur Jack Snyder:

Arizona: Arizona G Resort (R. 1984); Arizona Biltmore GC (Links Cse, R. 1 1989), with Forrest Richardson; [The] Boulders GC (A.9 1974; R. 2 1978, NLE); Brookview CC (R. 1986, NLE); Camelback GC (Padre Cse, R.2 1980); Casa Grande GC (A.9 1989), with Forrest Richardson; Desert Forest GC (R.2 1978); London Bridge GC (R.4 1984); Mesa CC (R. 1986); Orange Tree CC (R.1 1977); Papago Park GC (R.); Pinewood CC (R. 1965); Scottsdale CC (R.4 1973); Stonecreek GC [FKA Anasazi GC] (R. 1986); Tucson CC (R. 1972); White Mountain CC (A.9 1959); Wickenburg CC (R. 5 1963); Wigwam CC (R.9 A.9 1961, NLE).
California: La Jolla CC (R.3 1965).
Hawaii: Keauhou Kona CC (R.3 1981); Makaha Inn & CC (West Cse, R.3 1981); Volcano G&CC (A.9 R.9 1969); Waialae CC (R.3 1969); Waiehu Muni (R.3 1968).
Pennsylvania: Oakmont CC (R.1 1952).
Utah: Rose Park GC (R.5 1963).

DANIEL GORDON SOUTAR
(1882–1937)

BORN: Carmyllie, Forfar, Scotland.
DIED: Sydney, Australia, at age 55.

"Des" Soutar learned golf on the links of Carnoustie, where he watched and mimicked the swings of Freddie Tait, Archie Simpson and Willie Smith. He apprenticed as a carpenter at age 14, but decided early on that he wanted to be a golf professional.

In 1903 Soutar moved to Australia at the urging of his boyhood friend and golf

rival Carnegie Clark (who would eventually also design many courses in that country). The two formed a clubmaking and teaching partnership and were soon hired by Royal Sydney GC. They became successful competitive golfers in their adopted homeland and won many tournaments. Soutar wrote *The Australian Golfer* in 1906, a book that offered everything from basic instruction on how to play the game to critiques on Australia's most prominent layouts.

Soutar moved to Manly GC in 1911, where he taught, among others, Joe Kirkwood (who became a popular trick-shot artist in America) and Jim Ferrier (a PGA Tour player for decades). He and Clark also formed the Australian PGA, and Soutar won its first annual championship. About the same time Soutar began laying out courses along the east coast of Australia and in nearby New Zealand. In his later years Soutar gave lessons in a downtown Sydney department store.

Courses by Des Soutar:

Australia: Elanora CC (1929); Glenora GC (1923); Kingston Heath GC (1925); New South Wales GC (1928), with Alister Mackenzie.
New Zealand: Christchurch CC (1926).

Courses remodeled or expanded by Des Soutar:

Australia: Royal Adelaide GC (R. A.4).

Baxter Spann, 1991
COURTESY BAXTER
SPANN

ROBERT BAXTER SPANN
(1953–)

BORN: Baton Rouge, Louisiana.

Baxter Spann obtained a Bachelor of Landscape Architecture degree from Louisiana State University in 1979. During his college summers, Spann worked in the field on construction projects for the golf design firm of Joseph S. Finger and Associates. After graduation, Spann became a full-time associate in the Houston, Texas–based firm, which was later renamed Finger, Dye and Associates when designer Ken Dye became a partner.

In 1987, Spann was offered a partnership in the firm and its name was changed to Finger Dye Spann, Inc. In 1990 Dye and Spann became the sole principals of the firm when Finger retired. Together they collaborated on some designs and did others individually.

Courses by Baxter Spann (All with Joe Finger unless otherwise indicated):

Colorado: Thorncreek GC (1992), with Ken Dye.

Texas: Clear Creek GC (1989), and Ken Dye; Desert View GC (1990), with Ken Dye; Laredo CC (1985); Stonebriar CC (1988); Timarron GC (1988).

Courses remodeled or expanded by Baxter Spann (All with Joe Finger unless otherwise indicated):

Louisiana: England AFB GC (A.9 1989), with Ken Dye.

South Carolina: Whispering Pines GC, Myrtle Beach AFB (A.9 1989), with Ken Dye.

Texas: Hearthstone CC (A.9 1985); Tanglewood-on-the-Texoma GC (R. 1988), with Ken Dye; Victoria CC (R. 1985).

William James Spear, 1990 COURTESY ASGCA

WILLIAM JAMES SPEAR (1929–), ASGCA

BORN: Iowa City, Iowa.

After attending the University of Iowa in his hometown and obtaining a degree in botany in 1950, Jim Spear transferred to Iowa State University, where he studied landscape architecture. Finishing in 1953, he joined the Chicago practice of golf architect Robert Bruce Harris and trained

under him for seven years. Spear entered private practice as a course designer in 1960. Over the next thirty years, operating from an office in St. Charles, Illinois, he designed and remodeled over fifty courses in the upper Midwest.

Courses by William James Spear:

Georgia: Turtle Cove GC (9 1971).

Illinois: Arrowhead CC (9 1960); Danville Elks C (1969); Hawthorn Ridge GC (1977); Highland Springs CC (1968); Highland Woods GC (1975); Lakeshore GC (1970); Lakewood G&CC (9 1966); Little Tam GC (9 Precision 1970); Marengo Ridge CC (9 1964, A.9 1991); Midland CC (1970); Park Place GC (9 1965); Randall Oaks GC (1965); Renwood CC (9 1977); Rock River CC (9 1966); St. Elmo GC (9 1969); Swan Hills GC (1971).

Indiana: Castlebrook G&CC (1979); Elbel Park GC (1964); Forest Park GC (9 1971); Grand Prairie GC (9 1962); Playland Park G Center (9 Par 3 1962).

Iowa: Amana Colonies G Cse (1990); Clinton Muni (1981); Palmer Hills GC (1974).

Michigan: Brookwood G (9 1964).

Minnesota: Willow Creek GC (1974).

North Dakota: Souris Valley GC (1967).

Ohio: Auglaize CC (9 1963); Edgecreek GC (1960).

Wisconsin: Hickory Grove CC (9 1966); Voyager Village GC (1971).

Courses remodeled or expanded by William James Spear:

Illinois: Crawford County GC (A.9 1965); Effingham CC (A.9 1968).

BERT STAMPS (1911–)

BORN: Visalia, California.

Bert Stamps began as a caddy at the old Rancho Country Club in Los Angeles. An excellent golfer, he turned professional at age 18 but soon applied for reinstatement as an amateur and once won seven local tournaments in succession. He again turned pro in 1932 and went to work in a pro shop. He was admitted to the PGA of America in 1938.

Stamps was stationed with the U.S. Army in the Far East during and after

Bert Stamps, circa 1975 COLLECTION RON WHITTEN

World War II. While there he won the Japanese Open in Osaka, an event instituted by occupation forces. Following military service, he became head professional at Cleveland (Tennessee) CC. Between 1945 and 1948 he competed sporadically on the PGA Tour and remodeled the Cleveland layout. He was soon hired to plan a new course in Baton Rouge, Louisiana. He continued to practice golf design on a part-time basis after returning to California in the 1950s.

Stamps was chosen Northern California PGA Professional of the Year in 1974. The same year he retired to become professional emeritus at Rancho Murieta CC near Sacramento, where he had designed and constructed its first eighteen. Even after retirement, Stamps continued to design and build courses throughout California.

Courses by Bert Stamps:

California: Belmont CC (1956); Cameron Park CC (1965); Delano GC (9 Precision); DeLaveaga CC; Elkhorn GC (1962); Feather River Park GC; Kings River G&CC (1955); Fresno Airways GC (1949, NLE); Lawrence Links (9); Lighthouse Marina & CC (Precision 1990); Mesquite CC (1986); Oak Ridge GC (1967); Paso Robles G&CC (1960); Phoenix Lake GC (9 1967); Rancho Murieta GC (North Cse 1971); San Luis Obispo CC (1959).

Louisiana: Baton Rouge CC (1950).

Nevada: Sahara CC (1962); Tropicana CC (1961, NLE).

Courses remodeled or expanded by Bert Stamps:

California: Cold Springs G&CC (A.9 1981); Kings CC (A.9 1961); Rio del Mar GC (R. 1957); Woodbridge G&CC (R. A.3rd 9 1974).

Tennessee: Cleveland CC (R. 1947, NLE).

**DONALD MacLENNAN ARKLAY STEEL
(1937–), BIGCA, PRESIDENT 1991**

BORN: Hillingdon, England.

Donald Steel attended Fettes College in Edinburgh. Well known as a rugby and cricket player, Steel also became a scratch amateur golfer and represented England in many international matches. He played on the Cambridge golf team, was the Berkshire, Bucks and Oxon Open champion in 1971 and won the President's Putter at Rye Golf Club in three different decades.

Within a few months of obtaining his agricultural degree from Cambridge, Steel became the first golf correspondent for the London *Sunday Telegram*, a position he held until 1990. He also wrote regularly for *Country Life* magazine beginning in

D. M. A. Steel, circa 1985 COURTESY D. M. A. STEEL

1983. Over the years he distinguished himself as a golf writer and historian. He edited eight editions of *The Golf Course Guide to the British Isles*, two versions of *The Golfer's Bedside Book* (two editions) and several editions of *The Guinness Book of Golf Facts and Feats* and coauthored *The Encyclopædia of Golf* with Peter Ryde and Herbert Warren Wind. He also contributed a chapter to *The World Atlas of Golf* and penned *The Classic Links* (1992).

In 1965 Steel joined the golf architecture firm of Cotton (C. K.), Pennink, Lawrie and Partners, Ltd., as a consultant trainee and was made a partner in 1971. After the deaths of the other partners, the firm was sold in 1987 to a private investor and Steel formed Donald Steel and Co., Ltd., hiring young architects Colin Mackenzie and Martin Ebert as his associates.

Courses by D. M. A. Steel:

Ontario: Red Tail G Cse (1992).
Belgium: Heerle's Hof GC (1992).
England: Abbey Park GC (1989); Barnham Broome Hotel G&CC (1977), with J. J. F. Pennink; Beacon Park GC

(1982); Blackhill Wood GC, with J. J. F. Pennink; Boothferry GC (1981); Bradley Park GC (1978); Breadsall Priory G&CC (New Cse 1991); Broome Park GC (1981), with J. J. F. Pennink; Bushey G & Squash C (9 1980), with J. J. F. Pennink; Canwell Park G&CC (1992); Carlisle Race Track GC; Crane Valley GC; Dudsbury GC (1992); Farnham Park GC (9 1974), with J. J. F. Pennink; Forest of Arden G&CC (New Cse); Goodwood Park Hotel G&CC (1989); Halifax Bradley Hall GC, with J. J. F. Pennink; Harrow School GC (9 Precision 1978), with J. J. F. Pennink; Hurlston GC (1990); Ingol G & Squash C (1984), with J. J. F. Pennink; Lambourne GC (1992); Liscombe Park GC (27); Mill Ride GC (1992); Northampton GC; Pitcheroak GC (1973); Portal GC (1991); Radley College GC (9); Shrigley Hall GC; Tudor Park G&CC; Uppingham Castle GC (1992); Waverton GC (1992); Woburn G&CC (Duchess Cse 1976), with J. J. F. Pennink and C. D. Lawrie.
France: Château des Vigiers GC (1992); Golf de Chantilly (New Cse).
Germany: Treudelberg GC (1992).
Italy: Gardagolf; Il Picciolo GC (1992).
Malaysia: Sri Menanti GC.
Netherlands: Havelte GC; Hoge Kleij GC; Rijswijk GC; Winterswijk GC; Zeewolde GC.
Portugal: Vila Sol GC (1991).
Scotland: Brunston Castle GC; Letham Grange G&CC (Cse No. 1 1986), with G. K. Smith; St. Andrews (Strathtyrum Cse 1993).
Sweden: Johannesberg CC (27 1992).
Tenerife: Amarilla G&CC (1987).

Courses remodeled or expanded by D. M. A. Steel:

England: Fulford GC (R.); Leckford and Longstock GC (A.9 1988); Puttenham GC (R.); Royal Birkdale GC (A.2 1987); Royal Lytham & St. Annes GC (R. 1987); Saunton GC (West Cse, R.); Sunningdale GC (Old Cse, R. 1986; New Cse, R. 1986); Thetford GC (R.).
Ireland: Lahinch CC (Castle Cse, R. A.9); Portmarnock GC (New Cse, A.9 1990).
Italy: Molinetto CC (R. 1992).
Netherlands: Geysteren G&CC (A.5); Noord Nederlanse G&CC (A.9 1987); Sallandsche GC "De Hoek" (A. 11).
Scotland: Deeside GC (A.9); Machrie Hotel GC (R.); Royal Dornoch GC (Struie Cse, R.); Sittingbourne and Milton

Regis GC (R. A.9); St. Andrews (Eden Cse, R. 1990; Jubilee Cse, R. 1987).
Sweden: Barsebacks GC (Forest Cse, A.9 1989).

**JAMES ALBERT STEER
(1885–)**

BORN: Middlesex, England.

J. A. Steer served as a clubmaker and teaching professional at a series of clubs, including Royal Lytham and St. Annes and Blackpool Golf Club. While he was best-known for the hand-crafted golf clubs bearing his name, he also designed several courses in and around his home base of Blackpool from the 1930s to the 1950s.

Courses by J. A. Steer:

England: Ashton & Lea GC; Blackpool North Shore GC (1932); Blundell GC; Chorley GC (1925); Fairhaven GC; Fleetwood GC (1932); Lowes Park GC (9 1930); Southport and Ainsdale GC (1923).
Isle of Man: Rowany GC.

Courses remodeled or expanded by J. A. Steer:

England: Blackpool–Stanley Park GC (R.); Davyhulme Park GC (R.); Deane GC (R.); Whalley GC (R.); Whitefield GC (R.).

John Steidel, 1991 COURTESY JOHN STEIDEL

**JOHN ROBERT STEIDEL
(1949–)**

BORN: Nyack, New York.

Following his graduation from the University of California at Berkeley in 1971, where he originally attended on a football scholarship and ultimately obtained a degree in landscape architecture, John Steidel spent three years as an assistant to golf architect Robert Muir Graves. He then did graduate work at California Polytechnic State University at Pomona in urban planning. In 1976 he became an assistant architect and project manager for the international firm of Thomson, Wolveridge, Fream and Associates, working primarily on the firm's projects in the Pacific Northwest. In 1980 Steidel established his own practice, based near Seattle, Washington.

Courses by John Steidel:

California: Bixby GC (9 1980), ass't Ronald Fream; Diablo Hills GC (9 Precision 1974), ass't Robert Muir Graves; El Cariso GC (1977), ass't Robert Muir Graves.

Montana: Marian Hills GC (1983); Shangri-La GC (9 1990).

Washington: Apple Tree G Cse (1992); Canyon Lakes GC (1981), ass't Peter Thomson, Michael Wolveridge and Ron Fream; Lynnwood Muni GC (Precision 1991); Riverbend GC (1989).

India: Coimbatore GC (1985), with *Max Wexler.*

Courses remodeled or expanded by John Steidel:

California: Almaden G&CC (R. 1979), ass't Ronald Fream, Peter Thomson and Michael Wolveridge; Rancho Bernardo GC (R. 4 1988); Rossmoor GC (North Cse, A.9 1975), ass't Robert Muir Graves; Sunnyside CC (R. 1990).

Idaho: Coeur d'Alene G Cse (R.15 1986); Hayden Lake CC (R. 2 1990).

Montana: Missoula CC (R.2 1987); Whitefish Lake GC (R. 1985).

Nebraska: Skyline Woods GC (R. 1987).

North Dakota: Williston Muni GC (A.9 1981), with *Theodore Wirth.*

Oregon: Portland GC (R.1 1987); Riverside G&CC (R.3 1989).

Texas: Las Colinas CC (R. 1985); Prestonwood CC (R. 1984).

Washington: Broadmoor GC (R.3 1984); Cedarcrest GC (R.3 1981); Everett G&CC (R.1 1981); Glendale CC (R. 1986); Indian Canyon GC (R. 1984); Lake Padden GC (R. 1991); Legion Memorial GC (1985); Liberty Lake GC (R.1 1981); Lopez Island GC (R. 1984); Maplewood GC (R.5 1987); Oakbrook G&CC (R. 1990); Overlake G&CC (R. 3 1984); Tacoma C&GC (R.5 1987); Walla Walla CC (R.4 1987); Walter E. Hall G Cse (R. 1986).

British Columbia: Vancouver GC (R.2 1990).

Wayne Stiles, circa 1945 COLLECTION RON WHITTEN

WAYNE E. STILES
(1884–1953) ASGCA, CHARTER MEMBER

BORN: Boston, Massachusetts.
DIED: Wellesley, Massachusetts, at age 68.

Wayne Stiles did not train formally for a career in landscape architecture. Instead he began working at age 18 as an office boy for landscape designer Franklin Brett. After being made a draftsman and finally a junior partner, Stiles opened his own landscape design and town planning office in Boston in 1915. Within a year he had branched into golf design.

Stiles formed a course-design partnership with John Van Kleek in 1924. The firm of Stiles and Van Kleek had offices in Boston, New York City and St. Petersburg, concentrating mainly on golf courses and their accompanying subdivisions. Over the years associates of the firm included professional golfer Walter Hagen (who was a consultant in course design), Thomas D. Church and Butler Sturdivant (both subsequent nationally known landscape architects) and Bruce Matthews (later a prominent course designer).

The firm dissolved before the Depression, when the real estate boom faded in Florida, but Stiles remained in practice almost exclusively as a golf course architect. During the Depression, he supervised Civil Conservation Corps projects for the National Park Service. After World War II he was active again in course architecture. Stiles served as president of the Boston Society of Landscape Architects for several years and was a member of the ASLA.

Courses by Wayne Stiles (All with John Van Kleek unless otherwise indicated):

Alabama: Charles Boswell G Cse [FKA Highland Park GC].

Connecticut: Paul Block Private Cse (9, NLE).

Florida: Highland Park C (1925); Holly Hill G&CC (NLE); Kenilworth Lodge GC (NLE); Lake Jovita CC; Palmetto

G&CC; Pasadena GC (1925), and Walter Hagen; Tarpon Springs CC (1927).

Georgia: Glen Arven CC (1929); Radium CC (1927).

Maine: Bath CC (9 1932 *solo*); Boothbay Region GC (9 1921 *solo*); North Haven C (1932 *solo*); Riverside Muni (9 1935 *solo*); Rockland (9 1932 *solo*); Wawenock GC (9 1926); Wilson Lake (9 1931 *solo*).

Massachusetts: Albemarle CC (9 *solo*); Berkshire Hunt & CC (1930); Cranwell School GC; D. W. Field Muni (1927); Duxbury YC (9 *solo*); Franconia Muni (1930 *solo*); Haverhill CC (*solo*); Larry Gannon Memorial GC (1932 *solo*); Marlborough CC (9); Marshfield CC (9 1922 *solo*, A.9 1931); Memorial Muni (NLE); Needham GC (9 1923 *solo*); Newton Commonwealth GC; Pine Brook CC; Putterham Meadows Muni; South Shore CC (1923); Stony Brae GC; Taconic GC (1927); Thorny Lea GC (1925); Unicorn CC; Wahconah CC (9 *solo*); Weld GC; Woodland CC (*solo*); Wyndhurst C (*solo*).

Missouri: Norwood Hills CC (East Cse 1923 *solo*; West Cse 1922 *solo*).

Nebraska: Omaha CC.

New Hampshire: Cochecho CC (9 1921 *solo*); CC of New Hampshire [FKA Kearsarge Valley CC] (9 1930); Dover CC (1923 *solo*, NLE); Hooper GC (9 1926); Laconia CC (9 1921 *solo*); Mojalaki CC [FKA Franklin CC] (9 1928); Nashua (9 1916 *solo*, A.9 1925).

New Jersey: Brigantine CC (1927); Wildwood G&CC (1924).

New York: South Shore CC; Woodstock CC (*solo*).

North Carolina: Hamilton Lakes CC.

South Carolina: Hartford Estate GC (*solo*, NLE).

Vermont: Barre CC (9 1923 *solo*); Brandon GC (9 *solo*, NLE); Brattleboro CC (9 1916 *solo*).

Courses remodeled or expanded by Wayne Stiles (All with John Van Kleek unless otherwise indicated):

Maine: Augusta CC (A.9 1926); Brunswick GC (R.9 1925); Prouts Neck GC (R.9 A.9 1923 *solo*).

Massachusetts: CC of Pittsfield (R. *solo*); Franklin CC (R.); Monoosnock CC (R.9); Oak Hill CC (A.9); Sharon CC (R.9 *solo*); Wellesley CC (R.9); Presidents CC [FKA Wollaston CC] (R.); Woods Hole GC (R. *solo*).

New Hampshire: Bethlehem CC (R.1920 *solo*); Crawford Notch CC (R., NLE); Mountain View House GC (R.); Wentworth Resort GC (R.9 A.9 1922 *solo*).

Pennsylvania: Gulph Mills GC (R. 1941 *solo*).

Vermont: Rutland CC (R.9 A.9 1928); Woodstock CC (R.9 A.9 1924).

EARL STONE
(1926–   )

BORN: Alachua, Florida.

Earl Stone graduated from Auburn University in 1949 after service in the U.S. Navy during World War II. He worked in the electrical appliance business and as a heating and air-conditioning contractor until the mid-1950s, when he began installing irrigation systems on golf courses. This led to jobs rebuilding greens and in 1958 to a commission to design and build an entire course. An admirer of golf architect Dick Wilson's work, Stone designed dozens of courses in the Southeast over the next thirty years.

Courses by Earl Stone:

Alabama: Camden State Park GC (9 1970); Deer Run GC (9 1980, A.9 1991); Eagle Point GC (1990); Frank House Muni (1972); Gulf Shores GC (1965); Gulf State Park GC (1972); Holly Hill CC (9 1966); Joe Wheeler State Park GC (1974); Lake Guntersville State Park GC (1972); Little Mountain State Park GC (1972); McFarland Park GC (1973); Oak Mountain State Park GC (1972); St. Andrews CC (9 1971, A.9 1976).

Arkansas: Rivercliff GC (9 1977).

Florida: Indian Bayou G&CC (1978, A.3rd 9 1991); Marcus Pointe GC (1990).

Kentucky: Western Hills Muni (1985).

Mississippi: Briarwood CC (1967); Broadwater Beach Hotel GC (Fun Cse [9 Par 3] 1967; Sun Cse 1968); Diamond Head Y&CC (Pine Cse 1977); Gulfport Naval Air Station GC (9 1978); Hickory Hill CC (1965); Longfellow House GC (9 Par 3 1981); Pine Burr CC (9 1977, A.9 1991); Riverside Muni (9 1974); Waynesboro CC (9 1960).

Bahrain: Bahrain National GC (1980).

Courses remodeled or expanded by Earl Stone:

Alabama: CC of Mobile (A.9 1966); Lake Forest CC (R.9 A.9 1978); Skyline CC (A.3rd 9 1974).

Florida: Foxwood CC (A.9 1985).

Kentucky: Hopkinsville CC (R. 1990).

Mississippi: Broadwater Beach Hotel GC (Sea Cse, R.9 A.9 1962); Rainbow Bay GC (R.12 A.6 1976).

DAVID STRATH
(1840–1879)

BORN: St. Andrews, Scotland.
DIED: En route to Australia at age 39.

Davie Strath served as greenkeeper at North Berwick from 1876 to 1878. He formalized the course and extended it to 18 holes, and his revisions to the Perfection (hole number 14) and the Redan (hole number 15) made those holes famous worldwide. The concepts of both holes were subsequently adapted repeatedly on courses throughout the world by many golf architects. A contemporary competitor of Young Tom Morris, Strath left North Berwick to seek his fortune in Australia. He developed consumption and died aboard a steamship enroute.

Herbert Strong, circa 1910
COLLECTION RON WHITTEN

HERBERT BERTRAM STRONG
(1879–1944)

BORN: Ramsgate, Kent, England.
DIED: Fort Pierce, Florida, at age 65.

Herbert Strong began his golf career as professional and clubmaker at St. George's Golf Club in Sandwich, Kent, England. In 1905 he emigrated to New York and became professional at Apawamis Club in Rye. Six years later he moved to Inwood Golf Club in Far Rockaway and, while there, remodeled the course. This led to

other design jobs, and within a few years Strong was devoting virtually all his time to golf course architecture. In the early 1920s he formed a short-lived design partnership with George Low, Sr., a prominent golfer and instructor.

Throughout his career, Strong did his own surveying and usually remained at the sites to supervise construction. He was assisted on some of his later jobs by his younger brother Leonard, who later became a prominent course superintendent. (Curiously, though Strong never made much of the fact, Leonard claimed Herbert had invented the first golf pull cart in the 1920s but someone else had obtained a patent on such a device before Herbert was able to apply.)

Like many architects of that era, Strong was a victim of the Depression. He lost a fortune when the golf course market collapsed, although he remained in the golf business until the end. In his day he had been a fine player and considered among the longest drivers, having nearly a dozen holes in one to his credit, including one of 320 yards. He was a charter member of the PGA and served as its first treasurer from 1917 to 1919.

Courses by Herbert Strong:

Florida: Clearwater CC (1920); Indian Hills G&CC; Lakewood CC; Ponte Vedra C (Ocean Cse 1932); Rio Mar CC (9 1919); Royal Park G&CC (NLE); Vero Beach CC (1929).

Maryland: CC of Maryland [FKA Rodgers Forge CC] (1923), with George Low; Sherwood Forest GC (1920); Woodholme CC (1927).

Michigan: Aviation CC.

New Jersey: Aviation Y&CC (1937, NLE); Braidburn CC (NLE); Brook Lake CC [FKA Florham Park CC]; Linwood CC.

New York: Engineers GC (1918); Huntington G & Marine C (1915); Island Hills CC; Island's End G&CC; Metropolis CC [FKA Century CC].

Ohio: Canterbury CC (1922); Lake Forest CC (1931).

Pennsylvania: Saucon Valley CC (Old Cse 1922).

Vermont: Lake Shore CC (9 1928, NLE).

Virginia: Army-Navy CC (Fairfax Cse).

West Virginia: Guyan G&CC (1918).

Ontario: Lakeview G&CC.

Quebec: Manoir Richelieu GC (1927); St. Andrews GC.

Cuba: Veradera Beach CC (NLE).

Courses remodeled or expanded by Herbert Strong:

New Jersey: Knickerbocker CC (R.); Mountain Ridge CC (R.).
New York: Beacon CC (R.9 A.9 1929); Deepdale GC (R., NLE); Inwood CC (R. 1911); Nassau CC (R. A.3 1924), with George Low.
Pennsylvania: CC of Harrisburg (R.).
Quebec: Laval sur le Lac GC (R.); Royal Quebec CC (Kent Cse, R.9 A.9 1923, NLE).

J. Hamilton Stutt, 1990 COURTESY J. HAMILTON STUTT

JOHN HAMILTON STUTT
(1924–) BIGCA, FOUNDING MEMBER; CHAIRMAN 1975; PRESIDENT 1980

BORN: Scotland.

J. Hamilton Stutt attended Glasgow Academy and received a B.S. degree in mathematics and botany from St. Andrews University, where he was a member of the golf and tennis teams. As a boy, he accompanied his father, John R. Stutt, and his father's business associate, James Braid, to many construction sites. Following service with the Royal Air Force during World War II, he entered his father's golf course and sports ground construction firm. At the same time he began studying civil engineering and surveying at Strathclyde University. Over the next fifteen years Stutt constructed many golf courses, several of them planned by golf architects P. M. Ross and J. S. M. Morrison. Ross and Morrison instructed and encouraged Stutt, and in the 1960s Stutt gradually gave up the family construction business to devote full time to golf course architecture.

Stutt wrote *Restoration of Derelict Land for Golf,* a booklet published by the Golf Development Council. In addition to his native tongue, Stutt spoke French, German, Spanish and Norwegian. Such fluency helped him land projects in Europe, Scandinavia and the Middle East.

Courses by J. Hamilton Stutt:

England: Barton-on-Sea GC (27 1990); Blyth GC (1976); Bodmin G&CC; Bramshott Hill GC (1974); Carlyon Bay GC; Country Club Hotels (9); Deane Muni (Precision); Ferndown GC (New Cse 1970); Hyde G&CC; Knighton Heath GC (1976); Meon Valley CC (27 1976); Middlesborough Muni (1977); Rushyford GC (1983); St. Mellion G&CC (Old Cse 1976); Solihull GC (1989); Vivary GC (Precision); Westwood GC; Woodbury Park G&CC.
France: Corsica GC (Par 3); Normandie GC (9); Piencort CC.
Ireland: Wexford GC (9 1961, A.9 1984).
Lebanon: Delhamyeh CC.
Scotland: Ardeer GC (1980); Cumbernauld GC (1977); Fort William GC (1974); Glennoch G&CC (1974); Glenrothes GC (1958), with Fraser Middleton; Murrayshall G&CC (1981).
Spain: Costa Brava GC (1962); Coto de Donana (1985).

Courses remodeled or expanded by J. Hamilton Stutt:

England: Ashley Wood GC (R.9 1983); Ashridge GC (R.); Bath GC (R.); Blandford GC (R.); Bristol & Clifton GC (R.); Broadstone GC (R.); Brockenhurst Manor GC (R.); Bude and North Cornwall GC (R.); Came Down GC (R.); Churston GC (R.); Coombe Hill GC (R.); Cowes GC (A.9); East Devon GC (R.); East Herts GC (R.); Elfordleigh G&CC (R.); Ellesborough GC (R.); Great Barr GC (R.); Hockley GC (R.); Knighton Heath GC (R.); Launceston GC (A.9); Lee-on-the-Solent GC (R.); Lewes GC (R.); Lyme Regis GC (R.); Marlborough GC (A.9); Middlesborough GC (R.); Morpeth GC (R.); Mullion GC (R.); Newton Abbot GC (R.); Parkstone GC (R.); Perranporth GC (R.); Ramsey GC (R. 1964); Royal Eastbourne GC (R.); Sham Castle GC (R.); South Herts GC (R.); Southampton GC (R. A.3rd 9); St. George's Hill GC (R.); Stoke Poges GC (R.); Tidworth Garrison GC (R.); Torquay GC (R.); Ventnor GC (R.); Weymouth GC (R. A.9); Whitby GC (R.).
France: International C du Lys (R. 1980).
Germany: Falkenstein GC (R.); Frankfurter GC (R. 1952), with J. S. F. Morrison.

Ireland: Dundalk GC (R.); Rosslare GC (R.); Waterford GC (R.).
Isle of Man: Shanklin & Sandown GC (R.).
Isle of Wight: Ryde GC (R.).
Scotland: Colville Park GC (R.); Inverurie GC (R.); Irvine GC (R.); Kirkcaldy GC (R.); Monifieth GC (R.); Prestwick GC (R. 1979); Prestwick St. Cuthbert GC (R.); Strathaven GC (R.).
Wales: Pyle and Kenfig GC (R.).

JOHN R. STUTT
(1897–1990)

BORN: Paisley, Scotland.
DIED: Scotland at age 93.

In 1923 John Stutt founded the landscape and sports ground construction firm of John R. Stutt Ltd. Soon branching into golf, Stutt had built some eighty-two courses by 1939, most to the plans of James Braid, with whom he had become associated in 1923.

The Braid-Stutt team lasted until Braid's death in 1950. In the beginning Braid did all the course planning, but he encouraged Stutt to take on some of the design work as well as construction. Eventually, Stutt became architect and builder of numerous courses of his own. A majority of his career, however, was spent building courses designed by Braid and other architects, including J. S. F. Morrison and Theodore Moone.

In the early 1930s Stutt invented, patented and manufactured one of the first turf aeration machines. After World War II he was joined in the business by his son J. Hamilton Stutt.

Courses by John R. Stutt (All with James Braid unless otherwise indicated):

England: Arcot Hall GC; Basingstoke GC; Clitheroe GC; Drayton Park GC; Exeter G&CC; Finchley GC (1929); Fulford Heath GC (1934); Hainault Forest GC (Cse No. 2 *solo*); Hoylake Muni (1933); Ipswich GC (9 1928); Kedleston Park GC (1947), and J. S. F. Morrison; Kingswood GC (1928); Mere G&CC (1934), and George Duncan; Middlesborough GC; Newton Abbott GC (1930); Orsett GC; Oswestry GC (1930); Perranporth GC (1927); Petersborough Milton GC (1938); Royal Blackheath GC (1923); Scarborough North Cliff GC (1927);

John R. Stutt, 1938
COURTESY J. HAMILTON
STUTT

Tiverton GC (1932); Torquay GC.
Ireland: Mullingar GC (1932); Newlands GC (1926).
Isle of Man: Ramsey GC (1935).
Northern Ireland: Carnalea GC (1927).
Scotland: Belleisle GC (1927); Blairgowrie GC (Wee Cse); Boat-of-Garten GC; Buchanan Castle GC (1936); Carnoustie GC (Burnside Cse 1926); Cawder GC (Cawder Cse 1933; Keir Cse 1933); Crow Wood GC (1925); Dalmahoy GC (East Cse 1926; West Cse 1926); Downfield GC (1932); Fort Augustus GC (9 1930); Glenbervie GC (1932); Hamilton GC; Hayston GC (1926); Hilton Park GC (Allender Cse 1937); Ingliston GC; Musselburgh GC (1937); Ratho Park GC (1928); Royal Musselburgh GC (1925); Seafield GC (1930); Stornoway GC (1947 solo); Taymouth Castle GC (1928).
Wales: Welshpool GC (1929).

Courses remodeled or expanded by John R. Stutt (All with James Braid unless otherwise indicated):

New York: St. Andrews GC (R. 1930).
Channel Islands: La Moye GC (R. 1938).
England: Berkhampsted GC (R.12 A.6 1927); Berwick-upon-Tweed GC (R. 1925); Bramley GC (R.); Bush Hill Park GC (R.); Cockermouth GC (R.2); Denham GC (R.); Enfield GC (R.); Leamington and County GC (R.); Littlestone GC (R.); Meyrick Park GC (R. solo); Parkstone GC (R. 1927); Queens Park GC (R.); Royal Cromer GC (R.); Ruislip GC (A.9 1938); Sherwood Forest GC (R. 1935); Thetford GC (R.); Wallasey GC (R. 1939).
Ireland: Ballybunion GC (Old Cse, R.9 A.9 1927); Howth GC (R.9 A.9 1929); Limerick GC (A.9 1928); Tullamore GC (R. 1938); Waterford GC (R.9 A.9 1934).
Northern Ireland: Bangor GC (R. 1932).

Scotland: Alyth GC (R.); Blairgowrie GC (Rosemount Cse, R.10 A.8 1934); Broomieknowe GC (R.); Bruntsfield Links (R.); Carnoustie GC (R. 1926; 1936); Cathcart Castle GC (R. solo); Cochrane Castle GC (R. A.9 1949); Crieff GC (R.); Dunfermline GC (R. solo); Eastwood GC (R. solo); Edzell GC (R. 1934); Forres GC (R.); Lanark GC (R. solo); Murcar GC (R.); Nairn GC (R. 1938); Newtonmore GC (R.); Prestwick GC (R. 1930); Royal Burgess G Society of Edinburgh (R. 1932); St. Andrews (New Cse, R.; Old Cse, R.); Scotscraig GC (R.); Stranraer GC (R. solo).

JOHN SUTHERLAND

John Sutherland served as secretary of Royal Dornoch Golf Club in Scotland for almost fifty years, from the 1880s to the late 1920s. A lifelong student of course architecture and greenkeeping, he exerted an enormous influence on Donald Ross during the years young Ross worked as pro-greenkeeper at Dornoch. The two made a point of walking the course every evening to see where improvements could be made. They constantly experimented with grasses and often discussed what constituted a good golf hole.

Sutherland also did some designing of his own, including a private course for his friend Andrew Carnegie, the American steel magnate, at Carnegie's Scottish estate, Skibo Castle.

Courses by John Sutherland:

Scotland: Skibo Castle GC (1898); Tarbat GC (9).

Courses remodeled or expanded by John Sutherland:

Scotland: Royal Dornoch GC (R.9 A.9); Tain GC (R.).

HOWARD SWAN

BORN: Newcastle upon Tyne, England.

After attending Leeds University and the University of Warwick, where he obtained a Master's degree, Howard Swan worked for two years in corporate planning for an American pharmaceutical firm. But he soon got bored with life in an

office and resigned to join Golf Landscapes Ltd., a company founded by his father, Alec Swan, a highly regarded golf course contractor. Howard constructed his first golf course in 1972 and, serving as company director, worked on over 150 projects thereafter. Swan's reputation grew as a knowledgeable turf and construction man. He lectured to golf superintendent associations on both sides of the Atlantic, became chairman of the National Turfgrass Council in 1984 and served as consultant in the establishment of genuine fescues during the creation of the Links at Spanish Bay in Pebble Beach, California.

As a contractor, Swan worked with many leading golf course architects, especially Sir Henry Cotton, a close friend of his father's and an active designer in Portugal. Swan also designed several courses in association with his father. Both men assisted Cotton in the establishment of the Henry Cotton Golf Foundation to develop simple, low-budget courses for beginners. After Alec's death in 1984, Howard continued to construct courses for Henry Cotton and worked with him on some of the great man's last designs. Soon after Cotton's death in 1987, Swan established his own design-and-construction company, The Howard Swan Practice.

Courses by Howard Swan:

England: Allerthorpe GC; Benton Hall GC (27); Bidford Grange GC; Birchwood Park GC (27); Brett Vale GC; Bridgedown CC; Bridlington Bay GC (27); Colne Valley GC (1991); GC at Dunton Hills; Gosfield Lake GC (27 1986), with Henry Cotton; Lexden West House GC; Little Hadham GC; [The] Links at Gainsborough Lea; Mistley Estate GC; Navestock Park GC; Prince's GC (White Cse); Sandwich Bay G&CC; Stapleford Abbotts C (27); Stratford Oaks GC.
Netherlands: C Aktief.

Howard Swan, 1990
COURTESY HOWARD
SWAN

Portugal: Camola GC (27); Dunas Douradas GC (9); G da Dona Rainha (27); Monte Vehlo GC (9); Ponte de Lima GC; Praia da Marinha GC (9); Quinta da Benamor (1987), with Henry Cotton; Quinta da Boavista (9 Precision); Quinta da Boina GC; Quinta das Navalhas GC; Vila Anica GC.

Courses remodeled or expanded by Howard Swan:

England: Burnham on Crouch GC (A.9 1991); Clandon GC (R.); Market Harborough GC (A.9); Romsey GC (R.9 A.9)

Portugal: Estoril Sol GC (R. 1990); Pinheiros Altos GC (R. 1992), with *Peter McEvoy.*

J. H. Taylor, circa 1930 COURTESY *GOLF WORLD*

JOHN HENRY TAYLOR (1871–1963)

BORN: Devonshire, England.
DIED: Devonshire, England, at age 92.

J. H. Taylor, one of British golf's "Great Triumvirate," originally trained as a gardener at the boyhood home of Horace Hutchinson. He served as assistant greenkeeper at Westward Ho! and later as club professional and greenkeeper at Burnham, Winchester, Wimbledon, and for many years at Royal Mid-Surrey. He won the British Open five times, as well as many other major championships.

Taylor used his enormous influence to promote public golf courses in England. He had laid out several courses before World War I and continued to plan new ones as part of a design-and-build partnership with F. G. Hawtree. Founded in 1922, the firm of Hawtree & Taylor was active until World War II. Taylor had little formal education, having left school by age 11, but he was an avid reader and insisted on writing his memoirs, *Golf, My Life's Work,* without the assistance of a ghostwriter.

Courses by J. H. Taylor (All with F. G. Hawtree unless otherwise indicated):

Egypt: Heliopolis Sporting C (9 1905 *solo*).

England: Addington Court GC (Lower Cse 1931; Old Cse 1931); Addington Palace GC (1923); Batchwood Hall GC (1936); Bigbury GC (1923); Came Down GC (1890 *solo*); Chadwell Springs GC (9 1905 *solo*); Chigwell GC (1925); Clevedon GC (1909 *solo*); Cock Moor Woods GC (1926); Easingwold GC (1930); Eastbourne Downs GC (1908 *solo*); Elfordleigh GC (1932); Gorleston GC (1926); Hainault Forest GC (Cse No. 1, 9 1920 *solo*, A.9 1927); Harborne Church Farm GC (1926); Harpenden GC (1931); Heaton Park GC (1911 *solo*); High Post GC (1922); Highwoods GC (1925); Hill Barn GC (1935); Hollingbury Park GC (1922); Ifield G&CC (1927); Knowle GC; Marston Green Muni; Pinner Hill GC (1929); Pype Hayes Muni (1932); Queens Park GC (1905 *solo*); Richmond Park GC (Dukes Cse 1923; Princes Cse 1923); Rose Hill GC (1927); Royal Ascot GC (1905 *solo*); Royal Mid-Surrey GC (Ladies Cse *solo*); Royal Winchester GC (*solo*); Ruislip GC (1938); Salisbury & South Wilts GC (1894 *solo*); Seaford GC (1906 *solo*); Selsdon Park Hotel GC (1929); Southampton GC (27 1935); Southcliffe and Canwick GC; Stratford-on-Avon GC (1928); Swinton Park GC (1926); Tinsley Park GC (1922); Warren GC (9 1911 *solo*); Wells-by-the-Sea GC (9 Par 3); Welwyn Garden City GC (1922); White Webbs Muni (1932); Woodlands Manor GC (1928); Woolacombe Bay Hotel GC (9 Par 3); Wyke Green GC (1928).

France: Nivelle GC (1907 *solo*).
Ireland: Arklow GC (1926).
Scotland: Hilton Park GC (Hilton Cse 1922).
Sweden: Bastad GC (1928).
Wales: Holywell GC (9 1907 *solo*); Rhuddlan GC (1930).

Courses remodeled or expanded by J. H. Taylor (All with F. G. Hawtree unless otherwise indicated):

England: Aldeburgh GC (R. 1906 *solo*); Coventry GC (R. *solo*); Filton GC (R.9 A.9); Hull GC (R.); Ipswich GC (A.9 1931); Littlehampton GC (R.9 A.9); Notts GC (R. *solo*); Rickmansworth Public GC (R. 1937); Royal Birkdale GC (R. 1932); Royal Mid-Surrey GC (R. 1911, with Peter W. Lees, R. 1928); Sidmouth GC (R. A.9 1908 *solo*); Sonning GC (R.9 A.9); West Middlesex GC (A.9); West Wiltshire GC (R. *solo*); Willingdon GC (R. *solo*); York GC (R. *solo*).

Scotland: Machrihannish GC (R. 1914 *solo*); Morton Hall GC (R. 1906 *solo*); Royal Dornoch GC (R. 1907 *solo*); Williamswood GC (R.).

Wales: Ashburnham GC (R. 1914); Royal Porthcawl GC (R. A.4 1925).

ALEC TERNYEI, NÉ ELEK VIKTOR TERNYEY (1909–1983)

BORN: Briarcliff, New York.
DIED: Port St. Lucie, Florida, at age 74.

The son of Hungarian immigrants, Elek Ternyey became a caddy at age 9 and within a year was working for the club professional, cleaning up after clubmaking sessions. By observing the clubmaker and by salvaging old parts, Ternyey soon became adept at clubmaking and repaired many a club for fellow caddies. Leaving high school at age 16, Ternyey turned professional and worked as an apprentice to Englewood (New Jersey) Country Club professional Cyril Walker. He became a member of the PGA of America at 18 and, in the manner of star golfer Gene Sarazen, modified his name to Alec Ternyei. The "Alec" he once explained, had a Scottish ring to it, while the "Ternyei" was a concession to those who constantly misspelled his last name.

After stints at Knickerbocker Country Club and the Maidstone Club, Ternyei got his first head professional job in 1931 at Rivervale Country Club in New Jersey. Over the next twenty-five years he worked as professional at several New Jersey clubs, played in local and regional PGA events and earned a fine reputation as an expert clubmaker. He also served in the air force during World War II.

In the late 1950s Ternyei designed and built his first golf course. He resigned his professional duties in the 1960s to devote his full energies to golf architecture and prided himself on the fact that he personally constructed the dozen courses he designed in the New Jersey area. In 1970 Ternyei retired to a teaching professional position in Florida.

Courses by Alec Ternyei:

Florida: Crystal Lago CC (1972).
New Jersey: Beacon Hill CC (1962); Beaver Brook GC (1965); Glenhurst CC (1966); Green Pond GC (9 1964); High Mountain CC (1968); Pines GC (1963); Princeton Hills G Academy (1970).

Courses remodeled or expanded by Alec Ternyei:

New Jersey: Englewood CC (R. 1961).
Pennsylvania: Turbot Hills GC (A.9 1957).

WILLIAM G. TEUFEL
(1926–), ASGCA

BORN: Fairbanks, Alaska.

William Teufel attended Washington State University and obtained a Bachelor of Science degree in landscape architecture from the University of Oregon. In 1956 Teufel established a landscape architecture firm in Seattle. In the early 1960s his company, William G. Teufel and Associates, branched into golf course architecture, primarily in the planning of golf course residential development layouts.

William Teufel,
1990 COURTESY ASGCA

Courses by William Teufel:

Washington: Braeburn GC (9 Par 3 1965); Fairwood G&CC (1966); Hat Island G&CC (1969); Quincy G&CC (1986); Tam O'Shanter CC (9 1965); Twin Lakes G&CC (9 1965); Useless Bay G&CC (1968; R. 1982); Wing Point G&CC (9 1963).

Courses remodeled or expanded by William Teufel:

Montana: Green Meadow CC (A.9 1974).
Washington: Bellingham G&CC (R.); Enumclaw GC (A.9 1978); Fort Lewis GC (A.3rd 9 1979); Foster G Links (R. 1986); Inglewood CC (R. 1985); Kit-

sap G&CC (R. 1981); Vashon Island G&CC (R. 1983).

DAVID C. THOMAS
(1934–)

BORN: Newcastle upon Tyne, England.

David Thomas competed on the British, European and American professional golf circuits for over two decades with mixed success. He won the Belgian, Dutch and French opens, but was never able to win the British Open, losing it in a play-off in 1958 and by a stroke in 1966. A four-time member of Ryder Cup teams, Thomas represented his adopted homeland of Wales in a dozen World Cup competitions.

In the late 1960s Thomas became interested in golf course design. Teaming with fellow professional golfer Peter Alliss, he laid out and built several courses, including The Belfry, home of the British PGA and a three-time Ryder Cup site. Thomas and Alliss abandoned course architecture for a time in the late 1970s to concentrate on the more lucrative business of course construction. In the 1980s the two dissolved the partnership and each practiced course architecture on his own and in tandem with new partners. By the 1990s Thomas had teamed with former U.S. and British Open champion Tony Jacklin on a series of courses.

Courses by David Thomas (All with Peter Alliss unless otherwise indicated):

Brazil: Golf Hotel do Frade (1980).
England: [The] Belfry GC (Barbazon Cse 1979; Derby Cse 1979); Chapel-en-le-Firth GC; Dewsbury District GC; Hessle GC; Hill Valley G&CC (27 1975); King's Lynn GC (1975); Slaley Hall GC (1989 *solo*); Thorpe Wood GC (1975).
France: Cannes-Mougins GC (1978).
Ivory Coast: President CC (1980).
Japan: Top Players CC (1989 *solo*).

David Thomas,
circa 1970 COURTESY
GOLF WORLD

Northern Ireland: Clandeboye GC (Dufferin Cse 1973), and T. J. A. Macauley.
Scotland: Blairgowrie GC (Lansdowne Cse, 9 1974).

Courses remodeled or expanded by David Thomas (All with Peter Alliss unless otherwise indicated):

France: Golf de la Baule (R. 1977).
Ireland: Dundalk GC (R. A.9 1975).
Northern Ireland: Ballyclare GC (R.9 A.9 1973), and T. J. A. Macauley.
Scotland: Blairgowrie GC (Rosemount Cse, R. 1974); Haggs Castle GC (R.); Turnberry GC (Ailsa Cse, R. 1976).

George C. Thomas,
Jr., circa 1920
COLLECTION RON
WHITTEN

GEORGE CLIFFORD THOMAS, JR.
(1873–1932)

BORN: Philadelphia, Pennsylvania.
DIED: Beverly Hills, California, at age 58.

George C. Thomas, Jr., scion of a prominent Philadelphia family, was educated at Episcopal Academy and at the University of Pennsylvania. He worked with his father in the banking firm of Drexel & Co. until 1907, but his early avocation was gardening. He was a nationally recognized authority on the care and breeding of roses and wrote several books about them.

Thomas was a marginal golfer but was interested in the landscaping aspects of golf course design. His first course, a nine-hole layout at Marion, Massachusetts, was staked out in the early 1900s. Thomas went on to design other courses in the East and to study the various techniques of prominent architects. He worked as a club committeeman with Donald Ross at Flourtown Country Club and Sunnybrook Country Club in Pennsylvania and with A. W. Tillinghast on a second course for Philadelphia Cricket Club. He also observed the works in progress of his friends Hugh Wilson at Merion and George Crump at Pine Valley. In 1908 Thomas designed Mount Airy Country Club (later Whitemarsh Valley Country Club), built on his family estate at Chestnut Hill, Pennsylvania. The family home served for years as the clubhouse.

During World War I, Thomas served in Europe with the U.S. Army Corps as captain of a unit rumored to have been totally outfitted at his expense. In 1919 he moved to California, ostensibly to carry on his rose breeding. He devoted much of his time, however, to course architecture and over the next 10 years designed and built some twenty-five courses, many with the assistance of William P. Bell. Throughout his career, Thomas never accepted a fee for his services as course designer.

Thomas's classic work, *Golf Architecture in America: Its Strategy and Construction*, was published in 1927 and later republished half a century later as one of the game's classics. Soon after the book's initial appearance, Thomas began to lose interest in the subject. He spent his last years working on a book about Pacific game fish.

Courses by George C. Thomas, Jr.

California: Baldwin Hills GC (1926, NLE), with William P. Bell; Bel-Air CC (1927), with William P. Bell and Jack Neville; El Caballero CC (1926, NLE), with William P. Bell; Fox Hills GC (1926, NLE), with William P. Bell; Griffith Park GC (Harding Cse 1926); Los Angeles CC (North Cse 1921); Ojai Valley Inn & CC (1925), with William P. Bell; Palos Verdes CC (1924), with William P. Bell; Red Hill CC (9 1921); Riviera CC (1927), with William P. Bell; Saticoy Regional G Cse [FKA Saticoy G&CC] (1926).
Massachusetts: Marion GC (9).
New Jersey: Spring Lake G&CC (1910).
Pennsylvania: Whitemarsh Valley CC [FKA Mount Airy CC] (1908).

Courses remodeled or expanded by George C. Thomas, Jr.:

California: La Cumbre G&CC (R.9 A.9 1920), with William P. Bell; Griffith Park GC (Wilson Cse, R. 1923; South Cse, R. 1921).

JOHN ALEXANDER THOMPSON (1920–   )

BORN: Winnipeg, Manitoba, Canada.

Jack Thompson (no relation to legendary Canadian golf architect Stanley Thompson) graduated from the American School of Landscape Design in Chicago in 1938. After World War II he formed a garden supply and landscape contracting firm in Canada.

While a contractor, Thompson formed an association with Alexander Mann, a golf course designer and turfgrass consultant from Aberdeen, Scotland. Thompson worked closely with Mann on the renovation and redesign of numerous courses from 1946 until Mann's death in 1952 and credited the Scot with providing his formal education in golf course architecture. After 1952 Thompson returned full-time to his landscape contracting business until 1966, when he branched into golf course and landscape architecture. In the 1980s Thompson served as superintendent of parks for the city of Regina, Saskatchewan.

Courses by John A. Thompson:

Alberta: Black Bull G&CC (9).
Manitoba: Carmen G&CC; Hecla GC (1975); Minnedosa G&CC (9); Selkirk G&CC.
Saskatchewan: Craig GC (9).

Courses remodeled or expanded by John A. Thompson:

Manitoba: Southwood G&CC (R.); Steinback Fly Inn GC (A.9); Tor Hill GC (R. 1982).

STANLEY THOMPSON (1894–1952), ASGCA, CHARTER MEMBER; PRESIDENT 1949

BORN: Scotland.
DIED: Toronto, Ontario, Canada, at age 58.

Stanley Thompson emigrated with his family to Toronto before the First World War. He was one of five brothers (Nicol, William, Matthew, Stanley and Frank), all

Stanley Thompson, 1949 COLLECTION RON WHITTEN

of whom became internationally known professional or amateur golfers. Stanley attended Ontario Agricultural College in Guelph but left in 1915 to serve with the Canadian Expeditionary Force in France.

In 1921 Thompson entered practice as a course architect and landed a few modest projects in Ontario. After courses in Winnipeg and Toronto, Thompson produced in quick succession two of his greatest triumphs, Jasper Park and Banff Springs, both in the Canadian Rockies. Banff was built for the Canadian Pacific Railway and officially opened by the Prince of Wales. Jasper was done for the Canadian National Railway and opened by Field Marshal Haig. Both dramatic mountain layouts met with worldwide acclaim. They exhibited a degree of strategic design unprecedented in North America, and Thompson's fame spread as a result. Even Winston Churchill, hardly a golf devotee, enjoyed his rounds at Banff on his visits to Canada between the wars.

Thompson, nicknamed "the Toronto Terror," was one of the more colorful figures in golf design history. Many close to him felt he was a genius and recognized depth beneath his flamboyance. He made and spent fortunes. But he was also conscientious in the training of a number of assistants who later made names for themselves in course architecture, including Robert Trent Jones (who became his partner in the firm of Thompson, Jones & Co. Ltd.), Howard Watson, C. E. Robinson, Norman Woods, Kenneth Welton, Robert Moote and Geoffrey S. Cornish.

Shortly after his death in 1952, the Ottawa *Citizen* eulogized him with these words: "Stanley Thompson has left a mark on the Canadian landscape from coast to coast. No man could ask for a more handsome set of memorials."

In 1980 Stanley Thompson was inducted posthumously into the Canadian Hall of Fame.

Courses by Stanley Thompson:

Florida: Nealhurst GC (27, NLE).
Minnesota: North Oaks CC.
New York: Midvale G&CC (1931), with Robert Trent Jones.
Ohio: Beechmont GC; Chagrin Valley G&CC (1925); Geneva on the Lake GC (NLE); Sleepy Hollow GC (1923); Squaw Creek CC (1924); Trumbull CC.
Alberta: Banff Springs Hotel GC (1927); Beaver GC; Jasper Park Lodge GC (1925); Mayfair GC.

British Columbia: Capilano G&CC
(1937).

Manitoba: Clear Lake GC; Glendale
G&CC; Niakwa G&CC; Pine Ridge
GC.

New Brunswick: Fundy National Park GC
(9).

Nova Scotia: Cape Breton Highlands GC,
"Keltic Lodge" (1935); Digby Pines GC
(1932); Halifax G&CC, "Old Ashburn"
(1922); Lingan GC.

Ontario: Allandale GC (9); Aurora GC
(9); Bayview GC; Beach Grove G&CC
(1922); Big Bay G&CC (9); Bigwin
Inn GC; Briars G&CC (9 1922); Bur-
lington G&CC; Cataraqui G&CC;
Cedarbrook G&CC (1922); Carleton
Yacht & GC; Chedoke GC (New Cse
1950); Civic GC (9); Credit Valley GC
(9); Dundas Valley G&CC; Erie
Downs G&CC; Essex GC; Fort Wil-
liam G&CC (1925); Glen Mawr GC
(1931); Highland GC (1921); Humber
Valley G&CC (1921); Huntsville
Downs G&CC (1926); Islington GC
(1921); Kawartha GC; Kenogamisis
GC (9); Kenora G&CC (9); Ladies
G&TC (1924); Marathon GC (9);
Mardon Lodge GC (9); Minaki Lodge
GC (9 1928); Muskoka Beach GC
(1922); Muskoka Lakes G&CC (9);
North Bay G&CC (9 1922); Oakdale
GC; Orchard Beach G&CC (9 1926);
Owen Sound GC (9); Peninsula Park
GC (9); Rio Vista GC (9); St. Andrews
GC (27, NLE); St. Catharines G&CC;
St. George's G&CC (27 1929); St.
Thomas G&CC; Saugeen GC (9);
Shore Acres GC; Sir Harry Oakes
Private Cse (9); Sunningdale GC
(Old Cse 1937); Thunder Bay GC;
Uplands G&CC (1922); Wasaga GC
(9); Westmount G&CC (1935);
Whirlpool GC (1949); Willow-
dale GC.

Prince Edward Island: Green Gables GC
(1939).

Quebec: Arvida GC (9); International C;
Ki-8-AB GC (9); Marlborough GC (27,
NLE); Model City GC (NLE); Noranda
Mines GC (9 1934); Saguenay CC (9
1927); Seigniory C.

Saskatchewan: Tor Hill GC (1931);
Waskesiu Lake GC.

Brazil: Gavea G&CC; Itanhanga CC
(1922); São Paulo CC; Therezopolis
CC (1932).

Colombia: San Andres GC (1946);
Medellin GC.

Jamaica: Constant Spring GC (1930);
Manchester GC (9).

**Courses remodeled or expanded by
Stanley Thompson:**

Florida: Floridale GC (R., NLE); Hyde
Park GC (R.).

Minnesota: Somerset CC (R.).

New York: Bartlett CC (R.); Bonnie Briar
CC (R. 1936), with Robert Trent
Jones; Fort Erie G&CC (R.9 A.9);
Lockport CC (R.); Onondaga G&CC
(R.); Stafford CC (R. 1931), with Rob-
ert Trent Jones.

Alberta: Calgary G&CC (R.); Edmonton
CC (R.); Waterton Lakes GC (R.
1935).

British Columbia: Pacific National Exhibition GC (9).

Manitoba: Assiniboine GC (R.); Southwood G&CC (R. 1926)

New Brunswick: Monkton GC (R.).

Nova Scotia: Sydney GC (R. 1923); Truro
GC (R.).

Ontario: Brampton GC (R.9); Brantford
G&CC (R.); Brockville CC (R.9);
Chedoke GC (Old Cse, R.), Cutten
Field CC (R.); Hamilton G&CC (R.
1950); Lake Shore G&CC (R.); Mis-
sissauga G&CC (R. 1928); Norway
Point GC (R.9); Oshawa GC (R.); Pe-
terborough G&CC (R.); Sault Ste.
Marie GC (R.); Thornhill GC (R.
1922); Waterloo GC (R.); York Downs
(R., NLE).

Quebec: Beaconsfield GC (R. 1940).

Saskatchewan: Hillcrest GC (R.); Regina
G&CC (R. 1925).

PETER WILLIAM THOMSON, C.B.E.
(1929–   )

BORN: Melbourne, Australia.

Five-time British Open champion and
winner of seventy-five other professional
golf tournaments, Peter Thomson was as
close to being a Renaissance Man of Golf
as any person in the late twentieth century. He was a lively and sometimes acer-
bic writer and columnist for the Melbourne *Herald* and *Melbourne Age*. He was
a respected critic of golf courses and
coauthored *The World Atlas of Golf*. He
served as a member of the Australian Parliament, as a television commentator on
golf broadcasts, as president of the Australian PGA, as special adviser for the Asia
golf circuit (which he was instrumental in
founding) and as a member of the India
Golf Union.

Thomson was also deeply involved in
golf course architecture. In his younger

*Peter Thomson,
1985* COURTESY *GOLF
DIGEST*

days he served as a consultant to British
designer John D. Harris and in 1964 became his partner. After Harris's death, he
teamed with another Harris associate,
American Ronald Fream, for a short time.
He then formed a partnership with yet
another Harris associate, Michael Wolveridge, in the design and remodeling of
courses throughout the Far East and Australia. Wolveridge handled the routings,
Thomson the green designs, and together
they devised various strategies for each
hole. During the mid-1980s Thomson
played the U.S. Senior Tour for seven
months each year, but devoted the remainder of each year to golf architecture.

As outspoken on design as on any other
subject, Thomson decried the use of water
on modern courses, calling it "out of proportion and common sense." He was opposed to USGA green specifications,
feeling green bases primarily of sand were
too firm, causing shots by average golfers
to "splash on the green and then run like a
rat across it." He also advocated use of a
variety of turfgrasses around the edges of
greens and the elimination of all sand-
bunker rakes. His personal test of a good
golf design: "If my grandmother can't play
it, it's a lousy course."

**Courses by Peter Thomson (All with
Michael Wolveridge unless otherwise
indicated):**

California: Bixby GC (9 Precision 1980),
with Ronald Fream.

Washington: Canyon Lakes G&CC
(1981), with Ronald Fream; Indian
Summer GC (1991); Kayak Point GC
(1974), with Ronald Fream; Tapps Island GC (9 1981), with Ronald Fream.

Australia: Alice Springs GC (1987); Collier Park GC (1984); Darwin GC
(1983); Desert Springs CC (1984);
Fairway Park GC (1984); Gold Coast
CC (1984); Hall's Head Resort GC
(1984); Iwasaki Resort GC (1984);

Lake Ross GC (1984); Midlands GC (1975); North Lakes CC; Tasmanian Casino CC (1982); Thurgoona GC (27 1983); Tura Beach CC (1982).
England: Telford Hotel G&CC (1979), with John Harris.
Fiji: Fijian Hotel GC (9 Precision 1973), with Ronald Fream.
Hong Kong: Royal Hong Kong GC (Eden Cse 1968), with John Harris.
India: Bangladore GC (1982); Gulmarg GC (1973), with John Harris; Karnataka GC (1984).
Indonesia: Bali Handara CC (1975), with John Harris and Ronald Fream; Jagorawi G&CC (1978), with Ronald Fream; National GC, with Ronald Fream.
Japan: Chigusa CC (27 1973), with John Harris; Fujioka CC (1971), with *Tameshi Yamada;* Hammamatsu CC; Ibusuki CC (New Cse 1978); Korakuen CC (27 1974), with John Harris and Ronald Fream; Meihan Kokusai CC (1975); Naie GC (1976); Nambu Fuji GC (1974), with John Harris; Takaha Royal CC (1976); Three Lakes CC (1976); Tokuyama CC (1975); Yoro CC (1977); Zen CC (1977).
Mauritius: Case Noyale GC (1972), with John Harris.
New Zealand: Harewood GC (1967), with John Harris; Karori GC (1968), with John Harris; Maramarua GC (1969), with John Harris; Taieri GC (1967), with John Harris; Wairakei International GC (1975), with John Harris.
Portugal: Estoril Sol GC (9 Precision 1976), with John Harris and Ronald Fream.
Scotland: Inverness GC (1968), with John Harris.
Singapore: Sentosa Island GC (Serapong Cse 1983), and Ronald Fream.
St. Kitts: Royal St. Kitts GC (1977), with John Harris and Ronald Fream.
Tonga: Tonga GC.
Trinidad and Tobago: Balandra Beach GC (1982), and Ronald Fream; St. Andrews GC (1975), with John Harris and Ronald Fream.
Tunisia: El Kantaoui GC (1977), with John Harris and Ronald Fream.

Courses remodeled or expanded by Peter Thomson (All with Michael Wolveridge unless otherwise indicated):

California: Almaden G&CC (R. 1979), with Ronald Fream; Hacienda CC (R. 1978), with Ronald Fream; Marine Memorial GC (R. 1980), with Ronald

Fream; Miramar Memorial GC (R. 1981), with Ronald Fream; San Juan Hills CC (R. 1981), with Ronald Fream.
Nevada: Edgewood Tahoe GC (R. 1980), with Ronald Fream.
Oregon: Sunriver CC (South Cse, R. 1978), with Ronald Fream.
Washington: Broadmoor GC (R.2 1982), with Ronald Fream; Cedarcrest GC (R. 1982), with Ronald Fream; Manito G&CC (R. 1979), with Ronald Fream; Seattle GC (R.2 1981), with Ronald Fream; West Seattle GC (R. 1979), with Ronald Fream.
Alberta: Glendale CC (R.3 1981), with Ronald Fream.
Australia: Cottlesloe GC (R.); Kingston Heath GC (R.); Kooyonga GC (R.); Lake Karrinyup CC (R. A.3rd 9 1977); Metropolitan GC (R.); Middlemore GC (R.); New South Wales GC (R.); Peninsula G&CC (R.); Royal Adelaide GC (R.); Royal Canberra GC (R.); Royal Perth GC (R.); Royal Sydney GC (R. 1987); Sorrento GC (R.); Southern GC (R. A.9 1978); Victoria GC (R. 1983); Yarrawonga GC (A.9 1980).
Hong Kong: Royal Hong Kong GC (New Cse, R. 1970; Old Cse, R. 1976), with John Harris.
India: Bombay Presidency GC (R. 1980); Delhi GC (R. A.9 1974), with John Harris; Royal Calcutta GC (R. 1969), with John Harris.
Indonesia: Kebayoran GC (R. 1980), with Ronald Fream; Yani GC (R.).
Malaysia: Awana GC, Gentling Highlands (R. 1984), with Ronald Fream.
New Zealand: Akarana GC (R. 1972); Ashburton GC (R. 1977); Auckland GC (R.); Hastings GC (R. 1972); Miramar GC (R. 1977); Nelson GC (R. 1967), with John Harris; North Shore GC (R. 1969), with John Harris; Rarotonga GC (A.9 1984); Russley GC (R. 1967), with John Harris; Timaru GC (R. 1968), with John Harris.

ALBERT WARREN TILLINGHAST (1874–1942)

BORN: North Philadelphia, Pennsylvania.
DIED: Toledo, Ohio, at age 67.

A. W. Tillinghast, known in his day as "Tillie the Terror," was an outstanding golf architect and one of the most colorful characters in the history of golf.

The only child of a wealthy Philadelphia

A. W. Tillinghast, circa 1920
COLLECTION RON WHITTEN

couple, Tillinghast was a spoiled, pampered youth. He ran with a local gang of boys—called the Kelly Street Gang—who seemed bent on engaging in the most scandalous behavior that could be attempted in the late 1880s.

At the age of 20 Tillinghast abruptly left the band of ruffians, joined a more refined social circle and married a lovely young woman named Lillian. He then worked hard to develop an aristocratic image. He took on the trappings of a connoisseur and raconteur, collected beautiful pieces of furniture, china and art and wrote self-published novels full of maudlin prose. He lived the life of a sportsman, dabbling in cricket, billiards, polo and bridge.

Tillinghast also became enthralled with golf during a visit to St. Andrews, Scotland. He took lessons from Old Tom Morris and returned each summer for several years to visit the grand old man of the game. In the States Tillinghast competed in the U.S. Amateur on several occasions between 1905 and 1915, acquitting himself well in matches lost to such golfing luminaries as Walter Travis, Chandler Egan and Chick Evans.

In 1907, at the behest of Charles Worthington (who had made a fortune with his pump company), Tillinghast somewhat audaciously laid out a golf course on the Worthington family's farm at Shawnee-on-Delaware, Pennsylvania. He was 32 years old.

It was about the first honest work Tillie had ever done in his life, and he found that he not only enjoyed it, but also that he was good at it. He formed a design-and-construction firm that immediately became a success, and Tillinghast was a millionaire from his own efforts by the mid-1920s.

He honed his aristocratic image even further during his years as a golf designer. From his home in Harrington Park, New Jersey, Tillie routinely rode a chauffeured limousine to his office in midtown Manhattan. Not one to slave over working drawings and detailed plans, Tillie preferred to tromp through the thick brush of a course site—always dressed in the garb of a Wall Street banker—and lay out the course with his perceptive eye and uncanny intuition. During course construction he would routinely appear in his three-piece suit, plant a shooting stick in the shade, settle his bulk on it, sip from a flask and shout directions all day long to the laborers.

His glorious career, which included outstanding designs such as Winged Foot and Baltusrol, lasted until the Great Depression, when a series of ill-advised investments (into such things as a Broadway show) left Tillinghast nearly a pauper. He then worked for the PGA of America, touring members' courses and recommending changes. Most clubs were struggling to simply avoid foreclosure and had little need for an expert's keen opinion on the weaknesses of their courses. Still, Tillie dutifully performed his assignments, emphasizing the savings that could result if clubs followed his suggestions.

Tillinghast gave that up after a couple of seasons and, figuring that Hollywood was the last bastion of wealth in America, moved to Beverly Hills and opened an antique shop. His own family's furniture and art collections supplied most of the stock. When this venture failed, so did his health. He moved in with a daughter in Toledo, Ohio, where he died shortly after, nearly forgotten by the golfing world.

Tillinghast was an accomplished artist and prolific golf writer as well as an architect. He also coined the word "birdie" to describe a hole shot in one less stroke than par. He was a frequent contributor to *Golf Illustrated* of pre–World War II days and for a short time before its demise served as editor.

Courses by A.W. Tillinghast:

California: San Francisco GC (1915).
Florida: Atlantic Beach CC (1918, NLE); Davis Shores CC (1926, NLE).
Kansas: Indian Hills CC (1926).
Maryland: Baltimore CC (East Cse 1926).
Massachusetts: Berkshire Hills CC (1926).
Minnesota: Golden Valley GC (1924).
New Jersey: Alpine CC (1931); Baltusrol GC (Lower Cse 1922; Upper Cse 1922); Forest Hill Field C; Myosotis CC (NLE); Norwood CC (NLE);

Ridgewood CC (27 1929); Shackamaxon G&CC (1917); Somerset Hills CC (1917); Suburban GC (1922); Wilton Grove CC (1916).
New York: Bethpage State Park GC (Black Cse 1936; Blue Cse 1935; Red Cse 1935); Binghamton CC (1918); CC of Ithaca (NLE); Elmwood CC (1928); Fenway GC (1924); Fresh Meadow CC (NLE); Harmon CC (9 1918); Jackson Heights GC (9 Par 3 1925, NLE); North Hempstead GC (1916); North Shore CC; Old Oaks CC (routing); Oswego CC (9); Port Jervis CC (9 1922); Rainey Estate GC (3); Southward Ho! CC (1924); Sunningdale CC (1918); Winged Foot GC (East Cse 1923; West Cse 1923).
North Carolina: Myers Park CC (9 1921).
Ohio: Lakewood CC (1920).
Oklahoma: Oaks CC (1924); Tulsa CC (1920).
Pennsylvania: Cedarbrook CC (NLE); Irem Temple CC; New Castle CC (1923); Philadelphia Cricket C, Flourtown (1922); Shawnee CC (1908); Sunnehanna CC (1923); Wyoming Valley CC (1923).
Rhode Island: Beavertail CC (NLE); Clarke Estate GC (9 1928).
South Carolina: Rock Hill CC (9).
Tennessee: Johnson City CC; Kingsport CC.
Texas: Brackenridge Park GC (1915); Brook Hollow GC (1921); Cedar Crest GC (1919); Fort Sam Houston GC; Oak Hill CC [FKA Alamo CC] (1921).
Vermont: Marble Island G&YC (9).
Virginia: Belmont Park GC [FKA Hermitage CC] (1916).
Quebec: Anglo-American C; Elm Ridge CC (NLE).

Courses remodeled or expanded by A.W. Tillinghast:

Connecticut: Brooklawn CC (R. 1928); CC of Fairfield (R. 2 1925).
Illinois: Glen Oak CC (R. 1935); Westmoreland CC (R. 1925).
Massachusetts: Sankaty Head GC (R.).
Minnesota: Rochester G&CC (R.9 A.9 1925).
Missouri: Swope Park GC (R. 1934).
New Jersey: Essex County CC (East Cse, R.; West Cse, R.); Hollywood GC (R., NLE); Seaview GC (Bay Cse, R.); Spring Lake G&CC (R.); Suburban GC (R.); Upper Montclair CC (R., NLE).
New York: Bethpage State Park GC (Green Cse, R. 1935); Bluff Point CC

(R. 1916); Bonnie Briar CC (R.); Elmira CC (A.9 1922); Hempstead G&CC (R. 1924); Island Hills CC (R. 1927); Knollwood CC (R.); Meadow Brook C (R., NLE); Metropolis CC (R.); Mount Kisco CC (R. 1920); Quaker Ridge CC (R.9 A.9 1926); Rockaway Hunting C (R. A.7 1933); Rockwood Hall CC (R. A.5 1929); Sands Point CC (R.9 A.9); Scarsdale GC (R. A.6 1929); Sleepy Hollow GC (R. A.5 1933); St. Albans CC (R.); Sunningdale CC (R.); Wolferts Roost CC (R.); Wykagyl CC (R. 1931).
Ohio: Inverness C (R. 1930).
Pennsylvania: Aronimink GC (R., NLE); Bedford Springs CC (R.); Conyngham Valley CC (R.); Fox Hill CC (R.); Galen Hall GC (R. 1917); Nemacolin CC (R.); Old York Road CC (R., NLE); Wanango CC (R.); Williamsport CC (R.).
Rhode Island: Newport CC (R.9 A.9).
Texas: Corsicana CC (R. 1921); San Antonio CC (R.).
Virginia: Roanoke CC (R.).
Wisconsin: Blackhawk CC (R. 1937).
Ontario: Scarboro G&CC (R. 1926).

Bancroft Timmons, 1982 COURTESY BANCROFT TIMMONS

WALLACE BANCROFT TIMMONS (1915–1983)

BORN: Maryland.
DIED: Birmingham, Alabama, at age 68.

Bancroft Timmons gained his first golf course experience as a boy when he maintained the Ocean City (Maryland) Golf Club after school and on weekends for $15 a week. A fine athlete, Timmons pursued a baseball career and played several seasons in a semipro league around the Eastern Shore. In the late 1930s Timmons joined the Automobile Association of America, working as office manager in Virginia and later West Virginia. When he was transferred to the Alabama Motorists Association in Birmingham in 1948, Timmons was surprised by the lack of courses in the area. He helped organize Green Valley Country Club and laid out its original nine. Timmons practiced golf design as a hobby in the Birmingham area for over thirty years, often donating his services and, on at least one occasion, parcels of land. Timmons never professed to be a course architect, preferring to call his role that of "golf promoter."

Courses by Bancroft Timmons:

Alabama: Buxahatchee CC; Cahawba Falls CC (9); Chace Lake CC (1966); Green Valley CC (9 1960); Pine Crest CC (9); Shades Valley CC; Terry Walker G&CC (1961).

HOWARD C. TOOMEY
(–1933)

An engineer specializing in railroad construction, Howard Toomey formed the partnership of Toomey and Flynn with William S. Flynn shortly after World War I and was responsible for much of the firm's construction.

Courses by Howard Toomey (All with William S. Flynn):

Florida: Boca Raton Hotel & C (1928; North Cse 1928, NLE); Cleveland Heights G&CC (1925); Indian Creek CC (1930); Normandy Shores GC (1916).
Illinois: Mill Road Farm GC (1924, NLE).
New Jersey: Seaview GC (Pines Cse, 9 1931); Springdale CC (1928); Woodcrest CC.
New York: Shinnecock Hills GC (1931).
Ohio: [The] Country Club, Cleveland (1931).
Pennsylvania: Green Valley CC (1924); Huntingdon Valley CC (1927); Lehigh CC (1926); Philadelphia CC (1927); Philmont CC (North Cse 1924); Rolling Green CC (1926).
Virginia: CC of Virginia (James River Cse 1928).

Courses remodeled or expanded by Howard Toomey (All with William S. Flynn):

Massachusetts: [The] Country Club (A.3rd 9 1927).
Pennsylvania: Merion GC (East Cse, R. 1925).

Walter Travis, 1916
COLLECTION RON WHITTEN

WALTER JAMES TRAVIS
(1862–1927)

BORN: Maldon, Australia.
DIED: Denver, Colorado, at age 65.

Educated at public schools and at Trinity College in Australia, Walter Travis emigrated to the United States at age twenty-three. Although he did not take up golf until he was thirty-five, he was soon the winner of the U.S. Amateur (1900, 1901 and 1903) and the British Amateur (1904) and was runner-up in the 1902 U.S. Open. In addition, he was founder and editor of *American Golfer* magazine and author of *The Art of Putting* and *Practical Golf.* He was known in golf circles as the "Grand Old Man."

Travis, unlike his contemporary C. B. Macdonald, often criticized British golf and in turn was not often treated kindly by the British press. He was originally appointed to Macdonald's select committee for The National Golf Links but was later dropped from it.

Walter Travis created many distinguished courses in the Eastern United States after learning the design trade as a consultant to John Duncan Dunn. He was particularly fond of the state of Vermont and was buried at Manchester near Ekwanok, one of his favorites.

Courses by Walter J. Travis:

Connecticut: Round Hill C (1922).
Georgia: Jekyll Island GC (Oceanside Course 1926, 9, NLE); Sea Island GC (Plantation Nine 1927).
Michigan: Lochmoor C (1919).
New Jersey: Canoe Brook CC (South Cse 1917); North Jersey CC (1915); White Beeches G&CC.
New York: Cherry Valley GC (1907); CC of Troy; Garden City CC (1916); Old Country Club (NLE); Onondaga G&CC; Orchard Park CC (1928); Stafford CC (1928); Westchester CC (South Cse 1922; West Cse 1922); Yahnundasis GC.

Ohio: Youngstown CC.
Pennsylvania: CC of Scranton (9 1927).
South Carolina: Camden CC [FKA Kirkwood Hotel GC] (1923).
Vermont: Ekwanok CC, with John Duncan Dunn; Equinox G Links (1925).
Washington, D.C.: West Potomac Park GC (9 1920), with Dr. Walter S. Harban.
Ontario: Cherry Hill GC (1917); Lookout Point G&CC; Welland CC.

Courses remodeled or expanded by Walter J. Travis:

Connecticut: CC of New Canaan (R.9).
Kentucky: Louisville CC (R.9 A.9).
Maine: Cape Arundel GC (R.9 A.9 1922), with John Duncan Dunn.
Maryland: Columbia CC (R.).
Massachusetts: Essex CC (R.), with John Duncan Dunn.
New Jersey: Hollywood GC (R. 1915).
New York: Garden City GC (R. 1926); Grover Cleveland Muni (R. 1926); Oak Ridge GC (R. 1925, NLE).

Kevin Tucker, 1991
COURTESY KEVIN TUCKER

THOMAS KEVIN TUCKER
(1950–)

BORN: Mt. Vernon, Indiana.

Kevin Tucker graduated from Mississippi State University at Starkville in 1973 with a Bachelor's degree in landscape architecture. He worked for two landscape architects in Florida before forming Kevin Tucker & Associates in 1975. While primarily practicing landscape architecture, Tucker did handle the designs of several courses in the southeastern United States.

Courses by Kevin Tucker:

Kentucky: Hartland GC (1989).
Mississippi: Castlewoods CC (9); Timbervale GC.
Tennessee: Cotton Run GC; Dorchester GC, with *Bob Greenwood*; Long Hollow GC (1983); Sycamore Valley GC (9).

Courses remodeled or expanded by Kevin Tucker:

Georgia: Bowden GC (R.).
Illinois: Metropolis GC (A.9).
Mississippi: Copiah-Lincoln Junior College GC (R.9 A.9); Tupelo CC (R.).
Tennessee: Chickasaw CC (R.); Cookeville CC (A.10); Houston Levee CC (A.3rd 9); Lakewood CC (A.12).

William H. Tucker, 1927 COLLECTION RON WHITTEN

WILLIAM HENRY TUCKER (1871–1954)

BORN: Redhill, Surrey, England.
DIED: Albuquerque, New Mexico, at age 83.

William H. Tucker learned the art of sod rolling from his father, an employee of the Wimbledon Commons. He served as professional at two English clubs as a teenager and then worked on course-construction crews for Tom Dunn and Young Willie Dunn in England, France and Switzerland.

In 1895 Tucker emigrated to the United States, joining his brother Samuel, who was professional at St. Andrews Golf Club in New York. They formed the equipment firm of Tucker Brothers, and their handmade Defiance-brand clubs were sold for years. When St. Andrews moved to a new site, Tucker was hired to club member Harry Tallmadge for the design and construction of a new course and to serve as greenkeeper. After the opening of the course, Tucker remained as its greenkeeper and soon rearranged some holes and built several new ones.

Tucker laid out several other courses in the New York area while at St. Andrews and later at Ardsley Country Club. He also worked in the early 1900s as pro-greenkeeper at Chevy Chase Club near Washington, D.C., where he collaborated with Dr. Walter S. Harban, the wealthy and eccentric dentist to presidents who dabbled in course design and maintenance. In the 1920s Tucker and his son, William H. Tucker, Jr., established full-time golf architecture and course-construction firms with offices in New York, Los Angeles and Portland, Oregon. Among their assistants were Frank James and Gregor MacMillan.

After World War II, Tucker retired to Albuquerque, New Mexico, where he designed, built and maintained the University of New Mexico course. He once estimated that he had designed or remodeled over 120 courses in his career.

Tucker was also a nationally known turfgrass expert and in his New York days had been called upon to install and nurture the original turf at such sports facilities as Yankee Stadium and the West Side Tennis Club, better known as Forest Hills.

Courses by William H. Tucker:

Colorado: Green Gables CC (9 1928); Overland Park Muni (9).
Maryland: Argyle CC, with Dr. Walter S. Harban; Bannockburn G&CC (NLE), with Dr. Walter S. Harban.
Nebraska: CC of Lincoln (1923); Hillcrest CC (1925); Pioneer Park GC (1932).
New Jersey: Phelps Manor GC (1924); Preakness Hills CC (1927).
New Mexico: Portales CC (9); Riverside CC (1946), with William H. Tucker, Jr.; University of New Mexico GC (North Cse 1951, 9 NLE).
New York: Antlers CC (1928); Clearview GC (1925); Douglaston Park GC [FKA North Hills CC] (1926); Maidstone C (9 1896); St. Andrews GC (1898, with *Harry Tallmadge*; R. 1900).
Vermont: Woodstock CC (1906, NLE).
Washington: Jackson Park Muni; Linden G&CC (9); Olympia G&CC (9); Roche Harbor GC; Sands Point CC (1928).

Courses remodeled or expanded by William H. Tucker:

New York: Ardsley CC (A.9).
Pennsylvania: Bala GC (R.9).

WILLIAM HENRY TUCKER, JR. (1895–1962)

BORN: New York.
DIED: Los Angeles, California, at age 67.

William H. Tucker, Jr., was the son of pioneer golf course architect and builder William H. Tucker. He joined his father's business after service in World War I and, except for a stint in World War II, he worked most of his life on the design, construction and maintenance of courses for his father.

Tucker Jr. did not work under his own name until his father's death in 1954, although some of the courses that bore the name of his father were actually his own designs. He practiced on his own for slightly less than a decade, designing courses mainly in the Southwest from his base in Los Angeles.

Courses by William H. Tucker, Jr.:

Arizona: Glendale Muni (NLE).
California: Anderson Tucker Oaks GC (9 1964); Elkins Ranch GC (1962); Fletcher Hills CC (1960); Ontario National GC.
New Mexico: Riverside CC (1946), with William H. Tucker.

JAMES WALKER TUFTS (1835–1902)

BORN: Charlestown, Massachusetts.
DIED: Pinehurst, North Carolina, at age 67.

James Tufts, a cousin of Charles Tufts (who donated the land for the campus of Tufts University in Medford, Massachusetts), became an apprentice druggist at the age of 16. By age 21 the enterprising Tufts owned three stores and was on his way to becoming a tycoon in the soda fountain business. One of the first to foresee the coming popularity of soda fountains, Tufts installed them in his stores and developed and marketed extracts and dispensers. Using his own efficient method of silver plating, he also created a line of silver-plated accessories that sold nationwide. In 1891 Tufts consolidated his booming business with several others to become the American Soda Fountain Company.

But Tufts remained as head of his organization for only four years. Turning the operation over to his son, he moved south for his health, settling in central North Carolina. There he bought 5,000 acres of barren sandhills for $7,500. Many claimed this proved Tarheel woodsmen to be better businessmen than Yankee merchants, but Tufts was so enamored with the place that he dreamed of developing it into a resort. He hired eminent landscape architect Frederick Law Olmsted to lay out a formal village, built several hotels and negotiated for a railroad spur. The resort was named Pinehurst.

Pinehurst proved a popular winter retreat, and in 1898 Tufts and a friend, Dr. D. LeRoy Culver, laid out a primitive nine-hole course for guests. A year later they added nine more. It was the beginning of what would become the largest golf resort in the world.

In 1900 Tufts met a young Scottish professional golfer in Massachusetts and hired him to become winter pro at Pinehurst and to develop its courses. The young golfer, Donald J. Ross, began an association with Pinehurst in the winter of 1901 that would last the rest of his life. James W. Tufts died in 1902 while his proudest accomplishment, Pinehurst, was still evolving.

LEONARD TUFTS
(1870–1945)

BORN: Medford, Massachusetts.
DIED: Pinehurst, North Carolina, at age 75.

Leonard Tufts, who attended the Massachusetts Institute of Technology, worked for his father, James Walker Tufts, in the soda fountain business after leaving college. Though not yet 26 at the time of his father's retirement, Leonard was placed on the executive staff of the giant American Soda Fountain Company. But he was more interested in the new Pinehurst resort his father was building in North Carolina.

Tufts assisted his father and Dr. D. LeRoy Culver in building Pinehurst's first course in 1898. Although this was his only active golf course design experience, he was instrumental in the early 1900s in convincing Donald Ross to rebuild the course and eventually add several others to the resort. Tufts became nationally known for his cattle-breeding experiments, begun originally in an effort to supply fresh milk and butter to the Pinehurst guests.

Tufts resigned his control of Pinehurst in 1930 due to ill health, but he continued to reside there and assisted his eldest son, Richard, in running the resort. He died of pneumonia in 1945, leaving three sons and a daughter.

PETER VAIL TUFTS

BORN: Pinehurst, North Carolina.

Peter Tufts, son of Richard S. Tufts and Alice Vail Tufts and godson of Donald

Ross, worked his way up to the management of Pinehurst. Beginning as a manager of laundry and garage facilities, he worked on course-maintenance crews, served as club manager and was finally appointed golf operations manager at Pinehurst in the 1960s. When the resort was sold in 1971, he resigned his position and he and his father searched for a new location in which to carry on their family traditions. They established Seven Lakes Golf Club in nearby West End, North Carolina, a residential housing complex.

Peter Tufts designed and supervised construction of the Seven Lakes course, his first experience in golf architecture. When the course opened in 1976, he was quick to downplay any comparison with Donald Ross works. Nevertheless Tufts, who grew up playing Ross's courses in the company of the great designer, professed his admiration for Ross designs and announced his hope of someday reestablishing the Ross philosophy of course design.

In 1977 Tufts opened his course-design firm and soon landed a few promising contracts, including partial renovation of the famous Pinehurst No. 2. There he set about restoring some of the original Ross mounds, removing the Bermuda roughs and redefining the fairway contours. For a man who had hoped to someday practice the art as Donald Ross had it was the fulfillment of a dream.

RICHARD SISE TUFTS
(1896–1980)

BORN: Medford, Massachusetts.
DIED: Pinehurst, North Carolina, at age 84.

Richard Tufts, son of Leonard Tufts and Gertrude Sise Tufts, learned his golf at Pinehurst from Donald Ross. Starting at the age of 8, he ultimately became the most proficient golfer of the Tufts clan. Upon graduation from Harvard in 1917, he served with the U.S. Navy during World War I and then returned to Pinehurst to work with his father. He took over in 1930 after his father's retirement and continued as director of Pinehurst Inc. into the 1960s.

A lifelong friend of Donald Ross and devotee of his work, Tufts dabbled in course design after the great architect's death. He laid out a new Pinehurst No. 4 course in the early 1950s after the original No. 4 (a Ross design) had been abandoned during World War II as an austerity mea-

sure. He revised several holes of Pinehurst No. 2 for the 1962 U.S. Amateur, and he also assisted golf architect Ellis Maples with the routing of Pinehurst No. 5 in the 1960s.

Richard Tufts was involved in every facet of golf administration and was often consulted in setting up courses for championship play. At one time or another he served on every committee of the USGA and was its president in 1956–57. He was awarded the William Richardson Award in 1950 by the Golf Writers Association of America for outstanding contributions to the game and the Bob Jones Award in 1966 by the USGA for distinguished sportsmanship in golf. He also wrote many articles on golf, some pertaining to golf architecture, and was author of *The Principles Behind the Rules of Golf* (1960) and *The Scottish Invasion: A Brief Review of American Golf in Relation to Pinehurst* (1962).

In 1971 Tufts' two brothers, who owned a majority of the stock in Pinehurst Inc., voted to sell the grand old resort. Undaunted, Richard Tufts helped his son Peter start a new golf resort a short distance away. In the late 1970s he was pleased to see the Pinehurst management restore the courses, particularly the masterful No. 2.

Alfred H. Tull, 1965
COLLECTION RON WHITTEN

ALFRED H. TULL
(1897–1982), ASGCA

BORN: England.
DIED: Fort Myers, Florida, at age 85.

Alfred Tull moved with his family to Canada in 1907 and to the United States in 1914. He began his career with his brother William J. Tull in a construction firm that supervised the building of courses for golf architects Walter Travis, A. W. Tillinghast and Devereux Emmet. The Tulls also handled a couple of course designs on their own.

In 1924, however, Alfred Tull joined Emmet as a design associate and became a full partner in 1929 in the firm of Emmet, Emmet and Tull. Following Emmet's death in 1934. Tull entered private practice as a course architect.

Clients and others he worked with were struck by Tull's remarkable ability to lay out individual holes and establish a circuit by walking the land and staking the holes without resort to a topographical plan. Later he would place his circuit on a topo to convey his ideas to others.

Courses by Alfred H. Tull:

Arkansas: Rosswood CC (1961).
Connecticut: CC of Darien (1958); Fulton Estate GC (1933), with Devereux Emmet; Hob Nob Hill GC (1934, NLE), with Devereux Emmet; Keney Park GC (1927), ass't Devereux Emmet; Oak Hill G Cse (1967); Pilgrim's Harbor CC (9 1970); Pine Tree CC (9 1953); Rolling Hills CC (1965).
Delaware: Brandywine CC (1951); Du Pont CC (Du Pont Cse 1950; Nemours Cse 1938); Hercules CC (9 1937, A.9 1941, A.3rd 9 1966); Seaford G&CC (9 1941).
Maryland: Norbeck CC (1952); Woodmont CC (1951; A.9 1955).
Massachusetts: Cape Cod CC (9 1929, with Devereux Emmet; A.9 1954); Jug End Inn GC (9 1961); Ledgemont CC (1948).
New Jersey: Ashbrook GC (1951); Canoe Brook CC (North Cse 1949); Cooper River CC (1929, NLE), with Devereux Emmet; Greenacres CC (1932), with Devereux Emmet; Mendham G&TC (1967); Rockleigh GC (Rockleigh Cse 1958).
New York: Bethpage State Park GC (Yellow Cse 1958); Broadmoor CC (1929, NLE), with Devereux Emmet; Concord Hotel GC (Challenger Cse, 9 1951; International Cse 1951); Graham F. Vanderbilt Estate GC (4); Hampshire CC (1927), ass't Devereux Emmet; Harbor Hills CC (1955); Harrison Williams Private Cse (3 1932), with Devereux Emmet; Huntington Crescent CC (1931; West Cse 1931, NLE), with Devereux Emmet; Indian Hills GC (9 Par 3 1965); Lake Anne CC (9 1963); Mayflower GC (1930, NLE), with Devereux Emmet; Morningside Hotel GC (1961); Muttontown G&CC (1959); Nassau CC (1927), ass't Devereux Emmet; Nevele GC (1963); Pine Ridge CC (1954); Poxebogue GC (9 1962); Rockwood Hall CC (1929), with Devereux Emmet;

Schuyler Meadows C (1928), ass't Devereux Emmet; Seawane C (1927), ass't Devereux Emmet; South Shore GC (1927); Sunken Meadow Park GC (1968); Tennanah Lake House GC (1960); Vanderbilt Estate GC (9 1929, NLE), with Devereux Emmet; Vernon Hills CC (1928), ass't Devereux Emmet.
North Carolina: Hog Back Mountain C (9 1931, NLE), with Devereux Emmet; Old Fort CC (9).
Pennsylvania: Lawrence Park GC (1941); Radley Run CC (1964); Valley Forge V.A. Hospital GC (1943).
South Carolina: Georgetown CC (9 1956).
Virginia: Brook Manor CC (1955); Westwood CC (1953).
Newfoundland: Blomidon Club (1967).
Bahamas: Carnival's Crystal Palace GC [FKA Cable Beach Hotel & GC] (1928), ass't Devereux Emmet.
Bermuda: Southampton Princess GC (Par 3 1964).
Dominican Republic: Campo de G Bella Vista (1958).
Puerto Rico: Ponce GC (9 1953).
Virgin Islands: Estate Carlton GC (9 1960).

Courses remodeled or expanded by Alfred H. Tull:

Alabama: CC of Mobile (R. 1967).
Connecticut: CC of New Canaan (A.9 1947); Hunter Memorial GC (R. 1968); Silver Spring CC (R.); Silvermine CC (R.).
Delaware: Henry F. Du Pont Private Cse (R. 1929), with Devereux Emmet.
Maryland: Congressional CC (Blue Cse, R. 1951); Green Hill Y&CC (R. 1951).
Massachusetts: Belmont CC (R. 1969); Green Hill Muni (R. 1962).
New Jersey: Fairmont CC (R. 1968); Galloping Hills GC (R. 1953); Passaic County GC (A.9 1955); White Beeches G&CC (R. 1950).
New York: Apawamis C (R. 1962); Bonnie Briar CC (R. 1928), ass't Devereux Emmet; R. 1964); Elmwood CC (R. 1954); Fairview CC (R. 1964); Glen Head CC (R. 1968); Huntington CC (R. 1928), ass't Devereux Emmet; Maidstone C (R. 1965); Middle Bay CC (R. 1955); Old Country Club (R. 1928, NLE), ass't Devereux Emmet; Pelham CC (R. 1954); Red Hook GC (R. 1967); Rockland CC (R. 1965); Waccabuc CC (R. 1967); Westchester CC (West Cse, R. 1969); Wheatley

Hills CC (R. 1929), with Devereux Emmet; Willow Ridge CC (R. 1947).
Oklahoma: Walnut Hills CC (R. 1968).
Bermuda: St. George Hotel GC (R. 1928), ass't Devereux Emmet.
Puerto Rico: Berwind CC (A.9, NLE).

HERBERT JAMES TWEEDIE
(–1921)

BORN: Hoylake, Cheshire, England.
DIED: Chicago, Illinois.

H. J. Tweedie came to the United States with his brother L.P. in 1887. Both avid golfers from Royal Liverpool Club, they settled in Chicago and managed the A. G. Spalding & Bros. sporting goods store. The Tweedies became friends of C. B. Macdonald and were members of his original Chicago Golf Club. When Chicago Golf Club was moved to Wheaton, Illinois, Tweedie and others organized Belmont Golf Club at the old site and built a new course there. Over the next ten years Tweedie built a number of Chicago-area clubs. He also continued to manage the Spalding concern until his death, when his son Douglas assumed the position.

Courses by II. J. Tweedie:

Illinois: Belmont GC (9 1898); Bryn Mawr GC; Exmoor CC; Flossmoor CC [FKA Homewood CC] (1898); Glen View GC (1904); La Grange CC (9 1899, NLE); Midlothian CC (1898); Park Ridge CC (1906); Ridge CC (1902); Rockford CC (1899); Washington Park CC (NLE); Westward Ho CC (NLE).
Indiana: CC of Indianapolis (9 1900, NLE), with *Alvin Lockard.*
Wisconsin: Maple Bluff CC (1900, NLE).

Courses remodeled or expanded by H. J. Tweedie:

Illinois: Onwentsia C (A.9 1898), with James Foulis, Robert Foulis and H. J. Whigham.

KENNETH TYSON
(–1983)

DIED: Tacoma, Washington.

A golf professional and course superintendent in the Pacific Northwest for thirty-four years, Ken Tyson completed Lake Spanaway to the plans of A. Vernon

Macan after Macan's death, then owned and operated a succession of golf courses that he designed or remodeled himself.

Courses designed by Ken Tyson:

Washington: Gold Mountain GC (1976); Lake Spanaway GC (1967), with A. Vernon Macan; Madrona Links (9 1978).

Courses remodeled or expanded by Ken Tyson:

Washington: Elks Allenmore GC (R.); Everett Muni (R.).

LAWRENCE E. VAN ETTEN (1865–1951)

BORN: Kingston, New York.
DIED: New Rochelle, New York, at age 85.

Lawrence Van Etten attended Princeton University, where he received an engineering degree in 1886 and later a law degree as well. For most of his life he worked as a civil engineer, planning and developing residential subdivisions in metropolitan New York.

Van Etten was also a prominent player in the early days of American golf and won many local titles. His golfing abilities and engineering training provided excellent course-design background, and he planned many in the New York area. Though most were eventually abandoned, Wykagyl in New Rochelle, where Van Etten maintained a lifelong membership, has retained his design in modified form since its inception.

Courses by Lawrence Van Etten:

New Jersey: Deal GC (1898).
New Hampshire: Province Lake CC (9 1913).
New York: Knollwood CC (1898); Pelham Bay Park GC (Pelham Cse); Pelham CC (9 1908, NLE); Wykagyl CC (1905).

JOHN R. VAN KLEEK (–1957)

DIED: Tryon, North Carolina.

After graduating with a degree in landscape architecture from Cornell University, John Van Kleek formed a partnership with Wayne Stiles of Boston, Massachusetts, in 1924. Van Kleek managed the firm's St. Petersburg, Florida, office. The firm was one of the nation's busiest during the mid and late 1920s, but the failing real estate market in the South in 1929 forced Stiles and Van Kleek to dissolve their partnership. Stiles maintained his Boston practice. Van Kleek landed a job working for Robert Moses and the New York City Parks Department, remodeling the city's existing courses and adding several new ones. After World War II Van Kleek branched into South America, designing several courses in Colombia and Venezuela. He also began designing courses in the southeastern United States again.

Courses by John Van Kleek (All with Wayne Stiles unless otherwise indicated):

Alabama: Charles Boswell G Cse [FKA Highland Park GC].
Connecticut: Paul Block Private Cse (9, NLE).
Florida: Highland Park C (1925); Holly Hill G&CC (NLE); Kenilworth Lodge GC (NLE); Lake Jovita CC; Palmetto G&CC; Pasadena GC (1923), and Walter Hagen; Tarpon Springs CC (1927).
Georgia: Glen Arven CC (1929); Radium CC (1927).
Maine: Wawenock GC (9 1926).
Massachusetts: Berkshire Hunt & CC (1930); Cranwell School GC; D. W. Field Muni (1927); Marlborough CC (9); Memorial Muni (NLE); Newton Commonwealth GC; Pine Brook CC; Putterham Meadows Muni; Taconic GC (1927); Thorny Lea GC (1925); Unicorn CC; Weld GC.
Nebraska: Omaha CC.
New Hampshire: CC of New Hampshire [FKA Kearsarge Valley CC] (9 1930); Hooper GC (9 1926); Mojalaki CC [FKA Franklin CC] (9 1928).
New Jersey: Brigantine CC (1927); Wildwood G&CC (1924).
New Mexico: Albuquerque CC (1929 solo).
New York: Forest Park GC (1934 solo); IBM CC, Johnson City (Country Club Cse 1937 solo); Kissena GC (1934 solo); Pelham Bay Park GC (Split Rock Cse 1934 solo); Silver Lake GC (1929 solo); South Shore CC; Whiteface Inn & GC (1935 solo).
North Carolina: Hamilton Lakes CC; Lake Lure Muni (9 1935 solo).
Colombia: CC of Bogotá (East Cse 1950 solo; West Cse 1947 solo).
Venezuela: Carabelleda G&YC (9 1949 solo).

Courses remodeled or expanded by John Van Kleek (All with Wayne Stiles unless otherwise indicated):

Maine: Augusta CC (A.9 1926); Brunswick GC (R.9 1925).
Massachusetts: Franklin CC (R.); Monoosnock CC (R.9); Oak Hill CC (A.9); Wellesley CC (R.9); Presidents CC [FKA Wollaston CC] (R.).
New Hampshire: Crawford Notch CC (R., NLE); Mountain View House GC (R.); Nashua CC (A.9 1925).
New York: Dyker Beach GC (R. 1935 solo); La Tourette Muni (R.9 A.9 1935 solo); Pelham Bay Park GC (Pelham Cse, R. 1934 solo).
Vermont: Rutland CC (R.9 A.9 1928); Woodstock CC (R.9 A.9 1924).

Harry Vardon, circa 1902 COURTESY GOLF WORLD

HARRY VARDON (1870–1937)

BORN: Grouville, Isle of Jersey.
DIED: London, England, at age 67.

Harry Vardon was one of Britain's "Great Triumvirate" of professional golfers. He won a record six British Opens and one U.S. Open. Despite demand for his services as a course architect, his planning was limited by chronic poor health.

Courses by Harry Vardon:

England: Brocton Hall GC (1923); Copt Heath GC (9 1910); Hanbury Manor GC (9 1908); Hendon GC; Letchworth GC (1905); Little Aston GC (1908); Mendip GC (9 1908); Moore Place GC (1909); Saffron Walden GC (1919); Sandy Lodge GC (1910), with H. S. Colt; Tadmarton Heath GC (9 1922);

Woodhall Spa GC (1905); Worthing GC (Lower Cse 1905; Upper Cse, 9 1905).

France: Montreux GC (9).
Scotland: Kingussie GC.
Wales: Aberystwyth GC (1911); Knighton GC (1908); Llandrindod Wells GC (1905).

Courses remodeled or expanded by Harry Vardon:

England: City of Newcastle GC (R.); Ganton GC (R. 1899); Hendon GC (R., NLE); Royal Cinque Ports GC (R.); South Herts GC (R.); West Herts GC (R. 1910).
Ireland: Bundoran GC (R.); Rosapenna GC (R. 1906), with James Braid.
Northern Ireland: Royal County Down GC (R. 1908; R. 1919).

TOM VARDON
(1874–1938)

BORN: Grouville, Isle of Jersey.
DIED: Minneapolis, Minnesota, at age 64.

Tom Vardon, younger brother of the legendary Harry Vardon, decided at an early age to become a golf professional. After landing an assistant's job in England, he found one for Harry.

They both played competitively, but Tom never had much success. After the turn of the century, he sailed for America, where he landed the head professional position at Onwentsia Club near Chicago. In 1914 he moved to a similar position at White Bear Yacht Club near Minneapolis, where he remained the rest of his life. While in Minnesota, Vardon designed some fine courses throughout that and surrounding states.

Courses by Tom Vardon:

North Dakota: Minot CC (1929).
Wisconsin: Spooner Lake GC (9 1930).

LORRIE A. VIOLA
(1961–)

As a high school student in Troy, Ohio, Lorrie Viola so excelled in gymnastics, swimming and diving that she was chosen her school's athlete of the year. After spending a year on Mexico's Yucatán peninsula studying architecture, Viola en-

Lorrie Viola, 1990
COURTESY LORRIE VIOLA

rolled at Michigan State University, interned in the office of golf architect Bill Newcomb and graduated in 1983 with a Bachelor's degree in landscape architecture. She then landed a job in Jack Nicklaus's Florida design office and worked as a design associate under the direction of Bob Cupp, Tom Pearson, Scott Miller and Gene Bates. In 1985, Viola was hired by the newly formed firm of George and Jim Fazio, and in 1986 she joined the design team of Gary Player and Karl Litten. When that firm disbanded, Viola remained in Litten's employ as his principal design associate, handling all aspects of course architecture from planning and drafting to field supervision.

In 1991 Lorrie Viola fulfilled her longtime dream and established her own golf architecture firm, based in southern Florida.

Courses by Lorrie Viola:

California: Pacific GC (27 1988), ass't Gary Player and Karl Litten.
Florida: Alaqua CC (1989), ass't Karl Litten and Gary Player; Hawk's Nest GC (1986), ass't Jim Fazio; Landings GC (Precision 1990); Pine Ridge GC (1990), ass't Karl Litten; Polo Trace CC (1990), ass't Karl Litten; St. Lucie West CC (1987), ass't Jim Fazio; Westchester G&CC (Regulation Cse 1988; Par 3 Cse 1988), ass't Karl Litten; Wycliffe G&CC (1989), ass't Karl Litten and Bruce Devlin.
Maine: Woodlands CC (1989), ass't George and Jim Fazio.
Missouri: Whitmoor CC (West Cse 1990), ass't Karl Litten.
Cayman Islands: Britannia GC (Precision 1985), ass't Jack Nicklaus.
England: Leek Wooten GC (1992), ass't Karl Litten.
United Arab Emirates: Dubai Creek GC (1992), ass't Karl Litten.

GEORGE VON ELM
(1901–1961)

BORN: Salt Lake City, Utah.
DIED: Pocatello, Idaho, at age 60.

George Von Elm was well known as an amateur golfer between the First and Second World wars and had an impressive record in both the British and U.S. opens. After his retirement from active competition, Von Elm designed several courses in the Western United States.

Courses by George Von Elm:

California: Shadow Mountain GC (1960).
Idaho: Blackfoot Muni (9 1957).

Courses remodeled or expanded by George Von Elm:

California: Hacienda CC (R. 1959).
Idaho: Sun Valley GC (R.9 A.9 1962).

Robert von Hagge, 1991 COURTESY ROBERT VON HAGGE

ROBERT VON HAGGE, NÉ ROBERT BERNHARDT HAGGE
(1930–), FAGCA

BORN: Texas.

Robert von Hagge, the adopted son of Indiana superintendent Bernhardt F. "Ben" Hagge, literally grew up on a golf course. Ben Hagge had constructed courses in the 1920s for such architects as William Diddel, Donald Ross and George O'Neil and also tried a few designs himself.

After two years at Annapolis, young Bob Hagge transferred to Purdue University, where he graduated with a degree in agricultural engineering in 1951. He then spent a few years on the PGA Tour, worked as a club professional in the Catskill Mountains of New York and tried his hand at acting in Hollywood. During that time he was involved in successive (unsuccessful) marriages to golfing sisters Alice and Marlene Bauer. In 1957 he joined the golf architectural firm of Dick Wilson Inc. in Florida. Training under

Wilson, he quickly proved adept at course design and building.

Hagge established his own practice in Delray Beach, Florida, in 1963, and soon gained a reputation as an elaborate showman. He changed his surname to von Hagge and toured golf course sites in a gold lamé cape. Some of his early works, particularly El Conquistador in Puerto Rico, were equally spectacular and attracted widespread attention.

In the mid-1960s von Hagge was hired to redesign The Lakes GC in Australia at the recommendation of professional golfer Bruce Devlin. Von Hagge and Devlin became friends and colleagues, forming a course-design partnership in Australia in 1968. The following year, the firm of von Hagge and Devlin was established in the United States. They practiced together for nearly twenty years, based first in Florida and later in Texas.

In June of 1987 Devlin left the partnership to prepare for a bid on the Senior PGA Tour. Von Hagge then formed von Hagge Design Associates. The new design group included young architects Rick Baril, Alan Lenz, Kelly Moran and Mike Smelek. Under von Hagge's personal guidance, the round table of architects provided design input on each of the firm's projects, although von Hagge remained the architect of record.

Courses by Robert von Hagge (All with Bruce Devlin unless otherwise indicated):

Alabama: Lakeview GC (1988 *solo*).

Arizona: Moon Valley CC (1958), ass't Dick Wilson.

California: Blackhawk CC (Lakeside Cse 1981); La Costa CC (Green Cse, 9 1964; Orange Cse, 9 1964), ass't Dick Wilson and Joe Lee; Tierra del Sol GC (1978).

Colorado: Eagle Vail CC (1975).

Delaware: Wilmington CC (North Cse 1962), ass't Dick Wilson.

Florida: Admirals Cove GC (East Cse 1987 *solo*; West Cse 1988 *solo*); Bay Hill C (1961), ass't Dick Wilson and Joe Lee; Bay Point Y&CC (Lagoon Legend Cse 1986); Bayshore Muni (1969); Boca Del Mar G&CC (1972); Boca Lago G&CC (East Cse 1975; West Cse 1975); Boca Rio GC (1967 *solo*); Boca West CC (Cse No. 3 1974); Boynton Beach Muni (27 1984); Briar Bay GC (9 Precision 1975); Cape Coral CC (1962), ass't Dick Wilson; Carolina CC [FKA Holiday Springs CC] (1975); C at Emerald Hills (1969); Colony West GC (Cse No. 1 1970; Cse No. 2 [Precision] 1974); Cypress Creek CC (1964 *solo*); Cypress Lake CC (1960), ass't Dick Wilson; Doral CC (Blue Cse 1962, ass't Dick Wilson; Gold Cse 1969; Green Cse [9 Par 3] 1967 *solo*; Red Cse 1962, ass't Dick Wilson; White Cse 1967); Doral Park CC (Silver Cse 1984); East Lake Woodlands G&CC (North Cse 1979); Eastwood Muni (1978); [The] Fountains G&RC (North Cse 1970; South Cse 1972; West Cse 1981); Golden Gate CC (1965), ass't Dick Wilson; Hillcrest G&CC (1966 *solo*); Hole-in-the-Wall GC (1958), ass't Dick Wilson; Hunters Run GC (East Cse 1979; North Cse 1979; South Cse 1979); Indian Spring CC (East Cse 1975; West Cse 1980); Key Biscayne GC (1972); Marco Shores CC (1974); Oak Tree CC (1961), ass't Dick Wilson; Ocean Reef C (Harbor Cse 1976); Palm-Aire CC (Palms Cse 1969; Sabals Cse [Precision] 1969); Palm-Aire West CC (Champions Cse 1961), ass't Dick Wilson; Palmetto GC (1960), ass't Dick Wilson; Pine Tree CC (1962), ass't Dick Wilson and Joe Lee; Poinciana G&RC (1973); Pompano Beach CC (Pines Cse 1967 *solo*); Royal Oak G&CC (1964), ass't Dick Wilson; Sherbrooke G&CC (1979); Tequesta CC (1958), ass't Dick Wilson; TPC at Prestancia (Club Cse [FKA CC of Sarasota] 1976); Winter Springs GC [FKA Big Cypress GC] (1973); Woodlands CC (East Cse 1969; West Cse 1969); Woodmont CC (Cypress Cse 1976; Pines Cse 1976).

Georgia: Callaway Gardens GC (Mountainview Cse 1963), ass't Dick Wilson; Jekyll Island GC (Oleander Cse 1961), ass't Dick Wilson and Joe Lee.

Idaho: Quail Hollow GC [FKA Shamanah GC] (1983).

Illinois: Cog Hill GC (Cses No. 3 and 4 1964), ass't Dick Wilson and Joe Lee.

Indiana: Carolina Trace GC (9 1969 *solo*, NLE).

Kentucky: Boone Aire GC (1968).

Massachusetts: [The] Ridge C (1990 *solo*).

Mississippi: CC of Jackson (27 1963), ass't Dick Wilson.

Missouri: Hidden Lake GC (9 1969 *solo*); [The] Oaks GC (1980).

New Jersey: Crystal Springs G&CC (1991 *solo*).

New Mexico: Tanoan GC (27 1978).

New York: Garrison GC (1963), ass't Dick Wilson.

North Carolina: Brandywine Bay GC (1983).

Ohio: Coldstream CC (1960), ass't Dick Wilson and Joe Lee; Quail Hollow Inn & CC (1975).

Oklahoma: Shawnee G&CC (9 1982).

Pennsylvania: Laurel Valley CC (1960), ass't Dick Wilson.

Tennessee: Nashville G&AC [FKA Crockett Springs National G&CC] (1972).

Texas: Chase Oaks GC (Blackjack Cse 1986; Sawtooth Cse, 9 1986); [The] Cliffs GC (1988); C at Falcon Point (1985); C at Sonterra (North Cse 1985); Crown Colony CC (1979); Gleneagles CC (King's Cse 1985; Queen's Cse 1985); Hollytree CC (1982); Northgate CC (1985); Northshore CC (1985); Raveneaux CC (1980); TPC at The Woodlands [FKA Woodlands Inn & CC (East Cse)] (1982); Vista Hills CC (1975); Walden on Lake Conroe CC (1976); Walden on Lake Houston GC (1985); Wedgewood GC (routing 1983); Willow Creek GC (1982).

West Virginia: Fincastle CC (1963), ass't Dick Wilson.

Wisconsin: Brookfield Hills GC (Precision 1971).

Australia: Campbelltown GC (1976); [The] Lakes GC (1970); Magnolia Hills CC (1975); Ocean Shores GC.

Bahamas: Cape Eleuthera GC (1971, NLE); Lucayan GC (1964), ass't Dick Wilson; Lyford Cay C (1960), ass't Dick Wilson; Paradise Island CC (1962), ass't Dick Wilson.

Cuba: Villa Real CC (1957, NLE), ass't Dick Wilson.

France: Golf d'Abbesse (1992 *solo*); Golf de Courson Monteloup (North Cse 1991 *solo*; South Cse 1991 *solo*); Golf de Seignosse (1990 *solo*); Golf International Les Bordes (1987); Le Golf National (1990), with *Hubert Chesneau* and *Pierre Thevenin*; Le Kempferhof GC (27 1992 *solo*); Royal Mougins GC (1992 *solo*).

Japan: Daisifu Central CC (1971); Horai CC (1990 *solo*); Katsuragaoka CC (1992 *solo*); Kawaguchi-ko GC (1979); Maoi Resort GC (1992 *solo*); Nishinashuno CC (1992 *solo*).

Mexico: Isla Navidad GC (27 1992 *solo*); Las Misiones CC (1991 *solo*).

Puerto Rico: El Conquistador Hotel & C (1967 *solo*, NLE).

Spain: Emporda GC (1992 *solo*).
Tahiti: Travelodge GC (9 1972).

Courses remodeled or expanded by Robert von Hagge (All with Bruce Devlin unless otherwise indicated):

Arizona: Tucson National GC (R. A.3rd 9 1979).

California: Bel-Air CC (R. 1961), ass't Dick Wilson.

Florida: Boca Rio GC (R. 1992 *solo*); Doral CC (Blue Cse, R. 1971; Gold Cse, R. 1982; Red Cse, R. 1985); Ocean Reef C (Dolphin Cse, R. 1969); Pompano Beach CC (Palms Cse, R. 1967 *solo*).

Georgia: Sea Island GC (A.3rd 9 1959), ass't Dick Wilson.

Michigan: Pine Lake CC (R.9 *solo*).

Ohio: Camargo C (R. 1963 *solo*); Columbus CC (R. 1961), ass't Dick Wilson; Scioto CC (R. 1961), ass't Dick Wilson and Joe Lee.

Oklahoma: Quail Creek CC (R. 1986 *solo*).

Pennsylvania: Aronimink GC (R. 1961), ass't Dick Wilson; Penn Hills C (R.9 A.9 1960), ass't Dick Wilson.

Texas: Ranchland Hills GC (R. 1983); Rayburn G&CC (A.3rd 9 1984); [The] Woodlands Inn & CC (North Cse, A.9 1983; West Cse, A.9 1983).

BRENT H. WADSWORTH

A graduate landscape architect, Brent Wadsworth joined golf architect Edward Lawrence Packard in a golf and landscape architect partnership in 1954. Packard and Wadsworth was dissolved in 1957 when Wadsworth left to form his own firm specializing in golf course construction. He occasionally participated in course designs after that, including laying out Fox Bend GC, Oswego, Illinois, a daily-fee course near his corporate headquarters that was built to showcase the company's talents.

By the 1990s the Wadsworth company was the nation's largest and most respected golf contracting firm. In 1990 Wadsworth was inducted into the Illinois Golf Hall of Fame.

Courses by Brent Wadsworth (All with Edward Lawrence Packard unless otherwise indicated):

Illinois: Belk Park GC (9 1957); Coal Creek CC (9 1958); Fox Bend CC

(1970 *solo*); Granite City GC (9 1958); Vermillion Hills CC (9 1959); Westlake CC (9 1958).

Michigan: Spring Meadows CC (1965).

Missouri: Whiteman AFB GC (9 1956).

New York: Wayne CC (9 1957).

Ohio: Silver Lake CC (1959).

Wisconsin: Skyline GC (9 1956).

Courses remodeled or expanded by Brent Wadsworth (All with Edward Lawrence Packard unless otherwise indicated):

Illinois: Calumet CC (R.12 1957); Danville CC (A.9 1958); Greenville CC (R. 1958); Sunset Hills CC (A.9 1957).

Indiana: Gary CC (R. 1958).

Iowa: Fort Dodge CC (R.9 1958).

Minnesota: Westfield CC (R. 1960).

Missouri: Cape Girardeau CC (R.2 A.2 1957).

Ohio: Twin Base GC, Wright-Patterson AFB (R. 1958).

Wisconsin: Watertown CC (A.9 1961).

C. D. Wagstaff, 1948 COLLECTION RON WHITTEN

CHARLES DUDLEY WAGSTAFF
(1894–1977)

BORN: Tipton, Indiana.

DIED: Boca Raton, Florida, at age 82.

C. D. Wagstaff attended the University of Illinois, where he was captain of the varsity gymnastics team, and graduated in 1918 with a B.S. degree in landscape architecture.

After serving in the U.S. Navy for two years, the diminutive Wagstaff (5′ 3″, 110 pounds) moved to Glenview, Illinois, where he formed a landscape and golf course architecture business in 1923. Over the next forty-six years he worked on many prominent landscaping projects, including the Chicago World's Fair of 1933, the Great Lakes Exposition in Cleveland in 1936 and the La Gorce Island housing project in Florida.

But Wagstaff devoted much of his attention to golf course design and construction, creating such well-known Illinois layouts as Tam O'Shanter, Kildeer [which later became Twin Orchards Country Club] and, after World War II, 36 holes for the University of Illinois. In his later years Wagstaff was assisted by Donald R. Anderson and by his son Charles Jr. C. D. Wagstaff disbanded his firm in 1969 and retired to Florida, where he died in 1977.

Courses by C. D. Wagstaff:

Illinois: Bonnie Dundee GC; Brookridge CC; Brookwood CC; Ellsbert Farm GC (3 1964); Grigsby CC; Indian Boundary CC; Mauh-Na-Tee-See CC; Naval Training Center GC, Great Lakes (9); Olympic G&CC (1927); Park Hills GC (East Cse 1953; West Cse 1964); Park Lake GC; Sandy Hollow Muni; Tam O'Shanter CC (1925, NLE); Twin Orchards CC [FKA Kildeer CC] (Red Cse 1928; White Cse 1928); Twin Ponds GC (9 Par 3 1964); University of Illinois GC (Blue Cse 1964; Orange Cse 1950); Wheeling GC; Winnetka Park GC.

Iowa: Emeis Park GC (1961); Sheaffer Memorial GC (1962); Starhaven GC (3 1969).

Michigan: Leland CC (1965); Sugarloaf Mountain GC (1966).

Missouri: Greenbriar Hills CC (9 1937, A.9 1958).

North Carolina: Sippihaw CC (9 1961).

Courses remodeled or expanded by C. D. Wagstaff:

Illinois: Barrington Hills CC (R.); Hickory Hills CC (A.9 Precision 1963); Mission Hills CC (A. Par 3, NLE); Rockford CC (R.); Silver Ridge GC (R. 1949); Sunset Ridge CC (R.); Winnetka Park GC (A.18 Par 3 1961).

ROBERT C. WALKER
(1948–), ASGCA

BORN: Sherman, Texas.

Robert Walker received a B.S. degree in engineering and architecture from East Texas State University in 1971 and later undertook postgraduate studies in soil science and parks and recreation at Texas A&M University. He was employed in 1972 with the Club Corporation of America, where he worked with golf architects Ralph Plummer and Joe Finger. In 1974 he joined the firm of Edwin B. Seay Inc., which soon associated with Arnold Palmer. In 1979 the Palmer Course Design Company was formed, with Seay and Walker serving as its principal designers. In 1986 Walker left Palmer Course Design and formed his own architectural firm, based in Florida.

Courses by Bob Walker (All as assistant to Arnold Palmer and Ed Seay unless otherwise indicated):

Arizona: Arrowhead CC (1987).
California: Aviara CC (1991); Ironwood CC (Short Cse [9 Par 3] 1975).
Colorado: Lone Tree GC (1986).
Florida: Adios GC (1985); Grenelefe G&RC (East Cse 1977), ass't Ed Seay; Julington Creek GC (1989 *solo*); Marsh Landing CC (1986); Matanzas Woods GC (1986); Orange Park CC (routing 1987 *solo*); PGA National (The General Cse 1985); Pine Lakes GC (1980); [The] Plantation at Ponte Vedra (1987); Saddlebrook G&TC (Palmer Cse 1986); Sawgrass GC (1974, ass't Ed Seay; A.3rd 9 1985); Spessard Holland GC (Precision 1977); St. Johns County G Cse (1989 *solo*); Suntree CC (Challenge Cse 1987).
Georgia: [The] Landings at Skidaway Island (Marshwood Cse 1979).
Maryland: Prince Georges G&CC (1981).
Michigan: Shanty Creek GC (The Legend Cse 1985).
North Carolina: River Run G&CC (1991), with *Ray Floyd*.
Texas: Barton Creek C (Lakeside Cse) [FKA Hidden Hills GC] (1986); GC at Fossil Creek GC (1987).

Bob Walker, 1990
COURTESY ASGCA

Utah: Jeremy Ranch GC (1981).
British Columbia: Whistler Village GC (1980).
China: Chung-Shan GC (1985).
Japan: Aso GC (1987); Furano Kogen GC (1976); Minakami Kogen GC (Lower Cse 1986; Upper Cse 1986); Niseko GC (1986); Niseko Kogen GC (1986); Tsugaru Kogen GC (1986).
Mexico: Nuevo Vallarta GC (27 1980).

Courses remodeled or expanded by Bob Walker (All as assistant to Arnold Palmer and Ed Seay unless otherwise indicated):

Alabama: Anniston CC (R. 1975), ass't Ed Seay.
Arizona: Scottsdale CC (R. 1986).
Florida: Hidden Hills CC (R. 1986); Jacksonville Beach GC (R. 1987 *solo*); Mill Cove GC (R. 1991 *solo*); Oak Bridge GC (R. 1982), ass't Ed Seay; San Jose CC (R. 1990 *solo*).

DAVID L. WALLACE

David Wallace's first golf design experience was his collaboration with Mark Mahannah on the addition of a second course at Sandpiper Resort in Florida, where he was employed as superintendent of grounds. In the 1970s, based in Tampa, Wallace created a score of courses along Florida's west coast.

Courses by David Wallace:

Florida: Burnt Store Village GC (1970); Club Med Sandpiper GC (Saints Cse 1963); Cove Cay G&TC (1972); Deltona G&CC (1964); Grenelefe G&RC (West Cse 1973); High Point CC (Par 3 1972); Lake Region Y&CC (1964); Lely Community GC; Lely G&CC (1975); Lucerne GC (Par 3 1967); Marco Island CC (1966); Mission Valley G&CC (1969); Port Charlotte CC (9 1962); Royal Poinciana GC (Cypress Cse 1970; Pines Cse 1969); Southridge GC (1968); Spring Hill G&CC (1969); Willow Brook GC (1968).

Courses remodeled or expanded by David Wallace:

Florida: Gasparilla Inn & CC (R.); Riviera CC (A.9 1968); Rocky Point GC (A.9).

Laurie Waters, 1958
COLLECTION RON WHITTEN

LAWRENCE BUDDO WATERS (1875–1960)

BORN: St. Andrews, Scotland.
DIED: Salisbury, Rhodesia, at age 85.

A native of St. Andrews, Laurie Waters apprenticed under Old Tom Morris. In 1896 he emigrated to South Africa in search of a better climate for his health. Waters served as club professional at several South African clubs, most notably Royal Salisbury, where he worked for seventeen years before retiring in 1939. Waters won the first South African Open in 1903 as well as three others, introduced grass greens to the country, laid out several courses and became known as the "Father of South African Golf."

Courses by Laurie Waters:

South Africa: Durban CC (1920), with *George Waterman*; Royal Johannesburg GC (West Cse 1920).
Zimbabwe: Royal Salisbury GC (1922); Ruma CC (1948), with *George Waterman*.

HOWARD WATSON (1907–1992), ASGCA, PRESIDENT 1958

BORN: Dresden, Ontario, Canada.
DIED: LaChute, Quebec, Canada, at age 85.

Howard Watson attended the University of Toronto, majoring in bacteriology at the School of Agriculture in Guelph. He met golf architect Stanley Thompson through classmate Edwin I. Wood, who later became a prominent Canadian landscape architect. Thompson started Watson and another classmate, C. E. "Robbie" Robinson, on their respective careers on the same day in June 1929 at Royal York

Golf Club, then under construction in Toronto. Both went on to become well-known designers. In 1930 Watson was sent to work with Robert Trent Jones in Rochester, New York, in the newly formed Thompson, Jones & Co. As the Depression progressed, he became involved in a variety of occupations in addition to his work at Thompson, Jones. He worked as greenkeeper at Port Arthur (Ontario) Golf Club, as a turf consultant in Toronto and as a diamond driller, mucker boss and blasting foreman at Noranda Mines in Quebec. During the war years he served overseas with the Royal Canadian Engineers.

Watson remodeled the Noranda Mines course and did his first solo design in Seaforth, Ontario, in the thirties. In 1945 Watson rejoined Stanley Thompson, remaining until 1949, when he established Canadian Golf Landscaping Ltd. in Quebec. He was joined in this business by his son John in 1969.

Courses by Howard Watson:

Florida: Pembroke Lakes G&CC (27 1974), with John Watson.
New York: O'Brien Estate GC (1962).
Vermont: A. D. Dana Estate GC (9 1966).
Manitoba: Pinawa GC (9 1964).
New Brunswick: Pokemouche GC (9 1974), with John Watson.
Ontario: Aguasabon GC (1955); Bay of Quinte GC (1964); Board of Trade CC (East Cse 1963; West Cse 1963); Brian Thicke Estate GC (1974); Cherry Downs GC (27 1962); Chrysler Memorial Park GC (9 1958); Crang Estate GC (9 1953); Deep River GC (9 1952); Don Valley Muni (1956; R. A.9 1973, with John Watson); Downsview G&CC (27 1955); F. A. McConnel Private Cse (3 1954); Flemingdon Park GC (9 1959); Hylands GC (North Cse 1968; South Cse 1968); Kanata Lakes G&CC (9 1966); Manderly GC (1962); Mantiouwadge GC (1971); Pine Valley GC (1960, NLE); R. H. Storrer Estate GC (1966); Rideau View CC (1957); Ridgetown GC, with John Watson; Scarlett Woods GC (1972); Seaforth GC (9 1933); Spruce Needles GC (1959); Sumner Heights GC (9 1968); Tam O'Shanter Muni (1974), with John Watson; Woodbine Downs GC (1960).
Quebec: Asbestos G&CC (1966); Bonaventure GC (9 1973), with John Watson; Bonniebrook GC (1966); Car-

ling Lake GC (1961); Cedarbrook GC (1959); Champlain GC (1963); Chicoutimi GC (1955); C de G Berthier (1959); C de G Bromont (1963); C de G Cap Rouge (1959); C de G Chambly (1960); C de G Charny (R.9 A.9 1971), with John Watson; C de G Chicoutina (Cse No. 1; Cse No. 2); C de G de Joliette (1951); C de G du Bic (1962); C de G Granby-St. Paul (New Cse), with John Watson; C de G Lac Beauport (1961); C de G Laprairie (27 1964); C de G Les Dunes (Cse No. 2 1952); C de G Longchamps (1969), with John Watson; C de G St. Michel (St. Michel Cse 1960; Vaudrevil Cse 1960); C de G St. Patrick, with John Watson; C de G Valle du Parc (1972); C de G Vieilles Forges (1974), with John Watson; C d'Golf Triangle Dor (1968); Concordia GC (1962); Cowansville GC (1963); Dorval GC (1974); Douglas H. Keen Estate GC (9 1974); Grey Rocks GC; Harve des Isles GC (1966); Hillsdale G&CC (Dale Cse 1958; Hill Cse 1953); Hudson G & Curling C (1969); Ile Bourdon GC (1969); Lac Thomas GC (9 1962); Le Chantecler GC; Le Seigneurie de Vaudrevil GC (1969); Lennoxville GC (1964); Leonard Wheatley Private Cse (3 1962); Mont Adstock GC (9 1972), with John Watson; Mont St. Anne GC (Cse No. 1 1972; Cse No. 2, 9 1974), with John Watson; Mont Ste. Marie GC (9 1967); Mountain Ranches GC (1963); Nun's Island GC (1967); Pinegrove G&CC (27 1958); Royal Quebec CC (Quebec Cse, 9 1958); St. Georges GC (1959); St. Laurent GC (1971); St. Luc GC (1974); St. Marguerite GC (9

Howard Watson, 1956 COLLECTION RON WHITTEN

1954); Salzbourg GC (1954); Shawinigan G&CC (1962); Wentworth GC (1969).
Colombia: Club Campestre de Cucuta (1958); CC de Manizales (1953); CC El Rodeo (1953); CC Militar (1954).
Jamaica: Caymanas G&CC (1955).

Courses remodeled or expanded by Howard Watson:

Maine: Aroostook Valley GC (R.9 A.9 1958).
New York: Wheatley Hills CC (A.9 1962).
Ontario: Carleton Yacht & GC (R.1 1980); Forest Hills GC (R.27 1956); Idylwylde GC (R.9 A.9 1961); Mississauga G&CC (R.3 A.3rd 9 1973); North Bay G&CC (R.9 A.9 1963); Rosedale CC (R. 1951); Thornhill GC (R. 1954); Toronto GC (R.9 A.5 1962).
Quebec: Beaconsfield G&CC (R.6 1970); Candiac GC (R. 1974), with John Watson; C de G Alpin (R. 1942); C de G Baie Comeau (A.9 1973), with John Watson; C de G Chaudiere (R.5 1973), with John Watson; C de G Granby-St. Paul (Old Cse, R. 1974), with John Watson; C de G Grand Pabos (R.9 A.9 1972); C de G Les Dunes (Cse No. 1, R. 1952); C de G Port (R. 9 1953); C de G Ste. Marie (R.2 1970), with John Watson; C de G Victoriaville (R.9 A.9 1960); Fort Preval GC (R.9 A.5 1974), with John Watson; Grandmere GC (R.3 1967); Green Valley GC (R. 1965); Islesmere G&CC (A.9 1965); Kanawaki GC (R.9 1963; R.3 1976, with John Watson); Ki-8-EB GC (R.2 1974); Knowlton GC (R.9 A.9 1969); Lachute GC (R.9 A.18 1956); Larrimac GC (R.9 1973); Laval sur le Lac GC (R.9 1966); Levis GC (R. 1956); Lorette GC (R.9 1962); Marlborough GC (R. 1964, NLE); Mont Ste. Marie GC (R.2 1970), with John Watson; Mont Tremblant GC (R.9 1974); New Glasgow GC (R. 1974); Noranda Mines GC (R.9 1935); Riviere du Loup GC (R.9 A.9 1974), with John Watson; Royal Ottawa GC, Hull (R.27 A.9 1966); Royal Quebec CC (Quebec Cse, R.9 1966; A.2 1974, with John Watson); Thetford Mines G & Curling C (R.9 A.9 1971), with John Watson; Val Morin GC (R. 1971, A.9 1973, with John Watson); Whitlock G&CC (A.9 1961, R. 1970).
Jamaica: Upton G&CC (R.9 1961).

John Watson, 1980
COURTESY ASGCA

JOHN WATSON
(1933–   ), ASGCA, PRESIDENT 1985

BORN: Toronto, Ontario, Canada.

John Watson served for sixteen years as a pilot in the Royal Canadian Air Force, resigning his commission in 1967 to accept a flight test position with North American Rockwell. In 1969 he joined the practice of his father, golf architect Howard Watson, training under and working with him on some twenty projects.

Watson entered private practice on his own under the firm name of John Watson Golf Design Ltd. in 1975. He was joined by his son Scott Watson in the business in 1990.

Courses by John Watson:

Florida: Pembroke Lakes G&CC (27 1974), with Howard Watson.
New Brunswick: Memramcook GC (1987); Pokemouche GC (9 1974, with Howard Watson; R.9 1977; A. 9 1983).
Ontario: Amberwood Village GC (9 1979); Ridgetown GC, with Howard Watson; Scarlett Woods GC (1971), with Howard Watson; Tam O'Shanter Muni (1974), with Howard Watson.
Quebec: Bonaventure GC (9 1973, with Howard Watson; A.9 1976); C de G Adstock (9), with Howard Watson; C de G Deaux (1985); C de G des Saules (9 1985); C de G Gaspesien (9 1987); C de G Granby–St. Paul (New Cse 1973), with Howard Watson; C de G Longchamps (1969), with Howard Watson; C de G Montcalm (9 1978, A.9 1986); C de G Montevilla (9 1983); C de G St. Luc (9 1977, A.9 1985); C de G Terrebonne (9 1977, A.9 1985; A.3rd 9 1985); C de G Vielles Forges (1976); Como GC (9 1988, A.9 1991); Deux Montagnes GC (1985); Estrimont GC (1986); Le Versant GC (Cse No. 1 1988; Cse No. 2, 9 1988, A.9 1990; Cse No. 3, 9 1990,

A.9 1991); Manoir Inverness GC (9 1988, A.9 1991); Mont Adstock GC (9 1972), with Howard Watson; Mont Ste. Anne GC (Cse No. 1 1972, with Howard Watson; Cse No. 2, 9 1974, with Howard Watson, A.9 1980); Mont Ste. Marie GC (9 1978, A.9 1980); St. Laurent GC (1971), with Howard Watson; Val Morin GC (9 1973), with Howard Watson; Val Niegette GC (9 1980).

Courses remodeled or expanded by John Watson:

Massachusetts: Mount Pleasant GC, Lowell (R.3 1987).
Ontario: Carlton Yacht & GC (R.1 1980, R.3 1989); Don Valley Muni (R. A.9 1973), with Howard Watson; Fort William G&CC (R.16 1985); Hylands GC (North Cse, R.2 1981); St. Andrews GC (R.3 1981, R.6 1986); Strathcona GC (R.3 1985).
Prince Edward Island: Summerside GC (R.3 1988).
Quebec: Beaconsfield GC (R.3 1989, R.3 1991); Bonniebrook GC (R.3 1988); Candiac GC (R.2 1978); Chanbay GC (A.3 1986); Château Montebello GC (R.9 1989, R.9 1991); C de G Alpin (R.3 1976); C de G Baie Comeau (R.2 A.9 1973), with Howard Watson; C de G Charny (A.9 1976); C de G de Joliette (R.10 1982); C de G du Bic (R.6 1986, R.2 1989); C de G Chaudiere (A.5 1973), with Howard Watson; C de G Ste. Marie (R.2 1970), with Howard Watson; C de G St. Patrick (R.9 A.9 1974), with Howard Watson; C de G Sorel Tracy (R.4 1977); Fort Preval GC (R.5 1974), with Howard Watson; Green Valley GC (R.7 1980); Hillsdale G&CC (Dale Cse, R.1 1976; Hill Cse, R.1 1974); Kanawaki GC (R.3 1972, R.5 1989), with Howard Watson; Ki-8-EB GC (R.3 1977, R.5 1989); Larrimac GC (R.3 1976); Laval sur le Lac GC (R.3 1984); Les Dunes GC (R.1 1988); Les Jardin du Sable GC (R.6 1988); L'esterel GC (R.1 1988); Massawippi GC (R.3 1986); Milby GC (R.4 1986, R. 6 1988); Mont Adstock (R.9 1976); Mountain Acres GC (R.3 1990); Napierville GC (R.4 1988, A.4 1990); Noranda GC (R.9 1989); Pinegrove (R.8 1988); Riviere du Loup GC (R.9 A.9 1974), with Howard Watson; Rosemere G&CC (R.3 1979); Royal Ottawa GC (R.4 A.2 1986); Royal Quebec GC (Quebec Cse, R.9 1966, with Howard Watson; Royal Cse, A.2

1974, with Howard Watson); St. Luc GC (A.9); Thetford Mines Golf & Curling Club (R.9 A.9 1971), with Howard Watson; Thurso GC (R.9 1987).

RICHARD WATSON
(1932–   )

BORN: Fairbury, Nebraska.

Dick Watson attended Fairbury Junior College and Doane College and received a B.S. degree in zoology from the University of Nebraska. He then served four years with the U.S. Navy, learning to play golf while stationed in Pensacola, Florida. Upon his return to Nebraska, he was employed as district sales manager with a major pharmaceutical company and continued to play golf. Watson competed successfully in many local and regional tournaments and won the 1962 Lincoln Publinks title.

In 1963 Watson resigned to build and operate a par-3 course in Lincoln. He retained Denver golf architect Henry Hughes to assist him with the project. Hughes stayed in Nebraska to build several small-town courses, and Watson collaborated on both design and construction phases. The two formed a partnership in the mid-1960s, planning several courses in the Midwest.

In 1970 Hughes retired to Colorado and Watson continued to practice on his own in Nebraska. He had designed or remodeled some forty courses by the end of the 1970s, when he gradually began to concentrate on constructing layouts for other architects.

Courses by Richard Watson (All with Henry B. Hughes unless otherwise indicated):

California: Suncrest CC (9 Precision 1980 *solo*).
Iowa: Beacon Hills GC (9 Precision *solo*); Lake Panorama National GC (1972 *solo*); Lake Panorama Par 3 GC (9 Par 3 1973 *solo*).
Kansas: Belleville CC (9 1968); Indian Hills Muni (9 1977 *solo*); Rolling Meadows GC (1981 *solo*); Scott City CC (9 1968).
Kentucky: Doe Valley G&CC (1973 *solo*).
Missouri: Nehai Tonkayea GC (9 Par 3 1977 *solo*).
Montana: Larchmont Muni (1982), with *Keith Hellstrom.*

Nebraska: Ashland CC (9 1968; A.9 1982 *solo*); Atkinson-Stuart GC (9 1969); Bloomfield-Wausa GC (9 1969); Colonial GC (9 Par 3 1964, NLE); Friend CC (9 1967); Mid-County GC (9 1968); Pine Lake GC (9 Par 3 1973 *solo*); Tara Hills GC (9 Precision 1978 *solo*); Wayne CC (1969).
South Dakota: Lakeview Muni (9 1979 *solo*); Mitchell CC (9 *solo*).
Texas: Colony Creek CC (1985 *solo*); Sinton Muni (9 1968); Treasure Hills CC (1986 *solo*).
Virginia: Massanutten Village GC (1975 *solo*); [The] Summit GC at Lake Holiday (1972 *solo*).
Wyoming: Midway GC (9 1970); Riverton CC (9 *solo*).

Courses remodeled or expanded by Richard Watson:

Kansas: Great Bend Petroleum C (A.9 1981).

Scott Gordon Watson
(1966–)

Scott Watson, son of designer John Watson and grandson of Howard Watson, was a third-generation golf course architect. After graduating from Carleton University in Ottawa, Ontario, Scott joined his father's company in 1990 and became actively engaged in both design and inspection of construction.

Courses by Scott Watson (All as assistant to John Watson):

Quebec: Le Versant GC (Cse No. 3, 9 1990, A.9 1991).

Courses remodeled or expanded by Scott Watson (All as assistant to John Watson):

Quebec: Beaconsfield CC (R.3 1991); Château Montebello GC (R.9 1991); Como GC (A.9 1991); Le Versant GC (Cse No. 2, A.9 1990); Manoir Inverness GC (A.9 1991); Mountain Acres GC (R.3 1990); Napierville GC (A.4 1990).

William Watson

Willie Watson emigrated to the United States from Scotland in 1898 to help Robert Foulis lay out and build the original nine holes at Minikahda Country Club in Minneapolis. He remained at Minikahda as pro-greenkeeper during the summer months and served as golf instructor at Hotel Green GC in Pasadena, California, during the winter, where he began laying out golf courses on his own.

Prior to World War I, most of Watson's design work was done in Minnesota, Michigan and Illinois. Following the war he was based in Los Angeles, where he was assisted by construction superintendents Joe Mayo and Sam Whiting. In 1931 he returned to Michigan when golf course construction was severely curtailed by the Depression. Watson served as a club professional in Charlevoix, Michigan, during the last years of his life.

Courses by Willie Watson:

California: Coronado GC (3 1922, NLE); Diablo G&CC (1914); East Bay CC (NLE); Fort Washington G&CC (1923); Harding Park GC (1925); Hillcrest CC (1920); Hotel Green GC (9 1901, NLE); Lake Arrowhead CC (NLE); Mira Vista G&CC [FKA Berkeley CC] (1921); Mount Diablo CC; Olympic C (Lake Cse 1924; Ocean Cse 1924); Orinda CC (1924); Sunset Canyon GC (9 Par 3 1921, NLE).
Colorado: Colorado Springs CC (9).
Illinois: Olympia Fields CC (Cse No. 3 1919, NLE); South Shore GC, Momence (9 1928).
Michigan: Belvedere GC (1927).
Minnesota: Interlachen CC (1910); Minikahda C (9 1906), with Robert Foulis.

Courses remodeled or expanded by Willie Watson:

California: Annandale CC (R. 1928); Brentwood CC (R.); Burlingame CC (R. 1923).
Michigan: Kalamazoo CC (R. 1915).

Willie Watson, circa 1925 COLLECTION RON WHITTEN

William R. Watts
(1932–)

BORN: Miami, Florida.

Billy Watts attended the University of Miami, where he was a member of the golf team. A lifelong amateur golfer, he won more than thirty local and regional titles in southern Florida. In the late 1950s Watts designed and built Sunrise Country Club, which he owned and managed. Over the next twenty years he designed a dozen other courses along the Gold Coast of Florida.

Courses by Bill Watts:

Florida: Arrowhead CC (1968); Broken Woods G&RC (Precision); Don Shula's Hotel & C [FKA Miami Lakes Inn & CC] (Championship Cse 1963); Deer Creek G&CC (1971); Foxcroft CC (1968); Hollywood Lakes CC (East Cse 1965; West Cse 1967); Lago Mar CC (1970); Sun 'n Lake CC (Precision 1969); Sunrise CC (1960).
Georgia: Innsbruck GC (1987); Sky Valley CC.

Ernest W. Way
(1878–1943)

BORN: Westward Ho!, Devonshire, England.
DIED: Miami, Florida, at age 65.

Ernest Way was the son of an English cabinetmaker and brother of golfers Ed, Jack and Bert Way. He and Jack emigrated to the United States around 1905 to join their elder brother Bert, already a successful golf professional in America. After brief jobs at golf clubs in Pittsburgh and Richmond, Virginia, Ernest moved to Detroit Golf Club, whose course Bert had just built. He remained as head professional at Detroit until 1919 and during his tenure supervised construction of the club's two Donald Ross courses. Jack meantime became the professional of Canterbury Country Club near Cleveland, where he remodeled the course and added three holes in the early 1920s.

A charter member of the Michigan PGA and a member of both the PGA of America and the GCSAA, Ernest resigned from Detroit Golf Club to design and build courses in Michigan in the 1920s. He returned to his position as course superintendent at Detroit in the 1930s, but ill health forced him to retire in 1937. He then moved to Florida, where he resided until his death.

Courses by Ernest Way:

Florida: Hotel Indiatlantic GC (NLE).
Michigan: Belle Isle Muni (9 1922); Birch Hill GC (NLE); Edgewood CC; Pontiac CC.

Bert Way, circa 1915 COLLECTION RON WHITTEN

WILLIAM HERBERT "BERT" WAY (1873–1963)

BORN: Westward Ho!, Devonshire, England.
DIED: Miami, Florida, at age 90.

Bert Way and his brothers grew up alongside the Royal North Devon GC, where they caddied and played as youngsters. All developed into proficient golfers and, after learning the craft of clubmaking from their father, moved one by one to America to further their careers. The first of his family to emigrate to the United States, the 6' 3" Bert took a roundabout route. He had quit school after the sixth grade to work in the golf shop of Young Willie Dunn, Royal North Devon's pro. But after Dunn left, Way grew tired of his job and worked at various odd jobs about Britain for several years until Willie Dunn summoned him to Dunn's new pro shop in Biarritz, France. Bert lasted one winter in France before moving back to England, but in 1896, when he heard Dunn had moved to America, Bert Way soon followed.

There he found one of the few available club professional jobs in the United States, at the Meadowbrook Hunt Club in New York, where he worked for $100 a month. His duties left him plenty of time to work on his game, and he soon became a successful tournament golfer. In 1899 he was joint runner-up in the U.S. Open, though a distant eleven shots behind the winner, Willie Smith.

In 1898 Bert relocated to Detroit, Michi-

gan, where he laid some of that area's earliest courses. Two years later he was hired by the Euclid Club of Cleveland, Ohio, to design and build its course and serve as professional. While there he introduced the game of golf to John D. Rockefeller, who happened to own the land on which the course was laid.

When Euclid lost its lease ten years later, Way designed a new course for the membership, Mayfield Country Club. He remained as its professional until 1951. Bert continued to design and remodel courses while at Mayfield, his best-known creation being the original Firestone CC in Akron, which was considerably toughened by Robert Trent Jones in the 1950s.

A member of the PGA of America, Bert was especially active in Senior golf activities. He served as PGA Senior president in 1946, won several Senior events and was at one time the oldest living PGA professional. He died in Miami in August of 1963, just two weeks short of his 91st birthday.

Courses by Bert Way:

Kentucky: Sundowner GC (9 1953).
Michigan: CC of Detroit (1898, NLE); Detroit GC (1905, NLE).
Ohio: Aurora CC (1926); Dover Bay CC (9 1904); Euclid Heights CC (1900, NLE); Firestone CC (South Cse 1929); Firestone Public GC (1929, NLE); Mayfield CC (1911), with Herbert Barker.

Bobby Weed, 1983 RON WHITTEN

ROBERT WEED (1955–), ASGCA

BORN: South Carolina.

As a youngster, Bobby Weed built a driving range in a field on his father's farm. After high school he attended Presbyterian College in South Carolina and then obtained a degree from the Turf School at Lake City Community College in Florida.

He soon joined the construction crew of Long Cove Club, being built by Pete Dye on Hilton Head Island, and stayed on as its first golf course superintendent. Within a year Dye brought him south to Jacksonville to serve as construction superintendent at the TPC of Sawgrass. Again Weed remained as superintendent, and from 1983 to 1985 he oversaw all golf course improvements to the Stadium course. After helping Dye add the Valley course to the club and assisting him in several other designs, Weed became chief construction superintendent over all TPC courses being constructed across the United States. In 1988 Weed became chief in-house course designer for the newly formed PGA Tour Design Services, Inc.

Courses by Bobby Weed:

Florida: Cypress Links (1988), ass't Pete Dye; GC of Jacksonville (1989); GC of Miami (South Cse [Precision] 1990), TPC at Sawgrass (Valley Cse 1987), ass't Pete Dye and Jerry Pate; TPC of Tampa Bay at Cheval (1991).
Georgia: River's Edge GC (1989).
Nevada: TPC of Summerlin (1992), with *Fuzzy Zoeller*.
North Carolina: Landfall C (Dye Cse 1988), ass't Pete Dye and P. B. Dye.

Courses remodeled or expanded by Bobby Weed:

Connecticut: TPC at River Highlands (R. A.11 1991).
Florida: Amelia Island G Links (R. Oakmarsh 9 1990); GC of Miami (R. East and West Cses 1989); TPC at Sawgrass (R. Stadium Cse 1984), ass't Pete Dye.

REINHOLD WEISHAUPT (1943–), ESGCA, FOUNDING MEMBER

BORN: Wolfsberg, Austria.

Reinhold Weishaupt studied landscape architecture in Vienna and worked for firms in Scandinavia, Switzerland and Germany before establishing his own office in Stuttgart, Germany. In 1981 he received a German Federation of Landscape Architects prize for his work in landscape planning. In the mid-1980s Weishaupt expanded his landscape architecture business to include golf course design. A founding member of the ESGCA, he coauthored the society's publication, *Golf Course Construction Guidelines.*

Courses by Reinhold Weishaupt:

Germany: Aschaffenburg GC (1991); Bensheim GC (9 1989); Pforzheim GC (1989); Tutzing GC (1985); Weiden GC (1991); Wiesloch Hohenhardter Hof GC (1986).

Courses remodeled or expanded by Reinhold Weishaupt:

Germany: Hohenstaufen GC (A.9 1991); Mainsondheim GC (A.9 1989, A.3rd 9 1990); Saarbrücken GC (R.9 1990).
Switzerland: Schoenenberg G&CC (A.9 1991).

THOMAS DANIEL WEISKOPF (1942–)

BORN: Massillon, Ohio.

Tom Weiskopf enjoyed a fine career in professional golf with fifteen PGA Tour victories, the British Open crown of 1973, two Ryder Cup appearances and many other championships around the world. He turned his attention to golf course architecture in the early 1980s, teaming with Jay Morrish in 1984 to form one of the most successful partnerships of all time. One of their collaborations, Troon Golf & Country Club in Arizona (named for the site of Weiskopf's British Open triumph), won *Golf Digest*'s Best New Private Course of 1986. Another, Shadow Glen near Kansas City, Kansas, was the magazine's Best New Private Course of 1989, and the duo's Forest Highlands Golf Club was runner-up. In the early 1990s Morrish and Weiskopf became the first Americans to design a course in Scotland.

Courses by Tom Weiskopf (All with Jay Morrish):

Arizona: Estancia GC (1993); [The] Foothills GC (1988); Forest Highlands GC (1988); TPC of Scottsdale (Desert Cse 1987; Stadium Cse 1986); Troon G&CC (1985); Troon North GC (1990).
California: Marbella G&CC.
Georgia: Harbor C (1991).
Hawaii: [The] Kings' GC (1990).
Kansas: Shadow Glen GC (1989); Willowbend GC (1987).
Missouri: CC of St. Albans (1992).
Ohio: Double Eagle C (1992).
South Carolina: Bloody Point C (1991).
Texas: Bentwater CC (1989); Buffalo Creek G Cse (1992); Mira Vista CC (1987).
Scotland: Loch Lomond GC (1992).

GRANT WENCEL (1957–)

BORN: Wichita, Kansas.

Grant Wencel, a 1981 landscape architecture graduate of Kansas State University, worked for golf course architects Richard Phelps, Roger Packard and Willard Byrd before establishing his own golf design firm in Atlanta in 1988.

Courses by Grant Wencel:

Illinois: Cantigny GC (27 1988), ass't Roger Packard.

Courses remodeled or expanded by Grant Wencel:

Tennessee: Brainerd Muni (R.); Brown Acres GC (R.); Creek's Bend GC (R.).

H. J. Whigham, circa 1926
COLLECTION RON WHITTEN

HENRY JAMES WHIGHAM (1869–1954)

BORN: Prestwick, Scotland.
DIED: Southampton, New York, at age 85.

H. J. Whigham, descended from one of Prestwick's oldest golfing families, was the son of a golfing friend whom Charles Blair Macdonald first met as an undergraduate at St. Andrews University. An Oxford graduate, Whigham traveled to the United States in 1895 to lecture on English literature and political economy at the university level. Shortly after his arrival, he became drama critic for the Chicago *Tribune*, a post from which he took time off in 1896 and 1897 to win consecutive U.S. Amateur Championships.

From 1896 to 1907 Whigham served as war correspondent for several British and American newspapers, covering the Battle of San Juan (where he was captured), the Boer War, the Boxer Rebellion, the Macedonian Rebellion and the Russo-Japanese War. He returned to the United States in 1908 and became editor of *Metropolitan* and *Town and Country* magazines. He was author of *How to Play Golf* and other books on a variety of subjects, from *The Persian Problem* (1903) to one on the New Deal in 1936.

In his first years in the United States, Whigham had staked out the original Onwentsia Club in Chicago in collaboration with H. J. Tweedie and James and Robert Foulis. After his marriage in 1909 to C. B. Macdonald's daughter Frances, he assisted his father-in-law in planning The National Golf Links of America. Whigham took a friendly interest in Macdonald's design work and studied the work of other early golf architects on the East Coast. He did little other design work himself.

Tom Weiskopf (left), with design partner Jay Morrish, 1991 COURTESY JAY MORRISH

JACK WHITE
(1873–1949)

BORN: Dirleton, Scotland.
DIED: London, England, at age 76.

Jack White, professional golfer at Sunningdale in England for many years, won the British Open in 1904. He assisted Willie Park, Jr., with the design and construction of several courses and consulted on modifications to numerous established layouts in the London area. He also laid out a few original designs himself.

ROBERT WHITE
(1874–1959), ASGCA, CHARTER MEMBER

BORN: St. Andrews, Scotland.
DIED: Myrtle Beach, South Carolina, at age 85.

In 1894 Robert White emigrated from St. Andrews to the United States to study agronomy. For a short period around 1895 he served as pro-greenkeeper at Myopia Hunt Club in Massachusetts and in 1902 moved to Ravisloe Country Club in Illinois. Later he was professional at Wykagyl in New Rochelle, New York. During his career, White laid out a number of courses at which he remained as pro-superintendent. He also planned and revised many others.

White became the first president of the PGA of America in 1916, was a founding member of the ASGCA, a pioneer in scientific turfgrass management and a leading golf businessman.

Courses by Robert White:

Connecticut: Fairchild Wheeler GC (Black Cse 1922; Red Cse, 1933); Shorehaven GC (1924); Silver Spring CC.
Kentucky: Louisville CC (9).
Massachusetts: North Salem Links (9 1895, NLE).
New Jersey: Green Brook CC (1923); Harkers Hollow GC; Lake Hopatcong GC (1918); Manasquan River G&CC.
New York: Richmond County CC (1916); Rockland CC (1928).
Pennsylvania: Berkleigh CC (1926); Glen Brook CC (1924); Longue Vue C (1920); Skytop C (1927); Wiscasset GC (9 1924); Wolf Hollow CC [FKA Water Gap CC](1923).

Robert White, circa 1950 COURTESY HIMMELBACH COMMUNICATIONS, INC.

South Carolina: Kingstree CC (1925); Pine Lakes International GC (1927).
Washington, D.C.: East Potomac Park GC (9).

Course remodeled or expanded by Robert White:

Connecticut: Greenwich CC (R.2 1925).
Illinois: Ravisloe CC (R.).
New Jersey: Colonia CC (A.9 1937); Echo Lake CC (R.6 1919).
New York: Rockland CC (R.9 1929); Wykagyl CC (R. 1923).
Ohio: Cincinnati CC (R.9 A.9).
Pennsylvania: Buck Hill Inn & CC (A.3rd 9).

SAM WHITING
(1880–1956)

DIED: San Francisco, California, at age 76.

Sam Whiting was an English professor at the University of California at Berkeley when he was hired in 1921 to serve as a clubmaker and teaching professional at the newly founded Berkeley CC. He soon switched to Lakeside G&CC across the bay. In 1924, when Lakeside's course was sold to the Olympic Club of San Francisco, Whiting was hired as superintendent of construction of the new Lake and Pacific (later Ocean) courses of Olympic, which superimposed the old Lakeside layout by architect Willie Watson. Whiting also supervised construction of another nearby Watson design, Harding Park Municipal.

After the courses opened, Whiting remained as course superintendent. Within two years the club sought to eliminate several blind shots from Watson's design. Golf architect Max Behr was hired, with Whiting again supervising construction; several holes were remodeled, and a few new ones were added. Drawing on his construction experiences, Whiting began designing courses on his own, doing among others Sonoma National (1928, now called

Sonoma GC), Stockton G&CC, and Hillview in San Jose, and doing some remodeling at Del Paso.

But Olympic was Sam Whiting's true love. He was responsible for the massive tree-planting program that eventually made Olympic one of the tightest courses in the country. He also made minor design changes to both courses, most notably on the Ocean eighteen. He continued as superintendent at Olympic until poor health forced his retirement in 1954. It was a disappointment to him that he was unable to handle the course for the U.S. Open scheduled there in the following year.

RODERICK K. WHITMAN

Rod Whitman attended Sam Houston State University in Huntsville, Texas, where he played on the golf team during his senior year and graduated in 1979. After his college days Whitman worked on the course-maintenance crew at nearby Waterwood National under course superintendent Bill Coore. He helped Coore with renovation of several holes and learned to operate various course-construction equipment in the process.

After serving as a construction superintendent to Pete Dye during the building of a new Austin Country Club, Whitman designed and built his first course, Wolf Creek in Alberta. More jobs with Pete Dye followed, and then in 1987 he was reunited with Bill Coore on a job in France, Médoc, which was declared one of Europe's Top 50 courses by *Golf World* soon after it opened.

Based in Alberta, Whitman continued to work actively in Europe during the early 1990s.

Courses by Rod Whitman:

Colorado: Glenmoor CC (1985), ass't Perry Dye.

Rod Whitman, 1991 COURTESY ROD WHITMAN

Texas: Austin CC (1983), ass't Pete
Dye; Stonebridge CC (1988), ass't Pete
Dye.
Alberta: Wolf Creek G Resort (18 1983,
A.3rd 9 1990 *solo*).
France: G du LePian Médoc (1991 *solo*);
G du Médoc (1989), with Bill Coore.
Germany: Schloss Langenstein CC (1992
solo).

**Courses remodeled or expanded by Rod
Whitman:**

Indiana: Crooked Stick GC (R. 1986),
ass't Pete Dye.
Texas: Waterwood National GC (R.
1981), ass't Bill Coore.
Alberta: Devon G & Curling C (R.4 1980
solo).

RONALD EDWARD WHITTEN
(1950–   )

BORN: Omaha, Nebraska.

Ron Whitten's interest in golf design
began in 1967 when, as a high school student, he visited the Chicago Golf Club and
the Beverly Country Club in Illinois. Intrigued by their differences, he began
studying golf course architecture as a
hobby, compiling information about
courses and course architects and eventually establishing one of the world's most
complete data banks on the subject.

Whitten received a Bachelor of Science
degree in education in 1972 from the University of Nebraska and a Juris Doctor
degree in 1977 from the Washburn University School of Law in Kansas. He then
worked for twelve years as a practicing
trial attorney, serving at different times as
an assistant district attorney, an assistant
city attorney and as a private practitioner
in Topeka, Kansas.

In 1974 Whitten contributed to Frank
Hannigan's article in the USGA *Golf Journal* on golf architect A. W. Tillinghast.
Four years later he began work with
coauthor Geoffrey S. Cornish on a history
on course architecture, *The Golf Course*,
which first appeared in 1981. He then
wrote extensively on golf design, and his
articles appeared in every major American
golf magazine as well as magazines in
Great Britain and France. He contributed
chapters to William Davis's *100 Greatest
Golf Courses—And Then Some* and Harry
Valerien's *Golf Encyclopedia*.

In 1985 he became contributing editor
on golf architecture for *Golf Digest* and in
1990 left the practice of law to become the
magazine's full-time architecture editor.
In that capacity he spent time with nearly
every practicing golf architect in America,
wrote numerous articles and coordinated
Golf Digest's various lists of golf course
rankings. He also conceived and conducted two popular amateur "Armchair
Architect" competitions for the magazine.

Ben Wihry, 1972
COURTESY *GOLF WORLD*

BENJAMIN J. WIHRY
(1913–   ), ASGCA

BORN: Haverhill, Massachusetts.

Ben Wihry received a Bachelor of Science degree from the University of Massachusetts in 1935 and a landscape architecture degree from the same university in
1941. He was employed as a recreational
planner for the U.S. Forest Service from
1935 to 1940 and from 1941 to 1946
served with the U.S. Army Corps of Engineers.

In 1946 Wihry entered private practice
in planning, engineering and landscape
architecture. His firm, Miller, Wihry, Lee
Inc. of Louisville, Kentucky, branched
into golf course architecture around 1964,
after Wihry had worked with and studied
course design under his friend and former
classmate, Edward Lawrence Packard.

Courses by Benjamin Wihry:

Indiana: Elks Lodge GC (9 1969).
Kentucky: Barren River State Park GC (9
1979); Bobby Nichols GC (9 1964);
Chenoweth GC (9 1967); Danville CC
(1974); Eagle's Nest CC (1979); East-
ern Kentucky University GC (1972);
Elizabethtown CC (1968), with *Mor-
gan Boggs*; Hunting Creek CC (1965);
Long Run GC (9 1965); Rough River
Dam State Park GC (9 1973); Sun Val-
ley GC (9 1972).
Tennessee: Nashboro Village CC (1974);
Paris Landing State Park GC (1970);
Swan Lake CC (1977); Winfield Dunn
GC (1973).

**Courses remodeled or expanded by
Benjamin Wihry:**

Kentucky: Iroquois GC (R.3 A.9 1964);
Lexington CC (R.4 A.5 1975);
Louisville CC (R.1 A.1 1974); Seneca
Muni (R.8 1972); Shelbyville CC (A.2
1974).

WILLARD G. WILKINSON
(1889–1979), ASGCA

BORN: Wimbledon, England.
DIED: Phoenix, Arizona, at age 90.

After service with the Royal Flying
Corps during World War I, Willard Wilkinson moved to the United States, where
he attended Rutgers University and then
went to work as assistant to golf architect
A. W. Tillinghast. Eventually he became
vice president of A. W. Tillinghast Golf
Construction Company Inc. and during
those years supervised construction at
Winged Foot, Baltusrol and other renowned layouts.

In 1924 Wilkinson entered private
practice, aided by his former employer,
who generously arranged for him to complete three Tillinghast courses and receive
the fees still due on them. He went on to
design eighty-seven courses and remodel
sixteen in the continental United States,
Hawaii (where he resided for many years),
the Philippines, Guam, Japan and Tahiti.
He was assisted by his son, Colonel Robert
N. Wilkinson (USAF, Ret.), during several
of the years when his practice was based in
Honolulu. Wilkinson moved to Arizona
shortly after his retirement in 1969.

Courses by Willard Wilkinson:

Hawaii: Hilo Muni (1951); Kauai Surf
G&CC (9 1967, NLE); Pacific Palisades GC (Par 3 1962); Pali GC
(1957); Walter Nagorski G Cse [FKA
Fort Shafter GC](9 1950).

*Willard Wilkinson,
1966* COLLECTION RON
WHITTEN

New Jersey: Galloping Hills GC; Jumping Brook GC (1925); Locust Grove GC (1925); Oak Ridge GC (1928); Prescott Hills GC (1926).
New York: Cortland CC (1947); Malone GC (9 1939); Tupper Lake CC (9 1932, A.9 1941).
Japan: Hayana International GC (1967).
Philippines: Binicitan GC; Subic Bay GC (1966).
Tahiti: Atimoona G&CC (1965).

Courses remodeled or expanded by Willard Wilkinson:

Hawaii: Mid-Pacific CC (R.9 A.9 1949).
New Jersey: Echo Lake CC (R.3 1928).
New York: Bellevue CC (R. A.3 1947).

GEORGE B. WILLIAMS
(1947–)

BORN: Hearne, Texas.

George Williams received a Bachelor's degree in mechanical engineering in 1970 and a Master's degree in landscape architecture, with emphasis on golf course design, in 1976, both from Texas A&M University. He then worked in course construction in several states, first with Gunderson's Construction Company of Rapid City, South Dakota, and later with Wadsworth Golf Construction of Oldsmar, Florida.

In 1986, after some independent course design and consulting work, Williams formed a golf design partnership with Garrett Gill, a former Texas A&M classmate.

Courses by George B. Williams (All with Garrett Gill):

California: David L. Baker GC (1987); Micke Grove G Links (1992).
Minnesota: Inverwood G Links (27 1991); Majestic Oaks GC (South Cse 1991); Willinger GC (1991).

Courses remodeled or expanded by George B. Williams (All with Garrett Gill):

California: Aptos Seascape (R.); Camarillo Springs CC (R.); Chula Vista Muni (R.); El Dorado Park GC (R.); El Toro G Cse (A.9 1991); Mountain Shadows GC (North and South Cses, R.); MountainGate CC (R.); Yorba Linda CC (R.).
Colorado: Applewood GC (R.).
Georgia: Alfred "Tup" Holmes G Cse

(R.); Bobby Jones GC (R.); North Fulton Muni (R.).
Iowa: Ottumwa Muni (R.).
Minnesota: Brookview GC (R.); Keller GC (R.).
New Jersey: Brigantine G Links (R.); Rancocas GC (R.).
New Mexico: Tanoan CC (R.).
Nevada: Sahara CC (R.).
Texas: Maxwell GC (R.); Mesquite Muni (R.); Pecan Valley CC (R.); World Houston GC (R.).

JOHN HAROLD WILLIAMS, SR.
(1920–)

BORN: Alabama.

Harold Williams attended the University of Alabama and served in the military for four and a half years during World War II. He became a professional golfer in 1945, joining the PGA of America and becoming a charter member of the Alabama PGA. Williams owned and operated Meadowbrook Golf Club in Tuscaloosa, Alabama, until 1962. He played frequently on the PGA Tour during that time and won the Alabama Open once, the Mississippi Open twice and the Alabama PGA Championship on several occasions. He began designing golf courses in Alabama on a part-time basis in the late 1950s.

Courses by Harold Williams:

Alabama: Canoe Creek CC; [The] Country Club, Reform (9); Grayson Valley CC; Harry Pritchett GC [FKA University of Alabama GC] (9 1959), with *Thomas H. Nicol*; Indian Hills CC (1960), with *Thomas H. Nicol*; Indian Oaks CC (1968); Pine Harbor G&RC; Terrapin Hills GC.

Courses remodeled or expanded by Harold Williams:

Alabama: Anniston CC (R.).

JOSEPH B. WILLIAMS

Joseph Williams served as superintendent at the Santa Clara (California) Country Club in the 1960s and then designed Shorecliffs Country Club in San Clemente and became its superintendent. He later planned several more courses in the Southwest.

Courses by Joseph B. Williams:

California: Bishop CC (9 1963); Golden Hills GC (1966); Navy GC (Destroyer Cse); Richard Nixon Estate GC (1 1970); Shorecliffs CC (1964); Tahoe Donner GC (1975).
Utah: Roosevelt Muni (1973); Tri-City GC; Valley View GC (1979), with *William Hull*.

Tom Williamson, circa 1935 COURTESY NOTTS G. C.

TOM WILLIAMSON
(1880–1950)

BORN: England.
DIED: Hollingwell, England, at age 70.

Tom Williamson's career as a pro-greenkeeper and clubmaker at Notts Golf Club spanned more than half a century, from 1896 until his death in 1950. He laid out numerous courses on the side and in 1919 claimed to have worked on all but one of the courses within a fifty-mile radius of Nottingham. Over the years he designed or remodeled some sixty courses and was assisted by his brother Hugh on the construction of several. Williamson was an early advocate of Plasticine models of new greens.

Courses by Tom Williamson:

England: Ashover GC: Beeston Fields GC (1923); Garforth GC (1913); Hillsborough GC (1920); Ladbrook Park GC (1908); Longcliffe GC (1905); Louth GC (1919); Mapperley GC (1913); Matlock GC (1907); Melton Mowbray GC (1925); Nuneaton GC (1906); Radcliffe-on-Trent GC (1909); Retford GC (1921); Rothley Park GC (1911); Rushcliffe GC (1910); Scraptoft GC (1928); Serlby Park GC (1905); Sleaford GC (1905); Southwell GC (NLE); Stanton-on-the-Wolds GC (1928); Tipworth GC; Trentham Park GC (1936); Wellingborough GC; Wollaton Park GC (1927); Worksop GC (1914).

Courses remodeled or expanded by Tom Williamson:

England: Belton Park GC (R.); Birstall GC (R.); Bulwell Forest GC (R.); Burton-on-Trent GC (R.); Buxton and High Peak GC (R.); Cavendish GC (R. 1925); Chatsworth GC (R.); Chesterfield GC (R.); Chilwell Manor GC (R.); Edgbaston GC (R.); Erewash Valley GC (R.); Grimsby GC (R.); Leek GC (R.); Lees Hall GC (R.); Mullion GC (R.); Notts GC (R.); Radcliffe-on-Trent GC (R.); Renishaw GC (R.); Rushden & District GC (R. 1919); Sandilands GC (R.); Sherwood Forest GC (R.); Sickleholme GC (R.); West Runton GC (R., NLE).
Switzerland: Zurich G&CC (R.).

DICK WILSON NÉ LOUIS SIBBETT WILSON (1904–1965)

BORN: Philadelphia, Pennsylvania.
DIED: Boynton Beach, Florida, at age 61.

Dick Wilson was a fine athlete as a youth and attended the University of Vermont on a football scholarship. As a youngster, he had served as water boy for a construction crew at Merion in Pennsylvania. After leaving college Dick returned to Merion and worked on Toomey and Flynn's crew during the revision of Merion's East Course in 1925.

Wilson remained with Toomey and Flynn, becoming a construction superintendent and later a design associate. He was credited with making major contributions to Flynn's design of Shinnecock Hills GC on Long Island, which opened in 1931, but in truth he supervised its construction to Flynn's plans. In the early 1930s Wilson moved to Florida to construct Indian Creek Club in Miami Beach for Flynn. But Toomey's death and the decline of business due to the Depression forced Wilson to take a job as pro-greenkeeper at Delray Beach Country Club. He remained there until World War II, teaching the game to visiting tourists. Among the frequent visitors to Wilson's course were Mr. and Mrs. Paul Dye of Ohio, parents of Pete and Roy Dye.

He spent the war years constructing and camouflaging airfields. In 1945 Wilson formed his own golf design company in association with a Miami earth-moving firm, the Troup Brothers. His early postwar works, especially West Palm Beach

Dick Wilson, 1958
COURTESY *GOLF WORLD*

Country Club and NCR Country Club in Dayton, Ohio, established Wilson as one of the most sought after architects of the 1950s and 1960s. Wilson designed relatively few courses in his later years so he could give personal attention to each work bearing his name. He maintained a staff of loyal and talented assistants who handled much of the actual design and construction on some projects, including Joseph L. Lee (who was made his full partner a short time before Wilson's death), Robert von Hagge, Bob Simmons, Ward Northrup and Frank Batto.

Courses by Dick Wilson:

Arizona: Moon Valley CC (1958).
Arkansas: Blytheville CC (9 1957).
California: La Costa CC (North Cse, 9 1964; South Cse, 9 1964), with Joe Lee; Sunnylands GC (9 1962), with Joe Lee.
Delaware: Bidermann GC, with Joe Lee; Wilmington CC (North Cse 1962).
Florida: Bay Hill C (1961), with Joe Lee; Blackburn Estate GC (3); Cape Coral CC (1963); Cypress Lake CC (1960); Doral CC (Blue Cse 1962; Red Cse 1962); Golden Gate CC (1965); Harder Hall Hotel GC (1958); Hole-in-the-Wall GC (1958); JDM CC (East Cse 1964; North Cse, 9 1964; South Cse, 9 1964), with Joe Lee; Lone Palm GC (1965), with Joe Lee; Melreese GC (1962), with Joe Lee; Palm Beach Par 3 GC (9 Par 3 1961); Oak Tree CC [FKA Tamarac CC] (1961); Palm-Aire West CC (Champions Cse) [FKA DeSoto Lakes G&CC] (1958); Palmetto GC (1960); Pine Tree CC (1962), with Joe Lee; Royal Oak G&CC (1964); Tequesta CC (1958), with Joe Lee; West Palm Beach CC (1947); Westview CC (9 1949).
Georgia: Callaway Gardens GC (Mountainview Cse 1963), with Joe Lee; Canongate GC (1965), with Joe Lee; Jekyll Island GC (Oleander Cse 1961),

with Joe Lee; Mystery Valley CC (1965), with Joe Lee; Sea Island GC (Retreat Nine 1959), with Joe Lee.
Illinois: Cog Hill GC (Cse No. 3 1964; Cse No. 4 1964), with Joe Lee.
Louisiana: Oakbourne CC (1958).
Mississippi: CC of Jackson (27 1963).
Nevada: Desert Rose GC [FKA Winterwood GC] (1964), with Joe Lee.
New Jersey: Bedens Brook C, with Joe Lee.
New York: Cavalry C (1966), with Joe Lee; Deepdale CC (1956; R. 1962); Garrison GC [FKA North Redoubt C] (1963); Meadow Brook C (1955).
Ohio: Coldstream CC (1960), with Joe Lee; NCR CC (North Cse 1954; South Cse 1954).
Pennsylvania: Laurel Valley CC (1960); Radnor Valley CC (1953); Westmoreland CC (1948).
Tennessee: Town and Country GC (Par 3 1963).
Virginia: Elizabeth Manor GC (1951); Glen Oak CC (9 1951); Hidden Valley CC (1952); Kinderton CC (1947); Suffolk CC (1950).
West Virginia: Fincastle CC (1963); [The] Greenbrier GC (Lakeside Cse 1962).
Quebec: Royal Montreal GC (Black Cse, 9 1959; Blue Cse 1959; Red Cse 1959).
Bahamas: Bahamas Princess Hotel & CC (Emerald Cse 1965), with Joe Lee; Lucayan G&CC (1964), with Joe Lee; Lyford Cay C (1960), with Joe Lee; Paradise Island G&CC (1962), with Joe Lee; Treasure Cay GC (1966), with Joe Lee.
Cuba: Villa Real GC (1957).
Venezuela: Lagunita CC (1958).

Courses remodeled or expanded by Dick Wilson:

California: Bel-Air CC (R. 1961).
Florida: Dunedin CC (R. 1960); Gulfstream GC (R. 1958), with Joe Lee; Indian Creek CC (R.), with Joe Lee; Lake Worth Muni (R.); Lakewood CC (R. 1957); Riviera CC (R. 1962); Seminole GC (R. 1947).
Georgia: Callaway Gardens GC (Lakeview Cse, A.9 1963), with Joe Lee.
Illinois: Cog Hill CC (Cse No. 1, R. 1963; Cse No. 2, R. 1963), with Joe Lee.
New Jersey: Hollywood GC (R. A.2 1962).
New York: Scarsdale GC (R. 1956); Winged Foot GC (West Cse, R.3 1958).
Ohio: Columbus CC (R. 1962); Inverness

C (R. 1956); Moraine CC (R. 1955);
Scioto CC (R. 1963), with Joe Lee.
Pennsylvania: Aronimink GC (R. 1961);
Merion GC (East Cse, R. 1965); Penn
Hills C (R.9 A.9 1956).
Texas: Colonial CC (R. 1956).
Australia: Metropolitan GC (R.11 A.8
1961); Royal Melbourne GC (East Cse,
R. 1959; West Cse, R. 1959).
Mexico: Club Campestre (R.).

*Hugh Wilson, circa
1900* COLLECTION RON
WHITTEN

HUGH IRVINE WILSON
(1879–1925)

BORN: Philadelphia, Pennsylvania.
DIED: Bryn Mawr, Pennsylvania, at age 45.

Hugh Wilson graduated in 1902 from
Princeton University, where he was captain of the golf team. Following college, he
joined a Philadelphia insurance brokerage
firm and eventually became its president.

A lifelong amateur golfer, Wilson was a
member of Aronimink Golf Club and Merion Cricket Club. In 1910 he was chosen
to make a survey of great British courses in
preparation for a new Merion course. Wilson spent seven months in England and
Scotland, returning with armloads of
sketches and notes and proceeded, with
the assistance of Richard S. Francis, to lay
out a new course for Merion in Ardmore.
With the exception of later changes to four
holes and some rebunkering, Merion East
remained as Wilson designed it in 1912.

Wilson also planned the West Course at
Merion and Cobbs Creek Municipal in
Philadelphia. With the assistance of his
brother Alan, he finished the remaining
four holes at Pine Valley after George
Crump's death in 1919. He was close
friends with William S. Flynn, Merion's
first superintendent, and the two planned
to form a design partnership in the early
1920s. But Wilson grew increasingly ill
and died at age 45 before the two were able
to complete any plans. They had been consulted on a design for The Kittansett Club

in Marion, Massachusetts, but that design
was not used. They had also talked about
various changes to Merion, changes Flynn
accomplished after Wilson's death.

Courses by Hugh Wilson:

Pennsylvania: Cobbs Creek Muni (1917);
Merion GC (East Cse 1912; West Cse
1914).

Courses remodeled or expanded by Hugh Wilson:

New Jersey: Pine Valley GC (A.4 1921),
with *Alan Wilson.*

THOMAS WINTON
(1871–1944)

BORN: Montrose, Scotland.
DIED: Tuckahoe, New York, at age 73.

Tom Winton, descended from a Scottish golfing family, was the son of James
Winton, longtime pro and clubmaker at
Montrose. Tom's brothers all became professionals and clubmakers. Tom studied
under his father as well but moved to London at the turn of the century. There he
became involved in golf course construction, working for several architects on
construction of such courses as Coombe
Hill and South Herts.

At the outbreak of World War I, Winton
joined Willie Park, Jr.'s crew and moved to
the United States. But business was slow
there also, so Winton took a position as
superintendent for the Westchester (New
York) County Parks Commission, where
he remained for many years. He was in
charge of maintaining the county's golf
courses and other parks and with constructing new facilities. In this capacity he
designed several public courses in the
New York suburbs.

Winton soon found additional design
jobs and in the 1920s was active along the
Eastern Seaboard, laying out courses and
supervising their construction. When design business fell off in the Depression, he
continued in his Parks Commission position and also served as a maintenance consultant for several New York clubs.

Courses by Tom Winton:

Connecticut: Mill River CC (1923).
Massachusetts: Woods Hole GC.
New Jersey: Cranmoor CC (1925); Hope-
well Valley GC (1927).
New York: Amityville CC; Colgate Uni-
versity GC (NLE); Corning CC;

*Tom Winton, circa
1930* COLLECTION RON
WHITTEN

Kingsridge CC (1929); Maplemoor CC
(1927), with *Archie Capper;* Mohansic
Park GC (1925); Mount Kisco CC;
Saxon Woods GC (1930); Sprain
Brook GC (27 1928); Westport GC
(1928).
Virginia: Lynn Haven CC.

Courses remodeled or expanded by Tom Winton:

Kentucky: Big Spring CC (R.).
Maryland: Congressional CC (Blue Cse,
R. 1927).
Massachusetts: Fall River CC (R.6 A.3
1918).
New York: Apawamis C (R.); Hollow
Brook G&CC (R.); Maplemoor CC
(R.); Siwanoy CC (R.); Sleepy Hollow
GC (R.); Sunset Hill GC (R. 1929);
Westchester CC (South Cse, R.).

THEODORE J. WIRTH
(1927–)

BORN: New Orleans, Louisianna.

Theodore Wirth attended St. Thomas
College, Kansas University and Iowa State
University, where he received a B.S. degree in landscape architecture in 1950. After working as a park planner with the
National Park Service for ten years, he
entered private practice as a landscape architect in Montana in the early 1960s.
Wirth served as president of the National
Council of Parks and Recreation Consultants and as vice president of the ASLA.
Branching into golf course design in the
late 1960s, he had planned several courses
in the Montana area by the end of the
1970s.

Courses by Theodore Wirth:

Montana: Ennis GC (9); Laurel G&RC
(1968); Riverside GC; Valley View GC.
Wyoming: Powell Muni (9 1971).

W. DERRELL WITT

After obtaining a landscape architecture degree from LSU and a Master's in architecture from Houston University, Derrell Witt worked for a large engineering firm in Houston until he founded his own landscape design and land-planning business, Enviroplan, in 1983. His first golf design work was in association with Rick Forester, a former owner of Houston's Bear Creek Golf World who created Cypresswood GC. Forester then recommended Witt to Houston resident Bruce Devlin, who had dissolved his long-time partnership with Robert von Hagge and was handling some designs on his own. In 1990 Witt joined Forester in the newly formed Mahaffey-Forester Inc.

Courses by Derrell Witt:

South Carolina: Secession GC (1991), ass't Bruce Devlin.
Texas: Cypresswood GC (Creek Cse 1988; Cypress Cse 1988), ass't Rick Forester; First Colony GC (1990), ass't Carlton Gipson; Greatwood GC (1990), ass't Carlton Gipson; Old Orchard GC (27 1991), ass't Carlton Gipson.

Courses remodeled or expanded by Derrell Witt:

Texas: Brae Burn CC (R. 1990); Pirates GC (R. 1990), ass't Carlton Gipson; TPC at The Woodlands (R. 1986), ass't Carlton Gipson.

GORDON C. WITTEVEEN

A graduate of Ontario (Canada) Agricultural College in Guelph, Gordon Witteveen was course superintendent at Northwood CC in Toronto and Board of Trade CC in Woodbridge, Ontario. He also served as national president of the CGCSA. While at Board of Trade, he altered some holes and designed an additional nine-hole precision course for the club. Working alone and sometimes with well-known Toronto landscape architect Alexander Budrevics, Witteveen designed and remodeled several other Ontario courses in the 1970s and 1980s.

Courses by Gordon Witteveen:

Ontario: Board of Trade CC (South Cse [9 Precision] 1981); Loch March GC (1987); Lyndway GC (9 1991); Mona

Hills (9 1990); Nottawasaga Inn GC (1986); Sawmill GC (1977); Warkworth GC (9 1969, A.9 1977).

Courses remodeled or expanded by Gordon Witteveen:

Ontario: Bay of Quinte GC (R.3); Board of Trade CC (East Cse, R.4).

Skip Wogan, circa 1950 COURTESY PHIL WOGAN

EUGENE F. WOGAN
(1890–1957)

BORN: Roxbury, Massachusetts.
DIED: Manchester, Massachusetts, at age 67.

"Skip" Wogan attended public schools in Watertown, Massachusetts, and after graduation went to work as assistant professional under Donald Ross at Essex Country Club in Manchester.

Upon Ross's resignation from Essex in 1913, Wogan succeeded him and remained as its head professional and grounds manager until his death. He helped found the New England Professional Golfers Organization, which later became the New England Chapter of the PGA of America, and served as chapter president in 1926–27 and again in 1940–41. His contributions as an administrator to the NEPGA were honored in 1954, when the chapter established the Eugene Wogan Trophy, an annual award presented to a section member with the year's best tournament record.

While at Essex, Skip Wogan also conducted a design practice on the side, planning a number of courses in Massachusetts and other Eastern states. Wogan's son Philip became a course architect and two other sons, Louis and Richard, became contractors specializing in golf construction.

Courses by Skip Wogan:

Maine: Mingo Springs GC (9 1925); Webhannett GC (9 1913, A.9 1925); Willowdale GC (9 1924).

Massachusetts: Arlmont CC (9); Bellevue CC (9); Blue Hill CC (9 1950, A.9 1955, with Phil Wogan; Bristol County CC (9); Cape Ann GC (9); Herring Run CC (9); Labour-in-Vain GC (9, NLE); Merrimack GC; Rockland CC (Par 3 1955), with Phil Wogan; Walpole CC (9, NLE).
New Jersey: Picatinny Arsenal GC.

Courses remodeled or expanded by Skip Wogan:

Massachusetts: Bear Hill GC (R.); Beverly G&TC (R.); Essex CC (R.); Sankaty Head GC (R. 1925); Tedesco CC (R.).

PHILIP A. WOGAN
(1918–   ), ASGCA

BORN: Beverly, Massachusetts.

Philip Wogan attended North Carolina State, Penn State, Lehigh University and Boston University, where he received a Bachelor's degree in biology and a Master's degree in education. From 1947 to 1956 he taught biology on the high school level and during the same years assisted his father, Skip Wogan, in golf course design on a part-time basis.

In 1956 Wogan retired from teaching to devote full time to golf architecture. After his father's death in 1957, he continued the practice on his own. Employing his joint background in biology and course design, he became a leading authority on the relationship of golf courses to the environment and prepared the ASGCA's widely distributed paper on the subject.

Courses by Phil Wogan:

Maine: Bar Harbor GC (1968); Bucksport G&CC (9 1969); Martindale CC (9 1963); Natanis GC (1990); Val Halla CC (9 1965, A.9 1986).
Massachusetts: CC of Billerica (9 1971, A.9 1991); CC of Halifax (1969); [The] Georgetown C (1992); Juniper

Phil Wogan, 1990 COURTESY ASGCA

Hills GC (New Cse 1991); Maplegate CC (1991); New Meadows GC (9 1963); Oxford CC (9); Pembroke CC (1973); Pine Hill Estates GC (9 Par 3); Quail Hollow GC (9 1991); Rockland CC (Par 3 1955), with Skip Wogan; Rowley CC (9 1970).

New Hampshire: Charmingfare Links (1964); East Kingston GC (9); Hoodkroft CC (9 1971); Lochmere G&CC (9 1992).

Rhode Island: Lindbrook CC (Par 3 1968; R. 1986); Pond View GC (9); Spring Haven GC (9 Par 3).

Courses remodeled or expanded by Phil Wogan:

Massachusetts: Blue Hill CC (A.9 1955), with Skip Wogan; Essex CC (R.); Franklin CC (A.10 1974); Juniper Hills GC (R.4 1972); Myopia Hunt C (R.1 1981); Putterham Meadows Muni (R.2 1962); Rockport GC (R.2); William F. Devine GC (R.18 1989).

New Hampshire: Cochecho CC (A.9 1965); Farnum Hill CC (A.9 1991); John H. Cain GC (R.7 A.11 1991); Manchester CC (R.4 1985); North Conway CC (A.9 1974); Rochester CC (A.9 1964).

New York: Onondaga G&CC (R.2 1982), with Samuel Mitchell.

MICHAEL STEPHEN WOLVERIDGE (1937–)

BORN: Essex, England.

After playing for a time on the PGA Tour in the United States, Michael Wolveridge joined the golf design firm of British architect John Harris in the late 1960s. Beginning in 1970, Wolveridge worked closely with Harris's design partner, professional golfer Peter Thomson, on projects in Japan, New Zealand and elsewhere in the Pacific Rim. Wolveridge continued to work as a primary design associate after the firm expanded in 1974 to include American Ronald Fream.

After Harris's death in 1977 the company reorganized and Wolveridge was made a full partner with Thomson and Fream. Thomson, Wolveridge, Fream and Associates worked on an international scale in course design and construction, with Thomson and Wolveridge teaming in Australia, Japan and New Zealand and Fream handling projects in the United States and Europe. Fream left after a few years, but Wolveridge and Thomson continued to work as a team. By the late 1980s they were as active as any firm down under.

Courses by Michael Wolveridge (All with Peter Thomson unless otherwise indicated):

California: Bixby GC (9 Precision 1980), and Ronald Fream.

Washington: Canyon Lakes G&CC (1981), and Ronald Fream; Indian Summer GC (1991); Kayak Point GC (1974), and Ronald Fream; Tapps Island GC (9 1981), and Ronald Fream.

Australia: Alice Springs GC (1987); Collier Park GC (1984); Darwin GC (1983); Desert Springs CC (1984); Fairway Park GC (1984); Gold Coast CC (1984); Hall's Head Resort GC (1984); Iwasaki Resort GC (1984); Lake Ross GC (1984); Midlands GC (1975); North Lakes CC; Tasmanian Casino C (1982); Thurgoona GC (27 1983); Tura Beach CC (1982).

England: Southwood GC (9 1977), ass't John Harris; Telford Hotel G&CC (1979), ass't John Harris and Peter Thomson; Washington GC (1969), ass't John Harris.

Fiji: Fijian Hotel GC (9 Precision 1973), and Ronald Fream.

Hong Kong: Royal Hong Kong GC (Eden Cse 1968), ass't John Harris and Peter Thomson.

India: Bangalore GC (1982); Gulmarg GC (1973); Karnataka GC (1984).

Indonesia: Bali Handara CC (1975), ass't John Harris, Peter Thomson and Ronald Fream; Jagorawi G&CC (1978), and Ronald Fream; National GC, and Ronald Fream.

Japan: Chigusa CC (27 1973), ass't John Harris and Peter Thomson; Fujioko CC (1971), ass't Peter Thomson and *Tameshi Yamada;* Hammamatsu CC; Ibusuki CC (New Cse 1978); Korakuen CC (27 1974), ass't John Harris, Peter Thomson and Ronald Fream; Naie GC (1976); Nambu Fuji GC (1974), ass't John Harris and Peter Thomson; Takaha Royal CC (1976); Three Lakes CC (1976); Tokuyama CC (1975), ass't John Harris and Peter Thomson; Yoro CC (1977); Zen C (1977).

Mauritius: Case Noyale GC (1972), ass't John Harris and Peter Thomson.

New Zealand: Harewood GC (1967), ass't John Harris and Peter Thomson; Karori GC (1968), ass't John Harris and Peter Thomson; Maramarua GC (1969), ass't John Harris and Peter Thomson; Taieri G (1967), ass't John Harris and Peter Thomson; Wairakei International GC (1975), ass't John Harris and Peter Thomson.

Portugal: Estoril Sol GC (9 Precision 1976), ass't John Harris, Peter Thomson and Ronald Fream.

Scotland: Douglaston GC (1977), ass't John Harris; Inverness GC (1968), ass't John Harris and Peter Thomson.

Singapore: Sentosa Island GC (Serapong Cse 1983), and Ronald Fream.

St. Kitts: Royal St. Kitts GC (1977), ass't John Harris, Peter Thomson and Ronald Fream.

Tonga: Tonga GC.

Trinidad and Tobago: Balandra Beach GC (1982), and Ronald Fream; St. Andrews GC (1975), ass't John Harris, Peter Thomson and Ronald Fream.

Tunisia: El Kantaoui GC (1977), ass't John Harris, Peter Thomson and Ronald Fream.

Courses remodeled or expanded by Michael Wolveridge (All with Peter Thomson unless otherwise indicated):

California: Almaden G&CC (R. 1979), and Ronald Fream; Hacienda CC (R. 1978), and Ronald Fream; Marine Memorial GC (R. 1980), and Ronald Fream; Mirimar Memorial GC (R. 1981), and Ronald Fream; San Juan Hills GC (R. 1981), and Ronald Fream.

Nevada: Edgewood Tahoe C (R. 1980), and Ronald Fream.

Oregon: Sunriver CC (South Cse, R. 1978), and Ronald Fream.

Washington: Cedarcrest GC (R. 1982), and Ronald Fream; Manito G&CC (R. 1979), and Ronald Fream; Seattle GC (R.2 1981), and Ronald Fream; West Seattle GC (R. 1979), and Ronald Fream.

Alberta: Glendale CC (R.3 1981), and Ronald Fream.

Australia: Cottlesloe GC (R.); Kingston Heath GC (R.); Kooyonga GC (R.); Lake Karrinyup CC (R. A.3rd 9 1977); Metropolitan GC (R.); Middlemore GC (R.); New South Wales GC (R.); Peninsula G&CC (R.); Royal Adelaide GC (R.); Royal Canberra GC (R.); Royal Perth GC (R.); Royal Sydney GC (R.); Sorrento GC (R.); Southern GC (R.

A.9 1978); Victoria GC (R. 1983); Yarrawonga GC (A.9 1980).

Hong Kong: Royal Hong Kong GC (New Cse, R. 1970; Old Cse, R. 1976), ass't John Harris and Peter Thomson.

India: Bombay Presidency GC (R. 1980); Delhi GC (R. A.9 1974), ass't John Harris and Peter Thomson; Royal Calcutta GC (R. 1969), ass't John Harris and Peter Thomson.

Indonesia: Kebayoran GC (R. 1980), and Ronald Fream; Yani GC (R.).

Malaysia: Awana GC, Genting Highlands GC (R. 1984), and Ronald Fream.

New Zealand: Akarana GC (R. 1972), ass't John Harris and Peter Thomson; Ashburton GC (R. 1977); Auckland GC (R.); Hastings GC (R. 1972), ass't John Harris and Peter Thomson; Miramar GC (R. 1977); Nelson GC (R. 1967), ass't John Harris and Peter Thomson; North Shore GC (R. 1969), ass't John Harris and Peter Thomson; Rarotonga GC (A.9. 1984); Russley GC (R. 1967), ass't John Harris and Peter Thomson; Timaru GC (R. 1968), ass't John Harris and Peter Thomson.

Spain: Real Sociedad Hipica Espanola (R.), ass't John Harris.

Norman Woods, 1966 COLLECTION RON WHITTEN

NORMAN H. WOODS
(1908–1987)

Norman Woods attended the Ontario Agricultural College at Guelph in the early 1930s and later became associated with golf architect Stanley Thompson. He worked on over fifty projects for the legendary designer over a period of fifteen years.

After Thompson's death in 1952 Woods began his own practice in British Columbia and worked on an estimated 200 designs and remodelings during the next twenty-five years.

Courses by Norman H. Woods:

Montana: Hilands GC (9 1950), with Gregor MacMillan; Marias Valley G&CC (1971); Signal Point CC (9).
Pennsylvania: Lords Valley CC (1963).
Washington: Capital City GC; Nile CC.
Alberta: Broadmoor CC; Glendale GC; Henderson Lake GC; Indian Hills GC; Stoney Plain GC; Willow Park CC.
British Columbia: Harrison GC (9 1961); Hirsch Creek CC; Kokanee Springs CC (1968); Lake Point Course (9); Mission GC; Pine Hills G&CC (9 Precision); Tsawwassen G&CC (1966), with *Jack Reimer.*
Manitoba: Falcon Beach Lake CC; Grand Beach GC; Rossmere G&CC; St. Charles CC (West Nine 1954).

Courses remodeled or expanded by Norman H. Woods:

Washington: Lake Wilderness CC (A.9).
British Columbia: Gorge Vale GC; Kimberly GC (A.9 1980); Penticton G&CC (A.9); Revelstoke GC (R. A.9 1976); Shaughnessy G&CC (R. 1969); Shuswap Lake Estates G&CC (R. 1977).
Manitoba: Birds Hill GC (R.).

CHARLES CAMPBELL WORTHINGTON
(1854–1944)

C. C. Worthington was famed as a pump manufacturer and later as a developer of mowing and other types of golf course maintenance equipment. Around 1900 he laid out several rudimentary courses on estates in the Eastern United States. These included a six-hole course on his own estate at Irvington-on-Hudson, New York, Manwallimink at Shawnee-on-Delaware, Pennsylvania (built in 1898 on one of his properties that was reportedly the largest private estate east of the Mississippi at the time) and the nine-hole Calendo Golf Club in Pennsylvania.

Worthington started A. W. Tillinghast on his road to fame as a course architect when he hired him to design a course at Shawnee-on-Delaware in 1907. This was Tillinghast's first project. Worthington was also the grandfather of several men whose careers in the development and

production of maintenance equipment were significant in the business world of golf. They included Edmund Ross Sawtelle, Chester Sawtelle, Charles Sawtelle and Edward Worthington, Jr.

GEORGE WRIGHT
(1847–1937)

BORN: Yonkers, New York.
DIED: Boston, Massachusetts, at age 90.

The founder of Wright and Ditson Sporting Goods in Boston, Massachusetts, George Wright laid out several informal courses in the 1890s in parks and vacant lots in the Boston area. Among these were a course at Franklin Park (later renamed William F. Devine Golf Course), the original Allston Golf Club and an early version of Wollaston Golf Club. Wright built them in an attempt to popularize the then recently imported game of golf and thus increase the sales of playing equipment imported from Great Britain. His promotional efforts led local sportswriters to later declare Wright the "Father of Golf in New England."

Rodney Wright, 1991 COURTESY RODNEY WRIGHT

RODNEY WRIGHT
(1951–), ASGCA

BORN: Atlanta, Georgia.

Rodney Wright, after obtaining a bachelor's degree in landscape architecture from the University of Georgia in 1974, started in golf course architecture with the firm of Ron Kirby and Denis Griffiths in Atlanta. He spent the next dozen years working on a variety of golf projects throughout the United States, Europe, Asia and Africa.

After advancing to the level of senior designer for Kirby, Griffiths, Wright left the company in 1987 and moved to Honolulu, where he joined the land-planning firm of Belt, Collins and Associates. There he met fellow in-house designer Robin Nelson and the two formed Nelson and Wright, Golf Course Architects, a division of Belt, Collins, and handled golf projects around the Pacific Rim as well as in Europe.

Courses by Rodney Wright (All with Robin Nelson unless otherwise indicated):

Hawaii: Ewa Beach International CC (1992); Waikapu Sandalwood G Cse (1992); West Loch Muni (1990).
Australia: Caves Beach GC (Cliffs Cse 1991; Lakeside Cse 1991).
France: Champs de Bataille GC (1990); Montgriffon GC (Coulonges Cse 1992; Luzarches Cse 1992).
Guam: Guam First Green GC (1993); Mangilao GC (1992); Togcha Beach GC (1992).
Indonesia: Bali G&RC (1991).
Japan: Busena Resort GC (1992).
Thailand: Friendship Meadows CC (1992); Royal Hills GC (1993).

Courses remodeled or expanded by Robin Nelson (All with Rodney Wright unless otherwise indicated):

California: San Geronimo Valley GC (R. 1991).
Hawaii: Frances I'l Brown GC, Mauna Lani Resort (North Cse, A.9 1991; South Cse, A.9 1991); Hickam AFB GC (R. 1987); Kapalua GC (Bay Cse, R. 1986; Village Cse, R. 1987), and Hale Irwin; Mauna Kea GC (R.); Mid-Pacific CC (R.); Oahu CC (R. 1986); Sheraton Makaha Resort & CC (R. 1987).
France: Chantilly GC (Old Cse, R.); Lann-Rohou GC (A.9 1989).
Malaysia: Kelab Golf di Raja Trengganu (R.9 1986).
Okinawa: Naha CC (R. 1990).
Singapore: Sentosa Island GC (Serapong Cse, R.)

PATRICK H. WYSS
(1949–   )

BORN: Columbus, Ohio.

An Ohio State University graduate in landscape architecture, Pat Wyss worked for Gunderson Golf Course Construction

Pat Wyss, 1991
COURTESY PAT WYSS

Company for over a decade, constructing such courses as the South Course at The Broadmoor, the CC of Muirfield Village and a remodeling of Cherry Hills CC for the 1978 U.S. Open. In 1981 Wyss formed a landscape architecture and course-design business in Rapid City, South Dakota. His firm included Sandra Doran as an assistant golf course architect.

Courses by Pat Wyss:

Iowa: Shoreline G Cse (1990).
Nebraska: Brentwood Falls G Cse (9 Precision 1992); Legend Buttes G Cse (9 1991).
South Dakota: Ellsworth AFB GC (9 1990); Hart Ranch GC (9 1986); La-Croix Links (9 Par 3 1987); Rapid City Executive G Cse (9 Precision 1985); Yankton Muni (1992).
Wyoming: Hay Creek Centennial G Cse (1992).

Courses remodeled or expanded by Pat Wyss:

Colorado: Lowry AFB GC (R. 1989).
South Dakota: Hillsview G Cse (R. 1989).

ARTHUR M. YOUNG
(1917–   )

BORN: Kalamazoo, Michigan.

Arthur Young attended Northwestern University and was employed as a CPA with Swift & Co. in Chicago. He served in the U.S. Army during World War II and the Korean War and then resigned his accounting position to build his first golf course in Shelbyville, Michigan, in the early 1950s. After operating that course for several years as a member of the PGA of America, Young designed and built

other small-town courses in Michigan.

Young moved to Florida in the late 1960s and designed and built several precision courses, which he owned and operated. In the 1970s he retired to operate Crane Creek, a course he helped Charles Ankrom design.

Courses by Arthur Young:

Florida: Holiday CC, Lake Park (Precision 1969); Indian Pines GC (Precision 1971); Martin Downs CC (Crane Creek Cse 1976), with Chuck Ankrom; Pine Lakes GC, Stuart (Precision 1971).
Michigan: Orchard Hills GC (1955, A.9 1960); Whiffletree Hill GC (1970).

Courses remodeled or expanded by Arthur Young:

Michigan: Duck Lake GC (A.9).

Michael Young, 1991 COURTESY MICHAEL YOUNG

MICHAEL YOUNG
(1952–   )

The golf design bug bit Mike Young when he was still in high school. While attending Georgia State University on a golf scholarship, Young worked on course-construction crews. He also managed to tour some of the great courses of Scotland. Upon graduation in 1973 with a degree in chemistry, Young began working as a sales representative for the Toro Corporation, a major golf course machinery producer. He later handled similar services for the John Deere Corporation. In 1987 he gave up his sales business and entered golf architecture full-time, establishing Mike Young Designs, based in Watkinsville, Georgia.

Courses by Mike Young:

Georgia: Countryland G Cse (1991); [The] Fields GC (1990); Lane Creek G Cse (1992).

Courses remodeled or expanded by Mike Young:

Georgia: Hunter Pope G Cse (A.9 1989); Marietta GC [FKA Marietta CC] (R. 1991).

Al Zikorus, 1990
COURTESY ASGCA

ALBERT ZIKORUS
(1921–), ASGCA

BORN: Needham, Massachusetts.

After caddying at Needham and Wellesley country clubs, Al Zikorus attended the Winter School for turfgrass managers at the University of Massachusetts and then served overseas in the U.S. Army Air Force. After the war he worked as superintendent at Ould Newbury and Wellesley in Massachusetts and finally Woodbridge Country Club in Connecticut.

In the early 1950s Zikorus worked for course designer William F. Mitchell for a short time and then with golf architect Orrin Smith. When Smith retired in 1955 Zikorus took over the practice and ultimately planned many courses on his own. Several of his early designs were built by his brothers Walter and Edward, who operated a course-construction company.

Courses by Al Zikorus:

Connecticut: Deercrest CC (1957), ass't Orrin Smith; Elmcrest CC (1964); Glastonbury Hills CC (1965); Great Hills CC (9 1960); Harry Greens GC (9 Par 3 1965); Heritage Village CC (1966); Highland Greens GC (9 Par 3 1961); Hillandale CC (1960); Portland GC West (1991); Riverview CC (1961); Stonington CC (9 1991); Stony Brook CC (9 1964); Tashua Knolls G&RC (1971); Timberlin GC (1971); Tunxis Plantation CC (Cse No. 1 1961; Cse No. 2, 9 1961, A.9 1989); Wallingford CC (6 1961); Washington CC (9 1964); Woodhaven CC (1968).

Maryland: [The] Chesapeake C (9 1991).
Massachusetts: Billerica GC (9 Par 3 1952), ass't William F. Mitchell; Hampden CC (1964); Ludlow Muni (9), ass't Orrin Smith; Twin Hills CC; Walpole CC (1973); Wyckoff Park GC (1966).
New Hampshire: Pease AFB GC (1960).
New Jersey: Lakeshore CC (1965).
New York: Bel Aire CC (1963); Canyon C (1963); Cedar Brook CC (1960); Lakeover CC (1967); Plattsburg AFB GC (1960); Segalla CC (1992).
South Carolina: Green River CC (9 1966).

Courses remodeled or expanded by Al Zikorus:

Connecticut: Alling Memorial GC (R. 1972); Banner Lodge GC (A.9 1965); Crestbrook CC (A.9 1980); East Hartford GC (A.9 1956), ass't Orrin Smith; Greenwoods CC (R.1 1961); Hartford GC (R. 1989); Highfield CC (R. 1964); High Ridge CC (R.2 1951), ass't William F. Mitchell; Hunter Memorial GC (R. 1987); Minnechaug GC (R.9 1951), ass't William F. Mitchell; New Haven CC (R.1 1957); Pautipaug CC (R. 1989); Pine Orchards CC (A.4 1961); Racebrook CC (R.2 1957); Redding CC (R. 1989); Rockledge CC (R.9 1954, ass't Orrin Smith; R. 1989); Rockrimmon CC (A.9 1953), ass't Orrin Smith; Stanley GC (A.9 1958), ass't Orrin Smith; Tumble Brook GC (R. 1989); Wepaug CC (R.13 1961); Woodway CC (R.1 1961).
Florida: Pelican Bay CC (North Cse, R. 1988).
Massachusetts: Cohasset GC (R.9 1971); Colonial GC (R.5 1954), ass't William F. Mitchell; Framingham CC (A.5 1954), ass't Orrin Smith; Quincy CC (R.), ass't Orrin Smith; Red Hill CC (A.9 1951), ass't William F. Mitchell; Winthrop GC (R. 1950), ass't William F. Mitchell.
New York: Lake Success GC (R.9 A.9 1958), ass't Orrin Smith; Orange County CC (R.3 1961); Somers CC (R.9 A.9 1961).
Rhode Island: Kirkbrae CC (R.1 1988).
Virginia: Langley AFB GC (A.9 1969).

BENJAMIN W. ZINK

A charter member of the GCSAA, Ben Zink served as superintendent at Acacia

Country Club and later at Kirtland Country Club, both in Ohio. In the 1950s and 1960s, his design firm, Ben W. Zink and Son, planned a number of courses in Ohio and Florida.

Courses by Ben Zink:

Florida: Palm River CC (1960).
Ohio: Aqua Marine Swim C (Par 3); Erie Shores GC (1958); Hemlock Springs GC; Pebble Brook CC; Shawnee Hills GC (9 1957); Shelby CC; Tomahawk CC (1963).

Courses remodeled or expanded by Ben Zink:

Ohio: Lander Haven CC (A.9 1955).

Herwig Zisser, 1991
COURTESY HERWIG ZISSER

HERWIG ZISSER

Trained as a civil engineer, German Herwig Zisser began designing golf courses in the mid-1980s, handling everything from indoor driving ranges to private 18-hole regulation layouts. The bulk of his early work occurred in Austria.

Courses by Herwig Zisser:

Austria: Castle of Ebreichsdorf GC (1987); Frauenthal GC (9 1988); Thal GC (9 1990; 9 Par 3 1990).
Hungary: International G Centre (1992).

Courses remodeled or expanded by Herwig Zisser:

Austria: Innsbruck GC (Lans-Sperberegg Cse, R. 1987; Rinn Cse, R. 1987); Wels GC (R.9 A.9 1990).

PART THREE

A Master List of Golf Courses Cross-Referenced to Designers

Generally, listings are alphabetized according to the course name without regard to appellations such as COUNTRY CLUB, GOLF COURSE, etc. Thus, all courses named ADDINGTON appear before courses named ADDINGTON COURT.

When there is more than one course of the same name, we take into consideration their appellations and list them in the following order: COUNTRY CLUB first, then GOLF AND COUNTRY CLUB, then GOLF CLUB and finally GOLF COURSE.

When there is more than one course with the same name and appellation (e.g., ALPINE CC), we list them in the following geographical order: alphabetically by American state, alphabetically by Canadian province and, finally, alphabetically by foreign country.

Punctuation, capitalization or spaces do not affect the alphabetical order in which the name appears. For example, BELLE ISLE and BELLEISLE appear next to one another on the listing, alphabetized only in accordance with the above rules.

Whenever possible, we've attempted to list credits within a listing in chronological order. But to best determine the various order in which architects added or remodeled holes to an individual course, we suggest you also consult the lists following the profiles of the respective architects involved with a particular course.

In order to avoid confusion, we have listed only ARCHITECTS OF RECORD on this master list of courses. Associates of architects may have in many cases handled most or all of a particular design, but while those designs are included in the listing of that associate's profile, they are not included in this master list because often more than one associate claims credit for the design, one for the routing, another for the working drawings and yet another for the field supervision. The fact remains that all associates perform their work for and under the supervision of their employer, the ARCHITECT OF RECORD.

In cases where two or more architects worked in a formal partnership, all partners' names are listed. We have attempted where possible to list in first position the partner most responsible for that particular design.

If an architect's name appears in italics on the master list, that person is not profiled in Part Two. In such case, the year of the work is also listed.

Abbreviations are the same as explained in Part II.

With some 25,000 links and courses in existence around the world, there are many layouts yet to be identified and included in the master list. This compilation is an ongoing project. The authors welcome additions, deletions and corrections so that an even more accurate and complete listing can be prepared.

AACHENER GC
Aachener, Germany
H. S. Colt, C. H. Alison, S. F. Morrison

AALBORG GC
Denmark
(A.9) John Harris

ABBEYDALE GC
Yorkshire, England
Herbert Fowler

ABBEY HILL GC
Buckinghamshire, England
J. J. F. Pennick, C. D. Lawrie

ABBEY LEIX GC
Ireland
(R.) Eddie Hackett

ABBEY PARK GC
Redditch, England
D. M. A. Steel

ABBEY SPRINGS GC
Fontana, Wisconsin
Ken Killian, Dick Nugent

ABC GC
Japan
Takeshi Sato, Shoichi Suzuki

ABENAQUI CC
Rye Beach, New Hampshire
A. H. Fenn
(R.3) Manny Francis
(R.) Geoffrey S. Cornish, William G. Robinson

ABERCROMBIE CC
England
(R.) H. S. Colt

ABERCROMBIE CC
Nova Scotia
(A.9) Clinton E. Robinson

ABERDEEN G&CC
Boynton Beach, Florida
Desmond Muirhead

ABERDEEN PROVING GROUNDS GC
Aberdeen, Maryland
Edmund B. Ault

ABERDOUR GC
Aberdour, Scotland
(A.3) Fraser Middleton

ABERDOVEY GC
Aberdovey, Wales
(R.) H. S. Colt
(R.) James Braid
(R.) Herbert Fowler

ABERGELE AND PENSARE GC
Clwyd, Wales
F. G. Hawtree, Fred W. Hawtree

ABERYSTWYTH GC
Dyfed, Wales
Harry Vardon

ABIDJAN GC
Abidjan, Ivory Coast
Pier Mancinelli

ABIKO GC
Abiko, Japan
Rokuro Akaboshi, *Shiro Akaboshi*

ABILENE CC
Abilene, Kansas
(R.) *Dewitt "Maury" Bell*

ABILENE CC
Abilene, Texas
(R.1) Marvin Ferguson

ABINGDON CC
Abingdon, Illinois
Tom Bendelow

ABINGTON CC
Pennsylvania
Robert Strange

ABITIBI GC
Iroquois Falls, Ontario
Willie Park, Jr.

ABOYNE GC
Aberdeenshire, Scotland
(R.) Martin Hawtree

ABRIDGE GC
Abridge, England
Henry Cotton

ABUJA GC
Abuja, Nigeria
Kurt Rossknecht

ACACIA CC [NLE]
Harlem, Illinois
William B. Langford, Theodore J. Moreau
(R.) Robert Bruce Harris

ACACIA CC
South Euclid, Ohio
Donald Ross, Sandy Alves

ACADEMIE DE GOLF DU TREMBLAY
France
Robert Berthet

ACADIAN HILLS CC
Lafayette, Louisiana
Luca Barbato
(R.) Jay Riviere

ACAPULCO CC
Acapulco, Mexico
John Bredemus
(R. A.9) Percy Clifford

ACAPULCO PRINCESS CC
Acapulco, Mexico
Ted Robinson

A. C. READ GC (MAINSIDE CSE)
Pensacola, Florida
(R.) Bill Amick

A. C. READ (SEASIDE CSE)
Pensacola, Florida
Bill Amick

ACRES OF FUN GC
Greenfield, Indiana
NKA Riley Village GC

ACTON GC
Acton, England
Willie Park, Jr.

ADAM SPRINGS G&CC
Cobb, California
Jack Fleming

ADAMS PARK MUNI
Bartlesville, Oklahoma
Floyd Farley

A. D. DANA ESTATE GC
Stowe, Vermont
Howard Watson

ADDINGTON GC (NEW CSE)
Surrey, England
J. F. Abercromby

ADDINGTON GC (OLD CSE)
Surrey, England
J. F. Abercromby

ADDINGTON COURT GC (LOWER CSE)
Surrey, England
Fred G. Hawtree, J. H. Taylor

ADDINGTON COURT GC (UPPER CSE)
Surrey, England
Fred W. Hawtree

ADDINGTON PALACE GC
Surrey, England
F. G. Hawtree, J. H. Taylor

ADDISON PINNACLE GC
New York
Geoffrey S. Cornish, William G. Robinson

ADIOS CC
Deerfield Beach, Florida
Arnold Palmer, Ed Seay
ADIRONDACK G&CC
Peru, New York
Brian Silva, Geoffrey S. Cornish
ADIRONDACKS C [NLE]
Lake Placid, New York
Alister Mackenzie
ADLER CREEK GC
Medford, Oregon
Robert Muir Graves
ADMIRALS COVE GC (EAST CSE)
Jupiter, Florida
Robert von Hagge
ADMIRALS COVE GC (WEST CSE)
Jupiter, Florida
Robert von Hagge
ADOBE CREEK GC
Petaluma, California
Robert Trent Jones, Jr.
ADOLFO SIRO GC
Argentina
Mungo Park II
ADRIATIC GC
Cervia, Italy
Marco Croze
ADVENTURE INN GC [NLE]
Hilton Head Island, South
Carolina
George W. Cobb
AFANDOU GC
Rhodes, Greece
Donald Harradine
A-GA-MING GC
Elk Rapids, Michigan
Roy Wetmore
(A.9) *Leroy Phillips, Chick
Harbert*
AGATE BEACH GC
Newport, Oregon
Frank Stenzel
(R.9) Fred Federspiel
AGAWAM HUNT C
Providence, Rhode Island
Willie Park, Jr.
(R.) Donald Ross
(R.) Geoffrey S. Cornish
AGESTA GC
Sweden
(A.13) Jan Sederholm
AGUASABON GC
Terrace Bay, Ontario
Howard Watson
AHAUS G&CC
Ahaus, Germany
Karl F. Grohs, *Rainer
Preissmann*
A. H. BLANK GC
Des Moines, Iowa
Edward Lawrence Packard
(A.9) Edward Lawrence
Packard, Roger Packard
AHWATUKEE CC
Phoenix, Arizona
Fred Bolton
AHWATUKEE LAKES CC
Phoenix, Arizona
Gary Panks
AHWAZ GC
Ahwaz, Iran
Neil Coles, *Brian Huggett, Roger
Dyer*

AICHI CC
Nagoya, Japan
Seichi Inouye
AIRCO GC
Clearwater, Florida
Chic Adams
AIRDRIE GC
Lanarkshire, Scotland
James Braid
AIRPORT GC [NLE]
Oklahoma City, Oklahoma
Arthur Jackson
AIRPORT G CSE
Columbus, Ohio
Jack Kidwell
AIRPORT INN GC
Florida
(A.9) *William Bulmer*
AIX-LES-BAINS GC
Aix-les-Bains, France
V. Bernard
AIZUBANDAI CC
Japan
Seisui Chin
AJIGASAWA GC (A CSE)
Aomori, Japan
Arnold Palmer, Ed Seay
AJIGASAWA GC (B CSE)
Aomori, Japan
Arnold Palmer, Ed Seay
AJONCS D'OR GC
St. Quay Portrieux, France
G. Desheulles, J. Bourret
AKAGI KOKUSAI CC
Japan
Shigeru Ishii
AKAIGAWA CC
Hokkaido, Japan
Takeaki Kaneda
AKARANA GC
New Zealand
(R.) C. H. Redhead
(R.) Peter Thomson, Michael
Wolveridge
AKITA TAIHEIZAN CC
Akita, Japan
Katsumi Takizawa
AKKESHI GC
Japan
Hideo Takemura
ALABANG G&CC
Alabang, Philippines
Robert Trent Jones, Jr.
ALACANTE GC
Alacante, Spain
Robert Dean Putman
ALAMANCE CC
Burlington, North Carolina
Donald Ross
(R.) Willard Byrd
ALAMEDA MUNI (EARL FRY CSE)
Alameda, California
William P. Bell
ALAMEDA MUNI (JACK CLARK CSE)
Alameda, California
William F. Bell
(R.) Desmond Muirhead
(R.) Robert Muir Graves
AL AMIN TEMPLE CC
Little Rock, Arkansas
William B. Langford, Theodore
J. Moreau

ALAMO CC
San Antonio, Texas
NKA Oak Hills CC
ALAMOSA GC
Alamosa, Colorado
(A.9) Richard Phelps
ALAND GC
Finland
Jan Sederholm
ALANWOOD GC
Sarver, Pennsylvania
X. G. Hassenplug
ALAQUA GC
Longwood, Florida
Karl Litten, Gary Player
ALASKAN MOTOR INN GC
Kewaunee, Wisconsin
Ed Kabat
ALASSIO GC
Alassio, Italy
John Harris
ALA WAI GC
Waikiki, Hawaii
Donald MacKay
(R.) Bob Baldock
(R.) Robin Nelson, Rodney
Wright
ALBANY CC
Albany, Minnesota
(A.9) Willie Kidd, Sr.
ALBANY CC [NLE]
Albany, New York
Devereux Emmet
(R.) Willie Ogg
ALBANY CC
Voorheesville, New York
Robert Trent Jones
(R.2) Brian Silva, Geoffrey S.
Cornish
ALBARELLA GC
Rosolina, Italy
John Harris
ALBEMARLE CC
West Newton, Massachusetts
Wayne Styles
ALBERNI GC
Port Alberni, British Columbia
William G. Robinson
ALBERTVILLE G&CC
Albertville, Alabama
Leon Howard
ALBUQUERQUE CC
Albuquerque, New Mexico
John Van Kleek
(R.) Warren Cantrell
(R.) Leon Howard
ALBURG CC
Alburg, Vermont
Walter Barcomb, R. B. Ellison
ALCESTER GC
Alcester, North Dakota
Ralph Gobel
ALCOMA CC
Pennsylvania
Emil Loeffler, *John McGlynn*
(R.) Ferdinand Garbin
ALDEBURGH GC
Suffolk, England
Willie Fernie
(R.) Willie Park, Jr.
(R.) J. H. Taylor
ALDEN PINES GC
Pineland, Florida
Gordon G. Lewis

ALDERBROOK G&CC
Union, Washington
Ray L. Goss, *Glen Proctor*
ALDERNEY GC
Channel Islands
J. J. F. Pennink
ALDERWOOD CC [NLE]
Portland, Oregon
A. Vernon Macan
(R.) A. Vernon Macan
ALEXANDRIA G&CC
Alexandria, Mississippi
Tom Bendelow
ALEXANDRIA GC
Alexandria, Minnesota
Gerry Pirkl, *Donald G. Brauer*
ALFA RESORT TOMAMU GC
Hokkaido, Japan
Isao Aoki
ALFRED "TUP" HOLMES GC
Atlanta, Georgia
(R.) Garrett Gill, George B.
Williams
ALGONA CC
Algona, Iowa
Willie Dunn, Jr.
ALGONQUIN CC
Glendale, Missouri
Robert Foulis
(R.) Dick Nugent, Ken Killian
(R.) Geoffrey S. Cornish,
Brian Silva
ALGONQUIN HOTEL GC
St. Andrews, New Brunswick
Donald Ross
A. L. GUSTIN JR. MEMORIAL GC
Columbia, Missouri
Floyd Farley
ALHAMBRA G&CC
Orlando, Florida
Bill Amick
ALHAMBRA MUNI
Alhambra, California
William F. Bell
(R.9 A.9) Algie Pulley
ALICE CC
Alice, Texas
Ralph Plummer
ALICE SPRINGS GC
Northwest Territories, Australia
Peter Thomson, Michael
Wolveridge
ALINGSÅS GC
Alingsås, Sweden
Jan Sederholm
[THE] ALISAL GC
Solvang, California
William F. Bell
(R.) Jack Darray, Jr., Stephen
Halsey
[THE] ALISAL RANCH GC
Solvang, California
Jack Daray, Jr., Stephen Halsey
ALIWAL NORTH GC
Aliwal North, South Africa
John Watt
ALADDIN CC [NLE]
Columbus, Ohio
Donald Ross
ALADDIN HOTEL GC [NLE]
Las Vegas, Nevada
Bob Baldock

ALL-AMERICAN GC
Sharpes, Florida
Robert Trent Jones
ALLANDALE GC
Ontario
Stanley Thompson
ALLEGHENY CC
Sewickley, Pennsylvania
Tom Bendelow
(R. A.3) Herbert Fowler
(R.3) Donald Ross
(R.) Ed Seay
ALLEN CC
Louisiana
Vernon Meyer
ALLENDALE CC
New Bedford, Massachusetts
Geoffrey S. Cornish
ALLERTHORPE GC
Yorkshire, England
Howard Swan
ALLESTREE PARK GC
Derbyshire, England
J. S. F. Morrison
ALLIANCE CC
Alliance, Ohio
(R.) Ferdinand Garbin
ALLING MEMORIAL GC
New Haven, Connecticut
Robert D. Pryde
(R.) Al Zikorus
ALLOWACE GC
Japan
Kazumi Miura
ALLSTON CC [NLE]
Allston, Massachusetts
George Wright
ALL-VIEW GC
Columbia, Maryland
Edmund B. Ault
(R.) Desmond Muirhead
ALMADEN G&CC
San Jose, California
Jack Fleming
(R.) Peter Thomson, Michael
Wolveridge, Ronald Fream
(R.1) Robert Muir Graves
ALMANOR WEST GC
Lake Almanor West, California
Doug Pohlson
ALMERE GC
Netherlands
J. F. Dudok van Heel
ALMERIMAR GC
Almeria, Spain
Ron Kirby, Gary Player
ALNMOUTH GC
Northumberland, England
Mungo Park
(R.) P. M. Ross
(R.) J. S. F. Morrison
ALOHA GOLF
Spain
Javier Arana
ALONDRA PARK GC (CSE NO. 1)
Lawndale, California
William P. Bell, William H.
Johnson
(R.) Ted Robinson
ALONDRA PARK GC (CSE NO. 2)
Lawndale, California
Cecil B. Hollingsworth

ALPENA GC
Alpena, Michigan
Warner Bowen
ALPINE CC
Comstock Park, Michigan
Mark DeVries
ALPINE CC
Alpine, New Jersey
A. W. Tillinghast
(R.) William Gordon
ALPINE CC
Cranston, Rhode Island
Geoffrey S. Cornish
ALPINE CC
American Fork, Utah
William H. Neff
ALPINE BAY Y&CC
Alpine, Alabama
Robert Trent Jones
ALPINE LAKE RESORT GC
Terra Alta, West Virginia
(A.6) Ron Forse
ALPINE RESORT GC
Egg Harbor, Wisconsin
Francis H. "Fritz" Schaller
ALPINO DI STRESA GC
Italy
James Gannon
ALTADENA TOWN & CC
Altadena, California
William P. Bell
ALTA MESA CC
Mesa, Arizona
Dick Phelps
ALTA SIERRA CC
Grass Valley, California
Bob Baldock
ALTA VISTA CC
Placentia, California
Harry Rainville
(A.9) Harry Rainville, David
Rainville
ALTO LAKES G&CC
New Mexico
Milt Coggins
(A.9) Arthur Davis, Ron
Kirby, Gary Player
ALTON CC
Alton, Iowa
Joel Goldstrand
ALTON GC
Hampshire, England
Willie Park, Jr.
ALTON BEACH GC [NLE]
Miami, Florida
Willie Park, Jr.
ALTON JONES ESTATE GC
Albemarle, Virginia
James Root
ALTÖTTING-BURGHAUSEN GC
Bayern, Germany
Götz Mecklenburg
ALTUS GC
Oklahoma
Ralph Plummer
(A.9) Floyd Farley
ALVA G&CC
Alva, Oklahoma
Floyd Farley
ALVAMAR CC
Lawrence, Kansas
Bob Dunning
(A.9) *Melvin Anderson*
(R.1) Ken Kavanaugh

ALVAMAR GC
Lawrence, Kansas
Bob Dunning
ÄLVKARLEBY GC
Sweden
Jan Sederholm
ALWOODLEY GC
Leeds, England
Alister Mackenzie, H. S. Colt
ALYTH GC
Tayside, Scotland
Old Tom Morris
(R.) James Braid, John R.
Stutt
AMAGASE ONSEN CC
Japan
Hiromasa Shimamura
AMANA COLONIES G CSE
Amana, Iowa
William James Spear
AMARILLA G&CC
Tenerife
D. M. A. Steel
AMARILLO CC
Amarillo, Texas
William A. McConnell
(R.) Warren Cantrell
(R.) Jay Morrish
AMARILLO PUBLIC G CSE
Amarillo, Texas
Joseph S. Finger
AMBASSADOR HOTEL GC [NLE]
Los Angeles, California
Herbert Fowler
AMBERWOOD VILLAGE GC
Stittsville, Ontario
John Watson
AMBO CHESTERFIELD GC
Missouri
Walter F. Ambo
AMBRIDGE CC
Ambridge, Pennsylvania
Emil Loeffler, *John McGlynn*
AMELIA ISLAND PLANTATION GC
Fernadina Beach, Florida
Pete Dye
AMERICAN GOLFERS C
Fort Lauderdale, Florida
Robert Trent Jones
AMERICAN LEGION GC
Albany, Georgia
(R.) Hugh Moore
AMERICAN LEGION GC
Shenandoah, Iowa
Chic Adams
**AMERICANA LAKE GENEVA GC
(BRUTE CSE)**
Lake Geneva, Wisconsin
Robert Bruce Harris
**AMERICANA LAKE GENEVA GC
(BRIARPATCH CSE)**
Lake Geneva, Wisconsin
Pete Dye, Jack Nicklaus
AMERY GC
Amery, Wisconsin
(R.9 A.9) Don Herfort
AMES G&CC
Ames, Iowa
Don Sechrest
AMHERST CC
Amherst, New Hampshire
William F. Mitchell
(A.9) *Robert Currier*

AMHERST G&CC
Amherst, Nova Scotia
(R.) C. E. Robinson
AMHERST CC
Amherst, Massachusetts
Walter Hatch
AMHERST AUDUBON GC
Williamsville, New York
William Harries
AMITYVILLE CC
Amityville, New York
Tom Winton
AMMONOOSUC INN & GC
Lisbon, New Hampshire
NKA Lisbon Village CC
AMPFIELD PAR 3 CC
England
Henry Cotton
AM SACHSENWALD GC
Germany
Karl F. Grohs, *Rainer
Preissmann*
AMSTERDAM MUNI
Amsterdam, New York
Robert Trent Jones
AM WIENERBERG G CSE
Vienna, Austria
Gerold Hauser, *Günther Hauser*
ANACONDA CC
Anaconda, Montana
Gregor MacMillan
ANACONDA HILLS GC
Great Falls, Montana
William Howard Neff
ANAHEIM "DAD MILLER" GC
Anaheim, California
Bob Baldock
ANAHEIM HILLS GC
Anaheim, California
Richard Bigler
ANASAZI GC
Paradise Valley, Arizona
NKA Stonecreek GC
ANCALA CC
Scottsdale, Arizona
Perry Dye
ANCHORAGE G CSE
Anchorage, Alaska
William Newcomb
ANCIL HOFFMAN GC
Sacramento, California
William F. Bell
ANDERSON CC
Anderson, Indiana
(R.9 A.9) William H. Diddel
ANDERSON CC
Anderson, South Carolina
Tom Bendelow
ANDERSON GC
Fort Knox, Kentucky
Buck Blankenship, *Morgan
Boggs*
ANDERSON GC
Killeen, Texas
Perry Maxwell, Press Maxwell
ANDERSON AFB GC
Guam
Joe Lee
ANDERSON TUCKER OAKS GC
Anderson, California
William H. Tucker, Jr.
ANDORRA SPRINGS GC
Lafayette Hill, Pennsylvania
Horace W. Smith

ANDOVER CC
Andover, Massachusetts
W. H. "Pipe" Follett
ANDOVER G&CC
Lexington, Kentucky
Clyde Johnston
ANDREWS AFB GC (EAST CSE)
Camp Springs, Maryland
Frank Murray, Russell Roberts
ANDREWS AFB GC (WEST CSE)
Camp Springs, Maryland
Frank Murray, Russell Roberts
ANDREWS CC
Andrews, Texas
Warren Cantrell
ANDROSCOGGIN VALLEY CC
Gorham, New Hampshire
Alex Chisholm
   (A.9) *Horace Smith*
ANDROS ISLAND CC [NLE]
Bahamas
George W. Cobb
ÄNGELHOLM GC
Ängelholm, Sweden
Jan Sederholm
ANGEL PARK GC (MOUNTAIN CSE)
Las Vegas, Nevada
Arnold Palmer and Ed Seay
(routing); *Gary Vickers*
ANGEL PARK GC (PALM CSE)
Las Vegas, Nevada
Arnold Palmer and Ed Seay
(routing);
Gary Vickers
ANGEL PARK GC (PUTTING CSE)
Las Vegas, Nevada
Gary Panks
ANGLESEY GC
Wales
Fred W. Hawtree, Martin
Hawtree
ANGLO-AMERICAN CLUB
Lac L'Achign, Quebec
A. W. Tillinghast
ANGUS LEA GC
Hillsboro, New Hampshire
Ed Bedell
ANJOU G&CC
Angers, France
F. W. Hawtree, Martin Hawtree
ANKARA GC
Ankara, Turkey
George Wadsworth
ANKENY G&CC
Ankeny, Iowa
Leo Johnson
ANNANDALE GC
Jackson, Mississippi
Jack Nicklaus
ANNANDALE GC
Pasadena, California
   (R.) Walter Fovargue
   (R.) Norman Macbeth
   (R.4) *Jack Croke*
   (R.) Willie Watson
   (R.2 A.2) William P. Bell
   (R.) Robert Trent Jones
   (R.) David Rainville
ANNANHILL GC
Ayrshire, Scotland
Fraser Middleton
ANNAPOLIS ROADS GC
Annapolis, Maryland
Charles Banks

ANNECY GC
Annecy, France
Charles Blandford (1950)
ANNISTON CC
Anniston, Alabama
   (R.) Harold Williams
   (R.) Ed Seay
ANSLEY GC
Atlanta, Georgia
Ward Northrup
ANTELOPE HILLS GC (NORTH CSE)
Prescott, Arizona
Lawrence Hughes
ANTELOPE HILLS GC (SOUTH CSE)
Prescott, Arizona
Gary Panks
ANTELOPE VALLEY CC
Palmdale, California
William F. Bell
ANTIGO & BASS LAKE CC
Antigo, Wisconsin
Edward Lawrence Packard
ANTIOCH GC
Chicago, Illinois
   (R.) Mike Hurdzan
   (R.) Dave Esler
ANTLERS CC
New York
William H. Tucker
[THE] ANTLERS G CSE [NLE]
Raquette Lake, New York
Seymour Dunn
ANTLERS CC
Wheaton, Illinois
NKA Arrowhead GC
ANTONIO GC
Toronto, Ontario
Clinton E. Robinson
ANTRIM DELLS GC
Atwood, Michigan
Bruce Matthews, Jerry Matthews
ANTWERP GC
Antwerp, Belgium
Seymour Dunn
AOMORI ROYAL GC
Aomori, Japan
Mitsuaki Kobayashi
APACHE CC
Mesa, Arizona
NKA Arizona G Resort
APACHE WELLS CC
Mesa, Arizona
Arthur Jack Snyder
   (A.9) Milt Coggins
APAWAMIS C [NLE]
Rye, New York
   (A.9) William F. Davis
APAWAMIS C
Rye, New York
Willie Dunn, Jr., *Maturin Ballou*
   (R.) Tom Winton
   (R.) *Peter W. Lees*
   (A.9) Tom Bendelow
   (A.3) Donald Ross
   (R.) Alfred H. Tull
   (R.) George Fazio, Tom Fazio
APOLLO BEACH G & SEA C
Apollo Beach, Florida
Robert Trent Jones
APPANOOSE G&CC
Iowa
   (R.) Charles Calhoun

APPI KOGEN CC
Japan
Tsuyoshi Arai
APPLE CREEK G&CC
Bismarck, North Dakota
Robert Bruce Harris
   (R.) Don Herfort
APPLE ORCHARD CC
Bartlett, Illinois
   (R.) David Gill
APPLE RIDGE CC
Mahwah, New Jersey
Hal Purdy
APPLE TREE G CSE
Yakima, Washington
John Steidel
APPLE VALLEY CC
Apple Valley, California
William P. Bell, William F. Bell
   (A.9) William F. Bell
APPLE VALLEY CC
Bartlett, Illinois
Edward Lawrence Packard
APPLE VALLEY GC
Howard, Ohio
William Newcomb
APPLE VALLEY GC
Lake Lure, North Carolina
Dan Maples
APPLE VALLEY GC
Lewiston, Maine
Arthur David Chapman
APPLEWOOD GC
Golden, Colorado
Press Maxwell
   (R.) Garrett Gill, George B.
   Williams
APPLEWOOD G CSE
Omaha, Nebraska
Dave Bennett, Leon Howard
APRIL SOUND CC
Conroe, Texas
Carlton Gipson
APTOS SEASCAPE GC
Aptos, California
NKA Rio Del Mar GC
AQUA CALIENTE GC
Tijuana, Mexico
NKA Tijuana CC
AQUA MARINE SWIM C
Avon Lake, Ohio
Ben W. Zink
ARASHIYAMA GC
Nakijin, Okinawa
Kowashi Arai (1991)
ARBORETUM GC
Buffalo Grove, Illinois
Dick Nugent
ARBOR HILLS CC
Ann Arbor, Michigan
Arthur Ham
ARBUTUS RIDGE G&CC
Cobble Hill, British Columbia
William G. Robinson
   (A.9) William G. Robinson,
   John F. Robinson
ARCACHON GC
France
Charles Blandford
   (A.9) *P. Hirrigoyan*
ARCADIA GC
Arcadia, Florida
Ted Eller

ARCADIAN SHORES G&RC
Myrtle Beach, South Carolina
Rees Jones
ARCOLA CC
Paramus, New Jersey
Herbert H. Barker, *Harry Auch-
terlonie*
   (R.) Robert Trent Jones
ARCOT HALL GC
Northumberland, England
James Braid, John R. Stutt
ARDEE GC
Ardee, Ireland
   (R.9 A.9) Eddie Hackett
ARDEER GC
Ayrshire, Scotland
J. Hamilton Stutt
ARDSLEY CC
Ardsley-on-Hudson, New York
Willie Dunn, Jr.
   (A.9) William H. Tucker
   (R.) Stephen Kay
ARENZANO G&TC
Arenzano, Italy
Donald Harradine
ARGYLE CC
Chevy Chase, Maryland
William H. Tucker, Dr. Walter
S. Harban
   (R.) Edmund B. Ault, Al
   Jamison
ARIKIKAPAKAPA GC
New Zealand
Charles H. Redhead
ÄRILA GC
Navekvam, Sweden
Nils Sköld, Sund Linde
ARIMA ROYAL CC
Japan
Fukuichi Kato
ARIMA ROYAL GC
Hyogo, Japan
O. Ueda
ARISPIE LAKE CC
Princeton, Illinois
John Darrah
ARIZONA BILTMORE GC (ADOBE
CSE)
Phoenix, Arizona
William P. Bell
ARIZONA BILTMORE GC (LINKS CSE)
Phoenix, Arizona
William Johnston
   (R.1) Forrest Richardson,
   Arthur Jack Snyder
ARIZONA CC
Phoenix, Arizona
Ernest Suggs, Willie Wansa
   (R.) Gary Panks
   (R.4) Joseph S. Finger
   (R.) Johnny Bulla
   (R.) Tom Clark, Bill Love
ARIZONA CITY CC
Arizona City, Arizona
Arthur Jack Snyder
ARIZONA G RESORT
Mesa, Arizona
Arthur Jack Snyder
   (R.) Arthur Jack Snyder
ARKANSAS CITY CC
Arkansas City, Kansas
Perry Maxwell
   (A.9) *Dick Metz*

ARKLOW GC
County Wicklow, Ireland
F. G. Hawtree, J. H. Taylor
(A.9) Eddie Hackett

ARLINGTON GC [NLE]
Arlington Heights, Illinois
David Gill

ARLINGTON LAKES GC
Arlington Heights, Illinois
David Gill, Garrett Gill

ARLINGTON PARK GC
Arlington Heights, Illinois
David Gill

ARLMONT CC
Arlington, Massachusetts
Skip Wogan

ARMOUR FIELDS GC [NLE]
Kansas City, Missouri
Smiley Bell

ARMY GC
England
Colonel R. E. Bagot
(R.) C. K. Cotton, J. J. F.
Pennink

ARMY-NAVY CC (ARLINGTON CSE)
Arlington, Virginia
Major Richard D. Newman
(R.) Donald Ross
(R.5) Buddy Loving, Algie
Pulley
(R.3) Edmund B. Ault
(R.5) Edmund B. Ault, Tom
Clark, Bill Love

ARMY-NAVY CC (FAIRFAX CSE)
Fairfax, Virginia
Herbert Strong
(R.) George W. Cobb
(R.) Edmund B. Ault
(R.2) Buddy Loving, Algie
Pulley
(R.2) Edmund B. Ault, Brian
Ault, Bill Love

AROEIRA CLUB DE CAMPO
Aroeira, Portugal
J. J. F. Pennink

AROMA PARK GC
Kankakee, Illinois
William B. Langford

ARONIMINK GC [NLE]
Philadelphia, Pennsylvania
Alex Findlay

ARONIMINK GC
Newton Square, Pennsylvania
Donald Ross
(R.) Donald Ross
(R.) A. W. Tillinghast
(R.) Dick Wilson
(R.) George Fazio, Tom Fazio
(R.) Robert Trent Jones

AROOSTOOK VALLEY GC
Fort Fairfield, Maine
(R.9 A.9) Howard Watson

ARROWBROOK CC
Chesterfield, Indiana
John Darrah

ARROWBROOK CC
Bordentown, New Jersey
Hal Purdy

ARROWHEAD CC
Glendale, Arizona
Arnold Palmer, Ed Seay

ARROWHEAD CC
San Bernardino, California
Clark Glasson
(R.) Robert Muir Graves

ARROWHEAD CC
Fort Lauderdale, Florida
Bill Watts

ARROWHEAD CC
Jasper, Georgia
Arthur Davis

ARROWHEAD CC
Chillicothe, Illinois
William James Spear

ARROWHEAD GC
Tuscumbia, Alabama
(R.9 A.9) Arthur L. Davis

ARROWHEAD GC
Littleton, Colorado
Robert Trent Jones, Jr.

ARROWHEAD GC
Wheaton, Illinois
Stanley Pelchar
(A.3rd 9) David Gill

ARROWHEAD GC
Alexandria, Minnesota
Gerry Pirkl, *Donald G. Brauer*

ARROWHEAD GC
Mebane, North Carolina
Ed Riccoboni

ARROWHEAD GC
Molalla, Oregon
Kip Kappler

ARROWHEAD PARK GC
Minster, Indiana
Bob Simmons
(A.9) John F. Robinson

ARROWHEAD STATE PARK GC
Eufaula, Oklahoma
Floyd Farley
(R.9 A.9) Dave Bennett

ARROW WOOD CC
Roanoke, Virginia
Ellis Maples

ARROYO DEL OSO GC
Albuquerque, New Mexico
Arthur Jack Snyder
(A.3rd 9) Richard Phelps

ARROYO DUNES G CSE
Yuma, Arizona
Warner Brown

ARROYO SECO GC
Banning, California
William H. Johnson

ARTESIA CC
Artesia, New Mexico
Ralph Plummer

ARTHUR PACK GC
Tucson, Arizona
Dave Bennett, *Lee Trevino*

ARTHUR RAYMOND GC
Columbus, Ohio
Robert Trent Jones

ARTONDALE G&CC
Gig Harbor, Washington
NKA Gig Harbor G&CC

ARUBA GC
Aruba
(R.9) *C. H. Anderson*

ARVIDA GC
Arvida, Quebec
Stanley Thompson

ASAGIRI JAMBOREE GC
Japan
Masujiro Yamamoto

ASAHI CC
Asahi, Japan
Junji Shiba

ASBESTOS G&CC
Quebec
Howard Watson

ASBURY PARK GC
Neptune, New Jersey
NKA Shark River GC

ASCARTE PARK MUNI
El Paso, Texas
George Hoffman

ASCHAFFENBURG GC
Aschaffenburg, Germany
Reinhold Weishaupt

ASHBOURNE GC
Ashbourne, England
(R.) J. J. F. Pennink

ASHBROOK GC
Scotch Plains, New Jersey
Alfred H. Tull

ASHBURNHAM GC
Wales
Charles Gibson
(A.9) *William Tate*
(R.) F. G. Hawtree, J. H.
Taylor
(R. A.1) C. K. Cotton

ASHBURTON GC
Ashburton, New Zealand
(R.) Peter Thomson, Michael
Wolveridge

ASHEBORO CC
Asheboro, North Carolina
(A.9) Russell Breeden

ASHEVILLE CC
Asheville, North Carolina
Donald Ross

ASHEVILLE MUNI
Asheville, North Carolina
NKA Buncombe County G Cse

ASHFORD CASTLE GC
County Galway, Ireland
Eddie Hackett

ASHIYA CC
Hyogo, Japan
Y. Yasuda, Y. Sato

ASHLAND CC
Ashland, Nebraska
Henry B. Hughes, Richard
Watson
(A.9) Richard Watson

ASHLEY WOOD GC
Dorset, England
Tom Dunn
(R.9) J. Hamilton Stutt

ASHLUDIE GC
Angus, Scotland
Willie Park, Jr.

ASHOVER GC
Derbyshire, England
Tom Williamson

ASHRIDGE GC
Hertfordshire, England
Sir Guy Campbell, C. K.
Hutchison, S. V. Hotchkin
(R.) J. Hamilton Stutt
(R.) Tom Simpson

ASHTON & LEA GC
Preston, England
J. A. Steer

ASHTON-IN-MAKERFIELD GC
Ashton-in-Makerfield, England
(A.9) Fred W. Hawtree

ASIAGO GC
Asiago, Italy
A. Girardi

ASKERNISH GC
Western Isles, Scotland
Old Tom Morris

ASKERSUNDS GC
Ammeberg, Sweden
Ronald Fream

ASO GC (A CSE)
Kumamoto, Japan
Arnold Palmer, Ed Seay

ASO GC (B CSE)
Kumamoto, Japan
Arnold Palmer, Ed Seay

ASPEN GROVE GC
Winfield, British Columbia
V. Nortraten

ASPEN MUNI
Aspen, Colorado
Frank Hummel

ASPEN VALLEY GC
Flagstaff, Arizona
Jeff Hardin, Greg Nash
(R.9) Gary Panks

ASPETUCK VALLEY CC
Weston, Connecticut
Hal Purdy

ASPLEY GUISE & WOBURN SANDS GC
Buckinghamshire, England
Sandy Herd, *Charles Willmott*

ASSINIBOINE GC
Winnipeg, Manitoba
(R.) Stanley Thompson
(R.) C. E. Robinson

ASSOCIATION SPORTIVE DU G DE MÉRIBEL
Méribel, France
Michael G. Fenn

ASTORHURST CC
Bedford, Ohio
Harold Paddock

ASTORIA G&CC
Warrenton, Oregon
George Junor

ASUKA CC
Okayama, Japan
Shunsuke Kato

ASUNCIÓN CC
Asunción, Paraguay
Alberto Serra

ATACOCITA CC
Humble, Texas
Ralph Plummer

ATALAYA PARK HOTEL G&CC
Spain
Bernhard von Limburger

ATASCADERO CC [NLE]
California
John Duncan Dunn

ATHENS CC
Athens, Alabama
William Burton

ATHENS CC
Athens, Georgia
Donald Ross
(R.) Hugh Moore
(A.3rd 9) George W. Cobb,
John LaFoy

ATHENS CC
Athens, Ohio
Donald Ross

ATHLONE GC
Athlone, Ireland
(R.) C. K. Cotton

ATIMOONA G&CC
Tahiti
Willard Wilkinson

ATKINSON-STUART GC
Atkinson, Nebraska
Henry B. Hughes, Richard Watson

ATLANTA ATHLETIC C
Atlanta, Georgia
NKA East Lake CC

ATLANTA ATHLETIC C (HIGHLANDS CSE)
Duluth, Georgia
Robert Trent Jones
(A.9) Joseph S. Finger
(R.) George Fazio, Tom Fazio
(R.) Tom Fazio
(R.) Arnold Palmer, Ed Seay

ATLANTA ATHLETIC C (RIVERSIDE CSE)
Duluth, Georgia
Robert Trent Jones

ATLANTA CC
Marietta, Georgia
Willard Byrd, Joseph S. Finger
(R.) Jack Nicklaus

ATLANTA NATIONAL GC
Atlanta, Georgia
P. B. Dye, Pete Dye

ATLANTIC BEACH CC [NLE]
Florida
A. W. Tillinghast

ATLANTIC CITY CC [NLE]
Atlantic City, New Jersey
John Reid
(R. A.13) Willie Park, Jr.

ATLANTIC CITY CC
Northfield, New Jersey
William S. Flynn
(R.) Al Janis

ATLANTIC CITY ELECTRIC COMPANY GC
Somers Point, New Jersey
Hal Purdy

ATLANTIC GC
Southampton, New York
Rees Jones

ATLANTIC PINES CC [NLE]
New Jersey
James McMillan

ATLANTIDE GC
Ile Perrot, Quebec
Graham Cooke

ATLANTIS GC
Atlantis, Florida
William F. Mitchell
(A.3rd 9) Bob Simmons
(R.) Ted McAnlis

ATLANTIS GC
Tuckerton, New Jersey
NKA Ocean County G Cse

ATLANTIS INN & CC
Atlantis, Florida
Bob Simmons

ATLAS VALLEY GC
Flint, Michigan
Tom Bendelow

ATOKA GC
Atoka, Oklahoma
Floyd Farley

ATSUGISHI GC
Hokkaido, Japan
Hideo Takemura

ATTIGHOF GC
Brandoberndorf, Germany
Wolfgang Siegmann

ATVIDABERG GC
Sweden
Douglas Brazier

ATWOOD GC
Rockford, Illinois
Charles Maddox

AUBURN CC
Auburn, New York
Tom Bendelow

AUBURN CENTER GC
Auburn, Oregon
Wayne Larson, Sue Larson

AUBURN HILLS G CSE
Auburn, Alabama
Ward Northrup

AUBURN VALLEY G&CC
Auburn, California
Bob Baldock

AUCKLAND GC
Middlewood, New Zealand
F. G. Hood
(R.) C. H. Alison
(R.) Peter Thomson, Michael Wolveridge
(R.) C. H. Redhead

AUDUBON CC
Naples, Florida
Joe Lee

AUDUBON CC [NLE]
Louisville, Kentucky
Tom Bendelow

AUDUBON CC
Louisville, Kentucky
William B. Langford, Theodore J. Moreau

AUDUBON STATE PARK GC
Henderson, Kentucky
Edward Lawrence Packard

AUGLAIZE CC
Defiance, Ohio
William James Spear

AUGSBURG GC
Augsburg, Germany
Bernhard von Limburger
(R.) Donald Harradine, *Peter Harradine*

AUGUSTA CC
Augusta, Maine
Donald Ross
(A.9) Wayne Stiles, John Van Kleek
(R.) Orrin Smith

AUGUSTA CC
Augusta, Georgia
David Ogilvie
(R.) Donald Ross
(R.) Seth Raynor
(R.) Hugh Moore
(R.) Bob Cupp

AUGUSTA CC
Augusta, Kansas
Charles Bland

AUGUSTA CC
Staunton, Virginia
Fred Findlay

AUGUSTA GOLFERAMA [NLE]
Augusta, Georgia
Luther O. "Luke" Morris

AUGUSTA NATIONAL GC
Augusta, Georgia
Alister Mackenzie, Robert Tyre "Bobby" Jones, Jr.
(R.) Perry Maxwell
(R.3) Robert Trent Jones
(R.) George W. Cobb
(R.) George W. Cobb, John LaFoy
(R.) George Fazio
(R.1) Joseph S. Finger, Byron Nelson
(R.) Jay Morrish, Bob Cupp
(R.) Jack Nicklaus

AUGUSTA NATIONAL GC (PAR 3 CSE)
Augusta, Georgia
George W. Cobb
(R. A.2) Tom Fazio

AURORA CC
Aurora, Illinois
Tom Bendelow

AURORA CC
Louisiana
Tom Bendelow

AURORA CC
Aurora, Missouri
Horton Smith (9 1931)

AURORA CC
Aurora, Ohio
Bert Way

AURORA GC
Aurora, Ontario
Stanley Thompson

AURORA HIGHLANDS GC
Aurora, Ontario
René Muylaert, *Charles Muylaert*

AURORA HILLS GC
Aurora, Colorado
Henry B. Hughes

AUSABLE VALLEY G CSE
Ausable, New York
Seymour Dunn

AUSTIN CC
Austin, Minnesota
William H. Livie

AUSTIN CC [NLE]
Austin, Texas
(A.9) John Bredemus

AUSTIN CC
Austin, Texas
Pete Dye

AUSTRALIAN GC
Kensington, Australia
Alister Mackenzie
(R.) Sloan Morpeth
(R.) Jack Nicklaus

AUTOMOBILE C OF PEORIA [NLE]
Peoria, Illinois
Tom Bendelow

AVA G&CC
Ava, Missouri
Floyd Farley

AVALON GC
Bellingham, Washington
Robert Muir Graves

AVALON LAKES GC
Warren, Ohio
Pete Dye

AVIARA GC
Carlsbad, California
Arnold Palmer, Ed Seay

AVIATION CC
Detroit, Michigan
Herbert Strong

AVIATION Y&CC
Chaptico, Maryland
NKA Wicomico Shores GC

AVILA G&CC
Tampa, Florida
Ron Garl
(R.) Jack Nicklaus

AVON CC
Avon, Connecticut
Robert J. Ross
(R.18 A.9) Geoffrey S. Cornish, William G. Robinson

AVONDALE CC
Palm Desert, California
Jimmy Hines

AVONDALE GC
Avondale, New Zealand
(R.) C. H. Redhead

AVONDALE-ON-HAYDEN GC
Hayden Lake, Idaho
Mel "Curley" Hueston

AVON FIELDS GC
Cincinnati, Ohio
William B. Langford, Theodore J. Moreau
(R.) William H. Diddel

AVON OAKS CC
Avon, Ohio
Harold Paddock
(R.) Geoffrey S. Cornish, William G. Robinson

AWAJISHIMA CC
Japan
Sozaburo Uenishi

AWANA GC
Genting Highlands, Malaysia
(R.) Ronald Fream, Peter Thomson, Michael Wolveridge

AYDEN G&CC
Ayden, North Carolina
C. Stroud

AZALEA CITY GC
Mobile, Alabama
Robert Bruce Harris

AZALEA SANDS GC
North Myrtle Beach, South Carolina
Gene Hamm

AZUMA KOGEN GC
Fukushima Prefecture, Japan
Tadakado Shimoyama

AZUMINO CC
Japan
Makoto Murakami, Seiha Chin

AZUMINO TOYOSHINA GC
Nagano, Japan
Tsuneo Tanaka

AZUZA GREENS GC
Pomona, California
Bob Baldock

BABERTON GC
Edinburgh, Scotland
Willie Park, Sr.

BABE DIDRIKSON ZAHARIAS MUNI
Port Arthur, Texas
Leon Howard

BABE ZAHARIAS G CSE
Tampa, Florida
Ron Garl
BABSON PARK G&YC [NLE]
Babson Park, Florida
Seth Raynor
BACK ACRES CC
Senatobia, Mississippi
(R.9 A.9) John Darrah
BÄCKAVATTNETS GC
Sweden
Ake Persson
BACK O'BEYOND GC
Brewster, New York
Edward Ryder, *Val Carlson*
BACON PARK GC
Savannah, Georgia
Donald Ross
(R.9 A.3) J. Porter Gibson
(R. A.3rd 9) Ron Kirby, Denis
Griffiths
BAD DRIBURGER GC
Bad Driburger, Germany
Karl Hoffmann, Bernhard von
Limburger
BAD GASTEIN GC
Bad Gastein, Austria
Bernhard von Limburger
BAD GLEICHENBERG GC
Bad Gleichenberg, Austria
Gerold Hauser, *Günther Hauser*
BAD GRIESBACH G RESORT
Germany
Kurt Rossknecht
BAD KISSINGEN GC
Bad Kissingen, Germany
C. S. Butchart
BAD KLEIN KIRCHHEIM GC
Bad Klein Kirchheim, Austria
Donald Harradine
BAD NEUENAHR-AHRWEILER G&CC
Bad Neuenahr, Germany
Joan Dudok van Heel
BAD RAGAZ GC [NLE]
Bad Ragaz, Switzerland
(R.) Donald Harradine
BAD RAGAZ GC
Bad Ragaz, Switzerland
Fred W. Hawtree
BAD RAPPENAU GC
Germany
Karl F. Grohs, *Rainer
Preissmann*
BAD SALZGITTER GC
Bad Salzgitter, Germany
Wolfgang Siegmann
BAD TÜRKHEIM GC
Germany
Kurt Rossknecht
BAD TATZMANNSDORF GC
Austria
Kurt Rossknecht
BAD UBERKINGEN GC
Baden, Germany
Götz Mecklenburg
BAD WALDSEE GC
Germany
Bernhard von Limburger
BAD WÖRISHOFEN GC
Bad Wörishofen, Germany
Donald Harradine

BAEDERWOOD GC
Pennsylvania
John Reid
(R.) C. H. Alison, H. S. Colt
BAHAMAS CC
Nassau, Bahamas
Devereux Emmet
**BAHAMAS PRINCESS HOTEL & CC
(EMERALD CSE)**
Freeport, Bahamas
Dick Wilson, Joe Lee
**BAHAMAS PRINCESS HOTEL & CC
(RUBY CSE)**
Freeport, Bahamas
Joe Lee
BAHAMAS REEF CC
Bahamas
Byrecton Scott
BAHIA DE BANDERAS GC
Mexico
Percy Clifford
BAHNFYRE GC [NLE]
St. Louis, Missouri
Marvin Ferguson
BAHRAIN EQUESTRIAN & RACING C
Manama, Bahrain
Earl Stone
BAINBRIDGE CC
Bainbridge, Georgia
Les Hall
BAITING HOLLOW CC
Riverhead, New York
NKA Fox Hills G&CC
BAJA CC
Ensenada, Mexico
Enrique Valenzula
BAJAMAR GC
Baja, Mexico
Percy Clifford
BAKER GC
Baker, Oregon
George Junor
BAKER NATIONAL GC
Medina, Minnesota
Michael Hurdzan
BAKERSFIELD CC
Bakersfield, California
William F. Bell, William P. Bell
BALA GC
Philadelphia, Pennsylvania
Willie Dunn, Jr.
(R.) William H. Tucker
(R.9 A.9) William S. Flynn
BALANDRA BEACH GC
Trinidad and Tobago
Peter Thomson, Michael
Wolveridge, Ronald Fream
BALBIRNIE PARK GC
Scotland
Fraser Middleton
BALBOA GC
Hot Springs Village, Arkansas
Tom Clark, Edmund B. Ault
BALBOA PARK GC
San Diego, California
William P. Bell
(R.) Stephen Halsey, Jack
Daray, Jr.
BALBRIGGAN GC
Balbriggan, Ireland
(R.) Eddie Hackett
(A.9) *Bobby Browne*

BALD HEAD ISLAND CC
Bald Head Island, North
Carolina
George W. Cobb
BALD MOUNTAIN GC
Detroit, Michigan
Wilfrid Reid, William Connellan
BALD MOUNTAIN GC
Lake Lure, North Carolina
William B. Lewis
BALDOC CC
Erwin, Pennsylvania
Orrin Smith
BALD PEAK COLONY C
Moultonboro, New Hampshire
Donald Ross
BALDWIN HILLS GC [NLE]
Los Angeles, California
George C. Thomas, Jr., William
P. Bell
BALFOUR G&CC
Balfour, British Columbia
Les Furber, *Jim Eremko*
BALI G&RC
Nusa Dua, Bali, Indonesia
Robin Nelson, Rodney Wright
BALI HANDARA CC
Pancasari, Indonesia
John Harris, Peter Thomson,
Ronald Fream
BALI INTERNATIONAL GC
Bali, Indonesia
George Hadi
BALLAGHADERREEN GC
Ballaghaderreen, Ireland
Paddy Skerritt
**BALLEN ISLES CC OF JDM (EAST
CSE)**
Palm Beach Gardens, Florida
Dick Wilson, Joe Lee
**BALLEN ISLES CC OF JDM (NORTH
CSE)**
Palm Springs Gardens, Florida
Dick Wilson, Joe Lee
(A.9) Joe Lee
**BALLEN ISLES CC OF JDM (SOUTH
CSE)**
Palm Springs Gardens, Florida
Dick Wilson, Joe Lee
(A.9) Joe Lee
BALLINA GC
Ballina, Ireland
(R.) Eddie Hackett
BALLINASLOE GC
Ireland
(R.) Eddie Hackett
BALLINROBE GC
Ballinrobe, Ireland
(R.) Eddie Hackett
BALLOCHMYLE GC
Scotland
(A.9) Fraser Middleton
BALLSTON SPA & CC
Ballston Spa, New York
(R.9 A.9) Pete Craig
BALLWIN MUNI GC
Ballwin, Missouri
Homer Herpel
(R.) Bob Lohmann
BALLYBOFEY & STRANORLAR GC
Ireland
(A.9) Eddie Hackett

BALLYBUNION GC (NEW CSE)
County Kerry, Ireland
Robert Trent Jones
BALLYBUNION GC (OLD CSE)
County Kerry, Ireland
M. Smyth, P. Murphy
(R.9 A.9) James Braid, John
R. Stutt
(R.) Tom Simpson, Molly
Gourlay
(R.) Eddie Hackett
BALLYCLARE GC
County Antrim, Northern
Ireland
(R.9 A.9) Peter Alliss, David
Thomas, T. J. A. Macauley
BALLYLIFFINS GC
Ireland
(R.) Eddie Hackett
BALMACEWAN GC
New Zealand
(R.) C. H. Redhead
BALMORAL GC
Morin Heights, Ontario
Graham Cooke
BALMORAL BELFAST GC
Northern Ireland
P. M. Ross
BALMORE GC
Glasgow, Scotland
James Braid
BALNAGASK GC
Aberdeen, Scotland
Fred W. Hawtree, Martin
Hawtree
BALSAMS HOTEL GC
Dixville Notch, New Hampshire
Donald Ross
**BALTIMORE CC (ROLAND PARK CSE)
[NLE]**
Baltimore, Maryland
Willie Dunn, Jr.
BALTIMORE CC (EAST CSE)
Timonium, Maryland
A. W. Tillinghast
(R.) Brian Silva, Geoffrey S.
Cornish
BALTIMORE CC (WEST CSE)
Timonium, Maryland
Edmund B. Ault
(R.) Bob Cupp, *Tom Kite*
BALTINGLASS GC
Ireland
(R.) Eddie Hackett
BALTUSROL GC [NLE]
Springfield, New Jersey
Louis Keller
BALTUSROL GC (LOWER CSE)
Springfield, New Jersey
A. W. Tillinghast
(R.) Robert Trent Jones
(R.) Rees Jones
BALTUSROL GC (UPPER CSE)
Springfield, New Jersey
A. W. Tillinghast
BAMM HOLLOW CC
Middleton, New Jersey
Hal Purdy, Malcolm Purdy
(R.) Nicholas Psiahas
(R.1) Karl Litten
BANCROFT GC
Zimbabwe
Robert G. Grimsdell

BANDON-BY-THE-SEA GC
Bandon, Oregon
  (R.) Robert Muir Graves
BANDON FACE ROCK GC
Bandon, Oregon
  Lee Smith
BANDON GC
Bandon, Ireland
  (R.) Eddie Hackett
  (R.) J. J. F. Pennink
BANFF SPRINGS GC [NLE]
Banff, Alberta
Donald Ross
BANFF SPRINGS GC
Banff, Alberta
Stanley Thompson
  (A.3rd 9) William G.
  Robinson, Geoffrey S.
  Cornish
BANGLADORE GC
India
Peter Thomson, Michael
Wolveridge
BANGOR GC
Bangor, Northern Ireland
  (R.) P. M. Ross
  (R.) James Braid, John R.
  Stutt
  (R.1) T. J. A. Macauley
BANGOR MUNI
Bangor, Maine
Geoffrey S. Cornish
  (A.3rd 9) Geoffrey S.
  Cornish, Brian Silva
BANGPOO GC
Thailand
Arnold Palmer, Ed Seay
BANKS LAKE GC
Grand Coulee, Washington
Keith Hellstrom (9 1985)
BANKSVILLE CC
New York
  (A.9) Edward Ryder
BANNER LODGE GC
Moodus, Connecticut
  (A.9) Al Zikorus
BANNING MUNI
Banning, California
William F. Bell
BANNOCKBURN G&CC [NLE]
Glen Echo, Maryland
William H. Tucker, Dr. Walter
S. Harban
  (R.) Donald Ross
BANSTEAD DOWNS GC
England
Wilfrid Reid
BANTRY GC
County Cork, Ireland
Eddie Hackett
BANYAN GC
Hilo, Hawaii
Colonel Alex Kahapea
BANYAN GC
West Palm Beach, Florida
Joe Lee, Rocky Roquemore
BARABOO CC
Baraboo, Wisconsin
Edward Lawrence Packard
BARBADOS G&CC
Christchurch, Barbados
John Harris

BARBARA WORTH GC
Holtville, California
  (R.) Lawrence Hughes
BARBAROUX GC
Nice, France
P. B. Dye
BARCOVEN GC
Ontario
  (R.) Clinton E. Robinson
BARDMOOR CC (EAST CSE) [NLE]
Largo, Florida
William H. Diddel
  (R.) Edmund B. Ault, Tom
  Clark
BARDMOOR CC (NORTH CSE)
Largo, Florida
William H. Diddel
BARDMOOR CC (SOUTH CSE)
Largo, Florida
William H. Diddel
BAREFOOT BAY G&CC
Sebastian, Florida
Joe Lee
BARGOED GC
South Wales, Wales
  (A.9) H. S. Colt, C. H. Alison,
  J. S. F. Morrison
BAR HARBOR GC
Trenton, Maine
Phil Wogan
BAR-K GC
Lago Vista, Texas
Leon Howard
BARLASSINA CC
Milan, Italy
Donald Harradine
  (R.) John Harris
BARNEHURST GC
Kent, England
James Braid
BARNHAM BROOM HOTEL G&CC
(OLD CSE)
Norwich, England
J. J. F. Pennink, D. M. A. Steel
BARNTON GC
England
Willie Park, Jr.
BARON EDWARD DE ROTHSCHILD
ESTATE GC
France
Tom Simpson
BARON HENRI DE ROTHSCHILD
ESTATE GC
France
Tom Simpson
BARQUISMETO CC
Barquismeto, Venezuela
Joe Lee, Rocky Roquemore
BARRANQUILLA CC [NLE]
Barranquilla, Colombia
Frank Applebye
BARRANQUILLA CC
Barranquilla, Colombia
Ward Northrup
BARRE CC
Barre, Vermont
Wayne Stiles
  (A.9) Michael Hurdzan
BARREN RIVER STATE PARK GC
Glasgow, Kentucky
Benjamin Wihry
BARRHEAD GC
Barrhead, Alberta
Les Furber, *Jim Eremko*

BARRIE GC
Barrie, Ontario
Robert Moote, David L. Moote
BARRIE NATIONAL PINES G&CC
Barrie, Ontario
Thomas McBroom
BARRINGTON CC
Aurora, Ohio
Jack Nicklaus
BARRINGTON GC
Bangkok, Thailand
Gary Roger Baird
BARRINGTON HALL GC
Macon, Georgia
Tom Clark
BARRINGTON HILLS CC
Barrington, Illinois
George O'Neil, Joseph A.
Roseman, *Jack Croke*
  (R.) C. D. Wagstaff
  (R.1) William B. Langford
  (R.) Edward Lawrence
  Packard
  (R.) Roger Packard
BARSEBACKS GC (FOREST CSE)
Landskrona, Sweden
Ture Bruce
  (A.9) D. M. A. Steel
BARSEBACKS GC (SEA CSE)
Landskrona, Sweden
Ture Bruce
BARTLETT CC
Olean, New York
  (R.) Stanley Thompson
  (R.) Robert Trent Jones
BARTLETT HILLS G&CC
Bartlett, Illinois
Charles Maddox, *Frank P.
MacDonald*
  (R.1) Ken Killian
  (R.) Bob Lohmann
BARTON CC [NLE]
Barton, Vermont
Andrew Freeland
BARTON CREEK C (CRENSHAW/
COORE CSE)
Austin, Texas
Bill Coore, Ben Crenshaw
BARTON CREEK C (FAZIO CSE)
Austin, Texas
Tom Fazio
BARTON CREEK C (LAKESIDE CSE)
Spicewood, Texas
Arnold Palmer, Ed Seay
BARTON HILLS CC
Ann Arbor, Michigan
Donald Ross
  (R.) William H. Diddel
  (R.) William Newcomb
  (R.) Arthur Hills
BARTON-ON-SEA GC [NLE]
Hampshire, England
  (A.9) H. S. Colt
BARTON-ON-SEA GC
Hampshire, England
J. Hamilton Stutt
BARWICK GC
Delray Beach, Florida
John Strom, John Carpenter
BASEL G&CC
Basel, Switzerland
Karl Hoffmann, Bernhard von
Limburger

BASH RECREATION GC [NLE]
Dublin, Ohio
Jack Kidwell
BASILDON GC
Essex, England
J. J. F. Pennink
BASINGSTOKE GC
Hampshire, England
James Braid, John R. Stutt
BASIN HARBOR GC
Vergennes, Vermont
Alex "Nipper" Campbell
  (A.9) William F. Mitchell
  (R.) Geoffrey S. Cornish
BASKING RIDGE GC
Basking Ridge, New Jersey
Alex Findlay
  (R.) Arthur Hills
BAS RIDGE GC
Hinsdale, Massachusetts
  (R.) Rowland Armacost
BASSITT CC
Martinsville, Virginia
  (R.) Gene Hamm
BASS RIVER GC
South Yarmouth, Massachusetts
  (R.) Donald Ross
BASS ROCKS GC
Gloucester, Massachusetts
Herbert Leeds
BASTAD GC
Sweden
F. G. Hawtree, J. H. Taylor
BATCHWOOD HALL GC
St. Albans, England
F. G. Hawtree, J. H. Taylor
BATH CC
Bath, Maine
Wayne Stiles
BATH GC
Avon, England
Tom Dunn
  (R.) J. Hamilton Stutt
BATHGATE GC
East Lothian, Scotland
Willie Park
BATO KORAKUEN GC
Kitakata, Japan
Karl Litten
BATON ROUGE CC
Baton Rouge, Louisiana
Bert Stamps
  (R.) Joe Lee
  (R.) Joseph S. Finger
BATON ROUGE MUNI [NLE]
Baton Rouge, Louisiana
Tom Bendelow
BATTLE CREEK CC
Battle Creek, Michigan
Willie Park, Jr.
  (R.) William Newcomb
BATTLECREEK GC
Salem, Oregon
Lynn Baxter
BATTLEGROUND CC
Freehold, New Jersey
James Gilmore Harrison
(routing); Hal Purdy
BATTLEMENT MESA CC
Battlement Mesa, Colorado
Ken Dye, Joseph S. Finger
BAVARIAN HILLS GC
St. Marys, Pennsylvania
Bill Love, Brian Ault

Bay Beach GC
Fort Myers Beach, Florida
(R.) Gordon Lewis

Bayberry Hills G Cse
Yarmouth, Massachusetts
Brian Silva, Geoffrey S. Cornish

Bay City CC [NLE]
Bay City, Michigan
(R.9 A.9) Robert Bruce Harris

Bay City CC
Bay City, Michigan
Edward Lawrence Packard

[The] Bay C
Ocean City, Maryland
Russell Roberts

Bayerwald G und Land C
Waldkirchen, Germany
Donald Harradine

Bay Forest G Cse
LaPorte, Texas
Jay Riviere

Bay Hill C
Orlando, Florida
Dick Wilson, Joe Lee
(A.3rd 9) Bob Simmons
(R.) Arnold Palmer

Bay Hills GC
Arnold, Maryland
Edmund B. Ault

Bay Hills GC
Plattsmouth, Nebraska
Larry Hagewood

Baymeadows GC
Jacksonville, Florida
Desmond Muirhead

Baymeadows GC
San Francisco, California
Jack Fleming

Bay Oaks CC
Clear Lake City, Texas
Arthur Hills

Bay of Quinte GC
Bellville, Ontario
Howard Watson
(A.9) Clinton E. Robinson
(R.3) Gordon Witteveen

[The] Bayou C
Largo, Florida
Tom Fazio

Bayou Barriere GC
New Orleans, Louisiana
Jimmy Self

Bayou Bend CC
Crowley, Louisiana
(R.) Jay Riviere

Bayou de Siard CC
Monroe, Louisiana
Perry Maxwell, Press Maxwell
(R.) John Cochran
(R.) Ron Prichard

Bayou G&CC
Oregon
William Sander

Bayou GC
Texas City, Texas
Joseph S. Finger

Bay Park GC
East Rockaway, New York
David Gordon

Bay Pointe GC
West Bloomfield, Michigan
Ernest Fuller

Bay Point Y&CC (Club Meadows Cse)
Panama City Beach, Florida
Willard Byrd

Bay Point Y&CC (Lagoon Legend Cse)
Panama City Beach, Florida
Robert von Hagge, Bruce Devlin

Bayreuth GC
Bayreuth, Germany
Bernhard von Limburger

Bay Ridge GC
Sister Bay, Wisconsin
William E. Davis

Bayshore GC [NLE]
Miami Beach, Florida
H. C. C. Tippetts
(R.) Red Lawrence

Bayshore Muni
Miami Beach, Florida
Robert von Hagge, Bruce Devlin

Bayside CC
San Diego, California
William P. Bell

Bayside CC [NLE]
Rhode Island
Seth Raynor

Bayside Links [NLE]
New York
Tom Wells
(R.) Alister Mackenzie

Bayside Muni
Eureka, California
H. Chandler Egan

Baytree GC
Winter Haven, Florida
Dean Refram

Bay Tree G Plantation (Gold Cse)
North Myrtle Beach, South Carolina
Russell Breeden (routing);
George Fazio, Tom Fazio

Bay Tree G Plantation (Green Cse)
North Myrtle Beach, South Carolina
Russell Breeden (routing);
George Fazio, Tom Fazio

Bay Tree G Plantation (Silver Cse)
North Myrtle Beach, South Carolina
Russell Breeden (routing);
George Fazio, Tom Fazio

Bay Valley GC
Bay City, Michigan
Desmond Muirhead, Jack Nicklaus

Bayview G&CC
Thornhill, Ontario
Clinton E. Robinson
(R.) Robert Moote

Bay View GC
Honolulu, Hawaii
Jimmy Ukauka

Bayview GC
Ontario
Stanley Thompson

Bay West Lodge & CC
Florida
Chic Adams

Baywood CC
Houston, Texas
Joseph S. Finger
(R.) Jay Riviere

Baywood G&CC
Arcata, California
Bob Baldock
(R.) Robert Muir Graves

[The] Beach C
Berlin, Maryland
Brian Ault

Beach Grove G&CC
Walkerville, Ontario
Stanley Thompson
(R.) Clinton E. Robinson

Beachview GC
Sanibel Island, Florida
Truman Wilson

Beachwood GC
North Myrtle Beach, South Carolina
Gene Hamm

Beacon CC
Beacon, New York
(R.9 A.9) Herbert Strong

Beacon Hall GC
Aurora, Ontario
Bob Cupp

Beacon Hill CC [NLE]
Atlantic Heights, New Jersey
Seymour Dunn

Beacon Hill CC
Atlantic Heights, New Jersey
Alec Ternyei

Beacon Hills GC
Creston, Iowa
Richard Watson

Beacon Light GC
Columbus, Ohio
Wright McCallip

Beacon Park GC
West Lancashire, England
D. M. A. Steel

Beacon Ridge G&CC
Seven Lakes, North Carolina
Gene Hamm

Beaconsfield G&CC
Montreal, Quebec
Willie Park, Jr.
(R.) Stanley Thompson
(R.) Clinton E. Robinson
(R.6) Howard Watson
(R.6) John Watson

Beaconsfield GC
Beaconsfield, England
H. S. Colt

Beacon Woods CC
New Port Richey, Florida
Bill Amick

Beamish Park GC
England
Sir Guy Campbell, Henry Cotton

Bear Creek CC
Redmond, Washington
Jack Frei

Bear Creek GC
Golden, Colorado
Arnold Palmer, Ed Seay

Bear Creek GC
Oregon
Shirley Stone

Bear Creek GC
Hilton Head Island, South Carolina
Rees Jones
(R.) Arthur Hills

Bear Creek GC
Wildomar, California
Jack Nicklaus

Bear Creek G&RC (East Cse)
Dallas–Fort Worth, Texas
Ted Robinson

Bear Creek G&RC (West Cse)
Dallas–Fort Worth, Texas
Ted Robinson

Bear Creek G World (Executive Cse)
Houston, Texas
Bruce Littell

Bear Creek G World (Masters Cse)
Houston, Texas
Ralph Plummer (routing); Jay Riviere
(R.) Rick Forester

Bear Creek G World (Presidents Cse)
Houston, Texas
Jay Riviere

Bear Hill GC
Wakefield, Massachusetts
Alex Findlay
(R.) Skip Wogan
(R.) William F. Mitchell

Bear Lakes CC (Lakes Cse)
West Palm Beach, Florida
Jack Nicklaus

Bear Lakes CC (Links Cse)
West Palm Beach, Florida
Jack Nicklaus

Bear Lake West GC
Fish Haven, Idaho
Keith Downs

Bear's Paw CC
Naples, Florida
Jack Nicklaus

Bearspaw CC
Calgary, Alberta
Bill Newis

Bear Valley GC
Kodiak, Alaska
Richard L. Blackburn, Wayne Berry (9 1985)

Bear Valley GC
California
Bob Baldock

Beatrice CC
Beatrice, Nebraska
Tom Bendelow

Beau Chene G&RC (Magnolia Cse)
Manderville, Louisiana
Joe Lee, Rocky Roquemore

Beau Chene G&RC (Oak Cse)
Manderville, Louisiana
Joe Lee, Rocky Roquemore

Beauclerc CC
Jacksonville, Florida
Robert Trent Jones
(A.9) George W. Cobb

Beau Desert GC
Staffordshire, England
Herbert Fowler

BEAUMONT CC
  Holidayburg, Pennsylvania
  James Gilmore Harrison
BEAUMONT CC
  Beaumont, Texas
  Alex Findlay
BEAU RIVAGE PLANTATION GC
  Wilmington, North Carolina
  Joe Gessner (1988)
BEAVER GC
  Edmonton, Alberta
  Stanley Thompson
BEAVER BROOK G&CC
  Knoxville, Tennessee
  Lon Mills
BEAVER BROOK GC
  Clinton, New Jersey
  Alec Ternyei
    (R.) Nicholas Psiahas
BEAVER CREEK CC
  Lake Montezuma, Arizona
  Arthur Jack Snyder
BEAVER CREEK CC
  Hagerstown, Maryland
  Reuben Hines
BEAVER CREEK GC
  Avon, Colorado
  Robert Trent Jones, Jr.
BEAVER CREEK MEADOWS CC
  Ohio
  *Bruce Weber, Mark Weber, Steve
  Weber*
BEAVER DAM GC
  Beaver Dam, Nevada
  Neal Matthews, G. R. Fisby
BEAVER HILL CC
  Martinsville, Virginia
  Ferdinand Garbin
BEAVER HILLS CC
  Cedar Falls, Iowa
  Edward Lawrence Packard
BEAVER ISLAND GC
  Grand Island, New York
  William Harries, *A. Russell
  Tryon*
BEAVER LAKE GC
  Asheville, North Carolina
  NKA Asheville CC
BEAVER LAKES CC
  Aliquippa, Pennsylvania
  Ferdinand Garbin
BEAVER MEADOW CC
  New York
  Russell D. Bailey
BEAVER MEADOWS MUNI
  Concord, New Hampshire
  Willie Campbell
    (R.9 A.9) Geoffrey S.
    Cornish, William G.
    Robinson
BEAVERS BEND STATE PARK GC
  Broken Bow, Oklahoma
  Floyd Farley
BEAVER RUN G CSE
  Grimes, Iowa
  Jerry Raible
BEAVERSTOWN GC
  Ireland
  Eddie Hackett
BEAVERTAIL CC [NLE]
  Conanicuit, Rhode Island
  A. W. Tillinghast

BEAVER VALLEY CC
  Beaver Falls, Pennsylvania
  Emil Loeffler, *John McGlynn*
    (R.9 A.9) James Gilmore
    Harrison, Ferdinand Garbin
BEBINGTON GC
  England
    (A.9) Fred W. Hawtree
BECK CREEK GC
  Lebanon, Pennsylvania
  Ron Forse
BECKENHAM PLACE PARK GC
  England
  Tom Dunn
BECKETT RIDGE G&CC
  Cincinnati, Ohio
  Jack Kidwell, Michael Hurdzan
BEDALE GC
  England
    (R.) J. J. F. Pennick
    (A.6) Martin Hawtree, Simon
    Gidman
BEDENS BROOK C
  Skillman, New Jersey
  Dick Wilson, Joe Lee
    (R.) Stephen Kay
BEDFORD AFB GC
  Bedford, Massachusetts
  Manny Francis
    (R.) Brian Silva, Geoffrey S.
    Cornish
BEDFORD G&TC
  Bedford, New York
    (R.9 A.9) Devereux Emmet
    (R.9) Geoffrey S. Cornish
BEDFORD SPRINGS CC
  Bedford, Pennsylvania
  Arthur M. Goss
    (R.) A. W. Tillinghast
    (R.) Donald Ross
    (R.) James Gilmore Harrison
BEDFORD VALLEY CC
  Battle Creek, Michigan
  William F. Mitchell
    (R.) Charles Darl Scott
BEDINGTONSHIRE GC
  Northumberland, England
  J. J. F. Pennink
BEDOUIN HILLS GC
  Saudi Arabia
  John Arnold
BEDWELL PARK GC
  England
  Fred W. Hawtree, Martin Haw-
  tree
BEECH GROVE G&CC
  Ontario, Canada
  Stanley Thompson
    (R.) Thomas McBroom
BEECHMONT CC
  Cleveland, Ohio
  Stanley Thompson
BEECH MOUNTAIN GC
  Banner Elk, North Carolina
  Willard Byrd
BEECH PARK RATHCOOLE GC
  County Dublin, Ireland
  Eddie Hackett
BEECHWOOD CC
  Ahoskie, North Carolina
  Russell Breeden
BEECHWOOD GC
  LaPorte, Indiana
  William H. Diddel

BEECHWOOD GC
  Niagara Falls, Ontario
    (R.9 A.9) Robert Moote,
    David L. Moote
BEEKMAN GC
  Hopewell Junction, New York
  Cortlandt Fish
BEESON PARK GC
  Winchester, Indiana
  William H. Diddel
BEESTON FIELDS GC
  Nottinghamshire, England
  Tom Williamson
BEEVILLE CC
  Beeville, Texas
  George Albrecht
BEIJING GC
  Beijing, China
  Brad Benz, Mike Poellot
BEL-AIR CC
  Los Angeles, California
  George C. Thomas, William P.
  Bell, Jack Neville
    (R.3) William H. Johnson
    (R.) William F. Bell
    (R.) Dick Wilson
    (R.1) George Fazio
    (R.1) Robert Trent Jones, Jr.
BELAIR CC
  Gunma, Japan
  Takeo Aiyama
BEL AIRE CC
  Armonk, New York
  Al Zikorus
BEL AIRE CC
  Greensboro, North Carolina
  R. Brame
BEL AIRE G&CC
  Bowie, Maryland
  Frank Murray, Russell Roberts
BEL CAMPO GC
  Avon, Connecticut
  Joseph Brunoli
[THE] BELFRY GC (BRABAZON CSE)
  Sutton Coldfield, West
  Midlands, England
  Peter Alliss, David Thomas
[THE] BELFRY GC (DERBY CSE)
  Sutton Coldfield, West
  Midlands, England
  Peter Alliss, David Thomas
BELGRADE HOTEL GC [NLE]
  Belgrade Lakes, Maine
  Alex Findlay
BELHAM RIVER VALLEY GC
  Montserrat, British West Indies
  Edmund B. Ault
BELK PARK GC
  Wood River, Illinois
  Edward Lawrence Packard,
  Brent Wadsworth
    (A.9) Edward Lawrence
    Packard
BELLACH GC
  Austria
  Bernhard von Limburger
BELLAIRE GC
  Phoenix, Arizona
  Red Lawrence, Jeff Hardin, Greg
  Nash

BELLA VISTA CC
  Bella Vista, Arkansas
  Joseph S. Finger
    (R.) Edmund B. Ault
    (R.) Tom Clark
BELLA VISTA GC
  Howie-in-the-Hills, Florida
  Lloyd Clifton, *Kenneth Ezell,
  George Clifton*
BELL BEACH GC
  Okinawa, Japan
  Takeo Aiyama
BELLEAIR CC (EAST CSE)
  Clearwater, Florida
  Donald Ross
    (R.) Hal Purdy, Malcolm
    Purdy
BELLEAIR CC (WEST CSE)
  Clearwater, Florida
  John Duncan Dunn
    (R.9 A.9) Donald Ross
    (R.) Hal Purdy, Malcolm
    Purdy
BELLECLAIRE G LINKS
  Bayside, New York
  Tom Wells
BELLEFONTE CC
  Ashland, Kentucky
    (R.) James Gilmore Harrison,
    Ferdinand Garbin
BELLE GLADE G&CC
  Belle Glade, Florida
  Karl Litten, Gary Player
BELLE HAVEN CC
  Alexandria, Virginia
  Leonard Macomber
    (R.) George W. Cobb
    (R.) Edmund B. Ault
BELLEISLE GC
  Ayrshire, Scotland
  James Braid, John R. Stutt
BELLE ISLE MUNI
  Detroit, Michigan
  Ernest Way
BELLE MEADE CC
  Nashville, Tennessee
  Donald Ross
    (R.) Robert Trent Jones
    (R.) Gary Roger Baird
BELLE MEADE CC
  Thompson, Georgia
  Boone A. Knox, Nick Price
BELLERIVE CC [NLE]
  Normandy, Missouri
  Robert Foulis
BELLERIVE CC
  Creve Coeur, Missouri
  Robert Trent Jones
    (R.1) Ron Kirby, Denis
    Griffiths
BELLES SPRINGS GC
  Pennsylvania
  Edmund B. Ault
BELLE TERRE CC
  LaPlace, Louisiana
  David Pfaff
BELLEVIEW MIDO CC
  Clearwater, Florida
  Donald Ross
BELLEVIEW-BILTMORE HOTEL & C
  Clearwater, Florida
  NKA Belleair CC

BELLEVILLE CC [NLE]
Belleville, Kansas
Mike Ahern
BELLEVILLE CC
Belleville, Kansas
Henry B. Hughes, Richard
Watson
BELLEVILLE G&CC
Belleville, Ontario
(A.9) Clinton E. Robinson
BELLEVUE CC
Atchinson, Kansas
James Dalgleish
BELLEVUE CC
Melrose, Massachusetts
Skip Wogan
BELLEVUE CC
Sewickley, Pennsylvania
John Moorhead
BELLEVUE CC
Syracuse, New York
Donald Ross
(R. A.3) Willard Wilkinson
(R.14 A.4) Frank Duane
BELLEVUE MUNI
Bellevue, Washington
David W. Kent
BELLINGHAM GC
Bellingham, Washington
John Ball
(R.) *Bill Overdorf*
(R.) William Teufel
(R.) William G. Robinson,
John F. Robinson
BELLPORT GC
Bellport, New York
Seth Raynor
(R.) Robert Trent Jones
BELLWOOD CC
Texas
Tyrus Stroud
BEL-MAR GC
Belvidere, Illinois
Tom Bendelow
BEL-MEADOW G&CC
Mount Clare, West Virginia
Robert Trent Jones
BELMONT CC
Fresno, California
Bert Stamps
(R.) Bob Baldock
(R.) Robert Dean Putman
BELMONT CC
Belmont, Massachusetts
Donald Ross
(R.) Orrin Smith
(R.) Alfred H. Tull
BELMONT CC
Perrysburg, Ohio
Robert Bruce Harris
(R.) Arthur Hills (1974)
(R.) Arthur Hills (1990)
BELMONT GC
Illinois
H. J. Tweedie
BELMONT GC
Langley, British Columbia
Les Furber, *Jim Eremko*
BELMONT HILLS CC
St. Clairsville, Ohio
Devereux Emmet

BELMONT HOTEL & C
Warwick, Bermuda
Devereux Emmet
(A.9) Devereux Emmet
BELMONT PARK GC
Richmond, Virginia
A. W. Tillinghast
(R.) Donald Ross
(R.) David Gordon
(R.) Edmund B. Ault
BELOIT CC
Beloit, Wisconsin
Stanley Pelchar
BELTON MUNI
Belton, Missouri
Bob Baldock
BELTON PARK GC
England
(R.) Tom Williamson
BELVEDERE CC
Hot Springs, Arkansas
Herman Hackbarth
BELVEDERE CC [NLE]
West Palm Beach, Florida
Sheffield A. Arnold
BELVEDERE GC
Charlevoix, Michigan
Willie Watson
(R.) *Ray Didier* (1961)
(R.) William Newcomb
BELVEDERE GC
Edmonton, Alberta
(R.) William G. Robinson,
John F. Robinson
BELVEDERE G & WINTER C
Prince Edward Island
(R.) Clinton E. Robinson
BELVEDERE PLANTATION CC
Hampstead, North Carolina
Russell T. Burney
BELVOIR PARK GC
Belfast, Northern Ireland
H. S. Colt, C. H. Alison
BENBROOK MUNI
Fort Worth, Texas
NKA Pecan Valley Muni
BEND G&CC
Bend, Oregon
H. Chandler Egan
(A.9) Bob Baldock, Robert L.
Baldock
BEND MUNI
Bend, Oregon
Gene "Bunny" Mason
BENDIX ESTATE GC
Illinois
Jack Kohr
BEN GEREN GC
Fort Smith, Arkansas
Marvin Ferguson
BENGHAZI GC
Libya
J. J. F. Pennink
BENNETT VALLEY GC
Santa Rosa, California
Ben Harmon
BENODET-DE-L'ODET GC
Benodet, France
Robert Berthet
BENONA SHORES GC
Shelby, Michigan
Warner Bowen

BENSHEIM GC
Germany
Reinhold Weishaupt
BENSON GC
Benson, Minnesota
(A.9) Joel Goldstrand
BENSON PARK GC
Omaha, Nebraska
Edward Lawrence Packard
BENT BROOK GC
Bessemer, Alabama
Ward Northrup
BENT CREEK CC
Louisville, Kentucky
Bob Simmons
BENT CREEK GC
Eden Prairie, Minnesota
(R.) Don Herfort
BENT CREEK GC
Jackson, Missouri
Gary Kern, Ron Kern
BENT CREEK G RESORT
Gatlinburg, Tennessee
Arthur Davis, Ron Kirby, Gary
Player
BENTLEY VILLAGE CC
Naples, Florida
Ward Northrup
BENT OAK GC
Oak Grove, Missouri
Bob Simmons
BENTON CC
Benton, Illinois
Robert Bruce Harris
BENTON G&CC
Benton, Kentucky
Alex McKay
BENTON HALL GC
Witham, Essex, England
Howard Swan
BENT PINE GC
Vero Beach, Florida
Joe Lee
BENT TREE CC
Jasper, Georgia
Joe Lee
BENT TREE GC
Sunbury, Ohio
Denis Griffiths
BENT TREE GC
Dallas, Texas
Desmond Muirhead
(R.) Dick Nugent
BENT TREE G&RC
Sarasota, Florida
William B. Lewis
BENTWATER CC (CSE No. 1)
Houston, Texas
Jay Morrish, Tom Weiskopf
BENTWATER CC (CSE No. 2)
Bentwater, Texas
Scott Miller
BENTWINDS G&CC
Fuquay-Varina, North Carolina
Tom Hunter
BENTWOOD CC
San Angelo, Texas
Billy Martindale
BENVENUE CC
Rocky Mount, North Carolina
Donald Ross
(R.) Donald Ross

BERGAMO L'ALBENZA GC
Bergamo, Italy
J. S. F. Morrison
(A.9) C. K. Cotton, John
Harris
BERGEN PARK GC
Springfield, Illinois
(R.) Edward Lawrence
Packard
BERGEN POINT MUNI
Babylon, New York
William F. Mitchell
BERGISCH LAND UND GC
Germany
(R.) Bernhard von Limburger
BERKELEY CC
Berkeley, California
NKA Mira Vista G&CC
BERKELEY CC
Moncks Corner, South Carolina
George W. Cobb
BERKELEY HILLS CC
Norcross, Georgia
Arthur Davis, Ron Kirby, Gary
Player
(A.3rd 9) Joe Lee, Rocky
Roquemore
BERKELEY TOWNSHIP GC
New Jersey
Nicholas Psiahas
BERKHAMPSTED GC
Hertfordshire, England
C. J. Gilbert
(R.) Willie Park, Willie Park
Jr.
(R.12 A.6) James Braid, John
R. Stutt
BERKLEIGH CC
Kutztown, Pennsylvania
Robert White
BERKSDALE GC
Bella Vista, Arkansas
Edmund B. Ault
BERKSHIRE CC
Reading, Pennsylvania
Willie Park, Jr.
[THE] BERKSHIRE GC (BLUE CSE)
Surrey, England
Herbert Fowler, Tom Simpson
(R.) J. S. F. Morrison
[THE] BERKSHIRE GC (RED CSE)
Surrey, England
Herbert Fowler, Tom Simpson
(R.) J. S. F. Morrison
BERKSHIRE HILLS CC
Pittsfield, Massachusetts
A. W. Tillinghast
(R.4) Geoffrey S. Cornish,
William G. Robinson
BERKSHIRE HUNT & CC
Lenox, Massachusetts
Wayne Stiles, John Van Kleek
BERLIN G&CC
Berlin, Germany
C. S. Butchart
BERMUDA DUNES CC
Bermuda Dunes, California
William F. Bell
(A.9) Bob Baldock, Robert L.
Baldock
BERMUDA RUN G&CC
Clemmons, North Carolina
Ellis Maples
(A.3rd 9) Dan Maples

BERNARDO HEIGHTS CC
Rancho Bernardo, California
Ted Robinson
BERRIEN HILLS CC
Benton Harbor, Michigan
(R.) Ken Killian, Dick Nugent
BERRY HILLS CC
Charleston, West Virginia
William Gordon
BERWICK-UPON-TWEED GC
Northumberland, England
Willie Park
(A.9) Fred W. Hawtree
(R.) James Braid, John R.
Stutt
BERWIND CC [NLE]
Rio Grande, Puerto Rico
(A.9) Alfred H. Tull
BERWIND CC
Rio Grande, Puerto Rico
Frank Murray
BEST GC
Netherlands
J. F. Dudok van Heel
BETCHWORTH PARK GC
Dorking, Surrey, England
H. S. Colt
(R.) Tom Simpson
BETHEL INN & CC
Bethel, Maine
(A.11) Geoffrey S. Cornish,
Brian Silva
BETHEL ISLAND GC
Bethel Island, California
Bob Baldock
BETHEMONT GC
Bethemont, France
Jim Engh, *Bernhard Langer*
BETHESDA CC
Bethesda, Maryland
Fred Findlay
(R.9 A.9) Edmund B. Ault
(R.1) Lindsay Ervin
BETHESDA NAVAL HOSPITAL GC
Bethesda, Maryland
(R.9) Edmund B. Ault
BETHLEHEM CC
New Hampshire
W. Lillywhite
(R.9 A.9) Donald Ross
(R.) Wayne Stiles
BETHLEHEM MUNI
Bethlehem, Pennsylvania
William Gordon, David Gordon
BETHLEHEM STEEL C
Hellertown, New York
William Gordon, David Gordon
BETHLEHEM STEEL C
Bethlehem, Pennsylvania
(R. A.9) William Gordon,
David Gordon
BETHPAGE STATE PARK GC (BLACK
CSE)
Farmingdale, New York
A. W. Tillinghast
BETHPAGE STATE PARK GC (BLUE
CSE)
Farmingdale, New York
A. W. Tillinghast
(R.) Frank Duane

BETHPAGE STATE PARK GC (GREEN
CSE)
Farmingdale, New York
Devereux Emmet
(R.) A. W. Tillinghast
(R.) Frank Duane
BETHPAGE STATE PARK GC (RED
CSE)
Farmingdale, New York
A. W. Tillinghast
(R.) Frank Duane
BETHPAGE STATE PARK GC (YELLOW
CSE)
Farmingdale, New York
Alfred H. Tull
(R.) Frank Duane
BEUERBERG GC
Beuerberg, Germany
Donald Harradine
BEVERLY CC
Chicago, Illinois
Donald Ross
(R.4) William B. Langford
(R.) Bob Lohmann
BEVERLY GC
Copetown, Ontario
Clinton E. Robinson
BEVERLY G&TC
Beverly, Massachusetts
(R.) Skip Wogan
BEVERLY SHORES CC
Indiana
Charles Maddox, *Frank P.
MacDonald*
BEVICO CC
Memphis, Tennessee
John W. Frazier
BEY-LEA GC
Toms River, New Jersey
Hal Purdy
BIDDEFORD AND SACO CC
Saco, Maine
Donald Ross
(A.9) Brian Silva, Geoffrey S.
Cornish
BIDE-A-WEE CC
Portsmouth, Virginia
Fred Findlay, *R. F. Loving, Sr.*
BIDERMANN GC
Wilmington, Delaware
Dick Wilson, Joe Lee
BIDFORD GRANGE GC
Warwickshire, England
Howard Swan
BIELEFELDER GC
Bielefeld, West Germany
Donald Harradine
BIG BAY G&CC
Lake Simcoe, Ontario
Stanley Thompson
BIGBURY GC
England
F. G. Hawtree, J. H. Taylor
BIG CANYON CC
Newport Beach, California
Robert Muir Graves
(R.) Desmond Muirhead
(1976)
(R.) Desmond Muirhead
(1992)

BIG CYPRESS AT ROYAL PALM CC
Florida
Chuck Ankrom
BIG CYPRESS GC
Lakeland, Florida
Ron Garl
BIG ELM GC
Kentucky
Robert Lee
BIG FOOT CC
Fontana, Wisconsin
Tom Bendelow
(R.) Roger Packard
(R.) Dick Nugent
BIGGAR GC
Lanarkshire, Scotland
Willie Park
BIGHORN GC
Palm Desert, California
Arthur Hills
BIG OAKS CC
Chicago, Illinois
Edward B. Dearie, Jr.
BIG ONE CC
Shiga, Japan
Mitsuaki Kobayashi
BIG PINE GC
Attica, Indiana
Robert Beard
BIG RUN GC
Lockport, Illinois
Harry B. Smead (1930)
(R.) Dick Nugent
BIG SKY GC
Big Sky, Montana
Frank Duane, Arnold Palmer
BIG SPRING CC
Louisville, Kentucky
George Davies
(R.) Tom Winton
(R.) William H. Diddel
(R.) Edward Lawrence
Packard
(R.) Arthur Hills
BIG SPRING CC [NLE]
Big Spring, Texas
(A.9) John Bredemus
BIG SPRING CC
Big Spring, Texas
Warren Cantrell
BIG TEE GC
Buena Park, California
William H. Johnson
BIGWIN ISLAND GC
Lake of Bays, Ontario
Stanley Thompson
BIGWOOD GC
Sun Valley, Idaho
Robert Muir Graves
(R.) Robert Muir Graves
BILLERICA GC [NLE]
Billerica, Massachusetts
William F. Mitchell
BILLERUD GC
Sweden
Nils Sköld, Douglas Brazier
BILLINGHAM GC
Durham, England
J. J. F. Pennink
BILLINGS G&CC
Billings, Montana
Tom Bendelow

BILLINGS MUNI
Billings, Montana
Dave Bennett
BILL ROBERTS MUNI
Helena, Montana
Robert Muir Graves
BILOXI CC [NLE]
Biloxi, Mississippi
Tom Bendelow
(R.) Jack Daray
BILTMORE CC
Barrington, Illinois
Leonard Macomber
(R.) William B. Langford
(R.) Edward Lawrence
Packard
(R.) Bob Lohmann
BILTMORE FOREST GC
Asheville, North Carolina
Donald Ross
BILTSE DUINEN GC
Netherlands
J. F. Dudok van Heel
BINBROOK GC
Hamilton, Ontario
René Muylaert
BINDER PARK GC
Battle Creek, Michigan
Charles Darl Scott
BINGHAMTON CC
Endwell, New York
A. W. Tillinghast
(R.) William Gordon, David
Gordon
BINGLEY ST. IVES GC
Bingley, England
Alister Mackenzie
BING MALONEY G CSE
Sacramento, California
Michael J. McDonagh
(A.3rd 9) Ronald Fream
BINICITAN GC
Manila, Philippines
Willard Wilkinson
BINKS FOREST CC
Wellington, Florida
Gene Bates, Johnny Miller
BIRCH BAY VILLAGE GC
Blaine, Washington
(R.) Robert Muir Graves
BIRCH HILL GC [NLE]
Detroit, Michigan
Ernest Way
BIRCH HILLS GC
Brea, California
Harry Rainville, David Rainville
BIRCH POINT CC
St. David, Maine
Ben Gray
BIRCHWOOD CC
Westport, Connecticut
Orrin Smith
(R.) William F. Mitchell
BIRCHWOOD GC
Sharon, Ohio
(R.9 A.9) Ferdinand Garbin
BIRCHWOOD GC
Kieler, Wisconsin
Bob Lohmann
BIRCHWOOD GC
Cheshire, England
T. J. A. Macauley

BIRCHWOOD FARM G&CC
Harbor Springs, Michigan
Bruce Matthews, Jerry Matthews
BIRCHWOOD PARK GC
Kent, England
Howard Swan
BIRD BAY EXECUTIVE GC
Venice, Florida
R. Albert Anderson
BIRD CREEK GC
Port Austin, Michigan
Jerry Matthews
BIRDLAND G&CC (CHAMPIONSHIP
CSE)
Bad Buk, Hungary
Gerold Hauser, *Günther Hauser*
BIRDLAND G&CC (SHORT CSE)
Bad Buk, Hungary
Gerold Hauser, *Günther Hauser*
BIRDS HILL GC
Manitoba
Tom Bendelow
(R.) Norman H. Woods
BIRDWOOD GC
Charlottesville, Virginia
Lindsay Ervin
BIRKDALE GC
Chesterfield, Virginia
Dan Maples
BIRMINGHAM CC
Birmingham, Michigan
Tom Bendelow
(R.) Wilfrid Reid, William
Connellan
(R.) William H. Diddel
(R.3) Bruce Matthews, Jerry
Matthews
(R.) Arthur Hills
BIRMINGHAM VA HOSPITAL GC
California
William P. Bell
BIRNAMWOOD GC
Burnsville, Minnesota
Don Herfort
BIRNAM WOOD GC
Santa Barbara, California
Robert Trent Jones
(R.) Robert Trent Jones, Jr.
BIRR GC
Birr, Ireland
(R.) Eddie Hackett
BIRSTALL GC
England
(R.) Tom Williamson
BISHOP CC
Bishop, California
Joseph B. Williams
(A.9) Gary Roger Baird
BISHOPVILLE CC
Bishopville, South Carolina
Ed Riccoboni
BITTERROOT RIVER CC
Montana
William F. Bell
BIXBY GC
Long Beach, California
Ronald Fream, Peter Thomson,
Michael Wolveridge
BJÖRN BORG SPORTS C
Vallentuna, Sweden
Ake Persson
BLACKBERRY FARM GC
Cupertino, California
Robert Muir Graves

BLACK BULL G&CC
Ma-Me-O Beach, Alberta
Jack Thompson
BLACKBURN ESTATE GC
Fort Myers, Florida
Dick Wilson
BLACK BUTTE RANCH GC (BIG
MEADOWS CSE)
Sisters, Oregon
Robert Muir Graves
BLACK BUTTE RANCH GC (GLAZE
MEADOWS CSE)
Sisters, Oregon
Gene "Bunny" Mason
BLACK CANYON GC [NLE]
Phoenix, Arizona
Arthur Jack Snyder
BLACK DIAMOND RANCH G&CC
Lecanto, Florida
Tom Fazio
BLACKFOOT MUNI
Blackfoot, Idaho
George Von Elm
BLACK HALL C
Old Lyme, Connecticut
Robert Trent Jones
BLACKHAWK CC (FALLS CSE)
Danville, California
Ted Robinson
BLACKHAWK CC (LAKESIDE CSE)
Danville, California
Robert von Hagge, Bruce Devlin
BLACKHAWK CC
Janesville, Wisconsin
(R.) A. W. Tillinghast
(R.) Ken Killian, Dick Nugent
(R.) Bob Lohmann
BLACKHAWK GC
Galena, Ohio
Jack Kidwell
BLACKHAWK GC
Pflugerville, Texas
Charles Howard, Hollis Stacy
(1992)
BLACKHEAD MOUNTAIN LODGE &
CC
Round Top, New York
Nicholas Psiahas
BLACKHILL WOOD GC
Staffordshire, England
J. J. F. Pennink, D. M. A. Steel
BLACKHORSE GC
Downers Grove, Illinois
Charles Maddox
BLACK KNIGHT CC
Beckley, West Virginia
(R.) Ferdinand Garbin
BLACK LAKE CC
Nipomo, California
Joe Novak
BLACKLEDGE CC
Hebron, Connecticut
Geoffrey S. Cornish, William G.
Robinson
BLACKLICK WOODS GC (GOLD CSE)
Reynoldsburg, Ohio
Jack Kidwell
BLACKLICK WOODS GC (GREEN
CSE)
Reynoldsburg, Ohio
Jack Kidwell

BLACKLION GC
County Levon, Ireland
Eddie Hackett
(R.) Eddie Hackett
BLACKMOOR GC
Hampshire, England
H. S. Colt
(A.5) H. S. Colt, C. H. Alison
(R.) H. S. Colt, C. H. Alison
BLACKMOOR GC
Myrtle Beach, South Carolina
Gary Player
BLACK MOUNTAIN CC
Black Mountain, North Carolina
(R.9 A.9) *Ross Taylor*
BLACK MOUNTAIN G&CC
Henderson, Nevada
Bob Baldock
(R.) Bob Baldock, Robert L.
Baldock
BLACKPOOL NORTH SHORE GC
Blackpool, England
J. A. Steer
BLACKPOOL-STANLEY PARK GC
Lancashire, England
Alister Mackenzie
(R.) J. A. Steer
BLACK RIVER CC
Port Huron, Michigan
Fred L. Riggin
(A.9) Wilfrid Reid, William
Connellan
(R.9 A.9) William H. Diddel
BLACKROCK CC
Edenton, North Carolina
Dick Phelps, Hale Irwin
BLACK ROCK GC
Hagerstown, Maryland
Robert L. Elder
BLACKSBURG CC
Blacksburg, Virginia
Ferdinand Garbin
BLACKWELL GC
Worcestershire, England
Herbert Fowler
BLACKWELL GRANGE GC
England
(R.) J. J. F. Pennink
BLACKWOLF RUN GC (MEADOW
VALLEYS CSE)
Kohler, Wisconsin
Pete Dye
BLACKWOLF RUN GC (RIVER CSE)
Kohler, Wisconsin
Pete Dye
BLACKWOOD CC
Douglasville, Pennsylvania
William Gordon, David Gordon
BLACKWOOD CC
Gloucester Township, New
Jersey
Alex Findlay
BLAIR ACADEMY GC
New Jersey
Duer Irving Sewall
BLAIRGOWRIE GC (LANSDOWNE
CSE)
Perthshire, Scotland
Peter Alliss, David Thomas

BLAIRGOWRIE GC (ROSEMOUNT
CSE)
Scotland
Tom Dunn
(R.9 A.9) Alister Mackenzie
(R.10 A.8) James Braid, John
R. Stutt
(R.) Peter Alliss, David
Thomas
BLAIRGOWRIE GC (WEE CSE)
Perthshire, Scotland
James Braid, John R. Stutt
BLAIR HAMPTON GC
Minden, Ontario
Robert Moote, *David S. Moote*
BLAIRMORE AND STRONE GC
Argyll, Scotland
James Braid
BLAIRSVILLE CC
Pennsylvania
James Gilmore Harrison,
Ferdinand Garbin
BLANDFORD GC
England
(R.) J. Hamilton Stutt
BLED GC
Bled, Yugoslavia
Donald Harradine
B. L. ENGLAND GC
Beesley Point, New Jersey
Hal Purdy
BLIND BROOK C
Port Chester, New York
Charles Blair Macdonald, Seth
Raynor (routing); George Low
(R.) Geoffrey S. Cornish,
Brian Silva
(R.1) Stephen Kay
BLOEMFONTEIN GC
South Africa
John Watt
BLOMIDON C
Corner Brook, Newfoundland
Alfred H. Tull
BLOODY POINT C
Daufuskie Island, South
Carolina
Jay Morrish, Tom Weiskopf
BLOOMFIELD HILLS CC
Bloomfield Hills, Michigan
Tom Bendelow
(R.) Donald Ross
(R.) Robert Trent Jones
(1968)
(R.) Robert Trent Jones
(1978)
(R.) Arthur Hills
BLOOMFIELD-WAUSA GC
Bloomfield, Nebraska
Henry B. Hughes, Richard
Watson
BLOOMINGDALE GOLFERS C
Valrico, Florida
Ron Garl
BLOOMINGTON CC
Bloomington, Illinois
William B. Langford
(R.) Edward Lawrence
Packard
BLOOMINGTON CC
Bloomington, Minnesota
Paul Coates

BLOOMINGTON CC
St. George, Utah
William H. Neff
BLOOMINGTON DOWNS G CENTRE
Richmond Hill, Ontario
Robert Heaslip
BLOOMSBURG CC
Bloomsburg, Pennsylvania
(R.) James Gilmore Harrison
BLOSSOM TRAILS GC
Benton Harbor, Michigan
Bruce Matthews
BLOWING ROCK CC
Blowing Rock, North Carolina
(R.9 A.9) Donald Ross
(R.) Tom Jackson
BLOXWICH GC
England
J. Sixsmith
BLUE ASH GC
Cincinnati, Ohio
Jack Kidwell, Michael Hurdzan
BLUEBERRY HILL GC
Warren, Pennsylvania
James Gilmore Harrison,
Ferdinand Garbin
(A.9) Ferdinand Garbin
BLUEBONNET CC
Navasota, Texas
Jay Riviere
(R.) Rick Forester
BLUEBONNET HILLS GC
Manor, Texas
Jeff Brauer
BLUE DANUBE GC
Budapest, Hungary
Dr. Ferenc Gati (9 1988)
BLUEFIELD CC
Bluefield, West Virginia
(R.) I. C. "Rocky" Schorr
BLUEGRASS CC
Hendersonville, Tennessee
Robert Bruce Harris
(R. A.2) Robert Bruce Harris
BLUE HERON HILLS CC
Macedon, New York
Peter Craig, *Richard Bator*
BLUE HERON PINES GC
Atlantic City, New Jersey
Stephen Kay
BLUE HILL CC
Canton, Massachusetts
Skip Wogan
(A.9) Skip Wogan, Phil
Wogan
(R.6) Manny Francis
(R.) Brian Silva, Geoffrey S.
Cornish
BLUE HILL GC
Orangetown, New York
(R.) Frank Duane
(R.) Edmund B. Ault
(R.) Stephen Kay
BLUE HILL GC [NLE]
Nassau, Bahamas
C. C. Shaw
BLUE HILLS CC
Kansas City, Missouri
NKA Metro GC
BLUE HILLS CC
Kansas City, Missouri
Bob Dunning

BLUE KNOB RESORT GC
Claysburg, Pennsylvania
Ferdinand Garbin
BLUE LAKE ESTATES GC
Marble Falls, Texas
Joseph S. Finger
BLUE LAKE SPRINGS GC
Arnold, California
Bob Baldock
BLUE MOUND G&CC [NLE]
Milwaukee, Wisconsin
Tom Bendelow
BLUE MOUND G&CC
Wauwautosa, Wisconsin
Seth Raynor
(R.3) David Gill
(R.) Ken Killian, Dick Nugent
(R.) Bob Lohmann
BLUE MOUNTAIN G&CC
Collingwood, Ontario
Clinton E. Robinson
(A.9) William G. Robinson,
John F. Robinson
BLUE MOUNTAIN GC
Mars Hill, North Carolina
William B. Lewis
BLUE MOUNTAIN GC
Linglestown, Pennsylvania
David Gordon
BLUE RIDGE CC
Linville, North Carolina
Charles Mahannah, *Lee Trevino*
BLUE RIDGE CC
Pennsylvania
(R.) James Gilmore Harrison,
Ferdinand Garbin
(R.) William F. Mitchell
BLUE RIVER G CSE
Kansas City, Missouri
James Dalgleish
BLUE ROCK GC
South Yarmouth, Massachusetts
Geoffrey S. Cornish
BLUE ROCK SPRINGS GC
Vallejo, California
Jack Fleming
BLUE SKIES CC
Yucca Valley, California
Roscoe Smith
BLUE SPRINGS G&CC
Blue Springs, Missouri
John S. Davis
BLUEWATER BAY GC
Niceville, Florida
Tom Fazio
(A.3rd 9) Tom Fazio
BLUFF CREEK G CSE
Chaska, Minnesota
Gerry Pirkl, *Donald G. Brauer*
BLUFF POINT GC
Lake Champlain, New York
(R.) A. W. Tillinghast
(R.) George Low
(R.) Ron Forse
[THE] BLUFFS ON THOMPSON CREEK CC
St. Francisville, Louisiana
Arnold Palmer, Ed Seay
BLUMISBERG G&CC
Bern, Switzerland
Bernhard von Limburger
BLUNDELL GC
England
J. A. Steer

BLUSH HILL CC
Waterbury, Vermont
Andrew Freeland
BLYTH GC
Northumberland, England
J. Hamilton Stutt
BLYTHE MUNI
Blythe, California
William F. Bell
BLYTHEFIELD CC
Grand Rapids, Michigan
William B. Langford, Theodore
J. Moreau
(R.6) Bruce Matthews, Jerry
Matthews
(R.2) Jerry Matthews
BLYTHEVILLE CC
Blytheville, Arkansas
Dick Wilson
(R.9 A.9) Joseph S. Finger
BOARD OF TRADE CC (EAST CSE)
Woodbridge, Ontario
Howard Watson
(R.4) Gordon Witteveen
BOARD OF TRADE CC (SOUTH CSE)
Woodbridge, Ontario
Gordon Witteveen
BOARD OF TRADE CC (WEST CSE)
Woodbridge, Ontario
Howard Watson
(R.9 A.9) Arthur Hills
BOAR'S HEAD INN GC
Charlottesville, Virginia
Buddy Loving
BOAT-OF-GARTEN GC
Invernesshire, Scotland
James Braid, John R. Stutt
BOBBY JONES GC
Atlanta, Georgia
(R.) Garrett Gill, George B.
Williams
BOBBY JONES MUNI (AMERICAN CSE)
Sarasota, Florida
Donald Ross
(R.) R. Albert Anderson
(R.) Ron Garl
BOBBY JONES MUNI (BRITISH CSE)
Sarasota, Florida
Donald Ross
BOBBY JONES MUNI (GILLESPIE CSE)
Sarasota, Florida
Lane Marshall
BOBBY NICHOLS GC
Louisville, Kentucky
Benjamin Wihry
BOB O'LINK CC
Highland Park, Illinois
Donald Ross
(R. A.4) C. H. Alison, H. S.
Colt
(R.) Edward Lawrence
Packard
(R.) Ken Killian, Dick Nugent
BOB O'LINK CC
Novi, Michigan
Wilfrid Reid, William Connellan
BOCA G&TC
Boca Raton, Florida
Joe Lee
BOCA DEL MAR G&TC
Boca Raton, Florida
Robert von Hagge, Bruce Devlin
(R.) Chuck Ankrom

BOCA DELRAY G&CC
Delray Beach, Florida
Karl Litten
BOCA GREENS GC
Boca Raton, Florida
Joe Lee
BOCA GROVE PLANTATION GC
Boca Raton, Florida
Karl Litten
BOCA LAGO G&CC (EAST CSE)
Boca Raton, Florida
Robert von Hagge, Bruce Devlin
BOCA LAGO G&CC (WEST CSE)
Boca Raton, Florida
Robert von Hagge, Bruce Devlin
BOCA POINTE CC
Boca Raton, Florida
Bob Cupp, Jay Morrish
BOCA RATON HOTEL & C (LAKEVIEW CSE)
Boca Raton, Florida
Dick Bird
BOCA RATON HOTEL & C (NORTH CSE) [NLE]
Boca Raton, Florida
William S. Flynn, Howard
Toomey
BOCA RATON HOTEL & C (SOUTH CSE)
Boca Raton, Florida
NKA Boca Raton Resort & CC
BOCA RATON MUNI
Boca Raton, Florida
Chuck Ankrom
BOCA RATON RESORT & CC
Boca Raton, Florida
William S. Flynn, Howard
Toomey
(R.) Red Lawrence
(R.) Robert Trent Jones
(R.) Joe Lee
BOCA RIO GC
Boca Raton, Florida
Robert von Hagge
(R.) Robert von Hagge
BOCA TEECA CC
Boca Raton, Florida
Mark Mahannah, Charles
Mahannah
BOCA WEST C (CSE NO. 1)
Boca Raton, Florida
Desmond Muirhead
(R.) Desmond Muirhead
BOCA WEST C (CSE NO. 2)
Boca Raton, Florida
Desmond Muirhead
BOCA WEST C (CSE NO. 3)
Boca Raton, Florida
Robert von Hagge, Bruce Devlin
BOCA WEST C (CSE NO. 4)
Boca Raton, Florida
Joe Lee
BOCA WOODS CC (NORTH CSE)
Boca Raton, Florida
Karl Litten
BOCA WOODS CC (SOUTH CSE)
Boca Raton, Florida
Joe Lee
BOCAIRE CC
Boca Raton, Florida
Rocky Roquemore

BOCHUMER GC
Bochum, Germany
Karl F. Grohs, *Rainer Preissmann*

BODEGA HARBOUR G LINKS
Bodega Bay, California
Robert Trent Jones, Jr.

BODENSEE GC
Lindau, Germany
Robert Trent Jones

BODENSTOWN GC
County Kildare, Ireland
Eddie Hackett

BODMIN G&CC
Cornwall, England
J. Hamilton Stutt

BOGEY GC
St. Louis, Missouri
Robert Foulis

BOGNOR REGIS GC
Sussex, England
James Braid

BOGSTAD GC
Bogstad, Norway
(R.) Jan Sederholm

BOGUE BANKS CC
Atlantic Beach, North Carolina
Maurice Brackett

BOILING SPRINGS GC
Woodward, Oklahoma
Don Sechrest

BOIS DE SIOUX GC
Wahpeton, North Dakota
Robert Bruce Harris

BOIS LE ROE GC
France
Robert Berthet

BOLDMERE GC
England
Carl Bretherston

BOLEN GC
Ohio
Robert Morrison

BOLIVAR GC
Bolivar, Missouri
Lou Stoy

BOLLING AFB GC
Virginia
Edmund B. Ault, Al Jamison

BOLOGNA GC
Bologna, Italy
Henry Cotton

BOLTON GC
Bolton, Lancashire, England
(R.) Alister Mackenzie

BOLTON FIELD GC
Columbus, Ohio
Jack Kidwell
(A.3rd 9) Jack Kidwell

BOMBAY PRESIDENCY C
Bombay, India
C. R. Clayton
(R.) Peter Thomson, Michael Wolveridge

BOMOSEEN GC
Castleton, Vermont
Henry Duskett

BOMUN LAKE GC
Kyongju, South Korea
Edward Lawrence Packard, Roger Packard

BON AIR CC
Glen Rock, Pennsylvania
William Gordon, David Gordon

BON AIR GC
Kentucky
Taylor Boyd

BON AIR-VANDERBILT HOTEL GC (HILL CSE)
Augusta, Georgia
(R.) Donald Ross

BON AIR-VANDERBILT HOTEL GC (LAKE CSE) [NLE]
Augusta, Georgia
Seth Raynor

BONANZA VALLEY GC
Brooten, Minnesota
Joel Goldstrand

BONAVENTURE CC (EAST CSE)
Fort Lauderdale, Florida
Joe Lee

BONAVENTURE CC (WEST CSE)
Fort Lauderdale, Florida
Charles Mahannah

BONAVENTURE GC
Fauvel, Quebec
Howard Watson, John Watson
(A.9) John Watson

BONDUES GC (RED & BLUE CSE)
Lille, France
Fred W. Hawtree

BONDUES GC (WHITE & GREEN CSE)
Lille, France
Robert Trent Jones
(A.9) Robert Trent Jones, Jr.

BONITA GC
Bonita, California
William F. Bell

BONITA BAY C (CREEKSIDE CSE)
Bonita Springs, Florida
Arthur Hill

BONITA BAY C (MARSH CSE)
Bonita Springs, Florida
Arthur Hill

BONITA SPRINGS G&CC
Bonita Springs, Florida
William Maddox

BONMONT GC
Switzerland
Donald Harradine

BONMUNT CATALUNYA GC
Reus, Spain
Robert Trent Jones, Jr.

BONNET CREEK GC (EAGLE PINES CSE)
Lake Buena Vista, Florida
Pete Dye

BONNET CREEK GC (OSPREY RIDGE CSE)
Lake Buena Vista, Florida
Tom Fazio

BONNEVILLE MUNI
Salt Lake City, Utah
William F. Bell, William P. Bell
(A.9) William F. Bell

BONN-GODESBERG GC
Germany
John Harris

BONNIE BRAE GC
Greenville, South Carolina
Russell Breeden

BONNIE BRIAR CC
Larchmont, New York
Archie Capper
(R.) A. W. Tillinghast
(R.) Devereux Emmet
(R.) Robert Trent Jones, Stanley Thompson
(R.) Alfred H. Tull

BONNIE BROOK GC
Waukegan, Illinois
James Foulis

BONNIEBROOK GC
St. Colomban, Quebec
Howard Watson
(R.3) John Watson

BONNIE CREST CC
Montgomery, Alabama
Weldon W. Doe

BONNIE DUNDEE GC
Dundee, Illinois
C. D. Wagstaff

BONNIE VIEW CC
Baltimore, Maryland
(R.) Edmund B. Ault

BONNIE VIEW GC
Eaton, Michigan
Henry Chisholm
(R.4 A.2) Bruce Matthews, Jerry Matthews

BONNYDUNE GC [NLE]
Tuftonboro, New Hampshire
W. H. Crawford

BON VIVANT CC
Bourbonnais, Illinois
Ray Didier

BOOKCLIFF CC
Grand Junction, Colorado
Henry B. Hughes
(A.5) Press Maxwell

BOOMERANG GC
Greeley, Colorado
William Howard Neff

BOONE CC
Boone, North Carolina
Ellis Maples

BOONE AIRE GC
Florence, Kentucky
NKA Boone Links GC

BOONE LINKS GC
Florence, Kentucky
Robert von Hagge
(A.3rd 9) Michael Hurdzan

BOONE VALLEY GC
Clayton, Missouri
P. B. Dye

BOONSBORO CC
Lynchburg, Virginia
Fred Findlay
(R.) Rees Jones

BOONVILLE GC
Boonville, Indiana
Tom Bendelow

BOOTHBAY REGION CC
Boothbay, Maine
Wayne Stiles

BOOTHFERRY GC
Yorkshire, England
D. M. A. Steel

BOOTLE GC
Lancashire, England
Tom Simpson

BOOTS RANDOLPH GC
Lake Barkley State Park, Kentucky
Edward Lawrence Packard

BORAS GC
Sweden
Douglas Brazier

BORDEAUX-CAMEYRAC GC
France
J. Quenot

BORDEAUX-LAC GC
France
J. Bourret

BORDEN G&CC
Amiens, France
P. M. Ross
(R.9) J. J. F. Pennink

BORRIS GC
County Carlow, Ireland
Colonel J. H. Curry
(R.) Eddie Hackett

BORTH AND YNSLAS GC
Wales
(R.) H. S. Colt
(R.) J. S. F. Morrison

BOSCOBEL G&CC
South Carolina
Fred Bolton

BOSJÖKLOSTER GC
Sweden
Douglas Brazier

BOSKOGENS GC
Sweden
Anders Amilon (1963)

BOSO CC OKAMI
Japan
Hirochika Tomizawa

BOSQUES DEL LAGO CC (EAST CSE)
Mexico City, Mexico
Joseph S. Finger

BOSQUES DEL LAGO CC (WEST CSE)
Mexico City, Mexico
Joseph S. Finger

BOSQUES DE SAN ISIDRO GC
Guadalajara, Mexico
Lawrence Hughes

BOSTON CORNERS G CSE
Boston Corners, New York
Stephen Kay

BOTANY WOODS GC
Greenville, South Carolina
George W. Cobb

BOUGHTON RIDGE GC
Bollingbrook, Illinois
Roger Packard

BOULDER CC [NLE]
Boulder, Colorado
Tom Bendelow

BOULDER CC
Boulder, Colorado
Press Maxwell

BOULDER CITY GC
Boulder City, Nevada
Harry Rainville, David Rainville
(A.9) Greg Nash

BOULDER CREEK GC
Boulder Creek, California
Jack Fleming

BOULDER RIDGE CC
Lake in the Hills, Illinois
Bob Lohmann, *Fuzzy Zoeller*

[THE] BOULDERS C (NORTH CSE)
Carefree, Arizona
Jay Morrish

[THE] BOULDERS C (SOUTH CSE)
Carefree, Arizona
Jay Morrish

[THE] BOULDERS GC [NLE]
Carefree, Arizona
Red Lawrence
(R.2 A.9) Arthur Jack Snyder

BOUNDARY OAKS GC
Walnut Creek, California
Robert Muir Graves

BOUNTIFUL MUNI
Bountiful, Utah
William H. Neff, William
Howard Neff

BOW CREEK GC
Virginia Beach, Virginia
Fred Sappenfield

BOWDEN MUNI
Macon, Georgia
Hugh Moore
(A.9) Ward Northrup
(R.) Kevin Tucker

BOWES CREEK G CSE
South Elgin, Illinois
(R.) Dave Esler

BOWIE MUNI
Bowie, Texas
Leon Howard

BOWLING GREEN CC [NLE]
Bowling Green, Kentucky
William B. Langford, Theodore
J. Moreau

BOWLING GREEN CC
Bowling Green, Kentucky
Buck Blankenship

BOWLING GREEN GC
Milton, New Jersey
Geoffrey S. Cornish, William G.
Robinson

BOWLING GREEN UNIVERSITY GC
Bowling Green, Ohio
(R.) Arthur Hills
(R.9 A.9) X. G. Hassenplug

BOWMAN'S MOUNT HOOD GC
Mount Hood, Oregon
George Walle, Ralph Shattuck
(A.9) *Gene Bowman*

BOWMAN'S MOUNT HOOD GC
(RIPPLING RIVER CSE)
Mount Hood, Oregon
Gene Bowman

BOWMANVILLE CC
Ontario
Clinton E. Robinson

BOWNESS GC
Calgary, Alberta
Willie Park, Jr.

BOWRING PARK GC
Liverpool, England
Fred W. Hawtree

BOYCE HILL GC
England
(R.9) F. G. Hawtree

BOYLE GC
County Roscommon
Eddie Hackett

BOYNE HIGHLANDS GC (EXECUTIVE
CSE)
Harbor Springs, Michigan
(R.) *Everett Kircher, Stephen
Kircher* (1990)

BOYNE HIGHLANDS GC (HEATHER
CSE)
Harbor Springs, Michigan
Robert Trent Jones

BOYNE HIGHLANDS GC (MOOR CSE)
Harbor Springs, Michigan
William Newcomb

BOYNE HIGHLANDS GC (DONALD
ROSS MEMORIAL CSE)
Harbor Springs, Michigan
William Newcomb, *Everett
Kircher, Jim Flick, Stephen
Kircher*

BOYNE MOUNTAIN GC (ALPINE CSE)
Boyne Falls, Michigan
William Newcomb

BOYNE MOUNTAIN GC (EXECUTIVE
CSE)
Boyne Falls, Michigan
William Newcomb

BOYNE MOUNTAIN GC (MONUMENT
CSE)
Boyne Falls, Michigan
William Newcomb

BOYNTON BEACH MUNI
Boynton Beach, Florida
Robert von Hagge, Bruce Devlin
(R.) Chuck Ankrom

BOX GROVE CC
Markham, Ontario
NKA IBM CC, Markham

BRACKENRIDGE PARK GC
San Antonio, Texas
A. W. Tillinghast
(R.6) John Bredemus

BRACKENWOOD MUNI
Cheshire, England
Fred W. Hawtree

BRADENTON CC
Bradenton, Florida
Donald Ross
(R.) Gordon Lewis

BRADFORD CC
Bradford, Massachusetts
Brian Silva, Geoffrey S. Cornish

BRADFORD GC
Bradford, Pennsylvania
James Gilmore Harrison,
Ferdinand Garbin

BRADFORD GC (MANOR CSE)
Yorkshire, England
(R.) Herbert Fowler
(A.13) Old Tom Morris

BRADLEY PARK GC
Huddersfield, England
D. M. A. Steel

BRAE BURN CC
West Newton, Massachusetts
Donald Ross
(R.) Donald Ross
(R.2) Geoffrey S. Cornish,
William G. Robinson
(R.) Brian Silva, Geoffrey S.
Cornish

BRAE BURN CC
Purchase, New York
Frank Duane
(R.) Stephen Kay

BRAE BURN CC
Bellaire, Texas
John Bredemus
(R.) Ralph Plummer
(R.4) Joseph S. Finger
(R.4) Marvin Ferguson
(R.) Derrell Witt

BRAE BURN CC
Bellevue, Washington
Al Smith

BRAE BURN GC
Plymouth, Michigan
Wilfrid Reid, William Connellan

BRAEBURN GC
Redmond, Washington
William Teufel

BRAE BURN LINKS [NLE]
Copley, Ohio
L. M. Latta

BRAELINN GC
Peachtree City, Georgia
Rocky Roquemore

BRAEMAR CC (EAST CSE)
Tarzana, California
Ted Robinson

BRAEMAR CC (WEST CSE)
Tarzana, California
Ted Robinson

BRAEMAR CC
Edina, Minnesota
Dick Phelps
(A.3rd 9) Gerry Pirkl, *Donald
G. Brauer*

BRAIDBURN CC [NLE]
Florham Park, New Jersey
Herbert Strong

BRAID HILLS GC
Edinburgh, Scotland
Robert Ferguson, Peter McEwan

BRAIDWOOD GC
Braidwood, Illinois
Homer Fieldhouse

BRAINERD MUNI
Chattanooga, Tennessee
Donald Ross
(R.) Grant Wencel

BRAINROE GC
County Wicklow, Ireland
Fred W. Hawtree, Martin Haw-
tree

BRAINTREE GC
Essex, England
Fred W. Hawtree

BRAINTREE MUNI
South Braintree, Massachusetts
(R. A.11) Samuel Mitchell

BRAMLEY GC
England
Charles H. Mayo
(R.) James Braid, John R.
Stutt

BRAMPTON GC
Ontario
(R.9) Stanley Thompson

BRAMPTON PARK GC
Cambridge, England
(R.) Martin Hawtree, Simon
Gidman

BRAMSHAW GC (MANOR CSE)
England
Tom Dunn
(R.) *W. Wiltshire*

BRAMSHOTT HILL GC
Hampshire, England
J. Hamilton Stutt

BRANCEPETH CASTLE GC
Durham, England
H. S. Colt, C. H. Alison, Alister
Mackenzie

BRANCHTON MEADOWS GC
Branchton, Ontario
William G. Robinson, John F.
Robinson

BRANCHWOOD GC
Bella Vista, Arkansas
Edmund B. Ault

BRANDERMILL CC
Midlothian, Virginia
Ron Kirby, Gary Player

BRANDLHOF G&CC
Saalfelden, Austria
(R.) Jeremy Pern

BRANDON GC
Ireland
Eddie Hackett

BRANDON GC [NLE]
Brandon, Vermont
Wayne Stiles

BRANDON WOOD GC
Coventry, England
J. J. F. Pennink

BRANDYWINE CC
Wilmington, Delaware
Alfred H. Tull
(R.7) Brian Ault, Bill Love

BRANDYWINE CC
Maumee, Ohio
Arthur Hills

BRANDYWINE CC
Peninsula, Ohio
Earl F. Yesberger

BRANDYWINE BAY GC
Morehead City, North Carolina
Robert van Hagge, Bruce Devlin

BRANSON BAY GC
Mason, Michigan
Phil Shirley

BRANTFORD G&CC
Brantford, Ontario
George Cumming, Nicol
Thompson
(R.) Clinton E. Robinson
(R.) Stanley Thompson

BRASÍLIA GC
Brasília, Brazil
Robert Trent Jones

BRATTLEBORO CC
Brattleboro, Vermont
Wayne Stiles
(R.) William F. Mitchell

BRAY GC
Bray, Ireland
(R.9) Cecil Barcroft

BRAYS ISLAND PLANTATION GC
Sheldon, South Carolina
Ron Garl

BRAYSIDE GC AT COURTLAND HILLS
Rockford, Michigan
Mark DeVries

BRAZORIA BEND GC
Houston, Texas
Frank Cope

BREADSALL PRIORY GC (NEW CSE)
Derby, England
D. M. A. Steel

BREADSALL PRIORY GC (OLD CSE)
Derby, England
William Cox
[THE] BREAKERS GC
Palm Beach, Florida
Alex Findlay
   (R.9) William B. Langford,
   Theodore J. Moreau
   (A.9) William B. Langford
   (R.) Joe Lee
BREAKERS BEACH CC [NLE]
Northbrook, Illinois
Leonard Macomber
BREAKERS WEST GC
West Palm Beach, Florida
Willard Byrd
BREAN GC
England
A. H. Clarke
BREATHNACH CC
Akron, Ohio
Harold Paddock
BRECHIN GC
Angus, Scotland
James Braid
BRECHTEL MEMORIAL PARK GC
New Orleans, Louisiana
   (R.9 A.9) Richard W.
   LaConte, Ted McAnlis
BRECKENRIDGE GC
Breckenridge, Texas
Tom Bendelow
BRECKENRIDGE G CSE
Breckenridge, Colorado
Jack Nicklaus
BREEZY BEND CC
Manitoba
   (R.) Geoffrey S. Cornish,
   William G. Robinson
BREITENLOO GC
Oberwil, Switzerland
J. J. F. Pennink
   (R.) Donald Harradine
BRENTWOOD CC
Brentwood, Tennessee
Gary Roger Baird
BRENTWOOD CC
Los Angeles, California
   (R.) Max Behr
   (R.) Willie Watson
   (R.3) Ronald Fream
   (R.) Robert Muir Graves
BRENTWOOD GC
Jacksonville, Florida
Donald Ross
BRENTWOOD GC
Milwaukee, Wisconsin
Harry B. Smead
BRENTWOOD FALLS G CSE
La Vista, Nebraska
Pat Wyss
BRENTWOOD LAKES GC
Victoria, British Columbia
William G. Robinson, John F.
Robinson
BRESLAU GC
Breslau, Germany
Karl Hoffmann
BREST-IROISE GC
Landerneau, France
Michael Fenn

BRETON BAY G&CC
Leonardtown, Maryland
J. Porter Gibson
BRETTON WOODS GC
Germantown, Maryland
Edmund B. Ault
BRETT VALE GC
Raydon, Suffolk, England
Howard Swan
BRETWOOD GC
Keene, New Hampshire
Geoffrey S. Cornish, William G.
Robinson
   (A.3rd 9) *Hugh Barrett*
BREWSTER GREEN GC [NLE]
Brewster, Massachusetts
Orrin Smith
   (A.2) Geoffrey S. Cornish,
   William G. Robinson
BRIAN THICKE ESTATE GC
Orangeville, Ontario
Howard Watson
BRIAR BAY GC
Miami, Florida
Robert van Hagge, Bruce Devlin
BRIARBROOK CC
Carl Junction, Missouri
Jim Latimer
BRIARCLIFF G&CC
Rainier, Washington
Fred Federspiel
BRIAR CREEK CC
Sylvania, Georgia
Bill Amick
BRIARCREST CC
Bryan, Texas
Marvin Ferguson
BRIARDALE GREENS MUNI
Euclid, Ohio
Richard W. LaConte, Ted
McAnlis
BRIAR HALL CC
Briarcliff Manor, New York
Devereux Emmet
BRIAR RIDGE CC
Munster, Indiana
Roger Packard
BRIARS G&CC
Jackson Point, Ontario
Stanley Thompson
   (A.9) Clinton Robinson
   (R.) Douglas Carrick
BRIARWOOD CC
Deerfield, Illinois
C. H. Alison, H. S. Colt
   (R.) Robert Bruce Harris
   (R.) Bob Lohmann
   (R.) Dave Esler
BRIARWOOD CC
Baton Rouge, Louisiana
   (R.) Stephen Kay
BRIARWOOD CC
Meridian, Mississippi
Earl Stone
BRIARWOOD CC
Billings, Montana
Brad Benz, Mike Poellot
BRIARWOOD GC
Broadview Heights, Ohio
Ted McAnlis
BRIARWOOD GC
Sun City West, Arizona
Jeff Hardin, Greg Nash

BRIARWOOD WEST GC
York, Pennsylvania
Bill Love
BRICKENDON GRANGE G&CC
England
C. K. Cotton, J. J. F. Pennink
BRICK LANDING PLANTATION GC
Ocean Isle Beach, North
Carolina
Michael Brazeal (1987)
BRIDGEDOWN CC
Arkley, Hertfordshire, England
Howard Swan
BRIDGEPORT CC
Bridgeport, West Virginia
James Gilmore Harrison,
Ferdinand Garbin
BRIDGEPORT FAIRWAYS GC
Connestoga, Ontario
Clinton E. Robinson
BRIDGESTONE CC
Saga, Japan
T. Miyoshi
BRIDGEWATER G&CC
Bridgewater, Nova Scotia
Graham Cooke
BRIDGTON HIGHLANDS GC
Maine
Ralph Barton
   (R.) Orrin Smith
   (A.2) Geoffrey S. Cornish,
   Brian Silva
BRIDLINGTON BAY GC
East Yorkshire, England
Howard Swan
BRIDPORT AND WEST DORSET GC
England
James Braid
BRIERGATE CC
Deerfield, Illinois
NKA Briarwood CC
BRIERWOOD GC
Shallotte, North Carolina
Benjamin Ward
BRIGANTINE CC
New Jersey
Wayne Stiles, John Van Kleek
   (R.) Garrett Gill, George B.
   Williams
BRIGGSWOOD G CSE
Webster, Iowa
Jerry Raible
BRIGHAM CITY G&CC
Brigham City, Utah
Mick Riley
   (A.9) William Howard Neff
BRIGHT LEAF GC
Harrodsburg, Kentucky
Buck Blankenship
BRIGHTMOOR CC
Dearborn, Michigan
Donald Ross
BRIGHTON AND HOVE GC
Sussex, England
Tom Dunn
   (R.) Willie Park, Jr.
   (A.9) James Braid
BRIGHTON CREST CC
Friant, California
Gene Bates, Johnny Miller
BRIGHTON DALE GC
Kansasville, Wisconsin
Edmund B. Ault
   (R. A.2) Steve Halberg

BRIGHTON PARK GC
Tonawanda, New York
William Harries, *A. Russell
Tyron*
BRIGHTWOOD G&CC
Dartmouth, Nova Scotia
Willie Park, Jr.
   (R.) Donald Ross
   (R.) Robert Moote
BRIGHTWOOD HILLS GC
New Brighton, Minnesota
Leo Johnson
BRIGODE GC
Lille, France
M. Baker
BRIONI GC
Italy
Archie Kitts, M. Lauber
   (R. A.2) *M. Lauber*
BRISTOL & CLIFTON GC
Avon, England
   (R.) J. Hamilton Stutt
BRISTOL COUNTY CC
Massachusetts
Skip Wogan
BRISTOL GC [NLE]
Bristol, Vermont
George Frazer
BRISTOL HARBOR VILLAGE GC
Canandaigua, New York
Robert Trent Jones
BRISTOLWOOD GC
Bristol, Pennsylvania
George Fazio
BRITANNIA GC
Cayman Islands
Jack Nicklaus
BROAD BAY POINT G&CC
Virginia Beach, Virginia
Tom Clark, Edmund B. Ault
BROADMOOR CC
Indianapolis, Indiana
Donald Ross
BROADMOOR CC
Shareville, Indiana
R. Albert Anderson
BROADMOOR CC [NLE]
New Rochelle, New York
Devereux Emmet, Alfred H. Tull
BROADMOOR CC
Moore, Oklahoma
Floyd Farley
BROADMOOR CC
Sherwood Park, Alberta
Norman H. Woods
[THE] BROADMOOR GC (EAST CSE)
Colorado Springs, Colorado
Donald Ross
   (A.9) Robert Trent Jones
[THE] BROADMOOR GC (SOUTH
CSE)
Colorado Springs, Colorado
Arnold Palmer, Ed Seay
[THE] BROADMOOR GC (WEST CSE)
Colorado Springs, Colorado
Donald Ross
   (A.9) Robert Trent Jones
BROADMOOR GC
Caledonia, Michigan
   (A.) Mark DeVries
BROADMOOR GC
Portland, Oregon
George Junor
   (R.) *William Sander*

BROADMOOR GC
Seattle, Washington
A. Vernon Macan
(R.3) John Steidel
BROADMORE CC
Nampa, Idaho
T. R. Scott
BROADSTONE GC
Dorset, England
Tom Dunn
(R. A.8) H. S. Colt
(R.) Herbert Fowler
(R.) Willie Park, Willie Park,
Jr.
(R.) J. Hamilton Stutt
BROADVIEW GC
Pataskala, Ohio
Jack Kidwell
BROADWATER BEACH HOTEL GC
(FUN CSE)
Gulfport, Mississippi
Earl Stone
BROADWATER BEACH HOTEL GC
(SEA CSE)
Gulfport, Mississippi
Charles G. Nieman
(R.9 A.9) Earl Stone
BROADWATER BEACH HOTEL GC
(SUN CSE)
Gulfport, Mississippi
Earl Stone
BRO-BALSTA GC
Bro, Sweden
Peter Nordwall
BROCKENHURST MANOR GC
England
H. S. Colt
(R.) J. Hamilton Stutt
BROCK PARK GC
Texas
A. C. Ray
BROCKTON CC
Brockton, Massachusetts
Alex Findlay
BROCKVILLE CC
Ontario
(R.9) Stanley Thompson
(A.9) Clinton E. Robinson
BROCKWAY GC
Kings Beach, California
NKA Woodvista G Cse
BROCTON HALL GC
Staffordshire, England
Harry Vardon
(R.) *Reginald Beale*
BRODAUER MÜHLE GC
Grömitz, Germany
Wolfgang Siegmann
BROEKPOLDER GC
Vlaardingen, Netherlands
J. J. F. Pennink
BROKEN SOUND GC (CLUB CSE)
Boca Raton, Florida
Joe Lee
BROKEN SOUND GC (OLD CSE)
Boca Raton, Florida
Joe Lee
BROKEN WOODS G&RC
Coral Springs, Florida
Bill Watts
(R.2) Edmund B. Ault

BROMBOROUGH GC
England
(R.) Fred W. Hawtree, A. H.
F. Jiggens
BROMLEY GC
England
Tom Dunn
BROMME MANOR GC
Wiltshire, England
Fred W. Hawtree, Martin
Hawtree
BRONDERSLEV GC
Denmark
E. Schnack
BROOKDALE CC
Tacoma, Washington
Al Smith
BROOKE HILLS PARK GC
Wellsburg, West Virginia
X. G. Hassenplug
BROOKFIELD CC
Clarence, New York
William Harries
BROOKFIELD HILLS GC
Brookfield, Wisconsin
Robert von Hagge, Bruce Devlin
BROOKFIELD WEST G&CC
Atlanta, Georgia
George W. Cobb
BROOKHAVEN CC (CHAMPIONSHIP
CSE)
Dallas, Texas
Press Maxwell
BROOKHAVEN CC (MASTERS CSE)
Dallas, Texas
Press Maxwell
(R.) Jeff Brauer, Larry Nelson
BROOKHAVEN CC (PRESIDENTS CSE)
Dallas, Texas
Press Maxwell
BROOKHAVEN GC
New York
George Pulver
BROOK HILL GC
Brookville, Indiana
Gary Kern
BROOKHILL GC
Rantoul, Illinois
Edward Lawrence Packard
(A. 9) Roger Packard
BROOKHILLS GC
Springfield, Illinois
Leon Howard
BROOK HOLLOW GC
Dallas, Texas
A. W. Tillinghast
(R.) Ralph Plummer
(R.) Jay Morrish
BROOK LAKE CC
Florham Park, New Jersey
Herbert Strong
(R.9) *Duer Irving Sewall*
(R. A.9) Hal Purdy, Malcolm
Purdy
(R. A.5) Geoffrey S. Cornish,
Brian Silva
BROOKLAWN CC
Fairfield, Connecticut
(R.) A. W. Tillinghast
BROOKLEA CC
Rochester, New York
Donald Ross
(R.) William Harries
(R.) Bob Cupp

BROOKLEA GC
Midland, Ontario
(R.) Robert Moote
BROOKLEDGE GC
Cuyahoga Falls, Ohio
Arthur Hills
BROOKE MANOR CC
Brooke, Virginia
Alfred H. Tull
BROOKMEADOW GC
Canton, Massachusetts
Samuel Mitchell
BROOKRIDGE G&CC
Overland Park, Kansas
Chic Adams
BROOKRIDGE GC
Park Ridge, Illinois
C. D. Wagstaff
(R.) Charles Maddox, *Frank
P. MacDonald*
BROOKS CC
Okoboji, Iowa
Warren Dickenson
BROOKSHIRE CC
Williamstown, Michigan
Bruce Matthews
BROOKSHIRE GC
Carmel, Indiana
William H. Diddel
BROOKSIDE CC
Canton, Ohio
Donald Ross
(R.2) Jack Kidwell, Michael
Hurdzan
(R.) Robert Trent Jones
BROOKSIDE CC
Pottstown, Pennsylvania
(R.9 A.9) William Gordon,
David Gordon
(R.) James Gilmore Harrison,
Ferdinand Garbin
BROOKSIDE G&CC
Stockton, California
Robert Trent Jones, Jr.
BROOKSIDE GC
Kingsley, Iowa
Leo Johnson
BROOKSIDE GC
Saline, Michigan
David Snider
BROOKSIDE GC [NLE]
Reno, Nevada
Bob Baldock
BROOKSIDE GC
Oklahoma City, Oklahoma
Floyd Farley
BROOKSIDE GC
Agincourt, Ontario
René Muylaert
BROOKSIDE G CSE
Ashland, Ohio
(A.9) Stephen Burns
BROOKSIDE MUNI (CSE NO. 1)
Pasadena, California
William P. Bell
BROOKSIDE MUNI (CSE NO. 2)
Pasadena, California
William P. Bell
(R.) Desmond Muirhead
BROOKSIDE PARK GC
Ashland, Ohio
X. G. Hassenplug
(A.9) Jack Kidwell, Michael
Hurdzan

BROOKSTONE G&CC
Acworth, Georgia
Jeff Brauer, Larry Nelson
BROOKSVILLE G&CC
Brooksville, Florida
William F. Mitchell
BROOKTREE MUNI
Owatonna, Minnesota
Gerry Pirkl, *Donald G. Brauer*
BROOKTRAILS GC
Willets, California
Robert Muir Graves
BROOK VALLEY G&CC
Greenville, North Carolina
Ellis Maples
BROOKVIEW CC
Golden Valley, Minnesota
Charles Maddox
(R.9) *Fred Sicora*
(R.) Dick Phelps
(R.) Gerry Pirkl, *Donald G.
Brauer, Paul S. Fjare*
(A. Par 3 9) Gerry Pirkl,
Donald G. Brauer, Emil Perret
BROOKVIEW MUNI
Golden Valley, Minnesota
Don Herfort
(R.) Garrett Gill, George B.
Williams
BROOKVILLE CC
Surprise, Arizona
Gary Grandstaff
(R.) Arthur Jack Snyder
BROOKVILLE CC
Glen Head, New York
Seth Raynor
BROOKVILLE MUNI
Indianapolis, Indiana
William Newcomb
BROOKWOOD CC
Addison, Illinois
C. D. Wagstaff
(R.) Edward Lawrence
Packard, Roger Packard
BROOKWOOD CC
Rochester, Michigan
William Newcomb
BROOKWOOD GC
Buchanan, Michigan
William James Spear
BROOKWOODS GC
Quinton, Virginia
Algie Pulley
BROOME PARK GC
Kent, England
J. J. F. Pennink, D. M. A. Steel
BROOMIEKNOWE GC
Midlothian, Scotland
Ben Sayers
(R.) James Braid, John R.
Stutt
(A.4) Martin Hawtree
BRORA GC
Sutherland, Scotland
James Braid
BROWN ACRES GC
Chattanooga, Tennessee
(R.) Grant Wencel
BROWN COUNTY GC
Green Bay, Wisconsin
Edward Lawrence Packard
BROWN DEER PARK GC
Milwaukee, Wisconsin
George Hansen

BROWN'S LAKE GC
Burlington, Wisconsin
(R.2) David Gill
BROWN'S MILL GC
Atlanta, Georgia
George W. Cobb
BROWN'S RUN CC
Middleton, Ohio
William Gordon, David Gordon
(R.) Hal Purdy
(R.) Arthur Hills
BROWNSVILLE CC
Brownsville, Texas
Don Sechrest
BROWNWOOD CC
Brownwood, Texas
Leon Howard
BRUCE DODSON ESTATE GC [NLE]
Kansas City, Missouri
James Dalgleish
BRUCE MEMORIAL GC
Greenwich, Connecticut
Robert Trent Jones
BRUDENELL G&CC
Montague, Prince Edward
Island
Clinton E. Robinson
BRUNN GC
Brunn, Austria
Gerold Hauser, *Günther Hauser*
BRUNSSUM GC
Netherlands
J. F. Dudok van Heel
BRUNSWICK CC
Brunswick, Georgia
Donald Ross
BRUNSWICK CC
Brunswick, Maine
(R.9) Wayne Stiles, John Van
Kleek
(A.9) Geoffrey S. Cornish,
William G. Robinson
BRUNSWICK NAVAL AIR STATION GC
Brunswick, Maine
(R.9) *Mark Verhey*
BRUNSWICK PLANTATION GC
Calabash, North Carolina
Willard Byrd
BRUNTSFIELD LINKS [NLE]
Davidson's Main, Scotland
(R.) Willie Park, Mungo Park
BRUNTSFIELD LINKS
Davidson's Main, Scotland
Willie Park, Jr.
(R.) James Braid, John R.
Stutt
(R. A.7) Fred W. Hawtree
BRYAN MUNI
Bryan, Texas
(R.13) I. F. "Fred" Marberry
(R.6) Marvin Ferguson
BRYAN PARK GC (CHAMPIONS CSE)
Browns Summit, North Carolina
Rees Jones
BRYAN PARK GC (PLAYERS CSE)
Browns Summit, North Carolina
George W. Cobb, John LaFoy
BRYANSTON CC
South Africa
C. H. Alison
BRYCE RESORT GC
Basye, Virginia
Edmund B. Ault

BRYNHILL GC
Glamorganshire, Wales
Willie Park, Jr.
(R.) C. K. Cotton
(R.) Willie Park, Jr.
BRYN LLAWEN GC
Ivyville, Pennsylvania
Garrett J. Renn
BRYN MAWR GC [NLE]
Chicago, Illinois
H. J. Tweedie
BRYN MAWR GC
Lincolnwood, Illinois
William B. Langford, Theodore
J. Moreau
(R.) William B. Langford
(R.) Edward Lawrence
Packard
(R.) Bob Cupp, Jay Morrish
(R.) Roger Packard
BRYN MEADOWS G&CC
Wales
Edgar Jeffries
BRYNWOOD CC
Milwaukee, Wisconsin
William H. Diddel
(R.6) David Gill
(R.) Ken Killian, Dick Nugent
(R.1 A.2) Bruce Matthews,
Jerry Matthews
(R.) Bob Lohmann
BUCCANEER HOTEL GC
Virgin Islands
Robert Joyce
BUCHANAN CASTLE GC
Stirlingshire, Scotland
James Braid, John R. Stutt
BUCHANAN FIELDS GC
Concord, California
Jack Fleming
(R.) Robert Muir Graves
BUCK CREEK G PLANTATION
Longs, South Carolina
Tom Jackson
BUCKEYE HILLS CC
Washington Court House, Ohio
X. G. Hassenplug
BUCK HILL INN & CC
Buck Hill Falls, Pennsylvania
Donald Ross
(A.9) Robert White
(R.) William Gordon, David
Gordon
BUCKINGHAM CC
Dallas, Texas
Ralph Plummer
BUCKINGHAM G&CC
Kelseyville, California
James Young
BUCKMEADOW GC
Amherst, New Hampshire
Jake Young
BUCKNELL UNIVERSITY GC
Lewisburg, Pennsylvania
(A.9) Edmund B. Ault
BUCKNER CHILDREN'S HOME G CSE
Dallas, Texas
Leon Howard
BUCKS COUNTY GC
Jamison, Pennsylvania
William Gordon, David Gordon
BUCKSPORT G&CC
Bucksport, Maine
Phil Wogan

BUDE AND NORTH CORNWALL GC
England
Tom Dunn
(R.) J. Hamilton Stutt
BUDOCK VEAN HOTEL GC
England
James Braid
BUENAVENTURA GC
Ventura, California
William P. Bell, William F. Bell
BUENAVENTURA LAKES CC
Kissimmee, Florida
Buddy Blanton
BUENAVENTURA LAKES WEST CC
Kissimmee, Florida
Ward Northrup
BUENA VISTA CC
Buena, New Jersey
William Gordon, David Gordon
BUENA VISTA GC
Taft, California
Lance Hopper
BUENA VISTA GC
Vincennes, Indiana
William B. Langford
BUFFALO G CSE
Buffalo, Wyoming
Frank Hummel
BUFFALO CREEK GC
Manatee, Florida
Ron Garl
BUFFALO CREEK G CSE
Rockwall, Texas
Jay Morrish, Tom Weiskopf
BUFFALO DUNES MUNI
Garden City, Kansas
Frank Hummel
BUFFALO GROVE GC
Buffalo Grove, Illinois
Ken Killian, Dick Nugent
BUFFALO HILL GC
Kalispell, Montana
(R. A.9) Robert Muir Graves
(R.) William G. Robinson,
John F. Robinson
BUFORD ELLINGTON GC
Horton State Park, Tennessee
Charles M. Graves
BUHL CC
Buhl, Idaho
(R.) Robert Muir Graves
BUKIT JAMBUL CC
Malaysia
Robert Trent Jones, Jr.
BULAWAYO GC
South Africa
(R.) C. H. Alison
BULL BAY GC
Gwynedd, Wales
Herbert Fowler
(R.) James Braid
BULL CREEK G CSE
Columbus, Georgia
Joe Lee
(A.3rd 9) Ward Northrup
BULLDOG SPORTS COMPLEX
Stuart, Florida
Charles Ankrom
BULLS EYE CC
Wisconsin Rapids, Wisconsin
Leonard Macomber
(A.9) Edward Lawrence
Packard

BULL VALLEY GC
Woodstock, Illinois
Dick Nugent
BULWELL FOREST GC
England
Tom Dunn
(R.) Tom Williamson
BUMI SERPONG DAMAI GC
Jakarta, Indonesia
Jack Nicklaus
BUNCOMBE COUNTY G CSE
Asheville, North Carolina
Donald Ross
BUNDORAN GC
County Donegal, Ireland
C. S. Butchart
(R.) Harry Vardon
BUNKER HILL CC
Maryland
Charles B. Schalestock
BUNKER HILL GC
Brush, Colorado
Frank Hummel
BUNKER HILL GC
Medina, Ohio
Walter Kennedy
BUNKER HILLS G CSE (EAST CSE)
Coon Rapids, Minnesota
David Gill
BUNKER HILLS G CSE (WEST CSE)
Coon Rapids, Minnesota
David Gill
(A.2nd 9) Joel Goldstrand
BUNKER HILLS G CSE (EXECUTIVE
CSE) [NLE]
Coon Rapids, Minnesota
Joel Goldstrand
BUNN PARK GC
Springfield, Illinois
(R.) Edward Lawrence
Packard
BURAPHA GC
Bangkok, Thailand
Gary Panks, *David Graham*
BURG OVERBACH GC
Munich, Germany
Karl F. Grohs, *Rainer
Preissmann*
BURHILL GC
Surrey, England
Tom Dunn
(R.9) Willie Park, Jr.
(A.9) H. S. Colt
BURKE LAKE PARK GC
Annandale, Virginia
Dave Bennett, Leon Howard
BURKE MEMORIAL GC
South Bend, Indiana
(R.) Ken Killian, Dick Nugent
BURLEIGH CC
Burleigh, Australia
James D. Scott
BURLINGAME CC [NLE]
Hillsborough, California
Tom Nicoll
BURLINGAME CC
Hillsborough, California
Herbert Fowler, *Harold Sampson*
(R.) Willie Watson
(R.) Robert Muir Graves
BURLINGTON CC
Burlington, North Carolina
Donald Ross

BURLINGTON CC
Burlington, Vermont
Donald Ross
BURLINGTON CC
Burlington, Wisconsin
James Foulis
BURLINGTON COUNTY CC
Mount Holly, New Jersey
John Finley
BURLINGTON G&CC
Hamilton, Ontario
Stanley Thompson
(R.) Robert Moote
BURLINGTON GC
Burlington, Iowa
Ben Knight
(R.9 A.9) Edward Lawrence
Packard
BURL OAKS GC
Minitrista, Minnesota
(R.) Joel Goldstrand
BURNABY MOUNTAIN GC
British Columbia
(R.) Clinton E. Robinson
BURNET PARK MUNI
New York
Larry Murphy
BURNHAM AND BARROW GC
Somerset, England
(R.) C. H. Alison
(R.) J. S. F. Morrison
(A.9) Fred W. Hawtree
BURNHAM-ON-CROUCH GC
Essex, England
(A.9) Howard Swan
BURNHAM WOODS CC
Burnham, Illinois
Stanley Pelchar
BURNING RIDGE GC (EAST CSE)
Myrtle Beach, South Carolina
Gene Hamm
BURNING RIDGE GC (WEST CSE)
Myrtle Beach, South Carolina
Gene Hamm
BURNING TREE C
Bethesda, Maryland
C. H. Alison, H. S. Colt
(R.) William S. Flynn
(R.) Robert Trent Jones
(R.) Edmund B. Ault
BURNINGTREE CC
Decatur, Alabama
George W. Cobb
BURNING TREE CC
Greenwich, Connecticut
Hal Purdy
(R.) Stephen Kay
BURNING TREE G&CC
Mount Clemens, Michigan
Lou Powers
BURNING TREE GC
White Oak, Ohio
Edward Lawrence Packard
BURNS PARK MUNI
North Little Rock, Arkansas
(R.) Joseph S. Finger
BURNTISLAND GOLF HOUSE C
Scotland
(R.) Willie Park, Jr.
BURNT STORE VILLAGE GC
Punta Gorda, Florida
David Wallace
(R.) Gordon Lewis

BURNT STORE MARINA GC (MARINA
CSE)
Punta Gorda, Florida
Ron Garl
BURNT STORE MARINA GC (SOUTH
CSE)
Punta Gorda, Florida
Mark McCumber
BURSWOOD ISLAND GC
Perth, Australia
Robin Nelson, Rodney Wright
BURTON-ON-TRENT GC
England
(R.) Tom Williamson
BURY ST. EDMUNDS GC
England
Ted Ray
(R.) J. J. F. Pennink
(R.) Martin Hawtree, Simon
Gidman
BUSCOT PARK GC
England
Tom Dunn
BUSENA RESORT GC
Busena, Okinawa
Robin Nelson, Rodney Wright
BUSHEY G & SQUASH C
Hertfordshire, England
J. J. F. Pennink, D. M. A. Steel
BUSHFIELD CC
Mount Holly, Virginia
Edmund B. Ault, Al Jamison
BUSHFOOT GC
Northern Ireland
John Harris
BUSH HILL PARK GC
England
(R.) James Braid, John R.
Stutt
BUTLER CC
Butler, Pennsylvania
Tom Bendelow
(R.) Emil Loeffler, *John
McGlynn*
(R.9 A.9) Leonard Macomber
(R.) Edmund B. Ault
(R.) Ferdinand Garbin
BUTLER COUNTY GC
Ohio
Tom Bendelow
BUTLER NATIONAL GC
Oak Brook, Illinois
George Fazio, Tom Fazio
(R.) Dick Nugent
BUTTE CC
Butte, Montana
Alex Findlay
BUTTE CREEK CC
Chico, California
Bob Baldock
BUTTE DES MORTS GC
Appleton, Wisconsin
Frank Taylor
(R.) Bob Lohmann
BUTTERFIELD CC
Hinsdale, Illinois
William B. Langford, Theodore
J. Moreau
(R.) Edward Lawrence
Packard
(R.) Ken Killian, Dick Nugent
BUTTERMILK FALLS GC
Georgetown, Ohio
Jack Kidwell, Michael Hurdzan

BUTTERNUT FARM GC
Stow, Massachusetts
Brian Silva, Geoffrey S. Cornish
BUTTERNUT HILLS GC
Sarona, Wisconsin
Carl Marshall
BUTTERNUT RIDGE CC
North Olmstead, Ohio
Harold Paddock
BUTTONVILLE GC
Ontario
NKA Markham G&CC
BUXAHATCHEE CC
Calera, Alabama
Bancroft Timmons
BUXTEHUDE GC
Daensen, Germany
Wolfgang Siegmann
BUXTON AND HIGH PEAK GC
Derbyshire, England
(R.) Alister Mackenzie
(R.) Tom Williamson
BYRNCLIFF CC
Varysborg, New York
William Harries
BYRNEWOOD GC
New Jersey
J. E. Wells
BYRON MEADOWS CC
Batavia, New York
William Harries

CÀ AMATA GC
Italy
Marco Croze
CABARRUS CC
Concord, North Carolina
George W. Cobb
CABINET VIEW CC
Libby, Montana
Gregor MacMillan
CABLE BEACH HOTEL & GC
Nassau, Bahamas
NKA Carnival's Crystal Palace
GC
CABOOL-MOUNTAIN GROVE CC
Cabool, Missouri
Floyd Farley
CACAPON SPRINGS GC
Berkley Springs, West Virginia
Robert Trent Jones
CACTUS HEIGHTS GC
South Dakota
Clifford A. Anderson
CÀ'DEGLI ULIVI GC
Verona, Italy
Jim Engh
CÀ'DELLA NAVE GC
Italy
Arnold Palmer, Ed Seay
CADILLAC CC
Cadillac, Michigan
Paul Blick
(R.1) Bruce Matthews, Jerry
Matthews
CADRON VALLEY CC
Conway, Arkansas
Jim Miller
CAERNARVONSHIRE GC
Wales
(R.) J. J. F. Pennink

CAESAREA G&C
Israel
Fred Smith
CAHAWBA FALLS CC
Centerville, Alabama
Bancroft Timmons
CAHIR PARK GC
County Tipperary, Ireland
Eddie Hackett
CAIRNDNU GC
Northern Ireland
J. S. F. Morrison, H. S. Colt,
C. H. Alison
(R.) Eddie Hackett
CAIRO CC
Cairo, Georgia
R. Albert Anderson
CALABASAS PARK CC
Calabasas Park, California
Robert Trent Jones
CALAIS GC
Calais, France
(R.) J. J. F. Pennink
CALA SERENA GOLF TRAINING
CENTER
Mallorca, Spain
Karl F. Grohs, *Rainer
Preissmann*
CALATAGAN GC
Philippines
Robert Trent Jones, Jr.
CALCOT PARK GC
Reading, England
H. S. Colt, J. S. F. Morrison
CALDWELL GC
Caldwell, Idaho
Delwin Jones
CALDWELL GC
Glasgow, Scotland
George Fernie
CALEDON CC
Caledon, Ontario
René Muylaert
CALEDON GC
South Africa
(R.9 A.9) *Ken B. Elkin*
CALEDONIAN GC
Chiba-ken, Japan
Mike Poellot
CALENDO GC
Pennsylvania
C. C. Worthington
CALERO HILLS CC
San Jose, California
Jack Fleming
CALGARY G&CC
Alberta
Willie Park, Jr.
(R.) Stanley Thompson
(R.) C. E. Robinson
(R.) William G. Robinson
CALGARY MUNI
Calgary, Alberta
Tom Bendelow
CALGARY ST. ANDREWS GC
Calgary, Alberta
Willie Park, Jr.
CALHOUN C
St. Matthews, South Carolina
Ellis Maples
CALIFORNIA C
Hallandale, Florida
Charles Mahannah

CALIFORNIA CC
Whittier, California
William F. Bell
(R.9 A.9) Max Behr
CALIFORNIA GC
California, Missouri
Chet Mendenhall
CALIFORNIA GC
Cincinnati, Ohio
William H. Diddel
(A.5) Jack Kidwell, Michael
Hurdzan
CALIFORNIA GC OF SAN FRANCISCO
South San Francisco, California
A. Vernon Macan
(R.) Alister Mackenzie
(R.) Robert Trent Jones
CALIMESA G&CC
Calimesa, California
William F. Bell
CALIS GC
Calis, Colombia
(R.) C. E. Robinson
CALLAN GC
County Kilkenny, Ireland
P. Mahon
(R.) Eddie Hackett
CALLANDER GC
Stirlingshire, England
Old Tom Morris
CALLAWAY GARDENS GC
(GARDENSVIEW CSE)
Pine Mountain, Georgia
Joe Lee
CALLAWAY GARDENS GC (LAKEVIEW
CSE)
Pine Mountain, Georgia
J. B. McGovern
(A.9) Dick Wilson, Joe Lee
CALLAWAY GARDENS GC
(MOUNTAINVIEW CSE)
Pine Mountain, Georgia
Dick Wilson, Joe Lee
CALLAWAY GARDENS GC (SKYVIEW
CSE)
Pine Mountain, Georgia
Joe Lee
CALLEMONT RESORT GC
Myerstown, Pennsylvania
Robert L. Elder
CALOOSA CC
Sun City Center, Florida
Mark Mahannah, Charles
Mahannah
CALUMET CC [NLE]
Homewood, Illinois
(R.) James Foulis
CALUMET CC
Homewood, Illinois
Donald Ross
(R.12) Edward Lawrence
Packard, Brent Wadsworth
CALUSA CC
Miami, Florida
Mark Mahannah
CALUSA LAKES GC
Nokomis, Florida
Ted McAnlis
CALVADA VALLEY G&CC
Pahrump, Nevada
William F. Bell
CALVERTON G CENTRE
England
Martin Hawtree, Simon Gidman

CAMARGO C
Cincinnati, Ohio
Seth Raynor
(R.) Robert von Hagge
(R.1) Jack Kidwell
CAMARILLO SPRINGS CC
Camarillo, California
Ted Robinson
(R.) Garrett Gill, George B.
Williams
CAMBERLEY HEATH GC
Surrey, England
H. S. Colt
(R.) Tom Simpson
CAMBRIAN GC
San Jose, California
George E. Santana
CAMBRIDGE GC
Cambridge, Ontario
Clinton E. Robinson
CAMBRIDGE GC
New Zealand
(R.) C. H. Redhead
CAMBRIDGESHIRE HOTEL GC
England
Fraser Middleton
CAMDEN CC
Camden, South Carolina
Walter Travis
(R.) Donald Ross
CAMDEN STATE PARK GC
Camden, Alabama
Earl Stone
CAME DOWN GC
England
J. H. Taylor
(R.) J. Hamilton Stutt
CAMELBACK GC (INDIAN BEND CSE)
Scottsdale, Arizona
Arthur Jack Snyder
CAMELBACK GC (PADRE CSE)
Scottsdale, Arizona
Red Lawrence
(R.2) Arthur Jack Snyder
CAMELIA HILLS CC
Chiba, Japan
K. Yasuda, S. Kawamura
CAMELOT CC
Mesa, Arizona
Milt Coggins
CAMELOT CC
Lomira, Wisconsin
Homer Fieldhouse
CAMELOT G&CC
Ottawa, Ontario
Thomas McBroom
CAMELOT INN & GC
Rogersville, Tennessee
Robert Thomason
CAMERON PARK CC
Shingle Springs, California
Bert Stamps
CAMINO DEL MAR CC
Boca Raton, Florida
Joe Lee
CAMOLA GC
Algarve, Portugal
Howard Swan
CAMPBELL RIVER G&CC
British Columbia
Jock McKinn, Ben Fellows

CAMPBELLTOWN GC
Sydney, Australia
Robert von Hagge, Bruce Devlin
(R.) Robin Nelson
CAMP CHIC-A-MEE GC
Levering, Michigan
Elmer Dankert
CAMP CROWDER GC
Camp Crowder, Missouri
Smiley Bell
CAMP DAVID G CSE
Camp David, Maryland
Robert Trent Jones
CAMPERDOWN GC
Australia
Colin Campbell
CAMPERDOWN GC
Scotland
Fraser Middleton
CAMPESTRE DE GOLF LORETO
Loreto, Mexico
Mario Schjetnan, Pedro Guereca
CAMPESTRE DE LAGUNERO
Mexico
Percy Clifford
CAMPOBELLO ISLAND GC [NLE]
New Brunswick
Franklin D. Roosevelt
CAMPOBELLO PROVINCIAL PARK GC
New Brunswick
Geoffrey S. Cornish, William G.
Robinson
CAMPO CARLO MAGNO GC
Italy
(R.) Henry Cotton
CAMPO DE GOLF BELLA VISTA
Ciudad Trujillo, Dominican
Republic
Alfred H. Tull
CAMPO DE GOLF EL SALER
Spain
Javier Arana
CAMPO DE GOLF LOS CABOS
San Jose del Cabo, Baja, Mexico
Jerry Martin
CAMPO DE GOLF SOMOSAGUAS
Madrid, Spain
John Harris
CANAAN VALLEY STATE PARK GC
Davis, West Virginia
Geoffrey S. Cornish, William G.
Robinson
CAÑADA HILLS CC
Tucson, Arizona
NKA Sheraton El Conquistador
GC
CANDIAC GC
Quebec
(R.) Howard Watson, John
Watson
(R.2) John Watson
CANDLESTONE GC
Belding, Michigan
Bruce Matthews, Jerry Matthews
CANDLEWOOD CC
Whittier, California
Harry Rainville, David Rainville
(R.6) Ted Robinson
CANDO GC
North Dakota
Leo Johnson
CANDYWOOD GC
Vienna, Ohio
Homer Fieldhouse

CANE PATCH PAR 3 GC
Myrtle Beach, South Carolina
Edmund B. Ault
(A.3rd 9) Tom Clark
CANLUBANG G CSE
Philippines
Robert Trent Jones, Jr.
CANMORE GC
Canmore, Alberta
Bill Newis
CANNES-MOUGINS GC
France
Peter Alliss, David Thomas
CANNON GC
Cannon Falls, Minnesota
(A.9) Joel Goldstrand
CANOA HILLS GC
Green Valley, Arizona
Dave Bennett
CANOE BROOK CC (NORTH CSE)
Milburn, New Jersey
Alfred H. Tull
(R.) Carroll P. Bassett
(R.) William Gordon, David
Gordon
(R.) Robert Trent Jones
CANOE BROOK CC (SOUTH CSE)
Summit, New Jersey
C. H. Alison, H. S. Colt
(R.) Walter J. Travis
(R.) William Gordon, David
Gordon
(R.) Rees Jones
CANOE CREEK CC
Gadsen, Alabama
Harold Williams
CANON DEL ORO CC
Sedona, Arizona
Arthur Jack Snyder
CANONGATE GC
Orlando, Florida
Joe Lee
CANONGATE GC
Palmetto, Georgia
Dick Wilson, Joe Lee
CANONGATE ON LANIER GC
Cumming, Georgia
Joe Lee, Rocky Roquemore
CANONGATE ON WHITE OAK GC
(CHEROKEE CSE)
Newnan, Georgia
Joe Lee, Rocky Roquemore
CANONGATE ON WHITE OAK GC
(SEMINOLE CSE)
Newnan, Georgia
Rocky Roquemore
CANONS BROOK GC
England
Henry Cotton
CANTERBURY CC
Shaker Heights, Ohio
Herbert Strong
(R.) Geoffrey S. Cornish,
William G. Robinson
CANTERBURY GC
Kent, England
H. S. Colt
CANTERBURY GC
New Zealand
A. R. Blank
CANTERBURY GREEN GC
Fort Wayne, Indiana
Robert Beard

CANTERBURY PLACE GC
Crystal Lake, Illinois
Bob Lohmann
CANTERWOOD G&CC
Gig Harbor, Washington
Robert Muir Graves
CANTIGNY GC
Wheaton, Illinois
Roger Packard
CANTON PARK DISTRICT GC
Canton, Ohio
(A.9) Edward Lawrence
Packard
CANTON PUBLIC G CSE
Canton, Connecticut
Robert J. Ross
CANWELL PARK G&CC
Sussex, England
D. M. A. Steel
CANYAMEL GC
Majorca, Spain
Pepe Gancedo
CANYON CC
Palm Springs, California
William F. Bell
(R.) William F. Mitchell
(R.) Robert Muir Graves
CANYON C
Armonk, New York
Al Zikorus
CANYON CREEK CC
San Antonio, Texas
NKA Club at Sonterra (South
Cse)
CANYON CREEK GC
Clinton, Iowa
Robert Bruce Harris
CANYON GATE CC
Las Vegas, Nevada
Theodore Robinson
CANYON LAKE CC
Canyon Lake, California
Ted Robinson
CANYON LAKES CC
Danville, California
Ted Robinson
CANYON LAKES G&CC
Kennewick, Washington
Peter Thomson, Michael
Wolveridge, Ronald Fream
CANYON MEADOWS G&CC
Calgary, Alberta
(R.) William G. Robinson
CANYON MESA GC
Sedona, Arizona
Arthur Jack Snyder
CANYON RIDGE CC
New Jersey
Gerald C. Roby
CANYON SOUTH G CSE
Palm Springs, California
William F. Bell
(R.) William F. Mitchell
CANYON SPRINGS GC
Twin Falls, Idaho
Max Mueller
CAPADEPERA GC
Mallorca, Spain
Dan Maples
CAPE ANN GC
Essex, Massachusetts
Skip Wogan

CAPE ARUNDEL GC
Kennebunkport, Maine
(R.9 A.9) John Duncan Dunn,
Walter J. Travis
**CAPE BRETON HIGHLANDS NATIONAL
PARK GC**
Keltic Lodge, Nova Scotia
Stanley Thompson
CAPE COD CC
North Falmouth, Massachusetts
Devereux Emmet, Alfred H. Tull
(A.9) Alfred H. Tull
CAPE CORAL CC
Cape Coral, Florida
Dick Wilson
CAPE CORAL EXECUTIVE GC
Cape Coral, Florida
Sid Clarke
CAPE ELEUTHERA GC
Eleuthera, Bahamas
Robert von Hagge, Bruce Devlin
CAPE FEAR CC
Wilmington, North Carolina
Donald Ross
(R.) Donald Ross
(R.) John LaFoy
CAPE G&RC
Wilmington, North Carolina
Gene Hamm
[THE] CAPE GC
Cape Schanck, Australia
Robert Trent Jones, Jr.
CAPE GIRARDEAU CC
Cape Girardeau, Missouri
Al Linkogel
(R.2 A.2) Edward Lawrence
Packard, Brent Wadsworth
(R.9 A.9) David Gill
(R.) Ron Kern, Gary Kern
CAPEHART GC
Offutt AFB, Nebraska
NKA Willow Lakes GC
CAPE HAZE GC
Rotonda West, Florida
John LaFoy
CAPE MAY NATIONAL GC
Cape May, New Jersey
Karl Litten
CAPE NEDDICK CC
Ogunquit, Maine
Donald Ross
CAPE ROYALE CC
Texas
Bruce Littell
CAPILANO G&CC
West Vancouver, British
Columbia
Stanley Thompson
CAPITAL CITY C
Atlanta, Georgia
Herbert Barker
(R.) George W. Cobb
(R.9) Joseph S. Finger
(R.) Arthur Hills
(R.) Bob Cupp
CAPITAL CITY CC
Tallahassee, Florida
John Budd
(R.) R. Albert Anderson
CAPITAL CITY GC
Olympia, Washington
Norman H. Woods

CAPITOL HILLS CC
Philippines
Francisco D. Santana
CAPRICORN INTERNATIONAL GC
Yeppoon, Australia
Karl Litten
CAPRI ISLES GC
Venice, Florida
Lane Marshall
CAPROCK G&CC
Lubbock, Texas
Warren Cantrell
CAPTAINS GC
Brewster, Massachusetts
Brian Silva, Geoffrey S. Cornish
CARABELLEDA G&YC
Macuto, Venezuela
John Van Kleek
CARACAS CC
Caracas, Venezuela
Charles Banks
CARAMBOLA BEACH GC
Frederiksted, Virgin Islands
Robert Trent Jones
(R.) D. J. DeVictor
CARDIFF G&CC
Edmonton, Alberta
William G. Robinson, John F.
Robinson
CARDINAL CREEK GC
Scott AFB, Illinois
(R.) Gary Kern
CARDINAL GC
Greensboro, North Carolina
Pete Dye
CARDROSS GC
Dumbartonshire, Scotland
Willie Fernie
CARD SOUND GC
North Key Largo, Florida
Robert von Hagge, Bruce Devlin
(R.) Ted McAnlis
CAREZZA GC
Italy
Marco Croze
CARIARI INTERNATIONAL CC
San Jose, Costa Rica
George Fazio, Tom Fazio
CARIBOU CC
Caribou, Maine
(R.) *Ben Gray*
CARILLON GC
Plainfield, Illinois
Greg Martin (1990)
CARIMATE PARCO GC
Como, Italy
Pier Mancinelli
CARL E. SMOCK GC
Indianapolis, Indiana
Bob Simmons
CARLETON GLEN GC
Michigan
Joseph E. Milosch
CARLETON Y&CC
Manotick, Ontario
Stanley Thompson
(R.3) John Watson
CARLING LAKE GC
Pine Hill, Quebec
Howard Watson
CARLINVILLE GC
Carlinville, Illinois
Edward Lawrence Packard

CARLISLE GC
Cumberland, England
Theodore Moone
(R.) J. J. F. Pennink
(R.) P. M. Ross
CARLISLE RACE TRACK GC
Cumbria, England
D. M. A. Steel
CARLOW GC
Ireland
(R.) Eddie Hackett
(R.) Tom Simpson, Molly
Gourlay
CARLTON OAKS CC
California
William W. Mast
(R.) Perry Dye
CARLTON YACHT & GC
Ontario
(R.1) Howard Watson
(R.1) John Watson
CARLYON BAY GC
Cornwall, England
J. Hamilton Stutt
CARMACK LAKE GC
Converse, Texas
Donald Carmack
CARMEL CC (NORTH CSE)
Charlotte, North Carolina
George W. Cobb
(R.) Rees Jones
CARMEL CC (SOUTH CSE)
Charlotte, North Carolina
Ellis Maples
(R.) Rees Jones
CARMEL HIGHLAND G&TC
San Diego, California
William F. Bell
(R. A.3) Jack Daray, Jr.,
Stephen Halsey
CARMEL MOUNTAIN RANCH GC
Rancho Bernardo, California
Ronald Fream
CARMEL VALLEY GC
Carmel, Maine
Ted Johns, Sr.
CARMEL VALLEY G&CC
Carmel, California
NKA Golf Club at Quail Lodge
CARMEL VALLEY RANCH GC
Carmel, California
Pete Dye
CARMEN G&CC
Manitoba
Jack Thompson
CARMONEY GC
Calgary, Alberta
Les Furber, *Jim Eremko*
CARNALEA GC
Northern Ireland
James Braid, John R. Stutt
CARNIVAL'S CRYSTAL PALACE GC
Nassau, Bahamas
Devereux Emmet

CARNOUSTIE GC
Angus, Scotland
Allan Robertson
(R.) Willie Park, Jr.
(R.) Old Tom Morris
(A.9) Old Tom Morris
(R.) James Braid, John R.
Stutt (1926)
(R.) James Braid, John R.
Stutt (1936)
CARNOUSTIE GC (BURNSIDE CSE)
Angus, Scotland
James Braid, John R. Stutt
CARNOUSTIE G&CC
Burns Lake, British Columbia
Mel Forbes, Peggy Forbes
CARNTON GC
Franklin, Tennessee
(A.9) Leon Howard
CARO GC
Caro, Michigan
F. L. Clark
CAROLINA CC
Margate, Florida
Robert von Hagge, Bruce Devlin
(R.1) Karl Litten
CAROLINA CC
Raleigh, North Carolina
(R.) John LaFoy
CAROLINA CC
Spartanburg, South Carolina
Tom Jackson
CAROLINA G&CC
Charlotte, North Carolina
Donald Ross
(R.) Gene Hamm
CAROLINA LAKES GC
Shaw AFB, South Carolina
Ed Riccoboni
CAROLINA PINES CC
New Bern, North Carolina
Ron Borsset
CAROLINA PINES GC [NLE]
Raleigh, North Carolina
Donald Ross
CAROLINA SANDS GC
White Lake, North Carolina
Willard Byrd
CAROLINA SHORES GC
Calabash, North Carolina
Tom Jackson
CAROLINA SPRINGS G&CC
Fountain Inn, South Carolina
Russell Breeden
CAROLINA TRACE G&CC (LAKE CSE)
Sanford, North Carolina
Robert Trent Jones
CAROLINA TRACE G&CC (CREEK CSE)
Sanford, North Carolina
Robert Trent Jones
CAROLINA TRACE GC [NLE]
West Harrison, Indiana
Robert von Hagge
CAROLINE CC
Denton, Maryland
Edmund B. Ault
CARPERS VALLEY GC
Winchester, Virginia
Fred Findlay

CARRADAM CC
Irwin, Pennsylvania
James Gilmore Harrison,
Ferdinand Garbin
CARRICK-ON-SHANNON GC
Ireland
(R.) Eddie Hackett
CARRICK-ON-SUIR GC
Ireland
(R.) Eddie Hackett
CARROL LAKE GC
McKenzie, Tennessee
R. Albert Anderson
CARROLL CC
Carroll, Iowa
Jack Hawkins
(R.9 A.9) Gerry Pirkl, *Donald
G. Brauer*
CARROLL COUNTY GC
Berryville, Arkansas
Herman Hackbarth
CARROLL MEADOWS GC
Carrollton, Ohio
John F. Robinson
CARROLL PARK MUNI
Baltimore, Maryland
Gus Hook
CARROLLTON CC
Pennsylvania
(R.9) Marvin Ferguson
CARROLLWOOD VILLAGE G&TC
Tampa, Florida
Edmund B. Ault
CARSON CITY MUNI [NLE]
Carson City, Nevada
Bob Baldock
CARSTAIRS G&CC
Alberta
William G. Robinson
CARSWELL AFB GC
Texas
Charles B. Akey
CARTER CAVES STATE PARK GC
Olive Hill, Kentucky
Hal Purdy
CARTER CC
Lebanon, New Hampshire
NKA Farnum Hill CC
CARTERSVILLE CC
Cartersville, Georgia
(R.9 A.9) Arthur Davis, Ron
Kirby, Gary Player
CARTHAGE MUNI
Carthage, Missouri
Tom Bendelow
(R.9 A.9) Don Sechrest
CARVOEIRO GC
Carvoeiro, Portugal
Ronald Fream
CASA BLANCA GC
Laredo, Texas
Leon Howard
CASA DE CAMPO (LINKS CSE)
La Romana, Dominican
Republic
Pete Dye
CASA DE CAMPO (TEETH OF THE DOG CSE)
La Romana, Dominican
Republic
Pete Dye
CASA DE MAR G&CC
Nevada
Bob Baldock

CASA DEL MAR CC
Dyer, Indiana
Harry Collis
CASA GRANDE GC
Casa Grande, Arizona
Gary Panks
(A.9) Arthur Jack Snyder,
Forrest Richardson
CASAVIEW CC [NLE]
Dallas, Texas
Leon Howard
CASCADE GC
Cascade, Idaho
Bob Baldock
CASCADE CANYON GC
St. Adele, Quebec
Cal Olson
CASCADE FAIRWAYS GC
Orem, Utah
William H. Neff
CASCADE HILLS CC
Grand Rapids, Michigan
Jack Daray
(R.) David Gill
(R.) Edward Lawrence
Packard
(R.) Bruce Matthews, Jerry
Matthews
(R.9) Jerry Matthews
CASCADES GC
Jackson, Michigan
Tom Bendelow
CASCADES GC
Hot Springs, Virginia
William S. Flynn
(R.) Robert Trent Jones
CASE LEASING GC
Celina, Michigan
Robert Beard
CASE NOYALE GC
Port Louis, Mauritius
John Harris, Peter Thomson
CASEY GC
Pacific, Missouri
Gary Kern
CASINO BEACH CC
South Africa
Robert Trent Jones, Jr.
CASINO C
San Salvador, El Salvador
Fred W. Hawtree
CASLANO GC
Switzerland
(R.) Edmund B. Ault
CASPER CC [NLE]
Casper, Wyoming
Tom Bendelow
CASPER CC
Casper, Wyoming
James Mason
(R.9 A.9) Bob Baldock
(R.) Robert Muir Graves
CASPER MUNI
Casper, Wyoming
(R.) Robert Muir Graves
CASSELBERRY GC
Casselberry, Florida
Paul McClure
(R.9 A.9) Lloyd Clifton
CASSVILLE GC
Cassville, Missouri
DeWitt "Maury" Bell (9 1962)

CASTA DEL SOL GC
Mission Viejo, California
Ted Robinson
CASTINE GC
Castine, Maine
Willie Park, Jr.
CASTLE GC
Dublin, Ireland
H. S. Colt, C. H. Alison
(R.) Eddie Hackett
(R.) H. S. Colt
CASTLE AFB GC
Atwater, California
NKA Rancho del Ray GC
CASTLEBAR GC
Ireland
(R.9 A.9) Eddie Hackett
(R.4) *Paddy Skerritt*
CASTLEBROOK G&CC
Lowell, Indiana
William James Spear
CASTLE CREEK CC
Escondido, California
Jack Daray
(R.) Jack Daray, Jr., Stephen
Halsey
CASTLE EDEN AND PETERLEE GC
England
(R.) Henry Cotton
CASTLEFALFI GC (BLUE CSE)
Florence, Italy
Pier Mancinelli
CASTLEFALFI GC (RED CSE)
Florence, Italy
Pier Mancinelli
CASTLE HARBOUR GC
Tuckerstown, Bermuda
Charles Banks
CASTLE HAWK GC
Lancashire, England
E. Jones
CASTLE INN GC [NLE]
Bermuda
Devereux Emmet
CASTLENAUD GC
Villeneuve-sur-Lot, France
Robert Berthet
CASTLE OF EBREICHSDORF GC
Ebreichsdorf, Austria
Herwig Zisser
CASTLE PINES GC
Castle Rock, Colorado
Jack Nicklaus
CASTLEREA GC
Ireland
(R.) Eddie Hackett
CASTLEROCK GC
County Londonderry, Northern
Ireland
Ben Sayers
(R.) Eddie Hackett
(A.9) J. J. F. Pennink
CASTLE ROCK GC
Pembroke, Virginia
Ferdinand Garbin
CASTLE ROCK G CSE
New Lisbon, Wisconsin
*Art Johnson, Jim Van Pee, Gary
Van Pee (1991)*
CASTLE SHANNON GC
Hopedale, Ohio
Gary Grandstaff

CASTLETOWN GC
Isle of Man
Old Tom Morris
(R.) Alister Mackenzie
(R.) P. M. Ross
CASTLETROY GC
County Limerick, Ireland
Ronnie Deakin
(R.) Eddie Hackett
CASTLE VIEW TOWN & CC
Atlanta, Georgia
Chic Adams
CASTLEWOODS CC
Brandon, Mississippi
Jim Lipe
CASTLEWOODS CC
Jackson, Mississippi
Kevin Tucker
(A.9) Dave Bennett
CASTLEWOOD GC (HILL CSE)
Pleasanton, California
William P. Bell
(R.) Ronald Fream
CASTLEWOOD GC (VALLEY CSE)
Pleasanton, California
William P. Bell
(R.) Ronald Fream
CASTRO CC
Texas
Leon Howard
CASTROP-RAUXEL GC
Frohlinde, Germany
Karl F. Grohs, *Rainer Preissmann*
CASWELL PINES CC
North Carolina
Gene Hamm
CATALINA GC
Avalon, California
John Duncan Dunn
CATARAQUI G&CC
Kingston, Ontario
Stanley Thompson
CATATONK GC
Candor, New York
Hal Purdy
CATAWBA CC
Newton, North Carolina
Donald Ross
CATAWBA ISLAND GC
Port Clinton, Ohio
William J. Rockefeller
CATHCART CASTLE GC
Scotland
(R.) John R. Stutt
CATHEDRAL CANYON CC
Cathedral City, California
David Rainville
CAT ISLAND CC
Fripp Island, South Carolina
George W. Cobb, *Byron Comstock*
CATSKILLS VILLAGE GC [NLE]
New York
John Duncan Dunn
CATTAILS GC
South Lyon, Michigan
Donald Childs (1991)
CAUSEWAY C
Southwest Harbor, Maine
Alonzo Yates

CAVALIER G&YC
Virginia Beach, Virginia
Charles Banks
(R.) Tom Clark
CAVALIERS CC
New Castle, Delaware
Frank Murray, Russell Roberts
CAVALRY C
Manlius, New York
Dick Wilson, Joe Lee
CAVE CREEK MUNI
Phoenix, Arizona
Arthur Jack Snyder
CAVENDISH GC
Derbyshire, England
Alister Mackenzie
(R.) Tom Williamson
CAVES BEACH GC (CLIFFS CSE)
Caves Beach, New South Wales, Australia
Robin Nelson, Rodney Wright
CAVES BEACH GC (LAKESIDE CSE)
Caves Beach, New South Wales, Australia
Robin Nelson, Rodney Wright
CAVES VALLEY GC
Owings Mill, Maryland
Tom Fazio
CAWDER GC (CAWDER CSE)
Scotland
James Braid, John R. Stutt
CAWDER GC (KEIR CSE)
Scotland
James Braid, John R. Stutt
CAYMANAS G&CC
Spanish Town, Jamaica
Howard Watson
CAZENOVIA CC
New York
Seymour Dunn
(A.9) Hal Purdy
CBC PORT HUENEME GC
Port Hueneme, California
Jack Daray
(R.9 A.9) Jack Daray, Jr., Stephen Halsey
CEANN SIBEAL GC
County Kerry, Ireland
Eddie Hackett
CEDAR GC
Bush Prairie, Washington
(R.) Robert Muir Graves
CEDAR BEND GC
Oregon
John Zoller
CEDAR BRAE G&CC
East Toronto, Ontario
Clinton E. Robinson
CEDAR BROOK CC
Brookville, New York
Al Zikorus
(R.) Ron Garl
CEDAR BROOK CC
Elkin, North Carolina
Ellis Maples
CEDARBROOK CC [NLE]
Philadelphia, Pennsylvania
A. W. Tillinghast
(R.) Donald Ross
CEDARBROOK CC
Blue Bell, Pennsylvania
William F. Mitchell

CEDARBROOK G&CC
Toronto, Ontario
Stanley Thompson
CEDAR BROOK GC
Pennsylvania
Michael Hurdzan, Jack Kidwell
CEDARBROOK GC
Smithton, Pennsylvania
James Gilmore Harrison, Ferdinand Garbin
CEDAR BROOK GC
London, Ontario
Robert Moote
CEDARBROOK GC
Ste. Sophie, Quebec
Howard Watson
CEDAR CREEK CC
Shell Knob, Missouri
Skeeter Lewis
CEDAR CREEK CC
Onalaska, Wisconsin
Bob Lohmann
CEDAR CREEK GC
Leo, Indiana
Robert Beard
CEDAR CREEK GC
Battle Creek, Michigan
Robert Beard
CEDAR CREEK GC
Aiken, South Carolina
Arthur Hills
CEDAR CREEK MUNI
San Antonio, Texas
Ken Dye
CEDAR CREST GC
Antioch, Illinois
George O'Neil
CEDARCREST GC
McLeansville, North Carolina
H. Lowdermilk
CEDAR CREST GC
Dallas, Texas
A. W. Tillinghast
(R.) John Bredemus
CEDARCREST GC
Marysville, Washington
(R.) Peter Thomson, Michael Wolveridge, Ronald Fream
(R.2) John Steidel
CEDARDELL GC
Plano, Illinois
Leonard Macomber
CEDAR GLEN G&CC
Ontario
(A.9) John F. Robinson
CEDAR GLEN GC
Massachusetts
(R.) Orrin Smith
CEDAR GLEN GC
New Baltimore, Michigan
(R.9 A.9) Jerry Matthews
CEDAR GROVE GC
Hillsboro, North Carolina
Gene Hamm
CEDAR HILL CC
Livingston, New Jersey
(R.) Nicholas Psiahas
CEDAR HILLS GC [NLE]
Omaha, Nebraska
Harold Glissmann
CEDARHOLM MUNI
Minnesota
Paul Coates

CEDARHURST CC
Ohio
William H. Livie
CEDAR KNOB CC
Somers, Connecticut
Geoffrey S. Cornish
CEDAR KNOLL CC
Ashland, Kentucky
James Gilmore Harrison
CEDAR LAKE GC
Howe, Indiana
R. Albert Anderson
CEDAR LINKS GC
Medford, Oregon
Dale Coverstone
(A.9) Robert Muir Graves
CEDAR POINT C
Norfolk, Virginia
Arthur Jack Snyder
(R.) Tom Clark
CEDAR RAPIDS CC [NLE]
Cedar Rapids, Iowa
Tom Bendelow
CEDAR RAPIDS CC
Cedar Rapids, Iowa
Donald Ross
(R.) Bob Lohmann
CEDAR RIDGE CC
Broken Arrow, Oklahoma
Joseph S. Finger
CEDAR RIDGES GC
Rangely, Colorado
Frank Hummel
CEDAR ROCK CC
Lenoir, North Carolina
Ellis Maples
CEDAR ROCKS CC
Wheeling, Pennsylvania
Emil Loeffler, *John McGlynn*
CEDARS G&CC
Dade City, Florida
Steve Smyers
CEDARS CC
Chatham, Virginia
Gene Hamm
CEDAR SPRINGS GC
Waupacas, Wisconsin
Homer Fieldhouse
CEDAR VALLEY GC
Guthrie, Oklahoma
Floyd Farley
CEDAR VALLEY GC
Antigua
Ralph Aldridge
CEDARWOOD CC
Matthews, North Carolina
Ellis Maples
CELLE-GARSSEN GC
Celle, Germany
Dr. Wolfgang Siegmann
CELY GC
France
Jack Nicklaus
CENTENNIAL CC
Chattanooga, Tennessee
Arthur Davis
CENTENNIAL GC [NLE]
Littleton, Colorado
Jack Fleming
CENTENNIAL GC
Acworth, Georgia
Jeff Brauer, Larry Nelson

CENTENNIAL ACRES GC
Sunfield, Michigan
Warner Bowen
CENTENNIAL DOWNS GC
Littleton, Colorado
Dick Phelps
CENTERBROOK G CSE
Brooklyn, Minnesota
Donald G. Brauer, Paul S. Fjare
(9 Par 3 1987)
CENTER SQUARE CC
Pennsylvania
Edmund B. Ault
CENTER VALLEY C
Allentown, Pennsylvania
Geoffrey S. Cornish, Brian Silva
CENTERVILLE G&CC
Centerville, Iowa
Tom Bendelow
CENTERVILLE MUNI GC
Centerville, Ohio
Gene Bates
CENTO GC
Ferrara, Italy
Marco Croze
CENTRAL CITY CC
Kentucky
Harold England
CENTRALIA CC
Centralia, Missouri
Chet Mendenhall
CENTRAL OTAGO GC
Arrowhead, New Zealand
B. V. Wright
CENTRAL VALLEY GC
New York
Hal Purdy
CENTRE HILLS GC
Aurora, Colorado
Richard Phelps
CENTRE HILLS CC
State College, Pennsylvania
Alex Findlay
    (R.) James Gilmore Harrison
    (A.9) Robert Trent Jones
CENTRO DEPORTIVO GC
Acapulco, Mexico
Percy Clifford
CENTURY GC
West Palm Beach, Florida
Joe Lee
CENTURY GC
White Plains, New York
C. H. Alison, H. S. Colt
    (R.) Robert Trent Jones
CENTURY HILLS CC
Rocky Hills, Connecticut
Geoffrey S. Cornish, William G.
Robinson
CENTURY MIKI GC
Hyogo, Japan
Fukuichi Kato
CENTURY VILLAGE GC
Deerfield Beach, Florida
Joe Lee
CENTURY XXI C
Germantown, Maryland
Algie Pulley
CERRITOS IRON-WOOD NINE GC
Cerritos, California
Ted Robinson
CERROMAR BEACH GC (NORTH CSE)
Dorado Beach, Puerto Rico
Robert Trent Jones

CERROMAR BEACH GC (SOUTH CSE)
Dorado Beach, Puerto Rico
Robert Trent Jones
CERRO PLATA GC
San Jose, California
Hale Irwin, Dick Phelps
CERVINO GC
Cervinia, Italy
Donald Harradine
    (A.9) Fred W. Hawtree
C. F. B. BORDEN GC
Ontario
    (R.) Clinton E. Robinson
CHABRE GC
Somerset, Wisconsin
John R. Nelson
CHACE LAKE CC
Montgomery, Alabama
Bancroft Timmons
CHADRON CC
Chadron, Nebraska
Frank Hummel
CHADWELL SPRINGS GC
Hertfordshire, England
J. H. Taylor
CHADWICK MANOR GC [NLE]
Warwick, England
H. S. Colt, J. S. F. Morrison
CHAGRIN VALLEY CC
Chagrin Falls, Ohio
Stanley Thompson
CHAIN O'LAKES GC
South Bend, Indiana
NKA Burke Memorial GC
CHALK MOUNTAIN G CSE
Atascadero, California
Robert Muir Graves
CHALON-SUR-SAÔNE GC
Chalon-sur-Saône, France
M. Rio
CHAMBERLAIN CC
Chamberlain, South Dakota
Robert Bruce Harris
CHAMBERLAIN PARK GC
Auckland, New Zealand
C. H. Redhead
CHAMBERSBURG CC
Chambersburg, Pennsylvania
    (R.) David Gordon, William
    Gordon
    (A.9) Edmund B. Ault
CHAMBERS COUNTY GC
Anahuac, Texas
Leon Howard
CHAMONIX GC
Chamonix, France
Robert Trent Jones
CHAMPAIGN CC
Champaign, Illinois
Tom Bendelow
    (R.) Edward Lawrence
    Packard
CHAMPION HILLS C
Hendersonville, North Carolina
Tom Fazio
CHAMPION LAKES GC
Bolivar, Pennsylvania
Paul E. Erath
CHAMPION LAKES G&CC
Fruitvale, British Columbia
Dave Barr (9 1991)
[THE] CHAMPIONS C
Omaha, Nebraska
Jeff Brauer

CHAMPION'S C OF ATLANTA
Alpharetta, Georgia
D. J. DeVictor, *Steve Melnyk*
CHAMPIONS GC (CYPRESS CREEK
CSE)
Houston, Texas
Ralph Plummer
CHAMPIONS GC (JACKRABBIT CSE)
Houston, Texas
George Fazio
CHAMPIONS G&CC
Rogers, Arkansas
Don Sechrest
CHAMPIONS GC
Lexington, Kentucky
Arthur Hills
CHAMPIONS OF COLUMBUS G CSE
Columbus, Ohio
Robert Trent Jones
CHAMPLAIN CC
St. Albans, Vermont
Duer Irving Sewall
    (R.9 A.9) Graham Cooke
CHAMPLAIN GC
Ville, Brossard, Quebec
Howard Watson
CHAMPS DE BATAILLE GC
Normandy, France
Robin Nelson, Rodney Wright
CHANBAY GC
Austin, Quebec
John Watson
CHANG AN G&CC
Taipei, Taiwan
Jack Nicklaus
CHANNAHON GC
Channahon, Illinois
Dick Nugent
CHANTILLY GC (OLD CSE)
Chantilly, France
Tom Simpson
    (R.) Robin Nelson, Rodney
    Wright
CHANTILLY GC (NEW CSE)
Chantilly, France
D. M. A. Steel
CHANTILLY MANOR CC
Rising Sun, Maryland
Russell Roberts
CHANTILLY NATIONAL G&CC
Centerville, Virginia
Edmund B. Ault, Al Jamison
CHANUTE AFB GC
Rantoul, Illinois
Edward Lawrence Packard
CHAPARRAL CC
Palm Desert, California
Ted Robinson
CHAPARRAL CC
Sequin, Texas
Leon Howard
CHAPEL-EN-LE-FIRTH GC
Derbyshire, England
David Thomas
CHAPEL HILL CC [NLE]
Chapel Hill, North Carolina
Fred Findlay
    (R.) George W. Cobb
CHAPEL HILL CC
Chapel Hill, North Carolina
Gene Hamm
CHAPEL HILLS GC
Douglasville, Georgia
Rocky Roquemore

CHAPEL HILLS GC
Ashtabula, Ohio
Richard W. LaConte
CHAPEL WOODS GC
Lee's Summit, Missouri
Ray Bondurant
CHAPPAQUA CC [NLE]
Chappaqua, New York
Tom Bendelow
CHAPPELL G&RC
Ontario
    (R.9 A.9) Gerry Pirkl, *Donald
    G. Brauer*
CHAPPELL CC
Chappell, Nebraska
Frank Hummel
CHAPPAQUA CC [NLE]
Mount Kisco, New York
Donald Ross
CHAPULTEPEC CC
Mexico
Willie Smith, *Alex Smith*
    (R.) Percy Clifford
CHARBONNEAU GC
Wilsonville, Oregon
Ted Robinson
CHARDONNAY C (SHAKESPEARE CSE)
Napa, California
Algie Pulley
CHARDONNAY C (VINEYARD CSE)
Napa, California
Algie Pulley
CHARLEMAGNE GC
Henri Chapelle, Belgium
Wolfgang Siegmann
CHARLES BOSWELL G CSE
Birmingham, Alabama
Wayne Stiles, John Van Kleek
CHARLES CITY CC [NLE]
Charles City, Iowa
William H. Livie
CHARLES CITY CC
Charles City, Iowa
Dick Phelps
CHARLES RIVER CC
Newton Centre, Massachusetts
Donald Ross
    (R.) William F. Mitchell
CHARLES M. SCHWAB ESTATE GC
[NLE]
Loretto, Pennsylvania
Devereux Emmet
CHARLES T. MYERS GC
Charlotte, North Carolina
Bill Love
CHARLESTON AFB GC
Charleston, South Carolina
George W. Cobb
CHARLESTON MUNI
Charleston, South Carolina
John E. Adams
CHARLESTON NATIONAL CC
Mount Pleasant, South Carolina
Rees Jones
CHARLEVILLE GC
Ireland
    (R.) Eddie Hackett
CHARLIE CHAPLIN ESTATE GC
[NLE]
Beverly Hills, California
Alister Mackenzie

CHARLOTTE CC
Charlotte, Michigan
Tom Bendelow
(R.) Jeff Gorney
CHARLOTTE CC
Charlotte, North Carolina
(R.) Donald Ross (1925)
(R.) Donald Ross (1947)
(R.) Hugh Moore
(R.) Robert Trent Jones
(1962)
(R.) Robert Trent Jones
(1984)
CHARMINGFARE LINKS
Candia, New Hampshire
Phil Wogan
CHARNITA CC
Pennsylvania
Edmund B. Ault
CHARNWOOD FOREST GC
Leicester, England
James Braid
[THE] CHARTER C
Palm Desert, California
Fred Bliss
CHARTIERS CC
Pittsburgh, Pennsylvania
Willie Park, Jr.
(R.) Emil Loeffler, *John McGlynn*
(R.) X. G. Hassenplug
(R.) Arthur Hills
CHARTWELL CC
Severna, Maryland
Edmund B. Ault, Al Jamison
CHASE HAMMOND MUNI
Muskegan, Michigan
Mark DeVries
CHASE OAKS GC (BLACKJACK CSE)
Plano, Texas
Robert von Hagge, Bruce Devlin
CHASE OAKS GC (SAWTOOTH CSE)
Plano, Texas
Robert von Hagge, Bruce Devlin
CHASKA GC
Greenville, Wisconsin
Edward Lawrence Packard,
Roger Packard
CHÂTEAU DE LA BAWETTE GC
Belgium
T. J. A. Macauley
CHÂTEAU DES VIGIERS GC
Dordogne, France
D. M. A. Steel
CHÂTEAU ELAN GC
Braselton, Georgia
Denis Griffiths
CHÂTEAU MONTEBELLO GC
Montebello, Quebec
Stanley Thompson
(R.18) John Watson
CHÂTEAU WHISTLER GC
Whistler Mountain, British
Columbia
Robert Trent Jones, Jr.
CHATELLERAULT GC
France
Jean Garaialde
CHATHAM CC
Chatham, Virginia
Gene Hamm
Chatham G&CC
Ontario
Clinton E. Robinson

CHATMOSS CC
Martinsville, Virginia
Ellis Maples
CHATSWORTH GC
England
(R.) Tom Williamson
CHATTAHOOCHE CC
Abbeville, Alabama
Bill Amick
CHATTAHOOCHEE GC
Gainesville, Georgia
Robert Trent Jones
(R.) Denis Griffiths
CHATTANOOGA G&CC
Chattanooga, Tennessee
Donald Ross
(R.) Alex McKay
(R.4) Arthur Davis
(R.) Gary Roger Baird
CHATUGE SHORES CC
Haysville, North Carolina
John V. Townsend
CHAUTAUQUA GC (CSE NO. 1)
Chautauqua, New York
Seymour Dunn
(R.9 A.9) Donald Ross
(R.) X. G. Hassenplug
CHAUTAUQUA GC (CSE NO. 2)
Chautauqua, New York
X. G. Hassenplug
CHEATHAM GC
Williamsburg, Virginia
Jack Daray, Jr., Stephen Halsey
CHEAT LAKE GC
Morgantown, West Virginia
James Gilmore Harrison
CHEDOKE GC (NEW CSE)
Hamilton, Ontario
Stanley Thompson
CHEDOKE GC (OLD CSE)
Hamilton, Ontario
(R.) Stanley Thompson
CHEECA LODGE GC
Islamorada, Florida
Bob Cupp, Jay Morrish
CHELMSFORD GC
Essex, England
(R.) H. S. Colt
(R.) John Harris
CHEMAY ESTATE GC
France
Seymour Dunn
CHEMNITZER GC
Slauv-Floeha, Germany
Karl Hoffmann, Bernhard von
Limburger
CHEMUNG HILLS CC
Howell, Michigan
(R.) Arthur Hills
(A.9) William Newcomb
CHENAL CC
Little Rock, Arkansas
Robert Trent Jones, Jr.
CHENANGO VALLEY GC
Binghampton, New York
Hal Purdy
CHENEQUA GC
Hartland, Wisconsin
Tom Bendelow
(A.9) Edward Lawrence
Packard
CHENNAULT GC
Monroe, Louisiana
Winnie Cole

CHENOWETH GC
Jeffersontown, Kentucky
Benjamin Wihry
CHERAW STATE PARK G CSE
Cheraw, South Carolina
Tom Jackson
CHEROKEE CC
Knoxville, Tennessee
Donald Ross
(R.) Alex McKay
(R.) Dan Maples
CHEROKEE CC
Jacksonville, Texas
John Bredemus
CHEROKEE G&TC
Madison, Wisconsin
David Gill
(R.) Bob Lohmann
CHEROKEE GC
Centre, Alabama
Neil R. Bruce
CHEROKEE GC
Louisville, Kentucky
Tom Bendelow
(R.) Alex McKay
(R.) Edward Lawrence
Packard
CHEROKEE GROVE GC
Grove, Oklahoma
Vince Bizik
CHEROKEE HILLS CC
Murphy, North Carolina
Bill Wells (1969)
CHEROKEE HILLS CC
Bellefontaine, Ohio
Wilton Ede
CHEROKEE NATIONAL G&CC
Gaffney, South Carolina
J. Porter Gibson
CHEROKEE TOWN & CC (HILLSIDE
CSE)
Dunwoody, Georgia
David Gill
(R.) Willard Byrd
CHEROKEE TOWN & CC (RIVERSIDE
CSE)
Dunwoody, Georgia
Willard Byrd
(A.9) Joe Lee, Rocky Roque-
more
CHEROKEE VILLAGE CC (NORTH
CSE)
Hardy, Arkansas
Edmund B. Ault
CHEROKEE VILLAGE CC (SOUTH
CSE)
Hardy, Arkansas
Edmund B. Ault
CHERRY DOWNS GC
Claremont, Ontario
Howard Watson
CHERRY HILL C
Fort Erie, Ontario
A. W. Tillinghast
CHERRY HILL GC
Massachusetts
David Maxon
CHERRY HILL GC
Ontario, Ontario
Walter J. Travis
(R.) Clinton E. Robinson

CHERRY HILLS CC
Englewood, Colorado
William S. Flynn
(R.2 A. Par 3 9) Press
Maxwell
(R.) Arnold Palmer, Ed Seay
(R.) Geoffrey S. Cornish,
Brian Silva
CHERRY HILLS CC
Flossmoor, Illinois
Harry Collis, Jack Daray
(A.9) David Gill
(R.) Gary Kern
CHERRY HILLS CC (CSE NO. 2)
[NLE]
Flossmoor, Illinois
Joe Meister
CHERRY HILLS CC
Glencoe, Missouri
Al Linkogel, *Ray Freeborg*
(R.) Gary Kern
CHERRY HILLS CC
Sun City, California
Milt Coggins
CHERRY HILLS GC
Hyogo Prefecture, Japan
Robert Trent Jones, Jr.
CHERRY ISLAND GC
Sacramento, California
Robert Muir Graves
CHERRY LANE GC
Meridian, Idaho
Bob Baldock, Robert L. Baldock
CHERRY LODGE GC
Kent, England
John Day
CHERRY POINT GC
Havelock, North Carolina
George W. Cobb
CHERRY RIDGE GC
Elyria, Ohio
Harold Paddock
CHERRY VALLEY CC
Garden City, New York
Walter Travis
(R.) Devereux Emmet
(R.) Robert Trent Jones
(R.2) Stephen Kay
CHERRY VALLEY CC
New Jersey
(R.) Willie Park, Jr.
(R.12) Frank Duane
CHERRY VALLEY GC
Skillman, New Jersey
Rees Jones
CHESAPEAKE CC
Chesapeake, Virginia
Michael Malyn
CHESAPEAKE C
North East, Maryland
Al Zikorus
CHESAPEAKE HILLS CC
Lusby, Maryland
James Thompson
CHESTER CC
Chester, Illinois
Bill Amick
CHESTER GC
Greenville, South Carolina
Russell Breeden
CHESTER GC
Chester, Nova Scotia
(A.9) William G. Robinson

CHESTER GC
Chester, England
Fred W. Hawtree, A. H. F.
Jiggens
CHESTERFIELD GC
Derbyshire, England
(R.) Tom Williamson
(A.9) H. S. Colt
(R.) H. S. Colt
CHESTER RIVER Y&CC
Chestertown, Maryland
Alex Findlay
(A.9) Edmund B. Ault
CHESTER VALLEY CC
Malvern, Pennsylvania
Perry Maxwell
(R.) George Fazio
CHESTER W. DITTO MUNI
Arlington, Texas
Ken Killian, Dick Nugent
CHESTNUT CREEK CC
Hardy, Virginia
Russell Breeden
CHESTNUT HILL CC
Newton, Massachusetts
Samuel Mitchell
CHESTNUT HILL CC
Ravenna, Ohio
Harold Paddock
CHESTNUT HILL G&CC
Richmond Hill, Ontario
René Muyleart
CHESTNUT PARK GC
Herts, England
Fred W. Hawtree
CHESTNUT RIDGE CC
Lutherville, Maryland
Alex McKay
(R.9 A.9) Russell Roberts
(R.) Clyde Johnston
CHESTNUT RIDGE CC
Indiana, Pennsylvania
James Gilmore Harrison,
Ferdinand Garbin
CHESTUEE G&CC
Etowah, Tennessee
Bill Amick
CHEVAL POLO & CC
Lutz, Florida
Karl Litten
(R.) Steve Smyers
CHEVIOT HILLS GC [NLE]
Raleigh, North Carolina
Harold Long
CHEVIOT HILLS GC
Raleigh, North Carolina
Gene Hamm
CHEVRY II GC
Magny-en-Vexin, France
John Harris
CHEVY CHASE CC
Glendale, California
William F. Bell, William P. Bell
(R.9) Harry Rainville, David
Rainville
CHEVY CHASE CC
Chevy Chase, Maryland
Donald Ross
(R.) C. H. Alison, H. S. Colt
(R.) Robert Trent Jones
(R.) Tom Clark
CHEVY CHASE CC [NLE]
Kansas City, Missouri
James Dalgleish

CHEVY CHASE CC
Wheeling, Illinois
Tom Bendelow
(R.) Ken Killian, Dick Nugent
CHEYENNE CC [NLE]
Cheyenne, Wyoming
Tom Bendelow
CHEYENNE CC
Cheyenne, Wyoming
Herbert Lockwood
CHIANGMAI CC
Chiangmai, Thailand
Denis Griffiths
CHIBA CC (KAWAMA CSE)
Chiba, Japan
Kinya Fujita
CHIBA CC (NODA CSE)
Chiba, Japan
Kinya Fujita
CHIBA CC (UMESATO CSE)
Chiba, Japan
K. Yasuda
CHIBA CENTRAL GC
Chiba, Japan
Kazumi Miura
CHIBA ISUMI GC
Chiba, Japan
Shiro Kawamura
CHIBA SPORTS SHINKO CC
Chiba, Japan
Hale Irwin
CHIBA YOMIURI CC
Chiba, Japan
Tsuneo Abe
CHIBURI LAKE RESORT GC
Tochigi-ken, Japan
Mike Poellot
CHICAGO GC
Belmont, Illinois
NKA Downers Grove GC
CHICAGO GC
Wheaton, Illinois
Charles Blair Macdonald
(R.) Seth Raynor
CHICAGO G & SADDLE C [NLE]
Chicago, Illinois
Charles Maddox, *Frank P.
MacDonald*
CHICASAKI GC
Kanagawa, Japan
Osamu Ueda
**CHI CHI RODRIGUEZ YOUTH
FOUNDATION GC**
Clearwater, Florida
Denis Griffiths
CHICKAMING GC
Lakeside, Michigan
Harry Collis
CHICKASAW CC
Memphis, Tennessee
William B. Langford
(R.) Kevin Tucker
CHICKASAW POINT GC
Fair Play, South Carolina
Russell Breeden
CHICKASHA CC
Chickasha, Oklahoma
Woody Kerr
CHICK EVANS GC
Morton Grove, Illinois
(R.) Dick Nugent
CHICOPEE MUNI
Chicopee, Massachusetts
Geoffrey S. Cornish

CHICOPEE WOODS G CSE
Gainesville, Georgia
Denis Griffiths
CHICOUTIMI GC
Chicoutimi, Quebec
Howard Watson
CHIEMING GC
Chieming, Germany
J. F. Dudok van Heel
CHIEMSEE GC
Prien, Germany
Donald Harradine
(A.9) J. F. Dudok van Heel
CHIGUSA CC
Japan
John Harris, Peter Thomson
CHIGWELL GC
Essex, England
F. G. Hawtree, J. H. Taylor
CHIHUAHUA CC
Mexico
Percy Clifford
CHILLIWACK G&CC
British Columbia
Ernest Brown
CHILWELL MANOR GC
England
(R.) Tom Williamson
CHIMNEY ROCK GC
Napa, California
Bob Baldock
(R.) *Martin Blumberg*
CHIMNEY ROCK GC
Wells, Nevada
Arthur Jack Snyder
CHINA FLEET GC
Saltash, England
Martin Hawtree
CHINA LAKE GC
Ridgecrest, California
William F. Bell
CHINGFORD GC
England
Willie Dunn, Jr.
CHINGUACOUSY CC
Caledon, Ontario
NKA Caledon CC
CHIPPANEE GC
Bristol, Connecticut
Herbert Lagerblade
CHIPPENDALE GC
Farmington, Minnesota
Joel Goldstrand
CHIPPENHAM GC
England
(R.) J. J. F. Pennink
CHIPPEWA CC
Barberton, Ohio
James Gilmore Harrison,
Ferdinand Garbin
(A.9) Ferdinand Garbin
CHIPPEWA CC
Pennsylvania
(R.9 A.9) James Gilmore
Harrison, Ferdinand Garbin
(A.9) Ferdinand Garbin
CHIPPING SODBURY GC
Avon, England
Fred W. Hawtree
CHISAGO LAKES GC
Lindstrom, Minnesota
Donald G. Brauer, Paul S. Fjare
(R.) Joel Goldstrand

CHISELHURST GC
Kent, England
Tom Dunn
(R.) Willie Park, Jr.
(R.) J. S. F. Morrison
CHITA CC
Japan
Yasuzo Kaneko
CHITOSE AIRPORT GC
Chitose, Japan
(R.) Ronald Fream
CHIYODA CC
Ibaragi, Japan
Hideyo Sugimoto
CHOCKOYETTE CC
Roanoke Rapids, North Carolina
Ellis Maples
CHOMONIX G CSE
Lino Lakes, Minnesota
Don Herfort
(R.9 A.9) Gerry Pirkl
CHONAN CC
Japan
Shiro Kawamura
CHORLEY GC
Lancashire, England
J. A. Steer
(R.) Fred W. Hawtree, A. H. F.
Jiggens
CHRISTCHURCH CC [NLE]
Christchurch, New Zealand
Denis O'Rourke, L. B. Wood
CHRISTCHURCH CC
Shirley, New Zealand
Des Soutar
(R.) *Arthur Ham*
(R.) Sloan Morpeth
CHRISTIANA CC
Elkhart, Indiana
William B. Langford, Theodore
J. Moreau
(A.9) William B. Langford
CHRISTINA LAKE GC
Grand Forks, British Columbia
Reg Stone, Roy Stone
(A.9) Les Furber, *Jim Eremko*
CHRISTMAS LAKE G&CC
Santa Claus, Indiana
Edmund B. Ault
CHRISTMAS VALLEY GC
Oregon
Joe Ward
CHRISTOWN G&CC
Phoenix, Arizona
Milt Coggins
CHRYSLER MEMORIAL PARK GC
Morrisburg, Ontario
Howard Watson
CHULA VISTA MUNI
Bonita, California
Harry Rainville
(R.) Jack Daray, Jr.
(R.) Garrett Gill, George B.
Williams
CHULMLEIGH GC
North Devon, England
*J. W. D. Goodban, W. G.
Mortimer*
CHUNG JU CC
Chungchong Pukdo, Korea
Shunsuke Kato

CHUNG-NAM CC
Seoul, Korea
Gary Roger Baird
CHUNG-SHAN GC
China
Arnold Palmer, Ed Seay
CHURCHILL VALLEY CC
Churchill, Pennsylvania
(R.) James Gilmore Harrison,
Ferdinand Garbin
CHURCH STRETTON GC
Shropshire, England
James Braid
CHURSTON GC
Devon, England
H. S. Colt
(R.) J. Hamilton Stutt
CHURUBUSCO CC
Mexico City, Mexico
John Bredemus
(R.) Manny Francis
(R.) Robert Trent Jones, Jr.
CHYUODO HAREGAMINE CC
Japan
Seiichi Kanai
CIELO VISTA GC
El Paso, Texas
Marvin Ferguson
CIMARRON CC
Mission, Texas
Dave Bennett
CIMARRON GC
East Oakdale, Minnesota
Don Herfort
CIMARRON HILLS GC
Colorado Springs, Colorado
Press Maxwell
CIMARRON VALLEY G CSE
Satanta, Kansas
Larry Flatt
CIMARRONE AT CARTWHEEL BAY GC
Jacksonville, Florida
David Postlethwait
CINCINNATI CC
Cincinnati, Ohio
(R.9 A.9) Robert White
(R.A.4) William Newcomb
CIRCLE BAR GC
Westfir, Oregon
Clarence Sutton
CIRCLE R GOLF RANCH CC
Escondido, California
NKA Castle Creek CC
CIRCLESTONE CC
Adel, Georgia
Sid Clarke
CIRENCESTER GC
Gloucestershire, England
John Harris
CITICORP G CSE
Westchester, New York
(R.) Gene Hamm
CITRUS HILLS G&CC (MEADOWS
CSE)
Hernando, Florida
Phil Friel
CITRUS HILLS G&CC (OAKS CSE)
Hernando, Florida
Mike Andrijiszyn
CITRUS SPRINGS CC
Florida
Charles Almony

CITY OF DERRY GC
Londonderry, Northern Ireland
Willie Park, Jr.
(A.9) Eddie Hackett
CITY OF NEWCASTLE GC
Northumberland, England
Old Tom Morris
(R.) Harry Vardon
(R.) Alister Mackenzie
CITY PARK GC
Pueblo, Colorado
Tom Bendelow
(R.) John Cochran
CITY PARK GC (CSE No. 1)
New Orleans, Louisiana
Richard Koch
(R.) Ralph Plummer
(R.3) Bill Amick
CITY PARK GC (CSE No. 2)
New Orleans, Louisiana
Richard Koch
CITY PARK GC
Portsmouth, Virginia
(R.) Tom Clark
CIVIC GC
Kitchener, Ontario
Stanley Thompson
CIVITAN PARK MUNI
Farmington, New Mexico
Arthur Jack Snyder
CLACTON-ON-SEA GC
Essex, England
Jack White
CLAIRVILLE GC
Toronto, Ontario
William G. Robinson
CLANDEBOYE GC (AVA CSE)
County Down, Northern Ireland
William Rennick Robinson
(R.) Bernhard von Limburger,
T. J. A. Macauley
CLANDEBOYE GC (DUFFERIN CSE)
County Down, Northern Ireland
Peter Alliss, David Thomas, T. J.
A. Macauley
CLANDON GC
Essex, England
(R.) Howard Swan
CLANWILLIAM GC
Clanwilliam, South Africa
Polly Burger
CLAPP PARK GC
Wichita, Kansas
(R.9) Don Sechrest
CLAREMONT CC
Claremont, New Hampshire
(R.) Orrin Smith
CLAREMONT GC
Oakland, California
Jim Smith
(R.) Alister Mackenzie
(R.) Brad Benz, Mike Poellot
(R.) Robert Muir Graves
CLAREMORRIS GC
Claremorris, Ireland
(R.) Eddie Hackett
CLARENDON CC
Manning, South Carolina
Ed Riccoboni
CLARKE ESTATE GC
Rhode Island
A. W. Tillinghast

CLARKESDALE CC
Clarkesdale, Mississippi
William B. Langford, Theodore
J. Moreau
CLARK ESTATE GC
Windlesham, England
Tom Simpson
CLARKSBURG GC
Clarksburg, West Virginia
(R.9 A.9) Edmund B. Ault
CLARKSTON G&CC
Clarkston, Washington
(R.) *Keith Hellstrom* (1974)
CLARKSVILLE CC
Clarksville, Tennessee
George W. Cobb
CLASSIC CC
Spanaway, Washington
William Overdorf (1991)
[THE] CLASSIC GC
Palm Springs, California
Maury Miller, *D. A. Weibring*
[THE] CLASSICS GC
Naples, Florida
Gary Player
CLAY CENTER CC
Clay Center, Kansas
Floyd Farley
CLAY COUNTY CC
Henrietta, Texas
Bruce Littell
CLAY COUNTY G&CC
Flora, Illinois
Robert Bruce Harris
CLAYCREST GC
Liberty, Missouri
Chet Mendenhall
CLEARBROOK CC
Saugutuck, Michigan
Charles Darl Scott
CLEARBROOK GC
Cranbury, New Jersey
Hal Purdy, Malcolm Purdy
CLEAR CREEK GC
Huntington, Indiana
Tom Bendelow
CLEAR CREEK GC
Killeen, Texas
Leon Howard
CLEAR CREEK G CSE
Houston, Texas
Baxter Spann, Ken Dye, Joseph
S. Finger
CLEARCREST CC [NLE]
Evansville, Indiana
Robert Bruce Harris
CLEARCREST CC
Evansville, Indiana
Roger Packard
CLEARFIELD-CURWENSVILLE CC
Pennsylvania
Alex Findlay
CLEAR LAKE GC
Houston, Texas
Milt Coggins (routing); George
Fazio
(A.9) Jay Riviere
CLEAR LAKE GC
Riding Mountain National Park,
Manitoba
Stanley Thompson
CLEAR LAKE GC
Salem, Oregon
Felix Riedel

CLEAR LAKE RIVIERA GC
Lower Lake, California
Edward Defilice
CLEARVIEW CC
Lincoln Park, New Jersey
Hal Purdy
CLEARVIEW GC
Bayside, New York
William H. Tucker
CLEARWATER CC
Clearwater, Florida
Herbert Strong
(R.) George Low
(R.) Perry Maxwell
(R.) Joe Lee
CLEARWATER G PARK
Clearwater, Florida
Ron Garl
CLEARWATER BAY CC
Hong Kong
Brad Benz, Mike Poellot
CLEARWATER GREENS GC
Clearwater, Kansas
Dave Trufelli
CLEARY LAKE PARK GC
Prior Lake, Minnesota
(R.) Don Herfort
CLEBURNE MUNI
Cleburne, Texas
Leon Howard
CLEGHORN PLANTATION G&CC
Rutherfordton, North Carolina
George W. Cobb
CLEMSON UNIVERSITY GC
Clemson, South Carolina
George W. Cobb, John LaFoy
CLERBROOK CC
Clermont, Florida
Dean Refram
CLERMONT GC
Clermont, Indiana
Tom Bendelow
CLEVEDON GC
Avon, England
J. H. Taylor
CLEVELAND CC
Shelby, North Carolina
(R.) John LaFoy
CLEVELAND CC [NLE]
Cleveland, Tennessee
(R.) Bert Stamps
CLEVELAND CC
Cleveland, Tennessee
Gene Hamm
CLEVELAND GC
Redcar, England
(R. A.9) Old Tom Morris
(R.) J. S. F. Morrison
CLEVELAND HEIGHTS G&CC
Lakeland, Florida
William S. Flynn, Howard
Toomey
(R.3 A.9) Ron Garl
CLEWISTON CC
Clewiston, Florida
R. Albert Anderson
CLIFFSIDE CC
Simsbury, Connecticut
Geoffrey S. Cornish
CLIFFSIDE GC
Gallipolis, Ohio
Michael Hurdzan

[THE] CLIFFS GC
Possum Kingdom Lake, Texas
Robert von Hagge
[THE] CLIFFS AT GLASSY GC
Glassy Mountain, South
Carolina
Tom Jackson
CLIFTON HIGHLANDS GC
Prescott, Wisconsin
Homer Fieldhouse
CLIFTON PARK MUNI
Baltimore, Maryland
Gus Hook
CLIFTON SPRINGS CC
Clifton Springs, New York
Pete Craig
CLINGENDAEL GC
Netherlands
John Duncan Dunn
CLINTON CC
Clinton, Connecticut
Geoffrey S. Cornish, William G.
Robinson
   (R.) Al Zikorus
CLINTON CC
Clinton, Iowa
Tom Bendelow
CLINTON CC [NLE]
Lock Haven, Pennsylvania
Alex Findlay
CLINTON CC
Lock Haven, Pennsylvania
Edmund B. Ault
CLINTON MUNI
Clinton, Iowa
William James Spear
CLINTON SPRINGS CC
Wheeling, West Virginia
William Gordon, David Gordon
CLINTON VALLEY CC
Detroit, Michigan
David T. Millar
CLITHEROE GC
Lancashire, England
James Braid, John R. Stutt
CLONGOWES WOOD COLLEGE GC
County Kildaire, Ireland
Eddie Hackett
CLONMEL GC
Clonmel, Ireland
   (A.9) Eddie Hackett
CLONTARF GC
Clontarf, Ireland
   (R.) Eddie Hackett
CLOVELLY CC
South Africa
Campbell Ross
CLOVERLEAF GC
Pennsylvania
Wynn Tredway
CLOVERNOOK CC
Cincinnati, Ohio
William B. Langford, Theodore
J. Moreau
   (R.) William H. Diddel
   (R.) Arthur Hills
CLUB AKTIEF
Netherlands
Howard Swan
CLUB AT EMERALD HILLS
Hollywood, Florida
Robert von Hagge, Bruce Devlin
   (R.) Chuck Ankrom

CLUB AT FALCON POINT
Katy, Texas
Robert von Hagge, Bruce Devlin
CLUB AT HIDDEN CREEK
Pensacola, Florida
Ron Garl
CLUB AT MORNINGSIDE
Rancho Mirage, California
Jack Nicklaus
CLUB AT NEVILLEWOOD
Pittsburgh, Pennsylvania
Jack Nicklaus
CLUB AT PELICAN BAY
Naples, Florida
Arthur Hills
CLUB AT SONTERRA (NORTH CSE)
San Antonio, Texas
Robert von Hagge, Bruce Devlin
CLUB AT SONTERRA (SOUTH CSE)
San Antonio, Texas
Press Maxwell
CLUB ATLAS CAMPO DE GOLF
Guadalajara, Mexico
Joseph S. Finger
CLUB CAMPESTRE
Mexico City, Mexico
   (R.) Dick Wilson
CLUB CAMPESTRE AGUNERO
Mexico
Percy Clifford
CLUB CAMPESTRE CARTAGENA
Colombia
Ward Northrup
CLUB CAMPESTRE CELAYENSE
Mexico
Luis Nieto
CLUB CAMPESTRE DE BUCARAMANGA
Chile
Mark Mahannah, *Jaime Saenz*
CLUB CAMPESTRE DE CÚCUTA
Cúcuta, Colombia
Howard Watson
CLUB CAMPESTRE DE HERMOSILLA
San Buenaventura, Mexico
Lawrence Hughes
CLUB CAMPESTRE DE LEÓN
Mexico
Mario Schjetnan
   (R.9) Joseph S. Finger
CLUB CAMPESTRE DE LIVRAMENTO
Brazil
Jose Maria Gonzales
CLUB CAMPESTRE DE MORELIA
Morelia, Mexico
Percy Clifford
CLUB CAMPESTRE DE PELOTAS
Brazil
Pable Miguel
CLUB CAMPESTRE DE QUERETARO
Mexico
Percy Clifford
CLUB CAMPESTRE DE SALTILLO
Mexico
George Hoffman
CLUB CAMPESTRE COAZACOALCOS
Vera Cruz, Mexico
Mario Schjetnan
CLUB CAMPESTRE HUATULCO
Oaxaca, Baja California, Mexico
Mario Schjetnan, *Pedro Guereca*
CLUB CAMPESTRE LOMAS DE
COCOYOC
Morales, Mexico
Mario Schjetnan

CLUB CAMPESTRE TORREON
Mexico
Percy Clifford
CLUB CHILUCA
Mexico City, Mexico
Larry Hughes
CLUB CURITIBANO
Brazil
Luis Dedini, Frederico German
CLUB D'AMIENS
France
P. M. Ross
CLUB DE CAMPO DE MALAGA
Torremolinos, Spain
Tom Simpson, P. M. Ross
CLUB DE CAMPO DE SÃO PAULO
Brazil
*Gastão Almeida Silva, Jose Maria
Gonzales*
CLUB DE GOLF ACOZAC
Mexico
Lawrence Hughes
CLUB DE GOLF ALPIN
Quebec
   (R.) Howard Watson
   (R.3) John Watson
CLUB DE GOLF AVANDARA
Mexico
Percy Clifford
CLUB DE GOLF BAIE COMEAU (OLD
CSE)
Hauterire, Quebec
Clinton E. Robinson
   (A.9) Howard Watson, John
Watson
   (R.2 A.9) John Watson
   (A.4) John Watson
CLUB DE GOLF BAIE COMEAU (NEW
CSE)
Hauterire, Quebec
Graham Cooke
CLUB DE GOLF BARU
Colombia
Percy Clifford
CLUB DE GOLF BEATTIE
Lasarre, Quebec
Graham Cooke
CLUB DE GOLF BELLAVISTA
Mexico City, Mexico
Percy Clifford
   (R.) Manny Francis
CLUB DE GOLF BELVEDERE
Val d'Or, Quebec
Graham Cooke
CLUB DE GOLF BERTHIER
Berthierville, Quebec
Howard Watson
CLUB DE GOLF BRASÍLIA
Brasília, Brazil
Robert Trent Jones
CLUB DE GOLF BROMONT
Shefford, Quebec
Howard Watson
CLUB DE GOLF BUGAMBILLIAN
Guadalajara, Mexico
Percy Clifford
CLUB DE GOLF CAMPESTRE DEL
LAGO
Mexico City, Mexico
Percy Clifford
CLUB DE GOLF CAP ROUGE
Quebec
Howard Watson

CLUB DE GOLF CERDANA
Puigcerda, Spain
Javier Arana
CLUB DE GOLF CERRO ALTO
Mexico
Percy Clifford
CLUB DE GOLF CHAMBLY
Quebec
Howard Watson
CLUB DE GOLF CHARNY
Quebec
   (A.9) Howard Watson, John
Watson
   (R.9) Howard Watson
CLUB DE GOLF CHAUDIERE
Quebec
   (R.5) Howard Watson, John
Watson
CLUB DE GOLF CHICOUTINA (CSE
NO. 1)
Quebec
Howard Watson
CLUB DE GOLF CHICOUTINA (CSE
NO. 2)
Quebec
Howard Watson
CLUB DE GOLF CHILUCA
Mexico City, Mexico
Lawrence Hughes
CLUB DE GOLF COSTALITA
Malaga, Spain
Pepe Gancedo
CLUB DE GOLF DEAUX
St. Eustache, Quebec
John Watson
CLUB DE GOLF DE CARACAS
Caracas, Venezuela
Dave Bennett
CLUB DE GOLF DE JOLIETTE
Quebec
Howard Watson
   (R.10) John Watson
CLUB DE GOLF DE MEXICO
Mexico
Lawrence Hughes, Percy
Clifford
CLUB DE GOLF DES PINS
des Pins, Quebec
   (A.9) Graham Cooke
CLUB DE GOLF DES SAULES
Rimouski, Quebec
John Watson
CLUB DE GOLF DOS MARES
Ensenada, Mexico
Percy Clifford
CLUB DE GOLF DU BIC
Rimouski, Quebec
Howard Watson
   (R.5) John Watson
   (R.2) John Watson
CLUB DE GOLF ERANDENI
Mexico
Percy Clifford
CLUB DE GOLF GASPESIEN
Ste. Anne des Morts, Quebec
John Watson
CLUB DE GOLF GRANBY–ST. PAUL
(NEW CSE)
Quebec
Howard Watson, John Watson

CLUB DE GOLF GRANBY–ST. PAUL
(OLD CSE)
Quebec
(R.) Howard Watson, John
Watson
CLUB DE GOLF GRAND PABOS
Quebec
(R.9 A.9) Howard Watson
CLUB DE GOLF HACIENDA
Mexico City, Mexico
Percy Clifford
(R.) *Harry C. Offutt*
CLUB DE GOLF HERMOSILLO [NLE]
Mexico
John Bredemus
CLUB DE GOLF ILE PERROT
Quebec
(R.) Robert Moote
CLUB DE GOLF LA CANADA
Mexico City, Mexico
Percy Clifford
CLUB DE GOLF LAC BEUPORT
Quebec
Howard Watson
CLUB DE GOLF LAPRAIRIE
Montreal, Quebec
Howard Watson
CLUB DE GOLF LA VILLA RICA
Vera Cruz, Mexico
Percy Clifford
CLUB DE GOLF LE MIRAGE (NORD
CSE)
Terrebonne, Quebec
Graham Cooke
CLUB DE GOLF LE MIRAGE (SUD
CSE)
Terrebonne, Quebec
Graham Cooke
CLUB DE GOLF LE PORTAGE
Cape Breton, Nova Scotia
Robert Moote, David L. Moote
CLUB DE GOLF LE PORTAGE
L'Assomtion, Quebec
Howard Watson
CLUB DE GOLF LES DUNES
(CSE NO. 1)
Quebec
(R.) Howard Watson
CLUB DE GOLF LES DUNES (CSE
NO. 2)
Sorel, Quebec
Howard Watson
(R.1) John Watson
CLUB DE GOLF LLAVANERAS
Spain
James Gannon
(R.) Fred W. Hawtree
CLUB DE GOLF LONGCHAMPS
Sherbrooke, Quebec
Howard Watson, John Watson
CLUB DE GOLF LOS MONTEROS
Spain
Javier Arana
CLUB DE GOLF MALINALCO
Malinalco, Mexico
Stephen Burns
CLUB DE GOLF MARINA VALLARTA
Puerto Vallarta, Mexico
Joseph S. Finger
CLUB DE GOLF MERIDA
Yucatán, Mexico
Felix Terán

CLUB DE GOLF MIJAS (LOS LAGOS
CSE)
Fuengirola, Malaga, Spain
Robert Trent Jones
CLUB DE GOLF MIJAS (LOS OLIVOS
CSE)
Fuengirola, Malaga, Spain
Robert Trent Jones
CLUB DE GOLF MONTCALM
St. Liguori, Quebec
John Watson
CLUB DE GOLF MONTE CASTILLO
Mexico
Percy Clifford
CLUB DE GOLF MONTEVILLA
Montebello, Quebec
John Watson
CLUB DE GOLF MORELIA
Mexico
Percy Clifford
CLUB DE GOLF OBREGON
Sonora, Mexico
Percy Clifford
CLUB DE GOLF PANAMA
Panama
Jay Riviere
CLUB DE GOLF PIRAMIDES
Mexico
Percy Clifford
CLUB DE GOLF POINENTE MAGALUF
Mallorca, Spain
John Harris
CLUB DE GOLF PORT
Quebec
(R.9) Howard Watson
CLUB DE GOLF PUEBLA
Puebla, Mexico
Adolfo Cazares
CLUB DE GOLF RANCHITOS
Morales, Mexico
Percy Clifford
CLUB DE GOLF RIO SECO
Valles, Mexico
Percy Clifford
CLUB DE GOLF ST. CÉSAIRE
St. Césaire, Quebec
Graham Cooke
CLUB DE GOLF ST. FRANÇOIS
Laval, Quebec
Graham Cooke
CLUB DE GOLF ST. LUC
Quebec
John Watson
CLUB DE GOLF STE. MARIE
Quebec
(R.2) Howard Watson, John
Watson
CLUB DE GOLF ST. MICHEL (ST.
MICHEL CSE)
Quebec
Howard Watson
CLUB DE GOLF ST. MICHEL
(VAUDREUIL CSE)
Quebec
Howard Watson
CLUB DE GOLF ST. PATRICK
Quebec
Howard Watson, John Watson
(R.9 A.9) John Watson
CLUB DE GOLF SAN ANDRES DE
LLAVANERAS
Barcelona, Spain
James Gannon
(R.) Fred W. Hawtree

CLUB DE GOLF SAN CARLOS
Toluca, Mexico
Percy Clifford
CLUB DE GOLF SAN GASPER
Mexico
Percy Clifford
CLUB DE GOLF SAN LUIS
Mexico
Percy Clifford
CLUB DE GOLF SANTA ANITA
Mexico
Lawrence Hughes
CLUB DE GOLF SANTO DOMINGO
Chile
A. Macdonald
CLUB DE GOLF SANTA FE
Morelos, Mexico
Roy Dye
CLUB DE GOLF SOREL TRACY
Quebec
(R.6 A.9) John Watson
(R.4) John Watson
CLUB DE GOLF TABASHINES
Morales, Mexico
Percy Clifford
CLUB DE GOLF TEQUISQUIAPAN
Queretaro, Mexico
Joseph S. Finger
CLUB DE GOLF TERRAMAR
Stiges, Spain
Tom Simpson
(A.9) Fred W. Hawtree
CLUB DE GOLF TERREBONNE
Quebec
John Watson
(A.3rd 9) John Watson
CLUB DE GOLF ULZAMA
Spain
Javier Arana
CLUB DE GOLF VALLE DU PARC
Grand'mère, Quebec
Howard Watson
CLUB DE GOLF VALLESCONDIDO
Mexico City, Mexico
Percy Clifford
CLUB DE GOLF VICTORIAVILLE
Quebec
(R.9 A.9) Howard Watson
CLUB DE GOLF VIDAGO
Portugal
P. M. Ross
CLUB DE GOLF VIELLE FORGES
Trois-Rivières, Quebec
John Watson, Howard Watson
CLUB DE GOLF XALAPA
Vera Cruz, Mexico
Percy Clifford
CLUB DE LA CORDELIERE
Chaource, France
Tom Simpson
CLUB DE LYON [NLE]
Lyon, France
(R.) Michael G. Fenn
CLUB DE MANS MULSANNE
Le Mans, France
J. J. F. Pennink
CLUB DE PALMOLA
Toulouse, France
Michael G. Fenn
CLUB DE ROUEN
Rouen, France
Willie Park, Jr.

CLUB DE VALESCURE
France
John Harris
CLUB D'GOLF TRIANGLE DOR
St. Remi, Quebec
Howard Watson
CLUB DEL LAGO
Conroe, Texas
Jay Riviere, *Dave Marr*
CLUB DEPORTIVO COCOYOC
Morelos, Mexico
Mario Schjetnan
CLUB JURICA
Queretaro, Mexico
Larry Hughes
CLUB LAGOS DE CAUJARAL
Barranquilla, Columbia
Joe Lee
CLUB MED MONTARGIS
France
Martin Hawtree, Simon Gidman
CLUB MED SANDPIPER GC (FAMILY
CSE)
Port St. Lucie, Florida
Chuck Ankrom
CLUB MED SANDPIPER GC (SAINTS
CSE)
Port St. Lucie, Florida
David Wallace
CLUB MED SANDPIPER GC (SINNERS
CSE)
Port St. Lucie, Florida
Mark Mahannah, Charles
Mahannah
(R.) Chuck Ankrom
CLUB MED SANDPIPER GC
(WILDERNESS CSE)
Port St. Lucie, Florida
LeRoy Phillips
CLUB PORTALES DEL CENTENARIO
Argentina
Angel Reartes
CLUB SANTIAGO MANZANILLO
Mexico
Lawrence Hughes
CLUB TEQUISQUIAPAN
Queretaro, Mexico
Joseph S. Finger
CLUB 700
Soju, Korea
David Rainville
CLUSTERED SPIRES G CSE
Frederick, Maryland
Bill Love, Brian Ault
CLYNE GC
Wales
H. S. Colt
COACHMAN'S INN GC
Edgerton, Wisconsin
R. C. Greaves
COAL CREEK CC
Atkinson, Illinois
Edward Lawrence Packard,
Brent Wadsworth
COAL CREEK G CSE
Louisville, Colorado
Dick Phelps
COAL RIDGE CC
West Virginia
NKA Pete Dye G Cse
COATESVILLE CC
Pennsylvania
Alex Findlay

COBBLESTONE CC
Stuart, Florida
Roy Case (1989)
COBBLESTONE CREEK CC
Victor, New York
Michael Hurdzan
COBBLY KNOB G LINKS
Gatlinburg, Tennessee
NKA Bent Creek G Resort
COBBOSSEE COLONY GC
Monmouth, Maine
Royal Cantrell
COBBS CREEK MUNI
Philadelphia, Pennsylvania
Hugh Wilson
COBB'S GLEN CC
Anderson, South Carolina
George W. Cobb, John LaFoy
COBTREE MANOR GC
Maidstone, England
Martin Hawtree
COCHECHO CC
Dover, New Hampshire
Wayne Stiles
(A.9) Phil Wogan
COCHITI LAKE GC
Cochiti Lake, New Mexico
Robert Trent Jones, Jr.
COCHRANE CASTLE GC
Renfrewshire, Scotland
Charles Hunter
(R.) Willie Fernie
(A.10) James Braid, John R.
Stutt
(R.) James Braid, John R.
Stutt
COCKERMOUTH GC
England
(R.2) James Braid, John R.
Stutt
COCK MOOR WOODS GC
Birmingham, England
F. G. Hawtree, J. H. Taylor
COCOA BEACH MUNI [NLE]
Cocoa Beach, Florida
Mark Mahannah, Charles
Mahannah
COCOA BEACH CC
Cocoa Beach, Florida
Chuck Ankrom
COESFELD GOLF UND LAND C
Coesfeld, Germany
Wolfgang Siegmann
COEUR D'ALENE GC
Coeur d'Alene, Idaho
Mel "Curley" Hueston
(R.4) John Steidel
COEUR D'ALENE RESORT GC
Coeur d'Alene, Idaho
Scott Miller
COFFEYVILLE CC
Coffeyville, Kansas
Smiley Bell
(R.) Bob Dunning
COFFIN MUNI
Indianapolis, Indiana
William H. Diddel
(R.) William H. Diddel
(R.) Ron Kern
COG HILL GC (CSE NO. 1)
Lemont, Illinois
Bert F. Coghill
(R.) Dick Wilson, Joe Lee

COG HILL GC (CSE NO. 2)
Lemont, Illinois
Bert F. Coghill
(R.) Dick Wilson, Joe Lee
COG HILL GC (CSE NO. 3)
Lemont, Illinois
Dick Wilson, Joe Lee
COG HILL GC (CSE NO. 4)
Lemont, Illinois
Dick Wilson, Joe Lee
(R.) Joe Lee
(R.) Rocky Roquemore
COHANZICK CC
Bridgeton, New Jersey
Alex Findlay
COHASSET GC
Quincy, Massachusetts
Donald Ross
(R.9) Al Zikorus
(R.) Brian Silva, Geoffrey S.
Cornish
COHERIE CC
Clinton, North Carolina
Ellis Maples
COIMBATORE GC
Coimbatore, India
John Steidel, *Max Wexler*
COIROUX GC
Aubazine, France
H. Chesneau
COKATO TOWN & CC
Cokato, Minnesota
Paul Coates
COLCHESTER GC
Essex, England
James Braid
COLD ASHBY GC
Northamptonshire, England
Fred W. Hawtree
COLD NORTON GC
England
Fred W. Hawtree
COLD SPRING HARBOR CC
Cold Spring Harbor, New York
Seth Raynor
(R.) Robert Trent Jones
COLD SPRINGS G&CC
Placerville, California
(A.9) Bert Stamps
COLDSTREAM CC
Cincinnati, Ohio
Dick Wilson, Joe Lee
COLDSTREAM GC
East Hempstead, New York
Devereux Emmet
COLDWATER CC
Coldwater, Michigan
Robert Beard
COLD WATER CANYON GC
Wisconsin Dells, Wisconsin
J. C. Wilson
COLE PARK GC
Fort Campbell, Kentucky
(R.) Edward Lawrence
Packard
COLFAX GC
Colfax, Iowa
(R.) Charles Calhoun
COLGATE UNIVERSITY GC [NLE]
Hamilton, New York
Tom Winton
COLLATTIN GC
Ireland
(R.) Eddie Hackett

COLL CREEK CC
Pennsylvania
Chester Ruby
COLLEGE GC
Delhi, New York
Pete Craig
COLLEGE HILL GC
Poughkeepsie, New York
(R.) William F. Mitchell
COLLEGE OF THE SEQUOIAS GC
Fresno, California
Bob Baldock
COLLETON RIVER PLANTATION GC
Hilton Head, South Carolina
Jack Nicklaus
COLLIER PARK GC
Perth, Australia
Peter Thomson, Michael
Wolveridge
COLLINDALE GC
Fort Collins, Colorado
Frank Hummel
COLLINGTREE PARK GC
Northampton, England
Johnny Miller, Gene Bates
COLLY CREEK GC
Topeka, Kansas
(A.9) Larry Flatt
COLNE VALLEY GC
East Anglia, England
Howard Swan
COLOGNE G UND LAND C
Cologne, Germany
Karl Hoffmann, Bernhard von
Limburger
COLONIA CC
New Jersey
Tom Bendelow
(A.9) Robert White
(R.) Hal Purdy
(R.) Frank Duane
COLONIAL CC
Thomasville, North Carolina
(R.) Gene Hamm
COLONIAL CC
Harrisburg, Pennsylvania
William Gordon, David Gordon
COLONIAL CC [NLE]
Memphis, Tennessee
William B. Langford
COLONIAL CC (NORTH CSE)
Cordova, Tennessee
Joseph S. Finger
COLONIAL CC (SOUTH CSE)
Cordova, Tennessee
Joseph S. Finger
(R.) Bob Cupp
COLONIAL CC
Fort Worth, Texas
John Bredemus
(A.3) Perry Maxwell
(R.) Dick Wilson
(R.) Robert Trent Jones
(R.) Jay Morrish, Bob Cupp
COLONIAL G&CC
Hanrahan, Louisiana
Ernest Penfold
COLONIAL GC
Lynnfield, Massachusetts
(R.5) William F. Mitchell
(1963)
(A.9) William F. Mitchell
(1967)

COLONIAL GC [NLE]
Lincoln, Nebraska
Henry B. Hughes, Richard
Watson
COLONIAL GC
Uniontown, Pennsylvania
William Gordon, David Gordon
COLONIAL BEND GC
Arlington, Texas
Jeff Brauer
COLONIAL GARDENS GC
Ohio
James Root
COLONIAL OAKS GC
Fort Wayne, Indiana
Richard Chilcote, Pat Riley
COLONIAL PALMS GC
Miami, Florida
John E. O'Connor
COLONIAL PARK GC
Clovis, New Mexico
Warren Cantrell
(A.9) *Ray Hardy*
COLONIAL VALLEY GC
Grants Pass, Oregon
John Nelson
COLONIE CC
Albany, New York
Geoffrey S. Cornish
COLONIE MUNI
New York
William F. Mitchell
(A.9) Robert Trent Jones
COLONY CC
Algonac, New York
C. H. Alison, H. S. Colt
COLONY G CSE
Murrietta, California
David Rainville
COLONY CREEK CC
Victoria, Texas
Richard Watson
COLONY WEST GC (CSE NO. 1)
Tamarac, Florida
Robert von Hagge, Bruce Devlin
COLONY WEST GC (CSE NO. 2)
Tamarac, Florida
Robert von Hagge, Bruce Devlin
COLORADO SPRINGS CC
Colorado Springs, Colorado
Willie Watson
(A.9) Dick Phelps
COLUMBIA CC
Chevy Chase, Maryland
Walter Harban
COLUMBIA CC
Chevy Chase, Maryland
Herbert Barker
(R.) Walter J. Travis
(R.) William S. Flynn
(R.) George Fazio, Tom Fazio
COLUMBIA CC
Columbia, Missouri
Tom Bendelow
(R.) Smiley Bell
(R.) Edward Lawrence
Packard
(A.9) Roger Packard
COLUMBIA CC
Columbia, South Carolina
Ellis Maples
COLUMBIA G&CC
Hudson, New York
Hal Purdy

COLUMBIA GC
Columbia, Illinois
Al Linkogel
COLUMBIA G CSE
Minneapolis, Minnesota
(R.) Edward Lawrence
Packard
COLUMBIA G CSE
Columbia, Missouri
Smiley Bell
COLUMBIA-EDGEWATER CC
Portland, Oregon
A. Vernon Macan
(R.) William F. Bell
(R.) Robert Muir Graves
COLUMBIA HILLS CC
Columbia Station, Ohio
Harold Paddock
COLUMBIA LAKES CC
West Columbia, Texas
Jack B. Miller
(R.) Tom Fazio
COLUMBIAN C
Carrollton, Texas
Ralph Plummer
(A.9) Leon Howard
(R.6) Joseph S. Finger
COLUMBINE CC
Littleton, Colorado
Henry B. Hughes
(R.) Press Maxwell
(R.) Henry B. Hughes
COLUMBUS CC
Columbus, Indiana
William H. Diddel
COLUMBUS CC
Columbus, Mississippi
John W. Frazier
(R.9) Brian Ault
COLUMBUS CC
Columbus, Ohio
Tom Bendelow
(R.9 A.9) Donald Ross
(A.4) C. H. Alison, H. S. Colt
(R.) Orrin Smith
(R.2) Robert Bruce Harris
(R.) Dick Wilson
(R.) Geoffrey S. Cornish,
Brian Silva
COLUMBUS PARK GC
Chicago, Illinois
Tom Bendelow
COLVILLE ELKS GC
Colville, Washington
Reg Stone, Roy Stone (9 1950)
COLVILLE PARK GC
Scotland
James Braid
(R.) J. Hamilton Stutt
COLWOOD NATIONAL GC
Portland, Oregon
A. Vernon Macan
COMBAT CENTER GC
Twenty Nine Palms, California
David W. Kent
COMMACK HILLS G&CC
New York
Alex McKay
COMMANCHE TRAIL GC
Big Spring, Texas
William Cantrell
COMMONWEALTH GC
Victoria, Australia
S. Berriman

COMMONWEALTH NATIONAL GC
Horsham, Pennsylvania
Arnold Palmer, Ed Seay
COMMUNITY GC
Dayton, Ohio
Willie V. Hoare
(A.9) *Earl Shock*
COMO PARK MUNI
St. Paul, Minnesota
(R.) Don Herfort
COMPTON GC
Los Angeles, California
William H. Johnson
COMSTOCK CC
Davis, California
Bob Baldock
COMSTRIJEN GC
Netherlands
T. J. A. Macauley
COMTE DE ROUGEMONT ESTATE GC
France
Tom Simpson
CONCHO VALLEY GC
St John's, Arizona
Arthur Jack Snyder
(A.9) Arthur Jack Snyder,
Forrest Richardson
CONCORD CC
Concord, Massachusetts
Donald Ross
(A.9) William F. Mitchell
CONCORD CC
Concord, New Hampshire
NKA Beaver Meadows Muni
CONCORD CC
Concord, New Hampshire
Ralph Barton
(R.) Geoffrey S. Cornish,
Brian Silva
CONCORD GC
Chattanooga, Tennessee
Arthur Davis
CONCORD GREEN GC
Libertyville, Illinois
Ken Killian, Dick Nugent
CONCORD HOTEL GC (CHALLENGER
CSE)
Kiamesha Lake, New York
Alfred H. Tull
CONCORD HOTEL GC
(CHAMPIONSHIP CSE)
Kiamesha Lake, New York
Joseph S. Finger
CONCORD HOTEL GC
(INTERNATIONAL CSE)
Kiamesha Lake, New York
Alfred H. Tull
CONCORDIA GC
Monroe, New Jersey
Brian Ault, Tom Clark, Bill Love
CONCORDIA GC
Ste. Thérèse, Quebec
Howard Watson
CONCORDVILLE CC
Pennsylvania
(A.4) Geoffrey S. Cornish,
William G. Robinson
CONDON GC
Condon, Oregon
Don Lehman
CONERO GC
Italy
Marco Croze

CONESTOGA CC
Lancaster, Pennsylvania
William Gordon
(R.) Ferdinand Garbin
CONESTOGA G&TC
Ontario
Clinton E. Robinson
(A.9) William G. Robinson,
John F. Robinson
CONEWANGO VALLEY CC
Pennsylvania
Clinton E. Robinson
(R.) Edmund B. Ault
CONFEDERATE HILLS CC
Highland Springs, Virginia
NKA The Lakes GC
CONGLETON GC
England
Fred W. Hawtree, A. H. F.
Jiggens
CONGRESSIONAL CC (BLUE CSE)
Bethesda, Maryland
Devereux Emmet
(R.) Tom Winton
(R.) Donald Ross
(R.) Alfred H. Tull
(R.9 A.9) Robert Trent Jones
(R.) Robert Trent Jones
(R.2) Edmund B. Ault
(R.) Rees Jones
CONGRESSIONAL CC (GOLD CSE)
Bethesda, Maryland
Devereux Emmet
(A.9) George Fazio, Tom
Fazio
CONGRESS LAKE C
Hartville, Ohio
Willie Park, Jr.
(R.) Donald Ross
(R.) William Newcomb
CONNEAUT SHORES CC
Conneaut, Ohio
J. Thomas Francis
CONNECTICUT GC
Easton, Connecticut
Geoffrey S. Cornish, William G.
Robinson
CONNELL LAKE G&CC
Inverness, Florida
William L. Campbell
CONNEMARA GC
County Galway, Ireland
Eddie Hackett
CONNERSVILLE CC
Connersville, Indiana
William H. Diddel
(A.9) Robert Simmons
CONNESTEE FALLS CC
Brevard, North Carolina
George W. Cobb
CONCHAS LAKE GC
Conchas Lake, New Mexico
Leon Howard
CONSTANT SPRINGS GC
Jamaica
Stanley Thompson
CONTEA DI GRADELLA GC
Milan, Italy
Pier Mancinelli
CONTINENTAL CC
Wildwood, Florida
Ron Garl

CONTINENTAL G CSE
Scottsdale, Arizona
Jeff Hardin, Greg Nash
CONTRA COSTA CC
Pleasant Hill, California
(R.) Robert Muir Graves
CONWAY FARMS GC
Lake Forest, Illinois
Tom Fazio
CONYNGHAM VALLEY CC
Pennsylvania
(R.) A. W. Tillinghast
COODEN BEACH GC
Sussex, England
Willie Park, Jr.
COOKE MUNICIPAL GC
Prince Albert, Saskatchewan
(A.9) *Hubert Cooke*
COOKEVILLE G&CC
Cookeville, Tennessee
Hooper Elblen, Tom Thaxton
(A.10) Kevin Tucker
COOMBE HILL GC
Surrey, England
J. F. Abercromby, Willie Park,
Jr.
(R.) J. Hamilton Stutt
COONSKIN PARK GC
Charleston, West Virginia
X. G. Hassenplug
COOPER COLONY CC
Hollywood, Florida
Pat Pattison
COOPER HILL GC
New Jersey
W. F. Pease
COOPER RIVER CC [NLE]
Camden, New Jersey
Devereux Emmet, Alfred H. Tull
COOSA CC
Rome, Georgia
(R.) George W. Cobb
(R.) Arthur Davis
COOSA PINES CC
Coosa Pines, Alabama
(A.11) John LaFoy
COOS CC
Coos Bay, Oregon
H. Chandler Egan
COPELAND HILLS CC
Columbiana, Ohio
R. Albert Anderson
COPENHAGEN GC
Copenhagen, Denmark
C. H. Alison, J. S. F. Morrison
(R.) John Harris
COPIAH-LINCOLN JUNIOR COLLEGE
GC
Brookhaven, Mississippi
(R.9 A.9) Kevin Tucker
COPPER CREEK GC
Copper Mountain, Colorado
Dick Phelps, Brad Benz
(R.9 A.9) Perry Dye
COPPER GC
Copper, Utah
Mick Riley
COPPER HILL CC
Flemington, New Jersey
(R.) Mike Hurdzan
COPT HEATH GC
Warwickshire, England
Harry Vardon
(A.9) H. S. Colt

COPTHORNE GC
Sussex, England
James Braid

COQUILLE VALLEY ELKS CC
Oregon
Clarence Sutton

CORAL CREEK G&CC
Fisherville, Ontario
Clinton E. Robinson

CORAL GABLES BILTMORE GC
Coral Gables, Florida
Donald Ross
(R.) William B. Langford
(R.) Mark Mahannah

CORAL HARBOUR GC [NLE]
Nassau, Bahamas
George Fazio

CORAL OAKS G CSE
Cape Coral, Florida
Arthur Hills

CORAL OCEAN POINT GC
Saipan
Larry Nelson

CORAL RIDGE CC
Fort Lauderdale, Florida
Robert Trent Jones

CORBALLIS GC
County Dublin, Ireland
Fred W. Hawtree, A. H. F.
Jiggens
(R.) Eddie Hackett

CORDILLERA RESORT GC
Edwards, Colorado
Hale Irwin, Dick Phelps

CORDOVA BAY GC
Victoria, British Columbia
William G. Robinson

CORFU G&CC
Corfu, Greece
Donald Harradine

CORHAMPTON GC
Corhampton, England
(R.9 A.9) J. J. F. Pennink, C.
D. Lawrie

CORK GC
County Cork, Ireland
David Brown
(R.9) Tom Dunn
(R.9 A.9) Alister Mackenzie
(R.) C. K. Cotton, J. J. F.
Pennink, C. D. Lawrie

CORNELL UNIVERSITY GC
Ithaca, New York
NKA Robert Trent Jones G Cse

CORNING CC
Corning, New York
Tom Winton

CORNWELLS CC
Cornwells Heights,
Pennsylvania
William Gordon, David Gordon

CORONADO G&CC
El Paso, Texas
Lawrence Hughes
(R.) Marvin Ferguson

CORONADO GC
Scottsdale, Arizona
Arthur Jack Snyder
(A. 9) Milt Coggins

CORONADO GC
Hot Springs Village, Arkansas
Edmund B. Ault

CORONADO GC [NLE]
Coronado, California
Willie Watson

CORONADO GC
Coronado, California
Jack Daray
(R.9 A.9) William F. Bell
(R.) Jack Daray, Jr., Stephen
Halsey

CORONADO BEACH GC
Panama City, Panama
George Fazio, Tom Fazio

CORPUS CHRISTI CC [NLE]
Corpus Christi, Texas
Tom Bendelow
(R.9) John Bredemus

CORPUS CHRISTI CC
Corpus Christi, Texas
Robert Trent Jones

CORPUS CHRISTI G CENTER
Corpus Christi, Texas
NKA Gabe Losano Sr. G Center

CORRAL DE TIERRA CC
Salinas, California
Bob Baldock
(R.) Gary Roger Baird
(R.) Robert Muir Graves

CORRY MUNI
Corry, Pennsylvania
Edmund B. Ault

CORSICA GC
Corsica, France
J. Hamilton Stutt

CORSICANA CC
Corsicana, Texas
Willie Lorimer (1914)
(R.) A. W. Tillinghast

CORTEZ GC
Hot Springs Village, Arkansas
Edmund B. Ault

CORTEZ MUNI
Cortez, Colorado
Press Maxwell

CORTLAND CC
Cortland, New York
Willard Wilkinson

CORVALLIS CC
Corvallis, Oregon
(A.9) Fred Federspiel

COSHOCTON T&CC
Coshocton, Ohio
Tom Bendelow

COSTA BRAVA GC
Gerona, Spain
J. Hamilton Stutt

COSTA DEL SOL G&RC
Miami, Florida
Bob Cupp

**COSTA MESA G&CC (LOS LAGOS
CSE)**
Costa Mesa, California
William F. Bell
(R.) Ronald Fream

**COSTA MESA G&CC (MESA LINDA
CSE)**
Costa Mesa, California
William F. Bell
(R.) Ronald Fream

COSTA TEGUISE GC
Lanzarote, Canary Islands
John Harris

COSTEBELLE G LINKS
Hyères, France
Willie Park, Jr.

COTO DE CAZA GC
Coto de Caza, California
Robert Trent Jones, Jr.

COTO DE DONANA
Seville, Spain
J. Hamilton Stutt

COTSWOLD HILLS GC
England
M. D. Little

COTTESMORE GC (NEW CSE)
England
M. Rogerson

COTTON BAY C
Eleuthera, Bahamas
Robert Trent Jones

COTTON CREEK GC
Gulf Shores, Alabama
Arnold Palmer, Ed Seay

COTTON DIKE GC
Dataw Island, South Carolina
Tom Fazio
(A.2) Tom Fazio

COTTON RUN GC
Tennessee
Kevin Tucker

COTTON VALLEY CC
Texas
Lee Singletary

COTTONWOOD CC
Sunlakes, Arizona
Jeff Hardin, Greg Nash

COTTONWOOD CC
El Cajon, California
NKA Rancho San Diego GC

COTTONWOOD CC
Glendive, Montana
Leo Johnson

COTTONWOOD CREEK MUNI
Waco, Texas
Joseph S. Finger, Ken Dye

COTTONWOOD C
Salt Lake City, Utah
(R.9 A.9) William H. Neff

COTTONWOOD G&CC
Calgary, Alberta
Bill Newis

COTTLESLOE GC
Australia
(R.) Peter Thomson, Michael
Wolveridge

COUBERT GC
France
Tom Dunn

COUNCIL BLUFFS CC [NLE]
Council Bluffs, Iowa
(R.) *Henry C. Glissmann*,
Harold Glissmann

COUNCIL FIRE GC
Chattanooga, Tennessee
Bob Cupp

COUNCIL GROVE CC
Council Grove, Kansas
(R.9) Leo Johnson

[THE] COUNTRY CLUB
Reform, Alabama
Harold Williams

[THE] COUNTRY CLUB
Brookline, Massachusetts
Willie Campbell
(A.3)Willie Campbell
(R.2 A.3rd 9) William S.
Flynn
(R.2) Geoffrey S. Cornish
(R.2) Geoffrey S. Cornish,
William G. Robinson
(R.) Rees Jones

[THE] COUNTRY CLUB
Cleveland, Ohio
William S. Flynn, Howard
Toomey

[THE] COUNTRY CLUB
Donora, Pennsylvania
Tom Bendelow

[THE] COUNTRY CLUB
Meadville, Pennsylvania
(R.) Ferdinand Garbin

[THE] COUNTRY CLUB
Salt Lake City, Utah
Harold B. Lamb
(R.) William F. Bell, William
P. Bell
(R.) Ralph Plummer

[THE] COUNTRY CLUB
Johannesburg, South Africa
Fred W. Hawtree
(R.12) Martin Hawtree

**COUNTRY CLUB AT MUIRFIELD
VILLAGE**
Dublin, Ohio
Jack Nicklaus

COUNTRY CLUB AT THE LEGENDS
Eureka, Missouri
Robert Trent Jones

**COUNTRY CLUB AT WOODLOCH
SPRINGS**
Hawley, Pennsylvania
Rocky Roquemore, Jeff Burton

COUNTRY CLUB CASTELGANDOLFO
Rome, Italy
Robert Trent Jones

**COUNTRY CLUB CIDADE DO RIO
GRANDE**
Brazil
Luis A. Dias, Jessiel Magalhaes

COUNTRY CLUB DE MANIZALES
Calais, Colombia
Howard Watson

COUNTRY CLUB DE SANTIAGO [NLE]
Santiago, Cuba
Devereux Emmet

**COUNTRY CLUB DU CHÂTEAU DE
TAULANE**
France
John Harris, C. K. Cotton

COUNTRY CLUB EL RODEO
Medellin, Colombia
Howard Watson

COUNTRY CLUB GLENMOOR
Japan
Perry Dye

[THE] COUNTRY CLUB JAPAN
Chiba, Japan
Shunsuke Kato

COUNTRY CLUB KHOA YAI
Nakornratchasima, Thailand
Jack Nicklaus

COUNTRY CLUB LAKES
Dumfries, Virginia
Buddy Loving, Algie Pulley

COUNTRY CLUB LAKES
Japan
Isao Aoki
COUNTRY CLUB MILITAR
Melgar, Columbia
Howard Watson
COUNTRY CLUB OF ALABAMA
Eufaula, Alabama
Ron Kirby, Denis Griffiths
COUNTRY CLUB OF ASHLAND
Ashland, Ohio
Willie Park, Jr.
COUNTRY CLUB OF AUSTIN
Austin, Texas
NKA Riverside GC
COUNTRY CLUB OF BELOIT [NLE]
Beloit, Wisconsin
Tom Bendelow
COUNTRY CLUB OF BILLERICA
Billerica, Massachusetts
Phil Wogan
COUNTRY CLUB OF BIRMINGHAM
(EAST CSE)
Birmingham, Alabama
Donald Ross
   (R.) George W. Cobb
   (R.) John LaFoy
COUNTRY CLUB OF BIRMINGHAM
(WEST CSE)
Birmingham, Alabama
Donald Ross
   (R.) Robert Trent Jones
   (R.) Pete Dye, P. B. Dye
COUNTRY CLUB OF BOGOTÁ [NLE]
Bogotá, Colombia
Charles Banks
COUNTRY CLUB OF BOGOTÁ (EAST
CSE)
Bogotá, Colombia
John Van Kleek
COUNTRY CLUB OF BOGOTÁ (WEST
CSE)
Bogotá, Colombia
John Van Kleek
COUNTRY CLUB OF BREVARD
Brevard, Florida
R. Albert Anderson
COUNTRY CLUB OF BRISTOL [NLE]
Bristol, Tennessee
Alex Findlay
COUNTRY CLUB OF BRISTOL
Bristol, Tennessee
Alex McKay
COUNTRY CLUB OF BUFFALO
Williamsville, New York
Donald Ross
   (R.) Robert Trent Jones
   (R.) Geoffrey S. Cornish,
   William G. Robinson
COUNTRY CLUB OF CALLAWASSIE
Callawassie Island, South
Carolina
Tom Fazio
   (A.3rd 9) Tom Fazio
COUNTRY CLUB OF CALLAWASSIE
(PUTTING CSE)
Callawassie Island, South
Carolina
Denis Griffiths
COUNTRY CLUB OF CASTLE PINES
Castle Rock, Colorado
Jack Nicklaus

COUNTRY CLUB OF CHAPALA
Chapala, Mexico
Harry C. Offutt
COUNTRY CLUB OF CHARLESTON
[NLE]
Charleston, South Carolina
Tom Bendelow
COUNTRY CLUB OF CHARLESTON
James Island, South Carolina
Seth Raynor
   (R.) John LaFoy
COUNTRY CLUB OF COLORADO
Colorado Springs, Colorado
Roy Dye
COUNTRY CLUB OF COLUMBUS
Columbus, Georgia
Donald Ross
COUNTRY CLUB OF CORAL SPRINGS
Coral Springs, Florida
Edmund B. Ault
COUNTRY CLUB OF CULPEPER
Culpeper, Virginia
Fred Findlay, *R. F. Loving, Sr.*
COUNTRY CLUB OF CUZCATLAN
San Salvador, El Salvador
Fred W. Hawtree
COUNTRY CLUB OF DARIEN
Darien, Connecticut
Alfred H. Tull
   (R.) Hal Purdy, Malcolm
   Purdy
   (R.3) Geoffrey S. Cornish,
   Brian Silva
COUNTRY CLUB OF DECATUR
Decatur, Illinois
Tom Bendelow
   (R.) Edward Lawrence
   Packard, Roger Packard
   (R.) Dick Nugent
COUNTRY CLUB OF DETROIT [NLE]
Detroit, Lake St. Clair, Michigan
Bert Way
COUNTRY CLUB OF DETROIT
Grosse Pointe Farms, Michigan
H. S. Colt
   (R.) C. H. Alison, H. S. Colt
   (R. A.9 Par 3) Robert Trent
   Jones
   (R.) Bruce Matthews, Jerry
   Matthews
   (R.) Arthur Hills
   (R.) Geoffrey S. Cornish,
   Brian Silva
COUNTRY CLUB OF EDISTO
Edisto Island, South Carolina
Tom Jackson
   (R.1) Tom Fazio
COUNTRY CLUB OF FAIRFAX
Fairfax, Virginia
William Gordon
   (A.9) Robert Trent Jones
   (R.) Buddy Loving, Algie
   Pulley
COUNTRY CLUB OF FAIRFIELD
Fairfield, Connecticut
Seth Raynor
   (R.2) A. W. Tillinghast
   (R.2) Geoffrey S. Cornish
   (R.) Robert Trent Jones

COUNTRY CLUB OF FARMINGTON
Farmington, Connecticut
Willie Park, Jr.
   (R.) Devereux Emmet
   (R.) Orrin Smith
   (R.1) Geoffrey S. Cornish
   (R.) Bob Cupp
COUNTRY CLUB OF FLORIDA
Delray Beach, Florida
Robert Bruce Harris
   (R.) Arthur Hills
COUNTRY CLUB OF FORT COLLINS
Fort Collins, Colorado
Henry B. Hughes
   (R.) John Cochran
COUNTRY CLUB OF GREEN VALLEY
Green Valley, Arizona
Red Lawrence
COUNTRY CLUB OF HALIFAX
Halifax, Massachusetts
Phil Wogan
COUNTRY CLUB OF HANOVER
Hanover, Germany
Dan Maples
COUNTRY CLUB OF HARRISBURG
Harrisburg, Pennsylvania
William S. Flynn
   (R.) Herbert Strong
COUNTRY CLUB OF HAVANA [NLE]
Havana, Cuba
Donald Ross
COUNTRY CLUB OF HILTON HEAD
Hilton Head Island, South
Carolina
Rees Jones
COUNTRY CLUB OF HUDSON
Hudson, Ohio
Harold Paddock
   (R.) Geoffrey S. Cornish
COUNTRY CLUB OF INDIANAPOLIS
[NLE]
Indianapolis, Indiana
Arthur Tweedie, Alvin Lockard
COUNTRY CLUB OF INDIANAPOLIS
Indianapolis, Indiana
Tom Bendelow
   (R.) William H. Diddel
   (R.) Pete Dye
   (R.) Dean Refram
COUNTRY CLUB OF ITHACA [NLE]
Ithaca, New York
A. W. Tillinghast
   (R.) Robert Trent Jones
COUNTRY CLUB OF ITHACA
Ithaca, New York
Geoffrey S. Cornish
COUNTRY CLUB OF JACKSON
Jackson, Michigan
Arthur Ham
   (A.9) Arthur Hills
   (R.) Jeff Gorney
COUNTRY CLUB OF JACKSON [NLE]
Jackson, Mississippi
Tom Bendelow
COUNTRY CLUB OF JACKSON
Jackson, Mississippi
Dick Wilson
   (R.9) Edmund B. Ault
   (R.) John LaFoy
COUNTRY CLUB OF JOHNSTON
COUNTY
Smithfield, North Carolina
   (R.9 A.9) Ellis Maples

COUNTRY CLUB OF LANSING
Lansing, Michigan
William B. Langford, Theodore
J. Moreau
   (R.) Edward Lawrence
   Packard
   (R.) Edward Lawrence
   Packard, Roger Packard
   (R.1) Jerry Matthews (1984)
   (R.11) Jerry Matthews (1990)
COUNTRY CLUB OF LAUREL
Laurel, Mississippi
Seymour Dunn
COUNTRY CLUB OF LEXINGTON
Lexington, South Carolina
Ed Riccoboni
COUNTRY CLUB OF LINCOLN
Lincoln, Nebraska
William H. Tucker
   (R.2) David Gill
   (R.3) Pete Dye
COUNTRY CLUB OF LITTLE ROCK
Little Rock, Arkansas
Herman Hackbarth
   (R.) William H. Diddel
   (R.3) Joseph S. Finger
   (R.) Edmund B. Ault (1968)
   (R.) Edmund B. Ault (1980)
COUNTRY CLUB OF LOUISIANA
Baton Rouge, Louisiana
Jack Nicklaus
COUNTRY CLUB OF MARYLAND
Baltimore, Maryland
Herbert Strong, George Low
COUNTRY CLUB OF MIAMI (EAST &
WEST CSES)
Hialeah, Florida
NKA GC of Miami
COUNTRY CLUB OF MIAMI (NORTH
CSE) [NLE]
Hialeah, Florida
Robert Trent Jones
COUNTRY CLUB OF MIAMI (SOUTH
CSE) [NLE]
Hialeah, Florida
Bill Dietsch
COUNTRY CLUB OF MISSOURI
Columbia, Missouri
Marvin Ferguson
COUNTRY CLUB OF MOBILE
Mobile, Alabama
Donald Ross
   (R.) Alfred H. Tull
   (R.) Willard Byrd
   (A.3rd 9) Earl Stone
COUNTRY CLUB OF MONTREAL
St. Laurent, Quebec
Albert Murray
   (R.) Roy Dye
COUNTRY CLUB OF MORRISTOWN
Morristown, Tennessee
William B. Langford
COUNTRY CLUB OF MOUNT DORA
Mount Dora, Florida
Lloyd Clifton, *Kenneth Ezell,*
George Clifton
COUNTRY CLUB OF NAPLES
Naples, Florida
William H. Diddel
   (R.) Ward Northrup
   (R.) Gordon Lewis

COUNTRY CLUB OF NEW BEDFORD
New Bedford, Massachusetts
Willie Park, Jr.
   (R.9 A.9) Donald Ross
COUNTRY CLUB OF NEWBERRY
Newberry, South Carolina
   (R.) Russell Breeden
COUNTRY CLUB OF NEW CANAAN
New Canaan, Connecticut
Willie Park, Jr.
   (R.9) Walter J. Travis
   (A.9) Alfred H. Tull
   (R.) Robert Trent Jones
COUNTRY CLUB OF NEW HAMPSHIRE
North Sutton, New Hampshire
Wayne Stiles, John Van Kleek
   (R.9 A.9) William F. Mitchell
COUNTRY CLUB OF NEW SEABURY
(BLUE CSE)
South Mashpee, Massachusetts
William F. Mitchell
   (R.) Rees Jones
COUNTRY CLUB OF NEW SEABURY
(GREEN CSE)
South Mashpee, Massachusetts
William F. Mitchell
   (R.) Rees Jones
COUNTRY CLUB OF NORTHAMPTON
COUNTY
Easton, Pennsylvania
   (R.12 A.6) David Gordon
COUNTRY CLUB OF NORTH
CAROLINA (CARDINAL CSE)
Pinehurst, North Carolina
Willard Byrd
   (A.9) Willard Byrd, Robert
   Trent Jones
COUNTRY CLUB OF NORTH
CAROLINA (DOGWOOD CSE)
Pinehurst, North Carolina
Willard Byrd, Ellis Maples
   (R.) Willard Byrd
   (R.) Robert Trent Jones
   (R.) Rees Jones
COUNTRY CLUB OF NORTH PORT
CHARLOTTE
North Port Charlotte, Florida
NKA Sabal Trace G&CC
COUNTRY CLUB OF NORWOOD
Norwood, Massachusetts
Samuel Mitchell
COUNTRY CLUB OF ORANGEBURG
Orangeburg, South Carolina
Ellis Maples
COUNTRY CLUB OF ORLANDO
Orlando, Florida
Donald Ross
   (R.) Robert Trent Jones
   (R.) Brian Silva, Geoffrey S.
   Cornish
COUNTRY CLUB OF OZARK
Ozark, Alabama
Ron Garl
COUNTRY CLUB OF PADUCAH [NLE]
Paducah, Kentucky
Tom Bendelow
COUNTRY CLUB OF PADUCAH
Paducah, Kentucky
Robert Trent Jones
COUNTRY CLUB OF PEORIA
Peoria, Illinois
F. M. Birks

COUNTRY CLUB OF PETERSBURG
[NLE]
Petersburg, Virginia
Donald Ross
COUNTRY CLUB OF PETERSBURG
Petersburg, Virginia
Edmund B. Ault
COUNTRY CLUB OF PITTSFIELD
Pittsfield, Massachusetts
Donald Ross
   (R.) Wayne Stiles
COUNTRY CLUB OF ROCHESTER
[NLE]
Rochester, New York
Alex Findlay
COUNTRY CLUB OF ROCHESTER
Rochester, New York
Donald Ross
   (R. A.3) Robert Trent Jones
   (R.) Arthur Hills
COUNTRY CLUB OF ST. ALBANS
Cherry Hill, Missouri
Tom Weiskopf, Jay Morrish
COUNTRY CLUB OF SALISBURY
Salisbury, North Carolina
   (R.) Donald Ross
COUNTRY CLUB OF SAPPHIRE
Sapphire Valley, North Carolina
George W. Cobb
   (R.1) John LaFoy
COUNTRY CLUB OF SARASOTA
Sarasota, Florida
NKA TPC at Prestancia
COUNTRY CLUB OF SAVANNAH
[NLE]
Savannah, Georgia
Tom Bendelow
COUNTRY CLUB OF SCRANTON
Clarks Summit, Pennsylvania
Walter J. Travis
   (R.) Geoffrey S. Cornish,
   Brian Silva
   (A.9) Michael Hurdzan
COUNTRY CLUB OF SEBRING
Sebring, Florida
Ron Garl
COUNTRY CLUB OF SILVER SPRINGS
SHORES
Ocala, Florida
Desmond Muirhead
COUNTRY CLUB OF SOUTH CAROLINA
Florence, South Carolina
Ellis Maples
COUNTRY CLUB OF SPARTANBURG
Spartanburg, South Carolina
   (R.9 A.9) George W. Cobb
   (R.) John LaFoy
COUNTRY CLUB OF TERRE HAUTE
Terre Haute, Indiana
Tom Bendelow
   (R.9 A.9) William H. Diddel
COUNTRY CLUB OF THE NORTH
Beaver Creek, Ohio
Jack Nicklaus
COUNTRY CLUB OF THE ROCKIES
Avon, Colorado
Jack Nicklaus
COUNTRY CLUB OF THE SOUTH
Alpharetta, Georgia
Jack Nicklaus
COUNTRY CLUB OF TROY
Troy, New York
Walter J. Travis

COUNTRY CLUB OF VIRGINIA (JAMES
RIVER CSE)
Richmond, Virginia
William S. Flynn
   (R.) Fred Findlay
   (R.) George O'Neil
   (R.3) Buddy Loving
COUNTRY CLUB OF VIRGINIA
(TUCKAHOE CREEK CSE) [NLE]
Richmond, Virginia
Edmund B. Ault
COUNTRY CLUB OF VIRGINIA
(TUCKAHOE CREEK CSE)
Richmond, Virginia
Joe Lee, Rocky Roquemore
COUNTRY CLUB OF VIRGINIA
(WESTHAMPTON CSE) [NLE]
Richmond, Virginia
Herbert Barker
COUNTRY CLUB OF VIRGINIA
(WESTHAMPTON CSE)
Richmond, Virginia
Donald Ross
   (R.) Fred Findlay
COUNTRY CLUB OF WATERBURY
Waterbury, Connecticut
Donald Ross
COUNTRY CLUB OF WHISPERING
PINES (EAST CSE)
Whispering Pines, North
Carolina
Ellis Maples
COUNTRY CLUB OF WHISPERING
PINES (SOUTH CSE)
Whispering Pines, North
Carolina
NKA Whispering Woods CC
COUNTRY CLUB OF WHISPERING
PINES (WEST CSE)
Whispering Pines, North
Carolina
Ellis Maples
COUNTRY CLUB OF YORK
York, Pennsylvania
Donald Ross
   (R.) William S. Flynn
COUNTRY GOLD CC
Kaufman, Texas
Leon Howard
COUNTRY HILLS GC (LINKS CSE)
Calgary, Alberta
Dave Bennett
COUNTRY HILLS GC (RIDGE CSE)
Calgary, Alberta
Dave Bennett
COUNTRY HILLS G CSE
Hendersonville, Tennessee
Leon Howard
COUNTRYLAND G CSE
Cumming, Georgia
Mike Young
COUNTRY LAKES VILLAGE CC
Naperville, Illinois
Rolf C. Campbell
COUNTRY MEADOWS GC
Peoria, Arizona
Jeff Hardin, Greg Nash
COUNTRY OAKS GC
Thomasville, Georgia
Willard Byrd
COUNTRYSIDE CC
Clearwater, Florida
Edward Lawrence Packard,
Roger Packard

COUNTRYSIDE GC
De Kalb, Illinois
   (R.) Ken Killian, Dick Nugent
   (R.) Bob Lohmann
COUNTRYSIDE WEST GC
De Kalb, Illinois
Edward Lawrence Packard
COUNTRYSIDE GC
Mundelein, Illinois
Bob Lohmann
COUNTRY SQUIRE INN GC
Eugene, Oregon
Gary Washburn
COUNTRY VIEW GC
Brooks, Maine
Ralph Brown
COUNTRY VIEW GC
St. Paul, Minnesota
Don Herfort
COUNTRY VIEW G CSE
Lancaster, Texas
Ron Garl
COUNTY CAVEN GC
Ireland
   (A.9) Eddie Hackett
COUNTY LONGFORD GC
Ireland
   (A.9) Eddie Hackett
COUNTY LOUTH GC
Ireland
   (R.) Cecil Barcroft, N.
   Halligan
   (R.) Tom Simpson, Molly
   Gourlay
COUNTY SLIGO GC
Ireland
H. S. Colt, C. H. Alison
   (R.) Eddie Hackett
COURTHOUSE CC
Fairfax, Virginia
Reuben Hines
COURTOWN GC
County Wexford, Ireland
C. K. Cotton, John Harris
   (R.) Eddie Hackett
COVE CAY G&TC
Clearwater, Florida
David Wallace
COVE CREEK CC
Stevensville, Maryland
Lindsay Ervin
COVENTRY GC
Coventry, England
Peter Paxton
   (R.) J. H. Taylor
COVERED BRIDGE GC
Morganville, New Jersey
   (R.) Hal Purdy, Malcolm
   Purdy
COVERED BRIDGE GC
Hartland, New Brunswick
William G. Robinson, John F.
Robinson
[THE] COVES AT BIRD ISLAND GC
Afton, Oklahoma
Jay Morrish
COWAL GC
Argyll, Scotland
James Braid
COWANSVILLE GC
Quebec
Howard Watson

COWDRAY PARK GC
England
J. F. Abercromby, Herbert
Fowler
(R.2) Herbert Fowler
COWES GC
England
(A.9) J. Hamilton Stutt
COWESSESS G&CC
Broadview, Saskatchewan
(R.) Bill Newis
COWICHAN G&CC
Duncan, British Columbia
A. Vernon Macan
(A.9) Ken Worthington
(R.) William G. Robinson,
John F. Robinson
CRAB MEADOW GC
Northport, New York
William F. Mitchell
(R.3) Stephen Kay
CRACKERNECK CC
Blue Springs, Missouri
Charles Maddox, William
Maddox
CRACKLEWOOD GC
Mt. Clemens, Michigan
Jerry Matthews
CRADOC GC
Powys, Wales
J. J. F. Pennink
CRAG BURN C
Elma, New York
Robert Trent Jones
(R.) Rees Jones
CRAGIE BRAE GC
Leroy, New York
James Gilmore Harrison,
Ferdinand Garbin
CRAIG GC
Regina, Saskatchewan
Jack Thompson
CRAIG GOWAN GC
Woodstock, Ontario
Clinton E. Robinson
CRAIGIE HILL GC
Perth, Scotland
J. Anderson
CRAIGOWAN G&CC
Woodstock, Ontario
Clinton E. Robinson
CRAIG RANCH GC
Las Vegas, Nevada
John F. Stinson, John C. Stinson
CRAIG WOOD CC
Lake Placid, New York
Seymour Dunn
CRAIL GC
Fife, Scotland
Old Tom Morris
CRAMER MOUNTAIN CC
Cramerton, North Carolina
Dan Maples
CRANBERRY VALLEY GC
Harwich, Massachusetts
Geoffrey S. Cornish, William G.
Robinson
CRANBERRY VILLAGE C
Collingwood, Ontario
Thomas McBroom
CRANBROOK GC
British Columbia
Reid Geddes, Arch Finlay, Frank
Fergie

CRANBROOK GC
Kent, England
John Harris
CRANBURY GC
Cranbury, New Jersey
(R.) Stephen Kay
CRANDON GC
Crandon, Wisconsin
Charles Maddox, Frank
MacDonald
CRANE ATHLETIC C [NLE]
Kansas City, Missouri
James Dalgleish
CRANE COUNTY CC
Crane, Texas
(R.) Leon Howard
CRANE CREEK CC
Boise, Idaho
Bob Baldock
(R.2) Robert Muir Graves
CRANE VALLEY GC
Hampshire, England
D. M. A. Steel
CRANG ESTATE GC
Toronto, Ontario
Howard Watson
CRANMOOR CC
Toms River, New Jersey
Tom Winton
CRANS-SUR-SIERRE GC
Switzerland
Sir Arnold Lunn
(R.9 A.9) Elysee Bonvin
CRANSTON CC
Cranston, Rhode Island
Geoffrey S. Cornish, William G.
Robinson
CRANWELL SCHOOL GC
Lenox, Massachusetts
Wayne Stiles, John Van Kleek
CRATER CC
Virginia
Fred Findlay
CRAWFORD CC
Crawford, New York
(R.) Seth Raynor
CRAWFORD COUNTY GC
Robinson, Illinois
Tom Bendelow
(A.9) William James Spear
CRAWFORD NOTCH CC [NLE]
New Hampshire
A. H. Fenn
(R.) Wayne Stiles, John Van
Kleek
CRAWFORDSVILLE CC
Crawfordsville, Indiana
(A.9) Jeff Gorney
CRAWFORDSVILLE MUNI
Crawfordsville, Indiana
William H. Diddel
(R.5 A.13) Gary Kern
CRAY VALLEY GC
Kent, England
John Day
CREAM RIDGE GC
New Jersey
Frank Miscoski
CREDIT ISLAND GC
Davenport, Iowa
William B. Langford, Theodore
J. Moreau

CREDIT VALLEY G&CC
Toronto, Ontario
Stanley Thompson
(R.) Clinton E. Robinson
(R.3) Robert Moote, David S.
Moote
[THE] CREEK C
Locust Valley, New York
Charles Blair Macdonald, Seth
Raynor
(R.) William S. Flynn
[THE] CREEK AT QUALCHAN G CSE
Spokane, Washington
William G. Robinson, John F.
Robinson
CREEK G LINKS
Cave Springs, Missouri
Paul Hughes, Reed Hughes
CREEK'S BEND GC
Chattanooga, Tennessee
(R.) Grant Wencel
CREIGIAU GC
Wales
(A.9) Fraser Middleton
CRESCENT CC
Crescent, Missouri
NKA [The] Players C at St.
Louis
CRESCENT DRIVE GC
Winnipeg, Canada
Günter A. Schoch
CRESCENT HILL GC
Louisville, Kentucky
(R.) Alex McKay
CRESCENT OAKS CC
Palm Harbor, Florida
Steve Smyers
CRESS CREEK CC
Naperville, Illinois
David Gill
CRESTBROOK CC
Watertown, Connecticut
Geoffrey S. Cornish
(A.9) Al Zikorus
CREST CREEK G&CC
Shepherdstown, Maryland
Robert L. Elder
CREST HILLS CC
Cincinnati, Ohio
Bob Simmons
CRESTMONT CC
West Orange, New Jersey
Donald Ross
(R.3) Frank Duane
(R.) Robert Trent Jones
CRESTVIEW CC
Agawam, Massachusetts
Geoffrey S. Cornish
CRESTVIEW CC
Crestview, Florida
NKA Foxwood CC
CRESTVIEW CC (NORTH CSE)
Wichita, Kansas
Robert Trent Jones
CRESTVIEW CC (SOUTH CSE)
Wichita, Kansas
Robert Trent Jones
(A.9) Robert Trent Jones, Jr.
CRESTVIEW GC
Muncie, Indiana
Robert Beard
CRESTVIEW HILLS GC
Waldport, Oregon
Willard Hill

CRESTWICKE CC
Bloomington, Illinois
Edward Lawrence Packard,
Roger Packard
CRESTWOOD CC
Pittsburg, Kansas
(R.3 A.9) Floyd Farley
CRESTWOOD CC
Rehoboth, Massachusetts
Geoffrey S. Cornish
CRESTWOOD HILLS GC
Anita, Iowa
Kenneth Turner
CREWE GC
Cheshire, England
(R.) J. S. F. Morrison
CRICKENTREE G CSE
Columbia, South Carolina
Ken Killian
CRIEFF GC
Perthshire, Scotland
Willie Park
(R.) James Braid, John R.
Stutt
CRIPPLE CREEK CC
Cripple Creek, Colorado
Dewitt "Maury" Bell
CRIPPLE CREEK G&CC
Bethany Beach, Delaware
Algie Pulley
CRISPIN CENTER GC
Oglebay Park, Wheeling, West
Virginia
Robert Biery (1936)
CROARA GC
Croara dei Gazzola, Italy
R. Buratti
(A.9) Marco Croze
CROASDAILE CC
Durham, North Carolina
George W. Cobb
CROCKERY HILLS GC
Nunica, Michigan
(R.5 A.9) Bruce Matthews,
Jerry Matthews
CROCKETT SPRINGS NATIONAL
G&CC
Brentwood, Tennessee
NKA Nashville G&AC
CROFTON GC
Crofton, Maryland
Edmund B. Ault
CROHAM HURST GC
Surrey, England
James Braid, F. G. Hawtree
CROOKED CREEK G&CC
Miami, Florida
Frank Murray
(R.) Bob Cupp
CROOKED CREEK GC
Hendersonville, North Carolina
Alex Guin, Stewart Goodin
CROOKED CREEK GC
Saginaw, Michigan
Donald Bray
(R.2) Jerry Matthews
CROOKED RIVER RANCH GC
Redmond, Oregon
Gene "Bunny" Mason
CROOKED STICK GC
Carmel, Indiana
Pete Dye
(R.) Pete Dye (1978)
(R.) Pete Dye (1986)

CROOKHILL PARK GC
Yorkshire, England
J. J. F. Pennink
CROSS CREEK CC
Fort Myers, Florida
Arthur Hills
CROSS CREEK CC
Atlanta, Georgia
Arthur Davis
CROSS CREEK CC
Mount Airy, North Carolina
Joe Lee, Rocky Roquemore
CROSS CREEK GC
Titusville, Pennsylvania
(R.9 A.9) Ferdinand Garbin
CROSS CREEK PLANTATION GC
Seneca, South Carolina
P. B. Dye
[THE] CROSSINGS GC
Richmond, Virginia
Joe Lee
CROSSMOOR GC
Netherlands
J. F. Dudok van Heel
CROSS ROADS CC
Lawrenceville, Illinois
Tom Bendelow
CROSS ROADS GC
Seattle, Washington
Al Smith
CROWBOROUGH BEACON GC
Sussex, England
(R.2) H. S. Colt
CROW CANYON CC
Danville, California
Ted Robinson
CROWFIELD G&CC
Goose Creek, South Carolina
Tom Jackson
CROWN COLONY CC
Lufkin, Texas
Robert von Hagge, Bruce Devlin
CROWN ISLE GC
Courtenay, British Columbia
Graham Cooke
CROWN MINES GC
South Africa
(R.) C. H. Alison
(R.) Gary Player, Sid Brews,
Van Vincent
CROWN POINT CC
Springfield, Vermont
William F. Mitchell
CROW RIVER CC
Hutchinson, Minnesota
Robert Prochnow
CROW VALLEY CC
Bettendorf, Iowa
John Cochran
CROW WOOD GC
Glasgow, Scotland
James Braid, John R. Stutt
CRUDEN BAY G&CC
Aberdeen, Scotland
Herbert Fowler, Tom Simpson
CRUMPIN-FOX C
Bernardston, Massachusetts
Robert Trent Jones
CRYSTALAIRE CC
Llano, California
William F. Bell
CRYSTAL DOWNS CC [NLE]
Frankfort, Michigan
Eugene Goebel

CRYSTAL DOWNS CC
Frankfort, Michigan
Alister Mackenzie, Perry
Maxwell
(R.) Geoffrey S. Cornish,
Brian Silva
CRYSTAL HIGHLANDS GC
Crystal City, Missouri
Michael Hurdzan
CRYSTAL LAGO CC [NLE]
Pompano Beach, Florida
Alec Ternyei
CRYSTAL LAKE CC
Crystal Lake, Illinois
George O'Neil, Joseph A.
Roseman, Jack Croke
(R.) Ken Killian, Dick Nugent
(R.) Bob Lohmann
CRYSTAL LAKE CC
Pompano Beach, Florida
Pat Pattison
(R.) Rees Jones
CRYSTAL LAKE CC
St. Louis, Missouri
William H. Diddel
CRYSTAL LAKE GC
Beulah, Michigan
Bruce Matthews, Jerry Matthews
(A.9) Jerry Matthews
CRYSTAL LAKES CC
Montana
(A.9) William G. Robinson
CRYSTAL LAKES GC
Okeechobee, Florida
Chuck Ankrom
CRYSTAL MOUNTAIN GC
Thomasville, Michigan
Robert Meyer
CRYSTAL SPRINGS CC
Caledonia, Michigan
Ernie Schrock (1989)
CRYSTAL SPRINGS G&CC
Hamburg, New Jersey
Robert von Hagge
CRYSTAL SPRINGS GC
Haverhill, Massachusetts
Geoffrey S. Cornish
CRYSTAL SPRINGS GC
Pineville, North Carolina
John J. Criscione, Gene Thomas
CRYSTAL SPRINGS GC
Burlingame, California
Herbert Fowler
(R.) William P. Bell
(R.) William F. Bell
(R.) Robert Muir Graves
CRYSTAL TREE G&CC
Orland Park, Illinois
Robert Trent Jones, Jr.
CRYSTAL WOODS GC
Woodstock, Illinois
(R.) Bob Lohmann
CUDDINGTON GC
England
H. S. Colt, J. S. F. Morrison, C.
H. Alison
CUERNAVACA CC
Cuernavaca, Mexico
I. D. Gonzales
CULLASAJA C
Highlands, North Carolina
Arnold Palmer, Ed Seay

CULLEN GC
Scotland
(R.) Old Tom Morris
CULVER MILITARY ACADEMY GC
Culver, Indiana
William B. Langford
CUMBERLAND CC
Carlisle, Pennsylvania
James Gilmore Harrison,
Ferdinand Garbin
CUMBERLAND GC
Cumberland, Maryland
(R.11) X. G. Hassenplug
CUMBERLAND GC
Cumberland, Wisconsin
(R.9 A.9) Don Herfort
CUMBERLAND LAKE CC
Birmingham, Alabama
Bill Amick
CUMBERNAULD GC
Dumbartonshire, Scotland
J. Hamilton Stutt
CUMMAQUID GC
Massachusetts
(A.9) Henry Mitchell
CUMMINGS COVE GC
Hendersonville, North Carolina
Bob Cupp
CURRENT RIVER CC
Doniphan, Missouri
Floyd Farley
CURRIE PARK GC
Wauwautosa, Wisconsin
George Hansen
CURTIS CREEK CC
Rensselaer, Indiana
Leonard Macomber
CUSTER GC
South Dakota
John W. Gillum
CUSTER HILL GC
Fort Riley, Kansas
Robert Trent Jones
CUTTEN FIELD CC
Guelph, Ontario
Chick Evans
(R.) Stanley Thompson
CUTTER SOUND CC
Stuart, Florida
Mark McCumber
CUYUNA CC
Deerwood, Minnesota
(R.9 A.9) Don Herfort
CYPRESS CC
Tochigi, Japan
Shunsuke Kato
CYPRESS GC
Cypress, California
Perry Dye
CYPRESS BAY GC
North Myrtle Beach, South
Carolina
Russell Breeden
CYPRESS CREEK CC
Boynton Beach, Florida
Robert von Hagge
CYPRESS CREEK CC
Orlando, Florida
Lloyd Clifton
CYPRESS CREEK OF LAKE ALFRED
GC
Lake Alfred, Florida
Steve Smyers

CYPRESS GREENS CC
Sun City Center, Florida
Ron Garl
CYPRESS HILLS GC
Colma, California
Jack Fleming
CYPRESS KNOLL GC
Palm Coast, Florida
Gary Player
CYPRESS LAKE CC
Fort Myers, Florida
Dick Wilson
(R.) Arthur Hills
CYPRESS LAKES CC
New South Wales, Australia
Steve Smyers
CYPRESS LAKES GC
Travis AFB, California
Joseph S. Finger (routing);
Robert Dean Putnam
CYPRESS LAKES GC
Hope Hills, North Carolina
L. B. Floyd
CYPRESS LINKS
Jupiter, Florida
Pete Dye
CYPRESS PINES CC
Lehigh Acres, Florida
Bob Petrucka
CYPRESS POINT C
Pebble Beach, California
Alister Mackenzie, Robert
Hunter
CYPRESS POINT CC
Virginia Beach, Virginia
Tom Clark, Brian Ault
CYPRESS RUN CC
Tarpon Springs, Florida
Edward Lawrence Packard
CYPRESS TREE GC (WEST CSE)
Maxwell AFB, Montgomery,
Alabama
Joseph S. Finger
CYPRESSWOOD G&RC
Winter Haven, Florida
Ron Garl
CYPRESSWOOD GC (CREEK CSE)
Spring, Texas
Rick Forester
CYPRESSWOOD GC (CYPRESS CSE)
Spring, Texas
Rick Forester

DACCA GC
Dacca, Bangladesh
J. J. F. Pennink
DACHSTEIN TAUERN GC
Schladming, Austria
Jim Engh, Bernhard Langer
DA-DE-CO GC
Ottawa, Illinois
Edward Lawrence Packard
DAD MILLER MUNI
Anaheim, California
Dick Miller, Wynn Priday
DAE JEON CC
Taejon, Korea
Mark McCumber
DAHLGREEN GC
Chaska, Minnesota
Gerry Pirkl, Donald G. Brauer

DAIFUJI GC
Shizuoka, Japan
Dr. N. Marumo
DAIHAKONE CC
Kanagawa, Japan
Hatohiko Asaka, Mitsuaki Otani
DIAKOGA CC
Japan
Seiha Chin
DAISIFU CENTRAL CC
Fukoka, Japan
Robert von Hagge, Bruce Devlin
DAKOTA DUNES CC
Dakota Dunes, South Dakota
Arnold Palmer, Ed Seay
DALE GC
Shetland, Scotland
Fraser Middleton
DALEWOOD G & CURLING C
Port Hope, Ontario
Clinton E. Robinson
DALLAS ATHLETIC C (BLUE CSE)
Mesquite, Texas
Ralph Plummer
(R.) Jack Nicklaus
DALLAS ATHLETIC C (GOLD CSE)
Mesquite, Texas
Ralph Plummer
(R.) Jack Nicklaus
DALLAS CC
Dallas, Texas
Tom Bendelow
(R.) Ralph Plummer
(R.) Jay Morrish
D'ALLEGRE ESTATE GC
France
Seymour Dunn
DALMAHOY GC (EAST CSE)
Midlothian, Scotland
James Braid, John R. Stutt
DALMAHOY GC (WEST CSE)
Midlothian, Scotland
James Braid, John R. Stutt
DALMILLING GC
Ayrshire, Scotland
Fraser Middleton
DALTON G&CC
Dalton, Georgia
(R.) Ron Kirby
DALTON RANCH GC
Durango, Colorado
Ken Dye
DAMAI BEACH GC
Sarawak, Malaysia
Arnold Palmer, Ed Seay
DAMAI INDAH GC
Jakarta, Indonesia
Jack Nicklaus
DANDRIDGE GC
Dandridge, Tennessee
Ellis Maples, Dan Maples
DANVILLE CC
Danville, Illinois
William H. Diddel
(A.9) Edward Lawrence
Packard, Brent Wadsworth
DANVILLE CC
Danville, Kentucky
Benjamin Wihry
DANVILLE CC
Danville, Pennsylvania
William Gordon, David Gordon

DANVILLE CC
Danville, Virginia
(R.) Gene Hamm (1958)
(R.) Gene Hamm (1961)
DANVILLE ELKS C
Danville, Illinois
William James Spear
DANVILLE VA HOSPITAL GC
Danville, Illinois
Charles Maddox
DARBY CREEK GC
Marysville, Ohio
Brian Silva, Geoffrey S. Cornish
D'ARCY RANCH GC
Okotoks, Alberta
Ken Dye
DARENTH VALLEY GC
England
R. Tempest
DARLEY GC
Troon, Scotland
Willie Fernie
(R.) James Braid
DARLINGTON CC
South Carolina
(A.9) *Roland Robertson*
DARLINGTON GC
Durham, England
Alister Mackenzie
(R.) J. J. F. Pennink
DARLINGTON G CSE
Mahwah, New Jersey
Nicholas Psiahas
DARMSTADT TRAISA GC
Darmstadt, Germany
(R.) Karl F. Grohs, *Rainer Preissmann*
DARTFORD GC
England
(R.) J. J. F. Pennink
DARTMOUTH G&CC
Blackawton, England
Jeremy Pern
DARWIN GC
Darwin, Australia
Peter Thomson, Michael Wolveridge
DAUPHIN G&CC
Manitoba
(A.9) William G. Robinson
DAVENPORT CC
Pleasant Valley, Iowa
C. H. Alison, H. S. Colt
(R.2) Ted Lockie
(R.) Bob Lohmann
DAVENPORT GC
Cheshire, England
Fraser Middleton
DAVID L. BAKER GC
Fountain Valley, California
Garrett Gill, George B. Williams
DAVISON CC
Davison, Michigan
Frederick A. Ellis
DAVIS PARK GC
Kaysville, Utah
William H. Neff
(R.) William Howard Neff
DAVIS SHORES CC [NLE]
St. Augustine, Florida
A. W. Tillinghast
DAVOS GC
Switzerland
(R.9 A.9) Donald Harradine

DAVYHOLME PARK GC
Manchester, England
(R.) J. A. Steer
DAWN HILL CC
Siloam Springs, Arkansas
Virgil Brookshire
DAWSON CC
Dawson, Georgia
Hugh Moore
DAYNE GLASS MUNI
Mountain View, Missouri
Bob Stevens
DAYTONA BEACH G&CC (NORTH CSE)
Daytona Beach, Florida
Amos Deatherage
DAYTONA BEACH G&CC (SOUTH CSE)
Daytona Beach, Florida
Donald Ross
DAYTON CC
Dayton, Ohio
Donald Ross
(R.) Geoffrey S. Cornish,
William G. Robinson
DAYTON GC
Aurora, Missouri
Horton Smith
DAYTON VALLEY CC
Dayton, Nevada
Arnold Palmer, Ed Seay
DEACONSBANK GC
Glasgow, Scotland
James Braid
DEAL GC
Deal Beach, New Jersey
Lawrence Van Etten
DEANE GC
Lancashire, England
(R.) J. A. Steer
DEANE MUNI
Somerset, England
J. Hamilton Stutt
DEANGATE RIDGE GC
Kent, England
Fred W. Hawtree
DeANZA DESERT CC
Borrego Springs, California
Lawrence Hughes
DeANZA PALM SPRINGS MOBILE CC
Cathedral City, California
Ted Robinson
DEARBORN CC
Dearborn, Michigan
Donald Ross
(R.) Clinton E. Robinson
(R.1) Jerry Matthews
DEARBORN HILLS CC
Dearborn, Michigan
Walter Hagen, *Mike Brady*
(R.) Warner Bowen
DEARHURST GC
Hidden Valley, Ontario
Clinton E. Robinson
DeBARY PLANTATION GC
DeBary, Florida
Lloyd Clifton, *Kenneth Ezell,
George Clifton*
DeBELL GC
Burbank, California
William F. Bell, William H.
Johnson
(R.) William F. Bell
(R.) Richard Bigler

DEBORDIEU COLONY CC [NLE]
Pawley's Island, South Carolina
Wallace F. Pate (9 Reversible
1982)
DEBORDIEU GC
Pawley's Island, South Carolina
Pete Dye, P. B. Dye
DECATUR CC
Decatur, Alabama
(R.9 A.9) David Gill
DECATUR GC
Decatur, Indiana
Robert Bruce Harris
DeCORDOVA BEND GC
Granbury, Texas
Dave Bennett, Leon Howard
DEDHAM HUNT & POLO C
Dedham, Massachusetts
Alex Findlay
(R.) Willie Ogg
(R.2) Geoffrey S. Cornish,
William G. Robinson
DE DOMMEL GC
Hertogenbosch, Netherlands
J. F. Dudok van Heel
DEEP CLIFF GC
Cupertino, California
Clark Glasson
DEEP CREEK GC
Port Charlotte, Florida
Mark McCumber
DEEPDALE GC [NLE]
Great Neck, New York
Charles Blair Macdonald, Seth
Raynor
(R.) Herbert Strong
DEEPDALE GC
Manhasset, New York
Dick Wilson
(R.) Dick Wilson
DEEP RIVER GC
Greensboro, North Carolina
W. W. Pegg
DEEP RIVER GC
Ontario
Howard Watson, Robert Moote
DEEP SPRINGS GC
Madison, North Carolina
Ellis Maples
(R.9 A.9) Ellis Maples, Dan
Maples
DEER CREEK G&CC
Deerfield Beach, Florida
Bill Watts
DEER CREEK G&T RESORT
Davenport, Florida
Ward Northrup
DEER CREEK GC
Park Forest, Illinois
Edward Lawrence Packard,
Roger Packard
DEER CREEK GC
Overland Park, Kansas
Robert Trent Jones, Jr.
DEER CREEK GC
Ajax, Ontario
(R.) Robert Heaslip
DEER CREEK G CSE
House Springs, Missouri
Brooks McCarthy (1989)

DEER CREEK STATE PARK GC
Mount Sterling, Ohio
Jack Kidwell, Michael Hurzdan
DEERCREST CC
Greenwich, Connecticut
Orrin Smith
DEERCROFT CC
Wagram, North Carolina
J. Williams
DEERFIELD CC
Deerfield Beach, Florida
William F. Mitchell
DEERFIELD CC
Madison, Mississippi
Joseph S. Finger
DEERFIELD CC
Brockport, New York
Pete Craig
DEERFIELD CC
Weston, West Virginia
(R.9 A.9) Jack Kidwell,
Michael Hurzdan
DEERFIELD PARK GC
Riverside, Illinois
Edward Lawrence Packard
DEERHURST HIGHLANDS GC
Huntsville, Ontario
Bob Cupp, Thomas McBroom
DEERHURST INN & CC
Huntsville, Ontario
Clinton E. Robinson
(R.) Thomas McBroom
DEERING BAY Y&CC
Miami, Florida
Arnold Palmer, Ed Seay
DEERING GC [NLE]
Portland, Maine
Waldron T. Bates
DEER LAKE GC
Springfield, Missouri
Bill Amick
DEER PARK GC
Utica, New Jersey
Hal Purdy
DEER PARK GC
Valentine, Nebraska
Leon Pounders
DEERPATH PARK GC
Lake Forest, Illinois
Alex Pirie
(R.) Ken Killian, Dick Nugent
(1971)
(R.) Ken Killian, Dick Nugent
(1981)
(R.) Dick Nugent
DEER RIDGE GC
Kitchener, Ontario
Thomas McBroom
DEER RUN CC
Casselberry, Florida
(R.) Lloyd Clifton
DEER RUN GC
Moulton, Alabama
Earl Stone
DEER RUN GC
Lehigh, Florida
Gordon G. Lewis
DEER RUN GC
Horton, Michigan
Bruce Gilpin (9 1964)
DEER RUN GC
West Deer, Pennsylvania
Ron Forse

DEER RUN GC (CARDINAL CSE)
Newport News, Virginia
Edmund B. Ault
(R.) Ron Kirby, Denis
Griffiths
DEER RUN GC (DEER RUN CSE)
Newport News, Virginia
Edmund B. Ault
(R.9 A.9) Ron Kirby, Denis
Griffiths
DEER TRACE G LINKS
Linn Valley Lakes, Kansas
(R.) Larry Flatt
DEER TRACK CC (NORTH CSE)
Myrtle Beach, South Carolina
J. Porter Gibson
DEER TRACK CC (SOUTH CSE)
Myrtle Beach, South Carolina
J. Porter Gibson
DEER TRAIL CC
Woodville, Texas
Leon Howard
DEERWOOD CC
Jacksonville, Florida
George W. Cobb
(R.) Willard Byrd
DEERWOOD GC
Kingwood, Texas
Joseph S. Finger, Ken Dye
DEESIDE GC
Scotland
(A.9) D. M. A. Steel
DEFENCE GC
Bloemfontein, South Africa
Robert Grimsdell
DEGRAY STATE PARK GC
Bismarck, Arkansas
Leon Howard, *Charles Howard*
DEJIMA CC
Ibaragi, Japan
Larry Nelson
DEL-AIRE CC
Delray Beach, Florida
Joe Lee
DELAMERE FOREST GC
Cheshire, England
Herbert Fowler
(R.) Fred W. Hawtree
DELANO GC
Delano, California
Bert Stamps
DELAPRE GC
England
John Jacobs
DELAVEAGA CC
Santa Cruz, California
Bert Stamps
(R.2) Ronald Fream
DELAWARE CC
Delaware, Indiana
(R.) Gary Kern
DELAWARE CC
Delaware, Ohio
Donald Ross
DEL BOSQUE CC
Mexico
Percy Clifford
DELBROOK GC
Delavan, Wisconsin
(R.) Bob Lohmann
DELCASTLE GC
Wilmington, Delaware
Edmund B. Ault

DELHAMYEH CC
Beirut, Lebanon
J. Hamilton Stutt
DELHI GC
Delhi, India
(R. A.9) John Harris, Peter
Thomson
DELKENHEIM GC
West Germany
Bernhard von Limburger
DELLWOOD CC
New York
(R.) William F. Mitchell
(R.) Robert Trent Jones
DELLWOOD NATIONAL GC
White Bear Lake, Minnesota
Don Herfort
DEL MAR CC
Ellwood City, Pennsylvania
Emil Loeffler, *John McGlynn*
DELMAR CC [NLE]
California
Charles Maud
DEL PASO CC
Sacramento, California
John L. Black
(R.) Herbert Fowler
(R.) Sam Whiting
(R.) William F. Bell
(R.) Gary Roger Baird
(R.) Robert Muir Graves
DELPHOS CC
Ohio
Leonard Schmutte
DELRAY BEACH G&CC
Delray Beach, Florida
Donald Ross
(R.) Robert Bruce Harris
(A.3rd 9) Red Lawrence
DELRAY DUNES G&CC
Delray Beach, Florida
Pete Dye
(R.) Pete Dye
DEL RIO G&CC
Brawley, California
William P. Bell
(R.) Robert Muir Graves
DEL SAFARI CC
Palm Desert, California
NKA Avondale CC
DELSJOE GC
Göteborg, Sweden
Douglas Brazier
DELTONA G&CC
Deltona, Florida
David Wallace
DELTURA CC
North Fort Myers, Florida
Ron Garl
DEMOR HILLS CC
Morenci, Michigan
Harold Paddock
DEMPSTER GC [NLE]
Chicago, Illinois
Tom Bendelow
DENBIGH GC
Wales
J. Stockton
DEN BRAE GC
Sanbornton, New Hampshire
Henry Homan

DENHAM GC
Denham, England
H. S. Colt
(R.) James Braid, John R.
Stutt
DENISON CC
Denison, Iowa
William Ada
DENNIS HIGHLANDS GC
Dennis, Massachusetts
Michael Hurdzan, Jack Kidwell
DENNIS PINES MUNI
Dennis, Massachusetts
Henry Mitchell
DENTON CC
Denton, Texas
Ralph Plummer
(R.) Dick Nugent
DENTON GC
Manchester, England
B. Allen
(R.) T. J. A. Macauley
DENVER CC
Denver, Colorado
James Foulis
(R.) Harry Collis
(R.) William S. Flynn
(R.) William H. Diddel
(R.) Press Maxwell
(R.3) John Cochran
(R.) Ed Seay
(R.) Bill Coore
DEREHAM GC
England
E. C. Gray
DERRICK C
Edmonton, Alberta
William Brinkworth
DERRYDALE GC
Brampton, Ontario
René Muylaert
DESARU RESORT GC
Malaysia
Robert Trent Jones, Jr.
DE SCHOOT GC
Sint Oedenrode, Netherlands
J. F. Dudok van Heel
DESERT AIR CC
Rancho Mirage, California
Jimmy Hines
DESERT AIRE CC
Palmdale, California
Ted Robinson
DESERT AIRE G&CC
Mattawa, Washington
(A.9) *Jim Krause*
DESERT DUNES G CSE
Desert Hot Springs, California
Robert Trent Jones, Jr.
DESERT FALLS CC
Palm Desert, California
Ronald Fream
DESERT FOREST GC
Carefree, Arizona
Red Lawrence
(R.2) Arthur Jack Snyder
DESERT HIGHLANDS GC
Scottsdale, Arizona
Jack Nicklaus
DESERT HIGHLANDS GC (PUTTING
CSE)
Scottsdale, Arizona
Gary Panks

DESERT HILLS GC
Green Valley, Arizona
Dave Bennett

DESERT HORIZONS CC
Indian Wells, California
Ted Robinson

DESERT INN CC
Las Vegas, Nevada
Lawrence Hughes
(R.) *Donald Collett*
(R.) Tom Clark
(R.) Richard Bigler

DESERT ISLAND CC
Rancho Mirage, California
Desmond Muirhead
(R.) Stan Leonard, *Philip Tattersfield*
(R.) Robert Muir Graves

DESERT LAKES G CSE
Fort Mohave, Arizona
Bob Baldock

DESERT MOUNTAIN GC (COCHISE CSE)
Carefree, Arizona
Jack Nicklaus

DESERT MOUNTAIN GC (GERONIMO CSE)
Carefree, Arizona
Jack Nicklaus

DESERT MOUNTAIN GC (RENEGADE CSE)
Carefree, Arizona
Jack Nicklaus

DESERT PRINCESS CC
Cathedral City, California
David Rainville

DESERT ROSE GC
Las Vegas, Nevada
Dick Wilson, Joe Lee
(R.) Jeff Brauer

DESERT SANDS G&CC
Mesa, Arizona
Arthur Jack Snyder

DESERT SPRINGS CC
Alice Springs, Australia
Peter Thomson, Michael Wolveridge

DES MOINES G&CC (BLUE CSE)
West Des Moines, Iowa
Pete Dye
(R.) Roger Packard

DES MOINES G&CC (RED CSE)
West Des Moines, Iowa
Pete Dye
(R.) Roger Packard

DESOTO GC
Hot Springs Village, Arkansas
Edmund B. Ault

DESOTO LAKES G&CC
Sarasota, Florida
NKA Palm-Aire West CC
(Champions Cse)

DETROIT CC
Detroit Lakes, Minnesota
Tom Bendelow
(A.9) Don Herfort

DETROIT GC [NLE]
Detroit, Michigan
Bert Way

DETROIT GC (NORTH CSE)
Detroit, Michigan
Donald Ross
(R.) Robert Trent Jones
(R.) Arthur Hills

DETROIT GC (SOUTH CSE)
Detroit, Michigan
Donald Ross
(R.2) Donald Ross
(R.) Robert Trent Jones

DETWILER GC
Toledo, Ohio
Arthur Hills

DEUX MONTAGNES GC
Quebec
John Watson

DEVIL'S HEAD RESORT GC
Merrimac, Wisconsin
Arthur Johnson

DEVIL'S KNOB GC
Wintergreen, Virginia
Ellis Maples, Dan Maples

DEVIL'S PAINTBRUSH G LINKS
Caledon, Ontario
Michael Hurdzan

DEVIL'S PULPIT GC
Caledon, Ontario
Michael Hurdzan

DEVIL'S RIDGE GC
Holly Springs, North Carolina
John LaFoy

DEVON CC
Pennsylvania
Lemuel C. Altemus

DEVON G & CURLING C
Devon, Alberta
(R.4) Rod Whitman

DEVONSHIRE GC
Chatsworth, California
William H. Johnson

DEWSBURY DISTRICT GC
England
Peter Alliss, David Thomas

DEXTER MUNI GC
Dexter, Maine
Bill Nadeau

DIABLO CREEK GC
Concord, California
Bob Baldock
(R.5) Robert Muir Graves

DIABLO G&CC
Diablo, California
Willie Watson
(R.2) Robert Muir Graves

DIABLO HILLS GC
Walnut Creek, California
Robert Muir Graves

DIAMOND BAR GC
California
William F. Bell

DIAMONDHEAD GC
Hot Springs, Arkansas
Norman Henderson

DIAMOND HEAD Y&CC (CARDINAL CSE)
Bay St. Louis, Mississippi
Bill Atkins (1972)

DIAMOND HEAD Y&CC (PINE CSE)
Bay St. Louis, Mississippi
Earl Stone

DIAMOND HILL GC
Dover, Florida
Chic Adams

DIAMOND OAKS CC
Roseville, California
Ted Robinson

DIAMOND OAKS G&CC
Fort Worth, Texas
Charles B. Akey

DIAMOND RIDGE GC
Woodlawn, Maryland
Edmund B. Ault

DIBOLL MUNI
Texas
Dave Bennett, Leon Howard
(A.9) Leon Howard

DIGBY PINES GC
Digby, Nova Scotia
Stanley Thompson
(R.) William G. Robinson

DIGHTON GC
Dighton, Massachusetts
Samuel Mitchell

DINALAND GC
Vernal, Utah
Bill Johnston

DINARD GC
France
(R.) Willie Park, Jr.

DINSLAKEN-HÜNXERWALD GC
Germany
Karl F. Grohs, *Rainer Preissmann*

DINSMORE CC [NLE]
Staatsburg, New York
Robert P. Huntington

DINSMORE GC
Staatsburg, New York
Hal Purdy

DIPLOMAT CC
Hollywood, Florida
Red Lawrence

DIPLOMATIC C
Bucharest, Rumania
Donald Harradine

DISCOVERY BAY CC
Byron, California
Ted Robinson

DISCOVERY BAY GC
Lantau Island, Hong Kong
Robert Trent Jones, Jr.

DISNEYLAND HOTEL GC [NLE]
Anaheim, California
Desmond Muirhead

DIVERSEY GC [NLE]
Chicago, Illinois
Tom Bendelow

DIVI BAHAMAS GC
New Providence Island, Bahamas
Joe Lee

DIX HILLS GC
New York
(R.) Stephen Kay

DIXIE GC
Laurel, Mississippi
Charles N. Clark

DIXIE RED HILLS GC
St. George, Utah
Ernie Schneider

DIXON CC
Dixon, Illinois
Tom Bendelow

DIXON LANDING CC [NLE]
Milpitas, California
Algie Pulley

DIX RIVER CC
Stanford, Kentucky
Buck Blankenship

DIXVILLE NOTCH GC
New Hampshire
George Thom

DJAKARTA GC
Batavia, Indonesia
Tom Simpson

DJURSHOLM GC
Djursholm, Sweden
Nils Sköld

DJURSLANDS GC
Denmark
Frederick Dreyer

DOBBINS AFB GC
Georgia
Chic Adams

DR. GIL MORGAN G CSE
Wewoka, Oklahoma
Floyd Farley

DOBSON RANCH GC
Mesa, Arizona
Red Lawrence, Jeff Hardin, Greg Nash

DODGE CITY CC
Dodge City, Kansas
Harry Robb
(A.9) Don Sechrest

DODGE COUNTY GC
Eastman, Georgia
Sid Clarke (9)

DODGE POINT GC
Dodgeville, Wisconsin
Homer Fieldhouse

DODGER PINES CC
Vero Beach, Florida
Dick Bird, Walter O'Malley, Ira Hoyt

DOERING ESTATE GC
Chicago, Illinois
William G. Langford, Theodore J. Moreau

DOE VALLEY G&CC
Brandenberg, Kentucky
Richard Watson

DOGWOOD HILLS GC
Osage Beach, Missouri
Herman Hackbarth

DOGWOOD LAKES CC
Bonifay, Florida
James Root

DOI CC
Japan
Taizo Kawada

DOLPHIN HEAD GC
Hilton Head Island, South Carolina
Arthur Davis, Ron Kirby, Gary Player

DOMAINE DE FONCOUVERTE GC
France
Gary Player

DOMAINE DES PRINCES GC
Brussels, Belgium
Jack Nicklaus

[THE] DOMINION C
Glen Allen, Virginia
Bill Love, *Curtis Strange*

DOMINION CC
San Antonio, Texas
Bill Johnston

DOM PEDRO GC
Algarve, Portugal
KNA Villamoura II GC

DONABATE GC
Ireland
(R.) Eddie Hackett

DONALSONVILLE CC
Donalsonville, Georgia
Bill Amick
DONAVESCHINGEN GC
Germany
Karl Hoffmann
DONCASTER GC
Doncaster, England
(R.) J. J. F. Pennink
(R.7) Fred W. Hawtree,
Martin Hawtree
DONEGAL HIGHLANDS GC
Donegal, Pennsylvania
James Gayton (routing); Ron
Forse
DONEGAL TOWN GC
County Donegal, Ireland
Eddie Hackett
DON HAWKINS MUNI
Birmingham, Alabama
Herbert Barker
(R.9 A.9) Jack Daray
DONNERSBERG GC
Rheinland, Germany
Götz Mecklenburg
DONNERSKIRCHEN GC
Neusiedler See, Austria
Kurt Rossknecht
DONNEYBROOK GC [NLE]
San Bernadino, California
William H. Johnson
DON SHULA'S HOTEL & C
(CHAMPIONSHIP CSE)
Miami Lakes, Florida
Bill Watts
DON SHULA'S HOTEL & C
(EXECUTIVE CSE)
Miami Lakes, Florida
John E. O'Connor
DON VALLEY MUNI
Toronto, Ontario
Howard Watson
(R. A.3rd 9) Howard Watson,
John Watson
DOOKS GC
Ireland
(R.) Eddie Hackett
DOON VALLEY GC
Kitchener, Ontario
Clinton E. Robinson
DOORNSCHE GC [NLE]
Utrecht, Netherlands
John Duncan Dunn
DORADO CC
Tucson, Arizona
Ted Robinson
DORADO BEACH GC (EAST CSE)
Dorado, Puerto Rico
Robert Trent Jones
DORADO BEACH GC (WEST CSE)
Dorado, Puerto Rico
Robert Trent Jones
DORADO DEL MAR GC
Dorado, Puerto Rico
James Gilmore Harrison,
Ferdinand Garbin
(R.) Edmund B. Ault
DORADO SANDS GC
Dorado Beach, Puerto Rico
Ron Garl

DORAL CC (BLUE CSE)
Miami, Florida
Dick Wilson
(R.) Robert von Hagge, Bruce
Devlin
DORAL CC (GOLD CSE)
Miami, Florida
Robert von Hagge, Bruce Devlin
(R.) Robert von Hagge, Bruce
Devlin
DORAL CC (GREEN CSE)
Miami, Florida
Robert von Hagge
DORAL CC (RED CSE)
Miami, Florida
Dick Wilson
(R.) Robert von Hagge, Bruce
Devlin
DORAL CC (WHITE CSE)
Miami, Florida
Robert von Hagge
DORAL PARK SILVER GC
Miami, Florida
Robert von Hagge, Bruce Devlin
DORCHESTER GC
Fairfield Glade, Tennessee
Kevin Tucker, *Bob Greenwood*
DORCHESTER G&CC
London, Ontario
Robert Moote, David L. Moote
DORCHESTER GC
Dorchester, Quebec
(A.9) Graham Cooke
DORKING GC
Surrey, England
James Braid
DORLON PARK GC
Columbiana, Ohio
Richard W. LaConte
DORNICK HILLS G&CC
Ardmore, Oklahoma
Perry Maxwell
(R.) Dick Nugent
DORTMUNDER GC
Dortmund, Germany
Bernhard von Limburger
DORVAL GC
Dorval, Quebec
Howard Watson
DORVAL MUNI (DORVAL CSE)
Dorval, Quebec
Graham Cooke
DORVAL MUNI (OAKVILLE CSE)
Dorval, Quebec
Graham Cooke
DOS RIOS CC
Gunnison, Colorado
John Cochran
(A.9) Dick Phelps, Brad Benz
DOTHAN CC
Dothan, Alabama
Hugh Moore
DOUBLE EAGLE C
Galena, Ohio
Jay Morrish, Tom Weiskopf
DOUBLE EAGLE CC
Albuquerque, New Mexico
Red Lawrence
DOUBLE EAGLE GC
Eagle Bend, Minnesota
Joel Goldstrand
DOUBLEGATE PLANTATION CC
Albany, Georgia
George W. Cobb

DOUGLAS G&CC
Douglas, Georgia
(A.9) Don Cottle
DOUGLAS G & SOCIAL C
Douglas, Arizona
A. H. Jolly
DOUGLAS GC
County Cork, Ireland
(R.9) Alister Mackenzie
(R.) Eddie Hackett
DOUGLAS MUNI
Isle of Man
Alister Mackenzie
DOUGLASDALE ESTATES GC
Calgary, Alberta
William G. Robinson, John F.
Robinson
DOUGLAS H. KEEN ESTATE GC
Austin, Quebec
Howard Watson
DOUGLAS MUNI
Isle of Man
Alister Mackenzie
DOUGLASTON GC
Glasgow, Scotland
John Harris
DOUGLASTON PARK GC
Douglaston, New York
William H. Tucker
(R.1) Robert Bruce Harris
(R.5) Frank Duane
DOVE CANYON CC
Dove Canyon, California
Jack Nicklaus
DOVER BAY CC
Ohio
Bert Way
DOVER CC
Dover, Delaware
(A.9) Edmund B. Ault
DOVER CC
Dover, New Hampshire
Wayne Stiles
(R.) Orrin Smith, William F.
Mitchell
DOWNERS GROVE GC
Belmont, Illinois
Charles Blair Macdonald
(R.3) David Gill
DOWNEY VA HOSPITAL GC
Chicago, Illinois
Charles Maddox
DOWNFIELD GC
Dundee, Scotland
James Braid, John R. Stutt
(R.) C. K. Cotton
DOWNING MUNI
Erie, Pennsylvania
James Gilmore Harrison,
Ferdinand Garbin
DOWNINGTOWN INN GC
Downingtown, Pennsylvania
George Fazio
DOWNPATRICK GC
County Down, Ireland
(R. A.8) Martin Hawtree,
Simon Gidman
DOWNSHIRE GC
Berkshire, England
Fred W. Hawtree
DOWNSVIEW G&CC
Toronto, Canada
Howard Watson, Robert Moote

DOWS CC
Dows, Iowa
Arthur E. Cott
DOYLESTOWN CC
Doylestown, Pennsylvania
William S. Flynn
(R.) James Blaukovitch
DRAGON HILLS GC
Thailand
Jim Engh, *Isao Aoki*
DRAGON LAKE GC
British Columbia
Jack Reimer
DRAGON VALLEY GC
Yongpyeong, South Korea
Ronald Fream
DRAYTON PARK GC
Birmingham, England
James Braid, John R. Stutt
DRAYTON VALLEY GC
Alberta
Robert Milligan
DRETZKA PARK GC
Madison, Wisconsin
Evert Kincaid
DRIFFIELD GC
England
C. H. Websdale
DRIFTWOOD G&CC
Bayou La Batre, Alabama
Telfair Ghioto
DRÖBAK GC
Norway
Gerold Hauser, *Günther Hauser*
DROMOLAND CASTLE GC
Ireland
B. E. Wiggington
DROTTNINGHOLMS GC
Sweden
Nils Sköld, Rafael Sundblom
DRUID HILLS CC
Atlanta, Georgia
Herbert Barker
(R.) Ron Kirby
(R.) Arthur Hills
DRUID HILLS GC
Fairfield Glade, Tennessee
Leon Howard
DRUMLINS GC
Syracuse, New York
Leonard Macomber
DRUMOIG G CSE
Leuchars, Scotland
Jack Nicklaus
DRY CREEK GC
Galt, California
Jack Fleming
DRYDEN G&CC
Ontario
Clinton E. Robinson
DRYDEN PARK MUNI
Modesto, California
William F. Bell, William P. Bell
(R.) Jack Daray, Jr., Stephen
Halsey
DUAMYRE CC [NLE]
Enfield, Massachusetts
Orrin Smith
DUBAI CREEK GC
Dubai, United Arab Emirates
Karl Litten
DUBB'S DREAD GC
Butler, Pennsylvania
John Aubrey

DUBLIN AND COUNTY GC
Dublin, Ireland
Eddie Hackett
DUBLIN CC
Dublin, Georgia
(R.9 A.9) George W. Cobb
DUBLIN SPORTS C
County Dublin, Ireland
Eddie Hackett
DUBOIS CC
DuBois, Pennsylvania
(R.9 A.9) X. G. Hassenplug
DUBSDREAD CC
Orlando, Florida
Tom Bendelow
(R.) Lloyd Clifton, *Kenneth Ezell, George Clifton*
DUBS DREAD GC
Piper, Kansas
Bob Dunning
DUBUQUE G&CC
Dubuque, Iowa
Tom Bendelow
(R.9) Roger Packard
DUC DE GRAMONT ESTATE GC
France
Tom Simpson
DUCK CREEK CC
Ravenna, Ohio
Richard W. LaConte
DUCK CREEK PARK GC
Davenport, Iowa
William B. Langford
(R.) Robert Bruce Harris
DUCK LAKE GC
Albion, Michigan
Tom Bendelow
(A.9) Arthur Young
DUCK WOODS GC
Kitty Hawk, North Carolina
Ellis Maples
(R.7) Brian Ault, Tom Clark
DUDDINGTON GC
Edinburgh, Scotland
Willie Park, Willie Park, Jr.
DUDSBURY GC
Hampshire, England
D. M. A. Steel
DUFF HOUSE ROYAL GC
Banff, Scotland
(R.) Alister Mackenzie, *Charles A. Mackenzie*
DUGWAY GC
Utah
William F. Bell
DUKE OF MARLBOROUGH GC
Upper Marlboro, Maryland
NKA Marlboro CC
DUKE ESTATE GC [NLE]
Somerville, New Jersey
Robert Trent Jones
DUKE UNIVERSITY GC
Durham, North Carolina
Robert Trent Jones
DULLATUR GC
Glasgow, Scotland
James Braid
DUMFRIES AND GALLOWAY GC
Scotland
(R.) Theodore Moone
DUMFRIES & COUNTY GC
Scotland
(R.) P. M. Ross

DUNAS DOURADAS GC
Algarve, Portugal
Howard Swan
DUNBAR GC
East Lothian, Scotland
Old Tom Morris
(R. A.3) Willie Park
DUNBLANE GC
Perthshire, Scotland
Old Tom Morris
DUNDALK GC
County Louth, Ireland
James Braid
(R.) J. Hamilton Stutt
(R. A.9) Peter Alliss, David Thomas
DUNDAS VALLEY G&CC
Ontario
Stanley Thompson
(R.) Clinton E. Robinson
DUNDEE CC
Dundee, Illinois
Harry Collis, *Jack Croke*
DUNDEE GC [NLE]
Omaha, Nebraska
Henry C. Glissmann, Harold Glissmann
DUNDEE PARK GC [NLE]
Omaha, Nebraska
Harry Lawrie
DUNDEE RESORT GC
Cape Breton, Nova Scotia
Robert Moote, David L. Moote
DUNEDIN CC
Dunedin, Florida
Donald Ross
(R.) Dick Wilson
(R.) Arthur Hills
DUNEDIN GC [NLE]
Otago, New Zealand
Charles R. Howden
[THE] DUNES C
New Buffalo, Michigan
Dick Nugent
DUNES G&BC
Myrtle Beach, South Carolina
Robert Trent Jones
(R.) Robert Trent Jones
DUNES GC
Sanibel Island, Florida
Mark McCumber
DUNES HOTEL CC
Las Vegas, Nevada
William F. Bell
DUNES WEST GC
Mt. Pleasant, South Carolina
Arthur Hills
DUNFERMLINE GC
Scotland
(R.) John R. Stutt
DUNFEY'S GC
Hyannis, Massachusetts
Geoffrey S. Cornish, William G. Robinson
DUNGENESS GC
Sequim, Washington
Jack Reimer (1970)
DUNGRAVAN GC
County Waterford, Ireland
Eddie Hackett
(R.) Eddie Hackett
DUNHAM MUNI
Cincinnati, Ohio
Arthur Hills

DUN LAOGHAIRE GC
Dublin, Ireland
H. S. Colt, C. H. Alison
(R.) Eddie Hackett
DUNMAGLAS GC
Charlevoix, Michigan
Larry Mancour (1992)
DUNMURRY GC
Northern Ireland
T. J. A. McAuley
(R.) J. J. F. Pennink
DUNNIKIER PARK GC
Fife, Scotland
Fraser Middleton
DUN ROAMIN GC
Gilbertsville, Massachusetts
Manny Francis
DUN ROVIN CC
Northville, Michigan
Bruce Matthews
DUNSTABLE DOWNS GC
Bedfordshire, England
James Braid
DUNWOODY CC
Dunwoody, Georgia
Willard Byrd
DUPAGE GC
DuPage, Illinois
Robert Trent Jones, Jr.
DU PONT CC
Wilmington, Delaware
NKA Green Hill Muni
DU PONT CC (DU PONT CSE)
Wilmington, Delaware
Alfred H. Tull
(R.) William Gordon, David Gordon
(R.) Geoffrey S. Cornish, William G. Robinson
DU PONT CC (LOUVIERS CSE)
Wilmington, Delaware
William Gordon, David Gordon
(R.) Geoffrey S. Cornish, William G. Robinson
DU PONT CC (MONTCHANIN CSE)
Newark, Delaware
William Gordon, David Gordon
(R.) Geoffrey S. Cornish, William G. Robinson
DU PONT CC (NEMOURS CSE)
Wilmington, Delaware
Alfred H. Tull
(R.) William Gordon, David Gordon
(R.) Geoffrey S. Cornish, William G. Robinson
DU PONT GC
Martinsville, Virginia
(R.9 A.9) Gene Hamm
DUQUESNE GC
Duquesne, Pennsylvania
(R.) Ferdinand Garbin
DURAND-EASTMAN PARK GC
Rochester, New York
Robert Trent Jones
DURANT CC
Durant, Oklahoma
Leon Howard
DURBAN CC
Durban, South Africa
Laurie Waters, *George Waterman*
(R.) S. V. Hotchkin
(R.) Robert G. Grimsdell

DÜREN GC
Bad Düren, Germany
Bernhard von Limburger
(A.9) J. J. F. Pennink
DUSSELDORFER GC
Dusseldorf, Germany
Fred W. Hawtree
DUSTON CC
Hopkinton, New Hampshire
George Dunn, Jr.
(R.) *Jerome Lewis*
DUTCH ELM GC
Arundel, Maine
Lucian Bourque
DUWAYNE MOTEL GC
Chicago, Illinois
Charles Maddox
DUXBURY PARK GC
Lancashire, England
Fred W. Hawtree, Martin Hawtree, A. H. F. Jiggens
DUXBURY YC
Duxbury, Massachusetts
Wayne Stiles
(R.) William F. Mitchell
(A.9) Geoffrey S. Cornish, William G. Robinson
DUXHURST FARM GC
Reigate, England
Jim Engh
DWAN GC
Bloomington, Minnesota
David Gill
D. W. FIELD MUNI
Brockton, Massachusetts
Wayne Stiles, John Van Kleek
(A.2) Samuel Mitchell
DWIGHT D. EISENHOWER MEMORIAL GC
Crownsville, Maryland
Edmund B. Ault
DYERSBURG MUNI
Dyersburg, Tennessee
Scott Nall
DYESS AFB GC
Abilene, Texas
Leon Howard
DYKE GC
England
(R.) F. G. Hawtree, Fred W. Hawtree
DYKEMAN PARK MUNI
Logansport, Indiana
William B. Langford, Theodore J. Moreau
DYKER BEACH GC
Brooklyn, New York
Tom Bendelow
(R.) John Van Kleek
DYKER MEADOW GC [NLE]
Brooklyn, New York
Tom Bendelow
DYSART G&CC
Dysart, Iowa
Dick Phelps

EAGLE BEND GC
Big Fork, Montana
William Hull (1988)
EAGLE BLUFF CC
Hurley, Wisconsin
Homer Fieldhouse

EAGLE BROOK CC
Geneva, Illinois
Roger Packard
EAGLE CC
Broomfield, Colorado
Leon Howard
(R.9 A.9) Dick Phelps
EAGLE GC
Delhi, India
Stephen Kay
EAGLE CREEK GC
Cave Creek, Arizona
Bill Johnston
EAGLE CREEK GC
Dunrobin, Ontario
Kenneth Skodacek, Ken Venturi
EAGLE CREEK G&TC
Naples, Florida
Edward Lawrence Packard
(R.) Gordon Lewis
EAGLE CREEK G CSE
Dover AFB, Delaware
Edmund B. Ault, Al Jamison
EAGLE CREEK MUNI
Indianapolis, Indiana
Pete Dye
(R.) Perry Dye
EAGLE CREEK RESORT & GC
Shelbyville, Illinois
Ken Killian
EAGLE CREST CC
Escondido, California
Stephen Halsey, Jack Daray, Jr.
EAGLE CREST GC
Cline Falls, Oregon
Gene "Bunny" Mason
EAGLE CREST GC
Garner, North Carolina
J. Baucom
EAGLEGLEN GC
Elmendorf AFB, Alaska
Robert Trent Jones
EAGLE GLEN GC
Farwell, Michigan
Jerry Matthews
EAGLEHEAD G&CC
New Market, Maryland
William F. Mitchell
EAGLE HILLS GC
Eagle, Idaho
C. Edward Trout
(A.9) Bob Baldock, Robert L. Baldock
EAGLE LANDING G&RC
Hanahan, South Carolina
Bill Amick
EAGLE LODGE GC
Lafayette Hill, Pennsylvania
Rees Jones
EAGLE MOUNTAIN GC
Brigham City, Utah
William Howard Neff
EAGLE NEST GC
North Myrtle Beach, South Carolina
Gene Hamm
EAGLE POINT GC
Birmingham, Alabama
Earl Stone
EAGLE RIDGE CC
Fort Myers, Florida
Gordon G. Lewis

EAGLE RIDGE G&CC
Spartanburg, South Carolina
Russell Breeden, *Dan Breeden*
EAGLE RIDGE GC (EAST CSE)
Galena, Illinois
Roger Packard
EAGLE RIDGE GC (NORTH CSE)
Galena, Illinois
Roger Packard
EAGLE RIDGE GC (SOUTH CSE)
Galena, Illinois
Roger Packard
EAGLE RIVER CC
Eagle River, Wisconsin
(R.3 A.9) Don Herfort
EAGLE ROCK GC
Sheppton, Pennsylvania
Arnold Palmer, Ed Seay
EAGLE ROCK GC
Edmonton, Alberta
Sid Puddicome (1990)
EAGLE RUN GC
Omaha, Nebraska
Jeff Brauer
EAGLE SPRINGS G CSE
St. Louis, Missouri
David Gill
EAGLE VAIL GC
Avon, Colorado
Robert von Hagge, Bruce Devlin
EAGLE VALLEY MUNI
Carson City, Nevada
Arthur Jack Snyder
EAGLE WATCH GC
Woodstock, Georgia
Arnold Palmer, Ed Seay
EAGLESTICKS GC
Zanesville, Ohio
Michael Hurdzan
EAGLEWOOD CC
Hobe Sound, Florida
Ward Northrup
[THE] EAGLES GC
Odessa, Florida
Ron Garl
(A.3rd 9) Ron Garl
EAGLESCLIFFE GC
County Durham, England
James Braid
(R.) Henry Cotton
EAGLE'S LANDING CC
Stockbridge, Georgia
Tom Fazio
EAGLE'S LANDING G CSE
Ocean City, Maryland
Mike Hurdzan
EAGLESMERE CC
Pennsylvania
(R.) William S. Flynn
EAGLE'S NEST CC
Somerset, Kentucky
Benjamin Wihry
EAGLE'S NEST CC
Blue Mountain Lake, New York
Willie Dunn, Jr.
EAGLE'S NEST GC
Sewell, New Jersey
William Gordon, David Gordon
EAGLE'S NEST GC
Seoul, Korea
Robert Dean Putman
EAGLES NEST G CSE
Silverthorne, Colorado
Dick Phelps

EARL F. ELLIOT PARK GC
Rockford, Illinois
Edward Lawrence Packard
EARL GREY GC
Alberta
(R.) Clinton E. Robinson
EARLINGTON G&CC
Washington
Frank James
(R.) *David Craig*
EARLVILLE ISLAND GC
Earlville, Illinois
Joe Meister
EARLYWINE PARK GC
Oklahoma City, Oklahoma
Floyd Farley
EASINGWOLD GC
North Yorkshire, England
F. G. Hawtree, J. H. Taylor
EAST AURORA CC
East Aurora, New York
(R.9 A.9) William Harries, *A. Russell Tryon*
EAST BAY CC [NLE]
Oakland, California
Willie Watson
EAST BAY CC
Largo, Florida
William F. Mitchell
EAST BAY G CSE
Provo, Utah
William Howard Neff
(R.1) William Howard Neff
EAST BERKSHIRE GC
East Berkshire, England
Peter Paxton
EAST CORK GC
County Cork, Ireland
John Harris
(R.) Eddie Hackett
EAST DEVON GC
Budleigh Salterton, Devon, England
(R.) J. Hamilton Stutt
EAST DORSET GC
East Dorset, England
(R.) Martin Hawtree
EAST HARTFORD GC
East Hartford, Connecticut
Orrin Smith
EAST HERTS GC
Hertfordshire, England
D. Hunt, D. Lewis
(R.) J. Hamilton Stutt
EAST KILBRIDE GC
Lanarkshire, Scotland
Fred W. Hawtree
EAST KINGSTON GC
East Kingston, New Hampshire
Phil Wogan
EAST LAKE CC
Atlanta, Georgia
Tom Bendelow
(R.) Donald Ross
(R.) George W. Cobb
EAST LAKE CC (CSE NO. 2) [NLE]
Atlanta, Georgia
Donald Ross
(R.) Chic Adams
EASTLAKE CC
Chula Vista, California
Theodore Robinson

EAST LAKES GC
Palm Beach Gardens, Florida
George Fazio, Tom Fazio
EAST LAKE WOODLANDS G&CC (NORTH CSE)
Oldsmar, Florida
Robert von Hagge, Bruce Devlin
EAST LAKE WOODLANDS G&CC (SOUTH CSE)
Oldsmar, Florida
Tom Jackson
EAST LIVERPOOL CC
East Liverpool, Ohio
Willie Park, Jr.
(A.9) Sandy Alves
EAST LONDON GC [NLE]
South Africa
George Peck
EAST LONDON CC
South Africa
C. H. Alison
(R.) S. V. Hotchkin
EAST MOUNTAIN MUNI
Waterbury, Connecticut
William Gordon, David Gordon
EAST ORANGE MUNI
East Orange, New Jersey
Tom Bendelow
EAST PARK GC
London, Ontario
Clinton E. Robinson
EAST POTOMAC PARK GC
Washington, D.C.
Robert White
(R.) William S. Flynn
EAST RIDGE CC [NLE]
Lincoln, Nebraska
Orrin Smith
EAST RIDGE CC
Shreveport, Louisiana
Press Maxwell
(R.) Dave Bennett
EAST SHORE CC
Culver, Indiana
William B. Langford, Theodore J. Moreau
EAST SUSSEX NATIONAL GC (EAST CSE)
East Sussex, England
Bob Cupp
EAST SUSSEX NATIONAL GC (WEST CSE)
East Sussex, England
Bob Cupp
EASTBOURNE DOWNS GC
Sussex, England
J. H. Taylor
EASTERN HILLS CC
Garland, Texas
Ralph Plummer
(R.9) Marvin Ferguson
EASTERN KENTUCKY UNIVERSITY GC
Richmond, Kentucky
Benjamin Wihry
EASTERN SHORE Y&CC
Onancock, Virginia
Russell Roberts
(R.) Edmund B. Ault
EASTERN STAR CC
Bangkok, Thailand
Robert Trent Jones, Jr.

EASTHAM LODGE GC
Cheshire, England
Fred W. Hawtree, Martin Hawtree, A. H. F. Jiggens
EASTMAN G LINKS
Grantham, New Hampshire
Geoffrey S. Cornish, William G. Robinson
EASTMORELAND GC
Portland, Oregon
H. Chandler Egan
(R.) *John Junor*
EASTHAMPSTEAD PARK GC
Wokingham, England
Fred W. Hawtree
EASTON CC
Easton, Massachusetts
Samuel Mitchell
EASTOVER CC
New Orleans, Louisiana
Joe Lee, Rocky Roquemore
EASTPOINTE CC
Palm Beach Gardens, Florida
George Fazio, Tom Fazio
EASTPORT MARINA & CC
North Myrtle Beach, South Carolina
Denis Griffiths
EASTWARD HO! CC
Chatham, Massachusetts
Herbert Fowler
EASTWOOD CC
Tochigi Prefecture, Japan
Robert Trent Jones, Jr.
EASTWOOD G&CC
Orlando, Florida
Lloyd Clifton, *Kenneth Ezell, George Clifton*
EASTWOOD GC
Renfrewshire, Scotland
Theodore Moone
(R.) John R. Stutt
EASTWOOD MUNI
Fort Myers, Florida
Robert von Hagge, Bruce Devlin
EASTWOOD FAIRWAYS GC
Louisiana
Tommy Moore
EASTWOOD HILLS G CSE [NLE]
Kansas City, Missouri
James Dalgleish
EATON CANYON GC
California
William F. Bell
EATON GC
Cheshire, England
Fred W. Hawtree
EBELTOFT GC
Ebeltoft, Denmark
Frederic Dreyer
EBERHART-PETRO MUNI
Mishawaka, Indiana
Jack Jernigan
EBONY HILL GC
Edinburg, Texas
John Bredemus
ECHO FARMS G&CC
Wilmington, North Carolina
Gene Hamm
(R.) Johnny Johnston, Clyde Johnston
ECHO HILLS GC
Hemet, California
Ed Dover

ECHO HILLS GC
Kansas
(R.) *Bert Henderson*
ECHO HILLS GC
Ohio
(A.9) John F. Robinson
ECHO LAKE CC
Detroit, Michigan
William H. Diddel
ECHO LAKE CC
Westfield, New Jersey
Donald Ross, George Low
(R.6) Robert White
(R.3) Willard Wilkinson
(R.3 A.3) Geoffrey S. Cornish, William G. Robinson
ECHO MESA GC
Sun City West, Arizona
Greg Nash
ECHO VALLEY G&CC
Des Moines, Iowa
Edward Lawrence Packard
EDEN CC DO BRAZIL
Marica, Brazil
Francisco Nobre Guedes
EDEN ISLES CC
Slidell, Louisiana
Edmund B. Ault
(R.1) Edmund B. Ault
EDENVALE GC
Eden Prairie, Minnesota
NKA Bent Creek GC
EDELWEISS GC
Japan
Perry Dye
EDGBASTON GC
Warwickshire, England
H. S. Colt
(R.) Tom Williamson
EDGEBROOK GC [NLE]
Illinois
James Foulis
EDGEBROOK GC
Sandwich, Illinois
Ken Killian, Dick Nugent
EDGEBROOK GC
South Dakota
Donald K. Rippel
EDGECREEK GC
Van Wert, Ohio
William James Spear
EDGEMONT GC
Philadelphia, Pennsylvania
Tony Pedone
EDGEWATER GC
Richland, California
T. R. Fritz
EDGEWATER GC [NLE]
Chicago, Illinois
Harry Turpie
EDGEWATER GC
Biloxi, Mississippi
NKA Rainbow Bay GC
EDGEWATER MUNI [NLE]
Pasco, Washington
A. Vernon Macan
(R.) Bob Baldock
EDGEWOOD CC
Virden, Illinois
Charles Maddox
EDGEWOOD CC
Anderson, Indiana
Marion Collins

EDGEWOOD CC
Southwick, Massachusetts
Geoffrey S. Cornish
EDGEWOOD CC
Union Lakes, Michigan
Ernest Way
(R.) Arthur Hills
EDGEWOOD CC
Pittsburgh, Pennsylvania
Donald Ross
(R.) Emil Loeffler, *John McGlynn*
(R.) James Gilmore Harrison, Ferdinand Garbin
(R.) Arthur Hills
EDGEWOOD CC
Charleston, West Virginia
George W. Cobb
EDGEWOOD GC
Cromwell, Connecticut
NKA TPC at River Highlands
EDGEWOOD GC
Polo, Illinois
Tom Bendelow
EDGEWOOD G CSE
Fargo, North Dakota
(R.) Robert Bruce Harris
EDGEWOOD IN THE PINES GC
Hazelton, Pennsylvania
David Gordon
EDGEWOOD TAHOE CC
Stateline, Nevada
George Fazio
(R.) Ronald Fream, Peter Thomson, Michael Wolveridge
EDGEWOOD VALLEY CC
LaGrange, Illinois
William H. Diddel
(R.) Roger Packard
EDINA CC
Edina, Minnesota
Tom Bendelow
(R.) Geoffrey S. Cornish, Brian Silva
EDINBURG CC
Edinburg, Texas
NKA Ebony Hill GC
EDINBURGH USA G CSE
Brooklyn Park, Minnesota
Robert Trent Jones, Jr.
EDISON CC
Rexford, New York
Devereux Emmet
EDMONDSTOWN GC
Ireland
(R.) Eddie Hackett
EDMONTON G&CC
Edmonton, Alberta
William Brinkworth
(R.) Stanley Thompson
(R.) William G. Robinson, John F. Robinson
EDMONTON PETROLEUM G&CC
Edmonton, Alberta
Mark McCumber
EDMORE GC
Edmore, Michigan
Carol O. Hegenauer
EDMUND ORGILL GC
Millington, Tennessee
Press Maxwell

EDMUNSTON GC
Edmunston, New Brunswick
(R. A.11) Albert Murray
EDWALTON GC
Nottinghamshire, England
J. J. F. Pennink
EDWIN R. CARR ESTATE GC
Virginia
Edmund B. Ault, Al Jamison
EDZELL GC
Edzell, Scotland
Archie Simpson
(R.) James Braid, John R. Stutt
EFFINGHAM CC
Effingham, Illinois
(A.9) William James Spear
EFFINGHAM GC
Surrey, England
H. S. Colt, J. S. F. Morrison
E. GAYNOR BRENNAN GC
Stamford, Connecticut
Maurice McCarthy
EGLIN AFB GC
Niceville, Florida
William B. Langford, Theodore J. Moreau
(A.3rd 9) Chuck Ankrom
EGWANI FARMS GC
Rockford, Tennessee
D. J. DeVictor
EGYPT VALLEY CC (RIDGE CSE)
Ada, Michigan
Arthur Hills
EGYPT VALLEY CC (VALLEY CSE)
Ada, Michigan
Arthur Hills
EHIME HIGH LAND GC
Ehime Prefecture, Japan
Yoshimasa Fujii
EICHENRIED GC
Munich, Germany
Kurt Rossknecht
EIFEL-HILLESHEIM GC
Hillesheim, Germany
(A.9) Karl F. Grohs, *Rainer Preissmann*
EINDHOVEN GC
Netherlands
H. S. Colt, C. H. Alison, J. S. F. Morrison
EISENHOWER GC (BLUE CSE)
US Air Force Academy, Colorado
Robert Trent Jones
EISENHOWER GC (SILVER CSE)
US Air Force Academy, Colorado
Frank Hummel
EISENHOWER COLLEGE GC
Seneca, New York
George W. Cobb
EISENHOWER PARK GC (BLUE CSE)
East Meadow, New York
Robert Trent Jones
EISENHOWER PARK GC (RED CSE)
East Meadow, New York
Devereux Emmet
EISENHOWER PARK GC (WHITE CSE)
East Meadow, New York
Robert Trent Jones
EKANA G&CC
Oviedo, Florida
Joe Lee

EKERÖD GC
Sweden
Jan Sederholm

EKSJÖ GC
Eksjö, Sweden
Anders Amilon

EKWANOK CC
Manchester, Vermont
John Duncan Dunn, Walter J.
Travis
(R.8) Geoffrey S. Cornish

ELANORA CC
Australia
Des Soutar

ELBA DELL'ACQUABONE GC
Italy
G. Albertini

ELBA GC
Elba, Italy
Pier Mancinelli

ELBEL PARK GC
South Bend, Indiana
William James Spear
(R.) William Newcomb

EL BOSQUE CC
Mexico
Percy Clifford

EL BOSQUE GC
Valencia, Spain
Robert Trent Jones

ELBOW HARBOUR GC
Elbow, Saskatchewan
Les Furber, *Jim Eremko*

EL CABALLERO CC [NLE]
Tarzana, California
George C. Thomas, Jr., William
P. Bell

EL CABALLERO CC
Tarzana, California
William H. Johnson
(R.) Robert Trent Jones

EL CAMINO CC
Oceanside, California
William H. Johnson

EL CAMPO CC
Texas
Jay Riviere

EL CARISO GC
Sylmar, California
Robert Muir Graves

EL CHAPARRAL GC
Urbanizacion El Chaparral,
Spain
Pepe Gancedo

EL CID G&CC
Mazatlan, Mexico
Manore Orthoco
(A.9) Lawrence Hughes

ELCONA CC
Elkhart, Indiana
William H. Diddel
(R.) Bruce Matthews, Jerry
Matthews
(R.) Arthur Hills

EL CONQUISTADOR CC
Bradenton, Florida
Mark Mahannah
(R.) Ted McAnlis

EL CONQUISTADOR GC [NLE]
Valparaiso, Florida
George O'Neil

EL CONQUISTADOR HOTEL & C
[NLE]
Fujardo, Puerto Rico
Robert von Hagge

ELDEN HILLS GC
Flagstaff, Arizona
Bob Baldock
(R.) Bill Johnston

ELDON CC
Eldon, Missouri
Skeeter Lewis

EL DORADO CC
El Dorado, Arkansas
Herman Hackbarth

ELDORADO CC
Palm Desert, California
Lawrence Hughes

EL DORADO CC
Greenwood, Indiana
NKA Royal Oak CC

EL DORADO CC
El Dorado, Kansas
Smiley Bell

EL DORADO CC
McKinney, Texas
Gary Roger Baird

ELDORADO GC
Mason, Michigan
Bruce Matthews, Jerry Matthews
(A.9) Bruce Matthews, Jerry
Matthews

EL DORADO GC
Humble, Texas
George Fazio

EL DORADO G CSE
Long Beach, California
(R.12) Ted Robinson
(R.) Garrett Gill, George B.
Williams

EL DORADO HILLS GC
El Dorado Hills, California
Robert Trent Jones

ELEPHANT BUTTE G&CC
Truth or Consequence, New
Mexico
Dick Phelps, Brad Benz

ELEPHANT HILLS GC
Victoria Falls, Zimbabwe
Gary Player, Sid Brews, *Dr. Van
Vincent*

ELFORDLEIGH G&CC
Devon, England
F. G. Hawtree, J. H. Taylor
(R.) J. Hamilton Stutt

ELGIN CC [NLE]
Elgin, Illinois
(R.9 A.9) Tom Bendelow

ELGIN CC
Elgin, Illinois
Edward Lawrence Packard
(R.) Ken Killian, Dick Nugent

ELGIN HOUSE GC
Port Carling, Ontario
Clinton E. Robinson

ELGIN WING PARK GC
Elgin, Illinois
Tom Bendelow

ELIE GOLF HOUSE C
Fife, Scotland
Old Tom Morris
(R.) James Braid

ELIZABETH CITY GC
Elizabeth City, North Carolina
J. Porter Gibson

ELIZABETH MANOR GC
Portsmouth, Virginia
Dick Wilson

ELIZABETHTOWN CC
Elizabethtown, Kentucky
Benjamin Wihry, *Morgan Boggs*

EL KANTAOUI GC
Soussenord, Tunisia
John Harris, Peter Thomson,
Ronald Fream

ELK CITY G&CC
Elk City, Oklahoma
Bob Dunning
(R.) Don Sechrest

ELK COUNTY CC
Ridgeway, Pennsylvania
Devereux Emmet
(R.9) X. G. Hassenplug

ELKHART GC
Elkhart, Kansas
(R.9) Leo Johnson

ELKHORN GC
Orcutt, California
Ed Burns

ELK HORN GC
Stockton, California
Bert Stamps
(R.) Robert Muir Graves

ELKHORN GC
Sun Valley, Idaho
Robert Trent Jones, Robert
Trent Jones, Jr.

ELKHORN VALLEY GC
Orcutt, Oregon
Don Cutler

ELKINS LAKE GC
Huntsville, Texas
Ralph Plummer

ELKINS RANCH GC
Fillmore, California
William H. Tucker, Jr.

ELK ISLAND NATIONAL PARK GC
Alberta
William Brinkworth

ELK RAPIDS GC
Elk Rapids, Michigan
Donald Ross

ELKRIDGE CC
Baltimore, Maryland
Tom Bendelow
(R.) Robert Trent Jones
(R.) Edmund B. Ault

ELK RIDGE G CSE
Atlanta, Michigan
Jerry Matthews

ELK RIVER CC
Elk River, Minnesota
Willie Kidd

ELK RIVER GC
Banner Elk, North Carolina
Jack Nicklaus

ELK RUN G CSE
Maple Valley, Washington
Jack Frei (9 Precision 1989)

ELKS CC
Elkhart, Indiana
Hal Purdy
(R. A.3) *Gene Conway*

ELKS CC
Marion, Indiana
William H. Diddel

ELKS CC
Seymour, Indiana
Harold England

ELKS CC
West Lafayette, Indiana
William H. Diddel

ELKS CC
Benton Harbor, Michigan
Charles Maddox

ELKS CC
Columbus, Nebraska
Dick Phelps

ELKS CC
Columbus, Ohio
Donald Ross

ELKS CC
McDermott, Ohio
Donald Ross

ELKS CC
Hamilton, Ohio
John Duncan Dunn

ELKS CC
Duncan, Oklahoma
Perry Maxwell
(A.9) Floyd Farley

ELKS GC
Pontiac, Illinois
(A.9) Edward Lawrence
Packard

ELKS GC
Alberta
(R.) *Claude Muret*

ELKS ALLENMORE GC
Washington
(R.) Kenneth Tyson

ELKS LODGE GC
Jeffersonville, Indiana
Benjamin Wihry

ELKS LODGE GC
Calgary, Alberta
(R.) William G. Robinson,
John F. Robinson

ELK VIEW CC
Pennsylvania
Donald Ross

ELLENDALE CC
Houma, Louisiana
Joseph S. Finger

ELLESBOROUGH GC
Buckinghamshire, England
James Braid
(R.) J. Hamilton Stutt

ELLESMERE GC
England
(R.) J. J. F. Pennink

ELLINGTON RIDGE CC
Connecticut
Geoffrey S. Cornish
(R.) Brian Silva, Geoffrey S.
Cornish

ELLINWOOD CC
Athol, Massachusetts
Donald Ross
(A.9) Geoffrey S. Cornish,
William G. Robinson

ELLIS CC
Ellis, Kansas
Dewey Longworth

ELLIS PARK MUNI [NLE]
Cedar Rapids, Iowa
Tom Bendelow

ELLIS PARK MUNI
Cedar Rapids, Iowa
William Woods
(R.9 A.9) William B.
Langford

ELLSWORTH AFB G CSE
Ellsworth AFB, South Dakota
Pat Wyss

ELLWOOD GREENS CC
Genoa, Illinois
NKA [The] Oak C of Genoa

EL MACERO CC
El Macero, California
Bob Baldock
(R.) Robert Muir Graves

ELMA MEADOWS GC
Elma, New York
William Harries, *A. Russell
Tryon*

ELMBROOK GC
Traverse City, Michigan
(R.3) Jerry Matthews

ELMCREST CC
Cedar Rapids, Iowa
(R.) Bob Lohmann

ELMCREST CC
East Longmeadow, Connecticut
Al Zikorus

EL MERRIE DEL CC [NLE]
Florida
John Duncan Dunn

ELMGATE CC
Glenview, Illinois
NKA Glenview Park GC

ELMHURST CC
Oskaloosa, Iowa
Tom Bendelow

ELMHURST G LINKS
Winnipeg, Manitoba
Donald Ross
(R.3) Clinton E. Robinson
(R.2) Geoffrey S. Cornish,
William G. Robinson
(R.9 A.9) John Robinson

ELMIRA CC
Elmira, New York
Willie Dunn, Jr.
(A.9) A. W. Tillinghast
(A.7) Ferdinand Garbin
(R.2) Stephen Kay

EL MIRADOR HOTEL GC [NLE]
Palm Springs, California
Gregor MacMillan

EL MONTE GC
Ogden, Utah
Mick Riley

EL MORRO GC
Puerto La Cruz, Venezuela
Edward Lawrence Packard,
Roger Packard

ELM PARK G & SPORTS C
Ireland
(R.) Eddie Hackett
(R.) John Harris

ELMRIDGE CC
Pawcatuck, Connecticut
Joseph Rustica

ELM RIDGE CC [NLE]
Montreal, Quebec
A. W. Tillinghast

ELM RIDGE CC (CSE NO. 1)
Ile Bizard, Quebec
William Gordon, David Gordon
(R.) Clinton E. Robinson

ELM RIDGE CC (CSE NO. 2)
Ile Bizard, Quebec
William Gordon, David Gordon

ELMSFORD CC [NLE]
Elmsford, New York
Donald Ross

ELMWOOD CC
White Plains, New York
A. W. Tillinghast
(R.) Alfred H. Tull
(R.1) Frank Duane

ELMWOOD G&CC
Marshalltown, Iowa
Tom Bendelow

ELMWOOD G&CC
Swift Current, Saskatchewan
(R.) William Brinkworth

ELMWOOD PARK GC
Sioux Falls, South Dakota
Edward Lawrence Packard
(A.9) Charles Maddox
(R.) Don Herfort

ELMWOOD PARK G CSE
Omaha, Nebraska
Tom Bendelow
(R.) Dave Bennett

EL NIGUEL CC
San Bernardino, California
David W. Kent

EL PARAISO GC
Costa del Sol, Spain
Arthur Davis, Ron Kirby, Gary
Player
(R) J. F. Dudok van Heel

EL PASO CC [NLE]
El Paso, Texas
Tom Bendelow

EL PASO CC
El Paso, Texas
Jack Harden
(R.) Ronald Fream

EL PRADO CC (BUTTERFIELD STAGE
CSE)
Chino, California
Harry Rainville, David Rainville

EL PRADO CC (CHINO CREEK CSE)
Chino, California
Harry Rainville, David Rainville

EL QORTINE INTERNATIONAL GC
Monastir, Tunisia
Ronald Fream

EL RANCHO VERDE CC
Rialto, California
Harry Rainville, David Rainville

EL RENO GC
El Reno, Oklahoma
Floyd Farley

EL RINCON C
Bogotá, Colombia
Robert Trent Jones

EL RIO GC
Tucson, Arizona
William P. Bell

EL RIVINO CC
Riverside, California
Joseph Calwell

ELSBERT FARM GC
Chicago, Illinois
C. D. Wagstaff

ELTHAM WARREN GC
England
Tom Dunn

EL TORO G CSE
Irvine, California
William Foley
(A.9) Garrett Gill, George B.
Williams

ELY CITY GC
England
Henry Cotton

ELY PARK GC
Binghamton, New York
Ernest E. Smith

ELYRIA CC
Elyria, Ohio
William S. Flynn
(R.2) Jack Kidwell, Michael
Hurdzan

EMBASSY C
Armonk, New York
Orrin Smith

EMBASSY WOODS AT BRETONNE
PARK GC
Naples, Florida
Mark McCumber

EMEIS PARK GC
Davenport, Iowa
C. D. Wagstaff

EMERALD BAY G&CC
Destin, Florida
Bob Cupp

EMERALD DUNES GC
West Palm Beach, Florida
Jim Fazio (routing); Tom Fazio

EMERALD GREEN GC
Rocky Hill, New York
William F. Mitchell

EMERALD HILLS CC
Hollywood, Florida
NKA [The] C at Emerald Hills

EMERALD HILLS GC
Redwood City, California
Ellis W. Van Gorder

EMERALD HILLS GC
Arnolds Park, Iowa
Leo Johnson

EMERALD HILLS ELKS GC
Redwood City, California
Clark Glasson

EMERALD LINKS GC
Greeley, Ontario
Graham Cooke

EMERALD PARK G&CC
Regina, Saskatchewan
William G. Robinson, John F.
Robinson

EMERALD RIVER G CSE
Laughlin, Nevada
Tom Clark

EMERALD VALLEY GC
Creswell, Oregon
Bob Baldock
(R.) Robert Muir Graves

EMIRATES GC
Dubai, United Arab Emirates
Karl Litten

EMFULENI CC
Vanderbuipark, South Africa
Robert Grimsdell

EMMA GC
Missouri
Chet Mendenhall

EMMETTSBURG G&CC
Emmettsburg, Iowa
Henry C. Glissmann, Harold
Glissmann

EMORYWOOD CC
North Carolina
(R.9) Ellis Maples
(R.) Willard Byrd

EMPIRE G&CC
Vernal, Utah
Mick Riley

EMPORDA GC
Pals, Spain
Robert von Hagge

EMPORIA CC
Emporia, Kansas
Bob Peebles
(A.9) Harry Robb

EMPORIA CC
Emporia, Virginia
Jim Reynolds

EMPORIA MUNI
Emporia, Kansas
Frank Hummel

EMPORIUM CC
Emporium, Pennsylvania
(R.9 A.9) Ferdinand Garbin

EMPRESS JOSEPHINE GC
Martinique
Robert Trent Jones

ENCANTO MUNI
Phoenix, Arizona
William P. Bell
(A.3rd 9) William P. Bell,
William F. Bell
(R.) Gary Panks

ENCINAL GC
Alameda, California
William Lock

ENDERLIN GC
North Dakota
(R.9) Don Herfort

ENDWELL GREENS GC
Johnson City, New York
Geoffrey S. Cornish, William G.
Robinson

ENFIELD GC
Enfield, England
Tom Dunn
(R.) James Braid, John R.
Stutt

ENGADINE GC
St. Moritz, Switzerland
M. Verdieri

ENGER PARK GC
Duluth, Minnesota
(R.18 A.9) Dick Phelps

ENGINEERS GC
Roslyn, New York
Herbert Strong
(R.) Devereux Emmet
(R.) William Gordon, David
Gordon
(R.3) Frank Duane (1970)
(R.18) Frank Duane (1977)

ENGLAND AFB GC
Alexandria, Louisiana
(A.9) Baxter Spann, Ken Dye

ENGLEWOOD CC
Englewood, New Jersey
(R.) Donald Ross
(R.) Alec Ternyei

ENGLEWOOD G&CC
Englewood, Florida
R. Albert Anderson
(R.) Steve Smyers

ENGLEWOOD MUNI
Englewood, Colorado
Dick Phelps, Brad Benz

ENGLISH HILLS GC
Walker, Michigan
Mark DeVries
(A.9) Jerry Matthews

ENGLISH TURN G&CC
New Orleans, Louisiana
Jack Nicklaus

ENIWA CC
Hokkaido, Japan
Hirochika Tomizawa

EN-JOIE CC
Endicott, New York
Ernest E. Smith
(R.) William F. Mitchell
(R.2) Pete Dye

ENKOEPING GC
Sweden
Nils Sköld

ENMORE PARK GC
Somerset, England
Fred W. Hawtree, A. H. F.
Jiggens

ENNIS GC
Ennis, Montana
Theodore Wirth

ENNIS GC
Ennis, Ireland
(R.) Eddie Hackett

ENNISCORTHY GC
Enniscorthy, Ireland
(R.) Eddie Hackett

ENNISCRONE GC
County Sligo, Ireland
Eddie Hackett

ENNISKILLEN GC
County Fermanagh, Northern
Ireland
(A.1) T. J. A. Macauley
(R.) Eddie Hackett

ENOCH HILLS G&CC
Edmonton, Alberta
NKA Indian Lakes G&CC

ENOSHIMA GC
Kanagawa, Japan
Dr. N. Marumo

ENT AFB G CSE
Colorado Springs, Colorado
Dick Phelps

ENTERPRISE MUNI GC
Glen Dale, Maryland
Robert L. Elder

ENUMCLAW GC
Enumclaw, Washington
(A.9) William Teufel

ENZESFELD G&CC
Austria
John Harris

EQUINOX G LINKS [NLE]
Manchester, Vermont
George A. Orvis

EQUINOX G LINKS
Manchester, Vermont
Walter J. Travis
(R.) William F. Mitchell
(R.) Rees Jones

ERDING-GRUNBACH GC
Bayern, Germany
Donald Harradine
(A.9) Götz Mecklenburg

EREWASH VALLEY GC
Derbyshire, England
Tom Dunn
(R.) Tom Williamson

ERIE DOWNS G&CC
Ontario
Stanley Thompson

ERIE MACCAUNE CC
Erie, Pennsylvania
James Gilmore Harrison

ERIE SHORES GC
North Madison, Ohio
Ben W. Zink

ERROL ESTATES INN & CC
Apopka, Florida
Joe Lee

ERSKINE MUNI
South Bend, Indiana
William H. Diddel
(R.) William Newcomb

ESPOO GC
Espoo, Finland
Jan Sederholm

ESBJERG GC
Denmark
Frederic Dreyer

ESCANABA CC
Michigan
Tom Bendelow

ESCHENRIED GC
Munich, Germany
Götz Mecklenburg

ESCONDIDO CC
Escondido, California
Harry Rainville, David Rainville

ESCORPION GC
Valencia, Spain
Ron Kirby, Gary Player

ESEEOLA LODGE GC [NLE]
North Carolina
Alex Findlay

ESKILSTUNA GC
Sweden
Douglas Brazier

ESLÖV GC
Eslöv, Sweden
Ture Bruce, Anders Amilon

ESQUIRE CC
Huntington, West Virginia
X. G. Hassenplug

ESSEN-HEIDHAUSEN GC
Essen, Germany
(R.) Karl F. Grohs, *Rainer
Preissmann*

ESSEX CC [NLE]
Manchester, Massachusetts
Herbert Leeds
(R.) John Duncan Dunn,
Walter J. Travis

ESSEX CC
Manchester, Massachusetts
Donald Ross
(R.) Skip Wogan
(R.) Phil Wogan

ESSEX CC
Hempstead, New York
Donald Ross

ESSEX COUNTY CC (EAST CSE)
West Orange, New Jersey
Tom Bendelow
(A.9 NLE) Alex Findlay
(R.) *David S. Hunter*
(R.) A. W. Tillinghast
(R.) Donald Ross
(R.) Robert Trent Jones

ESSEX COUNTY CC (WEST CSE)
West Orange, New Jersey
Charles Banks
(R.) A. W. Tillinghast
(R.9) Frank Duane

ESSEX FELLS CC
New Jersey
Donald Ross
(R.) Hal Purdy, Malcolm
Purdy

ESSEX G&CC
LaSalle, Ontario
Donald Ross
(R.) Arthur Hills
(A.2) Bruce Matthews, Jerry
Matthews

ESSEX GC
St. Thomas, Ontario
Stanley Thompson

ESTATE CARLTON GC
St. Croix, Virgin Islands
Alfred H. Tull

ESTELA GC
Oporto, Portugal
Doarta Souta Miaor

ESTES PARK GC
Estes Park, Colorado
Henry B. Hughes

**ESTORIA PALACIO GC [FKA ESTORIL
GC]**
Portugal
Jean Gassiat
(R.9 A.9) P. M. Ross

ESTORIL SOL GC
Estoril, Portugal
John Harris, Peter Thomson,
Michael Wolveridge, Ronald
Fream
(R.) Howard Swan

ESTRIMONT GC
Mont Orford, Quebec
John Watson

ETHELWOOD CC
Richmond, Virginia
William Gordon, David Gordon

ETON COLLEGE GC
Windsor, England
J. J. F. Pennink

ETOWAH VALLEY CC
Etowah, North Carolina
Edmund B. Ault

EUCLID HEIGHTS CC [NLE]
Cleveland, Ohio
Bert Way

EUCLID HILL CC
Orland Park, Illinois
NKA Silver Lake GC (North
Cse)

EUFAULA CC
Eufaula, Alabama
(A.9) Don Cottle

EUGENE CC [NLE]
Eugene, Oregon
H. Chandler Egan

EUGENE CC
Eugene, Oregon
Robert Trent Jones
(R.) Gary Roger Baird

EUGENE GRACE ESTATE GC
Bethlehem, Pennsylvania
Perry Maxwell

EUNHWASAM CC
Seoul, Korea
Arnold Palmer, Ed Seay

EUREKA GC
Eureka, Kansas
(R.9) Leo Johnson

EUREKA MUNI
Eureka, California
Bob Baldock

EURODISNEY GC
Paris, France
Ronald Fream

EUROPA SPORT REGION GC
Austria
Donald Harradine

EUSTIS CC [NLE]
Florida
C. S. Butchart

EVAN HEIGHTS GC
Georgia
(R.9) Arthur Davis

EVANSTON GC [NLE]
Kansas City, Missouri
Tom Bendelow

EVANSTON GC [NLE]
Kansas City, Missouri
James Dalgleish

EVANSTON GC
Skokie, Illinois
Donald Ross
(R.) Ken Killian, Dick Nugent
(R.) Bob Cupp

EVANSVILLE CC
Evansville, Indiana
William H. Diddel

EVERETT G&CC
Everett, Washington
*Frank Fifield, Frank Pendleton,
Allen Hibbard (9 1910)*
(A.9) Frank James
(R.) *Ken Tucker, Boyd Gourley*
(R.6) Ted Robinson
(R.1) John Steidel

EVERETT MUNI
Everett, Washington
Al Smith
(R.) Kenneth Tyson

[THE] EVERGLADES C
Palm Beach, Florida
Seth Raynor
(R.) William B. Langford,
Theodore J. Moreau
(R.) George Fazio, Tom Fazio
(R.) Ron Kirby, Denis
Griffiths

EVERGREEN CC
Hudson, Michigan
Robert Beard

EVERGREEN CC
Haymarket, Virginia
Buddy Loving, Algie Pulley

EVERGREEN CC
Mount Angel, Oregon
Bill Schaefer

EVERGREEN GC
Elkhorn, Wisconsin
Ken Killian, Dick Nugent

EVERGREEN VALLEY GC [NLE]
East Stoneham, Maine
Robert Trent Jones

EVIAN GC
Evian, France
Willie Park, Jr.
(R.) Michael Fenn
(R.) Robert Berthet
(R.) Cabell Robinson

EWA BEACH INTERNATIONAL CC
Ewa Beach, Oahu, Hawaii
Robin Nelson, Rodney Wright
EXCELSIOR SPRINGS CC
Excelsior Springs, Missouri
Tom Bendelow
    (R.) Smiley Bell
    (R.) Chet Mendenhall
    (A.9 Par 3, NLE) Perry
    Maxwell
EXETER CC
New Hampshire
    (R.) Manny Francis
EXETER CC
Exeter, Rhode Island
Geoffrey S. Cornish
EXETER G&CC
Countess Wear, Devon, England
James Braid, John R. Stutt
EXETER MUNI
Exeter, California
Bob Baldock
EXMOOR CC
Highland Park, Illinois
H. J. Tweedie
    (R.) Donald Ross
    (R.) Ken Killian, Dick Nugent
    (R.) Bob Lohmann
[THE] EXPERIENCE AT KOELE
Lanai, Hawaii
Ted Robinson, *Greg Norman*

F. A. MCCONNEL PRIVATE CSE
Catedon, Ontario
Howard Watson
FAIRACRES GC
Loveland, Ohio
Don Siebern (1965)
FAIRBANKS G&CC
Fairbanks, Alaska
    (R.) Robert Muir Graves
FAIRBANKS RANCH CC
Rancho Santa Fe, California
Ted Robinson
FAIRBORN CC
Ohio
William H. Diddel
FAIRBURY CC
Fairbury, Nebraska
    (R.1) Jeff Brauer
FAIRCHILD'S BEL AIR GREENS
Palm Springs, California
Len Gerkin
FAIRCHILD WHEELER GC (BLACK CSE)
Bridgeport, Connecticut
Robert White
FAIRCHILD WHEELER GC (RED CSE)
Bridgeport, Connecticut
Robert White
FAIRFIELD CC
Cincinnati, Ohio
    (R.) Mike Hurdzan
FAIRFIELD CC
Winnsboro, South Carolina
Robert Renaud
FAIRFIELD HARBOUR GC
New Bern, North Carolina
Dominic Palumbo
FAIRFIELD MOUNTAINS GC
Lake Lure, North Carolina
NKA Bald Mountain GC

FAIRFIELD OCEAN RIDGE GC
Edisto Island, South Carolina
NKA CC of Edisto
FAIRFIELD PAGOSA GC
Pagosa Springs, Colorado
Johnny Bulla
    (A.3rd 9) D. J. DeVictor
FAIRFIELD PLANTATION CC
Carrollton, Georgia
Willard Byrd
FAIRGREEN CC
New Smyrna Beach, Florida
Bill Amick
FAIRHAVEN GC
Lytham and St. Annes, England
J. A. Steer
FAIRHOPE MUNI
Fairhope, Alabama
Horace Smith
FAIRINGTON G&TC
Decatur, Georgia
NKA Metropolitan G&TC
FAIRLAWN CC
East Poland, Maine
Chic Adams, *Frank Bartasius*
FAIRLAWN CC
Akron, Ohio
William B. Langford
    (R.) Edward Lawrence
    Packard
    (R.) Arthur Hills
FAIRLESS HILLS GC
Morrisville, Pennsylvania
Marion V. Packard
FAIRMEDE CC [NLE]
Florida
John Duncan Dunn
FAIRMONT CC
New Jersey
    (R.) Alfred H. Tull
FAIRMONT FIELD C
Fairmont, West Virginia
    (R.) Gary Grandstaff
FAIRMONT HOT SPRINGS CC
Fairmont Hot Springs, British
Columbia
C. L. Wilder
FAIRMOUNT CC
Chatham, New Jersey
Hal Purdy
FAIR OAKS RANCH G&CC
Boerne, Texas
Ron Kirby, Gary Player
    (A.3rd 9) Ron Kirby, Denis
    Griffiths
FAIRVIEW CC
Greenwich, Connecticut
Robert Trent Jones
FAIRVIEW CC [NLE]
Elmsford, New York
Donald Ross
    (R.) Alfred H. Tull
FAIRVIEW G&CC
Quentin, Pennsylvania
Frank Murray, Russell Roberts
FAIRVIEW GC
New Jersey
William F. Mitchell
FAIRVIEW GC
Wayne, Indiana
Donald Ross
    (A.9) *Everett A. Monroe*

FAIRVIEW MOUNTAIN GC
Oliver, British Columbia
Les Furber, *Jim Eremko*
FAIRVIEW MUNI
St. Joseph, Missouri
    (R.2) *Melvin Anderson*
FAIRWAY GC
Orlando, Florida
Bill Amick
FAIRWAY GLEN GC
Santa Clara, California
Bob Baldock
FAIRWAY OAKS G&CC
Abilene, Texas
Ron Garl
FAIRWAY PARK GC
Maridurah, Australia
Peter Thomson, Michael
Wolveridge
FAIRWAY PINES GC
Painesville, Ohio
X. G. Hassenplug
FAIRWAY VILLAGE GC
Vancouver, Oregon
Gene "Bunny" Mason
FAIRWAYS CC
Warrington, Pennsylvania
William Gordon, David Gordon
FAIRWAY-TO-THE-STARS GC [NLE]
Las Vegas, Nevada
Louis Prima
FAIRWAY WOODLANDS GC
Punta Gorda, Florida
Gordon Lewis
FAIRWINDS G&CC
Nanoose Bay, British Columbia
Les Furber, *Jim Eremko*
FAIRWINDS G CSE
Fort Pierce, Florida
Jim Fazio
FAIRWOOD G&CC
Renton, Washington
William Teufel
FAIRWOOD PARK GC
Swansea, Wales
Fred W. Hawtree
FAIRYLAND CC
Lookout Mountain, Georgia
NKA Lookout Mountain GC
FAKENHAM GC
Norfolk, England
J. J. F. Pennink, C. D. Lawrie
FALCON BEACH LAKE CC
Manitoba
Norman H. Woods
FALCON FAIRWAYS GC
Homestead AFB, Florida
Mark Mahannah
    (R.9 A.9) Bob Cupp
FALCONHEAD GC
Burneyville, Oklahoma
Bob Dunning, *Waco Turner*
FALCON RIDGE CC
Mesa, Arizona
Robert Trent Jones, Jr.
FALCON'S LAIR GC
Walhalla, South Carolina
Harry Bowers
FALKENBERG GC
Sweden
    (A.11) Jan Sederholm

FALKENSTEIN GC
Hamburg, Germany
H. S. Colt, C. H. Alison, J. S. F.
Morrison
    (R.) Bernhard von Limburger
    (R.) J. Hamilton Stutt
FALKOEPING GC
Sweden
Nils Sköld
FALLBROOK CC
Fallbrook, California
Harry Rainville
FALL CREEK FALLS STATE PARK GC
Pikesville, Tennessee
Joe Lee, Rocky Roquemore
FALLEN TIMBER GC
Midway, Pennsylvania
NKA Quicksilver GC
FALLING CREEK GC
Kinston, North Carolina
Gene Hamm
FALLING RIVER CC
Appomattox, Virginia
Fred Findlay, *R. F. Loving, Sr.*
FALL RIVER CC
Fall River, Massachusetts
A. H. Fenn
    (R.6 A.3) Tom Winton
    (A.9) Geoffrey S. Cornish,
    William G. Robinson
FALL RIVER VALLEY G&CC
Fall River Mills, California
Clark Glasson
[THE] FALLS CC
Lake Worth, Florida
Joe Lee
[THE] FALLS CC
International Falls, Minnesota
    (R.) Don Herfort
[THE] FALLS G&CC
New Ulm, Texas
Jay Riviere, *Dave Marr*
[THE] FALLS G&RC
Lake Toxaway, North Carolina
Gene Bates
FALLS ROAD MUNI
Maryland
Edmund B. Ault, Al Jamison
FALLSVIEW HOTEL GC
Ellenville, New York
Robert Trent Jones
FALMOUTH CC
Falmouth, Maine
Brian Silva, Geoffrey S. Cornish
FALSTERBO GC
Sweden
Gunnar Bauer
FALUN-BORLÄNGE GC
Falun, Sweden
Nils Sköld
FAR CORNER FARM GC
West Boxford, Massachusetts
Geoffrey S. Cornish, William G.
Robinson
FARGO CC
Fargo, North Dakota
    (A.9) Robert Bruce Harris
    (R.) Dick Nugent
    (R.) Joel Goldstrand
FARIBAULT CC
Minnesota
Willie Kidd

FARIES PARK GC
Decatur, Illinois
Edward Lawrence Packard

[THE] FARM GC
Rocky Face, Georgia
Tom Fazio

FARMER'S G AND HEALTH C
Sanborn, Minnesota
Joel Goldstrand

FARMINGTON CC
Farmington, Michigan
(R.) William Newcomb
(R.) Bruce Matthews, Jerry
Matthews

FARMINGTON CC
Farmington, New Mexico
Warren Cantrell

FARMINGTON CC
Germantown, Tennessee
Press Maxwell

FARMINGTON CC
Charlottesville, Virginia
Fred Findlay
(A.9) R. F. Loving, Sr., Buddy
Loving
(R.) Buddy Loving

FARMINGTON GC [NLE]
Farmington, Maine
George Purrington

FARMINGTON WOODS CC
Farmington, Connecticut
Desmond Muirhead

FARM NECK GC
Martha's Vineyard,
Massachusetts
Geoffrey S. Cornish, William G.
Robinson
(A.9) Patrick Mulligan

FARMS CC
Wallingford, Connecticut
Geoffrey S. Cornish

[THE] FARMS RESORT GC
Vermont
Geoffrey S. Cornish, William G.
Robinson

FARNHAM PARK GC
Folly Hill, England
Henry Cotton
(R.9 A.9) Martin Hawtree

FARNHAM PARK GC
Stoke Poges, England
J. J. F. Pennink, D. M. A. Steel
(A.9) Fred W. Hawtree,
Martin Hawtree

FARNUM HILL CC
Lebanon, New Hampshire
Donald Ross
(R.) Orrin Smith
(A.9) Phil Wogan

FARRINGDON PLACE G CSE
Brantford, Ontario
Doug Carrick

FARWELL CC
Farwell, Texas
Warren Cantrell

FAUQUIER SPRINGS CC
Warrenton, Virginia
Reuben Hines

FAWN CLUB G CSE
Lake Placid, New York
Seymour Dunn

FAWN BROOK GC
Ajax, Ontario
Robert Heaslip

FAWN CREEK GC
Alamosa, Iowa
Gordon Cunningham

FAWN CREST GC
Michigan
Ron Weber

FEATHER BAY G&CC
Brownwood, Texas
Bill Johnston

FEATHER RIVER INN GC
Blairsden, California
Harold Sampson

FEATHER RIVER PARK GC
Blairsden, California
Bert Stamps

FEATHER SOUND CC
St. Peterburg, Florida
Joe Lee
(R.) Bob Cupp

FEILDING GC
New Zealand
C. H. Redhead

FELDAFING GC
Germany
Karl Hoffmann, Bernhard von
Limburger

FELIXSTOWE FERRY GC [NLE]
Suffolk, England
Tom Dunn
(R.) Willie Fernie

FELIXSTOWE FERRY GC
Suffolk, England
Alister Mackenzie
(R. A.4) Tom Simpson
(R.) Sir Guy Campbell, Henry
Cotton

FELLOWS CREEK GC
Canton, Michigan
Bruce Matthews, Jerry Matthews
(A.9) Jerry Matthews

FENDRICH GC
Evansville, Indiana
William H. Diddel
(R.) Edmund B. Ault

FENWAY CC
White Plains, New York
A. W. Tillinghast

FERMOY GC
County Cork, Ireland
John Harris
(R.) Eddie Hackett

FERNADINA BEACH GC
Florida
Ed Matteson
(A.3rd 9) Joe Lee

FERNCLIFFE CC
New Hampshire
Alex Findlay

FERNDOWN GC (NEW CSE)
Dorset, England
J. Hamilton Stutt

FERNDOWN GC (OLD CSE)
Dorset, England
Harold Hilton

FERNIE G&CC
Fernie, British Columbia
(R.) Bill Newis

FERNWOOD CC
McComb, Mississippi
George C. Curtis

FERNWOOD RESORT GC
Pennsylvania
Nicholas Psiahas

FIANNA HILLS GC
Fort Smith, Arkansas
James L. Holmes

FIDDLER'S ELBOW CC (NORTH CSE)
Bedminster, New Jersey
Hal Purdy

FIDDLER'S ELBOW CC (SOUTH CSE)
Bedminster, New Jersey
Hal Purdy
(A.9) Brian Silva, Geoffrey S.
Cornish

FIDDLERS GREEN GC
Eugene, Oregon
John Zoller

FIDDLESTICKS CC (LONG MEAN CSE)
Fort Myers, Florida
Ron Garl

FIDDLESTICKS CC (WEE FRIENDLY CSE)
Fort Myers, Florida
Ron Garl

FIELD C OF OMAHA
Omaha, Nebraska
Harry Lawrie

FIELDS FERRY GC
Calhoun, Georgia
Arthur Davis

[THE] FIELDS GC
LaGrange, Georgia
Mike Young

FIG GARDEN GC
Fresno, California
Nick Lombardo
(R.) Robert Dean Putman

FIJIAN HOTEL GC
Fiji
Ronald Fream, Peter Thomson,
Michael Wolveridge

FILTON GC
England
(R.9 A.9) F. G. Hawtree, J. H.
Taylor

FINCASTLE CC
Bluefield, West Virginia
Dick Wilson
(R.) John LaFoy

FINCHLEY GC
London, England
James Braid, John R. Stutt

FINGER LAKES GC
Ithaca, New York
David Gordon

FINHAM PARK GC
England
(R.3) Fred W. Hawtree

FINKBINE GC
Iowa City, Iowa
Robert Bruce Harris
(R.) Dick Nugent

FINLEY GC
Chapel Hill, North Carolina
(R.3) George W. Cobb

FIORANELLO GC
Italy
D. Mezzacane

FIRCREST GC
Tacoma, Washington
A. Vernon Macan

FIRE FIGHTERS GORMLEY GREEN GC
(CIRCLE CSE)
Gormley, Ontario
(R.9) René Muylaert, Charles
Muylaert

FIRE FIGHTERS GORMLEY GREEN GC
(CREEK CSE)
Gormley, Ontario
René Muylaert

FIREFLY GC
Seekonk, Massachusetts
Donald Hoenig

FIRE LAKE GC
Shawnee, Oklahoma
Don Sechrest

FIRENZE GC
Ugolino, Italy
Charles Blandford
(R.) Pier Mancinelli

FIRESTONE CC (NORTH CSE)
Akron, Ohio
Robert Trent Jones

FIRESTONE CC (SOUTH CSE)
Akron, Ohio
Bert Way
(R.) Robert Trent Jones
(R.) Jack Nicklaus

FIRESTONE CC (WEST CSE)
Akron, Ohio
Brian Silva, Geoffrey S. Cornish

FIRESTONE FARMS G&CC
New Springfield, Ohio
John F. Robinson

FIRESTONE PUBLIC GC [NLE]
Arkon, Ohio
Bert Way

FIRETHORN GC
Lincoln, Nebraska
Pete Dye

FIREWHEEL G PARK (LAKE CSE)
Garland, Texas
Dick Phelps

FIREWHEEL G PARK (OLD CSE)
Garland, Texas
Dick Phelps, Brad Benz, Mike
Poellot

FIRST COLONY G CSE
Sugar Land, Texas
Carlton Gipson

FISHERS ISLAND GC
Fishers Island, New York
Seth Raynor

FITZSIMONS GC
Denver, Colorado
Joseph Wheeler

FIVE-BY-80 GC
Menlo, Iowa
Harold Glissmann

FIVE HUNDRED C
Japan
Chohei Miyazawa

FIVE PONDS G CSE
Warminster, Pennsylvania
X. G. Hassenplug

FJÄLLBACKA GC
Sweden
Eric Röhss

FJUGSTAD GC
Norway
Jan Sederholm

FLAGSTAFF HILL GC
Australia
D. N. Hillan

FLAGTREE CC
Fairmont, North Carolina
J. Porter Gibson

FLAINE LES CARROZ GC
France
Robert Berthet

FLAMINGO ISLAND C
Naples, Florida
Robert Trent Jones

FLANDERS VALLEY GC (RED & GOLD CSE)
New Jersey
Hal Purdy

FLANDERS VALLEY GC (WHITE & BLUE CSE)
New Jersey
Hal Purdy
(R.4 A.9) Rees Jones

FLAT CREEK GC
Peachtree City, Georgia
Joe Lee
(A.3rd 9) Joe Lee, Rocky Roquemore

FLATIRONS CC
Boulder, Colorado
Robert Bruce Harris

FLAXMERE GC
Hastings, New Zealand
John Harris

FLEETWOOD GC
Lancashire, England
J. A. Steer

FLEMINGDON PARK GC
Toronto, Ontario
Howard Watson

FLEMING PARK GC
Hampshire, England
J. J. F. Pennink

FLETCHER HILL CC
Santee, California
William H. Tucker, Jr.

FLINDERS GC
Victoria, Australia
(R. A.2) Alister Mackenzie

FLINT GC
Flint, Michigan
Willie Park, Jr.
(R.1) Jerry Matthews

FLINT GC
Wales
James Braid

FLINT ELKS CC
Flint, Michigan
(A.9) *Larry Mancour* (1970)

FLORA CC
Flora, Illinois
Robert Bruce Harris

FLORENCE CC
Florence, South Carolina
(R.) John LaFoy

FLORHAM PARK CC
Florham Park, New Jersey
Hal Purdy

FLORIDA CC [NLE]
Jacksonville, Florida
Donald Ross

FLORIDALE GC [NLE]
Milford, Florida
William S. Flynn
(R.) Stanley Thompson

FLOSSMOOR CC
Flossmoor, Illinois
H. J. Tweedie
(R.) Harry Collis

FLOURTOWN CC
Philadelphia, Pennsylvania
(R.) Donald Ross
(R.) Perry Maxwell

FLOYDADA CC
Floydada, Texas
Curt Wilson

FLOYD CC
Floyd, Virginia
Gene Hamm

FLUSHING GC [NLE]
Flushing, New York
Tom Bendelow

FLUSHING VALLEY CC
Flushing, Michigan
Wilfrid Reid, William Connellan

FOLGARIA GC
Trentino, Italy
Marco Croze

FOLKESTONE GC [NLE]
Kent, England
H. S. Colt

FOLMONT RESORT GC
Somerset, Pennsylvania
Ferdinand Garbin

FONDERLAC CC
Ohio
(A.9) William Newcomb

FONTAINEBLEAU PARK CC (EAST CSE)
Miami, Florida
Mark Mahannah

FONTAINEBLEAU PARK CC (WEST CSE)
Miami, Florida
Mark Mahannah, Charles Mahannah

[THE] FOOTHILLS GC
Phoenix, Arizona
Jay Morrish, Tom Weiskopf

FOOTHILLS GC (FOOTHILLS CSE)
Lakewood, Colorado
Dick Phelps

FOOTHILLS GC (PAR 3 CSE)
Lakewood, Colorado
Dick Phelps

FOOTHILLS WEST GC
Phoenix, Arizona
Ken Kavanaugh

FORBES GC
Topeka, Kansas
Bob Baldock
(R.) L. J. "Dutch" McClellan

FORD'S COLONY CC (RED CSE)
Williamsburg, Virginia
Dan Maples

FORD'S COLONY CC (GOLD CSE)
Williamsburg, Virginia
Dan Maples

FORE LAKES GC
Salt Lake City, Utah
William H. Neff, William Howard Neff

FOREST CC (BEAR CSE)
Fort Myers, Florida
Gordon G. Lewis

FOREST CC (BOBCAT CSE)
Fort Myers, Florida
Gordon G. Lewis
(R.) Gene Bates

FOREST AKERS GC (WEST CSE)
East Lansing, Michigan
Bruce Matthews

FOREST COVE CC
Humble, Texas
John A. Plumbley

FOREST CREEK GC
Round Rock, Texas
Dick Phelps

FOREST DALE GC
Salt Lake City, Utah
Mick Riley
(R.) William Howard Neff

FOREST HEIGHTS CC
Statesboro, Georgia
George W. Cobb

FOREST HEIGHTS CC
Jamestown, New York
Alfred A. Schardt

FOREST HIGHLANDS GC
Flagstaff, Arizona
Jay Morrish, Tom Weiskopf

FOREST HILL FIELD C [NLE]
Bloomfield, New Jersey
Tom Bendelow

FOREST HILL FIELD C
Bloomfield, New Jersey
A. W. Tillinghast
(R.) Charles Banks
(R.) Rees Jones

FOREST HILL GC
West Palm Beach, Florida
Hans Schmeisser

FOREST HILL GC
Augusta, Georgia
Donald Ross
(R.) Arnold Palmer, Ed Seay

FOREST HILLS CC
Tampa, Florida
J. Franklyn Meehan

FOREST HILLS CC
Rockford, Illinois
Charles Maddox
(R.) Bob Lohmann

FOREST HILLS CC
Richmond, Indiana
William H. Diddel

FOREST HILLS CC
Clarkson Valley, Missouri
(R.2) Denis Griffiths
(R.) Dick Nugent

FOREST HILLS CC
Columbia, Missouri
John Gavin

FOREST HILLS CC
Cullowhee, North Carolina
George W. Cobb

FOREST HILLS GC
Michigan
Harry E. Flora
(R.8 A.10) Mark DeVries
(R.1) Jerry Matthews

FOREST HILLS GC [NLE]
Cornelius, Oregon
William Martin

FOREST HILLS GC
Cornelius, Oregon
William F. Bell, William P. Bell

FOREST HILLS GC
Ontario
(R.27) Howard Watson

FOREST HOTEL G&CC
Ontario
Norm Anders

FOREST LAKE CC
Bloomfield Hills, Michigan
William H. Diddel
(R. A.4) William H. Diddel
(R.) Arthur Hills

FOREST LAKE CC
Great Falls, Virginia
NKA River Bend G&CC

FOREST LAKES C
Columbia, South Carolina
Maurice McCarthy
(R.) John B. FaFoy

FOREST LAKES CC
Sarasota, Florida
R. Albert Anderson

FOREST LITTLE GC
County Dublin, Ireland
Fred W. Hawtree, A. H. F. Jiggens
(R.) Eddie Hackett

FOREST MEADOWS GC
Murphys, California
Robert Trent Jones, Jr.

FOREST OAKS CC
Greensboro, North Carolina
Ellis Maples

FOREST OF ARDEN GC (OLD CSE)
Warwickshire, England
J. B. Tomlinson

FOREST OF ARDEN GC (NEW CSE)
Warwickshire, England
D. M. A. Steel

FOREST PARK CC
Martinsville, Virginia
(R.9 A.9) Gene Hamm

FOREST PARK GC
Brazil, Indiana
William H. Diddel

FOREST PARK GC
Adams, Massachusetts
Alex Findlay

FOREST PARK GC
Bronx, New York
Tom Bendelow
(R.) John Van Kleek
(R.) Lindsay Ervin

FOREST PARK GC
Brazil, Indiana
Pete Dye

FOREST PARK MUNI
Noblesville, Indiana
William Newcomb

FOREST PARK MUNI
Valparaiso, Indiana
William James Spear

FOREST PARK MUNI
Baltimore, Maryland
Alex "Nipper" Campbell
(R.) Gus Hook

FOREST PARK MUNI
St. Louis, Missouri
Robert Foulis

FOREST PRESERVE NATIONAL GC
Oak Forest, Illinois
Ken Killian, Dick Nugent

FOREST RIDGE GC
Broken Arrow, Oklahoma
Randy Heckenkemper

FOREZ GC
Meaux, France
Michel Gayon

FORFAR GC
Angus, Scotland
James Braid

FORGE POND GC
Brinktown, New Jersey
Hal Purdy

FORMBY GC
Formby, England
Willie Park, Jr.
(R.) H. S. Colt

FORMOSA FIRST GC
Taipai, Taiwan
Arnold Palmer, Ed Seay

FORMOSA YANGMEI G&CC
Yangmei, Taiwan
Arnold Palmer, Ed Seay

FORRES GC
Morayshire, Scotland
(R.) *Andrew Kirkaldy*
(R.) Willie Park
(R.) James Braid, John R. Stutt

FORREST CROSSING GC
Franklin, Tennessee
Gary Roger Baird

FORSBACKA GC
Forsbacka, Sweden
Nils Sköld
(R.2) Jan Sederholm

FORSGATE CC (EAST CSE)
Jamesburg, New Jersey
Charles Banks
(A.3) Carlton Gipson

FORSGATE CC (WEST CSE)
Jamesburg, New Jersey
Hal Purdy

FORSYTH CC
Winston-Salem, North Carolina
Donald Ross
(R.) Willard Byrd
(R.) Dan Maples

FORT AUGUSTUS GC
Invernesshire, Scotland
James Braid, John R. Stutt

FORT BELVOIR GC
Fort Belvoir, Virginia
Robert Trent Jones
(R.9 A.9) Edmund B. Ault

FORT BENNING GC (LAKESIDE CSE)
Fort Benning, Georgia
Lester Lawrence

FORT BENNING GC (PINESIDE CSE)
Fort Benning, Georgia
Lester Lawrence
(A.9) Robert Trent Jones

FORT BRAGG OFFICERS GC
Fort Bragg, North Carolina
C. C. McCuison

FORT CARSON GC
Colorado Springs, Colorado
Dick Phelps

FORT COBB LAKE STATE PARK GC
Lake Cobb, Oklahoma
Floyd Farley
(A.9) Don Sechrest

FORT DEVENS GC
Massachusetts
Melvin B. Lucas, Jr.

FORT DODGE CC
Fort Dodge, Iowa
Tom Bendelow
(R.9) Edward Lawrence Packard, Brent Wadsworth

FORT DOUGLAS VA HOSPITAL GC
Salt Lake City, Utah
Mick Riley

FORT DU PONT MUNI
Washington, D.C.
William Gordon

FORT ERIE GC
Buffalo, New York
Tom Bendelow
(R.9 A.9) Stanley Thompson

FORT EUSTIS GC
Maryland
George W. Cobb

FORT FRANCES GC
Fort Frances, Ontario
Clinton E. Robinson

FORT GEORGE ISLAND GC [NLE]
Fort George, Florida
Donald Ross

FORT HARRISON GC
Indiana
William H. Diddel

FORT HAYS CC
Hays, Kansas
Dewey Longworth
(R.9) Chet Mendenhall

FORT HUACHUCA GC
Sierra Vista, Arizona
Milt Coggins
(A.9) Gary Panks

FORT IRWIN GC
California
(R.) Desmond Muirhead

FORT JACKSON GC (OLD CSE)
Columbia, South Carolina
George W. Cobb
(R.4) John LaFoy

FORT JACKSON GC (NEW CSE)
Columbia, South Carolina
Arthur Davis

FORT JAY GC
Governors Island, New York
Fred J. Roth
(R.) Nicholas Psiahas

FORT KENT GC
Fort Kent, Maine
Ben Gray

FORT LAUDERDALE CC (NORTH CSE)
Fort Lauderdale, Florida
Joseph A. Roseman
(R.) Red Lawrence
(R.) Chuck Ankrom

FORT LAUDERDALE CC (SOUTH CSE)
Fort Lauderdale, Florida
Red Lawrence
(R.) Chuck Ankrom

FORT LEAVENWORTH GC
Fort Leavenworth, Kansas
(A.9) *Art F. Hall*

FORT LEONARD WOOD GC
Fort Leonard Wood, Missouri
NKA Piney Valley GC

FORT LEWIS GC
Olympia, Washington
(A.3rd 9) William Teufel

FORT McCLELLAN GC
Alabama
George W. Cobb

FORT McMURRAY GC
Fort McMurray, Alberta
Bill Newis

FORT McPHERSON GC
Georgia
(R.) George W. Cobb

FORT MEADE GC (MEADE CSE)
Fort Meade, Maryland
Major Robert B. McClure

FORT MEADE GC (PARKS CSE)
Fort Meade, Maryland
George W. Cobb

FORT MITCHELL CC
Covington, Kentucky
Tom Bendelow
(R.) Arthur Hills (1971)
(R.) Arthur Hills (1982)

FORT MONMOUTH GC
New Jersey
Seymour Dunn

FORT MORGAN MUNI
Fort Morgan, Colorado
(R.9 A.9) Henry B. Hughes

FORT MYERS CC
Fort Myers, Florida
Donald Ross

FORT ORD GC (BAYONET CSE)
Fort Ord, California
Major Robert B. McClure,
Lawson Little

FORT PREVAL GC
Preval, Quebec
William F. Mitchell
(R.9) Howard Watson
(A.5) Howard Watson, John Watson

FORT RILEY OFFICER'S GC
Fort Riley, Kansas
Major Richard D. Newman

FORTROSE AND ROSEMARKIE GC
Fortrose, Scotland
(R.) James Braid

FORT ROYAL GC
County Donegal, Northern Ireland
T. J. A. Macauley

FORT SAM HOUSTON GC
San Antonio, Texas
A. W. Tillinghast

FORT SHAFTER GC
Honolulu, Hawaii
NKA Walter Nagorski G Cse

FORT SHERIDAN GC
Illinois
Edward B. Dearie, Jr.

FORT SILL GC
Fort Sill, Oklahoma
Lefty Mace
(R.) Don Sechrest

FORT SMITH CC
Fort Smith, Arkansas
Alex Findlay

FORTROSE AND ROSEMARKIE GC
Invernesshire, Scotland
James Braid

[THE] FORTRESS GC
Frankenmuth, Michigan
Dick Nugent

FORTUNE HILLS GC
Freeport, Bahamas
Joe Lee

FORT WALTON BEACH MUNI
Fort Walton Beach, Florida
Bill Amick

FORT WASHINGTON G&CC
Pinedale, California
Willie Watson
(R.) Bob Baldock

FORT WAYNE CC
Fort Wayne, Indiana
(R.) William H. Diddel
(R.3) Bruce Matthews, Jerry Matthews
(R.) Rees Jones
(R.) Arthur Hills

FORT WILLIAM G&CC
Fort William, Ontario
Stanley Thompson
(R.13) John Watson

FORTWILLIAM GC
Belfast, Northern Ireland
C. S. Butchart

FORT WILLIAM GC
Invernesshire, Scotland
J. Hamilton Stutt

FORT WORTH CC [NLE]
Fort Worth, Texas
Tom Bendelow

FORTY-NINER CC
Tucson, Arizona
William F. Bell

FORT YUKON AFB GC
Fort Yukon, Alaska
Richard Carpenter, Charles F. Scholer

FOSTER G LINKS
Washington
(R.) William Teufel

FOSTORIA CC
Fostoria, Ohio
(R. A.10) Jack Kidwell

FOUNTAIN GROVE GC
Santa Rosa, California
Ted Robinson

FOUNTAIN HEAD CC
Hagerstown, Maryland
Donald Ross
(R.) Edmund B. Ault

FOUNTAINHEAD STATE PARK GC
Oklahoma
Floyd Farley

FOUNTAIN LAKES GC
Estero, Florida
Gordon Lewis

FOUNTAIN OF THE SUN GC
Mesa, Arizona
Red Lawrence

FOUNTAINS GC
Escondido, California
David Rainville

[THE] FOUNTAINS G&RC (NORTH CSE)
Lake Worth, Florida
Robert von Hagge, Bruce Devlin

[THE] FOUNTAINS G&RC (SOUTH CSE)
Lake Worth, Florida
Robert von Hagge, Bruce Devlin

[THE] FOUNTAINS G&RC (WEST CSE)
Lake Worth, Florida
Robert von Hagge, Bruce Devlin

FOUNTAIN VALLEY GC
Fredriksted, Virgin Islands
NKA Carambola Beach GC

FOURCHE VALLEY GC
Potosi, Missouri
Gary Kern, Ron Kern

FOUR HILLS CC
Albuquerque, New Mexico
Bob Baldock

FOUR LAKES GC
County Dublin, Ireland
Phil Lawlor
FOUR OAKS GC
Pittsburg, Kansas
(A.9) Floyd Farley
FOURQUEUX GC (FOREST CSE)
St. Germain-en-Laye, France
(R.9 A.9) T. J. A. Macauley,
Stephen Quenouille
FOURQUEUX GC (HILL CSE)
St. Germain-en-Laye, France
(R.9 A.9) T. J. A. Macauley,
Stephen Quenouille
FOUR SEASONS CC
Wrens, Georgia
R. Albert Anderson
FOUR SEASONS GC
Jennerstown, Pennsylvania
Ferdinand Garbin
(A.18 Par 3) Ferdinand
Garbin
FOUR SEASONS GC
Pembine, Wisconsin
Stanley Pelchar
FOUR SEASONS RESORT GC
Nevis, West Indies
Robert Trent Jones, Jr.
FOUR WAYS GC
Johannesburg, South Africa
Gary Player, Sid Brews, *Dr. Van
Vincent*
FOUR WINDS GC
East Lansing, Michigan
(R.3) Jerry Matthews
FOWLER'S MILL G CSE
Chesterland, Ohio
Roy Dye, Pete Dye
FOX ACRES CC
Red Feather Lake, Colorado
John Cochran
FOX BEND CC
Oswego, Illinois
Brent Wadsworth
FOXBOROUGH CC
Foxborough, Massachusetts
Geoffrey S. Cornish
(A.9) Geoffrey S. Cornish,
William G. Robinson
FOXBURY CC
Pennsylvania
James Gilmore Harrison
FOX CHAPEL GC
Pittsburgh, Pennsylvania
Seth Raynor, Charles Banks
(R.) James Gilmore Harrison
(R.) Paul E. Erath
(R.) X. G. Hassenplug
FOX CLIFF CC
Martinsville, Indiana
William H. Diddel
FOX CREEK CC
Ballwin, Missouri
Homer Herpel
FOXCREEK GC
Atlanta, Georgia
John LaFoy
FOX CREEK GC
Edwardsville, Illinois
Gary Kern, Ron Kern
FOX CREEK G CSE
Livonia, Michigan
Mark DeVries

FOXCROFT CC
Miramar, Florida
Bill Watts
FOX DEN CC
Knoxville, Tennessee
Willard Byrd
FOXFIRE CC
Naples, Florida
Arthur Hills
FOXFIRE CC (EAST CSE)
Pinehurst, North Carolina
Gene Hamm
FOXFIRE CC (WEST CSE)
Pinehurst, North Carolina
Gene Hamm
FOXFIRE GC
Sarasota, Florida
Lane Marshall
(A.3rd 9) Ted McAnlis
FOXFIRE GC
Lockbourne, Ohio
(A.6) Jack Kidwell
(A.9) Jack Kidwell, Michael
Hurdzan
FOXFIRE G CSE
Hempstead, Texas
Jack B. Miller, Lee Freeman
FOXHILL CC
Longmont, Colorado
Frank Hummel
FOX HILL CC
Pennsylvania
(R.) A. W. Tillinghast
FOX HILLS CC
Plymouth, Michigan
(R. A.3rd 9) Jim Lipe
FOX HILLS CC (GOLDEN FOX CSE)
Plymouth, Michigan
Arthur Hills
FOX HILLS CC
Mishicot, Wisconsin
Edward G. Lockie
FOX HILLS G&CC
Riverhead, New York
Robert Trent Jones
FOX HILLS GC
New York
Tom Bendelow
(R.) Donald Ross
FOX HILLS GC [NLE]
California
George C. Thomas, Jr., William
P. Bell
FOXHILLS GC (CHERTSEY CSE)
Surrey, England
Fred W. Hawtree
FOXHILLS GC (LONGCROSS CSE)
Surrey, England
Fred W. Hawtree
FOX HILLS NATIONAL GC
Mishicot, Wisconsin
Bob Lohmann
FOX HOLLOW GC
Rogers, Minnesota
Joel Goldstrand
FOX HOLLOW GC
Somerville, New Jersey
Hal Purdy
FOX LAKE CC
Fox Lake, Illinois
Harry Hall King
(R.) Ken Killian, Dick Nugent

FOX LAKE CC
Wisconsin
(A.9) Homer Fieldhouse
FOX MEADOWS CC
Memphis, Tennessee
Chic Adams
FOX RIDGE CC
Vincennes, Indiana
Charles Maddox
FOX RIVER CC
Green Bay, Wisconsin
Tom Bendelow
FOXROCK GC
Dublin, Ireland
Ben Sayers
(R.) H. S. Colt, C. H. Alison
(R.) Eddie Hackett
FOX RUN CC
Grayling, Michigan
Jeff Gorney
FOX RUN GC
Elk Grove, Illinois
William Newcomb
FOX RUN GC
Eureka, Missouri
Gary Kern, Ron Kern
FOX RUN GC
Ludlow, Vermont
Frank Duane
FOX RUN MUNI (SOUTH CSE)
Livonia, Michigan
Mark DeVries
FOX SQUIRREL CC
Boiling Springs Lake, North
Carolina
Ed Riccoboni
(R.) Russell Breeden
FOX VALLEY CC
Batavia, Illinois
Joe Meister
FOXWOOD CC
Crestview, Florida
Bill Amick
(A.9) Earl Stone
FRAMINGHAM CC
Framingham, Massachusetts
Orrin Smith
(R.5) Orrin Smith
(A.9) William F. Mitchell
(R.) Manny Francis
(A.2) Geoffrey S. Cornish,
William G. Robinson
(R.) Brian Silva, Geoffrey S.
Cornish
FRANCES I'I BROWN GC (NORTH
CSE)
Mauna Lani Resort, Hawaii
Homer Flint, Raymond F. Cain,
Robin Nelson
(A.9) Robin Nelson, Rodney
Wright
FRANCES I'I BROWN GC (SOUTH
CSE)
Mauna Lani Resort, Hawaii
Homer Flint, Raymond F. Cain,
Robin Nelson
(A.9) Robin Nelson, Rodney
Wright
FRANCES MILLER MEMORIAL GC
Murray, Kentucky
Jack Kidwell, Michael Hurdzan
FRANCIACORTA GC
Italy
Marco Croze

FRANCISCO GRANDE CC
Casa Grande, Arizona
Ralph Plummer
FRANCIS LAKE GC
Valdosta, Georgia
Willard Byrd
FRANCONIA MUNI
Springfield, Massachusetts
Wayne Stiles, John Van Kleek
(R.7) Geoffrey S. Cornish,
William G. Robinson
FRANCOURT FARMS GC
Elmira, New York
Pete Craig
FRANKEN-ABENBERG GC
Germany
Karl F. Grohs, *Rainer
Preissmann*
FRANKENMUTH GC [NLE]
Frankenmuth, Michigan
(R.2) Jerry Matthews
FRANKFORT CC
Frankfort, Kentucky
William H. Diddel
FRANKFORT CC
Frankfort, Indiana
Charles Maddox
FRANKFURTER GC
Frankfurt, Germany
H. S. Colt, C. H. Alison, J. S. F.
Morrison
(R.) Bernhard von Limburger
(R.) J. S. F. Morrison, J.
Hamilton Stutt
(R.) Karl F. Grohs, *Rainer
Preissmann*
FRANK G. CLEMENT GC
Dickson, Tennessee
George W. Cobb
FRANK HOUSE MUNI
Bessemer, Alabama
Earl Stone
FRANKLIN CANYON GC
Rodeo, California
Robert Muir Graves
FRANKLIN CC
Franklin, Massachusetts
(R.) Wayne Stiles
(R. A.2) William F. Mitchell
(A.10) Phil Wogan
FRANKLIN CC
Washington, Missouri
Ron Prichard
FRANKLIN COUNTY CC
West Frankfort, Illinois
William B. Langford, Theodore
J. Moreau
FRANKLIN HILLS CC
Franklin Woods, Michigan
Donald Ross
FRANKLIN PARK GC
Boston, Massachusetts
NKA William F. Devine GC
FRANK SEESTED PRIVATE CSE [NLE]
Kansas City, Missouri
James Dalgleish
FRASSANELLE GC
Padova, Italy
Marco Croze
FRAUENTHAL G CSE
Frauenthal, Austria
Herwig Zisser

Frear Park GC
Troy, New York
Robert Trent Jones

Fred Enke Muni
Tucson, Arizona
Brad Benz, Dick Phelps

Frederick GC
Frederick, Oklahoma
(R.) Arthur Jackson

Fredericksburg CC
Fredericksburg, Virginia
(R.9 A.9) James Gilmore
Harrison
(R.1) Bill Love

Fredericton GC
Fredericton, New Brunswick
(R.1) Clinton E. Robinson
(R.2) Geoffrey S. Cornish,
William G. Robinson

Fredriksberg GC
Sweden
Jan Sederholm

**Fred Wardnell Estate G Cse
[NLE]**
Detroit, Michigan
Donald Ross

Freeport CC
Freeport, Illinois
Harry Collis
(R.2) Robert Bruce Harris

Freestone CC
Teague, Texas
Leon Howard

Freiburger GC
Freiburg, Germany
Bernhard von Limburger
(A.9) Karl F. Grohs, *Rainer
Preissmann*

Fremont CC
Fremont, Ohio
(R.) Edward Lawrence
Packard
(R.) Arthur Hills

Fremont GC
Fremont, Nebraska
Tom Bendelow
(R.) Harold Glissmann
(R.7 A.11) David Gill

Fremont County GC
St. Anthony, Idaho
Marvin J. Aslett

Fremont Hills CC
Nixa, Missouri
Press Maxwell
(A.9) *Ken Kahmann* (1986)

French Lick G&TC (Hill Cse)
French Lick, Indiana
Donald Ross
(R.) Hal Purdy

French Lick G&TC (Valley Cse)
French Lick, Indiana
Tom Bendelow
(R.) Sandy Alves
(R.) Hal Purdy

**Frenchman's Creek GC (North
Cse)**
North Palm Beach, Florida
Gardner Dickinson, Bob Cupp
(R.) Bob Cupp, Jay Morrish

**Frenchman's Creek GC (South
Cse)**
North Palm Beach, Florida
Gardner Dickinson, Bob Cupp
(R.) Bob Cupp, Jay Morrish
(R.) Chuck Ankrom

Fresh Meadow CC
Great Neck, New York
C. H. Alison, H. S. Colt
(R.) Orrin Smith

Fresh Meadow CC [NLE]
Port Washington, New York
A. W. Tillinghast

Fresh Meadow G&CC
Illinois
(R.) William B. Langford
(R.) *Ray Didier* (1956)

Fresh Pond Muni
Cambridge, Massachusetts
Walter I. Johnson
(R.9) Geoffrey S. Cornish,
William G. Robinson

Freshwater Bay GC
England
(R.) F. G. Hawtree

Fresno Airways GC [NLE]
Fresno, California
Bert Stamps

Fresno Airways G Cse
Fresno, California
Robert Dean Putman

Fresno West GC
Kerman, California
Bob Baldock

Friend CC
Friend, Nebraska
Henry B. Hughes, Richard
Watson

Friendly Hills CC
Whittier, California
Jimmy Hines

Friendship CC
Japan
Soichi Murayama

Friendship Meadows CC
Bangkok, Thailand
Robin Nelson, Rodney Wright

Frilford Heath GC (Green Cse)
England
(R.9 A.9) C. K. Cotton, J. J. F.
Pennink

Frilford Heath GC (Red Cse)
England
(R.9 A.9) C. K. Cotton, J. J. F.
Pennink

Frinton GC
Frinton-on-Sea, England
Tom Dunn
(R.) Willie Park, Willie Park,
Jr.

Fripp Island CC
Fripp Island, South Carolina
NKA Ocean Point G Links

Frisch Auf Valley CC
LaGrange, Texas
Jay Riviere

Frontier GC
Canby, Oregon
Joe Sisul

Frosty Valley CC
Danville, Pennsylvania
William Gordon, David Gordon
(R.) Ferdinand Garbin

Fruitport CC
Muskegon, Michigan
David Snyder

Frye Island GC
Frye Island, Maine
Geoffrey S. Cornish, William G.
Robinson

Fuchu CC
Tokyo, Japan
S. Tomizawa

Fuji-Chuo
Mount Fuji, Japan
Desmond Muirhead

Fuji CC
Fuji, Japan
C. H. Alison
(R.) Rokuro Akaboshi, *Shiro
Akaboshi*

Fuji CC (Shuga Cse)
Gifu, Japan
Gary Player, *Hirochika
Tomizawa*

Fuji CC (Tomioka Cse)
Gunma, Japan
Hirochika Tomizawa

Fuji Kawaguchiko CC
Fuji, Japan
Sho Okubo

Fuji Lakeside GC
Fuji, Japan
Makoto Harada

Fuji Oyama GC
Fuji, Japan
Pete Nakamura

Fuji Shiokawa CC
Gifu, Japan
Gary Player

Fujioka CC
Magoya, Japan
Peter Thomson, *Tameshi
Yamada*

Fukuo CC
Mie, Japan
Yasuzo Kaneko

Fulford GC
Yorkshire, England
Alister Mackenzie
(R.) D. M. A. Steel

Fulford Heath GC
England
James Braid, John R. Stutt

Fullerton G&CC
Fullerton, California
William F. Bell

Fullerton Muni
Fullerton, California
(A.9) Ted Robinson

Fulton Estate GC
Salisbury, Connecticut
Devereux Emmet, Alfred H. Tull

Fulwell GC
Middlesex, England
C. H. Alison
(R.) J. S. F. Morrison

Funabashi GC
Chiba, Japan
Seichi Inouye

Fundy National Park GC
Alma, New Brunswick
Stanley Thompson

Furano GC
Furano, Japan
Arnold Palmer, Ed Seay

Furano Kogen GC
Furano, Japan
Arnold Palmer, Ed Seay

Fureso GC
Birkerod, Denmark
Jan Sederholm

Furnace Brook CC
Massachusetts
(R.) William F. Mitchell

Furnace Creek GC
Death Valley, California
William P. Bell
(A.9) William F. Bell

Furnas GC
Azores Islands
P. M. Ross

Furth-im-Wald GC
Nordbayern, Germany
Bernhard von Limburger
(R.) Kurt Rossknecht

Fuso CC
Japan
*Yoshitaro Kawanami, Mitso
Komatsubara*

Futurama GC
Sarasota, Florida
R. Albert Anderson

Gabe Lozano Sr. G Center
Corpus Christi, Texas
Leon Howard

Gables GC [NLE]
Florida
John Duncan Dunn

Gabriola G&CC
British Columbia
(A.) *Dan Kitsul*

Gadsden CC
Quincy, Florida
Joe Lee

Gagetown GC
Oromocto, New Brunswick
Clinton E. Robinson

Gaines County GC
Seminole, Texas
C. William Keith

Gainesville G&CC
Gainesville, Florida
George W. Cobb

Gainesville Muni [NLE]
Gainesville, Georgia
Donald Ross

Gainesville Muni
Gainesville, Texas
Ralph Plummer

Gainey Ranch GC
Scottsdale, Arizona
Brad Benz, Mike Poellot

Galaglades G&CC
Cambridge, Ontario
Clinton E. Robinson

Galbraith Muni
Oakland, California
(R.) Robert Muir Graves

Galen Hall GC
Wernersville, Pennsylvania
Alex Findlay
(R.) A. W. Tillinghast
(R.) William Gordon, David
Gordon

Galion CC
Galion, Ohio
(A.9) Jack Kidwell

GALLAGHERS CANYON GC
  Kelowna, British Columbia
  William G. Robinson
GALLIVARE GC
  Gallivare, Sweden
  Jan Sederholm
GALLOPING HILLS GC
  Union, New Jersey
  Willard Wilkinson
    (R.) Robert Trent Jones
    (R.) Alfred H. Tull
GALLS GC
  Minnesota
    (R.) Don Herfort
GALLUP MUNI
  Gallup, New Mexico
  Leon Howard
GALT G & CURLING C
  Galt, Ontario
  Robert Moote, *David S. Moote*
GALVESTON CC
  Galveston, Texas
  John Bredemus
    (R.6) Joseph S. Finger
GALVESTON MUNI [NLE]
  Galveston, Texas
  Donald Ross
GALWAY GC
  County Galway, Ireland
    (R.) Alister Mackenzie
GAMBEL G LINKS [NLE]
  Carefree, Arizona
  Roy Dye, Gary Grandstaff
GARNSTEAD PARK GC
  Yorkshire, England
  Ted Eltherington
GANTON GC
  Ganton, England
  Tom Dunn
    (R.) Harry Vardon
    (R.) H. S. Colt
    (R.) C. K. Hutchison
    (R.) Herbert Fowler
    (R.) *Ted Ray*
    (R.) James Braid
    (R.) *Harold Hilton*
    (R.) C. K. Cotton
GARDAGOLF
  Italy
  D. M. A. Steel
GARDEN GC
  Ibaraki, Japan
  Mitsuaki Kobayashi
GARDEN CITY CC
  Garden City, Kansas
    (R.) Smiley Bell
GARDEN CITY CC
  Garden City, New York
  Walter J. Travis
    (R.6) Frank Duane
    (R.) Brian Silva, Geoffrey S.
  Cornish
GARDEN CITY GC
  Garden City, New York
  Devereux Emmet
    (R.) Walter J. Travis
    (R.) Robert Trent Jones
  (1935)
    (R.) Robert Trent Jones
  (1958)
GARDEN OF EDEN GC [NLE]
  Momence, Illinois
  Stanley Pelchar

GARDEN VALLEY G RESORT
  Lindale, Texas
  Leon Howard
GARDINER'S BAY CC
  Gardiner's Bay, New York
  C.A. Fox
    (R.9 A.9) Seth Raynor
    (R.) William F. Mitchell
GARDNER MUNI
  Gardner, Massachusetts
    (R.2) Samuel Mitchell
GARFIELD MUNI
  Chicago, Illinois
  Tom Bendelow
GARFORTH GC
  Yorkshire, England
  Tom Williamson
    (R.1) *Charles A. Mackenzie*
GARLAND GC (MONARCH CSE)
  Lewiston, Michigan
  Ron Otto (1989)
GARLAND GC (REFLECTIONS CSE)
  Lewiston, Michigan
  Ron Otto (1991)
GARLAND GC (SWAMPFIRE CSE)
  Lewiston, Michigan
  Ron Otto (1989)
GARLENDA GC
  Italy
  John Harris
GARMISCH-PARTENKIRCHEN GC
  Garmisch, Germany
  Karl Hoffmann, Bernhard von
  Limburger
    (R.) Donald Harradine
GARNER LAKE GC
  Edwardsburg, Michigan
  Bruce L. Dustin
GARRATS HALL G
  England
  Wilfrid Reid
GARRETT CC
  Garrett, Indiana
  Tom Bendelow
GARRISON GC
  Garrison, New York
  Dick Wilson
GARRISON G & CURLING C
  Kingston, Ontario
    (A.9) Thomas McBroom
GARRISONS LAKE GC
  Smyrna, Delaware
  Edmund B. Ault
GARY CC
  Merrillville, Indiana
  William B. Langford, Theodore
  J. Moreau
    (R.) Edward Lawrence
  Packard, Brent Wadsworth
    (R.) R. Albert Anderson
GARY PLAYER CC
  Sun City, Bophuthatswana
  Ron Kirby, Gary Player
GASCHWITZ GC
  Leipzig, Germany
  Karl Hoffmann, Bernhard von
  Limburger
GASPARILLA INN & CC
  Gasparilla Island, Florida
    (R.) David Wallace
GASSIN GC
  St. Tropez, France
  Pier Mancinelli

GASTON CC
  Gastonia, North Carolina
  Ellis Maples
GASTONIA NATIONAL GC
  Gaston, North Carolina
  J. Porter Gibson
GATES FOUR G&CC
  Fayetteville, North Carolina
  Willard Byrd
GATES PARK GC
  Waterloo, Iowa
  Robert Bruce Harris
GATEWAY GC
  Fort Myers, Florida
  Tom Fazio
GATEWAY GC
  Land O'Lakes, Wisconsin
  Robert Bruce Harris
GATLINBURG G&CC
  Pigeon Forge, Tennessee
  William B. Langford
    (R.) Ellis Maples
GATOR CREEK GC
  Sarasota, Florida
  Joe Lee
GATOR HOLE GC
  North Myrtle Beach, South
  Carolina
  Rees Jones
GATOR TRACE GC
  Fort Pierce, Florida
  Arthur Hills
GATTON MANOR HOTEL & GC
  Surrey, England
  John Harris
[THE] GAUNTLET G&CC
  Wilmington, North Carolina
  P. B. Dye
GAUSS'S GREEN VALLEY GC
  Jackson, Michigan
  Lloyd Gauss, Gary Gauss
GAVEA G&CC
  Rio de Janeiro, Brazil
  Arthur Morgan Davidson
  (9 1921)
    (R.9 A.9) Stanley Thompson
GÄVLE GC
  Gävle, Sweden
  Nils Sköld (9 1947)
    (A.9) Jan Sederholm
GAY HILL CC
  Galax, Virginia
  Gene Hamm
GAYLORD CC
  Gaylord, Michigan
  Wilfrid Reid
    (R.) *Robert W. Bills, Donald L.
  Childs*
GELPENBERG GC
  Zweeloo, Netherlands
  J. J. F. Pennink
GELSENKIRCHEN GC
  Haus Leythe, Germany
  Karl F. Grohs, *Rainer
  Preissmann*
GEM LAKE GC
  Minnesota
  Paul Coates
GENEGANSLET GC
  Greene, New York
  Ernest E. Smith
GENE LIST MUNI
  Bellflower, California
  Harry Rainville

GENERAL BLANCHARD GC
  Davis Monthan AFB, Arizona
  Bob Baldock
GENERAL BUTLER STATE PARK GC
  Carrollton, Kentucky
  Hal Purdy
GENERAL ELECTRIC ATHLETIC
  ASSOCIATION GC
  Pittsfield, Massachusetts
  Rowland Armacost
GENERAL WASHINGTON CC
  Audubon, Pennsylvania
  William F. Mitchell
GENERALS GC
  Crownsville, Maryland
  Edmund B. Ault
GENEVA G&CC [NLE]
  Muscatine, Iowa
  Tom Bendelow
GENEVA G&CC
  Muscatine, Iowa
  David Gill, Garrett Gill
GENEVA G&CC
  Ontario
  Stanley Thompson
GENEVA G&CC [NLE]
  Switzerland
    (R.) Donald Harradine
GENEVA G&CC
  Geneva, Switzerland
  Robert Trent Jones
GENEVA GC
  Geneva, Illinois
    (R.) Dick Nugent
GENEVA FARM GC
  Street, Maryland
  Robert L. Elder
GENEVA LAKE Y&GC
  Lake Geneva, Wisconsin
    (R.) Tom Bendelow
GENEVA NATIONAL GC (PALMER
  CSE)
  Lake Como, Wisconsin
  Arnold Palmer, Ed Seay
GENEVA NATIONAL GC (TREVINO
  CSE)
  Lake Como, Wisconsin
  Charles Mahannah, *Lee Trevino*
GENEVA ON THE LAKE GC [NLE]
  Geneva, Ohio
  Stanley Thompson
GENEVA ON THE LAKE GC
  Geneva, Ohio
  James Gilmore Harrison
GEORGE GC
  Cape Province, South Africa
  Hendrick J. Raubenheimer
    (R.9 A.9) *Dr. C. M. Murray*
[THE] GEORGETOWN C
  Georgetown, Massachusetts
  Philip Wogan
GEORGETOWN CC
  Georgetown, South Carolina
  Alfred H. Tull
GEORGETOWN GC
  Ann Arbor, Michigan
  Charles Maddox, *Charles
  Maddox, Jr.*
GEORGETOWN GC
  Georgetown, Ontario
  Clinton E. Robinson
GEORGE WRIGHT MUNI
  Boston, Massachusetts
  Donald Ross

GEORGE YOUNG GC
    Iron River, Michigan
    George Young (1984)
GEORGIA VETERANS MEMORIAL
    STATE PARK G CSE
    Cordele, Georgia
    Denis Griffiths
GERMISTON GC
    Germiston, South Africa
    (R.) C. H. Alison
    (R.) Robert Grimsdell
GEYSTEREN G&CC
    Eindhoven, Netherlands
    J. J. F. Pennink
    (A.5) D. M. A. Steel
GIANT OAK CC
    Temperance, Michigan
    Arthur Hills
GIBSON ISLAND GC [9 NLE]
    Gibson Island, Maryland
    Charles Blair Macdonald, Seth
    Raynor
GIBSON WOODS MUNI
    Monmouth, Illinois
    Homer Fieldhouse
GIFFORD GC
    Lothian, Scotland
    Willie Watt (9 1903)
GIFU GC (TANIGUMI CSE)
    Gifu, Japan
    Dai Nihon Doboku
GIFU INAGUCHI GC
    Gifu, Japan
    Shunsuke Kato
GIFU KOKUSAI CC
    Gifu, Japan
    Yuko Moriguchi
GIFU MIYAMA CC
    Gifu, Japan
    Tetsuro Akabane
GIG HARBOR G&CC
    Gig Harbor, Washington
    (R.) Robert Muir Graves
GILLELEJE GC
    Gilleleje, Denmark
    Jan Sederholm
GILLESPIE GC [NLE]
    Sarasota, Florida
    John Hamilton Gillespie
GILLETTE CC
    Gillette, Wyoming
    Frank Hummel
GILWOOD G&CC
    Slave Lake, Alberta
    Les Furber, *Jim Eremko*
GLACIER GREENS GC
    Kalispell, Montana
    William G. Robinson, John F.
    Robinson
GLACIER VIEW GC
    West Glacier, Montana
    Bob Baldock, Robert L. Baldock
    (R.) Ronald Fream
GLADES CC (CSE NO. 1)
    Naples, Florida
    B. Dudley Gray
GLADES CC (CSE NO. 2)
    Naples, Florida
    B. Dudley Gray
GLADE SPRINGS CC
    Beckley, West Virginia
    George W. Cobb

GLADE VALLEY GC
    Walkersville, Maryland
    Robert L. Elder
GLADSTAN GC
    Payson, Utah
    William Howard Neff
GLADSTONE CC
    Michigan
    A. H. Jolly
GLAMORGANSHIRE GC
    Wales
    Willie Park, Jr.
    (R.) Tom Simpson
GLASGOW AFB GC
    Montana
    Bob Baldock
GLASGOW GC
    Glasgow, Scotland
    Old Tom Morris
GLASGOW KILLERMONT GC
    Glasgow, Scotland
    (R.) Willie Park, Jr.
GLASTONBURY HILLS CC
    Glastonbury, Connecticut
    Al Zikorus
    (R.4) Geoffrey S. Cornish,
    William G. Robinson
GLEN ABBEY GC
    New Smyrna Beach, Florida
    Dominic Palombo
GLEN ABBEY GC
    Oakville, Ontario
    Jack Nicklaus
GLEN ACRES CC
    Bothel, Washington
    George S. "Pop" Merrit
GLEN ARVEN CC
    Thomasville, Georgia
    Wayne Stiles, John Van Kleek
    (R.4) Hugh Moore
GLEN AVON GC
    California
    William H. Johnson
GLENBARD GC [NLE]
    Glen Ellyn, Illinois
    Robert Bruce Harris
GLENBERVIE GC
    Stirlingshire, Scotland
    James Braid, John R. Stutt
GLENBROOK CC
    Nevada
    (R.) Robert Muir Graves
GLENBROOK CC
    East Brunswick, New Jersey
    Hal Purdy
GLEN BROOK CC
    Stroudsburg, Pennsylvania
    Robert White
GLENBROOK GC
    Texas
    (R.) John Bredemus
GLENBURNIE G CSE [NLE]
    Lake George, New York
    Alex Findlay
    (R. A.3) Donald Ross
GLEN CANNON GC
    Brevard, North Carolina
    William B. Lewis
GLEN CEDARS GC
    Markham, Ontario
    René Muylaert
GLENCOE G&CC (FOREST CSE)
    Calgary, Alberta
    Robert Trent Jones, Jr.

GLENCOE G&CC (MEADOW CSE)
    Calgary, Alberta
    Robert Trent Jones, Jr.
GLENCOE GC
    Glencoe, Illinois
    (R.) Ken Killian, Dick Nugent
    (1964)
    (R.) Ken Killian, Dick Nugent
    (1978)
GLENCORSE GC
    Midlothian, Scotland
    Willie Park, Sr.
GLEN COVE MUNI
    Glen Cove, New York
    William F. Mitchell
GLENCRUITTEN GC
    Argyll, Scotland
    James Braid
GLENDALE CC
    Bellevue, Washington
    Al Smith
    (R.3) Peter Thomson,
    Michael Wolveridge, Ronald
    Fream
GLENDALE CC [NLE]
    Bloomingdale, Illinois
    Tom Bendelow
GLENDALE G&CC
    Bothel, Washington
    Al Smith
GLENDALE G&CC
    Winnipeg, Manitoba
    Stanley Thompson
    (R.) William G. Robinson,
    John F. Robinson
GLENDALE G&CC
    Glendale, Ontario
    (R.) Clinton E. Robinson
GLENDALE GC
    Edmonton, Alberta
    Norman H. Woods
GLENDALE LAKES GC
    Glendale Heights, Illinois
    Dick Nugent
GLENDALE MUNI [NLE]
    Glendale, Arizona
    William H. Tucker, Jr.
GLENDALE PARK MUNI
    Salt Lake City, Utah
    William F. Bell
GLENDORA CC
    Glendora, California
    E. Warren Beach
    (R.9) William H. Johnson
    (R.) Robert Trent Jones
GLENDOVEER GC (EAST CSE)
    Portland, Oregon
    John Junor (1923)
    (R.) *Frank Stenzel*
GLENDOVEER GC (WEST CSE)
    Portland, Oregon
    Frank Stenzel
GLENDOWER GC
    Bedfordview, South Africa
    C. H. Alison
GLENDOWIE GC
    New Zealand
    (R.) C. H. Redhead
GLENEAGLE CC
    Colorado Springs, Colorado
    Frank Hummel
GLENEAGLES CC (EAST CSE)
    Delray Beach, Florida
    Karl Litten

GLENEAGLES CC (WEST CSE)
    Delray Beach, Florida
    Karl Litten
GLENEAGLES CC (KING'S CSE)
    Plano, Texas
    Robert von Hagge, Bruce Devlin
GLENEAGLES CC (QUEEN'S CSE)
    Plano, Texas
    Robert von Hagge, Bruce Devlin
GLENEAGLES GC (RED COURSE)
    Lemont, Illinois
    Charles Maddox, *Frank P.
    MacDonald*
GLENEAGLES GC (WHITE CSE)
    Lemont, Illinois
    Charles Maddox, *Frank P.
    MacDonald*
GLENEAGLES GC
    Twinsburg, Ohio
    Ted McAnlis
GLENEAGLES GC
    West Vancouver, British
    Columbia
    A. Vernon Macan
GLEN EAGLES GC
    Bolton, Ontario
    René Muylaert
GLENEAGLES HOTEL GC
    (GLENDEVON CSE) [NLE]
    Perthshire, Scotland
    T. J. A. Macauley
GLENEAGLES HOTEL GC (KING'S
    CSE)
    Perthshire, Scotland
    James Braid, C. K. Hutchison
GLENEAGLES HOTEL GC
    (MONARCH'S CSE)
    Perthshire, Scotland
    Jack Nicklaus
GLENEAGLES HOTEL GC (PRINCE'S
    CSE)[NLE]
    Perthshire, Scotland
    *James Alexander, I. Marchbanks,
    T. Telford*
GLENEAGLES HOTEL GC (QUEEN'S
    CSE)
    Perthshire, Scotland
    James Braid, C. K. Hutchison
    (R.) *James Alexander*
GLENEAGLES HOTEL GC (WEE CSE)
    [NLE]
    Perthshire, Scotland
    George Alexander (9 1928)
GLENEAGLES INTERNATIONAL GC
    Daly City, California
    Jack Fleming
    (R.) Robert Muir Graves
GLEN ECHO CC
    Normandy, Missouri
    James Foulis, Robert Foulis
    (R.) Robert Foulis
GLENELG GC
    Australia
    V. Morcomb
GLEN FLORA GC
    Waukegan, Illinois
    Robert Bruce Harris
GLEN GARDEN CC
    Dallas, Texas
    (R.9 A.9) John Bredemus
GLEN GC
    Scotland
    (R.) P. M. Ross

GLENHARDIE CC
Wayne, Pennsylvania
David Gordon
GLENHAVEN CC
Oelwein, Iowa
Dick Phelps, *Emil Perret, Donald G. Brauer*
GLENHAVEN G&CC
Milpitas, California
Jack Fleming
GLEN HEAD CC [FKA WOMEN'S NATIONAL G&CC]
Glen Head, New York
Devereux Emmet
(R.) William S. Flynn
(R.) William F. Mitchell
(R.) Alfred H. Tull
(R.) Stephen Kay
GLENHURST CC
Watchung, New Jersey
Alec Ternyei
GLEN LAKES CC
Weeki Wachi, Florida
Ron Garl
GLEN LAKES CC
Dallas, Texas
(R.) Ralph Plummer
GLEN LAKES GC
Glendale, Arizona
Milt Coggins
GLEN LAWRENCE G&CC
Kingston, Ontario
W. C. Harvey, D. H. Green
(R.) Clinton E. Robinson
GLENMARY G & RECREATION C
Louisville, Kentucky
John Addington (1990)
GLEN MAWR GC
Toronto, Ontario
Stanley Thompson
GLENMOOR CC
Englewood, Colorado
Perry Dye
GLENMOOR CC
Canton, Ohio
Jack Nicklaus
GLENMOOR CC
Charlottesville, Virginia
John LaFoy
GLENMORE G&CC
Jordan, Utah
William H. Neff
GLENN DALE GC
Glenn Dale, Maryland
George W. Cobb
(R.) *Ray Shields, Roy Shields*
GLENN G&CC
Willows, California
Ben Harmon
GLENNOCH G&CC
Firth of Clyde, Scotland
J. Hamilton Stutt
GLEN OAK CC
Danville, Virginia
Dick Wilson
(A.9) Gene Hamm
GLEN OAK CC
Glen Ellyn, Illinois
Tom Bendelow
(R.) A. W. Tillinghast
(R.) William B. Langford, Theodore J. Moreau
(R.4) David Gill
(R.) Ken Killian

GLEN OAK CC
Waverly, Pennsylvania
James Gilmore Harrison, Ferdinand Garbin
GLEN OAK GC
East Amherst, New York
Robert Trent Jones
GLEN OAKS C
Floral Park, New York
NKA Towers CC
GLEN OAKS C
Old Westbury, New York
Joseph S. Finger
GLEN OAKS CC
Maiden, North Carolina
B. McRee
GLEN OAKS CC
Chiba, Japan
Mike Poellot, Brad Benz
GLEN OAKS GC
Clearwater, Florida
Hans Schmeisser
GLEN OAKS GC
Virginia
Gene Hamm
GLENORA GC
Glenora, Australia
Des Soutar
GLEN RIDGE CC [NLE]
Glen Ridge, New Jersey
Tom Bendelow
GLEN RIDGE CC
Glen Ridge, New Jersey
Willie Park, Jr.
(R.) Robert Trent Jones (1949)
(R.) Robert Trent Jones (1978)
GLENROCHIE CC
Abington, Virginia
Alex McKay
(A.9) Dan Maples
GLENROTHES GC
Fife, Scotland
J. Hamilton Stutt, Fraser Middleton
GLENS FALLS CC
Glens Falls, New York
Donald Ross
GLEN VIEW GC
Golf, Illinois
H. J. Tweedie
(R.) William S. Flynn
(R.) George O'Neil, Joseph A. Roseman
(R.) Dick Nugent
GLENVIEW MUNI
Cincinnati, Ohio
Arthur Hills
GLENVIEW NAVAL AIR STATION GC (CSE NO. 1)
Glenview, Illinois
Joseph A. Roseman
GLENVIEW NAVAL AIR STATION GC (CSE NO. 2)
Glenview, Illinois
Joseph A. Roseman

GLENVIEW PARK GC [FKA ELMGATE CC]
Glenview, Illinois
Joseph A. Roseman
(R.) Edward Lawrence Packard
(R.) Ken Killian
GLENVILLE GC
Glenville, West Virginia
(R.) Gary Grandstaff
GLENVISTA CC
Booysens, South Africa
Gary Player, Sid Brews, *Dr. Van Vincent*
GLENWOOD CC
Farmingdale, New York
Devereux Emmet
GLENWOOD CC
East Brunswick, New Jersey
Hal Purdy
GLENWOOD CC
Richmond, Virginia
Fred Findlay
GLENWOOD GC
Virginia Beach, Virginia
Rees Jones
GLENWOOD HALL CC
Perry Park, Kentucky
Buck Blankenship
(A.9) Bob Simmons
GLENWOODIE GC
Chicago Heights, Illinois
Harry Collis, Jack Daray
(R.) Joe Lee
GLENWOOD MUNI
Ashland, Ohio
X. G. Hassenplug
GLENWOOD MUNI
Columbia, South Carolina
R. B. Jennings
GLENWOOD PARK MUNI
Erie, Pennsylvania
Charles Hymers
GLENWOOD SPRINGS GC
Glenwood Springs, Colorado
Henry B. Hughes
GLIMMERGLASS STATE PARK GC
East Springfield, New York
Frank Duane
GLOUCESTER G&CC
Gloucester, England
John Day
GLYFADA GC
Athens, Greece
Donald Harradine
(R.) Robert Trent Jones
GLYNHIR GC
Llandeilo, Wales
Fred W. Hawtree
GMG HACHIOJI GC
Japan
Y. Kawanami, M. Komatsubara
GODERICH GC
Goderich, Ontario
(R.) Robert Moote
GODWIN GLEN GC [NLE]
South Lyon, Michigan
Bruce Matthews, Jerry Matthews
GÖTTINGEN GC
Göttingen, Germany
Donald Harradine
GOFFSTOWN CC
Goffstown, New Hampshire
William F. Mitchell

GOG MAGOG GC
Cambridgeshire, England
Willie Park, Jr.
(A.9) Fred W. Hawtree
GOLD CANYON GC
Apache Junction, Arizona
Jeff Hardin, Greg Nash
(A. 9) Ken Kavanaugh
GOLD COAST CC
Surfers' Paradise, Australia
Peter Thomson, Michael Wolveridge
GOLDEGG GC
Salzburg, Austria
J. F. Dudok van Heel
GOLDEN ACRES CC
Schaumberg, Illinois
William B. Langford, Theodore J. Moreau
GOLDEN AND DISTRICT G&CC
Golden, British Columbia
Bill Newis
GOLDEN EAGLE GC
Tallahassee, Florida
Tom Fazio
GOLDEN EAGLE GC
Rio Maior, Portugal
Rocky Roquemore, Jeff Burton
GOLDEN ERA GC
Hemet, California
Jack Daray, Jr., Stephen Halsey
GOLDEN GATE CC
Naples, Florida
Dick Wilson
GOLDEN GATE FIELDS GC
Albany, California
Jack Fleming
GOLDEN GATE GC
San Francisco, California
Jack Fleming
GOLDEN HILLS G&CC
Lexington, South Carolina
Ron Garl
GOLDEN HILLS G&TC
Ocala, Florida
Charles Pace, Lee Popple
GOLDEN HILLS GC
Tehachapi, California
Joseph B. Williams
GOLDEN HILLS G RESORT [FKA APACHE CC]
Mesa, Arizona
NKA Arizona G Resort
GOLDEN HILLS MUNI
California
Stephen Halsey, Jack Daray, Jr.
GOLDEN HORSESHOE GC (GOLD CSE)
Williamsburg, Virginia
Robert Trent Jones
GOLDEN HORSESHOE GC (GREEN CSE)
Williamsburg, Virginia
Rees Jones
GOLDEN HORSESHOE GC (SPOTSWOOD 9)
Williamsburg, Virginia
Robert Trent Jones
GOLDEN OCALA G&CC
Ocala, Florida
Ron Garl
GOLDEN PHEASANT CC
Medford, New Jersey
Richard E. Kidder (1964)

GOLDEN SANDS GC
Cecil, Wisconsin
Homer Fieldhouse
GOLDEN TEE GC
Sarasota, Florida
R. Albert Anderson
GOLDEN TEE GC
Sharonville, Ohio
R. Albert Anderson
GOLDEN TRIANGLE GC
Crofton, Maryland
NKA Walden GC
GOLDEN VALLEY G&CC
Nakorn Rajasima Province,
Thailand
Jack Nicklaus
GOLDEN VALLEY GC
Minneapolis, Minnesota
A. W. Tillinghast
(R.) Geoffrey S. Cornish,
Brian Silva
GOLDEN VALLEY GC
Japan
Robert Trent Jones, Jr.
GOLD FIELDS WEST GC
Carletonville, South Africa
Robert Grimsdell
GOLD HILLS CC
Redding, California
Bob Baldock, Robert L. Baldock
GOLDMAN HOTEL GC
East Orange, New Jersey
Frank Duane
GOLD MOUNTAIN GC
Gorst, Washington
Ken Tyson
GOLDWIN GC
Toyama, Japan
Shunsuke Kato
GOLF CITY PAR 3 GC
Corvallis, Oregon
Ed Burns
[THE] GOLF CLUB
New Albany, Ohio
Pete Dye
GOLF CLUB AT ASPETUCK
Easton, Connecticut
NKA Connecticut GC
GOLF CLUB AT FOSSIL CREEK
Fort Worth, Texas
Arnold Palmer, Ed Seay
GOLF CLUB AT HIDDEN VALLEY
Somerset, Pennsylvania
Lindsay Ervin (routing); Russell
Roberts
GOLF CLUB AT MARCO
Marco Island, Florida
Joe Lee
GOLF CLUB AT QUAIL LODGE
Carmel, California
Robert Muir Graves
GOLF CLUB AT SAGINAW GREENS
Ann Arbor, Michigan
William Newcomb
GOLF CLUB CASTELCONTURBIA
Arona, Italy
Robert Trent Jones
GOLF CLUB CASTEL D'AVIANO
Aviano, Italy
Marco Croze
GOLF CLUB CLEMENT ADER
Seine-et-Marne, France
Michel Gayon

GOLF CLUB COLLI BERICI
Vicenza, Italy
Marco Croze
GOLF CLUB CRANS
Crans-sur-Sierre, Switzerland
Jack Nicklaus
GOLF CLUB D'ESERY
Haute Savoie, France
Michel Gayon
GOLF CLUB D'ETIOLLES
Essonne, France
Michel Gayon
GOLF CLUB DI MONTEGALLO
Ancona, Italy
Bill Amick
GOLF CLUB ERLEN
Switzerland
Karl F. Grohs, *Rainer
Preissmann*
GOLF CLUB GUT ALTENTANN
Salzburg, Austria
Jack Nicklaus
GOLF CLUB KANAZAWA LINKS
Ishikawa, Japan
Katsumi Takizawa
GOLF CLUB LIGNANO
Udine, Italy
Marco Croze
GOLF CLUB MATILDE DI CANOSSA
Italy
Marco Croze
GOLF CLUB RYUGASAKI
Ibaraki, Japan
Shunsuke Kato
GOLF CLUB SEVEN LAKES
Ibaraki, Japan
Shunsuke Kato
GOLF CLUB AT DUNTON HILLS
Essex, England
Howard Swan
GOLF CLUB DE BOURBON
Bourbon, Réunion Island
Michel Gayon
GOLF CLUB DE BROTEL
Hières-sur-Amby, France
Michael G. Fenn
GOLF CLUB DE CERGY PONTOISE
Val d'Oise, France
Michel Gayon
GOLF CLUB DE CHAMBON SUR
LIGNON
Chambon-sur-Lignon, France
Michel Gayon
GOLF CLUB DE CHAMPAGNE
Nîmes, France
Donald Harradine
GOLF CLUB DE CHANTACO
St. Jean de Luz, France
J. S. F. Morrison, H. S. Colt, C.
H. Alison
GOLF CLUB DE COULANDRES
Montpellier, France
Donald Harradine
GOLF CLUB DE EPINAL
Epinal, France
Michel Gayon
GOLF CLUB DE FEUCHEROLLES
France
Mike Poellot
GOLF CLUB DE FONTENAILLES
Seine-et-Marne, France
Michel Gayon

GOLF CLUB DE FOREZ
Forez, France
Michel Gayon
GOLF CLUB DE LA BAROUGE
France
P. M. Ross
(A.9) Fred Hawtree
GOLF CLUB DE LA DOMANGERE
Vendée, France
Michel Gayon
GOLF CLUB DE LA VAUCOULEURS
(RIVER CSE)
Yvelines, France
Michel Gayon
GOLF CLUB DE LA VAUCOULEURS
(VALLEY CSE)
Yvelines, France
Michel Gayon
GOLF CLUB DE LES DRYADES
Les Dryades, France
Michel Gayon
GOLF CLUB DE L'ILE D'OR
L'Ile d'Or, France
Michel Gayon
GOLF CLUB DE LOU ROUCAS
Var, France
Michel Gayon
GOLF CLUB DE MAINTENON
Eure-et-Loire, France
Michel Gayon
GOLF CLUB DE MARSEILLE LA
SALETTE
Marseille, France
Michel Gayon
GOLF CLUB DE MEAUX BOUTIGNY
Meaux, France
Michel Gayon
GOLF CLUB DE PALS
Gerona, Spain
Fred W. Hawtree
GOLF CLUB DE PIERPONT
Belgium
J. F. Dudok van Heel
GOLF CLUB DE PORNIC
Pornic, France
Michel Gayon
GOLF CLUB DE QUIBERON
Quiberon, France
Michael G. Fenn
GOLF CLUB DE REIMS
Reims, France
Michael G. Fenn
GOLF CLUB DE SABLE
Sarthe, France
Michel Gayon
GOLF CLUB DE ST. CLOUD (GREEN
CSE)
St. Cloud, France
H. S. Colt
GOLF CLUB DE ST. CLOUD (YELLOW
CSE)
St. Cloud, France
J. S. F. Morrison, H. S. Colt
GOLF CLUB DE ST. DENIS
St. Denis, Réunion Island
Michel Gayon
GOLF CLUB DE URUGUAY
Montivideo, Uruguay
Alister Mackenzie
GOLF CLUB DE VALMARTIN
Valmartin, France
Michel Gayon

GOLF CLUB DE VILLETTE-D'ANTHON
France
Michael G. Fenn
GOLF CLUB DES ILES BORROMEES
Stresa, Italy
Marco Croze
GOLF CLUB D'AIX-LES-BAINS
Aix-les-Bains, France
Wilfrid Reid
GOLF CLUB D'ARCACHON
Arcachon, France
Charles Blandford (1952)
GOLF CLUB D'OZOIR-LA-FERRIÈRE
Ozoir-la-Ferrière, France
Tom Simpson
GOLF CLUB OF CYPRESS CREEK
Ruskin, Florida
Steve Smyers
GOLF CLUB OF DELRAY
Delray Beach, Florida
Bill Dietsch
GOLF CLUB OF GEORGIA (CREEKSIDE
CSE)
Alpharetta, Georgia
Arthur Hills
GOLF CLUB OF GEORGIA (LAKESIDE
CSE)
Alpharetta, Georgia
Arthur Hills
GOLF CLUB OF ILLINOIS
Algonquin, Illinois
Dick Nugent
GOLF CLUB OF INDIANA
Lebanon, Indiana
Charles Maddox
GOLF CLUB OF JACKSONVILLE
Jacksonville, Florida
Bobby Weed
GOLF CLUB OF KENTUCKY
Crestwood, Kentucky
Larry Fitch
GOLF CLUB OF LEBANON
Beirut, Lebanon
J. J. F. Pennink
GOLF CLUB OF MIAMI (EAST CSE)
Hialeah, Florida
Robert Trent Jones
(R.) Bobby Weed
GOLF CLUB OF MIAMI (WEST CSE)
Hialeah, Florida
Robert Trent Jones
(R.) Bobby Weed
GOLF CLUB OF MIAMI (SOUTH CSE)
Hialeah, Florida
Bobby Weed
GOLF CLUB OF NEWPORT
Newport, New York
Geoffrey S. Cornish, William G.
Robinson
GOLF CLUB OF OKLAHOMA
Broken Arrow, Oklahoma
Tom Fazio
GOLF CLUB OF TENNESSEE
Kingston Springs, Tennessee
Tom Fazio
GOLFCREST CC NLE
Houston, Texas
Ralph Plummer
GOLFCREST CC
Houston, Texas
Joseph S. Finger
GOLF DA DONA RAINHA
Obidos, Portugal
Howard Swan

GOLF D'ABBESSEE
  Dax, France
  Robert von Hagge
GOLF D'ABLEIGES
  Ableiges, France
  Jeremy Pern, *Jean Garaialde*
GOLF D'ALBI LASBORDES
  Lasbordes, France
  Jeremy Pern, *Jean Garaialde*
GOLF D'AMMERSCHWIHR
  Alsace, France
  Robert Berthet
GOLF D'ARCANGUES
  Biarritz, France
  Ronald Fream
GOLF D'ARC-EN-BARROIS
  Arc-en-Barrois, France
  Jeremy Pern
GOLF D'ARDON
  Orléans, France
  Cabell Robinson
GOLF D'ATIMAONA
  Papeete, Tahiti
  Bob Baldock
GOLF D'AVERNAS
  Belgium
  Martin Hawtree
GOLF D'AVRILLE
  Avrille, France
  Robert Berthet
GOLF DE BARBAROUX
  Brignoles, France
  P. B. Dye
GOLF DE BERCUIT
  Grez Doiceau, Belgium
  Robert Trent Jones
GOLF DE BESANÇON
  Besançon, France
  Michael G. Fenn
GOLF DE BIARRITZ
  Biarritz, France
  Willie Dunn, Jr., Tom Dunn
    (R.) H. S. Colt
GOLF DE BOMBEQUOILS
  Montpellier, France
  Martin Hawtree, Simon Gidman
GOLF DE BONDUES (RED CSE)
  Roubaix, France
  Fred W. Hawtree
    (R.) Robert Trent Jones
GOLF DE BONDUES (BLUE CSE)
  Roubaix, France
  Robert Trent Jones
    (A.9) Robert Trent Jones, Jr.
GOLF DE BORDEAUX
  Bordeaux, France
  Jean Bourret
GOLF DE BOURGOGNE
  Dijon, France
  Michael G. Fenn
GOLF DE BOURNEL
  France
  Robert Berthet
GOLF DE BRESSON
  Grenoble, France
  Robert Trent Jones, Jr.
GOLF DE BRUZ
  Bruz, France
  T. J. A. Macauley, *Stephen Quenouille*
GOLF DE CABO NEGRO
  Tetuan, Morocco
  Cabell Robinson

GOLF DE CAEN
  Caen, France
  Martin Hawtree
GOLF DE CANNES
  La Napoule, France
  Wilfrid Reid
    (R.) H. S. Colt
    (R.) Robert Berthet
GOLF DE CAP SKIRRING
  France
  Robert Berthet
GOLF DE CARQUEFOU
  Carquefou, France
  Martin Hawtree, Simon Gidman
GOLF DE CASTELNAUD
  Villeneuve-sur-Lot, France
  Robert Berthet
GOLF DE CHANTACO
  St. Jean de Luz, France
  J. S. F. Morrison, H. S. Colt
GOLF DE CHANTILLY (NEW CSE)
  Chantilly, France
  D. M. A. Steel
GOLF DE CHANTILLY (OLD CSE)
  Chantilly, France
  J. F. Abercromby
    (R.) Tom Simpson
GOLF DE CHÂTEAU DE PELLY
  France
  Jeremy Pern, *Jean Garaialde*
GOLF DE CHAUMONT EN VEXIN
  Paris, France
  Donald Harradine
GOLF DE CHIBERTA
  Biarritz, France
  Tom Simpson
GOLF DE CLARIS
  France
  Michael G. Fenn
GOLF DE CLERMONT-FERRAND
  Clermont-Ferrand, France
  Michael G. Fenn
GOLF DE COGNAC
  Cognac, France
  Jeremy Pern, *Jean Garaialde*
GOLF DE COURCHEVEL
  Courchevel, France
  Robert Berthet
GOLF DE COURSON-MONTELOUP
  (NORTH CSE)
  Courson-Monteloup, France
  Robert von Hagge
GOLF DE COURSON-MONTELOUP
  (SOUTH CSE)
  Courson-Monteloup, France
  Robert von Hagge
GOLF DE DIEPPE
  Dieppe, France
  Willie Park, Jr.
    (R.) Tom Simpson
GOLF DE DIGNE
  France
  Robert Berthet
GOLF DE DINARD
  Brittany, France
  Tom Dunn
GOLF DE DOMONT
  Paris, France
  Fred W. Hawtree
GOLF DE DUNKERQUE
  Nord, France
  Robert Berthet

GOLF DE FIAC
  Lavaur, France
  Fred W. Hawtree
GOLF DE FONTAINEBLEAU
  Fontainebleau, France
  Tom Simpson
    (R. A.4) Fred W. Hawtree
    (R.) Martin Hawtree, Simon
    Gidman
GOLF DE FREGATE
  Bandol, France
  Ronald Fream
GOLF DE GASSIN
  St. Tropez, France
  Ronald Fream
GOLF DE GRANVILLE
  Normandy, France
  H. S. Colt, C. H. Alison
GOLF DE HOSSEGOR
  Landes, France
  Tom Simpson, J. S. F. Morrison
GOLF DE LA BAROUGE
  Mazamet, France
  Tom Simpson, P. M. Ross
    (R.) P. M. Ross
    (A.9) Fred W. Hawtree,
    Martin Hawtree
GOLF DE LA BAULE
  France
    (R.) Peter Alliss, David
    Thomas
GOLF DE LA BRESSE
  Bourgen-Bresse, France
  Jeremy Pern, *Jean Garaialde*
GOLF DE LACANAU
  France
  Jeremy Pern, *Jean Garaialde*
GOLF DE LA CÔTE D'ARGENT
  MOLIETS
  Bordeaux, France
  Robert Trent Jones
GOLF DE LA GRANDE MOTTE (LONG
  CSE)
  Montpellier, France
  Robert Trent Jones
GOLF DE LA GRANDE MOTTE (SHORT
  CSE)
  Montpellier, France
  Robert Trent Jones
GOLF DE LA LARGUE
  France
  Jeremy Pern, *Jean Garaialde*
GOLF DE LANN-ROHOU
  Brest, France
  Michael G. Fenn
GOLF DE LA PALMERAIE
  Marrakesh, Morocco
  Robert Trent Jones
GOLF DE LA PORCELAINE
  Limoges, France
  Jeremy Pern, *Jean Garaialde*
GOLF DE LA RAMÉE
  France
  Martin Hawtree
GOLF DE LA SAINTE BAUME
  Ste. Baume, France
  Robert Berthet
GOLF DE LA SALLE
  France
  Robert Berthet
GOLF DE LA TOURNETTE
  Brussels, Belgium
  Bill Amick

GOLF DE LA WANTZENAU
  La Wantzenau, France
  Jeremy Pern, *Jean Garaialde*
GOLF DE L'ESTAJEAN
  France
  Jeremy Pern, *Jean Garaialde*
GOLF DE L'ESTEREL
  France
  Jeremy Pern, *Jean Garaialde*
GOLF DE L'ISLE FLEURIE
  Paris, France
  Martin Hawtree
GOLF DE L'ODEF
  France
  Robert Berthet
GOLF DE LYON
  Lyon, France
  Fred W. Hawtree
    (A.9) Michael G. Fenn
GOLF DE MALLAMOLLIERE
  Fribourg, Switzerland
  Jeremy Pern
GOLF DE MARIVAUX
  France
  T. J. A. Macauley, *Stephen Quenouille*
GOLF DE MASSANE
  Baillargues, France
  Ronald Fream
GOLF DE MEMILLON
  France
  Tom Simpson
GOLF DE METZ CHERISEY
  Metz, France
  Fred W. Hawtree
GOLF DE METZ
  Metz, France
  Robert Berthet
GOLF DE MONT DE MARSAN
  France
  Jeremy Pern
GOLF DE MONT GARNI
  Belgium
  T. J. A. Macauley
GOLF DE MORFONTAINE
  Senlis, France
  Tom Simpson
GOLF DE NANCY-AINGERAY
  France
    (R.) Michael G. Fenn
GOLF DE NANTES
  Nantes, France
  J. J. F. Pennink
GOLF DE NICE
  Nice, France
  Robert Berthet
GOLF DE NIORT-ROMAGNE
  France
  Robert Berthet
GOLF DE PARIS INTERNATIONAL
  Bouffemont, France
  Jack Nicklaus
GOLF DE PÉRIGUEUX
  Périgueux, France
  Robert Berthet
GOLF DE QUIMPER ET DE
  CORNOUIAILLE
  Quimper, France
  Fred W. Hawtree
    (A.9) Fred W. Hawtree,
    Martin Hawtree
GOLF DE REGINÉE
  Villers-la-Ville, Belgium
    (R.) Bill Amick

GOLF DE RIVIERA
Mandelieu, France
Robert Trent Jones
GOLF DE ROCHEFORT EN YVELINES
Paris, France
Fred W. Hawtree
GOLF DE ROUGEMONT
Rougemont, France
Robert Berthet
GOLF DE ROURET
France
Jeremy Pern, *Jean Garaialde*
GOLF DE ROYAN
Royan, France
Robert Berthet
GOLF DE ST. DONAT
Grasse, France
Robert Trent Jones, Jr.
GOLF DE ST. FRANÇOIS
Guadeloupe
Robert Trent Jones
GOLF DE ST. GERMAIN
Yvelines, France
H. S. Colt
GOLF DE ST. SAMSON
Pleumeur-Bodou, France
Fred W. Hawtree
GOLF DE SALBRIS
Salbris, France
Jeremy Pern, *Jean Garaialde*
GOLF DE SAUMANE
France
Jeremy Pern, *Jean Garaialde*
GOLF DE SEIGNOSSE
Seignosse, France
Robert von Hagge
GOLF DE SERAINCOURT
Meulan, France
Fred W. Hawtree
GOLF DE SPERONE
Corsica, France
Robert Trent Jones
GOLF DE STRASBOURG
Strasbourg, France
Donald Harradine
GOLF DE TÉOULA
Toulouse, France
Martin Hawtree
GOLF DE TOULOUSE
Toulouse, France
(A.9) Fred W. Hawtree
GOLF DE TOULOUSE-SEILH (RED
CSE)
Toulouse, France
Jeremy Pern, *Jean Garaialde*
GOLF DE TOULOUSE-SEILH (YELLOW
CSE)
Toulouse, France
Jeremy Pern, *Jean Garaialde*
GOLF DE TOURAINE
Tours, France
Michael G. Fenn
GOLF DE TOUR D'ALING
Arles, France
Jeremy Pern
GOLF DE VALBONNE
France
Donald Harradine
GOLF DE VALCROS
France
Fred W. Hawtree
GOLF DE VALESCURE
St. Raphael, France
Robert Trent Jones

GOLF DE VALLIÈRES
Vallières, France
Tom Simpson
GOLF DE VAUDREUIL
France
Fred W. Hawtree
GOLF DE VAUX DE CERNAY
France
Tom Simpson
GOLF DE VIDAUBAN
Vidauban, France
Robert Trent Jones
GOLF DE VILLARD-DE-LANS
France
Tom Simpson
GOLF DE VILLARE
France
Jeremy Pern, *Jean Garaialde*
GOLF DE VILLENNES
France
Robert Berthet
GOLF DE VITTEL
Vosges, France
(R.) J. S. F. Morrison
GOLF DE VOISINS
France
Tom Simpson
GOLF DEL SUR
Tenerife
Pepe Gancedo
GOLF DES BAUX DE PROVENCE
France
Martin Hawtree, Simon Gidman
GOLF DES CHÂTEAUX DE
VILLARCEAUX
France
John Harris
GOLF DES ETANGES DE FLAC
Lavaur, France
Martin Hawtree
GOLF D'ORMESSON
France
John Harris
GOLF DU CAP D'AGDE
Cap d'Agde, France
Ronald Fream
GOLF DU CHÂTEAU D'AVOISE
Montchanin, France
Martin Hawtree
GOLF DU CHÂTEAU DE TAULANE
France
Gary Player
GOLF DU CHARMEIL À ST. QUENTIN
Grenoble, France
Jeremy Pern, *Jean Garaialde*
GOLF DU CLAIR VALLON
Clairis, France
Michael G. Fenn
GOLF DU CLUB MED
Cannes, France
Cabell Robinson
GOLF DU CLUB MED
Agadir, Morocco
Cabell Robinson
GOLF DU LEPIAN MÉDOC
Bordeaux, France
Rod Whitman
GOLF DU MÉDOC
Bordeaux, France
Bill Coore, Rod Whitman
GOLF DU PARC CARELTON
Quebec
William F. Mitchell

GOLF DU PAYS DE BRIVE
Brive, France
Jeremy Pern
GOLF DU PETIT CHENE-MAZIERES
France
Robert Berthet
GOLF DU PRIEURE (EAST CSE)
Sailly, France
Fred W. Hawtree
GOLF DU PRIEURE (WEST CSE)
Sailly, France
Fred W. Hawtree
GOLF DU RHIN
Alsace, France
Donald Harradine
GOLF DU RONCEMAY
Yonne, France
Jeremy Pern, *Jean Garaialde*
GOLF DU TECHONOPOLE METZ
Lorraine, France
Robert Berthet
GOLF ESTEREL
St. Raphael, France
Robert Trent Jones
GOLF GIRONA
Spain
Martin Hawtree
GOLF GUADALAMINA (NORTH CSE)
Spain
Javier Arana
GOLF GUADALAMINA (SOUTH CSE)
Spain
Javier Arana
GOLF HAMMOCK CC
Sebring, Florida
Ron Garl
GOLF HILL G&CC
Fatogue, New York
Frank Duane
GOLF HOTEL DO FRADE
Frade, Brazil
Peter Alliss, David Thomas
GOLF ILE DE BERDER
France
Wilfrid Reid
GOLF INTERNATIONAL LES BORDES
St. Laurent, France
Robert von Hagge, Bruce Devlin
GOLF LA DUQUESA
Manilva, Spain
Robert Trent Jones
GOLF LA MARGHERITA
Turin, Italy
Marco Croze
GOLFLAND GC
Marietta, Georgia
Chic Adams
GOLFLAND GC
Hamilton, Ontario
(R.) Clinton E. Robinson
[THE] GOLF LINKS
Frostproof, Florida
Henry C. Higginbotham
GOLFMOHR GC
East Moline, Illinois
Ted Lockie
GOLF PARK G LINKS [NLE]
Florida
H. C. C. Tippetts
GOLF PROFESSIONALS C (CHAMPIONS
CSE)
Beaufort, South Carolina
Walter I. Rodgers

GOLF PROFESSIONALS C (PLAYERS
CSE)
Beaufort, South Carolina
Walter I. Rodgers
GOLF PUBLIC DE L'AILETTE
Aisne, France
Michel Gayon
GOLF PUBLIC DE SAVENAY
Loire Atlantique, France
Michel Gayon
GOLF PUY-DE-DÔME
Puy-de-Dôme, France
Michael G. Fenn
GOLF RENNES ST. JACQUES
France
Robert Berthet
GOLF RIO REAL
Spain
Javier Arana
GOLFVIEW G&RC
Fort Myers, Florida
Gordon Lewis
GOLF VILLAGE GC
Neenah, Wisconsin
Homer Fieldhouse
GOODLAND GC
Goodland, Kansas
Chet Mendenhall
GOODRICH CC
Goodrich, Michigan
(R.) Jeff Gorney
GOODWIN PARK MUNI
Hartford, Connecticut
(R.) Everett Pyle
GOODWOOD PARK HOTEL G&CC
West Sussex, England
D. M. A. Steel
GOODYEAR G&CC
Litchfield Park, Arizona
NKA Wigwam G&CC
GOODYEAR GC
Danville, Virginia
Gene Hamm
GOOSE CREEK CC
Leesburg, Virginia
William Gordon
GOOSE HUMMOCK G&CC
Gibbons, Alberta
William G. Robinson
GOOSE ISLAND LAKE GC
Texas
Bruce Littell
GOOSEPOND COLONY GC
Scottsboro, Alabama
George W. Cobb
GÖPPINGEN GC
Göppingen, Germany
Reinhold Weishaupt
GORDON LAKES GC
Fort Gordon, Georgia
Robert Trent Jones
GORDON TRENT GC
Martinsville, Virginia
Al Jamison, *Claude Bingham*
GORGE VALE GC
Victoria, British Columbia
A. Vernon Macan
(R.) Norman W. Woods
GORHAM CC
Gorham, Maine
Jim McDonald, Sr.
(R.) *Ernest Hawkes*

GORLESTON GC
  Suffolk, England
    F. G. Hawtree, J. H. Taylor
GORT GC
  Gort, Ireland
    (R.) Eddie Hackett
GOSFIELD LAKE GC
  Braintree, Essex, England
    Henry Cotton, Howard Swan
GOSHEN PLANTATION CC
  Augusta, Georgia
    Ellis Maples
GÖTEBORG GC
  Göteborg, Sweden
    (A.4) Jan Sederholm
GÖTTINGEN GC
  Mortheim, Germany
    Wolfgang Siegmann
GOTTS PARK GC
  England
    T. R. Trigg
GOUROCK GC
  Scotland
    Henry Cotton
GOVERNORS C
  Chapel Hill, North Carolina
    Jack Nicklaus
GOVERNORS LANDING CC
  Williamsburg, Virginia
    Tom Fazio
GOWAN BRAE GC
  Bathurst, New Brunswick
    Clinton E. Robinson
GOWANDA CC
  Gowanda, New York
    A. Russell Tryon
GOWRIE G&CC
  Gowrie, Iowa
    Charles Calhoun
GRACEWIL CC (EAST CSE)
  Grand Rapids, Michigan
    Maurie Wells
GRACEWIL CC (WEST CSE)
  Grand Rapids, Michigan
    Morris Wilson
GRACEWIL PINES GC
  Jackson, Michigan
    Morris Wilson
GRAFING-OBERELKOFEN GC
  Bayern, Germany
    Götz Mecklenburg
GRAHAM ACRES GC
  Whitecourt, Alberta
    Les Furber, Jim Eremko
GRAHAM F. VANDERBILT ESTATE GC
  Manhasset, New York
    Alfred H. Tull
GRAHAMSTOWN GC
  Grahamstown, South Africa
    (R.) Robert Grimsdell
GRAIN VALLEY GC
  Grain Valley, Missouri
    John S. Davis, Robert Stone
GRAMADO GC
  Brazil
    Alberto Serra
GRAMONT ESTATE GC
  France
    Tom Simpson
GRANADA GC
  Coral Gables, Florida
    William B. Langford,
    Theodore J. Moreau

GRANADA FARMS CC
  Granite, North Carolina
    Tom Jackson
GRANBURY GC
  Granbury, Texas
    Leon Howard
GRAND BAHAMAS HOTEL & CC
  Freeport, Bahamas
    Mark Mahannah
GRAND BEACH CC
  Michigan
    Tom Bendelow
    (A.27) William H. Livie
GRAND BEACH GC
  Grand Beach, Manitoba
    Norman H. Woods
GRAND BLANC GC
  Grand Blanc, Michigan
    Bruce Matthews, Jerry Matthews
    (A.3rd 9) Larry Mancour
GRANDE CACHE G&CC
  Grande Cache, Alberta
    Robert H. Krewusik (9 1980)
GRAND CYPRESS GC
  Orlando, Florida
    Jack Nicklaus
    (A.3rd 9) Jack Nicklaus
    (A.3 Golf Academy) Jack
    Nicklaus
GRAND FALLS GC
  New Brunswick
    (R.) Robert Moote
GRANDFATHER G&CC
  Linville, North Carolina
    Ellis Maples
GRAND FORKS CC
  Grand Forks, North Dakota
    Robert Bruce Harris
GRAND HARBOR GC
  Vero Beach, Florida
    Joe Lee
GRAND HAVEN GC
  Grand Haven, Michigan
    Bruce Matthews, Jerry Matthews
GRAND HOTEL GC
  Mackinac Island, Michigan
    (R.) Jerry Matthews
GRAND ISLAND MUNI
  Grand Island, Nebraska
    Frank Hummel
GRAND LAKE GC
  Grand Lake, Colorado
    (R.9 A.9) Dick Phelps, Brad
    Benz
GRAND LEDGE GC
  Grand Ledge, Michigan
    Stephen Lipkowitz
GRAND MARAIS GC
  East St. Louis, Illinois
    Joseph A. Roseman
GRAND' MÈRE GC
  Grand' Mère, Quebec
    (R.3) Howard Watson
GRAND NATIONAL GC (AUBURN
  CSE)
  Opelika, Alabama
    Robert Trent Jones
GRAND NATIONAL GC (OPELIKA
  CSE)
  Opelika, Alabama
    Robert Trent Jones
GRAND NATIONAL GC (SHORT CSE)
  Opelika, Alabama
    Robert Trent Jones

GRAND OAK GC
  West Harrison, Indiana
    Michael Hurdzan
GRAND PALMS G&CC
  Pembroke Pines, Florida
    Wade Northrup
GRAND PRAIRIE GC
  Kalamazoo, Indiana
    William James Spear
GRAND PRAIRIE GC
  Grand Prairie, Alberta
    (R. A.3rd 9) Bill Newis
GRAND PRAIRIE MUNI
  Grand Prairie, Texas
    Ralph Plummer
GRAND RAPIDS CC
  Grand Rapids, Michigan
    Willie Park, Jr.
GRAND TRAVERSE RESORT (RESORT
  CSE)
  Acme, Michigan
    Bill Newcomb
    (R.) Bob Cupp
GRAND TRAVERSE RESORT (THE
  BEAR CSE)
  Acme, Michigan
    Jack Nicklaus
GRANDVIEW CC
  Middlefield, Ohio
    (R.) Richard W. LaConte, Ted
    McAnlis
GRANDVIEW G&CC
  Dartmouth, Nova Scotia
    William G. Robinson
GRANDVIEW GC
  Sun City West, Arizona
    Greg Nash
GRANDVIEW GC
  Pfafftown, North Carolina
    W. Fleenor
GRANDVIEW GC
  Pennsylvania
    (R.) James Gilmore Harrison
GRANDVIEW GC
  Hortonville, Wisconsin
    Ted Lockie
GRANDVIEW GC
  Huntsville, Ontario
    Thomas McBroom
GRANDVIEW MUNI
  Springfield, Missouri
    Perry Maxwell, Press Maxwell
    (R.) Kyle Phillips
    (R.) Don Sechrest
GRANGE GC
  Dublin, Ireland
    Tom Hood
    (R.) W. Wiltshire
[THE] GRANGE GC
  Coventry, England
    (R.9 A.9) T. J. A. Macauley
GRANGEMOUTH MUNI
  Stirlingshire, Scotland
    Fred W. Hawtree
GRANGE-OVER-SANDS GC
  Cumbria, England
    Alister Mackenzie
GRANITE CITY GC
  Granite City, Illinois
    Edward Lawrence Packard,
    Brent Wadsworth
GRANIT HOTEL GC
  Kerhonkson, New York
    Lou Block

GRANLIDEN HOTEL GC [NLE]
  Lake Sunapee, New Hampshire
    Alex Findlay
GRANTOWN GC
  Morayshire, Scotland
    Willie Park
GRANT PARK GC
  Milwaukee, Wisconsin
    George Hansen
GRANT'S PASS CC
  Grant's Pass, Oregon
    (R. A.14) Bob Baldock,
    Robert L. Baldock
GRANTWOOD GC
  Solon, Ohio
    Harold Paddock
    (R.9) Ron Forse
GRANVILLE GC
  Granville, Ohio
    Donald Ross
GRAPEVINE MUNI
  Grapevine, Texas
    Joseph S. Finger, Ken Dye,
    Byron Nelson
    (R.1) Jeff Brauer
GRASMERE-BY-THE-SEA GC [NLE]
  Hamilton, Bermuda
    Nicol Thompson (9 1927)
GRASMERE GC
  Falmouth, Massachusetts
    Geoffrey S. Cornish, William G.
    Robinson
GRASSLANDS G&CC
  Lakeland, Florida
    Bob Cupp, Jerry Pate
GRASS VALLEY CC
  Crowder Mt., North Carolina
    (A.9) Ellis Maples
GRASSY BROOK GC
  Alder Creek, New York
    Geoffrey S. Cornish, William G.
    Robinson
GRASSY SPRAIN CC [NLE]
  Yonkers, New York
    Devereux Emmet
GRAY GABLES GC
  Laramie, Wyoming
    Herbert Lockwood
GRAYLING CC
  Grayling, Michigan
    (R.2 A.9) Jeff Gorney
GRAYSBURG HILLS GC
  Chuckey, Tennessee
    Rees Jones
GRAYS HARBOR CC
  Grays Harbor, Washington
    John Ball (1913)
    (R.) Walter Fovargue
GRAYSON COUNTY G CSE
  Denison, Texas
    Leon Howard
GRAYSON VALLEY CC
  Birmingham, Alabama
    Harold Williams
    (R.) John LaFoy
GREAT BARR GC
  Birmingham, England
    (R.) J. Hamilton Stutt
GREAT BEND PETROLEUM C
  Great Bend, Kansas
    (A.9) Richard Watson
GREAT CHEBEAGUE GC
  Great Chebeague Island, Maine
    George Spaulding

GREAT COVE GC
Pennsylvania
Edmund B. Ault
GREAT COVE GC
Roque Bluffs, Maine
Paul Browne
GREATE BAY CC
Somers Point, New Jersey
Willie Park, Jr.
  (R.) George Fazio
  (A.3) Ron Garl
GREAT GORGE GC
McAfee, New Jersey
George Fazio, Tom Fazio
GREAT HARBOUR CAY CC
Berry Island, Bahamas
Joe Lee
GREAT HILLS CC
Seymour, Connecticut
Al Zikorus
GREAT HILLS GC
Austin, Texas
Don January, Billy Martindale
GREAT ISLAND GC
Massachusetts
Alex Findlay
GREAT OAKS CC
Rochester, Michigan
William Newcomb
  (R.) Mark McCumber
GREAT OUTDOORS G CSE
Titusville, Florida
Ron Garl
GREAT SAND DUNES CC
Mosca, Colorado
John Sanford, John Ewseychik
(1990)
GREAT SMOKIES HILTON GC
Asheville, North Carolina
William B. Lewis
GREAT SOUTHWEST GC
Arlington, Texas
Ralph Plummer
  (R.) Ken Killian, Dick Nugent
GREAT WATERS GC
Greensboro, Georgia
Jack Nicklaus
GREATWOOD GC
Sugar Land, Texas
Carlton Gipson
GREELEY CC
Greeley, Colorado
Tom Bendelow
  (R.9 A.9) Press Maxwell
GREELY GLEN G&CC
Greely, Ontario
Graham Cooke
GREEN ACADEMY GC
Shirakawa, Japan
Karl Litten
GREEN ACRES CC
Northbrook, Illinois
George O'Neil
  (R.) Joseph A. Roseman
  (R.1) Ken Killian, Dick
  Nugent
  (R.) Roger Packard
GREEN ACRES CC
Kokomo, Indiana
Bob Simmons

GREENACRES CC
Lawrence, New Jersey
Devereux Emmet, Alfred H. Tull
  (R.) William Gordon, David
  Gordon
  (R.2) Brian Ault, Tom Clark,
  Bill Love
  (R.3) Stephen Kay
GREEN ACRES GC
Dexter, Georgia
Arthur Davis
GREEN ACRES GC
Canton, Maine
Laurence Poland
GREENACRES GC
Richmond, British Columbia
Henry Knoedler
GREENBRIAR GC
Lupton, Michigan
Jeff Gorney
GREENBRIAR HILLS CC
Kirkwood, Missouri
C. D. Wagstaff
  (R.) Don Sechrest
  (R.) Ron Prichard
[THE] GREENBRIER (OLD WHITE CSE)
White Sulphur Springs, West Virginia
Charles Blair Macdonald, Seth Raynor
[THE] GREENBRIER (LAKESIDE CSE) [NLE]
White Sulphur Springs, West Virginia
Alex Findlay
[THE] GREENBRIER (LAKESIDE CSE)
White Sulphur Springs, West Virginia
Dick Wilson
[THE] GREENBRIER (GREENBRIER CSE)
White Sulphur Springs, West Virginia
George O'Neil
  (R.) Jack Nicklaus
GREENBRIER CC
Chesapeake, Virginia
Rees Jones
GREENBRIER G&CC
Lexington, Kentucky
William Newcomb
GREENBRIER GC
New Bern, North Carolina
Rees Jones
GREEN BROOK CC
Caldwell, New Jersey
Robert White
  (R.) Maurice McCarthy
  (R.) Robert Trent Jones
  (R.) Hal Purdy, Malcolm
  Purdy
  (R.) Brian Silva, Geoffrey S.
  Cornish
GREENBRYRE CC
Saskatoon, Saskatchewan
Peter Semko, Sherrill Semko
GREENCASTLE CC
Burtonsville, Maryland
Robert L. Elder
GREENCASTLE GREENS GC
Greencastle, Pennsylvania
Robert L. Elder

GREENDALE MUNI
Alexandria, Virginia
Leon Howard, *Charles Howard*
GREENE CC
Yellow Springs, Ohio
William H. Diddel
GREENE COUNTY GC
Waynesburg, Pennsylvania
Emil Loeffler, *John McGlynn*
GREENE HILLS C
Standardsville, Virginia
Buddy Loving
GREENFIELD CC
Greenfield, Indiana
  (R.9 A.9) Gary Kern
GREENFIELD CC
Greenfield, Massachusetts
Alex Findlay
  (R.) Ralph Barton
GREENFIELD PARK GC
West Allis, Wisconsin
George Hansen
GREEN GABLES CC
Denver, Colorado
William H. Tucker
  (A.9) *James L. Haines*
GREEN GABLES GC
Charlottetown, Prince Edward Island
Stanley Thompson
  (R. A.9) Clinton E. Robinson
GREEN HARBOR CC
Marshfield, Massachusetts
Manny Francis
GREEN HAVEN GC
Minnesota
  (R.3) David Gill
GREEN HILL CC
Kagoshima, Japan
Minami Kyushu
GREEN HILL MUNI
Wilmington, Delaware
Wilfrid Reid
  (R.) Edmund B. Ault
GREEN HILL MUNI [NLE]
Worcester, Massachusetts
Willie Ogg
GREEN HILL MUNI
Worcester, Massachusetts
William F. Mitchell
  (R.) Alfred H. Tull
GREEN HILL Y&CC
Salisbury, Maryland
  (R.) Alfred H. Tull
GREEN HILLS CC
Millbrae, California
Alister Mackenzie, Robert Hunter, H. Chandler Egan
  (R.) Robert Muir Graves
  (R.) Gary Roger Baird
GREEN HILLS CC
Mount Vernon, Illinois
  (A.9) Gary Kern
GREEN HILLS CC
Willard, Missouri
Floyd Farley
GREEN HILLS CC
Rochester, New York
Pete Craig, *Joseph Demino*
GREEN HILLS CC
Riddleton, Tennessee
Robert Renaud

GREEN HILLS CC
West Virginia
Edmund B. Ault
GREENHILLS CC
Lambeth, Ontario
René Muylaert, *Charles Muylaert*
GREEN HILLS G&CC
Selma, Indiana
William H. Diddel
  (R.) William H. Diddel
GREEN HILLS GC
Linwood, Michigan
William Newcomb
GREEN ISLAND CC
Columbus, Georgia
George W. Cobb
  (R.) Joe Lee, Rocky
  Roquemore
  (R.) Arthur L. Davis
GREENISLAND GC
Northern Ireland
  (R.9 A.9) Fraser Middleton
GREEN KNOLL GC
Somerset, New Jersey
William Gordon, David Gordon
GREEN LAKES STATE PARK GC
Fayetteville, New York
Robert Trent Jones
  (R.) William F. Mitchell
GREENLEA GC
Boring, Oregon
Walt Markham
GREENLEAF G&RC
Invergrove, Minnesota
Donald G. Brauer, Emil Perret
GREEN MEADOW CC
Helena, Montana
Gregor MacMillan
  (R.) Gregor MacMillan
  (A.9) William Teufel
  (R.) Robert Muir Graves
GREEN MEADOW CC
Rye, New York
NKA Willow Ridge CC
GREEN MEADOW CC
Marysville, Tennessee
William B. Langford
  (R.) Willard Byrd
GREEN MEADOW GC
Farmingdale, Maine
  (A.9) Brian Silva, Geoffrey S.
  Cornish
GREEN MEADOW GC (CSE NO. 1)
Hudson, New Hampshire
Phil Friel, David Friel
GREEN MEADOW GC (CSE NO. 2)
Hudson, New Hampshire
Phil Friel, David Friel
GREEN MEADOWS CC
Augusta, Georgia
Bill Amick
GREEN MEADOWS CC
Katy, Texas
Jay Riviere
GREEN OAKS CC
Verona, Pennsylvania
Donald Ross
  (R.) Emil Loeffler, *John
  McGlynn*
GREEN OAKS G CSE
Ypsilanti, Michigan
Robert W. Bills, Donald L. Childs

GREENOCK CC
Lee, Massachusetts
Donald Ross
GREENOCK GC
Renfrewshire, Scotland
James Braid
GREENORE GC
Greenore, Ireland
(R.) Eddie Hackett
GREEN PARK–NORWOOD GC [NLE]
Blowing Rock, North Carolina
Seth Raynor
GREEN POND CC
Bethlehem, Pennsylvania
Alex Findlay
GREEN POND GC
New Jersey
Alec Ternyei
GREEN RIDGE CC [NLE]
Grand Rapids, Michigan
Tom Bendelow
(R.) Bruce Matthews (1930)
(R.) Bruce Matthews (1950)
(R.) William Newcomb
GREEN RIVER CC (ORANGE CSE)
Corona, California
Lawrence Hughes
GREEN RIVER CC (RIVERSIDE CSE)
Corona, California
Cary Bickler
GREEN RIVER CC
Chesterfield, South Carolina
Al Zikorus
GREEN RIVER CC
Waynesboro, Tennessee
Robert Renaud
GREEN RIVER GC
Normandie, France
Ronald Fream
[THE] GREENS AT EAGLEBROOK
Scarborough, Maine
Jimmy Jones
GREENSBORO CC (CARLSON FARMS CSE)
Greensboro, North Carolina
Ellis Maples
(R.1) John LaFoy
GREENSBORO CC (IRVING PARK CSE)
Greensboro, North Carolina
Donald Ross
(R.) George W. Cobb
GREENSBURG CC
Greensburg, Pennsylvania
Tom Bendelow
GREEN'S FOLLY CC
South Boston, Virginia
Gene Hamm
GREENS G&RC
Oklahoma City, Oklahoma
Don Sechrest
GREENSHIRE GC
Waukegan, Illinois
Ken Killian, Dick Nugent
GREEN SPRING G CSE
Washington City, Utah
Gene Bates
GREEN SPRING VALLEY HUNT C
Garrison, Maryland
(R.9 A.9) Robert Trent Jones
GREEN TREE GC
California
William F. Bell

GREENTREE CC
Carmel, Indiana
NKA Twin Lakes GC
GREENTREE GC
Mays Landing, New Jersey
Horace Smith
(R.) Robert Muir Graves
GREEN VALLEY CC
Birmingham, Alabama
Bancroft Timmons
(R.9 A.9) George W. Cobb
(R.) Ward Northrup
GREEN VALLEY CC
Suisun, California
Elmer G. Border
(R.) Robert Muir Graves
GREEN VALLEY CC
Clermont, Florida
R. Albert Anderson
(A.9) Lloyd Clifton, *Kenneth Ezell, George Clifton*
GREEN VALLEY CC
Lafayette Hills, Pennsylvania
(R.) J. B. McGovern
GREEN VALLEY CC [NLE]
Roxborough, Pennsylvania
Willie Park, Jr.
GREEN VALLEY CC
Portsmouth, Rhode Island
Manny Raposa
GREEN VALLEY CC
Greenville, South Carolina
George W. Cobb
GREEN VALLEY CC
Kingsport, Tennessee
Lon Mills
GREEN VALLEY CC
St. George, Utah
Mark Dixon Ballif
GREEN VALLEY GC
Green Valley, North Carolina
Gene Hamm
GREEN VALLEY GC
Greensboro, North Carolina
George W. Cobb
GREEN VALLEY GC
Kings Mountain, North Carolina
Ellis Maples
GREEN VALLEY GC
Quebec
George Cumming
(R.) Howard Watson
(R.7) John Watson
GREEN VALLEY GC
Bangkok, Thailand
Robert Trent Jones, Jr.
GREEN VALLEY MUNI
Sioux City, Iowa
David Gill
GREENVIEW GC
Centralia, Illinois
Tom Bendelow
GREENVIEW GC
Central Square, New York
Hal Purdy
GREENVIEW COVE GC
West Palm Beach, Florida
Ted McAnlis
GREENVILLE CC
Greenville, Illinois
(R.) Edward Lawrence Packard, Brent Wadsworth

GREENVILLE CC
Greenville, Kentucky
Alex McKay
GREENVILLE CC
Greenville, Mississippi
Jack Daray
GREENVILLE CC
Greenville, Pennsylvania
James Gilmore Harrison
(R.9 A.9) Ferdinand Garbin
GREENVILLE CC (CHANTICLEER CSE)
Greenville, South Carolina
Robert Trent Jones
GREENVILLE CC (RIVERSIDE CSE)
Greenville, South Carolina
William B. Langford
(R.) George W. Cobb
(R.) Russell Breeden
GREENVILLE MUNI
Greenville, Mississippi
Leon Howard
GREENWAY PARK GC
Broomfield, Colorado
Dick Phelps
GREENWICH CC [NLE]
Greenwich, Connecticut
Julian W. Curtis, Edwin Curtis
GREENWICH CC
Greenwich, Connecticut
Seth Raynor
(R.) Donald Ross
(R.2) Robert White
(R.) Robert Trent Jones
GREENWOOD CC
Greenwood, South Carolina
George W. Cobb
GREENWOODS CC
Connecticut
(R.1) Al Zikorus
GRENADA G&CC
St. George, Grenada
Ewart Hughes
GRENELEFE G&RC (EAST CSE)
Haines City, Florida
Arnold Palmer, Ed Seay
GRENELEFE G&RC (SOUTH CSE)
Haines City, Florida
Ron Garl
GRENELEFE G&RC (WEST CSE)
Haines City, Florida
Robert Trent Jones (routing);
David Wallace
GRENLAND GC
Norway
Jan Sederholm
GRESHAM G&CC
Gresham, Oregon
Eddie Hogan, Sam Walsborn
GREVERUD G CSE
Oppegard, Oslo, Norway
Gerold Hauser, *Günther Hauser*
GREYLOCK GLEN CC [NLE]
Adams, Massachusetts
Geoffrey S. Cornish, William G. Robinson
GREYNOLD PARK GC
Miami Beach, Florida
Mark Mahannah
GREY OAKS CC
Naples, Florida
Lloyd Clifton, *Kenneth Ezell, George Clifton*

GREY ROCKS GC
St. Jovite, Quebec
Howard Watson
GREYSTONE GC
Birmingham, Alabama
Bob Cupp, *Hubert Green*
GREYSTONE GC
Douglasville, Georgia
Don Cottle
GREYSTONE GC
White Hall, Maryland
Joe Lee
GREYSTONE GC
Romeo, Michigan
Jerry Matthews
GREYSTONE GC
Milton, Ontario
Doug Carrick
GREYSTONES GC
County Wicklow, Ireland
(R.) C. H. Alison, H. S. Colt
(R.) Eddie Hackett
GRIFFIN CC
Griffin, Georgia
(A.9) Willard Byrd
GRIFFITH PARK GC (COOLIDGE CSE)
Los Angeles, California
William H. Johnson
GRIFFITH PARK GC (HARDING CSE)
Los Angeles, California
George C. Thomas, Jr.
(R.9) William H. Johnson
GRIFFITH PARK GC (LOS FELIZ CSE)
Los Angeles, California
William H. Johnson
GRIFFITH PARK GC (ROOSEVELT CSE)
Los Angeles, California
William H. Johnson
GRIFFITH PARK GC (WILSON CSE)
Los Angeles, California
Tom Bendelow
(R.) George C. Thomas, Jr.
(R.) William H. Johnson
GRIFFITHS PARK GC
Akron, Ohio
Harold Paddock
GRIGSBY CC
Chicago, Illinois
C. D. Wagstaff
GRIMBALL GC
Savannah, Georgia
Ron Kirby, Denis Griffiths
GRIMSBY GC
Lincolnshire, England
S. V. Hotchkin
(R.) Tom Williamson
(R.) Fred W. Hawtree
GRINDSTONE NECK GC
Winter Harbor, Maine
(R.) Alex Findlay
(A.5) *Charles Clarke*
GROSSE ILE G&CC
Grosse Ile, Michigan
Donald Ross
(R.) Wilfrid Reid, William Connellan
(R.) Arthur Hills
GROSSINGER'S GC
Grossinger, New York
Andrew Carl Salerno
(R.) William F. Mitchell
(R.9 A.9) Joseph S. Finger

GROVE CITY CC
Grove City, Pennsylvania
Tom Bendelow
GROVE PARK GC
Jackson, Mississippi
Sonny Guy
GROVE PARK INN CC
Asheville, North Carolina
Willie Park, Jr.
(R.9 A.9) Herbert Barker
(R.) Donald Ross
(R.) Russell Breeden
GROVEPORT GC
Ohio
(A.9) Jack Kidwell
(R.) Jack Kidwell, Michael
Hurdzan
GROVER CLEVELAND MUNI
Buffalo, New York
(R.) Walter J. Travis
GROVER KEATON MUNI
Dallas, Texas
Dave Bennett
GRUNOW ESTATE GC
Lake Geneva, Wisconsin
Alfred F. Hackbarth
GUADALAJARA CC
Guadalajara, Mexico
John Bredemus
(R.) Lawrence Hughes
GUAM CC
Santa Rita, Guam
Mark Rathert
GUAM FIRST GREEN GC
Pulantat, Guam
Robin Nelson, Rodney Wright
GUAM INTERNATIONAL CC
Dededo, Guam
Ronald Fream
GUARAPIRANGA G&CC
São Paulo, Brazil
Gastão Almeida Silva
GUARUJA GC
Brazil
Nuno Duarte Sottomayer
GUATAPARO GC
Valencia, Venezuela
Joe Lee, Rocky Roquemore
GUGGENHEIM ESTATE GC "TRIL-
LORA"
Port Washington, New York
William Mackie
GUILFORD GC
British Columbia
Jack Reimer
GUILIN-LIJIANG G&CC
Guilin, China
Ronald Fream
GULF HARBORS GC
New Port Richey, Florida
Don Rawley
GULF HILLS GC
Ocean Springs, Mississippi
Jack Daray
(R.) Tom Clark
GULFPORT NAVAL AIR STATION GC
Gulfport, Mississippi
Earl Stone
GULF SHORES GC
Gulf Shores, Alabama
Earl Stone
(R.) Gary Roger Baird

GULF STATE PARK GC
Gulf Shores, Alabama
Earl Stone
GULFSTREAM GC
Delray Beach, Florida
Donald Ross
(R.) Dick Wilson
(R.3) Mark Mahannah
GULLANE GC (CSE NO. 1)
East Lothian, Scotland
Willie Park
(R.) Willie Park, Jr.
GULLANE GC (CSE NO. 2)
East Lothian, Scotland
Willie Park, Jr.
GULLANE GC (CSE NO. 3)
East Lothian, Scotland
Willie Park, Jr.
GULLBRINGA GC
Sweden
Douglas Brazier
GULL LAKE CC
Richland, Michigan
William F. Mitchell
GULL LAKE VIEW GC (EAST CSE)
Augusta, Michigan
Charles Darl Scott
GULL LAKE VIEW GC (WEST CSE)
Augusta, Michigan
Darl Scott, Charles Darl Scott
(R.) Charles Darl Scott
GULMARG GC
Kashmir, India
John Harris, Peter Thomson
GULPH MILLS GC
King of Prussia, Pennsylvania
Donald Ross
(R.) William S. Flynn
(R.) Perry Maxwell
(R.) Wayne Stiles
(R.) J. B. McGovern
(R.7) William Gordon, David
Gordon
(R.4) Robert Trent Jones
GUNPOWDER CC
Maryland
Robert Milligan
GUS WORTHAM MUNI
Houston, Texas
Willie Maguire
(R.4) John Bredemus
(R.) Ralph Plummer
GUTHRIE CC
Guthrie, Oklahoma
Alex Findlay
GUT NEUHOF GC
Frankfurt, Germany
Gerold Hauser, *Günther Hauser*
GUT STEINBERG GC
Germany
Bernhard von Limburger
GUYAN G&CC
Huntington, West Virginia
Herbert Strong
(R.3) X. G. Hassenplug
(R.) Brian Silva, Geoffrey S.
Cornish
GWEEDORE GC
Gweedore, Ireland
(R.) Eddie Hackett
GYPSY HILL GC
Staunton, Virginia
(A.9) Gene Hamm

HAAGSCHE GC [NLE]
Netherlands
Tom Dunn
(A.9) J. F. Abercromby
HAAGSCHE G&CC
Netherlands
H. S. Colt, C. H. Alison, J. S. F.
Morrison
(R.) Sir Guy Campbell
[THE] HABITAT GC
Melbourne, Florida
Chuck Ankrom
HACIENDA CC
La Habra, California
Max Behr
(R.) William P. Bell
(R.) George Von Elm
(R.2) Ted Robinson
(R.) Robert Trent Jones
(R.) Peter Thomson, Michael
Wolveridge, Ronald Fream
HACIENDA HILLS G&CC
Lady Lake, Florida
Lloyd Clifton, *Kenneth Ezell,*
George Clifton
HACIENDA HOTEL PAR 3 GC [NLE]
Bakersfield, California
Bob Baldock
HACIENDA HOTEL PAR 3 GC [NLE]
Las Vegas, Nevada
Bob Baldock
HACIENDA SAN GASPAR GC
Cuernavaca, Mexico
Joseph S. Finger
HACKBERRY CREEK CC
Irving, Texas
Joseph S. Finger, Ken Dye
HACKENSACK CC [NLE]
Hackensack, New Jersey
Tom Bendelow
HACKENSACK GC
Oradell, New Jersey
Seth Raynor, Charles Banks
(R.) William Gordon, David
Gordon
HADLEY WOOD GC
Hertfordshire, England
Alister Mackenzie
HAGERSTOWN MUNI
Hagerstown, Maryland
Frank Murray, Russell Roberts
HAGGIN OAKS GC (NORTH CSE)
Sacramento, California
Michael J. McDonagh
HAGGIN OAKS MUNI (SOUTH CSE)
Sacramento, California
Alister Mackenzie
HAGGS CASTLE GC
Scotland
(R.) Peter Alliss, David
Thomas
HAGLEY GC
Russley, New Zealand
J. A. Clements
(R.) *F. W. Hobbs*
HAIG POINT GC
Daufuskie Island, South
Carolina
Rees Jones
(A.3rd 9) Rees Jones
HAINAULT FOREST GC (CSE NO. 1)
Essex, England
J. H. Taylor(A.9) F. G. Hawtree,
J. H. Taylor

HAINAULT FOREST GC (CSE NO. 2)
Essex, England
John R. Stutt
HAKONE CC
Kanagawa, Japan
Rokuro Akaboshi, *Shiro
Akaboshi*
HAKUHO CC
Japan
Sho Okubo
HAKUSAN VILLAGE GC
Mei, Japan
Shoichi Suzuki
HALEAKALA RANCH GC [NLE]
Maui, Hawaii
Charles Dole
HALF MOON BAY G LINKS
Half Moon Bay, California
Frank Duane, Arnold Palmer
(R.) Robert Muir Graves
HALF MOON-ROSE HALL GC
Montego Bay, Jamaica
Robert Trent Jones
HALF SINKE GC
Richmond, Virginia
NKA [The] Crossings GC
HALIE PLANTATION GC
Gainesville, Florida
Joe Lee
HALIFAX BRADLEY HALL GC
Yorkshire, England
J. J. F. Pennink, D. M. A. Steel
HALIFAX G&CC (NEW ASHBURN
CSE)
Nova Scotia
Geoffrey S. Cornish, William G.
Robinson
HALIFAX G&CC (OLD ASHBURN
CSE)
Nova Scotia
Stanley Thompson
HALIFAX PLANTATION GC
Daytona Beach Shores, Florida
Bill Amick
HALLAMSHIRE GC
Sheffield, England
(R.) J. S. F. Morrison
HALLBROOK CC
Leawood, Kansas
Tom Fazio
HALLOUD MUNI
Virginia
(A.9) Russell Breeden
HALLOWES GC
Yorkshire, England
George Duncan
HALL'S HEAD RESORT GC
Mandurah, Australia
Peter Thomson, Michael
Wolveridge
HALMSTAD GC (NORTH CSE)
Halmstad, Sweden
Rafael Sundblom
HALMSTAD GC (SOUTH CSE)
Halmstad, Sweden
J. J. F. Pennink
HAMAMATSU SEASIDE GC
Japan
Tomiichi Fukuda
HAMBURGER GC
Lüneburg, Germany
Herbert E. Gaertner

HAMBURGER LAND UND GC
  Hamburg, Germany
  H. S. Colt, C. H. Alison, J. S. F.
  Morrison
HAMBURG-AHRENSBURG GC
  Hamburg, Germany
  Bernhard von Limburger
    (R.) Robert Trent Jones
HAMBURG-FALKENSTEIN GC
  Germany
    (R.) Bernhard von Limburger
HAMBURG-WALDORFER GC
  Hoisbuettel, Germany
  Bernhard von Limburger
    (R.) Bernhard von Limburger
HAMILTON CC
  Hamilton, Montana
  Gregor MacMillan
    (A.9) Edward A. Hunnicut
HAMILTON CC
  Hamilton, Ohio
  Donald Ross
HAMILTON G&CC
  Ancaster, Ontario
  H. S. Colt
    (R.) William H. Diddel
    (A.3rd 9) Clinton E.
  Robinson
    (R.) Rees Jones
    (R.2) Tom Clark
    (R.) Thomas McBroom
HAMILTON G&CC (LADIES 9)
  Ancaster, Ontario
  H. S. Colt
HAMILTON GC
  Lanarkshire, England
  James Braid, John R. Stutt
HAMILTON GC
  St. Andrews, New Zealand
  F. G. Hood, Harry T. Gillies,
  Arthur D. S. Duncan
    (R.) C. H. Redhead
HAMILTON LAKES CC
  Chimney Rock, North Carolina
  Wayne Stiles, John Van Kleek
HAMILTON MUNI
  Evansville, Indiana
  William H. Diddel
HAMILTON PROPER G CSE
  Indianapolis, Indiana
  Arthur Hills
HAMLET OF DELRAY BEACH GC
  Delray Beach, Florida
  Joe Lee, Rocky Roquemore
HAMMAMATSU CC
  Japan
  Peter Thomson, Michael
  Wolveridge
HAMMAMET GC
  Hammamet, Tunisia
  Ronald Fream
HAMMAMET II GC
  Hammamet, Tunisia
  Ronald Fream
HAM MANOR GC
  Sussex, England
  H. S. Colt, C. H. Alison, J. S. F.
  Morrison
HAMMERSLEY HILL GC
  Pawling, New York
  William F. Mitchell
HAMMOCK CC
  Larchmont, New York
  Nicholas Demane

HAMMOCK DUNES GC
  Palm Coast, Florida
  Tom Fazio
HAMMOND CC
  Hammond, Indiana
  Tom Bendelow
HAMPDEN CC
  Hampden, Maine
  Ham Robbins
    (R.) Wally Pearson
HAMPDEN CC
  Hampden, Massachusetts
  Al Zikorus
HAMPSHIRE CC
  Dowagiac, Michigan
  Edward Lawrence Packard
HAMPSHIRE CC
  Mamaroneck, New York
  Devereux Emmet
    (R.) Edmund B. Ault
    (R.4) Frank Duane
HAMPSTEAD CC
  Hampstead, England
  Tom Dunn
[THE] HAMPTON C
  St. Simons Island, Georgia
  Joe Lee
HAMPTON GC
  Hampton, Virginia
  Donald Ross
    (R.) Edmund B. Ault
HAMPTON COVE GC (HIGHLAND
  CSE)
  Huntsville, Alabama
  Robert Trent Jones
HAMPTON COVE GC (LOWLAND
  CSE)
  Huntsville, Alabama
  Robert Trent Jones
HAMPTON COVE GC (SHORT CSE)
  Huntsville, Alabama
  Robert Trent Jones
HAMPTON MUNI
  Rochester, Michigan
  William Newcomb
HAMPTON HILLS GC
  Riverhead, New York
  Frank Duane
HAMPTON PARK GC
  Hampton, Virginia
  Michael Hurdzan
HAMPTON RHODES GC
  Hampton, Virginia
  NKA Hampton GC
[THE] HAMPTONS G&CC
  Calgary, Alberta
  Bill Newis
HAMPTON VALLEY GC
  Allison Park, Pennsylvania
  X. G. Hassenplug
HANANOKI GC
  Gifu, Japan
  Taizo Kawada
HANANOMORI GC
  Miyagi Prefecture, Japan
  Jack Nicklaus
HANA RANCH G PARK
  Hawaii
    (R.3) Robin Nelson, Rodney
  Wright
HANAYASHIKI GC (HIRONO CSE)
  Hyogo, Japan
  R. Shimaumura

HANAYASHIKI GC (YOKAWA CSE)
  Hyogo, Japan
  O. Ueda
HANBURY MANOR GC
  London, England
  Harry Vardon
    (R.9 A.9) Jack Nicklaus, Jr.
HANCOCK MUNI
  Hancock, New York
  Robert Trent Jones
HANDSWORTH GC
  Handsworth, England
    (R.) H. S. Colt (1912)
    (R.) H. S. Colt (1919)
HANGING ROCK GC
  Banner Elk, North Carolina
  Gardner Gidley
HANGING ROCK GC
  Salem, Virginia
  Russell Breeden
HANGING TREE GC
  Westfield, Indiana
  Gary Kern, Ron Kern
HANGMAN VALLEY MUNI
  Spokane, Washington
  Bob Baldock, Robert L. Baldock
HANINGE GC
  Sweden
  Jan Sederholm
HANKLEY COMMON GC
  Surrey, England
    (R.9 A.9) James Braid
    (R.) H.S. Colt
HANNA G&CC
  Hanna, Alberta
    (R.9) Les Furber, Jim Eremko
HANNASTOWN CC
  Greensburg, Pennsylvania
  Emil Loeffler, John McGlynn
HANNIBAL CC [NLE]
  Hannibal, Missouri
  Tom Bendelow
HANNO GC
  Saitama, Japan
  Ichisuke Izumi
HANNO GREEN CC
  Saitama, Japan
  Fujita Kogyo
HANOVER CC
  Ashland, Virginia
  Jim Reynolds
HANOVER CC
  Dartmouth College, Hanover,
  New Hampshire
    (A.9) Ralph Barton (NLE)
    (R.) Orrin Smith
    (R.) Geoffrey S. Cornish,
  William G. Robinson
HANOVER CC
  Abbottstown, Pennsylvania
    (R.) William Gordon
    (R.) Ferdinand Garbin
HANOVER GC
  Garbsen, Germany
  Herbert E. Gaertner
    (R.) Karl Hoffmann, Bernhard
  von Limburger
HAPPY ACRES CC
  Webster, New York
  James Gilmore Harrison,
  Ferdinand Garbin

HAPPY HOLLOW C
  Omaha, Nebraska
  William B. Langford, Theodore
  J. Moreau
    (R.) James L. Holmes
    (R.) William H. Diddel
    (R.) David Gill
    (R.) Bob Lohmann
HAPPY HUNTING C
  Lenexa, Kansas
  Bob Dunning
HAPPY TRAILS G CSE
  Surprise, Arizona
  Ken Kavanaugh
    (A.9) Greg Nash
HAPPY VALLEY CC
  Lynn, Massachusetts
  NKA Larry Gannon Memorial
  GC
HAPPY VALLEY CC
  Wilson, North Carolina
  Willard Byrd
HAPPY VALLEY CC
  Sapporo, Japan
  Ronald Fream
HAPUNA BEACH GC
  Kamuela, Hawaii
  Ed Seay, Arnold Palmer
HARBOR C
  Greensboro, Georgia
  Jay Morrish, Tom Weiskopf
HARBOR CITY MUNI
  Eau Gallie, Florida
  R. Albert Anderson
    (R.) Bill Amick
HARBOR HILLS G&CC
  Lady Lake, Florida
  Lloyd Clifton, Kenneth Ezell,
  George Clifton
HARBOR HILLS CC
  Port Jefferson, New York
  Alfred H. Tull
HARBORNE CHURCH FARM GC
  Birmingham, England
  F. G. Hawtree, J. H. Taylor
HARBORNE GC
  England
    (R.) H. S. Colt
HARBOR PARK GC
  Wilmington, California
  William H. Johnson
HARBOR POINT GC
  Harbor Springs, Michigan
  David Foulis
    (R.15 A.3) David Gill
HARBOUR POINTE GC
  New Bern, North Carolina
  Rees Jones
    (A.9) D. J. DeVictor
HARBOUR POINTE GC
  Everett, Washington
  Arthur Hills
HARBOUR RIDGE Y&CC (GOLDEN
  MARSH CSE)
  Stuart, Florida
  Joe Lee
HARBOUR RIDGE Y&CC (RIVER
  RIDGE CSE)
  Stuart, Florida
  P. B. Dye, Pete Dye

HARBOUR TOWN G LINKS
Hilton Head Island, South
Carolina
Pete Dye, Jack Nicklaus
(R.) Pete Dye
HARBOUR TREES GC
Noblesville, Indiana
Pete Dye
(R.) Bob Lohmann
HARDELOT GC (PINES CSE)
France
John Duncan Dunn
(R.) Tom Simpson, P. M. Ross
HARDELOT GC (DUNES CSE)
Hardelot, France
Paul Rolin (1991)
HARDER HALL HOTEL GC
Sebring, Florida
Dick Wilson
(R.) Gordon G. Lewis
HARDING PARK GC
San Francisco, California
Willie Watson
(R.) Jack Fleming
(A.3rd 9) Jack Fleming
HARD LABOR CREEK STATE PARK
GC
Madison, Georgia
James B. McCloud
HARDSCRABBLE CC
Fort Smith, Arkansas
Herman Hackbarth
(R.) James L. Holmes
(R.) Marvin Ferguson
HAREWOOD GC [NLE]
New Zealand
A. R. Blank
HAREWOOD GC
Christchurch, New Zealand
John Harris, Peter Thomson
HARKER HEIGHTS MUNI
Harker Heights, Texas
Dave Bennett, Leon Howard
HARKERS HOLLOW GC
Phillipsburg, New Jersey
Robert White
HARLEM GC [NLE]
Forest Park, Illinois
Tom Bendelow
HARLEM HILLS CC
Rockford, Illinois
Harry Collis
HARLINGEN CC
Harlingen, Texas
Dave Bennett, Leon Howard
(R.) Dick Nugent
HARLINGEN MUNI [NLE]
Harlingen, Texas
John Bredemus
HARMON CC
Lebanon, New York
A. W. Tillinghast
HARMONY FARM CC [NLE]
Jane Lew, West Virginia
Arthur Jack Snyder
HARMONY LANDING CC
Goshen, Kentucky
Hal Purdy
HARNEY'S GC
Falmouth, Massachusetts
Paul Harney
HAROLD LLOYD ESTATE GC [NLE]
Beverly Hills, California
Alister Mackenzie

HARPENDEN GC
Hertsfordshire, England
F. G. Hawtree, J. H. Taylor
HARRINGTON G&CC
Harrington, Washington
Robert Dean Putman
HARRISON GC
Harrison Hotel, British
Columbia
Norman H. Woods
HARRISON HEIGHTS GC [NLE]
Omaha, Nebraska
Henry C. Glissman, Harold
Glissman
HARRISON HILLS CC
Attica, Indiana
William B. Langford, Theodore
J. Moreau
HARRISON LAKE GC
Columbus, Indiana
Bob Simmons
(R.) Gary Kern, Ron Kern
HARRISON WILLIAMS PRIVATE CSE
Bayville, New York
Devereux Emmet, Alfred H. Tull
HARROGATE GC
Yorkshire, England
Sandy Herd, George Duncan
(R.) George Duncan
(R.) Alister Mackenzie
HARROW SCHOOL GC
Middlesex, England
J. J. F. Pennink, D. M. A. Steel
HARRY BROWNSON CC
Shelton, Connecticut
Edward Ryder, Val Carlson
HARRY GREENS GC
Prospect, Connecticut
Al Zikorus
HARRY PRITCHETT GC
Tuscaloosa, Alabama
Harold Williams, Thomas H.
Nicol
HARSENS ISLAND GC
Harsens Island, Michigan
Wilfrid Reid, William Connellan
HARSTAD GC
Norway
Jan Sederholm
HARTEPOOL GC
Durham, England
Willie Park, Jr.
HARTFORD CC
Hartford, Wisconsin
(R.9 A.9) Ken Killian, Dick
Nugent
HARTFORD ESTATE GC
Charleston, South Carolina
Wayne Stiles
HARTFORD GC [NLE]
West Hartford, Connecticut
Donald Ross
(R.9 A.9) Devereux Emmet
(R.14 A.4) Donald Ross
(R.) William Gordon, David
Gordon
(R.2) Robert Trent Jones
(R.2) Geoffrey S. Cornish,
William G. Robinson
(R.) Al Zikorus
HARTLAND GC
Bowling Green, Kentucky
Kevin Tucker

HARTLAND POINT GC
Hartland, Nova Scotia
(R. A.3) William G. Robinson
HART RANCH GC
Pennington, South Dakota
Pat Wyss
HARTSBOURNE CC
Hertfordshire, England
F. G. Hawtree, Fred W. Hawtree
HARTWELLVILLE CC [NLE]
Hartwellville, Vermont
William S. Flynn
HARUNA CC
Japan
Mitsuo Komatsubara
HARVE DES ISLES GC
Montreal, Quebec
Howard Watson
HARVE ELKS CC
Harve, Montana
(R.) William H. Diddel
HARVEST HILLS GC
Calgary, Alberta
Dave Bennett
HARZ GC
Bad Harzburg, Germany
Bernhard von Limburger
HÄSSLEHOLMS GC
Skyrup, Sweden
Jan Sederholm
HASTINGS AND ST. LEONARDS GC
[NLE]
Sussex, England
Tom Dunn
(A.9) H. S. Colt
HASTINGS GC
Bridge Pa, New Zealand
W. A. Kiely, H. Stewart
(R.) C. H. Redhead
(R.) John Harris
HASTINGS CC
Hastings, Michigan
Jack Daray
(R.) Bruce Matthews
(R.3) Jerry Matthews
HASTINGS CC
Hastings, Minnesota
Paul Coates
(R.) Don Herfort
(R.3) Craig Schreiner
HASTINGS GC [NLE]
Sussex, England
Tom Dunn
HASTINGS GC
Sussex, England
J. J. F. Pennink
(R.) Peter Thomson, Michael
Wolveridge
HATCHFORD BROOK MUNI
Birmingham, England
Fred W. Hawtree
HATCH POINT CC
Victoria, British Columbia
William G. Robinson
HATHERLY CC
Scituate, Massachusetts
(R.2 A.3) Samuel Mitchell
HAT ISLAND G&CC
Washington
William Teufel
HATTIESBURG CC
Hattiesburg, Mississippi
Press Maxwell

HAULOVER BEACH GC
Miami, Florida
Mark Mahannah
HAUS OEFTE GC
Essen, Germany
Karl Hoffmann, Bernhard von
Limburger
(R.) Karl F. Grohs, Rainer
Preissmann
HAVANA CC
Havana, Florida
Bill Amick
HAVANA BILTMORE GC [NLE]
Havana, Cuba
Donald Ross
(R.) Mark Mahannah
HAVELTE GC
Holland
D. M. A. Steel
HAVEN CC
Green Valley, Arizona
Arthur Jack Snyder
HAVENHURST GC
New Haven, Indiana
Robert Beard
HAVERHILL G&CC
Haverhill, Massachusetts
Wayne Stiles, John Van Kleek
HAWAII CC
Honolulu, Oahu, Hawaii
Red Uldrick
HAWAII KAI G CSE (CHAMPIONSHIP
CSE)
Honolulu, Oahu, Hawaii
William F. Bell
HAWAII KAI G CSE (EXECUTIVE
CSE)
Honolulu, Oahu, Hawaii
Robert Trent Jones
(R.) William F. Bell
HAWAII PRINCE GC
Ewa Beach, Oahu, Hawaii
Arnold Palmer, Ed Seay
HAWK CREEK GC
Neskowin, Oregon
Harold Schlicting
HAWKHURST G&CC
Kent, England
J. J. F. Pennink
HAWK'S NEST CC
Vero Beach, Florida
Jim Fazio
HAWK'S NEST GC
Wooster, Ohio
Stephen Burns
HAWK VALLEY GC
Bowmansville, Pennsylvania
William Gordon, David Gordon
HAWTHORNE CC
Maryland
Edmund B. Ault, Al Jamison
HAWTHORNE HILLS CC
Indianapolis, Indiana
William H. Diddel
HAWTHORNE HILLS CC
Lima, Ohio
Harold Paddock
HAWTHORNE HILLS GC
Mequon, Wisconsin
(R.) Bob Lohmann
HAWTHORNE RIDGE GC
Aledo, Illinois
William James Spear

HAWTHORNE VALLEY CC
Cleveland, Ohio
Donald Ross
HAWTHORNE VALLEY G&CC
Mississauga, Ontario
Clinton E. Robinson
HAYAKITA CC
Sapporo, Japan
Larry Nelson
HAYANA INTERNATIONAL GC
Japan
Willard Wilkinson
HAY CREEK CENTENNIAL G CSE
Wright, Wyoming
Pat Wyss
HAYDEN LAKE CC
Hayden Lake, Idaho
(R.1) John Steidel
HAYLING GC
England
(R.) Tom Simpson
HAYSTACK CC
Wilmington, Vermont
Desmond Muirhead
HAYSTON GC
Glasgow, Scotland
James Braid, John R. Stutt
HAYWARD GC
Hayward, California
Dick Fry
(R.) Robert Muir Graves
HAZELDEN CC
Brook, Indiana
Tom Bendelow
HAZEL GROVE GC
Cheshire, England
(R.) T. J. A. Macauley
HAZELHEAD MUNI (CSE NO. 1)
Aberdeen, Scotland
Alister Mackenzie
HAZELHEAD MUNI (CSE NO. 2)
Aberdeen, Scotland
Brian Huggett, Neil Coles
HAZELTINE NATIONAL GC
Chaska, Minnesota
Robert Trent Jones
(R.) Robert Trent Jones
(R.) Rees Jones
HEAD OF THE BAY CC
Plymouth, Massachusetts
Ray Richard
HEADINGLEY GC
Leeds, England
Willie Park
(R.) Alister Mackenzie
HEARTHSTONE CC
Houston, Texas
Jay Riviere
(A.9) Baxter Spann, Ken Dye,
Joseph S. Finger
HEART RIVER GC
Dickinson, North Dakota
Abe Espinosa
(R.9 A.9) Dick Phelps, Brad
Benz
HEARTWELL GC
Long Beach, California
William F. Bell
HEATHER FARMS GC
Walnut Creek, California
Bob Baldock
HEATHER GARDENS CC
Aurora, Colorado
Dick Phelps

HEATHER GLEN GC
Little River, South Carolina
Willard Byrd
(A.3rd 9) Clyde Johnston
HEATHER HIGHLANDS GC
Holly, Michigan
Robert Bruce Harris
HEATHER HILL GC
Bradenton, Florida
R. Albert Anderson
HEATHER DOWNS CC (NORTH CSE)
Toledo, Ohio
(R.) Arthur Hills
HEATHER DOWNS CC (SOUTH CSE)
Toledo, Ohio
(R.) Arthur Hills
HEATHER HILLS CC
Indianapolis, Indiana
Pete Dye
HEATHERHURST G CSE
Fairfield Glade, Tennessee
Gary Roger Baird
HEATHER RIDGE CC
Aurora, Colorado
Dick Phelps
[THE] HEATHERS GC
Bloomfield Hills, Michigan
William Newcomb
HEATHERWOOD GC
Birmingham, Alabama
Arthur Davis
HEATHERWOODE GC
Springboro, Ohio
Denis Griffiths
HEATH GC
Ireland
(R.) Eddie Hackett
HEATHROW CC
Heathrow, Florida
Ron Garl
HEATON PARK GC
Lancashire, England
J. H. Taylor
HECHINGEN-HOHENZOLLERN GC
Hechingen, Germany
Götz Mecklenburg
HECLA GC
Manitoba
Jack Thompson
HEDELAND GC
Denmark
Jan Sederholm
HEERLE'S HOF GC
Meerle, Belgium
D. M. A. Steel
HEIDELBERG CC
Heidelberg, Pennsylvania
John H. Guenther, Jr.
HEIDELBERG G & SPORTS C
Heidelberg, Germany
Bernhard von Limburger
(R.) Donald Harradine
HEIGHT PARK CC
Davis, Oregon
Ernest Schneiter
HEILBRONN HOHENLOHE GC
Heilbronn, Germany
(A.9) Karl F. Grohs, Rainer
Preissmann
HEJAZ SHRINE RECREATION C
Greenville, South Carolina
Russell Breeden

HELENA CC
Helena, Arkansas
Herman Hackbarth
HELENSBURGH GC
Scotland
Old Tom Morris
HELFRICH MUNI
Evansville, Indiana
Tom Bendelow
HELIOPOLIS SPORTING C
Cairo, Egypt
J. H. Taylor
HELL'S POINT GC
Virginia Beach, Virginia
Rees Jones
HELSIGNØR GC
Helsignør, Denmark
Anders Amilon
(R.) Jorn Larsen
HELSINKI GC
Sweden
Ture Bruce
HEMET WEST GC
Hemet, California
Harry Rainville
HEMLOCK GC
Walnut Cove, North Carolina
D. L. Robertson
HEMLOCK SPRINGS GC
Harpersfield, Ohio
Ben W. Zink
HEMPSTEAD G&CC
Hempstead, New York
Peter W. Lees
(R.9 A.9) A. W. Tillinghast
HEMPSTEAD CC
Hempstead, Texas
Leon Howard
HEMPSTEAD GC AT LIDO
Long Beach, New York
Robert Trent Jones
(R.) Stephen Kay
HENBURY CC
England
(R.) F. G. Hawtree
HENDAYE GC
Hendaye, France
John Duncan Dunn
HENDERSON CC
Henderson, North Carolina
(A.9) Gene Hamm
HENDERSON G&CC
Henderson, Kentucky
William B. Langford, Theodore
J. Moreau
HENDERSON LAKE GC
Lethbridge, Alberta
Norman H. Woods
HENDERSONVILLE CC
Hendersonville, North Carolina
Donald Ross
(R.) Tom Fazio
HENDON GC [NLE]
London, England
Willie Park, Willie Park, Jr.
(R.) Harry Vardon
HENDON GC
Middlesex, England
H. S. Colt
HENDRICKS COUNTY GC
Danville, Indiana
William H. Diddel

HENDRICKS FIELD GC
Belleville, New Jersey
Tom Bendelow
(A.9) Willie Norton
HENDRY ISLES GC
Moore Haven, Florida
B. Dudley Gray
HENLEY GC
England
James Braid
(R.) Robert Muir Graves
HENRY F. DU PONT PRIVATE CSE
[NLE]
Wilmington, Delaware
(R.) Devereux Emmet, Alfred
H. Tull
HENRY HOMBERG G CSE
Port Arthur, Texas
Leon Howard
HENRY STAMBAUGH MUNI
Youngstown, Ohio
Herbert Lagerblade (9 1923)
HENSON CREEK GC
Fort Washington, Maryland
Edmund B. Ault
HERCULES CC
Wilmington, Delaware
Alfred H. Tull
(A.3rd 9) Alfred H. Tull
(A.4) Geoffrey S. Cornish,
Brian Silva
HERCULES POWDER C [NLE]
Wilmington, Delaware
(R.) William S. Flynn
HERETAUNGA GC
Wellington, New Zealand
Alister Mackenzie
HERITAGE GC
Pawley's Island, South Carolina
Dan Maples
HERITAGE HARBOUR GC
Annapolis, Maryland
Edmund B. Ault
HERITAGE HILLS C (EAST HILL CSE)
Somers, New York
Geoffrey S. Cornish, William G.
Robinson
HERITAGE HILLS C (WEST HILL
CSE)
Somers, New York
Geoffrey S. Cornish, William G.
Robinson
HERITAGE HILLS CC
La Jolla, California
Joe Lee, Rocky Roquemore
HERITAGE HILLS GC
Lakeville, Massachusetts
Geoffrey S. Cornish, William G.
Robinson
HERITAGE HILLS GC
McCook, Nebraska
Dick Phelps, Brad Benz
HERITAGE HILLS GC
Claremore, Oklahoma
Don Sechrest
HERITAGE HILLS G RESORT
York, Pennsylvania
Russell Roberts
HERITAGE PARK GC
Primghar, Iowa
Joel Goldstrand
HERITAGE PARK G CSE
Olathe, Kansas
Don Sechrest

HERITAGE POINTE GC
Calgary, Alberta
Ron Garl

HERITAGE RIDGE GC
Stuart, Florida
Ted McAnlis
(R.9 A.9) Chuck Ankrom

HERITAGE VILLAGE CC
Southbury, Connecticut
Al Zikorus
(A.9) *Theodore Manning*

HERMANN PARK GC
Houston, Texas
John Bredemus
(R.9) Ralph Plummer

HERMANUS GC
South Africa
Archie Tosh
(R.) *Ken B. Elkin*
(R.) Robert Grimsdell

HERMITAGE CC
Richmond, Virginia
NKA Belmont Park GC

HERMITAGE CC
Manakin-Sabot, Virginia
Edmund B. Ault
(A.3rd 9) Arthur Hills

HERMITAGE GC
Ireland
(R.) Eddie Hackett

HERMITAGE G CSE
Old Hickory, Tennessee
Gary Roger Baird

HERMITAGE WOODS GC
Nashville, Tennessee
James King

HERMON MEADOW GC
Hermon, Maine
Winn Pike

HERNDON CENTENNIAL MUNI
Herndon, Virginia
Edmund B. Ault

HERON LAKES GC (RED CSE)
Portland, Oregon
Robert Trent Jones
(A.9) Robert Trent Jones, Jr.

HERON LAKES GC (WHITE CSE)
Portland, Oregon
Robert Trent Jones

HERON POINT GC
Myrtle Beach, South Carolina
(R.9 A.9) Willard Byrd

HERON POINT GOLF LINKS
Ancaster, Ontario
Thomas McBroom

HERRENALB-BERNBACH GC
Germany
Bernhard von Limburger

HERRERIA GC
El Escorial, Spain
A. Lucena

HERRING RUN CC
Taunton, Massachusetts
Skip Wogan

HERRLJUNGA GC
Herrljunga, Sweden
Jan Sederholm

HERSHEY CC (EAST CSE)
Hershey, Pennsylvania
George Fazio

HERSHEY CC (WEST CSE)
Hershey, Pennsylvania
Maurice McCarthy

HERSHEY POCONO GC
White Haven, Pennsylvania
NKA Mountain Laurel GC

HERSHEY'S MILL GC
Malvern, Pennsylvania
David Gordon

HESPERIA G&CC
Hesperia, California
William F. Bell

HESSIAN HILLS CC [NLE]
Croton-on-Hudson, New York
C. S. Butchart

HESSLE GC
Hessle, England
Peter Alliss, David Thomas

HESSTON MUNI
Hesston, Kansas
Frank Hummel

HEXHAM GC
Hexham, England
(R.) C. K. Cotton, J. J. F.
Pennink

HEYSHAM GC
Lancashire, England
Sandy Herd, F. G. Hawtree

HEYTHROP COLLEGE GC
England
Tom Simpson

HIAWATHA CC
Syracuse, New York
(R.) William F. Mitchell

HIAWATHA GC
Mount Vernon, Ohio
Jack Kidwell

HI CEDARS GC
Orting, Washington
Roy L. Goss, *Glen Proctor*

HICKAM AFB GC
Oahu, Hawaii
Bob Baldock
(R.) Robin Nelson, Rodney
Wright

HICKLETON GC
Yorkshire, England
Brian Huggett, Neil Coles, *Roger
Dyer*

HICKMAN GC
Wayne, New Jersey
Hal Purdy

HICKORY FLAT GC
West Lafayette, Ohio
Jack Kidwell

HICKORY GROVE CC
Oelwein, Iowa
Tom Bendelow

HICKORY GROVE CC
Fennimore, Wisconsin
William James Spear

HICKORY HEIGHTS GC
Pittsburgh, Pennsylvania
Michael Hurdzan

HICKORY HILL GC
Lawrence, Massachusetts
Manny Francis

HICKORY HILL GC
Wixom, Michigan
George Catto

HICKORY HILLS CC
Palos Park, Illinois
James Foulis
(A.9) William B. Langford
(R.) C. D. Wagstaff

HICKORY HILLS CC
Liberty, Kentucky
Buck Blankenship

HICKORY HILLS CC
Grand Rapids, Michigan
Mark DeVries

HICKORY HILLS CC
Gautier, Mississippi
Earl Stone

HICKORY HILLS CC
Springfield, Missouri
(R.) Bob Dunning
(R.) Edmund B. Ault

HICKORY HILLS CC
Georgesville, Ohio
Jack Kidwell, Michael Hurdzan

HICKORY HILLS GC
Jackson, Michigan
(R.9 A.9) William Newcomb

HICKORY KNOB STATE PARK GC
McCormack, South Carolina
Tom Jackson

HICKORY MEADOWS GC
Whitakers, North Carolina
R. Sapp

HICKORY POINT GC
Decatur, Illinois
Edward Lawrence Packard

HICKORY RIDGE CC
Amherst, Massachusetts
Geoffrey S. Cornish, William G.
Robinson

HIDA TAKAYAMA CC
Japan
Shigeru Uchida

HIDDEN CREEK GC
Reston, Virginia
Edmund B. Ault

HIDDEN GREENS GC
Hastings, Minnesota
Joel Goldstrand

HIDDEN HILLS CC
Jacksonville, Florida
David Gordon
(R.) Arnold Palmer, Ed Seay

HIDDEN HILLS CC
Stone Mountain, Georgia
Joe Lee, Rocky Roquemore

HIDDEN HILLS ON LAKE TRAVIS GC
Spicewood, Texas
NKA Barton Creek C (Lakeside
Cse)

HIDDEN LAKE GC
Osage Beach, Missouri
Robert von Hagge

HIDDEN LAKES CC
Derby, Kansas
Floyd Farley

HIDDEN VALLEY CC
Reno, Nevada
William F. Bell

HIDDEN VALLEY CC
Willow Springs, North Carolina
Henry Dupree

HIDDEN VALLEY CC
Pittsburgh, Pennsylvania
Edmund B. Ault
(R.9 A.9) James Gilmore
Harrison, Ferdinand Garbin
(R.) Joe Lee

HIDDEN VALLEY CC
Reading, Pennsylvania
James Gilmore Harrison

HIDDEN VALLEY CC
Gaston, South Carolina
Russell Breeden

HIDDEN VALLEY CC [NLE]
Salt Lake City, Utah
William P. Bell

HIDDEN VALLEY CC
Draper, Utah
William F. Bell
(A.9) William H. Neff,
Howard Neff

HIDDEN VALLEY CC
Salem, Virginia
Dick Wilson

HIDDEN VALLEY GC
Boca Raton, Florida
Pat Pattison

HIDDEN VALLEY GC
Miami, Florida
Bob Cupp

HIDDEN VALLEY GC
Lawrenceburg, Indiana
Jack Kidwell, Michael Hurdzan

HIDDEN VALLEY GC
Gaylord, Michigan
William H. Diddel

HIDDEN VALLEY GC
Eureka, Missouri
Tim Boyd

HIDDEN VALLEY GC
New Philadelphia, Ohio
James Gilmore Harrison,
Ferdinand Garbin

HIDDEN VALLEY GC
Cottage Grove, Oregon
Ray Vincent

HIDDEN VALLEY GC
Pottstown, Pennsylvania
James Gilmore Harrison,
Ferdinand Garbin

HIDDEN VALLEY GC
Edmonton, Alberta
Ron Garl

HIDDEN VALLEY GC
Ontario
Clinton E. Robinson

HIDDEN VALLEY G LINKS
Clever, Missouri
Mario Alfonzo

HIDDEN VALLEY LAKE G&CC
Middletown, California
William F. Bell

HIDEAWAY GC
Fort Myers, Florida
Ron Garl

HIDEOUT GC
Lake Ariel, Pennsylvania
Bob Baldock

HIGASHI IBARAGI CC
Ibaragi, Japan
Arthur Hills

HIGASHI MATSUYAMA GC
Saitama, Japan
Kinya Fujita

HIGASHI UTSUNOMIYA CC
Japan
Mitsuaki Kobayashi

HIGBY HILLS CC
Utica, New York
Geoffrey S. Cornish, William G.
Robinson

HIGH ELMS GC
Kent, England
Fred W. Hawtree, Martin Hawtree
HIGHFIELD CC
Middlebury, Connecticut
(R.9 A.9) Orrin Smith
(R.) Al Zikorus
HIGHGATE GC
England
(R.) C. S. Butchart
HIGH HAMPTON INN GC
Cashiers, North Carolina
J. Victor East
(R.) George W. Cobb
(R.) George W. Cobb, John LaFoy
HIGHLAND CC
LaGrange, Georgia
Donald Ross
(A.9) Joseph S. Finger
HIGHLAND CC [NLE]
Fort Thomas, Kentucky
Tom Bendelow
HIGHLAND CC
Fort Thomas, Kentucky
William H. Diddel
(R.) Willard Byrd
(R.) Edmund B. Ault
(A.9) Arthur Hills
HIGHLAND CC
Omaha, Nebraska
William B. Langford, Theodore J. Moreau
(R.) David Gill
HIGHLAND CC
Fayetteville, North Carolina
Donald Ross
HIGHLAND CC
Pittsburgh, Pennsylvania
Emil Loeffler, John McGlynn
(R.) James Gilmore Harrison
(R.) Ferdinand Garbin
(R. A.3) Ferdinand Garbin
HIGHLAND G&CC [NLE]
Indianapolis, Indiana
Tom Bendelow
HIGHLAND G&CC
Indianapolis, Indiana
Willie Park, Jr. (routing);
William H. Diddel
(R.) Bob Lohmann
HIGHLAND GC
Tacoma, Washington
Ted Robinson
HIGHLAND GC
London, Ontario
Stanley Thompson
HIGHLAND MUNI
Pocatello, Idaho
Perley A. Hill
HIGHLAND BURNE GC [NLE]
Michigan
Warner Bowen
HIGHLAND CREEK CC
Charlotte, North Carolina
Lloyd Clifton, Kenneth Ezell, George Clifton
HIGHLAND GREENS GC
Prospect, Connecticut
Al Zikorus
HIGHLAND HILLS GC
Roann, Indiana
Bud Camp

HIGHLAND HILLS GC
Dewitt, Michigan
(A.9) Bruce Matthews, Jerry Matthews
HIGHLAND HILLS MUNI
Greeley, Colorado
(A.9) Frank Hummel
HIGHLAND LAKE GC
Richmond, Indiana
Bob Simmons
HIGHLAND LAKE ESTATES GC
Jackson, Mississippi
Ward Northrup
HIGHLAND LAKES GC
Palm Harbor, Florida
Lloyd Clifton
HIGHLAND LAKES GC
Kingsland, Texas
Dave Bennett, Leon Howard
(R.) Dave Bennett
HIGHLAND LINKS
Norfolk, Virginia
Luther O. "Luke" Morris
HIGHLAND LINKS COLONY
Holderness, New Hampshire
Joe Clark, Sr.
HIGHLAND MEADOWS CC
Sylvania, Ohio
Sandy Alves
(R.) Arthur Hills
HIGHLAND PARK CC
New York
(A.9) Geoffrey S. Cornish, William G. Robinson
HIGHLAND PARK GC
Birmingham, Alabama
NKA Charles Boswell G Cse
HIGHLAND PARK GC
Lake Wales, Florida
Wayne Stiles, John Van Kleek
HIGHLAND PARK GC
Highland Park, Illinois
(R.) C. H. Alison, H. S. Colt
(R.3) William B. Langford, Theodore J. Moreau
(R.5) Ken Killian, Dick Nugent
HIGHLAND PARK GC
Mason City, Iowa
David Gill
HIGHLAND PARK GC
St. Paul, Minnesota
(A.9) Gerry Pirkl, Donald G. Brauer, Emile Perret
HIGHLAND PARK GC (BLUE CSE)
Cleveland, Ohio
Sandy Alves
HIGHLAND PARK GC (RED CSE)
Cleveland, Ohio
Sandy Alves
HIGHLAND RIDGE CC
Sebring, Florida
Steve Smyers
HIGHLANDS CC
Highlands, North Carolina
Donald Ross
HIGHLANDS G&CC
Post Falls, Idaho
Jim Krause (1991)
[THE] HIGHLANDS CC
Grand Rapids, Michigan
Tom Bendelow
(R.9 A.9) Donald Ross

[THE] HIGHLANDS GC
Waikoloa Village, Hawaii
Arnold Palmer, Ed Seay
[THE] HIGHLANDS GC
Hutchinson, Kansas
Leo Johnson
HIGHLANDS GC
Edmonton, Alberta
William Brinkworth
HIGHLANDS G CSE
Bella Vista, Alabama
Tom Clark
HIGHLANDS FALLS CC
Highlands, North Carolina
Bill Amick
(R.5 A.13) Joe Lee, Rocky Roquemore
(R.) Tom Fazio
HIGHLAND SPRINGS CC
Ohio
Harold Paddock
HIGHLAND SPRINGS CC
Springfield, Missouri
Robert Trent Jones, Jr.
HIGHLAND SPRINGS GC
Rock Island, Illinois
William James Spear
HIGHLAND SPRINGS GC
Wellsburg, Pennsylvania
James Gilmore Harrison, Ferdinand Garbin
HIGHLAND WOODS GC
Hoffman Estates, Illinois
William James Spear
HIGH MEADOWS GC
Roaring Gap, North Carolina
George W. Cobb
(R.) John LaFoy
HIGH MOUNTAIN CC
Franklin Lakes, New Jersey
Alec Ternyei
HIGH POINT CC
Naples, Florida
David Wallace
HIGH POINT CC
Montague, New Jersey
Gerald C. Roby
HIGH POINTE GC
Williamsburg, Michigan
Tom Doak
HIGH POST GC
Wiltshire, England
F. G. Hawtree, J. H. Taylor
HIGH RIDGE CC
Stamford, Connecticut
(R.2) William F. Mitchell
HIGH RIDGE CC
Boynton Beach, Florida
Joe Lee
HIGH RIDGE GC
Norwalk, Connecticut
(R.) William F. Mitchell
HIGH VISTA CC
Arden, North Carolina
Tom Jackson
HIGHWOOD G&CC
High River, Alberta
(R.18 A.3rd 9) William G. Robinson
HIGHWOODS GC
Bexhill-on-Sea, England
F. G. Hawtree, J. H. Taylor

HIJIRI MEADOW CC
Japan
Takeaki Kaneda
HILAMAN PARK GC
Tallahassee, Florida
Edward Lawrence Packard, Roger Packard
HILAND GC
Glens Falls, New York
Stephen Kay
HILANDS GC
Billings, Montana
Gregor MacMillan, Norman H. Woods
(R.) Robert Muir Graves
HI-LINE GC
Goshen College, Indiana
John Ingold
HILLANDALE CC
Trumbull, Connecticut
Al Zikorus
HILLANDALE GC
Huntington, New York
Hal Purdy
HILLANDALE CC
Durham, North Carolina
Donald Ross
(R.) Perry Maxwell
(R.) George W. Cobb
HILL BARN GC
Sussex, England
F. G. Hawtree, J. H. Taylor
HILLCREST CC
Los Angeles, California
Willie Watson
(A.9) William F. Bell, William P. Bell
(R.6) Robert Muir Graves
HILLCREST CC (PAR 3 CSE)
Los Angeles, California
William F. Bell, William P. Bell
HILLCREST CC
Durango, Colorado
(R.9 A.9) Henry B. Hughes
HILLCREST CC
Boise, Idaho
A. Vernon Macan
(R.6) Robert Muir Graves
HILLCREST CC
Long Grove, Illinois
Robert Bruce Harris
(R.) Ken Killian, Dick Nugent
HILLCREST CC
Indianapolis, Indiana
William H. Diddel
(R.) Gary Kern
HILLCREST CC
Kansas City, Missouri
Donald Ross
(R.4) Marvin Ferguson
(R.) Bill Amick
HILLCREST CC
Lincoln, Nebraska
William H. Tucker
HILLCREST CC [NLE]
Cincinnati, Ohio
William B. Langford, Theodore J. Moreau
HILLCREST CC
Bartlesville, Oklahoma
Perry Maxwell
(R.9) Floyd Farley
(R.) Arnold Palmer, Ed Seay

HILL CREST CC
New Kensington, Pennsylvania
Emil Loeffler, *John McGlynn*
(A.9) James Gilmore Harrison

HILLCREST CC
Lubbock, Texas
Ralph Plummer

HILLCREST CC [NLE]
San Antonio, Texas
John Bredemus

HILLCREST G&CC
Hollywood, Florida
Robert von Hagge

HILLCREST G&CC
Batesville, Indiana
D. Robertson Smith
(R.9) William H. Diddel
(R.9) Michael Hurdzan, Jack
Kidwell
(A.9) Michael Hurdzan

HILLCREST G&CC
Yankton, South Dakota
(A.9) Homer Fieldhouse

HILLCREST GC
Sun City West, Arizona
Jeff Hardin, Greg Nash

HILLCREST GC
Durango, Colorado
Frank Hummel

HILLCREST GC
Washington, Illinois
Al Linkogel

HILLCREST GC
Millinocket, Maine
(R.) *Larry H. Striley*

HILLCREST GC
Saskatchewan
(R.) Stanley Thompson

HILL CREST GC
Tochigi, Japan
Eiichi Motohashi

HILLCREST GC
Tokyo, Japan
Desmond Muirhead

HILLCREST MUNI
Coffeyville, Kansas
Smiley Bell

HILLCREST MUNI
Owensboro, Kentucky
Alex McKay

HILLCREST ACRES GC
Barrington, Illinois
David Gill

HILLCREST EAST GC
Florida
Mark Mahannah

HILLDALE GC
Hoffman Estates, Illinois
Robert Trent Jones

HILLENDALE CC
Phoenix, Maryland
William Gordon, David Gordon
(R.) Edmund B. Ault
(R.) George Fazio

HILLERØD GC
Hillerød, Denmark
(R.9 A.9) Jan Sederholm

HILLMAN'S GC
New Jersey
Geoffrey S. Cornish

HILLMOOR CC
Lake Geneva, Wisconsin
James Foulis

HILL MUNI
Chickasha, Oklahoma
Donald Sparks

HILLSBORO CC
Boca Raton, Florida
W. C. Nicolaysen, Mark M.
Nicolaysen

HILLSBORO CC
Hillsboro, Illinois
(R.9 A.9) Edward Lawrence
Packard

HILLSBORO ELKS GC
Hillsboro, Ohio
Ted Cox

HILLSBORO PINES GC
Deerfield Beach, Florida
Joe Lee

HILLSBOROUGH GC
Yorkshire, England
Tom Williamson

HILLSDALE GC
Bellwood, Illinois
Tom Bendelow

HILLSDALE G&CC
Hillsdale, Michigan
Tom Bendelow
(R.9 A.9) Harold Paddock
(R.) *Arthur Ham*

HILLSDALE G&CC (DALE CSE)
Ste. Thérèse, Quebec
Howard Watson
(R.1) John Watson

HILLSDALE G&CC HILL CSE)
Ste. Thérèse, Quebec
Howard Watson
(R.1) John Watson

HILLSGROVE GC
Rhode Island
Geoffrey S. Cornish

HILL'S HEART OF THE LAKES GC
Brooklyn, Michigan
(A.9) Jeff Gorney

HILLSIDE GC
England
(R.9 A.9) Fred W. Hawtree

HILLSIDE G&TC [NLE]
Plainfield, New Jersey
Tom Bendelow

HILLSIDE MUNI [NLE]
Illinois
Tom Bendelow

[THE] HILLS OF LAKEWAY GC
Lakeway, Texas
Jack Nicklaus
(A.3 Golf Academy) Jack
Nicklaus

HILLSVIEW GC
California
(A.9) Richard Bigler

HILLSVIEW G CSE
Pierre, South Dakota
Charles Maddox
(R.) Pat Wyss

HILLTOP GC
Coshocton, Ohio
(R.) Ferdinand Garbin

HILLTOP LAKES GC
Normangee, Texas
Ralph Plummer
(A.9) Leon Howard

HILLTOP & MANWOOD FARM GC
Birmingham, England
Fred W. Hawtree, Martin
Hawtree

HILL VALLEY G&CC
England
Peter Alliss, David Thomas

HILLVIEW CC
Franklin, Indiana
Bob Simmons
(R.) Ron Kern, Gary Kern

HILLVIEW CC
North Reading, Massachusetts
William F. Mitchell

HILLVIEW G CSE
San Jose, California
Sam Whiting

HILLWOOD CC
Nashville, Tennessee
Bubber Johnson

HILLY DALE CC
Carmel, New York
Orrin Smith

HILO MUNI
Hilo, Hawaii
Willard Wilkinson

HILTON HEAD NATIONAL GC
Hilton Head Island, South
Carolina
Gary Player

HILTON PARK GC (ALLENDER CSE)
Dunbarton, Scotland
James Braid, John R. Stutt

HILTON PARK GC (HILTON CSE)
Scotland
F. G. Hawtree, J. H. Taylor

HILVERSUMSE GC
Hilversum, Netherlands
John Duncan Dunn

HIMBERG GUTENHOF GC
Vienna, Austria
Kurt Rossknecht

HIMMERLANDS G&CC (CSE NO. 1)
Aars, Denmark
Jan Sederholm

HIMMERLANDS G&CC (CSE NO. 2)
Aars, Denmark
Jan Sederholm

HINCKLEY GC
Leicestershire, England
Jeremy Pern, *Ray Wilson*

HINCKLEY HILLS GC
Hinckley, Ohio
Harold Paddock

HINDMAN PARK GC
Little Rock, Arkansas
Dave Bennett, Leon Howard

HINSDALE GC
Hinsdale, Illinois
Donald Ross
(R.) Edward Lawrence
Packard, Roger Packard
(R.) Dick Nugent
(R.) Bob Lohmann

HINSDALE PAR 3 GC
Hinsdale, Illinois
Edward Lawrence Packard

HINTLESHAM PARK GC
Ipswich, England
F. W. Hawtree, Martin Hawtree

HIRAKATA CC
Osaka, Japan
Seichi Inouye

HIRAKAWA CC
Chiba, Japan
Koukichi Yasuda

HIRONA CC
Japan
C. H. Alison

HIROSHIMA CC
Hiroshima, Japan
Dr. N. Marumo

HIROSHIMA GC
Hiroshima, Japan
Robert Trent Jones, Jr.

HIRSCH CREEK CC
Kitimat, British Columbia
Norman H. Woods
(A.9) Les Furber, *Jim Eremko*

HISAYAMA CC
Japan
Yoshimasa Fujii

HITACHI TAKASUZU GC
Japan
Eichi Motohashi

HIWAN GC
Evergreen, Colorado
Press Maxwell

HOBART CC
Hobart, Oklahoma
Bob Dunning

HOBBIT'S GLEN GC
Columbia, Maryland
Edmund B. Ault

HOBBLE CREEK GC
Springville, Utah
William F. Bell

HOBBS CC
Hobbs, New Mexico
(R.9 A.9) Warren Cantrell

HOBE SOUND CC [NLE]
Hobe Sound, Florida
Ernest E. Smith

HOBE SOUND GC
Hobe Sound, Florida
Joe Lee

HOB NOB HILL GC [NLE]
Salisbury, Connecticut
Devereux Emmet, Alfred H. Tull

HOCKLEY GC
Hampshire, England
(R.) J. Hamilton Stutt

HOCKLEY VALLEY RESORT GC
Orangeville, Ontario
Thomas McBroom

HODGE PARK MUNI
Kansas City, Missouri
Larry Runyon, Michael H. Malyn

HODOGAYO G&CC
Yokohama, Japan
Walter Fovargue
(R.) Rokuro Akaboshi, *Shiro*
Akaboshi

HOEBRIDGE GC
Woking, Surrey, England
John Jacobs

HOEBRIDGE GC (SHORT CSE)
Woking, Surrey, England
Martin Hawtree, Simon Gidman

HOEGBO GC
Sweden
Nils Sköld

HOGAN PARK GC
Midland, Texas
(A.3rd 9) Ron Kirby

HOG BACK MOUNTAIN C [NLE]
Tryon, North Carolina
Devereux Emmet, Alfred H. Tull

HOGE DIJK GC
Netherlands
J. F. Dudok van Heel
HOGE KLEIJ GC
Netherlands
D. M. A. Steel
HOG NECK GC
Easton, Maryland
Lindsay Ervin
HOHENHARDTER HOF GC
Baden-Württemberg, Germany
Donald Harradine
HOHENSTAUFEN GC
Göppingen, Germany
Donald Harradine
(A.9) Reinhold Weishaupt
HOISDORF GC
Germany
H. Pieters
HOKKAIDO CC (CLASSIC CSE)
Hokkaido, Japan
Jack Nicklaus
HOKKAIDO CC (OHNUMA CSE)
Hokkaido, Japan
Robert Trent Jones, Jr.
HOKKAIDO CC (EAGLE CSE)
Hokkaido, Japan
Shunsuke Kato
HOKKAIDO CC (LION CSE)
Hokkaido, Japan
Shunsuke Kato
HOKKAIDO LINKS CC
Hokkaido, Japan
Isami Doi
HOLBÆK GC
Denmark
Jan Sederholm
HOLDEN HILLS GC
Holden, Massachusetts
(R.) William F. Mitchell
HOLDREDGE CC
Holdredge, Nebraska
(A.9) Jeff Brauer
HOLE-IN-THE-WALL GC
Naples, Florida
Dick Wilson
(R.) Arthur Hills
HOLIDAY CC
Lake Park, Florida
Arthur Young
HOLIDAY CC
Stuart, Florida
NKA Pine Lakes GC
HOLIDAY BEACH GC
Breckenridge, Kentucky
Morgan Boggs
HOLIDAY GREENS GC
Mount Pleasant, Michigan
William Newcomb
HOLIDAY HILLS CC
Branson, Missouri
Bob Dunning, Larry Gardner
HOLIDAY HILLS CC
Mineral Well, Texas
(R.) Leon Howard
HOLIDAY HILLS GC
Philippines
Seichi Inouye
HOLIDAY INN GC
Crete, Illinois
Arthur David, Ron Kirby
HOLIDAY INN GC
Sarnia, Ontario
Clinton E. Robinson

HOLIDAY ISLAND GC
Holiday Island, Arkansas
John Allen
HOLIDAY PARK GC
Saskatoon, Saskatchewan
Clinton E. Robinson
HOLIDAY SPRINGS CC
Margate, Florida
NKA Carolina CC
HOLLAND LAKE GC
Sheridan, Michigan
Warner Bowen
(R.1) Jerry Matthews
HOLLINGBURY PARK GC
Sussex, England
F. G. Hawtree, J. H. Taylor
HOLLOW ACRES GC
Delphi, Indiana
R. Albert Anderson
HOLLOW BROOK G&CC
Peekskill, New York
Mungo Park II
(R.) Tom Winton
[THE] HOLLOWS GC
Montpelier, Virginia
Brian Ault, Tom Clark
HOLLYBROOK G&TC
(CHAMPIONSHIP CSE)
Pembroke Pines, Florida
William F. Mitchell
HOLLYBROOK G&TC (PAR 3 CSE)
Pembroke Pines, Florida
Leon Howard
HOLLYDOT AT COLORADO CITY GC
Colorado City, Colorado
Holland Duell (9 1958)
(A.9) DeWitt "Maury" Bell
(1972)
(A.3rd 9) Frank Hummel
HOLLY FOREST GC
Sapphire, North Carolina
Tom Jackson
HOLLY HILL CC
Frederick, Maryland
Russell Roberts
HOLLY HILL CC
Holly Hill, South Carolina
Ed Riccoboni
HOLLY HILL G&CC [NLE]
Davenport, Florida
Wayne Stiles, John Van Kleek
HOLLY HILLS CC
Bay Minette, Alabama
Earl Stone
HOLLY HILLS CC
Cordova, Tennessee
Marvin Ferguson
HOLLY LAKE RANCH GC
Hawkins, Texas
Leon Howard
HOLLY RIDGE GC
South Sandwich, Massachusetts
Geoffrey S. Cornish, William G.
Robinson
HOLLY TREE CC
Greenville, South Carolina
George W. Cobb, John LaFoy
HOLLYTREE CC
Tyler, Texas
Robert von Hagge, Bruce Devlin
HOLLYWOOD GC
Fort Walton Beach, Florida
Bill Amick

HOLLYWOOD GC [NLE]
Deal, New Jersey
Tom Bendelow
HOLLYWOOD GC
Deal, New Jersey
Isaac Mackie
(R.) Walter J. Travis
(R.) A. W. Tillinghast
(R.) Dick Wilson
(R.) Geoffrey S. Cornish,
Brian Silva
HOLLYWOOD BEACH HOTEL CC
Hollywood, Florida
H. C. C. Tippets (1925)
(R.) Mark Mahannah
HOLLYWOOD LAKES CC (EAST CSE)
[NLE]
Hollywood, Florida
Bill Watts
HOLLYWOOD LAKES CC (WEST CSE)
[NLE]
Hollywood, Florida
Bill Watts
HOLMES PARK MUNI
Lincoln, Nebraska
Floyd Farley
HOLSTEBRO GC
Holstebro, Denmark
E. Schnack
HOLSTON HILLS CC
Knoxville, Tennessee
Donald Ross
(R.3) Alex McKay
HOLSTON HILLS CC
Marion, Virginia
Edmund B. Ault
HOLYHEAD GC
Holyhead, Wales
James Braid
HOLYWELL GC
Clywed, Wales
J. H. Taylor
HOMBRE G CSE
Panama City Beach, Florida
Wes Burnham (1989)
HOMELINKS GC
Olmstead Falls, Ohio
Harold Paddock
HOME PARK GC
Surrey, England
James Braid
HOMESTEAD AFB GC
Miami, Florida
NKA Falcon Fairways GC
HOMESTEAD CC [NLE]
Prairie Village, Kansas
James Dalgleish
HOMESTEAD CC
Spring Lake, New Jersey
Donald Ross
HOMESTEAD GC
Tipp City, Ohio
Bill Amick
[THE] HOMESTEAD GC
Hot Springs, Virginia
Donald Ross
(R.) William Flynn
HOMESTEAD RESORT & GC
Midway, Utah
Bruce Summerhays (1990)
HOMESTEAD SPRINGS GC
Groveport, Ohio
Harlan "Bud" Rainier

HOMINY HILL GC
Colts Neck, New Jersey
Robert Trent Jones
HOMOSASSA CC [NLE]
Homosassa, Florida
Harry Collis
HONESDALE GC
Honesdale, Pennsylvania
(R.) Mike Hurdzan
HONEY BEE GC
Virginia Beach, Virginia
Rees Jones
HONEY RUN G&CC
York, Pennsylvania
Edmund B. Ault
HONEYWELL GC
Wabash, Indiana
William H. Diddel
(A.9) Arthur Hills
HONJO MIKAHO KOGEN CC
Gunma, Japan
Takeshi Sato
HONOLULU CC
Honolulu, Oahu, Hawaii
Frank Duane, Arnold Palmer
[THE] HONORS CSE
Ooltewah, Tennessee
Pete Dye
HOODKROFT CC
Derry, New Hampshire
Phil Wogan
HOOD RIVER GC
Hood River, Oregon
H. Chandler Egan, Hugh Junor
HOOKS G&CC
Hook, Sweden
Sig Edberg
(A.9) Jan Sederholm
(R.) Ture Bruce
HOOK & SLICE GC
Oklahoma City, Oklahoma
Floyd Farley
HOOPER GC
Walpole, New Hampshire
Wayne Stiles, John Van Kleek
HOOSIER LINKS
New Palestine, Indiana
Charles Maddox
HOPEDALE CC
Hopedale, Massachusetts
(R.) Geoffrey S. Cornish
HOPE G&CC
Hope, British Columbia
Gordon McKay
HOPE PLANTATION G&CC
Johns Island, South Carolina
Clyde Johnston
HOPE VALLEY CC
Durham, North Carolina
Donald Ross
(R.) Perry Maxwell
(R.) Dan Maples
HOPEWELL CC
Hopewell, Virginia
Fred Findlay
HOPEWELL VALLEY GC
Hopewell Junction, New Jersey
Tom Winton
(R.1) Stephen Kay
HOPEWOOD GC
England
H. S. Colt

HOPKINSVILLE G&CC
Hopkinsville, Kentucky
John Darrah
(R.) Earl Stone
HOP MEADOW CC
Simsbury, Connecticut
Geoffrey S. Cornish
HORAI CC
Tochigi Prefecture, Japan
Robert von Hagge
HORIN CC
Chiba, Japan
Hideyo Sugimoto
HORIZON CC
Rancho Santa Fe, California
Robert Trent Jones, Jr.
HORIZON CC
Belen, New Mexico
Red Lawrence
HORIZON CITY CC
El Paso, Texas
Jack Harden
HORNBY TOWERS GC
Ontario
Robert Moote, *David S. Moote*
HORSENS GC
Denmark
Jan Sederholm
HORSESHOE BAY CC (APPLEROCK CSE)
Horseshoe Bay, Texas
Robert Trent Jones
HORSESHOE BAY CC (RAM ROCK CSE)
Horseshoe Bay, Texas
Robert Trent Jones
HORSESHOE BAY CC (SLICK ROCK CSE)
Horseshoe Bay, Texas
Robert Trent Jones
HORSESHOE BEND CC
Roswell, Georgia
Joe Lee, Rocky Roquemore
(R.) Denis Griffiths
HORSESHOE GC
Cummings Cove, North Carolina
Bob Cupp
HORSESHOE VALLEY GC
Barrie, Ontario
René Muylaert, *Charles Muylaert*
HORSE THIEF G&CC
Tehachapi, California
Bob Baldock, Robert L. Baldock
HORTON SMITH MUNI
Springfield, Missouri
Tom Talbot
(R.) Don Sechrest
HOST FARMS GC (CHAMPIONSHIP CSE)
Lancaster, Pennsylvania
William Gordon, David Gordon
(R.8) Tom Clark
HOST FARMS GC (EXECUTIVE CSE)
Lancaster, Pennsylvania
Geoffrey S. Cornish, William G. Robinson
HOTCHKISS SCHOOL GC
Lakeville, Connecticut
Seth Raynor
(R.) Charles Banks

HOTEL FRASCATI GC [NLE]
Bermuda
Devereux Emmet
HOTEL GREEN GC [NLE]
Pasadena, California
Willie Watson
HOTEL HERSHEY GC
Hershey, Pennsylvania
Maurice McCarthy
HOTEL INDIATLANTIC GC [NLE]
Melbourne, Florida
Ernest Way
HOT SPRINGS G&CC (ARLINGTON CSE)
Hot Springs, Arkansas
William H. Diddel
(R.) Smiley Bell
HOT SPRINGS G&CC (MAJESTIC CSE)
Hot Springs, Arkansas
Willie Park, Jr.
(R.) William H. Diddel
(R.) Smiley Bell
HOT SPRINGS G&CC (PINEVIEW CSE)
Hot Springs, Arkansas
Bert Meade
HOUGHTON GC
South Africa
A. M. Copland
(R.) Sid Brews
HOUND EAR CC
Blowing Rock, North Carolina
George W. Cobb
(R.) Tom Jackson
HOUNDSLAKE CC
Aiken, South Carolina
Joe Lee, Rocky Roquemore
HOUNSLOW HEATH GC
Middlesex, England
Fraser Middleton
HOUSTON CC
Houston, Texas
NKA Gus Wortham Muni
HOUSTON CC
Houston, Texas
Robert Trent Jones
(R.) Bill Coore, Ben Crenshaw
HOUSTON G ACADEMY
Houston, Texas
Bruce Littell
HOUSTON LAKE CC
Perry, Georgia
O. C. Jones
HOUSTON LEVEE CC
Germantown, Tennessee
George C. Curtis
(A.3rd 9) Kevin Tucker
HOVERINGHAM GC
Yorkshire, England
E. Baker, M. Baker
HOWELL PARK GC
Farmingdale, New Jersey
Frank Duane
(R.) Geoffrey S. Cornish, Brian Silva
HOWSTRAKE GC
Isle of Man
(R.) T. J. A. Macauley
HOWTH CASTLE GC
County Dublin, Ireland
Fred W. Hawtree

HOWTH GC
Howth, Ireland
Cecil Bancroft
(R.9 A.9) James Braid, John R. Stutt
HOYLAKE MUNI GC
Hoylake, Merseyside, England
James Braid, John R. Stutt
HOYT PARK GC
Portland, Oregon
Ed Erickson, David Duval
H. P. WHITNEY ESTATE GC
Manhasset, New York
Charles Blair Macdonald, Seth Raynor
H. SMITH RICHARDSON MUNI
Fairfield, Connecticut
Hal Purdy, Malcolm Purdy
(R.2) Stephen Kay
HUBBARD HEIGHTS CC
Stamford, Connecticut
NKA E. Gaynor Brennan GC
HUBBELRATH GC (EAST CSE)
Dusseldorf, Germany
Bernard von Limburger
(R.) Karl F. Grohs, *Rainer Preissmann*
HUBBELRATH GC (WEST CSE)
Dusseldorf, Germany
Bernhard von Limburger
HUDDERSFIELD GC
Yorkshire, England
Tom Dunn
(R.) Herbert Fowler
(R.) Tom Simpson
HUDDLE PARK GC (BLUE CSE)
Johannesburg, South Africa
Robert Grimsdell
HUDDLE PARK GC (YELLOW CSE)
Johannesburg, South Africa
Robert Grimsdell
HUDDLE PARK GC (WHITE CSE)
Johannesburg, South Africa
Robert Grimsdell
HUDSON CC
Hudson, Wisconsin
Leo J. Feser
(R.9 A.9) Don Herfort
HUDSON G & CURLING C
Hudson Heights, Quebec
Howard Watson
HUDSON RIVER GC [NLE]
Yonkers, New York
Donald Ross
HUESTON WOODS STATE PARK GC
Oxford, Ohio
Jack Kidwell
HUGHES C
Houston, Texas
A. B. "Monk" Keith
HUGUENOT MANOR GC
New Paltz, New York
Hal Purdy
HUIS TEN BOSCH CC
Nagasaki Prefecture, Japan
Jack Nicklaus
HULL GC
Hull, England
(R.) F. G. Hawtree, J. H. Taylor
HULMAN LINKS OF TERRE HAUTE
Terre Haute, Indiana
David Gill, Garrett Gill

HULTA GC
Sweden
Jan Sederholm
HUMBERSTONE HEIGHTS GC
Leicestershire, England
Fred W. Hawtree, Martin Hawtree
HUMBER VALLEY G&CC
Toronto, Ontario
Stanley Thompson
(R.) Thomas McBroom
HUMEWOOD CC
Port Elizabeth, South Africa
S. V. Hotchkin
HUNSLEY HILLS CC
Canyon, Texas
Henry B. Hughes
HUNSTANTON GC
Norfolk, England
George Fernie
(R.9 A.9) James Braid
(R.3) *James Sherlock*
HUNTER ARMY BASE GC
Savannah, Georgia
George W. Cobb
HUNTERCOMBE GC
Oxfordshire, England
Willie Park, Jr.
HUNTER MEMORIAL GC
Meriden, Connecticut
Robert D. Pryde
(R.) Alfred H. Tull
(R.) Al Zikorus
HUNTER POPE G CSE
Monticello, Georgia
(A.9) Mike Young
HUNTER'S CREEK CC
Kissimmee, Florida
Lloyd Clifton
HUNTER'S GREEN CC
Tampa, Florida
Tom Fazio
HUNTER'S POINT GC
Lebanon, Tennessee
Robert Renaud
HUNTERS RIDGE CC
Bonita Springs, Florida
Gordon Lewis
HUNTERS RUN GC (EAST CSE)
Boynton Beach, Florida
Robert von Hagge, Bruce Devlin
HUNTERS RUN GC (NORTH CSE)
Boynton Beach, Florida
Robert von Hagge, Bruce Devlin
HUNTERS RUN GC (SOUTH CSE)
Boynton Beach, Florida
Robert von Hagge, Bruce Devlin
HUNTING CREEK CC
Prospect, Kentucky
Benjamin Wihry
(R.) Arthur Hills
HUNTINGDALE GC
Victoria, Australia
C. H. Alison, *S. Berriman*
HUNTINGDON VALLEY CC [NLE]
Philadelphia, Pennsylvania
(R.) Emil Loeffler
HUNTINGDON VALLEY CC
Abington, Pennsylvania
William S. Flynn, Howard Toomey

HUNTING HILLS CC
Roanoke, Virginia
Fred Findlay, Buddy Loving, *R. F. Loving, Sr.*
(R.) Buddy Loving
HUNTINGTON CC
Huntington, New York
Devereux Emmet
(R.) Devereux Emmet
(R.) Robert Trent Jones
(R.) William F. Mitchell
HUNTINGTON CC
Huntington, West Virginia
Tom Bendelow
HUNTINGTON GC [NLE]
Huntington, New York
Tom Bendelow
HUNTINGTON GC
Ontario
(R.) Clinton E. Robinson
HUNTINGTON G & MARINE C
Huntington, New York
Herbert Strong
HUNTINGTON CRESCENT CC
Huntington, New York
Devereux Emmet, Alfred H. Tull
(R.) Orrin Smith
(R.2) Stephen Kay
HUNTINGTON CRESCENT CC (WEST CSE) [NLE]
Huntington, New York
Devereux Emmet, Alfred H. Tull
(R.) Orrin Smith
HUNTINGTON ELKS CC
Martha, West Virginia
X. G. Hassenplug
HUNTINGTON PARK GC
Shreveport, Louisiana
Tommy Moore
HUNTSVILLE CC
Huntsville, Alabama
Robert Bruce Harris
(R.) John LaFoy
HUNTSVILLE MUNI
Huntsville, Alabama
Denis Griffiths, Ron Kirby
HUNTSVILLE DOWNS G&CC
Huntsville, Ontario
Stanley Thompson
HUNT VALLEY INN & CC
Hunt Valley, Maryland
Edmund B. Ault
(A.9) Algie Pulley
HURLBURT FIELD GC
Hurlburt Field, Florida
Dave Bennett
HURLINGHAM G&CC
Argentina
George Gadd, Arthur Havers
HURLSTON GC
Ormskirk, England
D. M. A. Steel
HURON CC
Huron, South Dakota
(R.9 A.9) Dick Phelps, Brad Benz
HURON GC
Ypsilanti, Michigan
Karl Litten
HURON BREEZE G&CC
Au Gres, Michigan
William Newcomb

HURON HILLS GC
Ann Arbor, Michigan
Tom Bendelow
HURON PINES G&CC
Blind River, Ontario
Clinton E. Robinson
(A.9) Thomas McBroom
HURRICANE CREEK CC
Anna, Texas
Leon Howard
HURSTBORNE CC
Louisville, Kentucky
Chic Adams
(R.) Arthur Hills
HUTCHISON CC [NLE]
Hutchinson, Kansas
Tom Bendelow
HUTT GC
New Zealand
J. R. Callender, Tom Wilford
(R.) John Harris
(R.) C. H. Redhead
HUYTON & PRESCOT GC
England
(R.) Fred W. Hawtree, A. H. F. Jiggens
HVIDE KLIT GC
Denmark
Anders Amilon
HV-JAC GC
Delaware, Ohio
Jack Kidwell
HYANNISPORT C
Hyannisport, Massachusetts
Alex Findlay
(R.) Donald Ross
(R.) Ron Forse
HYATT PATTAYA GC
Thailand
Ichisuke Izumi
HYATT REGENCY COOLUM GC
Sunshine Coast, Australia
Robert Trent Jones, Jr.
HYDEAWAY GC
Tecumseh, Ontario
Nick Panasi
HYDE G&CC
Dorset, England
J. Hamilton Stutt
HYDE ESTATE GC
France
Tom Simpson
HYDE MANOR GC [NLE]
Vermont
Horace Rollins, George Sargent
HYDE PARK GC
Jacksonville, Florida
Donald Ross
(R.) Stanley Thompson
HYDE PARK CC [NLE]
Cincinnati, Ohio
Tom Bendelow
HYDE PARK GC
Cincinnati, Ohio
Donald Ross
(R.) Arthur Hills
HYDE PARK MUNI (NORTH CSE)
Niagara Falls, New York
William Harries
(R.) William Gordon, David Gordon

HYDE PARK MUNI (SOUTH CSE)
Niagara Falls, New York
William Harries
(R.9 A.9) William Gordon, David Gordon
HYLAND GREENS CC
Bloomington, Minnesota
Paul Coates
HYLAND HILLS CC
Westminster, Colorado
Henry B. Hughes
(A.3rd 9) Frank Hummel
HYLAND HILLS GC
Southern Pines, North Carolina
Tom Jackson
HYLANDS GC (NORTH CSE)
Ottawa, Ontario
Howard Watson
(R.1) John Watson
HYLANDS GC (SOUTH CSE)
Ottawa, Ontario
Howard Watson
HYLANDS PARK GC
Chelmsford, England
Martin Hawtree, Simon Gidman
HYLLIEKROKEN GC
Sweden
Jan Sederholm
HYPERION FIELD C
Grimes, Iowa
Tom Bendelow
(R.) *Warren Dickenson*
(R.) Roger Packard
HY POINTE CC
Grand Rapids, Michigan
Jack Daray
HYTHE IMPERIAL GC
Kent, England
P. M. Ross

IBARAKI GC (EAST CSE)
Osaka, Japan
Seichi Inouye
IBARAKI GENERAL CC
Ibaraki, Japan
Katsunari Takahashi
IBIS GC
Niigata, Japan
Yoichi Akiyama
IBIS G&CC (LEGEND CSE)
Palm Beach Gardens, Florida
Jack Nicklaus
IBIS G&CC (HERITAGE CSE)
Palm Beach Gardens, Florida
Jack Nicklaus, Jr.
IBIS G&CC (TRADITION CSE)
Palm Beach Gardens, Florida
Tom Pearson
IBM CC (COUNTRY CLUB CSE)
Johnson City, New York
John Van Kleek
IBM CC
Poughkeepsie, New York
Robert Trent Jones
(R.) Robert Trent Jones
(R.) Stephen Kay
IBM CC
Sands Point, New York
(R.) Robert Trent Jones
(R.9) Hal Purdy
(R.1) Frank Duane

IBM CC
Markham, Ontario
Jimmy Johnstone (1951)
IBM GC
San Jose, California
Jack Fleming
IBUSUKI CC (NEW CSE)
Kagoshima, Japan
Peter Thomson, Michael Wolveridge
ICHON G&CC
Ichon, Korea
Cal Olson
IDA GROVE G&CC
Ida Grove, Iowa
Harold Glissmann
IDAHO FALLS CC
Idaho Falls, Idaho
William F. Bell
IDLE HOUR CC
Lexington, Kentucky
Donald Ross
IDLE HOUR G&CC
Macon, Georgia
(R.) Willard Byrd
(R.2) Brian Silva, Geoffrey S. Cornish
IDLEWILD CC
Flossmoor, Illinois
Al Naylor
(R.) William B. Langford
IDYLLWILD CC [NLE]
California
John Duncan Dunn
IDYLWYLDE GC
Ontario
(R.9 A.9) Howard Watson
(R.1) Robert Moote
IFIELD G&CC
Sussex, England
F. G. Hawtree, J. H. Taylor
IGA UENO CC
Nara, Japan
Arnold Palmer, Ed Seay
IKAHO CC
Gunma, Japan
Shunsuke Kato
IKOMA KOGEN KOBAYASHI MIYAZAKI GC
Miyazaki-ken, Japan
Mike Poellot
ILE BOURDON GC
Montreal, Quebec
Howard Watson
ILKLEY GC
West Yorkshire, England
(R.) Alister Mackenzie
ILLAHE HILLS CC
Salem, Oregon
William F. Bell
(R.) Robert Muir Graves
ILLINI CC
Springfield, Illinois
Tom Bendelow
(R.9 A.9) Robert Bruce Harris
(R.) Edward Lawrence Packard
ILLINOIS STATE UNIVERSITY GC
Normal, Illinois
Robert Bruce Harris
ILLINOIS VALLEY GC
Cave Junction, Oregon
Bob Baldock, Robert L. Baldock

IL PICCIOLO GC
Sicily
D. M. A. Steel

IM CHIEMGAU GC
Chieming, Germany
J. F. Dudok van Heel

IMMINGHAM GC
Lincolnshire, England
J. J. F. Pennink
(A.9) Fred W. Hawtree,
Martin Hawtree
(R.9) Martin Hawtree

IMPERIAL CC
Teheran, Iran
Jack Armitage

IMPERIAL CC
Ibaraki Prefecture, Japan
Mark Rathert

IMPERIAL GC
Brea, California
Harry Rainville, David Rainville

IMPERIAL GC (EAST CSE)
Naples, Florida
Arthur Hills

IMPERIAL GC (WEST CSE)
Naples, Florida
Ward Northrup

IMPERIAL GC
Imperial, Texas
(R.) Leon Howard

IMPERIALAKES CC
Mulberry, Florida
Ron Garl

IMPERIAL LAKES GC
Palmetto, Florida
Ted McAnlis

IMPERIAL SPORTS C
Teheran, Iran
Fred W. Hawtree

IMPERIAL WING GC
Gifu Prefecture, Japan
Mike Poellot

INCLINE GREEN GC
Incline Village, Nevada
Robert Trent Jones

INCLINE VILLAGE GC
Incline Village, Nevada
Robert Trent Jones
(R.) Robert Muir Graves
(R.) Robert Trent Jones, Jr.

INDEPENDENCE CC
Independence, Kansas
Tom Manley
(R.) Smiley Bell
(R.) Don Sechrest

INDEPENDENCE GREEN GC
Farmington, Michigan
Bruce Matthews, Jerry Matthews

INDIANA CC
Indiana, Pennsylvania
Willie Park, Jr.
(A.9) James Gilmore
Harrison, Ferdinand Garbin
(R.) Edmund B. Ault

INDIANA UNIVERSITY GC
Bloomington, Indiana
Jim Soutar

INDIAN BAYOU G&CC
Destin, Florida
Earl Stone

INDIAN BOUNDARY CC
Chicago, Illinois
C. D. Wagstaff
(R.) Dick Nugent

INDIAN CANYON GC
Spokane, Washington
H. Chandler Egan

INDIAN CREEK CC
Miami Beach, Florida
William S. Flynn, Howard
Toomey
(R.) Dick Wilson

INDIAN CREEK CC
Abilene, Texas
Ralph Plummer

INDIAN CREEK GC
Jupiter, Florida
Lamar K. Smith

INDIAN CREEK G CSE (CREEK CSE)
Carrollton, Texas
Dick Phelps, Brad Benz, Mike
Poellot

INDIAN CREEK G CSE (LAKES CSE)
Carrollton, Texas
Dick Phelps

INDIANFIELD G&CC
Caro, Michigan
William Newcomb

INDIAN FOOTHILLS GC
Marshall, Missouri
Tom Talbot, Lloyd Thompson

INDIAN HEAD NAVAL ORDINANCE
GC
Indian Head, Maryland
(R.9) Edmund B. Ault

INDIAN HILL C
Winnetka, Illinois
(R.) Donald Ross

INDIAN HILL GC
California
(R.) William P. Bell

INDIAN HILLS CC
Tuscaloosa, Alabama
Harold Williams, *Thomas H.
Nicol*

INDIAN HILLS CC
Riverside, California
(R.) Bob Baldock, Robert L.
Baldock

INDIAN HILLS CC
Newington, Connecticut
Robert J. Ross

INDIAN HILLS CC
Marietta, Georgia
Joe Lee, Rocky Roquemore

INDIAN HILLS CC
Prairie Village, Kansas
A. W. Tillinghast
(R.) Floyd Farley
(R.) Bob Dunning
(R.2) Tom Clark

INDIAN HILLS CC
Bowling Green, Kentucky
William B. Langford

INDIAN HILLS CC
North St. Paul, Minnesota
Don Herfort

INDIAN HILLS G&CC
Fort Pierce, Florida
Herbert Strong

INDIAN HILLS GC
Fairfield Bay, Arkansas
Leon Howard, *Charles Howard*
(R.) Edmund B. Ault

INDIAN HILLS GC
Mt. Vernon, Illinois
Thomas A. Puckett

INDIAN HILLS GC
Okemos, Michigan
(R.) Bruce Matthews, Jerry
Matthews

INDIAN HILLS GC [NLE]
Omaha, Nebraska
Henry C. Glissmann, Harold
Glissmann

INDIAN HILLS GC
Pine Bush, New York
Alfred H. Tull

INDIAN HILLS GC
Brookings, South Dakota
Donald G. Brauer, Emil Perret

INDIAN HILLS GC
Calgary, Alberta
Norman H. Woods

INDIAN HILLS GC
Ontario
Russ Axford

INDIAN HILLS MUNI
Chapman, Kansas
Richard Watson

INDIAN ISLAND PARK GC
Riverhead, New York
William F. Mitchell

INDIAN LAKE G&CC
Manistique, Michigan
John Barr
(R.3) Bruce Matthews, Jerry
Matthews

INDIAN LAKE GC
Central City, Pennsylvania
(A.9) X. G. Hassenplug,
Arnold Palmer

INDIAN LAKE ESTATES CC
Indian Lake Estates, Florida
(R.9 A.9) George W. Cobb

INDIAN LAKES CC (IROQUOIS TRAIL
CSE)
Bloomingdale, Illinois
Robert Bruce Harris

INDIAN LAKES CC (SIOUX TRAIL
CSE)
Bloomingdale, Illinois
Robert Bruce Harris

INDIAN LAKES CC
Winterburn, Alberta
William G. Robinson

INDIAN LAKES G&CC (INDIAN CSE)
Edmonton, Alberta
William G. Robinson

INDIAN LAKES G&CC (LAKES CSE)
Edmonton, Alberta
William G. Robinson, John F.
Robinson

INDIAN LAKES GC
Florida
William L. Campbell

INDIAN LAKES GC
Batesville, Indiana
Robert Renaud

INDIAN MEADOW CC
Westboro, Massachusetts
Geoffrey S. Cornish

INDIAN OAKS CC
Anniston, Alabama
Harold Williams

INDIAN OAKS CC
Phenix City, Alabama
Willard Byrd

INDIAN PALMS CC
Indio, California
Jackie Cochran, Helen Detweiler
(9 1948)

INDIAN PINES GC
Fort Pierce, Florida
Arthur Young

INDIAN PINES GC
Rockledge, Florida
Robert Renaud

INDIAN PINES G&TC
Mi-Wuk Village, California
Clark Glasson

INDIAN RIDGE CC
Andover, Massachusetts
Geoffrey S. Cornish

INDIAN RIDGE GC
Hobart, Indiana
Stanley Pelchar

INDIAN RIVER COLONY C
Melbourne, Florida
Gordon Lewis

INDIAN RIVER GC
Indian River, Michigan
Wilfrid Reid, William Connellan

INDIAN RIVER PLANTATION GC
Stuart, Florida
Chuck Ankrom

INDIAN RUN GC
Portage, Michigan
Charles Darl Scott
(A.9) Bruce Matthews, Jerry
Matthews

INDIAN SPRING C (CHIEF CSE)
Silver Spring, Maryland
William Gordon, David Gordon
(R.) Edmund B. Ault

INDIAN SPRING C (VALLEY CSE)
Silver Spring, Maryland
William Gordon, David Gordon

INDIAN SPRING CC (EAST CSE)
Boynton Beach, Florida
Robert von Hagge, Bruce Devlin

INDIAN SPRING CC (WEST CSE)
Boynton Beach, Florida
Robert von Hagge, Bruce Devlin

INDIAN SPRING CC [NLE]
Laurel, Maryland
Donald Ross

INDIAN SPRING GC
Saybrook, Illinois
(A.9) Edward Lawrence
Packard

INDIAN SPRINGS CC
Palm Springs, California
John Gurley, Hoagy Carmichael

INDIAN SPRINGS CC (RIVER CSE)
Broken Arrow, Oklahoma
George Fazio

INDIAN SPRINGS CC (WINDMILL
CSE)
Broken Arrow, Oklahoma
Don Sechrest

INDIAN SPRINGS GC
Mechanicsburg, Ohio
Jack Kidwell

INDIAN SUMMER GC
Olympia, Washington
Peter Thomson, Michael
Wolveridge

INDIAN TRAIL CC
Palm Beach, Florida
Mark Mahannah

INDIAN TRAILS G CSE
Grand Rapids, Michigan
(R.) Jeff Gorney
INDIAN TREE GC
Arvada, Colorado
Dick Phelps
INDIAN VALLEY CC
Burlington, North Carolina
Ellis Maples
INDIAN VALLEY CC
Telford, Pennsylvania
William Gordon, David Gordon
INDIAN VALLEY GC
Navato, California
Robert Nyberg
INDIAN VALLEY GC
Cincinnati, Ohio
William H. Diddel
INDIAN VILLAGE CC
Lafayette, Indiana
Edward Lawrence Packard
INDIAN WELLS CC
Indian Wells, California
Harry Rainville, David Rainville
(R.) Ted Robinson
INDIAN WELLS GC
Burlington, Ontario
René Muylaert
INDIAN WELLS GC
Myrtle Beach, South Carolina
Gene Hamm
INDIAN WELLS G RESORT (EAST
CSE)
Indian Wells, California
Ted Robinson
INDIAN WELLS G RESORT (WEST
CSE)
Indian Wells, California
Ted Robinson
INDIANWOOD G&CC
Indiantown, Florida
Ted McAnlis
INDIAN WOOD G&CC
Matteson, Illinois
Harry Collis
INDIANWOOD G&CC (NEW CSE)
Lake Orion, Michigan
Bob Cupp, Jerry Pate
INDIANWOOD G&CC (OLD CSE)
Lake Orion, Michigan
Wilfrid Reid, William Connellan
(R.) Arthur Hills
(R.) Bob Cupp, Jerry Pate
INDIES INN GC
Duck Key, Florida
Carl H. Anderson
INDIGO CREEK GC
Myrtle Beach, South Carolina
Willard Byrd
INDIGO LAKES CC
Daytona Beach, Florida
Lloyd Clifton
(R.) Lloyd Clifton, *Kenneth Ezell, George Clifton*
INDIGO RUN GC
Hilton Head Island, South
Carolina
Willard Byrd
INDIO MUNI
Indio, California
Lawrence Hughes

INDUSTRY HILLS GC (EISENHOWER
CSE)
Industry, California
William F. Bell
INDUSTRY HILLS GC (ZAHARIAS
CSE)
Industry, California
William F. Bell
INGAROE GC
Sweden
Nils Sköld
INGERSOL MUNI
Rockford, Illinois
Tom Bendelow
INGESTRE GC
Staffordshire, England
Fred W. Hawtree, Martin Hawtree
INGLESIDE AUGUSTA CC
Staunton, Virginia
Fred Findlay
INGLESIDE CC [NLE]
San Francisco, California
Robert Johnstone
INGLEWOOD CC
Kenmore, Washington
A. Vernon Macan, Robert
Johnstone
(R.) William Teufel
INGLEWOOD GC
Inglewood, California
Ted Robinson
INGLISTON GC
Scotland
James Braid, John R. Stutt
INGOL G & SQUASH C
Lancashire, England
J. J. F. Pennink, D. M. A. Steel
INKSTER VALLEY GC
Detroit, Michigan
(R.) Gary Roger Baird
INLAND WINDS GC
Loring AFB, Maine
William F. Mitchell
INNELLAN GC
Argyllshire, Scotland
Willie Park, Willie Park, Jr.
INNERLEITHEN GC
Pebbleshire, Scotland
Willie Park
INNIS ARDEN GC
Greenwich, Connecticut
J. Kennedy Tod
(R.) Robert Trent Jones
(R.) Frank Duane
(R.3) Geoffrey S. Cornish,
Brian Silva
INNISBROOK GC (COPPERHEAD CSE)
Tarpon Springs, Florida
Edward Lawrence Packard,
Roger Packard
INNISBROOK GC (ISLAND CSE)
Tarpon Springs, Florida
Edward Lawrence Packard
INNISBROOK GC (SANDPIPER CSE)
Tarpon Springs, Florida
Edward Lawrence Packard,
Roger Packard
INNISFAIL G&CC
Innisfail, Alberta
(A.9) William G. Robinson,
John F. Robinson

INN OF THE MOUNTAIN GODS GC
Mescalero, New Mexico
Ted Robinson
INNSBRUCK GC
Helen, Georgia
Bill Watts
INNSBRUCK-IGLS GC (LANS-
SPERBEREGG CSE)
Sperberegg, Austria
(R.) Gerold Hauser, *Günther
Hauser*
(R.) Herwig Zisser
INNSBRUCK-IGLS GC (RINN CSE)
Innsbruck, Austria
(R.9 A.9) Gerold Hauser,
Günther Hauser
(R.) Herwig Zisser
INTERCOLLEGIATE GC [NLE]
New York
Devereux Emmet
INTERCONTINENTAL GC
Germany
Bernhard von Limburger
INTERLACHEN CC
Winter Park, Florida
Joe Lee
INTERLACHEN CC
Edina, Minnesota
Willie Watson
(R.) Donald Ross
(R. A.2) Willie Kidd
(R.) Robert Trent Jones
(R.) Gerry Pirkl, *Donald G.
Brauer*
(R.) Brian Silva, Geoffrey S.
Cornish
INTERLAKEN GC
Fairmount, Minnesota
(R.9 A.9) Don Herfort
INTERLAKEN-UNTERSEEN GC
Switzerland
Donald Harradine
INTERNATIONAL C
Richford, Quebec
Stanley Thompson
INTERNATIONAL C DU LYS (CHÊNES
CSE)
Chantilly, France
Tom Simpson
(R.) J. Hamilton Stutt
INTERNATIONAL C DU LYS
(BOULEAUX CSE)
Chantilly, France
Tom Simpson
(R.9 A.9) Robert Berthet
INTERNATIONAL GC
Orlando, Florida
Joe Lee
INTERNATIONAL GC
Bolton, Massachusetts
Geoffrey S. Cornish
(R.) Robert Trent Jones
(R.) Brian Silva, Geoffrey S.
Cornish
INTERNATIONAL GC DÜSSELDORF
Düsseldorf, Germany
Karl F. Grohs, *Rainer
Preissmann*
INTERNATIONAL G CENTRE
Sopron, Hungary
Herwig Zisser
INTERNATIONAL TOWN & CC
Fairfax, Virginia
(R.) Edmund B. Ault

INTERSTATE PARK GC [NLE]
New York
John Duncan Dunn
INTERVALE GC
Manchester, New Hampshire
Alex Findlay
INVERALLOCHY GC
Aberdeen, Scotland
James Gibbs
INVERCARGILL GC
Otatara, New Zealand
R. C. Butters
(R.) Sloan Morpeth
INVERGORDON GC
Invergordon, Scotland
(A.9) Fraser Middleton
INVERNESS C
Toledo, Ohio
Bernard Nicholls
(R.9 A.9) Donald Ross
(R.) A. W. Tillinghast
(R.) Dick Wilson
(R.) Robert Bruce Harris
(R.) Arthur Hills
(R. A.4) George Fazio, Tom
Fazio
(R.) Arthur Hills
INVERNESS CC
Birmingham, Alabama
George W. Cobb
INVERNESS CC
Gregory, Michigan
(R.9) Jerry Matthews
INVERNESS GC
Englewood, Colorado
Press Maxwell
INVERNESS GC
Palatine, Illinois
(R.) Edward Lawrence
Packard
INVERNESS GC
Invernesshire, Scotland
John Harris, Peter Thomson
INVERRARY CC (EAST CSE)
Lauderhill, Florida
Robert Trent Jones
INVERRARY CC (SOUTH CSE)
Lauderhill, Florida
Robert Trent Jones
INVERRARY CC (WEST CSE)
Lauderhill, Florida
Robert Trent Jones
INVERURIE GC
Inverurie, Scotland
(R.) J. Hamilton Stutt
INVERWOOD G LINKS
Minnesota
Garrett Gill, George B. Williams
INWOOD CC
Inwood, New York
*Dr. William Exton, Arthur
Thatcher*
(R.) Herbert Strong
(R.) Hal Purdy
(R.) Frank Duane
INWOOD FOREST CC
Houston, Texas
Donald Collett
(A.9) Jay Riviere
INWOOD GC
Joliet, Illinois
(R.) Edward Lawrence
Packard

IOLA CC [NLE]
Iola, Kansas
Harry Robb
IOLA COMMUNITY GC
Iola, Wisconsin
Edward Lawrence Packard
IOWA CITY CC [NLE]
Iowa City, Iowa
Tom Bendelow
IPSWICH CC
Ipswich, Massachusetts
Robert Trent Jones
IPSWICH GC
Purdis Heath, England
James Braid, John R. Stutt
(A.9) F. G. Hawtree, J. H.
Taylor
(A.3rd 9) Fred W. Hawtree,
A. H. F. Jiggens
IREM TEMPLE CC
Wilkes-Barre, Pennsylvania
A. W. Tillinghast
IRONDEQUOIT CC
Rochester, New York
Donald Ross
(A.9) J. B. McGovern
IRONHEAD G&CC
Lake Wabamum, Alberta
Les Furber
IRONHORSE G&CC
West Palm Beach, Florida
Arthur Hills
IRON HORSE G CSE
North Richland Hills, Texas
Dick Phelps
IRON MASTERS CC
Roaring Springs, Pennsylvania
Edmund B. Ault
IRON MOUNTAIN GC
Mission, Ontario
William L. Overdorf
IRON RIVER CC
Iron River, Michigan
William B. Langford, Theodore
J. Moreau
IRONSHORE CC
Montego Bay, Jamaica
Robert Moote, David S. Moote
IRONTON CC
Ironton, Ohio
Harold Paddock
IRONWOOD CC
Normal, Illinois
Roger Packard
IRONWOOD CC (NORTH CSE)
Palm Desert, California
Ted Robinson
IRONWOOD CC (SHORT CSE)
Palm Desert, California
Arnold Palmer, Ed Seay
IRONWOOD CC (SOUTH CSE)
Palm Desert, California
Desmond Muirhead
(R.) Ted Robinson
IRONWOOD GC
Yuma, Arizona
Arthur Jack Snyder
IRONWOOD GC
Byron Center, Michigan
George Woolferd
IRONWOOD GC
Hinckley, Ohio
Harold Paddock

IRONWOOD GC
Cookeville, Tennessee
L. Wesley Flatt
IRONWOOD GC
Exeter, Ontario
(A.9) John F. Robinson
IROQUOIS GC
Louisville, Kentucky
Robert Bruce Harris
(A.9) Edward Lawrence
Packard
(R.3 A.9) Benjamin Wihry
I ROVERI GC
Turin, Italy
Robert Trent Jones
IRVINE COAST CC
Newport Beach, California
William F. Bell, William P. Bell
(R.) William F. Bell
(R.) Harry Rainville, David
Rainville
IRVINE GC
Irvine, Scotland
(R.) J. Hamilton Stutt
IRVINE RAVENSPARK GC
Ayrshire, Scotland
J. Walker
IRWIN CC
Pennsylvania
(R.) James Gilmore Harrison
ISABERGS GC
Gislaved, Sweden
Anders Amilon, Ture Bruce
ISAO AOKI GC
Hyogo, Japan
Karl Litten, Isao Aoki
IS ARENAS GC
Oristano, Sardinia
Pier Mancinelli
ISEWAN CC
Gifu, Japan
(R.) Larry Nelson
ISLA DE LA PIEDRA GC
Mazatlan, Mexico
Robert Trent Jones, Jr.
ISLA DEL SOL CC
St. Petersburg, Florida
Mark Mahannah, Charles
Mahannah
ISLA NAVIDAD GC
Barra de la Navidad, Mexico
Robert von Hagge
ISLAND GC
Fort Walton Beach, Florida
Bill Amick
ISLAND GC
Cork, Ireland
Alister Mackenzie
(R.) Eddie Hackett
ISLAND G LINKS [NLE]
Garden City, New York
Devereux Emmet
ISLAND'S END G&CC
Greenport, New York
Herbert Strong
ISLAND DUNES GC
Jensen Beach, Florida
Joe Lee
ISLAND GREEN GC
Myrtle Beach, South Carolina
William Mooney

ISLAND HILLS CC
Sayville, New York
Herbert Strong
(R.) William F. Mitchell
ISLAND OF RHODES GC
Rhodes, Greece
Donald Harradine
ISLAND VALLEY GC
Rochester, New York
Pete Craig
ISLAND VIEW GC
Waconia, Minnesota
Willie Kidd
(R.) Joel Goldstrand
ISLAND WEST GC
Hilton Head Island, South
Carolina
Clyde Johnston, Fuzzy Zoeller
ISLE DAUPHINE CC
Alabama
Charles Maddox
ISLE OF PURBECK GC (PURBECK
CSE)
Dorset, England
(A.9) H. S. Colt
ISLESMERE G&CC
Quebec
Willie Park, Jr.
(A.9) Howard Watson
ISLES OF SCILLY GC
Isles of Scilly, England
Horace Hutchinson
ISLEWORTH G&CC
Windemere, Florida
Arnold Palmer, Ed Seay
ISLINGTON GC
Toronto, Ontario
Stanley Thompson
(R.) Thomas McBroom
ISOGO CC
Yokohama, Japan
S. Tachi
IS MOLAS GC
Sardinia
Pier Mancinelli
ITAKO CC
Itako, Japan
Sho Okubo
ITANHANGA CC
Tijuca, Brazil
Stanley Thompson
(R.) Robert Trent Jones
ITASCA CC
Itasca, Illinois
(R.) Robert Bruce Harris
ITŌ GC
Itō, Japan
Masujiro Yamamoto
ITO INTERNATIONAL GC
Shizuoko, Japan
Kinya Fujita
IVANHOE C
Ivanhoe, Illinois
Dick Nugent
IVES GROVES GC
Racine, Wisconsin
David Gill
IVES HILL CC
Watertown, New York
Maurice McCarthy
(R.) Peter W. Lees
(A.9) Geoffrey S. Cornish,
William G. Robinson

IVEY RANCH CC
Thousand Palms, California
William F. Bell
IVINGHOE GC
Ivinghoe, England
R. Garrad
IVY CREEK FARM GC
Virginia
Bill Love
IVY HILL CC
Forrest, Virginia
J. Porter Gibson
IVY HILLS CC
Cincinnati, Ohio
Steve Smyers
IWAKI G AND SPORT C
Iwaki City, Japan
Maury Miller, Byron Nelson, D.
A. Weibring
IWAMIZAWA LINKS GC
Iwamizawa, Japan
Isami Toi
IWASAKI RESORT GC
Yeppoon, Australia
Peter Thomson, Michael
Wolveridge
IYANOUGH HILLS GC
Hyannis, Massachusetts
Geoffrey S. Cornish, William G.
Robinson
IYO GC
Iyo, Japan
Tsuneo Abe
IZATY'S G&YC
Onamia, Minnesota
(R.) Perry Dye
IZCARAGUA CC
Caracas, Venezuela
Joe Lee, Rocky Roquemore
IZMIR HILTON INTERNATIONAL GC
Izmir, Turkey
Algie M. Pulley, Simon Gidman
IZU GC
Shizuoka, Japan
Shunsuke Kato

JABLONNA GC
Warsaw, Poland
J. J. F. Pennink
JACARANDA CC (EAST CSE)
Fort Lauderdale, Florida
Mark Mahannah
JACARANDA CC (WEST CSE)
Fort Lauderdale, Florida
Mark Mahannah, Charles
Mahannah
JACK NICKLAUS SPORTS CENTER
(BRUIN CSE)
Mason, Ohio
Desmond Muirhead, Jack
Nicklaus
JACK NICKLAUS SPORTS CENTER
(GRIZZLY CSE)
Mason, Ohio
Desmond Muirhead, Jack
Nicklaus
JACK-O-LANTERN RESORT GC
Woodstock, New Hampshire
(R.9 A.9) Bob Keating
JACKPOT GC
Jackpot, Nevada
Robert Muir Graves

JACKSON CC
    Jackson, Illinois
        (A.9) David Gill
JACKSON CC
    Jackson, Tennessee
        (R.) John LaFoy
JACKSON HEIGHTS GC [NLE]
    Jamaica, New York
    A. W. Tillinghast
JACKSON HOLE G&TC
    Jackson, Wyoming
    Bob Baldock
        (R.) Robert Trent Jones
JACKSON LAKES GC
    Lemoore, California
    Charles Hudson
JACKSON PARK MUNI
    Seattle, Washington
    William H. Tucker
        (R.) Al Smith
JACKSONVILLE CC
    Jacksonville, Illinois
    Tom Bendelow
        (A.9) Edward Lawrence
    Packard
JACKSONVILLE CC
    Jacksonville, North Carolina
    George W. Cobb
JACKSONVILLE G&CC
    Jacksonville, Florida
    Clyde Johnston, *Fuzzy Zoeller*
JACKSONVILLE BEACH GC
    Jacksonville, Florida
        (R.) Robert Walker
JAGORAWI G&CC
    Jakarta, Indonesia
    Peter Thomson, Michael
    Wolveridge, Ronald Fream
JAMES BAIRD STATE PARK GC
    Pleasant Valley, New York
    Robert Trent Jones
JAMES CONNALLY GC
    Waco, Texas
    Ralph Plummer
JAMES D. ROTHSCHILD ESTATE GC
    England
    Tom Simpson
JAMES H. AGER, JR. G CSE
    Lincoln, Nebraska
    Floyd Farley
JAMES ISLAND GC
    Sydney, British Columbia
    William G. Robinson
JAMES L. KEY MUNI
    Atlanta, Georgia
    Willie Ogg
JAMES RIVER CC
    Newport News, Virginia
    James McMenamin
JAMESTOWN CC
    St. James, Missouri
    Floyd Farley
JAMESTOWN CC
    Jamestown, North Dakota
    Robert Bruce Harris
JAMESTOWN PARK GC
    Jamestown, North Carolina
    John V. Townsend
JANLEY HILLS GC
    New York
    Pete Craig
JAPAN MEMORIAL GC
    Kobe City, Japan
    Jack Nicklaus

JASPER MUNI
    Jasper, Indiana
    William Newcomb
        (A.9) Gary Kern
JASPER PARK GC [NLE]
    Jasper, Alberta
    Sir Arthur Conan Doyle
JASPER PARK GC
    Jasper, Alberta
    Stanley Thompson
        (R.) William Brinkworth
JAWBONE CREEK GC
    Harlowton, Montana
    Frank Hummel
JAYCEE MEMORIAL G CSE
    Pine Bluff, Arkansas
    Leon Howard
J. C. LONG ESTATE GC
    Mount Pleasant, South Carolina
    George W. Cobb
JDM CC
    Palm Beach Gardens, Florida
    NKA BallenIsles CC of JDM
JEDBURGH GC
    Roxburghshire, Scotland
    Willie Park
JEFFERSON CC
    Monticello, Florida
    Bill Amick
JEFFERSON G&CC
    Blacklick, Ohio
    Robert Trent Jones, Jr.
JEFFERSON CITY CC
    Jefferson City, Missouri
    Robert Foulis
        (R.9 A.9) Edward Lawrence
    Packard
JEFFERSON HIGH SCHOOL GC
    Jefferson, Kentucky
    Hal Purdy
JEFFERSON-LAKESIDE CC
    Richmond, Virginia
    Donald Ross
JEFFERSON LANDING GC
    Jefferson, North Carolina
    Larry Nelson, *Dennis Lehmann*
JEFFERSON PARK GC
    Fairfax, Maryland
    Algie Pulley
JEFFERSON PARK MUNI
    Seattle, Washington
    Robert Johnstone, *Jim Barnes*
JEKYLL-HYDE GC
    Mulberry, Florida
    NKA [The] Reservation GC
JEKYLL ISLAND GC [NLE]
    Jekyll Island, Georgia
    Willie Dunn, Jr.
JEKYLL ISLAND GC (INDIAN MOUNDS
    CSE)
    Jekyll Island, Georgia
    Joe Lee, Rocky Roquemore
JEKYLL ISLAND GC (OCEANSIDE
    CSE)
    Jekyll Island, Georgia
    Walter J. Travis
        (R.3) Hugh Moore
JEKYLL ISLAND GC (OLEANDER CSE)
    Jekyll Island, Georgia
    Dick Wilson
JEKYLL ISLAND GC (PINE LAKES
    CSE)
    Jekyll Island, Georgia
    Joe Lee

JENNINGS MILL CC
    Athens, Georgia
    Bob Cupp
JENNY WILEY STATE PARK GC
    Pikeville, Kentucky
    Hal Purdy
JEREMY RANCH GC
    Park City, Utah
    Arnold Palmer, Ed Seay
JERSEY VILLAGE GC
    Jersey Village, Texas
    Bob Simmons
JERRY'S FARM C
    Annandale, Minnesota
    Joel Goldstrand
JESTER PARK GC
    Granger, Iowa
    Dick Phelps
JESUP G&CC
    Jesup, Iowa
    Charles Calhoun
JETPORT GC
    Huntsville, Alabama
    Bob Baldock, Robert L. Baldock
JIDDA GC
    Jidda, Saudi Arabia
    George Wadsworth
JOCKEY C (BLUE CSE)
    San Isidro, Argentina
    Alister Mackenzie
        (R.) Ronald Fream
JOCKEY C (RED CSE)
    San Isidro, Argentina
    Alister Mackenzie
        (R.) Ronald Fream
JOE LEWIS THE CHAMP GC
    Blue Island, Illinois
    James Foulis
        (R.) Dick Nugent
JOENKOEPINGS GC
    Sweden
    Nils Sköld
JOETSU KOKUSAI CC (TOKAMACHI
    CSE)
    Niigata Prefecture, Japan
    Mike Poellot, Brad Benz
JOE WHEELER STATE PARK GC
    Rogersville, Alabama
    Earl Stone
JOHANNESBERG GC
    Stockholm, Sweden
    D. M. A. Steel
JOHANNESBURG CC [NLE]
    Transvaal, South Africa
        (R.) C. H. Alison
JOHN BLUMBERG MUNI
    Winnipeg, Manitoba
    Clinton E. Robinson
JOHN C. BEASLEY MUNI
    Beeville, Texas
    Leon Howard
JOHN CONRAD GC
    Midwest City, Oklahoma
    Floyd Farley
JOHN F. KENNEDY MUNI
    Denver, Colorado
    Henry B. Hughes
JOHN H. CAIN GC
    Newport, New Hampshire
    Willie Park, Jr.
        (R.) Ralph Barton
        (R.) Orrin Smith
        (R.7 A.11) Phil Wogan

JOHN KNOX VILLAGE GC
    Lees Summit, Missouri
    Larry Runyon, Michael H. Malyn
JOHN O'GAUNT GC (CARTHAGENA
    CSE)
    Bedfordshire, England
    Willie Dunn, Jr.
        (R.) Fred W. Hawtree
JOHN'S ISLAND C (NORTH CSE)
    Vero Beach, Florida
    Pete Dye
JOHN'S ISLAND C (SOUTH CSE)
    Vero Beach, Florida
    Pete Dye
        (R.) Joe Lee
JOHN'S ISLAND C (WEST CSE)
    Wabasso, Florida
    Tom Fazio
JOHNSON CITY CC
    Johnson City, Tennessee
    A. W. Tillinghast
        (R.) John LaFoy
JOHNSON PARK GC
    Racine, Wisconsin
    Todd Sloan
JOHNSTOWN ELKS CC
    Johnstown, Pennsylvania
    James Gilmore Harrison
JOLIET CC
    Joliet, Illinois
    Tom Bendelow
JOLLY ACRES GC
    South Dakota
    Clifford A. Anderson
JONATHAN'S LANDING GC
    Jupiter, Florida
    George Fazio, Tom Fazio
JONATHAN PAR 3 GC
    Chaska, Minnesota
    Robert Trent Jones
JONESBORO CC
    Jonesboro, Arkansas
    William M. Martin
JONESCO GC
    Gray, Georgia
    Ernie Schrock
JONES CREEK GC
    Evans, Georgia
    Rees Jones
JOONDALUP GC
    Australia
    Robert Trent Jones, Jr.
JOPLIN CC [NLE]
    Joplin, Missouri
    Tom Bendelow
        (R.) Orrin Smith
JORDAN POINT CC
    Hopewell, Virginia
    Russell Breeden
JUAN DE FUCA MUNI G CSE
    Victoria, British Columbia
    Dick Phelps
JUAREZ CC
    Juarez, Mexico
    George Hoffman
JUG END INN GC
    Egremont, Massachusetts
    Alfred H. Tull
JULIANA WUPPERTAL GC
    Germany
    M. Peters
JULINGTON CREEK GC
    Jacksonville, Florida
    Robert Walker

JUMPING BROOK GC
Neptune, New Jersey
Willard Wilkinson
   (R.) Nicholas Psiahas

JUNIATA GC
Philadelphia, Pennsylvania
Edmund B. Ault

JUNIPER CC
Redmond, Oregon
Fred Sparks

JUNIPER HILLS GC
Frankfort, Kentucky
Buck Blankenship

JUNIPER HILLS GC (OLD CSE)
Northborough, Massachusetts
Homer Darling
   (A.9) Geoffrey S. Cornish
   (R.4) Phil Wogan

JUNIPER HILLS GC (NEW CSE)
Northborough, Massachusetts
Phil Wogan

JUNKO CC
Venezuela
Charles Banks

JUPITER DUNES GC
Jupiter, Florida
Bob Erickson
   (R.) Ward Northrup

JUPITER HILLS C (HILLS CSE)
Jupiter, Florida
George Fazio
   (R.) George Fazio, Tom Fazio
   (A.3) George Fazio, Tom
   Fazio

JUPITER HILLS C (VILLAGE CSE)
Jupiter, Florida
George Fazio, Tom Fazio

JUPITER ISLAND C
Jupiter, Florida
William H. Diddel
   (R.) George Fazio, Tom Fazio

JUPITER WEST GC [NLE]
Jupiter, Florida
Ward Northrup
   (R.) Karl Litten

JURONG CC
Jurong, Singapore
   (R.) Ronald Fream

JURUPA HILLS CC
Riverside, California
William F. Bell

KAANAPALI KAI GC [NLE]
Lahaina, Hawaii
Arthur Jack Snyder

KAGOSHIMA GC
Kagoshima, Japan
Y. Yasuda

KAHKWA C
Erie, Pennsylvania
Donald Ross

KAHLER GLEN GC
Leavenworth, Washington
Roy Goss

KAH-NEE-TA GC
Warm Springs, Oregon
William P. Bell
   (A.9) Gene "Bunny" Mason

KAIFUYO CC
Yamanashi, Japan
Hiroshi Umezawa

KAISERGOLF ELLMAU
Tirol, Austria
Gerold Hauser, *Günther Hauser*

KAKOGAWA GC
Kakogawa City, Japan
Mitsuaki Otani

KALAMAZOO CC
Kalamazoo, Michigan
Tom Bendelow
   (R.) Willie Watson
   (R.) William Newcomb

KALAMAZOO ELKS CC
Kalamazoo, Michigan
   (R.2) Bruce Matthews, Jerry
   Matthews

KALISPELL G&CC
Kalispell, Montana
Gregor MacMillan

KALMAR GC
Sweden
Rafael Sundblum

KALONA GC
Kalona, Iowa
   (R.9) Charles Calhoun

KALUA KOI GC
Maunaloa, Molokai, Hawaii
Ted Robinson

KALUNDBORG GC
Kalundborg, Denmark
Jan Sederholm

KAMIRAG GC
Cebu Island, Philippines
Ron Kirby, Denis Griffiths

KAMO GC
Aichi, Japan
Tetsuro Akabane

KANANASKIS COUNTRY GC (MOUNT KIDD CSE)
Kananaskis Village, Alberta
Robert Trent Jones

KANANASKIS COUNTRY GC (MOUNT LORETTE CSE)
Kananaskis Village, Alberta
Robert Trent Jones

KANATA LAKES G&CC
Ottawa, Ontario
Howard Watson
   (R.9 A.9) Thomas McBroom

KANAWAKI GC
Quebec
Albert Murray, *Charles Murray*
   (R.) Clinton E. Robinson
   (R.9) Howard Watson
   (R.3) Howard Watson, John
   Watson
   (R.5) John Watson

KANEFF G&CC
Brampton, Ontario
Ted Baker

KANEGASAKI GC
Oaza-Nagasawa, Japan
Arnold Palmer, Ed Seay

KANEOHE KLIPPER GC
Kaneohe Bay, Hawaii
William P. Bell
   (R.) *Jimmy Ukauka*

KANKAKEE CC
Kankakee, Illinois
Tom Bendelow
   (R.8 A.10) John Darrah

KANKAKEE ELKS CC
St. Anne, Illinois
William B. Langford, Theodore
J. Moreau

KANNAMI SPRINGS CC
Japan
Perry Dye

KANON VALLEY CC
Oneida, New York
Hal Purdy

KANSAI CLASSIC GC
Japan
Takeshi Sato

KANSAS CITY CC
Shawnee Mission, Kansas
Tom Bendelow
   (R.2) Floyd Farley
   (R.) Bob Dunning
   (R.) Rees Jones

KANSAI GC
Hyogo, Japan
Shoichi Suzuki

KAPALUA GC (BAY CSE)
Kapalua, Maui, Hawaii
Frank Duane, Arnold Palmer
   (R.) Robin Nelson, Rodney
   Wright, Hale Irwin

KAPALUA GC (PLANTATION CSE)
Kapalua, Maui, Hawaii
Bill Coore, Ben Crenshaw

KAPALUA GC (VILLAGE CSE)
Kapalua, Maui, Hawaii
Arnold Palmer, Ed Seay
   (R.) Robin Nelson, Rodney
   Wright, Hale Irwin

KAPRUN-ZELL AM SEE GC
Austria
Donald Harradine

KAPUK GC
Jakarta, Indonesia
Robert Trent Jones, Jr.

KARASAWA GC
Japan
Seisui Chin

KARLOVY VARY GC [NLE]
Karlovy Vary, Czechoslovakia
Willie Brown (9 1904)

KARLOVY VARY GC
Karlovy Vary, Czechoslovakia
M. C. Noskowski (1935)

KARLSHAMNS GC
Karlshamn, Sweden
Douglas Brazier

KARLSKOGA GC
Karlskoga, Sweden
Nils Sköld
   (A.9) Jan Sederholm

KARLSKRONA GC
Karlskrona, Sweden
Anders Amilon
   (R. A.8) Jan Sederholm

KARLSTAD GC
Karlstad, Sweden
Nils Sköld

KARNATAKA GC
Bangalore, India
Peter Thomson, Michael
Wolveridge

KARORI GC
Wellington, New Zealand
John Harris, Peter Thomson

KARSTEN G CSE AT ASU
Tempe, Arizona
Perry Dye, Pete Dye

KARTNER GC
Dellach, Austria
E. Leitner

KARUIZAWA GC
Nagano, Japan
Yuji Kodera

KARUIZAWA GOLF (HIGASHI CSE)
Karuizawa, Japan
Robert Trent Jones

KARUIZAWA GOLF (KARUIZAWA CSE)
Karuizawa, Japan
Robert Trent Jones, Jr.

KARUIZAWA GOLF (KITA CSE)
Karuizawa, Japan
Robert Trent Jones

KARUIZAWA GOLF (MINAMI CSE)
Karuizawa, Japan
Robert Trent Jones

KARUIZAWA GOLF (NISHI CSE)
Karuizawa, Japan
Robert Trent Jones

KARUIZAWA NINE HUNDRED C
Karuizawa, Japan
Hirochika Tomizawa

KASHIWAZAKI CC
Kashiwazaki, Japan
Ayako Okamoto

KASHIWAZAKI SEASIDE GC
Kashiwazaki, Japan
Tomiichi Fukuda

KASSEL-WILHELMSHOHE GC
Kassel, Germany
Bernhard von Limburger
   (A.9) Donald Harradine, *Peter Harradine*

KASS INN & CC
New York
   (A.9) Ernest E. Smith

KASUGABARA GC
Fukuoka, Japan
T. Hirayama

KASUGADAI CC
Japan
Sho Sato

KASUGAI CC (EAST CSE)
Nagoya, Japan
Seichi Inouye

KASUGAI CC (WEST CSE)
Nagoya, Japan
Seichi Inouye

KASUMIGASEKI CC (EAST CSE)
Saitama, Japan
Kinya Fujita
   (R.) C. H. Alison

KASUMIGASEKI CC (WEST CSE)
Saitama, Japan
Kinya Fujita
   (R.) C. H. Alison

KATAHDIN CC
Milo, Maine
Larry H. Striley

KATKE GC
Ferris State University
Big Rapids, Michigan
Robert Beard

KATKE COUSINS GC
Oakland University
Rochester, Michigan
Robert Beard

KATRINEHOLMS GC
Katrineholms, Sweden
Nils Sköld

KATSURA GC
Hokkaido Prefecture, Japan
Robert Trent Jones, Jr.

KATSURAGAOKA CC
   Ibaragi Prefecture, Japan
   Robert von Hagge
KATSURA TOKYU GC
   Japan
   Chohei Miyazawa
KAUAI LAGOONS G&CC (KIELE
   CSE)
   Lihue, Kauai, Hawaii
   Jack Nicklaus
KAUAI LAGOONS G&CC (LAGOONS
   CSE)
   Lihue, Kauai, Hawaii
   Jack Nicklaus
KAUAI SURF G&CC [NLE]
   Kauai, Hawaii
   Willard Wilkinson
      (A.9) *Raymond F. Cain*
KAUFMAN GC
   Wyoming, Michigan
   Bruce Matthews, Jerry Matthews
KAWAGOE CC
   Kawagoe, Japan
   Pete Nakamura
KAWAGOE GREEN CROSS GC
   Saitama-ken, Japan
   Mike Poellot
KAWAGUCHI G & ATHLETIC C
   Saitama, Japan
   K. Kasugai
KAWAGUCHI-KO GC
   Mount Fuji, Japan
   Robert von Hagge, Bruce Devlin
KAWAKAMI VILLAGE CC
   Japan
   Makoto Murakami
KAWANA GC (FUJI CSE)
   Shizuoka, Japan
   C. H. Alison
      (R.) Kinya Fujita
KAWANA GC (OSHIMA CSE)
   Shizuoka, Japan
   Komei Otani
      (R.) C. H. Alison
KAWARTHA GC
   Peterboro, Ontario
   Stanley Thompson
KAWASAKI KOKUSAI CC
   Kanagawa, Japan
   Seichi Inouye
KAYAK POINT GC
   Stanwood, Washington
   Peter Thomson, Michael
   Wolveridge, Ronald Fream
KAZUSA GC
   Tokyo, Japan
   Jack Nicklaus
KEARNEY CC
   Kearney, Nebraska
      (R.) Harold Glissmann
      (R.9 A.9) Leo Johnson
KEARNEY HILL G LINKS
   Lexington, Kentucky
   P. B. Dye, Pete Dye
KEARSARGE VALLEY CC
   North Sutton, New Hampshire
   NKA CC of New Hampshire
KEAUHOU KONA CC
   Kailua-Kona, Hawaii
   William F. Bell
      (R.3) Arthur Jack Snyder
      (A.3rd 9) William F. Bell

KEBAYORAN GC
   Jakarta, Indonesia
      (R.) Peter Thomson, Michael
      Wolveridge, Ronald Fream
KEBO VALLEY C
   Bar Harbor, Maine
   Herbert Leeds
      (A.9) *Andrew E. Liscombe*
      (R.) *Waldron T. Bates*
KEDLESTON PARK GC
   Derbyshire, England
   James Braid, John R. Stutt, J. S.
   F. Morrison
KEENE CC
   Keene, New Hampshire
      (R.) Manny Francis
KEERBERGEN GC
   Keerbergen, Belgium
   Tom Simpson
      (R.) J. J. F. Pennink
KEESLER AFB GC
   Gulfport, Mississippi
   Joseph S. Finger
KEFFERVILLE CC
   Stockbridge, Vermont
   Bob Labbance
KEIGHLEY GC
   Keighley, England
      (R.) Tom Simpson
KEITH HILLS CC
   Buies Creek, North Carolina
   Ellis Maples, Dan Maples
KELAB GOLF DI RAJA DARUL EHSAN
   Ampang Jay, Malaysia
   Ronald Fream
KELAB GOLF DI RAJA TRENGGANU
   Trengganu, Malaysia
      (R.9) Robin Nelson, Rodney
      Wright
KELLER GC
   St. Paul, Minnesota
   Paul Coates
      (R.1) Don Herfort
      (R.) Garrett Gill, George B.
      Williams
KELLOGG GC
   Peoria, Illinois
   Edward Lawrence Packard,
   Roger Packard
KELLY GREENS G&CC
   Fort Myers, Florida
   Gordon Lewis
KELLY RIDGE G LINKS
   Oroville, California
   Homer Flint
KELOWNA G&CC
   Kelowna, British Columbia
   A. Vernon Macan
KELOWNA SPRINGS GC
   Kelowna, British Columbia
   Les Furber, *Jim Eremko*
KELSEY CITY GC [NLE]
   West Palm Beach, Florida
   William B. Langford, Theodore
   J. Moreau
KELSO ELKS GC [NLE]
   Kelso, Washington
      (R.) Robert Muir Graves
KELSO GC
   Roxboroughshire, Scotland
   James Braid
KEMMERER GC
   Kemmerer, Wyoming
   Dick Phelps

KEMPER LAKES GC
   Hawthorn Woods, Illinois
   Ken Killian, Dick Nugent
      (R.) Ken Killian
KEMPSVILLE MEADOWS G&CC
   Norfolk, Virginia
   Ellis Maples
KEMPTON PARK CC
   South Africa
   Fred Stegman
KENATA LAKES G&CC
   Kenata, Ontario
   Thomas McBroom
KENDALE LAKES G&CC
   Miami, Florida
   Charles Mahannah
KENDALE LAKES WEST CC
   Miami, Florida
   Charles Mahannah
KENDALLVILLE ELKS CC
   Kendallville, Indiana
   Tom Bendelow
KENDRICK MUNI
   Sheridan, Wyoming
   Edward A. Hunnicutt
      (A.9) Frank Hummel
KENDUSKEAG VALLEY GC
   Kenduskeag, Maine
   Bob Girvan
KENEY PARK GC
   Hartford, Connecticut
   Devereux Emmet
      (R.) Robert J. Ross
      (R.) Everett Pyle
      (R.3) Geoffrey S. Cornish,
      William G. Robinson
KENILWORTH GC
   Warwickshire, England
   Roger Dyer
KENILWORTH LODGE GC [NLE]
   Sebring, Florida
   Wayne Stiles, John Van Kleek
KENJO SHONAI CC
   Japan
   Hiromasa Shimamura
KENLOCH G LINKS
   Lombard, Illinois
   David Gill
KEN MCDONALD MUNI
   Tempe, Arizona
   Arthur Jack Snyder
KENMURE GC
   Flat Rocks, North Carolina
   Joe Lee, Rocky Roquemore
KENNEMER G&CC
   Netherlands
   H. S. Colt, C. H. Alison, J. S. F.
   Morrison
KENOGAMISIS GC
   Geraldton, Ontario
   Stanley Thompson
KENORA G&CC
   Kenora, Ontario
   Stanley Thompson
      (R.7 A.11) Robert Moote
KENOSEE LAKES GC
   Saskatchewan
      (A.9) Clinton E. Robinson
KENOSHA CC
   Kenosha, Wisconsin
   Donald Ross
      (R.) Stephen Kay

KENSINGTON GC
   Milford, Michigan
   H. A. Lemley
KENSINGTON GC
   South Africa
      (R.) Ron Kirby, Denis
      Griffiths
KENT CC
   Grand Rapids, Michigan
   E. C. Simonds
      (R.9 A.9) Donald Ross
      (R.9) James Foulis
      (R.4) Jerry Matthews
KENTLAND GC
   Kentland, Indiana
   Tom Bendelow
KENTON COUNTY GC (NORTH CSE)
   Independence, Kentucky
   Jack Kidwell, Michael
   Hurdzan
KENTON COUNTY GC (SOUTH CSE)
   Independence, Kentucky
   Taylor Boyd (1968)
      (R.) Jack Kidwell, Michael
      Hurdzan
KENTON STATION GC
   Maysville, Kentucky
   Harold England (9 1967)
KENTUCK GC
   North Bend, Oregon
   Don Houston, Wallace Wickett
KENTUCKY DAM VILLAGE GC
   Gilbertsville, Kentucky
   Perry Maxwell, Press Maxwell
KENTVILLE GC
   Kentville, Nova Scotia
   Willie Park, Jr.
KENWICK HALL GC
   Louth, England
   Jim Engh
KEN-WO G&CC
   New Minas, Nova Scotia
      (A.9) Clinton E. Robinson
KENWOOD CC (KENDALE CSE)
   Cincinnati, Ohio
   William H. Diddel
      (R.) William H. Diddel
      (R.) Jack Kidwell, Michael
      Hurdzan
KENWOOD CC (KENVIEW CSE)
   Cincinnati, Ohio
   William H. Diddel
      (R.) Jack Kidwell, Michael
      Hurdzan
KENWOOD G&CC
   Bethesda, Maryland
      (R.) Edmund B. Ault
KEOKUK CC
   Keokuk, Iowa
   Tom Bendelow
      (R.) William B. Langford
KEOWEE KEY CC
   Seneca, South Carolina
   George W. Cobb, John LaFoy
KEPPEL C
   Singapore
      (R.) Ronald Fream
KERIGOLF
   Kerimaa-Savonlinna, Finland
   Ronald Fream
KERN CITY GC
   Bakersfield, California
   Arthur Jack Snyder

KERN RIVER CC
Bakersfield, California
William F. Bell, William P. Bell
KERN VALLEY GC
Kernville, California
William F. Bell
KERNWOOD CC
Salem, Massachusetts
Donald Ross
(R.) William F. Mitchell
(R.) Geoffrey S. Cornish,
William Robinson
(R.) Brian Silva, Geoffrey S.
Cornish
KERRVILLE HILLS CC
Kerrville, Texas
Donald Collett
KESWICK C OF VIRGINIA
Keswick, Virginia
Fred Findlay
(R.) Arnold Palmer, Ed Seay
KESWICK GC
Cumbria, England
Eric Brown
KETTENRING CC
Defiance, Ohio
Tom Bendelow
(A.9) William Newcomb
KETTLE HILLS GC
Richfield, Wisconsin
Bob Lohmann (routing); Don
Zimmermann (1987)
KEY BISCAYNE GC
Key Biscayne, Florida
Robert von Hagge, Bruce Devlin
KEY BISCAYNE HOTEL CC
Miami Beach, Florida
Mark Mahannah
KEY COLONY GC [NLE]
Key Biscayne, Florida
Mark Mahannah
KEY COLONY BEACH GC
Miami, Florida
John O'Connor
KEYSTONE HEIGHTS G&CC
Keystone Heights, Florida
Donald Ross
(R.) R. Albert Anderson
KEY ROYALE GC
Holmes Beach, Florida
James C. Cochran
KEYSTONE RANCH GC
Dillon, Colorado
Robert Trent Jones, Jr.
KEY WEST GC [NLE]
Key West, Florida
William B. Langford, Theodore
J. Moreau
KEY WEST RESORT GC
Key West, Florida
Rees Jones
KI-8-EB GC
Three Rivers, Quebec
Stanley Thompson
(R.) Clinton E. Robinson
(R.2) Howard Watson
(R.2) John Watson (1977)
(R.5) John Watson (1989)
KIAHUNA PLANTATION GC
Poipu Beach, Hawaii
Robert Trent Jones, Jr.

KICKINGBIRD GC
Edmond, Oklahoma
Floyd Farley
(R.) Gary Kern, Ron Kern
(R.) Lee Singletary (1992)
KIEL GC
Kiel, Germany
(R.) Bernhard von Limburger
KIIRE CC
Kagoshima, Japan
Shunsuke Kato
KILBUCK GC
Anderson, Indiana
William H. Diddel
KILCOCK GC
Kilcock, Ireland
Bobby Browne
KILDARE GC
Straffan, Ireland
Arnold Palmer, Ed Seay
KILKENNY GC
County Kilkenny, Ireland
Tom Simpson
KILLARNEY GC
Johannesburg, South Africa
Robert Grimsdell, Tommy
Tomsett
(R.) Tommy Tomsett
KILLARNEY GC [NLE]
County Kerry, Ireland
Willie Park
KILLARNEY G & FISHING C
(KILLEEN CSE)
County Kerry, Ireland
Sir Guy Campbell
(R.12 A.6) Fred W. Hawtree
KILLARNEY G & FISHING C
(MAHONEY'S POINT CSE)
County Kerry, Ireland
Sir Guy Campbell
(R.6 A.12) Fred W. Hawtree
KILLARNEY RACETRACK GC
Killarney, Ireland
Eddie Hackett
KILLEARN CC
Tallahassee, Florida
Bill Amick
(A.3rd 9) Bill Amick
KILLEEN MUNI
Killeen, Texas
Jay Riviere
KILLINEY GC
Killiney, Ireland
(R.) Eddie Hackett
KILLINGTON GC
Killington, Vermont
Geoffrey S. Cornish
KILLYMOON GC
County Tyrone, Northern
Ireland
Fred W. Hawtree
KILMARNOCK GC
Barassie, Scotland
John Allan
(R.) Theodore Moone
KILN CREEK CC
Newport News, Virginia
Tom Clark
KILSPINDLE GC
Scotland
(R.) Willie Park, Jr.
KIMBERLAND MEADOWS GC
New Meadows, Idaho
Bob Baldock, Robert L. Baldock

KIMBERLEY GC
Kimberley, British Columbia
(A.9) Norman H. Woods
(A.3) Ted Nagel
(R.) Bill Newis
KIMBERLING HILLS CC
Kimberling, Missouri
Mel Taylor, Hobe Jennings
KIMBERTON GC
Pennsylvania
George Fazio
(R.) James Blaukovitch
KINCHELO MEMORIAL GC
Kinross, Michigan
Bob Baldock
KINDERSLEY GC
Kindersley, Saskatchewan
William Kinnear
KINDERTON CC
Clarksville, Virginia
Dick Wilson
KING CITY GC
King City, California
Bob Baldock
(R.) Robert Dean Putman
KING DAVID CC
Cape Town, South Africa
Robert G. Grimsdell
KING EMMANUAL PRIVATE CSE
Italy
Seymour Dunn
KING FIELD CC
Chiba-ken, Japan
Mike Poellot
KINGFISHER GC
Kingfisher, Oklahoma
Floyd Farley
KINGHORN GC
Fife, Scotland
Old Tom Morris
KING JAMES VI GC
Perth, Scotland
Old Tom Morris
KING LEOPOLD PRIVATE CSE
Belgium
Seymour Dunn
KINGMAN GC
Kingman, Arizona
Milt Coggins
KINGS CC
California
William Lock (9 1923)
(A.9) Bert Stamps
[THE] KINGS' GC
Waikaloa Beach, Hawaii
Jay Morrish, Tom Weiskopf
KINGS BAY Y&CC [NLE]
Miami, Florida
Mark Mahannah, Charles
Mahannah
KINGSBERY C [NLE]
Vermont
Ralph Barton
KINGS CREEK CC
Rehoboth Beach, Delaware
Dominic Palombo (1990)
KINGS CROSSING G&CC
Corpus Christi, Texas
Bill Coore
KING'S GRANT G&CC
Fayetteville, North Carolina
Jim Holmes (1990)

KINGS GRANT GC
Charleston, South Carolina
Russell Breeden
KINGSKNOWE GC
Edinburgh, Scotland
James Braid
KING'S LYNN GC
England
Peter Alliss, David Thomas
KINGSMILL GC (PLANTATION CSE)
Williamsburg, Virginia
Arnold Palmer, Ed Seay
KINGSMILL GC (RIVER CSE)
Williamsburg, Virginia
Pete Dye
(R.7) Edmund B. Ault
KINGS MILL GC
Waldo, Ohio
Jack Kidwell
KINGS NORTON GC
Worcestershire, England
Fred W. Hawtree, Martin
Hawtree
KINGS POINT EXECUTIVE GC (CSE
No. 1)
Delray Beach, Florida
Robert Trent Jones
KINGS POINT EXECUTIVE GC (CSE
No. 2)
Delray Beach, Florida
Robert Trent Jones
KINGSPORT CC
Pennsylvania
Maurice McCarthy
KINGSPORT CC
Kingsport, Tennessee
A. W. Tillinghast
KINGSRIDGE CC
Port Chester, New York
Tom Winton
KINGS RIVER G&CC
Kingsbury, California
Bert Stamps, Nick Lombardo
(R.) Bob Baldock
KINGSTHORPE GC [NLE]
Northamptonshire, England
H. S. Colt, C. H. Alison
KINGSTON HEATH GC
Cheltenham, Australia
Des Soutar
(R.) Peter Thomson, Michael
Wolveridge
(R.) Alister Mackenzie
KINGSTREE CC
Greenleyville, South Carolina
Robert White
KINGSVILLE GC
Kingsville, Ontario
(A.9) Robert Moote, David S.
Moote
KINGSWAY CC
Lake Suzy, Florida
Ron Garl
KINGSWAY GC
Massachusetts
Brian Silva, Geoffrey S. Cornish
KINGSWOOD CC
Wolfeboro, New Hampshire
Donald Ross
(R.) Tom Clark
KINGSWOOD G&CC
La Salle, Manitoba
David Grant, Jim Thomas

KINGSWOOD GC
Bella Vista, Arkansas
Edmund B. Ault
KINGSWOOD GC
Surrey, England
James Braid, John R. Stutt
KINGTON GC
Herefordshire, England
C. K. Hutchison, Sir Guy Campbell, S. V. Hotchkin
KINGUSSIE GC
Invernesshire, Scotland
Harry Vardon
KING VALLEY GC
King City, Ontario
Douglas Carrick
KINGWOOD CC
Clayton, Georgia
Larry McClure
KINGWOOD CC (ISLAND CSE)
Kingwood, Texas
Joseph S. Finger
KINGWOOD CC (KINGS CROSSING CSE)
Kingwood, Texas
Ken Dye
KINGWOOD CC (LAKE CSE)
Kingwood, Texas
Bruce Littell
KINGWOOD CC (MARSH CSE)
Kingwood, Texas
Joseph S. Finger
KINNODAI CC
Japan
Seisui Chin
KINOJO GC
Okayama, Japan
Robert Trent Jones, Jr.
KINSDOWN GC
England
Tom Dunn
KINSTON CC
Kinston, North Carolina
(R.) Ellis Maples
(R.) Russell Breeden, *Dan Breeden*
KINUGAWA CC
Japan
Pete Nakamura
KINUGAWA SHINRIN CC
Tochigi, Japan
Hirochika Tomizawa
KINWEST GC
Dallas, Texas
(R.) Joseph S. Finger
KIOKAWA GC (EAST CSE)
Atsugi Prefecture, Japan
Jun Mizutani
(R.) Bob Cupp, Jay Morrish
KIOKAWA GC (WEST CSE)
Atsugi Prefecture, Japan
Jun Mizutani
(R.) Bob Cupp, Jay Morrish
KIPLINGEBERG GC
Sweden
Jan Sederholm
KIRA CC
Japan
Shigeru Ishii
KIRBYWOOD CC
Cleveland, Texas
Bruce Littell

KIRCHBROMBACH GC
Germany
Karl F. Grohs, *Rainier Preissmann*
KIRKBRAE CC
Lincoln, Rhode Island
Geoffrey S. Cornish
(R.3) Samuel Mitchell
(R.1) Al Zikorus
KIRKCALDY GC
Scotland
(R.) J. Hamilton Stutt
KIRKISTOWN CASTLE GC
Northern Ireland
James Braid
KIRRIEMUIR GC
Perthshire, Scotland
James Braid
KIRTLAND CC
Willoughby, Ohio
C. H. Alison, H. S. Colt
(R.) Pete Dye
KISHWAUKEE CC
De Kalb, Illinois
Tom Bendelow
(A.9) David Gill
(R.) Bob Lohmann
KISSENA GC
Flushing, New York
John Van Kleek
(R.) Stephen Kay
KISSIMMEE GC [NLE]
Kissimmee, Florida
John Hamilton Gillespie
KISSIMMEE BAY CC
Kissimmee, Florida
Lloyd Clifton, *Kenneth Ezell, George Clifton*
KISSING CAMELS GC
Colorado Springs, Colorado
Press Maxwell
KITAKATA GC
Miyazaki, Japan
Tsurugi Sokuryo Sekkei
KITSAP G&CC
Bremerton, Washington
(R.) William Teufel
KITTANNING CC
Pennsylvania
Emil Loeffler, *John McGlynn*
KITTANSETT C
Marion, Massachusetts
William S. Flynn (routing);
Frederic C. Hood
(R.1) Stephen Kay
KITTYHAWK MUNI (EAGLE CSE)
Dayton, Ohio
Robert Bruce Harris
KITTYHAWK MUNI (HAWK CSE)
Dayton, Ohio
Robert Bruce Harris
KITTYHAWK MUNI (KITTY CSE)
Dayton, Ohio
Robert Bruce Harris
KITZBÜHEL-SCHWARZSEE GC
Tirol, Austria
Gerold Hauser, *Günther Hauser*
KITZENBERG GC
Germany
(R.) Bernhard von Limburger
KIYOHARU CC
Japan
Yukitada Nakamura

KJEKSTAD GC
Norway
Jan Sederholm
KLEIBURG GC
Brielle, Netherlands
J. J. F. Pennink
KLINGENBURG-GUNZBERG GC
Germany
Donald Harradine
KLINGER LAKE CC
Sturgis, Michigan
Maurie Wells
(R.) William Newcomb
KNEBWORTH GC
Hertfordshire, England
Willie Park, Jr.
KNICKERBOCKER CC [NLE]
Tenafly, New Jersey
Maurice McCarthy
KNICKERBOCKER CC
Tenafly, New Jersey
Donald Ross
(R.) Herbert Strong
(R.6) Geoffrey S. Cornish, William G. Robinson
KNIGHTON GC
Powys, Wales
Harry Vardon
KNIGHTON HEATH GC
Dorset, England
J. Hamilton Stutt
(R.) J. Hamilton Stutt
KNOB HILL CC
Freehold, New Jersey
James Gilmore Harrison, Ferdinand Garbin
KNOLE PARK GC
Kent, England
Herbert Fowler, J. F. Abercromby
(R.) Tom Simpson
KNOLL GC
Omaha, Nebraska
(A.9) *William B. Kubly*
KNOLL GC
Boonton, New Jersey
Charles Banks
KNOLL EAST GC
Boonton, New Jersey
Hal Purdy
KNOLLS GC
Lincoln, Nebraska
Floyd Farley
KNOLLWOOD C
Lake Forest, Illinois
C. H. Alison, H. S. Colt
(R.) Edward Lawrence Packard, Roger Packard
(R.) Roger Packard
KNOLLWOOD CC
Granada Hills, California
William F. Bell, William H. Johnson
(R.) *David W. Kent*
KNOLLWOOD CC
West Bloomfield, Michigan
(R.1 A.1) Bruce Matthews, Jerry Matthews
KNOLLWOOD CC
Elmsford, New York
Lawrence Van Etten
(R.) A. W. Tillinghast
(R.) Charles Banks
(R.) Stephen Kay

KNOLLWOOD GC [NLE]
Irving, Texas
Perry Maxwell, Press Maxwell
KNOWLE GC
Gloucestershire, England
F. G. Hawtree, J. H. Taylor
KNOWLTON GC
Knowlton, Quebec
(R.9 A.9) Howard Watson
KNOXVILLE MUNI
Knoxville, Tennessee
(R.) D. J. DeVictor
KOBE GC
Kobe, Japan
Arthur Hesketh Groome (1904)
KOBUCHIZAWA CC
Yamanashi, Japan
Takeadi Kaneda
KOCHI KUROSHIO CC
Kochi, Japan
Takeadi Kaneda
KODAMA SPRING CC
Saitama, Japan
Mitsuo Yoshizaki
KOERUNDA-NYÄSHAMNS GC
Oesmo, Sweden
Ake Persson
KOGA GC
Fukuoka, Japan
O. Ueda
KOGA G LINKS
Koga, Japan
Takeadi Kaneda
KOGANEI CC
Tokyo, Japan
Walter Hagen
KOGASHI CC
Japan
Hiroshi Umezawa
KOHLERHOF GC
Bonn, Germany
J. F. Dudok van Heel
KOKANEE SPRINGS CC
Crawford Bay, British Columbia
Norman H. Woods
KOKKEDAL GC
Rungsted, Denmark
J. J. F. Pennink
(R.) Jan Sederholm
KOKOMO CC
Kokomo, Indiana
Tom Bendelow
(R.9 A.9) William H. Diddel
KOLDING GC
Kolding, Denmark
M. Steengaard
(R.9 A.9) Jan Sederholm
KOLN-REFRATH GC
Bergisch, Germany
Bernhard von Limburger
KOMONO GC
Nagoya, Japan
Jack Nicklaus
KONA INTERNATIONAL CC
Kailua-Kona, Hawaii
Robin Nelson, Rodney Wright
KONA MANSION INN GC
Moultonboro, New Hampshire
N.P. Neilsen
KONINKLIJKE GC
Ostend, Belgium
Willie Park, Jr.

KONSTANZ GC
Konstanz, Germany
Bernhard von Limburger
(A.9) Karl F. Grohs, *Rainer
Preissmann*
KO OLINA GC
Ewa Beach, Oahu, Hawaii
Ted Robinson
KOORALBYN VALLEY GC
Australia
Desmond Muirhead
KOOYONGA GC
Australia
(R.) Peter Thomson, Michael
Wolveridge
KORAKUEN CC
Sapporo, Japan
John Harris, Peter Thomson,
Ronald Fream
KORIYAMA ATAMI CC
Fukushima, Japan
Takaichi Fukuda
KORNWESTHEIM GC
Germany
Bernhard von Limburger
KORSLOETS GC
Sweden
Douglas Brazier, Peter Nordvall
(A.9) Jan Sederholm
KORSØR GC
Korsør, Denmark
Anders Amilon
KORYO CC
Kanuma, Japan
Shunsuke Kato
KOTOMI GC
Kotomi, Japan
Yoshimasa Fujii
KOUNTZE PLACE GC [NLE]
Omaha, Nebraska
Harry Lawrie
KREFELDER GC
Krefeld, Germany
Karl Hoffmann, Bernhard von
Limburger
KRISTALL LAKE CC
Bangkok, Thailand
Gary Roger Baird
KRISTIANSTAD GC
Kristianstad, Sweden
Douglas Brazier, Sune Linde
KRONBERG GC
Frankfort, Germany
Herbert E. Gaertner
(R.) Bernhard von Limburger
(R.) J. F. Dudok van Heel
KRUEGER MUNI
Beloit, Wisconsin
Stanley Pelchar
KRUSENBERG GC
Sweden
Jan Sederholm
KUEHN PARK GC
Sioux Falls, South Dakota
Don Herfort
KUILIMA GC
Oahu, Hawaii
NKA Turtle Bay GC
KUJIGAWA CC
Ibaraki, Japan
Shunsuke Kato
KUJI TAIVO GC
Ibaraki, Japan
Ginjiro Nakabe

KUKUIOLONO GC
Kauai, Hawaii
Walter Duncan McBryde (9)
KUMAMOTO GC
Kumamoto, Japan
Y. Yasuda
KUMLA GC
Kumla, Sweden
Jan Sederholm
KUNGSBACKA GC
Kungsbacka, Sweden
J. J. F. Pennink
KUNO CC
Chiba, Japan
Shunsuke Kato
KURABONE GC
Japan
Robert Muir Graves
KURHESSISCHER GC OBERAULA
Germany
Karl F. Grohs, *Rainer
Preissmann*
KUSATSU CC
Kusatsu, Japan
Mitsuaki Kobayashi
KUSHIRO CC
Kushiro, Japan
Naoto Sugaya
KUSTEN HOHE KLINT GC
Cuxhaven, Germany
G. Bruns
KUTSHERS HOTEL GC
Monticello, New York
William F. Mitchell
KUWANA CC
Mie, Japan
Seichi Inouye
KVARNBY GC
Sweden
Jan Sederholm
KWINIASKA GC
Vermont
Paul J. O'Leary, Brad Caldwell
KYALAMI CC
Bramley, South Africa
Tommy Tomsett, Koos deBeers
KYO CC
Chiba, Japan
Taiyo Ryokuka
KYOTO GC
Kyoto, Japan
O. Ueda
KYU-KARUIZAWA GC
Nagano-ken, Japan
(R.12) Mike Poellot
KYUSHU SHIMA CC
Japan
Seichi Inouye

LA BILBANIA GC
Bilbao, Spain
Robert Dean Putman
LABOUR-IN-VAIN GC [NLE]
Ipswich, Massachusetts
Skip Wogan
LA BRETÊCHE GC
Pontchateau, France
M. Baker
LABUAN GC
Labuan, Malaysia
Robert Muir Graves

LA CALA G&CC (RED CSE)
La Cala de Mijas, Spain
Cabell Robinson
LA CALA G&CC (YELLOW CSE)
La Cala de Mijas, Spain
Cabell Robinson
LA CANADA GC
Guardiare, Spain
Robert Trent Jones
LA CANADA-FLINTRIDGE CC
La Canada, California
Lawrence Hughes
LACANAU-L'ARDILOUSE GC
France
John Harris, J. J. F. Pennink
LA CEIBA GC
Yucatán, Mexico
Jaime Saenz, Felix Teran
LACHUTE GC
Lachute, Quebec
Stanley Thompson
(R.9 A.18) Howard Watson
LA CITA G&CC
Titusville, Florida
Ron Garl
LACKLAND AFB GC
Lackland AFB, Texas
(R.) Joseph S. Finger
LAC LA BICHE G&CC
Lac La Biche, Alberta
Sid Puddicome (1991)
LA COLINA CC
Bogotá, Columbia
Jeff Hardin, Greg Nash
LACOMA GC
East Dubuque, Illinois
Gordon Cunningham
LACOMBE GC
Lacombe, Alberta
(A.9) William G. Robinson,
John F. Robinson
LA COMMANDERIE GC
Laumusse-Crottet, France
M. Preneuf
LACONIA CC
Laconia, New Hampshire
Wayne Stiles
(A.9) Ralph Barton
(R.) Orrin Smith
LA CONTENTA CC
Valley Springs, California
Richard Bigler
LA CORUNA GC
Spain
A. Lucena
LA COSTA CC (NORTH CSE)
Carlsbad, California
Dick Wilson, Joe Lee
(A.9) Joe Lee
LA COSTA CC (SOUTH CSE)
Carlsbad, California
Dick Wilson, Joe Lee
(A.9) Joe Lee
LACROIX LINKS
Rapid City, South Dakota
Pat Wyss
LA CROSSE CC
La Crosse, Wisconsin
(R.) Edward Lawrence
Packard
(R.) Dick Nugent
(R.) Bob Lohmann

LAC THOMAS GC
St. Didace, Quebec
Howard Watson
LA CUMBRE G&CC
Santa Barbara, California
Tom Bendelow
(R.9 A.9) George C. Thomas,
Jr., William P. Bell
(R.) William F. Bell
(R.) Robert Muir Graves
LACUNA CC
Lantana, Florida
Joe Lee
LADBROOK PARK GC
Warwickshire, England
H. S. Colt
(R.) Tom Williamson
LADERA GC
Albuquerque, New Mexico
Dick Phelps, Brad Benz
LADIES GC OF TORONTO
Ontario
Stanley Thompson
LADYBANK GC
Fife, Scotland
Old Tom Morris
LADY BIRD JOHNSON MUNI
Fredericksburg, Texas
George Hoffman
(A.9) Jeff Brauer
LAEM CHABANG INTERNATIONAL CC
Sriracha District, Thailand
Jack Nicklaus
LAFAYETTE CC (BATTLEGROUND
CSE)
Battleground, Indiana
Bob Simmons
LAFAYETTE CC (LAFAYETTE CSE)
Lafayette, Indiana
Tom Bendelow
(R.) William H. Diddel
LAFAYETTE CC
Lafayette, Louisiana
(R.) Ralph Plummer
LAFAYETTE CC
Syracuse, New York
Seymour Dunn
(A.9) *Augie Nordone*
LAFAYETTE MUNI
Lafayette, Indiana
Bob Simmons
LAFAYETTE C
Minnetonka Beach, Minnesota
Tom Bendelow
LAFAYETTE MUNI
Lafayette, Colorado
Dick Phelps, Hale Irwin
LA FLORIDA CC
Santa Fe, Colombia
Charles Mahannah
LA FONTAINE GC
Huntington, Indiana
Harry B. Smead
(A.9) *Gordon Ludwig, Robert
Stoffel*
(R.) Robert Bruce Harris
LA FORTERESSE GC
France
P. Fromager, M. Adam
LA FORTUNE PARK MUNI
Tulsa, Oklahoma
Floyd Farley

LA FORTUNE PARK MUNI (PAR 3
CSE)
Tulsa, Oklahoma
Floyd Farley

LAGAN GC
Sweden
Anders Amilon, Ake Persson

LAGO AZUL GC
Brazil
Alberto Serra

LAGO MAR CC
Fort Lauderdale, Florida
Bill Watts

LAGO MAR EL PENON GC
Colombia
Charles Mahannah

LAGOON PARK GC
Montgomery, Alabama
Charles M. Graves

LA GORCE CC
Miami, Florida
H. C. C. Tippetts
(R.) Robert Trent Jones

LAGO VISTA CC
Lake Travis, Texas
Dave Bennett, Leon Howard

LA GRANGE CC [NLE]
La Grange, Illinois
H. J. Tweedie

LA GRANGE CC
La Grange, Illinois
Donald Ross
(R.) Edward B. Dearie, Jr.
(R.) Edward Lawrence
Packard
(R.) Roger Packard
(R.) Bob Lohmann

LAGUNA CC
Laguna, California
William P. Bell

LAGUNA CC
Mexicali, Mexico
Percy Clifford

LAGUNA HILLS GC
Laguna Hills, California
Harry Rainville, David Rainville
(R.) Robert Muir Graves

LAGUNA SECA G RANCH
Laguna Seca, California
Robert Trent Jones

LAGUNITA CC
Caracas, Venezuela
Dick Wilson

LA HERLIÈRE CC
Arras, France
Fred W. Hawtree

LAHINCH GC (CASTLE CSE)
County Clare, Ireland
John Harris
(R. A.9) D. M. A. Steel

LAHINCH GC (OLD CSE)
County Clare, Ireland
Old Tom Morris
(R. A.5) *Charles Gibson*
(R. A.11) Alister Mackenzie
(R.) *John Burke, Bill
McCavery*

LAHOLMS GC
Laholm, Sweden
Jan Sederholm

LA JOLLA CC
La Jolla, California
William P. Bell
(R.3) Arthur Jack Snyder
(R.3) Ted Robinson
(R.) Rees Jones

LAKE ACWORTH GC
Acworth, Georgia
Ken Dye

LAKE AJAY GC
Florida
Ward Northrup

LAKE ANNA CC [NLE]
Palos Park, Illinois
Stanley Pelchar

LAKE ANNE CC
Monroe, New York
Alfred H. Tull

LAKE ARBOR GC
Arvada, Colorado
Clark Glasson

LAKE ARLINGTON GC
Arlington, Texas
Ralph Plummer

LAKE ARROWHEAD CC [NLE]
Lake Arrowhead, California
Willie Watson

LAKE ARROWHEAD CC
Lake Arrowhead, California
William F. Bell
(R.2) William F. Bell
(R.2) Algie Pulley

LAKE ARROWHEAD GC
Nekoosa, Wisconsin
Ken Killian, Dick Nugent

LAKE BARRINGTON SHORES GC
Barrington, Illinois
Roger Packard

LAKE BARTON GC
Great Bend, Kansas
Harry Robb

LAKE BONAVENTURE CC
St. Paul, Virginia
Alex McKay

LAKE BREEZE GC
Winneconne, Wisconsin
Homer Fieldhouse

LAKE BUENA VISTA C
Lake Buena Vista, Florida
Joe Lee, Rocky Roquemore
(R.) Joe Lee

LAKE CHABOT GC
Oakland, California
William Lock
(R.) Robert Muir Graves

LAKE CHABOT GC (EXECUTIVE CSE)
Oakland, California
Robert Dean Putman

LAKE CHABOT VALLEJO GC
Vallejo, California
Jack Fleming

LAKE CHARLES G&CC
Lake Charles, Louisiana
Ralph Plummer
(R.) Jay Riviere

LAKE CITY CC
Lake City, Florida
Willard Byrd

LAKE CITY CC
Lake City, South Carolina
Ed Riccoboni

LAKE COUNTRY ESTATES GC
Fort Worth, Texas
Ralph Plummer
(A.9) Don January, Billy
Martindale

LAKE CREEK CC
Storm Lake, Iowa
Homer Fieldhouse

LAKE D'ARBONNE G&CC
Farmerville, Louisiana
Tom Clark

LAKE DON PEDRO G&CC
La Grange, California
William F. Bell

LAKE DOSTER GC
Plainwell, Michigan
Charles Darl Scott

LAKE ELSINORE GC [NLE]
California
John Duncan Dunn

LAKE ESTES GC
Estes Park, Colorado
Henry B. Hughes

LAKE FAIRFAX GC
Virginia
Edmund B. Ault, Al Jamison

LAKE FAIRWAYS GC
North Fort Myers, Florida
Ron Garl

LAKE FOREST CC
Hudson, Ohio
Herbert Strong
(R.) James Gilmore Harrison

LAKE FOREST G&CC
Lake St. Louis, Missouri
(R.9 A.9) Gary Kern

LAKE FOREST GC
Middletown, Kentucky
Arnold Palmer, Ed Seay

LAKE FOREST GC [NLE]
Kansas
Floyd Farley

LAKE FOREST Y&CC
Daphne, Alabama
(R.9 A.9) Earl Stone

LAKE GARRETT GC
Seattle, Washington
George S. "Pop" Merrit

LAKE GENEVA CC
Lake Geneva, Wisconsin
Robert Foulis

LAKE GEORGE CC
Lake George, New York
Alex Findlay

LAKE GREEN GC
Japan
Tetsuro Akabane

LAKE GUNTERSVILLE STATE PARK
GC
Guntersville, Alabama
Earl Stone

LAKE HEFNER GC (NORTH CSE)
Oklahoma City, Oklahoma
Perry Maxwell, Press Maxwell
(R.) Floyd Farley

LAKE HEFNER GC (SOUTH CSE)
Oklahoma City, Oklahoma
Floyd Farley

LAKE HICKORY CC
North Carolina
Willard Byrd

LAKE HILLS CC
Billings, Montana
George H. Schneider

LAKE HILLS G&CC
St. John, Indiana
Charles Maddox, *Frank P.
MacDonald*

LAKE HOPATCONG GC
New Jersey
Robert White

LAKE HOUSTON GC
Huffman, Texas
Jay Riviere

LAKEHURST GC
Lakehurst Naval Air Station,
New Jersey
(R.) Nicholas Psiahas

LAKE ISABELLA GC
Weidman, Michigan
Bruce Matthews, Jerry Matthews

LAKE ISLE CC
Eastchester, New York
Devereux Emmet

LAKE JAMES CC
Angola, Indiana
Robert Beard

LAKE JOVITA CC [NLE]
Florida
Wayne Stiles, John Van Kleek

LAKE KARRINYUP CC
Perth, Australia
Alister Mackenzie, Alex Russell
(R. A.9) Peter Thomson,
Michael Wolveridge

LAKE KEZAR C
Lovell, Maine
Donald Ross

LAKE KIOWA CC
Gainesville, Texas
Leon Howard

LAKE LACKAWANNA GC
Byram, New Jersey
William Gordon, David Gordon

LAKELAND PAR 3 GC
Lakeland, Florida
Hans Schmeisser
(R.) Ron Garl

LAKELAND VILLAGE GC
Allyn, Washington
Eugene "Bunny" Mason

LAKE LANIER ISLANDS HOTEL & GC
Lake Lanier, Georgia
Joe Lee, Rocky Roquemore

LAKE LAWN CC
Fort Myers, Florida
Ken Craig

LAKE LAWN GC
Irwin, Pennsylvania
Ferdinand Garbin

LAKE LAWN GC
Delavan, Wisconsin
Tom Bendelow
(R.) Dick Nugent

LAKE LINDERO CC
Agoura, California
Ted Robinson

LAKE LORRAINE CC
Shalimar, Florida
NKA Shalimar Pointe CC

LAKE LUCERNE GC
Cleveland, Ohio
Clyde W. Colby

LAKE LURE MUNI
Lake Lure, North Carolina
John Van Kleek

LAKE MARION GC
Santee, South Carolina
Ed Riccoboni

LAKE MERCED G&CC [NLE]
Daly City, California
William Lock (1923)
(R.) Alister Mackenzie

LAKE MERCED G&CC
Daly City, California
Robert Muir Graves

LAKE MOHAWK GC
Sparta, New Jersey
Duer Irving Sewall

LAKEMONT CC
Ohio
William J. Rockefeller

LAKE MONTICELLO GC
Palmyra, Virginia
Buddy Loving, Algie Pulley

LAKE MOREY INN GC
Lake Morey, Vermont
George Salling
(R.) *Allen Avery, Brian Smith, Bill Ross*

LAKE NONA GC
Orlando, Florida
Tom Fazio

LAKE NORCONIAN C [NLE]
California
John Duncan Dunn

LAKE OAKS CC (REGULATION CSE)
Waco, Texas
Warren Cantrell

LAKE OAKS CC (EXECUTIVE CSE)
Waco, Texas
Warren Cantrell

LAKE OF THE HILLS GC
Haslett, Michigan
Bruce Matthews, Jerry Matthews

LAKE OF THE NORTH GC
Mancelona, Michigan
Bruce Matthews, Jerry Matthews
(A.9) William Newcomb

LAKE OF THE WOODS GC
Mahomet, Illinois
Robert Bruce Harris

LAKE OF THE WOODS GC
Ypsilanti, Michigan
Leo J. Bishop

LAKE OF THE WOODS GC
Locust Grove, Virginia
(R.1) Tom Clark

LAKE OSWEGO MUNI
Lake Oswego, Oregon
Shirley Stone

LAKEOVER CC
Bedford Village, New York
Al Zikorus

LAKE PADDEN MUNI
Bellingham, Washington
Roy L. Goss, *Glen Proctor*

LAKE PANORAMA NATIONAL GC
Panora, Iowa
Richard Watson

LAKE PANORAMA PAR 3 GC
Panora, Iowa
Richard Watson

LAKE PAOAY GC
Ilocos Norte, Philippines
Ron Kirby, Denis Griffiths

LAKE PARK GC
Germantown, Wisconsin
James Jones

LAKE PLACID C [NLE]
Sebring, Florida
Seymour Dunn

LAKE PLACID C (LOWER CSE)
New York
Seymour Dunn

LAKE PLACID C (PRACTICE CSE)
New York
Seymour Dunn

LAKE PLACID C (UPPER CSE)
New York
Alex Findlay
(R.) Alister Mackenzie

LAKE PLATTE GC
Platte, South Dakota
Lee Tappe

LAKE POINT C
Fort St. John, British Columbia
Norman W. Woods

LAKEPOINTE CC [NLE]
St. Clair Shores, Michigan
(A.6) Bruce Matthews, Jerry Matthews

LAKEPOINTE STATE PARK GC
Eufaula, Alabama
Thomas H. Nicol

LAKEPORT CC [NLE]
Laconia, New Hampshire
Ralph Barton

LAKE QUIVIRA CC
Lake Quivira, Kansas
William B. Langford, Theodore Moreau
(R.) Floyd Farley
(R.) Chet Mendenhall
(R.4) Bill Love

LAKE REGION Y&CC
Winter Haven, Florida
David Wallace
(R.) Hugh Moore
(R.) Dean Refram

LAKERIDGE G&CC
Lakeview, Oregon
Charles Sullivan

LAKE RIDGE GC
Seattle, Washington
Robert Johnstone

LAKE RIDGE G CSE
Reno, Nevada
Robert Trent Jones

LAKE ROSS GC
Marulan, Australia
Peter Thomson, Michael Wolveridge

LAKES CC
Palm Desert, California
Ted Robinson

[THE] LAKES G&CC
Westerville, Ohio
David Postlethwait, Ed Sneed
(1991)

[THE] LAKES GC
Highland Springs, Virginia
Buddy Loving, Algie Pulley
(R.) Mike Hurdzan

[THE] LAKES GC
Sydney, Australia
Robert von Hagge, Bruce Devlin

[THE] LAKES AT SYCAMORE
Fort Wayne, Indiana
Dick Phelps, Hale Irwin

LAKE ST. CLAIR CC
Detroit, Michigan
William H. Diddel

LAKE ST. GEORGE G&CC
Ontario
(R.9 A.9) Clinton E. Robinson

LAKE SAMANISH STATE PARK GC
Issaquah, Washington
Al Smith

LAKE SAN MARCOS CC
Lake San Marcos, California
Harry Rainville, David Rainville

LAKES EAST GC
Sun City, Arizona
Jeff Hardin

LAKE SHASTINA G&CC
Weed, California
Robert Trent Jones

LAKE SHAWNEE GC
Topeka, Kansas
Larry W. Flatt

LAKE SHORE CC
Glencoe, Illinois
Tom Bendelow
(R.) Ken Killian, Dick Nugent

LAKESHORE CC
Council Bluffs, Iowa
(A.9) David Gill

LAKESHORE CC
Madisonville, Kentucky
Buck Blankenship

LAKE SHORE CC [NLE]
Burlington, Vermont
Herbert Strong

LAKESHORE CC
Oradell, New Jersey
Al Zikorus

LAKE SHORE G&CC
Ontario
(R.) Stanley Thompson

LAKESHORE GC
Durham, North Carolina
J. M. Utley, Sr.

LAKE SHORE GC
Erie, Pennsylvania
Tom Bendelow

LAKESHORE GC
Taylorsville, Illinois
William James Spear

LAKESIDE CC
Atlanta, Georgia
George W. Cobb

LAKESIDE CC
Houston, Texas
Ralph Plummer
(R.14) Joseph S. Finger
(R.) Ron Prichard

LAKESIDE CC
Manitowoc, Wisconsin
William H. Diddel

LAKESIDE G&CC [NLE]
San Francisco, California
Wilfrid Reid, Walter G. Fovargue and *James Donaldson*

LAKESIDE GC
Fort Wayne, Indiana
Robert Beard

LAKESIDE GC
Meridian, Mississippi
Sonny Guy

LAKESIDE GC
Moore, Oklahoma
Duffy Martin

LAKESIDE GC OF HOLLYWOOD
North Hollywood, California
Max Behr
(R.) Robert Muir Graves
(R.) David Rainville

LAKESIDE GREENS GC
Lake Milton, Ohio
Edmund B. Ault

LAKESIDE HILLS GC
Olathe, Kansas
Charles Nash

LAKESIDE MEMORIAL GC
Stillwater, Oklahoma
Labron Harris, Sr.

LAKE SPANAWAY GC
Tacoma, Washington
A. Vernon Macan, Kenneth Tyson

LAKE SUCCESS GC
New York
(R.9 A.9) Orrin Smith
(R.1) Stephen Kay

LAKE SUNAPEE GC
New London, New Hampshire
Donald Ross
(R.) Orrin Smith

LAKE SURF CC
Vass, North Carolina
NKA Woodlake CC

LAKES WEST GC
Sun City, Arizona
Milt Coggins

LAKE TAHOE CC
Lake Tahoe, California
(A.9) *Larry Mancour* (1964)

LAKE TARLETON C [NLE]
Pike, New Hampshire
Donald Ross

LAKE TEXOMA STATE PARK GC
Kingston, Oklahoma
Floyd Farley

LAKE TOXAWAY CC
North Carolina
R. D. Heinitsh (1963)

LAKE VALLEY GC
Boulder, Colorado
Press Maxwell

LAKE VALLEY G&CC
Camdenton, Missouri
Floyd Farley
(R.) Gary Kern, Ron Kern

LAKE VENICE CC
Venice, Florida
Mark Mahannah
(R.) *Carl Rohmann*

LAKEVIEW CC
Lodi, Illinois
Charles Maddox

LAKEVIEW CC [NLE]
Oklahoma
Leslie Brownlee

LAKEVIEW CC
North East, Pennsylvania
James Gilmore Harrison, Ferdinand Garbin

LAKEVIEW CC
Virginia
Fred Findlay, Buddy Loving, *R. F. Loving, Sr.*

LAKE VIEW CC
Niigata-ken, Japan
Mike Poellot

Lakeview G&CC
Toronto, Ontario
Herbert Strong

Lakeview G Challenge
Vancouver, Washington
Duke Wager (9 Par 3)

Lakeview GC
Foley, Alabama
Robert von Hagge

Lakeview GC
Delray Beach, Florida
Bill Dietsch

Lakeview GC
Oelwein, Iowa
Harold Glissmann

Lakeview GC
Burnham, Maine
Ronello Reynolds

Lakeview GC
Ralston, Nebraska
Harold Glissmann

Lake View GC
Johnson City, Tennessee
Alex McKay

Lakeview GC
Harrisonburg, Virginia
Russell Roberts

Lakeview GC
Roanoke, Virginia
Fred Sappenfield

Lakeview GC
Rotorua, New Zealand
A. C. Relph

Lakeview G & YC
Cha Am, Thailand
Roger Packard

Lakeview Hills CC (North Cse)
Lexington, Michigan
William Newcomb (routing);
Jeff Gorney

Lakeview Hills CC (South Cse)
Lexington, Michigan
Walter Hagen
(R.1) Jerry Matthews

Lakeview Inn & CC
Morgantown, West Virginia
NKA Sheraton Lakeview Resort
& GC

Lakeview Motor Inn GC
Roanoke, Virginia
Buddy Loving

Lakeview Muni
Brandon, South Dakota
Richard Watson

Lake View Park GC
Rochester, Indiana
James Merdigh

Lake Wales CC
Lake Wales, Florida
Donald Ross
(A.9) *William L. Campbell*

Lake Waneawega GC
Illinois
Tom Bendelow

Lakeway GC (Live Oak Course)
Lake Travis, Texas
Leon Howard

Lakeway GC (Yaupon Cse)
Lake Travis, Texas
Leon Howard

Lakeway G Cse
Bellingham, Washington
Frank James

Lake Whitney CC
Whitney, Texas
Leon Howard

Lake Wilderness CC
Maple Valley, Washington
Ray Coleman
(A.9) Norman H. Woods
(R.) Robert Muir Graves

Lake Wildwood GC
Grass Valley, California
William F. Bell
(R.) Robert Muir Graves

Lake Windsor GC
Madison, Wisconsin
Marvin Busse
(R.) Bob Lohmann

Lakewood CC
Denver, Colorado
Tom Bendelow
(R.) Donald Ross
(R.) Press Maxwell

Lakewood CC
St. Petersburg, Florida
Herbert Strong
(R.) Dick Wilson
(R.) Gordon Lewis

Lakewood CC
Hutchinson, Kansas
NKA [The] Highlands GC

Lakewood CC
Russell Springs, Kentucky
Harold England

Lakewood CC
New Orleans, Louisiana
Robert Bruce Harris

Lakewood CC
Rockville, Maryland
Edmund B. Ault, Al Jamison

Lakewood CC
Westlake, Ohio
A. W. Tillinghast
(R.1) Jack Kidwell, Michael
Hurdzan
(R.) Brian Silva, Geoffrey S.
Cornish

Lakewood CC
Tullahoma, Tennessee
Bubber Johnson, Pete Grandison
(A.12) Kevin Tucker

Lakewood CC [NLE]
Dallas, Texas
Tom Bendelow

Lakewood CC
Dallas, Texas
Ralph Plummer
(R.) Leon Howard

Lake Wood CC
Bangkok, Thailand
Mike Poellot

Lakewood G&CC
Havana, Illinois
William James Spear

Lakewood GC
Phenix City, Alabama
Lester Lawrence

Lakewood GC (Azalea Cse)
Point Clear, Alabama
Joe Lee
(A.9) Ron Garl

Lakewood GC (Dogwood Cse)
Point Clear, Alabama
Perry Maxwell, Press Maxwell
(R.) Robert Trent Jones

Lakewood GC
California
William P. Bell

Lakewood GC
Naples, Florida
Arthur Hills

Lakewood GC
Madison, Maine
Alex Chisholm

Lakewood GC
Fenton, Missouri
(R.) Hale Irwin

Lakewood GC
Lakewood, New Jersey
Willie Dunn, Jr.

Lakewood GC
Statesville, North Carolina
F. Britton

Lakewood GC (East Cse)
Kanagawa, Japan
Ted Robinson

Lakewood GC (West Cse)
Kanagawa, Japan
Ted Robinson

Lakewood Oaks GC
Lees Summit, Missouri
Jay Riviere
(R.4) Don Sechrest

Lakewood on the Green GC
Cadillac, Michigan
*Norman Smith, Pete Smith (9
1980)*

Lakewood Shores G&CC
Oscoda, Michigan
Bruce Matthews, Jerry Matthews

Lakewood Recreation C
Rising Star, Texas
Leon Howard

Lake Worth GC
Lake Worth, Florida
William B. Langford,
Theodore J. Moreau
(R.) Dick Wilson
(R.) Ward Northrup

Lake Wright GC
Norfolk, Virginia
Al Jamison

Lakey Hill GC
Dorset, England
Brian Bramford, G. T. Halloway

Lakota Hills GC
West Chester, Ohio
(R.9 A.9) Jack Kidwell

La Mandria GC
Turin, Italy
J. S. F. Morrison
(A.9) John Harris

La Manga Campo de G (North Cse)
Costa Blanca, Spain
Robert Dean Putman

La Manga Campo de G (South Cse)
Costa Blanca, Spain
Robert Dean Putman

La Mantarraya GC
Las Hadas, Mexico
Roy Dye

Lamar CC
Lamar, South Carolina
Ed Riccoboni

Lamberhurst GC
Lamberhurst, England
C. K. Cotton, J. J. F. Pennink

Lambourne GC
Buckinghamshire, England
D. M. A. Steel

Lambton G&CC
Ontario
(R.) Clinton E. Robinson
(R.) Stanley Thompson
(R.) Graham Cooke

Lam Luk Ka CC
Bangkok, Thailand
Roger Packard

Lamont Hill GC
Pomona, Kansas
Melvin Anderson

La Moraleja GC
Madrid, Spain
Desmond Muirhead, Jack
Nicklaus

La Moye GC
Channel Islands
George Boomer
(R.) James Braid, John R.
Stutt
(R.) Henry Cotton
(R.) *David Melville*

Lanark GC
Lanarkshire, Scotland
Old Tom Morris
(R.) John R. Stutt

Lancaster CC
Lancaster, New York
Charles G. Nieman

Lancaster CC
Lancaster, Ohio
Donald Ross
(A.9) Jack Kidwell
(R.) Ken Killian
(R.) Ron Forse

Lancaster CC
Lancaster, Pennsylvania
William S. Flynn
(R.12 A.6) William Gordon,
David Gordon

Lancaster CC
Lancaster, South Carolina
Donald Ross
(R.) Russell Breeden

Lancaster GC [NLE]
Lancaster, New Hampshire
Ralph Barton

Landa Park GC
New Braufels, Texas
(A.9) Dave Bennett, Leon
Howard

Lander Haven CC
Ohio
(A.9) Ben W. Zink

Landfall GC (Jack Nicklaus Cse)
Wrightsville Beach, North
Carolina
Jack Nicklaus

Landfall GC (Pete Dye Cse)
Wrightsville Beach, North
Carolina
P. B. Dye, Pete Dye

Land Harbour GC
Blowing Rock, North Carolina
Tom Jackson

[The] Landings GC
Warner Robins, Georgia
Tom Clark, Bill Love

[THE] LANDINGS AT SKIDAWAY
ISLAND (DEER CREEK CSE)
Skidaway Island, Georgia
Tom Fazio
[THE] LANDINGS AT SKIDAWAY
ISLAND (MAGNOLIA CSE)
Skidaway Island, Georgia
Frank Duane, Arnold Palmer
[THE] LANDINGS AT SKIDAWAY
ISLAND (MARSHWOOD CSE)
Skidaway Island, Georgia
Arnold Palmer, Ed Seay
[THE] LANDINGS AT SKIDAWAY
ISLAND (OAKRIDGE CSE)
Skidaway Island, Georgia
Arthur Hills
[THE] LANDINGS AT SKIDAWAY
ISLAND (PALMETTO CSE)
Skidaway Island, Georgia
Arthur Hills
[THE] LANDINGS AT SKIDAWAY
ISLAND (PLANTATION CSE)
Skidaway Island, Georgia
Willard Byrd
L AND N GC
Brooks, Kentucky
Alex McKay
LAND O'GOLF GC
Miami, Florida
John E. O'Connor
LAND-O-LAKES GC
Whiteville, North Carolina
H. White
LAND-O-LAKES G&CC
Coaldale, Alberta
Les Furber, Jim Eremko
LANDSKRONA GC
Landskrona, Sweden
Ture Bruce
LANDS WEST GC
Douglasville, Georgia
Ward Northrup
LANE CREEK G CSE
Watkinsville, Georgia
Mike Young
LANE TREE GC
Goldsboro, North Carolina
John LaFoy
LANGARA GC
British Columbia
A. Vernon Macan
LANGENHAGEN GC
Langenhagen, Germany
Wolfgang Siegmann
LANGHORNE GC
Langhorne, Pennsylvania
Alex Findlay
(R.) George Fazio
LANGLAND BAY GC
West Glamorgan, Wales
J. J. F. Pennink
LANGLEY AFB GC
Langley, Virginia
Edmund B. Ault
(A.9) Al Zikorus
LANGSTON GC
Washington, D.C.
(A.9) William Gordon
LANNEMEZAN GC
Lannemezan, France
Pierre Hirrigoyan

LANN ROHOU GC
Brest, France
Michael G. Fenn
(A.9) Robin Nelson, Rodney
Wright
LANSDOWN GC
Bath, England
Tom Dunn
(R.) H. S. Colt
(A.2) C. H. Alison
LANSDOWNE G RESORT
Leesburg, Virginia
Robert Trent Jones, Jr.
L'ANSE GC
L'Anse, Michigan
Edward Lawrence Packard
LANSING SPORTMAN'S C
Lansing, Illinois
(A.9) Ken Killian, Dick
Nugent
LAN-YAIR GC
Spartanburg, South Carolina
Russell Breeden
LANZO INTELVI GC
Lanzo, Italy
Donald Harradine
LA PALMA CC [NLE]
Arizona
Harry Collis
LA PALOMA GC
Tucson, Arizona
Jack Nicklaus
LA PENAZA GC
Zaragoza, Spain
Fred W. Hawtree
LA POINTE DU DIAMANT GC
Martinique
Robert Moote, David S. Moote
LA PORTE CC
Pine Lake, Indiana
William B. Langford
LA PURISIMA GC
Lompoc, California
Robert Muir Graves
LA QUERCE GC
Rome, Italy
Jim Fazio
LA QUINTA CC
California
Lawrence Hughes
LA QUINTA HOTEL GC (CITRUS
CSE)
La Quinta, California
Pete Dye
LA QUINTA HOTEL GC (DUNES CSE)
La Quinta, California
Pete Dye
LA QUINTA HOTEL GC (MOUNTAIN
CSE)
La Quinta, California
Pete Dye
LA RAINBOW CC
Okayama, Japan
Ronald Fream
LARAMIE CC [NLE]
Chicago, Illinois
Harry Collis
LARCHMONT MUNI
Missoula, Montana
Richard Watson, Keith Hellstrom
LARCH TREE CC
Trotwood, Ohio
Jack Kidwell

LAREDO CC
Laredo, Texas
Joseph S. Finger, Baxter Spann
LAREDO AFB GC
Laredo AFB, Texas
Dave Bennett, Leon Howard
LARIMORE GC
Larimore, North Dakota
Charles Maddox
LA RINCONADA CC
Saratoga, California
(R.) Robert Dean Putman
(R.) Robert Muir Graves
LARNE GC
County Antrim, Northern
Ireland
Willie Park
LA ROCCA GC
Parma, Italy
Marco Croze
LA ROMANA CC
Dominican Republic
Pete Dye
LARRIMAC GC
Quebec
(R.9) Howard Watson
(R.3) John Watson
LARRY GANNON MEMORIAL GC
Lynn, Massachusetts
Wayne Stiles
LA SABANA GC
Bogotá, Colombia
Charles Mahannah
LAS COLINAS SPORTS C
(COTTONWOOD VALLEY CSE)
Irving, Texas
Robert Trent Jones, Jr.
(A.9) Jay Morrish
(R.) John Steidel
LAS COLINAS SPORTS C (TPC CSE)
Irving, Texas
Robert Trent Jones, Jr.
(R.9 A.9) Jay Morrish, Byron
Nelson, Ben Crenshaw
LAS HUERTAS CC
Mexico
Percy Clifford
LAS LOMAS ÉL BOSQUE GC
Madrid, Spain
Robert Dean Putman
LAS MONTAÑAS GC
Jamul, California
Forrest Richardson, Arthur Jack
Snyder
LAS MISIONES GC
Monterrey, Mexico
Robert von Hagge
LAS POSAS CC
Camarillo, California
Lawrence Hughes
LAS POSITAS MUNI GC
Livermore, California
Robert Muir Graves
(R. A.3rd 9) Robert Muir
Graves
LAS PRADERAS DE LUJAN GC
Argentina
Angel Reartes
LAS SIERRAS GC
Taos, New Mexico
Jeff Hardin
LAST HILL G&CC
Eckville, Alberta
Les Furber, Jim Eremko

LAST OAK RESORT GC
Broadview, Saskatchewan
Bill Newis
LAS VEGAS CC
Las Vegas, Nevada
Edmund B. Ault
(R.) Ron Garl
LAS VEGAS GC
Las Vegas, Nevada
William P. Bell
(A.9) William F. Bell
(R.) Jeff Brauer, Jim Colbert
LA TIERRA BONITA GC
Porter, Oklahoma
Art Lopez
LA TOURETTE MUNI
Staten Island, New York
David L. Rees
(R.9 A.9) John Van Kleek
(R.4) Frank Duane
LATROBE CC
Latrobe, Pennsylvania
Emil Loeffler, John McGlynn
(A.9) James Gilmore
Harrison, Ferdinand Garbin
LA TUQUE G & CURLING C
Quebec
(R.9 A.9) Howard Watson
LAUDERDALE LAKES CC
Fort Lauderdale, Florida
Hans Schmeisser
LAUDER GC
Berwickshire, Scotland
Willie Park, Sr., Willie Park, Jr.
LAUGHLIN AFB GC
Del Rio, Texas
Joseph S. Finger
LAUNCESTON GC
Launceston, England
(A.9) J. Hamilton Stutt
LAURA S. WALKER STATE PARK G
CSE
Waycross, Georgia
Stephen Burns
LAUREL GC
Laurel, Virginia
Fred Findlay
LAUREL G&RC
Laurel, Montana
Theodore Wirth
(R.) Robert Muir Graves
LAUREL CREEK CC
Moorestown, New Jersey
Arnold Palmer, Ed Seay
LAUREL GREENS GC
Latrobe, Pennsylvania
X. G. Hassenplug
LAUREL HEIGHTS G&CC
Orangeville, Ontario
Douglas Carrick
LAUREL HILL GC
Gold Hill, Oregon
Harvey Granger
LAUREL OAK CC
Gibbsboro, New Jersey
Gary Renn, C. H. Evans
LAUREL OAK CC
Sarasota, Florida
Gary Player
LAUREL PINES CC
Laurel, Maryland
George W. Cobb

LAUREL RIDGE CC
  Waynesville, North Carolina
  Bob Cupp
LAURELTON GC (NORTH CSE)
  [NLE]
  New York
  Devereux Emmet
LAURELTON GC (SOUTH CSE)
  [NLE]
  New York
  Devereux Emmet
LAUREL VALLEY CC
  Ligonier, Pennsylvania
  Dick Wilson
    (R.) Paul E. Erath
    (R.) Arnold Palmer, Ed Seay
LAUREL VIEW MUNI
  Hamden, Connecticut
  Geoffrey S. Cornish, William G.
  Robinson
LAURELWOOD GC
  Eugene, Oregon
  Clarence Sutton
LAUSANNE GC
  Lausanne, Switzerland
    (R.) Donald Harradine
LAVA HILLS G&CC
  St. George, Utah
  NKA Southgate GC
LAVA LAVA GC
  American Samoa
  Tolani Teleso
LAVAL SUR LE LAC GC
  Laval, Quebec
  Willie Park, Jr.
    (R.) Herbert Strong
    (R.) Clinton E. Robinson
    (R.9) Howard Watson
    (R.3) John Watson
    (A.2nd 9) Graham Cooke
LA VECCHIA PIEVACCIA GC
  Italy
  Marco Croze
LA VISTA G&CC
  Wichita Falls, Texas
  Larry Flatt
LAWRENCE CC
  Lawrence, Kansas
  Bob Peebles
LAWRENCE GC
  Lawrence, New York
  Devereux Emmet
LAWRENCEBURG CC
  Lawrenceburg, Tennessee
    (R.4 A.9) Arthur Davis
LAWRENCE COUNTY CC
  Lawrenceville, Illinois
    (R.1) Ken Kavanaugh
LAWRENCE HARBOUR CC
  New Jersey
  Willie Dunn, Jr.
LAWRENCE LINKS
  North Highland, California
  Bert Stamps
LAWRENCE PARK GC
  Erie, Pennsylvania
  Alfred H. Tull
LAWRENCE PARK VILLAGE CC
  New York
    (R.) Joseph S. Finger
LAWRENCEVILLE CC
  Lawrenceville, Virginia
  Fred Findlay, *R. F. Loving, Sr.*

LAWRENCEVILLE SCHOOL GC
  Lawrenceville, New Jersey
  John Reid
    (R.) William Gordon, David
    Gordon
LAWRENCE WELK VILLAGE GC
  Escondido, California
  David Rainville
LAWSONIA GC (LINKS CSE)
  Green Lake, Wisconsin
  William B. Langford, Theodore
  J. Moreau
LAWSONIA GC (NEW CSE)
  Green Lake, Wisconsin
  Rocky Roquemore
LAWTON CC
  Lawton, Oklahoma
  Perry Maxwell, Press Maxwell
    (A.9) Floyd Farley
LAYTONSVILLE GC
  Laytonsville, Maryland
  Robert L. Elder
LAZY H GC
  California
  Bob Baldock
L.B. HOUSTON MUNI
  Dallas, Texas
  Dave Bennett, Leon Howard
    (R.) Dave Bennett
L.B. RAMEY GC
  Kingsville, Texas
  Dennis W. Arp
LEAMINGTON AND COUNTY GC
  Warwickshire, England
  H. S. Colt, C. H. Alison
    (R.) James Braid, John R.
    Stutt
LEANING TREE GC
  West Richfield, Ohio
  Richard W. LaConte, Ted
  McAnlis
LEATHEM SMITH LODGE GC
  Sturgeon Bay, Wisconsin
  William B. Langford, Theodore
  J. Moreau
LEATHERSTOCKING CC
  Cooperstown, New York
  Devereux Emmet
LEAVENWORTH CC
  Leavenworth, Kansas
  Tom Bendelow
LEAWOOD SOUTH CC
  Leawood, Kansas
  Bob Dunning
    (R.5) Tom Clark
LEBANON CC
  Lebanon, Missouri
  George Bassore
    (A.9) Maury Miller
LEBANON CC [NLE]
  Lebanon, Pennsylvania
  Alex Findlay
LEBANON CC
  Lebanon, Pennsylvania
  Frank Murray, Russell Roberts
    (R.) Ferdinand Garbin
    (R.) Ron Forse
LE BETULLE GC
  Biella, Italy
    (R.) J. S. F. Morrison
    (R.) John Harris

LE BLAINVILLIER GC (LE ROYAL
  CSE)
  Blainville, Quebec
  Graham Cooke
LE BLAINVILLIER GC (L'HERITAGE
  CSE)
  Blainville, Quebec
  Graham Cooke
LE CHANTECLER GC
  Quebec
  Howard Watson
LE CHÂTEAU MONTEBELLO GC
  Montebello, Quebec
  Stanley Thompson
LE CHIOCCIOLE GC
  Cherasco, Italy
  Marco Croze
LECKFORD AND LONGSTOCK GC
  Hampshire, England
  H. S. Colt, J. S. F. Morrison
    (R.) Michael G. Fenn
    (A.9) D. M. A. Steel
LE COUDRAY GC
  Evry, France
  C. K. Cotton
LEDGEMONT CC
  Seekonk, Massachusetts
  Alfred H. Tull
LEDGES CC
  Roscoe, Illinois
  Edward Lawrence Packard
LEDGEVIEW G&CC
  Abbotsford, British Columbia
  Wally Shamenski
    (R.14) Les Furber, *Jim
    Eremko*
LEDUC G&CC
  Leduc, Alberta
    (R.8) Les Furber, *Jim Eremko*
LEEDS CASTLE GC
  Leeds, England
  Sir Guy Campbell, C. K.
  Hutchison, S. V. Hotchkin
LEEK GC
  Leek, England
    (R.) Tom Williamson
LEEK WOOTEN GC
  Leek, England
  Karl Litten
LEE-ON-THE-SOLENT GC
  Lee-on-the-Solent, England
  John Duncan Dunn
    (R.) J. Hamilton Stutt
LEE PARK GC
  Liverpool, England
  C. K. Cotton, J. J. F. Pennink
LEE PARK GC
  South Dakota
    (A.9) *Clifford A. Anderson*
    (R.) *Gary L. Nelson*
LEES HALL GC
  Yorkshire, England
  Sandy Herd
    (R.) Tom Williamson
LEE WIN GC
  Salem, Ohio
  Jack Kidwell
LEEWOOD GC
  Eastchester, New York
  Devereux Emmet
LE FRONDE GC
  Avigliana, Italy
  John Harris

[THE] LEGACY GC AT GREEN
  VALLEY
  Henderson, Nevada
  Arthur Hills
LEGACY G LINKS
  Aberdeen, North Carolina
  Jack Nicklaus, Jr.
[THE] LEGEND GC
  Glendale, Arizona
  Arnold Palmer, Ed Seay
LEGEND BUTTES G CSE
  Crawford, Nebraska
  Pat Wyss
LEGEND LAKE GC
  Chardon, Ohio
  Reece Alexander
[THE] LEGENDS C OF TENNESSEE
  Franklin, Tennessee
  Bob Cupp, *Tom Kite*
[THE] LEGENDS GC (HEATHLAND
  CSE)
  Myrtle Beach, South Carolina
  Tom Doak
[THE] LEGENDS GC (MOORLAND
  CSE)
  Myrtle Beach, South Carolina
  P. B. Dye
[THE] LEGENDS GC (PARKLAND
  CSE)
  Myrtle Beach, South Carolina
  Tom Doak
[THE] LEGENDS OF INDIANA GC
  Franklin, Indiana
  Jim Fazio
LEGION MEMORIAL GC
  Everett, Washington
  H. Chandler Egan
    (R.) John Steidel
LE GOLF NATIONAL
  Paris, France
  Robert von Hagge, *Hubert
  Chesneau, Pierre Thevenin*
LEHIGH CC
  Emmaus, Pennsylvania
  William S. Flynn, Howard
  Toomey
    (R.) William Gordon, David
    Gordon
LEHIGH ACRES CC (NORTH CSE)
  Lehigh, Florida
  R. Albert Anderson
LEHIGH ACRES CC (SOUTH CSE)
  Lehigh, Florida
  R. Albert Anderson
    (R.) Gordon Lewis
LEICESTER HILL CC
  Leicester, Massachusetts
    (R.) William F. Mitchell
LEISURE LAKES G&CC
  Lake Placid, Florida
  J. R. "Buddy" Simpson
LEISURE TOWN GC
  California
    (R.) Robert Muir Graves
LEISURE VILLAGE GC
  Laguna Hills, California
  Edward Lawrence Packard
LEISURE VILLAGE GC
  Woodlake, New Jersey
  Edward Lawrence Packard
LEISURE WORLD GC (CHAMPIONSHIP
  CSE)
  Mesa, Arizona
  Jeff Hardin, Greg Nash

LEISURE WORLD GC (EXECUTIVE
CSE)
Mesa, Arizona
Jeff Hardin, Greg Nash
LEISURE WORLD GC
Silver Spring, Maryland
Desmond Muirhead
LE KEMPFERHOF GC
Strasbourg, France
Robert von Hagge
LEKSAND GC
Leksand, Sweden
Nils Sköld
LELAND CC
Leland, Michigan
C. D. Wagstaff
(R.9 A.9) Rees Jones
LELAND MEADOWS PAR 3 GC
Long Bain, California
Bob Baldock
LELY COMMUNITY GC
Naples, Florida
David Wallace
LELY G&CC
Naples, Florida
David Wallace
LEMON BAY BEACH CC
Englewood, Florida
James Petrides (1982)
LEMONTREE GC
Belleville, Michigan
Clinton E. Robinson
LEMOORE MUNI
Lemoore, California
Bob Baldock
LENAPE HEIGHTS GC
Ford City, Pennsylvania
Ferdinand Garbin
(A.9) X. G. Hassenplug
LENIOR CC
Lenior, North Carolina
Donald Ross
LENOX GC
Lenox, Massachusetts
Devereux Emmet
LENOX HILLS CC
Farmingdale, New York
NKA Bethpage State Park GC
(Green Cse)
LENNOXVILLE GC
Lennoxville, Quebec
Howard Watson
LENZERHEIDE VALBELLA GC
Lenzerheide, Switzerland
James Gannon
(A.9) Fred W. Hawtree
LEONARD LITWIN PRIVATE CSE
Long Island, New York
Stephen Kay
LEONARD WHEATLEY PRIVATE CSE
Hillhead, Quebec
Howard Watson
LEO PALACE RESORT GC
Yona Hills, Guam
Jack Nicklaus
LE PETAW GC
Hokkaido, Japan
Maury Miller, *D. A. Weibring*
LE PORTAGE GC
Cheticamp, Nova Scotia
Robert Moote, David L. Moote
LE RICHOCET GC
Chicoutimi, Quebec
Graham Cooke

LE ROVEDINE GC
Milan, Italy
Marco Croze
LEROY CC
Leroy, Illinois
Tom Bendelow
LEROY KING PRIVATE CSE
Hesston, Kansas
Floyd Farley
LE SEIGNEURIE DE VAUDREUIL GC
Louisville, Quebec
Howard Watson
LES JARDIN DU SABLE GC
Cherry River, Quebec
(R.6) John Watson
LESLIE PARK GC
Ann Arbor, Michigan
Edward Lawrence Packard
L'ESTEREL GC
L'Esterel, Quebec
(R.1) John Watson
LESTER PARK GC
Duluth, Minnesota
(R.18 A.9) Dick Phelps
LES TERRASSES DE GENEVE G&CC
Bossey, France
Robert Trent Jones, Jr.
LE SUEUR CC
Le Sueur, Minnesota
Joel Goldstrand
LES VIEUX CHÊNES GC
Youngsville, Louisiana
Marvin Ferguson
LETCHWORTH GC
Hertfordshire, England
Harry Vardon
LETHAM GRANGE GC (CSE NO. 1)
Angus, Scotland
D. M. A. Steel, *G. K. Smith*
LETHAM GRANGE GC (CSE NO. 2)
Angus, Scotland
T. J. A. Macauley
LETHBRIDGE GC
Lethbridge, Alberta
Tom Bendelow
(R. A.9) William G. Robinson
LE TOUQUET GC [NLE]
Le Touquet, France
Allen Stoneham
LE TOUQUET GC (FOREST CSE)
France
H. S. Colt
(R.) P. M. Ross
(R.) Peter Alliss, *Clive Clark*
LE TOUQUET GC (SEA CSE)
France
H. S. Colt, J. S. F. Morrison, C.
H. Alison
LE TRIOMPHE GC
Lafayette, Louisiana
Robert Trent Jones, Jr.
LETTERKENNY GC
County Donegal, Ireland
Eddie Hackett
LEVERKUSEN GC
Germany
Karl F. Grohs, *Rainer
Preissmann*
LE VERSANT GC (CSE NO. 1)
Terrebonne, Quebec
John Watson
LE VERSANT GC (CSE NO. 2)
Terrebonne, Quebec
John Watson

LE VERSANT GC (CSE NO. 3)
Terrebonne, Quebec
John Watson
LÉVIS GC
Lévis, Quebec
(R.) Howard Watson
LEWES GC
Sussex, England
(R.) J. Hamilton Stutt
LEW GALBRAITH MUNI
Oakland, California
Bob Baldock
(R.) Robert Muir Graves
LEWIS ESTATES G&CC
Edmonton, Alberta
William G. Robinson, John F.
Robinson
LEWISTON CC
Lewiston, Idaho
Bob Baldock, Robert L. Baldock
LEWISTOWN CC
Lewistown, Pennsylvania
Edmund B. Ault
LEWISTOWN ELKS CC
Lewistown, Montana
William H. Diddel
LEW WENTZ MEMORIAL GC
Ponca City, Oklahoma
Arthur Jackson
(R.9 A.9) Floyd Farley
LEXDEN WEST HOUSE GC
Colchester, Essex, England
Howard Swan
LEXINGTON CC
Lexington, Kentucky
Tom Bendelow
(R.4 A.5) Benjamin Wihry
LEXINGTON G&CC
Lexington, Virginia
Ellis Maples
LEXINGTON MUNI
Lexington, North Carolina
Dugan Aycock
LEXINGTON VA HOSPITAL GC
Lexington, Kentucky
Bob Baldock
LIBERAL CC
Liberal, Kansas
Dewey Longworth
LIBERAL HILLS GC
Fukushima, Japan
Shunsuke Kato
LIBERTY HILLS CC
Liberty, Missouri
Ray Pettegrew
LIBERTY LAKE GC
Spokane, Washington
Mel "Curley" Hueston
(R.1) John Steidel
LIBERTYVILLE CC [NLE]
Libertyville, Illinois
Leonard Macomber
LICK CREEK GC
Pekin, Illinois
Edward Lawrence Packard,
Roger Packard
LICKING SPRINGS G & TROUT C
Newark, Ohio
Jack Kidwell
LIDKOEPING GC
Lidkoeping, Sweden
Douglas Brazier

LIDO DI VENEZIA GC
Venice, Italy
(R.9 A.9) C. K. Cotton, John
Harris
LIDO GC [NLE]
Lido Beach, New York
Charles Blair Macdonald, Seth
Raynor
LIDO G CSE CENTER
Oakville, Ontario
Clinton E. Robinson
LIDO SPRINGS GC
Lido Beach, New York
William F. Mitchell
LIGHTHOUSE MARINA & CC
Sacramento, California
Bert Stamps
LIGONIER CC
Ligonier, Pennsylvania
(R.9 A.9) X. G. Hassenplug
LILLESHALL HALL GC
England
H. S. Colt, J. S. F. Morrison
LIMBURG GC
Hasselt, Belgium
Fred W. Hawtree
LIMEKILN GC
Ambler, Pennsylvania
Al Janis
LIMERICK GC
Limerick, Ireland
James Braid
(A.9) James Braid, John R.
Stutt
(R.) Eddie Hackett
LIMOGES GC
Limoges, France
J. Bourret, Hubert Chesneau
LIMON GC
Limon, Colorado
Henry B. Hughes
LINCOLN GC
Ludington, Michigan
(A.2) Jerry Matthews
LINCOLN ELKS GC
Lincoln, Illinois
Tom Bendelow
LINCOLN GREENS GC
Springfield, Illinois
Robert Bruce Harris
LINCOLN HILLS CC
Ruidoso, New Mexico
Ralph Plummer
LINCOLN HILLS CC
Marshfield, Wisconsin
Edward Lawrence Packard
LINCOLN HILLS GC
Birmingham, Michigan
Bruce Matthews, Jerry Matthews
(R.1) Jerry Matthews
LINCOLN HOMESTEAD STATE PARK G
CSE
Springfield, Kentucky
(R.) Perry Maxwell, Press
Maxwell
LINCOLN PARK GC
San Francisco, California
Tom Bendelow
(R.9 A.9) Herbert Fowler
(R.) Jack Fleming
LINCOLN PARK GC
Grand Junction, Colorado
(R.) Richard Phelps

LINCOLN PARK GC
  Milwaukee, Wisconsin
  Tom Bendelow
    (R.) George Hansen
LINCOLN PARK MUNI
  Chicago, Illinois
  Edward B. Dearie, Jr.
LINCOLN PARK MUNI
  Grand Forks, North Dakota
    (R.) Don Herfort
LINCOLN PARK MUNI (EAST CSE)
  Oklahoma City, Oklahoma
  Arthur Jackson
    (R.) Perry Maxwell
    (R.) Floyd Farley
LINCOLN PARK MUNI (WEST CSE)
  Oklahoma City, Oklahoma
  Arthur Jackson
    (R.) Perry Maxwell
    (R.) Floyd Farley
LINCOLNSHIRE CC (CSE NO. 1)
  Crete, Illinois
  Tom Bendelow
    (R.) Ken Killian, Dick Nugent
LINCOLNSHIRE CC (CSE NO. 2)
  Crete, Illinois
  Tom Bendelow
    (R.) Ken Killian, Dick Nugent
LINCOLNSHIRE FIELDS GC
  Champaign, Illinois
  Edward Lawrence Packard
LINDALE GREENS GC
  Sacramento, California
  Bob Baldock
LINDAU-BAD SCHACHEN GC
  Lindau, Germany
  Bernhard von Limburger
    (A.9) Kurt Rossknecht
LINDBROOK CC
  Hope Valley, Rhode Island
  Phil Wogan
    (R.) Phil Wogan
LINDE GC
  Lindesberg, Sweden
  Jan Sederholm
LINDEMAN ISLAND GC
  Queensland, Australia
  Ted Ashby
LINDEN GC
  Linden, Alabama
  Neil R. Bruce
LINDEN G&CC
  Puyallup, Washington
  William H. Tucker
LINDERHOF CC
  Glen, New Hampshire
  J. R. Blais
LINDRICK GC
  England
  Tom Dunn
    (R.) Fred W. Hawtree
LINDSAY ARMS GC
  St. George, Ontario
    (A.9) Robert Heaslip
LINDSAY MUNI
  Lindsay, California
  Bob Baldock
LINGAN GC
  Sydney, Nova Scotia
  Stanley Thompson
    (A.9) Clinton E. Robinson
LINK HILLS CC
  Greenville, Tennessee
  Robert Trent Jones

LINKOPINGS GC
  Linkopings, Sweden
  Gunnar Bauer
    (R.) Douglas Brazier, Rafael
    Sundblum
    (R.) Ronald Fream
[THE] LINKS GC
  Highlands Ranch, Colorado
  Dick Phelps
[THE] LINKS GC [NLE]
  Roslyn, New York
  Charles Blair Macdonald, Seth
  Raynor
    (R.) Perry Maxwell
[THE] LINKS GC
  Newmarket, England
  S. V. Hotchkin
[THE] LINKS AT FISHER ISLAND
  Fisher Island, Florida
  P. B. Dye
[THE] LINKS AT GAINSBOROUGH LEA
  Lincolnshire, England
  Howard Swan
[THE] LINKS AT MONARCH BEACH
  Laguna Niguel, California
  Robert Trent Jones, Jr.
[THE] LINKS AT NATURAL BRIDGE
  Natural Bridge, Virginia
  Algie Pulley
[THE] LINKS AT NICHOLS PARK
  Jacksonville, Illinois
  David Gill, Garrett Gill
[THE] LINKS AT PINEWOOD
  Walled Lake, Michigan
  Ernest Fuller
[THE] LINKS AT PORTO CARRAS
  New Marmoras, Greece
  Geoffrey S. Cornish, William G.
  Robinson
[THE] LINKS AT SIERRA BLANCA
  Ruidoso, New Mexico
  Jeff Brauer
[THE] LINKS AT SPANISH BAY
  Pebble Beach, California
  Robert Trent Jones, Jr., Frank
  "Sandy" Tatum, Tom Watson
[THE] LINKS AT SPRUCE GROVE
  Spruce Grove, Alberta
  William G. Robinson, John F.
  Robinson
[THE] LINKS AT STONO FERRY
  Hollywood, South Carolina
  Ron Garl
[THE] LINKS OF AMHERST
  Amherst, New Hampshire
  Geoffrey S. Cornish, Brian Silva
[THE] LINKS OF LAKE BERNADETTE
  Zephyrhills, Florida
  Dean Refram
[THE] LINKS OF NOVI
  Novi, Michigan
  Jerry Matthews
LINKS O'TRYON
  Gowensville, South Carolina
  Tom Jackson
LINN CC
  Linn, Missouri
  Chet Mendenhall
LINRICK GC
  Columbia, South Carolina
  Russell Breeden

LINVILLE GC
  Linville, North Carolina
  Donald Ross
    (R.) Richard S. Tufts
LINVILLE RIDGE CC
  Linville, North Carolina
  George W. Cobb, John LaFoy
LINWOOD CC
  Linwood, New Jersey
  Herbert Strong
LINZ ST. FLORIAN GC
  Linz, Austria
  Donald Harradine
[THE] LION AT TANGLEWOOD GC
  South Lyon, Michigan
  William Newcomb
LIONS MUNI
  Columbus, Georgia
  Nolan Murrah
LION'S MUNI
  Austin, Texas
    (R.) Leon Howard
LION'S PAW G LINKS
  Sunset Beach, North Carolina
  Willard Byrd
LIPHOOK GC
  England
  A. C. M. Croome, J. F.
  Abercromby
    (R.) Tom Simpson
    (R. A.2) J. S. F. Morrison
LISBON BISSELL GC
  North Dakota
    (R.9) Don Herfort
LISBON SPORTS C
  Lisbon, Portugal
  F. G. Hawtree
    (A.9) Fred W. Hawtree
LISBON VILLAGE CC
  Lisbon, New Hampshire
  Ralph Barton
LISBURN GC
  Belfast, Northern Ireland
  F. W. Hawtree
LISCOMBE PARK GC
  England
  D. M. A. Steel
L'ISLE D'ABEAU GC
  France
  Robert Berthet
LISMORE GC
  County Waterford, Ireland
  Eddie Hackett
    (R.) Eddie Hackett
LISTOWEL GC
  Listowel, Ontario
    (R.8 A.10) Robert Moote,
    David L. Moote
LITCHFIELD CC
  Pawleys Island, South Carolina
  Willard Byrd
LITHIA SPRINGS CC
  Georgia
  Johnny Suggs
[THE] LITTLE C
  Delray Beach, Florida
  Joe Lee
[THE] LITTLE C
  Tequesta, Florida
  Mark Mahannah
[THE] LITTLE CSE
  Norcross, Georgia
  Ron Kirby

LITTLE AMERICA GC
  Cheyenne, Wyoming
  William H. Neff
LITTLE ASHTON GC
  Staffordshire, England
  Harry Vardon
    (R.) M. J. Lewis
    (R.) H. S. Colt
LITTLE CHALFONT GC
  England
  R. Garrad
LITTLE CROW CC
  Spicer, Minnesota
  Don Herfort
LITTLE CYPRESS G&CC
  Wauchulla, Florida
  R. Albert Anderson
LITTLE HADHAM GC
  Bishop's Stortford, Hertford-
  shire, England
  Howard Swan
LITTLEHAMPTON GC
  Littlehampton, England
    (R.9 A.9) F. G. Hawtree, J. H.
    Taylor
LITTLE HARBOR CC
  Wareham, Massachusetts
  Samuel Mitchell
LITTLE HAY GC
  Hertfordshire, England
  Fred W. Hawtree, Martin Haw-
  tree
LITTLE KNOLL GC
  Napa, California
  Clark Glasson
LITTLE LAKES GC
  Worcestershire, England
  Michael Cooksey
LITTLE MILL CC
  Marlton, New Jersey
  Garrett J. Renn
    (A.9) David Gordon
LITTLE MOUNTAIN CC
  Ellenwood, Georgia
    (R.) Arthur Davis, Ron Kirby
LITTLE MOUNTAIN STATE PARK GC
  Gunthersville, Alabama
  Earl Stone
LITTLE SIOUX G&CC
  Sioux Rapids, Iowa
  Harold McCullough
LITTLE ST. ANDREWS GC [NLE]
  Shrewsbury, Massachusetts
  Geoffrey S. Cornish
LITTLESTONE GC
  Kent, England
  W. Laidlaw Purves
    (R.) F. W. Maude
    (R.) Tom Dunn
    (R.) James Braid, John R.
    Stutt
LITTLE TAM GC
  Niles, Illinois
  William James Spear
LITTLE TRAVERSE BAY GC
  Harbor Springs, Michigan
  Jeff Gorney
LITTLE TURTLE C
  Columbus, Ohio
  Roy Dye, Pete Dye
LIVELY GC
  Ontario
    (R.9 A.9) Robert Moote

LIVEOAKS CC
Jackson, Mississippi
George C. Curtis

LIVERMORE VA HOSPITAL GC
Livermore, California
Bob Baldock

LIVERPOOL MUNI
Liverpool, England
J. Large

LIVINGSTON GC
Livingston, Alabama
Paul Hogren (9 1967)

LIVINGSTON G&CC
Edinburgh, Scotland
J. J. F. Pennink, C. D. Lawrie

LJUNGHUSENS GC
Sweden
Douglas Brazier
(R.) Ronald Fream
(R.) Jan Sederholm

LLANDRINDON WELLS GC
Powys, Wales
Harry Vardon

LLANERCH CC
Havertown, Pennsylvania
Alex Findlay
(R.) J.B. McGovern

LLANGEFNI GC
Anglesey, Wales
Martin Hawtree

LLANO GRANDE GC
Mercedes, Texas
John Bredemus

LLOYDMINSTER G&CC
Lloydminster, Alberta
Bill Newis

LOBLOLLY PINES GC
Hobe Sound, Florida
P. B. Dye

LOCHGREEN GC
Troon, Scotland
Willie Fernie
(R.) James Braid

LOCHIEL GC
Lochiel, New Zealand
W.A. Kiely

LOCHINVAR GC
Houston, Texas
Jack Nicklaus

LOCHLAND CC
Hastings, Nebraska
David Gill

LOCH LEDGE G&CC
Yorktown Heights, New York
Nat Squire

LOCH LLOYD CC
Belton, Missouri
Don Sechrest

LOCH LOMOND GC
Scotland
Jay Morrish, Tom Weiskopf

LOCH MARCH GC
Kanata, Ontario
Gordon Witteveen

LOCHMERE G&CC
Tilton, New Hampshire
Phil Wogan

LOCHMERE GC
Cary, North Carolina
Gene Hamm

LOCHMOOR C
Grosse Pointe Woods, Michigan
Walter J. Travis
(R.) C. H. Alison, H. S. Colt
(R.) Edward Lawrence
Packard
(R.) Arthur Hills

LOCHMOOR GC
North Fort Myers, Florida
William F. Mitchell

LOCKHAVEN CC
Alton, Illinois
Robert Bruce Harris

LOCKPORT CC
Lockport, New York
(R.) Stanley Thompson

LOCKWOOD G LINKS
Holden Beach, North Carolina
Willard Byrd

LOCUST GROVE GC
Rahway, New Jersey
Willard Wilkinson

LOCUST HILL CC
Rochester, New York
Seymour Dunn
(R.) Robert Trent Jones

LOCUST TREE CC
New Paltz, New York
Hal Purdy

LOCUST VALLEY CC
Coopersburg, Pennsylvania
William Gordon, David Gordon

[THE] LODGE GC
Laurinburg, North Carolina
Thomas Jackson

[THE] LODGE OF FOUR SEASONS GC
Lake Ozark, Missouri
Robert Trent Jones

[THE] LODGE OF FOUR SEASONS GC (EXECUTIVE CSE)
Lake Ozark, Missouri
Homer Herpel

LOGAN G&CC
Logan, Utah
Mick Riley

LOGANSPORT CC
Logansport, Indiana
Bob Simmons

LOG CABIN C
Clayton, Missouri
Robert Foulis
(R.) Robert Foulis

LOG CABIN CC [NLE]
Kansas City, Missouri
James Dalgleish

LOGO DE VITA GC
Greensburg, Pennsylvania
Ferdinand Garbin

LOHERSAND GC
Rendsburg, Germany
Bernhard von Limburger

LOHOLM GC
Sweden
Jan Sederholm

LOMA LINDA CC (NORTH CSE)
Joplin, Missouri
Don Sechrest

LOMA LINDA CC (SOUTH CSE)
Joplin, Missouri
Scott Brown (1992)

LOMAS SANTA FE CC
Solana Beach, California
William F. Bell
(R.) Robert Muir Graves

LONDON BRIDGE GC
Lake Havasu City, Arizona
Lawrence Hughes
(R.4) Arthur Jack Snyder

LONDONDERRY CC
Londonderry, New Hampshire
Forrest Kimball

LONDON GC
London, Kentucky
John Darrah

LONDON HUNT & CC
London, Ontario
Robert Trent Jones

LONDON SCOTTISH GC [NLE]
England
Willie Dunn
(R. A.9) Tom Dunn

LONE OAK CC
Nicholasville, Kentucky
Buck Blankenship

LONE PALM GC
Lakeland, Florida
Dick Wilson, Joe Lee

LONE PINE GC
New Jersey
Donald Ross

LONE PINE GC
Washington, Pennsylvania
X. G. Hassenplug
(R.) X. G. Hassenplug

LONE PINE GC
West Palm Beach, Florida
Richard W. LaConte, Ted
McAnlis

LONESOME PINE GC
Big Stone Gap, Virginia
(R.) John LaFoy

LONE TREE GC
Littleton, Colorado
Arnold Palmer, Ed Seay

LONE TREE G CSE
Antioch, California
Bob Baldock

LONG BAY C
Longs, South Carolina
Jack Nicklaus

LONG BEACH HOTEL GC [NLE]
New York
John Duncan Dunn

LONGBOAT KEY C (HARBORSIDE CSE)
Sarasota, Florida
Willard Byrd

LONGBOAT KEY C (ISLANDSIDE CSE)
Sarasota, Florida
William F. Mitchell
(R.) Willard Byrd

LONG BRANCH CC
Long Branch, New Jersey
Martin J. O'Loughlin

LONGCLIFFE GC
Leicestershire, England
Tom Williamson

LONG COVE C
Hilton Head Island, South
Carolina
Pete Dye

LONG CREEK G&CC
Avonlea, Saskatchewan
Bill Newis
(A.9) John F. Robinson

LONGFELLOW HOUSE GC
Pascagoula, Mississippi
Earl Stone

LONGFIT NEW TOWNE GC
Agana Heights, Guam
Jeff Brauer, Larry Nelson

LONG HOLLOW GC
Gallatin, Tennessee
Kevin Tucker

LONG LAKE HILL GC
Korea
Desmond Muirhead

LONGLEAF CC
Pinehurst, North Carolina
Dan Maples

LONGMEADOW CC
Springfield, Massachusetts
Donald Ross
(R.) William F. Mitchell
(R.) Geoffrey S. Cornish,
Brian Silva

LONG MEADOW GC
Lowell, Massachusetts
Alex Findlay

LONG MEADOWS CC
Jersey Village, Texas
NKA Jersey Village GC

LONGNIDDRY GC
East Lothian, Scotland
H. S. Colt, C. H. Alison
(R.) P. M. Ross

LONG POINT C
Amelia Island, Florida
Tom Fazio

LONG RUN GC
Anchorage, Kentucky
Benjamin Wihry

LONGSHORE PARK GC
Westport, Connecticut
Orrin Smith

LONGUE VUE C
Verona, Pennsylvania
Robert White
(R.) Ferdinand Garbin
(R.) Geoffrey S. Cornish,
Brian Silva

LONGVIEW LAKES G CSE
Lees Summit, Missouri
Brad Benz, Mike Poellot

LONGVIEW MUNI
Timonium, Maryland
(R.3) Edmund B. Ault, Bill
Love

LONGWOOD CC
Dyer, Indiana
Harry Collis

LOOKOUT MOUNTAIN GC
Lookout Mountain, Georgia
Seth Raynor, Charles Banks

LOOKOUT POINT G&CC
Fonthill, Ontario
Walter J. Travis

LOPE C
Tochigi, Japan
Tadashi Sasaki

LORAIN CC
Lorain, Ohio
Tom Bendelow

LORD MOUNTBATTEN ESTATE GC
England
Herbert Fowler, Tom Simpson

LORDS VALLEY CC
Hawley, Pennsylvania
Norman H. Woods

LORETTE GC
Quebec
(R.9) Howard Watson

Los Alamitos GC
Los Alamitos, California
(R. A.12) William F. Bell

Los Altos G&CC
Los Altos, California
Tom Nicoll
(R.) Tom Nicoll, Clark
Glasson
(R. 9) Robert Muir Graves
(R.) Clark Glasson
(R.) Ronald Fream

Los Altos Muni
Albuquerque, New Mexico
Bob Baldock

Los Andes GC
Lima, Peru
George Hardmann

Los Angeles CC (North Cse)
Los Angeles, California
George C. Thomas, Jr.
(R.) William P. Bell
(R.) Robert Muir Graves

Los Angeles CC (South Cse)
Los Angeles, California
Herbert Fowler
(R.) George C. Thomas, Jr.
(R.) Robert Muir Graves

Los Angeles Royal Vista GC
Walnut, California
William F. Bell

Losantiville CC
Cincinnati, Ohio
Tom Bendelow
(R.) Hal Purdy

Los Banos CC
Los Banos, California
Bob Baldock

Los Caballeros GC
Wickenburg, Arizona
Jeff Hardin, Greg Nash

Los Coyotes CC
Buena Park, California
William F. Bell
(R.6) Ted Robinson

Los Flamingos CC
Puerto Vallarta, Mexico
Percy Clifford

Los Gatos G&CC
San Jose, California
Clark Glasson

Los Leones GC
Chile
A. Macdonald

Los Prados GC
Las Vegas, Nevada
Jeff Hardin

Los Rios CC
Plano, Texas
Don January, Billy Martindale

Los Robles Greens GC
Thousand Oaks, California
Bob Baldock

Los Serranos Lakes CC (North Cse)
Chino, California
John Duncan Dunn
(R.) Harry Rainville, David
Rainville

Los Serranos Lakes CC (South Cse)
Chino, California
William Eaton

Lost Brook GC
Norwood, Massachusetts
Samuel Mitchell

Lost Creek CC
Lima, Ohio
(R.) Hal Purdy

Lost Creek GC
Sturgeon Bay, Wisconsin
James Keyes, Bob Peterson

Lost Creek GC
Austin, Texas
Dave Bennett, *Terry Dill*
(R.12) Jeff Brauer

Lost Diamond Valley CC
Flat Rock, North Carolina
Dick Phelps, Brad Benz

Lost Lake Woods GC
Lincoln, Michigan
(A.9) Ken Killian, Dick
Nugent

Lost Pines GC
Bastrop, Texas
Leon Howard

Lost Tree C
Singer Island, Florida
Mark Mahannah, Charles
Mahannah
(R.) Bob Cupp, Jay Morrish

Los Verdes G&CC
Rancho Palos Verdes, California
William F. Bell

Lotte Minayoshidai CC
Chiba, Japan
Hirochika Tomizawa

Loudun–St. Hilaire GC
Loudun, France
T. J. A. Macauley, *Stephen
Quenouille*

Loudun G&CC
Purcellville, Virginia
Edmund B. Ault, Al Jamison

Loughrea GC
Loughrea, Ireland
(R.) Eddie Hackett

Louisiana State University GC
Baton Rouge, Louisiana
NKA Webb Memorial G Cse

Louis Stoner Private Cse
West Hartford, Connecticut
Orrin Smith

Louisville CC
Louisville, Kentucky
Robert White
(R.9 A.9) Walter J. Travis
(R.) William B. Langford,
Theodore J. Moreau
(R.) William H. Diddel
(R.1 A.1) Benjamin Wihry

Louth GC
Lincolnshire, England
Tom Williamson
(R.) C. K. Cotton, J. J. F.
Pennink

Louvain-La-Neuve GC
Belgium
J. F. Dudok van Heel

Loveland GC
Loveland, Colorado
(R.) Dick Phelps
(A.9) Frank Hummel

Lovington Muni
Lovington, New Mexico
Warren Cantrell

Low Laithes GC
Huddersfield, England
Alister Mackenzie

Lower Cascades GC
Hot Springs, Virginia
Robert Trent Jones

Lowes Park GC
Bury, Lancashire, England
J. A. Steer

Lowestoft GC
Lowestoft, England
J. J. F. Pennink

Lowry AFB GC
Denver, Colorado
Bob Baldock
(R.) Pat Wyss

Loxahatchee C
Jupiter, Florida
Jack Nicklaus

Lubbock CC
Lubbock, Texas
(R.9 A.9) Warren Cantrell
(R.) Joseph S. Finger, Ken
Dye

Lucan GC
Lucan, Ireland
(R.) Eddie Hackett

Lucayan G&CC
Freeport, Bahamas
Dick Wilson, Joe Lee

Lucerne GC
Winter Haven, Florida
David Wallace

Lucerne-in-Maine GC [NLE]
Lucerne, Maine
Donald Ross

Lucerne-in-Quebec GC
Montebello, Quebec
Stanley Thompson

Lucky Hills CC
Franklin, Pennsylvania
X. G. Hassenplug

Luden Riverside CC
Pennsylvania
Alex Findlay

Ludersburg GC
Hamburg, Germany
Jim Engh, *Bernhard Langer*

Ludington Hills GC
Ludington, Michigan
Tom Bendelow
(R.4) Bruce Matthews, Jerry
Matthews

Ludlow CC
Ludlow, Massachusetts
Donald Ross

Ludlow Muni
Chicopee, Massachusetts
Orrin Smith

Luffenham Heath GC
England
James Braid

Luffness New GC
East Lothian, Scotland
Old Tom Morris
(R.) Tom Simpson
(R.) Willie Park, Jr.

Lugano GC
Magliaso, Switzerland
(R.) Donald Harradine
(R.) Pier Mancinelli
(R.) Cabell Robinson

Luisita GC
Tarlac, Philippines
Robert Trent Jones

Lullingstone Park GC
Kent, England
Fred W. Hawtree

Lu Lu Temple CC
North Hills, Pennsylvania
Donald Ross

Lumby GC
British Columbia
Reggie Betts

Lum International GC
Lum, Michigan
Joseph Hawald

Lunds Akademiska GC
Lund, Sweden
(R.9 A.9) J. S. F. Morrison

Luray GC [NLE]
Luray, Virginia
Fred Findlay

Luray Caverns CC
Luray, Virginia
Hal Purdy, Malcolm Purdy

Lurgin GC
Netherlands
(R.) J. J. F. Pennink

Lusaka GC
Lusaka, Zambia
J. J. F. Pennink

Lusk GC
Lusk, Wyoming
Frank Hummel

Lutterworth GC
Lutterworth, England
(A.9) Fred W. Hawtree

Luverne GC
Luverne, Minnesota
(R.) Joel Goldstrand

Lyckorna GC
Ljungskile, Sweden
Anders Amilon

Lyford Cay C
New Providence Island,
Bahamas
Dick Wilson, Joe Lee

Lyman Meadow GC
Middlefield, Connecticut
Robert Trent Jones

Lyme Regis GC
Dorset, England
(R.) J. Hamilton Stutt

Lynchburg CC
Lynchburg, Virginia
Gene Hamm

Lyndway GC
Lyndhurst, Ontario
Gordon Witteveen

Lynnfield Center GC
Lynnfield, Massachusetts
(R.) William F. Mitchell

Lynnhaven [NLE]
Kansas City, Missouri
Orrin Smith

Lynn Haven CC
Norfolk, Virginia
Tom Winton

Lynnwood Muni
Lynnwood, Washington
John Steidel

Lynrock GC
Eden, North Carolina
Gene Hamm

LYNWOOD G&CC
Martinsville, Virginia
George W. Cobb
LYNWOOD GC
London, Ontario
Robert Moote, *David S. Moote*
LYON-CHARBONNIÈRE GC
France
Pier Mancinelli
LYONS DEN GC
Akron, Ohio
Bill Lyons
LYONS TOWN & CC
Lyons, Kansas
Dewey Longworth
LYONS VA HOSPITAL GC
New Jersey
Robert Trent Jones
LYON-VERGER GC
France
M. Preneuf
LYSEGARDENS GC
Kungälv, Sweden
Eric Röhss

MACARENA GC
Colombia
Mark Mahannah
MACCAUVLEI CC
Transvaal, South Africa
S. V. Hotchkin, *George Peck*
MACCRIPINE CC
Pinetops, North Carolina
Leo Greene
MACDILL AFB GC (NEW CSE)
Tampa, Florida
Ron Garl
MACDILL AFB GC (OLD CSE)
Tampa, Florida
(R.) Ron Garl
MACDONALD ESTATE GC
Bal Harbour, Florida
Robert Trent Jones
MACDONALD PARK MUNI
Wichita, Kansas
James Dalgleish
(R.) Orrin Smith
(R.) William H. Diddel
(R.) Bob Dunning
MACE MEADOWS GC
Jackson, California
Jack Fleming
MACGREGOR DOWNS CC
Cary, North Carolina
Willard Byrd
MACHRIE HOTEL GC
Scotland
Willie Campbell
(R.) D. M. A. Steel
MACHRIHANISH GC
Argyllshire, Scotland
Charles Hunter
(R. A.6) Old Tom Morris
(R.) J. H. Taylor
(R.) Sir Guy Campbell
MACHYNLLETH GC
Powys, Wales
James Braid
MACKENZIE'S GC [NLE]
Franconia, New Hampshire
Ralph Barton

MACKTOWN GC
Rockton, Illinois
R. Welch
MACOMB GC
Macomb, Illinois
Robert Bruce Harris
MACTAQUAC PROVINCIAL PARK GC
New Brunswick
William F. Mitchell
MADARAO TOKYU GC
Nagano, Japan
Nagao Kurosawa
MADDEN GC
Dayton, Ohio
Alex "Nipper" Campbell
MADDEN INN & GC (EAST CSE)
Brainerd, Minnesota
James Dalgleish
(R.) Don Herfort
MADDEN INN & GC (PAR 3 CSE)
Brainerd, Minnesota
Jim Madden
MADDEN INN & GC (WEST CSE)
Brainerd, Minnesota
Paul Coates
(R.) *Jim Madden*
MADELINE ISLAND G LINKS
La Pointe, Wisconsin
Robert Trent Jones
MADERA G&CC
Madera, California
Bob Baldock
MADERA MUNI
Madera, California
Robert Dean Putman
MADGE LAKE GC
Quebec
(R.) William F. Mitchell
(R.9) Clinton E. Robinson
MADISON CC
Madison, Connecticut
Willie Park, Jr.
(R.) Brian Silva, Geoffrey S.
Cornish
MADISON CC
Madison, Florida
Hans Schmeisser
MADISON CC
Madison, Ohio
Sandy Alves
MADISON CC
Madison, South Dakota
Joel Goldstrand
MADISON MEADOWS GC
Ennis, Montana
Frank Hummel
MADISON PARK MUNI
Peoria, Illinois
Tom Bendelow
MADISONVILLE GC
Madisonville, Texas
Leon Howard
MAD RIVER GC
Toronto, Ontario
Bob Cupp
MADRONA LINKS
Gig Harbor, Washington
Ken Tyson
MAGGIE VALLEY CC
Maggie Valley, North Carolina
William Prevost, Emmett Mitchell
MAGNOLIA CC
Magnolia, Arkansas
Herman Hackbarth

MAGNOLIA GC
Magnolia, Massachusetts
Ralph Barton
MAGNOLIA GROVE GC (CROSSINGS CSE)
Mobile, Alabama
Robert Trent Jones
MAGNOLIA GROVE GC (FALLS CSE)
Mobile, Alabama
Robert Trent Jones
MAGNOLIA GROVE GC (SHORT CSE)
Mobile, Alabama
Robert Trent Jones
MAGNOLIA HILLS CC
Suncoast, Australia
Robert von Hagge, Bruce Devlin
MAGNOLIA POINT G&CC
Green Cove Springs, Florida
Mark McCumber
MAGNOLIA RIDGE CC
Liberty, Texas
Ralph Plummer
MAGNOLIA VALLEY G&CC
New Port Richey, Florida
Phil Leckey
(R. A.4) Bill Amick
MAHACHIA GC
Bangkok, Thailand
Greg Nash
MAHOGANY RUN GC
St. Thomas, Virgin Islands
George Fazio, Tom Fazio
MAHONEY GC
Lincoln, Nebraska
Floyd Farley
MAHONING VALLEY CC [NLE]
Lansford, Pennsylvania
Maurice McCarthy
MAHONING VALLEY CC
Leighton, Pennsylvania
William Gordon, David Gordon
MAHON MUNI
County Cork, Ireland
Eddie Hackett
MAHOPAC GC [NLE]
Lake Mahopac, New York
Tom Bendelow
MAHOPAC GC
Lake Mahopac, New York
Devereux Emmet
(R.) Stephen Kay
MAIBARA CC
Chiba, Japan
Mitsuaki Kobayashi
MAIDENHEAD GC
Maidenhead, England
Tom Dunn
(R.) Willie Park, Jr.
MAIDSTONE C
East Hampton, New York
William H. Tucker
(A.9) Willie Park, Jr., *John A. Park*
(A.9) *C. Wheaton Vaughan*
(R.11) Willie Park, Jr., *John A. Park*
(R.) Perry Maxwell
(R.) Alfred H. Tull
MAINLANDS GC
Tamarac, Florida
William Boorman
MAINPRIZE REGIONAL PARK GC
Estevan, Saskatchewan
John F. Robinson

MAINSONDHEIM GC
Germany
(A.9) Reinhold Weishaupt
(A.3rd 9) Reinhold Weishaupt
MAJESTIC OAKS GC (NORTH CSE)
Ham Lake, Minnesota
Charles Maddox
MAJESTIC OAKS GC (SOUTH CSE)
Ham Lake, Minnesota
Garrett Gill, George B. Williams
MAJESTIC OAKS GC
Salt Lake City, Utah
William H. Neff
MAJETTE DUNES G&CC
Panama City, Florida
Jack Cunningham (1989)
MAKAHA VALLEY CC
Waianae, Oahu, Hawaii
William F. Bell
(R.) Arthur Jack Snyder
MAKENA GC (OLD COURSE)
Kihei, Maui, Hawaii
Robert Trent Jones, Jr.
MAKENA GC (NEW COURSE)
Kihei, Maui, Hawaii
Robert Trent Jones, Jr.
MAKETEWAH CC
Cincinnati, Ohio
Donald Ross
MAKILA GC
Bassussarry-Biarritz, France
Rocky Roquemore, Jeff Burton
MÁLAGA GC
Málaga, Spain
Tom Simpson
MALAHIDE GC
County Dublin, Ireland
N. Hone
(R.) Eddie Hackett
MALDEN GC
Surrey, England
Sandy Herd, *H. Bailey*
MALIBU GC
Malibu, California
William F. Bell
MALKINS BANK GC
Cheshire, England
Fred W. Hawtree, A. H. F. Jiggens
MALLARD HEAD CC
Mooresville, North Carolina
J. Porter Gibson
MALLOW GC
Mallow, Ireland
(R.9 A.9) John Harris
MALMÖ GC
Malmö, Sweden
Jan Sederholm
(A.7) Jan Sederholm
MALONE GC
Belfast, Northern Ireland
Fred W. Hawtree
MALONE GC (OLD CSE)
Malone, New York
Willard Wilkinson
(A.9) Albert Murray
MALONE GC (NEW CSE)
Malone, New York
Robert Trent Jones
MALTON & NORTON GC
England
(A.9) Fred W. Hawtree, Martin Hawtree

MALVERN GC
England
(A.9) Fred W. Hawtree
MALVERN HILLS CC
North Carolina
(R.) Ross Taylor
MANADA GC
Grantville, Pennsylvania
David Gordon
MANAGO CC
Japan
Arnold Palmer, Ed Seay
MANAKI G&CC
Ontario
(R.) Clinton E. Robinson
MANAKIKI G&CC
Willoughby, Ohio
Donald Ross
(R.) Craig Schreiner
MANASQUAN RIVER G&CC
Brielle, New Jersey
Robert White
MANATEE COUNTY GC
Bradenton, Florida
Lane Marshall
MANAWATU GC
New Zealand
C. T. Munro, C. T. G. Still
(R.) C. H. Redhead
(R.) H. G. Babbage
MANCHESTER CC
Manchester, Connecticut
Tom Bendelow
MANCHESTER CC
Manchester, New Hampshire
Donald Ross
(R.4) Phil Wogan
MANCHESTER CC
Manchester, Vermont
Geoffrey S. Cornish, William G.
Robinson
MANCHESTER CC
Lancashire, England
H. S. Colt
(R.) Alister Mackenzie
MANDARIN G&CC
Newmarket, Ontario
Douglas Carrick
MANDARIN GC
Mandarin, North Dakota
Don Herfort
MANDERLEY GC
North Gower, Ontario
Howard Watson
M AND W GC
Winnsboro, Texas
Leon Howard
MANGILAO GC
Mangilao, Guam
Robin Nelson, Rodney Wright
MANGROVE BAY GC
St. Petersburg, Florida
Bill Amick
MANHATTAN CC [NLE]
Manhattan, Kansas
Mike Ahearn
MANHATTAN CC
Manhattan, Kansas
Smiley Bell
(R.1) Jeff Brauer
MANHATTAN CC [NLE]
Freeport, New York
Devereux Emmet

MANHATTAN WOODS GC
New York
Brian Silva, Geoffrey S. Cornish,
M. Kubayashi
MANILA G&CC
Makati, Philippines
Bob Baldock
MANILA SOUTHWOODS G&CC
Manila, Phillipines
Jack Nicklaus
MANISTEE G&CC
Manistee, Michigan
Tom Bendelow
(R.9 A.9) Bruce Matthews
(R.) Jeff Gorney
MANITO G&CC
Spokane, Washington
A. Vernon Macan
(R.) Peter Thomson, Michael
Wolveridge, Ronald Fream
MANITOU RIDGE GC
White Bear Lake, Minnesota
(R.) Don Herfort
MANITOUWADGE GC
Manitouwadge, Ontario
Howard Watson
MANKATO GC
Mankato, Minnesota
William B. Langford, Theodore
J. Moreau
(A.9) William B. Langford
(R.) Gerry Pirkl, Donald G.
Brauer
MANLEY'S GC
Albion, Michigan
Robert Beard
MANNHEIM-VIERNHEIM GC
Mannheim, Germany
Karl Hoffmann, Bernhard von
Limburger
MANNITTO HAVEN G CSE
Pittsburgh, Pennsylvania
George Beljan (9 1960)
MANOIR INVERNESS GC
Lac Brome, Quebec
(A.9) John Watson
(A.3rd 9) John Watson
MANOIR RICHELIEU GC
Murray Bay, Quebec
Herbert Strong
MANOR CC
Sinking Springs, Pennsylvania
Alex Findlay
(R.) William S. Flynn
MANOR PARK CC
Rockville, Maryland
Harry Collis
(R.) Reuben Hines
(R.4) Edmund B. Ault, Brian
Ault, Bill Love
MANOR HOUSE HOTEL GC
England
J. F. Abercromby, Herbert
Fowler
(R.) James Alexander
MANTECA PARK GC
Manteca, California
Jack Fleming

MANUFACTURERS G&CC
Oreland, Pennsylvania
William S. Flynn
(R.1) William Gordon
(A.9) William Gordon, David
Gordon
(R.) Tom Clark
MANWALLIMINK GC [NLE]
Shawnee-on-Delaware,
Pennsylvania
C. C. Worthington
MAOI RESORT GC
Hokkaido, Japan
Robert von Hagge
MAPLE CC
Morioka, Japan
Takeaki Kaneda, Tsuyoshi Arai
MAPLE BLUFF CC
Madison, Wisconsin
(R.) George B. Ferry
(R.) Ken Killian, Dick Nugent
MAPLE CITY G&CC
Chatham, Ontario
Clinton E. Robinson
MAPLECREST CC
Goshen, Indiana
(R.) Gary Kern
MAPLE CREST CC
Kenosha, Wisconsin
Leonard Macomber
MAPLE CREST GC
La Grange, Illinois
William B. Langford
MAPLECREST GC [NLE]
Downers Grove, Illinois
Robert Bruce Harris
MAPLEDALE CC
Dover, Delaware
Russell Roberts
MAPLE DOWNS G&CC
Ontario
William F. Mitchell
MAPLEGATE CC
Bellingham, Massachusetts
Phil Wogan
MAPLE GROVE GC
Washington Island, Wisconsin
Leland Thompson
MAPLE HILL GC
Augusta, Michigan
Robert Beard
MAPLE HILL GC
Hemlock, Michigan
Carl O. Hegenauer (9 1951)
(R.1) Jerry Matthews
MAPLE HILLS GC
Grandville, Michigan
George Woolferd
MAPLEHURST CC
Frostburg, Maryland
James Gilmore Harrison
MAPLE LANE GC
Livermore, Maine
Arthur David Chapman
MAPLE LANE GC (COURSE NO. 2)
Sterling Heights, Michigan
Clarence Wolfrom
MAPLE LEAF GC
North Sutton, New Hampshire
Sherman J. Felch
MAPLE LEAF G CSE
Linwood, Michigan
Robert W. Bills, Donald L. Childs

MAPLE LEAF ESTATES CC
Port Charlotte, Florida
Ward Northrup
MAPLEMOOR CC
White Plains, New York
Archie Capper
(R.) Tom Winton
MAPLE RIDGE GC
Calgary, Alberta
Dick Phelps, Claude Muret
(A.9) Les Furber, Jim Eremko
MAPLE RIVER GC
West Fargo, North Dakota
Edward Lawrence Packard
[THE] MAPLES OF BALLANTRAE
G&GC
Whitchurch, Ontario
Robert Moote, David L. Moote
MAPLE POINT GC
Japan
Perry Dye
MAPLE VALLEY G&CC
Stewartville, Minnesota
Wayne Idso
MAPLEVIEW G&CC [NLE]
Renton, Washington
Frank James
MAPLE VILLAGE GC
Omaha, Nebraska
NKA Warren Swiggart GC
MAPLEWOOD CC
Bethlehem, New Hampshire
Alex Findlay
(R.9 A.9) Donald Ross
MAPLEWOOD CC
Renton, Washington
Al Smith
(R.5) John Steidel
MAPPERLEY GC
Nottinghamshire, England
Tom Williamson
MARACAIBO GC
Maracaibo, Venezuela
James Baird Wilson
MARACAY GC
Maracay, Venezuela
C. H. Anderson
MARAMARUA GC
Pokeno, New Zealand
John Harris, Peter Thomson
MARAYUI G&CC
Mar del Plata, Argentina
Ronald Fream
MARBELLA G&CC
Marbella, Spain
Robert Trent Jones
MARBELLA G&CC
San Juan Capistrano, California
Jay Morrish, Tom Weiskopf
MARBLE ISLAND G&YC
Essex Junction, Vermont
A. W. Tillinghast
MARCELINE GC
Marceline, Missouri
Floyd Farley
MARCO ISLAND CC
Marco Island, Florida
David Wallace
(R.) Pete Dye
MARCO SHORES CC
Marco Island, Florida
Robert von Hagge, Bruce Devlin

Marco Simone GC
Rome, Italy
Jim Fazio

Marcus Pointe GC
Pensacola, Florida
Earl Stone

Mar de Plata GC
Argentina
Juan Dentone
(R.) Alister Mackenzie

Mardon Lodge GC
Barrie, Ontario
Stanley Thompson

Mare Island GC
Vallejo, California
(R.) Robert Muir Graves

Marengo Ridge CC
Marengo, Illinois
William James Spear

Margara GC
Allessandria, Italy
John Harris

Margarethenhof am Tegernsee GC
Germany
J. J. F. Pennink

Margarita Village G Cse
Hemet, California
Ted Robinson

Margate CC
Natal, South Africa
Arthur Lawrence Mandy

Mariah Hills G Cse
Dodge City, Kansas
Frank Hummel
(R.) Larry W. Flatt

Marian Hills GC
Malta, Montana
John Steidel

Marianské Lázné GC
Marianské Lázné, Czechoslovakia
Willie Brown

Marias Valley G&CC
Shelby, Montana
Norman H. Woods
(R.) Robert Muir Graves

Marienbad GC
Marianské Lázné, Czechoslovakia
(R.) Bernhard von Limburger

Marienburger GC
Cologne, Germany
Bernhard von Limburger

Mariestad GC
Mariestad, Sweden
S. Meistedt

Marietta CC
Marietta, Georgia
Bob Cupp

Marietta CC
Marietta, Ohio
Perl O. Hart
(R.) Edmund B. Ault

Marietta G Cse
Marietta, Georgia
(R.) Mike Young

Marigola GC
Italy
F. Pregazzi

Marina del Ray GC
Venice, California
Harry Rainville

Marina Velca GC
Italy
R. Russo

Marin G&CC
Novato, California
Lawrence Hughes
(R.) Robert Muir Graves

Marine Corps GC
Nebo, California
Lawrence Hughes

Marine Drive GC
Vancouver, British Columbia
A. Vernon Macan

Marine Memorial GC
Camp Pendelton, California
William P. Bell
(R.) Peter Thomson, Michael Wolveridge, Ronald Fream

Marine Memorial GC
Santa Ana, California
William P. Bell

Marine Park GC
Brooklyn, New York
Robert Trent Jones

Mariner Sands CC (Gold Cse)
Stuart, Florida
Tom Fazio

Mariner Sands CC (Green Cse)
Stuart, Florida
Frank Duane, Arnold Palmer

Marion CC
Marion, Kansas
(R.) Mark Rathert

Marion CC
Marion, Ohio
(R.) Jack Kidwell, Michael Hurdzan

Marion GC
Marion, Massachusetts
George C. Thomas, Jr.

Marion Oaks CC
Marion Oaks, Florida
John Denton

Marion Oaks GC
Howell, Michigan
Harry Bowers (routing), *Frank Godwin*

Mariposa Pines GC
California
Bob Baldock, Robert L. Baldock

Maritim Timmendorfer Strand GC
Germany
Bernhard von Limburger

Maritzburg GC
Pietermaritzburg, South Africa
Robert Grimsdell

Mariya CC
Japan
Perry Dye

Market Harborough GC
Leicester, England
(A.9) Howard Swan

Markgraflerland GC
Germany
Karl F. Grohs, *Rainer Preissmann*

Markham G&CC
Buttonville, Ontario
René Muylaert, *Charles Muylaert*

Markischer GC
Kemnitz-Phoeben, Germany
Wolfgang Siegmann

Marks GC
Sweden
(R. A.9) Jan Sederholm

Marktl-Inn GC
Germany
Kurt Rossknecht

Mark Twain GC
Elmira, New York
Donald Ross

Marland Estate GC [NLE]
Ponca City, Oklahoma
Arthur Jackson

Marlboro CC
Upper Marlboro, Maryland
Algie Pulley

Marlborough CC
Marlboro, Massachusetts
Wayne Stiles, John Van Kleek
(A.9) Geoffrey S. Cornish, William G. Robinson

Marlborough GC [NLE]
Montreal, Quebec
Stanley Thompson
(R.) Howard Watson

Marlborough GC
Wiltshire, England
J. S. F. Morrison
(A.9) J. Hamilton Stutt

Marlton GC
Marlton, Maryland
Robert L. Elder

Marlwood GC
Bristol, England
Martin Hawtree, Simon Gidman

Marquette G&CC
Marquette, Michigan
William B. Langford, Theodore J. Moreau
(A.9) David Gill

Marquette Park GC
Chicago, Illinois
William B. Langford
(R.) Dick Nugent

Marrakesh CC
Palm Desert, California
Ted Robinson

Marrakesh CC
Marrakesh, Morocco
G. Golias

Marriott's Desert Springs GC (Palm Cse)
Palm Desert, California
Ted Robinson

Marriott's Desert Springs GC (Putting Cse)
Palm Desert, California
Ted Robinson

Marriott's Desert Springs GC (Valley Cse)
Palm Desert, California
Ted Robinson

Marriott's Griffin Gate GC
Lexington, Kentucky
Rees Jones

Marriott's Lincolnshire GC
Lincolnshire, Illinois
George Fazio, Tom Fazio
(R.2) Ken Killian, Dick Nugent

Marriott's Orlando World GC
Orlando, Florida
Joe Lee

Marriott's Rancho Las Palmas CC
Rancho Mirage, California
Ted Robinson

Marsden GC
Huddersfield, England
Alister Mackenzie

Marsden Park GC
Lancashire, England
C. K. Cotton
(A.9) Fred W. Hawtree

Marseille-Aix GC
Aix-en-Provence, France
Peter Gannon
(A.9) J. J. F. Pennink

Marshall GC [NLE]
Marshall, Michigan
Tom Bendelow

Marshall GC
Marshall, Minnesota
J. W. Whitney

Marshall Lakeside CC
Marshall, Texas
(A.9) *Lee Singletary*

Marshall Park GC
Moundsville, West Virginia
X. G. Hassenplug

Marsh Creek CC
St. Augustine, Florida
Mark McCumber

Marshfield CC
Marshfield, Massachusetts
Wayne Stiles
(R.) Brian Silva, Geoffrey S. Cornish

Marshfield CC
Marshfield, Missouri
(A.9) Larry Flatt

Marsh Harbour G Links
Calabash, North Carolina
Dan Maples

Mars Hill CC
Mars Hill, Maine
Alton McQuade

Marsh Landing GC
Ponte Vedra, Florida
Arnold Palmer, Ed Seay

Marsh Point G Links
Kiawah Island, South Carolina
Ron Kirby, Gary Player

Marston Green Muni [NLE]
Birmingham, England
F. G. Hawtree, J. H. Taylor

Marston Green GC
England
Carl Bretherston

Martin County G&CC
Stuart, Florida
(R.9 A.9) William B. Langford
(R.) Ernest E. Smith
(R.) Ron Garl

Martindale CC
Auburn, Maine
(A.9) Phil Wogan
(R.) Brian Silva, Geoffrey S. Cornish

Martindale CC
Buenos Aires, Argentina
Ken Dye

Martin Downs CC (Crane Creek Cse)
Stuart, Florida
Chuck Ankrom, Arthur Young

MARTIN DOWNS CC (TOWER CSE)
Stuart, Florida
Chuck Ankrom
MARTINGHAM G&TC
St. Michaels, Maryland
Pete Dye, Roy Dye
MARTIN MEMORIAL GC
Weston, Massachusetts
William F. Mitchell
(A.9) Samuel Mitchell
MARTINSVILLE CC
Martinsville, Indiana
William H. Diddel
MARUMASU NORTH HILL GC
Hokkaido, Japan
Masashi Ozaki
MARVIN RUPP GC
Stryker, Ohio
Robert Beard
MARY CALDER GC
Savannah, Georgia
George W. Cobb
MARYLAND BICYCLE C [NLE]
Maryland
David Ogilvie
MARYLAND G&CC
Belair, Maryland
Frank Murray, Russell Roberts
MARYSVILLE CC
Marysville, Kansas
Edward Lunz (9 1926)
MARYSVILLE GC
Corvallis, Oregon
Fred Federspeil
MARYSVILLE G CSE
Marysville, Michigan
Robert W. Bills, Donald L. Childs
MARYVALE GC
Phoenix, Arizona
William F. Bell
MARYWOOD CC
Battle Creek, Michigan
Maurice McCarthy
MASCOUTIN GC
Berlin, Wisconsin
Edward Lawrence Packard,
Roger Packard
MASHIKO CC
Japan
Tsuyoshi Arai
MASON CITY CC
Mason City, Iowa
Tom Bendelow
MASON HILLS GC
Mason, Michigan
Henry Chisholm
MASPALOMAS GC (NORTH CSE)
Canary Islands
Ron Kirby, Gary Player
MASPALOMAS GC (SOUTH CSE)
Canary Islands
P. M. Ross
MASSACRE CANYON INN & CC
[NLE]
Gilman Hot Springs, California
William H. Johnson
MASSANUTTEN VILLAGE GC
McGaheysville, Virginia
Frank Duane
(A.9) Richard Watson
MASSAREENE GC
Northern Ireland
(R.) Eddie Hackett
(A.9) Fred W. Hawtree

MASSAWIPPI GC
Quebec
(R.7) John Watson
MASSENA GC
Massena, New York
Albert Murray
MASTERS GC
Hyogo, Japan
Fukuichi Kato
MASUKE GC
Hokkaido, Japan
Adachi Kensetsu, Doto Sekkei
MATANZAS WOODS GC
Palm Coast, Florida
Arnold Palmer, Ed Seay
MATHER GC
Sacramento, California
Jack Fleming
MATLOCK GC
Derbyshire, England
Tom Williamson
MATSUNA CC
Aichi, Japan
Yahagi Ryokuka
MATTICKS FARM GC
Cordova Bay, British Columbia
William G. Robinson, John F.
Robinson
MATTOON G&CC
Mattoon, Illinois
(A.9) Edward Lawrence
Packard, Roger Packard
MAUH-NA-TEE-SEE CC
Rockford, Illinois
C. D. Wagstaff
(R.) Bob Lohmann
MAUI CC
Paia, Maui, Hawaii
Alex Bell, *William McKewan*
MAUI LU GC [NLE]
Maui, Hawaii
J. Gordon Gibson
MAUMEE BAY STATE PARK GC
Oregon, Ohio
Arthur Hills
MAUMELLE G&CC
Maumelle, Arkansas
Edmund B. Ault
(R.9) Gary Kern
MAUNA KEA BEACH HOTEL GC
Kamuela, Hawaii
Robert Trent Jones
(R.) Robert Trent Jones, Jr.
(R.) Robin Nelson, Rodney
Wright
MAUNA LANI GC
South Kohala, Hawaii
See Francis I'ie Brown GC
MAUNGAKIEKIE GC
Mount Roskill, New Zealand
C. H. Alison
(R.) C. H. Redhead
MAURITZBERG SLOTTS G RESORT
Norrkoeping, Sweden
Gene Bates
MAX STARKE PARK GC
Seguin, Texas
John Bredemus
(A.9) Ralph Plummer
(R.) *Shelly Mayfield*
MAXSTOKE PARK GC
Birmingham, England
F. G. Hawtree, Fred W. Hawtree

MAXWELL MUNI
Abilene, Texas
Dave Bennett
(R.) Garrett Gill, George B.
Williams
MAXWELTON GC
Syracuse, Indiana
William B. Langford
MAXWELTON BRAES GC
Bailey Harbor, Wisconsin
George O'Neil, Joseph A.
Roseman
MAYACOO LAKES CC
West Palm Beach, Florida
Desmond Muirhead, Jack
Nicklaus
(R.) Jack Nicklaus
MAYAPPLE G LINKS
Carlisle, Pennsylvania
Ron Garl
MAYFAIR CC (EAST CSE)
Uniontown, Ohio
Edmund B. Ault
MAYFAIR CC (WEST CSE)
Uniontown, Ohio
Edmund B. Ault
MAYFAIR G&CC [NLE]
Edmonton, Alberta
J. Munro Hunter
MAYFAIR G&CC
Edmonton, Alberta
Stanley Thompson
(R.) Les Furber, *Jim Eremko*
MAYFAIR LAKES GC
Richmond, British Columbia
Les Furber, *Jim Eremko*
MAYFIELD CC
South Euclid, Ohio
Bert Way, Herbert Barker
(R.) William Newcomb
MAYFIELD CC
Clarion, Pennsylvania
X. G. Hassenplug
MAYFIELD G&CC
Mayfield, Kentucky
Scott Nall
MAYFLOWER GC
Japan
Eichi Motohashi
MAYFLOWER GC [NLE]
New York, New York
Devereux Emmet, Alfred H. Tull
MAYLANDS GC
Essex, England
J. S. F. Morrison, H. S. Colt
MAYS LANDING GC
Atlantic City, New Jersey
Hal Purdy
MAYSVILLE CC
Maysville, Kentucky
William Newcomb
MAYVILLE CC
Mayville, Wisconsin
(A.9) Bob Lohmann
MAYWOOD CC [NLE]
Hillside, Illinois
Tom Bendelow
MOLLEAEN GC
Denmark
Jan Sederholm
MCALESTER CC [NLE]
McAlester, Oklahoma
Arthur Jackson

MCALESTER CC
McAlester, Oklahoma
Floyd Farley
(R.9) Bob Dunning
MCALLEN CC
McAllen, Texas
Jay Riviere
MCCALL LAKE GC
Calgary, Alberta
Bill Newis
MCCANN MEMORIAL GC
Poughkeepsie, New York
William F. Mitchell
MCCLEERY GC
Vancouver, British Columbia
A. Vernon Macan
MCCLOSKEY HOSPITAL GC
Fort Worth, Texas
NKA Temple Junior College GC
MCCONNELL AFB GC
Wichita, Kansas
Floyd Farley
MCCOOK CC
Salem, South Dakota
Emil Belzer
MCCORMICK RANCH GC (PALM
CSE)
Scottsdale, Arizona
Desmond Muirhead
(R.) Tom Fazio
MCCORMICK RANCH GC (PINE CSE)
Scottsdale, Arizona
Desmond Muirhead
(R.) Tom Fazio
MCCORMICK WOODS GC
Port Orchard, Washington
Jack Frei
MCFARLAND PARK GC
Florence, Alabama
Earl Stone
MCGREGOR GC
Saratoga Spa, New York
Devereux Emmet
MCGUIRE AFB GC
New York
Edmund B. Ault
MCGUIRE'S EVERGREEN GC
Cadillac, Michigan
Bruce Matthews
MCHENRY GC
McHenry, Illinois
Harry Hall King
(R.1) Ken Killian, Dick
Nugent
MCINNIS PARK G CSE
Marin, California
Fred Bliss
MCINTIRE PARK GC
Charlottesville, Virginia
Fred Findlay, *R. F. Loving, Sr.*
MCKELLAR GC
Memphis, Tennessee
Charles M. Graves
MCKENZIE RIVER GC
Lewisburg, Oregon
*Ken Omlid, Earl Omlid, Lloyd
Omlid*
MCKINNEY MUNI
McKinney, Texas
Ralph Plummer, Bob Dunning
MCLAREN PARK GC
Daly City, California
NKA Gleneagles International
GC

McMillen Park GC
Fort Wayne, Indiana
Hal Purdy

McMinnville CC
McMinnville, Tennessee
Edward Lawrence Packard

McNary GC
Salem, Oregon
Fred Federspiel, *Fred Sparks*
(R.) Robert Muir Graves

Meadia Heights GC
Lancaster, Pennsylvania
(R.) *Chester Ruby*
(R.) Ferdinand Garbin

Meadow Brook C
Jericho, New York
Dick Wilson

Meadowbrook C
Dayton, Ohio
Alex "Nipper" Campbell
(A.9) William H. Diddel

Meadowbrook CC
West Memphis, Arkansas
(R.) Joseph S. Finger

Meadowbrook CC
Hamden, Connecticut
(R.) William F. Mitchell

Meadowbrook CC
Northville, Michigan
Willie Park, Jr.
(R.6 A.12) Harry Collis, Jack Daray
(R.1) Bruce Matthews, Jerry Matthews
(R.) Arthur Hills
(R.2) Jerry Matthews

Meadow Brook CC [NLE]
St. Louis, Missouri
Robert Foulis

Meadowbrook CC
Ballwin, Missouri
Robert Bruce Harris
(R.) Gary Kern

Meadowbrook CC
Tulsa, Oklahoma
Press Maxwell
(A.9) *Charles Bland*
(R.) Don Sechrest

Meadowbrook CC
Richmond, Virginia
Fred Findlay, *R. F. Loving, Sr.*
(R.) Edmund B. Ault

Meadowbrook CC
Charlestown, West Virginia
Alex McKay

Meadowbrook CC
Racine, Wisconsin
(A.9) Todd Sloan
(R.) David Gill

Meadowbrook G&CC
Prairie Village, Kansas
(R.) Bob Dunning
(R.5) Don Sechrest

Meadowbrook G&CC
Gormley, Ontario
(R.) Thomas McBroom

Meadowbrook GC
Gainesville, Florida
Steve Smyers

Meadowbrook GC
Hartley, Iowa
Everett Dunn

Meadow Brook GC
Reading, Massachusetts
Alex Findlay
(R.9) Geoffrey S. Cornish

Meadowbrook GC
Hopkins, Minnesota
James Foulis
(A.9) Ken Killian, Dick Nugent

Meadowbrook GC
Omaha, Nebraska
Floyd Farley

Meadowbrook GC
Rutherfordton, North Carolina
William B. Lewis

Meadow Brook GC
Phoenixville, Pennsylvania
Leon Campbell

Meadowbrook GC
Rapid City, South Dakota
David Gill, Garrett Gill

Meadowbrook G Cse
Fort Worth, Texas
(R.9 A.9) John Bredemus
(R.) Ralph Plummer

Meadow Brook Hunt C [NLE]
Westbury, New York
Devereux Emmet
(R.) A. W. Tillinghast

Meadowbrook Muni (Cse No. 1)
Lubbock, Texas
Ralph Plummer
(R.) Warren Cantrell
(R.) Bob Lohmann

Meadowbrook Muni (Cse No. 2)
Lubbock, Texas
Ralph Plummer
(R.) Warren Cantrell
(R.) Bob Lohmann

Meadowbrook Muni
Salt Lake City, Utah
Mick Riley

Meadow C
Fairfax, California
Alister Mackenzie, Robert Hunter
(R.) Robert Muir Graves

Meadow Greens CC
Eden, North Carolina
Ellis Maples

Meadow Heights GC
Jackson, Michigan
Tom Bendelow

Meadow Hills GC
Nogales, Arizona
Red Lawrence

Meadow Hills GC
Denver, Colorado
Henry B. Hughes
(R.) Dick Phelps, Brad Benz

Meadowink GC
Murraysville, Pennsylvania
Ferdinand Garbin

Meadow Lake CC
San Diego, California
Tom Sanderson

Meadow Lake CC [NLE]
Overland Park, Kansas
William B. Langford

Meadow Lake CC
Columbia Falls, Montana
(R.9 A.9) Dick Phelps

Meadow Lake GC
Meadow Lake, Saskatchewan
(R.) Les Furber, *Jim Eremko*

Meadow Lake Acres CC
New Bloomfield, Missouri
Edmund B. Ault, Al Jamison

Meadowlands CC
Blue Bell, Pennsylvania
(R.) William Gordon, David Gordon

Meadowlands GC
Willoughby, Ohio
Sandy Alves

Meadow Lark CC
Great Falls, Montana
William H. Diddel

Meadowlark CC
Huntington Beach, California
William P. Bell

Meadow Links GC
Manitowoc, Wisconsin
Tom Bendelow

Meadowmont G&CC
Arnold, California
Dick Fry

Meadow Oaks G&CC
Hudson, Florida
Bill Amick

Meadowood GC
Cascade, Michigan
Mark DeVries

Meadowood GC
Spokane, Washington
Robert Muir Graves

Meadowood G&TC
Fort Pierce, Florida
Chuck Ankrom
(R.) Arnold Palmer, Ed Seay

Meadowood Resort GC
St. Helena, California
Jack Fleming

Meadows CC (Groves Cse)
Sarasota, Florida
Arthur Hills

Meadows CC (Highlands Cse)
Sarasota, Florida
Frank Duane
(A.9) *Patrick Mulligan, Rod Robinson*

Meadows CC (Meadows Cse)
Sarasota, Florida
Frank Duane
(A.9) *Patrick Mulligan, Rod Robinson*

[The] Meadows GC
Littleton, Colorado
Dick Phelps, Brad Benz, Mike Poellot

Meadow Springs GC
Richland, Washington
Jack Reimer
(R.9 A.9) Robert Muir Graves

Meadow Springs G Cse
Perth, Australia
Robert Trent Jones, Jr.

Meadow Valley GC
Caliente, Nevada
Richard Bigler

Meadowview GC
Kingsport, Tennessee
(R.) Rees Jones

Meaford GC
Meaford, Ontario
(R.2) Robert Heaslip

Meaux-Boutigny GC
France
Michel Gayon

Meceola CC
Big Rapids, Michigan
Jack Daray
(R.) Jeff Gorney

Mechaneer GC
Fort Carson, Colorado
Dick Phelps

Mechanicsville CC [NLE]
Mechanicsville, New York
Devereux Emmet

Medellin GC
Medellin, Colombia
Stanley Thompson
(R.) C. E. Robinson

Medford Lakes CC
Medford Lakes, New Jersey
Alex Findlay
(A.9) Hal Purdy

Medford Village GC
Medford, New Jersey
William Gordon, David Gordon

Medicine Hat G&CC
Medicine Hat, Alberta
Tom Bendelow
(R.16) Les Furber, *Jim Eremko*

Medicine Lodge Muni
Medicine Lodge, Kansas
(R.9) Chet Mendenhall

Medinah CC (Cse No. 1)
Medinah, Illinois
Tom Bendelow
(R.) Edward Lawrence Packard

Medinah CC (Cse No. 2)
Medinah, Illinois
Tom Bendelow

Medinah CC (Cse No. 3)
Medinah, Illinois
Tom Bendelow
(R.) Harry Collis
(A.2) Roger Packard
(R.) Bob Lohmann

Mediolanum GC
Italy
Marco Croze

Meeker GC
Meeker, Colorado
Henry B. Hughes

Megunticook GC
Rockport, Maine
Alex Findlay

Mehr Shahr GC [NLE]
Iran
Pier Mancinelli

Meihan Kokusai CC
Sapporo, Japan
Peter Thomson, Michael Wolveridge

Meisho GC
Japan
Hideo Takemura

Melbourne CC
Melbourne, Arkansas
Orrin Smith

Melbourne G&CC
Melbourne, Florida
Bill Amick

MELBOURNE GC [NLE]
  Melbourne, Florida
  Donald Ross
MELODY FARM CC [NLE]
  Lake Forest, Illinois
  George O'Neil, Jack Daray, *Jack Croke*
MELODY HILL GC
  Harmony, Rhode Island
  Samuel Mitchell
MELREESE GC
  Miami, Florida
  Dick Wilson, Joe Lee
    (R. A.4) Robert Trent Jones
MELROSE CC
  Cheltenham, Pennsylvania
  Perry Maxwell
    (R.) Clinton E. Robinson
MELROSE GC
  Daufuskie Island, South Carolina
  Jack Nicklaus
MELROSE GC
  Roxburghshire, Scotland
  Willie Park
MEL'S EXECUTIVE GC
  Arcata, California
  Mel Babica
MELTON MOWBRAY GC
  Leicestershire, England
  Tom Williamson
MEMORIAL MUNI [NLE]
  Springfield, Massachusetts
  Wayne Stiles, John Van Kleek
MEMORIAL PARK CC
  La Moure, North Dakota
  Joel Goldstrand
MEMORIAL PARK GC
  Houston, Texas
  John Bredemus
MEMPHIS CC [NLE]
  Memphis, Tennessee
  James Foulis
    (A.9) Tom Bendelow
MEMPHIS CC
  Memphis, Tennessee
  Donald Ross
    (R.) John LaFoy
MENAGGIO E. CADENABBIA GC
  Milan, Italy
  John Harris
    (R. A.5) J. J. F. Pennink
MENARD AOYAMA CC
  Japan
  Shigeru Uchida, Teruo Sugihara
MENARD GC
  Petersburg, Illinois
  Charles Maddox
MENDHAM G&TC
  Mendham, New Jersey
  Alfred H. Tull
MENDIP GC
  Avon, England
  Harry Vardon
    (A.9) C. K. Cotton, J. J. F. Pennink
MENDAKOTA CC
  Mendota Heights, Minnesota
    (R.3) Gerry Pirkl, *Donald G. Brauer, Emil Perret*
MENDOTA HEIGHTS PAR 3 GC
  Mendota Heights, Minnesota
  Paul Coates

MENIFEE LAKES G&CC
  Menifee, California
  Ted Robinson
MENLO CC
  Redwood City, California
  Tom Nicoll
    (R.) Herbert Fowler
    (R.) Robert Trent Jones
MENNEZALES GC
  Colombia
    (R.) C. E. Robinson
MEON VALLEY CC
  Hampshire, England
  J. Hamilton Stutt
MERCEDES GC
  Mercedes, Texas
  NKA Llano Grande GC
MERCED G&CC
  Slater, California
  Bob Baldock
    (R.) Robert Muir Graves
MERCER COUNTY ELKS CC
  Celina, Ohio
  Harold Paddock
MERCER ISLAND G&CC [NLE]
  Mercer Island, Washington
  Robert Johnstone
MERCER OAKS GC
  Trenton, New Jersey
  Bill Love, Brian Ault
MERE G&CC
  Surrey, England
  James Braid, John R. Stutt, George Duncan
MERIDIAN GC
  Englewood, Colorado
  Jack Nicklaus
MERIDIAN GC
  Oklahoma City, Oklahoma
  Floyd Farley
MERIDIAN HILLS CC
  Indianapolis, Indiana
  William H. Diddel
    (R.) George Fazio, Tom Fazio
MERIDIAN VALLEY CC
  Kent, California
  Ted Robinson
MERION GC (EAST CSE)
  Ardmore, Pennsylvania
  Hugh Wilson
    (R.) William S. Flynn, Howard Toomey
    (R.) Perry Maxwell
    (R.) Dick Wilson
MERION GC (WEST CSE)
  Ardmore, Pennsylvania
  Hugh Wilson
    (R.) Perry Maxwell
[THE] MERIT C
  Gurnee, Illinois
  Bob Lohmann
MERIWETHER NATIONAL GC
  Hillsboro, Oregon
  Fred Federspiel
MERRICK ROAD PARK GC
  Merrick, New York
  Frank Duane
MERRILL HILLS GC
  Waukesha, Wisconsin
    (R.) Edward Lawrence Packard
MERRIMACK GC
  Methuen, Massachusetts
  Skip Wogan

MERRITT G&CC
  Merritt, British Columbia
  Jack Reimer
MERRY HILL G&CC
  Ontario
  Clinton E. Robinson
MERU GC
  Meru, Kenya
  E. B. Horn
MESA CC
  Mesa, Arizona
  William F. Bell, William P. Bell
    (R.) Arthur Jack Snyder
MESA DEL SOL GC
  Yuma, Arizona
  Arnold Palmer, Ed Seay
MESA VERDE CC
  Costa Mesa, California
  William F. Bell
    (R.) David Rainville
    (R.) Ronald Fream
MESHINGOMESIA CC
  Marion, Indiana
  Clarence Lamboley
    (R.) William H. Diddel
MESQUITE CC
  Palm Springs, California
  Bert Stamps
MESQUITE MUNI
  Mesquite, Texas
  Leon Howard
    (R.) Garrett Gill, George B. Williams
MESSALONKEE GC
  Waterville, Maine
  Burton R. Anderson
METACOMET GC
  East Providence, Rhode Island
  Donald Ross
    (R.2) Geoffrey S. Cornish
METAIRIE CC
  Metairie, Louisiana
  Jack Daray
METAMORA G&CC
  Metamora, Michigan
  Robert W. Bills, Donald L. Childs (1991)
METEDECONK NATIONAL GC
  Jackson, New Jersey
  Robert Trent Jones
    (A.3rd 9) Robert Trent Jones
METFIELD GC
  Bella Vista, Arkansas
  Edmund B. Ault
METRO GC [NLE]
  Kansas City, Missouri
    (R.) Orrin Smith
    (R.) Floyd Farley
METROPOLIS GC
  Metropolis, Illinois
    (A.9) Kevin Tucker
METROPOLIS CC
  White Plains, New York
  Herbert Strong
    (R.) A. W. Tillinghast
    (R.2) Joseph S. Finger
METROPOLITAN GC
  Australia
  J.B. Mackenzie
    (R.11 A.8) Dick Wilson
    (R.) Peter Thomson, Michael Wolveridge

METROPOLITAN G&TC
  Decatur, Georgia
  Robert Trent Jones
METROWEST CC
  Orlando, Florida
  Robert Trent Jones
MEXICALI G&CC
  Mexicali, Mexico
  Lawrence Hughes
MEXICO CITY CC
  Mexico City, Mexico
  Willie Smith
    (R.) John Bredemus
MEYRICK PARK GC
  Hampshire, England
  Tom Dunn
    (R.) John R. Stutt
MIACOMET G LINKS
  Nantucket, Massachusetts
  Alex Findlay
MIAMI CC [NLE]
  Miami, Florida
  Donald Ross
MIAMI G&CC
  Miami, Oklahoma
  John Embry
    (A.9) Don Sechrest
MIAMI G LINKS [NLE]
  Miami, Florida
  Alex Findlay
MIAMI BEACH PAR 3 GC
  Miami Beach, Florida
  William S. Flynn
MIAMI BILTMORE GC (NORTH CSE)
  Coral Gables, Florida
  NKA Coral Gables Biltmore GC
MIAMI BILTMORE GC (SOUTH CSE)
  Coral Gables, Florida
  NKA Riviera CC
MIAMI LAKES INN & CC
  Miami Lakes, Florida
  NKA Don Shula's Hotel & C
MIAMI PARK GC
  Johore, Malaysia
  Robin Nelson, Rodney Wright
MIAMISBURG MUNI
  Miamisburg, Ohio
  Alex "Nipper" Campbell
MIAMI SHORES CC
  Miami, Florida
  Red Lawrence
MIAMI SHORES GC
  Troy, Ohio
  Donald Ross
    (R.9) Jack Kidwell, Michael Hurzdan
MIAMI SPRINGS GC
  Miami Springs, Florida
  Thomas "Tubby" Palmer
    (R.10) Bill Dietsch
MIAMI VALLEY CC
  Dayton, Ohio
  Donald Ross
    (R.) Jack Kidwell, Michael Hurzdan
MIAMI VIEW GC
  Miamitown, Ohio
  William H. Diddel
MICHAYWE HILLS GC (LAKE CSE)
  Gaylord, Michigan
  Jerry Matthews
MICHAYWE HILLS GC (PINE CSE)
  Gaylord, Michigan
  Robert W. Bills, Donald L. Childs

MICHELBOOK CC
McMillan, Oregon
Shirley Stone
(A.9) Robert Muir Graves
MICKE GROVE G LINKS
Lodi, California
Garrett Gill, George B. Williams
MICK RILEY GC
Murray, Utah
Mick Riley
MID CAROLINA GC
Prosperity, South Carolina
Russell Breeden
MID CITY GC [NLE]
Chicago, Illinois
William B. Langford, Theodore
J. Moreau
(R.) William B. Langford
MID-COUNTY GC
Arapahoe, Nebraska
Henry B. Hughes, Richard
Watson
MIDDLE BASS ISLAND GC
Sandusky, Ohio
Sandy Alves
MIDDLE BAY CC
Oceanside, New York
Alfred H. Tull
(R.) Hal Purdy
(R.) Stephen Kay
MIDDLEBURG GC
Middleburg, Pennsylvania
Edmund B. Ault
MIDDLE ISLAND CC
Middle Island, New York
Baier Lustgarten
MIDDLEMARCH GC
Middlemarch, New Zealand
C. H. Redhead
MIDDLEMORE GC
Australia
(R.) Peter Thomson, Michael
Wolveridge
MIDDLEMORE GC
New Zealand
(R.) C. H. Redhead
MIDDLESBOROUGH GC
England
James Braid, John R. Stutt
(R.) J. Hamilton Stutt
MIDDLESBOROUGH MUNI
Yorkshire, England
J. Hamilton Stutt
MIDDLETON GC
Salem, Massachusetts
Geoffrey S. Cornish, William G.
Robinson
MIDDLETON PARK GC
Yorkshire, England
T. R. Trigg
MID KENT GC
Gravesend, England
Willie Park, Jr.
MIDLAND CC [NLE]
Kewanee, Illinois
Tom Bendelow
MIDLAND CC
Kewanee, Illinois
William James Spear

MIDLAND CC
Midland, Michigan
(R.) Bruce Matthews, Jerry
Matthews
(R.) Edward Lawrence
Packard
(R.5) Jerry Matthews
MIDLAND CC
Midland, Texas
Ralph Plummer
(R.) Ron Kirby
(R.) Dick Nugent
MIDLAND FARMS CC
Pinehurst, North Carolina
Tom Jackson
MIDLAND G&CC
Midland, Ontario
Nicol Thompson
(A.9) J. Ross Parrott
MIDLAND HILLS CC
St. Paul, Minnesota
Seth Raynor
(R.) Paul Coates
MIDLAND HILLS CC
Carbondale, Illinois
William H. Diddel
MIDLANDS GC
Victoria, Australia
Peter Thomson, Michael
Wolveridge
MIDLAND TRAIL GC
Middletown, Kentucky
Edward Lawrence Packard
MIDLAND VALLEY CC
St. Louis, Missouri
Robert Foulis
(R.) William H. Diddel
MIDLAND VALLEY GC
Aiken, South Carolina
Ellis Maples
MIDLANE CC
Wadsworth, Illinois
Robert Bruce Harris
(R.) Bob Lohmann
MIDNIGHT SUN G CENTER
Paltamo, Finland
Ronald Fream
MIDLOTHIAN CC
Midlothian, Illinois
H. J. Tweedie
(R.) Ken Killian, Dick Nugent
MID OCEAN C
Tuckerstown, Bermuda
Charles Blair Macdonald, Seth
Raynor, Charles Banks, Ralph
Barton
(R.) Robert Trent Jones
(R.) John LaFoy
MIDO GC
Japan
Naoto Sugaya
MIDO GC (YOTEI CSE)
Hokkaido, Japan
Tadashi Sugaya
MIDONO CC
Gunma, Japan
Shunsuke Kato

MID-PACIFIC CC
Honolulu, Oahu, Hawaii
Seth Raynor, Charles Banks
(R.9 A.9) Willard Wilkinson
(R.) Bob Baldock, Robert L.
Baldock
(R.) Robin Nelson, Rodney
Wright
MID PINES CC
Southern Pines, North Carolina
Donald Ross
MID-RIVERS Y&CC
Stuart, Florida
Charles Prynne Martyn
MIDVALE G&CC
Penfield, New York
Robert Trent Jones, Stanley
Thompson
MIDWAY GC [NLE]
Groton, Massachusetts
Geoffrey S. Cornish
MIDWAY GC
Amherst, Ohio
Ted McAnlis
MIDWAY GC
Greybull, Wyoming
Henry B. Hughes, Richard
Watson
MIDWAY PAR 3 G CSE
Myrtle Beach, South Carolina
Edmund B. Ault
MIDWEST CC (EAST CSE)
Oak Brook, Illinois
(R.) Robert Bruce Harris
MIDWEST CC (WEST CSE)
Oak Brook, Illinois
(R.9 A.9) Robert Bruce Harris
MIDWEST CITY MUNI
Oklahoma City, Oklahoma
Floyd Farley
MIDWICK CC [NLE]
Monterey Park, California
Norman Macbeth
MIE HAKUSAN CC
Japan
Shoichi Suzuki
MIGHTY PEACE GC
Peace River, Alberta
(A.9) Bill Newis
MIHO CC
Ibaragi Perfecture, Japan
Robert Trent Jones, Jr.
MILAN G&CC
Milan, Tennessee
George C. Curtis
MILANO GC
Milan, Italy
Charles Blandford
(R.) John Harris
MILBURN G&CC
Overland Park, Kansas
William B. Langford
(R.) Orrin Smith
(R.) Floyd Farley
(R.) Bill Love
MILBY GC
Quebec
(R.9) John Watson
MILER CC
Summerville, South Carolina
Ed Riccoboni
MILE SQUARE GC
Fountain Valley, California
Harry Rainville, David Rainville

MILES CITY TOWN & CC
Miles City, Montana
(R.) Robert Muir Graves
MILES GRANT CC
Stuart, Florida
Mark Mahannah, Charles
Mahannah
(R.) Edmund B. Ault
MILFORD GC
Milford, Illinois
Edward Lawrence Packard
MILHAM MUNI
Kalamazoo, Michigan
David T. Millar
MILILANI GC
Mililani, Oahu, Hawaii
Bob Baldock
MILITARY GC
Wright-Patterson AFB, Ohio
Edward Lawrence Packard,
Brent Wadsworth
(R.9 A.9) Alex McKay
MILLBROOK C
Windsor, Connecticut
Geoffrey S. Cornish
MILLBROOK CC
Greenwich, Connecticut
(R.3) Frank Duane
(R.) Stephen Kay
MILLBURN GC
Short Hills, New Jersey
Hal Purdy
MILL COVE GC
Jacksonvile, Florida
Arnold Palmer, Ed Seay
MILL CREEK CC
Bothell, Washington
Ted Robinson
MILL CREEK CC
Burlington, West Virginia
James Spencer
MILL CREEK G&CC
Salado, Texas
(R.5 A.13) Robert Trent
Jones, Jr.
MILL CREEK GC
Rochester, Indiana
James R. Neidigh
MILLCREEK GC
Ostrander, Ohio
Dwight Black
MILL CREEK GC (NORTH CSE)
Youngstown, Ohio
Donald Ross
MILL CREEK GC (SOUTH CSE)
Youngstown, Ohio
Donald Ross
MILL CREEK GC
Nashville, Tennessee
Leon Howard
MILLCROFT G&CC
Burlington, Ontario
Thomas McBroom
MILLEDGEVILLE CC
Milledgeville, Georgia
George W. Cobb
MILL HILL GC
London, England
J. F. Abercromby
(R.) H. S. Colt
MILLINGTON NAVAL AIR STATION
GC
Millington, Tennessee
(R.) William H. Diddel

MILL QUARTER PLANTATION GC
Powhattan, Virginia
Edmund B. Ault
MILLRACE CC
Jonesville, Michigan
Arthur Hills
MILL RACE G&CC
Wellesley, Ontario
John F. Robinson
MILL RACE GC
Benton, Pennsylvania
Geoffrey S. Cornish, William G.
Robinson
MILL RIDE GC
Ascot, England
D. M. A. Steel
MILL RIVER CC
Oyster Bay, New York
Gerald C. Roby
   (R.4) Frank Duane
MILL RIVER CC
Stratford, Connecticut
Tom Winton
MILL RIVER GC
O'Leary, Prince Edward Island
Clinton E. Robinson
MILL ROAD FARM GC [NLE]
Lake Forest, Illinois
William S. Flynn, Howard
Toomey
MILLSAPS GC
Mississippi
Ken Bottorf
MILL STONE CC
Milford, Connecticut
   (R.) William F. Mitchell
MILLTOWN GC
Milltown, Ireland
   (R.) Eddie Hackett
MILNEGAVIE GC
Scotland
   (R.) *Willie Auchterlonie*
MILNE MEMORIAL PARK GC
Dysart, Iowa
*Donald G. Brauer, Donald K.
Rippel*
MILTON-FREEWATER GC
Milton-Freewater, Oregon
George McRae
MILTON-HOOSIC GC
Canton, Massachusetts
Willie Park, Jr.
MILWAUKEE CC [NLE]
Milwaukee, Wisconsin
James Foulis
   (A.9) Tom Bendelow
MILWAUKEE CC
Milwaukee, Wisconsin
C. H. Alison, H. S. Colt
   (R.) Robert Trent Jones
MIMOSA HILLS CC
Morganton, North Carolina
Donald Ross
MINAGAWAJO CC
Tochigi-ken, Japan
   (R.) Mike Poellot
MINAKAMI KOGEN GC (LOWER CSE)
Japan
Arnold Palmer, Ed Seay
MINAKAMI KOGEN GC (NEW CSE)
Japan
Arnold Palmer, Ed Seay

MINAKAMI KOGEN GC (UPPER CSE)
Japan
Arnold Palmer, Ed Seay
MINAKI LODGE GC
Minaki, Ontario
Stanley Thompson
MINAMI CC
Gifu, Japan
Billy Dunk
MINAMI GC
Kaneohe, Oahu, Hawaii
Dick Nugent
MINAMIKARUIZAWA GC
Nagano, Japan
Hatohiko Asaka
MINAMIMOBARA CC
Chiba, Japan
Haruo Yasuda
MINAMI NAGANO GC
Japan
*Toshiharu Kurakami, Shoichi
Asami*
MINCHINHAMPTON GC (NEW CSE)
Gloucestershire, England
Fred W. Hawtree
MINCHINHAMPTON GC (OLD CSE)
Gloucestershire, England
R. B. Wilson
MINERAL SPRINGS GC
Martinsville, Indiana
William H. Diddel
MINES RESORT GC
Sungei Besi, Kuala Lumpur, Ma-
laysia
Robert Trent Jones, Jr.
MINGO SPRINGS GC
Rangeley, Maine
Skip Wogan
   (R.) *Thomas Bates, Sy
Pillsbury*
MINIKAHDA C
Minneapolis, Minnesota
Robert Foulis, Willie Watson
   (R.9 A.9) *Robert Taylor, C. T.
Jaffray*
   (R.) Donald Ross
   (R.) Ralph Plummer
   (R.) Mike Hurdzan
MINNEAPOLIS GC
St. Louis Park, Minnesota
Tom Bendelow
   (R.) Gerry Pirkl, *Donald G.
Brauer, Emil Perret*
   (R.) Geoffrey S. Cornish,
Brian Silva
MINNECHAUG GC
Glastonbury, Connecticut
Graham Clark (routing); Geof-
frey S. Cornish
   (R.9) William F. Mitchell, Al
Zikorus
MINNEDOSA G&CC
Minnedosa, Manitoba
Jack Thompson
MINNEHAHA CC [NLE]
Sioux Falls, South Dakota
Tom Bendelow

MINNEHAHA CC
Sioux Falls, South Dakota
William B. Langford, Theodore
J. Moreau
   (R.) Edward Lawrence
Packard
   (R.6) Ken Killian, Dick
Nugent
   (R.) Dick Nugent
MINNESOTT CC
Arapahoe, North Carolina
Russell T. Burney (1969)
MINNESTRISTA GC
Muncie, Indiana
William H. Diddel
MINNETONKA CC
Excelsior, Minnesota
   (R.3) Don Herfort
MINNEWASTA G&CC
Morden, Manitoba
Les Furber, *Jim Eremko*
MINO CC
Mino, Japan
Pete Nakamura
MINOCQUA CC
Minocqua, Wisconsin
   (R.9 A.9) Edward Lawrence
Packard
MINOR PARK GC
Kansas City, Missouri
Larry W. Flatt
MINOT CC
Minot, North Dakota
Tom Vardon
MINT VALLEY MUNI
Longview, Washington
Ronald Fream
MIRABEL GC
Quebec
Gaston Alarie
MIRACLE HILL GC
Omaha, Nebraska
Floyd Farley
MIRAMAR GC
New Zealand
   (R.) Peter Thomson, Michael
Wolveridge
MIRAMAR MEMORIAL GC
San Diego, California
Kenneth Welton, Jack Daray, Jr.
   (R.) Peter Thomson, Michael
Wolveridge, Ronald Fream
MIRAMICHI G&CC
New Brunswick
   (A.9) Clinton E. Robinson
   (R.) John F. Robinson
MIRA VISTA CC
Fort Worth, Texas
Jay Morrish, Tom Weiskopf
MIRA VISTA G&CC
Berkeley, California
Willie Watson
   (R.) Robert Muir Graves
MIRROR LAKE GC
Idaho
Edward A. Hunnicutt
MIRROR LAKES CC
Lehigh Acres, Florida
Mark Mahannah
MISHIMA SPRINGS CC
Shizuoka, Japan
Mitsuo Yoshizaki

MISQUEMICUT GC
Westerly, Rhode Island
   (R.) Donald Ross
MISSING LINKS G LINKS
Mequon, Wisconsin
Gene Bates, *Charles Pasternak*
MISSION CC
Odessa, Texas
Ken Killian, Dick Nugent
MISSION CC
Mission, Texas
Ralph Plummer
MISSION GC
British Columbia
Norman H. Woods
MISSION BAY GC
San Diego, California
Ted Robinson
MISSION CREEK G&CC
Kelowna, British Columbia
*Dan Kitsul, Vic Welder, Ruth
Welder*
MISSION DEL LAGO MUNI
San Antonio, Texas
Denis Griffiths
MISSION HILLS CC
Fairway, Kansas
Tom Bendelow
   (R.) William H. Diddel
   (R.2) Floyd Farley
   (R.) Bob Dunning
   (R.7) Tom Clark
MISSION HILLS CC [NLE]
Northbrook, Illinois
   (R.) C. D. Wagstaff
MISSION HILLS CC
Northbrook, Illinois
Edward Lawrence Packard,
Roger Packard
MISSION HILLS G&CC (DINAH
SHORE CSE)
Rancho Mirage, California
Pete Dye
MISSION HILLS G&CC (NEW CSE)
Rancho Mirage, California
Arnold Palmer, Ed Seay
MISSION HILLS G&CC (OLD CSE)
Rancho Mirage, California
Desmond Muirhead
MISSION HILLS GC
Plymouth, Michigan
Al Watrous
   (A.9) Jerry Matthews
MISSION HILLS GC
Kanchanaburi Province,
Thailand
Jack Nicklaus
MISSION HILLS NORTH G CSE
Rancho Mirage, California
Gary Player
MISSION HILLS RESORT GC
Rancho Mirage, California
Pete Dye
MISSION INN & CC (EL CAMPEON
CSE)
Howey-in-the-Hills, Florida
Captain Charles Clarke
   (R. A.3) Tom Line
MISSION INN & CC (LAS COLINAS
CSE)
Howey-in-the-Hills, Florida
Gary Koch (1992)

MISSION LAKES CC
Desert Hot Springs, California
Ted Robinson
MISSION MOUNTAIN CC
Ronan, Montana
Gary Roger Baird
(A.9) Frank Hummel
MISSION TRAILS G CSE
San Diego, California
William P. Bell
(A.9) Robert Muir Graves
MISSION VALLEY G&CC
Laurel, Florida
David Wallace
MISSION VIEJO CC
Mission Viejo, California
Robert Trent Jones
(R.2) Jerry Martin
MISSISSAUGA G&CC
Port Credit, Ontario
George Cumming, *Percy Barrett*
(R.) Stanley Thompson
(R.3) Howard Watson
(R. A.3) William G.
Robinson, John F. Robinson
MISSISSENEWA CC
Peru, Indiana
Tom Bendelow
MISSISSIPPI GC
Carleton, Ontario
(A.9) Graham Cooke
MISSISSIPPI NATIONAL G LINKS
Red Wing, Minnesota
Gordon Cunningham (1987)
MISSISSIPPI STATE UNIVERSITY GC
Starkville, Mississippi
Marvin Ferguson (routing),
Brian Ault
MISSISSIPPI VALLEY STATE UNIVERSITY GC
Greenwood, Mississippi
Leon Howard
MISSOULA CC
Missoula, Montana
Frank James
(R.) Robert Muir Graves
(R.) John Steidel
MISTER GOLF G CSE
Gilbertsville, Kentucky
Hal Purdy
MISTLEY ESTATE GC
Manningtree, Essex, England
Howard Swan
MISTY CREEK CC
Sarasota, Florida
Ted McAnlis
MISUGI GC
Mie, Japan
Shunsuke Kato
MITCHELL CC
Mitchell, South Dakota
Richard Watson
MITCHELL CREEK CC
Traverse City, Michigan
Bruce Matthews, Jerry Matthews
MITCHELSTOWN GC
Mitchelstown, Ireland
(R.) Eddie Hackett
MITO GC
Mito, Japan
Takeo Aiyama
MITO INTERNATIONAL CC
Tokyo, Japan
Jack Nicklaus

MITO LAKES CC
Ibaraki, Japan
Pete Nakamura, *Shinichi Kodaira*
MITSUKAIDO GC
Japan
Kokichi Yasuda
MITTELRHEINSCHER GC
Bad Ems, West Germany
Tom Simpson
(R.) Karl Hoffmann
MIYAKOJIMA G CSE
Takamatsu Resort, Miyakojima, Japan
Mark Rathert
MOANALUA GC
Honolulu, Oahu, Hawaii
Donald MacIntyre
MOBERLY LAKE GC
Chetwynd, British Columbia
William G. Robinson, John F. Robinson
MOBRAY CC
Cape Province, South Africa
S. V. Hotchkin
MOCCASIN BEND GC
Chattanooga, Tennessee
(R.) Alex McKay
MOCCASIN CREEK GC
Aberdeen, South Dakota
Charles Maddox
MOCHIZUKI CC
Japan
Yoshitaro Kawanami
MOCHIZUKI TOKYU GC
Nagano, Japan
Chohei Miyazawa, Nagao Kurosawa
MODEL CITY COMMERCIAL CSE [NLE]
Montreal, Quebec
Stanley Thompson
MODENA G&CC
Modena, Italy
Jim Engh, *Bernhard Langer*
MODESTO MUNI
Modesto, California
Ian MacDonald
MODESTO CREEKSIDE G CSE
Modesto, California
Stephen Halsey, Jack Daray, Jr.
MOFFAT GC
Moffat, Scotland
Ben Sayers
MOFFET FIELD GC
Sunnyvale, California
Bob Baldock
(R.9 A.9) Robert Muir Graves
MOHANSIC PARK GC
Yorktown Heights, New York
Tom Winton
MOHAWK CC
Tiffon, Ohio
(R. A.3rd 9) William J. Rockefeller
MOHAWK GC
Schenectady, New York
Devereux Emmet
MOHAWK HILLS GC
Carmel, Indiana
Gary Kern

MOHAWK PARK MUNI (PECAN VALLEY CSE)
Tulsa, Oklahoma
Floyd Farley
MOHAWK PARK MUNI (WOODBINE CSE)
Tulsa, Oklahoma
William H. Diddel
(R.) Perry Maxwell
(R.) Floyd Farley
MOHICAN HILLS GC
Wooster, Ohio
Jack Kidwell
(A.9) Jack Kidwell, Michael Hurzdan
MOJALAKI CC
Franklin, New Hampshire
Wayne Stiles, John Van Kleek
MOJI GC
Fukuoka, Japan
O. Ueda
MOLINETTO CC
Milan, Italy
(R.) D. M. A. Steel
MÖLLE GC
Mölle, Sweden
Ture Bruce
MOLNDALS GC
Göteborg, Sweden
Ronald Fream
MOLOKAI HIGHLANDS GC
Molokai, Hawaii
Ken Killian
MOLYHILLS GC
Fraser Lake, British Columbia
Gerry Wreggit
MONAGH LEA GC
Portland, Oregon
Robert G. Duncan
MONA HILLS GC
Hockley Valley, Ontario
Gordon Witteveen
MONARCH CC
Palm City, Florida
Arnold Palmer, Ed Seay
MONASTERY GC
Orange City, Florida
Pete Craig
MONASTIR INTERNATIONAL GC
Monastir, Tunisia
Ronald Fream
MONCTON G&CC
Moncton, New Brunswick
Stanley Thompson
(A.9) Clinton E. Robinson
(R.) William G. Robinson, John F. Robinson
MONIFIETH GC
Monifieth, Scotland
(R.) Willie Park, Jr.
(R.) J. Hamilton Stutt
MONKSTOWN GC
Ireland
(R.) Eddie Hackett
MONMOUTH CC
Monmouth, Illinois
Tom Bendelow
MONMOUTHSHIRE GC
Wales
James Braid

MONONGAHELA VALLEY CC
Monongahela, Pennsylvania
Tom Bendelow
(R.9 A.9) Emil Loeffler, *John McGlynn*
MONOOSNOCK CC
Leominster, Massachusetts
(R.9) Wayne Stiles, John Van Kleek
MONROE CC
Monroe, North Carolina
Donald Ross
MONROE CC
Pittsford, New York
Donald Ross
(R.2) Geoffrey S. Cornish, William G. Robinson
(R.) Arthur Hills
(R.) Brian Silva, Geoffrey S. Cornish
MONROE COUNTY GC
Churchville, New York
Hal Purdy
MONROE CREEK GC
Pennsylvania
Edmund B. Ault
MONROE G&CC
Monroe, Georgia
Chic Adams
(A.9) Bill Amick
(R.) Don Cottle
MONROE G&CC
Monroe, Michigan
Donald Ross
(R.) Clinton E. Robinson
MONSANTO EMPLOYEES GC
Pensacola, Florida
Bill Amick
MONT ADSTOCK GC
Thetford Mines, Quebec
Howard Watson, John Watson
(R.9) John Watson
MONT D'ARBOIS GC
Megève, France
Henry Cotton
MONT STE. ANNE GC (CSE NO. 1)
Ste. Anne de Beaupré, Quebec
Howard Watson, John Watson
MONT STE. ANNE GC (CSE NO. 2)
Ste. Anne de Beaupré, Quebec
Howard Watson, John Watson
(A.9) John Watson
MONT STE. MARIE GC
Ste. Marie de Bauce, Quebec
Howard Watson
(R.2) Howard Watson, John Watson
(A.9) John Watson
MONT TREMBLANT GC
Quebec
(R.9) Howard Watson
MONT VERNON GC [NLE]
New Hampshire
Alex Findlay
MONTAGUE GC
Randolph, Vermont
(A.3) Geoffrey S. Cornish, William G. Robinson
MONTAMMY CC
Alpine, New Jersey
Frank Duane
(R.4) Joseph S. Finger

MONTAUK DOWNS GC [NLE]
Montauk, New York
H. C. C. Tippetts
   (R.) *Carl H. Anderson*
MONTAUK DOWNS G&RC
Montauk Point, New York
Robert Trent Jones
MONTAZAN TABARKA G RESORT
Tabarka, Tunisia
Ronald Fream
MONTCLAIR CC
Chattanooga, Tennessee
Joe Lee
   (R.9 A.9) Arthur Davis
MONTCLAIR CC
Dumfries, Virginia
Algie Pulley
MONTCLAIR GC [NLE]
Montclair, New Jersey
Tom Bendelow
   (A.9) *Tom Anderson*
MONTCLAIR GC
Montclair, New Jersey
Donald Ross
   (A.4th 9) Charles Banks
   (R.) Robert Trent Jones
   (R.) Robert Trent Jones
   (R.) Rees Jones
MONTEBELLO GC
Montebello, California
Max Behr
   (R.5) William F. Bell
MONTE CARLO CC
Fort Pierce, Florida
NKA Meadowood G&TC
MONTE CARLO CC
Monaco
Willie Park, Jr.
   (R.) F. G. Hawtree
   (R. A.2) Fred W. Hawtree
MONTECITO CC
Santa Barbara, California
Max Behr
MONTE CRISTO CC
Edinburg, Texas
Don Sechrest
MONTE GORDO GC
Portugal
Henry Cotton
MONTE MAYOR GC
Málaga, Marbella, Spain
Pepe Gancedo
MONTEREY CC
Palm Desert, California
Ted Robinson
MONTEREY HILLS GC
California
William F. Bell, William P. Bell
MONTEREY PENINSULA CC (DUNES CSE)
Pebble Beach, California
Seth Raynor, Charles Banks
   (R.) Alister Mackenzie,
   Robert Hunter
MONTEREY PENINSULA CC (SHORE CSE)
Pebble Beach, California
Bob Baldock, Jack Neville
   (R.) Robert Bruce Harris
MONTEREY YACHT & CC
Stuart, Florida
Leon Howard

MONTERRA G CSE
Collingwood, Ontario
Thomas McBroom
MONTERREY CC
Monterrey, Mexico
John Bredemus
MONTE S. PIETRO GC
Bolzano, Italy
Marco Croze
MONTE VEHLO GC
Algarve, Portugal
Howard Swan
MONTGOMERY BELL STATE G CSE
Burns, Tennessee
   (R.) Gary Roger Baird
MONTGOMERY CC
Montgomery, Alabama
John M. "Jock" Inglis
   (R.) John LaFoy
MONTGOMERY CC
Laytonsville, Maryland
Robert L. Elder
MONTGOMERY CC
Troy, North Carolina
Russell Breeden
MONTGOMERY GC
Montgomery, Minnesota
Joel Goldstrand
MONTGOMERY VILLAGE CC
Gaithersburg, Maryland
Edmund B. Ault
MONTGRIFFON GC (COULONGES CSE)
Luzarches, France
Robin Nelson, Rodney Wright
MONTGRIFFON GC (LUZARCHES CSE)
Luzarches, France
Robin Nelson, Rodney Wright
MONTICCHIA GC
Italy
T. J. A. Macauley
MONTICELLO CC
Monticello, Indiana
Pete Dye
MONTICELLO CC
Monticello, Kentucky
Robert Thomason
MONTICELLO CC
Monticello, Minnesota
   (A.9) Joel Goldstrand
MONTOUR HEIGHTS CC [NLE]
Pittsburgh, Pennsylvania
Emil Loeffler, *John McGlynn*
   (A.9) James Gilmore
   Harrison, Ferdinand Garbin
MONTOUR HEIGHTS CC
Corapolis, Pennsylvania
P. B. Dye, Pete Dye
MONTPELIER CC
Montpelier, Vermont
   (R.) *Les Heon*
MONTREAL MUNI (YELLOW CSE)
Montreal, Quebec
Albert Murray
MONTREUX GC
France
Harry Vardon
   (R.) Donald Harradine
MONTROSE GC
Montrose, Colorado
Henry B. Hughes

MONTROSE GC (BLOOMFIELD CSE)
Montrose, Scotland
   (R.) Willie Park, Jr.
MONTROSE GC (MEDAL CSE)
Montrose, Scotland
   (R.) Willie Park, Jr.
MOODY AFB GC
Valdosta, Georgia
Joseph S. Finger
MOONBROOK CC
Jamestown, New York
Willie Park, Jr.
   (A.9) William Harries
   (R.) William Gordon, David
   Gordon
   (R.) Robert Trent Jones
MOON LAKE GC
Hoffman Estates, Illinois
Ken Killian, Dick Nugent
MOON LAKE GC
Saskatoon, Saskatchewan
Les Furber, *Jim Eremko*
MOON VALLEY CC
Phoenix, Arizona
Dick Wilson
MOOR ALLERTON GC [NLE]
Yorkshire, England
Alister Mackenzie
MOOR ALLERTON GC
Yorkshire, England
Robert Trent Jones
MOORE ESTATE GC
Roslyn, New York
Charles Blair Macdonald, Seth
Raynor
MOORE PLACE GC
Oxney, England
Harry Vardon
MOORESTOWN FIELD C
Moorestown, New Jersey
Alex Findlay
MOORESVILLE GC
Mooresville, North Carolina
J. Porter Gibson
MOORHEAD CC
Moorhead, Minnesota
   (R.) Joel Goldstrand
MOORHEAD VILLAGE GREEN G CSE
Moorhead, Minnesota
Gerry Pirkl, *Donald G. Brauer*
MOORINGS GC
Vero Beach, Florida
Pete Dye
MOORINGS OF MANATEE GC
Rustin, Florida
Ward Northrup
MOOR PARK GC (HIGH CSE)
Hertfordshire, England
H. S. Colt
MOOR PARK GC (WEST CSE)
Hertfordshire, England
H. S. Colt, C. H. Allison
[THE] MOORS GC
Pensacola, Florida
John LaFoy
[THE] MOORS OF PORTAGE GC
Portage, Michigan
Arthur Hills
MOORS VALLEY GC
Wimborne, England
Martin Hawtree, Simon Gidman

MOORTOWN GC
Yorkshire, England
Alister Mackenzie
   (R.) J. S. F. Morrison
MOOSBURG GC
Poirtschach-Moosburg, Austria
Gerold Hauser, *Günther Hauser*
MOOSE CC
Sidney, Ohio
Hal Purdy
MORA GC
Mora, Sweden
Sune Linde
MORAGA CC
Moraga, California
Robert Muir Graves
   (A.9) Algie Pulley
MORAINE CC
Kettering, Ohio
Alex "Nipper" Campbell
   (R.) Dick Wilson
MORAVIAN HILLS CC
Mount Clemens, Michigan
   (R.1) Jerry Matthews
MORAY GC (NEW CSE)
Morayshire, Scotland
Henry Cotton
MORAY GC (OLD CSE)
Morayshire, Scotland
Old Tom Morris
MOREHEAD CITY CC
Morehead City, North Carolina
C. C. McCuiston, Philip Ball
   (1952)
MORENO VALLEY RANCH GC
Moreno Valley, California
Pete Dye
MORGAN RIVER GC
Dataw Island, South Carolina
Arthur Hills
MORNINGSIDE HOTEL GC
Hurleyville, New York
Alfred H. Tull
MORNINGSTAR GC
Parksville, British Columbia
Les Furber, *Jim Eremko*
MORPETH GC
Morpeth, England
   (R.) J. Hamilton Stutt
MORRIS CC [NLE]
Morris, Illinois
William B. Langford, Theodore
J. Moreau
MORRIS CC
Morris, Illinois
John Darrah
MORRIS COUNTY GC
Morristown, New Jersey
Tom Bendelow
   (R.) H. J. Whigham
   (R.6 A.12) Seth Raynor
   (R.) Hal Purdy
   (R.) Rees Jones
MORRIS PARK CC
South Bend, Indiana
Robert E. Dustin
MORRIS WELLS GC
Glenville, West Virginia
Gary Grandstaff
MORRIS WILLIAMS MUNI
Austin, Texas
Leon Howard

MORRO BAY GC
Morro Bay, California
(R.) Robert Muir Graves

MORRO DO CHAPÉU GC
Morro do Chapéu, Brazil
Yukichi Suguihara

MORSUM-SYLT GC
Sylt, Germany
Bernhard von Limburger

MORTIMER SINGER ESTATE GC
England
Herbert Fowler

MORTONHALL GC
Edinburgh, Scotland
(R.) J. H. Taylor
(R.5 A.9) Fred W. Hawtree,
Martin Hawtree

MOSELEM SPRINGS CC
Fleetwood, Pennsylvania
George Fazio

MOSELEY GC
England
(R.) H. S. Colt

MOSES LAKE GC
Moses Lake, Washington
Mel "Curley" Hueston

MOSHOLU GC
Bronx, New York
(R.) Stephen Kay

**MOSS CREEK PLANTATION GC
(NORTH CSE)**
Hilton Head Island, South
Carolina
Tom Fazio

**MOSS CREEK PLANTATION GC
(SOUTH CSE)**
Hilton Head Island, South
Carolina
George Fazio, Tom Fazio

MOSSEL BAY GC
South Africa
Archie Tosh
(R.) Robert Grimsdell

MOSSWOOD MEADOWS GC
Monroe City, Missouri
David Gill, Garrett Gill

MOTALA GC
Motala, Sweden
(A.9) Jan Sederholm

MOTZENER SEE GC
Germany
Kurt Rossknecht

MOUNDBUILDERS CC
Newark, Ohio
Tom Bendelow

MOUNT AIRY LODGE & CC
Mt. Pocono, Pennsylvania
Hal Purdy, Malcolm Purdy,
Chandler Purdy

MOUNT BRENTON GC
Chemainus, British Columbia
(A.9) William G. Robinson

MOUNT BRUNO GC
Montreal, Quebec
Willie Park, Jr.

**MOUNT CARLETON PROVINCIAL PARK
GC**
Mount Carleton, New
Brunswick
John F. Robinson

MOUNT CHARRON GC
Huntsville, Alabama
Luther O. "Luke" Morris

MOUNT COBB MUNI
Scranton, Pennsylvania
James Gilmore Harrison,
Ferdinand Garbin

MOUNT CROTCHED CC
Francestown, New Hampshire
NKA Tory Pines G Resort

MOUNT DIABLO CC
Diablo, California
Willie Watson

MOUNT DORA GC [NLE]
Mount Dora, Florida
(R.9 A.9) Harold Paddock

MOUNT HAWLEY CC
Peoria, Illinois
(R.) Edward Lawrence
Packard, Roger Packard

MOUNT HOPE G&CC
Ontario
Clinton E. Robinson

MOUNT JULIET G&CC
Kilkenny, Ireland
Jack Nicklaus

MOUNT KINABALU GC
Kundasang, Malaysia
Robert Muir Graves

MOUNT KINEO GC
Kineo, Maine
Art Townley
(R.) Orrin Smith

MOUNT KISCO CC
Mount Kisco, New York
Tom Winton
(R.) A. W. Tillinghast

MOUNT LEBANON CC
Pittsburgh, Pennsylvania
James Gilmore Harrison

MOUNT LOMOND G&CC
Ogden, Utah
Mick Riley

MOUNT MANOR INN & GC
Marshall's Creek, Pennsylvania
Russell Scott, Jr.

MOUNT MITCHELL GC
Burnsville, North Carolina
Fred W. Hawtree

MOUNT ODIN PARK GC
Greensburg, Pennsylvania
(R.9 A.9) X. G. Hassenplug

MOUNT OGDEN GC
Ogden, Utah
(R.1) William Howard Neff

MOUNT PLEASANT CC
Boylston, Massachusetts
William F. Mitchell

MOUNT PLEASANT CC
Lowell, Massachusetts
(R.3) John Watson

MOUNT PLEASANT CC
Mount Pleasant, Michigan
Mark DeVries
(A.9) Bruce Matthews, Jerry
Matthews

MOUNT PLEASANT MUNI
Baltimore, Maryland
Gus Hook

MOUNT RANCHES GC
Rigaud, Quebec
Howard Watson

MOUNT ST. HELENA GC
Calistoga, California
Jack Fleming

MOUNT SNOW GC
Mount Snow, Vermont
Geoffrey S. Cornish, William G.
Robinson

MOUNT VERNON CC
Mount Vernon, Ohio
Tom Bendelow
(R.) Jack Kidwell, Michael
Hurdzan

MOUNT WASHINGTON GC
Bretton Woods, New Hampshire
A. H. Fenn
(R.9 A.9) Alex Findlay
(R. A.3rd 9) Donald Ross
(A.3rd 9) Brian Silva,
Geoffrey S. Cornish

MOUNT WOODSON GC
Ramona, California
Lee Schmidt, Brian Curley

MOUNT WHITNEY CC
Lone Pine, California
Bob Baldock

MOUNTAIN ACRES GC
Laurentians, Quebec
(R.3) John Watson

MOUNTAIN AIR CC
Burnsville, North Carolina
Scott Pool (1991)

MOUNTAIN BROOK C
Birmingham, Alabama
Donald Ross
(R.) George W. Cobb
(R.) John LaFoy

MOUNTAINBROOK GC
North Carolina
P. Almond

MOUNTAIN CREEK C
Gastonia, North Carolina
Ellis Maples

MOUNTAINDALE CC [NLE]
California
Robert Johnstone

MOUNTAIN DELL GC (CSE NO. 1)
Salt Lake City, Utah
William F. Bell

MOUNTAIN DELL GC (CSE NO. 2)
Salt Lake City, Utah
William Howard Neff

MOUNTAINGATE CC
Los Angeles, California
Ted Robinson
(A.3rd 9) Ted Robinson
(R.) Garrett Gill, George B.
Williams

MOUNTAIN GLEN GC
Newland, North Carolina
George W. Cobb

MOUNTAIN HARBOUR Y&CC
Hayesville, North Carolina
Willard Byrd

MOUNTAIN LAKE C
Lake Wales, Florida
Seth Raynor
(R.) William H. Diddel

MOUNTAIN LAKE GC
Mountain Lake, Minnesota
Joel Goldstrand

MOUNTAIN LAUREL GC
White Haven, Pennsylvania
Geoffrey S. Cornish, William G.
Robinson

**MOUNTAIN MEADOWS G&CC
[NLE]**
Los Angeles, California
William P. Bell

MOUNTAIN MEADOWS GC
Pomona, California
Ted Robinson

MOUNTAIN MEADOWS GC
Elkford, British Columbia
Reg Stone, Roy Stone

MOUNTAIN RANCH GC
Fairfield Bay, Arkansas
Brian Ault, Tom Clark, Edmund
B. Ault

MOUNTAIN RIDGE CC [NLE]
New Jersey
David S. Hunter
(R.) Herbert Strong

MOUNTAIN RIDGE CC
West Caldwell, New Jersey
Donald Ross

MOUNTAIN SHADOWS CC
Scottsdale, Arizona
Arthur Jack Snyder

**MOUNTAIN SHADOWS GC (NORTH
CSE)**
Rohnert Park, California
Gary Roger Baird
(R.) Garrett Gill, George B.
Williams

**MOUNTAIN SHADOWS GC (SOUTH
CSE)**
Rohnert Park, California
Bob Baldock
(R.) Garrett Gill, George B.
Williams

MOUNTAIN SPRINGS G&CC
Sonora, California
Robert Muir Graves

MOUNTAIN SPRINGS G&CC
Linville, North Carolina
Ellis Maples, Dan Maples

MOUNTAIN VALLEY GC
Waynesville, North Carolina
George W. Cobb

MOUNTAIN VIEW CC
Thousand Palms, California
NKA Ivey Ranch CC

MOUNTAIN VIEW CC
Alamogordo, New Mexico
C. William Keith

MOUNTAIN VIEW GC
Boring, Oregon
Jack Beaudoin, Jack Waltmire

MOUNTAIN VIEW GC
Fairfield, Pennsylvania
Edmund B. Ault, Brian Ault,
Tom Clark

MOUNTAIN VIEW GC
Jordan, Utah
William H. Neff

MOUNTAIN VIEW GC
Sequim, Washington
Ray Coleman

MOUNTAIN VIEW HOUSE GC
Whitefield, New Hampshire
Ralph Barton
(R.) Wayne Stiles, John Van
Kleek

MOUNTRATH GC
Mountrath, Ireland
(R.) Eddie Hackett

MOWBRAY CC
South Africa
(R.) S. V. Hotchkin
(R.) *Ken Elkin*

MOWSBURY MUNI
Bedfordshire, England
Fred W. Hawtree, Martin Hawtree

MOYOLA PARK GC
County Derry, Northern Ireland
Don Patterson

MUIRFIELD GC
East Lothian, Scotland
Old Tom Morris
(R.) H. S. Colt, C. H. Alison
(R.) Tom Simpson

MUIRFIELD G LINKS [NLE]
New York
John Duncan Dunn

MUIRFIELD VILLAGE GC
Dublin, Ohio
Jack Nicklaus, Desmond Muirhead

MULBERRY HILL GC
East Hungtington, Pennsylvania
Ferdinand Garbin

MÜLHEIM GC
Mülheim, Germany
Karl F. Grohs, *Rainer Preissmann*

MULLET BAY GC
St. Marten
Joe Lee

MULLETT LAKE G&CC
Mullett Lake, Michigan
Tom Bendelow

MULLINGAR GC
County Westmeath, Ireland
James Braid, John R. Stutt
(R.) Eddie Hackett

MULLION GC
Mullion, England
(R.) Tom Williamson
(R.) J. Hamilton Stutt

MULRANY GC
Ireland
(R.) Eddie Hackett

MULTNOMAH GC [NLE]
Beavertown, Oregon
William Lock

MÜNCHENER GC
Munich, Germany
Bernhard von Limburger

MUNCIE ELKS GC
Muncie, Indiana
William Barnes

MÜNSTER-WILKINGHEGE GC
Münster, Germany
(A.9) Wolfgang Siegmann

MURASAKINO CC
Gifu, Japan
Seibu Kensetsu

MURASAKIZUKA GC
Japan
Pete Nakamura

MURCAR GC
Aberdeen, Scotland
Archie Simpson
(R.) James Braid, John R. Stutt

MURHOF GC
Frohnleiten, Austria
Bernhard von Limburger
(A.9) J. F. Dudok van Heel

MURIWAI GC
Muriwai, New Zealand
H. G. Babbage

MURORAN GC
Hokkaido, Japan
E. Hagiwara

MURRAYFIELD GC
Edinburgh, Scotland
Willie Park, Willie Park, Jr.

MURRAY MUNI
Regina, Saskatchewan
Claude Muret

MURRAY PARKWAY GC
Murray, Utah
Robert Muir Graves

MURRAYSHALL G&CC
Perthshire, Scotland
J. Hamilton Stutt

MURRIETA GC
Murrieta, California
NKA Rancho California CC

MÜRSTATTEN GC
Graz, Austria
J. F. Dudok van Heel

MUSASHI CC (SASAI CSE)
Saitama, Japan
Seichi Inouye

MUSASHI CC (TOYOOKA CSE)
Saitama, Japan
Seichi Inouye

MUSASHI FUJI CC
Saitama, Japan
K. Yasuda, S. Kawamura

MUSASHI KYURYO CC
Saitama, Japan
Eiichi Motohashi

MUSASHINO CC
Japan
Ichisuke Izumi

MUSGROVE MILL GC
Clinton, South Carolina
Arnold Palmer and Ed Seay
(routing), *Ken Tomlinson*

MUSKEGO LAKES CC
Hales Corner, Wisconsin
(R.) Edward Lawrence Packard, Roger Packard

MUSKEGON CC
Muskegon, Michigan
Donald Ross
(R.3) Bruce Matthews, Jerry Matthews
(R.2) Jerry Matthews

MUSKERRY GC
County Cork, Ireland
(R.) Alister Mackenzie
(R.) Eddie Hackett

MUSKOGEE CC [NLE]
Muskogee, Oklahoma
Leslie Brownlee

MUSKOGEE CC
Muskogee, Oklahoma
Perry Maxwell
(R.) Don Sechrest

MUSKOKA BEACH GC
Gravenhurst, Ontario
Stanley Thompson

MUSKOKA LAKES G&CC
Port Carling, Ontario
Stanley Thompson
(R.) Tom McBroom

MUSQUEAM GC
Vancouver, British Columbia
Jack Ellis

MUSSELBURGH GC
Mussleburgh, Scotland
James Braid, John R. Stutt

MUSWELL HILL GC
London, England
Willie Park, Sr.

MUTHAIGA GC
Nairobi, Kenya
T. J. Anderson, Peter Whitelaw

MUTTONTOWN G&CC
East Norwich, New York
Alfred H. Tull
(R.1) Frank Duane
(R.) Robert Trent Jones
(R.) Joseph S. Finger

MYAKKA PINES GC
Englewood, Florida
Lane Marshall

MYERLEE CC
Fort Myers, Florida
Arthur Hills

MYERS PARK CC
Charlotte, North Carolina
A. W. Tillinghast
(R.) Donald Ross
(R.) Ellis Maples
(R.) Rees Jones

MYLORA GC
Richmond, British Columbia
Jack Reimer

MYOKO PINE VALLEY CC
Niigata, Japan
Seibu Kensetsu

MYOKO SUNSHINE GC
Niigata, Japan
Sumitomo Kensetsu

MYOPIA HUNT C
Hamilton, Massachusetts
Herbert Leeds
(R.) Geoffrey S. Cornish
(R.1) Phil Wogan
(R.) Geoffrey S. Cornish, Brian Silva

MYOSOTIS CC [NLE]
Eatontown, New Jersey
A. W. Tillinghast

MYRICK HILLS CC
Littleton, North Carolina
C. Scott, B. May

MYRTLE BEACH NATIONAL GC (NORTH CSE)
Myrtle Beach, South Carolina
Frank Duane, Arnold Palmer

MYRTLE BEACH NATIONAL GC (SOUTH CSE)
Myrtle Beach, South Carolina
Frank Duane, Arnold Palmer
(R.) Michael Hurdzan

MYRTLE BEACH NATIONAL GC (WEST CSE)
Myrtle Beach, South Carolina
Frank Duane, Arnold Palmer

MYRTLE POINT GC
Powell River, British Columbia
Les Furber, *Jim Eremko*

MYRTLE WEST GC
North Myrtle Beach, South Carolina
Tom Jackson

MYRTLEWOOD GC (PALMETTO CSE)
Myrtle Beach, South Carolina
Edmund B. Ault

MYRTLEWOOD GC (PINES CSE)
Myrtle Beach, South Carolina
George W. Cobb

MYSTERY VALLEY CC
Lithonia, Georgia
Dick Wilson, Joe Lee

NACHI KATSUURA GC
Wakayama, Japan
Shunsuke Kato

NADI GC
Fiji
(A.9) John Harris

NAGANO CC
Nagano, Japan
Hirochika Tomizawa

NAGA-WAUKEE PARK GC
Pewaukee, Wisconsin
Edward Lawrence Packard

NAGOYA GC
Aichi, Japan
M. Otani

NAGOYA HIROHATA GC
Japan
Junji Shiba

NAGS HEAD G LINKS
Nags Head, North Carolina
Jerry Turner, Bob Moore, Vance Heafner

NAHA CC
Okinawa
(R.) Robin Nelson, Rodney Wright

NAHABINO GC
Moscow, Russian Federation
Robert Trent Jones, Jr.

NAIE GC
Sapporo, Japan
Peter Thomson, Michael Wolveridge

NAIRN GC
Nairnshire, Scotland
Archie Simpson
(R.) Old Tom Morris
(R.) James Braid, John R. Stutt

NAIRN DUNBAR GC
Scotland
(A.9) Fraser Middleton

NAIVASHA SPORTING C
Naivasha, Kenya
(R.) *T.J. Anderson, S.J.O. Armstrong, A. K. Gibson*

NAKAGAWA GC
Tochigi, Japan
Taisei Kensetsu

NAKAIZU GREENS C
Shizuoka, Japan
Shoichi Asami

NAKAJO GC
Niigata, Japan
Kikuo Arai

NAKATSUGAWA CC
Nakatsugawa, Japan
Charles Mahannah, *Lee Trevino*

NAKOMA CC
Madison, Wisconsin
Tom Bendelow
(R.) Dick Nugent, Ken Killian

NAKURA CC
Aichi, Japan
Pete Nakajima

NAMBU FUJI GC
Kwate, Japan
John Harris, Peter Thomson
NAMPA MUNI
Nampa, Idaho
Bob Baldock, Robert L. Baldock
NAMPONT ST. MARTIN GC
Nampont St. Martin, France
(A.9) Robert Berthet
NANAIMO G&CC
Nanaimo, British Columbia
A. Vernon Macan
NANFONG GC
Taiwan
Charles Mahannah, *Lee Trevino*
NANTICOKE GC
Milton, Ontario
NKA Oakville Executive GC
NANTON GC
Nanton, Alberta
Les Furber, *Jim Eremko*
NANTUCKET GC [NLE]
Nantucket, Massachusetts
Donald Ross
NAPA MUNI
Napa, California
Bob Baldock, Jack Fleming, Ben
Harmon
NAPA VALLEY CC
Napa, California
(R.) Robert Muir Graves
(R.9 A.9) Ronald Fream
NAPERBROOK GC
Naperville, Illinois
Roger Packard
NAPERVILLE CC
Naperville, Illinois
Tom Bendelow
(R.5) David Gill
(R.) Edward Lawrence
Packard, Roger Packard
NAPIER GC
Napier, New Zealand
(R.) C. H. Redhead
NAPIERVILLE GC
Napierville, Quebec
(R.4 A.4) John Watson
NAPLES BEACH HOTEL GC
Naples, Florida
(R.) Mark Mahannah
(R.) Ron Garl
NAPLES SHORES CC
Naples, Florida
Chuck Ankrom
NAPOLEON MUNI
Napoleon, Ohio
William J. Rockefeller
NAPOLI G&CC
Naples, Italy
Jack Nicklaus
NAPPANEE MUNI
Nappanee, Indiana
Gary Kern
NARA SPORTS SHINKO CC
Nara, Japan
Hale Irwin
NARA INTERNATIONAL GC
Hyogo, Japan
O. Ueda
NARASHINO CC (KINGS CSE)
Chiba, Japan
Kinya Fujita

NARASHINO CC (QUEENS CSE)
Chiba, Japan
Kinya Fujita
NARA WAKAKUSA GC
Osaka, Japan
Johnny Miller
NARITA GC
Chiba, Japan
Taizo Kawada
NARROWSBURG GC
Syracuse, New York
Hal Purdy
NARUO CC
Japan
Rokuro Akaboshi, *Shiro
Akaboshi*
(R.) C. H. Alison
NARUO GC
Inagawa, Hyogo, Japan
H. C. Crane
NASHAWTUC CC
Concord, Massachusetts
Geoffrey S. Cornish
NASHBORO VILLAGE CC
Nashville, Tennessee
Benjamin Wihry
NASHUA CC
Nashua, New Hampshire
Wayne Stiles, John Van Kleek
(R.) William F. Mitchell
NASHVILLE G&AC
Brentwood, Tennessee
Robert von Hagge, Bruce Devlin
NASSAU CC [NLE]
Nassau, New York
Tom Bendelow
(R.9) Tom Bendelow
NASSAU CC
Glen Cove, New York
Devereux Emmet
(R. A.3) Herbert Strong,
George Low
(R.) Frank Duane
(R.) Geoffrey S. Cornish,
Brian Silva
NASSAU G LINKS [NLE]
Bahamas
Alex Findlay
NASSAWANGO CC
Snow Hill, Maryland
Russell Roberts
NASU GC
Tochiga Prefecture, Japan
Kinya Fujita, Seichi Inouye
NASU HIGHLANDS GC
Tochiga Prefecture, Japan
Robert Trent Jones, Jr.
NATANIS GC
Vassalboro, Maine
Paul Browne
(A.9) Philip Wogan
NATCHEZ TRACE CC
Sautillo, Mississippi
John W. Frazier
NATICK CC
Natick, Massachusetts
(R.4 A.9) Samuel Mitchell
NATIONAL GC
Woodbridge, Ontario
George Fazio, Tom Fazio
NATIONAL GC
Jakarta Pusat, Indonesia
Peter Thomson, Michael
Wolveridge, Ronald Fream

[THE] NATIONAL GC OF AUSTRALIA
Cape Schank, Australia
Robert Trent Jones, Jr.
NATIONAL G LINKS OF AMERICA
Southampton, New York
Charles Blair Macdonald
(R.1) Perry Maxwell
(R.) Robert Trent Jones
(R.) Robert Trent Jones
NATIONAL CITY GC
National City, California
Harry Rainville
NATIONAL TOWN & CC [NLE]
Lake Wales, Florida
Leonard Macomber
NATIONAL TOWN & CC [NLE]
Cleveland, Ohio
Leonard Macomber
[THE] NATURAL GC
Gaylord, Michigan
Jerry Matthews
NAUTICAL INN GC
Lake Havasu City, Arizona
Red Lawrence
NAVAJO FIELDS CC [NLE]
Worth, Illinois
Harry Collis
NAVAL ACADEMY GC
Annapolis, Maryland
Harry Collis
(A.9) William S. Flynn
NAVAL AIR STATION GC
New Orleans, Louisiana
Dick Metz
NAVAL TRAINING CENTER GC
Orlando, Florida
(A.3rd 9) Ward Northrup
NAVAL TRAINING CENTER GC
Great Lakes, Illinois
C.D. Wagstaff
(A.9) Ken Killian, Dick
Nugent
NAVATANEE CC
Thailand
Robert Trent Jones, Jr.
NAVESINK CC
Red Bank, New Jersey
Hal Purdy
(R.) Geoffrey S. Cornish,
Brian Silva
NAVESTOCK PARK GC
Essex, England
Howard Swan
NAVY GC (CRUISER CSE)
Cypress, California
Ted Robinson
NAVY GC (DESTROYER CSE)
Cypress, California
Joseph B. Williams
NAVY GC (NORTH CSE)
Mission Gorge, San Diego,
California
Jack Daray
(R.6) Ted Robinson
(R.) Jack Daray, Jr., Stephen
Halsey
NAVY GC (SOUTH CSE)
Mission Gorge, San Diego,
California
Jack Daray, Jr., Stephen Halsey
NAVY-MARINE GC
Pearl Harbor, Hawaii
William P. Bell
(R.) Bob Lohmann

NAVY POSTGRADUATE SCHOOL GC
Monterey, California
Robert Muir Graves
(R.4) Robert Muir Graves
NCR CC (NORTH CSE)
Dayton, Ohio
Dick Wilson
NCR CC (SOUTH CSE)
Dayton, Ohio
Dick Wilson
NEAH-KAH-NIE GC
Manzanita, Oregon
Barney Lucas
NEALHURST GC [NLE]
Jacksonville, Florida
Stanley Thompson
NECKARTAL GC
Stuttgart, Germany
Bernhard von Limburger
NEEDHAM GC [NLE]
Needham, Massachusetts
John Graham
NEEDHAM GC
Needham, Massachusetts
Wayne Stiles
(R.) Orrin Smith
(R.) Brian Silva, Geoffrey S.
Cornish
NEEDHAM CLASSIC GC
Hokkaido, Japan
Naomichi Sugaya
NEEDLES MUNI
Needles, California
Harry Rainville, David Rainville
NEEDWOOD GC
Rockville, Maryland
Lindsay Ervin
NEFYN AND DISTRICT GC
Wales
(R.) Fred W. Hawtree, A. H.
F. Jiggens
NEHAI TONKAYEA GC
Marceline, Missouri
Richard Watson
NEIPSIC PAR 3 GC [NLE]
Glastonbury, Connecticut
Geoffrey S. Cornish, William G.
Robinson
NELSON GC
Nelson, British Columbia
(R.9 A.9) Bill Newis
NELSON GC
England
(A.9) Fred G. Hawtree,
A. H. F. Jiggens
NELSON GC
New Zealand
W.A. Kiely
(R.) John Harris, Peter
Thomson
NELSON PARK GC
Decatur, Illinois
Tom Bendelow
NEMACOLIN CC
Beallsville, Pennsylvania
Emil Loeffler, *John McGlynn*
(R.) A. W. Tillinghast
(R.) Ron Forse
NEMACOLIN WOODLANDS GC
Farmington, Pennsylvania
(R.3 A.3) Ron Forse

NEMADJI GC
Spooner, Wisconsin
Stanley Pelchar
(A.9) Don Herfort

NEMAHA G&CC [NLE]
Oklahoma
Floyd Farley

NEMUNOSATO GC
Mie, Japan
Hal Sutton, Mitsuo Ito

NENAGH GC
Nenagh, Ireland
(A.9) Eddie Hackett

NES GC
Nes, Norway
Gerold Hauser, *Günther Hauser*

NESKOWIN BEACH GC
Neskowin, Oregon
Ercel Kay

NETTUNO GC
Nettuno, Italy
Marco Croze

NEUCHÂTEL GC
Neuchâtel, Switzerland
Karl Hoffmann, Bernhard von
Limburger

NEUMANN PARK GC
Cincinnati, Ohio
William H. Diddel
(A.3rd 9) Jack Kidwell,
Michael Hurdzan

NEUSTADT GC
Neustadt, Germany
Karl Hoffmann, Bernhard von
Limburger

NEU-ULM GC
Ulm, Germany
Bernhard von Limburger
(R.9 A.9) Karl F. Grohs,
Rainer Preissmann

NEVELE GC
Ellenville, New York
Alfred H. Tull
(R.) George Fazio, Tom Fazio

NEVELE MEADE GC
Prospect, Kentucky
Steve Smyers

NEVILL GC
Tunbridge Wells, England
(R.) H. S. Colt
(R.) J. S. F. Morrison

NEW GC
Deauville, France
Tom Simpson, P. M. Ross
(A.9) Henry Cotton

NEW ALBANY CC
New Albany, Ohio
Jack Nicklaus

NEWARK CC
Newark, Delaware
Wilfrid Reid
(A.9) Frank Murray, Russell
Roberts

NEWARK ATHLETIC C [NLE]
Newark, New Jersey
Alex Findlay

NEWAUKUM VALLEY GC
Chehalis, Washington
John H. Date, Henry M. Date

NEW BERN G&CC
New Bern, North Carolina
(R.9 A.9) Ellis Maples

NEWBIGGEN-BY-THE-SEA GC
Northumberland, England
Willie Park

NEWBOLD COWYN GC
Warwickshire, England
Frederick Gibberd

NEWBRIDGE CC
Largo, Maryland
Russell Roberts

NEWBURGH CC
Newburgh, New York
(R.9) Hal Purdy

NEW CASTLE CC
New Castle, Pennsylvania
A. W. Tillinghast

NEWCASTLE GC
Australia
Eric L. Apperly

NEWCASTLE-UNDER-LYME GC
Staffordshire, England
Fred W. Hawtree, Martin Haw-
tree

NEWCASTLE WEST GC
Ireland
(R.) Eddie Hackett

**[THE] NEW COURSE AT GRAND
CYPRESS**
Orlando, Florida
Jack Nicklaus

NEW ENGLAND CC
Bellingham, Massachusetts
Gary Kern, Ron Kern, Hale
Irwin

NEW FOREST GC
New Forest, England
Peter Swan

NEW GLASGOW GC
Quebec
(R.) Howard Watson

NEW HAVEN CC [NLE]
New Haven, Connecticut
Robert D. Pryde

NEW HAVEN CC
Hamden, Connecticut
Willie Park, Jr.
(R.1) Al Zikorus

NEWLANDS GC
County Dublin, Ireland
James Braid, John R. Stutt
(R.) Eddie Hackett

NEWLANDS G&RC
Langley, British Columbia
Clive Rogers
(R.) *William L. Overdorf*

NEW LONDON CC
New London, Connecticut
(R.5) Geoffrey S. Cornish,
William G. Robinson

NEW MEADOWS GC
Topsfield, Massachusetts
Phil Wogan

**NEW MEXICO MILITARY INSTITUTE
GC**
Roswell, New Mexico
Floyd Farley

NEW MEXICO STATE UNIVERSITY GC
Las Cruces, New Mexico
Floyd Farley

NEW MEXICO TECH G CSE
Socorro, New Mexico
James E. Voss

NEWNAN CC
Newnan, Georgia
(A.9) Denis Griffiths

NEW NANSO GC
Chiba, Japan
Shunsuke Kato

NEW ORLEANS CC
New Orleans, Louisiana
(R.9) Joe Lee
(R.) Ron Kirby, Denis
Griffiths

NEW ORLEANS VA HOSPITAL GC
New Orleans, Louisiana
Ralph Plummer, Bob Dunning

NEW PHILADELPHIA G&CC
New Philadelphia, Ohio
John F. Robinson

NEW PLYMOUTH GC
New Plymouth, New Zealand
(R.) C. H. Redhead

NEWPORT CC
Newport, Arkansas
(A.9) Edmund B. Ault

NEWPORT CC
Newport, New Hampshire
NKA John H. Cain GC

NEWPORT CC
Newport, Rhode Island
William F. Davis
(R.9 A.9) A. W. Tillinghast
(R.) Donald Ross
(R.) Orrin Smith

**NEWPORT CC (BEGINNERS CSE)
[NLE]**
Newport, Rhode Island
William F. Davis

NEWPORT CC
Newport, Vermont
Ralph Barton
(A.9) Michael Hurdzan

NEWPORT GC
Port Charlotte, Florida
Gordon Lewis

NEWPORT GC
Newport, Michigan
Alex Lilac, Sam Lilac, Bill Lilac

NEWPORT BEACH CC
Newport Beach, California
William P. Bell, William F. Bell
(R.) Harry Rainville, David
Rainville

NEWPORT BEACH GC
Newport Beach, California
Harry Rainville, David Rainville

NEWPORT ON LAKE HOUSTON GC
Crosby, Texas
Gary Darling

NEWPORTER INN GC
Newport Beach, California
William F. Bell

NEWPORT NEWS PARK GC
Newport News, Virginia
William Gordon

NEW PRAGUE GC
New Prague, Minnesota
(A.9) Don Herfort

NEW QUARTER PARK GC
Virginia
George W. Cobb, John LaFoy

NEWQUAY GC
Cornwall, England
(R.) H. S. Colt

NEW RICHMOND GC
New Richmond, Wisconsin
Willie Kidd
(R.5 A.9) Don Herfort

NEW ROSS GC
New Ross, Ireland
(R.) Eddie Hackett

NEW ST. ANDREWS GC
Ontawara, Japan
Jack Nicklaus, Desmond
Muirhead

NEW SMYRNA BEACH G CSE
New Smyrna Beach, Florida
Donald Ross

NEW SOUTH WALES GC
Sydney, Australia
Des Soutar, Alister Mackenzie
(R.) *Eric L. Apperly*
(R.) Peter Thomson, Michael
Wolveridge

NEWTON CC
Newton, Iowa
Harry Collis

NEWTON CC
Newton, Kansas
Harry Robb

NEWTON CC
Newton, New Jersey
(A.9) William Gordon, David
Gordon

NEWTON ABBOT GC [NLE]
Devonshire, England
Harold St. Maur

NEWTON ABBOT GC
Devonshire, England
James Braid, John R. Stutt
(R.) J. Hamilton Stutt

NEWTON COMMONWEALTH GC
Newton, Massachusetts
Donald Ross
(R.) Wayne Stiles, John Van
Kleek

NEWTONMORE GC
Inverness, Scotland
(R.) Old Tom Morris
(R.) James Braid, John R.
Stutt
(R.) Alister Mackenzie

NEWTONSTEWART GC
Northern Ireland
(R.) J. J. F. Pennink

NEW ULM GC
New Ulm, Minnesota
(A.9) Don Herfort

NEW YORK HOSPITAL GC
White Plains, New York
(R.) Robert Trent Jones

NEW ZEALAND GC [NLE]
Surrey, England
S. Mure Ferguson

NEW ZEALAND GC
Surrey, England
Tom Simpson

NIAGARA FALLS CC
Lewiston, New York
(R.) Robert Trent Jones
(R.) William Newcomb

NIAKWA G&CC
Winnipeg, Manitoba
Stanley Thompson

NIBLEY PARK GC
Salt Lake City, Utah
Harold B. Lamb
(R.) Mick Riley

NIIGATA FOREST GC
Nishi Nihon, Japan
Ron Kirby, Gary Player

NIKKO CC
Tochigi Prefecture, Japan
Seichi Inouye
NILE CC
Edmonds, Washington
Norman H. Woods
NINOUMI GC
Kyoto, Japan
Kokusai Kogyo
NIPPERSINK MANOR CC
Genoa City, Wisconsin
James Foulis
NISEKO GC
Sapporo, Japan
Arnold Palmer, Ed Seay
NISEKO KOGEN GC
Sapporo, Japan
Arnold Palmer, Ed Seay
NISHI BIWAKO GC
Japan
Arnold Palmer, Ed Seay
NISHI NIHON GC
Nōgata, Japan
Ron Kirby, Gary Player
NISHINOMIYA CC
Hyogo, Japan
Seichi Inouye, *O. Ueda, K.
Takeguchi*
NISHIWAKI CC
Nishiwaki, Japan
Tsuneo Abe
NISSEQUOGUE CC
St. James, New York
Edgar Senne
NIVELLE GC
France
J. H. Taylor
NOBEOKA GC
Miyazaki, Japan
Sato Kogyo
NOBLETON LAKES GC
Ontario
René Muylaert
NOB NORTH GC
Dalton, Georgia
Ron Kirby
NOBORIBETSU CC SATSUNAI
Hokkaido, Japan
K. Mochizuki
NOCONA HILLS CC
Nocona, Texas
Leon Howard, *Charles Howard*
NOGALES CC [NLE]
Nogales, Arizona
(R.) A. H. Jolly
NONAME GC
Albany, Georgia
Rocky Roquemore, Jeff Burton
NONGSA INDAH CC
Indonesia
Ronald Fream
NOORDBRABANTSE GC
Breda, Netherlands
J. S. F. Morrison
NOORDHOLLANDSE GC
Alkmaar, Netherlands
J. F. Dudok van Heel
NOORD NEDERLANDSE G&CC
Groningen, Netherlands
John Duncan Dunn
(A.9) D. M. A. Steel
NOORDWIJKSE GC
Netherlands
(R.) J. J. F. Pennink

NORANDA MINES GC
Quebec
Stanley Thompson
(R.9) Howard Watson
(R.9) John Watson
NORBECK CC
Rockville, Maryland
Alfred H. Tull
(R.) Edmund B. Ault
NORDCENTER G&CC
Aminnefors, Finland
Ronald Fream
NORDIC HILLS GC
Itasca, Illinois
Charles Maddox, *Frank P.
MacDonald*
NORDSEC-KURHOF GC
Wik-auf-Fuhr, Germany
J. J. F. Pennink
NORESUND GC
Sweden
Jan Sederholm
NORFOLK CC
Norfolk, Nebraska
(R.13 A.5) Floyd Farley
NORFOLK CC
Norfolk, Virginia
NKA Sewells Point GC
NORMANBY HALL GC
Scunthorpe, Lincolnshire,
England
Fred W. Hawtree, A. H. F.
Jiggens, Martin Hawtree
NORMANDALE GC
Edina, Minnesota
Leo J. Feser
NORMANDIE GC
France
J. Hamilton Stutt
NORMANDIE GC
St. Louis, Missouri
Robert Foulis
NORMANDY CC
Flossmoor, Illinois
Harry Collis
NORMANDY SHORES GC
Miami Beach, Florida
William S. Flynn, Howard
Toomey
(R.) Mark Mahannah
NORMANSIDE CC
Elsmere, New York
William Harries
NORRIS A. ALDEEN G CSE
Rockford, Illinois
Dick Nugent
NORRIS ESTATE GC
St. Charles, Illinois
Robert Trent Jones
NORRKOEPING GC
Norrkoeping, Sweden
Nils Sköld
NORRVIKEN GC
Norrvik, Sweden
Jan Sederholm
NORTH ADAMS GC
Massachusetts
(R.) Orrin Smith
NORTHAMPTON CC
Upper Marlboro, Maryland
Russell Roberts
NORTHAMPTON CC
Easton, Pennsylvania
(R.12 A.6) David Gordon

NORTHAMPTON GC
Northamptonshire, England
Old Tom Morris
(R.) Willie Park, Jr.
NORTHAMPTON GC
Harlestone, England
D. M. A. Steel
NORTHAMPTON VALLEY CC
Richboro, Pennsylvania
Edmund B. Ault
NORTHAMPTONSHIRE COUNTY GC
England
H. S. Colt
(R.) James Braid
(R.) C. K. Cotton
NORTH ANDOVER CC
North Andover, Massachusetts
Donald Ross
(R.) William F. Mitchell
NORTH BATTLEFORD G&CC
North Battleford, Saskatchewan
Ray Buffel
NORTHBAY CC
Madison, Mississippi
Ron Garl
NORTH BAY G&CC
North Bay, Ontario
Stanley Thompson
(R.9 A.9) Howard Watson
NORTH BERWICK GC (BURGH CSE)
North Berwick, Scotland
(R.) P. M. Ross
NORTH BERWICK GC (EAST LINKS)
North Berwick, Scotland
Ben Sayers
(A.9) Ben Sayers, James Braid
NORTH BERWICK GC (WEST LINKS)
North Berwick, Scotland
(A.9) David Strath
(R.) Tom Dunn
(R.) Sir Guy Campbell, C. K.
Hutchison, S. V. Hotchkin
NORTHBROOK CC
Luxemburg, Wisconsin
Ed Langert
NORTH CASTLE CC
Armonk, New York
Gilman P. Tiffany
NORTH COLVIN GC
New York
A. Russell Tryon
NORTH CONWAY CC
North Conway, New Hampshire
(R.9) Ralph Barton
(A.9) Phil Wogan
NORTH COUNTRY GC
Hokkaido, Japan
Isao Aoki
NORTHDALE G&CC
Tampa, Florida
Ron Garl
NORTH DOWNS GC
North Downs, England
(R.) J. J. F. Pennink
NORTHEAST HARBOR GC
Bar Harbor, Maine
J. G. Thorp
(A.9) Donald Ross
(R.9) Geoffrey S. Cornish,
William Robinson
NORTHEAST PARK GC
Winnipeg, Manitoba
Claude Muret

NORTH EASTWAY MUNI
Castleton, Indiana
Pete Dye
NORTHERNAIRE CC
Three Lakes, Wisconsin
Tom Bendelow
NORTHERN HILLS CC
San Antonio, Texas
Joseph Beleau
NORTHERN WAIROA GC
New Zealand
C. H. Redhead
NORTHERN SPY CC
Townsend, Massachusetts
Ted Manning, Mary Mills (1991)
NORTHFIELD CC
Northfield, Vermont
Les Heon
NORTHFIELD GC
East Northfield, Massachusetts
Alex Findlay
NORTHFIELD GC
Northfield, Minnesota
Paul Coates
(R.9 A.9) Don Herfort
NORTH FORELAND GC
Kingsgate, England
Herbert Fowler, Tom Simpson
(R.) Tom Simpson, J. S. F.
Morrison
(R.) J. S. F. Morrison
NORTH FORK CC
Cutchogue, New York
(R.) Gene Hamm
NORTH FORK CC
Johnstown, Pennsylvania
James Gilmore Harrison
NORTH FULTON MUNI
Atlanta, Georgia
H. Chandler Egan
(R.) Garrett Gill, George B.
Williams
NORTHGATE CC
Houston, Texas
Robert von Hagge, Bruce Devlin
NORTHGATE GC
Reno, Nevada
Brad Benz, Mike Poellot
NORTHGREEN VILLAGE GC
Rocky Mount, North Carolina
J. Porter Gibson
NORTH HALTON GC
Georgetown, Ontario
Robert Moote
(R.) Robert Moote
NORTH HANTS GC
Hampshire, England
James Braid
(R.) Tom Simpson
NORTH HAVEN C
Pulpit Harbor, Maine
Wayne Stiles, John Van Kleek
NORTH HEMPSTEAD CC
Port Washington, New York
A. W. Tillinghast
(R.) *Ed Erickson*
(R.) Robert Trent Jones
NORTH HILL CC
Duxbury, Massachusetts
William F. Mitchell
NORTH HILLS CC
Sherwood, Arkansas
(R.) Robert Trent Jones

North Hills CC
Manhasset, New York
Robert Trent Jones
   (R.) Stephen Kay

North Hills CC
Menominee Falls, Wisconsin
   (R.1) Robert Bruce Harris

North Hills GC
Douglaston, New York
NKA Douglaston Park GC

North Hills Muni
Corry, Pennsylvania
Edmund B. Ault
   (R.10) Bill Love

North Jersey CC
Wayne, New Jersey
Walter J. Travis
   (R.) Nicholas Psiahas
   (R.) Hal Purdy
   (R.) Robert Trent Jones

North Kent GC
Rockford, Michigan
Warner Bowen

North Kern CC
Bakersfield, California
William F. Bell

North Kingstown Muni
North Kingstown, Rhode Island
Walter I. Johnson

North Lakes CC
Victoria, Australia
Peter Thomson, Michael Wolveridge

Northland CC [NLE]
Duluth, Minnesota
Ward Ames, Jr.
   (R.9 A.9) Tom Bendelow

Northland CC
Duluth, Minnesota
Donald Ross
   (R.) Don Herfort

North Las Vegas GC
North Las Vegas, Nevada
Jack Walpole (9 Par 3 1971)

North Middlesex GC
England
C.S. Butchart

Northmoor CC [NLE]
Ravinia, Illinois
William B. Langford

Northmoor CC
Highland Park, Illinois
Donald Ross
   (R.) Edward Lawrence Packard
   (R.) Dick Nugent

Northmoor CC
Celina, Ohio
Alex "Nipper" Campbell

North Oaks CC
St. Paul, Minnesota
Stanley Thompson

North Olmstead GC
North Olmstead, Ohio
Earl Yesberger
   (R.) Bill Amick

North Otago GC [NLE]
Awamoa, New Zealand
Basil Smith

North Otago GC
Awamoa, New Zealand
Gilbert Martin, A. E. Conway

North Oxford GC
England
Tom Dunn

North Palm Beach CC
North Palm Beach, Florida
   (R.) Mark McCumber

North Park GC
Allison Park, Pennsylvania
   (R.) X. G. Hassenplug

North Park Community GC
Coloma, Michigan
George B. Ferry

North Port Charlotte CC
North Port Charlotte, Florida
NKA Sabal Trace G&CC

North Point GC
Sapporo, Japan
Takeaki Kaneda

North Port CC
North Port, Florida
LeRoy Phillips

Northport CC
Northport, New York
Devereux Emmet

Northport GC
Northport, Maine
George Nelson

North Port National G&CC
Lake Ozark, Missouri
Arnold Palmer, Ed Seay

Northport Point C
Northport, Michigan
Tom Bendelow

North Ranch CC
Westlake, California
Ted Robinson

North Redoubt C
Garrison, New York
NKA Garrison CC

North Ridge CC
Fair Oaks, California
William F. Bell, William P. Bell
   (R.) Robert Muir Graves

North Ridge CC (Lakes Cse)
Raleigh, North Carolina
George W. Cobb
   (A.9 R.9) Gene Hamm
   (R.) John LaFoy

North Ridge CC (Oaks Cse)
Raleigh, North Carolina
George W. Cobb
   (R.9 A.9) Gene Hamm
   (R.) John LaFoy

North River GC
Tuscaloosa, Alabama
Ron Kirby, Gary Player

North Salem Links [NLE]
Salem, Massachusetts
Robert White

North Shore CC
Glenview, Illinois
C. H. Alison, H. S. Colt
   (R.) Ken Killian, Dick Nugent
   (R.) Edward Lawrence Packard
   (R.) Roger Packard

North Shore CC
St. Louis, Missouri
Robert Foulis

North Shore CC [NLE]
St. Louis, Missouri
Robert Foulis

North Shore CC
St. Louis, Missouri
Chic Adams, Homer Herpel

North Shore CC
Glen Head, New York
A.W. Tillinghast

North Shore CC
Sneads Ferry, North Carolina
Jerry Turner, Bob Moore, Vance Heafner

Northshore CC
Portland, Texas
Robert von Hagge, Bruce Devlin

North Shore CC
Tacoma, Washington
Al Smith

North Shore CC
Mequon, Wisconsin
David Gill
   (R.) Dick Nugent

North Shore GC [NLE]
Kenilworth, Illinois
Tom Bendelow

North Shore GC
Menominee, Michigan
A. H. Jolly

North Shore GC
England
James Braid

North Shore C [NLE]
New Zealand
E. S. Douglas
   (A.9) *Basil Smith*

North Shore GC
New Zealand
H. G. Babbage
   (R.) John Harris, Peter Thomson

North Shore Acres GC [NLE]
Kenosha, Wisconsin
William B. Langford

Northstar at Tahoe GC
Truckee, California
Robert Muir Graves

Northumberland G&CC
Pugwash, Nova Scotia
Clinton E. Robinson
   (A.9) William G. Robinson

Northumberland GC
Northumberland, England
James Braid
   (R.) H. S. Colt, C. H. Alison

Northumberland Seaside G Links
Pugwash, Nova Scotia
   (R.9 A.9) William G. Robinson, John F. Robinson

Northway Heights G&CC
Ballston Lake, New York
Pete Craig

North West GC
Ireland
   (R.9 A.9) Eddie Hackett

Northwest Mississippi Junior College GC
Mississippi
John W. Frazier

Northwest Park GC
Wheaton, Maryland
Edmund B. Ault
   (A.3rd 9) Russell Roberts

Northwest Park Muni [NLE]
Oklahoma City, Oklahoma
Arthur Jackson

Northwood CC
Shreveport, Louisiana
   (A.9) Jeff Brauer

Northwood CC
Meridian, Mississippi
   (R.2) Brian Ault

Northwood C
Dallas, Texas
William H. Diddel
   (R.) Ralph Plummer
   (R.5) Marvin Ferguson
   (R.) Jay Morrish

Northwood G&CC
Lawrenceville, Georgia
Willard Byrd

Northwood G&CC
Toronto, Ontario
Stanley Thompson

Northwood GC
Guerneville, California
Alister Mackenzie, Robert Hunter
   (R.) Robert Muir Graves

Northwood GC
Northwood, England
Tom Dunn

North Woodmere GC
Woodmere, New York
David Gordon

Northwoods GC
Columbia, South Carolina
P. B. Dye

NorthWoods G Cse
Rhinelander, Wisconsin
Don Herfort

North Worcestershire GC
England
James Braid

Norton CC
Norton, Massachusetts
   (R.9 A.9) Brian Silva, Geoffrey Cornish

Norway CC
Norway, Maine
George Dunn, Jr.

Norway Point GC
Ontario
   (R.9) Stanley Thompson

Norwich Muni
Norwich, Connecticut
Donald Ross

Norwich Muni
Norwich, England
F. G. Hawtree, J. H. Taylor

Norwood CC
Norwood, Massachusetts
Samuel Mitchell

Norwood CC [NLE]
Long Branch, New Jersey
A. W. Tillinghast

Norwood GC
Huntington, Indiana
Hal Purdy

Norwood G Cse [NLE]
Winnipeg, Manitoba
Alexander Mann

Norwood Hills CC (East Cse)
St. Louis, Missouri
Wayne Stiles
   (R.) Gary Kern

Norwood Hills CC (West Cse)
St. Louis, Missouri
Wayne Stiles

NOSE CC
Japan
Sozaburo Uenishi
NOSHIRO CC
Noshiro, Japan
Hideyo Sugimoto
NOTO GC
Japan
Shozo Ozasa
NOTTAWASAGE INN GC
Alliston, Ontario
Gordon Witteveen
NOTTINGHAM CC
Nottingham, Pennsylvania
(R.) Edmund B. Ault
NOTTINGHAM CITY GC
Nottingham, England
Tom Dunn
(R.) Willie Park, Jr.
NOTTS GC
Nottinghamshire, England
Willie Park, Jr.
(R.) J.H. Taylor
(R.) Tom Williamson
NOYAC G&CC
Sag Harbor, New York
William F. Mitchell
NUBBINS RIDGE CC
Knoxville, Tennessee
Alex McKay
NUEVA ANDALUCIA GC (LAS BRISAS
CSE)
Marbella, Málaga, Spain
Robert Trent Jones
NUEVA ANDALUCIA GC (LOS
NARANJOS CSE)
Marbella, Málaga, Spain
Robert Trent Jones
NUEVA ANDALUCIA GC (PAR 3 CSE)
Marbella, Málaga, Spain
Robert Trent Jones
NUEVO VALLARTA GC
Mexico
Arnold Palmer, Ed Seay
NUKADA GC
Japan
Shoichi Suzuki
NUMATA FORUM GC
Gunma Prefecture, Japan
Scott Miller
NUN'S ISLAND GC
Montreal, Quebec
Howard Watson
NUNEATON GC
Warwickshire, England
Tom Williamson
NUREMORE GC
Ireland
(R.) Eddie Hackett
NYBRO GC
Nybro, Sweden
Jan Sederholm
NYERI GC
Kenya
*G. Sandbach Baker, Reggie
McClure*
NYU GC
Fukui, Japan
Jim Fazio

OAHU CC
Honolulu, Oahu, Hawaii
Alex Bell
(R.) Robin Nelson, Rodney
Wright
[THE] OAK C OF GENOA
Genoa, Illinois
Charles Maddox
OAKBOURNE CC
Lafayette, Louisiana
Dick Wilson
(R.) Jay Riviere
(R.) Joseph S. Finger, Ken
Dye
OAKBROOK G&CC
Olympia, Washington
(R.) John Steidel
OAK BROOK GC
Oak Brook, Illinois
Roger Packard
OAK BROOK HILLS GC
Oak Brook, Illinois
Dick Nugent
OAK CLIFF CC
Dallas, Texas
Press Maxwell
OAKCREST CC
Maryland
Edmund B. Ault, Al Jamison
OAKDALE G&CC
Oakdale, California
Bob Baldock
OAKDALE G&CC
Downsview, Ontario
Stanley Thompson
(A.9) Clinton E. Robinson
(R.) Robert Moote
OAKDALE GC
Florence, South Carolina
Roland "Robby" Robertson
OAKDALE GC
Yorkshire, England
Alister Mackenzie
(R.7) Fred W. Hawtree,
A. H. F. Jiggens
OAKFIELD CC
Grand Lake, Nova Scotia
Clinton E. Robinson
OAK FORD GC
Sarasota, Florida
Ron Garl
OAK FOREST CC
Longview, Texas
Billy Martindale
OAK GABLES GC
Ancaster, Ontario
John F. Robinson
OAK GLEN GC
Stillwater, Minnesota
Don Herfort
OAK GROVE CC
Oxford, Indiana
William H. Diddel
OAK GROVE CC
Terrell, Texas
Ralph Plummer
OAK HARBOR G&TC
Baudette, Minnesota
Gerry Pirkl, *Donald G. Brauer,
Emil Perret*
OAK HARBOR YACHT & CC
Slidell, Louisiana
Lee Schmidt

OAK HILL CC
Fitchburg, Massachusetts
Donald Ross
(A.9) Wayne Stiles, John Van
Kleek
(R.) Orrin Smith
(R.5) Geoffrey S. Cornish,
William G. Robinson
OAK HILL CC (EAST CSE)
Rochester, New York
Donald Ross
(R.) Robert Trent Jones
(R.) Robert Trent Jones
(R. A.3) George Fazio, Tom
Fazio
OAK HILL CC (WEST CSE)
Rochester, New York
Donald Ross
OAK HILL GC
Middlebury, Indiana
William H. Diddel
OAK HILL GC
Milford, New Jersey
William Gordon, David Gordon
OAK HILL GC
Oak Creek, Wisconsin
R. Albert Anderson
OAK HILLS CC
Montgomery, Alabama
Joseph S. Finger, Byron Nelson
OAK HILLS CC [NLE]
Palos Heights, Illinois
David McIntosh
OAK HILLS CC
Palos Heights, Illinois
Edward Lawrence Packard
OAK HILLS CC
Omaha, Nebraska
Robert Popp
(R.2) Jeff Brauer
OAK HILLS CC
San Antonio, Texas
A. W. Tillinghast
(R.6 A.3) Joseph S. Finger
(R.2) Ron Kirby
(R.) Jay Morrish
OAK HILLS CC
Richmond, Virginia
Reuben Hines
OAK HILLS CC
Chiba, Japan
Robert Trent Jones, Jr.
OAK HILLS G&CC
Ada, Oklahoma
(R.) *John Embry*
OAK HILLS GC
Spring Hill, Florida
Charles Almony
OAK HILLS GC
Farmington, Missouri
John Ball
OAK HILLS GC
Charlotte, North Carolina
G. W. Picklesimer
OAK HILLS GC
Columbia, South Carolina
D. J. DeVictor, *Steve Melynk*
OAK HILLS G CSE
Norwalk, Connecticut
Alfred H. Tull
OAK HOLLOW GC
High Point, North Carolina
Pete Dye

OAKHURST CC
Clayton, California
Ron Fream
OAKHURST CC
Grove City, Ohio
Jack Kidwell
OAKHURST G LINKS [NLE]
White Sulphur Springs, West
Virginia
George Grant, Lionel Torrin
OAK ISLAND G & BEACH C
Southport, North Carolina
George W. Cobb
OAK KNOLL GC
Streamwood, Illinois
Bob Lohmann
OAK KNOLL GC
Independence, Oregon
Bill Ashby
OAK KNOLLS GC
Kent, Ohio
Howard Morette
OAK LAKE GC
New Kensington, Pennsylvania
(A.9) Ferdinand Garbin
OAKLAND CC
Oakland, Maryland
Edmund B. Ault
OAKLAND ACRES CC
Grinnell, Iowa
Cliff Thompson
OAKLAND CITY GC
Oakland City, Indiana
William B. Langford
OAKLAND GC [NLE]
Bayside, New York
Tom Bendelow
(R.) Seth Raynor
OAKLAND GREENS GC
Ontario
(A.9) Clinton E. Robinson
OAKLAND HILLS CC
Battle Creek, Michigan
George V. Nickolaou
OAKLAND HILLS CC (NORTH CSE)
Birmingham, Michigan
Donald Ross
(R.) Robert Trent Jones
OAKLAND HILLS CC (SOUTH CSE)
Birmingham, Michigan
Donald Ross
(R.) Robert Trent Jones
(1950)
(R.) Robert Trent Jones
(1972)
(R.) Robert Trent Jones
(1984)
(R.) Arthur Hills
OAKLAND HILLS GC
Portage, Michigan
Stuart Dustin, Lucien Axtell
OAK LANE CC
Woodbridge, Connecticut
Geoffrey S. Cornish
OAKLAWN GC
Chicago, Illinois
William B. Langford
OAK LAWN GC
Elkhart, Indiana
William H. Diddel
OAK LEAF CC
Reinbeck, Iowa
(R.) Charles Calhoun

Oakley CC [NLE]
Watertown, Massachusetts
Willie Campbell
Oakley CC
Watertown, Massachusetts
Donald Ross
Oak Meadow G&TC
Evansville, Indiana
Ken Killian, Dick Nugent
Oakmont CC
Glendale, California
Max Behr
(R.) William P. Bell
(R.) William F. Bell
(R.) David Rainville
Oakmont CC (East Cse)
Santa Rosa, California
Ted Robinson
Oakmont CC (West Cse)
Santa Rosa, California
Ted Robinson
Oakmont CC
Oakmont, Pennsylvania
Henry C. Fownes, William C.
Fownes, Jr.
(R.) William C. Fownes, Jr.,
Emil Loeffler
(R.1) Arthur Jack Snyder
(R.) Robert Trent Jones
(R.) Arnold Palmer, Ed Seay
(R.) Ferdinand Garbin
(R.) Arthur Hills
Oakmont CC
Corinth, Texas
Roger Packard, Don January
Oakmont GC
Osaka, Japan
Jack Nicklaus
Oakmont East GC
Oakmont, Pennsylvania
Emil Loeffler, *John McGlynn*
(R.) James G. Harrison,
Ferdinand Garbin
Oakmoore GC
Stockton, California
Donald A. Crump
Oak Mountain State Park GC
Pelham, Alabama
Earl Stone
Oak n' Spruce GC
South Lee, Massachusetts
Geoffrey S. Cornish
Oak Park CC
Oak Park, Illinois
Donald Ross
(R.) Edward B. Dearie, Jr.
(R.) William H. Diddel
(R.) Dick Nugent
Oak Pointe GC (Honors Cse)
Brighton, Michigan
Arthur Hills
Oak Ridge CC
Fort Lauderdale, Florida
Hans Schmeisser
Oak Ridge CC
Hopkins, Minnesota
William D. Clark
Oak Ridge CC
Madisonville, Texas
Leon Howard
Oak Ridge CC
Richardson, Texas
Jack Kidwell, Michael Hurdzan

Oakridge CC
Farmington, Utah
William F. Bell
Oak Ridge G&CC
Ashburn, Ontario
Thomas McBroom
Oak Ridge GC
San Jose, California
Bert Stamps
Oak Ridge GC
Agawam, Massachusetts
George Fazio, Tom Fazio
Oak Ridge GC
Clark, New Jersey
Willard Wilkinson
Oak Ridge GC [NLE]
Tuckahoe, New York
(R.) Walter Travis
Oak Run GC
Dahinda, Illinois
William Newcomb
Oaks CC
Murray, Kentucky
Scott Nall
Oaks CC
St. Joseph, Michigan
Arthur Hills
Oaks CC
Tulsa, Oklahoma
A. W. Tillinghast
(R.) Perry Maxwell
[The] Oaks Cse
Covington, Georgia
Michael Hirsch, Dick Schulz
(1990)
Oaks G&CC (Blue Heron Cse)
Sarasota, Florida
Willard Byrd
Oaks G&CC (Eagle Cse)
Sarasota, Florida
Willard Byrd
[The] Oaks GC
Muscle Shoals, Alabama
Gary Roger Baird
[The] Oaks GC
Osage Beach, Missouri
Robert von Hagge, Bruce Devlin
Oak Shore CC [NLE]
Mississippi
Jack Daray
Oaks North GC
Rancho Bernardo, California
Ted Robinson
[The] Oaks of St. George GC
St. George, Ontario
David L. Moote, Robert Moote
Oaks Park GC
Surrey, England
John Day
Oak Tree CC
Tehachapi, California
Ted Robinson
(R.) Robert Muir Graves
Oak Tree CC
Fort Lauderdale, Florida
Dick Wilson
Oak Tree CC (East Cse)
Edmond, Oklahoma
Pete Dye
Oak Tree CC (West Cse)
Edmond, Oklahoma
Pete Dye

Oak Tree GC
Edmond, Oklahoma
Pete Dye
Oak Tree GC
West Middlesex, Pennsylvania
Edmund B. Ault
(R.2) Edmund B. Ault
Oak Valley GC
Beaumont, California
Lee Schmidt, Brian Curley
Oak Village GC
Japan
Desmond Muirhead
Oakville CC
Mount Carroll, Illinois
Tom Bendelow
Oakville G&CC
Oakville, Ontario
(R.) Clinton E. Robinson
(R. A.2) Thomas McBroom
Oakville Executive GC
Milton, Ontario
René Muylaert, *Charles Muylaert*
Oakway GC
Eugene, Oregon
(R.) *John Zoller*
Oakwood C
Cleveland, Ohio
Arthur Boggs
(A.9) Tom Bendelow
(R.) Donald Ross
(A.6) Sandy Alves
(R.2) Ted McAnlis
Oakwood CC
Sun Lakes, Arizona
Ken Kavanaugh
Oakwood CC
Coal Valley, Illinois
Pete Dye
Oakwood CC
Kansas City, Missouri
Tom Bendelow
(A.9) Orrin Smith
(R.) William H. Diddel
(R.) Scott Miller
Oakwood CC
Canton, Ohio
(R.) Edmund B. Ault
Oakwood CC
Enid, Oklahoma
Perry Maxwell, Press Maxwell
Oakwood Park GC
Franklin, Wisconsin
Edward Lawrence Packard
Oakwoods CC
North Wilkesboro, North
Carolina
(R.) Tom Jackson
Oarai GC
Ibaraki, Japan
Kinya Fujita, Seichi Inouye
Oasis CC
Palm Desert, California
David Rainville
Oasis Par 3 GC
Plymouth, Michigan
William Newcomb
Obara CC
Japan
Taizo Kawada
Obere Alp G&CC
Germany
Karl F. Grohs, *Rainer
Preissmann*

Oberau GC
Gut Buchwies, Germany
Donald Harradine
Oberfranken GC
Bayreuth, Germany
Bernhard von Limburger
Oberschwaben Bad Waldsee GC
Bad Waldsee, Germany
Bernhard von Limburger
(R.) Donald Harradine
Oberstaufen-Steibis GC
Germany
Kurt Rossknecht
O'Brien Estate GC
Plattsburg, New York
Howard Watson
Ocala Muni
Ocala, Florida
John Duncan Dunn
(R.) William Gordon
(R.) Lloyd Clifton, *Kenneth
Ezell, George Clifton*
[The] Ocean Cse
Kiawah Island, South Carolina
Pete Dye
Ocean G Links
Daytona Beach, Florida
Bill Amick
Ocean Links [NLE]
Newport, Rhode Island
Seth Raynor
Ocean Acres GC
Manahawkin, New Jersey
Hal Purdy
Ocean City CC [NLE]
Ocean City, New Jersey
Willie Park, Jr.
**Ocean City G & Yacht C
(Bayside Cse)**
Berlin, Maryland
Russell Roberts
**Ocean City G & Yacht C
(Seaside Cse)**
Berlin, Maryland
William Gordon, David Gordon
Ocean County G Cse
Tuckerton, New Jersey
George Fazio
Ocean Dunes G Links
Florence, Oregon
Fred Federspiel
(R.9 A.9) William G.
Robinson
Ocean Edge GC
Brewster, Massachusetts
Brian Silva, Geoffrey S. Cornish
Ocean Harbour G Links
Calabash, North Carolina
Clyde Johnston
Ocean Isle Beach GC
Ocean Isle Beach, North
Carolina
Russell Breeden, *Dan Breeden*
Ocean Meadows GC
Goleta, California
Harry Rainville, David Rainville
Ocean Palm CC
Flagler Beach, Florida
Fred Bolton
(R.) Lloyd Clifton
Ocean Pines G&CC
Ocean City, Maryland
Robert Trent Jones

OCEAN POINT G LINKS
Fripp Island, South Carolina
George W. Cobb
(R.) George W. Cobb, John
LaFoy
OCEAN REEF C (DOLPHIN CSE)
Key Largo, Florida
Mark Mahannah, Charles
Mahannah
(R.) Robert von Hagge, Bruce
Devlin
OCEAN REEF C (HARBOR CSE)
North Key Largo, Florida
Robert von Hagge, Bruce Devlin
OCEAN SHORES GC
Brunswick Heads, Australia
Robert von Hagge, Bruce Devlin
OCEANSIDE CENTER CITY GC
Oceanside, California
William H. Johnson
OCEANSIDE G&CC
Ormond Beach, Florida
Alex Findlay
(R.9 A.9) William H. Diddel
OCEANSIDE MUNI
Oceanside, California
Richard Bigler
OCONOMOWOC CC
Oconomowoc, Wisconsin
Donald Ross
OCONTO GC
Oconto, Wisconsin
A. H. Jolly
OCOTILLO CC
Chandler, Arizona
Ted Robinson
OCOTILLO PARK GC
Hobbs, New Mexico
Warren Cantrell
(A.9) Marvin Ferguson
ODAKYU NISHIFUJI GC
Shizuoka, Japan
Shunsuke Kato
ODAWARA CC
Odawara, Japan
Arthur Davis, Ron Kirby, Gary
Player
ODENSE GC
Odense, Denmark
Jan Sederholm
ODESSA CC
Odessa, Texas
John Bredemus
(R.) *Charles Howard*
O'DONNELL GC
Palm Springs, California
Johnny Dawson, Tom O'Donnell
ODSHERRED GC
Denmark
(R.) Jan Sederholm
ODYSSEY GC
Tinley Park, Illinois
Harry Bowers, *Curtis Strange*
OFFATS BAYOU PARK GC [NLE]
Galveston, Texas
John Bredemus
OGDEN G&CC
Ogden, Utah
(R.) William Howard Neff
**OGLEBAY PARK GC (CRISPEN
CENTER CSE)**
Wheeling, West Virginia
Robert Biery (1936)

OGLEBAY PARK GC (PAR 3 CSE)
Wheeling, West Virginia
William Gordon, David Gordon
**OGLEBAY PARK GC (WHEELING
PARK CSE)**
Wheeling, West Virginia
Robert Biery (9 1928)
OGOSE CC
Japan
Akira Hotti
**OHIO STATE UNIVERSITY GC (GRAY
CSE)**
Columbus, Ohio
Alister Mackenzie
**OHIO STATE UNIVERSITY GC
(SCARLET CSE)**
Columbus, Ohio
Alister Mackenzie
OHIO UNIVERSITY GC
Athens, Ohio
(A.9) Jack Kidwell
OHIRADAI CC
Japan
Sho Sato
OHTAKE GC
Hiroshima, Japan
Mark McCumber
ŌIJAREDS GC (OLD CSE)
Flodda, Sweden
Eric Röhss, Douglas Brazier
ŌIJAREDS GC (NEW CSE)
Flodda, Sweden
Anders Amilon
ŌITA CC
Ōita, Japan
Hiromasa Shimamura
OJAI VALLEY INN & CC
Ojai, California
George C. Thomas, Jr., William
P. Bell
(R.) William F. Bell, William
P. Bell
(R.) Jay Morrish
OKAYAMA KASUMIBASHI GC
Okayama, Japan
T. Harada
OKEECHOBEE G&CC
Okeechobee, Florida
Mark Mahannah
OKEFENOKEE CC [NLE]
Waycross, Georgia
Bill Laffoon
OKEFENOKEE GC
Waycross, Georgia
Joe Lee, Rocky Roquemore
OKLAHOMA CITY G&CC
Oklahoma City, Oklahoma
Perry Maxwell
(R.) Perry Maxwell
(R.10) Floyd Farley
(R.) Don Sechrest
OKOBOJI VU GC
Spirit Lake, Iowa
E. G. McCoy
OLALLA VALLEY GC
Toledo, Oregon
Vernon Warren
OLCHING GC
Munich, Germany
J. F. Dudok van Heel
(R.) Kurt Rossknecht
OLD BALDY C
Saratoga, Wyoming
Henry B. Hughes

OLD CHANNEL TRAIL GC
Montague, Michigan
Robert Bruce Harris
(A.11) Bruce Matthews, Jerry
Matthews
OLD COUNTRY CLUB [NLE]
Flushing, New York
Walter J. Travis
(R.) Devereux Emmet
OLD DEL MONTE G&CC
Monterey, California
Charles Maud
(R.9 A.9) Herbert Fowler
(R.) Jack Neville
(R.) *Nick Lombardo*
OLD ELM C
Fort Sheridan, Illinois
H. S. Colt, Donald Ross
(R.) *Ray Didier*
OLD ELM GC
Abilene, Texas
Warren Cantrell
OLD FLATBUSH CC [NLE]
Brooklyn, New York
Maurice McCarthy
OLD FORT CC
Old Fort, North Carolina
Alfred H. Tull
OLD FORT GC
Murfreesboro, Tennessee
Leon Howard
OLD HICKORY GC
Beaver Dam, Wisconsin
Tom Bendelow
OLD LAKE GC
Aichi, Japan
Tadashi Shimamura
OLD LANDING GC
Rehoboth Beach, Delaware
Frank Murray, Russell Roberts
OLD LYME GC
Old Lyme, Connecticut
(R.) William F. Mitchell
OLD MARSH GC
Palm Beach Gardens, Florida
Pete Dye
OLD MILL G&CC
Winton, North Carolina
Robert Thomason
OLD MILL POND GC
New Brunswick
William G. Robinson
OLD MISSION G&CC [NLE]
Kansas City, Kansas
Harry Robb
OLD NORTH STATE C
Uwharrie Point, North Carolina
Tom Fazio
OLD OAKLAND GC
Oaklandon, Indiana
Charles Maddox, William
Maddox
OLD OAKS CC
Purchase, New York
A. W. Tillinghast (routing), C.
H. Alison, H. S. Colt
(R.) William F. Mitchell
(R.6) Frank Duane
(R.) William Newcomb
OLD ORCHARD GC
Richmond, Texas
Carlton Gipson

OLD ORCHARD GC
Ibaraki, Japan
Jim Fazio
OLD ORCHARD BEACH CC
Old Orchard Beach, Maine
Alex Chisholm
(R.) *George Dunn, Jr.*
OLD PINE GC [NLE]
St. Johnsbury, Vermont
Alex Findlay
OLD RANCH CC
Seal Beach, California
Ted Robinson
OLD RANFURLY GC
Renfrewshire, Scotland
Willie Park, Jr.
OLD SOUTH CC
Lothian, Maryland
Lindsay Ervin
OLD SOUTH G LINKS
Hilton Head Island, South
Carolina
Clyde Johnston
OLD SPANISH FORT CC [NLE]
Mobile, Alabama
Jack Daray
OLD TAPPAN GC
Old Tappan, New Jersey
Hal Purdy
OLD TOWN C
Winston-Salem, North Carolina
Perry Maxwell
OLD TRAIL GC (FAZIO CSE)
Jupiter, Florida
Tom Fazio
OLD TRAIL GC (HILLS CSE)
Jupiter, Florida
Arthur Hills
OLD WAKE GC
Wake Forest, North Carolina
Ron Forse
OLD WARSON CC
Ladue, Missouri
Robert Trent Jones
OLD WAVERLY GC
West Point, Mississippi
Bob Cupp, Jerry Pate
OLD WAYNE GC
Chicago, Illinois
Charles Maddox
OLD WESTBURY CC [NLE]
Garden City, New York
Devereux Emmet
OLD WESTBURY G&CC
Old Westbury, New York
William F. Mitchell
(R.2) Frank Duane
(R.) Stephen Kay
OLD YORK ROAD CC
Spring House, Pennsylvania
(R.) A. W. Tillinghast
**OLDE BARNSTABLE FAIRGROUNDS
GC**
Barnstable, Massachusetts
Brian Silva, Geoffrey S. Cornish
OLDE BEAU GC
Roaring Gap, North Carolina
Billy Satterfield (1990)
OLDE HICKORY GC
Lancaster, Pennsylvania
Edmund B. Ault
OLDE MILL GC
Hillsville, Virginia
Ellis Maples, Dan Maples

OLDE POINT CC
Hampstead, North Carolina
Jerry Turner

OLDENBURGISCHER GC
Germany
Bernhard von Limburger

OLDHAM COUNTY CC
La Grange, Kentucky
Buck Blankenship

OLE MONTEREY CC
Roanoke, Virginia
Fred Findlay

OLENTANGY CC
Columbus, Ohio
Charles Lorms

OLGIATA CC
Rome, Italy
C. K. Cotton, J. J. F. Pennink
(R.) Robert Trent Jones

OLHAIN GC
France
Robert Berthet

OLIVAS PARK MUNI
Ventura, California
William F. Bell

OLIVE BRANCH CC
Olive Branch, Mississippi
Edward Creasey

OLIVE GLENN GC
Cody, Wyoming
Bob Baldock, Robert L. Baldock

OLMOS BASIN GC
San Antonio, Texas
George Hoffman

OLMSTEAD AFB GC
Pennsylvania
Edmund B. Ault

OLNEY G&CC
Olney, Texas
Leon Howard

OLOMANA G LINKS
Waimanolo, Hawaii
Bob Baldock, Robert L. Baldock

OLYMPIA G&CC
Olympia, Washington
William H. Tucker
(A.9) Fred Federspiel

OLYMPIA FIELDS CC (CSE NO. 2)
[NLE]
Olympia Fields, Illinois
Tom Bendelow

OLYMPIA FIELDS CC (CSE NO. 3)
[NLE]
Olympia Fields, Illinois
Willie Watson

OLYMPIA FIELDS CC (NORTH CSE)
Olympia Fields, Illinois
Willie Park, Jr.
(R.) Jack Daray
(R.) Edward Lawrence
Packard
(R.3) Roger Packard

OLYMPIA FIELDS CC (SOUTH CSE)
Olympia Fields, Illinois
Tom Bendelow
(R.) Jack Daray
(R.) Edward Lawrence
Packard

OLYMPIA SPA & CC
Dothan, Alabama
Bob Simmons

OLYMPIC C (LAKE CSE)
San Francisco, California
Willie Watson
(R.) Max Behr
(R.) Sam Whiting
(R.) Robert Trent Jones

OLYMPIC C (OCEAN CSE)
San Francisco, California
Willie Watson
(R.) Max Behr
(R.) Sam Whiting
(R.) Jack Fleming
(R.) *John Fleming*
(R.) Robert Muir Graves

OLYMPIC G&CC
Arlington Heights, Illinois
C. D. Wagstaff

OLYMPIC GC
Hyogo, Japan
Kiyoshi Okawa

OLYMPIC HILLS GC
Eden Prairie, Minnesota
Charles Maddox

OLYMPIC STAFF CC
Yamanashi, Japan
Perry Dye

OLYMPIC VIEW G CSE
Metchosin, British Columbia
William G. Robinson

OMAGH GC
Omagh, Northern Ireland
(R.) Eddie Hackett

OMAHA CC
Omaha, Nebraska
Wayne Stiles, John Van Kleek
(R.) Perry Maxwell
(R.) Dave Bennett

OMI CC
Omi, Japan
Sozaburo Uenishi

OMURAWAN CC
Japan
Shozo Ozasa

ONEIDA G & RIDING C
Green Bay, Wisconsin
Stanley Pelchar
(R. A.2) Bob Lohmann

ONELOA G&CC (NORTH CSE)
Hawaii
Dan Maples

ONELOA G&CC (SOUTH CSE)
Hawaii
Dan Maples

ONEONTA CC
Oneonta, New York
William Harries

ONEOTA CC
Decorah, Iowa
William B. Langford
(R.9 A.9) Don Herfort

ONION CREEK CC
Austin, Texas
Jimmy Demaret
(R.7) Jay Morrish

ONO GC
Hyogo, Japan
O. Ueda

ONOMICHI CC
Onomichi, Japan
Katsumi Takizawa

ONONDAGA G&CC
Fayetteville, New York
Walter J. Travis
(R.) Stanley Thompson
(R.) Hal Purdy
(R.2) Phil Wogan, Samuel
Mitchell

ONOTOYO GC
Hyogo, Japan
O. Ueda

ONTARIO GC
Ontario, New York
George Swatt
(R.) Geoffrey S. Cornish,
Brian Silva

ONTARIO MUNI
Ontario, Oregon
Bob Baldock

ONTARIO NATIONAL GC
Ontario, California
William H. Tucker, Jr.

ONTONAGON GC
Ontonagon, Michigan
Harry E. Flora

ONWENTSIA C
Lake Forest, Illinois
James Foulis, Robert Foulis
(A.9) James Foulis, Robert
Foulis, H. J. Tweedie, H. J.
Whigham
(R.) Ken Killian, Dick Nugent

OOSTERHOUT GC
Netherlands
J. F. Dudok van Heel

OPEQUON CC
Martinsburg, West Virginia
Robert L. Elder

OPORTO GC
Oporto, Portugal
J. J. F. Pennink

OPOTIKI GC
Opotiki, New Zealand
C.H. Redhead

OPPDAL GC
Oppdal, Norway
Jan Sederholm

OPPERDORF ESTATE GC
Berlin, Germany
C. A. Butchart

OQUIRRH HILLS GC
Tooele, Utah
Mick Riley

OQUOSSOC GC [NLE]
Rangeley, Maine
A. H. Fenn

ORANGE BROOK CC (EAST CSE)
Hollywood, Florida
(R.) Red Lawrence

ORANGE BROOK CC (WEST CSE)
Hollywood, Florida
(R.9 A.9) Red Lawrence

ORANGE COUNTY CC
Middletown, New York
(R.3) Al Zikorus

ORANGE HILLS CC
Orange, Connecticut
(A.9) Geoffrey S. Cornish

ORANGE LAKE CC
Kissimmee, Florida
Joe Lee

ORANGE PARK CC
Orange Park, Florida
Bob Walker (routing), *Robert M.
Miller* (1990)

ORANGE TREE CC
Orlando, Florida
Bob Simmons
(R.1) Joe Lee

ORANGE TREE CC
Scottsdale, Arizona
Lawrence Hughes, Johnny Bulla
(R.) Gary Panks
(R.1) Arthur Jack Snyder

[THE] ORCHARD G&CC
Clarkesville, Georgia
Dan Maples

ORCHARD BEACH G&CC
Lake Simcoe, Ontario
Stanley Thompson

ORCHARD GARDENS GC
Burnsville, Minnesota
Dick Phelps

ORCHARD HILLS CC
Waukegan, Illinois
Charles Maddox, *Frank P.
MacDonald*

ORCHARD HILLS CC
Bryan, Ohio
R. Albert Anderson
(R.9 A.9) Arthur Hills

ORCHARD HILLS G&CC
Waukegan, Illinois
Robert Bruce Harris

ORCHARD HILLS G&CC
Chesterland, Ohio
Gordon Alves

ORCHARD HILLS G&CC
Washougal, Washington
William Sander

ORCHARD HILLS GC
Newnan, Georgia
Donald Cottle

ORCHARD HILLS GC
Shelbyville, Michigan
Arthur Young

ORCHARD LAKE CC
Orchard Lake, Michigan
C. H. Alison, H. S. Colt
(R.) Wilfrid Reid, William
Connellan
(R.) William H. Diddel
(R.) Arthur Hills

ORCHARD PARK CC
Buffalo, New York
Walter J. Travis
(R.) William Harries
(R.) Dick Nugent

ORCHARD RIDGE CC
Fort Wayne, Indiana
(R.) Charles Maddox, *Frank
P. MacDonald*

ORCHARD VALLEY GC
Aurora, Illinois
Ken Kavanaugh

[THE] ORCHARDS GC
South Hadley, Massachusetts
Donald Ross

ORCHID ISLAND G & BEACH C
Vero Beach, Florida
Arnold Palmer, Ed Seay

ÖREBRO GC
Örebro, Sweden
Nils Sköld

OREGON GC
West Linn, Oregon
Ken Kavanaugh, *Peter Jacobsen*

OREGON CITY GC
  Oregon City, Oregon
  George Junor, Joe Herberger
ORENCO WOODS GC
  Hillsboro, Oregon
  Darrell Brown
ORETI SANDS GC
  Invercargill, New Zealand
  Sloan Morpeth
ORIENT G&CC
  Taiwan
  Ronald Fream
ORILLIA GC
  Orillia, Ontario
  Robert Moote, *David S. Moote*
ORINDA CC
  Orinda, California
  Willie Watson
    (R.) Robert Muir Graves
ORIOLE G&TC
  Margate, Florida
  Bill Dietsch
ORISTO G&RC
  Edisto Island, South Carolina
  NKA CC of Edisto
ORKNEY GC
  West Transvaal, South Africa
  Robert Grimsdell
ORLEANS GC
  Orleans, Vermont
  Alex Reid
ORMOND G&CC
  Destrehan, Louisiana
  Dick Biddle
ORMSKIRK GC
  Ormskirk, England
  Harold Hilton
ORONO PUBLIC GC
  Wayzata, Minnesota
  Leo J. Feser
ORONOQUE VILLAGE GC
  Stratford, Connecticut
  Desmond Muirhead
ORO VALLEY G&CC
  Tucson, Arizona
  Robert Bruce Harris
    (R.) Dave Bennett
    (R.) Arthur Hills
ORSETT GC
  Essex, England
  James Braid, John R. Stutt
ORTONVILLE GC
  Ortonville, Minnesota
    (R.) Joel Goldstrand
ORYUJI GC
  Nara Prefecture, Japan
  O. Ueda
OSAKA GC
  Osaka, Japan
  O. Ueda
OSAWATOMIE MUNI
  Osawatomie, Kansas
    (A.9) Chet Mendenhall
OSCAR BLOM MUNI
  Springfield, Missouri
    (R.) Don Sechrest
OSCEOLA MUNI
  Pensacola, Florida
  Bill Melhorn
OSHAWA GC
  Oshawa, Ontario
    (R.) Stanley Thompson
    (R.6) Clinton E. Robinson

OSHKOSH CC
  Oshkosh, Wisconsin
  Tom Bendelow
OSIRIS CC
  Walden, New York
  Frank Duane
OSLO-OPPEGARD GC
  Norway
  Gerold Hauser, *Günther Hauser*
OSO BEACH GC
  Corpus Christi, Texas
  John Bredemus
OSPREY COVE GC
  St. Marys, Georgia
  Mark McCumber
OSPREY POINT G LINKS
  Kiawah Island, South Carolina
  Tom Fazio
OSPREY VALLEY G LINKS
  Caledon, Ontario
  Douglas Carrick
OSTERLENS GC
  Simrishann, Sweden
  T. Nordstrom
OSTERAKER GC
  Osteraker, Sweden
  Jan Sederholm
ÖSTERSUND-FRÖSÖ GC
  Fröson, Sweden
  Nils Sköld
OSTSCHWEIZISCHER GC
  Niederburen, Switzerland
  Donald Harradine
OSTWESTFALEN-LIPPE GC
  Bad Salzuflen, Germany
  Bernhard von Limburger
OSWEGO CC [NLE]
  Oswego, New York
  Tom Bendelow
OSWEGO CC
  Oswego, New York
  A. W. Tillinghast
    (A.9) Geoffrey S. Cornish,
    William G. Robinson
OSWEGO LAKE CC
  Lake Oswego, Oregon
  H. Chandler Egan
    (R.) Robert Muir Graves
OSWESTRY GC
  Shropshire, England
  James Braid, John R. Stutt
OTAGO GC
  Balmacewan, New Zealand
  J. A. Somerville
    (R.) *Arthur Ham*
    (R.) *C. H. Redhead*
    (R.) *E. S. Douglas*
OTAKI-JO GC (CASTLE CSE)
  Otaki, Japan
  Takeaki Kaneda
OTHELLO G&CC
  Othello, Washington
  Melvin "Curley" Hueston
    (R.) *Jack Reimer*
OTIS AFB GC
  Falmouth, Massachusetts
  Bob Baldock
OTTAWA CC
  Ottawa, Kansas
  Harry Robb
OTTAWA GC [NLE]
  Ottawa, Ontario
  William F. Davis

OTTAWA HUNT & GC
  Ottawa, Ontario
  Willie Park, Jr.
    (R.) Thomas McBroom
OTTAWA PARK GC
  Toledo, Ohio
  Sylvanus Pierson Jermain
    (R.) Arthur Hills
OTTER CREEK G CSE
  Columbus, Indiana
  Robert Trent Jones
OTTERKILL G&CC
  Newburgh, New York
  William F. Mitchell
OTTO KAHN ESTATE G CSE [NLE]
  Manhasset, New York
  Charles Blair Macdonald, Seth
  Raynor
OTTUMWA G&CC
  Ottumwa, Iowa
  Tom Bendelow
    (A.9) Chic Adams
    (R.) Garrett Gill, George B.
  Williams
OUDENAARDE GC
  Oudenaarde, Belgium
  M. Baker
OUGHTERARD GC
  Oughterard, Ireland
    (A.9) Eddie Hackett
OULD NEWBURY GC
  Newburyport, Massachusetts
  James Lowe, Sr., Ben Pearson
    (R.) Orrin Smith
    (R.) Manny Francis
OULU GOLFKERHO
  Oulu, Finland
  Ronald Fream
OUR CC
  Salem, Wisconsin
  William B. Langford, Theodore
  J. Moreau
OUTDOOR CC
  York, Pennsylvania
  Edmund B. Ault
OUTDOOR RECREATION PAR 3 GC
  New York
  George Swatt
OUTLAW GAP GC
  Huntsville, Texas
  Raymond Outlaw (9 Par 3)
OVERBROOK CC
  Radnor, Pennsylvania
  J. B. McGovern
OVERHILLS GC
  North Carolina
  Donald Ross
OVERLAKE G&CC
  Medina, Washington
  A. Vernon Macon
    (R.) Desmond Muirhead
    (R.) Robert Muir Graves
    (R.2) William G. Robinson
    (R.3) John Steidel
OVERLAND PARK MUNI
  Denver, Colorado
  William H. Tucker
    (A.9) William F. Bell
    (R.) Henry B. Hughes
OVERLAND PARK MUNI
  Overland Park, Kansas
  Floyd Farley

OVEROAKS CC
  Kissimmee, Florida
  Karl Litten, Gary Player
OVERPECK GC
  Teaneck, New Jersey
  Nicholas Psiahas
ÖVIKS PUTTOM GC
  Ömsköldsvik, Sweden
  Nils Sköld
OWATONNA GC
  Owatonna, Minnesota
  Joel Goldstrand
    (A.9) Gerry Pirkl
OWENSBORO CC
  Owensboro, Kentucky
    (R.) Joe Lee
OWEN SOUND GC
  Owen Sound, Ontario
  Stanley Thompson
    (R.9 A.9) Robert Moote
OWL'S CREEK GC
  Virginia Beach, Virginia
  Brook Parker
OWLS HEAD GC
  Mansonville, Quebec
  Graham Cooke
OWOSSO CC
  Owosso, Michigan
  Tom Bendelow
OXBOW CC
  Hickson, North Dakota
  Robert Trent Jones
OXBOW G&CC
  Port LaBelle, Florida
  LeRoy Phillips
OXBOW G&CC
  Belpre, Ohio
  Jack Kidwell, Michael Hurdzan
OXBOW PARK G&CC
  Oxbow, Saskatchewan
  John F. Robinson
OXFORD CC
  Chicopee Falls, Massachusetts
  Phil Wogan
OXFORD G&CC
  Woodstock, Ontario
  Clinton E. Robinson
OXFORD HILLS GC
  Oxford, Michigan
  Jim Hubbard
OXFORDSHIRE GC
  England
  Rees Jones
OXHEY GC [NLE]
  Oxhey, England
  H. S. Colt
OXMOOR G & STEEPLECHASE C
  Louisville, Kentucky
  David Pfaff
OXMOOR VALLEY GC (RIDGE CSE)
  Birmingham, Alabama
  Robert Trent Jones
OXMOOR VALLEY GC (SHORT CSE)
  Birmingham, Alabama
  Robert Trent Jones
OXMOOR VALLEY GC (VALLEY CSE)
  Birmingham, Alabama
  Robert Trent Jones
OXON RUN GC
  Hillcrest Heights, Maryland
  Reuben Hines
OXTON GC
  Nottinghamshire, England
  J. J. F. Pennink

OYSTER BAY G CSE
Woodbury, New York
Tom Fazio
OYSTER BAY G LINKS
Sunset Beach, North Carolina
Dan Maples
OYSTER HARBORS C
Osterville, Massachusetts
Donald Ross
(R.) Stephen Kay
OYSTER REEF GC
Hilton Head Island, South
Carolina
Rees Jones
OZAUKEE CC
Mequon, Wisconsin
William B. Langford, Theodore
J. Moreau
(R.3) David Gill
(R.) Bob Lohmann

PACIFIC CC
Japan
Soichi Murayama
PACIFIC GC
San Clemente, California
Karl Litten, Gary Player
PACIFIC CITY GC
Surfers Paradise, Australia
Jack Nicklaus
PACIFIC GROVE G LINKS
Pacific Grove, California
H. Chandler Egan
(A.9) Jack Neville
PACIFIC HARBOUR G&CC
Fiji
Robert Trent Jones
PACIFIC NATIONAL EXHIBITION GC
British Columbia
(R.) Stanley Thompson
PACIFIC PALISADES GC
Pearl City, Hawaii
Willard Wilkinson
PACKACHAUG HILLS CC
Worchester, Massachusetts
Orrin Smith
PACKANACK GC
Wayne, New Jersey
(A.9) Geoffrey S. Cornish
PADDOCK CC
Florissant, Missouri
Homer Herpel
PADOVA GC
Padova, Italy
John Harris
PADRE ISLES CC
Corpus Christi, Texas
Bruce Littell
PAGANICA CC
Hutchinson, Kansas
NKA [The] Highlands GC
PAGE BELCHER G CSE (OLDE PAGE
CSE)
Tulsa, Oklahoma
Leon Howard
PAGE BELCHER G CSE (STONE
CREEK CSE)
Tulsa, Oklahoma
Don Sechrest
PAGOSA PINES GC
Pagosa Springs, Colorado
NKA Fairfield Pagosa GC

PAINT BRANCH GC
College Park, Maryland
Edmund B. Ault
PAINT CREEK GC
Lake Orion, Michigan
(R.9 A.9) *Robert W. Bills,
Donald L. Childs* (1990)
PAINTED DESERT GC
Las Vegas, Nevada
Jay Morrish
PAINTED DUNES DESERT G CSE
El Paso, Texas
Ken Dye
PAINTED HILLS GC
Mesquite, Nevada
Cal Olson
PAJARO VALLEY CC
Watsonville, California
(R.) Robert Muir Graves
PALACIO DEL MAR GC
California
Gerry Pirkl
PALA MESA G&TC
Fallbrook, California
William H. Johnson
(R.) *Virgil C. "Dick" Rossen*
(R.) Ted Robinson
PALATINE HILLS GC
Palatine, Illinois
Edward Lawrence Packard
PALATKA MUNI
Palatka, Florida
Donald Ross
PALEMBANG GC
Sumatra, Indonesia
J. J. F. Pennink
PALHEIRO GC
Funchal, Portugal
Cabell Robinson
PALI GC
Kaneohe, Oahu, Hawaii
Willard Wilkinson
PALISADE STATE PARK GC
Manti, Utah
Keith Downs
PALISADES CC
Clermont, Florida
Joe Lee
PALISADES PARK GC [NLE]
Michigan
Tom Bendelow
PALLANZA GC
Lake Maggiore, Italy
F. G. Hawtree
PALMA CEIA G&CC
Tampa, Florida
Tom Bendelow
(R.) Donald Ross
(R.) Mark Mahannah, Charles
Mahannah
(R.4) John LaFoy
PALM-AIRE CC (CYPRESS CSE)
Pompano Beach, Florida
George Fazio, Tom Fazio
PALM-AIRE CC (OAKS CSE)
Pompano Beach, Florida
George Fazio, Tom Fazio
PALM-AIRE CC (PALMS CSE)
Pompano Beach, Florida
William F. Mitchell
(R.) Robert von Hagge, Bruce
Devlin

PALM-AIRE CC (SABALS CSE)
Pompano Beach, Florida
Robert von Hagge, Bruce Devlin
PALM-AIRE WEST CC (CHAMPIONS
CSE)
Sarasota, Florida
Dick Wilson
(R.) R. Albert Anderson
PALM-AIRE WEST CC (LAKES CSE)
Sarasota, Florida
Joe Lee
PALMA REAL GC
Ixtapa, Mexico
Robert Trent Jones
PALMARES GC
Algarve, Portugal
J. J. F. Pennink
(R.) J. F. Dudok van Heel
PALMAS DEL MAR GC
Humacao, Puerto Rico
Arthur Davis, Ron Kirby, Gary
Player
PALMA SOLA GC
Bradenton, Florida
Donald Ross
(R.) R. Albert Anderson
PALM BEACH CC
Palm Beach, Florida
Donald Ross
PALM BEACH GC [NLE]
Palm Beach, Florida
Alex Findlay
(R.) A. H. Fenn
PALM BEACH GARDENS MUNI
Palm Beach Gardens, Florida
Roy Case (1991)
PALM BEACH LAKES CC
West Palm Beach, Florida
William F. Mitchell
PALM BEACH NATIONAL G&CC
West Palm Beach, Florida
J. Porter Gibson
(R.) Joe Lee
PALM BEACH PAR 3 GC
Palm Beach, Florida
Dick Wilson
PALM BEACH POLO & CC (CYPRESS
CSE)
West Palm Beach, Florida
P. B. Dye, Pete Dye
PALM BEACH POLO & CC (OLDE
CSE)
West Palm Beach, Florida
George Fazio, Tom Fazio
(R.) Ted McAnlis
PALM BEACH POLO & CC (DUNES
CSE)
West Palm Beach, Florida
Ron Garl, Jerry Pate
PALMBROOK CC
Sun City, Arizona
Jeff Hardin
PALM DESERT CC
Palm Desert, California
William F. Bell
PALM DESERT CC (EXECUTIVE CSE)
Palm Desert, California
William W. Mast
(R.) Robert Muir Graves
PALM DESERT GREENS CC
Palm Desert, California
Ted Robinson

PALM DESERT RESORT CC
Palm Desert, California
Joe Mulleneaux
PALMER HILLS GC
Bettendorf, Iowa
William James Spear
PALMETTO CC
Benton, Louisiana
Perry Maxwell, Press Maxwell
PALMETTO CC
Aiken, South Carolina
Herbert Leeds
(R.) Alister Mackenzie
(R.) Rees Jones
PALMETTO G&CC
Florida
Wayne Stiles, John Van Kleek
PALMETTO GC
Perrine, Florida
Dick Wilson
PALMETTO DUNES CC (FAZIO CSE)
Hilton Head Island, South
Carolina
George Fazio, Tom Fazio
(R.) Clyde Johnston
PALMETTO DUNES CC (HILLS CSE)
Hilton Head Island, South
Carolina
Arthur Hills
PALMETTO DUNES CC (JONES CSE)
Hilton Head Island, South
Carolina
Robert Trent Jones
PALMETTO HALL PLANTATION GC
(BOB CUPP CSE)
Hilton Head Island, South
Carolina
Bob Cupp
PALMETTO HALL PLANTATION GC
(ARTHUR HILLS CSE)
Hilton Head Island, South
Carolina
Arthur Hills
PALMETTO PINE CC
Cape Coral, Florida
Arthur Hills
PALM GARDENS GC
Melbourne, Florida
Edward Ryder
PALM HARBOR GC
Flager Beach, Florida
Bill Amick
PALM HILLS G RESORT
Naha, Okinawa
Ronald Fream
PALMIA PUTTING CSE
Mission Viejo, California
Scott Miller
PALM LAKES GC
Fresno, California
Richard Bigler
PALM MEADOWS GC
Norton AFB, California
William F. Bell
PALM MEADOWS G CSE
Surfers Paradise, Australia
Robin Nelson, *Graham Marsh*
PALM RIVER CC
Naples, Florida
Ben W. Zink
PALMS OF TERRA CEIA GC
Palmetto, Florida
Ted McAnlis

PALM SPRINGS CC
Palm Springs, California
Joe Kirkwood, Paul J. Addessi
PALM SPRINGS MUNI
Palm Springs, California
William F. Bell
PALM SPRINGS RIVIERA GC [NLE]
Palm Springs, California
Don Crabtree
PALM SPRINGS RV RESORT & CC
Cathedral City, California
Ron Garl
PALM VALLEY CC (NORTH CSE)
Palm Desert, California
Ted Robinson
PALM VALLEY CC (SOUTH CSE)
Palm Desert, California
Ted Robinson
PALM VALLEY GC
Ponte Vedra, Florida
Jack Hord
PALM VIEW HILLS GC
Palmetto, Florida
Dick Hamilton
PALM VIEW MUNI
McAllen, Texas
Ralph Plummer
PALMYRA GC
Palmyra, Maine
Frank Randall
    (R.) *Dick Cayer*
PALO ALTO HILLS G&CC
Palo Alto, California
Clark Glasson
    (R.5) Robert Muir Graves
    (R.) Gary Roger Baird
    (R.) Ronald Fream
PALO ALTO MUNI
Palo Alto, California
William F. Bell, William P. Bell
    (R.) Robert Trent Jones, Jr.
PALO ALTO VA HOSPITAL GC
Palo Alto, California
Bob Baldock
PALOLO MUNI [NLE]
Hawaii
Alex Bell
PALOS CC
Palos Park, Illinois
Charles Maddox, *Frank P.
MacDonald*
PALOS HILLS GC
Palos Heights, Illinois
David Gill
PALOS VERDES CC
Palos Verdes Estates, California
George C. Thomas, Jr., William
P. Bell
    (R.) *David W. Kent*
    (R.) Ted Robinson
    (R.) Robert Muir Graves
    (R.) Arthur Hills
PANAMA CC
Lynn Haven, Florida
Donald Ross
PANAMA CITY CC
Panama City, Panama
Dick Wilson
PANAMA CITY BEACH GC
Panama City Beach, Florida
Bill Amick

PANNAL GC
Yorkshire, England
Sandy Herd
    (R.) *Charles A. Mackenzie*
PANORAMA CC
Conroe, Texas
Jack B. Miller
    (R.) Joseph S. Finger, Ken
Dye
PANORAMA RESORT G&CC
Invermere, British Columbia
Bill Newis
PANORAMA VILLAGE GC
Hemet, California
Harry Rainville, David Rainville
PANSHANGER GC
Hertfordshire, England
John Harris
PANTAI MENTIRI GC
Bandar Seri, Brunei, Borneo
Ronald Fream
PANTHER CREEK CC
Springfield, Illinois
Dick Phelps, Hale Irwin
PANTHER VALLEY CC
Allamuchy, New Jersey
Robert Trent Jones
PANYA HILL GC
Bangkok, Thailand
Ronald Fream
PANYA INDRA GC
Bangkok, Thailand
Ronald Fream
PANYA PARK CC
Chon Buri, Thailand
Ronald Fream
PAOLA CC
Paola, Kansas
James S. Watson
PAPAGO PARK GC
Phoenix, Arizona
William F. Bell
    (R.) Arthur Jack Snyder
PARADISE CANYON G&CC
Lethbridge, Alberta
Bill Newis
PARADISE HILLS G&CC
Albuquerque, New Mexico
NKA Double Eagle CC
PARADISE INN RANCH GC
Grants Pass, Oregon
Robert Muir Graves
PARADISE ISLAND G&CC
Nassau, Bahamas
Dick Wilson, Joe Lee
PARADISE PARK GC
Jamaica
    (R.) Robert Moote
PARADISE PEAK WEST GC
Scottsdale, Arizona
Gary Grandstaff
PARADISE PINES GC
Magalia, California
Bob Baldock
PARADISE POINT GC (GOLD CSE)
Camp LeJeune, North Carolina
Fred Findlay
    (R.7) Edmund B. Ault
PARADISE POINT GC (GREEN CSE)
Camp LeJeune, North Carolina
Fred Findlay

PARADISE POINTE GC
Smithville, Missouri
Tom Clark, Edmund B. Ault,
Brian Ault
PARADISE SPRINGS GC
Paradise Springs, Maine
Donald Ross
PARADISE VALLEY CC
Scottsdale, Arizona
Lawrence Hughes
    (R.) Geoffrey S. Cornish,
Gary Panks
PARADISE VALLEY CC
Englewood, California
Henry B. Hughes
PARADISE VALLEY CC
Las Vegas, Nevada
NKA Royal Kenfield GC
PARADISE VALLEY CC
Casper, Wyoming
Henry B. Hughes
PARADISE VALLEY GC
Fairfield, California
Robert Muir Graves
PARADISE VALLEY PARK GC [NLE]
Phoenix, Arizona
Milt Coggins
PARADISE VALLEY PARK GC
Phoenix, Arizona
Jeff Hardin
PARAMUS G&CC
Paramus, New Jersey
    (R.) Stephen Kay
PARAPARAUMU BEACH GC
New Zealand
James Watt
    (R.) Alex Russell
PARC DE LOISIRS GC
Caen, France
Martin Hawtree
PARCOURS DU CERF
Longueuil, Quebec
Graham Cooke
PARIS HILL CC
South Paris, Maine
    (R.) *Harvey Lamontagne*
PARIS LANDING STATE PARK GC
Buchanan, Tennessee
Benjamin Wihry
    (R.) Arthur L. Davis
PARISO SPRINGS CC
Soledad, California
Bob Baldock
[THE] PARK CC
Buffalo, New York
C. H. Alison, H. S. Colt
    (R.) Arthur Hills
PARK CITY GC
Park City, Utah
William H. Neff
    (R.9 A.9) Press Maxwell
    (R.) William Howard Neff
PARKE COUNTY G CSE
Rockville, Indiana
William H. Diddel
PARKERSBURG CC
Vienna, West Virginia
    (R.) Edmund B. Ault
PARK FOREST GC [NLE]
Illinois
Harry Collis
PARK HILLS CC
Pratt, Kansas
    (R.) Smiley Bell

PARK HILLS CC
Altoona, Pennsylvania
James Gilmore Harrison
PARK HILLS GC (EAST CSE)
Freeport, Illinois
C. D. Wagstaff
PARK HILLS GC (WEST CSE)
Freeport, Illinois
C. D. Wagstaff
PARKHURST CC [NLE]
Boynton Beach, Florida
William B. Langford,
Theodore J. Moreau
PARK LAKE GC
Des Plaines, Illinois
C. D. Wagstaff
PARK MAMMOTH GC
Park City, Kentucky
Buck Blankenship
PARK MEADOWS GC
Park City, Utah
Jack Nicklaus
PARKNASILLA GC
Parknasilla, Ireland
    (R.) Eddie Hackett
PARK PLACE GC
De Kalb, Illinois
William James Spear
PARKRIDGE CC
California
John Duncan Dunn
PARK RIDGE CC
Park Ridge, Illinois
H. J. Tweedie
    (R.) William B. Langford
    (R.4) David Gill
    (R.3) Ken Killian, Dick
Nugent
PARKSTONE GC
Dorset, England
Willie Park, Jr.
    (R.) James Braid, John R.
Stutt
    (R.) J. Hamilton Stutt
PARKVIEW GC
Milliken, Ontario
Clinton E. Robinson
PARKVIEW HEIGHTS GC
Mayfield Heights, Ohio
Richard W. LaConte
PARKVIEW MANOR GC
Hershey, Pennsylvania
Maurice McCarthy
PARKVIEW MUNI
Pekin, Illinois
Charles Maddox, *Frank P.
MacDonald*
    (R.9 A.9) Robert Bruce Harris
PARKWAY G CSE
Fremont, California
Robert Muir Graves
PARLOR CITY CC
Bluffton, Indiana
    (A.9) *Henry Culp*
PAR MAR PINES GC
Parkersburg, West Virginia
    (R.) James Root
PAR MOR GC
East Lansing, Michigan
Art Prior
PARQUE DA FLORESTA GC
Lagos, Portugal
Pepe Gancedo

PARRIS ISLAND GC
Beaufort, South Carolina
Fred Findlay
PARRY SOUND G&CC
Parry Sound, Ontario
Thomas McBroom
PAR THREE GC
Daytona Beach, Florida
John T. Williamson
PAR THREE GC
Lakeland, Florida
Hans Schmeisser
PAR THREE GC
North Olmstead, Ohio
Harold Paddock
PARTILLE GC
Partille, Sweden
Jan Sederholm
PARTRIDGE POINT GC
Ludington, Michigan
William Newcomb
PASADENA MUNI
Pasadena, Texas
Jay Riviere
PASADENA GC [NLE]
Pasadena, California
Max Behr
(R.) George O'Neil, *Jack Croke*
(R.) William P. Bell
PASADENA GC
St. Petersburg, Florida
Wayne Stiles, John Van Kleek, Walter Hagen
(R.) Bill Dietsch
(R.) Arnold Palmer, Ed Seay
PASATIEMPO GC
Santa Cruz, California
Alister Mackenzie
(R.) Clark Glasson
(R.) Gary Roger Baird
(R.) Robert Trent Jones, Jr.
(R.) Robert Muir Graves
PASCACK BROOK G&CC
Riverdale, New Jersey
John Handwerg, Jr.
(R.) Stephen Kay
PASO ROBLES G&CC
Paso Robles, California
Bert Stamps
PASO ROBLES GC [NLE]
Paso Robles, California
Tom Bendelow
PASSACONAWAY GC
Litchfield, New Hampshire
Brian Silva, Geoffrey S. Cornish
PASSAIC COUNTY GC
Wayne, New Jersey
(A.9) Alfred H. Tull
PASS CHRISTIAN CC
Pass Christian, Mississippi
Tom Bendelow
(R.) *Alex Cunningham*
PASTURES GC
Derbyshire, England
J. J. F. Pennink
PATRICK AFB GC
Cocoa Beach, Florida
Robert Trent Jones
(R.) Bill Amick
PATRIOTS POINT G LINKS
Charleston, South Carolina
Willard Byrd

PATRIZIALE ASCONA GC
Ascona, Switzerland
(R.) John D. Harris, C. K. Cotton
PATSHULL PARK GC
Staffordshire, England
John Jacobs
PATTERSON C
Fairfield, Connecticut
Robert Trent Jones
(R.1) Frank Duane
(R.2) Stephen Kay
PATTON BROOK GC
Southington, Connecticut
Geoffrey S. Cornish, William G. Robinson
PATTY JEWETT GC
Colorado Springs, Colorado
Willie Campbell (9 1910)
(A.9) Press Maxwell
PATUXENT GREENS CC
Laurel, Maryland
(R.) Buddy Loving
PAU GC
Pau, France
Willie Dunn
PAUL BLOCK PRIVATE CSE
Greenwich, Connecticut
Wayne Stiles, John Van Kleek
PAUL SMITH'S ADIRONDACK C
New York
Seymour Dunn
PAULS VALLEY MUNI
Pauls Valley, Oklahoma
Bob Dunning
PAUMA VALLEY CC
Pauma Valley, California
Robert Trent Jones
(R.1) Ted Robinson
PAUTIPAUG CC
Norwich, Connecticut
Geoffrey S. Cornish
(R.) Al Zikorus
PAWLEYS PLANTATION GC
Pawleys Island, South Carolina
Jack Nicklaus
PAWNEE BILL STATE PARK G CSE
Pawnee, Oklahoma
Leon Howard
PAWNEE PRAIRIE MUNI
Wichita, Kansas
Bob Dunning
PAWPAW CC
Bamberg, South Carolina
Russell Breeden
PAWTUCKET GC
Pawtucket, Rhode Island
Willie Park, Jr.
PAWTUCKETT GC
Charlotte, North Carolina
Russell Breeden
PAXON HOLLOW CC
Media, Pennsylvania
(R.) James Blaukovitch
PEACEFUL VALLEY CC
Colorado Springs, Colorado
Dave Bennett, *Lee Trevino*
PEACE PIPE CC
Denville, New Jersey
Sidney C. Lee
PEACE PORTAL GC
British Columbia
(R.) Stan Leonard, *Philip Tattersfield*

PEACH TREE CC
Marysville, California
Bob Baldock
PEACH TREE GC
Atlanta, Georgia
Robert Trent Jones, Robert Tyre "Bobby" Jones, Jr.
(R.) Joseph S. Finger
PEACH TREE GC
Bullard, Texas
Dr. C. R. Hurst, Buddy Bridges
PEACHTREE HILLS GC
Spring Hope, North Carolina
R. W. Renn
PEARL CC
Kaonohi, Oahu, Hawaii
Akiro Sato
(R.1) Robin Nelson
PEARL HARBOR GC [NLE]
Pearl Harbor, Oahu, Hawaii
Thomas O. Brandon
[THE] PEARL G LINKS (EAST CSE)
Sunset Beach, North Carolina
Dan Maples
[THE] PEARL G LINKS (WEST CSE)
Sunset Beach, North Carolina
Dan Maples
PEARL RIVER VALLEY CC
Poplarville, Mississippi
W.W. *Kilby*
PEASE AFB GC
Portsmouth, New Hampshire
Al Zikorus
PEBBLE BEACH G LINKS
Pebble Beach, California
Jack Neville, *Douglas S. Grant*
(R.) Herbert Fowler
(R.) H. Chandler Egan, Robert Hunter, *Roger Lapham*
(R.) Jack Neville, *Frank "Sandy" Tatum*
(R.) Ed Connor
(R.) Jack Nicklaus
PEBBLE BROOK CC
Manchester, Georgia
Arthur Davis, Ron Kirby
PEBBLE BROOK CC
Cleveland, Ohio
Ben W. Zink
PEBBLE BROOK G&CC (NORTH CSE)
Noblesville, Indiana
Gary Kern, Ron Kern
PEBBLE BROOK G&CC (SOUTH CSE)
Noblesville, Indiana
James Dugan
PEBBLEBROOK GC
Sun City West, Arizona
Jeff Hardin, Greg Nash
PEBBLE CREEK CC
Taylors, South Carolina
Tom Jackson
PEBBLE CREEK GC
Becker, Minnesota
Don Herfort
PEBBLE CREEK GC
Lexington, Ohio
William F. Mitchell
PEBBLEWOOD CC
Bridgman, Michigan
George B. Ferry
PECAN GROVE PLANTATION CC
Richmond, Texas
Carlton Gipson

PECAN HOLLOW GC
Lancaster, Texas
Billy Martindale
PECAN PLANTATION GC
Granbury, Texas
Leon Howard
PECAN VALLEY CC
San Antonio, Texas
Press Maxwell
(R.) Garrett Gill, George B. Williams
PECAN VALLEY MUNI (HILLS CSE)
Fort Worth, Texas
Ralph Plummer
(R.9 A.9) Dave Bennett
PECAN VALLEY MUNI (RIVER CSE)
Fort Worth, Texas
Ralph Plummer
PECKETTS CC [NLE]
Sugar Hill, New Hampshire
Ralph Barton
PEDERNALES CC
Spicewood, Texas
Leon Howard
PEDLEY PAR 3 GC
Los Angeles, California
William H. Johnson
PEEBLES GC
Lothian, Scotland
James Braid
(R.) H. S. Colt
PEEK 'N PEAK GC
Clymer, New York
Ferdinand Garbin
PEEL GC
Isle of Man
Sandy Herd
(R.) James Braid
PEEL VILLAGE GC
Brampton, Ontario
(R.) Robert Moote, David L. Moote
PEKIN CC
Pekin, Illinois
Edward Lawrence Packard
PELHAM BAY PARK GC (PELHAM CSE)
Bronx, New York
Lawrence Van Etten
(R.) John Van Kleek
PELHAM BAY PARK GC (SPLIT ROCK CSE)
Bronx, New York
John Van Kleek
PELHAM CC [NLE]
Pelham, New York
Lawrence Van Etten
PELHAM CC
Pelham Manor, New York
Devereux Emmet
(R.) Alfred H. Tull
(R.) Robert Trent Jones
(R.) Stephen Kay
PELHAM MANOR GC [NLE]
New York
Tom Bendelow
PELICAN BAY G&CC (NORTH CSE)
Daytona Beach, Florida
Bill Amick
(R.) Al Zikorus
PELICAN BAY G&CC (SOUTH CSE)
Daytona Beach, Florida
Lloyd Clifton

Pelican's Nest GC
Bonita Springs, Florida
Tom Fazio

Pelican GC
Clearwater, Florida
NKA Belleview Mido CC

Pelican Hill GC (Canyon Cse)
Newport Beach, California
Tom Fazio

Pelican Hill GC (Ocean Cse)
Newport Beach, California
Tom Fazio

Pella G&CC
Pella, Iowa
(R.) Charles Calhoun

Pembroke CC
Pembroke, Massachusetts
Phil Wogan

Pembroke GC
Pembroke, Ontario
(A.9) Graham Cooke

Pembroke Lakes G&CC
Hollywood, Florida
Howard Watson

Penas Rojas GC
Alicante, Spain
John Harris

Pendaries G&CC
Rociada, New Mexico
Donald K. Burns

Penderbrook GC
Fairfax, Virginia
Edmund B. Ault

Pender Island G&CC
British Columbia
Sandy Crawford

Pendleton CC
Pendleton, Oregon
Frank James

Penfield CC
Penfield, New York
Pete Craig

Penha Longa GC
Lisbon, Portugal
Robert Trent Jones, Jr.

Penina GC
Portugal
Henry Cotton
(A.3rd 9) Henry Cotton

[The] Peninsula C
Huntersville, North Carolina
Rees Jones

Peninsula G&CC
San Mateo, California
Donald Ross
(R.) Clark Glasson
(R.) Robert Muir Graves
(R.) Ronald Fream

Peninsula G&CC
Australia
(R.) Peter Thomson, Michael Wolveridge

Peninsula GC
Amityville, New York
Maurice McCarthy

Peninsula GC
Marathon, Ontario
Stanley Thompson

Peninsula Park GC
Portage, Ontario
Stanley Thompson

Peninsula State Park GC
Fish Creek, Wisconsin
Edward Lawrence Packard

Pennant Hills GC
Sydney, Australia
Eric B. Apperly

Pennbrook GC
Basking Ridge, New Jersey
NKA Basking Ridge GC

Penn Hills C
Bradford, Pennsylvania
(R.9 A.9) Dick Wilson

Pennhurst CC [NLE]
Turtle Creek, Pennsylvania
James Gilmore Harrison

Penn Oaks CC
West Chester, Pennsylvania
Russell Roberts

Penn State University GC (Blue Cse)
State College, Pennsylvania
Willie Park, Jr.
(R.) James Gilmore Harrison, Ferdinand Garbin

Penn State University GC (White Cse)
State College, Pennsylvania
James Gilmore Harrison, Ferdinand Garbin

Pennsylvania National G&CC
Fayetteville, Pennsylvania
Edmund B. Ault

Pennyrile Forest State Park GC
Dawson Springs, Kentucky
Edward Lawrence Packard

Penobscot Valley CC
Bangor, Maine
Donald Ross

Pen Park GC
Charlottesville, Virginia
Buddy Loving

Penrhos GC
Gwynedd, Wales
Fred W. Hawtree, Martin Hawtree

Penrose Park GC
Reidsville, North Carolina
Donald Ross

Pensacola CC
Pensacola, Florida
A. S. Butterworth
(A.9) W. A. Blunt

Penticton G&CC
Penticton, British Columbia
A. Vernon Macan
(A.9) Norman H. Woods
(R.) Les Furber, *Jim Eremko*

Penwortham GC
England
Tom Dunn

Peoria North Shore CC [NLE]
Peoria, Illinois
Tom Bendelow

Pepperdine G&CC
Sturgeon Bay, Wisconsin
Dave Truttman

Peppermill Palms G Cse
Arizona Strip, Arizona
William Hull (1989)

Pepper Pike C
Cleveland, Ohio
William S. Flynn

Pequabuc CC
Bristol, Connecticut
(A.3) Geoffrey S. Cornish, William G. Robinson

Perdido Bay CC
Pensacola, Florida
Bill Amick

Perham Lakeside CC
Perham, Minnesota
(A.9) Joel Goldstrand

Peri GC
Redding, California
Cal Olson

Peridia G&CC
Bradenton, Florida
William B. Lewis

Perranporth GC
Cornwall, England
James Braid, John R. Stutt
(R.) J. Hamilton Stutt

Perrin AFB GC
Sherman, Texas
Joseph S. Finger

Perry CC
Perry, Georgia
Sid Clarke

Perry G&CC
Perry, Florida
Walter Ripley

Perry Hollow GC
Wolfeboro, New Hampshire
Brian Silva, Geoffrey S. Cornish

Perry Park CC
Larkspur, Colorado
Dick Phelps

Persepolis GC
Iran
Jack Armitage

Persimmon Hill CC
Saluda, South Carolina
Fred Bolton

Persimmon Ridge GC
Anchorage, Kentucky
Arthur Hills

Perstorp GC
Sweden
Anders Amilon, Ake Persson

Perth GC
Perthshire, Scotland
Old Tom Morris

Petaluma G&CC
Petaluma, California
(R.) Gary Roger Baird

Petawawa GC
Petawawa, Ontario
(A.9) Graham Cooke

Pete Dye G Cse
West Virginia
Pete Dye

Pete Dye Royal GC
Japan
Perry Dye

Peterborough G&CC
Peterborough, Ontario
(R.) Stanley Thompson

Peter Hay GC
Pebble Beach, California
Leonard G. Feliciano

Peter Jans GC
Evanston, Illinois
Todd Sloan

Peter Pan CC [NLE]
California
John Duncan Dunn

Petersborough Milton GC
Northamptonshire, England
James Braid, John R. Stutt

Peterson Field GC
Colorado Springs, Colorado
Dick Phelps

Petoskey Bay View CC
Petoskey, Michigan
(R.) Jeff Gorney

Petrifying Springs GC
Kenosha, Wisconsin
Joseph A. Roseman

Petropolis CC
Petropolis, Brazil
Antonio F. Bennett

Peurunka GC
Laukaa, Finland
Ronald Fream

Pevero GC
Costa Smeralda, Sardinia
Robert Trent Jones

Pfalz GC
Neustadt, Germany
Bernhard von Limburger

Pforzheim GC
Pforzheim, Germany
Reinhold Weishaupt

PGA National GC (Champion Cse)
Palm Beach Gardens, Florida
Tom Fazio
(R.) Jack Nicklaus

PGA National GC (Estates Cse)
Lake Park, Florida
Karl Litten

PGA National GC (General Cse)
Palm Beach Gardens, Florida
Arnold Palmer, Ed Seay

PGA National GC (Haig Cse)
Palm Beach Gardens, Florida
Tom Fazio

PGA National GC (Squire Cse)
Palm Beach Gardens, Florida
Tom Fazio

PGA West GC (Nicklaus Private Cse)
La Quinta, California
Jack Nicklaus

PGA West GC (Nicklaus Resort Cse)
La Quinta, California
Jack Nicklaus

PGA West GC (Palmer Cse)
La Quinta, California
Arnold Palmer, Ed Seay

PGA West GC (Stadium Cse)
La Quinta, California
Pete Dye

Phalen Park GC
St. Paul, Minnesota
(R.) Don Herfort

Pharaoh's CC
Corpus Christi, Texas
Ralph Plummer

Pheasant Ridge CC
Gilford, New Hampshire
Geoffrey S. Cornish

Pheasant Ridge GC
Cedar Falls, Iowa
Gerry Pirkl, *Donald G. Brauer, Emil Perret, Paul S. Fjare*

Pheasant Run CC
Newmarket, Ontario
René Muylaert, *Charles Muylaert*

Pheasant Run Lodge GC
St. Charles, Illinois
William Maddox

PHEASANT VALLEY GC
Crown Point, Indiana
R. Albert Anderson
PHELPS MANOR GC
Teaneck, New Jersey
William H. Tucker
PHILADELPHIA CC
Philadelphia, Pennsylvania
NKA Bala GC
PHILADELPHIA CC
Gladwyne, Pennsylvania
William S. Flynn, Howard
Toomey
    (R.) William S. Flynn, Perry
    Maxwell
    (A.3rd 9) Tom Fazio
PHILADELPHIA CRICKET C [NLE]
Philadelphia, Pennsylvania
NKA Flourtown CC
PHILADELPHIA CRICKET C
Flourtown, Pennsylvania
A. W. Tillinghast
PHILIPPINES CC
Philippines
Bob Baldock
PHILLIPSBURG CC
Phillipsburg, Pennsylvania
Alex Findlay
PHILLIPS PARK MUNI
Aurora, Illinois
Spencer Meister
PHILMONT CC (NORTH CSE)
Huntingdon Valley,
Pennsylvania
William S. Flynn, Howard
Toomey
    (R.) William Gordon, David
    Gordon
PHILMONT CC (SOUTH CSE)
Huntingdon Valley,
Pennsylvania
Willie Park, Jr.
[THE] PHOENICIAN G&RC
Phoenix, Arizona
Arthur Jack Snyder
    (R.) Homer Flint
PHOENIX CC
Phoenix, Arizona
Harry Collis
    (R.14) Gary Panks
PHOENIX G&CC
Pattaya, Thailand
Denis Griffiths
PHOENIX LAKE GC
Sonora, California
Bert Stamps
PIANDISCOLE GC
Premeno, Italy
John Harris
PICACHO HILLS CC
Las Cruces, New Mexico
Joseph S. Finger
PICATINNY ARSENAL GC
Dover, New Jersey
Skip Wogan
PICHEROAK GC
Worchestershire, England
D. M. A. Steel
PICKAWAY CC
Circleville, Ohio
Jack Kidwell
PICKENS COUNTY CC
Georgia
    (R.) Robert Renaud

PICTURE BUTTE G & WINTER C
Picture Butte, Alberta
Les Furber, Jim Eremko
PIEDMONT CRESCENT CC
Graham, North Carolina
NKA Quarry Hills CC
PIENCORT CC
Normandy, France
J. Hamilton Stutt
PIERCE PARK MUNI
Flint, Michigan
Frederick A. Ellis
PIERRE MARQUES GC
Acapulco, Mexico
Percy Clifford
    (R.) Robert Trent Jones
PIKE CREEK VALLEY GC
Wilmington, Delaware
NKA Three Little Bakers GC
PIKEFOLD GC
Manchester, England
E. W. Philips
PIKE RUN CC
Donegal, Pennsylvania
    (R.) James Gilmore Harrison
PILAR GC
Buenos Aires, Argentina
Ron Fream
PILGRIM'S HARBOR CC
Wallingford, Connecticut
Alfred H. Tull
PILMOOR ESTATE GC
Kuala Lumpur, Malaysia
Ronald Fream
PILOT KNOB PARK GC
Pilot Mountain, North Carolina
Gene Hamm
PILTDOWN GC
England
    (R.) G. M. Dodd
PIMA G RESORT
Scottsdale, Arizona
William F. Bell
PINAWA GC
Manitoba
Howard Watson
PINCH BROOK GC
Florham Park, New Jersey
Rees Jones
PINE ACRES CC
Bradford, Pennsylvania
James Gilmore Harrison
PINE BLUFF CC
Pine Bluff, Arkansas
Herman Hackbarth
    (R.9 A.9) Joseph S. Finger
PINE BROOK CC
Weston, Massachusetts
Wayne Stiles, John Van Kleek
    (R.) Brian Silva, Geoffrey S.
    Cornish
PINE BROOK CC
Winston-Salem, North Carolina
Ellis Maples
PINEBROOK G&CC
Calgary, Alberta
    (R.) Bill Newis
PINE BURR CC
Wiggins, Mississippi
Earl Stone
PINE CLIFFS G&CC
Albufeira, Portugal
Martin Hawtree, Simon Gidman

PINE CREEK GC
La Crescent, Minnesota
Sylvester Krajewski
PINE CREEK G CSE
Colorado Springs, Colorado
Dick Phelps
PINE CREST CC
Gardendale, Alabama
Bancroft Timmons
PINECREST CC
Pelham, Georgia
    (R.) Hugh Moore
PINECREST CC
Longview, Texas
    (R.9 A.9) Press Maxwell
PINECREST CC (CSE NO. 2)
Fairfax, Virginia
Al Jamison
PINECREST G&CC
Huntley, Illinois
Ted Lockie
    (R.) Ken Killian, Dick Nugent
    (R.) Bob Lohmann
PINECREST G&CC
Winslow, New Jersey
Ralph Leopardi
PINECREST GC
Lansdale, Pennsylvania
Ron Prichard
PINECREST GC
Trinity, Texas
Jay Riviere
PINECREST GC
Annandale, Virginia
Leon Howard
PINECREST MUNI
Idaho Falls, Idaho
Frank James
PINECREST ON LOTELA GC
Avon Park, Florida
Donald Ross
PINE FOREST CC [NLE]
Houston, Texas
John Bredemus
    (R.9) Ralph Plummer
PINE FOREST CC
Houston, Texas
Jay Riviere
PINE FOREST GC
Bastrop, Texas
Billy Martindale
PINE GROVE CC
Iron Mountain, Michigan
    (A.9) Edward Lawrence
    Packard
    (R.) Don Herfort
PINEGROVE G&CC
Montreal, Quebec
Howard Watson
    (R.3) John Watson
PINE GROVE GC
Sudbury, Ontario
    (A.9) John F. Robinson,
    William G. Robinson
PINE HARBOR G&RC
Pell City, Alabama
Harold Williams
PINEHAVEN CC
Guilderland, New York
James Thomson, Armand Farina
PINE HILL GC [NLE]
Windsor, Connecticut
Everett Pyle

PINE HILL GC
Brewer, Maine
Charlie Emery
PINE HILL GC
Brutus, Michigan
Larry Holbert
PINE HILL ESTATES GC
Mashpee, Massachusetts
Phil Wogan
PINE HILLS CC
Decatur, Georgia
Joe Lee, Rocky Roquemore
PINE HILLS CC
Calhoun City, Mississippi
George C. Curtis
PINE HILLS G&CC
Penticton, British Columbia
Norman H. Woods
PINE HILLS GC
Ottawa, Illinois
Tom Bendelow
PINE HILLS GC
West Monroe, Louisiana
George C. Curtis
    (R.) Jay Riviere
PINE HILLS GC [NLE]
Bay St. Louis, Mississippi
Jack Daray
PINE HILLS GC
Carrol, Ohio
Jack Kidwell
PINE HILLS GC
Cleveland, Ohio
Harold Paddock
PINE HILLS GC
Woodville, Texas
Leon Howard
PINE HILLS GC [AKA SHEBOYGAN
CC]
Sheboygan, Wisconsin
Harry B. Smead (1928)
PINE HOLLOW CC
East Norwich, New York
William F. Mitchell
PINE HOLLOW GC
Clayton, North Carolina
Maurice Brackett (1960)
PINEHURST CC
Denver, Colorado
Press Maxwell
PINEHURST CC (CSE NO. 1)
Pinehurst, North Carolina
James W. Tufts, Leonard Tufts,
Dr. D. Leroy Culver
    (R.9 A.9) Donald Ross
    (R.) Donald Ross
PINEHURST CC (CSE NO. 2)
Pinehurst, North Carolina
Donald Ross
    (A.9) Donald Ross
    (R.) Donald Ross (1925)
    (R.) Donald Ross (1935)
    (R.) Richard S. Tufts
    (R.) Peter V. Tufts
PINEHURST CC (CSE NO. 3)
Pinehurst, North Carolina
Donald Ross
    (R.) Donald Ross
PINEHURST CC (CSE NO. 4) [NLE]
Pinehurst, North Carolina
Donald Ross

PINEHURST CC (CSE NO. 4)
Pinehurst, North Carolina
Richard S. Tufts
   (R.) Robert Trent Jones
PINEHURST CC (CSE NO. 5) [NLE]
Pinehurst, North Carolina
Donald Ross
PINEHURST CC (CSE NO. 5)
Pinehurst, North Carolina
Ellis Maples, Richard S. Tufts
   (R.) Robert Trent Jones
PINEHURST CC (CSE NO 6)
Pinehurst, North Carolina
George Fazio, Tom Fazio
PINEHURST CC (CSE NO. 7)
Pinehurst, North Carolina
Rees Jones
PINEHURST CC
Orange, Texas
Donald Ross
PINEHURST NATIONAL GC
Pinehurst, North Carolina
Jack Nicklaus
PINEHURST PLANTATION GC
Pinehurst, North Carolina
Arnold Palmer, Ed Seay
PINE ISLAND CC
Charlotte, North Carolina
Charles Mahannah
PINE ISLAND GC
Ocean Springs, Mississippi
Pete Dye
PINE KNOB GC
Clarkston, Michigan
Leo Bishop
PINEKNOLL CC
Sylvester, Georgia
Bill Amick
PINE KNOT G&CC
Dorchester, Ontario
John F. Robinson
PINE LAKE CC
Orchard Lake, Michigan
Willie Park, Jr.
   (R.1) Bruce Matthews, Jerry
   Matthews
   (R.) Robert von Hagge
   (R.) William Newcomb
   (R.16 A.2) Jerry Matthews
PINE LAKE CC
Charlotte, North Carolina
Gene Hamm
   (R.9 A.9) J. Porter Gibson
   (R.) John LaFoy
PINE LAKE CC
Anderson, South Carolina
James T. Shirley
PINE LAKE GC
Lincoln, Nebraska
Richard Watson
PINE LAKE GC
Ontario
   (A.9) Clinton E. Robinson
PINE LAKE GC
Japan
Robert Trent Jones
PINE LAKE G CSE
Haslett, Michigan
Bob Wilkins (1962)
PINE LAKES GC
Naples, Florida
Arthur Hills

PINE LAKES GC
Palm Coast, Florida
Arnold Palmer, Ed Seay
PINE LAKES GC
Stuart, Florida
Arthur Young
PINE LAKES INTERNATIONAL GC
Myrtle Beach, South Carolina
Robert White
PINE LAKES VENTURE GC
North Fort Myers, Florida
Ron Garl
PINELAND CC
Mullins, South Carolina
Gene Hamm
PINELAND PLANTATION G&CC
Mayesville, South Carolina
Russell Breeden
PINE MEADOW GC
Mundelein, Illinois
Joe Lee, Rocky Roquemore
PINE MEADOWS GC
Overgaard, Arizona
Milt Coggins
PINE MOUNTAIN GC
Iron Mountain, Michigan
   (A.9) William Newcomb
PINE MOUNTAIN GC
Connelly Springs, North
Carolina
P. Mallard
PINE MOUNTAIN LAKE CC
Groveland, California
William F. Bell
PINE NEEDLES CC
Fort Valley, Georgia
Sid Clarke
PINE NEEDLES LODGE & CC
Southern Pines, North Carolina
Donald Ross
PINE OAK GC
Ocala, Florida
Lou Bateman
   (R.9 A.18) Ron Garl
PINE OAKS GC
Ocala, Florida
Ron Garl
PINE OAKS GC
Easton, Massachusetts
Geoffrey S. Cornish, William G.
Robinson
PINE OAKS MUNI
Johnson City, Tennessee
Alex McKay
PINE ORCHARDS CC
Brantford, Connecticut
Robert D. Pryde
   (A.4) Al Zikorus
PINE RIDGE CC
Beverly Hills, Florida
Charles Almony
PINE RIDGE CC
Newcastle, New York
Alfred H. Tull
PINE RIDGE CC
Cleveland, Ohio
Harold Paddock
PINE RIDGE CC
Edgefield, South Carolina
Russell Breeden
PINE RIDGE G&CC
Roundup, Montana
Frank Hummel

PINE RIDGE G&CC [NLE]
Winnipeg, Manitoba
H. S. Colt
   (R.) Donald Ross
PINE RIDGE G&CC
Winnipeg, Manitoba
Stanley Thompson
   (R.) Clinton E. Robinson
PINE RIDGE GC
Waterville, Maine
James Schoenthaler
PINE RIDGE GC
Meadville, Pennsylvania
James Gilmore Harrison,
Ferdinand Garbin
PINE RIDGE MUNI
Lutherville, Maryland
Gus Hook
PINE RIVER CC
Alma, Michigan
   (A.9) Bruce Matthews, Jerry
   Matthews
PINERY GC
Parker, Colorado
David Bingaman
PINES CC
Morgantown, West Virginia
Edmund B. Ault
PINES GC
Hollywood, Florida
Hans Schmeisser
PINES GC
Zebulon, Georgia
Arthur Davis
PINES GC
Wyoming, Michigan
George Woolferd
PINES GC
Emerson, New Jersey
Alec Ternyei
PINES GC
Pinebluff, North Carolina
Frank B. Hicks
[THE] PINES AT GRAND VIEW GC
Nisswa, Minnesota
Joel Goldstrand
PINES HOTEL GC
South Fallsburg, New York
Robert Trent Jones
PINE SHORE GC
Berlin, Maryland
Al Janis
PINESTONE GC
Minden, Ontario
Jack Davison
PINETOP CC
Pinetop, Arizona
Milt Coggins
   (R.) Gary Panks
PINETOP LAKES G&CC
Pinetop, Arizona
Milt Coggins
PINE TRACE GC
Rochester Hills, Michigan
Arthur Hills
PINE TREE CC
Birmingham, Alabama
George W. Cobb
PINE TREE CC
Brooksville, Connecticut
Alfred H. Tull
PINETREE CC
Marietta, Georgia
Chic Adams

PINE TREE GC
Delray Beach, Florida
Dick Wilson, Joe Lee
   (R.) Joe Lee
   (R.1) Ed Connor
PINE TREE GC
Kernersville, North Carolina
Gene Hamm
PINE TREES GC
Santa Ana, California
Harry Rainville
PINETUCK GC
Rock Hill, South Carolina
   (R.) Rees Jones
PINE VALLEY CC
Fort Wayne, Indiana
Clyde Williams
PINE VALLEY GC
Southington, Connecticut
Orrin Smith
PINE VALLEY GC
Elizabethtown, Kentucky
   (A.9) Bill Amick
PINE VALLEY GC
Romeo, Michigan
   (R.) William Newcomb
PINE VALLEY GC
Pine Valley, New Jersey
H. S. Colt (routing), George
Crump
   (A.4) Hugh Wilson, *Alan*
   Wilson
   (R.) William S. Flynn
   (R.) Perry Maxwell
   (R.) Tom Fazio
PINE VALLEY GC (PRACTICE CSE)
Pine Valley, New Jersey
Tom Fazio
PINE VALLEY GC
Wadsworth, Ohio
   (R.9 A.9) Ted McAnlis
PINE VALLEY GC [NLE]
Woodbridge, Ontario
Howard Watson
PINE VALLEY G LINKS
Pelham, New Hampshire
   (R.) *Todd Madden*
PINEVIEW G&CC
Macclenny, Florida
Bill Amick
PINE VIEW GC (HEMLOCK CSE)
Three Rivers, Michigan
Ed Ruess
PINE VIEW G CSE
Ypsilanti, Michigan
Harley Hodges (1990)
PINEWAY GC
Lebanon, Oregon
Fred Federspiel
PINEWILD GC
Pinehurst, North Carolina
Gene Hamm
PINEWOOD CC
Munds Park, Arizona
Lawrence Hughes
   (R.) Arthur Jack Snyder
PINEWOOD CC
Asheboro, North Carolina
Russell Breeden
   (R.) Tom Jackson
PINEWOOD GC
Beaumont, Texas
Leon Howard

PINEWOOD CAMPS GC
  Canton, Maine
  George Dunn, Jr.
PINEY BRANCH GC
  Hampstead, Maryland
  Edmund B. Ault
PINEY POINT CC
  Norwood, North Carolina
  J. Porter Gibson
PINEY POINT GC [NLE]
  Houston, Texas
  Joseph S. Finger
PINEY VALLEY GC
  Fort Leonard Wood, Missouri
  Floyd Farley
PINEY WOODS CC
  Nacagdoches, Texas
  (A.9) Karl Litten
PINHEIROS ALTOS CC
  Quinta do Lago, Portugal
  Ron Fream
    (R.) Howard Swan, *Peter
    McEvoy*
[THE] PINNACLE C
  Payne Springs, Texas
  Don January, Billy Martindale
    (A.9) *Raymond Garcia, Ed
    McSpadden*
PINNACLE PEAK CC
  Scottsdale, Arizona
  Dick Turner
    (R.) Gary Grandstaff
PINNER HILL GC
  Middlesex, England
  F. G. Hawtree, J. H. Taylor
PINE OAK CC
  Gilmer, Texas
  Jim Lyles
PIN OAKS CC
  Tuskegee, Alabama
  Robert Leimbeck
PIN OAKS GC
  Auburn, Alabama
  Gene Rutherford
PIÑON HILLS G CSE
  Farmington, New Mexico
  Ken Dye
PIONEER PARK GC
  Lincoln, Nebraska
  William H. Tucker
    (R.) Jeff Brauer
PIPE O'PEACE GC
  Blue Island, Illinois
  NKA Joe Louis the Champ GC
PIPER'S LANDING G&CC
  Stuart, Florida
  Joe Lee
    (R.) Chuck Ankrom
PIPESTEM STATE PARK GC
  Pipestem, West Virginia
  Geoffrey S. Cornish, William G.
  Robinson
PIPESTEM STATE PARK GC (PAR 3
  CSE)
  Pipestem, West Virginia
  Geoffrey S. Cornish, William G.
  Robinson
PIPESTONE GC
  Miamisburg, Ohio
  Arthur Hills

PIPING ROCK C
  Locust Valley, New York
  Charles Blair Macdonald, Seth
  Raynor
    (R.) Pete Dye
PIPPY PARK GC
  St. John's, Newfoundland
  Graham Cooke
PIQUA CC
  Piqua, Ohio
  Donald Ross
    (A.9) Jack Kidwell
PIRATES MUNI
  Galveston, Texas
  John Plumbley
    (R.) Carlton Gipson
PISTAKEE HILLS CC
  McHenry, Illinois
  Harry Collis
[THE] PIT G LINKS
  Aberdeen, North Carolina
  Dan Maples
PITEA GC
  Pitea, Sweden
  (A.7) Jan Sederholm
PITLOCHRY GC
  Perthshire, Scotland
  Willie Fernie
    (R.) C. K. Hutchison
PITMAN GC
  Pitman, New Jersey
  Alex Findlay
PITREAVIE GC
  Fife, Scotland
  Alister Mackenzie
PITTSBURG G&CC
  Pittsburg, California
  Alister Mackenzie, Robert
  Hunter
    (A.9) Robert Muir Graves
PITTSBURGH FIELD C
  Pittsburgh, Pennsylvania
  Alex Findlay
    (R. A.2) Willie Park, Jr.
    (R.) Emil Loeffler, *John
    McGlynn*
    (R.) A. W. Tillinghast
    (R.) Robert Trent Jones
    (R.) X. G. Hassenplug (1962)
    (R.) X. G. Hassenplug (1972)
    (R.) X. G. Hassenplug (1985)
    (R.) Arthur Hills
P L CC
  Japan
  Tokuchika Mika
P L LONDON CC
  England
  Fred W. Hawtree, Martin Haw-
  tree
PLACID LAKES INN & CC
  Lake Placid, Florida
  Frank Murray
    (R.) Gordon Lewis
PLAINFIELD CC
  Plainfield, New Jersey
  Donald Ross
    (R. A.3) Donald Ross
PLAINFIELD GC (WEST CSE) [NLE]
  Plainfield, New Jersey
  Tom Bendelow
PLAINFIELD ELKS GC
  Plainfield, Indiana
  Pete Dye

PLAINFIELD WEST GC
  Plainfield, New Jersey
  Martin O'Loughlin
PLA-MOR GC
  Fort Smith, Arkansas
  Herman Hackbarth
PLANDOME CC
  Plandome, New York
  Orrin Smith
    (R.) Frank Duane
PLANO MUNI
  Plano, Texas
  Don January, Billy Martindale
    (R.) Jeff Brauer, *Jim Colbert*
[THE] PLANTATION AT PONTE VEDRA
  GC
  Ponte Vedra Beach, Florida
  Arnold Palmer, Ed Seay
PLANTATION BAY CC
  Ormond Beach, Florida
  Lloyd Clifton, *Kenneth Ezell,
  George Clifton*
PLANTATION CC
  Pharr, Texas
  Dave Bennett
PLANTATION G&CC (PANTHER CSE)
  Venice, Florida
  Ron Garl
PLANTATION G&CC (BOBCAT CSE)
  Venice, Florida
  Ron Garl
PLANTATION GC
  Fort Lauderdale, Florida
  Red Lawrence
PLANTATION GC
  Boise, Idaho
    (R.) Robert Muir Graves
PLANTATION G RESORT
  Crystal River, Florida
  Mark Mahannah
PLATTEVIEW CC
  Omaha, Nebraska
  Edward Lawrence Packard
PLATTSBURGH AFB GC
  Plattsburgh, New York
  Al Zikorus
PLAUSAWA VALLEY CC
  Concord, New Hampshire
  William F. Mitchell
    (A.9) Geoffrey Cornish, Brian
    Silva
PLAYA DORADO GC
  Playa Dorado, Dominican
  Republic
  Robert Trent Jones
PLAYA GRANADA GC
  Granada, Spain
  John Harris
[THE] PLAYERS C
  Lansing, Michigan
  Jerry Matthews
[THE] PLAYERS C AT ST. LOUIS
  Crescent, Missouri
  Roger Packard
[THE] PLAYERS C AT WOODLAND
  TERRACE
  Muncie, Indiana
  Gene Bates
PLAYLAND PARK G CENTER
  South Bend, Indiana
  William James Spear
PLEASANT HILL CC
  Scarborough, Maine
  Jimmy Jones

PLEASANT HILL GC
  Monroe, Ohio
  Jack Kidwell
PLEASANT HILLS GC
  San Jose, California
  Henry Duino
PLEASANT POINT PLANTATION CC
  Beaufort, South Carolina
  Russell Breeden
PLEASANT VALLEY CC
  Little Rock, Arkansas
  Joseph S. Finger
    (R.) Dick Nugent
PLEASANT VALLEY CC
  Sutton, Massachusetts
  Donald Hoenig
    (R.2) Geoffrey S. Cornish,
    William Robinson
    (R.3) Brian Ault, Tom Clark,
    Edmund B. Ault
PLEASANT VALLEY CC
  Mount Pleasant, Pennsylvania
  Emil Loeffler, *John McGlynn*
    (R.9) X. G. Hassenplug
    (R.) X. G. Hassenplug
PLEASANT VALLEY CC
  Weirton, West Virginia
  Horace W. Smith
PLEASANT VALLEY GC
  Medina, Ohio
  Jack Kidwell
PLEASANT VALLEY GC
  Clackamus, Oregon
  Barney Lucas, Shirley Stone
PLEASANT VALLEY PAR 3 G CSE
  Okanagan, British Columbia
  William G. Robinson
PLEASANT VIEW GC
  Norvelt, Pennsylvania
  Paul E. Erath
PLEASANT VIEW GC
  Independence, Kansas
  NKA Sycamore Valley GC
PLEASANT VIEW GC
  Pennsylvania
  Edmund B. Ault, Al Jamison
PLEASANT VIEW LODGE GC
  Freehold, New York
  Frank Duane
PLEASANT VUE GC
  Paris, Ohio
  James Gilmore Harrison,
  Ferdinand Garbin
    (A.9) Ferdinand Garbin
PLEASURE PARK GC
  Concord, Ontario
  Robert Moote
PLETTENBERG BAY CC [NLE]
  Cape Province, South Africa
    (A.9) Robert Grimsdell
PLETTENBERG BAY CC
  Cape Province, South Africa
  Fred W. Hawtree
PLOEMEUR OCEAN GC
  France
  T. J. A. Macauley, *Stephen
  Quenouille*
PLUMAS LAKE G&CC
  Marysville, California
  Donald McKee
    (R.9 A.9) Bob Baldock
PLUMAS PINES CC
  Blairsden, California
  Homer Flint

PLUM BROOK GC
Sandusky, Ohio
Tom Bendelow
PLUM CREEK G&CC
Castle Rock, Colorado
Pete Dye
PLUM HOLLOW G&CC
Southfield, Michigan
Wilfrid Reid, William Connellan
(R.) William Newcomb
(R.1) Bruce Matthews, Jerry
Matthews
(R.) Arthur Hills
PLUM TREE NATIONAL GC
Harvard, Illinois
Joe Lee
PLYMOUTH CC
Plymouth, Indiana
(R.) Gary Kern
PLYMOUTH CC
Plymouth, North Carolina
William S. Flynn
PLYMOUTH CC
Norristown, Pennsylvania
(R.) William S. Flynn
PLYMOUTH GC
Plymouth, Massachusetts
Donald Ross
PLYMOUTH GC [NLE]
Plymouth, New Hampshire
Ralph Barton
PLYMOUTH PARK GC
Niles, Michigan
Tom Bendelow
POCALLA SPRINGS CC
Sumter, South Carolina
Ed Riccoboni
POCANTICO HILLS GC
Tarrytown, New York
William S. Flynn
POCASSET GC
Pocasset, Massachusetts
Donald Ross
POCO DIABLO GC
Sedona, Arizona
Arthur Jack Snyder
POCONO FARMS CC
Tobyhanna, Pennsylvania
Art Wall
(A.9) Al Janis
POCONO MANOR INN & GC (EAST
CSE)
Pocono Manor, Pennsylvania
Donald Ross
POCONO MANOR INN & GC (WEST
CSE)
Pocono Manor, Pennsylvania
George Fazio
POHICK BAY CC
Lorton, Virginia
George W. Cobb, John LaFoy
POHLCAT G CSE
Mt. Pleasant, Michigan
Dan Pohl (1991)
POINCIANA G&RC
Kissimmee, Florida
Robert von Hagge, Bruce Devlin
POINCIANA PLACE GC
Medellin, Colombia
Charles Mahannah
POINT AQUARIUS CC
Conroe, Texas
Jay Riviere

[THE] POINTE CC
Lake Monroe, Indiana
Bob Simmons
[THE] POINTE AT LOOKOUT
MOUNTAIN GC
Phoenix, Arizona
Forrest Richardson (routing),
Bill Johnston
[THE] POINTE AT SOUTH MOUNTAIN
GC
Phoenix, Arizona
Forrest Richardson, Arthur Jack
Snyder
POINTE ROYALE CC
Branson, Missouri
Tom Clark
POINTE WEST GC
Amherstburg, Ontario
Thomas McBroom
POINT GREY G&CC
Vancouver, British Columbia
(R.) Geoffrey S. Cornish,
William G. Robinson
(R.) William G. Robinson,
John Robinson
POINT JUDITH CC
Narragansett, Rhode Island
William Davis
(R.9 A.9) Donald Ross
(R.9) Geoffrey S. Cornish,
William G. Robinson
POINT LOMA GC [NLE]
San Diego, California
Tom Bendelow
POINT MALLARD PARK GC
Decatur, Alabama
Charles M. Graves
POINT O'WOODS G&CC
Benton Harbor, Michigan
Robert Trent Jones
POINT PLEASANT GC
New Jersey
Tom Bendelow
POINT VENTURE YACHT & CC
Jonestown, Texas
Bruce Littell
(A.9) Leon Howard, Charles
Howard
POIPU BAY RESORT GC
Shipwreck Beach, Kauai, Hawaii
Robert Trent Jones, Jr.
POKEMOUCHE GC
Caraquet, New Brunswick
Howard Watson
(R.9 A.9) John Watson
POK-TA-POK GC
Cancun, Mexico
Robert Trent Jones, Jr.
POLAND CC
Youngstown, Ohio
Leonard Macomber
POLAND SPRING GC
Poland Spring, Maine
A. H. Fenn
(R.9 A.9) Donald Ross
POLE CREEK GC
Tabernash, Colorado
Ron Kirby, Denis Griffiths
POLISH PINES CC
Keyser, West Virginia
Algie Pulley
POLLENSA GC
Majorca, Spain
Pepe Gancedo

[THE] POLO C
Boca Raton, Florida
Karl Litten
POLO FIELDS G&CC
Cumming, Georgia
Joe Lee, Rocky Roquemore
POLO FIELDS G&CC
Louisville, Kentucky
William Newcomb
POLO TRACE G&TC
Delray Beach, Florida
Karl Litten
POLSON CC
Polson, Montana
Gregor MacMillan
(A.9) Frank Hummel
POLVADERO G&CC
Coalinga, California
(R.9) Bob Baldock
POMME DE TERRE G&CC
Wheatland, Missouri
Press Maxwell
POMONOK CC [NLE]
Flushing, New York
Devereux Emmet
POMPANO BEACH CC (PALMS CSE)
Pompano Beach, Florida
Red Lawrence
(R.) Robert von Hagge
POMPANO BEACH CC (PINES CSE)
Pompano Beach, Florida
Robert von Hagge
POMPANO PARK GC
Pompano Beach, Florida
Frank Murray
[THE] POMPEY C
Syracuse, New York
Hal Purdy
PONCA CITY CC
Ponca City, Oklahoma
Perry Maxwell
(R.) Don Sechrest
PONCE DE LEON GC
Hot Springs Village, Arkansas
Tom Clark
PONCE DE LEON RESORT & CC
St. Augustine, Florida
Donald Ross
(R.) William H. Diddel
(R.2 A.2) Willard Byrd
(R.) Joe Lee
PONCE GC
Ponce, Puerto Rico
Alfred H. Tull
POND A RIVER GC
Woodburn, Indiana
Robert Beard
POND DOWN WOODS GC
Jacksonville, Illinois
Gary Grandstaff
POND VIEW GC
Westerly, Rhode Island
Phil Wogan
PONDEROSA CC
Warren, Ohio
Homer Fieldhouse
PONDEROSA CC
Batesburg, South Carolina
Ed Riccoboni
PONDEROSA G CSE
Truckee, California
Bob Baldock

PONDEROSA PAR 3 GC
Burley, Idaho
Ernest Schneiter
PONDOK INDAH GC
Indonesia
Robert Trent Jones, Jr.
PONKAPOAG GC (CSE NO. 1)
Canton, Massachusetts
Donald Ross
(R.) Donald Ross
PONKAPOAG GC (CSE NO. 2)
Canton, Massachusetts
William F. Mitchell
PONOKA COMMUNITY GC
Ponoka, Alberta
William G. Robinson
PONTA GROSSA GC
Brazil
Kenji Oda
PONTE DE LIMA GC
Oporto, Portugal
Howard Swan
PONTE VEDRA C (LAGOON CSE)
Ponte Vedra Beach, Florida
Robert Trent Jones
(A.9) Joe Lee
(R.) Robert Walker
PONTE VEDRA C (OCEAN CSE)
Ponte Vedra Beach, Florida
Herbert Strong
(R.) Robert Trent Jones
(R.) Robert Walker
PONTIAC CC
Pontiac, Michigan
Ernest Way
PONT ST. MAXENCE GC
France
Wilfrid Reid
POOLESVILLE GC
Poolesville, Maryland
Edmund B. Ault, Al Jamison
POPLAR BLUFF MUNI
Poplar Bluff, Missouri
Edmund B. Ault
POPLAR CREEK GC
Hoffman Estates, Illinois
Dick Nugent, Ken Killian
(R.) Bob Lohmann
POPLAR FOREST GC
Lynchberg, Virginia
Ken Killian, Dick Nugent
POPLAR HILLS G&CC
Fort Nelson, British Columbia
William G. Robinson
POPPY HILLS GC
Pebble Beach, California
Robert Trent Jones, Jr.
POQUOY BROOK GC
Lakeville, Massachusetts
Geoffrey S. Cornish
PORTAGE CC
Akron, Ohio
William B. Langford
(R.) Geoffrey S. Cornish,
William G. Robinson
PORTAGE HILLS CC
Portage, Maine
Ben Gray
PORTAGE LA PRAIRIE GC
Manitoba
(R.9 A.9) Clinton E.
Robinson

PORTAGE PARK GC [NLE]
Houghton, Michigan
William B. Langford
PORTAGE LAKE GC
Houghton, Michigan
William Newcomb
(A.9) Jerry Matthews
PORTAGE YACHT & CC
Treasure Lake, Florida
Chic Adams
PORTALES CC
Portales, New Mexico
William H. Tucker
PORTAL GC
Tarporley, England
D. M. A. Steel
PORT ARMOR C
Lake Oconee, Georgia
Bob Cupp
PORT ARTHUR CC
Port Arthur, Texas
Ralph Plummer
PORT-AU-PECK GC
New York
Mungo Park II
PORT CARLING G&CC
Port Carling, Ontario
Thomas McBroom
PORT CHARLOTTE CC
Port Charlotte, Florida
David Wallace
(R.9 A.9) Mark Mahannah
(R.) Chuck Ankrom
PORT CHERRY HILLS CC
McDonald, Pennsylvania
Paul Erath
PORT COLBORNE GC
Port Colborne, Ontario
(R.) Robert Moote
(R.) Robert Moote, David S.
Moote
PORT ELIZABETH GC
Port Elizabeth, South Africa
S. V. Hotchkin
PORTERS NECK CC
Wrightsville Beach, North
Carolina
Tom Fazio
PORTERS PARK GC
Hertfordshire, England
C. S. Butchart
PORTER VALLEY CC
North Ridge, California
Ted Robinson
PORT HURON CC
Port Huron, Michigan
Wilfrid Reid, William Connellan
(R.) William Newcomb
PORT JERVIS CC
Port Jervis, New York
A.W. Tillinghast
PORTLAND CC
Falmouth, Maine
Donald Ross
(R.) Orrin Smith
(R.) Robert Trent Jones
PORTLAND GC
Portland, Connecticut
Geoffrey S. Cornish, William G.
Robinson

PORTLAND GC
Portland, Oregon
George Turnbull
(R.) Robert Trent Jones
(R.) Robert Muir Graves
(R.1) John Steidel
PORTLAND GC WEST
Portland, Connecticut
Al Zikorus
PORTLAND MEADOWS GC
Portland, Oregon
Eddie Hogan, Stan Terry
PORT LUDLOW GC
Port Ludlow, Washington
Robert Muir Graves
PORTMADOC GC
Portmadoc, Wales
James Braid
PORT MALABAR CC
Palm Bay, Florida
Chuck Ankrom
PORTMARNOCK GC (OLD CSE)
Dublin, Ireland
George Ross, W. C. Pickeman
(R.1) Henry M. Cairnes
(R.) H. S. Colt
(R.1) Eddie Hackett
PORTMARNOCK GC (NEW CSE)
Dublin, Ireland
Fred W. Hawtree
(A.9) D. M. A. Steel
PÔRTO ALEGRE CC
Pôrto Alegre, Brazil
Carlos Pereira Sylla, Joseph A.
Millender
PORTO D'ORRA GC
Cantanzaro, Italy
Marco Croze
PORT ROYAL GC (BARONY CSE)
Hilton Head Island, South
Carolina
George W. Cobb
(R.) Willard Byrd
PORT ROYAL GC (PLANTERS ROW
CSE)
Hilton Head Island, South
Carolina
Willard Byrd
PORT ROYAL GC (ROBBERS ROW
CSE)
Hilton Head Island, South
Carolina
George W. Cobb
(R.) Willard Byrd
PORT ROYAL GC
Southampton, Bermuda
Robert Trent Jones
PORTSCHACHER GC
Moosburg, Austria
Gerold Hauser, Günther Hauser
PORTSDOWN HILL GC
England
Fred W. Hawtree
PORTSMOUTH G&CC
Greenland, New Hampshire
Robert Trent Jones
PORTSMOUTH NAVAL YARD GC
[NLE]
Portsmouth, New Hampshire
A. H. Fenn
PORTSTEWART GC
County Londonderry, Northern
Ireland
Willie Park

PORT SUNLIGHT GC
England
Fred W. Hawtree
PORTUMNA GC
Portumna, Ireland
(R.) Eddie Hackett
POSSUM TROT GC
North Myrtle Beach, South
Carolina
Russell Breeden
POTOWATOMI CC
Michigan City, Indiana
Tom Bendelow
POTOWOMUT CC
East Greenwich, Rhode Island
(A.9) Walter I. Johnson
POTRERO G&CC [NLE]
Inglewood, California
Robert Johnstone
POTTAWATOMIE PARK GC
St. Charles, Illinois
Robert Trent Jones
POTTER PARK GC
Hamilton, Ohio
William H. Diddel
POULT WOOD GC
Kent, England
Fred W. Hawtree
POVERTY BAY GC
New Zealand
(R.) C. H. Redhead
POWDER HORN GC [NLE]
Lexington, Massachusetts
Geoffrey S. Cornish
POWDER RIVER CC
Broadus, Montana
Frank Hummel
POWELL MUNI
Powell, Wyoming
Theodore Wirth
POWELL RIVER GC
British Columbia
Les Furber
POWELTON C
Newburgh, New York
J. Taylor
(R.6 A.12) Devereux Emmet
(R.) Robert Trent Jones
(R.4) Geoffrey S. Cornish,
Brian Silva
POWFOOT GC
Powfoot, Scotland
James Braid
POXEBOGUE GC
Bridgehampton, New York
Alfred H. Tull
PRÀ DELLE TORRI GC
Italy
Marco Croze
PRAIA DE MARINHA GC
Portugal
Howard Swan
PRAIRIE CREEK GC
DeWitt, Michigan
William Newcomb
PRAIRIE DOG GC
Norton, Kansas
Frank Hummel
PRAIRIE DUNES CC
Hutchinson, Kansas
Perry Maxwell
(A.9) Press Maxwell
(R.4) Bill Coore, Ben
Crenshaw

PRAIRIE HILL GC [NLE]
Maple Hill, Kansas
L. J. "Dutch" McClellan
PRAIRIE OAKS G&CC
Sebring, Florida
NKA CC of Sebring
PRAIRIE VIEW GC
Cheyenne, Wyoming
Jim Church
PRAIRIE VIEW G CSE
Worthington, Minnesota
Joel Goldstrand
PRAIRIE VISTA G CSE
Bloomington, Illinois
Roger Packard
PRAIRIEWOOD GC
Fargo, North Dakota
Dick Phelps, Brad Benz
PRAIRIEWOOD G CSE
Holland, Michigan
Warner Bowen
PRATT ESTATE GC
Glen Cove, New York
Tom Bendelow
PREAKNESS HILLS CC
Paterson, New Jersey
William H. Tucker
(R.) Geoffrey S. Cornish,
Brian Silva
PREAKNESS VALLEY PARK GC
Wayne, New Jersey
Frank Duane
PREDATOR RIDGE G RESORT
Vernon, British Columbia
Les Furber, Jim Eremko
PRENDEN GC
Prenden, Germany
Wolfgang Siegmann
PRENTON GC
Cheshire, England
H. S. Colt
(R.) Alister Mackenzie
(R.) Fred W. Hawtree
PRESCOTT CC
Prescott, Arizona
Milt Coggins
PRESCOTT HILLS GC
Plainfield, New Jersey
Willard Wilkinson
PRESIDENT CC (NORTH CSE)
West Palm Beach, Florida
William F. Mitchell
PRESIDENT CC (SOUTH CSE)
West Palm Beach, Florida
William F. Mitchell
PRESIDENT CC
Yamoussoukro, Ivory Coast
Peter Alliss, David Thomas
PRESIDENT CC
Bangkok, Thailand
Robert Trent Jones, Jr.
PRESIDENT GC
Tochigi Prefecture, Japan
Jack Nicklaus
PRESIDENTIAL CC
North Miami Beach, Florida
Mark Mahannah, Charles
Mahannah
PRESIDENTS GC
North Quincy, Massachusetts
George Wright
(R.) Wayne Stiles
(R.) William F. Mitchell
(R.) George Fazio, Tom Fazio

PRESIDIO GC
San Francisco, California
Robert Johnstone
(R.) *William McEwan*
(R.) Herbert Fowler
(R.) Robert Muir Graves
(R.) Desmond Muirhead

PRESQUE ISLE CC
Presque Isle, Maine
Ben Gray

PRESS CC
Takasaki, Japan
Denis Griffiths

PRESTBURY GC
England
H. S. Colt, J. S. F. Morrison

PRESTIGE CC (EAST CSE)
Tochigi, Japan
Mike Poellot, Brad Benz

PRESTIGE CC (WEST CSE)
Tochigi, Japan
Mike Poellot, Brad Benz

PRESTON CC
Kingwood, West Virginia
Edmund B. Ault

PRESTON TRAIL GC
Dallas, Texas
Ralph Plummer, Byron Nelson
(R.) Jay Morrish, Bob Cupp
(R.1) Pete Dye
(R.) Joseph S. Finger, Ken Dye

PRESTONWOOD CC (CREEK CSE)
Dallas, Texas
Ralph Plummer
(R.) Joseph S. Finger, Ken Dye

PRESTONWOOD CC (HILLS CSE)
Dallas, Texas
Dave Bennett

PRESTONWOOD CC
Cary, North Carolina
Leon Howard, *Vance Heafner*

PRESTWICK CC [NLE]
Orland Park, Illinois
Charles Maddox, *Frank P. MacDonald*

PRESTWICK CC
Frankfort, Illinois
Edward Lawrence Packard
(R.) Dick Nugent

PRESTWICK CC
Danville, Indiana
Bob Simmons

PRESTWICK GC
Ayrshire, Scotland
Old Tom Morris
(A.6) Old Tom Morris
(R.) *Charles Hunter*
(R. A.4) James Braid
(R.) *Harold Hilton*
(R.) James Braid, John R. Stutt
(R.) J. Hamilton Stutt

PRESTWICK ST. CUTHBERT GC
Scotland
(R.) J. Hamilton Stutt

PRESTWICK ST. NICHOLAS GC
Ayrshire, Scotland
Charles Hunter

PRESTWICK GC
Myrtle Beach, South Carolina
P. B. Dye, Pete Dye

PRETORIA GC
Pretoria, South Africa
Clarrie Moore
(R.) C. H. Alison
(R.) Robert G. Grimsdell

PRETTY ACRES GC
New Orleans, Louisiana
Louis Prima

PRIDDIS GREENS G&CC
Calgary, Alberta
Bill Newis

[THE] PRINCE CSE
Princeville, Kauai, Hawaii
Robert Trent Jones, Jr.

PRINCE ALBERT PAR 3 GC
Prince Albert, Saskatchewan
William G. Robinson, John F. Robinson

PRINCE GEORGE CC
British Columbia
Ernest Brown

PRINCE GEORGES G&CC [NLE]
Landover, Maryland
Donald Ross

PRINCE GEORGES G&CC
Mitchellville, Maryland
Arnold Palmer, Ed Seay

PRINCE LAND GC
Japan
Hiroshi Umezawa

PRINCE RUPERT GC
Edmonton, Alberta
William Brinkworth

PRINCE'S GC (BLUE CSE)
Kent, England
Charles Hutchings, Percy Montagu Lucas
(R.) C. K. Hutchison
(R.) Sir Guy Campbell, J. S. F. Morrison

PRINCE'S GC (RED CSE)
Kent, England
Sir Guy Campbell, J. S. F. Morrison

PRINCE'S GC (WHITE CSE)
Kent, England
Howard Swan

PRINCESS ANNE CC
Virginia Beach, Virginia
(R.) Tom Clark

PRINCETON CC
Princeton, New Jersey
William Gordon, David Gordon

PRINCETON HILLS G ACADEMY
Princeton, New Jersey
Alec Ternyei

PRINCETON MEADOWS CC
Plainsboro, New Jersey
Joseph S. Finger

PRINCEVILLE MAKAI GC
Princeville, Kauai, Hawaii
Robert Trent Jones, Jr.

PRINEVILLE G&CC
Prineville, Oregon
Eddie Hogan, Ted Longworth, George Junor

PRINEVILLE MEADOWS G CSE
Prineville, Oregon
William G. Robinson

PROFILE C
Franconia, New Hampshire
A. H. Fenn
(R.) *J.M. Cornell*
(R.) Ralph Barton

PROGRESS DOWNS GC
Progress, Oregon
Ervin Thoresen

PROSPECT BAY CC
Graysonville, Maryland
Lindsay Ervin

PROSPECT HILL CC
Bowie, Maryland
George W. Cobb

PROSPECT HILL GC
Auburn, Maine
Arthur David Chapman

PROUTS NECK GC
Prouts Neck, Maine
Howard Hinckley (1907)
(R.9 A.9) Wayne Stiles
(R.) Geoffrey S. Cornish

PROVIDENCE CC
Matthews, North Carolina
Dan Maples

PROVINCE LAKE CC
East Wakefield, New Hampshire
Lawrence Van Etten
(A.9) Brian Silva, Geoffrey S. Cornish

PRUNERIDGE FARMS GC
Santa Clara, California
Jack Fleming
(R.) Robert Trent Jones, Jr.

PRYOR CREEK CC
Billings, Montana
Jack Daray, Jr., Stephen Halsey

PRYOR MUNI
Pryor, Oklahoma
Hugh Bancroft

PTARMIGAN G&CC
Fort Collins, Colorado
Jack Nicklaus

PUB-LINKS PAR 3 G CSE
Loveland, Colorado
Dick Phelps

PUCKERBRUSH GC
Willoughby, Ohio
R. Albert Anderson

PUCKRUP HALL GC
Tewkesbury, Gloucester, England
Simon Gidman

PUEBLO CC
Pueblo, Colorado
(R.9 A.9) Henry B. Hughes

PUEBLO EL MIRAGE CC
El Mirage, Arizona
Ken Killian

PUEBLO WEST G&CC
Pueblo, Colorado
Clyde B. Young

PUERTO AZUL GC
Pasay City, Philippines
Ron Kirby, Gary Player

PUERTO DEL SOL GC
Albuquerque, New Mexico
Arthur Jack Snyder

PUKALANI CC
Pukalani, Maui, Hawaii
Bob Baldock, Robert L. Baldock

PUKEKOHE GC
Pukekohe, New Zealand
C. H. Redhead

PULGAS PANDAS CC
Aguacaliente, Mexico
Joseph S. Finger

PUMPKIN RIDGE GC (GHOST CREEK CSE)
Portland, Oregon
Bob Cupp, John Fought

PUMPKIN RIDGE GC (WITCH HOLLOW CSE)
Portland, Oregon
Bob Cupp, John Fought

PUNDERSON LAKE GC
Cleveland, Ohio
Jack Kidwell

PUNTA ALA GC
Italy
G. Cavalsani

PUNTA BORINQUEN CC
Puerto Rico
Ferdinand Garbin

PUNTA DEL ESTE GC
Canteril, Uruguay
Alister Mackenzie

PUNTA GORDA CC
Punta Gorda, Florida
(R.) Donald Ross
(R.) R. Albert Anderson

PUNXSUTAWNEY CC
Punxsutawney, Pennsylvania
James Gilmore Harrison

PUPUKE GC
New Zealand
(R.) C. H. Redhead

PURDUE UNIVERSITY GC (SOUTH CSE)
West Lafayette, Indiana
William H. Diddel
(R.) Edward Lawrence Packard

PURDUE UNIVERSITY GC (NORTH CSE)
West Lafayette, Indiana
Kenneth Welton

PURLEY CHASE GC
Warwickshire, England
J. B. Tomlinson

PURLEY DOWNS GC
Surrey, England
S.V. Hotchkin

PURMEREND GC
Purmerend, Netherlands
T. J. A. Macauley

PURPLE HAWK CC
Cambridge, Minnesota
Don Herfort
(R.) Joel Goldstrand

PURPLE SAGE GC
Evanston, Wyoming
Mick Riley

PURPLE SAGE MUNI
Caldwell, Idaho
A. Vernon Macan

PURPOODOCK C
Cape Elizabeth, Maine
Larry Rowe
(A.9) *Jim McDonald, Sr.*
(R.) Brian Silva, Geoffrey S. Cornish

PUSLINCH LAKE GC
Ontario
(R.) Robert Moote

PUT-IN-BAY GC [NLE]
Pennsylvania
Frederick Stafford

PUTNAM CC
Lake Mahopac, New York
William F. Mitchell
(R.) James Blaukovitch
PUTTENHAM GC
Surrey, England
(R.) D. M. A. Steel
PUTTERHAM MEADOWS MUNI
Brookline, Massachusetts
Wayne Stiles, John Van Kleek
(R.2) Phil Wogan
PWLLHELI CC
Pwllheli, Wales
Old Tom Morris
(R.9 A.9) James Braid
PYECOMBE GC
England
(R.4) Fred W. Hawtree,
Martin Hawtree
PYLE AND KENFIG GC
Wales
H. S. Colt, C. H. Alison
(A.9) P. M. Ross
(R.) J. Hamilton Stutt
PYMA VALLEY GC
Andover, Ohio
J. Thomas Francis
PYPE HAYES MUNI
Warwickshire, England
F. G. Hawtree, J. H. Taylor
[THE] PYRAMIDS GC
La Quinta, California
Robert Trent Jones, Jr.
PYRMONTER GC
Bad Byrmont, West Germany
Donald Harradine

QETTARA GC
Marrakesh, Morocco
Cabell Robinson
QUABOAG CC
Monson, Massachusetts
(R.2) Geoffrey S. Cornish,
William G. Robinson
QUAIL BROOK GC
Somerset, New Jersey
Edmund B. Ault
QUAIL CHASE G CSE
Louisville, Kentucky
David Pfaff
QUAIL CREEK CC
Green Valley, Arizona
Ken Kavanaugh
QUAIL CREEK CC (CREEK CSE)
Naples, Florida
Arthur Hills
QUAIL CREEK CC (QUAIL CSE)
Naples, Florida
Arthur Hills
QUAIL CREEK G&CC
Oklahoma City, Oklahoma
Floyd Farley
(R.) Robert von Hagge
QUAIL CREEK GC
North Liberty, Iowa
Leo Johnson
(A.9) Joel Goldstrand
QUAIL CREEK GC
South St. Louis, Missouri
Gary Kern, Hale Irwin
QUAIL CREEK GC
Myrtle Beach, South Carolina
Gene Hamm

QUAIL HEIGHTS CC
Lake City, Florida
Jerry Cooper
QUAIL HOLLOW CC
Charlotte, North Carolina
George W. Cobb
(R.) Tom Jackson
(R.) Arnold Palmer, Ed Seay
QUAIL HOLLOW G&CC
Zephyrhills, Florida
Charles E. Griffin
QUAIL HOLLOW GC
Boise, Idaho
Robert von Hagge, Bruce Devlin
QUAIL HOLLOW GC
Oakham, Massachusetts
Phil Wogan
QUAIL HOLLOW INN & CC
Painesville, Ohio
Robert von Hagge, Bruce Devlin
QUAIL LAKE CC
Moreno, California
Desmond Muirhead
QUAIL RIDGE CC (NORTH CSE)
Delray Beach, Florida
Joe Lee
QUAIL RIDGE CC (SOUTH CSE)
Delray Beach, Florida
Joe Lee
QUAIL RIDGE CC
Spring Hill, Florida
Lee Duxstad
QUAIL RIDGE GC
Sanford, North Carolina
Mike Souchak, Sidney Davis
QUAIL RIDGE G&TC
Bloomington, Indiana
Bob Simmons
QUAIL RUN GC
Sun City, Arizona
Jeff Hardin, Greg Nash
QUAIL RUN GC
Santa Fe, New Mexico
Arthur Jack Snyder
QUAIL RUN G CSE
Columbus, Nebraska
Frank Hummel
QUAIL VALLEY CC (EL DORADO
CSE)
Missouri City, Texas
Jack B. Miller
(A.9) Jay Riviere
QUAIL VALLEY CC (EXECUTIVE CSE)
Missouri City, Texas
Jay Riviere
QUAIL VALLEY CC (LA QUINTA
CSE)
Missouri City, Texas
Jack B. Miller
QUAIL VILLAGE GC
Naples, Florida
William Maddox
QUAIL WEST G&CC
Naples, Florida
Arthur Hills
QUAKER HILL GC
Pawling, New York
Robert Trent Jones
QUAKER MEADOWS GC
Morganton, North Carolina
Russell Breeden
QUAKER NECK CC
Pollocksville, North Carolina
Russell T. Burney (1967)

QUAKER RIDGE CC
Scarsdale, New York
John Duncan Dunn
(R.9 A.9) A.W. Tillinghast
(R.) Robert Trent Jones
(R.) Frank Duane
QUALICUM BEACH MEMORIAL GC
Vancouver Island, British
Columbia
A. Vernon Macan
QUALICUM HIGHLANDS GC
Qualicum, British Columbia
Douglas Carrick
QUARRY HILL GC [NLE]
Vermont
Walter Barcomb
QUARRY HILLS CC
Graham, North Carolina
Ellis Maples
QUARRY OAKS GC
Steinbach, Manitoba
Les Furber, Jim Eremko
QUASHNET VALLEY CC
Mashpee, Massachusetts
Geoffrey S. Cornish, William G.
Robinson
QUECHEE LAKES CC (HIGHLAND
CSE)
Quechee, Vermont
Geoffrey S. Cornish, William G.
Robinson
QUECHEE LAKES CC (LAKELAND
CSE)
Quechee, Vermont
Geoffrey S. Cornish, William G.
Robinson
QUEEN ELIZABETH PARK GC
British Columbia
A. Vernon Macan
QUEENSBORO LINKS
Astoria, New York
Devereux Emmet
QUEEN'S HARBOUR YACHT & CC
Jacksonville, Florida
Mark McCumber
QUEENS PARK GC
Bermuda
David Gordon
QUEENS PARK GC
Bournemouth, England
J. H. Taylor
(R.) James Braid, John R.
Stutt
QUEENSTOWN HARBOR G LINKS
Queenstown, Maryland
Lindsay Ervin
QUEEN'S VALLEY GC [NLE]
Kew Gardens, New York
Devereux Emmet, W. H. "Pipe"
Follett
QUERÉTARO CC
Querétaro, Mexico
Percy Clifford
QUICKSILVER GC
Midway, Pennsylvania
Don Nagode
(R.) Bob Murphy, Sean Parees
(1990)
QUIDNESSET CC
East Greenwich, Rhode Island
Geoffrey S. Cornish
(A.9) Geoffrey S. Cornish,
William G. Robinson

QUILCHENA G&CC
British Columbia
Desmond Muirhead
(R.6) Geoffrey S. Cornish,
William G. Robinson
(R.) William G. Robinson,
John F. Robinson
QUINCY CC
Quincy, Massachusetts
(R.) Orrin Smith
QUINCY G&CC
Quincy, Washington
William Teufel
QUINNATISSET CC
Thompson, Connecticut
(A.9) Geoffrey S. Cornish,
William G. Robinson
QUINTA DA BOINA GC
Portugal
Howard Swan
QUINTA DA BOAVISTA GC
Portugal
Howard Swan
QUINTA DA BENAMOR GC
Tavira, Portugal
Henry Cotton, Howard Swan
QUINTA DA MARINHA GC
Faro, Portugal
Robert Trent Jones
QUINTA DAS NAVALHAS GC
Portugal
Howard Swan
QUINTA DE ARAMBEPE GC
Bahia, Brazil
Pier Mancinelli
QUINTA DO LAGO GC (CSE NO. 1)
Algarve, Portugal
William F. Mitchell
QUINTA DO LAGO GC (CSE NO. 2)
Faro, Portugal
William F. Mitchell
(A.9) Joe Lee, Rocky
Roquemore
QUINTA DO PERU GC
Lisbon, Portugal
Rocky Roquemore, Jeff Burton
QUIT-QUI-OC GC
Elkhart Lake, Wisconsin
Tom Bendelow
QUOGUE FIELD C
Quogue, New York
James Hepburn, R. B. Wilson
(R.2) Stephen Kay

RABBIT CREEK GC
Louisburg, Kansas
Leon Andrews
RACCOON CREEK GC
Littleton, Colorado
Dick Phelps, Brad Benz
RACCOON RUN GC
Myrtle Beach, South Carolina
Gene Hamm
RACE BROOK CC
Orange, Connecticut
Robert D. Pryde
(R.) Orrin Smith
(R.2) Al Zikorus
RACEWAY GC
Thompson, Connecticut
Donald Hoenig

RACINE CC [NLE]
Racine, Wisconsin
Tom Bendelow

RACINE CC
Racine, Wisconsin
Joseph A. Roseman
(R.9 A.9) Todd Sloan
(R.) David Gill
(R.) Edward Lawrence
Packard, Roger Packard
(R.) Bob Lohmann

RACING CLUB DE FRANCE (VALLEY CSE)
La Boulie, France
Wilfrid Reid
(R.) Seymour Dunn
(R.) Willie Park, Jr.

RACKHAM PARK MUNI
Huntington, Michigan
Donald Ross
(R.9) Jerry Matthews

RADCLIFFE-ON-TRENT GC
Nottinghamshire, England
Tom Williamson
(R.) Tom Williamson
(R.) J. J. F. Pennink

RADISSON GREENS GC
Baldwinsville, New York
Robert Trent Jones

RADIUM CC
Albany, Georgia
Wayne Stiles, John Van Kleek
(R.) Hugh Moore

RADIUM HOT SPRINGS GC
British Columbia
Doug McIntosh, Bruce McIntosh

RADLEY COLLEGE GC
England
D. M. A. Steel

RADLEY RUN CC
West Chester, Pennsylvania
Alfred H. Tull

RADNOR VALLEY CC
Villanova, Pennsylvania
Dick Wilson
(R.4 A.14) William Gordon,
David Gordon

RADRICK FARMS GC
Ann Arbor, Michigan
Pete Dye
(R.1) Pete Dye

RAF CRANWELL GC
England
S.V. Hotchkin

RAFFLES CC
Jurong, Singapore
Robert Trent Jones, Jr.

[THE] RAIL GC
Springfield, Illinois
Robert Trent Jones

RAILSIDE G CSE
Byron Center, Michigan
Jerry Matthews

RAINBOW BAY GC
Biloxi, Mississippi
Jack Daray, Harry Collis
(R.12 A.6) Earl Stone

RAINBOW CANYON GC
Temecula, California
NKA Temecula Creek G Cse

RAINBOW LAKE GC
Geneva, Indiana
Henry Culp

RAINBOW'S END G&CC
Dunellon, Florida
Joe Lee

RAINEY ESTATE GC
Huntington, New York
A.W. Tillinghast

RAINIER G&CC
Rainier, Washington
Robert Johnstone

RAINTREE CC (NORTH CSE)
Matthews, North Carolina
Russell Breeden

RAINTREE CC (SOUTH CSE)
Matthews, North Carolina
Russell Breeden

RAINTREE GC
Pembroke Pines, Florida
Charles Mahannah

RAISIN RIVER CC
Monroe, Michigan
Charles Maddox

RALARA GC
Canary Islands
Tom Dunn

RALEIGH CC
Raleigh, North Carolina
Donald Ross

RALEIGH GOLF ASSOCIATION GC
Raleigh, North Carolina
George W. Cobb

RALPH G. COVER ESTATE GC
Maryland
Edmund B. Ault

RALPH MYHRE GC
Middlebury, Vermont
Ralph Myhre

RALSTON GC [NLE]
Ralston, Nebraska
Henry C. Glissmann, Harold
Glissmann

RAMAPO GC
Haverstraw, New York
Duncan Fountaine

RAMBLEWOOD CC
Mount Laurel, New Jersey
Edmund B. Ault

RAMSEY GC
Cambridgeshire, Isle of Man
James Braid, John R. Stutt
(R.) J. Hamilton Stutt

RAMSEY G&CC
Ramsey, New Jersey
Hal Purdy

RAMSGATE GC
Inman, South Carolina
Russell Breeden, *Dan Breeden*

RAMS HILL CC
Borrego Springs, California
Ted Robinson

RAMSHORN CC
Fremont, Michigan
Max Dietz
(A.9) Jerry Matthews

[THE] RANCH CC
Palm Springs, California
Joseph Calwell

[THE] RANCH CC
Westminster, Colorado
Dick Phelps

[THE] RANCH CC
McKinney, Texas
Arthur Hills

[THE] RANCH G&CC
Winterburn, Alberta
William G. Robinson, John F.
Robinson

[THE] RANCH GC
Edmonton, Alberta
Derek Johnson

RANCH AT ROARING FORK GC
Carbondale, Colorado
Milt Coggins

RANCH HILLS GC
Mulino, Oregon
Bob Blaine

RANCHLAND HILLS GC
Midland, Texas
Ralph Plummer
(R.) Robert von Hagge, Bruce
Devlin

RANCHO BERNARDO GC
San Diego, California
Ted Robinson
(R.) Stephen Halsey, Jack
Daray, Jr.

RANCHO BERNARDO INN GC
San Diego, California
William F. Bell
(R.3) Ted Robinson

RANCHO CALIFORNIA CC
Murrieta, California
Robert Trent Jones

RANCHO CAÑADA GC (EAST CSE)
Carmel, California
Robert Dean Putman

RANCHO CAÑADA GC (WEST CSE)
Carmel, California
Robert Dean Putman

RANCHO CC [NLE]
Los Angeles, California
Max Behr

RANCHO DEL RAY GC
Atwater, California
Bob Baldock

RANCHO DUARTE GC
Duarte, California
William F. Bell

RANCHO LAS PALMAS CC
Rancho Mirage, California
Ted Robinson

RANCHO MIRAGE CC
Palm Springs, California
Harold Heers
(R.) Robert Muir Graves

RANCHO MURIETTA GC (NORTH CSE)
Sloughhouse, California
Bert Stamps
(R.) Arnold Palmer, Ed Seay

RANCHO MURIETTA CC (SOUTH CSE)
Sloughhouse, California
Ted Robinson

RANCHO PALOS VERDE GC
Palos Verde, California
(R.) Robert Muir Graves

RANCHO PARK GC
Los Angeles, California
William P. Bell, William H.
Johnson

RANCHO PENASQUINTOS GC
San Diego, California
NKA Carmel Highland G&TC

RANCHO SAN DIEGO GC (IVANHOE CSE)
El Cajon, California
O.W. Moorman, A.C. Sears

RANCHO SAN DIEGO GC (MONTE VISTA CSE)
El Cajon, California
O.W. Moorman, A.C. Sears

RANCHO SAN JOAQUIN CC
Irvine, California
William F. Bell
(R.) Robert Muir Graves

RANCHO SANTA FE CC
Rancho Santa Fe, California
Max Behr
(R.) Harry Rainville, David
Rainville
(R.) Perry Dye

RANCHO SANTA FE FARMS GC
Rancho Santa Fe, California
Perry Dye, Pete Dye

RANCHO SANTA YNEZ CC
Solvang, California
Ted Robinson

RANCHO SOLANO G CSE
Fairfield, California
Gary Roger Baird

RANCHO VIEJO CC (EL ANGEL CSE)
Brownsville, Texas
Dennis W. Arp

RANCHO VIEJO CC (EL DIABLO CSE)
Brownsville, Texas
Dennis W. Arp

RANCOCAS GC
Willingboro, New Jersey
Robert Trent Jones
(R.) Garrett Gill, George B.
Williams

RANDALL OAKS GC
Dundee, Illinois
William James Spear
(R.) Bob Lohmann

RANDERS GC
Randers, Denmark
C. K. Cotton

RANDOLPH FIELD GC
San Antonio, Texas
Perry Maxwell, Press Maxwell
(R.3 A.9) Joseph S. Finger

RANDOLPH PARK GC (NORTH CSE)
Tucson, Arizona
William P. Bell
(R.4) Pete Dye

RANDOLPH PARK GC (SOUTH CSE)
Tucson, Arizona
William F. Bell

RANDPARK GC (RANDPARK CSE)
South Africa
Sid Brews

RANDPARK GC (WINDSOR PARK CSE)
South Africa
Robert Grimsdell

RANGE END GC
Dillsburgh, Pennsylvania
James Gilmore Harrison

RANK ESTATE GC
Sussex, England
Tom Simpson

RANSOM OAKS CC
East Amherst, New York
NKA Glen Oak GC

RANTAU PETRONAS GC (LINKS CSE)
Kertah, Malaysia
Ronald Fream
RAPID CITY EXECUTIVE G CSE
Rapid City, South Dakota
Pat Wyss
RAPOLANO TERME GC
Siena, Italy
Marco Croze
RARITAN VALLEY CC
Somerville, New Jersey
(R.) David Gordon
(R.9) Hal Purdy
RAROTONGA GC
Rarotonga, New Zealand
(A.9) Peter Thomson,
Michael Wolveridge
RASPBERRY RIDGE GC
Everson, Washington
Bill Overdorf (9 1984)
RASSBACH-THYRNAU GC
Germany
Götz Mecklenburg
RATHFARNHAM GC
Ireland
(R.) Eddie Hackett
RATHO PARK GC
Edinburgh, Scotland
James Braid, John R. Stutt
RATLIFF RANCH G LINKS
Odessa, Texas
Jeff Brauer
RATTLE RUN G&TC
St. Clair, Michigan
Lou Powers
RATTVIK GC
Rattvik, Sweden
Ture Bruce
RAVELSTON GC
Scotland
James Braid
RAVENEAUX CC
Spring, Texas
Robert von Hagge, Bruce Devlin
(R.) Ken Kavanaugh
RAVENSTEIN GC
Ravenstein, Belgium
George Pannall
RAVENWOOD C
Donelson, Tennessee
L.N. Adwell
[THE] RAVINES GC
Middleburg, Florida
Ron Garl
RAVINIA GREEN CC
Deerfield, Illinois
Edward Lawrence Packard
(R.) Ken Killian, Dick Nugent
(R.) Bob Lohmann
RAVISLOE CC
Homewood, Illinois
(R.) Robert White
(R.) Donald Ross
(R.) William B. Langford,
Theodore J. Moreau
RAWIGA CC
Seville, Ohio
Edward Lawrence Packard
RAYBURN G&CC (BLUE NINE)
Jasper, Texas
Robert Trent Jones
RAYBURN G&CC (GOLD NINE)
Jasper, Texas
Jay Riviere

RAYBURN G&CC (CREEK NINE)
Jasper, Texas
Robert von Hagge, Bruce Devlin
READING CC
Albertontul, South Africa
Koos deBeers
READING CC
Reading, Pennsylvania
Alex Findlay
REAL AUTOMOVIL CLUB DE ESPANA
Spain
Javier Arana
REAL CLUB DE GOLF DE MENORCA
Shangri-La, Spain
John Harris
REAL CLUB DE GOLF EL PRAT
Spain
Javier Arana
REAL CLUB DE LA PUERTO DE HIERRO (NEW CSE)
Madrid, Spain
John Harris
(R.) Henry Cotton
REAL CLUB DE LA PUERTO DE HIERRO (OLD CSE)
Madrid, Spain
J. S. F. Morrison, H. S. Colt,
C. H. Alison
(R.) Tom Simpson
(R.) John Harris
REAL CLUB DE SAN SEBASTIAN
Spain
Tom Simpson
REAL GOLD DE PEDRENA
Spain
J. S. F. Morrison, H. S. Colt,
C. H. Alison
REAL SOCIEDAD DE GOLF NEGURI LA GALEA
Spain
Javier Arana
REAL SOCIEDAD HIPICA ESPANOLA
Spain
Javier Arana
(R.) John Harris
REAMES G&CC
Klamath Falls, Oregon
H. Chandler Egan
(A.9) Bob Baldock
REBSAMEN PARK MUNI
Little Rock, Arkansas
Herman Hackbarth
RECREATION GC
Healdton, Oklahoma
Floyd Farley
RECREATION PARK GC
Long Beach, California
William F. Bell
RED APPLE INN GC
Heber Springs, Arkansas
Gary Panks
RED BANK G&CC
Red Bank, New Jersey
(R.) Seymour Dunn
REDBOURN GC
Hertfordshire, England
John Day
RED BULL G CSE
Kitzbuhel, Austria
Gerold Hauser, *Günther Hauser*
RED BUTTE CC
Gillette, Wyoming
Frank Hummel

RED CLOUD CC
Red Cloud, Nebraska
Harry Obitz
RED DEER G&CC
Alberta
(R.) William G. Robinson
REDDEMAN FARMS GC
Ann Arbor, Michigan
Bob Louhouse, Howard Smith
REDDING CC
West Redding, Connecticut
Edward Ryder
(A.9) Rees Jones
(R.1) Al Zikorus
REDDISH VALE GC
Cheshire, England
Alister Mackenzie
REDFORD MUNI
Detroit, Michigan
NKA Rogell G Cse
RED FOX CC
Tryon, North Carolina
Ellis Maples
REDHAWK CC
Temecula, California
Ron Fream
RED HILL CC
Cucamonga, California
George C. Thomas, Jr.
(A.9) William P. Bell
(R.) Harry Rainville, David Rainville
RED HILL CC
Massachusetts
(R.9 A.9) William F. Mitchell
RED HOOK CC
Red Hook, New York
(R.9) Alfred H. Tull
RED LAKE CC
Venice, Florida
R. Albert Anderson
REDLAND G&CC
Homestead, Florida
Red Lawrence
REDLANDS CC
Redlands, California
A. E. Sterling, J. H. Fisher (9 1897)
(R.) Alister Mackenzie
RED LODGE CC
Red Lodge, Montana
Bob Baldock, Robert L. Baldock
REDMOND G LINKS [NLE]
Redmond, Washington
Al Smith
RED MOUNTAIN RANCH GC
Mesa, Arizona
Perry Dye
RED OAKS G CSE
Madison Heights, Michigan
Robert W. Bills, Donald L. Childs
RED OAK VALLEY GC
Red Oak, Texas
Leon Howard
REDONDO BEACH GC
Redondo Beach, California
Tom Bendelow
RED RUN GC
Royal Oak, Michigan
Willie Park, Jr.
(R.) Emil Loeffler, *John McGlynn*
(R.) Clinton E. Robinson

RED TAIL G CSE
London, Ontario
D. M. A. Steel
RED WING CC
Red Wing, Minnesota
(R.9) Don Herfort
(R.) Joel Goldstrand
RED WING LAKE GC
Virginia Beach, Virginia
George W. Cobb
RED WOOD MEADOWS GC
Bragg Creek, Alberta
Stan Leonard, *Philip Tattersfield*
REDWOOD MEADOWS G&CC
Calgary, Alberta
Bill Newis
REDWOODS G&CC
Virginia
Dale Nolte
REEDSBURG CC
Reedsburg, Wisconsin
(A.9) Ken Killian, Dick Nugent
REEDY CREEK GC
Clayton, North Carolina
Gene Hamm
REEMS CREEK GC
Weaverville, North Carolina
Martin Hawtree, Simon Gidman
REEVES GC
Cincinnati, Ohio
William H. Diddel
REEVES GC (PAR 3 CSE)
Cincinnati, Ohio
Jack Kidwell
REFLECTION RIDGE CC
Wichita, Kansas
Karl Litten
REFLECTIONS GC
La Quinta, California
Ted Robinson
REGENSBURG G UND LAND C
Regensburg, Germany
Donald Harradine
REGINA G&CC
Regina, Saskatchewan
Fred Foord
(R.) Stanley Thomson
(R.) Clinton E. Robinson
(R.) Bill Newis
REGINA GC [NLE]
Regina, Saskatchewan
Gilpin Brown, James Benson
(A.5) *J. Kelso Hunter, William Rogers, H. G. Green*
REGINA GC
Regina, Saskatchewan
William Brinkworth
(R.) Clinton E. Robinson
REHOBOTH BEACH CC [NLE]
Rehoboth Beach, Delaware
Francis B. Warner
REHOBOTH BEACH CC
Rehoboth Beach, Delaware
Frank Murray, Russell Roberts
REHOBOTH GC
Rehoboth, Massachusetts
Geoffrey S. Cornish, William G. Robinson
REICHSWALD GC
Nuremburg, Germany
Bernhard von Limburger

REID MEMORIAL GC (NORTH CSE)
Springfield, Ohio
Jack Kidwell
REID MEMORIAL GC (SOUTH CSE)
Springfield, Ohio
Jack Kidwell
REIMS GC
Reims, France
(A.9) Michael G. Fenn
REINA CRISTINA GC
Spain
Javier Arana
REMUERA GC
Auckland, New Zealand
H. G. Babbage
(R.) H. G. Babbage
RENAISSANCE PARK G CSE
West Charlotte, North Carolina
Michael Hurdzan
REND LAKE GC
Benton, Illinois
Edward Lawrence Packard,
Roger Packard
RENFREW GC
Renfrewshire, Scotland
John Harris
RENISHAW GC
England
(R.) Tom Williamson
RENO CC [NLE]
Reno, Nevada
May Dunn Hupfel
RENO CC
Reno, Nevada
Lawrence Hughes
RENWOOD CC
Grays Lake, Illinois
William James Spear
[THE] RESERVATION GC
Mulberry, Florida
Warner Bowen
[THE] RESERVE G&CC
Fort Pierce, Florida
Jim Fazio, George Fazio
RESTIGOUCHE G&CC
New Brunswick
(A.9) Clinton E. Robinson
RESTON SOUTH GC
Reston, Virginia
Edmund B. Ault
RETFORD CC
Nottinghamshire, England
Tom Williamson
(R.) J. S. F. Morrison
RETREAT G&CC
Berryville, Virginia
Buddy Loving
REVELSTOKE GC
Revelstoke, British Columbia
Norman H. Woods
REYMERSWAEL GC
Netherlands
J. F. Dudok van Heel
REYNOLDS PARK GC
Winston-Salem, North Carolina
Perry Maxwell
(R.) Ellis Maples
REYNOLDS PLANTATION GC
Greensboro, Georgia
Bob Cupp, *Fuzzy Zoeller, Hubert Green*
RHEINBLICK-LOTTSTETTEN GC
Switzerland
Kurt Rossknecht

RHINELANDER CC
Rhinelander, Wisconsin
Charles Maddox, *Frank P. MacDonald*
(A.9) Harry Collis
RHODE ISLAND CC
West Barrington, Rhode Island
Donald Ross
(R.2) Geoffrey S. Cornish
RHODO DUNES GC
Florence, Oregon
NKA Ocean Dunes G Links
RHOS-ON-SEA GC
Rhos-on-Sea, Wales
(R.) Tom Simpson
R. H. STORRER ESTATE GC
Woodbridge, Ontario
Howard Watson
RHUDDLAN GC
Clwyd, Wales
F. G. Hawtree, J. H. Taylor
RHYL GC
Rhyl, Wales
James Braid
RIBAULT GC
Jacksonville, Florida
Luther O. "Luke" Morris
RIB MOUNTAIN LODGE GC
Wausau, Wisconsin
Edward Lawrence Packard
RICH ACRES GC
Richfield, Minnesota
Gerry Pirkl, *Donald G. Brauer, Paul S. Fjare*
RICHARD C. JONES MEMORIAL GC
Cedar Rapids, Iowa
Robert Everly
RICHARD NIXON ESTATE GC
San Clemente, California
Joseph B. Williams
RICHELIEU VALLEY CC (BLUE CSE)
Montreal, Quebec
William Gordon, David Gordon
(R.) Graham Cooke
RICHELIEU VALLEY CC (RED CSE)
Montreal, Quebec
William Gordon, David Gordon
(R.) Graham Cooke
RICHFORD CC
Richford, Vermont
Tom Devlin
RICHLAND CC [NLE]
Nashville, Tennessee
Donald Ross
(R.9) Joseph S. Finger
RICHLAND CC
Nashville, Tennessee
Jack Nicklaus
RICHLAND G&CC
Richland, Missouri
Don Falls
RICHMOND CC
British Columbia
A. Vernon Macon
RICHMOND CC
Richmond, California
(R.) Ronald Fream
RICHMOND CC
Richmond, Missouri
Chet Mendenhall
RICHMOND CC
Richmond, Rhode Island
Brian Silva, Geoffrey S. Cornish

RICHMOND GC
Richmond, England
Tom Dunn
(R.) Willie Park, Jr.
RICHMOND COUNTY CC
Staten Island, New York
Robert White
(R.4) Frank Duane
RICHMOND HILL G&CC
Richmond, Ontario
Clinton E. Robinson
RICHMOND PARK GC [NLE]
London, England
Willie Park, Jr.
RICHMOND PARK GC (DUKES CSE)
London, England
F. G. Hawtree, J. H. Taylor
RICHMOND PARK GC (PRINCES CSE)
London, England
F. G. Hawtree, J. H. Taylor
RICHMOND PINES CC
Rockingham, North Carolina
Donald Ross
(A.9) Gene Hamm
RICHTER PARK GC
Danbury, Connecticut
Edward Ryder
RICHTON PARK GC
Illinois
Harry Collis
RICHVIEW G&CC
Oakville, Ontario
Clinton E. Robinson
RICKMANSWORTH PUBLIC GC
Hertfordshire, England
H. S. Colt
(R.) F. G. Hawtree, J. H. Taylor
(R.) J. S. F. Morrison
RIDDELL'S BAY G&CC
Warwick, Bermuda
Devereux Emmet
RIDDER FARM GC
East Bridgewater, Massachusetts
Henry Homan
(A.9) Geoffrey S. Cornish
RIDEAU VIEW CC
Manotick, Ontario
Howard Watson
(A.9) Clinton E. Robinson
RIDENOOR PARK GC
Gahanna, Ohio
Jack Kidwell, Michael Hurdzan
[THE] RIDGE C
South Sandwich, Massachusetts
Robert von Hagge
RIDGE CC
Chicago, Illinois
H. J. Tweedie
(R.) Ken Killian, Dick Nugent
RIDGEFIELD GC [NLE]
Ridgefield, Connecticut
Tom Bendelow
RIDGEFIELD MUNI
Ridgefield, Connecticut
George Fazio, Tom Fazio
RIDGEFIELDS CC
Kingsport, Tennessee
Donald Ross
(R.) John LaFoy
RIDGE GC
Fort Quappelle, Saskatchewan
Brad Konecsni

RIDGEMARK G&CC (DIABLO CSE)
Hollister, California
Richard Bigler
RIDGEMARK G&CC (GABILAN CSE)
Hollister, California
Richard Bigler
RIDGEMONT CC
Greece, New York
(R.2) Brian Ault
RIDGEMOOR CC
Harwood Heights, Illinois
William B. Langford
(R.) William B. Langford,
Theodore J. Moreau
(R.) Edward B. Dearie, Jr.
(R.) Edward Lawrence
Packard
(R.) Edward Lawrence
Packard, Roger Packard
(R.) Bob Lohmann
THE RIDGES GC
Grand Junction, Colorado
Dick Phelps
RIDGES INN & CC
Wisconsin Rapids, Wisconsin
John Murgatroyd
RIDGETOWN GC
Ridgetown, Ontario
Howard Watson, John Watson
RIDGEVIEW GC
Ligonier, Pennsylvania
X. G. Hassenplug
RIDGEWAY CC [NLE]
Memphis, Tennessee
William B. Langford
RIDGEWAY CC
Germantown, Tennessee
Ellis Maples
RIDGEWAY CC
White Plains, New York
Pete Clark
(R.9) Frank Duane
(R.) Stephen Kay
RIDGEWOOD CC
Danbury, Connecticut
Devereux Emmett
(R.) *Carl H. Anderson*
(R.) Robert Trent Jones
RIDGEWOOD CC [NLE]
Ridgewood, New Jersey
(R.) Donald Ross
RIDGEWOOD CC
Paramus, New Jersey
A.W. Tillinghast
(R.) Rees Jones
RIDGEWOOD CC
Waco, Texas
(R.) Ralph Plummer
RIDGEWOOD MUNI
Cleveland, Ohio
Sandy Alves
RIDGLEA CC (CHAMPIONSHIP CSE)
Fort Worth, Texas
Ralph Plummer
(R.) Jay Morrish
RIDGLEA CC (NORTH CSE)
Fort Worth, Texas
John Bredemus
(R.6) Ralph Plummer
RIDING MOUNTAIN GC
Manitoba
(R.9 A.9) A.W. Creed

RIFLE CREEK GC
Rifle, Colorado
(A.9) Dick Phelps

RIGENEE GC
Belgium
Paul Rolin

RIJSWIJK GC
Rijswijk, Holland
D. M. A. Steel

RILEY VILLAGE GC
Greenfield, Indiana
Gary Kern

RINGGOLD CC
Ringgold, Virginia
Gene Hamm

RINGWAY GC
Manchester, England
H. S. Colt
(R.) H. S. Colt

RIO BRAVO GC
Bakersfield, California
Robert Muir Graves

RIO DEL MAR GC
Aptos, California
(R.) Clark Glasson
(R.) Bert Stamps
(R.) Garrett Gill, George B.
Williams

RIO GRANDE VALLEY GC
Texas
Ralph Plummer

RIO HONDO CC
Downey, California
John Duncan Dunn

RIO MAR CC
Vero Beach, Florida
Herbert Strong
(A.9) Ernest E. Smith
(R.) Joe Lee

RIO MAR GC
Palmer, Puerto Rico
George Fazio, Tom Fazio

RIO PINAR CC
Orlando, Florida
Mark Mahannah

RIO RANCHO G&CC
Albuquerque, New Mexico
Desmond Muirhead

RIO RICO G&CC
Rio Rico, Arizona
Robert Trent Jones, Jr.

RIO VERDE CC (QUAIL RUN CSE)
Rio Verde, Arizona
Fred Bolton, Milt Coggins
(A.9) Jeff Hardin, Greg Nash

RIO VERDE CC (WHITE WING CSE)
Rio Verde, Arizona
Fred Bolton, Milt Coggins
(A.9) Jeff Hardin, Greg Nash
(R.) Gary Panks

RIO VISTA GC
Bridgeburg, Ontario
Stanley Thompson

RIPON CITY GC
Yorkshire, England
George Lowe

RIP VAN WINKLE GC
Palenville, New York
Donald Ross

RISEBRIDGE GC
Essex, England
Fred W. Hawtree

RITTWOOD CC
Butler, Pennsylvania
James Gilmore Harrison

RIVA DEI TESSALI GC
Taranto, Italy
Marco Croze

RIVENDELL GC
Verona, Ontario
(A.9) Robert Heaslip

[THE] RIVER C
Bradenton, Florida
Ron Garl

[THE] RIVER C
Vero Beach, Florida
Pete Dye

[THE] RIVER C
Pawleys Island, South Carolina
Tom Jackson

RIVERBEND CC
Sugarland, Texas
Press Maxwell
(R.) Jay Riviere

RIVERBEND CC
Tequesta, Florida
George Fazio, Tom Fazio

RIVERBEND G&CC
Broderick, California
Jack Fleming

RIVER BEND G&CC
Great Falls, Virginia
Edmund B. Ault, Al Jamison

RIVER BEND GC
Ormond Beach, Florida
Lloyd Clifton, *Kenneth Ezell,
George Clifton*

RIVER BEND GC
Story City, Iowa
Charles Calhoun

RIVER BEND GC
Boiling Springs, North Carolina
Russell Breeden

RIVER BEND GC
New Bern, North Carolina
Gene Hamm

RIVERBEND GC
Miamisburg, Ohio
Robert Bruce Harris

RIVERBEND GC
Kent, Washington
John Steidel

RIVERBEND GC
Germantown, Wisconsin
Roger Packard

RIVER BEND G CSE
Red Deer, Alberta
William G. Robinson

RIVERBY HILLS GC
Bowling Green, Ohio
Harold Paddock

RIVERCHASE CC
Birmingham, Alabama
Joe Lee
(R.3) Denis Griffiths
(R.15) John LaFoy

RIVERCHASE CC
Coppell, Texas
Jim Fazio

RIVERCLIFF GC
Bull Shoals, Arkansas
Earl Stone

RIVER CREST CC
Fort Worth, Texas
Tom Bendelow
(R.) Ralph Plummer

RIVERDALE GC (DUNES CSE)
Brighton, Colorado
Perry Dye

RIVERDALE GC (KNOLLS CSE)
Brighton, Colorado
Henry B. Hughes

RIVERDALE GC
Little Rock, Arkansas
Herman Hackbarth

RIVERDALE GC
Riverdale, Montana
George H. Schneiter

RIVER FALLS PLANTATION GC
Duncan, South Carolina
Gary Player

RIVER FOREST CC
Elmhurst, Illinois
Charles Maddox, *Frank P.
MacDonald*
(R.) Edward Lawrence
Packard, Roger Packard

RIVERFOREST CC
Freeport, Pennsylvania
Wynn Tredway

RIVER GREENS GC
Avon Park, Florida
Jack Kidwell

RIVER GREENS GC
West Lafayette, Ohio
Jack Kidwell

RIVERGREENS GC
Gladstone, Oregon
John Junor

RIVERHILL C
Kerrville, Texas
Joseph S. Finger, Byron Nelson

RIVER HILLS CC
Valrico, Florida
Joe Lee

RIVER HILLS CC
Lake Wylie, South Carolina
Willard Byrd

RIVER HILLS CC
Robstown, Texas
Warren Cantrell
(A.9) Leon Howard

RIVER HILLS G&CC
Little River, South Carolina
Tom Jackson

RIVER HILLS G&CC
Saskatoon, Saskatchewan
William G. Robinson, John F.
Robinson

RIVER HILLS GC
California, Kentucky
Buck Blankenship, *Morgan
Boggs*

RIVER ISLAND C
Kodak, Tennessee
Arthur Hills

RIVER ISLAND GC
Porterville, California
Bob Baldock
(R.) Robert Muir Graves

RIVER ISLAND GC
Oconto Falls, Wisconsin
Edward Lawrence Packard

RIVERLANDS G&CC
Laplace, Louisiana
John Schneider, Henry Thomas

RIVERLAWN CC
Oceola, Arkansas
Joseph S. Finger

RIVERMEAD GC
Aylmer, Quebec
Kenneth F.P. Skodacek

RIVERMONT G&CC
Alpharetta, Georgia
Joe Lee, Rocky Roquemore
(R.) Bill Amick

RIVER NORTH G&CC
Macon, Georgia
Arthur Davis, Ron Kirby, Gary
Player

RIVER OAKS CC
Grand Island, New York
Desmond Muirhead

RIVER OAKS CC
Houston, Texas
Donald Ross
(R.) Ralph Plummer
(R.) Joseph S. Finger

RIVER OAKS GC
Calumet City, Illinois
Ken Killian, Dick Nugent
(R.) Dick Nugent

RIVER OAKS GC
Cottage Grove, Minnesota
Don Herfort

RIVER OAKS GC
Grandview, Missouri
Larry Runyon, Michael H. Malyn

RIVER OAKS G PLANTATION
Myrtle Beach, South Carolina
Gene Hamm
(A.3rd 9) Tom Jackson

RIVER PINES GC
Alpharetta, Georgia
Denis Griffiths

RIVER PLACE CC
Austin, Texas
Jay Morrish, *Tom Kite*

RIVER PLANTATION G&CC
Conroe, Texas
Jay Riviere

RIVER RANCH GC
Lake Wales, Florida
Joe Lee

RIVER RIDGE CC
Bradley, Virginia
Jerry Turner

RIVER RIDGE GC
Oxnard, California
William F. Bell

RIVER RUN G&CC
Davidson, North Carolina
Bob Walker, *Ray Floyd*

RIVER RUN GC
Berlin, Maryland
Gary Player

RIVER RUN G LINKS
Bradenton, Florida
Ward Northrup

RIVER'S BEND CC
Chester, Florida
Steve Smyers

RIVERS BEND GC
Everett, Pennsylvania
X. G. Hassenplug

RIVER'S EDGE GC
Fayetteville, Georgia
Bobby Weed

RIVER'S EDGE GC
Bend, Oregon
Robert Muir Graves

RIVER'S EDGE YACHT & CC
Fort Myers, Florida
Ron Garl
RIVERSHORE GC
Kamloops, British Columbia
Robert Trent Jones
RIVERSIDE C
Grand Prairie, Texas
Roger Packard
RIVERSIDE CC
Battle Creek, Michigan
Bruce Matthews, Jerry Matthews
(R.9 A.9) Roger Packard
RIVERSIDE CC
Lansing, Michigan
William B. Langford
RIVERSIDE CC
Menominee, Michigan
A. H. Jolly
RIVERSIDE CC
Bozeman, Montana
Theodore Wirth
(A.9) Dick Phelps, Brad Benz
RIVERSIDE CC
Carlsbad, New Mexico
William H. Tucker, William H.
Tucker, Jr.
(R.9 A.9) Brad Benz
RIVERSIDE CC
Syracuse, New York
Edward Lawrence Packard
RIVERSIDE CC
High Falls, North Carolina
J. Porter Gibson
RIVERSIDE CC
Lake Jackson, Texas
Ralph Plummer
RIVERSIDE CC
Provo, Utah
William F. Bell
(R.1) William Howard Neff
RIVERSIDE G&CC
Macon, Georgia
Chic Adams
RIVERSIDE G&CC
Swea City, Iowa
George Morton
RIVERSIDE G&CC
Portland, Oregon
James Henderson (9 1926)
(A.9) H. Chandler Egan
(R.) William F. Bell
(R.) John Steidel
RIVERSIDE G&CC
New Brunswick
(R.) Donald Ross
(R.) Clinton E. Robinson
RIVERSIDE G&CC
Saskatoon, Saskatchewan
William Kinnear
(R.) William G. Robinson
RIVERSIDE GC
Coyote, California
Jack Fleming
(A.9) William F. Bell
RIVERSIDE GC
Riverside, California
Charles Maud
(R.) Herbert Fowler

RIVERSIDE GC
North Riverside, Illinois
William B. Langford
(R.) William B. Langford
(R.) Edward Lawrence
Packard
(R.) Dick Nugent
RIVERSIDE GC
St. Francis, Kansas
Herman R. Johnson
RIVERSIDE GC
Chenango State Park, New York
L.D. Cox
RIVERSIDE GC
Austin, Texas
Perry Maxwell, Press Maxwell
RIVERSIDE GC
San Antonio, Texas
George Hoffman
RIVERSIDE GC
Ogden, Utah
Ernest Schneiter
RIVERSIDE GC
Mason, West Virginia
Jack Kidwell, Michael Hurdzan
RIVERSIDE G CSE
Chelais, Washington
(A.9) Roy Goss, *Glen Proctor*
RIVERSIDE INN & CC
Cambridge Springs,
Pennsylvania
William Baird
RIVERSIDE MUNI
Indianapolis, Indiana
William H. Diddel
RIVERSIDE MUNI
Portland, Maine
Wayne Stiles
(R.) William F. Mitchell
(A.3rd 9) Geoffrey S.
Cornish, William G.
Robinson
RIVERSIDE MUNI
Jackson, Mississippi
Earl Stone
RIVERSIDE MUNI
Victoria, Texas
Ralph Plummer
(R.) Jay Riviere
RIVERSIDE MUNI
Janesville, Wisconsin
Robert Bruce Harris
(R.) Bob Lohmann
RIVERSIDE OF FRESNO GC
Fresno, California
(R.9 A.9) William P. Bell
RIVERSIDE PARK GC [NLE]
San Antonio, Texas
George Hoffman
RIVERTON CC
Riverton, New Jersey
Donald Ross
RIVERTON GC
Henrietta, New York
Edmund B. Ault
RIVERTON GC
Riverton, Wyoming
Richard Watson
(R.9 A.9) Dick Phelps, Brad
Benz
RIVER VALE CC
River Vale, New Jersey
Orrin Smith
(R.) Hal Purdy

RIVER VALLEY CC
Canton, Michigan
William Klinger
RIVER VALLEY CC
Westfield, Pennsylvania
Geoffrey S. Cornish
RIVER VIEW C
Keosauqua, Iowa
Leo Johnson
RIVERVIEW CC
Milford, Connecticut
Al Zikorus
RIVERVIEW CC
Cleburne, Texas
Leon Howard
RIVERVIEW GC
Mesa, Arizona
Gary Panks
RIVERVIEW GC
Sun City, Arizona
Jeff Hardin
RIVERVIEW GC
New Cumberland, Pennsylvania
Royce Hewitt
RIVERVIEW HIGHLANDS GC
Riverview, Michigan
William Newcomb
(A.9) Arthur Hills
RIVERVIEW MUNI
Sterling, Colorado
Frank Hummel
RIVER WILDERNESS YACHT & CC
Parrish, Florida
Ted McAnlis
RIVERWOOD CC
Port Charlotte, Florida
Gene Bates
RIVERWOOD GC
Dundee, Oregon
George Junor
RIVERWOOD GC
Port Arthur, Texas
John Barlow
RIVERWOOD MUNI
Bismarck, North Dakota
Leo Johnson
RIVIERA AFRICAINE GC
Ivory Coast
Arthur Davis, Ron Kirby, Gary
Player
RIVIERA CC
Pacific Palisades, California
George C. Thomas, Jr., William
P. Bell
RIVIERA CC
Coral Gables, Florida
Donald Ross
(R.) Dick Wilson
(R.) Mark Mahannah
(A.9) David Wallace
(R.) Lloyd Clifton
RIVIERA CC
Lesage, West Virginia
(A.9) Buck Blankenship
RIVIERA MARIN GC
San Rafael, California
William F. Bell
RIVIÈRE DU LOUP GC
Quebec
(R.9 A.9) Howard Watson,
John Watson
ROADHAVEN GC
Apache Junction, Arizona
Greg Nash

ROADRUNNER DUNES GC
Twenty-nine Palms, California
Lawrence Hughes
ROANOKE CC
Williamston, North Carolina
Ellis Maples
(A.9) Gene Hamm
ROANOKE CC [NLE]
Roanoke, Virginia
Alex Findlay
(R.) A.W. Tillinghast
ROANOKE CC
Roanoke, Virginia
Gene Hamm
(R.5) Tom Clark
ROAN VALLEY CC
Mountain City, Tennessee
Ellis Maples, Dan Maples
ROARING GAP G&CC
Roaring Gap, North Carolina
Donald Ross
ROBBER'S ROOST GC
North Myrtle Beach, South
Carolina
Russell Breeden
ROBBINHEAD LAKES GC
Brandon, Mississippi
Sonny Guy
ROBERT A. BLACK GC
Chicago, Illinois
Ken Killian, Dick Nugent
ROBERT TRENT JONES GC
Lake Manassas, Virginia
Robert Trent Jones
ROBERT TRENT JONES G CSE
Ithaca, New York
Robert Trent Jones
ROBERT VAN PATTEN GC
Jonesville, New York
Armand Farina
ROBIN HOOD CC [NLE]
Illinois
George O'Neil
ROBIN HOOD GC
Birmingham, England
H. S. Colt
(R.) H. S. Colt
ROB ROY GC
Prospect Heights, Illinois
Edward B. Dearie, Jr.
ROCA LLISA GC
Ibiza, Spain
Fred W. Hawtree
ROCHDALE GC
Rochdale, England
(R.) J. J. F. Pennink
ROCHE HARBOR GC
San Juan, Washington
William H. Tucker
ROCHELLE CC
Rochelle, Illinois
Perry Maxwell
(R.9 A.9) David Gill
ROCHESTER CC
Gonic, New Hampshire
(R.) Orrin Smith
(A.9) Phil Wogan
(R.) Manny Francis
ROCHESTER G&CC [NLE]
Rochester, Minnesota
Harry Turpie
(R.9 A.9) A.W. Tillinghast
(R.2) Geoffrey S. Cornish,
Brian Silva

ROCHESTER GC
Rochester, Michigan
Tom Bendelow
ROCHFORD HUNDRED GC
England
(R.) F. G. Hawtree
[THE] ROCK GC
Drummond Island, Michigan
Harry Bowers
ROCKAWAY HUNTING C [NLE]
Cedarhurst, New York
Willie Dunn, Jr.
(A.9) Tom Bendelow
ROCKAWAY HUNTING C
Cedarhurst, New York
Devereux Emmet
(R. A.7) A. W. Tillinghast
(R.) Perry Maxwell
(R.) Press Maxwell
(R.) Brian Silva, Geoffrey S.
Cornish
ROCKAWAY RIVER CC
New Jersey
(A.9) George Low
(R.) Hal Purdy, Malcolm
Purdy
ROCK BARN GC
Conover, North Carolina
Russell Breeden
ROCK CHAPEL G&CC
Burlington, Ontario
John F. Robinson
ROCK CREEK G&CC
Jacksonville, North Carolina
Jerry Turner
ROCK CREEK G&CC
Cedar Mill, Oregon
William Sander
ROCK CREEK PARK GC
Washington, D.C.
(R.) William S. Flynn
ROCKDALE CC
Rockdale, Texas
Leon Howard
ROCKFISH CC
Hope Mills, North Carolina
C. C. McCuiston
ROCKFORD CC
Rockford, Illinois
H. J. Tweedie
(R.) C. D. Wagstaff
(R.) Bob Lohmann
ROCKFORD G&CC
Rockford, Iowa
Beryl Taylor
ROCK HILL CC
Rock Hill, South Carolina
A. W. Tillinghast
(A.9) J. Porter Gibson
ROCK HILL G&CC
Manorville, New York
Frank Duane
ROCK HILL GC
Ibaragi, Japan
Kokyu Kensetsu
ROCK ISLAND ARSENAL C
Rock Island, Illinois
(R.) David Gill
ROCK ISLAND CC [NLE]
Blue Island, Illinois
Tom Bendelow

ROCKLAND CC
Rockland, Maine
Wayne Stiles
(A.9) Roger Sorrent
ROCKLAND CC
Sparkhill, New York
Robert White
(R.9) Robert White
(R.) Alfred H. Tull
(R.) Robert Trent Jones
ROCKLAND GC
Rockland, Massachusetts
Skip Wogan, Phil Wogan
ROCKLAND LAKE GC (NORTH CSE)
Congers, New York
David Gordon
(R.) Stephen Kay
ROCKLAND LAKE GC (SOUTH CSE)
Congers, New York
David Gordon
ROCKLEDGE CC
West Hartford, Connecticut
(R.9 A.9) Orrin Smith
(R.) William F. Mitchell
(R.2) Al Zikorus
ROCKLEIGH GC (BERGEN CSE)
Hackensack, New Jersey
William Gordon, David Gordon
(R.) Robert Trent Jones
ROCKLEIGH GC (ROCKLEIGH CSE)
Hackensack, New Jersey
Alfred H. Tull
(R.) William Gordon, David
Gordon
ROCKPORT CC
Rockport, Texas
Bill Coore
ROCKPORT GC
Rockport, Massachusetts
Phil Wogan
ROCKRIMMON CC
Stamford, Connecticut
Robert Trent Jones
(A.9) Orrin Smith
ROCK RIVER CC
Sterling, Illinois
William James Spear
ROCK RIVER HILLS GC
Horizon, Wisconsin
Homer Fieldhouse
(A.9) Bob Lohmann
ROCK SPRING CC
West Orange, New Jersey
Charles Banks
(R.) Hal Purdy
ROCK SPRINGS CC
Alton, Illinois
Tom Bendelow
ROCKVILLE LINKS C
Rockville Centre, New York
Devereux Emmet
(R.1) Frank Duane
ROCKVILLE GC
Rockville, Indiana
William H. Diddel
ROCKWELL COLLEGE GC
Ireland
Eddie Hackett
ROCKWOOD CC
Independence, Missouri
John S. Davis
(A.9) Charles Dupree

ROCKWOOD HALL CC
Tarrytown, New York
Devereux Emmet, Alfred H. Tull
(R. A.5) A. W. Tillinghast
ROCKWOOD MUNI
Fort Worth, Texas
John Bredemus
(R.18 A.3rd 9) Ralph
Plummer
ROCKWOOD PARK GC
New Brunswick
(A.9) William G. Robinson,
John F. Robinson
ROCKY BAYOU CC
Niceville, Florida
Bill Amick
ROCKY POINT GC [NLE]
Tampa, Florida
Willie Black
(R.) Hans Schmeisser
(A.9) David Wallace
ROCKY POINT GC
Tampa, Florida
Ron Garl
ROCKY POINT GC [NLE]
Maryland
(R.) Orrin Smith
ROCKY POINT GC
Essex, Maryland
Russell Roberts
ROCKY RIDGE CC
St. George, Vermont
Walter Barcomb, Ernie
Farrington
RODGERS FORGE CC
Baltimore, Maryland
NKA CC of Maryland
ROEHAMPTON GC
London, England
Tom Simpson
ROGELL G CSE
Detroit, Michigan
Donald Ross
ROGERS PARK GC
Tampa, Florida
Willie Black
(R.) Ron Garl
ROGUE RIVER GC
Sparta, Michigan
Warner Bowen
ROGUE VALLEY CC
Medford, Oregon
H. Chandler Egan
(R.9 A.9) William F. Bell,
William P. Bell
(R.) Robert Muir Graves
ROHRENFELD GC
Ingolstadt, Germany
J. F. Dudok van Heel
ROKKO INTERNATIONAL GC
Hyogo, Japan
F. Kato
ROLLING ACRES CC
Beaver Falls, Pennsylvania
James Gilmore Harrison,
Ferdinand Garbin
(A.9) Ferdinand Garbin
ROLLING GREEN CC
Prattville, Alabama
R. Albert Anderson

ROLLING GREEN CC
Arlington Heights, Illinois
William H. Diddel
(R.6) David Gill
(R.) Roger Packard
ROLLING GREEN CC
Hamel, Minnesota
Charles Maddox
ROLLING GREEN CC
Springfield, Pennsylvania
William S. Flynn, Howard
Toomey
ROLLING GREEN G&CC
Sarasota, Florida
R. Albert Anderson
(A.9) Bill Dietsch
ROLLING GREEN GC
Huntsburg, Ohio
Richard W. LaConte
ROLLING GREEN GC
Easley, South Carolina
William B. Lewis
ROLLING GREEN GC
Green River, Wyoming
Henry B. Hughes
ROLLING GREENS GC
Newton, New Jersey
Nicholas Psiahas
ROLLING HILLS CC
Cabot, Arkansas
William T. Martin
ROLLING HILLS CC [NLE]
Rolling Hills, California
William F. Bell, William P. Bell
ROLLING HILLS CC
Rolling Hills Estate, California
Ted Robinson
ROLLING HILLS CC
Golden, Colorado
Press Maxwell
ROLLING HILLS CC
Wilton, Connecticut
Alfred H. Tull
(R.5) Brian Ault, Tom Clark
(R.2) Stephen Kay
ROLLING HILLS CC
Fort Lauderdale, Florida
William F. Mitchell
(A.9) Bill Dietsch
ROLLING HILLS CC
Newburgh, Indiana
William H. Diddel
(R.) Gary Kern
ROLLING HILLS CC
Wichita, Kansas
Walter Angle
(R.) Floyd Farley
ROLLING HILLS CC
Crystal Springs, Mississippi
George C. Curtis
ROLLING HILLS CC
Versailles, Missouri
George Gregory (1955)
ROLLING HILLS CC
Monroe, North Carolina
George W. Cobb
(R.) John LaFoy
ROLLING HILLS CC
Tulsa, Oklahoma
Perry Maxwell
(R.) Floyd Farley

Rolling Hills CC
Pittsburgh, Pennsylvania
James Gilmore Harrison,
Ferdinand Garbin
Rolling Hills CC
Arlington, Texas
C.M. Mimms
Rolling Hills CC
Moody, Texas
Leon Howard
Rolling Hills GC
Tempe, Arizona
Milt Coggins
(A.9) Gary Panks
Rolling Hills GC
Tucson, Arizona
William F. Bell
Rolling Hills GC
Weisner, Idaho
Frank James
Rolling Hills GC
Godfrey, Illinois
(A.9) Gary Kern, Ron Kern
Rolling Hills GC
Ionia, Michigan
Warner Bowen
Rolling Hills GC
Belfair, Washington
Donald A. Hogan
Rolling Hills G CSE
Aynor, South Carolina
Gene Hamm
Rolling Hills Par 3 GC [NLE]
Lenox, Massachusetts
Rowland Armacost
Rolling Meadows GC
Junction City, Kansas
Richard Watson
Rolling Road GC
Baltimore, Maryland
Willie Park, Jr.
Rolling Rock GC
Ligonier, Pennsylvania
Donald Ross
(R.9 A.9) P.B. Dye
Roman Hills GC
Splendora, Texas
Jay Riviere
Roman Nose State Park GC
Watonga, Oklahoma
Floyd Farley
Romeleasens GC
Veberöd, Sweden
Douglas Brazier
Romford GC
Romford, England
James Braid
Romsey GC
Romsey, England
(R.) J. J. F. Pennink, C. D.
Lawrie
(R.9 A.9) Howard Swan
Rondout GC
Accord, New York
Hal Purdy
Roodepoort Muni
Roodepoort, South Africa
Ron Kirby, Denis Griffiths
Rookery Park GC
Suffolk, England
J. J. F. Pennink, C. D. Lawrie
Roosevelt GC
Warm Springs, Georgia
Donald Ross

Roosevelt Muni
Roosevelt, Utah
Joseph B. Williams
Rosapenna GC
County Donegal, Ireland
Old Tom Morris
(R.) James Braid, Harry
Vardon
(R.) H. S. Colt
(R.) C. H. Alison, H. S. Colt
Rosário GC
Rosário, Brazil
José Maria Gonzales
Roscommon GC
Roscommon, Ireland
(R.) Eddie Hackett
Roscrea GC
Roscrea, Ireland
(R.) Eddie Hackett
Roseburg CC
Roseburg, Oregon
George Junor
(R.9 A.9) Gary Roger Baird
Rose City GC
Portland, Oregon
George Otten
Rose Creek Muni
Fargo, North Dakota
Dick Phelps
Rosedale CC
Toronto, Ontario
(R.9 A.9) Donald Ross
(R.) Howard Watson
(R.) Clinton E. Robinson
(R.) Bob Cupp
Rose Hill GC
Lickey Hill, England
F. G. Hawtree, J. H. Taylor
(R.) *Carl Bretherston*
Rose Hill Plantation GC
Hilton Head Island, South
Carolina
Gene Hamm
Rose Lake CC
Fairmont, Minnesota
Donald G. Brauer, Emil Perret
(A.9) Joel Goldstrand
Roseland G & Curling C
Windsor, Ontario
Donald Ross
Roselawn GC
Danville, Illinois
Tom Bendelow
Roselle GC
Roselle, New Jersey
Seth Raynor
Rosemere G&CC
Quebec
(R.3) John Watson
Rosemont GC
Akron, Ohio
Tom Bendelow
(A.9) Edward Lawrence
Packard
Rosemont G&CC
Winter Park, Florida
Lloyd Clifton
Rosendaelsche GC
Arnhem, Netherlands
John Duncan Dunn
(R.9 A.9) J. J. F. Pennink
Roseneath Farms GC
Pennsylvania
Alex Findlay

Rose Park GC
Salt Lake City, Utah
Mick Riley
(A.9) William F. Bell
(R.5) Arthur Jack Snyder
Roseville Cedarhold GC
Roseville, Minnesota
Gerry Pirkl, *Donald G. Brauer*
Roseville Rolling Green GC
Roseville, California
Jack Fleming
Rosewood Lakes G CSE
Reno, Nevada
Brad Benz
Roskilde GC
Roskilde, Denmark
Jan Sederholm
**Rossland Trail CC (Birchbank
CSE)**
Trail, British Columbia
Reg Stone
Rosslare GC
Rosslare, Ireland
(R.) J. Hamilton Stutt
Rossmere G&CC
Winnipeg, Manitoba
Norman H. Woods
Rossmoor GC (North CSE)
Walnut Creek, California
Desmond Muirhead
(A.9) Robert Muir Graves
Rossmoor GC (South CSE)
Walnut Creek, California
Harry Rainville, David Rainville
Rossmoor GC
Jamesburg, New Jersey
Desmond Muirhead
Rossmoor Leisure World GC
Laguna Hills, California
Desmond Muirhead
Rossmore GC
Ireland
(R.) Eddie Hackett
Ross on Rye GC
England
C. K. Cotton, J. J. F. Pennink
Ross Rogers Muni [NLE]
Amarillo, Texas
William A. McConnell
Ross Rogers Muni (East CSE)
Amarillo, Texas
Leon Howard
Ross Rogers Muni (West CSE)
Amarillo, Texas
Leon Howard, *Charles Howard*
Rosswood CC
Pine Bluff, Arkansas
Alfred H. Tull
Rotary GC
Osaka, Japan
Johnny Miller
Rother Valley GC
Yorkshire, England
Martin Hawtree, Simon Gidman
Rothesay GC
Island of Bute, Scotland
James Braid
Rothley Park GC
Leicestershire, England
Tom Williamson
Rothschild Estate GC
France
Seymour Dunn

**Rotonda G&CC (Oakland Hills
CSE)**
Cape Haze, Florida
Jim Petrides (1973)
**Rotonda G&CC (Pebble Beach
CSE)**
Cape Haze, Florida
D. J. DeVictor
Rotorua GC
Rotorua, New Zealand
C. H. Redhead
(R.) C. H. Redhead
Rotterdamsche GC
Netherlands
(R.) John Harris
Rough River Dam State Park GC
Falls of Rough, Kentucky
Benjamin Wihry
Round Hill C
Greenwich, Connecticut
Walter J. Travis
(R.) Robert Trent Jones
Round Hill C
South Dartmouth,
Massachusetts
Robert Trent Jones (routing),
Melvin Lucas, Jr.
Round Hill G&CC
Alamo, California
Lawrence Hughes
(R.) Robert Muir Graves
Round Meadow CC
Christiansburg, Virginia
J. Porter Gibson
Round Mountain GC
Round Mountain, Nevada
William Howard Neff
Round Valley CC
Morgan, Utah
Mark Dixon Ballif
Routenburn GC
Ayrshire, Scotland
James Braid
Rowany GC
Port Erin, Isle of Man
J. A. Steer
Rowlands Castle GC
England
H. S. Colt
Rowley CC
Rowley, Massachusetts
Phil Wogan
Roxboro CC
Roxboro, North Carolina
(A.9) Ellis Maples
Roxbury Run GC
Denver, New York
Hal Purdy, Malcolm Purdy
Roxiticus CC
Mendham, New Jersey
Hal Purdy
Royal CC
Miao-li, Taiwan
Robert Trent Jones, Jr.
Royal Aberdeen GC
Scotland
Willie Park
(R.) *Archie Simpson*
(R.) Tom Simpson
**Royal Aberdeen GC (Ladies
Course)**
Scotland
J. J. F. Pennink

ROYAL ADELAIDE GC
Australia
    (R.) Alister Mackenzie
    (R. A.4) Des Soutar
    (R.) Peter Thomson, Michael
    Wolveridge
ROYAL AMERICAN LINKS
Galena, Ohio
Michael Hurdzan
ROYAL AND ANCIENT GC OF ST. ANDREWS
St. Andrews, Fife, Scotland
See St. Andrews
ROYAL ANTWERP GC
Kapellenbos, Belgium
Willie Park, Jr.
    (R.18) P. M. Ross
    (A.9) Tom Simpson, P. M. Ross
ROYAL ASCOT GC
Berkshire, England
J. H. Taylor
ROYAL ASHDOWN FOREST GC (BLUE CSE)
Sussex, England
A. T. Scott
ROYAL ASHDOWN FOREST GC (RED CSE)
Sussex, England
A. T. Scott
ROYAL AUTOMOBILE C
Woodcote Park, Surrey, England
Herbert Fowler
ROYAL BELFAST GC
Belfast, Northern Ireland
H. S. Colt, C. H. Alison
ROYAL BELGIQUE GC
Belgium
    (R.) Wilfrid Reid
ROYAL BENIDINAT GC
Mallorca, Spain
Martin Hawtree
ROYAL BHUTAN GC
Thimphu, Bhutan
Stephen Kay
ROYAL BIRKDALE GC
Southport, England
George Lowe, *Charles Hawtree*
    (R.) F. G. Hawtree, J. H. Taylor
    (R.) Fred W. Hawtree (1967)
    (R.) Fred W. Hawtree (1974)
    (A.2) D. M. A. Steel
ROYAL BLACKHEATH GC [NLE]
England
    (R.) Willie Dunn
ROYAL BLACKHEATH GC
England
James Braid, John R. Stutt
ROYAL BROMONT GC
Bromont, Quebec
Graham Cooke
ROYAL BRUNEI G&CC
Jerudong Park, Brunei, Borneo
Ronald Fream
ROYAL BURGESS G SOCIETY OF EDINBURGH
Edinburgh, Scotland
Old Tom Morris
    (R.) Willie Park, Jr.
    (R.) James Braid, John R. Stutt

ROYAL CALCUTTA GC
Calcutta, India
    (R.) John Harris, Peter Thomson
ROYAL CANBERRA GC
Yarralumla, Australia
John Harris
    (R.) Peter Thomson, Michael Wolveridge
ROYAL CAPE GC
Cape Province, South Africa
C. H. Alison
ROYAL CINQUE PORTS GC
Deal, England
Tom Dunn
    (R.2) J. S. F. Morrison
    (R.) Harry Vardon
    (R.) Sir Guy Campbell, Henry Cotton
ROYAL COLWOOD G&CC
Victoria, British Columbia
A. Vernon Macan
ROYAL CC DE TANGIER
Tangier, Morocco
J. J. F. Pennink
ROYAL COUNTY DOWN GC
Newcastle, Northern Ireland
Old Tom Morris
    (R.) C. S. Butchart
    (R.) Seymour Dunn
    (R.) Harry Vardon (1908)
    (R.) Harry Vardon (1919)
ROYAL COUNTY DOWN GC (CSE No. 2)
Newcastle, Northern Ireland
C. S. Butchart
ROYAL CROMER GC
Norfolk, England
Old Tom Morris
    (R.) James Braid, John R. Stutt
ROYAL DORNOCH GC
Sutherland, Scotland
Old Tom Morris
    (R.9 A.9) John Sutherland
    (R.) J. H. Taylor
    (R. A.2) Donald Ross
    (R. A.4) George Duncan
    (R.) D. M. A. Steel
ROYAL DOWNS GC
Thornhill, Ontario
René Muylaert
ROYAL DUBLIN GC
Dublin, Ireland
    (R.) H. S. Colt, C. H. Alison
    (R.) Sir Guy Campbell, J. S. F. Morrison
    (R.2) Eddie Hackett
ROYAL EASTBOURNE GC
Sussex, England
Horace Hutchinson, *Charles Mayhewe*
    (R.) J. Hamilton Stutt
ROYALE GREEN GC
Coldspring, Texas
Bruce Littell
ROYAL FOX GC
St. Charles, Illinois
Dick Nugent
ROYAL GEMS G & SPORTS C
Bangkok, Thailand
Gary Roger Baird

ROYAL GC ARTIGUELOUVE
France
Jean Garialde
ROYAL GC DE BELGIQUE
Brussels, Belgium
Seymour Dunn
    (R.) Tom Simpson
ROYAL GC DES FAGNES
Balmoral Spa, Belgium
Tom Simpson, P. M. Ross
ROYAL GC DU SART TILMAN
Liège, Belgium
Tom Simpson
ROYAL GC LES BUTTES BLANCHES
Belgium
    (R.3) Fred W. Hawtree
ROYAL GOLF DAR ES SALAAM (BLUE CSE)
Rabat, Morocco
Robert Trent Jones
ROYAL GOLF DAR ES SALAAM (GREEN CSE)
Rabat, Morocco
Robert Trent Jones
ROYAL GOLF DAR ES SALAAM (RED CSE)
Rabat, Morocco
Robert Trent Jones
ROYAL GOLF DE FÈS
Fès, Morocco
Cabell Robinson
ROYAL GOLF D'EL JADIDA
El Jadida, Morocco
Cabell Robinson
ROYAL GOLF D'ERFOUD
Royal Palace, Erfoud, Morocco
Cabell Robinson
ROYAL GREENS GC
Roy, Utah
Keith Downs
ROYAL GUERNSEY GC
Channel Islands
P. M. Ross
ROYAL HAINAUT GC
Mons, Belgium
    (A.9) Martin Hawtree
ROYAL HAWAIIAN GC
Honolulu, Oahu, Hawaii
Perry Dye
ROYAL HILLS GC
Bangkok, Thailand
Robin Nelson, Rodney Wright
ROYAL HONG KONG GC (EDEN CSE)
Fanling, Hong Kong
John Harris, Peter Thomson
ROYAL HONG KONG GC (NEW CSE)
Hong Kong
L. S. Greenhill
    (R.) John Harris, Peter Thomson
ROYAL HONG KONG GC (OLD CSE)
Hong Kong
Captain H. N. Dumbleton
    (R.) John Harris, Peter Thomson
ROYAL HOST GC
Taiwan
Charles Mahannah, *Lee Trevino*
ROYAL HYLANDS GC
Knightstown, Indiana
Gary Kern
    (R.) Gary Kern, Ron Kern

ROYAL JOHANNESBURG CC (EAST CSE)
Johannesburg, South Africa
Robert G. Grimsdell
    (R.) C. H. Alison
ROYAL JOHANNESBURG GC (WEST CSE)
Johannesburg, South Africa
Laurie Waters
    (R.) Robert Grimsdell
    (R.) C. H. Alison
    (R.) Ron Kirby, Denis Griffiths
ROYAL KAANAPALI GC (NORTH CSE)
Lahaina, Maui, Hawaii
Robert Trent Jones
    (R.) Robert Trent Jones, Jr.
ROYAL KAANAPALI GC (SOUTH CSE)
Lahaina, Maui, Hawaii
Arthur Jack Snyder
ROYAL KENFIELD GC
Las Vegas, Nevada
Clark Glasson
    (R.) Bob Cupp, *Hubert Green*
ROYAL LAKES G&CC
Flowery Branch, Georgia
Arthur L. Davis
ROYAL LIVERPOOL GC
Hoylake, England
Robert Chambers, Jr., George Morris
    (R.) H. S. Colt
    (R.) J. J. F. Pennink
    (R.) Fred W. Hawtree
ROYAL LYTHAM & ST. ANNES GC
Lancashire, England
George Lowe
    (R.) Tom Simpson
    (R.) Herbert Fowler
    (R.2) Tom Simpson
    (R.) H. S. Colt, C. H. Alison
    (R.) H. S. Colt, J. S. F. Morrison
    (R.) J. S. F. Morrison
    (R.) C. K. Cotton, J. J. F. Pennink
    (R.) D. M. A. Steel
ROYAL LYTHAM & ST. ANNES GC (SHORT CSE)
Lancashire, England
J. J. F. Pennink, C. D. Lawrie
ROYAL MEADOWS GC
Kansas City, Missouri
Charles Stayton
ROYAL MELBOURNE GC
Long Grove, Illinois
Ted Robinson, *Greg Norman*
ROYAL MELBOURNE GC (EAST CSE)
Black Rock, Australia
Alex Russell
    (R.) Dick Wilson
ROYAL MELBOURNE GC (WEST CSE)
Black Rock, Australia
Alister Mackenzie, Alex Russell
    (R.) Dick Wilson
ROYAL MID-SURREY GC
Surrey, England
Tom Dunn
    (R.) *Reginald Beale*
    (R.) J. H. Taylor, Peter Lees
    (R.) F. G. Hawtree, J. H. Taylor
    (R.3) Fred W. Hawtree, Martin Hawtree

ROYAL MID-SURREY GC (LADIES CSE)
Surrey, England
J. H. Taylor

ROYAL MONTREAL GC (NORTH CSE) [NLE]
Dixie, Quebec
Willie Park, Jr.

ROYAL MONTREAL GC (SOUTH CSE) [NLE]
Dixie, Quebec
Willie Dunn, Jr.
   (R.) H. S. Colt
   (R.) Willie Park, Jr.

ROYAL MONTREAL GC (BLACK CSE)
Ile Bizard, Quebec
Dick Wilson

ROYAL MONTREAL GC (BLUE CSE)
Ile Bizard, Quebec
Dick Wilson
   (R.) Graham Cooke

ROYAL MONTREAL GC (RED CSE)
Ile Bizard, Quebec
Dick Wilson
   (R.) Graham Cooke

ROYAL MOUGINS GC
Mougins, France
Robert von Hagge

ROYAL MUSSELBURGH GC
East Lothian, Scotland
James Braid, John R. Stutt
   (R.) Mungo Park II

ROYAL NORTH DEVON GC
Westward Ho!, England
Old Tom Morris
   (R.) Herbert Fowler

ROYAL OAK CC
Greenwood, Indiana
Pete Dye
   (R.9 A.9) Gary Kern

ROYAL OAK G&CC
Titusville, Florida
Dick Wilson

ROYAL OAK GC
Royal Oak, Michigan
Bruce Matthews, Jerry Matthews

ROYAL OAK INN GC
Victoria, British Columbia
James P. Izatt

ROYAL OAKS CC
Dallas, Texas
Don January, Billy Martindale
   (R.) Arthur Davis
   (R.) Jay Morrish

ROYAL OAKS CC
Vancouver, Washington
Fred Federspiel
   (R.2) Ted Robinson
   (R.) Robert Muir Graves

ROYAL OAKS GC [NLE]
Clayton, California
Robert Muir Graves

ROYAL OAKS GC
Cartersville, Georgia
Arthur Davis, Ron Kirby, Gary Player

ROYAL OAKS GC
Lebanon, Pennsylvania
Ron Forse

ROYAL OAKS G CSE
Maryville, Tennessee
D. J. DeVictor

ROYAL OTTAWA GC
Hull, Quebec
Tom Bendelow
   (R.) Clinton E. Robinson
   (R.27) Howard Watson
   (A.9) Howard Watson
   (R.4 A.2) John Watson
   (R.) Graham Cooke

ROYAL PALACE GOLF D'AGADIR
Agadir, Morocco
Robert Trent Jones

ROYAL PALM BEACH G&CC
Palm Beach, Florida
Mark Mahannah, Charles Mahannah

ROYAL PALM HOTEL GC [NLE]
Fort Myers, Florida
John M. "Jock" Inglis

ROYAL PALMS GC
Mesa, Arizona
David Gill
   (R.) Gary Grandstaff

ROYAL PALM Y&CC
Boca Raton, Florida
Robert Trent Jones

ROYAL PARK G&CC [NLE]
Vero Beach, Florida
Herbert Strong

ROYAL PERTH GC
Perth, Australia
S. Cohen
   (R.) Peter Thomson, Michael Wolveridge

ROYAL PINE G&CC
Pinewald, New Jersey
Conrad Schupkagel

ROYAL PINES CC
Beaufort, South Carolina
NKA Golf Professionals C

ROYAL POINCIANA GC (CYPRESS CSE)
Naples, Florida
David Wallace

ROYAL POINCIANA GC (PINES CSE)
Naples, Florida
David Wallace

ROYAL PORT ALFRED GC
Port Royal, South Africa
   (R.) S. V. Hotchkin

ROYAL PORTHCAWL GC
Mid-Glamorgan, Wales
Charles Gibson
   (R.) James Braid
   (R.8 A.8) H. S. Colt
   (R. A.4) F. G. Hawtree, J. H. Taylor
   (R.) Tom Simpson
   (R.) C. K. Cotton

ROYAL PORTRUSH GC (DUNLUCE CSE)
Northern Ireland
H. S. Colt, J. S. F. Morrison
   (R.) J. S. F. Morrison

ROYAL PORTRUSH GC (VALLEY CSE)
Northern Ireland
   (R.) H. S. Colt, J. S. F. Morrison
   (R.) J. S. F. Morrison

ROYAL QUEBEC CC (KENT CSE) [NLE]
Montgomery Falls, Quebec
Albert Murray
   (R.9 A.9) Herbert Strong

ROYAL QUEBEC CC (QUEBEC CSE)
Boischatel, Quebec
Howard Watson
   (R.9) Howard Watson, John Watson
   (R.) Graham Cooke

ROYAL QUEBEC CC (ROYAL CSE)
Boischatel, Quebec
Willie Park, Jr.
   (A.2) Howard Watson, John Watson

ROYAL QUEENSLAND GC
Australia
   (R.) Alister Mackenzie

ROYAL RIVERSIDE G&CC
Fairmont Hot Springs, British Columbia
Bill Newis

ROYAL SALISBURY GC
Salisbury, Zimbabwe
Laurie Waters
   (R.) Fred W. Hawtree
   (A.2) Fred W. Hawtree

ROYAL SCOT CC
Green Bay, Wisconsin
Don Herfort

ROYAL SCOT GC
Lansing, Michigan
Jim Holmes
   (R.4) Jerry Matthews

ROYAL SELANGOR GC (NEW CSE)
Kuala Lumpur, Malaysia
J. J. F. Pennink
   (R.) Ronald Fream

ROYAL SELANGOR GC (OLD CSE)
Malaysia
   (R.) C. H. Alison
   (R.) Ronald Fream

ROYAL ST. DAVIDS GC
Harlech, Wales
Harold Finch-Hatton (1893)
   (R.) Fred W. Hawtree

ROYAL ST. GEORGE'S GC
Kent, England
W. Laidlaw Purves
   (R.9) H. S. Colt, C. H. Alison
   (R.) Alister Mackenzie
   (R.) J. J. F. Pennink

ROYAL ST. KITTS GC
St. Kitts
John Harris, Peter Thomson, Ronald Fream

ROYAL SWAN CC
Betterton, Maryland
Alex Findlay

ROYAL SYDNEY GC
Sydney, Australia
S. R. Robbie
   (R.) Alister Mackenzie
   (R.) Peter Thomson, Michael Wolveridge

ROYAL TARA GC
Ireland
   (R.9 A.9) John Harris
   (R.) Eddie Hackett

ROYAL TEE CC
Cape Coral, Florida
Gordon Lewis

ROYAL TROON GC
Ayrshire, Scotland
Charles Hunter
   (R.) Willie Fernie
   (R.) James Braid
   (R.) Alister Mackenzie
   (R.) J. S. F. Morrison

ROYAL VIRGINIA GC
Hadensville, Virginia
Algie Pulley

ROYAL WATERLOO GC [NLE]
Waterloo, Belgium
H. S. Colt, C. H. Alison

ROYAL WATERLOO GC (LA MARACHE CSE)
Ohain, Belgium
Fred W. Hawtree

ROYAL WATERLOO GC (LE LION CSE)
Ohain, Belgium
Fred W. Hawtree

ROYAL WEST NORFOLK GC
Norfolk, England
Horace Hutchinson, *Holcombe Ingleby*
   (R.) C. K. Hutchinson, Sir Guy Campbell, S. V. Hotchkin

ROYAL WIMBLEDON GC
Surrey, England
Willie Park
   (R.) H. S. Colt
   (R.) J. S. F. Morrison
   (R.) J. J. F. Pennink, C. D. Lawrie

ROYAL WINCHESTER GC
Hampshire, England
J. H. Taylor
   (R.) H. S. Colt

ROYAL WOODBINE GC
Toronto, Ontario
Michael Hurdzan

ROYAL WORLINGTON AND NEWMARKET GC
Suffolk, England
Tom Dunn
   (R.9) H. S. Colt

ROYAL ZOUTE GC
Belgium
Seymour Dunn
   (R.) J. S. F. Morrison

ROYAN GC
Royan, France
Robert Berthet

ROY ROGERS GC
Chatsworth, California
William H. Johnson

ROYSTON GC
Royston, England
Tom Dunn

ROZELLA FORD GC
Warsaw, Indiana
William H. Diddel
   (R.) Gary Kern

ROZENSTEIN GC
Netherlands
J. F. Dudok van Heel

RUBY VIEW MUNI [NLE]
Elko, Nevada
Pete Marich

RUBY VIEW MUNI
Elko, Nevada
Arthur Jack Snyder

RUFFLED FEATHERS GC
  Lemont, Illinois
  P. B. Dye, Pete Dye
RUISLIP GC
  Middlesex, England
  F. G. Hawtree, J. H. Taylor
    (A.9) James Braid, John R.
  Stutt
RUKA GC
  Finland
  Jan Sederholm
RUKUGO GC
  Tokyo, Japan
  K. Seiki
RUMA CC
  Zimbabwe
  Laurie Waters, George
  Waterman
RUM RIVER GC
  Princeton, Minnesota
  Willie Kidd
RUM RIVER HILLS GC
  Ramsey, Minnesota
  Joel Goldstrand
RUMSON CC
  Rumson, New Jersey
  Herbert H. Barker
RUNAWAY BAY CC
  St. Annes, Jamaica
  John Harris
RUNAWAY BAY GC
  Bridgeport, Texas
  Leon Howard
RUNGSTED GC
  Kyst, Denmark
  Charles A. Mackenzie
    (R.) Jan Sederholm
RUNNING FOX GC
  Chillicothe, Ohio
  Lawrence T. Cox
RUNNING HILLS CC
  Frye Island, Maine
  NKA Frye Island GC
RUSHCLIFFE GC
  Nottinghamshire, England
  Tom Williamson
    (R.) J. J. F. Pennink
RUSHDEN & DISTRICT GC
  North Hants, England
  C. Catlow
    (R.) Tom Williamson
RUSH GC
  Dublin, Ireland
  John Temple
    (R.) Eddie Hackett
RUSH LAKE GC
  Pinckney, Michigan
  Robert Herndon
RUSHVILLE CC
  Rushville, Illinois
  Jack Keywood
RUSHVILLE ELKS CC
  Rushville, Indiana
  William H. Diddel
RUSHYFORD GC
  Aycliffe, Durham, England
  J. Hamilton Stutt
RUSSELL COTTAGE GC [NLE]
  Kearsarge, New Hampshire
  Alex Findlay
RUSSLEY GC
  New Zealand
    (R.) John Harris, Peter
  Thomson

RUSUTSU KOGEN GC
  Hokkaido, Japan
  Masashi Ozaki
RUTGERS UNIVERSITY GC
  Piscataway, New Jersey
    (R.9 A.9) Hal Purdy
RUTH LAKE CC
  Hinsdale, Illinois
  William B. Langford, Theodore
  J. Moreau
    (R.) Edward Lawrence
  Packard
    (R.) Edward Lawrence
  Packard, Roger Packard
    (R.) Ken Killian, Dick Nugent
    (R.1) Dick Nugent
RUTH PARK GC
  University City, Missouri
  Robert Bruce Harris
RUTLAND CC
  Rutland, Vermont
  George Low
    (R.9 A.9) Wayne Stiles, John
  Van Kleek
RUTTGER'S BAY LAKE GC
  Deerwood, Minnesota
  James Dalgleish
    (R.9 A.9) Gerry Pirkl, Donald
  G. Brauer
RUUHIKOSKI GC
  Seinajoki, Finland
  Robert Trent Jones, Jr.
RYA GC
  Helsingborg, Sweden
  Anders Amilon
    (A.9) Jan Sederholm
RYAN HILL GC
  Osceola, Nebraska
  Harold Glissmann
RYDÖ BRUK GC
  Sweden
  Jan Sederholm
RYDE GC
  Isle of Wight
    (R.) J. Hamilton Stutt
RYE GC
  Deal, England
  H. S. Colt, Douglas Rolland
    (R.) Tom Simpson
    (R.) Sir Guy Campbell
    (A.9) J. J. F. Pennink
RYE GC
  Rye, New York
  Devereux Emmet
    (R.) Rees Jones
    (R.) Stephen Kay
RYUGASAKI GC
  Ibaraki, Japan
  Shunsuke Kato

SAARBRUCKEN GC
  Saarbrucken, Germany
  Donald Harradine
    (R.) Reinhold Weishaupt
SABAH G&CC
  Kota Kinabalu, Malaysia
  Robert Muir Graves
SABAL PALM CC
  Tamarac, Florida
  Frank Murray
SABAL POINT CC
  Longwood, Florida
  Ward Northrup

SABAL SPRINGS GC (PALM CSE)
  North Fort Myers, Florida
  Gordon Lewis
SABAL SPRINGS GC (SABAL CSE)
  North Fort Myers, Florida
  Gordon Lewis
SABAL TRACE G&CC
  North Port Charlotte, Florida
  Chuck Ankrom
SABLE OAKS GC
  South Portland, Maine
  Brian Silva, Geoffrey S. Cornish
SACRAMENTO CC [NLE]
  Sacramento, California
    (R.) Herbert Fowler
SADAQUADA GC
  Whitesboro, New York
    (R.) William F. Mitchell
SADDLEBROOK G&TC (PALMER
  CSE)
  Wesley Chapel, Florida
  Arnold Palmer, Ed Seay
SADDLEBROOK G&TC (SADDLE-
  BROOK CSE)
  Wesley Chapel, Florida
  Dean Refram
    (R.) Arnold Palmer, Ed Seay
SADDLE HILL CC
  Hopkinton, Massachusetts
  William F. Mitchell
SADDLEWORTH GC
  Oldham, England
    (R.9 A.9) Alister MacKenzie
SAFARI INN GC
  Miami, Florida
  Carl H. Anderson
SAFARI PINES CC
  Vero Beach, Florida
  Dick Bird
SAFFOLDS G CSE
  Savannah, Georgia
  Donald Ross
SAFFRON WALDEN GC
  Cambridgeshire, England
  Harry Vardon
SAGAMI CC
  Kanagawa, Japan
  Rokuro Akaboshi, Shiro
  Akaboshi
SAGAMIHARA GC (EAST CSE)
  Kanagawa, Japan
  Yuji Kodera
SAGAMIHARA GC (WEST CSE)
  Kanagawa, Japan
  Y. Murakami
SAGAMORE GC
  Bolton Landing, New York
  Donald Ross
SAGAMORE-HAMPTON GC
  North Hampton, New
  Hampshire
  C.S. Luff
    (A.9) R. D. Luff
SAGINAW CC
  Saginaw, Michigan
  Tom Bendelow
    (R.) William Newcomb
    (R.2) Bruce Matthews, Jerry
  Matthews
    (R.2) Jerry Matthews
SAGMÜHLE GC
  Germany
  Kurt Rossknecht

SAGUENAY CC
  Arvida, Quebec
  Stanley Thompson
SAHALEE CC
  Redmond, Washington
  Ted Robinson
    (R.) Robert Muir Graves
SAHARA CC
  Las Vegas, Nevada
  Bert Stamps
    (R.) Garrett Gill, George B.
  Williams
SAHORO CC
  Japan
  Isamu Toi
SAIL HO GC
  San Diego, California
  Jack Daray
SAILFISH POINT CC
  Stuart, Florida
  Jack Nicklaus
ST. ALBANS CC
  St. Albans, New York
  Willie Park, Jr.
    (R.) A. W. Tillinghast
ST. ALBANS GC
  Alexandria, Ohio
  Tony Price
ST. ANDRES DE BRUGES GC
  Montpellier, France
  Fred Hawtree
ST. ANDREWS (EDEN CSE)
  St. Andrews, Fife, Scotland
  H. S. Colt, Alister Mackenzie
    (R.) D. M. A. Steel
ST. ANDREWS (JUBILEE CSE)
  St. Andrews, Fife, Scotland
  Willie Auchterlonie
    (R.) D. M. A. Steel
ST. ANDREWS (NEW CSE)
  St. Andrews, Fife, Scotland
  Old Tom Morris
    (R.) H. S. Colt, J. S. F.
  Morrison
    (R.) James Braid, John R.
  Stutt
ST. ANDREWS (OLD CSE)
  St. Andrews, Fife, Scotland
    (R.) Allan Robertson
    (R.) Old Tom Morris
    (R.) Alister MacKenzie
    (R.) James Braid, John R.
  Stutt
ST. ANDREWS (STRATHTYRUM CSE)
  St. Andrews, Fife, Scotland
  D. M. A. Steel
ST. ANDREWS CC
  Mobile, Alabama
  Earl Stone
ST. ANDREWS CC (EAST CSE)
  Boca Raton, Florida
  Ted McAnlis
ST. ANDREWS CC (WEST CSE)
  Boca Raton, Florida
  Ted McAnlis
ST. ANDREWS G&CC (CSE NO. 1)
  West Chicago, Illinois
  Edward B. Dearie, Jr.
    (R.) Joe Lee
ST. ANDREWS G&CC (CSE NO. 2)
  West Chicago, Illinois
  Edward B. Dearie, Jr.
    (R.) Joe Lee

St. Andrews G&CC
Ocean Springs, Mississippi
James Thompson
St. Andrews GC [NLE]
Laguna Niquel, California
Norman Macbeth
St. Andrews GC
Hastings-on-Hudson, New York
William H. Tucker, *Harry Tall-madge*
  (R.) William H. Tucker
  (R.) *Morris Poucher*
  (R.) James Braid, John R. Stutt
  (R.) Jack Nicklaus
St. Andrews GC [NLE]
Memphis, Tennessee
David Patrick
St. Andrews GC
Calgary, Alberta
Willie Park, Jr.
St. Andrews GC [NLE]
Toronto, Ontario
Stanley Thompson
  (R.3) John Watson
St. Andrews GC
St. André, Quebec
Herbert Strong
St. Andrews GC [NLE]
Moka, Trinidad and Tobago
J. S. F. Morrison, H. S. Colt
St. Andrews GC
Maraval, Trinidad and Tobago
John Harris, Peter Thomson, Ronald Fream
St. Andrews G Cse [NLE]
Kansas City, Missouri
James Dalgleish
St. Andrews G Cse
Overland Park, Kansas
John Nash, Charles Nash
  (R.) Larry Flatt
St. Andrews South GC
Punta Gorda, Florida
Ron Garl
St. Ann GC
St. Louis, Missouri
Al Linkogel
St. Anne's GC
Ireland
  (R.9 A.9) Eddie Hackett
St. Arild GC
Sweden
Jan Sederholm
St. Aubin GC
Paris, France
M. Rio
St. Augustine CC [NLE]
St. Augustine, Florida
Alex Findlay
St. Augustine Links (North Cse)
St. Augustine, Florida
NKA Ponce de Leon Resort & CC
St. Augustine Links (South Cse) [NLE]
St. Augustine, Florida
Donald Ross
St. Augustine Shores CC
St. Augustine, Florida
John Denton
St. Austell GC
England
James Braid

St. Bernard CC
Richfield, Ohio
Earl F. Yesberger
St. Boswells GC
Roxburghshire, Scotland
Willie Park
St. Catharines G&CC
St. Catharines, Ontario
Stanley Thompson
  (R.) Clinton E. Robinson
St. Catherines Muni
St. Catherines, Ontario
René Muylaert
St. Charles CC
St. Charles, Illinois
Tom Bendelow
  (R.) Robert Trent Jones
  (R.) David Gill
St. Charles CC (North Nine)
Winnipeg, Manitoba
Alister Mackenzie
  (R.) Clinton E. Robinson
  (R.) William G. Robinson, Geoffrey S. Cornish
St. Charles CC (South Nine)
Winnipeg, Manitoba
Donald Ross
St. Charles CC (West Cse) [NLE]
Winnipeg, Manitoba
Tom Bendelow
St. Charles CC (West Nine)
Winnipeg, Manitoba
Norman H. Woods
  (R.) William G. Robinson, Geoffrey S. Cornish
St. Charles GC
St. Charles, Missouri
Al Linkogel
St. Clair CC
Belleville, Illinois
William B. Langford, Theodore J. Moreau
St. Clair CC
St. Clair, Michigan
Donald Ross
St. Clair CC [NLE]
Pittsburgh, Pennsylvania
Tom Bendelow
St. Clair CC
Pittsburgh, Pennsylvania
William Gordon, David Gordon
  (R.) James Gilmore Harrison, Ferdinand Garbin
  (A.3rd 9) Joe Lee
  (R. A.1) *Dominic Palombo*
St. Clair GC
New Zealand
  (R.) C. H. Redhead
St. Clair Shores CC
St. Clair Shores, Michigan
Bruce Matthews, Jerry Matthews
St. Cloud CC
St. Cloud, Minnesota
Tim Murphy
St. Creek GC
Aichi, Japan
Jack Nicklaus
St. Cyprien GC
Perpignan, France
J. B. Tomlinson

St. Davids GC
Philadelphia, Pennsylvania
Donald Ross
  (R.) A.W. Tillinghast
St. Deiniol GC
Wales
James Braid
St. Elena G&CC
Canlubang, Philippines
Robert Trent Jones, Jr.
St. Elmo GC
St. Elmo, Illinois
William James Spear
St. Enodoc GC
Cornwall, England
James Braid
St. Eurach GC
Munich, Germany
Donald Harradine
  (R.) Jim Engh, *Bernhard Langer*
St. George GC
St. George, Utah
David Bingaman
  (R.2) William Howard Neff
St. George Hotel GC [NLE]
Bermuda
  (R.) Devereux Emmet
St. George's G&CC
Stony Brook, New York
Devereux Emmet
St. George's G&CC [NLE]
Islington, Ontario
H. S. Colt, C. H. Alison
St. George's G&CC
Islington, Ontario
Stanley Thompson
  (R.4) Clinton E. Robinson
St. Georges GC
St. Georges de Beauc, Quebec
Howard Watson
St. George's GC
Bermuda
Robert Trent Jones
St. George's Hill GC
Surrey, England
H. S. Colt
  (R.) J. Hamilton Stutt
St. Helens GC
Warren, Oregon
Clarence Johnson, Gordon Johnson
St. Ives CC
Duluth, Georgia
Tom Fazio
St. James GC
St. James, Missouri
Chic Adams
St. James GC [NLE]
Montego Bay, Jamaica
William B. Langford
St. Janvier G&CC
Quebec
Gaston Alarie
St. Jerome GC
Quebec
Gaston Alarie
St. Johns County G Cse
Elkton, Florida
Bob Walker
St. Johnsbury CC
St. Johnsbury, Vermont
Mungo Park

St. Joseph CC
St. Joseph, Missouri
  (R.1) Bob Dunning
  (R.) Don Sechrest
St. Joseph's Bay CC
Port St. Joe, Florida
Bill Amick
St. Jude CC
Chicora, Pennsylvania
Emil Loeffler, *John McGlynn*
  (A.4) Ferdinand Garbin
St. Knuds GC
Denmark
C. K. Cotton, J. J. F. Pennink
St. Lakes GC
Mie, Japan
Perry Dye
St. Laurent GC
I'le d'Orléans, Quebec
Howard Watson, John Watson
St. Laurent-Ploemel GC
France
Michael G. Fenn
St. Lawrence University GC
Canton, New York
Devereux Emmet
  (A.12) Geoffrey S. Cornish, William G. Robinson
St. Leonard's School for Girls GC
Fife, Scotland
Old Tom Morris
St. Louis CC [NLE]
St. Louis, Missouri
James Foulis
St. Louis CC
Clayton, Missouri
Charles Blair Macdonald, Seth Raynor
  (R.) Robert Trent Jones
St. Luc GC
Quebec
Howard Watson
  (A.9) John Watson
St. Lucie River CC [NLE]
Port Sewall, Florida
William B. Langford, Theodore J. Moreau
St. Lucie West GC
Port St. Lucie, Florida
Jim Fazio
St. Malo-le-Tronchet GC
France
Hubert Chesneau
St. Marguerite GC
Sept Isles, Quebec
Howard Watson
St. Marys CC
St. Marys, Ohio
Tom Bendelow
St. Marys CC
St. Marys, Pennsylvania
Devereux Emmett
St. Marys GC
St. Marys, West Virginia
X. G. Hassenplug
St. Mellion G&CC (Old Cse)
Cornwall, England
J. Hamilton Stutt
St. Mellion G&CC (New Cse)
Plymouth, England
Jack Nicklaus

ST. MELLONS GC
St. Mellons, Wales
H. S. Colt, J. S. F. Morrison,
Henry Cotton
ST. MICHAEL GC
Sydney, Australia
Clement Glancey
ST. MICHAEL JUBILEE GC
England
Fred W. Hawtree
(A.9) Martin Hawtree, Simon
Gidman
ST. MICHAELS GC
South Africa
(R.) Sid Brews
ST. MICHAELS G LINKS
Fife, Scotland
Old Tom Morris
ST. NOM LA BRETÈCHE GC (BLUE
CSE)
France
Fred W. Hawtree
(R.) Pier Mancinelli
(R.) Ronald Fream
ST. NOM LA BRETÈCHE GC (RED
CSE)
France
Fred W. Hawtree
(R.) Pier Mancinelli
ST. OEDENRODE GC
Netherlands
J.F. Dudok van Heel
ST. OMER GC
St. Omer, France
J.F. Dudok van Heel
ST. PETERS-MORELL GC
Morel, Prince Edward Island
Thomas McBroom
ST. PÖLTEN-GOLDEGG GC
Austria
Gerold Hauser, *Günther Hauser*
ST. PIERRE G&CC (NEW CSE)
Gwent, Wales
William Cox
ST. PIERRE G&CC (OLD CSE)
Gwent, Wales
C. K. Cotton, J. J. F. Pennink
ST. QUEEN HOTEL GC
Channel Islands
Tony Jacklin
ST. QUENTIN-EN-YVELINES GC
France
J. Damonville
ST. SIMONS ISLAND C
St. Simons Island, Georgia
Joe Lee, Rocky Roquemore
ST. THOMAS G&CC
St. Thomas, Ontario
Stanley Thompson
(A.9) Clinton E. Robinson
SAKAIGAWA CC
Japan
Isao Aoki
SAKONNET GC
Little Compton, Rhode Island
Donald Ross
SAKURA CC
Sakura, Japan
Tetsuro Akabane
SALEM CC
Peabody, Massachusetts
Donald Ross

SALEM CC
Salem, Missouri
Floyd Farley
SALEM GC
North Salem, New York
Edward Ryder, *Val Carlson*
SALEM GC
Salem, Ohio
(A.9) Bob Simmons
(R.) Geoffrey S. Cornish
SALEM GC
Salem, Oregon
Ercel Kay
SALEM HILLS GC
Northville, Michigan
Bruce Matthews, Jerry Matthews
SALEMTOWNE GC
Salem, Oregon
Bill Schaefer
SALINA CC
Salina, Kansas
John J. Eberhardt
(R.) *Lee Singletary*
SALINA MUNI
Salina, Kansas
Floyd Farley
SALINAS CC
Salinas, California
Jack Fleming
(R.) Stephen Halsey, Jack
Daray, Jr.
SALINAS FAIRWAYS GC
Salinas, California
NKA Salinas CC
SALISBURY CC
Salisbury, Virginia
(R.) Edmund B. Ault
(R.) Rees Jones
SALISBURY & SOUTH WILTS GC
Wiltshire, England
J. H. Taylor
(R.6) Fred W. Hawtree,
Martin Hawtree
(A.3rd 9) Martin Hawtree,
Simon Gidman
SALISHAN G LINKS
Gleneden Beach, Oregon
Fred Federspiel
(R.) Robert Muir Graves
SALLANDSCHE GC "DE HOEK"
Deventer, Netherlands
J. J. F. Pennink
(A.11) D. M. A. Steel
SALMON ARM GC
Salmon Arm, British Columbia
Les Furber, *Jim Eremko*
SALMON BROOK CC [NLE]
Connecticut
(R.) Orrin Smith
SALMON CREEK CC
Rochester, New York
Pete Craig
SALMON FALLS GC
Bar Mills, Maine
Jimmy Jones
SALTCOATS GC
Saltcoats, Scotland
(R.) Old Tom Morris
SALT FORK STATE PARK GC
Cambridge, Ohio
Jack Kidwell

SALTSJÖBADEN GC
Saltsjöbaden, Sweden
A. Björklund
(A.9) *Douglas Brazier*
SALUDA VALLEY CC
Williamston, South Carolina
William B. Lewis
SALZBORG GC
Morin Heights, Quebec
Howard Watson
SALZBURG KLESHEIM GC
Salzburg, Austria
(R.9) Kurt Rossknecht
SALZKAMMERGUT GC
Bad Ischl, Austria
Kurt Rossknecht
(A.9) Gerold Hauser, *Günther
Hauser*
SAMOSET RESORT GC
Rockport, Maine
Robert Elder
(R.) Geoffrey S. Cornish,
Brian Silva
SAN ANDRES GC
Bogotá, Colombia
Stanley Thompson
SAN ANDRES GC
San Martín, Argentina
Mungo Park II
SAN ANGELO CC
San Angelo, Texas
John Bredemus
(R.) Warren Cantrell
SAN ANTONIO CC
San Antonio, Texas
Alex Findlay
(R.) A. W. Tillinghast
(R.15) Joseph S. Finger
(R.) Jay Morrish
SAN ANTONIO SHORES GC
Mexico
Bob Baldock, Robert L. Baldock
SAN BERNARDINO CC
San Bernardino, California
(R.5) Algie Pulley
(A.1) Jeff Brauer, *Jim Colbert*
SAN CARLOS G&CC
Sonora, Mexico
Roy Dye, Gary Grandstaff
SAN CARLOS PARK G&CC
Fort Myers, Florida
John E. O'Connor
SAN CLEMENTE MUNI
San Clemente, California
William P. Bell
(R.9 A.9) William F. Bell
SANCTUARY COVE GC
Gold Coast, Australia
Arnold Palmer, Ed Seay
SANDALFOOT COVE G&CC
Margate, Florida
NKA Carolina CC
SAN DAR ACRES GC
Bellville, Ohio
Jack Kidwell, Michael Hurdzan
SAND CREEK C
Chesterton, Indiana
Ken Killian, Dick Nugent
SAND CREEK MUNI
Idaho Falls, Idaho
William F. Bell

SANDELIE GC
West Linn, Oregon
Harvey Junor
(A.9) *William Kaiser*
SANDESTIN GC (BAYTOWNE CSE)
Destin, Florida
Tom Jackson
SANDESTIN GC (LINKS CSE)
Destin, Florida
Tom Jackson
SANDFORD SPRINGS GC
Newbury, England
Martin Hawtree, Simon Gidman
SANDIA MOUNTAIN GC
Albuquerque, New Mexico
Robert Dean Putman
SAN DIEGO CC
Chula Vista, California
William P. Bell
(R.1) Harry Rainville
(R.) Ronald Fream
SANDILANDS GC
Sutton-on-Sea, England
S. V. Hotchkin
(R.) Tom Williamson
SAN DIMAS CANYON GC
San Dimas, California
(R.) Jeff Brauer
SANDIWAY GC
Cheshire, England
S. Collins, Ted Ray
(R.) H. S. Colt, J. S. F.
Morrison
(R.3) Fred W. Hawtree
SANDMOOR GC
Leeds, England
Henry Barran
SANDOWN PARK GC
Surrey, England
John Jacobs, John Corby
SANDPIPER BAY CC
Port St. Lucie, Florida
NKA Club Med Sandpiper GC
SANDPIPER G&CC
Lakeland, Florida
Steve Smyers
SANDPIPER G LINKS
Goleta, California
William F. Bell
(R.) Robert Muir Graves
SANDPIPER BAY G&CC
Sunset Beach, North Carolina
Dan Maples
SANDRIDGE GC
Vero Beach, Florida
Ron Garl
SANDS CC
Somers Point, New Jersey
NKA Greate Bay CC
SANDS POINT CC
Sands Point, New York
George E. Reynolds
(R.9 A.9) A.W. Tillinghast
(R.) Robert Trent Jones
(R.) Frank Duane
(R.) Stephen Kay
SANDS POINT CC
Seattle, Washington
William H. Tucker
(R.) Robert Muir Graves
SANDS RV CC
Desert Hot Springs, California
Ron Garl

SAND SPRINGS MUNI
Idaho Falls, Idaho
William F. Bell
SAND SPRINGS MUNI
Sand Springs, Oklahoma
Floyd Farley
SANDWELL PARK GC
Birmingham, England
(R.) H. S. Colt
SANDWICH BAY G&CC
Kent, England
Howard Swan
SANDY BRAE G&CC
Clendenin, West Virginia
Edmund B. Ault
SANDY BURR CC
Wayland, Massachusetts
Donald Ross
SANDY CREEK CC
Panama City, Florida
Charles House (9)
SANDY HOLLOW MUNI
Rockford, Illinois
C. D. Wagstaff
(R.) David Gill
SANDY LANE HOTEL & GC
Barbados
Robertson Ward
SANDY LODGE GC
England
H. S. Colt, Harry Vardon
SANDY RIDGE CC
High Point, North Carolina
Gene Hamm
SANDY RIDGE GC
Midland, Michigan
Bruce Matthews, Jerry Matthews
SANDY RIVER GC
Farmington Falls, Maine
Roy Hazard
SANDY RUN CC
Oreland, Pennsylvania
J. Franklyn Meehan
SANDY RUN GC
Georgia
(R.) Arthur Davis, Ron Kirby
SAN FELIPE CC
Del Rio, Texas
John Bredemus
SAN FERNANDO VA HOSPITAL GC
California
William H. Johnson
SANFORD GC
Sanford, Maine
Alex Chisholm
SAN FRANCISCO GC
San Francisco, California
A.W. Tillinghast
(R.) William P. Bell
SAN GABRIEL CC
San Gabriel, California
Norman Macbeth
(R.) William F. Bell
(R.) Robert Trent Jones
SAN GERONIMO VALLEY GC
San Geronimo, California
A. Vernon Macon
(R.) Robert Muir Graves
(R.) Robin Nelson, Rodney
Wright
SAN GIL GC
San Juan El Rio, Mexico
Roy Dye

SAN GORGONIO GC
Banning, California
William H. Johnson
SAN IGNACIO G CSE
Green Valley, Arizona
Arthur Hills
SAN ISIDRO GC
San Isidro, Argentina
(R.3) Ronald Fream
SAN JOAQUIN CC
Bakersfield, California
(R.) Bob Baldock
(R.) Robert Muir Graves
(R.) Robert Dean Putman
SAN JOSE CC
San Jose, California
Tom Nicoll
(R.) Robert Muir Graves
(R.) Ed Seay
SAN JOSE CC
Jacksonville, Florida
Donald Ross
(R.) Bob Walker
SAN JOSE MUNI
San Jose, California
Robert Muir Graves
SAN JUAN GC
Monticello, Utah
Arthur Jack Snyder
SAN JUAN HILLS CC
San Juan Capistrano, California
Harry Rainville, David Rainville
(R.) Peter Thomson, Michael
Wolveridge, Ronald Fream
SANKATY HEAD GC
Nantucket, Massachusetts
H. Emerson Armstrong (1921)
(R.) Skip Wogan
(R.) A.W. Tillinghast
SANLANDO G&CC [NLE]
Florida
(R.) Robert Bruce Harris
SAN LORENZO GC
Vale do Lobo, Portugal
Joe Lee, Rocky Roquemore
SAN LUIS BAY INN & CC
Avila Beach, California
Desmond Muirhead
(A.9) Olin A. Dutra
(R.) Robert Muir Graves
SAN LUIS OBISPO CC
San Luis Obispo, California
Bert Stamps
(R.) Robert Muir Graves
SAN LUIS REY GC
Bonsall, California
William F. Bell
SAN MARCOS HOTEL & C
Chandler, Arizona
Harry Collis
(R.) Red Lawrence
SAN MARINO GC
Farmington, Michigan
Bruce Matthews, Jerry Matthews
SAN MICHELE GC
Italy
R. Conti, C. Siniscalchi
SAN MIGUEL GC
Azores
P. M. Ross
SAN PEDRO CC
California
William P. Bell

SAN PEDRO COMMUNITY HOTEL GC
San Pedro, California
William P. Bell
SAN PEDRO GC
San Pedro, Mexico
Willie Smith
SANPIA GC
Tokushima, Japan
Kazumi Miura
SANREMO GC
Sanremo, Italy
James Gannon
SAN RAMON ROYAL VISTA GC
San Ramon, California
Clark Glasson
SANRIZUKA GC
Japan
Kinya Fujita
SANSICARIO GC
Sansicario, Italy
Bill Amick
SANTA ANA CC
Santa Ana, California
John Duncan Dunn
(R.) Desmond Muirhead
(R.) Harry Rainville, David
Rainville
(R.) Ronald Fream
SANTA BARBARA CC [NLE]
Santa Barbara, California
Tom Bendelow
(R.) Walter Fovargue
SANTA BARBARA COMMUNITY GC
Santa Barbara, California
Lawrence Hughes
SANTA CLARA G&TC
Santa Clara, California
Robert Muir Graves
SANTA CROCE GC
Turin, Italy
Graham Cooke
SANTA CRUZ CC
Nogales, Arizona
Red Lawrence
SANTA CRUZ G&CC
Santa Cruz, California
Tom Bendelow
SANTA FE CC
Santa Fe, New Mexico
Tom Bendelow
SANTA FE HILLS GC [NLE]
Kansas City, Missouri
James Dalgleish
SANTA MARIA CC
Santa Maria, California
(R.) Bob Baldock
(R.) Robert Muir Graves
SANTA MARIA GC
Baton Rouge, Louisiana
Robert Trent Jones
SANTA MARTA GC
Santa Marta, Colombia
Mark Mahannah
SANTA MARTRETTA GC
Italy
P.L. Ariotti
SANTA MONICA SHORES GC
Santa Monica, California
George S. "Pop" Merrit
SANTA PONSA GC
Majorca, Spain
Folco Nardi
(R.) Pepe Gancedo

SANTA ROSA CC
Palm Desert, California
Leonard Gerkins
SANTA ROSA G&BC
Santa Rosa Beach, Florida
James Root
SANTA ROSA G&CC
Santa Rosa, California
Jack Fleming, Ben Harmon
(R.) Robert Trent Jones, Jr.
(R.) Robert Muir Graves
(R.) Fred Bliss
SANTA ROSA G&CC
Bradenton, Florida
R. Albert Anderson
SANTA SUSANA CC
California
William P. Bell
SANTA TERESA CC (SPANISH
DAGGER CSE)
Sunland Park, New Mexico
Dave Bennett, Lee Trevino
SANTA TERESA CC (YUCCA CSE)
Sunland Park, New Mexico
Dave Bennett, Lee Trevino
SANTA TERESA GC
San Jose, California
George E. Santana (1963)
(R.) Robert Muir Graves
SANTEE-COOPER CC
Santee, South Carolina
George W. Cobb
SANTEE NATIONAL GC
Santee, South Carolina
J. Porter Gibson
SANTIAGO GC
Orange, California
Ed Burns
SANTIAM GC
Salem, Oregon
Fred Federspiel
(R.) Robert Muir Graves
SANTIBURI GC
Chiang Rai, Thailand
Robert Trent Jones, Jr.
SANTO DA SERRA GC
Madeira Islands
Henry Cotton
SAN VICENTE CC
Ramona, California
Ted Robinson
SAN VITO DE NORMANNI GC
Brindisi, Italy
Pier Mancinelli
SANWA CC
Japan
Kazumi Miura
SÃO FERNANDO GC
Brazil
Luther Koonz
(R.) Alberto Serra
SÃO FRANCISCO GC
São Francisco, Brazil
José Maria Gonzales, Alberto
Serra
SÃO PAULO GC
São Paulo, Brazil
(R.) Stanley Thompson
SAPONA CC
Lexington, North Carolina
Ellis Maples

Sapphire Lakes CC
  Sapphire, North Carolina
  Russell Breeden, *Dan Breeden*
    (A.9) Tom Jackson
Sapporo CC
  Sapporo, Hokkaido, Japan
  Robert Trent Jones, Jr.
Sapporo GC
  Hokkaido, Japan
  Seichi Inouye
Sapporo Hiroshima GC
  Hokkaido, Japan
  Mike Poellot
Sapporo Kokusai CC
  Japan
  Naoto Sugaya
Sapporo Pacific CC
  Japan
  Isamu Toi
Sapporo Tokyu GC
  Hokkaido, Japan
  Chohei Miyagawa
Sapulpa City GC
  Sapulpa City, Oklahoma
    (R.9) *Joe Aycock*
Sara Bay CC
  Sarasota, Florida
  Donald Ross
    (R.) Joe Lee
Sarah Shank Muni
  Indianapolis, Indiana
    (R.9 A.9) William H. Diddel
Saranac GC
  Stahlstown, Pennsylvania
  Paul E. Erath
Saranac Inn G Cse
  Saranac Lake, New York
  Seymour Dunn
Saranac Lake GC
  Ray Brook, New York
  Alex Findlay
Sarasota GC
  Sarasota, Florida
  Wynn Tredway
Saratoga GC
  Saratoga, California
    (R.) Robert Muir Graves
Saratoga Spa GC
  Saratoga, New York
    (R. A.9) William F. Mitchell
Sarfvik GC (Cse No. 1)
  Espoo, Finland
  Jan Sederholm
Sarfvik GC (Cse No. 2)
  Espoo, Finland
  Jan Sederholm
Sarnia GC
  Sarnia, Ontario
  George Cumming
    (R.) Clinton E. Robinson
Sasakami Cayman G Park
  Sasakami, Japan
  Denis Griffiths
Sasebo Kokusai CC
  Japan
  Hiroshi Umezawa
Saskatoon GC (Blue Cse)
  Alto, Michigan
  Mark DeVries
Saskatoon GC (Red Cse)
  Alto, Michigan
  Mark DeVries

Saskatoon G&CC (East Cse)
  Saskatoon, Saskatchewan
  William Kinnear
Saskatoon G&CC (West Cse)
  Saskatoon, Saskatchewan
  William G. Robinson, John F. Robinson
Saticoy CC
  Camarillo, California
  William F. Bell
    (R.) Robert Muir Graves
Saticoy Regional G Cse
  Saticoy, California
  George C. Thomas, Jr.
Saucon Valley CC (Grace Cse)
  Bethlehem, Pennsylvania
  William Gordon, David Gordon
Saucon Valley CC (Junior Cse)
  Bethlehem, Pennsylvania
  William Gordon, David Gordon
Saucon Valley CC (Old Cse)
  Bethlehem, Pennsylvania
  Herbert Strong
    (R.) Perry Maxwell
    (R.) William Gordon
    (R.) William Gordon, David Gordon
Sauerland GC
  Neheim-Husten, Germany
  Bernhard von Limburger
Saugahatchee CC
  Opelika, Alabama
  Ward Northrup
Saugatuck CC [NLE]
  Saugatuck, Michigan
  George B. Ferry
Saugeen GC
  Port Elgin, Ontario
  Stanley Thompson
Saujana G&CC (Orchid Cse)
  Subang, Malaysia
  Ronald Fream
Saujana G&CC (Palm Cse)
  Subang, Malaysia
  Ronald Fream
Sault Ste. Marie CC
  Sault Ste. Marie, Michigan
    (A.9) Jerry Matthews
Sault Ste. Marie GC
  Sault Ste. Marie, Ontario
    (R.) Stanley Thompson
Saunton GC (East Cse)
  Saunton, England
  Tom Dunn
    (R.) C. K. Cotton, J. J. F. Pennink
Saunton GC (New Cse) [NLE]
  Devonshire, England
  Herbert Fowler
Saunton GC (West Cse)
  Devon, England
  J. J. F. Pennink
    (R.) D. M. A. Steel
Savanna C
  Port St. Lucie, Florida
  Chuck Ankrom
Savannah GC
  Savannah, Georgia
  Donald Ross
    (R.3) George W. Cobb, John LaFoy
[The] Savannahs GC
  North Merritt Island, Florida
  Gordon Lewis

Sawara Springs CC
  Chiba, Japan
  Mitsuo Yoshizaki
Sawgrass GC (Oakbridge Cse)
  Ponte Vedra Beach, Florida
  Bill Amick
    (R.) Ed Seay
Sawgrass GC (Oceanside Cse)
  Ponte Vedra Beach, Florida
  Ed Seay
    (R.) *Gardner Dickinson*
    (R.) Edmund B. Ault
    (R. A.3rd 9) Ed Seay
Sawmill GC
  Fenwick, Ontario
  Gordon Witteveen
Sawyer AFB GC
  Michigan
  Bob Baldock
Sawmill Creek GC
  Huron, Ohio
  George Fazio, Tom Fazio
Sawyerkill GC
  Saugerties, New York
  Hal Purdy
Saxon Woods GC
  Mamaroneck, New York
  Tom Winton
Sayama GC
  Sayama, Japan
  Hideo Takemura
Scarboro G&CC
  Scarborough, Ontario
    (R.) A.W. Tillinghast
    (R.) Stanley Thompson
Scarborough North Cliff GC
  Yorkshire, England
  James Braid, John R. Stutt
Scarborough South Cliff GC
  Scarborough, England
  Alister Mackenzie
Scarcroft GC
  Leeds, England
  Alister MacKenzie
Scarlett Woods GC
  Toronto, Ontario
  Howard Watson
    (A.9) Howard Watson, John Watson
Scarsdale GC
  Hartsdale, New York
  Willie Dunn, Jr.
    (R.9 A.9) A.W. Tillinghast
    (R.) Dick Wilson
    (R.) Robert Trent Jones
    (R.4) Frank Duane
    (R.) Geoffrey S. Cornish, Brian Silva
Scenic Hills G&CC
  Pensacola, Florida
  Chic Adams
Schalamar GC
  Lakeland, Florida
  Ron Garl
Schaumburg Park GC
  Schaumburg, Illinois
    (R.) Bob Lohmann
Schenectady CC
  Schenectady, New York
  Devereux Emmet
Schenectady Muni
  Schenectady, New York
  Arthur F. Knight

Schilling AFB GC [NLE]
  Salina, Kansas
  Leon Howard
Schloss Anholt GC
  Germany
  Bernhard von Limburger
Schloss Braunfels GC
  Germany
  Bernhard von Limburger
Schloss Egmating GC
  Germany
  Kurt Rossknecht
Schloss Fuschl G&CC
  Austria
  Bernhard von Limburger
Schloss Georgshausen GC
  Cologne, Germany
    (R.) Karl F. Grohs, *Rainer Preissmann*
Schloss Goldegg GC
  St. Polten, Austria
  Gerold Hauser, *Günther Hauser*
Schloss Klingenburg-Gunzburg GC
  Germany
  Donald Harradine
Schloss Langenstein CC
  Orsingen-Nenzingen, Germany
  Rod Whitman
Schloss Lüdersburg GC
  Lüdersburg, Germany
  Wolfgang Siegmann
Schloss Mittersill GC
  Austria
  Tom Simpson, Molly Gourlay
Schloss Moyland G&CC
  Germany
  Karl F. Grohs, *Rainer Preissmann*
Schloss Myllendonk GC
  Monchengladbach, Germany
  Bernhard von Limburger
    (A.9) Donald Harradine
Schloss Nippenburg GC
  Stuttgart, Germany
  Jim Engh, *Bernhard Langer*
Schloss Oberzwiesclau GC
  Bayern, Germany
  Götz Mecklenburg
Schloss Pahl GC
  Germany
  Kurt Rossknecht
Schloss Pichlarn GC
  Irdning, Austria
  Bernhard von Limburger
    (A.9) Donald Harradine
Schloss Reichertshausen GC
  Bayern, Germany
  Götz Mecklenburg
Schloss Rheden GC
  Germany
  Bernhard von Limburger
Schloss Schönborn GC
  Vienna, Austria
  Kurt Rossknecht
Schmallenberg GC
  Schmallenberg, Germany
  Karl F. Grohs, *Rainer Preissmann*
Schoenenberg G&CC
  Switzerland
  Donald Harradine
    (A.9) Reinhold Weishaupt

SCHÖNFELD GC
Austria
Gerold Hauser, *Günther Hauser*
SCHROON LAKE CC [NLE]
Schroon Lake, New York
Seymour Dunn
SCHROON LAKE G CSE
Schroon Lake, New York
Seymour Dunn
SCHUSS MOUNTAIN GC
Mancelona, Michigan
Warner Bowen
(R.) William Newcomb
SCHUYLER MEADOWS C
Loudonville, New York
Devereux Emmet
(R.) Geoffrey S. Cornish,
Brian Silva
SCHWARZE HEIDE GC
Bottrop-Kirchhellen, Germany
Wolfgang Siegmann
SCHWARZWALD-KONIGSFELD GC
Baden-Württemberg, Germany
Götz Mecklenburg
SCIOTO CC
Columbus, Ohio
Donald Ross
(R.1) *Marion A. Packard*
(R.) Dick Wilson, Joe Lee
(R.) Bob Cupp
SCONA LODGE GC
Alcoa, Tennessee
Robert Trent Jones
SCONTI GC
Big Canoe, Georgia
Joe Lee, Rocky Roquemore
(A.3rd 9) Rocky Roquemore,
Jeff Burton
SCOTCH MEADOWS CC
Morgantown, North Carolina
Russell Breeden
SCOTCH PINES GC
Payette, Idaho
William Graham
SCOTCH SETTLEMENT GC
Bradford, Ontario
Robert Moote, David L. Moote
SCOTCH VALLEY GC
Holidaysburg, Pennsylvania
James Gilmore Harrison
SCOTFIELD CC
Enfield, North Carolina
Leo Greene
(R.) Clement B. "Johnny"
Johnston, Clyde Johnston
SCOTHURST CC
Lumber Bridge, North Carolina
A. F. "Bud" Nash
SCOTSCRAIG GC
Fife, Scotland
Old Tom Morris
(R.) James Braid, John R.
Stutt
SCOTSDALE GC
Bella Vista, Arkansas
Tom Clark, Edmund B. Ault
SCOTSLAND GC
Oconomowoc, Wisconsin
Tom Burrows
SCOTT CITY CC
Scott City, Kansas
Henry B. Hughes, Richard
Watson

SCOTT LAKE CC
Comstock Park, Michigan
Bruce Matthews, Jerry Matthews
SCOTT PARK MUNI
Silver City, New Mexico
Arthur Jack Snyder
SCOTTSBLUFF CC
Scottsbluff, Nebraska
Frank Hummel
SCOTTSBURGH GC
South Africa
(R.) Robert G. Grimsdell
SCOTT SCHREINER MUNI
Kerrville, Texas
John Bredemus
(A.9) *Donald Collett*
SCOTTSDALE CC
Scottsdale, Arizona
Lawrence Hughes
(R.4) Arthur Jack Snyder
(R. A.3rd 9) Arnold Palmer,
Ed Seay
SCOVILL GC
Decatur, Illinois
(R.) Dick Nugent
SCRAPTOFT GC
Leicestershire, England
Tom Williamson
SCUNTHORPE GC
Lincolnshire, England
Fred W. Hawtree, A. H. F.
Jiggens
SEBRING SHORES CC
Sebring, Florida
Hans Schmeisser
SEABROOK ISLAND GC (CROOKED
OAKS CSE)
Seabrook Island, South Carolina
Robert Trent Jones
SEABROOK ISLAND GC (OCEAN
WINDS CSE)
Seabrook Island, South Carolina
Willard Byrd
SEACLIFF CC
Huntington Beach, California
Press Maxwell
(R.) Ronald Fream
SEACROFT GC
Lincolnshire, England
Tom Dunn
(R.9) Wilfrid Reid
(R.) Sir Guy Campbell
SEAFIELD GC
Scotland
James Braid, John R. Stutt
SEAFORD G&CC
Seaford, Delaware
Alfred H. Tull
SEAFORD GC [NLE]
Sussex, England
Tom Dunn
SEAFORD GC
Sussex, England
J. H. Taylor
(R.) J. S. F. Morrison
(R.) Willie Park, Jr.
SEAFORTH GC
Ontario
Howard Watson
SEA GULL GC
Pawleys Island, South Carolina
Gene Hamm

SEA ISLAND GC (MARSHSIDE NINE)
St. Simons Island, Georgia
Joe Lee, Rocky Roquemore
SEA ISLAND GC (PLANTATION NINE)
St. Simons Island, Georgia
Walter J. Travis
(R.) C. H. Alison, H. S. Colt
(R.) Robert Trent Jones
(R.) Rees Jones
SEA ISLAND GC (RETREAT NINE)
St. Simons Island, Georgia
Dick Wilson
SEA ISLAND GC (SEASIDE NINE)
St. Simons Island, Georgia
C. H. Alison, H. S. Colt
(R.) Robert Trent Jones
(R.) Rees Jones
SEA LINKS GC
Blaine, Washington
William G. Robinson, John F.
Robinson
SEAMOUNTAIN GC
Kau, Hawaii
Arthur Jack Snyder
(R.) Gene Bates, Johnny
Miller
SEA 'N AIR GC [NLE]
North Island, San Diego,
California
Jack Daray
SEA 'N AIR GC
North Island, San Diego,
California
Jack Daray, Jr., Stephen Halsey
SEA PALMS G&CC
St. Simons Island, Georgia
George W. Cobb
(A.3rd 9) Tom Jackson
SEA PINES PLANTATION GC (CLUB
CSE)
Hilton Head Island, South
Carolina
Frank Duane, Arnold Palmer
SEA PINES PLANTATION GC (OCEAN
CSE)
Hilton Head Island, South
Carolina
George W. Cobb
SEA PINES PLANTATION GC (SEA
MARSH CSE)
Hilton Head Island, South
Carolina
George W. Cobb
(R.) Clyde Johnston
SEA RANCH G LINKS
Sea Ranch, California
Robert Muir Graves
SEASCALE GC
Cumbria, England
Willie Campbell
(A.9) George Lowe
(R.) Sir Guy Campbell
SEASCAPE G LINKS
Kitty Hawk, North Carolina
Art Wall
SEASCAPE G&RC
Destin, Florida
Robert Logan
(R. A.4) Joe Lee
SEASIDE CC
Seaside, Oregon
H. Chandler Egan

SEASONS RIDGE GC
Lake Ozark, Missouri
Ken Kavanaugh
SEATON CAREW GC
England
(R.) Alister Mackenzie
SEATTLE GC
Seattle, Washington
John Ball, Robert Johnstone
(R.) Robert Johnstone
(R.) A. Vernon Macan
(R.) Ted Robinson
(R.2) Peter Thomson,
Michael Wolveridge, Ronald
Fream
SEA TRAIL G LINKS (DAN MAPLES
CSE)
Sunset Beach, North Carolina
Dan Maples
SEA TRAIL G LINKS (REES JONES
CSE)
Sunset Beach, North Carolina
Rees Jones
SEA TRAIL G LINKS (WILLARD BYRD
CSE)
Sunset Beach, North Carolina
Willard Byrd
SEAVIEW GC (BAY CSE)
Absecon, New Jersey
Donald Ross
(R.) A.W. Tillinghast
(R.) William Gordon, David
Gordon
(R.) Al Janis
SEAVIEW GC (PINES CSE)
Absecon, New Jersey
William S. Flynn, Howard
Toomey
(A.9) William Gordon, David
Gordon
(R. A.3) Al Janis
SEAVIEW GC
Nova Scotia
(R.9 A.9) Clinton E.
Robinson
(A.3rd 9) Robert Moote
SEA VIEW VILLAGE GC
Massachusetts
Geoffrey S. Cornish
SEAWANE C
Hewlitt Harbor, New York
Devereux Emmet
(R.) Frank Duane
(R.) Stephen Kay
SEBASTIAN MUNI
Sebastian, Florida
Chuck Ankrom
SEBRING CC
North Benton, Ohio
Ray Henry
SECESSION GC
Gibbes Island, South Carolina
P. B. Dye (routing), Bruce
Devlin
SEDALIA CC
Sedalia, Missouri
Floyd Farley
SEDGEFIELD CC
Greensboro, North Carolina
Donald Ross
(R.) Gene Hamm
(R.) Willard Byrd
(R.) Ed Connor

SEDGEFIELD CC (RED CSE) [NLE]
Greensboro, North Carolina
Donald Ross
SEDGEWOOD CC
Hopkins, South Carolina
Russell Breeden
SEDONA G RESORT
Sedona, Arizona
Gary Panks
SEEBURG GC
Berlin, Germany
Karl F. Grohs, *Rainer Preissmann*
SEEDY MILL GC
Litchfield, England
Martin Hawtree, Simon Gidman
SEEFELD-WILDMOOS GC
Seefeld, Austria
Donald Harradine
SEGALLA CC
Amenia, New York
Al Zikorus
SEGOVIA GC
Tokyo, Japan
Desmond Muirhead
SEGREGANSETT CC
Taunton, Massachusetts
(A.9) Geoffrey S. Cornish,
William G. Robinson
SEGUIN CC
Seguin, Texas
NKA Max Starke Park GC
SEHOY PLANTATION GC
Huntsboro, Alabama
Ellis Maples, Dan Maples
SEIGNIORY C
Montebello, Quebec
Stanley Thompson
SEINAN CC
Gunma, Japan
Pete Nakamura
SELKIRK G&CC
Selkirk, Manitoba
Jack Thompson
SELKIRK GC
Selkirkshire, Scotland
Willie Park
SELMA VALLEY CC
Selma, California
Bob Baldock
SELSDON PARK HOTEL GC
Surrey, England
F. G. Hawtree, J. H. Taylor
SELVA MARINA CC
Atlantic Beach, Florida
Ernest E. Smith
SEMI-AH-MOO G&CC
Everett, Washington
Arnold Palmer, Ed Seay
SEMINOLE GC
North Palm Beach, Florida
Donald Ross
(R.) Dick Wilson
(R.) Ed Connor
SEMINOLE GC
Tallahassee, Florida
R. Albert Anderson
(A.9) Bill Amick
SEMINOLE LAKE G&CC
Seminole, Florida
Chic Adams
SEMINOLE VALLEY GC
Chattahoochee, Florida
Bill Amick

SENAI MINAMI GC
Miyagi Prefecture, Japan
Jack Nicklaus
SENECA MUNI
Louisville, Kentucky
Alex McKay
(R.) Edward Lawrence
Packard
(R.8) Benjamin Wihry
SENE VALLEY, FOLKESTONE AND
HYTHE GC
England
Henry Cotton
SENGOKU GC
Fujiya Hotel, Kanagawa, Japan
Rokuro Akaboshi, *Shiro Akaboshi*
SENIOR ESTATES G&CC
Woodburn, Oregon
William Graham
SENNEVILLE CC
Montreal, Quebec
Willie Park, Jr.
SENSHU CC
Akita, Japan
Takeaki Kaneda
SENTOSA ISLAND GC (SENTOSA CSE)
Singapore
J. J. F. Pennink
SENTOSA ISLAND GC (SERAPONG
CSE)
Singapore
Peter Thomson, Michael
Wolveridge, Ronald Fream
(R.) Robin Nelson, Rodney
Wright
SENTRYWORLD GC
Stevens Point, Wisconsin
Robert Trent Jones, Jr.
SEPULVEDA GC (BALBOA CSE)
Encino, California
William F. Bell, William P. Bell,
William H. Johnson
SEPULVEDA GC (ENCINO CSE)
Encino, California
William F. Bell, William P. Bell,
William H. Johnson
SEPULVEDA VA HOSPITAL GC
Encino, California
William H. Johnson
SEQUOYAH CC
Oakland, California
(R.) Herbert Fowler
(R.13) Robert Muir Graves
SEQUOYAH STATE PARK GC
Hulbert, Oklahoma
Floyd Farley
SERLBY PARK GC
Yorkshire, England
Tom Williamson
SET C
Aix-en-Provence, France
Ronald Fream
SETH HUGHES GC [NLE]
Tulsa, Oklahoma
Floyd Farley
SETONAIKAI GC
Okayama, Japan
Shunsuke Kato
SETTINDOWN CREEK GC
Woodstock, Georgia
Bob Cupp

SETTLER'S HILL GC
Geneva, Illinois
Bob Lohmann
SEVE BALLESTEROS GC (IZUMI CSE)
Fukushima, Japan
Severiano Ballesteros
SEVEN BRIDGES GC
Woodridge, Illinois
Dick Nugent
SEVEN DEVILS GC
Boone, North Carolina
George Brownlaw
SEVEN HILLS CC
Hemet, California
Harry Rainville, David Rainville
SEVEN HILLS G&CC
Port Hardy, British Columbia
William L. Overdorf
SEVEN HILLS GC
Spring Hill, Florida
Denis Griffiths
SEVEN HILLS GC
Hartville, Ohio
William Newcomb
SEVEN LAKES CC
Palm Springs, California
Ted Robinson
SEVEN LAKES CC
Fort Myers, Florida
Ernest E. Smith
(R.) Edward Lawrence
Packard
(R.) Gordon Lewis
SEVEN LAKES GC
West End, North Carolina
Peter V. Tufts
SEVEN LAKES GC
Ibaraki, Japan
Shunsuke Kato
SEVEN OAKS CC
Bakersfield, California
Robert Muir Graves
SEVEN OAKS GC
Colgate University, Hamilton,
New York
Robert Trent Jones
SEVEN OAKS GC
Beaver, Pennsylvania
(R.) X. G. Hassenplug
SEVEN RIVERS CC
Crystal River, Florida
Bill Amick
SEVEN SPRINGS GC
Champion, Pennsylvania
X. G. Hassenplug
(R.9) Ferdinand Garbin
(R.2) Ron Forse
SEVEN SPRINGS G&CC (CSE NO. 1)
New Port Richey, Florida
James King
(R.) Ron Garl
SEVEN SPRINGS G&CC (CSE NO. 2)
New Port Richey, Florida
Ron Garl
SEVENTH MOUNTAIN GC
Bend, Oregon
Robert Muir Graves
SEVENTY-SIX FALLS CC
Albany, Kentucky
Harold England
SEVILLE G&CC
Brooksville, Florida
Arthur Hills

SEWARD CC
Seward, Nebraska
Harold Glissmann
SEWELLS POINT GC
Norfolk, Virginia
Donald Ross
(R.) William S. Flynn
(R.) Tom Clark
SEWICKLEY HEIGHTS CC
Sewickley, Pennsylvania
James Gilmore Harrison,
Ferdinand Garbin
(R.) Ferdinand Garbin
SEYMOUR CC
Seymour, Indiana
Victor George
SEYMOUR G&CC
North Vancouver, British
Columbia
James P. Izatt
(R.) William G. Robinson
SHACKAMAXON G&CC
Westfield, New Jersey
A.W. Tillinghast
SHADES VALLEY CC
Alabama
Bancroft Timmons
SHADOW BROOK CC
Tunkhannock, Pennsylvania
Karl Schmidt
SHADOW CREEK CC
Palm Springs, California
Clyde Johnston
SHADOW CREEK GC
North Las Vegas, Nevada
Tom Fazio, *Steve Wynn*
SHADOW GLEN GC
Olathe, Kansas
Jay Morrish, Tom Weiskopf
SHADOW HILLS CC
Junction City, Oregon
Alex Kindsfather
SHADOW LAKE G&RC
Rochester, New York
Pete Craig
SHADOWMOSS G&TC
Charleston, South Carolina
Russell Breeden
SHADOW MOUNTAIN GC
Palm Desert, California
George Von Elm
(R.) Ron Fream
SHADOW PINES GC
Penfield, New York
Gordon Odenbach
SHADOWRIDGE CC
Vista, California
David Rainville
SHADY ACRES GC
Springfield, Missouri
Herman Siler
SHADY HILLS GC
Marion, Indiana
William H. Diddel
SHADY HOLLOW CC
Massillon, Ohio
William F. Mitchell
(R.) Ron Forse
SHADY LAWN GC
Beecher, Illinois
R. Albert Anderson
(R.) Roger Packard

SHADY OAKS CC
Fort Worth, Texas
Robert Trent Jones, Lawrence
Hughes, Ralph Plummer
SHADY OAKS GC
Baird, Texas
Dave Bennett, Leon Howard
SHAFTSBURY GC
Fairfield Glade, Tennessee
Gary Roger Baird
SHAGANAPPI MUNI
Calgary, Alberta
Neil Little
SHAKER FARMS CC
Westfield, Massachusetts
Geoffrey S. Cornish
SHAKER HEIGHTS CC
Shaker Heights, Ohio
Donald Ross
(R.) Geoffrey S. Cornish
SHAKER HILLS GC
Harvard, Massachusetts
Brian Silva, Geoffrey S. Cornish
SHAKER RIDGE CC
Loudonville, New York
James Thomson
SHAKER RUN GC
Middletown, Ohio
Arthur Hills
SHALIMAR GC
Tempe, Arizona
(R.) Gary Grandstaff
SHALIMAR POINTE CC
Shalimar, Florida
Bill Amick
(R.) Joseph S. Finger, Ken
Dye
SHAMANAH GC
Boise, Idaho
NKA Quail Hollow GC
SHAMBOLEE GC
Petersburg, Illinois
Charles Maddox
SHAM CASTLE GC
Bath, England
(R.) J. Hamilton Stutt
SHAM-NA-PUM GC
Richland, Washington
Mel "Curley" Hueston
(R.) Robert Muir Graves
SHAMOKIN VALLEY CC
Pennsylvania
Alex Findlay
SHAMROCK GC
Columbus, Ohio
Michael Hurdzan
SHAMROCK GC
Ligonier, Pennsylvania
Ferdinand Garbin
SHAMROCK HILLS GC
Lee's Summit, Missouri
Jim Weaver
SHANDIN HILLS GC
San Bernardino, California
Cary A. Bickler
SHANGHAI INTERNATIONAL CC
Shanghai, China
Robert Trent Jones, Jr.
SHANGRI-LA CC (BLUE CSE)
Afton, Oklahoma
Don Sechrest
SHANGRI-LA CC (GOLD CSE)
Afton, Oklahoma
Don Sechrest

SHANGRI-LA GC
Whitefish, Montana
John Steidel
SHANKLIN & SANDOWN GC
Isle of Man
J. Cowper
(R.) J. Hamilton Stutt
SHANNON G&CC
Freeport, Bahamas
Joe Lee
SHANNON GC
County Clare, Ireland
John Harris
SHANNON GREEN GC
Fredericksburg, Virginia
Edmund B. Ault
SHANNON LAKE GC
Westbank, British Columbia
John Moore (1991)
SHANNOPIN CC
Ben Avon Heights, Pennsylvania
Emil Loeffler, *John McGlynn*
(R.) Ferdinand Garbin
SHANTY CREEK GC (DESKIN CSE)
Bellaire, Michigan
William H. Diddel
SHANTY CREEK GC (LEGEND CSE)
Bellaire, Michigan
Arnold Palmer, Ed Seay
SHARK RIVER GC
Neptune, New Jersey
Joseph "Scotty" I'Anson
(R. A.5) Hal Purdy
SHARON C
Sharon Center, Ohio
George W. Cobb
(R.) Geoffrey S. Cornish,
Brian Silva
SHARON CC
Sharon, Massachusetts
(R.9) Wayne Stiles
SHARON CC
Sharon, Pennsylvania
Tom Bendelow
SHARON HEIGHTS G&CC
Menlo Park, California
Jack Fleming
(R.) Robert Muir Graves
SHARON WOODS GC
Sharonville, Ohio
William H. Diddel
SHARP PARK GC
Pacifica, California
Alister Mackenzie
(R.) Robert Muir Graves
SHARPSTOWN CC
Houston, Texas
Ralph Plummer
(R.) Jay Riviere
SHASTA VALLEY CC
Montague, California
Clark Glasson
SHATTUCK GC
Shattuck, Oklahoma
Floyd Farley
SHATTUCK INN G CSE
Jaffrey, New Hampshire
Brian Silva, Geoffrey S. Cornish
SHAUGHNESSY G&CC
Vancouver, British Columbia
A. Vernon Macan
(R.) Norman H. Woods

SHAUGHNESSY HEIGHTS C [NLE]
Vancouver, British Columbia
A. Vernon Macan
SHAW HILL G&CC
Lancashire, England
(R.) T. J. A. Macauley
SHAWINIGAN G&CC
Shawinigan, Quebec
Howard Watson
SHAWNEE CC
Milford, Delaware
Edmund B. Ault, Al Jamison
(A.9) Edmund B. Ault, Bill
Love
SHAWNEE CC
Topeka, Kansas
Donald Ross
(R.) Chet Mendenhall
SHAWNEE CC
Lima, Ohio
Tom Bendelow
(R.) Jack Kidwell, Michael
Hurdzan
SHAWNEE CC
Shawnee-on-Delaware,
Pennsylvania
A.W. Tillinghast
(R.) *J. Franklin Meehan*
(R. A.3rd 9) William H.
Diddel
SHAWNEE G&CC
Shawnee, Oklahoma
Robert von Hagge, Bruce Devlin
SHAWNEE GC
Institute, West Virginia
(R.) Ron Kirby
SHAWNEE MUNI
Louisville, Kentucky
Alex McKay
SHAWNEE ELKS CC
Shawnee, Oklahoma
Perry Maxwell
SHAWNEE HILLS GC
Cleveland, Ohio
Ben W. Zink
SHAWNEE LOOKOUT GC
Cincinnati, Ohio
Jack Kidwell, Michael Hurdzan
SHAWNEE SLOPES GC
Alberta
Peter Olynyk, Ernie Tate
(R.) Robert Moote
SHAWNEE STATE PARK GC
Portsmouth, Ohio
Jack Kidwell, Michael Hurdzan
SHEAFFER MEMORIAL PARK GC
Fort Madison, Iowa
C. D. Wagstaff
SHEBOYGAN CC [AKA PINE HILLS
GC]
Sheboygan, Wisconsin
Harry B. Smead (1928)
SHEERNESS GC
Kent, England
Willie Park, Jr.
SHELBURNE FARMS LINKS [NLE]
Shelburne, Vermont
Willie Park, Jr.
SHELBY CC
Shelby, Ohio
Ben W. Zink
SHELBY OAKS GC
Sidney, Ohio
Ken Killian, Dick Nugent

SHELBYVILLE CC
Shelbyville, Kentucky
(A.2) Benjamin Wihry
SHELBYVILLE CC
Shelbyville, Tennessee
R. Albert Anderson
SHELBYVILLE ELKS CC
Shelbyville, Indiana
William H. Diddel
SHELRIDGE CC
Medina, New York
X. G. Hassenplug
SHENANDOAH CC
Baton Rouge, Louisiana
E. E. Evans
SHENANDOAH CC
Shenandoah, Virginia
Fred Findlay
SHENANDOAH G&CC
Walled Lake, Michigan
Bruce Matthews, Jerry Matthews
SHENANDOAH CROSSING FARM & C
Gordonsville, Virginia
Buddy Loving
SHENANDOAH VALLEY CC
Middleburg, Virginia
Buddy Loving
(R.) Rees Jones
SHENNECOSSETT GC
Groton, Connecticut
Donald Ross
(R.3) Donald Ross
SHENVALLEE C
New Market, Virginia
(R.9 A.9) Edmund B. Ault
SHEPARD HILLS CC
Roxbury, New York
(A.9) Geoffrey S. Cornish,
William G. Robinson
SHEPPARD AFB GC
Wichita Falls, Texas
(R.) *Spencer P. Ellis*
SHERATON EL CONQUISTADOR GC
(SUNRISE CSE)
Tucson, Arizona
Jeff Hardin, Greg Nash
SHERATON EL CONQUISTADOR GC
(SUNSET CSE)
Tucson, Arizona
Jeff Hardin
SHERATON INN GC
Greensburg, Pennsylvania
X. G. Hassenplug
SHERATON LAKEVIEW RESORT & CC
(LAKEVIEW CSE)
Morgantown, West Virginia
James Gilmore Harrison,
Ferdinand Garbin
SHERATON LAKEVIEW RESORT & CC
(MOUNTAINVIEW CSE)
Morgantown, West Virginia
Brian Ault, Tom Clark
SHERATON MAKAHA RESORT & CC
Waianae, Oahu, Hawaii
William F. Bell
(R.) Robin Nelson, Rodney
Wright
SHERATON SAVANNAH RESORT &
CC
Savannah, Georgia
Donald Ross
(R.) Willard Byrd

SHERATON STEAMBOAT SPRINGS GC
  Steamboat Springs, Colorado
  Robert Trent Jones, Jr.
SHERATON TARA HOTEL & GC
  Danvers, Massachusetts
  Robert Trent Jones
SHERBORNE GC
  Sherborne, England
  James Braid
SHERBROOKE G&CC
  Lake Worth, Florida
  Robert von Hagge, Bruce Devlin
SHEREWOGUE ESTATE GC [NLE]
  St. James, New York
  Devereux Emmet
SHERIDAN CC
  Sheridan, Arkansas
  William T. Martin
SHERIDAN PARK GC
  Kenmore, New York
  William Harries
    (R.) *A. Russell Tryon*
SHERINGHAM GC
  Sheringham, England
  Tom Dunn
SHERMAN GC
  Sherman, Texas
  Tom Bendelow
SHERRILL PARK MUNI (EAST CSE)
  Richardson, Texas
  Leon Howard
SHERRILL PARK MUNI (WEST CSE)
  Richardson, Texas
  Leon Howard, *Charles Howard*
SHERRY GOLF MONTECASTILLO
  Jerez, Spain
  Jack Nicklaus
SHERWOOD CC
  Thousand Oaks, California
  Jack Nicklaus
SHERWOOD G&CC
  Titusville, Florida
  Bill Amick
    (A.9) Lloyd Clifton
SHERWOOD GC
  Salisbury, Zimbabwe
  Robert G. Grimsdell
SHERWOOD FOREST CC
  Baton Rouge, Louisiana
  Ralph Plummer
SHERWOOD FOREST GC
  Sanger, California
  Bob Baldock, Robert L. Baldock
SHERWOOD FOREST GC
  Annapolis, Maryland
  Herbert Strong
    (R.4) Brian Ault
SHERWOOD FOREST GC
  Nottinghamshire, England
  Tom Dunn
    (R.) Tom Williamson
    (R.) James Braid, John R.
    Stutt
SHERWOOD HILLS GC
  Sardine Canyon, Utah
  Mark Dixon Ballif
SHERWOOD PARK GC
  Edmonton, Alberta
  William Brinkworth
SHEWANI CC
  Wateska, Illinois
  Dick Nugent

SHIFFERDECKER CC
  Joplin, Missouri
    (R.9 A.9) Smiley Bell
SHIFNAL GC
  Shifnal, England
    (R.) J. J. F. Pennink
SHIKOKU CC
  Japan
  Yasuzo Kaneko
SHILLELAGH GC
  Burlington, North Carolina
  W. Shoe, Jr.
SHILOH PARK GC
  Zion, Illinois
  Edward Lawrence Packard
SHIMODA FORUM GC
  Shimoda, Japan
  Scott Miller
SHIMODAJO CC
  Japan
  Kentaro Sato
SHIMONITA CC
  Gunma, Japan
  Shunji Kurakami
SHIMONOSEKI GC
  Yamaguchi, Japan
  O. Ueda
SHIMONOSEKI GOLDEN GC
  Yamaguchi, Japan
  Jack Nicklaus
SHIMOTSUKE CC
  Japan
  Arnold Palmer, Ed Seay
SHINGLE LAKE GC
  Marysville, California
  Bob Baldock
SHINNECOCK HILLS GC (WHITE
  CSE) [NLE]
  Southampton, New York
  William F. Davis
    (R.12 A.8) Willie Dunn, Jr.
SHINNECOCK HILLS GC
  Southampton, New York
  William S. Flynn, Howard
  Toomey
    (R.) William F. Mitchell
SHINNECOCK HILLS GC (RED CSE)
  [NLE]
  Southampton, New York
  Willie Dunn, Jr.
SHINRIN GC
  Aichi, Japan
  O. Ueda
SHINRIN KOEN GC
  Saitama, Japan
  K. Yasuda, S. Kawamura
SHINYO GC
  Japan
  Desmond Muirhead
SHIPLEY GC
  Yorkshire, England
  James Braid
    (R.) Alister MacKenzie
SHIPYARD GC
  Hilton Head Island, South
  Carolina
  George W. Cobb
    (A.3rd 9) Willard Byrd
SHIRAHAMA GC
  Wakayama, Japan
  G. Sato
SHIRAKAWA MEADOW GC
  Fukushima, Japan
  Shunsuke Kato

SHIRANUI CC
  Japan
  Teruo Sugihara
SHIREHAMPTON PARK GC
  Bristol, England
  A.N. Andrews
SHIRKEY CC
  Richmond, Missouri
  Chet Mendenhall
SHISHIDO INTERNATIONAL CC
  Ibaraki, Japan
  Gary Roger Baird
SHISHIDO KOKUSAI GC (SHIZU CSE)
  Ibaraki, Japan
  Gary Roger Baird
SHISKINE GC
  Isle of Arran, Scotland
  Willie Fernie
    (R.) Willie Park, Jr.
SHITADAJO CC
  Niigata, Japan
  Kentaro Sato
SHIUN CC
  Niigata, Japan
  Kinya Fujita
SHIZUKUISHI GC
  Iwate Prefecture, Japan
  Mike Poellot, Brad Benz
SHIZUOKA CC
  Shizuoka, Japan
  Kinya Fujita
SHOAFF PARK GC
  Fort Wayne, Indiana
  Hal Purdy
SHOAL CANYON GC
  Glendale, California
  William F. Bell
SHOAL CREEK
  Birmingham, Alabama
  Jack Nicklaus
SHOAL RIVER G&CC
  Crestview, Florida
  Dave Bennett
SHOOP PARK GC
  Racine, Wisconsin
  William B. Langford
SHOOTER'S HILL GC
  London, England
  Willie Park, Jr.
SHOREACRES
  Lake Bluff, Illinois
  Seth Raynor
SHORE ACRES CC [NLE]
  La Porte, Texas
  John Bredemus
SHORE ACRES GC
  Sebasco, Maine
  Alex Chisholm
SHOREACRES GC
  Ontario
  Stanley Thompson
SHORECLIFFS CC
  San Clemente, California
  Joseph B. Williams
    (R.) Bob Baldock, Robert L.
    Baldock
SHOREHAM GC
  Southdown, England
  Sir Guy Campbell, C. K.
  Hutchison, S. V. Hotchkin
SHOREHAVEN GC
  Norwalk, Connecticut
  Robert White

SHORELINE G CSE
  Carter Lake, Iowa
  Pat Wyss
SHORELINE G LINKS
  Mountain View, California
  Robert Trent Jones, Jr.
SHORE OAKS GC
  Little Silver, New Jersey
  Tom Pearson, Johnny Miller
SHORES CC
  Lake Hubbard, Texas
  Ralph Plummer
SHOREWOOD CC
  Dunkirk, New York
  William Harries
SHORT BEACH GC
  Connecticut
  Geoffrey S. Cornish, Brian Silva
SHORT HILLS CC
  East Moline, Illinois
  Ted Lockie
    (R.) Roger Packard
SHOWBOAT CC
  Las Vegas, Nevada
  NKA Royal Kenfield GC
SHOW LOW CC
  Show Low, Arizona
  Arthur Jack Snyder
SHREVEPORT CC
  Shreveport, Louisiana
    (R.9) Leon Howard
    (R.15 A.3) Joseph S. Finger
    (R.) Dave Bennett
SHREWSBURY GC
  Shrewsbury, England
    (R.) J. J. F. Pennink
SHRIGLEY HALL GC
  England
  D. M. A. Steel
SHUSWAP LAKE ESTATES G&CC
  Blind Bay, British Columbia
  Ernest Brown
    (R.) Norman H. Woods
SHUTTLE MEADOW CC
  New Britain, Connecticut
  Willie Park, Jr.
SIASCONSET GC
  Nantucket, Massachusetts
  Alex Findlay
SIBU GC
  Sarawak, Malaysia
  J. J. F. Pennink
SICKLEHOLME GC
  England
    (R.) Tom Williamson
SIDERURGIA GC
  Argentina
  Angel Reartes
SIDMOUTH GC
  Devon, England
  Charles Gibson
    (R. A.9) J. H. Taylor
SIEGEN OLPE GC
  Seigen, Germany
  Bernhard von Limburger
    (A.9) Karl F. Grohs, *Rainer
    Preissmann*
SIERRA ESTRELLA GC
  Goodyear, Arizona
  Red Lawrence
SIERRA LAVERNE CC
  LaVerne, California
  Dan Murray

SIERRA SKY RANCH GC
Oakhurst, California
Bob Baldock
SIERRA VIEW CC
Roseville, California
Jack Fleming
(A.9) Bob Baldock
SIERRA VISTA GC
White Sands, New Mexico
Leon Howard
SIGNAL HILL CC
Panama City, Florida
John Henry Sherman (1962)
SIGNAL HILL CC
Armonk, New York
Orrin Smith
SIGNAL POINT C
Niles, Michigan
Robert Bruce Harris
SIGNAL POINT CC
Fort Benton, Montana
Norman H. Woods
SIGTUNABYGDENS GC
Sigtuna, Sweden
Nils Sköld
SIGWICK INN & GC
Leesburg, Virginia
Edmund B. Ault
SIKSIKA RESORT G&CC
Calgary, Alberta
Bill Newis
SILER CITY CC
Siler City, North California
Ellis Maples
SILKEBORG GC
Silkeborg, Denmark
Frederic Dreyer
SILOTH-ON-SOLWAY GC
Cumbria, England
Willie Park, Willie Park, Jr.
SILVERADO CC (NORTH CSE)
Napa, California
Ben Harmon, *Johnny Dawson*
(R.) Robert Trent Jones
SILVERADO CC (SOUTH CSE)
Napa, California
Robert Trent Jones
(R.) Robert Muir Graves
SILVERBELL MUNI
Tucson, Arizona
Arthur Jack Snyder
SILVER CREEK CC
San Jose, California
Theodore Robinson
SILVER CREEK GC
White Mountain Lakes, Arizona
Gary Panks
SILVER CREEK GC
San Bernardino, California
William H. Johnson
SILVER CREEK GC
Swansboro, North Carolina
Gene Hamm
SILVERCREST G&CC
Decorah, Iowa
(R.) Charles Calhoun
SILVERHORN GC
Oklahoma City, Oklahoma
Randy Heckenkemper
SILVER K GC
Oxnard, California
William F. Bell

SILVER LAKE CC
Pontiac, Michigan
(R.3 A.2) Mark DeVries
SILVER LAKE CC
Akron, Ohio
Edward Lawrence Packard,
Brent Wadsworth
SILVER LAKE G&CC
Leesburg, Florida
Ernest E. Smith
SILVER LAKE GC (NORTH CSE)
Orland Park, Illinois
Leonard Macomber
(R.1) Ken Killian, Dick Nu-
gent
SILVER LAKE GC (SOUTH CSE)
Orland Park, Illinois
Charles Maddox, *Frank P.
MacDonald*
SILVER LAKE GC
Pomona, Kansas
Ted Haworth
SILVER LAKE GC
Staten Island, New York
John Van Kleek
SILVER LAKES CC
Helendale, California
Ted Robinson
SILVER LAKE SCHOOL GC
Pittsburgh, Pennsylvania
Ferdinand Garbin
SILVER LAKES GC
Pembroke Pines, Florida
Dick Nugent
SILVER LEAF GC
Rome, Georgia
Mike Hurdzan
SILVERMINE GC
Norwalk, Connecticut
John E. Warner, Jr.
(R.) Alfred H. Tull
SILVER PINES GC [NLE]
Florida
Lloyd Clifton
SILVER RIDGE GC
Oregon, Illinois
(R.) C. D. Wagstaff
SILVER SAGE GC
Mountain Home, Idaho
Bob Baldock
(A.9) Robert Muir Graves
SILVER SPRING CC
Ridgefield, Connecticut
Robert White
(R.) Alfred H. Tull
SILVER SPRING GC
Mechanicsburg, Pennsylvania
George Fazio
SILVER SPRING GC [NLE]
Ocala, Florida
Seymour Dunn
SILVER SPRINGS G&CC
Calgary, Alberta
Dick Phelps, *Claude Muret*
(R.) Les Furber, *Jim Eremko*
SILVER SPRINGS GC
Silver Springs, Maryland
Donald Ross
(R.) Edmund B. Ault, Al
Jamison
SILVER SPRING SHORES G&CC
Ocala, Florida
Desmond Muirhead

SILVERSWORD G&CC
Kihea, Maui, Hawaii
Bill Newis
SILVERWOOD G CSE
Saskatoon, Saskatchewan
John F. Robinson, William B.
Robinson
SIMILK BEACH GC
Anacortes, Washington
(R.) Bill Overdorf (1988)
SIM PARK MUNI
Wichita, Kansas
Harry Heimple, Jack Shearman
(R.) Bob Dunning
(R.) Don Sechrest
SIMSBURY FARMS MUNI
Simsbury, Connecticut
Geoffrey S. Cornish, William G.
Robinson
SINGAPORE ISLAND CC (ISLAND
CSE)
Singapore
C. K. Cotton, J. J. F. Pennink
SINGAPORE ISLAND GC (BUKIT CSE)
Singapore
James Braid
(R.) J. J. F. Pennink
SINGAPORE ISLAND GC (NEW CSE)
Singapore
John Harris, J. J. F. Pennink
SINGAPORE ISLAND GC (SIME CSE)
Singapore
J. J. F. Pennink
(R.) Ronald Fream
SINGING HILLS CC (OAK GLEN CSE)
El Cajon, California
Cecil B. Hollingsworth
(R.) Ted Robinson
SINGING HILLS CC (PINE GLEN CSE)
El Cajon, California
Cecil B. Hollingsworth
(R.) Ted Robinson
SINGING HILLS CC (WILLOW GLEN
CSE)
El Cajon, California
William F. Bell, William P. Bell,
William H. Johnson
(R.) Ted Robinson
SINGLETREE GC
Edwards, Colorado
Jay Morrish, Bob Cupp
SINKING VALLEY CC
Altoona, Pennsylvania
Edmund B. Ault
SINNISSIPPI PARK GC
Rockford, Illinois
Tom Bendelow
SINTON MUNI
Sinton, Texas
Henry B. Hughes, Richard
Watson
(A.9) Dave Bennett, Leon
Howard
SIOUX CITY CC
Sioux City, Iowa
Tom Bendelow
SIPPIHAW CC [NLE]
Fuquay-Varina, North Carolina
C. D. Wagstaff
(A.9) Gene Hamm
SIR ARCHIBALD BIRKMYRE ESTATE
GC
England
Tom Simpson

SIR HARRY OAKES PRIVATE CSE
Niagara Falls, Ontario
Stanley Thompson
SIR MORTIMER SINGER ESTATE GC
England
Tom Simpson
SIR PHILIP SASSOON ESTATE GC
England
Tom Simpson
SITTINGBOURNE AND MILTON GC
Kent, England
(R.) D. M. A. Steel
SITWELL PARK GC
Yorkshire, England
Alister Mackenzie
SIWANOY CC
Bronxville, New York
Donald Ross
(R.) Tom Winton
(R.) Robert Trent Jones
(R.) Geoffrey S. Cornish,
William G. Robinson
SKANEATELES CC
Skaneateles, New York
(A.9) Hal Purdy
SKELLEFTEÅ GC
Skellefteå, Sweden
Nils Sköld, B. Carlsson
(R.) Ronald Fream
SKENANDOA C
Clinton, New York
Russell D. Bailey
SKEPPARSLÖV GC
Sweden
R. Collijn
SKEPPTUNA GC
Skepptuna, Sweden
Jan Sederholm
SKERRIES GC
Skerries, Ireland
(A.9) Eddie Hackett
SKIBO CASTLE GC
Scotland
John Sutherland
SKIPPACK GC
Skippack, Pennsylvania
(R.) X. G. Hassenplug
SKLO BOHEMIA PODEBRADY GC
Czechoslovakia
J. J. F. Pennink
SKOKIE CC
Glencoe, Illinois
Tom Bendelow
(R.) Donald Ross
(R.) William B. Langford,
Theodore J. Moreau
(R.) Ken Killian, Dick Nugent
(R.) Rees Jones
SKOKIE PLAYFIELD GC [NLE]
Winnetka, Illinois
William B. Langford, Theodore
J. Moreau
SKYLAND GC
Crested Butte, Colorado
Robert Trent Jones, Jr.
SKYLAND LAKES G CSE
Fancy Gap, Virginia
Welch DeBoard (1988)
SKYLINE CC
Mobile, Alabama
Chic Adams
(A.3rd 9) Earl Stone

SKYLINE CC
Tucson, Arizona
Guy S. Greene
(R.) Tom Clark
SKYLINE GC
Pittsfield, Massachusetts
Rowland Armacost
SKYLINE GC
Black River Falls, Wisconsin
Edward Lawrence Packard,
Brent Wadsworth
SKYLINE GC
Osage, West Virginia
(R.18 A.9) Ferdinand Garbin
SKYLINE WOODS CC
Elkhorn, Nebraska
Frank Ervin
(R.) John Steidel
SKYLINKS GC
Long Beach, California
William F. Bell
SKYPARK GC
Florence, Alabama
Bob Baldock, Robert L. Baldock
SKYTOP C
Skytop, Pennsylvania
Robert White
SKY MEADOW CC
Nashua, New Hampshire
Bill Amick
SKY VALLEY CC
Dillard, Georgia
Bill Watts
SKY VALLEY GC
Hillsboro, Indiana
Gary Kern
SKYVIEW MUNI
Alliance, Nebraska
Henry Hughes
SKYWAY CC
Japan
Akira Hotti
SKYWEST PUBLIC GC
Hayward, California
Bob Baldock
SLADE VALLEY GC
County Dublin, Ireland
D. O'Brien, W. Sullivan
(R.) Eddie Hackett
SLALEY HALL GC
Northumberland, England
David Thomas
SLEAFORD GC
Lincolnshire, England
Tom Williamson
SLEEPING GIANT GC
Hamden, Connecticut
Ralph Barton
(R.) William F. Mitchell
SLEEPY HOLE MUNI
Portsmouth, Virginia
Russell Breeden
SLEEPY HOLLOW G&CC (LAKE CSE)
Dallas, Texas
Press Maxwell
(R.) Karl Litten
SLEEPY HOLLOW G&CC (RIVER CSE)
Dallas, Texas
Press Maxwell
(R.) Karl Litten
SLEEPY HOLLOW GC
Prospect, Kentucky
Harold England (9 1968)

SLEEPY HOLLOW GC
Scarboro-on-Hudson, New York
Charles Blair Macdonald, Seth Raynor
(R. A.5) A.W. Tillinghast
(R.) Tom Winton
(R.) Robert Trent Jones
(R.) Rees Jones
SLEEPY HOLLOW GC
Cleveland, Ohio
Stanley Thompson
SLEEPY HOLLOW GC
Hurricane, West Virginia
James Gilmore Harrison
SLIGO PARK GC
Silver Spring, Maryland
Edmund B. Ault, Al Jamison
SLOCAN LAKE GC
New Denver, British Columbia
James Greer, Neil Tatrie
SLUISPOLDER GC
Netherlands
J. F. Dudok van Heel
SMILEY'S SPORTLAND GC [NLE]
Kansas City, Kansas
Smiley Bell
SMILEY'S SPORTLAND GC
Overland Park, Kansas
Everett Tull
SMITH AND LAMBERTS GC
Llanelly, Wales
Martin Hawtree, Steven McFarlane
SMITHTOWN LANDING GC
Smithtown, New York
(R.) Stephen Kay
SMITHVILLE MUNI
Smithville, Tennessee
R. Albert Anderson
SMOKY HILL CC
Hays, Kansas
Dick Phelps
(A.9) Greg Nash
SMOKY MOUNTAIN CC
Newport, Tennessee
Alex McKay
SNAPFINGER WOODS GC
Decatur, Georgia
NKA Pine Hills CC
SNEE FARM CC
Charleston, South Carolina
George W. Cobb
SNOW CREEK GC
Mammoth Lakes, California
Theodore Robinson
SNOWMASS GC
Snowmass-at-Aspen, Colorado
Press Maxwell
(A.9) John Cochran
(R.) Arnold Palmer, Ed Seay
SNOWSNAKE GC
Harrison, Michigan
Jeff Gorney
SNYDER PARK CC
Springfield, Ohio
(R.4) Jack Kidwell
SOANGETAHA CC
Galesburg, Illinois
Tom Bendelow
SOBHU CC
Japan
(R.) Robert Trent Jones

SOBOBA SPRINGS CC
San Jacinto, California
Desmond Muirhead
SODEGAURA CC (SHINSODE CSE)
Japan
Ichisuke Izumi
SODERHAMN GC
Soderhamn, Sweden
Nils Sköld
SÖDERKÖPING GC
Söderköping, Sweden
Ronald Fream
SÖDERTÄLJE GC
Södertälje, Sweden
Nils Sköld
SODUS POINT HEIGHTS GC
Sodus Point, New York
(R.9) Robert Trent Jones
(R.7 A.11) Geoffrey S. Cornish, William G. Robinson
SOEDERASENS GC
Billesholm, Sweden
Ture Bruce
SOLDIERS FIELD GC
Rochester, Minnesota
Hugh Vincent Freehan
(R.) Gerry Pirkl, *Donald G. Brauer*
SOLIHULL GC
Warwickshire, England
J. Hamilton Stutt
SOLLEFTEA-LANGSELE GC
Sweden
Nils Sköld
SOLLENTUNA GC
Sollentuna, Sweden
Nils Sköld
SOLLEROD GC
Denmark
Anders Amilon
SOLTAU GC
Soltau, Germany
Wolfgang Siegmann
SOMBRERO CC
Marathon, Florida
Carl H. Anderson
SOMERSET CC
St. Paul, Minnesota
(R.) Stanley Thompson
(R.) Robert Bruce Harris
(R.) George W. Cobb, John LaFoy
(R.) Geoffrey S. Cornish, William G. Robinson
(R.) Geoffrey S. Cornish, Brian Silva
SOMERSET CC
Somerset, Pennsylvania
(A.9) Ferdinand Garbin
SOMERSET HILLS CC [NLE]
Bernardsville, New Jersey
Tom Bendelow
SOMERSET HILLS CC
Bernardsville, New Jersey
A.W. Tillinghast
(R.) Hal Purdy
SONDERJYLLANDS GC
Denmark
(A.9) Jan Sederholm
SONNING GC
Sonning, England
(R.9 A.9) F. G. Hawtree, J. H. Taylor

SONNY GUY MUNI
Jackson, Mississippi
Sonny Guy
SONOMA GC
Sonoma, California
Sam Whiting
(R.) Robert Muir Graves
SON SERVERA GC
Mallorca, Spain
John Harris
SON VIDA GC
Mallorca, Spain
Fred W. Hawtree
SOO NIPI PARK GC [NLE]
Lake Sunapee, New Hampshire
Alex Findley
(R.) Alex Findlay
SORACHIGAWA LAVENDER GC
Hokkaido, Japan
Toshio Hoshi
SORRENTO GC
Sorrento, Victoria, Australia
(R.) Peter Thomson, Michael Wolveridge
SORRENTO PAR 3 GC
Nokomos, Florida
R. Albert Anderson
SORRENTO VALLEY CC
Laurel, Florida
Ted McAnlis
SOTENÄS GC
Sweden
Jan Sederholm
SOTOGRANDE GC (NEW CSE)
Cadiz, Spain
NKA Valderrama GC
SOTOGRANDE GC (OLD CSE)
Cadiz, Spain
Robert Trent Jones
SOTOGRANDE GC (SHORT CSE)
Cadiz, Spain
Robert Trent Jones
SOTOGRANDE G&TC
Fort Worth, Texas
Dave Bennett, Leon Howard
SOULE PARK GC
Ojai, California
William F. Bell
(A.9) Bob Baldock, Robert L. Baldock
[THE] SOUND G LINKS
Hertford, North Carolina
Dan Maples
SOUND SHORE GC
Greenport, New York
Frank Duane
SOURABIA GC
Indonesia
Tom Simpson
SOURIS VALLEY GC
Minot, North Dakota
William James Spear
SOUTHAMPTON GC
Naples, Florida
Gordon Lewis
SOUTHAMPTON GC
Southampton, New York
Seth Raynor, Charles Banks
(R.) William F. Mitchell
SOUTHAMPTON GC
Hampshire, England
F. G. Hawtree, J. H. Taylor
(R. A.3rd 9) J. Hamilton Stutt

SOUTHAMPTON PRINCESS GC
Bermuda
Alfred H. Tull
(R.) Ted Robinson
SOUTH BEND CC
South Bend, Indiana
George O'Neil
(R.) William Newcomb
SOUTH BLUFF CC
Peru, Illinois
William B. Langford
SOUTH BOSTON CC [NLE]
South Boston, Virginia
Fred Findlay
SOUTHBRIDGE GC
Savannah, Georgia
Rees Jones
SOUTHBROOM GC
South Coast, Natal, South Africa
J. Naven
(R.4 A.14) A. L. Mandy
SOUTHCLIFFE AND CANWICK GC
Lincolnshire, England
F. G. Hawtree, J. H. Taylor
SOUTHERN DUTCHESS CC
Beacon, New York
(R.) Stephen Kay
SOUTHERNDOWN GC
Glamorgan, Wales
Willie Fernie
(R.) Willie Park, Jr.
(R.) Herbert Fowler
(R.) H. S. Colt
SOUTHERNESS GC
Stockbridge, Georgia
Clyde Johnston
SOUTHERNESS GC
Dumfrieshire, Scotland
P. M. Ross
SOUTHERN GC
Australia
(R. A.9) Peter Thomson,
Michael Wolveridge
SOUTHERN HILLS CC
Bowden, Indiana
James R. Neidigh
SOUTHERN HILLS CC
Hastings, Nebraska
Reuben Schneider
SOUTHERN HILLS CC
Tulsa, Oklahoma
Perry Maxwell
(R.) Robert Trent Jones
(R.) George Fazio, Tom Fazio
(A.3rd 9) Bill Coore, Ben
Crenshaw
SOUTHERN HILLS CC
Hot Springs, South Dakota
Dick Phelps, Brad Benz
SOUTHERN HILLS CC
Murfreesboro, Tennessee
Karl Litten
SOUTHERN LINKS GC
Okinawa
Yoshikazu Kato
SOUTHERN MANOR CC [NLE]
Boca Raton, Florida
William F. Mitchell
SOUTHERN PINES CC
Southern Pines, North Carolina
Donald Ross
(R.) William F. Mitchell
(R.) John LaFoy

SOUTHERN TRACE CC
Shreveport, Louisiana
Arthur Hills
SOUTHERN WOODS CC
Homosassa Springs, Florida
Hale Irwin, Dick Phelps
SOUTHFIELD GC
Oxford, England
James Braid
(R.) H. S. Colt
SOUTH FORK CC
Amagansett, New York
(R.3) Frank Duane
SOUTH GATE GC
South Gate, California
William H. Johnson
SOUTHGATE GC
St. George, Utah
John V. Lagant
(R.) William Howard Neff
SOUTH HAVEN CC
South Haven, Michigan
Tom Bendelow
SOUTH HERTS GC
London, England
Willie Park, Jr.
(R.) J. Hamilton Stutt
(R.) Harry Vardon
SOUTH HIGHLAND CC
Mayfield, Kentucky
Scott Nall
SOUTH HILL CC
La Crosse, Virginia
Fred Findlay
SOUTH HILLS CC
West Covina, California
William F. Bell, William P. Bell
(R.) Desmond Muirhead
SOUTH HILLS GC
Hanover, Pennsylvania
William Gordon, David Gordon
(R.) Edmund B. Ault
(R.) X. G. Hassenplug
SOUTHLAND CC
Stone Mountain, Georgia
Willard Byrd
SOUTH LAKES G CSE
Jenks, Oklahoma
Randy Heckenkemper
SOUTHMOOR CC
Charleston, West Virginia
(R.) William Gordon
SOUTHMOOR GC
Flint, Michigan
Bruce Matthews, Jerry Matthews
(R.1) Jerry Matthews
SOUTH MUSKOKA CURLING & GC
Bracebridge, Ontario
Clinton E. Robinson
SOUTH OCEAN BEACH HOTEL GC
New Providence Island,
Bahamas
NKA Divi Bahamas GC
SOUTH PARK GC
Pittsburgh, Pennsylvania
(R.) X. G. Hassenplug
SOUTH PINE CREEK GC
Fairfield, Connecticut
Geoffrey S. Cornish, William G.
Robinson
SOUTHPORT GC
Queensland, Australia
John Harris

SOUTHPORT AND AINSDALE GC [NLE]
England
James Braid
SOUTHPORT AND AINSDALE GC
Southport, England
J. A. Steer
SOUTHPORT MUNI GC
Lancashire, England
H. S. Colt, J. S. F. Morrison
SOUTH PORTLAND MUNI
South Portland, Maine
Larry Rowe
SOUTHRIDGE GC
Yuba City, California
Cal Olson
SOUTHRIDGE GC
Deland, Florida
David Wallace
SOUTH RIDGE GC [NLE]
Hickman Mills, Missouri
James Dalgleish
SOUTH RIDGE GREENS GC
Fort Collins, Colorado
Frank Hummel
SOUTH SEAS PLANTATION GC
Captiva Island, Florida
Ernest E. Smith
(R.) Gene Bates
SOUTH SHORE CC
Chicago, Illinois
Tom Bendelow
SOUTH SHORE CC
Syracuse, Indiana
(R.9 A.9) William H. Diddel
SOUTH SHORE CC
Hingham, Massachusetts
Wayne Stiles
SOUTH SHORE CC
Hamburg, New York
Wayne Stiles, John Van Kleek
SOUTH SHORE GC
Momence, Illinois
Willie Watson
SOUTH SHORE GC
Staten Island, New York
Alfred Tull
SOUTH SHORE HARBOUR GC
League City, Texas
Jay Riviere, Dave Marr
SOUTH SIDE GC
Decatur, Illinois
(R.) Robert Bruce Harris
(R.) Dick Nugent
SOUTH SUBURBAN GC
Littleton, Colorado
Dick Phelps
SOUTHVIEW CC
West St. Paul, Minnesota
(R.) Gerry Pirkl, Donald G.
Brauer, Emil Perret
(R.7) Dick Phelps
SOUTHVIEW GC
Belton, Missouri
John Nash
SOUTH WALES G&RC
Jeffersonton, Virginia
Edmund B. Ault
SOUTHWARD HO! CC
Bayshore, New York
A. W. Tillinghast
(R.) Stephen Kay

SOUTHWELL GC [NLE]
Nottinghamshire, England
Tom Williamson
SOUTHWEST PARK MUNI [NLE]
Oklahoma City, Oklahoma
Arthur Jackson
SOUTHWEST POINT G&CC
Kingston, Tennessee
Alex McKay
SOUTHWICK PARK GC
Hampshire, England
J. J. F. Pennink, C. D. Lawrie
SOUTHWIND CC
Garden City, Kansas
Don Sechrest
SOUTHWOOD G&CC
Winnipeg, Manitoba
Willie Park, Jr.
(R.9) Stanley Thompson
(R.) Jack Thompson
SOUTHWOOD GC
Hampshire, England
John Harris
(R.5 A.13) Martin Hawtree,
Simon Gidman
SOUTHWYCK GC
Pearland, Texas
Ken Kavanaugh
SPAARWOUDE GC
Velsen, Netherlands
J. J. F. Pennink
[THE] SPA GC
McAfee, New Jersey
Robert Trent Jones
SPA GC
Ballynahinch, Northern Ireland
R. R. Bell, A. Mathers
SPALLUMCHEEN G&TC
Vernon, British Columbia
Bill Simms, Cyril Foster
(R.) Les Furber, Jim Eremko
SPANGDAHLEM GC
Germany
Bernhard von Limburger
SPANISH HILLS G&CC
Camarillo, California
Bob Cupp
SPANISH OAKS GC
Ogden, Utah
Donald Collett, Gary Darling
SPANISH POINT GC
Northern Ireland
J. McAlister
SPANISH TRAIL G&CC (CANYON CSE)
Las Vegas, Nevada
Robert Trent Jones, Jr.
SPANISH TRAIL G&CC (SUNRISE CSE)
Las Vegas, Nevada
Robert Trent Jones, Jr.
SPANISH WELLS CC
Hilton Head Island, South
Carolina
George W. Cobb
SPANISH WELLS G&CC
Bonita Springs, Florida
Gordon G. Lewis
SPARROW HAWK G CSE
Jackson, Michigan
Floyd Hammond, John O'Leary (9
1964)

SPARROWS POINT CC
 Baltimore, Maryland
 William Gordon, David Gordon
SPARTANBURG GC
 Roebuck, South Carolina
 Tom Jackson
SPARTAN MEADOWS GC
 Elgin, Illinois
 Edward Lawrence Packard
SPARWOOD GC
 British Columbia
 Ernest Brown
SPEEDLINKS GC
 Shoemakersville, Pennsylvania
 Luther O. "Luke" Morris
SPEEDWAY 500 GC
 Indianapolis, Indiana
 William H. Diddel
  (A.3rd 9) William H. Diddel
  (R.) Pete Dye
SPEIDEL GC
 Wheeling, West Virginia
 Robert Trent Jones
SPENCER G&CC
 Spencer, Iowa
 David Gill
SPENCER T. OLIN COMMUNITY G
 CSE
 Alton, Illinois
 Arnold Palmer, Ed Seay
SPESSARD HOLLAND GC
 Melbourne, Florida
 Arnold Palmer, Ed Seay
SPESSART GC
 Wachtersbach, Germany
 Götz Mecklenburg
SPIRITWOOD ACRES G&CC
 Yorkton, Saskatchewan
 Simon P. Dilschneider
SPIVEY LAKE GC
 Jonesboro, Georgia
  (A.3rd 9) D. J. DeVictor
SPOKANE CC
 Spokane, Washington
 Robert Johnstone, *Jim Barnes*
  (R.) *Joe Novak*
  (R.) Robert Muir Graves
SPOOK ROCK GC
 Ramapo, New York
 Frank Duane
  (R.) Stephen Kay
SPOOKY BROOK GC
 Somerset, New Jersey
 Edmund B. Ault
SPOONCREEK GC
 Stuart, Virginia
 Gene Hamm
SPOONER LAKE GC
 Spooner, Wisconsin
 Tom Vardon
  (A.9) *Dr. Gordon Emerson*
SPORTING C DE BEAUVALLON
 France
 Pierre Mancinelli
SPORTS CENTER GC
 North Hollywood, California
 Joe Kirkwood, Jr.
SPORTSMAN G&CC
 Northbrook, Illinois
 Edward B. Dearie, Jr.
  (R.) Ken Killian, Dick Nugent
  (A.3rd 9) Roger Packard

SPORTSMAN'S GC
 Harrisburg, Pennsylvania
 James Gilmore Harrison,
 Ferdinand Garbin
SPOTSWOOD CC [NLE]
 Harrisonburg, Virginia
 Fred Findlay
SPOTSWOOD CC
 Harrisburg, Virginia
 Edmund B. Ault
  (A.9) Alex McKay
SPRAIN BROOK GC
 Yonkers, New York
 Tom Winton
SPRINGBROOK CC
 Lawrenceville, Georgia
 Perrin Walker
SPRINGBROOK GC
 Naperville, Illinois
 Edward Lawrence Packard,
 Roger Packard
SPRINGBROOK GC
 Leeds, Maine
 Al Biondi
SPRING BROOK CC
 Morristown, New Jersey
 Thomas Hucknell (1924)
SPRING BROOK CC
 Antigo, Wisconsin
 Charles Maddox, *Frank P.
 MacDonald*
SPRING CREEK GC
 Ripon, California
 Jack Fleming
SPRING CREEK GC
 Whitewater, Illinois
  (A.9) Ken Killian, Dick
 Nugent
  (R.) Bob Lohmann
SPRING CREEK GC
 Hershey, Pennsylvania
  (R.9) Maurice McCarthy
SPRINGDALE CC
 Princeton, New Jersey
 Gerald Lambert
  (R.) William S. Flynn,
 Howard Toomey
SPRINGDALE CC
 Canton, North Carolina
 Joseph Holmes
SPRINGFIELD CC
 Springfield, Massachusetts
 Donald Ross
  (R.) William F. Mitchell
  (A.7) Brian Silva, Geoffrey S.
 Cornish
SPRINGFIELD CC
 Springfield, Ohio
 Donald Ross
SPRINGFIELD CC
 Springfield, Oregon
 Sid Milligan
  (R.) Robert Muir Graves
SPRINGFIELD G&CC
 Springfield, Virginia
 Edmund B. Ault, Al Jamison
SPRINGFIELD GC
 Guelph, Ontario
 John F. Robinson
SPRINGFIELD GC
 Japan
 Robert Trent Jones, Jr.

SPRINGFIELD GC
 Rotorua, New Zealand
 Tom Galloway
SPRINGFIELD OAKS GC
 Davisburg, Michigan
 Mark DeVries
SPRINGFIELD ROYAL CC
 Cha-am, Thailand
 Jack Nicklaus
SPRINGHAVEN C
 Wallingford, Pennsylvania
 Ida Dixon
  (R.9 A.9) William S. Flynn
SPRING HAVEN GC
 Rhode Island
 Phil Wogan
SPRING HILL CC
 Tifton, Georgia
 Willard Byrd
SPRING HILL CC
 Richmond, Ohio
 James Gilmore Harrison,
 Ferdinand Garbin
SPRING HILL CC
 Albany, Oregon
 Fred Federspiel
SPRINGHILL GC
 Aurora, Colorado
  (R.9 A.9) Dick Phelps, Brad
 Benz
SPRING HILL G&CC
 Spring Hill, Florida
 David Wallace
SPRING HILLS GC
 Watsonville, California
 Ben Harmon
SPRINGHOUSE GC
 Nashville, Tennessee
 Jeff Brauer, Larry Nelson
SPRING LAKE CC
 Quincy, Illinois
 Edward Lawrence Packard
SPRING LAKE CC
 Lexington, Kentucky
 Buck Blankenship
SPRING LAKE CC
 Clarkston, Michigan
  (R.) William Newcomb
SPRING LAKE CC
 Spring Lake, Michigan
 Tom Bendelow
  (R.1) Bruce Matthews, Jerry
 Matthews
  (R.2) Jerry Matthews
  (R.) Jeff Gorney
SPRING LAKE CC
 York, South Carolina
 Fred Bolton
  (A.9) Robert Renaud
SPRING LAKE CC
 Rosebud, Texas
 Leon Howard
SPRING LAKE G&CC
 Sebring, Florida
 Frank Duane
SPRING LAKE G&CC
 Spring Lake Heights, New
 Jersey
 George C. Thomas
  (R.) A. W. Tillinghast
SPRING LAKES GC (CSE NO. 1)
 Stouffville, Ontario
 René Mulyaert, *Charles Mulyaert*

SPRING LAKES GC (CSE NO. 2)
 Stouffville, Ontario
 René Mulyaert, *Charles Mulyaert*
SPRING MEADOWS CC
 Linden, Michigan
 Edward Lawrence Packard,
 Brent Wadsworth
SPRING MEADOW GC
 Wall Township, New Jersey
  (R.) Nicholas Psiahas
SPRING ROCK CC
 Central Valley, New York
 Orrin Smith
[THE] SPRINGS C
 Rancho Mirage, California
 Desmond Muirhead
[THE] SPRINGS C
 Spring Green, Wisconsin
 Robert Trent Jones
  (A.3rd 9) Roger Packard,
 Andy North
[THE] SPRINGS G&CC
 Radium, British Columbia
 Les Furber, *Jim Eremko*
SPRINGS MILL CC
 Fort Mill, South Carolina
 Donald Ross
  (A.9) George W. Cobb
SPRINGTREE GC
 Sunrise, Florida
 Bill Dietsch
SPRINGVALE CC
 North Olmstead, Ohio
 James Gilmore Harrison
SPRING VALLEY CC
 Sharon, Massachusetts
 Geoffrey S. Cornish, Samuel
 Mitchell
SPRING VALLEY CC
 Elyria, Ohio
 Harold Paddock
SPRING VALLEY CC
 Columbia, South Carolina
 George W. Cobb
SPRING VALLEY CC
 Salem, Wisconsin
 William B. Langford, Theodore
 J. Moreau
SPRING VALLEY GC
 Reed City, Michigan
 Warner Bowen
SPRING VALLEY GC
 Union Center, Wisconsin
 R. Albert Anderson
SPRING VALLEY LAKE GC
 Victorville, California
 Robert Trent Jones
SPRUCE CREEK GC
 Daytona Beach, Florida
 Bill Amick
  (R.) Ron Garl
SPRUCE GROVE GC
 Edmonton, Alberta
 William G. Robinson
SPRUCE NEEDLES GC
 Timmins, Ontario
 Howard Watson
  (R.9 A.9) Clinton E.
 Robinson
SPRUCE PINES CC
 North Carolina
 Ross Taylor

SPYGLASS HILL G LINKS
Pebble Beach, California
Robert Trent Jones
SQUAW CREEK CC
Marion, Iowa
Herman Thompson
SQUAW CREEK CC
Vienna, Ohio
Stanley Thompson
(R.) Brian Ault
SQUAW CREEK CC
Fort Worth, Texas
Ralph Plummer
SQUAW CREEK GC
Glen Rose, Texas
Jeff Brauer
SQUAW CREEK G RESORT
Squaw Valley, California
Robert Trent Jones, Jr.
SQUAW MOUNTAIN INN GC
Greenville, Maine
(R.) *John S. Parsons*
(R.) *John A. Shirley*
SQUIRES GC
Fallbrook, California
William H. Johnson
SQUIRES GC
Ambler, Pennsylvania
George Fazio
SQUIRREL RUN G&RC
New Iberia, Louisiana
Joe Lee
SRI MENANTI GC
Malaysia
D. M. A. Steel
STADIUM CC
Schenectady, New York
James Thomson
STAFFORD CC
Stafford, New York
Walter J. Travis
(R.) Stanley Thompson,
Robert Trent Jones
STAGG HILL GC
Manhattan, Kansas
Ray B. Weisenburger, Richard H.
Morse
STAG ISLAND GC
Port Huron, Michigan
Tom Bendelow
[THE] STANDARD C [NLE]
Atlanta, Georgia
Robert Trent Jones
(R.1 A.1) Arthur Davis, Ron
Kirby
[THE] STANDARD C
Norcross, Georgia
Arthur Hills
STANDARD CC
Louisville, Kentucky
Robert Bruce Harris
(A.9) Edward Lawrence
Packard
STANDING STONE GC
Huntingdon, Pennsylvania
Geoffrey S. Cornish, William G.
Robinson
STANFORD UNIVERSITY GC
Palo Alto, California
William P. Bell
(R.) Robert Trent Jones
STANHOPE G&CC
Prince Edward Island
Clinton E. Robinson

STANISLAUS CC
Modesto, California
William Lock
STANLEY GC
New Britain, Connecticut
Robert J. Ross
(A.3rd 9) Orrin Smith
(R.27) Geoffrey S. Cornish,
William G. Robinson
STANLEY PARK GC
British Columbia
A. Vernon Macan
STANLY COUNTY CC
Badin, North Carolina
(R.) Ellis Maples
STANNUM GC
Grabo, Sweden
J. J. F. Pennink
STANSBURY PARK CC
Tooele, Utah
William H. Neff
STANTON HEIGHTS CC
Pittsburgh, Pennsylvania
Tom Bendelow
STANTON-ON-THE-WOLDS GC
Nottinghamshire, England
Tom Williamson
STANWICH C
Greenwich, Connecticut
William Gordon, David Gordon
(R.3) Brian Silva, Geoffrey S.
Cornish
STAPLEFORD ABBOTTS C
Essex, England
Howard Swan
STARDUST CC
San Diego, California
Lawrence Hughes
(R.6) Ted Robinson
STARDUST GC
Sun City West, Arizona
Jeff Hardin, Greg Nash
STAR FORT NATIONAL GC
Ninety Six, South Carolina
George W. Cobb
STARHAVEN GC
Keokuk, Iowa
C. D. Wagstaff
STAR HILL G&CC
Cape Carteret, North Carolina
Russell T. Burney
STARKE G&CC
Starke, Florida
R. Albert Anderson
STARKVILLE CC
Starkville, Mississippi
Sonny Guy
STARMOUNT FOREST CC
Greensboro, North Carolina
Perry Maxwell
(R.) George W. Cobb
STARNBERG GC
Hadorf, Germany
Kurt Rossknecht
STARR HOLLOW GC
Fort Worth, Texas
Joseph S. Finger
STATE LINE GC [NLE]
Texarkana, Texas
William B. Langford, Theodore
J. Moreau
STATES GC
Vicksburg, Michigan
Elmer Travis

STATESVILLE CC
Statesville, North Carolina
Alex McKay
STAUNTON CC
Staunton, Virginia
(R.) Buddy Loving
STAVANGER GC
Stavanger, Norway
Fred Smith
STAVERN GC
Norway
Jan Sederholm
STAVERTON PARK GC
Northamptonshire, England
John Harris
STEAD AFB GC
Nevada
Bob Baldock
STEED & EVANS GC
Fonthill, Ontario
René Muylaert
STEELE CANYON CC
El Cajon, California
Gary Player
STEINBACK FLY INN GC
Manitoba
Clinton E. Robinson
(A.9) Jack Thompson
STEPASIDE GC
Dublin, Ireland
Eddie Hackett
STEPHEN F. AUSTIN GC
San Felipe, Texas
Jay Riviere
STERLING CC
Sterling, Colorado
Henry B. Hughes
STERLING CC
Sterling, Kansas
Dewey Longworth
STERLING CC
Sterling, Massachusetts
Michael Hurdzan
STERLING GC
Sterling, Virginia
Edmund B. Ault
STERLING BLUFF GC
Richmond Hill, Georgia
P. B. Dye, Pete Dye
STERLING FARMS MUNI
Stamford, Connecticut
Geoffrey S. Cornish, William G.
Robinson
STEUBENVILLE CC
Steubenville, Ohio
(R.9 A.9) Ferdinand Garbin
STEVENAGE GC
Hertfordshire, England
John Jacobs
STEPHEN C. CLARK PRIVATE CSE
[NLE]
Cooperstown, New York
Devereux Emmet
STEVENS PARK GC
Dallas, Texas
(R.) Arthur Davis
STEVENS POINT CC
Stevens Point, Wisconsin
Edward Lawrence Packard
(R.) Edward Lawrence
Packard
STEVENSVILLE LAKE G&CC
Swan Lake, New York
William F. Mitchell

STILL MEADOW CC
Ohio
(R.) William H. Diddel
STILLWATER CC
Stillwater, Minnesota
Paul Coates
STILLWATER G&CC
Stillwater, Oklahoma
Don Sechrest
STILL WATERS CC
Dadeville, Alabama
George W. Cobb
STILLWATER VALLEY
Webster, Ohio
(A.9) John F. Robinson
(R.) Gene Bates
STINCHCOME HILL GC
England
James Braid
STIRLING GC
Scotland
(R.) Henry Cotton
STIRLING GC
Stirlingshire, Scotland
Old Tom Morris
STOCKBRIDGE GC
Stockbridge, Massachusetts
(R.) *Walter Nettleton*
(R.) *Joseph Franz*
STOCKDALE CC
Bakersfield, California
Lloyd Tevis
(R.9 A.9) Robert Muir Graves
STOCKGROVE GC
England
Fred W. Hawtree
STOCKHOLM GC
Stockholm, Sweden
H. S. Colt, C. H. Alison, J. S. F.
Morrison
(R.) *Nils Sköld*
STOCKSFIELD GC
England
(R.) J. J. F. Pennink
STOCKTON G&CC
Stockton, California
Sam Whiting
(R.) Robert Muir Graves
STOCKWOOD PARK GC
Bedfordshire, England
J. J. F. Pennink
STOKE POGES GC
Buckinghamshire, England
H. S. Colt, C. H. Alison
(R.) J. Hamilton Stutt
STOKE ROCHFORD GC
Lincolnshire, England
S. V. Hotchkin
STONEBRIAR CC
Frisco, Texas
Ken Dye, Baxter Spann
STONEBRIDGE CC
Blanchard, Idaho
James R. Kraus
STONEBRIDGE CC
Aurora, Illinois
Tom Fazio
STONEBRIDGE CC
Ann Arbor, Michigan
Arthur Hills
STONEBRIDGE CC
McKinney, Texas
Pete Dye

STONEBRIDGE G&CC
Boca Raton, Florida
Karl Litten
STONEBRIDGE GC
Memphis, Tennessee
George W. Cobb
STONEBROOKE G&CC
Shakopee, Minnesota
Tom L. Haugen
STONECREEK GC
Paradise Valley, Arizona
Roy Dye, Gary Grandstaff
(R.) Greg Nash
(R.) Arthur Jack Snyder
(R.) Arthur Hills
STONE CREEK GROVE GC
Anderson, South Carolina
J. Porter Gibson
STONEHAM GC
Hampshire, England
Willie Park, Jr.
STONE HARBOR GC
Cape May Court House, New
Jersey
(R.) Desmond Muirhead
STONEHAVEN GC
Stonehaven, Scotland
George Duncan
STONE HEDGE GC
Tunkhannock, Pennsylvania
James Blaukovitch
STONEHEDGE G CSE
Augusta, Michigan
Charles Darl Scott
STONEHENGE GC
Barrington, Illinois
Charles Maddox
STONEHENGE GC
Warsaw, Indiana
Ron Garl
STONEHENGE GC
Fairfield Glade, Tennessee
Joe Lee, Rocky Roquemore
STONEHENGE GC
Bon Air, Virginia
Edmund B. Ault
STONELEIGH G&CC
Round Hill, Virginia
Lisa Maki
STONE MOUNTAIN GC (STONEMONT
CSE)
Stone Mountain, Georgia
Robert Trent Jones
STONE MOUNTAIN GC (LAKEMONT
CSE)
Stone Mountain, Georgia
John LaFoy
STONERIDGE CC
Poway, California
David W. Kent
(R.9 A.9) Ted Robinson
STONES RIVER CC
Murfreesboro, Tennessee
(R.9) Arthur Davis
STONEWAL CC
Lake Park, Florida
NKA PGA National GC (Estates
Cse)
STONEY BROOK GC
Hopewell, New Jersey
Robert H. Kraeger
STONEY CREEK GC
Wintergreen, Virginia
Rees Jones

STONEYHOLME GC
Cumbria, England
J. J. F. Pennink
STONEY PLAIN GC
Alberta
Norman H. Woods
STONEY POINT G CSE
Greenwood, South Carolina
Tom Jackson
STONINGTON CC
Stonington, Connecticut
Al Zikorus
STONY BRAE GC
Quincy, Massachusetts
Wayne Stiles
STONY BROOK CC
Litchfield, Connecticut
Al Zikorus
STONYBROOK GC
England
(R.) Tom Bendelow
STONY CREEK GC
Rochester, Michigan
Robert Beard
STONEY CREEK METROPARK GC
Washington, Michigan
Robert W. Bills, Donald L. Childs
STONYCROFT HILLS CC
Bloomfield Hills, Michigan
(R.5) Bruce Matthews, Jerry
Matthews
STONY FORD GC
Goshen, New York
Hal Purdy
STORA LUNDBY GC
Grabo, Sweden
J. J. F. Pennink
STOREYCREEK GC
Campbell River, British
Columbia
Les Furber, *Jim Eremko*
STORK HILL GC
Hyogo, Japan
Pete Nakamura
STORNOWAY GC
Isle of Lewis, Scotland
John R. Stutt
(R.) J. J. F. Pennink
STORSTROMMEN GC
Nykøbing, Denmark
Anders Amilon
STOUFFER'S PINEISLE RESORT GC
Lake Lanier, Georgia
Arthur Davis, Ron Kirby
(R.) Arnold Palmer, Ed Seay
STOW ACRES CC (NORTH CSE)
Stow, Massachusetts
Geoffrey S. Cornish, William G.
Robinson
STOW ACRES CC (SOUTH CSE)
Stow, Massachusetts
(R.9 A.9) Geoffrey S.
Cornish, William G.
Robinson
STOWE CC
Stowe, Vermont
William F. Mitchell
STOWE SCHOOL GC
England
J. J. F. Pennink
STRABANE GC
Strabane, Northern Ireland
(A.9) Eddie Hackett

STRÄNGNÄS GC
Strängnäs, Sweden
Nils Sköld
(R.9) Jan Sederholm
STRANDHILL GC
Ireland
Eddie Hackett
STRANRAER GC
Scotland
(R.) John R. Stutt
STRANRAER GC
Wigtownshire, Scotland
James Braid
STRATFORD-UPON-AVON GC
Warwickshire, England
F. G. Hawtree, J. H. Taylor
STRATFORD OAKS GC
Stratford-upon-Avon, War-
wickshire, England
Howard Swan
STRATHAVEN GC
Strathaven, Scotland
(R.) J. Hamilton Stutt
STRATHCONA GC
Huntsville, Ontario
Clinton E. Robinson
(R.13) John Watson
STRATHLENE GC
Aberdeen, Scotland
George E. Smith
STRATHROY CC
Strathroy, Ontario
René Muylaert
STRATTON MOUNTAIN GC
Stratton Mountain, Vermont
Geoffrey S. Cornish, William G.
Robinson
(A.9) Geoffrey S. Cornish,
Brian Silva
STRATTON MOUNTAIN GOLF
ACADEMY
Stratton Mountain, Vermont
Geoffrey S. Cornish, William G.
Robinson
STREAMWOOD OAKS GC
Streamwood, Illinois
Bob Lohmann
STREETSVILLE GLEN GC
Ontario
Robert Moote, *David S. Moote*
STRESEHOLME GC
England
C. K. Cotton, J. J. F. Pennink
STROMBERG GC (PAR 3 CSE)
Stromberg, Germany
Karl F. Grohs, *Rainer
Preissmann*
STROMBERG-SCHINDELDORF GC
Stromberg, Germany
Karl F. Grohs, *Rainer
Preissmann*
STRÖMSTAD GC
Strömstad, Sweden
(A.9) Jan Sederholm
STRYKER GC
Fayetteville, North Carolina
Donald Ross
STUMPY LAKE GC
Norfolk, Virginia
Robert Trent Jones
STURGEON POINT GC
Ontario
Clinton E. Robinson

STURGEON VALLEY G&CC
St. Albert, Alberta
William G. Robinson
(A.9) William G. Robinson,
John F. Robinson
STUTTGARTER GC
Monsheim, Germany
Karl Hoffman, Bernhard von
Limburger
SUBANG GC
Kuala Lumpur, Malaysia
(R.) Mike Poellot, Brad Benz
SUBIC BAY GC
Philippines
Willard Wilkinson
SUBURBAN CC
Waukegan, Illinois
Joseph A. Roseman
SUBURBAN CC
Pikesville, Maryland
A. W. Tillinghast
(R.) Edmund B. Ault
(R.4) Edmund B. Ault, Bill
Love
SUBURBAN GC
Union, New Jersey
Tom Bendelow
(R.) A. W. Tillinghast
SUDBURY GC
Middlesex, England
Willie Park, Jr.
SUDDEN VALLEY G&CC
Bellingham, Washington
Ted Robinson
SUFFIELD CC
Suffield, Connecticut
Orrin Smith
SUFFOLK CC
Suffolk, Virginia
Dick Wilson
(R.) Russell Breeden
SUFFOLK COUNTY GC AT TIMBER
POINT
West Babylon, New York
William H. Mitchell
SUGARBUSH CC
Garrettsville, Ohio
Harold Paddock
SUGARBUSH GC
Warren, Vermont
Robert Trent Jones, Jr.
SUGAR CREEK CC
Sugarland, Texas
Robert Trent Jones
SUGARCREEK GC
Villa Park, Illinois
Rick Kepshire (9 Precision 1976)
SUGAR CREEK GC
St. Louis, Missouri
Ron Kern, Gary Kern
SUGAR CREEK GC
Elmore, Ohio
Ken Killian, Dick Nugent
SUGAR HILL G CSE
Sugar Hill, Georgia
Willard Byrd
SUGAR HOLLOW GC
Banner Elk, North Carolina
Frank Duane
SUGAR ISLE GC
New Carlisle, Ohio
Jack Kidwell

SUGARLOAF GC
Carrabassett Valley, Maine
Robert Trent Jones, Jr.

SUGARLOAF GC
Sugarloaf, Pennsylvania
Geoffrey S. Cornish, William G.
Robinson

SUGARLOAF MOUNTAIN GC
Cedar, Michigan
C. D. Wagstaff

SUGAR MILL CC
New Smyrna Beach, Florida
Joe Lee
    (A.3rd 9) Joe Lee, Rocky
    Roquemore

SUGARMILL WOODS G&CC
Homosassa, Florida
Ron Garl

SUGAR SPRINGS GC
Gladwin, Michigan
Bruce Matthews, Jerry Matthews

SUGAR TREE G&CC
Dennis, Texas
Phil Lumsden (1989)

SULLIVAN CC
Sullivan, Illinois
Robert Bruce Harris

SULLY-SUR-LOIRE GC
France
Jean Bourret (1963)

SULPHUR HILLS CC
Sulphur, Oklahoma
Floyd Farley

SUMMER BEACH G CSE
Amelia Island, Florida
Mark McCumber

SUMMERFIELD CC
Riverview, Florida
Ron Garl

SUMMERFIELD G&CC
Tigard, Oregon
Ted Robinson

SUMMERHEIGHTS GOLF LINKS
Cornwall, Ontario
    (A.3rd 9) Robert Heaslip

SUMMERLEA G&CC [NLE]
Montreal, Quebec
Willie Park, Jr.

**SUMMERLEA G&CC (CASCADES
CSE)**
Montreal, Quebec
Geoffrey S. Cornish

SUMMERLEA G&CC (DORION CSE)
Montreal, Quebec
Geoffrey S. Cornish

SUMMERSETT CC
Travelers Rest, South Carolina
    (R.) Tom Jackson

SUMMERSIDE G&CC
Summerside, Prince Edward
Island
    (R.3) John Watson

SUMMERTREE GC
New Port Richey, Florida
Arthur Davis

SUMMERTREE GC
Crown Point, Indiana
Bruce Matthews, Jerry Matthews

SUMMIT CHASE G&CC
Snellville, Georgia
Ward Northrup

SUMMIT CC
Pennsylvania
Edmund B. Ault

SUMMIT MUNI
Summit, New Jersey
Hal Purdy

[THE] SUMMIT GC
Cross Junction, Virginia
Tom Clark, Edmund B. Ault

SUMMIT GC
Richmond Hill, Ontario
    (R.) Bob Cupp
    (R.) Douglas Carrick

SUMMIT GC AT LAKE HOLIDAY
Winchester, Virginia
Richard Watson

SUMMIT HILLS CC
Crestview Hills, Kentucky
    (R.10 A.1) Jack Kidwell,
    Michael Hurzdan
    (R.) Arthur Hills
    (R.) Gene Bates

SUMMIT RIDGE CC
Canton, Georgia
Brendan Brogan (1992)

SUMMIT SPRINGS GC
Poland, Maine
Alex Findlay

SUMNER HEIGHTS GC
Cornwall, Ontario
Howard Watson

SUMNER HILLS GC
High Point, North Carolina
Clement B. "Johnny" Johnston,
Clyde Johnston

SUNAGAWA OASIS GC
Hokkaido, Japan
Kikuichi Nakajima

SUN AND FUN G & SWIM C
Decatur, Illinois
Charles Maddox

SUNBIRD GC
Chandler, Arizona
Gary Panks

SUN BLEST GC
Noblesville, Indiana
William H. Diddel

SUNBLEST G&CC
Fishers, Indiana
Gary Kern, Ron Kern

SUNBROOK GC
St. George, Utah
Ted Robinson

SUN CITY CC
Sun City, Arizona
Milt Coggins

**SUN CITY CENTER G&CC (KINGS
POINT CSE)**
Sun City Center, Florida
Robert Trent Jones

**SUN CITY CENTER G&CC (NORTH
CSE)**
Sun City Center, Florida
Milt Coggins
    (A.9) Mark Mahannah,
    Charles Mahannah

**SUN CITY CENTER G&CC (SOUTH
CSE)**
Sun City Center, Florida
Mark Mahannah

SUN CITY NORTH GC
Sun City, Arizona
Milt Coggins

SUN CITY SOUTH GC
Sun City, Arizona
Milt Coggins

SUN CITY SUMMERLIN GC
Las Vegas, Nevada
Greg Nash

SUN CITY VISTOSO GC
Tucson, Arizona
Greg Nash

SUNCREST CC
Palm Desert, California
Richard Watson

SUNCREST GC
Butler, Pennsylvania
James Gilmore Harrison
    (R.) Ferdinand Garbin

SUNDANCE GC
Nine Mile Falls, Washington
Dale Knott

SUNDANCE G&CC
Osseo, Minnesota
Ade Simonsen

SUNDOWN GC
Burlington, Iowa
Edmund B. Ault

SUNDOWN MUNI
Sweetwater, Texas
William Cantrell

SUNDOWNER GC
Ashland, Kentucky
Bert Way

SUNDRIDGE PARK GC (EAST CSE)
Kent, England
Willie Park, Sr., Willie Park, Jr.
    (R.) Sir Guy Campbell, C.K.
    Hutchison

SUNDRIDGE PARK GC (WEST CSE)
Kent, England
Willie Park, Willie Park, Jr.

SUNDRIM GC
Caledonia, Ontario
Tom Bendelow

SUNFIELD GC
Gunma, Japan
Michio Izumi

SUNFLOWER HILLS GC
Bonner Springs, Kansas
Edward L. Packard, Roger
Packard

SUN GREAT GC
Hyogo, Japan
Ken Sato

SUN HILLS CC
Toyko, Japan
Robert Trent Jones, Jr.

SUNKEN GARDENS MUNI
Sunnyvale, California
Clark Glasson
    (R.) Robert Muir Graves

SUNKEN MEADOW PARK GC
Northport, New York
Alfred H. Tull

SUNKIST CC
Biloxi, Mississippi
Roland "Robby" Robertson

SUN LAKE CC
Utsusonomiya, Japan
Ron Kirby, Denis Griffiths

SUN LAKES CC
Sun Lakes, Arizona
Jeff Hardin, Greg Nash

SUN LAKES CC
Banning, California
David Rainville

SUNLAND GC
Sequim, Washington
A. Vernon Macan

SUNLAND VILLAGE GC
Mesa, Arizona
Milt Coggins, Jeff Hardin, Greg
Nash

SUN MARINA TAMANIWA GC
Yamagata, Japan
Takashi Murakami

SUN MEADOW CC
Houston, Texas
Jay Riviere

SUNNE GC
Sunne, Sweden
    (A.9) Jan Sederholm

SUNNEHANNA CC
Johnstown, Pennsylvania
A. W. Tillinghast
    (R.) Ferdinand Garbin
    (R.1) Jerry Matthews

SUNNINGDALE CC
Scarsdale, New York
A. W. Tillinghast

SUNNINGDALE CC (NEW CSE)
London, Ontario
Clinton E. Robinson
    (R.) Douglas Carrick

SUNNINGDALE CC (OLD CSE)
London, Ontario
Stanley Thompson

SUNNINGDALE GC
Dover, New Hampshire
Geoffrey S. Cornish

SUNNINGDALE GC (NEW CSE)
Berkshire, England
H. S. Colt, C. H. Alison
    (R.) J. S. F. Morrison
    (R.) Tom Simpson
    (R.) C. K. Cotton
    (R.) D. M. A. Steel

SUNNINGDALE GC (OLD CSE)
Berkshire, England
Willie Park, Jr.
    (R.) H. S. Colt, C. H. Alison
    (R.) C. K. Cotton
    (R.) D. M. A. Steel

SUN 'N LAKE CC
Lake Placid, Florida
Bill Watts
    (R.) Gordon G. Lewis

SUN 'N LAKE GC
Sebring, Florida
Donald Dyer
    (A.3rd 9) Chuck Ankrom

SUN 'N SKY CC
Barstow, California
Ted Robinson

SUN 'N SURF GC
Boca Raton, Florida
Joe Kirkwood, Jr.

SUNNY ACRES CC
Roseville, Michigan
Lou Powers

SUNNY BRAE CC
Osage, Iowa
William H. Livie

SUNNYBROOK CC
Grandville, Michigan
Bruce Matthews

SUNNYBROOK CC
Plymouth Meeting,
Pennsylvania
William Gordon, David Gordon

SUNNYCREST CC
Rochester, New York
Pete Craig
SUNNYDALE GC
Courtenay, British Columbia
(R.) Les Furber
SUNNYFIELD GC
Gozenyama, Japan
Jack Nicklaus
SUNNY HILL GC
Greenville, New York
Hal Purdy
SUNNYHILL G&RC
Kent, Ohio
(R. A.9) Ferdinand Garbin
SUNNY JIM GC
Medford, New Jersey
NKA Medford Village GC
SUNNYBREEZE PALMS GC
Arcadia, Florida
R. Albert Anderson
SUNNYLANDS GC
Rancho Mirage, California
Dick Wilson, Joe Lee
SUNNYSIDE CC
Fresno, California
William P. Bell
(R.) Robert Dean Putman
(R.) John Steidel
SUNNYSIDE CC [NLE]
Waterloo, Iowa
Tom Bendelow
(R.) Robert Bruce Harris
SUNNYSIDE CC
Waterloo, Iowa
Edward Lawrence Packard
SUNNYSIDE CC
Texas
Bruce Littell
SUNNYSIDE GC
Decatur, Illinois
Tom Bendelow
SUNNYVALE GC
Sunnyvale, California
David W. Kent
SUNOL VALLEY GC (CYPRESS CSE)
Sunol, California
Clark Glasson
SUNOL VALLEY GC (PALM CSE)
Sunol, California
Clark Glasson
SUNPARK AKENO GC
Akeno-Lakewood, Japan
Theodore Robinson
SUNPORT CC
Albuquerque, New Mexico
Red Lawrence
SUNRISE CC
Rancho Mirage, California
Ted Robinson
SUNRISE CC
Fort Lauderdale, Florida
Bill Watts
SUN RISE CC
Yang Mei, Taiwan
Robert Trent Jones, Jr.
SUNRISE GC (NORTH CSE)
Las Vegas, Nevada
Cary Bickler (1992)
SUNRISE GC (SOUTH CSE)
Las Vegas, Nevada
Cary Bickler (1991)

SUNRISE LAKES PHASE 3 GC
Sunrise, Florida
Bill Dietsch
SUNRISE NATIONAL CC
Sarasota, Florida
R. Albert Anderson
SUNRISE VISTA GC
Nellis AFB, Nevada
Ted Robinson
SUNRIVER GC (NORTH CSE)
Sunriver, Oregon
Robert Trent Jones, Jr.
SUNRIVER GC (SOUTH CSE)
Sunriver, Oregon
Fred Federspiel
(R.) Peter Thomson, Michael
Wolveridge, Ronald Fream
SUN ROYAL GC
Japan
Fukuichi Kato
SUNSET CC
Moultrie, Georgia
Hugh Moore
SUNSET CC
Mount Morris, Illinois
(R.4) David Gill
SUNSET CC
St. Louis, Missouri
Robert Foulis, James Foulis
(R.) Edward Lawrence
Packard
(R.) Mike Hurdzan
SUNSET CC
Bartlesville, Oklahoma
Bob Dunning
SUNSET CC
Sumter, South Carolina
(R.) Ed Riccoboni
SUNSET G&CC
St. Petersburg, Florida
William H. Diddel
(R.) Hans Schmeisser
SUNSET GC
Hollywood, Florida
Red Lawrence
SUNSET G CENTER
Fort Erie, Ontario
René Muylaert
SUNSET CANYON GC [NLE]
Burbank, California
Willie Watson
SUNSET DUNES GC
Colton, California
Robert Trent Jones
SUNSET FIELDS GC [NLE]
California
William P. Bell
SUNSET HILL GC
Ossining, New York
(R.) Tom Winton
SUNSET HILLS CC
Thousand Oaks, California
Ted Robinson
SUNSET HILLS CC
Tarpon Springs, Florida
William H. Diddel
SUNSET HILLS CC
Carrollton, Georgia
Robert Trent Jones
(A.9) Ward Northrup

SUNSET HILLS CC
Edwardsville, Illinois
(A.9) Edward Lawrence
Packard, Brent Wadsworth
(R. A.6) Ron Kern, Gary Kern
SUNSET HILLS GC
Charlotte, North Carolina
B. Frazier
SUNSET HILLS GC
Guyton, Oklahoma
Bob Dunning
SUNSET LAKES GC
Sunset Hills, Missouri
Bob Lohmann
SUNSET OAKS CC
Rocklin, California
William F. Bell
SUNSET PARK GC [NLE]
New York
Tom Bendelow
SUNSET RANCH G&CC
Kelowna, British Columbia
J. Bruce Carr (1990)
SUNSET RIDGE CC
Northbrook, Illinois
William H. Diddel
(R.) C. D. Wagstaff
SUNSET VALLEY GC
Highland Park, Illinois
(R.) Ken Killian, Dick Nugent
(R.) Bob Lohmann
SUNSET VALLEY GC
Pequannock, New Jersey
Hal Purdy, Malcolm Purdy
SUNSHINE COAST G&CC
Roberts Creek, British Columbia
Ernest Brown, Roy Taylor
SUNSHORE GC
Chase, British Columbia
Ernest Brown
SUNTREE CC (CLASSIC CSE)
Melbourne, Florida
Ed Ryder
(R.) Richard W. LaConte
SUNTREE CC (CHALLENGE CSE)
Melbourne, Florida
Arnold Palmer, Ed Seay
SUN VALLEY CC
Sioux City, Iowa
Leo Johnson
SUN VALLEY GC
Sun Valley, Idaho
William P. Bell
(R.9 A.9) George Von Elm
(R. A.4) Robert Trent Jones,
Jr.
SUN VALLEY GC
Louisville, Kentucky
Benjamin Wihry
SUN VALLEY GC
Rehoboth, Massachusetts
Walter I. Johnson (routing);
Geoffrey S. Cornish
SUN VALLEY GC
Elsberry, Missouri
Gary Kern, Ron Kern
SUN VALLEY GC
Port Clinton, Ohio
Don Waggoner (1967)
SUN WILLOWS GC
Pasco, Washington
Robert Muir Graves

SUPERIOR NATIONAL GC
Lutsen, Minnesota
Don Herfort
SUPERSTITION SPRINGS GC
Mesa, Arizona
Greg Nash
SURBITON GC
Surbiton, England
Tom Dunn
SURF GC
Myrtle Beach, South Carolina
George W. Cobb
SURFER'S PARADISE GC
Queensland, Australia
Sloan Morpeth
SURPRISE PARK GC
Cedar Lake, Indiana
Stanley Pelchar
SURREY G CSE
Surrey, British Columbia
William B. Robinson, John F.
Robinson
SURREY PUBLIC GC
British Columbia
Heinz Knoedler
SUSQUEHANNA VALLEY CC
Hummels Wharf, Pennsylvania
(R.) William Gordon, David
Gordon
SUSSEX GC
New Brunswick
Clinton E. Robinson
SUSSEX PINES CC
Millsboro, Delaware
Edmund B. Ault
(A.9) Al Janis
SUTHERLIN KNOLLS GC
Sutherlin, Oregon
Vernon Warren
SUTTON CREEK G&CC
McGregor, Ontario
Robert Heaslip
SUTTON PARK GC
Yorkshire, England
L. Herrington
SUWANNEE CC
Live Oak, Florida
(R.) Walter Ripley
SUWANEE RIVER VALLEY CC
Jasper, Florida
Joe Lee
SUZUKANOMORI CC
Mie, Japan
Isao Aoki
SVENLJUNGA GC
Svenljunga, Sweden
Jan Sederholm
SWAIM FIELDS GC
Cincinnati, Ohio
William H. Diddel
SWAKOPMUND GC
Swakopmund, Namibia
Rees Jones
SWALLOW'S NEST GC
Sacramento, California
Bob Baldock
SWALLOW'S NEST GC
Clarkston, Washington
Bob Baldock
SWAN CREEK CC
Belair, Maryland
Frank Murray, Russell Roberts
(R.9) Edmund B. Ault

SWAN HILLS GC
Avon, Illinois
William James Spear
SWAN LAKE CC
Clarksville, Tennessee
Benjamin Wihry
SWAN POINT YACHT & CC
Issue, Maryland
Arthur Davis
(R.) Bob Cupp
SWAN VALLEY GC
Saginaw, Michigan
Carl Mueller
SWANNANOA GC
Waynesboro, Virginia
Fred Findlay
SWANSEA GC
Swansea, Massachusetts
Geoffrey S. Cornish
SWANSEA BAY GC
Wales
(R.6) Fred W. Hawtree,
Martin Hawtree
SWARTKOP CC
Pretoria, South Africa
Robert G. Grimsdell
SWARTZ CREEK MUNI
Flint, Michigan
Frederick A. Ellis
SWEETWATER CC
Sugar Land, Texas
Roger Packard
SWEETWATER GC
Bear Lake, Utah
William H. Neff, William
Howard Neff
SWEETWATER OAKS CC
Longwood, Florida
Lloyd Clifton
SWENSON PARK MUNI
Stockton, California
Jack Fleming
(A.9) Robert Muir Graves
SWINFORD GC
Swinford, Ireland
(R.) Eddie Hackett
SWINLEY FOREST GC
England
H. S. Colt
SWINTON PARK GC
Lancashire, England
F. G. Hawtree, J. H. Taylor
SWOPE PARK GC
Kansas City, Missouri
James Dalgleish
(R.) A. W. Tillinghast
(R.) Leon Howard
SYCAMORE GC
Rarenna, New York
Frank Duane
SYCAMORE CANYON G CSE
Arvin, California
Robert Dean Putman
SYCAMORE CREEK CC
Miamisburg, Ohio
Jack Ortman
(R.) Arthur Hills
SYCAMORE HILLS CC
Paris, Illinois
(R.8 A.10) Gary Kern
SYCAMORE HILLS GC
Fort Wayne, Indiana
Jack Nicklaus

SYCAMORE HILLS GC
Mount Clemens, Michigan
Jerry Matthews
SYCAMORE VALLEY GC
Independence, Kansas
Gene Schmidt
SYCAMORE VALLEY GC
Ashland City, Tennessee
Kevin Tucker
SYDNEY GC
Sydney, Nova Scotia
(R.) Stanley Thompson
SYLVANIA CC
Toledo, Ohio
Willie Park, Jr.
(R.6) Sandy Alves
(R.) Arthur Hills

TABLE MOUNTAIN GC
Oroville, California
Louis Bertolone
TABLE ROCK GC
Centerburg, Ohio
Jack Kidwell
(A.9) Jack Kidwell, Michael
Hurdzan
TABOADA GC
Guanajuato, Mexico
Dave Bennett
TÄBY GC
Täby, Sweden
Nils Sköld
TACHIKAWA INTERNATIONAL CC
Tokyo, Japan
M. Marumo
TACOMA C&GC
Tacoma, Washington
Stanley Thompson
(R.5) John Steidel
TACONIC GC
Williamstown, Massachusetts
Wayne Stiles, John Van Kleek
TADMARTON HEATH GC
Banbury, England
Harry Vardon
(A.9) C.K. Hutchison
TAHOE DONNER GC
Truckee, California
Joseph B. Williams
TAHOE PARADISE GC
Lake Tahoe, California
Fred R. Blanchard
TAHOE TAVERN GC
Tahoe, Nevada
May Dunn Hupfel
TAIERI GC
Mosgiel, New Zealand
John Harris, Peter Thomson
TAIHAPE GC
Taihape, New Zealand
H. G. Babbage
TAIHEIYO C (ICHIHARA CSE)
Chiba, Japan
Shunsuke Kato
TAIHEIYO C (KARUIZAWA CSE)
Gunma, Japan
Shunsuke Kato
TAIHEIYO C (TAKASAKI CSE)
Gunma, Japan
Shunsuke Kato
TAIHEIYO C (SAGAMI CSE)
Kanagawa, Japan
Shunsuke Kato

TAIHEIYO C (GOTEMBA CSE)
Shizuoka, Japan
Shunsuke Kato
TAIHEIYO C (MASHIKO CSE)
Tochigi, Japan
Shunsuke Kato
TAIN GC
Rosshire, Scotland
Old Tom Morris
(R.) John Sutherland
TAIWAN G&CC
Taipei, Taiwan
Rokuro Akaboshi, Shiro
Akaboshi
TAKAHA ROYAL CC
Fukuoka, Japan
Peter Thomson, Michael
Wolveridge
TAKAHIKO THREE CC
Japan
Kentaro Sato, Masashi Ozaki
TAKAMATSU CC
Kanawa, Japan
Dr. N. Marumo
TAKANODAI CC
Chiba, Japan
Seichi Inouye
TAKARAZUKA GC (NEW CSE)
Hyogo, Japan
G. Ohashi
TAKARAZUKA GC (OLD CSE)
Hyogo, Japan
K. Hiroka, K. Fukui
TAKASAKA CC
Saitama, Japan
T. Hirayama
TAKEO CC
Fukui, Japan
Makoto Murakami
TAKINOMIYA CC
Ehime, Japan
Shunsuke Kato
TALAMORE GC
Southern Pines, North Carolina
Rees Jones
TALLGRASS C
Wichita, Kansas
Arthur Hills
TALL PINES AT RIVER RIDGE GC
New Port Richey, Florida
Ron Garl
TALL PINES GC
Sewell, New Jersey
NKA Eagles Nest GC
TALL PINES GC
Paradise, California
Bob Baldock, Robert L. Baldock
TALL TIMBER GC
Langley, British Columbia
Stan Leonard, Wayne Lindberg,
Philip Tattersfield
TALL TIMBERS CC
Slingerlands, New York
Frank Duane
TALLULAH G&CC
Tallulah, Louisiana
Winnie Cole (1920)
TALLWOOD CC
Hebron, Connecticut
Michael Ovian, Karnig Ovian
TALLY MOUNTAIN C
Tallapoosa, Georgia
Joe Lee

TALVAS GC
Tochigi, Japan
Shunsuke Kato
TALVAS GOLF AND RESORT BATAM
(PRIVATE CSE)
Batam, Indonesia
Jeff Brauer, Larry Nelson
TALVAS GOLF AND RESORT BATAM
(RESORT CSE)
Batam, Indonesia
Jeff Brauer, Larry Nelson
TAMAN TUN ABDUL RAZAK GC
Ampangjaya, Malaysia
Ronald Fream
TAMARAC CC
Fort Lauderdale, Florida
NKA Oak Tree CC
TAMARAC GC
Reidville, North Carolina
Clement B. "Johnny" Johnston
TAMARACK CC
Port Chester, New York
Charles Banks
TAMARACK CC
Mount Lebanon, Pennsylvania
James Gilmore Harrison
TAMARACK GC
Plainfield, Illinois
David Gill
TAMARACK GC
New Brunswick, New Jersey
Hal Purdy, Malcolm Purdy
TAMARISK CC
Rancho Mirage, California
William F. Bell, William P. Bell
(R.) Ted Robinson
(R.) Ronald Fream
TAMARRON CC
Durango, Colorado
Arthur Hills
TAMCREST CC
Alpine, New Jersey
Frank Duane
(R.) Stephen Kay
TAMIMENT CC
Tamiment-on-the-Pocono,
Pennsylvania
Robert Trent Jones
TAMMY BROOK CC
Cresskill, New Jersey
Robert Trent Jones
TAM O'SHANTER C
Brookville, New York
(R.) Robert Trent Jones
(R.) Stephen Kay
TAM O'SHANTER CC [NLE]
Niles, Illinois
C. D. Wagstaff
(R.) Joseph A. Roseman
(R.) William B. Langford
TAM O'SHANTER CC
Orchard Lake, Michigan
Wilfrid Reid, William Connellan
(R.) Arthur Hills
TAM O'SHANTER CC (DALES CSE)
Canton, Ohio
Leonard Macomber
TAM O'SHANTER CC (HILLS CSE)
Canton, Ohio
Leonard Macomber
TAM O'SHANTER G&CC
Bellevue, Washington
William Teufel

Tam O'Shanter Muni
Toronto, Ontario
Howard Watson, John Watson
(R.) Thomas McBroom

Tampa Bay Hotel GC [NLE]
Tampa, Florida
Seymour Dunn

Tampa Palms CC
Tampa, Florida
Arthur Hills

Tampere GC
Tampere, Finland
(A.7) Jan Sederholm

Tampico CC
Tampico, Mexico
John Bredemus
(A.9) *Enrico Robles*

Tamworth Muni
Staffordshire, England
Fred W. Hawtree, Martin Hawtree, A. H. F. Jiggens

Tanagashima CC
Tanagashima, Japan
Karl Litten

Tanah Merah CC
Tanah Merah, Singapore
Ronald Fream

Tandragee GC
Northern Ireland
(A.9) Fred W. Hawtree, Martin Hawtree

Tandridge GC
England
H. S. Colt

Tanforan GC
San Mateo, California
Jack Fleming

Tangiers GC
Tangiers, Morocco
(R.) C. H. Alison

Tanglewood CC
Chagrin Falls, Ohio
William F. Mitchell

Tanglewood GC (East Cse)
Clemmons, North Carolina
Robert Trent Jones

Tanglewood GC (West Cse)
Clemmons, North Carolina
Robert Trent Jones
(R.) Robert Trent Jones

Tanglewood GC
Delaware, Ohio
Jack Kidwell

Tanglewood GC
Downling, Ohio
Richard Wyckoff

Tanglewood GC
Stroudsburg, Pennsylvania
George Fazio

Tanglewood G Cse
Taylorsville, Kentucky
Buck Blankenship

Tanglewood Manor GC
Pennsylvania
Chester Ruby

Tanglewood-on-the-Texoma GC
Pottsboro, Texas
Ralph Plummer
(R.) Ken Dye, Baxter Spann

Tannenhauf GC
Alliance, Ohio
James Gilmore Harrison, Ferdinand Garbin

Tanoan GC
Albuquerque, New Mexico
Robert von Hagge, Bruce Devlin
(R.) Garrett Gill, George B. Williams

Tansi Resort GC
Crossville, Tennessee
Robert Renaud

Tantallon CC
Tantallon, Maryland
Ted Robinson

Tan-Tara CC
North Tonawanda, New York
Dennis Schreckengost

Tapatio Springs CC
Boerne, Texas
Bill Johnston

Tapawingo GC
St. Louis, Missouri
Gary Player

Tapps Island GC
Sumner, Washington
Ronald Fream, Peter Thomson, Michael Wolveridge

Tapton Park GC
Derby, England
George Duncan

Tara G&CC
Bradenton, Florida
Ted McAnlis

Tara CC
McCormick, South Carolina
Tom Clark

Tara Ferncroft CC
Danvers, Massachusetts
NKA Sheraton Tara Hotel & GC

Tara Hills GC
Papillion, Nebraska
Richard Watson

Tarbat GC
Scotland
John Sutherland

Tarkio CC
Tarkio, Missouri
Chet Mendenhall

Tarpon Lake Village GC
Palm Harbor, Florida
Lane Marshall

Tarpon Springs CC
Tarpon Springs, Florida
Wayne Stiles, John Van Kleek
(R.) Mark Mahannah

Tarpon Woods GC
Palm Harbor, Florida
Lane Marshall

Tarratine C of Dark Harbor
Islesboro, Maine
Jamie Mackrell
(R.) Alex Findlay

Tarry Brae GC
South Fallsburgh, New York
William F. Mitchell

Tartan Park GC
St. Paul, Minnesota
Don Herfort
(A.11) Dick Nugent

Tascosa CC
Amarillo, Texas
Warren Cantrell

Tashua Knolls GC
Trumbull, Connecticut
Al Zikorus

Tasmania GC
Tasmania, Australia
Al Howard

Tasmanian Casino CC
Launceston, Australia
Peter Thomson, Michael Wolveridge

Tateno Classic GC
Japan
Yasuzo Kaneko

Tates Creek GC
Lexington, Kentucky
Buck Blankenship

Tate Springs GC
Bean Station, Tennessee
Donald Ross

Tatnuck CC [NLE]
Worcester, Massachusetts
Willie Campbell

Tatnuck CC
Worcester, Massachusetts
Donald Ross
(R.5) Geoffrey S. Cornish, William G. Robinson

Tatum Ranch GC
Phoenix, Arizona
Bob Cupp

Tatum Ridge G Links
Sarasota, Florida
Ted McAnlis

Taughannock G&CC
New York
Wester White

Taunus-Weilrod GC
Germany
Donald Harradine

Tavares Cove GC
West Palm Beach, Florida
William F. Mitchell

Tavistock CC
Haddonfield, New Jersey
Alex Findlay
(R.) James Gilmore Harrison, Ferdinand Garbin
(R.) Robert Trent Jones

Taylor Meadows GC
Taylor, Michigan
Arthur Hills

Taymouth Castle GC
Tayside, Scotland
James Braid, John R. Stutt

Tazewell County CC
Pounding Mill, Virginia
Ellis Maples, Dan Maples

Tchefuncta GC
Covington, Louisiana
Jack Daray
(A.9) Joe Lee

Teaford Lake GC
Bass Lake, California
Bob Baldock

Te Aroha GC
Te Aroha, New Zealand
C. H. Redhead

Te Awamutu GC
Te Awamutu, New Zealand
C. H. Redhead
(R.) H. G. Babbage

Tecolote Canyon GC
San Diego, California
Robert Trent Jones

Tecumseh CC
Tecumseh, Michigan
Leo J. Bishop

Tedesco CC
Salem, Massachusetts
(R.) Skip Wogan

Teeside GC
England
C. Robertson

Ted Makalena GC
Waipahu, Hawaii
Bob Baldock, Robert L. Baldock

Tega Cay CC
Fort Mill, South Carolina
William B. Lewis

Tegernseer GC
Bad Wiessee, Germany
Donald Harradine

Teignmouth GC
Devon, England
Alister Mackenzie
(R.) Martin Hawtree

Teijo GC
Finland
Jan Sederholm

Tejas GC [NLE]
Houston, Texas
Joseph S. Finger

Tekoa CC
Massachusetts
Donald Ross

Telemark GC
Cable, Wisconsin
Arthur Johnson

Telford Hotel G&CC
Great Hay, England
John Harris, Peter Thomson

Telgte-Hof Hahnes GC
Germany
Karl F. Grohs, *Rainer Preissmann*

Temecu CC
Temecula, California
Ted Robinson

Temecula Creek G Cse
Temecula, California
Virgil C. "Dick" Rossen
(A.3rd 9) Ted Robinson

Temple CC
Temple, Texas
Ralph Plummer
(R.9 A.9) Jay Riviere

Temple GC
Berkshire, England
Willie Park, Jr., *J. Hepburn*
(R.) Henry Cotton

Temple Hills CC
Columbia, Tennessee
Leon Howard

Temple Junior College GC
Temple, Texas
John Bredemus

Temple Terrace G&CC
Temple Terrace, Florida
Tom Bendelow
(R.) Hans Schmeisser

Tenby GC
Dyfed, Wales
C. K. Cotton

Tenerife GC
Canary Islands
A. Lucena

Tenison Muni (East Cse)
Dallas, Texas
Ralph Plummer
(R.) Arthur Davis

TENISON MUNI (WEST CSE)
Dallas, Texas
John Bredemus
(R.) Ralph Plummer
(R.) Arthur Davis
TENNANAH LAKE HOUSE GC
Roscoe, New York
Alfred H. Tull
TENNWOOD C
Hockley, Texas
Ralph Plummer
(R.18) Tom Fazio
TEQUESTA CC
Jupiter, Florida
Dick Wilson
(R.) Chuck Ankrom
TERESOPOLIS GC
Brazil
Stanley Thompson, Robert
Trent Jones
TERNESSE GC
Belgium
M. Baker
TERRACE HILLS GC
Algonquin, Illinois
Charles Maddox
TERRACE LAKES GC
Garden Valley, Idaho
Edward A. Hunnicutt
TERRACE PARK CC
Milford, Ohio
(R.) Arthur Hills (1977)
(R.) Arthur Hills (1984)
TERRADYNE RESORT & CC
Andover, Kansas
Don Sechrest
TERRAPIN HILLS GC
Fort Payne, Alabama
Harold Williams
TERRAS DE SÃO JOSE GC
São Paulo, Brazil
Frederick Bauer, Ricardo Rossi
TERRAVERDE GC
Fort Myers, Florida
Gordon Lewis
TERRE DU LAC CC
Bonne Terre, Missouri
R. Albert Anderson
TERRI PINES CC
Culman, Alabama
Tom Jackson
TERRY WALKER G&CC
Leeds, Alabama
Bancroft Timmons
TESHIKAGA CC
Hokkaido, Japan
Tsuneo Tanaka
TETON PINES G CSE
Jackson, Wyoming
Arnold Palmer, Ed Seay
TEUGEGA CC
Rome, New York
Donald Ross
(R.) William F. Mitchell
TEWKESBURY PARK GC
Gloucestershire, England
J. J. F. Pennink
TEXARKANA CC
Texarkana, Arkansas
William B. Langford, Theodore
J. Moreau
(R.) Leon Howard
(R.) Ron Prichard

TEXAS A&M UNIVERSITY GC
College Station, Texas
Ralph Plummer
(R.) Bruce Littell
TEXAS NATIONAL GC
Huntsville, Texas
Jack B. Miller
THAL G CSE
Thal, Austria
Herwig Zisser
THAMES GC
Thames, New Zealand
C. H. Redhead
THENDARA CC
Old Forge, New York
Donald Ross
(A.9) William Harries, A.
Russell Tryon
(R.1) Geoffrey S. Cornish,
William G. Robinson
THEODORE WIRTH GC
Minneapolis, Minnesota
Charles Erickson
(A.9) Edward Lawrence
Packard
THETFORD GC
Thetford, England
Charles H. Mayo
(R.) James Braid, John R.
Stutt
(R.) P. M. Ross
(R.) D. M. A. Steel
THETFORD MINES G & CURLING C
Quebec
(R.9 A.9) Howard Watson,
John Watson
THEYDON BOIS GC
Essex, England
James Braid
(A.2) Fred W. Hawtree,
Martin Hawtree
THISTLEDOWN GC
Owen Sound, Ontario
René Muylaert
THOMAS FORTUNE RYAN PRIVATE
CSE [NLE]
Oak Ridge, Virginia
Devereux Emmet
THOMAS MEMORIAL GC
Turners Falls, Massachusetts
Walter Hatch
THOMASTON CC
Thomaston, Georgia
Willard Byrd
THOMSON C
North Reading, Massachusetts
Geoffrey S. Cornish
THOMSON CC
Thomson, Georgia
Walter Ripley
(R.9) Robert Renaud
THORNAPPLE CC
Columbus, Ohio
Jack Kidwell
THORNAPPLE CREEK GC
Kalamazoo, Michigan
Mike Shields
THORNBLADE GC
Greer, South Carolina
Tom Fazio
THORNCREEK GC
Thornton, Colorado
Baxter Spann, Ken Dye

THORNDON PARK GC
Essex, England
(R.) J. S. F. Morrison
THORNGATE CC [NLE]
Deerfield, Illinois
Jack Croke
(R.) Robert Bruce Harris
(R.) Dick Nugent
THORNHILL GC
Ontario
(R.) Stanley Thompson
(R.) Howard Watson
(R.) Clinton E. Robinson
(R.) Robert Moote
THORNY LEA GC
Brockton, Massachusetts
Wayne Stiles, John Van Kleek
THORPENESS GC
Suffolk, England
James Braid
THORPE WOOD GC
England
Peter Alliss, David Thomas
THOUSAND ISLANDS C
Alexandria Bay, New York
Seth Raynor
(A.9) J. Webb
THREE LAKES CC
Kuwana, Japan
Peter Thomson, Michael
Wolveridge
THREE LITTLE BAKERS CC
Wilmington, Delaware
Edmund B. Ault
THREE PINES CC
Woodruff, South Carolina
Bill Amick
THREE RIDGES G CSE
Knoxville, Tennessee
Tom Clark
THREE RIVERS GC
Three Rivers, California
Robert Dean Putman
THREE RIVERS GC
Kelso, Washington
Robert Muir Graves
THUNDER BAY CC [NLE]
Ontario
Tom Bendelow
THUNDER BAY G&CC
Ontario
Stanley Thompson
(R.) Clinton E. Robinson
THUNDERBIRD CC
Phoenix, Arizona
Johnny Bulla, Charlene Suggs
THUNDERBIRD CC
Heber Springs, Arkansas
James T. Monk
THUNDERBIRD CC
Cathedral City, California
Lawrence Hughes
(R.) Harry Rainville, David
Rainville
(R.) Hal Purdy
(R.) Ted Robinson
THUNDERBIRD GC
Tyngsboro, Massachusetts
Geoffrey S. Cornish
THUNDERBIRD GC
Trumbarsville, Pennsylvania
Albert Stephen Cirino

THUNDER HILL CC
South Madison, Ohio
Fred Slagle
THUNDER HILLS GC
Dubuque, Iowa
Gordon Cunningham
THUNDERHOLLOW GC
Crossville, Tennessee
Ron Garl
THUNDER RIDGE CC
Rush, New York
Pete Craig, Joseph Demino
THURGOONA GC
Albury, Australia
Peter Thomson, Michael
Wolveridge
THURLES GC
Thurles, Northern Ireland
J. McAlister
(R.) Eddie Hackett
TIARA RADO GC
Grand Junction, Colorado
Tom Kolacny
(R.9 A.9) Dick Phelps
TIARE G&CC
Vanuatu
Cal Olson
TIBURON GC
Omaha, Nebraska
Dave Bennett, Lee Trevino
TICONDEROGA CC
Ticonderoga, New York
(R.9 A.9) Seymour Dunn
TIDES GC
St. Petersburg, Florida
David Gill
TIDES INN & CC (GOLDEN EAGLE
CSE)
Irvington, Virginia
George W. Cobb, John LaFoy
(R.) Buddy Loving
TIDES INN & CC (SHORT NINE)
Irvington, Virginia
Fred Findlay
TIDES INN & CC (TARTAN CSE)
Irvington, Virginia
Sir Guy Campbell
(A.9) George W. Cobb
(R. A.3) John LaFoy
TIDEWATER GC
Trenton, Maine
NKA Bar Harbor GC
TIDEWATER GC
Cherry Grove Beach, South
Carolina
Ken Tomlinson (1990)
TIDWORTH GARRISON GC
Wiltshire, England
(R.) J. Hamilton Stutt
TIERRA DEL SOL GC
California City, California
Robert von Hagge, Bruce Devlin
TIERRA GRANDE GC
Casa Grande, Arizona
Arthur Jack Snyder
TIERRAS DE SAN JOSE GC
Brazil
Frederico E. Bauer
TIERRE VERDE GC
Tierre Verde Island, Florida
Frank Murray
TIFTON GC
Darlington, South Carolina
Roland "Robby" Robertson

TIGER POINT G&CC (EAST CSE)
Gulf Breeze, Florida
Bill Amick
   (R.9 A.9) Ron Garl, Jerry Pate
TIGER POINT G&CC (WEST CSE)
Gulf Breeze, Florida
Bill Amick
TIJERAS ARROYO GC
Kirkland, New Mexico
Robert Dean Putman
TIJERAS CREEK GC
Rancho Santa Margarita,
California
Ted Robinson
TIJUANA CC
Tijuana, Mexico
William P. Bell
TILDEN PARK GC
Berkeley, California
William P. Bell
   (R.) Robert Muir Graves
TILGATE FOREST GC
Crawley, England
Brian Huggett, Neil Coles, *Roger Dyer*
TIMACUAN G&CC
Lake Mary, Florida
Ron Garl
TIMARRON GC
Dallas, Texas
Joseph S. Finger, Ken Dye,
Baxter Spann
TIMARU GC
Timaru, New Zealand
   (R.) John Harris, Peter
   Thomson
TIMBER CREEK G CSE
Watertown, Minnesota
Tim O'Connor (1987)
TIMBERLAKE GC
Sullivan, Illinois
Robert Bruce Harris
TIMBERLAKE PLANTATION GC
Chapin, South Carolina
Willard Byrd
TIMBERLANE CC
Gretna, Louisiana
Robert Trent Jones
TIMBERLIN GC
Berlin, Connecticut
Al Zikorus
TIMBERLINE RESORT GC
Canaan Valley, West Virginia
Ron Forse
TIMBERLINK GC
Ligonier, Pennsylvania
X. G. Hassenplug
TIMBER PINES GC (HILLS CSE)
Spring Hill, Florida
Ron Garl
TIMBER PINES GC (LAKES CSE)
Spring Hill, Florida
Ron Garl
TIMBER POINT CC
Great River, New York
H. S. Colt, C. H. Alison
TIMBER RIDGE CC
Minocqua, Wisconsin
Roger Packard
TIMBER RIDGE GC
East Lansing, Michigan
Jerry Matthews

TIMBERTON GC
Hattiesburg, Mississippi
Mark McCumber
TIMBER TRAILS CC
La Grange, Illinois
Robert Bruce Harris
   (R.) Robert Bruce Harris
TIMBERVALE GC
Batesville, Mississippi
Kevin Tucker
TIMMENDORFERSTRAND GC (CSE
No. 1)
Germany
Bernhard von Limburger
TIMMENDORFERSTRAND GC (CSE
No. 2)
Germany
Bernhard von Limburger
TIMPANOGAS MUNI [NLE]
Provo, Utah
Mike Riley
TIMUQUANA CC
Jacksonville, Florida
Donald Ross
   (R.) George W. Cobb
   (R.) David Gordon
TINKER AFB GC
Oklahoma City, Oklahoma
Floyd Farley
TINSLEY PARK GC
Yorkshire, England
F. G. Hawtree, J. H. Taylor
TIOGA GC
Nichols, New York
Hal Purdy
TIOMAN ISLAND RESORT GC
Kuantan, Malaysia
Ronald Fream
TIPPECANOE CC
Monticello, Indiana
Joseph A. Roseman
TIPPECANOE CC
Canfield, Ohio
R. Albert Anderson
   (R.) Geoffrey S. Cornish
TIPPECANOE LAKE CC
Leesburg, Indiana
   (R.) Gary Kern
TIPSINAH MOUNDS CC
Elbow Lake, Minnesota
Joel Goldstrand
TIPTON MUNI
Tipton, Indiana
William H. Diddel
TIPWORTH GC
England
Tom Williamson
TIRRENIA CC
Tirrenia, Italy
Henry Cotton
TITIRANGI GC
Titirangi, New Zealand
F. G. Hood, Gilbert Martin
   (R.) Alister Mackenzie
TITUSVILLE CC
Titusville, Pennsylvania
Emil Loeffler, *John McGlynn*
TIVERTON GC
Devon, England
James Braid, John R. Stutt
TOANA VISTA GC
Wendover, Nevada
Homer Flint

TOBAGO GC
Mount Irvine, Trinidad and
Tobago
John Harris
TOBO GC
Sweden
Douglas Brazier
TOCCOA G&CC
Toccoa, Georgia
   (R.) J. Porter Gibson
TODD VALLEY GC
Charleston, Maine
Don Todd
TOFTREES CC
State College, Pennsylvania
Edmund B. Ault
TOGCHA BEACH GC
Yona, Guam
Robin Nelson, Rodney Wright
TOGUS VA HOSPITAL GC [NLE]
Maine
Bob Baldock
TOHBETU GC
Hokkaido, Japan
Ronald Fream
TOHYA-KO RESORT GC
Hokkaido, Japan
Takeaki Kaneda
TOJO GC
Hyogo, Japan
Shunsuke Kato
TOKATEE GC
Blue River, Oregon
Ted Robinson
TOKUYAMA CC
Tokuyama, Japan
John Harris, Peter Thomson
TOKUSHIMA FOREST GC
Tokushima, Japan
Shoichi Suzuki
TOKYO GC
Tokyo, Japan
C. H. Alison
TOKYO KITA CC
Tochigi, Japan
Shunsuke Kato
TOKYO TOMIN GC (FUJI CSE)
Tokyo, Japan
Osamu Ueda
TOKYO TOMIN GC (TSUKUBA CSE)
Tokyo, Japan
Osamu Ueda
TOKYO ZAISHI GC
Tokyo, Japan
Desmond Muirhead
TOKYU SEVEN HUNDRED C
Chiba, Japan
Chohei Nagasawa
TOLEDO CC
Toledo, Ohio
Willie Park, Jr.
   (R.) Robert Bruce Harris
   (R.) Arthur Hills
TOLLISTON CC
Gary, Indiana
Tom Bendelow
TOMAC WOODS GC
Albion, Michigan
Robert Beard
TOMAHAWK CC
Welshfield, Ohio
Ben W. Zink

TOMAHAWK HILLS GC
Jamestown, Indiana
Gary Kern
TOMAHAWK HILLS GC
Shawnee, Kansas
Harry Robb
   (R.) *William V. Leonard, L.J.
   "Dutch" McLellan*
TOMAHAWK HOLLOW GC
Gambier, Ohio
R.C. Rowley
TOMAHAWK LAKE GC
Deadwood, South Dakota
Lawrence Hughes
TOMEI FUJI CC
Japan
Shigeru Ishii
TOMEI NEBA CC
Japan
Junji Shiba
TOM FRY GC
San Mateo, California
   (R.) Robert Muir Graves
TOMIOKA CC
Tomioka City, Gunma
Prefecture, Japan
Mark Rathert
TOMISATO GC
Chiba, Japan
Mike Poellot, Brad Benz
TOMOKA OAKS G&CC
Ormand Beach, Florida
J. Porter Gibson
TOM O'LEARY GC
Bismarck, North Dakota
David Gill, Garrett Gill
TOMS RIVER CC
Toms River, New Jersey
Paul Losi
TONAMI ROYAL GC
Toyama, Japan
Yasuzo Kaneko
TONE GC
Ibaragi, Japan
Shunsuke Kato
TONGA GC
Tonga
Peter Thomson, Michael
Wolveridge
TONGELREEP GC
Netherlands
J. F. Dudok van Heel
TONY BUTLER MUNI
Harlingen, Texas
Dennis W. Arp
TONY LEMA MEMORIAL GC
San Leandro, California
William F. Bell
TOOTING BEC C
England
Tom Dunn
   (R.) Willie Park, Jr.
TOPEKA CC
Topeka, Kansas
Tom Bendelow
   (R.9) *Bob Peebles*
   (R.9 A.9) Perry Maxwell
   (R.1 A.1) Chet Mendenhall
TOPEKA PUBLIC GC
Topeka, Kansas
*William V. Leonard, L.J. "Dutch"
McLellan*
   (R.3) Dick Nugent

TOP OF THE WORLD GC
Clearwater, Florida
Chic Adams

TOP OF THE WORLD GC
Lake George, New York
Charles Tuttle

TOP PLAYERS CC
Ibaraki, Japan
David Thomas

TOPSAIL GREENS GC
Hampstead, North Carolina
Russell T. Burney

TOQUA GC
Tellico Village, Tennessee
Tom Clark

TOREKOV GC
Torekov, Sweden
Nils Sköld

TORI CC
Tochigi-ken, Japan
Mike Poellot

TORIDE KOKUSAI GC
Ibaraki, Japan
Dr. N. Marumo

TORONTO GC
Toronto, Ontario
H. S. Colt
(R.9 A.5) Howard Watson

TORONTO HUNT C
Scarborough, Ontario
Willie Park, Jr.
(R.) Thomas McBroom

TOR HILL GC
Regina, Saskatchewan
Stanley Thompson
(R.) Jack Thompson

TORONTO HUNT C
Toronto, Ontario
Willie Park, Jr.

TORQUAY GC
Devonshire, England
James Braid, John R. Stutt
(R.) J. Hamilton Stutt

TORRANCE HOUSE GC
Lanarkshire, Scotland
Fred W. Hawtree, Martin Hawtree

TORREBY GC
Sweden
Douglas Brazier

TORREÓN GC
Torreón, Mexico
Percy Clifford

TORREQUEBRADA GC
Málaga, Spain
Pepe Gancedo

TORRESDALE-FRANKFORD CC
Philadelphia, Pennsylvania
Willie Campbell
(R.9 A.9) Donald Ross

TORREY PINES MUNI (NORTH CSE)
La Jolla, California
William F. Bell
(R.) David Rainville
(R.) Stephen Halsey, Jack Daray, Jr.

TORREY PINES MUNI (SOUTH CSE)
La Jolla, California
William F. Bell
(R.) David Rainville
(R.) Stephen Halsey, Jack Daray, Jr.

TORRINGTON CC
Goshen, Connecticut
Orrin Smith

TORWOODLEE GC
Selkirkshire, Scotland
Willie Park, Willie Park, Jr.

TORY PINES G RESORT
Francestown, New Hampshire
Donald Ross
(A.9) *Dick Tremblay*
(R.) *Mark Gagne, Lyman Doane II*

TOSHOEN GC
Tochigi, Japan
Iwao Nakijima

TOTEM PAR FOUR GC
Penticton, British Columbia
James P. Izatt

TOTSUKA CC (EAST CSE)
Kanawaga, Japan
S. Manno

TOTSUKA CC (WEST CSE)
Kanagawa, Japan
Seichi Inouye

TOTTERIDGE GC
Scotland
Willie Park, Jr.

TOULOUSE-PALMOLA GC
France
Michael G. Fenn

TOWER HILL GC
Somerset, England
Samuel Chisholm

TOWER TEE GC
St. Louis, Missouri
R. Albert Anderson

TOWER VUE GC
Pittsburgh, Pennsylvania
Edward Holowka

TOWERS CC
Floral Park, New York
W. H. "Pipe" Follett
(R.) Frank Duane

TOWN AND COUNTRY C
Blakely, Georgia
Hugh Moore

TOWN AND COUNTRY C
St. Paul, Minnesota
George McRee
(R.) Robert Foulis
(R.) Stan Thompson
(R.) Dick Nugent

TOWN AND COUNTRY C
Devil's Lake, North Dakota
William B. Langford, Theodore J. Moreau

TOWN AND COUNTRY C
Fond du Lac, Wisconsin
Tom Bendelow

TOWN AND COUNTRY GC
Ohio
Edmund B. Ault

TOWN AND COUNTRY GC
Chattanooga, Tennessee
Dick Wilson

TOWSON G&CC
Towson, Maryland
Geoffrey S. Cornish, William G. Robinson

TOYO RANTAN CC
Jiayi, Taiwan
Shunsuke Kato

TOYOTA HIGASHI GC
Nagoya, Japan
Karl Litten

TOY TOWN TAVERN GC [NLE]
Winchendon, Massachusetts
Donald Ross

TPC AT AVENEL
Potomac, Maryland
Edmund B. Ault, Brian Ault, Tom Clark, Bill Love, *Ed Sneed*

TPC AT EAGLE TRACE
Coral Springs, Florida
Arthur Hills

TPC AT MONTE CARLO
Fort Pierce, Florida
NKA Meadowood G&TC

TPC AT PIPER GLEN
Charlotte, North Carolina
Arnold Palmer, Ed Seay

TPC AT PRESTANCIA (CLUB CSE)
Sarasota, Florida
Robert von Hagge, Bruce Devlin

TPC AT PRESTANCIA (STADIUM CSE)
Sarasota, Florida
Ron Garl

TPC AT RIVER HIGHLANDS
Cromwell, Connecticut
Robert J. Ross, *Maurice Kearney*
(R.) Orrin Smith
(R.) Pete Dye, *David Postlethwait*
(R. A.11) Bobby Weed

TPC AT SAWGRASS (STADIUM CSE)
Ponte Vedra Beach, Florida
Pete Dye
(R.) Pete Dye

TPC AT SAWGRASS (VALLEY CSE)
Ponte Vedra Beach, Florida
Pete Dye, Jerry Pate

TPC AT SOUTHWIND
Germantown, Tennessee
Ron Prichard

TPC AT StarPass
Tucson, Arizona
Bob Cupp

TPC AT SUMMERLIN
Las Vegas, Nevada
Bobby Weed

TPC AT THE WOODLANDS
Woodlands, Texas
Robert von Hagge, Bruce Devlin
(R.) Carlton Gipson

TPC OF MICHIGAN
Dearborn, Michigan
Jack Nicklaus

TPC OF SCOTTSDALE (DESERT CSE)
Scottsdale, Arizona
Jay Morrish, Tom Weiskopf

TPC OF SCOTTSDALE (STADIUM CSE)
Scottsdale, Arizona
Jay Morrish, Tom Weiskopf

TPC OF TAMPA BAY AT CHEVAL
Lutz, Florida
Bobby Weed

TRABOLGAN GC
Ireland
Eddie Hackett

TRACY G&CC
Tracy, California
Bob Baldock

TRACY PARK G&CC
England
Grant Aitken

TRAFALGAR G&CC
Milton, Ontario
Clinton E. Robinson

[THE] TRAILS GC
Moore, Oklahoma
Leon Howard, *Charles Howard*

TRALEE GC [NLE]
County Kerry, Ireland
(R.) Eddie Hackett

TRALEE GC
County Kerry, Ireland
Arnold Palmer, Ed Seay

TRAMARK GC
Gulfport, Mississippi
Floyd Trehern

TRAMORE GC
County Waterford, Ireland
Willie Park, Willie Park, Jr.
(R.) John Harris

TRANÅS GC
Tranås, Sweden
Nils Sköld

TRAPPERS TURN GC
Wisconsin Dells, Wisconsin
Roger Packard, *Andy North*

TRAVELODGE GC
Papeete, Tahiti
Robert von Hagge, Bruce Devlin

TRAVERSE CITY CC
Traverse City, Michigan
Tom Bendelow
(R.) Bruce Matthews, Jerry Matthews
(R.) William Newcomb

TRAVIS POINTE CC
Ann Arbor, Michigan
William Newcomb

TREASURE CAY GC
Abaco, Bahamas
Dick Wilson, Joe Lee

TREASURE HILLS CC
Texas
Richard Watson

TREASURE ISLAND GC
Lubbock, Texas
Warren Cantrell

TREASURE LAKE CC
DuBois, Pennsylvania
Dominic Palombo

TREDYFFRIN CC
Paoli, Pennsylvania
Alex Findlay

TREE TOP GC
Manheim, Pennsylvania
Robert Hummer, Ken Brown, Tom Brown

TREETOPS GC
Gaylord, Michigan
Robert Trent Jones

TREETOPS NORTH GC (FAZIO CSE)
Gaylord, Michigan
Tom Fazio

TREETOPS NORTH GC (PAR 3 CSE)
Gaylord, Michigan
Rick Smith (9 Par 3 1992)

TREETOPS NORTH GC (SMITH CSE)
Gaylord, Michigan
Rick Smith (1993)

TREHAVEN GC
Ontario
(R.) Robert Moote

TRENT GC
Bolsouer, Ontario
René Muylaert

TRENTHAM PARK GC
Staffordshire, England
Tom Williamson
TRENT PARK GC
Enfield, England
John Day
TRES CERRITOS CC
Hemet, California
Cal Olson
TRES VIDAS EN LA PLAYA (EAST CSE)
[NLE]
Acapulco, Mexico
Robert Trent Jones
TRES VIDAS EN LA PLAYA (WEST
CSE) [NLE]
Acapulco, Mexico
Robert Trent Jones
TREUDELBERG GC
Hamburg, Germany
D. M. A. Steel
TREVOSE G&CC
England
H. S. Colt, C. H. Alison, J. S. F.
Morrison
    (R. A.9) Sir Guy Campbell
TREYBURN CC
Bahama, North Carolina
Tom Fazio
TRI-CITY GC
American Fork, Utah
Joseph B. Williams
TRICKLE CREEK GC
Kimberley, British Columbia
Les Furber, *Jim Eremko*
TRI-COUNTY CC
Corbin, Kentucky
    (R.9) *Robert Thomason*
TRI-COUNTY GC
Sulphur Springs, Indiana
Robert Beard
TRI-COUNTY GC
Granite Falls, North Carolina
William Pitts
TRI-COUNTY GC
Batesburg, South Carolina
Mike Serino, David Todd
TRI-PALM GC
Thousand Palms, California
Jim Petrides (1970)
TRIM GC
Trim, Ireland
    (R.) Eddie Hackett
TRIPLE A CC
St. Louis, Missouri
    (R.) Robert Foulis
TRIPLE CROWN CC
Boone, Kentucky
Gene Bates
TRIPOLI CC
Milwaukee, Wisconsin
Tom Bendelow
    (R.) Bob Lohmann
TRIPOLI GC
Tripoli, Libya
J. J. F. Pennink
TRI-WAY GC
Republic, Missouri
Press Maxwell
TROIA GC
Setubal, Portugal
Robert Trent Jones
TROLLHÄTTAN GC
Trollhättan, Sweden
Nils Sköld

TROON G&CC
Scottsdale, Arizona
Jay Morrish, Tom Weiskopf
TROON NORTH GC
Scottsdale, Arizona
Jay Morrish, Tom Weiskopf
TROON PORTLAND GC
Ayrshire, Scotland
Willie Fernie
TROPHY C (CREEK CSE)
Roanoke, Texas
Arthur Hills
TROPHY C (OAKS CSE)
Roanoke, Texas
Joe Lee, Ben Hogan
TROPICANA CC [NLE]
Las Vegas, Nevada
Bert Stamps
    (R.) Tom Clark, Brian Ault
TROSPER PARK GC
Oklahoma City, Oklahoma
Arthur Jackson
TROUT LAKE CC
Woodruff, Wisconsin
Charles Maddox, *Frank P.
MacDonald*
TROY CC
Troy, Ohio
    (R.9 A.9) Jack Kidwell,
    Michael Hurdzan
TRULL BROOK GC
North Tewksbury, Massa-
chusetts
Geoffrey S. Cornish
TRUMBARSVILLE GC
Trumbarsville, Pennsylvania
Albert Stephen Cirino
TRUMBULL CC
Warren, Ohio
Stanley Thompson
    (R.) William Newcomb
TRURO G&CC
Truro, Nova Scotia
    (R.) Stanley Thompson
    (R.9 A.9) Clinton E.
    Robinson
TRURO GC
Cornwall, England
H. S. Colt, J. S. F. Morrison
TRW CC
Chesterland, Ohio
NKA Fowler's Mill G Cse
TRYALL G & BEACH C
Jamaica
Ralph Plummer
    (R.) Jim Engh
TRYON CC
Tryon, North Carolina
Tom Bendelow
TRYSTING TREE GC
Corvallis, Oregon
Ted Robinson
TSAWWASSEN G&CC
British Columbia
Norman H. Woods, *Jack Reimer*
TSU CC
Mie, Japan
Kentaro Sato
TSU GC
Mie, Japan
Michio Izumi, Yuko Moriguchi
TSUGA CC
Japan
Yoshitaro Kawanami

TSUGARU KOGEN GC
Lake Tawata, Japan
Arnold Palmer, Ed Seay
TSUKUBA CC
Tokyo, Japan
Akiro Sato
TSUKUBA GAKUEN GC
Ibaragi, Japan
Masao Takema
TSUMEB GC
Tsumeb, South Africa
    (R.9 A.9) *Harry Hickson*
TSUTSUJIGAOKA CC
Japan
Katsumi Takizawa
TUALATIN CC
Tualatin, Oregon
H. Chandler Egan, *George Junor*
    (R.) Robert Muir Graves
    (R.) Bob Cupp, John Fought
TUAM GC
County Galway, Ireland
Eddie Hackett
TUBAC VALLEY CC
Tubac, Arizona
Red Lawrence
TUCKAWAY CC
Franklin, Wisconsin
Ken Killian, Dick Nugent
    (R.) Bob Lohmann
TUCSON CC
Tucson, Arizona
William F. Bell, William P. Bell
    (R.3) Red Lawrence
    (R.) Arthur Jack Snyder
TUCSON ESTATES GC (EAST CSE)
Tucson, Arizona
Red Lawrence
TUCSON ESTATES GC (WEST CSE)
Tucson, Arizona
Red Lawrence
TUCSON NATIONAL GC
Tucson, Arizona
Robert Bruce Harris
    (R.6) Red Lawrence
    (R. A.3rd 9) Robert von
    Hagge, Bruce Devlin
TUDOR PARK G&CC
Maidstone, England
D. M. A. Steel
TULARCITOS G&CC
Milpitas, California
Clark Glasson
TULARE GC
Tulare, California
Bob Baldock
TULLAMORE GC
County Offaly, Ireland
Lionel Hewson
    (R.) James Braid, John R.
    Stutt
    (R.) Eddie Hackett
TULSA CC
Tulsa, Oklahoma
A.W. Tillinghast
    (R. A.3) Floyd Farley
    (R.2) *James L. Holmes*
    (R.5) Jay Morrish
TUMBA G CSE
Moscow, Russian Federation
Sven Tumba (9 1989)

TUMBLE BROOK CC
Bloomfield, Connecticut
Willie Park, Jr.
    (A.9) Orrin Smith
    (A.3rd 9) George Fazio, Tom
    Fazio
    (R.2) Al Zikorus
TUMBLEBROOK GC
Pewaukee, Wisconsin
Edward Lawrence Packard
TUMWATER VALLEY GC
Olympia, Washington
Roy L. Goss, *Glen Proctor*
    (R.) Robert Muir Graves
TUNBRIDGE WELLS GC
Tunbridge Wells, England
C. K. Cotton
TUNXIS PLANTATION CC (CSE NO.
1)
Farmington, Connecticut
Al Zikorus
TUNXIS PLANTATION CC (CSE NO.
2)
Farmington, Connecticut
Al Zikorus
TUPELO CC
Tupelo, Mississippi
John W. Frazier
    (R.) Kevin Tucker
TUPPER LAKE CC
Tupper Lake, New York
Willard Wilkinson
TUPPER LAKE GC [NLE]
Tupper Lake, New York
Donald Ross
TURA BEACH CC
Meirmbula, Australia
Peter Thomson, Michael
Wolveridge
TURBOT HILLS GC
Milton, Pennsylvania
    (A.9) Alec Ternyei
TURF AND SURF GC
Tarpon Springs, Florida
Chic Adams
TURF VALLEY CC (NORTH CSE)
Ellicott City, Maryland
Edmund B. Ault, Al Jamison
TURF VALLEY CC (SOUTH CSE)
Ellicott City, Maryland
Edmund B. Ault
TURF VALLEY CC (WOODS NINE)
Ellicott City, Maryland
Edmund B. Ault, Al Jamison
TURIN HIGHLANDS GC
Turin, New York
William Harries
TURKEY CREEK CC
Gary, Indiana
Charles Maddox, *Frank P.
MacDonald*
TURKEY CREEK G&RC
Alachua, Florida
Ward Northrup
TURKEY RUN GC
Waveland, Indiana
Gary Kern
TURLOCK G&CC
Turlock, California
Bob Baldock, Jack Fleming
TURNBERRY G CSE
Pickerington, Ohio
Arthur Hills

TURNBERRY CC
Crystal Lake, Illinois
Edward Lawrence Packard,
Roger Packard
TURNBERRY GC (AILSA CSE)
Ayrshire, Scotland
Willie Fernie
(R.) C. K. Hutchison
(R.) P. M. Ross, James
Alexander
(R.) Peter Alliss, David
Thomas
TURNBERRY GC (ARRAN CSE)
Ayrshire, Scotland
Willie Fernie
(R.) James Alexander
TURNBERRY ISLE G&CC (NORTH
CSE)
North Miami, Florida
Robert Trent Jones
(R.) Donald Soffer
TURNBERRY ISLE G&CC (SOUTH
CSE)
North Miami, Florida
Robert Trent Jones
(R.) Donald Soffer
TURNER FIELD GC
Albany, Georgia
Hugh Moore
TURNER VALLEY G&CC
Calgary, Alberta
(R.10) Les Furber, Jim
Eremko
(R.) Bill Newis
TURNHOUSE GC
Edinburgh, Scotland
James Braid
(R.) Willie Park, Jr.
TURTLE BAY GC (NEW CSE)
Kahuku, Oahu, Hawaii
Arnold Palmer, Ed Seay
TURTLE BAY GC (OLD CSE)
Kahuku, Oahu, Hawaii
George Fazio, Tom Fazio
(R.) Robert Trent Jones, Jr.
TURTLE COVE GC
Atlanta, Georgia
William James Spear
TURTLE CREEK C
Jupiter, Florida
Joe Lee
TURTLE CREEK GC
Rockledge, Florida
Bob Renaud
TURTLE LAKE GC
Winchester, Wisconsin
Stanley Pelchar
TURTLE POINT G&CC
Laguna, Quays, Queensland,
Australia
Gary Panks, David Graham
TURTLE POINT G LINKS
Kiawah Island, South Carolina
Jack Nicklaus
TURTLE POINT YACHT & CC
Florence, Alabama
Robert Trent Jones
TUSCALOOSA CC
Tuscaloosa, Alabama
(R.) Arthur L. Davis
TUSCARORA CC
Danville, Virginia
Gene Hamm

TUSCARORA CC
Marcellus, New York
Seymour Dunn
TUSCAWILLA CC
Winter Springs, Florida
Joe Lee
(R.) Lloyd Clifton, Kenneth
Ezell, George Clifton
TUSCUMBIA CC
Green Lake, Wisconsin
Tom Bendelow
TUSTIN RANCH GC
Tustin, California
Ted Robinson
TUTZING GC
Weilheim, Germany
Reinhold Weishaupt
TUXEDO GC
Tuxedo Park, New York
Robert Trent Jones
(R.) Stephen Kay
TUXEDO MUNI
Manitoba
A. W. Creed
TUXEDO PARK C [NLE]
Tuxedo Park, New York
Henry Hewett
(R.) William S. Flynn
TWAIN HARTE GC
Twain Harte, California
Clark Glasson
TWENTY FIVE NASU GOLF GARDEN
Tochigi, Japan
Shiro Kawamura
TWENTY GREENS GC
Catoosa, Oklahoma
Richard Audrain
TWENTY VALLEY G&CC
Beamsville, Ontario
Clinton E. Robinson
TWICKENHAM GC
Middlesex, England
J. J. F. Pennink, C. D. Lawrie
TWIGGS MUNI
Providence, Rhode Island
Donald Ross
TWILIGHT GC
Denver, Colorado
Henry B. Hughes
TWIN BASE GC
Wright-Patterson AFB, Ohio
William H. Diddel
(R.) Edward Lawrence
Packard, Brent Wadsworth
(R.4) Jack Kidwell
TWIN CREEK CC
Dahlonega, Georgia
Arthur Davis
TWIN FALLS GC
Westbrook, Maine
Albert Young, Richard Young
TWIN FALLS STATE PARK GC
Mullens, West Virginia
Geoffrey S. Cornish, William G.
Robinson
(A.9) George W. Cobb, John
LaFoy
TWIN HILLS CC
Longmeadow, Massachusetts
Al Zikorus
TWIN HILLS CC
Joplin, Missouri
Smiley Bell

TWIN HILLS G&CC
Oklahoma City, Oklahoma
Perry Maxwell
(R.1) Floyd Farley
(R.) Don Sechrest
TWIN HILLS GC
Spencerport, New York
Pete Craig
(A.9) Geoffrey S. Cornish,
William G. Robinson
TWIN KNOLLS GC
Grass Lake, Michigan
Jim LaVernock
TWIN LAKES CC
Rathdrum, Idaho
Edward A. Hunnicutt
TWIN LAKES CC
Kent, Ohio
Sandy Alves
TWIN LAKES CC
Tacoma, Washington
Al Smith
TWIN LAKES CC
Twin Lakes, Wisconsin
Leonard Macomber
TWIN LAKES G&CC
Federal Way, Washington
William Teufel
TWIN LAKES GC
Mountain Home, Arkansas
Cecil B. Hollingsworth
TWIN LAKES GC
El Monte, California
William H. Johnson
(R.) Robert Muir Graves
TWIN LAKES GC
Carmel, Indiana
William H. Diddel
TWIN LAKES GC
Mansfield, Ohio
Jack Kidwell
TWIN LAKES GC
Mainland, Pennsylvania
Charles Bunton
(R.9 A.9) David Gordon
TWIN LAKES GC
St. George, Utah
Robert Muir Graves
TWIN LAKES GC
Centerville, Virginia
Charles B. Schalestock
TWIN LAKE VILLAGE GC
New London, New Hampshire
Henry Kidder
TWIN MOUNTAIN GC [NLE]
New Hampshire
A. H. Fenn
TWIN OAKS CC
Springfield, Missouri
Floyd Farley, Horton Smith
TWIN OAKS GC
St. John, Michigan
Warner Bowen
TWIN OAKS GC
Greensboro, North Carolina
Ellis Maples
TWIN ORCHARD CC [NLE]
Bensenville, Illinois
William B. Langford, Theodore
J. Moreau
TWIN ORCHARDS CC (RED CSE)
Long Grove, Illinois
C. D. Wagstaff
(R.) Ken Killian, Dick Nugent

TWIN ORCHARDS CC (WHITE CSE)
Long Grove, Illinois
C. D. Wagstaff
(R.) Edward Lawrence
Packard
TWIN PEAKS MUNI
Longmont, Colorado
Frank Hummel
TWIN PINES CC
Harrisonville, Missouri
Dewitt "Maury" Bell
TWIN PONDS GC
Crystal Lake, Illinois
C. D. Wagstaff
TWIN RIVERS G CSE
Terra Nova National Park,
Newfoundland
C. E. Robinson
(A.9) Douglas Carrick
TWIN RUN GC
Hamilton, Ohio
William H. Diddel
TWIN SHIELDS G&CC
Dunkirk, Maryland
Ray Shields, Roy Shields
TWIN VALLEY CC
Wadesboro, North Carolina
(A.9) Ron Kirby, Denis
Griffiths
TWIN WELLS G CSE
Irving, Texas
Brian Ault, Bill Love
TWISTED OAKS GC
Beverly Hills, Florida
Karl Litten
TWO BRIDGES CC
Lincoln Park, New Jersey
Nicholas Psiahas
TWO RIVERS MUNI
Nashville, Tennessee
Dave Bennett, Leon Howard,
Charles Howard
TYANDACA MUNI
Burlington, Ontario
Clinton E. Robinson
TYGART LAKE GC
Grafton, West Virginia
(R.) James Gilmore Harrison,
Ferdinand Garbin
TYLER'S CREEK GC
Alto, Michigan
Mark DeVries
TYNDALL AFB GC
Panama City Beach, Florida
Bob Baldock
(A.9) Joe Lee, Rocky Roque-
more
TYNEMOUTH GC
Northumberland, England
Willie Park, Jr.
TYNESIDE GC [NLE]
Newcastle, England
Mungo Park
TYNESIDE GC
Newcastle, England
H. S. Colt
TYNLEY PARK GC
England
W. Wiltshire
TYOGA CC
Wellsboro, Pennsylvania
Edmund B. Ault
(A.9) Tom Clark

TYRONE CC
  Tyrone, Pennsylvania
  Alex Findlay
      (R.) Edmund B. Ault
TYRONE HILLS CC
  Livingston, Michigan
  Bruce Matthews
TYRRELLS WOOD GC
  England
  James Braid

UCHIHARA CC
  Ibaraki, Japan
  Tsuyoshi Arai
UDINE GC
  Udine, Italy
  John Harris, Marco Croze
UDDEHOLM GC
  Sweden
  Nils Sköld (1965)
UGOLINO GC
  Florence, Italy
  Seymour Dunn
      (R.) Pier Mancinelli
U-GREEN NAKATSUGAWA GC
  Gifu, Japan
  Shozo Ozasa
UKIAH MUNI
  Ukiah, California
  Paul Underwood
UKIMA G LINKS
  Saitama, Japan
  K. Yasuda
ULEN CC
  Lebanon, Indiana
  William H. Diddel
ULLNA GC
  Sweden
  Sven Tumba (1980)
ULM-DO GC
  Germany
  Bernhard von Limburger
ULRICEHAMN GC
  Sweden
  Nils Sköld
ULRICHSBERG G CSE
  Ulrichsberg, Austria
  Kurt Rossknecht
ULVERSTON GC
  Cumbria, England
  Sandy Herd
      (R.) H. S. Colt
UNDERMOUNTAIN GC
  Boston Corners, New York
  John Shakshober
UNDERWOOD GC
  Underwood, North Dakota
  Don Herfort
UNDULATA GC
  Shelbyville, Kentucky
  Jack Ridge (1990)
UNICORN CC
  Stoneham, Massachusetts
  Wayne Stiles, John Van Kleek
      (R.) Orrin Smith
UNION CC [NLE]
  Dover, Ohio
  Tom Bendelow
UNION CC
  New Philadelphia, Ohio
  William Newcomb

UNION CITY CC
  Union City, Pennsylvania
  Tom Bendelow
UNION HILLS CC
  Sun City, Arizona
  Jeff Hardin, Greg Nash
UNION HILLS GC
  Pevely, Missouri
  Homer Herpel
      (A.9) Ron Kern, Gary Kern
UNIONTOWN CC
  Uniontown, Pennsylvania
  Emil Loeffler, *John McGlynn*
UNIONVILLE FAIRWAYS
  Ontario
  René Muylaert
UNIVERSITY GC
  Vancouver, British Columbia
  Davey Black
      (R.) Clinton E. Robinson
      (R.5) Les Furber, *Jim Eremko*
UNIVERSITY HEIGHTS GC
  Cleveland, Ohio
  Sandy Alves
UNIVERSITY OF ALABAMA GC
  Tuscaloosa, Alabama
  NKA Harry Pritchett GC
UNIVERSITY OF FLORIDA GC
  Gainesville, Florida
  Donald Ross
      (R.) Ron Garl
UNIVERSITY OF GEORGIA GC
  Athens, Georgia
  Robert Trent Jones
      (R.) John LaFoy
UNIVERSITY OF IDAHO GC
  Moscow, Idaho
  Frank James
      (R.9 A.9) Bob Baldock
UNIVERSITY OF ILLINOIS GC (BLUE
  CSE)
  Champaign, Illinois
  C. D. Wagstaff
UNIVERSITY OF ILLINOIS GC
  (ORANGE CSE)
  Champaign, Illinois
  C. D. Wagstaff
UNIVERSITY OF IOWA GC [NLE]
  Iowa City, Iowa
  Charles Kennett
UNIVERSITY OF MARYLAND GC
  College Park, Maryland
  George W. Cobb
UNIVERSITY OF MICHIGAN GC
  Ann Arbor, Michigan
  Alister Mackenzie, Perry
  Maxwell
UNIVERSITY OF MINNESOTA GC
  St. Paul, Minnesota
  Seth Raynor
      (R.) Gerry Pirkl, *Donald G.
      Brauer*
UNIVERSITY OF MISSISSIPPI GC
  Oxford, Mississippi
  Sonny Guy
UNIVERSITY OF MONTANA GC
  Missoula, Montana
  Gregor MacMillan
UNIVERSITY OF NEW MEXICO GC
  (NORTH CSE)
  Albuquerque, New Mexico
  William H. Tucker
      (A.9) William H. Tucker
      [NLE]

UNIVERSITY OF NEW MEXICO GC
  (SOUTH CSE)
  Albuquerque, New Mexico
  Red Lawrence
UNIVERSITY OF OKLAHOMA GC
  Norman, Oklahoma
  Perry Maxwell, Press Maxwell
UNIVERSITY OF SOUTHERN MISSIS-
  SIPPI GC
  Hattiesburg, Mississippi
  Sonny Guy
UNIVERSITY OF SOUTH FLORIDA GC
  Tampa, Florida
  William F. Mitchell
UNIVERSITY OF THE PHILIPPINES GC
  Philippines
  Francisco D. Santana
UNIVERSITY OF UTAH GC
  Salt Lake City, Utah
      (R.2) William Howard Neff
UNIVERSITY PARK CC
  Boca Raton, Florida
  Frank Murray
UNIVERSITY PARK CC
  University Park, Florida
  Ron Garl
UNIVERSITY PARK GC
  Muskegon, Michigan
  Bruce Matthews, Jerry Matthews
      (R.) Jeff Gorney
UNIVERSITY RIDGE GC
  Madison, Wisconsin
  Robert Trent Jones, Jr.
UNNA FRÖNDENBERG GC
  Germany
  Karl F. Grohs, *Rainer
  Preissmann*
UPLAND HILLS GC
  Upland, California
  David Rainville
UPLANDS G&CC
  Ontario
  Stanley Thompson
UPPER CANADA GC
  Morrisburg, Ontario
  Clinton E. Robinson
UPPER LANSDOWNE CC
  Asheville, Ohio
  Jack Kidwell
UPPER MAIN LINE CC
  Philadelphia, Pennsylvania
  William Gordon, David Gordon
UPPER MONTCLAIR CC [NLE]
  Clifton, New Jersey
      (R.) A. W. Tillinghast
UPPER MONTCLAIR CC
  Clifton, New Jersey
  Robert Trent Jones
UPPINGHAM CASTLE GC
  Uppingham, England
  D. M. A. Steel
UPSALA GC
  Sweden
  G. Paulsson
UPTON G&CC
  Jamaica
  John S. Collier
      (R.9) Howard Watson
UPTON BY CHESTER GC
  Cheshire, England
  J.W. Davies
URAKU GC
  Gotemba, Shizuoka, Japan
  Shunsuke Kato

URBAN GC
  Chicago Heights, Illinois
  Edward Lawrence Packard
URBAN HILLS CC
  Richton Park, Illinois
  Edward Lawrence Packard
URBANA CC
  Urbana, Ohio
  Paul Dye, Sr. (9 1929)
      (A.9) P. B. Dye
URBANA G&CC
  Urbana, Illinois
  Tom Bendelow
      (R.) Dick Nugent
U.S. NAVAL MEDICAL CENTER GC
  Maryland
      (R.) Edmund B. Ault
USELESS BAY G&CC
  Whidbey Island, Washington
  William Teufel
UTRECHT GC
  Utrecht, Netherlands
  H. S. Colt, C. H. Alison, J. S. F.
  Morrison
      (R.) J. J. F. Pennink

VACHE GRASSE CC
  Greenwood, Arkansas
  William M. Martin
VAIL GC
  Vail, Colorado
  Press Maxwell
VA-JO-WA GC
  Island Falls, Maine
  Vaughn Walker
      (A.9) *Warren Walker*
VAL DE CHER GC
  Montlucon, France
  M. Vigand
VALDERRAMA GC
  Cadiz, Spain
  Robert Trent Jones
VALDOSTA CC
  Valdosta, Georgia
  Joe Lee, Rocky Roquemore
VALE DO LOBO GC
  Portugal
  Henry Cotton
      (A.3rd 9) Henry Cotton
VALENCIA CC
  Valencia, California
  Robert Trent Jones
VAL HALLA CC
  Cumberland, Maine
  Phil Wogan
VALHALLA GC
  Louisville, Kentucky
  Jack Nicklaus
VALLEAIRE GC
  Hinckley, Ohio
  Harold Paddock
VALLE ALTO GC
  Monterrey, Mexico
  Lawrence Hughes
VALLE ARRIBA GC
  Venezuela
  James Baird Wilson
VALLEBROOK GC
  Lakefield, Minnesota
  Joel Goldstrand

VALLE GRANDE GC
Bakersfield, California
William P. Bell, William F. Bell
(A.9) William F. Bell

VALLE GRANDE GC
Bernalillo, New Mexico
Ken Killian

VALLE OAKS GC
Zephyr Hills, Florida
Ron Garl

VALLE VERDE CC [NLE]
Kingman, Arizona
Alex McLaren, Jock McLaren

VALLE VISTA CC
Kingman, Arizona
Fred Bolton

VALLE VISTA CC
Greenwood, Indiana
Bob Simmons

VALLEY C OF MONTECITO
Santa Barbara, California
Alister Mackenzie, Robert
Hunter
(R.) William P. Bell

VALLEY CC [NLE]
Scottsdale, Arizona
David Gill

VALLEY CC
Aurora, Colorado
William F. Bell
(R.) Dick Phelps
(R.) Gary Grandstaff

VALLEY CC
Valley, Nebraska
William B. Kubly

VALLEY CC
Hazelton, Pennsylvania
(R.) A.W. Tillinghast
(R.) Geoffrey S. Cornish

VALLEY CC
West Warwick, Rhode Island
W. H. "Pipe" Follett
(A.9) Geoffrey S. Cornish

VALLEY CC
Rizal, Philippines
Fred Smith, James D. Scott

VALLEY GC
Hines, Oregon
Shelby McCool

VALLEY BROOK CC
McMurray, Pennsylvania
Ferdinand Garbin
(R.) Robert Trent Jones

VALLEYBROOK G&CC
Hixson, Tennessee
Chic Adams

VALLEY FORGE GC
King of Prussia, Pennsylvania
Gordon Lewis

VALLEY FORGE VA HOSPITAL GC
Valley Forge, Pennsylvania
Alfred H. Tull

VALLEY GARDENS CC
Santa Cruz, California
Bob Baldock, Robert L. Baldock

VALLEY GREEN CC
Aurora, Illinois
Robert Bruce Harris

VALLEY GREEN GC
Greensburg, Pennsylvania
X. G. Hassenplug

VALLEY HI CC
Sacramento, California
William F. Bell

VALLEY HI GC
Colorado Springs, Colorado
Henry B. Hughes
(R.9) Dick Phelps
(R.) Frank Hummel

VALLEY HIGH GC
Houston, Minnesota
Homer Fieldhouse

VALLEY HILL CC
Huntsville, Alabama
(R.27) John LaFoy

VALLEY HILLS GC
Grain Valley, Missouri
Colonel John Davis

VALLEY INTERNATIONAL CC
Brownsville, Texas
Joseph S. Finger
(R.) *Dennis W. Arp*

VALLEY INTERNATIONAL CC (PAR 3
CSE)
Brownsville, Texas
Dennis W. Arp

VALLEY LEDGEMONT CC
West Warwick, Rhode Island
NKA Valley CC

VALLEY OAKS GC
Visalia, California
Robert Dean Putman

VALLEY OAKS GC
Clinton, Iowa
Robert Bruce Harris

VALLEY PINE GC
Lasker, North Carolina
Leo Green

VALLEY RANCH GC
Sun Valley, Idaho
Dick Phelps, Hale Irwin

VALLEY RIDGE GC
Calgary, Alberta
(A.9) Ken Dye

VALLEY SPRINGS GC
Oxen Hill, Maryland
Russell Roberts

VALLEY VIEW CC
White Sulphur Springs, West
Virginia
Russell Roberts

VALLEY VIEW GC
New Albany, Indiana
William H. Diddel
(A.9) Buck Blankenship

VALLEY VIEW GC
Bozeman, Montana
Theodore Wirth
(R.9 A.9) William G.
Robinson

VALLEY VIEW GC
Central City, Nebraska
Harold Glissmann

VALLEY VIEW GC
Fremont, Nebraska
Harold Glissmann

VALLEY VIEW GC [NLE]
Omaha, Nebraska
James Dalgleish

VALLEY VIEW GC
Utica, New York
(R.) Robert Trent Jones

VALLEY VIEW GC
Lancaster, Ohio
Harold Paddock

VALLEY VIEW GC
Layton, Utah
Joseph B. Williams, *William
Hull*

VALLEY VIEW GC
Moorefield, West Virginia
Russell Roberts

VALLROMANAS GC
Barcelona, Spain
Fred W. Hawtree

VAL MORIN GC
Quebec
(R.) Howard Watson
(A.9) Howard Watson, John
Watson

VAL NIEGETTE GC
Rimouski, Quebec
John Watson

VALPARAISO CC [NLE]
Valparaiso, Florida
William B. Langford, Theodore
J. Moreau

VALPARAISO CC
Valparaiso, Indiana
(R.9 A.9) John Darrah

VALPARAISO GC
Argentina
John "Jock" Anderson

VAN BUREN GC
Keosauqua, Iowa
NKA River View C

VAN BUSKIRK MUNI
Stockton, California
(A.9) Robert Muir Graves

VAN CORTLANDT PARK GC
Bronx, New York
T. McClure Peters
(R.9 A.9) Tom Bendelow
(R.) William F. Mitchell

VANCOUVER GC
Coquitlam, British Columbia
(R.) Clinton E. Robinson
(R.) *James P. Izatt*
(R.) William G. Robinson
(R.) John Steidel

VANDENBERG AFB GC
Vandenberg AFB, California
Robert Dean Putman

VANDERBILT ESTATE GC [NLE]
Manhasset, New York
Devereux Emmet, Alfred H. Tull

VAN NUYS GC (NORTH CSE)
Van Nuys, California
Joe Novak

VAN PATTEN GC
New York
James Thomson

VAN ZANDT CC
Canton, Texas
Leon Howard

VARA GC
Vara, Sweden
Jan Sederholm

VARBERG GC
Varberg, Sweden
Nils Sköld

VARESE GC
Varese, Italy
Charles Blandford
(R.) Donald Harradine

VARMERT GC
Kierspe, Germany
(A.9) Karl F. Grohs, *Rainer
Preissmann*

VÄRNAMO GC
Värnamo, Sweden
Nils Sköld

VASATORP GC
Helsingborg, Sweden
Ture Bruce

VASCO DA GAMA G RESORT
Cartaxo, Portugal
Bill Amick

VASHON ISLAND G&CC
Vashon, Washington
H. D. Williams
(R.) William Teufel

VASSAR G&CC
Vassar, Michigan
William Newcomb

VÄSTERÅS GC
Västerås, Sweden
Nils Sköld, Rafael Sundblum

VAUCOULEURS GC
Houdan, France
Michel Gayon

VAUGHN VALLEY GC
Ontario
René Muylaert

VAUGOUARD GC
France
P. Fromager, M. Adam

VÄXJÖ GC
Växjö, Sweden
Douglas Brazier

VECHTA GC
Vechta, Germany
Karl F. Grohs, *Rainer
Preissmann*

VEENKER MEMORIAL GC
Iowa State University, Ames,
Iowa
Perry Maxwell
(R. A.4) *Beryl Taylor*
(R.) Maury Miller

VEJLE GC
Vejle, Denmark
Frederic Dreyer
(R.) Jan Sederholm

VELDEN GC
Worthersee, Austria
Kurt Rossknecht

VENANGO TRAILS GC
Pittsburgh, Pennsylvania
James Gilmore Harrison

VENANGO VALLEY GC
Venango, Pennsylvania
Paul E. Erath

VENICE CC [NLE]
Venice, Florida
Carl H. Anderson

VENICE G&CC
Venice, Florida
Ted McAnlis

VENICE EAST GC
Venice, Florida
R. Albert Anderson

VENTANA CANYON G&RC (CANYON
CSE)
Tucson, Arizona
Tom Fazio

VENTANA CANYON G&RC
(MOUNTAIN CSE)
Tucson, Arizona
Tom Fazio

VENTNOR GC
Ventnor, England
Tom Dunn
(R.) J. Hamilton Stutt
VENTURA CC
Orlando, Florida
Mark Mahannah, Charles
Mahannah
VENTURA MUNI
Montalvo, California
William P. Bell
VERADERA BEACH CC [NLE]
Havana, Cuba
Herbert Strong
VERDAE GREENS GC
Greenville, South Carolina
Willard Byrd
VERDE VALLEY RANCH GC
Clarkdale, Arizona
Jeff Hardin
VEREENIGING CC
Transvaal, South Africa
C. H. Alison
VER HOVEN CC
Memphis, Michigan
Emil Beck
VERMILLION HILLS CC
Danville, Illinois
Edward Lawrence Packard,
Brent Wadsworth
VERNON G&CC
Vernon, British Columbia
Tom Bendelow
(R.5) Ernest Brown
VERNON HILLS CC
Mount Vernon, New York
Devereux Emmet
VERNON HILLS GC
Vernon Hills, Illinois
Ken Killian, Dick Nugent
(R.) Dick Nugent
VERNON VALLEY CC
Vernon, New Jersey
Nicholas Psiahas
VERNONIA G&CC
Vernonia, Oregon
George Junor
VERO BEACH CC
Vero Beach, Florida
Herbert Strong
(R.) Chuck Ankrom
VERONA GC
Verona, Italy
John Harris
VERSILIA GC
Italy
Marco Croze
VERULAM GC
England
(R.) James Braid
VESPER CC
Tyngsboro, Massachusetts
Alex Findlay
(R.9 A.9) Donald Ross
(R.) Manny Francis
(R.) Orrin Smith
VESPER HILLS CC
Otisco, New York
Geoffrey S. Cornish, William G.
Robinson
VESTAL HILLS CC [NLE]
Binghamton, New York
(R.) Robert Trent Jones

VESTAL HILLS CC
Binghamton, New York
Geoffrey S. Cornish
VESTAVIA CC
Vestavia, Alabama
(R.) George W. Cobb
(R.) John LaFoy
VESTFOLD GC
Vestfold, Norway
J. J. F. Pennink
(A.9) Jan Sederholm
VESTISCHER GC
Recklinghausen, Germany
Donald Harradine
(R.) Karl F. Grohs, *Rainer
Preissmann*
VETERANS MEMORIAL GC
Springfield, Massachusetts
Geoffrey S. Cornish
VETERANS MEMORIAL GC
Walla Walla, Washington
Frank James
VETLANDA GC
Vetlanda, Sweden
Jan Sederholm
VIA VERDE CC
San Dimas, California
Lawrence Hughes
VIBORG GC
Viborg, Denmark
Jan Sederholm
VICHY G&CC
Vichy, France
Jim Engh
VICTOR HILLS GC
Victor, New York
Pete Craig
VICTORIA CC
Victoria, Texas
George Hoffman
(A.9) John Bredemus
(R.) Joseph S. Finger, Baxter
Spann
VICTORIA GC
Riverside, California
Charles Maud, *Colonel W. E.
Pedley*
(R.) Walter G. Fovargue
(R.9 A.9) Max Behr
(R.) William P. Bell
(R.3) William H. Johnson
VICTORIA GC
Oak Bay, British Columbia
Harvey Coombe
(R.) A. Vernon Macan
(R.) Gary Panks
(R.) William G. Robinson,
John F. Robinson
VICTORIA GC
Cheltenham, Australia
Alister Mackenzie
(R.) Peter Thomson, Michael
Wolveridge
VICTORIA MUNI
Carson, California
William F. Bell
VICTORIA ESTATES GC
Port Charlotte, Florida
Ward Northrup
VICTORIA PARK GC (EAST CSE)
Guelph, Ontario
René Muylaert

VICTORIA PARK GC (WEST CSE)
Guelph, Ontario
René Muylaert
VICTORY HILLS CC
Kansas City, Kansas
James Dalgleish
VIEILLE TOULOUSE GC
Toulouse, France
F. W. Hawtree
(A.9) Michael G. Fenn
VIENNA GC
Vienna, Austria
Willie Park, Jr.
VIERUMÄKI GC
Finland
Jan Sederholm
VIKSJÖ GC
Viksjö, Sweden
Nils Sköld
VILA ANICA GC
Lagos, Portugal
Howard Swan
VILAMOURA GC
Algarve, Portugal
J. J. F. Pennink
VILAMOURA II GC
Algarve, Portugal
J. J. F. Pennink
(R. A.5) Robert Trent Jones
VILAMOURA III GC
Algarve, Portugal
Joe Lee, Rocky Roquemore
VILA SOL GC
Algarve, Portugal
D. M. A. Steel
VILLA CONDULMER GC
Venice, Italy
John Harris
(A.9) Marco Croze
VILLA DELRAY CC
Delray Beach, Florida
Frank Batto
VILLA DE PAZ CC
Phoenix, Arizona
Jeff Hardin, Greg Nash
VILLA D'ESTE GC
Como, Italy
James Gannon
(R.) John Harris
VILLA DU PARC CC
Mequon, Wisconsin
David Gill
(A.3rd 9) *Robert Chamberlain*
VILLA NOVA DE CACELA GC
Algarve, Portugal
Jack Nicklaus
VILLAGE CC
Lompoc, California
Ted Robinson
(R.) Stephen Halsey, Jack
Daray, Jr.
VILLAGE CC
Dallas, Texas
Press Maxwell
VILLAGE GREEN CC
Mundelein, Illinois
William B. Langford
VILLAGE GREEN G&CC
Inman, South Carolina
Russell Breeden
VILLAGE GREEN GC
Bradenton, Florida
William B. Lewis

VILLAGE GREEN GC
Sarasota, Florida
William B. Lewis
VILLAGE GREEN GC
Tavares, Florida
William B. Lewis
VILLAGE GREEN GC
Newaygo, Michigan
Bob Frain
VILLAGE GREEN GC
Syracuse, New York
Hal Purdy, Malcolm Purdy
VILLAGE GREEN GC
North Kingsville, Ohio
J. Thomas Francis
VILLAGE GREEN GC
Green Bay, Wisconsin
Robert Bruce Harris
VILLAGE GREENS CC
Gramling, South Carolina
Russell Breeden, *Dan Breeden*
VILLAGE GREENS GC
Ozaukie, Kansas
Buck Blankenship
(A.9) L. J. "Dutch" McClellan
VILLAGE GREENS OF WOODRIDGE
Woodridge, Illinois
Robert Bruce Harris
VILLAGE INN GC
McHenry, Maryland
Dominic Palombo
VILLAGE LINKS OF GLEN ELLYN
Glen Ellyn, Illinois
David Gill
VILLAGE OF OAK CREEK CC
Sedona, Arizona
Robert Trent Jones
VILLAGES AT COUNTRY CREEK GC
Estero, Florida
Gordon G. Lewis
[THE] VILLAGES G&CC
San Jose, California
Robert Muir Graves
(R.) Robert Muir Graves
VILLARS GC
Villars, Switzerland
(R.9) Donald Harradine
VILLA LA MOTTA GC
Travedona Monate, Italy
Pier Mancinelli
VILLA MONTERREY CC [NLE]
Scottsdale, Arizona
Milt Coggins
VILLA MONTERREY CC
Scottsdale, Arizona
Arthur Jack Snyder
VILLA OLIVIA CC
Bartlett, Illinois
Tom Bendelow
(R.) Bob Lohmann
(R.) Ken Killian, Dick Nugent
VILLA REAL GC [NLE]
Havana, Cuba
Dick Wilson
VILLA ROMA CC
Callicoon, New York
Lindsay Ervin (routing), *David
Postlethwait*
VILLERAY GC
St. Pierre de Perray, France
Hubert Chesneau, J. Bourret
VIMEIRO GC
Praia do Porto Novo, Portugal
J. F. F. Pennink

[THE] VINES G&CC
Fort Myers, Florida
Gordon G. Lewis

[THE] VINEYARD GC
Cincinnati, Ohio
Michael Hurdzan, Jack Kidwell

VINEYARDS G&CC (NORTH CSE)
Naples, Florida
Mark McCumber

VINEYARDS G&CC (SOUTH CSE)
Naples, Florida
Bill Amick

VINEYARDS GC
St. Helena, California
Bob Baldock, Robert L. Baldock

VINOY PARK C
St. Petersburg, Florida
David Gill

[THE] VINTAGE C (DESERT CSE)
Indian Wells, California
Tom Fazio

[THE] VINTAGE C (MOUNTAIN CSE)
Indian Wells, California
Tom Fazio

[THE] VINTAGE C
Bangkok, Thailand
Arthur Hills

VIRGINIA CC
Long Beach, California
William P. Bell
   (R.) Edward B. Dearie, Jr.
   (R.) Robert Muir Graves

VIRGINIA CC
Virginia, Illinois
Robert Bruce Harris

VIRGINIA GC
County Caven, Ireland
Tom Travers

VIRGINIA TECH GC
Blacksburg, Virginia
Buddy Loving

VISALIA CC
Visalia, California
   (R.) Desmond Muirhead
   (R.) Robert Muir Graves
   (R.) Robert Dean Putman

VISALIA PLAZA GC
Visalia, California
Robert Dean Putman
   (R.) Richard Bigler

VISBY GC
Sweden
Nils Sköld

VISTA CHICA GC
Valencia, California
Terry E. Van Gorder (9 Par 3)

VISTA HERMOSA GC
Cadiz, Spain
John Harris

VISTA HILLS CC
El Paso, Texas
Robert von Hagge, Bruce Devlin

VISTA PLANTATION GC
Vero Beach, Florida
Arthur Hills

VISTA ROYALE GC
Vero Beach, Florida
Arthur Hills
   (A.3rd 9) Arthur Hills

VISTA VALENCIA GC
Valencia, California
Terry E. Van Gorder (Precision)

VISTA VALLEY CC
Vista, California
Ted Robinson

VISTA VIEW VILLAGE GC
Zanesville, Ohio
Jack Kidwell

[THE] VISTAS C
Peoria, Arizona
Ken Kavanaugh

VITTEL GC
Vosges, France
James Braid

VIVARY GC
England
J. Hamilton Stutt

VIZCAYA CC
Miami, Florida
Frank Murray

VOLCANO G&CC
Volcano National Park, Hawaii
   (R.9 A.9) Arthur Jack Snyder

VOYAGER VILLAGE GC
Danbury, Wisconsin
William James Spear

VULPERA GC
Vulpera, Switzerland
Gordon Spencer

VUOKATTI GC
Sotkamo, Finland
Jan Sederholm

VFW GC
Indiana, Pennsylvania
James Gilmore Harrison
   (A.9) Edmund B. Ault

WABAMUN LAKE GC
Wabamun Lake, Alberta
Les Furber, *Jim Eremko*

WABASH VALLY GC
Geneva, Indiana
   (R.8 A.10) Gary Kern, Ron Kern

WABEEK CC
Bloomfield Hills, Michigan
Pete Dye, Jack Nicklaus, Roy Dye

WACCABUC CC
Waccabuc, New York
George Gullen, Fred Studwell (1912)
   (R.) Alfred H. Tull

WACHESAW PLANTATION GC
Pawleys Island, South Carolina
Tom Fazio

WACHUSETT CC
West Boylston, Massachusetts
Donald Ross

WACK WACK G&CC (EAST CSE)
Manila, Philippines
James Black
   (R.) Ron Kirby, Denis Griffiths

WACK WACK G&CC (WEST CSE)
Philippines
James Black

WADE HAMPTON GC
Cashiers, North Carolina
Tom Fazio

WADENA GC
Wadena, Minnesota
   (R.9) Don Herfort

WADESBORO CC [NLE]
Wadesboro, North Carolina
Arthur Ham

WAGON WHEEL GC
Rockton, Illinois
Edward Lawrence Packard

WAHCONAH CC
Dalton, Massachusetts
Wayne Stiles
   (A.9) Geoffrey S. Cornish, Rowland Armacost

WAIALAE CC
Honolulu, Oahu, Hawaii
Seth Raynor, Charles Banks
   (R.) Bob Baldock
   (R.3) Arthur Jack Snyder
   (R.) Robin Nelson, Rodney Wright
   (R.) Arnold Palmer, Ed Seay

WAIEHU MUNI
Waiehu, Maui, Hawaii
   (R.3) Arthur Jack Snyder

WAIKAPU SANDALWOOD G CSE
Wailuku, Maui, Hawaii
Robin Nelson, Rodney Wright

WAIKAPU VALLEY CC
Wailuku, Maui, Hawaii
Ted Robinson

WAIKELE GC
Honolulu, Hawaii
Theodore Robinson

WAIKOLOA BEACH GC
Kamuela, Hawaii
Robert Trent Jones, Jr.
   (R.) Robert Trent Jones, Jr.

WAIKOLOA VILLAGE GC
Kamuela, Hawaii
Robert Trent Jones, Jr.
   (R.) Robert Trent Jones, Jr.

WAILEA GC (BLUE CSE)
Maui, Hawaii
Arthur Jack Snyder
   (R.) Robert Trent Jones, Jr.

WAILEA GC (ORANGE CSE)
Maui, Hawaii
Arthur Jack Snyder
   (R.) Robert Trent Jones, Jr.

WAILUA MUNI
Lihue, Kauai, Hawaii
   (A.9) *Toyo Shirai* (1962)

WAIRAKEI INTERNATIONAL GC
Taupo, New Zealand
John Harris, Peter Thomson

WAITIKIRI GC
Christchurch, New Zealand
A.R. Blank

WAITOMO GC
New Zealand
C. H. Redhead
   (R.) H. G. Babbage

WAKAGI GC
Kyushi, Japan
Desmond Muirhead

WAKASU G LINKS
Tokyo, Japan
Ayako Okamoto

WAKEFIELD GC
Wakefield, England
Sandy Herd

WAKONDA C
Des Moines, Iowa
William B. Langford, Theodore J. Moreau
   (R.) Dick Nugent

WAKE FOREST CC
Wake Forest, North Carolina
Gene Hamm

WAKURA GC
Ishikawa, Japan
Tsuneo Tanaka

WALDEMERE HOTEL GC
Livingston Manor, New York
William F. Mitchell

WALDEN GC
Crofton, Maryland
Robert Trent Jones
   (R.9 A.9) Lindsay Ervin

WALDEN G&TC
Aurora, Ohio
William F. Mitchell

WALDEN LAKE POLO & CC
Plant City, Florida
Bob Cupp, Jay Morrish
   (A.3rd 9) Ron Garl

WALDEN ON LAKE CONROE CC
Montgomery, Texas
Robert von Hagge, Bruce Devlin

WALDEN ON LAKE HOUSTON GC
Humble, Texas
Robert von Hagge, Bruce Devlin

WALKING STICK GC
Pueblo, Colorado
Arthur Hills

WALLASEY GC
Cheshire, England
Old Tom Morris
   (R.) *Harold Hilton*
   (R.) James Braid, John R. Stutt
   (R.) *W. H. Davies*

WALLA WALLA CC
Walla Walla, Washington
W. W. Baker
   (A.9) Frank James
   (R.4) John Steidel
   (R.) Robert Muir Graves

WALLED LAKE CC
Walled Lake, Michigan
Harry Collis

WALLINGFORD CC
Wallingford, Connecticut
   (R.) Al Zikorus

WALLINWOOD SPRINGS GC
Jenison, Michigan
Jerry Matthews

WALLOON LAKE CC
Walloon Lake, Michigan
   (A.9) Jerry Matthews

WALNUT CREEK CC
South Lyon, Michigan
   (R.) Arthur Hills

WALNUT CREEK CC
Goldsboro, North Carolina
Ellis Maples

WALNUT CREEK CC
Oklahoma City, Oklahoma
Don January, Billy Martindale
   (R.9) Tom Clark

WALNUT CREEK GC
Mansfield, Texas
Don January, Billy Martindale
   (A.3rd 9) *Don Prigmore, Stan Wreyford*

WALNUT GROVE CC
Dayton, Ohio
William H. Diddel

WALNUT GROVE GC
New Albany, Indiana
William H. Diddel
WALNUT HILL CC
Columbus, Ohio
James Gilmore Harrison
WALNUT HILLS CC
East Lansing, Michigan
Joseph A. Roseman
(R.2) Bruce Matthews, Jerry
Matthews
(R.4) Jerry Matthews
(R.) Jeff Gorney
WALNUT HILLS CC
Oklahoma City, Oklahoma
Floyd Farley
(R.) Alfred H. Tull
WALNUT HILLS CC [NLE]
Fort Worth, Texas
Perry Maxwell
WALNUT HILLS GC
Chicago, Illinois
Stanley Pelchar
WALNUT LANE GC
Philadelphia, Pennsylvania
Alex Findlay
WALNUT WOODS CC
Gobles, Michigan
Warner Bowen
(A.9) *Ray Sudekis*
WALPOLE CC [NLE]
Walpole, Massachusetts
Skip Wogan
WALPOLE CC
Walpole, Massachusetts
Al Zikorus
WALSALL GC
Staffordshire, England
Alister Mackenzie
WALT DISNEY WORLD GC
(MAGNOLIA CSE)
Lake Buena Vista, Florida
Joe Lee, Rocky Roquemore
WALT DISNEY WORLD GC (PALM
CSE)
Lake Buena Vista, Florida
Joe Lee, Rocky Roquemore
WALT DISNEY WORLD GC (WEE
LINKS)
Lake Buena Vista, Florida
Ron Garl
WALTER E. HALL G CSE
Everett, Washington
(R.) John Steidel
WALTER NAGORSKI G CSE
Fort Shafter, Oahu, Hawaii
Willard Wilkinson
WALTER PEAK RESORT GC
New Zealand
Arnold Palmer, Ed Seay
WALTHAM CC [NLE]
Waltham, Massachusetts
Donald Ross
WALTHAM ABBEY GC
Hertfordshire, England
Howard Swan
WALTHOUR GC [NLE]
Savannah, Georgia
Donald Ross
WALTON HALL GC
Cheshire, England
J. J. F. Pennink

WALTON HEATH GC (NEW CSE)
Surrey, England
Herbert Fowler
WALTON HEATH GC (OLD CSE)
Surrey, England
Herbert Fowler
WAMEGO CC
Wamego, Kansas
"Chick" Trout (9 1922)
WAMPANOAG CC
West Hartford, Connecticut
Donald Ross
(R.) William F. Mitchell
(R.5) Geoffrey S. Cornish,
Brian Silva
WAMPATUCK CC
Canton, Massachusetts
Geoffrey S. Cornish
WANAKAH CC
Hamburg, New York
(R.) Bob Cupp, Jay Morrish
WANANGO CC
Reno, Pennsylvania
Donald Ross
(A.9) Tom Bendelow
(R.) A.W. Tillinghast
(R.) Ferdinand Garbin
WANGANUI GC
New Zealand
(R.) C. H. Redhead
WANNAMOISETT CC [NLE]
Rumford, Rhode Island
Willie Campbell
WANNAMOISETT CC
Rumford, Rhode Island
Donald Ross
(R.) Donald Ross
WANTAGE G CENTER
New Jersey
Nicholas Psiahas
WANUMETONOMY CC
Middletown, Rhode Island
Seth Raynor
WAPSIPINICON GC
Independence, Iowa
Tom Bendelow
WARKWORTH GC
Warkworth, Ontario
Gordon Witteveen
WARLEY PARK GC
Essex, England
R. Plumbridge
WAR MEMORIAL PARK GC
Little Rock, Arkansas
Herman Hackbarth
WARMLEY GC
England
Neil Coles, *Brian Huggett, Roger
Dyer*
WARM SPRINGS GC
Fremont, California
Jack Fleming
WARM SPRINGS GC
Warm Springs, Georgia
NKA Roosevelt GC
WARNER ROBINS AFB GC
Macon, Georgia
Hugh Moore
(R.) Arthur Davis, Ron Kirby
WARNER SPRINGS RANCH GC
Warner Springs, California
Harry Rainville, David Rainville

WARREN C
Singapore
(R.6 A.12) Ronald Fream
WARREN GC
Cheshire, England
J. H. Taylor
WARRENBROOK CC
Plainfield, New Jersey
Hal Purdy
WARREN HILLS GC
Salisbury, Zimbabwe
Robert G. Grimsdell
WARREN MEADOWS CC
Bowling Green, Kentucky
Bob Baldock, Robert L. Baldock
WARREN PARK GC
Illinois
Ken Killian, Dick Nugent
WARRENSBURG CC
Warrensburg, Missouri
Chet Mendenhall
WARREN SWIGGART GC
Omaha, Nebraska
Harold Glissmann
WARREN VALLEY CC (EAST CSE)
Wayne, Michigan
Donald Ross
(R.) Gary Roger Baird
WARREN VALLEY CC (WEST CSE)
Wayne, Michigan
Donald Ross
(R.) Gary Roger Baird
WARRINGTON CC
Cheshire, England
J. J. F. Pennink
(R.) J. J. F. Pennink
WARRINGTON CC
Warrington, Pennsylvania
William Gordon, David Gordon
WARRIORS PATH STATE PARK GC
Kingsport, Tennessee
George W. Cobb
WARSAW GC
England
Sir Guy Campbell, C. K.
Hutchison, S. V. Hotchkin
WARWICK CC
Warwick, Rhode Island
Donald Ross
(A.9) Geoffrey S. Cornish
WARWICK CC
Warwickshire, England
D. G. Dunkley
WARWICK HILLS G&CC
Grand Blanc, Michigan
James Gilmore Harrison,
Ferdinand Garbin
(R.) Joe Lee
WASAGA GC
Lake Huron, Ontario
Stanley Thompson
WASATCH MOUNTAIN GC
Midway, Utah
William H. Neff
(A.3rd 9) William H. Neff,
William Howard Neff
WASCANA G&CC
Regina, Saskatchewan
J. Kelso Hunter
(R.) Clinton E. Robinson
(R.) William G. Robinson,
John F. Robinson

WASCO VALLEY ROSE G CSE
Wasco, California
Robert Dean Putman
WASHINGTON CC
Washington Court House, Ohio
George Sargent
WASHINGTON G&CC
Arlington, Virginia
Donald Ross
(R.) Fred Findlay
(R.) Al Jamison
(R.) William S. Flynn
(R.5) Buddy Loving, Algie
Pulley
(R.) Tom Clark, Edmund B.
Ault, Brian Ault
WASHINGTON GC
Washington, Connecticut
Al Zikorus
WASHINGTON GC
Dunham, England
John Harris
WASHINGTON PARK CC [NLE]
Chicago, Illinois
H. J. Tweedie
WASHINGTON PARK MUNI
Racine, Wisconsin
Tom Bendelow
WASHINGTON STATE UNIVERSITY
GC
Pullman, Washington
Robert Muir Graves
WASHINGTON WILKES CC
Washington, Georgia
Donald Ross (routing)
(R.9) *Walter Ripley*
WASHINGTON YACHT & CC
Washington, North Carolina
William Gordon
(R.2 A.9) Gene Hamm
WASHINGTONIAN CC (COUNTRY
CLUB COURSE)
Gaithersburg, Maryland
Frank Murray, Russell Roberts
WASHINGTONIAN CC (NATIONAL
CSE)
Gaithersburg, Maryland
Frank Murray, Russell Roberts
WASHTENAW CC
Ypsilanti, Michigan
(R.1) Bruce Matthews, Jerry
Matthews
(R.5) Jerry Matthews
WASKESIU LAKE GC
Saskatchewan
Stanley Thompson
(R.) Clinton E. Robinson
WATERFORD GC
Venice, Florida
Ted McAnlis
WATERFORD GC
Warner Robins, Georgia
Don Cottle
WATERFORD GC
County Waterford, Ireland
Willie Park, Jr.
(R.9 A.9) James Braid, John
R. Stutt
(A.9) Cecil Barcroft
(R.) Eddie Hackett
(R.) J. Hamilton Stutt
WATERFORD PARK GC
Chester, West Virginia
X. G. Hassenplug

WATERLOO GC
Grass Lake, Michigan
Floyd Hammond (9 1962)
WATERLOO GC
Galt, Ontario
(R.) Stanley Thompson
WATER OAK GC
Leesburg, Florida
Mel Bishop
WATER'S EDGE GC
Penhook, Virginia
Buddy Loving
WATERTON LAKES GC
Waterton Lakes National Park,
Alberta
(R.) Stanley Thompson
WATERTOWN CC
Watertown, Wisconsin
(A.9) Edward Lawrence
Packard, Brent Wadsworth
WATERTOWN GC
Watertown, Connecticut
(R.) William F. Mitchell
(A.9) Geoffrey S. Cornish,
William G. Robinson
WATERVILLE CC
Waterville, Maine
Orrin Smith
(A.9) Geoffrey S. Cornish,
William G. Robinson
WATERVILLE G LINKS
County Kerry, Ireland
Eddie Hackett
WATERWAY HILLS GC
Myrtle Beach, South Carolina
Rees Jones
WATERWOOD GC
Ocean City, Delaware
Reginauld Giddings
WATERWOOD NATIONAL GC
Huntsville, Texas
Roy Dye
WATONA PARK G CSE
Madelia, Minnesota
Joel Goldstrand
WAUBEEKA SPRINGS G LINKS
Williamstown, Massachusetts
Rowland Armacost
WAUKEGAN WILLOW GC [NLE]
Techny, Illinois
Leonard Macomber
WAUKEWAN GC
Center Harbor, New Hampshire
Melvyn D. Hale
WAUKON G&CC
Waukon, Iowa
Charles Calhoun
WAUMBEK VILLAGE GC
New Hampshire
Willie Norton
(R.9 A.9) A. H. Fenn
(R.) Ralph Barton
WAUSAU GC
Wausau, Wisconsin
Edward Lawrence Packard
WAVELAND GC
Chicago, Illinois
Joseph A. Roseman
(R.9) Edward B. Dearie, Jr.

WAVELAND GC
Des Moines, Iowa
Tom Bendelow
(A.9) *Warren Dickenson*
(R.) Paul Coates
(R.) Edward Lawrence
Packard
WAVE OAK CC
Waverly, Pennsylvania
James Gilmore Harrison
WAVERLEY CC
Portland, Oregon
Jack Moffett
(R.) H. Chandler Egan
(R.) A. Vernon Macan
(R.) *William Junor*
(R.1) Robert Muir Graves
WAVERLY GC
Waverly, Iowa
(R.9 A.9) Dick Phelps
WAVERTON GC
England
D. M. A. Steel
WAWASEE GC
Syracuse, Indiana
Tom Bendelow
(R.9 A.9) William H. Diddel
WAWASHKAMO GC
Mackinac Island, Michigan
Alex Smith
(R.) *Frank Dufina*
WAWENOCK GC
Damariscotta, Maine
Wayne Stiles, John Van Kleek
WAWONA HOTEL GC
Yosemite, California
Walter G. Fovargue
WAWONOWIN CC
Ishpeming, Michigan
Tom Bendelow
(A.9) *Robert W. Bills, Donald
L. Childs*
WAYLAND CC
Wayland, Massachusetts
(R.) William F. Mitchell
WAYNE CC
Wayne, Nebraska
Henry B. Hughes, Richard
Watson
WAYNE CC [NLE]
Wayne, New Jersey
Robert Trent Jones
WAYNE CC
Lyons, New York
Edward Lawrence Packard,
Brent Wadsworth
(A.9) Edward Lawrence
Packard
WAYNE G CENTRE
Wayne, New Jersey
Nicholas Psiahas
WAYNE PUBLIC GC
Bothel, Washington
Al Smith
WAYNESBORO CC
Waynesboro, Georgia
George W. Cobb
(A.9) George W. Cobb, John
LaFoy
WAYNESBORO CC
Waynesboro, Mississippi
Earl Stone

WAYNESBORO CC
Waynesboro, Pennsylvania
Edmund B. Ault
WAYNESBORO CC
Waynesboro, Virginia
Fred Findlay
WAYNESBOROUGH CC
Paoli, Pennsylvania
George Fazio
WAYNESVILLE CC
Waynesville, North Carolina
Donald Ross (routing); *John
Drake*
(R.) *Ross Taylor*
(A.3rd 9) Tom Jackson
WAYZATA CC
Wayzata, Minnesota
Robert Bruce Harris
(R.) Geoffrey S. Cornish,
Brian Silva
WEAKLEY COUNTY CC
Sharon, Tennessee
George C. Curtis
WEATHERFORD GC
Weatherford, Oklahoma
Labron Harris, Sr.
WEATHERWAX GC (HIGHLANDS
CSE)
Middletown, Ohio
Arthur Hills
WEATHERWAX GC (MEADOWS CSE)
Middletown, Ohio
Arthur Hills
WEBB BROOK GC
Burlington, Massachusetts
William F. Mitchell
WEBB HILL GC
Wolfe City, Texas
Dave Bennett, Leon Howard
WEBB MEMORIAL GC
Baton Rouge, Louisiana
E. E. Evans, Al Michael
WEBER PARK GC
Skokie, Illinois
Ken Killian, Dick Nugent
WEBHANNETT GC
Kennebunkport, Maine
Skip Wogan
(R.4) Geoffrey S. Cornish,
William G. Robinson
WEDGEFIELD PLANTATION GC
North Georgetown, South
Carolina
J. Porter Gibson
WEDGEWOOD CC
Cabool, Missouri
Floyd Farley
WEDGEWOOD CC
Wilson, North Carolina
Edmund B. Ault
WEDGEWOOD CC
Medina, Ohio
Ed Bowers, Larry Fink
WEDGEWOOD G&CC
Lakeland, Florida
(R.) Ron Garl
WEDGEWOOD G&CC
Powell, Ohio
Robert Trent Jones, Jr.
WEDGEWOOD GC
Joliet, Illinois
Edward Lawrence Packard

WEDGEWOOD GC
Allentown, Pennsylvania
William Gordon, David Gordon
WEDGEWOOD GC
Conroe, Texas
Robert von Hagge, Bruce Devlin
(routing); Ron Pritchard, *Bill
Rogers*
WEDGEWOOD PARK CC
Port Elizabeth, South Africa
Robert Grimsdell
WEE BURN CC
Darien, Connecticut
Devereux Emmet
(R.4) Geoffrey S. Cornish,
William G. Robinson
WEEKS PARK G CSE
Wichita Falls, Texas
(R.10) Jeff Brauer
WEE-MA-TUK HILLS CC
Cuba, Illinois
Robert L. Jordan
WEEQUAHIC GC
Newark, New Jersey
George Low
(A.9) Hal Purdy
WEIDEN GC
Weiden, Germany
Reinhold Weishaupt
WEIDENBRUCK-GUTERSLOH GC
Germany
Bernhard von Limburger
WEIR PARK GC
Devonshire, England
James Braid
WEKIVA GC
Longwood, Florida
Ward Northrup
WELCOMBE HOTEL GC
Stratford-on-Avon, England
T. J. A. Macauley
WELD GC
Massachusetts
Wayne Stiles, John Van Kleek
WELKOM MUNI
South Africa
Ron Kirby, Denis Griffiths
WELLAND CC
Ontario, Ontario
Walter J. Travis
WELLESLEY CC
Wellesley, Massachusetts
Donald Ross
(R.9) Wayne Stiles
(A.9) Geoffrey S. Cornish
WELLINGBOROUGH GC
Northhamptonshire, England
Tom Williamson
(R.9 A.9) Fred W. Hawtree,
A. H. F. Jiggens, Martin Haw-
tree
WELLINGTON GC
West Palm Beach, Florida
Ted McAnlis
(R.) Johnny Miller, Gene
Bates
WELLINGTON GC
Wellington, New Zealand
J. S. Watson
WELLMAN CC
Johnsonville, South Carolina
Ellis Maples

WELLS GC
Gloucestershire, England
F. G. Hawtree
WELLS-BY-THE-SEA GC
England
F. G. Hawtree, J. H. Taylor
WELLSHIRE GC
Englewood, Colorado
Donald Ross
WELSCHAPSE DYK GC
Netherlands
J. F. Dudok van Heel
WELSHPOOL GC
Powys, Wales
James Braid, John R. Stutt
WELS GC
Weisskirchen, Austria
Gerold Hausen, *Günther Hauser*
(R.9 A.9) Herwig Zisser
WELWYN GARDEN CITY GC
Hertfordshire, England
F. G. Hawtree, J. H. Taylor
(R.) Fred W. Hawtree, Martin
Hawtree
WEMBLEY GC
Wembley, England
Willie Park, Jr.
WENATCHEE CC
Wenatchee, Washington
(A.9) A. Vernon Macan
WENDELL CC
Wendell, North Carolina
Ken Dye
WENHAM GC
Wenham, Massachusetts
(R.) Orrin Smith
WENTWORTH G&CC
Tarpon Springs, Florida
Steve Smyers
WENTWORTH GC
Ile Perrot, Quebec
Howard Watson
WENTWORTH GC (EAST CSE)
Surrey, England
H. S. Colt, C. H. Alison, J. S. F.
Morrison
WENTWORTH GC (SHORT NINE)
Surrey, England
C. K. Cotton, J. J. F. Pennink
WENTWORTH GC (WEST CSE)
Surrey, England
H. S. Colt, C. H. Alison, J. S. F.
Morrison
WENTWORTH-BY-THE-SEA GC
[NLE]
Portsmouth, New Hampshire
Alex Findlay
WENTWORTH-BY-THE-SEA GC
Portsmouth, New Hampshire
Donald Ross
(A.11) Geoffrey S. Cornish,
William G. Robinson
(R.) Bill Amick
WENTWORTH RESORT GC
Jackson, New Hampshire
(R.9 A.9) Wayne Stiles
WEPAUG CC
Orange, Connecticut
(R.13) Al Zikorus
WERMDÖ GC
Sweden
Nils Sköld

WESELERWALD GC
Schermbeck, Germany
Wolfgang Siegmann
WESSELMAN PAR 3 GC
Evansville, Indiana
Edmund B. Ault
WESTBANK RANCH G CSE
Glenwood Springs, Colorado
Dick Phelps
WEST BEND CC
West Bend, Wisconsin
William B. Langford, Theodore
J. Moreau
(A.9) David Gill
(R.) Roger Packard
(R.) Bob Lohmann
WEST BOGGS MUNI
Lakeview, Indiana
Edmund B. Ault
WEST BOLTON GC
West Bolton, Vermont
Marty Keene, Xen Wheeler
WESTBOROUGH CC
St. Louis, Missouri
Tom Bendelow
(R.) Gary Kern, Ron Kern
WEST BRANCH CC
West Branch, Michigan
William Newcomb
WESTBROOK CC
Great River, New York
Willie Dunn, Jr.
WESTBROOK VILLAGE CC
Peoria, Arizona
Ted Robinson
WEST BYFLEET GC
Surrey, England
C. S. Butchart
(R.) J. S. F. Morrison
WESTCHASE GC
Tyler, Texas
(R.) *Lee Singletary*
WEST CHASE GC
Tampa, Florida
Lloyd Clifton, *Kenneth Ezell,*
George Clifton
WESTCHESTER CC (SOUTH CSE)
Rye, New York
Walter J. Travis
(R.) William S. Flynn
(R.) Perry Maxwell
(R.) Tom Winton
(R.) Rees Jones
(R.) Stephen Kay
WESTCHESTER CC (WEST CSE)
Rye, New York
Walter J. Travis
(R.) William S. Flynn
(R.) Alfred H. Tull
(R.) Joseph S. Finger
(R.) Rees Jones
WESTCHESTER G&CC (REGULATION
CSE)
Boynton Beach, Florida
Karl Litten
WESTCHESTER G&CC (PAR 3 CSE)
Boynton Beach, Florida
Karl Litten
WESTCHESTER HILLS CC
White Plains, New York
Pete Clark
(R.) Stephen Kay

WEST END CC
New Orleans, Louisiana
Tom Bendelow
WEST END GC
Gainesville, Florida
John E. O'Connor
WESTERN G&CC
Redford, Michigan
Donald Ross
(R.) Edward Lawrence
Packard
(R.) Arthur Hills
WESTERN AVENUE GC
Los Angeles, California
William P. Bell
WESTERN GAILES GC
Ayrshire, Scotland
Willie Park, Willie Park, Jr.
(R.4) Fred W. Hawtree
WESTERN GREENBRIER HILLS GC
Rainelle, West Virginia
(R.) George W. Cobb, John
LaFoy
WESTERN GREENS GC
Wright, Michigan
Mark DeVries
WESTERN HILLS CC
Little Rock, Arkansas
Herman Hackbarth
WESTERN HILLS G&CC
Chino, California
Harry Rainville, David Rainville
WESTERN HILLS GC
Waterbury, Connecticut
William Gordon, David Gordon
WESTERN HILLS GC
Cincinnati, Ohio
Tom Bendelow
(R.) William H. Diddel
WESTERN HILLS GC
Fort Worth, Texas
Leon Howard
WESTERN HILLS MUNI
Hopkinsville, Kentucky
Earl Stone
WESTERN ILLINOIS UNIVERSITY GC
[NLE]
Macomb, Illinois
Robert Bruce Harris
WESTERN ILLINOIS UNIVERSITY GC
Macomb, Illinois
Ken Killian, Dick Nugent
WESTERN MARYLAND COLLEGE GC
Westminster, Maryland
Edmund B. Ault
WESTERN MICHIGAN UNIVERSITY
GC
Kalamazoo, Michigan
David T. Millar
WESTERN PARK GC
Leicester, England
Fred W. Hawtree
(R. A.8) Martin Hawtree,
Simon Gidman
WESTERN ROW GC
Mason, Ohio
William H. Diddel
WESTERN TURNPIKE GC
Guilderland, New York
James Thomson
WESTERN VILLAGE GC [NLE]
Tulsa, Oklahoma
Floyd Farley

WESTERN WOODS GC
Michigan
Warner Bowen
WESTFAELISCHER GC
Gütersloh, Germany
Bernhard von Limburger
WESTFIELD CC (NORTH CSE)
Westfield Center, Ohio
Geoffrey S. Cornish, William G.
Robinson
WESTFIELD CC (SOUTH CSE)
Westfield Center, Ohio
Nelson Monical
(R. A.11) Geoffrey S.
Cornish, William G.
Robinson
WESTFIELD G&CC
New Brunswick
(R.9 A.9) Clinton E.
Robinson
(R.) John F. Robinson
WESTFIELD GC
Winona, Minnesota
(R.) Edward Lawrence
Packard, Brent Wadsworth
WESTHAMPTON CC
Westhampton Beach, New York
Seth Raynor
WESTHAMPTON CC (ONECK CSE)
[NLE]
Westhampton Beach, New York
Charles Banks
WEST HERTS GC
Hertfordshire, England
Old Tom Morris
(R.) Harry Vardon
(R.) Alister Mackenzie
WEST HILL CC
Camillus, New York
Hal Purdy
WESTHILL GC
Aberdeenshire, Scotland
J. J. F. Pennink, C. D. Lawrie
WEST HILLS CC
Canton, Ohio
Leonard Macomber
WEST HILLS G CSE
Nora Springs, Iowa
Larry Flatt
WEST HILLS MUNI [NLE]
Portland, Oregon
H. Chandler Egan
WEST HOVE GC (NEW CSE)
Sussex, England
Martin Hawtree, Simon Gidman
WEST HOVE GC (OLD CSE)
Sussex, England
James Braid
WEST KENT GC
Kent, England
Herbert Fowler, J. F.
Abercromby
WEST LAKE CC
Augusta, Georgia
Ellis Maples
(R.) John LaFoy
WESTLAKE CC
Jerseyville, Illinois
Edward Lawrence Packard,
Brent Wadsworth
WESTLAKE GC
Lakeside, South Africa
Dr. C. M. Murray

WESTLAKE VILLAGE GC
Westlake Village, California
Ted Robinson
WEST LAKES GC
Boca Raton, Florida
Frank Batto
WEST LANCASHIRE GC
England
(R.) Fred W. Hawtree
(R.) C. K. Cotton
WESTLAND GC
Westland, Michigan
(R.) Bill Newcomb
WESTLAND HILLS GC
Jordan, Utah
William H. Neff
WEST LINKS PUBLIC GC
Overland Park, Kansas
Craig Schreiner
WEST LOCH MUNI
Ewa Beach, Oahu, Hawaii
Robin Nelson, Rodney Wright
WESTLOCK GC
Westlock, Alberta
Les Furber, *Jim Eremko*
WEST LOTHIAN GC
Bo'ness, Scotland
Willie Park
(A.9) Fraser Middleton
WEST MALLING GC
Kent, England
Max Faulkner
WEST MEADOWS GC
Englewood, Colorado
Dick Phelps, Brad Benz
WEST MEADOWS GC
Jacksonville, Florida
Sam Caruso
WEST MIDDLESEX GC
Middlesex, England
Willie Park
(A.9) F. G. Hawtree, J. H.
Taylor
WESTMINSTER GC
Fitchburg, Massachusetts
Manny Francis
WESTMOOR GC
Brookfield, Wisconsin
(R.5) William B. Langford
(R.9) David Gill
(R.) Bob Lohmann
WESTMORELAND CC
Wilmette, Illinois
Joseph A. Roseman
(R.) William B. Langford
(R.) A. W. Tillinghast
(R.) William H. Diddel
(R.) Ken Killian, Dick Nugent
WESTMORELAND CC
Verona, Pennsylvania
NKA Green Oaks CC
WESTMORELAND CC
Export, Pennsylvania
Dick Wilson
(R.) Robert Trent Jones
(R. A.12) Joseph S. Finger
(R.) Ron Forse
WESTMORELAND G&CC
Sedalia, Missouri
Edward Lawrence Packard

WESTMOUNT G&CC
Kitchener, Ontario
Stanley Thompson
(R. A.4) Clinton E. Robinson
(R.3) Robert Moote, David
Moote
WEST ONE'S CC
Japan
Perry Dye
WESTON G&CC
Toronto, Ontario
Willie Park, Jr.
WESTON GC
Weston, Massachusetts
Donald Ross ,
(A.2) Geoffrey S. Cornish
(R.) Bob Cupp
WESTONBIRT GC
Gloucestershire, England
Monty Hearn
WESTON HILLS CC
Fort Lauderdale, Florida
Robert Trent Jones, Jr.
WESTON LAKES CC
Fulshear, Texas
Carlton Gipson
WESTON-SUPER-MARE GC
Somerset, England
Tom Dunn
(R.) Alister Mackenzie
WEST ORANGE CC [NLE]
Oakland, Florida
Tom Bendelow
WEST ORANGE GC
Winter Garden, Florida
Lloyd Clifton
WEST ORANGE MUNI [NLE]
West Caldwell, New Jersey
David S. Hunter
WEST OTTAWA GC
Holland, Michigan
Bruce Matthews, Jerry Matthews
WEST PALM BEACH CC [NLE]
West Palm Beach, Florida
William B. Langford, Theodore
J. Moreau
WEST PALM BEACH CC
West Palm Beach, Florida
Dick Wilson
(R.) Ward Northrup
WESTPARK HOTEL & GC
Leesburg, Virginia
Edmund B. Ault
WEST PLAINS CC
West Plains, Missouri
Marvin Ferguson
WEST POINT GC
US Military Academy, New York
Robert Trent Jones
WESTPORT GC
Westport, New York
Tom Winton
WESTPORT GC
Denver, North Carolina
J. Porter Gibson
WESTPORT GC
County Mayo, Ireland
Fred W. Hawtree, Martin Haw-
tree, A. H. F. Jiggens
(R.) Eddie Hackett
WEST POTOMAC PARK GC
Washington, D.C.
Walter J. Travis, Dr. Walter S.
Harban

WEST RIDGE G CSE
West Valley City, Utah
William Howard Neff
WEST RUNTON GC [NLE]
England
(R.) Tom Williamson
WEST SAYVILLE GC
Sayville, New York
William F. Mitchell
WEST SEATTLE GC
Seattle, Washington
H. Chandler Egan
(R.) Peter Thomson, Michael
Wolveridge, Ronald Fream
WEST SHORE CC
Camp Hill, Pennsylvania
George Morris
(A.9) *Jack Norrie, Earl Moyer*
WEST SHORE G&CC
Grosse Ile, Michigan
George B. Ferry
(R.5) Jerry Matthews
WESTSIDE GC
Firebaugh, California
Bob Baldock
WEST SURREY GC
Surrey, England
Herbert Fowler
(R.) J. S. F. Morrison
WEST SUSSEX GC
Sussex, England
Sir Guy Campbell, C. K.
Hutchison, S. V. Hotchkin
WESTVIEW CC
Miami, Florida
Dick Wilson
(A.9) Mark Mahannah
WESTVIEW CC
Marshfield, Wisconsin
Edward Lawrence Packard
WESTVIEW GC
Ontario
(R.) Robert Moote
(R.9 A.9) Robert Moote,
David S. Moote
WESTVIEW PARK GC
DuBois, Wyoming
Frank Hummel
WESTWARD HO CC [NLE]
Oak Park, Illinois
H. J. Tweedie
WESTWARD HO CC
Sioux Falls, South Dakota
Edward Lawrence Packard
(R.1) Dick Nugent
(R.) Don Sechrest
WEST WILMETTE ILLUMINATED GC
Wilmette, Illinois
Joseph A. Roseman
WEST WILTSHIRE GC
England
(R.) J. H. Taylor
(R.) *Brian Huggett*, Neil
Coles, *Roger Dyer*
WEST WINDS GC
George AFB, California
Bob Baldock
WESTWOOD CC
Marietta, Georgia
Charles M. Graves
WESTWOOD CC
New Castle, Indiana
(A.9) Gary Kern, Ron Kern

WESTWOOD CC
St. Louis, Missouri
Harold Paddock
(R.) William H. Diddel
(R.1) Marvin Ferguson
WESTWOOD CC
Woodbury, New Jersey
Horace W. Smith
WESTWOOD CC
Rocky River, Ohio
C. H. Alison, H. S. Colt
(R.) Michael Hurdzan
WESTWOOD CC
Houston, Texas
John Bredemus
(A.9) Ralph Plummer
(R.3 A.5) Joseph S. Finger
WESTWOOD CC
Vienna, Virginia
Alfred H. Tull
(R.) Edmund B. Ault, Brian
Ault, Tom Clark
WESTWOOD CC
Williamsville, New York
William Harries
(R.) Geoffrey S. Cornish
(R.) Robert Moote
WESTWOOD GC
Newton, Iowa
(A.9) David Gill
WESTWOOD GC [NLE]
Richmond, Virginia
(R.) Donald Ross
WESTWOOD GC
Staffordshire, England
J. Hamilton Stutt
WESTWOOD G CSE [NLE]
Durham, North Carolina
Ellis Maples
WESTWOOD HEIGHTS GC
Omaha, Nebraska
Harold Glissmann
WESTWOOD PARK GC
Norman, Oklahoma
Floyd Farley
WESTWOOD SHORES GC
Trinity, Texas
Carlton Gipson
WESTWOOD WEST GC
Yakima, Washington
Mel "Curley" Hueston
WESTWOODS CC
Farmington, Connecticut
Geoffrey S. Cornish
WETHERSFIELD CC
Wethersfield, Connecticut
Robert D. Pryde
(R.9 A.9) Robert J. Ross
(R.1) Geoffrey S. Cornish,
William G. Robinson
(R.) Geoffrey S. Cornish,
Brian Silva
WEWOKA MUNI
Wewoka, Oklahoma
NKA Dr. Gil Morgan G Cse
WEXFORD GC
Hilton Head Island, South
Carolina
Willard Byrd
WEXFORD GC
County Wexford, Ireland
J. Hamilton Stutt
(R.) T. J. A. Macauley

WEXHAM PARK GC
Berkshire, England
Emil Lawrence
WEYMOUTH GC
Dorset, England
(R. A.9) J. Hamilton Stutt
WGC GC
Xenia, Ohio
(A.9) Jack Kidwell, Michael
Hurdzan
W G YOUNG CC
Gaastra, Michigan
W. G. Young
WHAKATANE GC
Whakatane, New Zealand
C. H. Redhead
WHALING CITY CC
New Bedford, Massachusetts
Donald Ross
(R.9 A.9) William F. Mitchell
WHALLEY GC
Lancashire, England
(R.) J. A. Steer
WHEATLAND GC
Wheatland, Wyoming
Frank Hummel
WHEATLEY GC
Yorkshire, England
Alister Mackenzie
(R.) George Duncan
WHEATLEY HILLS CC
East Williston, New York
Devereux Emmet
(R.) Devereux Emmet, Alfred
H. Tull
(R.) Alfred H. Tull
(A.9) Howard Watson
WHEELING CC
Wheeling, West Virginia
Devereux Emmet
WHEELING GC
Wheeling, Illinois
C. D. Wagstaff
WHETSTONE CC
Marion, Ohio
William F. Mitchell
WHICKHAM GC
Durham, England
Tom Dunn
(R.) J. S. F. Morrison
WHIFFLETREE HILL GC
Concord, Michigan
Arthur Young
WHIPPOORWILL CC [NLE]
Armonk, New York
Donald Ross
WHIPPOORWILL CC
Armonk, New York
Charles Banks
(R.) Geoffrey S. Cornish,
Brian Silva
WHIP-POOR-WILL CC
Hudson, New Hampshire
Manny Francis
WHIRLPOOL GC
Niagara Falls, Ontario
Stanley Thompson
(R.) Clinton E. Robinson
WHISKEY CREEK GC
Fort Myers, Florida
William B. Lewis
(R.) Gordon G. Lewis

WHISPER LAKES GC
Vero Beach, Florida
Karl Litten
WHISPERING FIRS GC
McChord AFB, Washington
Bob Baldock
WHISPERING FOREST GC
McCall, Idaho
Robert Muir Graves
WHISPERING HILLS GC
Conesis, New York
Pete Craig
WHISPERING LAKES GC
Pompano Beach, Florida
Pat Pattison
WHISPERING OAKS CC
Ridge Manor, Florida
Hans Schmeisser
(R.9 A.9) Willie Ogg
WHISPERING PALMS CC
Rancho Santa Fe, California
Harry Rainville
(A.3rd 9) Harry Rainville,
David Rainville
WHISPERING PINES GC
Annandale, Minnesota
Joel Goldstrand
WHISPERING PINES GC
Myrtle Beach AFB, South
Carolina
(A.9) Baxter Spann, Ken Dye
WHISPERING WILLOWS GC
Livonia, Michigan
Mark DeVries
WHISPERING WOODS CC
Whispering Pines, North
Carolina
Ellis Maples, Dan Maples
WHISTLER VILLAGE GC
British Columbia
Arnold Palmer, Ed Seay
WHITBURN GC
Durham, England
(R.) J. S. F. Morrison
WHITBY GC
Whitby, England
(R.) J. Hamilton Stutt
WHITE BARN GC
Pleasant View, Utah
Keith Downs
WHITE BEAR LAKE GC
Carlyle, Saskatchewan
Bill Newis
WHITE BEAR LAKE YACHT C
White Bear Lake, Minnesota
Donald Ross
(R.1) Don Herfort
WHITE BEECHES G&CC
Haworth, New Jersey
Walter J. Travis
(R.) Maurice McCarthy
(R.) Alfred H. Tull
(R.) William F. Mitchell
(R.) Brian Silva, Geoffrey S.
Cornish
WHITE BIRCH HILLS GC
Bay City, Michigan
Bruce Matthews
WHITE CITY VA HOSPITAL GC
White City, Oregon
Bob Baldock
WHITE CLIFFS GC [NLE]
Plymouth, Massachusetts
Geoffrey S. Cornish

WHITE CLIFFS OF PLYMOUTH GC
Plymouth, Massachusetts
Karl Litten, Gary Player
WHITECRAIGS GC
Glasgow, Scotland
Willie Fernie
WHITE DEER CC
Prudenville, Michigan
Glenn Guldner (1968)
WHITE DEER PARK & G CSE (OLD
CSE)
Montgomery, Pennsylvania
Kenneth J. Polakowski
(R.) Lindsay Ervin
WHITE DEER PARK & G CSE (NEW
CSE)
Montgomery, Pennsylvania
Lindsay Ervin
WHITE EAGLE GC
Naperville, Illinois
Arnold Palmer, Ed Seay
WHITEFACE INN & GC
Lake Placid, New York
John Van Kleek
WHITEFIELD GC
Manchester, England
(R.) J. A. Steer
WHITEFISH GC
Pequot Lakes, Minnesota
(A.9) Don Herfort
WHITEFISH LAKE GC
Pierson, Michigan
(A.3) Jerry Matthews
WHITEFISH LAKE GC
Whitefish, Montana
Gregor MacMillan
(R.9 A.9) Gregor MacMillan
(A.3rd 9) *Keith Hellstrom*
(R.) John Steidel
WHITEHAVEN CC
Memphis, Tennessee
John W. Frazier
WHITEHEAD GC
County Antrim, Northern
Ireland
C. S. Butchart
WHITE LAKE GC
Whitehall, Michigan
E. E. Roberts
(R.) Bruce Matthews, Jerry
Matthews
WHITE LAKES GC [NLE]
Topeka, Kansas
Harry Robb
WHITEMAN AFB GC
Sedalia, Missouri
Edward Lawrence Packard,
Brent Wadsworth
WHITE MANOR CC
Malvern, Pennsylvania
William Gordon, David Gordon
WHITEMARSH VALLEY CC
Chestnut Hill, Pennsylvania
George C. Thomas, Jr.
(R.) William S. Flynn
(R.) Donald Ross
WHITE MOUNTAIN CC
Pinetop, Arizona
Arthur A. Snyder
(A.9) Arthur Jack Snyder
WHITE MOUNTAIN GC
Ashland, New Hampshire
Geoffrey S. Cornish, William G.
Robinson

WHITE MOUNTAIN MUNI
Rock Springs, Wyoming
Dick Phelps, *Donald G. Brauer*
WHITE PATH CC
Ellijay, Georgia
Willard Byrd
WHITE PINES GC (EAST CSE)
Bensonville, Illinois
Jack Daray
(R.) Ken Killian, Dick Nugent
WHITE PINES GC (WEST CSE)
Bensonville, Illinois
Jack Daray
(R.) Ken Killian, Dick Nugent
WHITE PINES GC
Ely, Nevada
Bob Baldock
WHITE PLAINS GC
La Plata, Maryland
J. Porter Gibson
WHITE POINT BEACH GC
Hunts Point, Nova Scotia
Donald Ross
WHITE ROCK CC
Mooresville, Indiana
Henry Culp
WHITEWATER CREEK GC
Fayetteville, Georgia
Arnold Palmer, Ed Seay
WHITE WEBBS MUNI
Enfield, Middlesex, England
F. G. Hawtree, J. H. Taylor
WHITFORD CC
Exton, Pennsylvania
William Gordon, David Gordon
WHITINSVILLE CC
Whitinsville, Massachusetts
Donald Ross
WHITLOCK G&CC
Hudson Heights, Quebec
Willie Park, Jr.
(R. A.9) Howard Watson
WHITMOOR CC (EAST CSE)
St. Charles, Missouri
Karl Litten
WHITMOOR CC (WEST CSE)
St. Charles, Missouri
Karl Litten
WHITNALL CC
Hales Corner, Wisconsin
George Hansen
WHITNEY FARMS CC
Monroe, Connecticut
Hal Purdy, Malcolm Purdy
WHITSAND BAY HOTEL GC
Cornwall, England
Willie Fernie
WHITTIER NARROWS GC
Whittier, California
William F. Bell
WHITTINGTON BARRACKS GC
Lichfield, Staffordshire, England
(R.) H. S. Colt
(R.) J. S. F. Morrison
WIANNO CC
Wianno, Massachusetts
Leonard Biles
(R.) Donald Ross
WICHITA CC
Wichita, Kansas
William H. Diddel

WICHITA FALLS CC
Wichita Falls, Texas
(R.) Ralph Plummer
(R.2) Jeff Brauer

WICKENBURG CC
Wickenburg, Arizona
William F. Bell, William P. Bell
(R.) Arthur Jack Snyder

WICKER PARK GC
Hammond, Indiana
Tom Bendelow

WICKLOW GC
County Wicklow, Ireland
Michael Moran
(R.) Eddie Hackett

WICOMICO SHORES GC
Chaptico, Maryland
Edmund B. Ault
(R.) George W. Cobb
(A.9) Robert L. Elder

WIDNES MUNI
Lancashire, England
Fred W. Hawtree, A. H. F. Jiggens

WIDOW MAKER GC
Spartanburg, South Carolina
Russell Breeden, *Dan Breeden*

WIENER NEUSTADT-FÖHRENWALD GC
Wiener Neustadt, Austria
Gerold Hauser, *Günther Hauser*

WIENERWALD GC
Wienerwald, Austria
Gerold Hauser, *Günther Hauser*

WIESLOCH HOHENHARDTER HOF GC
Baden-Württemberg, Germany
Reinhold Weishaupt

WIGAN GC
Wigan, England
(R.) J. J. F. Pennink

WIGWAM CC [NLE]
Litchfield Park, Arizona
(R.9 A.9) Arthur Jack Snyder

WIGWAM G&CC (BLUE CSE)
Litchfield Park, Arizona
Robert Trent Jones

WIGWAM G&CC (GOLD CSE)
Litchfield Park, Arizona
Robert Trent Jones

WIGWAM G&CC (WEST CSE)
Litchfield Park, Arizona
Red Lawrence, Jeff Hardin, Greg Nash

WIJCHEN GC
Wijchen, Netherlands
J. F. Dudok van Heel

WIJDE WORMER GC
Netherlands
J. F. Dudok van Heel

WIKIUP G&TC
Santa Rosa, California
Clark Glasson

WILBRAHAM CC
Wilbraham, Massachusetts
Willie Ogg
(R.) Geoffrey S. Cornish, Brian Silva

WILCOX OAKS CC
Red Bluff, California
Ben Harmon

WILDCAT CLIFFS CC
Highlands, North Carolina
George W. Cobb

WILDCAT RUN CC
Estero, Florida
Arnold Palmer, Ed Seay

WILDCAT RUN GC
Cobourg, Ontario
Robert Moote

WILD COAST HOLIDAY INN GC
South Africa
Robert Trent Jones, Jr.

WILDCREEK GC
Sparks, Nevada
Dick Phelps, Brad Benz

WILD DUNES G LINKS (LINKS CSE)
Isle of Palms, South Carolina
Tom Fazio
(R.) Tom Fazio

WILD DUNES G LINKS (YACHT HARBOR CSE)
Isle of Palms, South Carolina
Tom Fazio

WILDERNESS CC
Naples, Florida
Arthur Hills

WILDERNESS GC
Carp Lake, Michigan
Elmer Dankert

WILDERNESS GC
Kent, England
James Braid

WILDERNESS VALLEY GC (BLACK FOREST CSE)
Gaylord, Michigan
Tom Doak

WILDERNESS VALLEY GC (RESORT CSE)
Gaylord, Michigan
Al Watrous

WILDEWOOD CC
Columbia, South Carolina
Russell Breeden

WILDFLOWER CC
Grove City, Florida
Lane Marshall

WILDFLOWER CC
Temple, Texas
Leon Howard, *Charles Howard*

WILDFLOWER CC
Niagara-on-the-Lake, Ontario
Charles Mahannah, *Lee Trevino*

WILD QUAIL G&CC
Dover, Delaware
Bill Love

WILDWING CC
Woodland, California
David Pfaff

WILD WING PLANTATION GC (HUMMINGBIRD CSE)
Myrtle Beach, South Carolina
Willard Byrd

WILD WING PLANTATION GC (WOOD STORK CSE)
Myrtle Beach, South Carolina
Willard Byrd

WILDWOOD CC
Louisville, Kentucky
William H. Diddel

WILDWOOD CC
Riverhead, New York
Frank Duane

WILDWOOD CC [NLE]
Raleigh, North Carolina
Gene Hamm

WILDWOOD CC
Fairfield, Ohio
Ted McAnlis
(R.) Arthur Hills

WILDWOOD CC
Beaumont, Texas
Leon Howard

WILDWOOD G&CC
Cape May Court House, New Jersey
Wayne Stiles, John Van Kleek

WILDWOOD GC
Rush, New York
Pete Craig
(R.) Geoffrey S. Cornish, Brian Silva

WILDWOOD GC
Middletown, Ohio
(R.3) Jack Kidwell, Michael Hurdzan

WILDWOOD GC
Allison Park, Pennsylvania
Emil Loeffler, *John McGlynn*
(R.) William Gordon, David Gordon
(R.3) Ron Forse

WILDWOOD MUNI
Charles City, Iowa
(R.) Charles Calhoun

WILDWOOD MUNI
Nebraska City, Nebraska
Robert Popp

WILDWOOD GREENS GC
Raleigh, North Carolina
Jerry Turner, Bob Moore, Vance Heafner

WILDWOOD PARK GC
Decatur, Illinois
Edward Lawrence Packard

WILKES-BARRE MUNI
Wilkes-Barre, Pennsylvania
Geoffrey S. Cornish, William G. Robinson

WILLAMETTE VALLEY CC
Canby, Oregon
Shirley Stone
(R.) William G. Robinson, John F. Robinson

WILLAPA HARBOR GC
Raymond, Washington
Walter Fovargue

WILLARD CC
Willard, Ohio
Harold Paddock
(A.9) Richard W. LaConte, Ted McAnlis

WILLBROOK PLANTATION GC
Pawleys Island, South Carolina
Dan Maples

WILLIAM F. DEVINE GC
Boston, Massachusetts
George Wright
(R.) Willie Campbell
(R.) Philip Wogan

WILLIAMS CC
Williams, Arizona
Gary Panks, *David Graham*

WILLIAMS CC
Weirton, West Virginia
Emil Loeffler, *John McGlynn*

WILLIAMSBURG CC [NLE]
Williamsburg, Virginia
Fred Findlay

WILLIAMSBURG CC
Williamsburg, Virginia
William Gordon, David Gordon

WILLIAMSBURG G&CC
Williamsburg, Kentucky
Robert Thomason

WILLIAMSBURG COLONY INN GC
Williamsburg, Virginia
Buddy Loving

WILLIAMSBURG INN GC [NLE]
Williamsburg, Virginia
Fred Findlay

WILLIAMSPORT CC
Williamsport, Pennsylvania
(R.) A. W. Tillinghast
(R.) David Gordon

WILLIAM S. SAHM MUNI
Indianapolis, Indiana
Pete Dye

WILLIAMSTON CC
Williamston, North Carolina
(R.4 A.9) Gene Hamm

WILLIAMWOOD GC
Glasgow, Scotland
James Braid
(R.) F. G. Hawtree, J. H. Taylor

WILLINGBORO CC
Willingboro, New Jersey
NKA Rancocas GC

WILLINGDON GC
East Sussex, England
(R.) J. H. Taylor
(R.) Alister Mackenzie

WILLINGER GC
Northfield, Minnesota
Garrett Gill, George B. Williams

WILLISTON MUNI
Williston, North Dakota
Lane Marshall, *Carl Thuesen*
(A.9) John Steidel, *Theodore Wirth*

WILLMAR CC
Willmar, Minnesota
(A.9) R. Albert Anderson

WILLOUGHBY GC
Stuart, Florida
Arthur Hills

WILLOWBEND CC
Cotuit, Massachusetts
Michael Hurdzan

WILLOWBEND GC
Wichita, Kansas
Jay Morrish, Tom Weiskopf

WILLOWBROOK CC
Huntsville, Alabama
Leon Howard

WILLOWBROOK CC
Belle Vernon, Pennsylvania
James Gilmore Harrison

WILLOW BROOK CC
Tyler, Texas
(R.9 A.9) Ralph Plummer
(R.9) Joseph S. Finger

WILLOWBROOK GC
Sun City, Arizona
George Fazio, Tom Fazio

WILLOWBROOK GC
Lakeside, California
Jack Daray, Jr., Stephen Halsey

WILLOW BROOK GC
Winter Haven, Florida
David Wallace

WILLOW BROOK GC
Moorestown, Maryland
William Gordon, David Gordon
WILLOW CREEK CC
High Point, North Carolina
Willard Byrd
WILLOW CREEK CC
Sandy, Utah
Henry B. Hughes
(R.) William Howard Neff
WILLOW CREEK CC
Rocky Mount, Virginia
Charles B. Schalestock
WILLOWCREEK GC
Sun City, Arizona
George Fazio, Tom Fazio
WILLOW CREEK GC
Des Moines, Iowa
(A.3rd 9) Dick Phelps
WILLOW CREEK GC
Rochester, Minnesota
William James Spear
WILLOW CREEK GC
Blowing Rock, North Carolina
Tom Jackson
WILLOW CREEK GC
Knoxville, Tennessee
William Oliphant (1988)
WILLOW CREEK GC
Spring, Texas
Robert von Hagge, Bruce Devlin
WILLOWDALE GC
Scarborough, Maine
Skip Wogan
(A.9) *Fred Nanney*
WILLOWDALE GC (COMMERCIAL
CSE)
Toronto, Ontario
Stanley Thompson
WILLOW GROVE GC
Solon, Ohio
George B. Ferry
WILLOW HAVEN CC
Durham, North Carolina
George W. Cobb
WILLOWICK CC
Cleveland, Ohio
(R.) Donald Ross
WILLOWICK GC
Santa Ana, California
William P. Bell
WILLOW LAKES G&CC (LAKEWOOD
CSE)
Jacksonville, Florida
Fred Bolton
WILLOW LAKES G&CC (TROON
CSE)
Jacksonville, Florida
Lloyd Clifton
WILLOW LAKES GC
Miami, Florida
Charles Mascaro
WILLOW LAKES GC
Offutt AFB, Nebraska
Robert Trent Jones
WILLOW LAKES GC
Pope AFB, North Carolina
George W. Cobb
WILLOW METRO GC
New Boston, Michigan
William Newcomb

WILLOW OAKS CC
Richmond, Virginia
William Gordon, David Gordon
(R.1) Algie Pulley
WILLOW PARK CC
Calgary, Alberta
Norman H. Woods
WILLOW PARK GC
Castro Valley, California
Bob Baldock
WILLOWPEG GC
Rincon, Georgia
Ward Northrup
WILLOW POINT G&CC
Alexander City, Alabama
Thomas H. Nicol
WILLOW RIDGE CC
Rye, New York
Maurice McCarthy
(R.) Alfred H. Tull
WILLOW RUN CC
Denver, Iowa
Gordon Cunningham
WILLOW RUN GC
Alexander, Ohio
Jack Kidwell
WILLOW RUN GC
Boardman, Oregon
Marty Leptich, Dallas Wilson
WILLOW RUN GC
Sioux Falls, South Dakota
Joel Goldstrand
WILLOWS G&CC
Saskatoon, Saskatchewan
Bill Newis
WILLOWS GC
Rexford, New York
William F. Mitchell
WILLOWS GC
British Columbia
*Bill Maxwell, Bill Mathers,
Marge Mathers*
WILLOW SPRINGS CC
Morrison, Colorado
Stanley A. Harwood
WILLOW SPRINGS CC
San Antonio, Texas
Emil Loeffler, *John McGlynn*
(R.9 A.9) John Bredemus
WILLOW SPRINGS G&CC
Roswell, Georgia
Randy Nichols
WILLOW SPRINGS G&CC
Milton, Ontario
Robert Heaslip
WILLOW SPRINGS GC
Baltimore, Maryland
Al Janis
WILLOW SPRINGS GC
Willow Springs, Missouri
Floyd Farley
WILLUNGA GC
Willunga, New Zealand
(R.3) Ronald Fream
WIL-MAR GC
Knightdale, North Carolina
Gene Hamm
WILMETTE GC
Wilmette, Illinois
Joseph A. Roseman
WILMETTE PARK GC
Glenview, Illinois
Joseph A. Roseman
(R.) Ken Killian, Dick Nugent

WILMINGTON CC (NORTH CSE)
Greenville, Delaware
Dick Wilson
WILMINGTON CC (SOUTH CSE)
Greenville, Delaware
Robert Trent Jones
WILMINGTON CC [NLE]
Wilmington, Vermont
Ralph Barton
WILMINGTON MUNI
Wilmington, North Carolina
Donald Ross
WILMSLOW GC
Wilmslow, England
(R.) Tom Simpson
WILSHIRE CC
Los Angeles, California
Norman Macbeth
WILSHIRE GC
Winston-Salem, North Carolina
G. Veach
WILSON CC
Wilson, North Carolina
Willard Byrd
WILSON GC
Columbus, Ohio
Jack Kidwell
WILSON LAKE CC
Wilton, Maine
Wayne Stiles, John Van Kleek
WILSON ROYAL GC (MASHIKO CSE)
Tochigi, Japan
Shunsuke Kato
WILTON GROVE CC
New Jersey
A. W. Tillinghast
WILTWYCK CC
Kingston, New York
Robert Trent Jones
(R.2) Geoffrey Cornish, Brian
Silva
WIMBLEDON COMMON GC
London, England
Willie Park, Jr.
WINBERIE GC
Port Clinton, Ohio
Arnold Palmer, Ed Seay
WINCHESTER CC
Winchester, Massachusetts
Donald Ross
(R.) Donald Ross
(R.) Stephen Kay
WINCHESTER GC
Winchester, Virginia
Fred Findlay, *Raymond F.
Loving, Sr.*
(R.) Edmund B. Ault
WINDANCE CC
Gulfport, Mississippi
Mark McCumber
WINDBER CC
Windber, Pennsylvania
James Gilmore Harrison,
Ferdinand Garbin
WINDBROOK GC
Parkville, Missouri
Buss Peele
(R.7 A.9) Dick Phelps
WINDCREST GC
San Antonio, Texas
George Hoffman

WINDERMERE CC
Windermere, Florida
Ward Northrup
(R.) Lloyd Clifton, *Kenneth
Ezell, George Clifton*
WINDERMERE G&CC
Edmonton, Alberta
Clinton E. Robinson
(R.) John F. Robinson,
William G. Robinson
WINDERMERE GC
Cumbria, England
George Lowe
WINDEMERE HOUSE GC
Ontario
George Cumming
WINDHAM CC
Windham, New York
Hal Purdy
WINDING BROOK CC
Valatie, New York
Paul Roth
WINDING CREEK GC
Zeeland, Michigan
Bruce Matthews, Jerry Matthews
WINDING HOLLOW CC
Columbus, Ohio
NKA Champions of Columbus
G CSE
WINDING HOLLOW CC
New Albany, Ohio
Arthur Hills
WINDMILL HILL GC
England
Henry Cotton
WINDMILL LAKES GC
Ravenna, Ohio
Edmund B. Ault
[THE] WINDSOR C
Vero Beach, Florida
Robert Trent Jones, Jr.
WINDSOR G&CC
Kenya
T. J. A. Macauley
WINDSOR GC
Windsor, California
Ronald Fream
WINDSOR GC
Windsor, New Zealand
A. R. Blank
WINDSOR FOREST CC
Savannah, Georgia
George W. Cobb
WINDSOR GARDENS GC
Denver, Colorado
Henry B. Hughes
WINDSOR PARKE GC
Jacksonville, Florida
Arthur Hills
WINDSTAR C
Naples, Florida
Tom Fazio
WINDSTONE G CSE
Ringgold, Georgia
Gary Roger Baird (routing), Jeff
Brauer
WINDTREE GC
Mount Juliet, Tennessee
John LaFoy
WINDWARD HILLS C&CC
Guam
William F. Bell

WindWatch GC
Hauppauge, New York
Joe Lee, Rocky Roquemore
Windyhill GC
Scotland
Henry Cotton
Windyke CC (East Cse)
Germantown, Tennessee
John W. Frazier
Windyke CC (West Cse)
Germantown, Tennessee
Bill Amick
Winfield CC
Winfield, Kansas
James Dalgleish
(R.9 A.9) *Dick Metz*
Winfield Dunn GC
Pickwick State Park, Tennessee
Benjamin Wihry
Wingate Park CC
Pretoria, South Africa
Arthur Frank Tomsett
(R.) C. H. Alison
Winged Foot GC (East Cse)
Mamaroneck, New York
A. W. Tillinghast
Winged Foot GC (West Cse)
Mamaroneck, New York
A. W. Tillinghast
(R.) Robert Trent Jones
(R.3) Dick Wilson
(R.) George Fazio, Tom Fazio
(R.) Tom Fazio
Winged Pheasant GC
Farmington, New York
Pete Craig
Wing Field GC
Nikko, Japan
Johnny Miller
Wingfield GC
Tochigi, Japan
Shunsuke Kato
Wingfield Pines GC
Upper St. Clair, Pennsylvania
Dominic Palombo
Wing Park GC
Elgin, Illinois
Tom Bendelow
Wingpointe G Cse
Salt Lake City, Utah
Arthur Hills
Wing Point G&CC
Bainbridge Island, Washington
William Teufel
(A.9) *Jack Frei* (1991)
Winnapaug GC
Westerly, Rhode Island
(R.9 A.9) Donald Ross
Winnemucca Muni
Winnemucca, Nevada
Bob Baldock
Winnipeg G&CC
Winnipeg, Manitoba
Alexander Mann (1929)
Winnipeg GC
Winnipeg, Manitoba
Willie Park, Jr.
Winnipeg Hunt C
Winnipeg, Manitoba
Willie Park, Jr.
Winnetka Park GC
Winnetka, Illinois
C. D. Wagstaff
(A 9) William B. Langford

Winona CC
Winona, Minnesota
Ben Knight
(A.9) Gerry Pirkl, *Donald G. Brauer*
Winsan GC
Bangkok, Thailand
Jack Nicklaus
Winslow Muni
Winslow, Arizona
Arthur Jack Snyder
Winston Lake Park GC
Winston-Salem, North Carolina
Ellis Maples
Winter Hill GC
Berkshire, England
J. J. F. Pennink, C. D. Lawrie
Winter Park GC [NLE]
Winter Park, Florida
John Duncan Dunn
Winter Pines GC
Winter Park, Florida
Lloyd Clifton
Winter Springs GC
Winter Springs, Florida
Robert von Hagge, Bruce Devlin
Winters Creek GC
Big Rapids, Michigan
(R.9) Bruce Matthews, Jerry Matthews
Winters Run GC
Bel Air, Maryland
Buddy Loving
Wintergreen Resort GC
Calgary, Alberta
Bill Newis
Winterswijk GC
Winterswijk, Netherlands
D. M. A. Steel
Winthrop GC
Winthrop, Massachusetts
(R.) William F. Mitchell
Winton CC
Amherst, Virginia
Edmund B. Ault
Winton Woods GC
Mt. Healthy, Ohio
William H. Diddel
(A.3rd 9) Michael Hurdzan
Wiscasset GC
Pennsylvania
Robert White
Wishaw GC
Lanarkshire, Scotland
James Braid
Wisley GC
London, England
Robert Trent Jones, Jr.
[The] Witch G Links
Conway, South Carolina
Dan Maples
Wittem G&CC
Wittem, Netherlands
Fred W. Hawtree
Wittenberg GC
Wittenberg, Germany
Karl Hoffman, Bernhard von Limburger
Wittsjö GC
Sweden
Nils Sköld, Anders Amilon

Woburn G&CC (Duchess Cse)
Buckinghamshire, England
J. J. F. Pennink, C. D. Lawrie, D. M. A. Steel
Woburn G&CC (Duke Cse)
Buckinghamshire, England
J. J. F. Pennink, C. D. Lawrie
Woking GC
Woking, England
Tom Dunn
Wolf Creek CC
Eden, Utah
Mark Dixon Ballif
Wolf Creek GC
Olathe, Kansas
Marvin Ferguson
Wolf Creek GC
Reidsville, North Carolina
Johnny Johnston
Wolf Creek GC
Bluefield, Virginia
Maurice Brackett
Wolf Creek G Resort
Ponoka, Alberta
Rod Whitman
(A.3rd 9) Rod Whitman
Wolferts Roost CC
Albany, New York
Harold F. Andrews
(R.9 A.9) A. W. Tillinghast
(R.) *Leonard Ranier*
(R.) Geoffrey S. Cornish, Brian Silva
Wolf Hollow CC
Delaware Water Gap, Pennsylvania
Robert White
Wolf Laurel GC
Mars Hill, North Carolina
NKA Blue Mountain GC
Wolf Run GC
Zionsville, Indiana
Steve Smyers
Wollaston CC
North Quincy, Massachusetts
NKA Presidents GC
Wollaston CC
Milton, Massachusetts
George Fazio, Tom Fazio
Wollaton Park GC
Nottinghamshire, England
Tom Williamson
Wolverine GC (New Cse)
Mount Clemens, Michigan
Jerry Matthews
Wolverine GC (Old Cse)
Mount Clemens, Michigan
Bruce Matthews, Jerry Matthews
Women's CC [NLE]
Waukegan, Illinois
Stanley Pelchar
Women's National G&CC
Glen Head, New York
NKA Glen Head CC
Wood Ranch GC
Simi Valley, California
Ted Robinson
Woodberry Forest GC
Virginia
Joe Walker
(R.) J. B. McGovern
(R.) Fred Findlay, *R. F. Loving, Sr.*

Woodbine Downs GC
Toronto, Ontario
Howard Watson
Woodbridge CC
Woodbridge, Connecticut
Orrin Smith
(R.1) Brian Ault
Woodbridge CC
Kings Mountain, North Carolina
J. Porter Gibson
Woodbridge G&CC
Lodi, California
Harold Sampson (1923)
(R. A.3rd 9) Bert Stamps
(R.) Robert Muir Graves
Woodbridge GC
Suffolk, England
Fred W. Hawtree
Woodbrook GC
Ireland
(R. A.2) Fred W. Hawtree, Martin Hawtree, A. H. F. Jiggens
Woodbury CC
Woodbury, New Jersey
Alex Findlay
(R.) Geoffrey Cornish, Brian Silva
Woodbury Park G&CC
Devon, England
J. Hamilton Stutt
Woodcliff GC
Fairport, New York
Gordon Odenback
Woodcote Park GC
Surrey, England
Herbert Fowler
Woodcreek CC (Brook Hollow Cse)
Wimberley, Texas
Bruce Littell
Woodcreek CC (Cypress Creek Cse) [NLE]
Wimberley, Texas
Leon Howard
Woodcrest C
Syosset, New York
William F. Mitchell
Woodcrest CC
Cherry Hill, New Jersey
William S. Flynn, Howard Toomey
(R.) Frank Duane
(R.1) Rees Jones
Woodcrest CC
Grand Prairie, Texas
Don January, Billy Martindale
Woodcrest Par 3 GC
Sarasota, Florida
R. Albert Anderson
Woodenbridge GC
Ireland
(R.) *Tom Travers*
Woodfield CC
Boca Raton, Florida
Joe Lee
Woodford Hills CC
Versailles, Kentucky
Buck Blankenship

WOODHALL SPA GC
Lincolnshire, England
Harry Vardon
(R.) H. S. Colt
(R.) S. V. Hotchkin
(R.) Sir Guy Campbell, C. K.
Hutchison, S. V. Hotchkin
WOODHAVEN CC
Palm Desert, California
Harold Heers
WOODHAVEN CC
Bethany, Connecticut
Al Zikorus
WOODHAVEN CC
Fort Worth, Texas
Leon Howard
WOODHILL CC
Wayzata, Minnesota
Donald Ross
(R.) Donald Ross
(R.) Geoffrey S. Cornish,
William G. Robinson
(R.) Geoffrey S. Cornish,
Brian Silva
WOODHOLME CC
Pikesville, Maryland
Herbert Strong
(R.) Edmund B. Ault (1964)
(R.) Edmund B. Ault (1975)
WOODLAKE CC (GOLD CSE)
Vass, North Carolina
Ellis Maples
WOODLAKE CC (GREEN CSE)
Vass, North Carolina
Dan Maples
WOODLAKE CC
San Antonio, Texas
Desmond Muirhead
WOODLAKE G&CC
Lakewood, New Jersey
Edward Lawrence Packard
WOODLAND CC
Carmel, Indiana
William H. Diddel
(R.) Gary Kern
WOODLAND CC
Newton, Massachusetts
Wayne Stiles
(R.) Donald Ross
(R.) Geoffrey S. Cornish
WOODLAND CC
North Kingston, Rhode Island
Geoffrey S. Cornish
WOODLAND CC
Weston, West Virginia
(R.) James Gilmore Harrison
WOODLAND GC
Cable, Ohio
(A.9) Jack Kidwell
WOODLAND G CSE
St. Paul, Alberta
Bill Garnier (9 Par 3 1988)
WOODLAND CREEK G CSE
Andover, Minnesota
Joel Goldstrand
WOODLAND HILLS CC
Woodland Hills, California
William P. Bell
WOODLAND HILLS GC
Eagle, Nebraska
Jeff Brauer
WOODLAND HILLS GC
Nacogdoches, Texas
Don January, Billy Martindale

[THE] WOODLANDS C
Falmouth, Maine
Jim Fazio
WOODLANDS CC (EAST COURSE)
Tamarac, Florida
Robert von Hagge, Bruce Devlin
WOODLANDS CC (WEST CSE)
Tamarac, Florida
Robert von Hagge, Bruce Devlin
WOODLANDS CC
Columbia, South Carolina
George W. Cobb, John LaFoy
(R.) Russell Breeden, *Dan
Breeden*
[THE] WOODLANDS INN & CC
(EAST CSE)
Woodlands, Texas
NKA TPC at The Woodlands
[THE] WOODLANDS INN & CC
(NORTH CSE)
Woodlands, Texas
Joe Lee
(A.9) Robert von Hagge,
Bruce Devlin
(R.) Carlton Gipson
[THE] WOODLANDS INN & CC
(PALMER CSE)
Woodlands, Texas
Arnold Palmer, Ed Seay
[THE] WOODLANDS INN & CC
(WEST CSE)
Woodlands, Texas
Joe Lee
(A.9) Robert von Hagge,
Bruce Devlin
(R.) Carlton Gipson
WOODLANDS MANOR GC
Sevenoaks, England
F. G. Hawtree, J. H. Taylor
WOODLAND TERRACE GC
East Holden, Maine
Burton R. Anderson
WOODLAWN CC
Farmer City, Illinois
Tom Bendelow
WOODLAWN CC
Mount Vernon, Virginia
Russell Roberts
(R.) Tom Marzolf
WOODLAWN GC
Fort Smith, Arkansas
Larry Campbell
WOODLAWN GC
Oklahoma City, Oklahoma
Floyd Farley
WOODLEY MUNI
Los Angeles, California
Ray Goates
WOODMAR CC [NLE]
Hammond, Indiana
(R.9) William H. Diddel
WOODMAR CC
Hammond, Indiana
Ken Killian, Dick Nugent
WOODMERE C
Woodmere, New York
Jack Pirie
(R.) *Gil Nicholls*
(R.) Robert Trent Jones
(R.) Brian Silva, Geoffrey
Cornish
WOODMONT CC (CYPRESS CSE)
Tamarac, Florida
Robert von Hagge, Bruce Devlin

WOODMONT CC (PINES CSE)
Tamarac, Florida
Robert von Hagge, Bruce Devlin
WOODMONT CC [NLE]
Bethesda, Maryland
(R.) William S. Flynn
WOODMONT CC
Rockville, Maryland
Alfred H. Tull
(R.) Bob Cupp
WOODMONT CC
Nashville, Tennessee
(A.9) Edmund B. Ault
WOODMONT CC
Milwaukee, Wisconsin
Alex Pirie
WOODMOOR CC
Monument, Colorado
Press Maxwell
WOODRIDGE CC
Lisle, Illinois
(R.) Edward Lawrence
Packard
WOODRUFF CC
Joliet, Illinois
(R.) Edward Lawrence
Packard
[THE] WOODS G CSE
Hedgesville, West Virginia
Ray Johnston (1989)
WOODS HOLE CC
Falmouth, Massachusetts
Tom Winton
(R.) Wayne Stiles
WOODSIDE PLANTATION C (PAR 3
CSE)
Aiken, South Carolina
Bob Cupp
WOODSIDE PLANTATION C
(PLANTATION CSE)
Aiken, South Carolina
Bob Cupp
WOODSIDE PLANTATION C
(WYSTERIA CSE)
Aiken, South Carolina
Rees Jones
WOODSON BEND CC
Burnside, Kentucky
Dave Bennett, *Lee Trevino*
WOODSON PARK CC [NLE]
Oklahoma City, Oklahoma
Arthur Jackson
WOODSTOCK CC
Japan
Seiha Chin
WOODSTOCK CC
Woodstock, New York
Wayne Stiles
WOODSTOCK CC
Woodstock, Vermont
William H. Tucker
(R.) Donald Ross
(R.9 A.9) Wayne Stiles, John
Van Kleek
(R.) Robert Trent Jones
(1969)
(R.) Robert Trent Jones
(1975)
WOODSTOCK G&CC
Woodstock, New Brunswick
(R.) John F. Robinson
WOODSTOCK GC
Indianapolis, Illinois
Tom Bendelow

WOODVISTA G CSE
Kings Beach, California
John Duncan Dunn
WOODWARD CC
Bessemer, Alabama
(R.) Ward Northrup
WOODWARD MUNI
Woodward, Oklahoma
Bob Dunning
WOODWAY CC
Darien, Connecticut
Willie Park, Jr.
(R.) Maurice McCarthy
(R.1) Al Zikorus
(R.4) Geoffrey S. Cornish,
William G. Robinson
WOOLACOMBE BAY HOTEL GC
England
F. G. Hawtree, J. H. Taylor
WOONSOCKET CC [NLE]
Woonsocket, Rhode Island
(A.9) Geoffrey S. Cornish,
Samuel Mitchell
WOOSTER CC
Wooster, Ohio
(A.9) William Newcomb
WORCESTER CC
Worcester, Massachusetts
Donald Ross
(R.) Geoffrey S. Cornish,
Brian Silva
WORCESTER G&CC
Worcester, England
Alister Mackenzie
WORCESTERSHIRE CC
Worcester, England
(R.) Alister Mackenzie
(A.9) Fred W. Hawtree,
A. H. F. Jiggens
WORKINGTON GC
Cumbria, England
James Braid
WORKSOP GC
Nottinghamshire, England
Tom Williamson
WORLD HOUSTON GC
Houston, Texas
(R.) Garrett Gill, George B.
Williams
WORLD OF RESORTS GC
Lago Vista, Texas
Leon Howard, *Charles Howard*
WORLD OF SPORTS GC
Florence, Kentucky
(R. A.10) Jack Kidwell,
Michael Hurdzan
WORPLESDON GC
Surrey, England
J. F. Abercromby
(R.) Willie Park, Jr., J. F.
Abercromby
(R.) H. S. Colt
WORPSWEDE GC
Worpswede, Germany
Wolfgang Siegmann
WORSLEY GC
Lancashire, England
James Braid
(A.9) Fred W. Hawtree,
A. H. F. Jiggens
WORTHING GC (LOWER CSE)
Sussex, England
Harry Vardon
(R.) H. S. Colt

WORTHING GC (UPPER CSE)
Sussex, England
Harry Vardon
(R.9 A.9) H. S. Colt
WORTHINGTON CC
Bonita Springs, Florida
Gordon Lewis
WORTHINGTON CC
Worthington, Minnesota
Leo Johnson
(R.) Joel Goldstrand
WORTHINGTON ESTATE CC [NLE]
Irvington-on-Hudson, New
York
C. C. Worthington
WORTHINGTON HILLS CC
Worthington, Ohio
Charles Lorms
(R.) Brian Silva, Geoffrey S.
Cornish
WÖRTHSEE GC
Wörthsee, Germany
Kurt Rossknecht
WRAG BARN GC
Highworth, England
Martin Hawtree, Simon Gidman
WRAY CC
Wray, Colorado
Frank Hummel
WRIGLEY ESTATE G CSE
Lake Geneva, Wisconsin
William P. Bell
WUPPERTAL GC
Wuppertal, Germany
Bernhard von Limburger
WÜRZBURG-HEIDINGSFELD GC
Würzburg, Germany
Karl F. Grohs, *Rainer
Preissmann*
WYANDOT MUNI
Worthington, Ohio
Donald Ross
WYANDOTTE CC [NLE]
Kansas City, Kansas
Orrin Smith
WYANDOTTE HILLS GC
Toivola, Michigan
Wilbert Poyhonen
WYANTENUCK GC
Great Barrington, Massachusetts
Robert D. Pryde
(R.3) Charles Banks
WYATON HILLS GC
Princeton, Illinois
John Darrah
WYCKOFF PARK GC
Holyoke, Massachusetts
Donald Ross
(R.) Al Zikorus
WYCLIFFE G&CC
Lake Worth, Florida
Karl Litten, Bruce Devlin
WYKAGYL CC
New Rochelle, New York
Lawrence Van Etten
(R.) Donald Ross
(R.) Robert White
(R.) A. W. Tillinghast
(R.) Hal Purdy
(R.) Stephen Kay
WYKE GREEN GC
Middlesex, England
F. G. Hawtree, J. H. Taylor

WYNDEMERE G&CC
Naples, Florida
Arthur Hills
WYNDEMERE GC
Columbia, South Carolina
P. B. Dye
WYNDHAM ROSE HALL GC
Montego Bay, Jamaica
Henry Smedley
WYNDHURST C
Lenox, Massachusetts
Wayne Stiles
WYNDON LINKS
Scottsdale, Pennsylvania
Ron Forse
WYNDWYCK CC
St. Joseph, Michigan
Arthur Hills
WYNLAKES CC
Montgomery, Alabama
Joe Lee, Rocky Roquemore
WYNSTONE CC
North Barrington, Illinois
Jack Nicklaus
WYOMING CC
Cincinnati, Ohio
Tom Bendelow
WYOMING VALLEY CC
Wilkes-Barre, Pennsylvania
A. W. Tillinghast
WYTHEVILLE GC
Wytheville, Virginia
Fred Findlay

XEN-WIE G&CC
Kaohsiung, Taiwan
Gary Roger Baird

[THE] YACHT & CC
Stuart, Florida
Charles Prynne Martin
(R.) Chuck Ankrom
YACHT CLUB ESTATES GC
Largo, Florida
Chic Adams
YADKIN CC
Yadkinville, North Carolina
Gene Hamm
YAHATA CC
Japan
Kinya Fujita
YAHANUNDASIS GC [NLE]
Utica, New York
George Low
YAHANUNDASIS GC
Utica, New York
Walter J. Travis
(R.5) William Gordon, David
Gordon
YAITA CC
Yaita, Japan
Masujiro Yamamoto
YAKIMA CC
Yakima, Washington
A. Vernon Macan
(R.) Frank James
(R.5) Ted Robinson
YALE UNIVERSITY GC
New Haven, Connecticut
Charles Blair Macdonald, Seth
Raynor, Charles Banks, Ralph
Barton

YAMAGUCHI CC
Yamaguchi, Japan
Seichi Inouye
YAMOUSSOUKRO GC
Ivory Coast
Pier Mancinelli
YAMPA VALLEY GC
Craig, Colorado
William H. Neff, William
Howard Neff
YANI GC
Indonesia
(R.) Peter Thomson, Michael
Wolveridge
YANKEE RUN GC
Brookfield, Ohio
William P. Jones
(R.2) Jerry Matthews
YANKTON MUNI
Yankton, South Dakota
Pat Wyss
YARDLEY CC
Yardley, Pennsylvania
Fred Findlay
YARRAWONGA GC
Victoria, Australia
(A.9) Peter Thomson,
Michael Wolveridge
YARRA YARRA GC
Melbourne, Australia
Alister Mackenzie, Alex Russell
YATSUGATAKE GC
Yamanashi Prefecture, Japan
Takeaki Kaneda
YATSUGATAKE KOGEN CC
Japan
Mitsuo Komatsubara
YEAMAN'S HALL C
Hanrahan, South Carolina
Seth Raynor
YELLOWSTONE G&CC
Billings, Montana
Robert Trent Jones
(R.) Robert Muir Graves
YELVERTON GC
Devon, England
Herbert Fowler
YOKKAICHI CENTRAL GC
Mie, Japan
Shoichi Asami
YOKOHAMA CC
Yokohama, Japan
Takeo Aiyama
YOLO FLIERS C
Woodland, California
Bob Baldock
YOMIURI CC (BLUE CSE)
Osaka, Japan
Seichi Inouye
YOMIURI CC (RED CSE)
Osaka, Japan
Seichi Inouye
YOMIURI CC
Tokyo, Japan
Seichi Inouye
YONGPYEONG GC
Yongpyeong Resort, South
Korea
Robert Trent Jones, Jr.
YORBA LINDA CC
Yorba Linda, California
Harry Rainville, David Rainville
(R.) Garrett Gill, George B.
Williams

YORK CC
York, Nebraska
Charles Johnston (9 1920)
YORK G&TC
York, Maine
(R.9 A.9) Donald Ross
YORK GC
York, England
(R.) J. H. Taylor
YORK DOWNS CC [NLE]
Toronto, Ontario
C. H. Alison, H. S. Colt
(R.) Stanley Thompson
YORK DOWNS G&CC
Toronto, Ontario
Geoffrey S. Cornish, William G.
Robinson
YORK LAKE GC
Yorkton, Saskatchewan
Les Furber, *Jim Eremko*
YORK TEMPLE CC
Worthington, Ohio
(R.1) Jack Kidwell, Michael
Hurdzan
YORKTOWN CC
Yorktown, Virginia
(R.) William Flynn
YORKTOWN GC
Belleville, Illinois
Pete Dye
YORO CC
Nagoya, Japan
Peter Thomson, Michael
Wolveridge
YOSEMITE LAKES GC
Coarse Gold, California
Bob Baldock
YOUCHE CC
Crown Point, Indiana
(R.9 A.9) John Darrah
(R.) Dick Nugent
YOUGHAL GC
Youghal, Ireland
(R.9 A.9) John Harris
YOUGHIOGHENY GC
McKeesport, Pennsylvania
Willie Park, Jr.
(R.3) Ferdinand Garbin
YOUNGSTOWN CC
Youngstown, Ohio
Walter J. Travis
(R.) Donald Ross
(R.) Geoffrey S. Cornish
YOUNTAKAH CC [NLE]
Delawanna, New Jersey
Tom Bendelow
YOUNTAKAH CC
Delawanna, New Jersey
Arthur Lockwood
YOWANI CC
Australia
Al Howard
YPRES GC
Ypres, Belgium
J. F. Dudok van Heel
YSTAD GC
Ystad, Sweden
Ture Bruce
YUGAWARA CC
Kanagawa, Japan
D. H. Kishida
YUMA G&CC
Yuma, Arizona
William F. Bell, William P. Bell

YUNOHANO GC
Kanagawa, Japan
Hatohiko Asaka, Mitsuaki Otani

ZAHRAM CC
Lebanon
John Arnold
ZANESVILLE CC
Zanesville, Ohio
Donald Ross
 (R.) Orrin Smith
 (R.5) Jack Kidwell, Michael
Hurdzan
Z. BOAZ GC
Fort Worth, Texas
Ralph Plummer
 (R.) Ralph Plummer

ZEBULON CC
Zebulon, North Carolina
Maurice Brackett (1958)
ZELLWOOD STATION CC
Zephyrhills, Florida
William Maddox
ZEN CC
Himeji, Japan
Peter Thomson, Michael
Wolveridge
ZOAR VILLAGE GC
Dover, Ohio
Geoffrey S. Cornish, William G.
Robinson
ZOATE GC
Italy
F. Marmori

ZOETERMEER GC
Zoetermeer, Netherlands
J. F. Dudok van Heel
ZOLLNER GC
Tri-State University, Indiana
Robert Beard
ZUIRYO CC
Gifu Prefecture, Japan
Robert Trent Jones, Jr.
ZUMIKON G&CC
Zurich-Zumikon, Switzerland
Tom Simpson
 (R.) Donald Harradine
 (R.) Tom Williamson
ZUNI MOUNTAIN GC
Grants, New Mexico
Warren Cantrell

ZURICH G&CC
Zumikon, Switzerland
Tom Simpson
 (R.) Tom Williamson
 (R.) Donald Harradine
ZURICH-HITTNAU G&CC
Switzerland
Bernhard von Limburger
ZUR VAHR GC (GARLSTEDT CSE)
Bremen, Germany
Bernhard von Limburger
1001 RANCH GC
Riverside, California
 (R.) Bob Baldock, Robert L.
Baldock
108 MILE RESORT GC
Caribou, British Columbia
Stan Leonard, *Philip Tattersfield*

PART FOUR

A Glossary of Design Terms

Art Principles including Harmony, Proportion, Balance, Rhythm and Emphasis are applicable to golf course design:

Harmony is exemplified when lines of greens, bunkers, mounds and backgrounds are similar.

Proportion is related to scale. For example, in mountain country bunkers are large to be in scale with their surroundings.

Balance can be formal or asymmetrical. Formal balance is achieved with similarly shaped bunkers placed symmetrically on either side of a green. Asymmetrical or informal balance is exemplified by a large feature on one side of a green and two mounds on the other. To explain these two kinds of balance, landscape architects use examples of two people of equal weight on either side of a seesaw, which is then equally balanced (formal) and for informal one large person on one end and two smaller persons whose combined weight equals the larger person's on the other.

Rhythm resembles ripples from a stone dropped into a still pond. One example on a golf course is the concentric mowing patterns established by a superintendent around his greens by different mowing heights.

Emphasis The eye is carried first to the most important part of the arrangement and then to other details.

Basic Considerations in golf course design can be depicted by an equilateral triangle with three aspects, namely the game itself, eye appeal and maintainability. Each aspect is represented by one side of

619

this triangle. Environmental aspects are represented by the space inside the triangle.

Classic Golf Holes are widely adapted or copied golf holes with the originals often found on the links of Scotland. Yet Charles Blair Macdonald, the first exponent of the use of classic holes and originator of the term, also created several classics. For example the Cape (the fifth at Mid Ocean Club in Bermuda and the fourteenth at The National Golf Links in Southampton, New York), where the green sits on a peninsula is a Macdonald original. A tremendous tee shot is required to allow a reasonably safe approach to the green. The prime example of a links classic is the Redan, the fifteenth hole at North Berwick, a par 3 with a deep bunker on the entire left side and a green tilting away from the shot. The correct shot on a Redan hole is a low curving shot that hits short of the green and then bounces and rolls toward the pin. High shots thrown directly at the flag won't stay on the putting surface, and any shot or putt from behind the green or from its front is difficult. A shot from the frontal hazard is even more treacherous, for the player must allow for the slope of the green when executing the shot.

Contour Mowing of Fairways involves establishing undulating lines between fairway and rough as contrasted to straight boundaries. With the advent of lightweight mowers, contouring has become universal and enhanced playing interest and eye appeal.

Design for Play
   Penal design generally involves compulsory carries over hazards with no alternate routes.
   Strategic design provides alternate routes so that the player is not required to carry the hazard. It also provides a premium for those who dare the hazard and succeed.
   Heroic design is a blend of strategic and penal. Hazards are placed on the diagonal so that the more a player carries the greater the reward. This is sometimes referred to as the "Bite off" theory.

Form Follows Function is an architectural axiom that is self-explanatory. Examples in course design are the longer the approach, the larger the putting surface, the shorter the approach the more severe the contouring of the putting surface and the closer to the green the deeper the bunker and steeper its face.

Shot Values is an important yet somewhat mysterious term. Golf architects Ken Killian and Dick Nugent have described it well as "a reflection of what the hole demands of the golfer and the relative reward or punishment it metes out for good and bad shots."

The Evolution
of Course Features

Greens were born at St. Andrews in the 1700s, when attention was focused on keeping some areas turfed. By the late 1800s greens were made by leveling tops of natural plateaus. At Sunningdale in 1901 Willie Park, Jr., was the first to move earth to create raised contoured putting surfaces, although both Allan Robertson and Old Tom Morris previously moved earth at St. Andrews in remodeling the seventeenth and the eighteenth holes respectively. Park's greens evolved into the sculptured greens of contemporary design.

Tees didn't exist until after 1875. Before that, a player teed his ball on the green. Then level areas were provided off the green, but they were too small to support grass. Artificial surfaces were tried, but it wasn't until after World War II that huge tees making it possible to maintain turf evolved. These large raised rectangular areas soon proved monotonous. Free forms introduced by golf course architect Edward Lawrence Packard solved this problem, as did the creation of alternate tees of various shapes and sizes.

Bunkers were originally scars on the links caused by livestock sheltering behind hillocks or gardeners quarrying seashells. In time numerous divots in hollows where balls came to rest in large numbers also caused some bunkers. Greenkeepers began to modify and stabilize the scars. This practice led to contemporary dramatic bunkering. Two bunker types arose from the links, namely the "pot" and the "raised." The "cop bunker" was totally a manmade creation, with earth removed from a hole placed directly in its front in the form of a huge steep mound.

Bunker placement theories have changed through history. Originally many were penal cross traps. Later they became lateral and strategic. With the coming of power golf, bunkers were sited further from the tees with their axes converging on the axis of the fairway, the rationale being that the further one hits the ball, the more accurate he or she should be.

Practice fairways existed by the late 1900s as golf professionals insisted on them in order to teach. As the years went on, these areas became increasingly elaborate. If real estate was available the fairways had tees at both ends and a variety of target greens and bunkers in between. Many practice fairways were landscaped with trees and other features.

Design experiments by golf architects have been endless, with varying degrees of success. One that ended favorably was the introduction by Alister Mackenzie of a green with enormous undulations at Sitwell Park in England. Although this green first met with a storm of protest it was eventually accepted and later adapted worldwide. Indeed it led to the "Maxwell rolls" on many North American courses by onetime Mackenzie partner Perry Maxwell. A similar cycle of initial opposition, gradual acceptance and final endorsement has greeted innovations in course design throughout its history. Not all experiments have been successful. Among failures were target areas requiring short irons from tees on dogleg par 4s and 5s, extremely sharp doglegs and bunkers extending into putting surfaces that required putts around them.

Computer planning of golf course designs originated in the 1970s, first in estimation of cuts and fills, then in planning irrigation and drainage, then in correlating holes with surrounding developments and finally in large-scale computer-aided design and drafting. Nearly every major design firm in the 1990s uses computers in some facet of their architecture.

Parallel Developments in Allied Fields

An evolutionary process parallel to the upward spiral of design is apparent in the increasing perfection of the greensward and conditioning of golf courses. This process was advanced by course superintendents and was supported by scientists, manufacturers and dealers. Superior conditioning in turn affected course design, as did improvements in playing equipment and the mechanics of the game. A chronological list of the highlights of these collateral developments follows.

• Ball makers, such as the Gourlays of Leith and Musselburgh and Allan Robertson of St. Andrews, made the earliest golf balls from leather and feathers. These were replaced by the gutta-percha after 1846. By that time, drivers, spoons, irons and putters were all in use. Club heads were made from hard-thorn wood.

• As golf spread in the British Isles and course designers resorted to penal cross bunkers and geometric features, greenkeepers saw to it that some of their greens were nestled among hillocks, sheltered from drying winds. These greens followed the natural contours of their locations, although some lost their contours by decades of top-dressing with sand. Before the last quarter of the nineteenth century, green areas were not cultivated. They were merely turf converted to "putting surfaces" and maintained by grazing, sanding and foot traffic.

• By the late 1800s greenkeepers were experimenting with different grasses and with methods for maintaining the turf. The pioneer in grass studies was seedsman Martin H. Sutton, who established Sutton's Grass Station in 1863 at Reading, England.

• The gutta-percha ball proved too hard for the hard-thorn club heads of the time. These hard woods were replaced by fruitwoods (apple, pear and beech) and iron heads. The ash shaft was superseded by hickory. A simple golf bag came into use for carrying the increasing number of clubs.

• As greens and other features became more natural and linkslike in the heathlands era in England, course conditioning improved. Greens were mowed. Fairways were still kept short by grazing sheep, but gasoline- and steam-propelled mowers (invented in England in 1896) were in evidence on golf courses by the early 1900s. British seed companies continued research and advisory services and expanded availability of their products and services to other parts of the British Empire and to the United States.

• With the universal adoption of the hard-core ball in the early 1900s, persimmon replaced fruitwoods in club heads.

• In America turfgrass research was initiated before the turn of the century in Connecticut, Michigan and Rhode Island. About the same time, the great "Scottish invasion" of greenkeepers and professionals into North America introduced techniques for course construction and maintenance.

• The rubber-cored "Haskell" ball was invented in the United States around 1900 and was soon adopted universally.

• In 1904 the center-shafted putter, another American invention, was introduced. It ushered in an age of invention that resulted in a decline of the skill needed to play golf. Further deterioration of the game was soon halted by regulations issued by the ruling bodies of golf. Actions in the field of course architecture also helped maintain the integrity of the game with features previously overlooked on the ancient links used as models.

• As American architects began to embellish natural features and artificially create others, greenkeepers also advanced the state of their art. Scientists became increasingly helpful. C. V. Piper, agrostologist of the United States Department of Agriculture, was consulted on establishment of grass at The National Golf Links of America, perhaps the first time a professional scientist contributed to the creation of a golf course.

• By 1910 the practice of mowing fairways using horses with leather boots pulling single mowers became common in America. In 1914

Charles Worthington introduced a horse-drawn three-unit mower and in 1919 designed and built a golf course tractor. By the end of World War I the use of multibladed reel mowers on greens became universal.

• British greenkeepers formed an association in 1912.

• Francis Ouimet's victory in the 1913 U.S. Open at The Country Club (Brookline, Massachusetts) inspired new interest in the game in America. This in turn led to a new demand for courses by Americans, a demand left unsatisfied until the boom that followed the war.

• Size and weight of the golf ball were regulated in 1915 although standards differed on each side of the Atlantic.

• In 1916 American professionals formed the Professional Golfers Association with Robert White as first president. White later became a founding member of the ASGCA.

• C. V. Piper and R. A. Oakley published *Turf for Golf Courses* in 1917, the first American book devoted to the subject.

• The Green Section of the United States Golf Association was established in 1920 to advise on turf problems of member courses. After World War II it was headed successively by Fred V. Grau, Alexander M. Radko, William H. Bengyfield and James T. Snow.

• Matched sets of numbered clubs were introduced in the 1920s, and steel shafts were legalized.

• In 1926 greenkeepers in the United States and Canada formed a continent-wide professional society, The National Greenkeepers Association, which later became The Golf Course Superintendents Association of America.

• In 1927 Lawrence S. Dickinson established a school for greenkeepers at the Stockbridge School of Massachusetts Agricultural College. In the mid-1950s the school was headed by Dr. Eliot C. Roberts, in 1959 by Dr. Joseph Troll, who presided over its expansion into the largest program of its type in the world, and in 1986 by Dr. Richard Cooper.

• In 1929 the British Board of Greenkeeping Research established a research station at Bingley, Yorkshire, England.

• During the Depression years professional Gene Sarazen developed a straight-faced sand wedge, which provided still another challenge for course architects. In an opposing move, the R&A and the USGA placed a limit of fourteen clubs for a round and ball velocity was limited.

• H. Burton Musser and Fred V. Grau established a turfgrass extension and research team in the 1930s at Pennsylvania State College. It was continued into the nineties at Penn State by the team of Joseph Duich, Donald Waddington, John C. Harper II and T. L. Watscke.

• In 1936 the National Golf Foundation, a nonprofit organization dedicated to the advancement of golf, was established by Herb and Joe Graffis, publishers of *Golfdom* magazine. Executive directors of the NGF since then have included Glen Morris, Rex McMorris, Harry Eckhoff, William Pack and Don A. Rossi, appointed in 1970, who greatly expanded the foundation's activities. He was followed by Frank Smith, David Hueber and Dr. Joseph Beditz, who has again expanded the foundation's activities.

• During the 1950s, the National Golf Foundation rescued American golf architects from a precarious situation. Prior to that time, owners turned to their architects for initial advice on the economic feasibility of a new course. The architect often found himself involved in a conflict of interest. But Harry Eckhoff, East Coast representative of the NGF, developed a procedure whereby the foundation provided feasibility data for groups contemplating new courses. If the project was deemed feasible, the foundation recommended hiring a course architect. The Eckhoff plan became standard. While the architect continued to give his client the benefit of his own economic observations, he was relieved of the ultimate responsibility of determining whether the project would be profitable.

• With the advent of scientific turf management and power golf in the quarter century after 1955, many hazards became antiquated, requiring their relocation.

• For better or worse, the powered golf cart was universally accepted in North America by the late 1950s. In providing for its use, the architect sometimes found that modifications required in his plans could result in the classic dilemma of "the tail waggin' the dog."

• The Golf Development Council was established in Britain in 1965 with roles similar to those of the National Golf Foundation in the United States.

• By the 1960s a growing number of contractors were specializing in golf course construction on both sides of the Atlantic, making it possible for architects and owners to bid their work competitively to skilled firms. In 1970 American contractors formed the Golf Course Builders of America.

• The inventors remained busy in the 1970s, which saw the introduction of graphite shafts, Surlyn-covered balls, balls with new dimple patterns and golf club heads weighted heel and toe. Once again, technology threatened the traditional parameters of the game and of golf course design.

• By 1980 golf course superintendents were beset by environmental problems. GCSAA presidents (1991) Stephen Cadanelli and William Roberts (1992) both said that when problems arise the GCSAA will "take the high road" through research and correction if needed. Independent studies gave correctly managed golf courses a clean bill of health.

Architects' Associations

The American Society of Golf Course Architects, founded by thirteen men in 1947, was the first professional organization of course designers in America. Robert Bruce Harris was elected the first president, and Donald Ross served as honorary president.

Qualifications for membership in the ASGCA included experience (six years on the job) and accomplishment (responsibility for five finished designs). Consequently, membership grew slowly. But over the years, the majority of prominent course architects in North America became members.

Critics of the ASGCA claimed it perpetuated only its own membership, not the art or practice of design. Perhaps, like any professional organization, the ASGCA in the beginning did concentrate on membership affairs, and its first few annual meetings were get-togethers at golf resorts for a few days of camaraderie and golf. But by the early 1950s the group was undertaking serious discussions of issues pertinent to course design and issuing public-policy statements on some issues.

For example, in 1953 the ASGCA resolved some basic standards for course architecture, favoring strategic design, the placement of hazards to provide minimum interference to high handicap golfers and green bunkering that didn't sacrifce the need for accuracy in the name of easy maintenance. The next year it publicized the membership's opposition to a federal tax on club memberships.

In 1956 the ASGCA stated its opposition to the rapid rise in the use of motorized golf carts, feeling they damaged courses, compromised design and maintenance and diminished much of the charm of the game by reducing exercise and companionship. The society urged the use of golf carts only by those with a medical need. It was a parting shot on a controversy that goes on today.

Still, despite public positions and promotion of the profession through articles, advertisements and appearances, the society remained a once-a-year activity for most members until 1970, the year of Edward Lawrence Packard's presidency.

The public relations firm of Selz, Seabolt, Inc., of Chicago was retained to conduct full-time relations for the society, and one of its staff members was named executive director of the ASGCA. He was Paul Fullmer, a Notre Dame graduate in journalism who happened to be married to the daughter of course architect Percy Clifford. Fullmer, who remained as executive director of the ASGCA, assisted in the institution of a number of dynamic changes under the direction of Packard and subsequent presidents.

Committees were formed to address problems and challenges of course design:

• The Foundation Committee under chairman Packard collected funds to establish a variety of research projects.

• The Environmental Committee, chaired by Philip Wogan, a graduate biologist, prepared a widely circulated white paper on the impact of golf courses and their construction on the environment. This committee remained active under subsequent chairmen. In 1991 president Tom Clark, working with this committee, initiated steps to untangle the web of permits required to develop a new golf course. The first step was an ASGCA publication by Tom Love addressing key environmental issues.

• The Design Committee, chaired by Edmund B. Ault, prepared comprehensive design standards for consideration by members.

• The Professional Development Committee, cochaired by David Gill and Dr. Michael Hurdzan, organized seminars at annual meetings and devised a limited form of certification for course architects.

• The Hall of Fame Committee, chaired by Roger Rulewich, established a display showing the history of course architecture at the World Golf Hall of Fame in Pinehurst, North Carolina.

• The Awards Committee, chaired by Rees Jones, initiated an annual Donald Ross Award for outstanding contributions to golf and its architecture. Recipients subsequently included Robert Trent Jones, a founding member of the Society; Herbert Warren Wind, noted writer; Herb and Joe Graffis, founders of the National Golf Foundation; Joe

Dye, former director of the USGA and PGA Tour Commissioner; and Gerald H. Micklem, former captain of the Royal and Ancient, president of the English Golf Union and chairman of the Rules Committee of the Royal and Ancient. The award to Micklem was presented at Gleneagles, Scotland, during the society's pilgrimage in 1980 to Dornoch, the home of Donald Ross. Later recipients included former Ohio governor James Rhodes, course architect and historian Geoffrey S. Cornish; USGA agronomist Alexander Radko; entertainer Dinah Shore; golf writer Peter Dobereiner, PGA Tour Commissioner Deane Beman; distinguished golf writers Charles Price and Dick Taylor, the multifaceted golf business person John Zoller, Michael Bonallak OBE, Secretary of the Royal and Ancient, and Paul Fullmer.

In 1972 the British formed an active association. By the late 1980s France had an association and in 1990 the European Association of Golf Architects was formed.

Organizations and Libraries

American Society of Golf Course Architects,
221 North LaSalle Street, Chicago, Illinois.
Paul Fullmer, Executive Secretary. This is a source of numerous publications produced by the society.

British Institute of Golf Course Architects,
Thorpe Hall GC, Thorpe Bay, Essex, England SS1 3A7. A. S. Furnival,
  Administrative Secretary.
Originally formed as the British Association of Golf Course Architects, the organization is active in the same manner as the ASGCA.

Club Managers Association of America,
Alexandria, Virginia.

Donald Ross Society,
PO Box 403, Bloomfield, Connecticut 06002.

European Society of Golf Course Architects,
PO Box 2, A-1233 Vienna.
Austria monitors golf design on the Continent.

Givens Memorial Library,
Pinehurst, North Carolina.

Golf Course Builders Association of America,
920 Airport Road, Suite 210, Chapel Hill, North Carolina 27514.

Golf Course Superintendents Association of America,
1421 Research Park Drive, Lawrence, Kansas 66049,
distributes publications related to design, construction and maintenance.

Golf Development Council,
The Quadrant, Richmond, Surrey, England, TW9 1BY,
offers services similar to the NGF in the United States.

National Golf Foundation,
1150 South U.S. Highway One, Jupiter, Florida 33477,
is the national clearinghouse for golf.
PGA World Golf Hall of Fame,
PO Box 1908, Pinehurst, North Carolina 28374.
Professional Golfers Association of America,
Palm Beach Gardens, Florida 33410,
distributes a wide array of golf publications.
Ralph W. Miller Golf Library,
City of Industry, California.
United States Golf Association,
Golf House, PO Box 2000, Far Hills, New Jersey 07931,
owns the world's largest golf library and distributes golf books. The
Green Section of the USGA has a video on green construction.

FACSIMILES

Facsimiles of several out of print books on golf course design can be
obtained from the following sources:

Classics of Golf, PO Box 10285, Stamford, Connecticut 06923–0001.
Grant Books, Victoria Square Droitwich, Worcestershire, England
  WR9 8DC.
The Old Golf Shop, Inc., 325 West 5th St., Cincinnati, Ohio 45202.
USGA Rare Book Collection, Golf House, PO Box 3000, Far Hills, New
  Jersey 07931–3000.

PERIODICALS NO LONGER IN CIRCULATION

Historical data is obtainable from two periodicals no longer in print
with which golf architects Max Behr, Walter Travis and A. W.
Tillinghast were associated. Both are found in university and other
libraries.
American Golfer
Golf Illustrated

SEMINARS

The Harvard Graduate School of Design Professional Development, 48
Quincy Street, Cambridge, Massachusetts 02138, conducts an annual
seminar on golf course design.

   The GCSAA and the PGA each conduct somewhat similar seminars
on design plus others on course construction and restoration.

Bibliography

Many of these books are out of print but are obtainable at libraries or through a book search. Facsimiles of several are now available.

Adams, John. *The Parks of Musselburgh.* Droitwich, Worcestershire, England: Grant Books, 1991.

Allen, Peter. *Play the Best Courses: Great Golf in the British Isles.* London: Stanley Paul, 1973.

Bartlett, Michael, and Tony Roberts. *The Golf Book.* New York: Arbor House, 1980.

Bauer, Aleck. *Hazards, Those Essential Elements in a Golf Course Without Which the Game Would Be Tame and Uninteresting.* Chicago: Toby Rubovitis, 1913.

Braid, James. *Advanced Golf.* London: Methuen, 1908.

Browning, Robert. *A History of Golf.* New York: E. P. Dutton, 1955.

Clark, Robert. *Golf: A Royal and Ancient Game.* London: Macmillan, 1899.

Colt, H. S., and C. H. Alison. *Some Essays on Golf Course Architecture.* New York: Charles Scribners Sons, 1920.

Colville, George M. *Five Open Champions and the Musselburgh Golf Story.* Musselburgh, Scotland: Colville Books, 1980.

Cornish, Geoffrey S., and Ronald E. Whitten. *The Golf Course.* New York: Rutledge Press, 1981, 1987.

Cousins, Geoffrey. *Golf in Britain.* London: Routledge and Kegan Paul, 1975.

Darwin, Bernard. *The Golf Courses of the British Isles.* London: Duckworth & Co., 1910.

————. *James Braid.* London: Hodder and Stoughton, 1952.

Darwin, Bernard, Sir Guy Campbell, and others. *A History of Golf in Britain.* London: Cassel and Co., 1952.

Davis, William H. *The World's Best Golf.* Trumbull, Conn.: *Golf Digest,* 1991.

————, and Editors of *Golf Digest. Great Golf Courses of the World.* Norwalk, Conn.: *Golf Digest,* 1974.

————. *100 Greatest Golf Courses—And Then Some.* Norwalk, Conn.: *Golf Digest,* 1982, 1983, 1986.

Dawe, Alan. *The Golf Courses of British Columbia.* British Columbia: A&J Publishing, 1985.

Doak, Tom. *The Anatomy of a Golf Course.* New York: Lyons and Burford, 1992.

Dobereiner, Peter. *The Glorious World of Golf.* New York: McGraw-Hill, 1973.

Evans, Webster. *Encyclopedia of Golf.* New York: St. Martin's Press, 1971.

Everard, H. S. C. *A History of the Royal and Ancient Golf Club, St. Andrews from 1754–1900.* Edinburgh: William Blackwood, 1907.

Gallup, Don and Jim. *Golf Courses of Colorado.* Colorado: Colorado Leisure Sports, 1984.

Glasheen, Carol and Pete. *New York City Area Golf Course Guide.* New York: Carol Glasheen, 1989.

Graffis, Herb. *Esquire's World of Golf—What Every Golfer Must Know.* New York: Esquire, Inc., in association with Trident Press, 1933, revised 1965.

————. *The P.G.A.* New York: Thomas Y. Crowell, 1975.

Grant, Donald. *Donald Ross of Pinehurst and Royal Dornoch.* Scotland: The Sutherland Press, 1973.

Grimsley, Will. *Golf—Its History, People & Events.* Englewood Cliffs, New Jersey: Prentice-Hall, 1966.

Hamilton, E. A., C. Preston, and A. Laney. *Golfing America.* Garden City, New York: Doubleday, 1958.

Hawtree, Fred W. *The Golf Course: Planning, Design, Construction & Maintenance.* London: E. & F. N. Spon, 1983.

————. *Colt & Co.* Woodstock, Oxford: Cambuc Archive, 1991.

Henderson, I. T., and D. I. Stirk. *Golf in the Making.* London: Henderson and Stirk, 1979.

Huggins, Percy, editor. *The Golfer's Handbook.* London: Macmillan Press, printed annually.

Hunter, Robert. *The Links.* New York, London: Charles Scribner's Sons, 1926.

Hutchinson, Horace G. *Golf*. Badminton Series. London: Longmans, Green & Co., 1895 and other years.

————. *Golf Greens and Greenkeeping*. London: George Newnes and *Country Life*, 1906.

————. *Fifty Years of Golf*. New York: Charles Scribners Sons, 1919.

Jenkins, Dan. *The Best 18 Holes in America*. New York: Delacorte Press, 1966.

Jones, Rees L., and Guy L. Rando. "Golf Course Developments." *Urban Land Institute Technical Bulletin* 70. Washington, D.C.: 1974.

Jones, Robert Trent, with Larry Dennis. *Golf's Magnificent Challenge*. New York: McGraw-Hill and Sammis Publication, 1989.

Jones, Robert Tyre. *Golf Is My Game*. Garden City, New York: Doubleday, 1960.

Kavanagh, L. V. *History of Golf in Canada*. Ontario: Fitzhenry & Whiteside, 1973.

Kelly, G. M. *Golf in New Zealand*. Wellington, New Zealand: The New Zealand Golf Association, 1971.

Labbance, Bob, and David Cornwell. *Vermont Golf Courses; A Player's Guide*. Shelburne, Vermont: New England Press, 1987.

————. *The Golf Courses of New Hampshire: From the Mountains to the Sea*. Stockbridge, Vermont: New England Golf Specialists, 1989.

————. *The Maine Golf Guide*. Stockbridge, Vermont: New England Golf Specialists, 1991.

Low, John L. *Concerning Golf*. London: Hodder and Stoughton, 1903.

Lyle, Sandy, and Bob Ferrier. *The Championship Courses of Scotland*. Tadworth, Surrey: World's Work, 1982.

Macdonald, Charles Blair. *Scotland's Gift—Golf*. New York, London: Charles Scribners Sons, 1928.

Mackenzie, Dr. Alister. *Golf Architecture*. London: Simpkin, Marshall, Hamilton, Kent & Co., 1920.

Mahoney, Jack. *The Golf History of New England*. Framingham, Mass.: New England Golf, Wellesley Press, 1973.

Martin, H. B. *Fifty Years of American Golf*. 2nd edition. New York: Argosy-Antiquarian, 1966.

McCormack, Mark H. *The Wonderful World of Professional Golf*. New York: Atheneum, 1973.

Miller, Dick. *America's Greatest Golfing Resorts*. Indianapolis: Bobbs-Merrill, 1977.

Montague, W. K. *The Golf of Our Fathers*. Grand Rapids, Minnesota: Grand Rapids Herald Review, 1952.

Morris, John, and Leonard Cobb. *Great Golf Holes of New Zealand*. New Zealand: Morris/Cobb Publications, 1971.

Mulvoy, Mark, and Art Spander. *Golf: The Passion and the Challenge*. New York: Rutledge Books for Prentice-Hall, 1977.

Murdoch, Joseph F. *The Library of Golf, 1743–1966*. Detroit: Gale Research Co., 1968, Supplement 1978.

———, and Janet Seagle. *A Guide to Information Sources*. Detroit: Gale Research Co., 1979.

Myers, Kent C. *Golf in Oregon*. Portland: Ryder Press, 1977.

Park, Willie, Jr. *The Game of Golf*. London: Longmans, Green & Co., 1896.

———. *The Art of Putting*. Edinburgh: James J. Gray, 1920.

Peper, George. *Golf Courses of the PGA Tour*. New York: Harry F. Abrams, 1986.

Phillips, Patrick L. *Developing With Recreational Amenities, Golf, Tennis, Skiing, Marinas*. Washington, D.C.: The Urban Land Institute, 1986.

Price, Charles. *The World of Golf*. New York: Random House, 1962.

———, editor. *The American Golfer*. New York: Random House, 1964.

Price, Robert. *Scotland's Golf Courses*. Aberdeen, Scotland: Aberdeen University Press, 1989.

Robertson, James K. *St. Andrews—Home of Golf*. St. Andrews, Fife, Scotland: J & G Innes, 1967.

Ryde, Peter, D. M. A. Steel, and H. W. Wind. *Encyclopedia of Golf*. New York: Viking Press, 1975.

Scharff, Robert, and Editors of *Golf Magazine*. *Encyclopedia of Golf*. New York: Harper & Row, 1970.

Scott, Tom. *The Concise Dictionary of Golf*. New York: Mayflower Books, 1978.

Simpson, Tom. *The Game of Golf*. Vol. IX. The Lonsdale Library, New York: A.S. Barnes, revised 1952.

Steel, Donald. *The Golf Course Guide*. Glasgow, London: Collins with *Daily Telegraph*, revised 1980.

———. *Golf Facts and Feats*. London: Guinness Superlatives, 1980.

———, Peter Ryde, and Herbert Warren Wind. *The Shell International Encyclopedia of Golf*. London: E. Bury Press and Pelham Books, 1975.

Strawn, John. *Driving the Green*. New York: HarperCollins, 1991.

Sutton, Martin H. F., editor. *The Book of the Links*. London: W. H. Smith & Sons, 1912.

———, editor. *Golf Course Design, Construction and Upkeep*. England: Sutton & Sons, 1950.

Taylor, Dawson. *St. Andrews, Cradle of Golf*. London: A. S. Barnes & Co., 1976.

Thomas, George C., Jr. *Golf Architecture in America—Its Strategy and Construction*. Los Angeles: The Times-Mirror Press, 1927.

Tufts, Richard S. *The Scottish Invasion*. North Carolina: Pinehurst Publishers, 1962.

Ward-Thomas, Pat. *The Royal and Ancient*. Edinburgh: Scottish Academic Press, 1980.

————, and others. *The World Atlas of Golf*. New York: Random House, 1976.

Wethered, H. N., and T. Simpson. *The Architectural Side of Golf*. London: Longmans, Green & Co., 1929 (2nd edition, *Design for Golf*, 1952).

Wind, Herbert Warren. *The Story of American Golf*. New York: Alfred A. Knopf, 1948 (1st edition), 1956 (2nd edition), 1975 (3rd edition).

————. *Herbert Warren Wind's Golf Book*. New York: Simon & Schuster, 1971.

————. *Following Through*. New York: Tickner & Fields, 1985.

————, editor. *The Complete Golfer*. New York: Simon & Schuster, 1954.

TURFGRASS SCIENCE BIBLIOGRAPHY

Beard, James B. *Turfgrass Science and Culture*. Englewood Cliffs, New Jersey: Prentice-Hall, 1973.

————. *Turf Management for Golf Courses*. Minneapolis: Burgess Publishing Co., 1982.

Daniel, W. H., and R. P. Freeborg. *Turf Managers Handbook*. Cleveland, Ohio: The Harvest Publishing Co., 1979.

Emmons, R. D. *Turfgrass Science and Management*. Albany, New York: Delmar Publishers, 1984.

Hanson, A. A., and F. W. Juska, editors. *Turfgrass Science*. Madison, Wisconsin: American Society of Agronomy, 1969.

Madison, John H. *Practical Turfgrass Management*. New York: Van Nostrand-Reinhold Co., 1971.

————. *Principles of Turfgrass Culture*. New York: Van Nostrand-Reinhold Co., 1971.

Musser, Burton H. *Turf Management*. New York: McGraw-Hill, 1950 (2nd edition), 1962.

Piper, C. V., and R. A. Oakley. *Turf for Golf Courses*. New York: The Macmillan Co., 1917 (2nd edition), 1929.

Turgeon, A. J. *Turfgrass Management*. Reston, Virginia: Reston Publishing Co., 1980.

PAMPHLETS AND VIDEOS

Bengeyfield, W. H., and USGA Green Section Staff. *Specifications for a Method of Putting Green Construction.* Far Hills, New Jersey: USGA, 1989.

Cornish, G. S., and W. G. Robinson. *Golf Course Design: An Introduction.* Reprinted by GCSAA, 1989.

Hawtree, F. W. *Elements of Golf Course Layout and Design.* Richmond, Surrey, England: Golf Development Council, 1980.

Hurdzan, Michael. *Evolution of the Modern Green.* American Society of Golf Course Architects, reprinted 1990.

Love, William R. *An Environmental Approach to Golf Course Development.* Chicago, Illinois: ASGCA, 1992.

Roberts, E., and B. Roberts. *Lawn and Sports Turf Benefits.* Pleasant Hill, Tennessee: The Lawn Institute, 1990.

(Video) Golf Course Superintendents Association of America. *Links with Nature: Golf Courses and the Environment.*

INDEPENDENT STUDIES

Cohen, S. Z., S. Nickerson, R. Maxey, A. Dupui, and Z. A. Senita. *A Groundwater Monitoring Study for Pesticides and Nutrients Associated with Golf Courses on Cape Cod.* Groundwater Monitoring Review. Summarized in *Golf Course Management*, February 1990.

Cooper, Richard J. *Evaluating the Runoff and Leaching Potential of Turfgrass Pesticides.* University of Massachusetts, Amherst. Golf Course Management, February 1990.

Petrovic, A. M. *The Fate of Nitrogenous Fertilizers Applied to Turfgrass.* Madison, Wisconsin: Journal of Environmental Quality. January/March 1990.

Watsche, T. L., and R. O. Mumma. *The Effect of Nutrients and Pesticides Applied to Turf on the Quality of Runoff and Percolating Water.* University Park, Pennsylvania: Pennsylvania State University, 1989.

Acknowledgments

The authors are grateful to the thousands who have contacted them about additions and amendments to this book's forerunner, *The Golf Course.*

Once again nearly every golf course architect in North America responded to our requests for updated information for *The Architects of Golf,* as did every colleague we reached in Great Britain, Ireland, the continent of Europe, Australia and Japan. Descendants of architects now deceased also responded, as did friends and strangers, course superintendents, professional golfers and others in the business world of golf.

Several names stand out. Literary agent Richard Pine of Arthur Pine Associates, whose positive attitude was immensely helpful; Paul Fullmer, executive secretary of the ASGCA; A. S. Furnival of the BIGCA; Gerold Hauser, President of the ESGCA together with W. Pete Jones, historical chairman of the Donald Ross Society. The works of John W. L. Adams of Henley-on-Thames, England, the authority of the Parks of Musselburgh, and Fred W. Hawtree, British golf course architect and writer, were also inspirations, as was John Strawn's *Driving the Green,* the first descriptive nonfiction account of golf course developments.

Several who assisted a decade ago with *The Golf Course* were still on hand to help. These include golf architect William G. Robinson, Naomi H. Gillison of West Vancouver, British Columbia, and Dr. T. T. Kozlowski of the University of Santa Barbara. Here is a partial list of others who contributed to *The Architects of Golf.*

John W. Allen, Kalamazoo CC, Kalamazoo, Michigan
Dr. Joe Beditz, president, National Golf Foundation, and staff

Cary Blair, Westfield Companies, Westfield Center, Ohio

J. M. Boyle, Regina, Saskatchewan

Jean Bryant, director, Ralph W. Miller Golf Library, City of Industry, California

Orin E. Burley, Wharton School of Business, Pennsylvania

Dr. John Cameron, Defiance, Ohio

Alec Campbell, New York, New York (son of Alec Campbell)

Constance Campbell, New York, New York (granddaughter of Alec Campbell)

Elmer O. Cappers, The Country Club, Massachusetts

George M. Colville, Musselburgh, Scotland (author of *Five Open Champions and the Musselburgh Golf Story*)

Martin J. Connelly, Wykagyl CC, New York

Sidney T. Cox, Ives Hill GC, New York

Ronald S. Crowley, Dover, New Hampshire

Allan J. Cumps, Amherst, Massachusetts

James Diorio, Purpooduck GC, Maine

Tom Doak, golf course architect, writer and photographer

Mrs. Gordon Dunn, Lake Placid, New York (daughter-in-law of Seymour Dunn)

Harry C. Eckhoff, National Golf Foundation

William Emerson, Paradise Valley CC, Arizona

Peter Engelhart, Berkeley, California (grandson of Max Behr)

John English, Eastward Ho! CC, Massachusetts

Martin Faberman, Verona, Pennsylvania

Gerald Faubel, Saginaw CC, Michigan

David Fearis, CC of Peoria, Illinois

G. Ward Fenley, *The Albuquerque Journal* (New Mexico)

John Fleming, Olympic CC, California (son of Jack Fleming)

Ronald J. Foulis, Washington, D.C. (son of Robert Foulis)

C. Edwin Francis, Portland, Oregon

Dave W. Gamble, The Pines Golf Course, Weidman, Michigan

Mrs. F. Paul Gardner, Indian Wells, California (daughter of George C. Thomas)

Lester George, Colonial Golf Design

Golf Digest staff, including Nick Seitz, editorial director, Jerry Tarde, editor, Stephen Szurlej, senior staff photographer, and Jim Moriarty, contributing writer/photographer

Golf World staff, including Terry Galvin, editor, and Ann Lockhart, associate editor-research

David Gordon, ASGCA

David Gourlay, Thornhill G&CC, Ontario, Canada

(The late) Herb Graffis, golf writer and former editor of *Golfdom*, Florida

(The late) Donald Grant, Royal Dornoch GC, Scotland

Robert Muir Graves, ASGCA

Alan Green, Hollywood GC, Deal, New Jersey

Harland C. Hackbarth, Fort Worth, Texas (son of Herman C. Hackbarth)

Joseph Hadwick, CC of Lincoln, Nebraska

Brinley M. Hall, Myopia Hunt Club, Massachusetts

J. Kennedy Hamill, Adventures in Golf, New Hampshire

Gil Hanse, golf course architect, writer and photographer

John C. Harper II, Pennsylvania State University

Mike Hassel-Shearer, Rye, New Hampshire

Martin Hawtree, BIGCA

Donald T. Hearn, Weston GC, Massachusetts

Steven Heath, Chestnut Hill, Massachusetts

C. Thomas Herbert, Riviera CC, California

Bruce Herd, Fort Myers, Florida

Aimee L. Herpel, University City, Missouri (widow of Homer Herpel)

Alan Hess, The CC of Virginia

Cyril Hewertson, O.B.E., Walton Heath GC, England

Dr. Thomas K. Hitch, Waialae CC, Hawaii

Arthur R. "Red" Hoffman of R.T. Jones, Inc.

Donald Hogan, Seattle, Washington

Edward Horton, Westchester CC, Rye, New York

Howard C. Hosmer, Locust Hill CC, Rochester, New York

Neil S. Hotchkin, Woodhall Spa GC, Lincolnshire, England (son of S. V. Hotchkin)

Henry B. Hughes, Denver, Colorado

W. D. Hughes, Golf Development Council, England

David Hull, The Columbus CC, Columbus, Ohio

Dr. Michael Hurdzan, ASGCA

Bill Johnson, Hanover CC, Hanover, New Hampshire

A. H. Jolly, Jr., San Diego, California

Harvey Junor, Portland GC, Portland, Oregon

Jack Kidwell, ASGCA

Ms. M. S. Kinney, Flossmoor CC, Flossmoor, Illinois

Dr. Brad Klein, University of Hartford, Connecticut

George Kruzik, Fort Worth, Texas

Bob Labbance, New England Golf Specialists

Mrs. Joseph M. Lagerman, Jr., Pennsylvania (daughter of architect William Flynn)

Thomas Langford, Chicago, Illinois (son of William B. Langford)

John P. LaPoint, Golf Resources Assoc., Inc., Grafton, Massachusetts

R. F. Loving, ASGCA

Norman Macbeth, Jr., Spring Valley, New York (son of Norman Macbeth)

Neil C. H. Mackenzie, town clerk, St. Andrews, Fife, Scotland

H. G. MacPherson, secretary, Royal Liverpool GC, England

Edward D. Magee, Jr., manager, Pine Valley GC, New Jersey

Charles Martineau, Whippoorwill Club, New York

D. Gardiner Mason, Chatham, Massachusetts

James Merkel, The Columbus CC, Ohio

John R. "Jack" McDermott, associate publisher, Director of Special Projects, the New York Times Company Magazine Group

Frank McGuiness, formerly Lake Placid Club, New York

(The late) John C. McHose, Esq., Wilshire CC, California

Eleanora F. Miller, Colorado Springs, Colorado (daughter of Robert Foulis)

Monroe Miller, Blackhawk CC, Madison, Wisconsin

Robert Miller, Interlachen CC, Minnesota

Robert V. Mitchell, CGCS, The Greenbrier, White Sulphur Springs, West Virginia

Hugh Moore, Jr., professional, Brunswick CC, Georgia (son of Hugh Moore)

Sherwood Moore, Captains GC, Massachusetts

Robert F. Moote, GCSAA

Rodney A. Morgan, Dartmouth College

George Morris, formerly Colonial CC, Pennsylvania (grandson of George Morris, brother of "Old Tom")

Harold Nathanson, Plymouth CC, Massachusetts

Gary L. Nelson, Lee Park GC, North Dakota

(The late) Jack Neville

Paul J. O'Leary, Ekwanok GC, Vermont

Albert William Olsen, Jr., Hotchkiss School, Connecticut

Warren Orlick, professional, Tam O'Shanter GC, Michigan

A. W. Patterson, Gulph Mills CC, Pennsylvania

David Patterson, Adventures in Golf, England

(The late) Ralph Plummer, ASGCA

Dr. William L. Quirin, Garden City, New York

Tom Rader, former superintendent, Shoreacres, Illinois

Fred Reese, Hot Springs G&TC, Virginia

W. H. Richardson, Royal Melbourne GC, Australia

David A. Root, Gary CC, Indiana

Warren Roseman, Glenview, Illinois (son of Joseph Roseman)

Dr. Max Rudicel, Kokomo, Indiana

Roger G. Rulewich, ASGCA

Leon St. Pierre, Longmeadow CC, Massachusetts

Chester Sawtelle, Sawtelle Brothers, Massachusetts

Janet Seagle, formerly USGA

Charles H. Seaver, Pebble Beach, California

Edwin B. Seay, ASGCA

Brian Silva, ASGCA

Arthur A. Snyder, retired superintendent, Arizona

Jack Snyder, ASGCA

Frank Socash, Elmira CC, New York

D.M.A. Steel, BIGCA

(The late) Leonard Strong (brother of Herbert Strong)

Mrs. Leonard Strong, Center Valley, Pennsylvania

E. Clinton Swift, Jr., Golf Photography International

Lee Tyler, Burlingame, California

Roger Ulseth, Glen Ellyn, Illinois

Mrs. C. D. Wagstaff, Boca Raton, Florida (widow of C. D. Wagstaff)

Herbert Watson, Hartford GC, Connecticut

Edward Weeks, Myopia Hunt Club, Massachusetts

Gordon Whitaker, British Transport Hotels

Katherine Cameron Winton, Bronxville, New York (daughter of Tom Winton)

Philip Wogan, ASGCA

Richard Wynn, Wildwood Park GC, Iowa

Tak Yanada, golf course architect, Tokyo, Japan

Bill Zmistowski, Boulder, Colorado (grandson of Wilfrid Reid)

Joan Zmistowski, West Palm Beach, Florida (daughter of Wilfrid Reid)

Index